Principles of Accounting

Chapters 14–28

ELEVENTH EDITION

Principles of Accounting Chapters 14–28

ELEVENTH EDITION

Belverd E. Needles, Jr., Ph.D., C.P.A., C.M.A.
DePaul University

Marian Powers, Ph.D.
Northwestern University

Susan V. Crosson, M.S. Accounting, C.P.A
Santa Fe College

Australia • Brazil • Canada • Mexico • Singapore • Spain • United Kingdom • United States

Principles of Accounting Chapters 14–28, Eleventh Edition
Belverd Needles, Marian Powers, Susan Crosson

Vice President of Editorial, Business: Jack W. Calhoun

Editor in Chief: Rob Dewey

Executive Editor: Sharon Oblinger

Supervising Developmental Editor: Katie Yanos

Sr. Marketing Manager: Kristen Hurd

Marketing Coordinator: Heather Mooney

Sr. Marketing Communications Manager: Libby Shipp

Content Project Manager: Darrell Frye

Media Editor: Bryan England

Editorial Assistant: Julie Warwick

Frontlist Buyer, Manufacturing: Doug Wilke

Production Service: S4Carlisle Publishing Services

Sr. Art Director: Stacy Jenkins Shirley

Cover and Internal Designer: Grannan Graphic Design

Cover Image: © Getty Images/Image Bank

Permissions Account Manager: John Hill

Library of Congress Control Number: 2009941722

Student Edition ISBN 10: 0-538-75587-3
Student Edition ISBN 13: 978-0-538-75587-0

South-Western Cengage Learning
5191 Natorp Boulevard
Mason, OH 45040
USA

Cengage Learning products are represented in Canada by Nelson Education, Ltd.

For your course and learning solutions, visit **www.cengage.com**
Purchase any of our products at your local college store or at our preferred online store **www.CengageBrain.com**

Printed in the United States of America
1 2 3 4 5 6 7 13 12 11 10 09

BRIEF CONTENTS

CONTENTS

CHAPTER 5 Financial Reporting and Analysis 180

SUPPLEMENT TO CHAPTER 5 How to Read an Annual Report 226

CHAPTER 6 The Operating Cycle and Merchandising Operations 266

SUPPLEMENT TO CHAPTER 6 Special-Purpose Journals 302

CHAPTER 7 Internal Control 318

CHAPTER 8 Inventories 350

CHAPTER 9 Cash and Receivables 390

CHAPTER 12 Contributed Capital 518

CHAPTER 13 Long-Term Liabilities 562

CHAPTER 14 The Corporate Income Statement and the Statement of Stockholders' Equity 614

CHAPTER 17 Partnerships 754

CHAPTER 18 The Changing Business Environment: A Manager's Perspective 794

CHAPTER 19 Cost Concepts and Cost Allocation 836

Accounting in Motion!

This revision of *Principles of Accounting* is based on an understanding of the nature, culture, and motivations of today's undergraduate students and on extensive feedback from many instructors who use our book. These substantial changes meet the needs of these students, who not only face a business world increasingly complicated by ethical issues, globalization, and technology but who also have more demands on their time. To assist them to meet these challenges, the authors carefully show them how the effects of business transactions, which are the result of business decisions, are recorded in a way that will be reflected on the financial statements. Instructors will find that building on the text's historically strong pedagogy, the authors have strengthened transaction analysis and its link to the accounting cycle.

Updated Content, Organization and Pedagogy

Strengthened Transaction Analysis

Maintaining a solid foundation in double-entry accounting, we increased the number of in-text journal entries and have used T accounts linked to these journal-entry illustrations throughout the financial accounting chapters. In Chapter 2, "Analyzing Business Transactions," for example, we clarified the relationship of transaction analysis to the accounting cycle. In Chapter 6, "The Operating Cycle and Merchandising Accounting," we include transaction illustrations for all transactions mentioned in the chapter. At the same time, we reduced excessive detail, shortened headings, simplified explanations, and increased readability in an effort to reduce the length of each chapter.

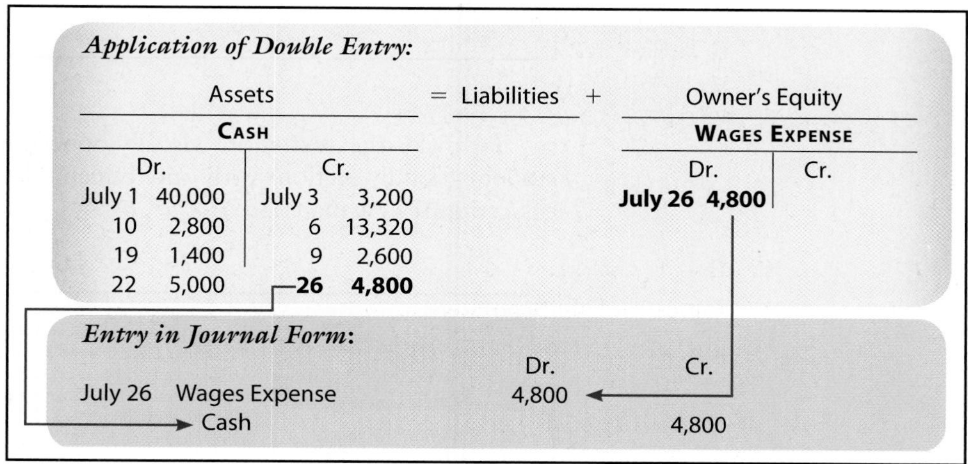

Content and Organization: Partnerships, Special-Purpose Journals, and Investments

Based on user input, Chapter 17 introduces a new topic of partnerships to the text. To make room for this, the investments chapter is now located in Appendix A with ample assignment material to provide greater flexibility of coverage.

Also based on user desires, we have inserted a supplement on special-purpose journals with assignment material after Chapter 6.

Strong Pedagogical System

Principles of Accounting originated the pedagogical system of ***Integrated Learning Objectives.*** The system supports both learning and teaching by providing flexibility in support of the instructor's teaching of first-year accounting. The chapter review and all assignments identify the applicable learning objective(s) for easy reference.

Each learning objective refers to a specific content area, usually either conceptual content or procedural techniques, in short and easily understandable segments. Each segment is followed by a "**Stop and Apply**" section that illustrates and solves a short exercise related to the learning objective.

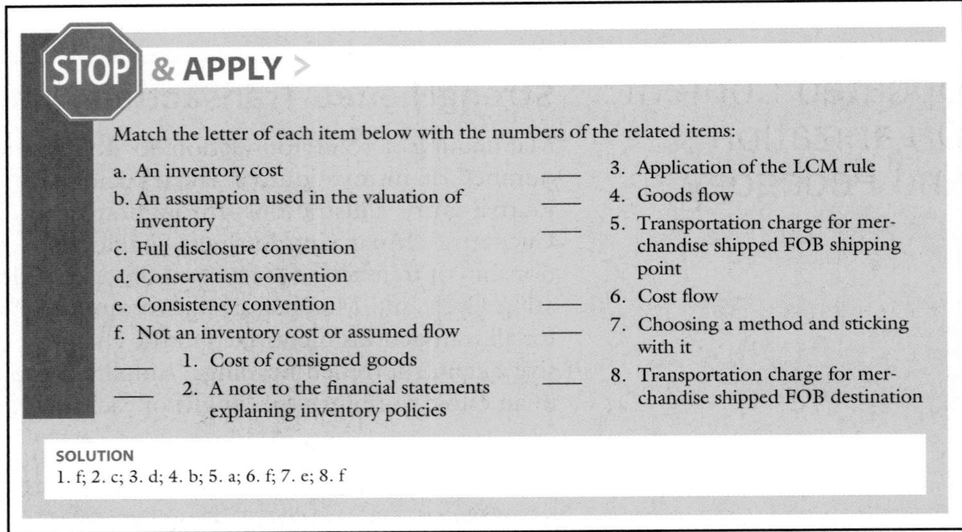

STOP & APPLY >

Match the letter of each item below with the numbers of the related items:

a. An inventory cost
b. An assumption used in the valuation of inventory
c. Full disclosure convention
d. Conservatism convention
e. Consistency convention
f. Not an inventory cost or assumed flow

____ 1. Cost of consigned goods
____ 2. A note to the financial statements explaining inventory policies
____ 3. Application of the LCM rule
____ 4. Goods flow
____ 5. Transportation charge for merchandise shipped FOB shipping point
____ 6. Cost flow
____ 7. Choosing a method and sticking with it
____ 8. Transportation charge for merchandise shipped FOB destination

SOLUTION
1. f; 2. c; 3. d; 4. b; 5. a; 6. f; 7. e; 8. f

To make the text more visually appealing and readable, it is divided into student-friendly sections with brief bulleted lists, new art, photographs, and end-of-section review material.

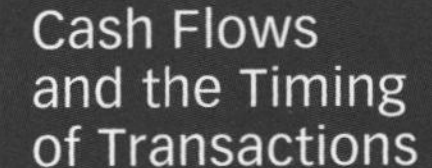

Cash Flows and the Timing of Transactions

LO5 Show how the timing of transactions affects cash flows and liquidity.

To avoid financial distress, a company must be able to pay its bills on time. Because the timing of cash flows is critical to maintaining adequate liquidity to pay bills, managers and other users of financial information must understand the difference between transactions that generate immediate cash and those that do not. Consider the transactions of Miller Design Studio shown in Figure 2-3. Most of them involve either an inflow or outflow of cash.

As you can see in Figure 2-3, Miller's Cash account has more transactions than any of its other accounts. Look at the transactions of July 10, 15, and 22:

- July 10: Miller received a cash payment of $2,800.
- July 15: The firm billed a customer $9,600 for a service it had already performed.
- July 22: The firm received a partial payment of $5,000 from the customer, but it had not received the remaining $4,600 by the end of the month.

Because Miller incurred expenses in providing this service, it must pay careful attention to its cash flows and liquidity.

One way Miller can manage its expenditures is to rely on its creditors to give it time to pay. Compare the transactions of July 3, 5, and 9 in Figure 2-3.

Study Note

After Step 1 has been completed, the Income Summary account reflects the account balance of the Design Revenue account before it was closed.

Further, to reduce distractions, the margins of the text include only **Study Notes**, which alert students to common misunderstandings of concepts and techniques; key ratio and cash flow icons, which highlight discussions of profitability and liquidity; and accounting equations.

Enhanced Real-World Examples Demonstrate Accounting in Motion

IFRS, Fair Value, and Other Updates

International Financial Reporting Standards and fair value have been integrated throughout the book where accounting standards have changed and also in the **Business Focus** features where applicable. All current events, statistics, and tables have been updated with the latest data.

FOCUS ON BUSINESS PRACTICE IFRS

IFRS: The Arrival of International Financial Reporting Standards in the United States

Over the next few years, international financial reporting standards (IFRS) will become much more important in the United States and globally. The International Accounting Standards Board (IASB) has been working with the Financial Accounting Standards Board (FASB) and similar boards in other nations to achieve identical or nearly identical standards worldwide. IFRS are now required in many parts of the world, including Europe. The Securities and Exchange Commission (SEC) recently voted to allow foreign registrants in the United States. This is a major development because in the past, the SEC required foreign registrants to explain how the standards used in their statements differed from U.S. standards. This change affects approximately 10 percent of all public U.S. companies. In addition, the SEC may in the near future allow U.S. companies to use IFRS.[11]

Use of Small, Diverse Companies

Each chapter begins with a **Decision Point**, a real-world scenario about a small company that challenges students to see the connection between accounting information and management decisions.

DECISION POINT ▸ A USER'S FOCUS
PENTE COMPUTER COMPANY

Pente Computer Company sells computer products for cash or on credit. The company's peak sales occur in August and September, when students are shopping for computers and computer-related supplies, and during the pre-holiday season in November and December. It is now January, and Andre Pente, the company's owner, has been reviewing the company's performance over the past two years. He has determined that in those years, approximately 1.5 percent of net sales have been uncollectible, and he is concerned that this year, the company may not have enough cash to cover operations before sales begin to increase again in late summer. In this chapter, we discuss concepts and techniques that would help Pente manage his cash and accounts receivable so that the company maintains its liquidity.

- ▸ How can Pente Computer Company manage its cash needs?
- ▸ How can the company reduce the level of uncollectible accounts and increase the likelihood that accounts receivable will be paid on time?
- ▸ How can the company evaluate the effectiveness of its credit policies and the level of its accounts receivable?

These company examples come full circle at the end of the chapter by linking directly to the **Review Problem**. Smaller, diverse company examples illustrate accounting concepts and encourage students to apply what they have learned.

▸ PENTE COMPUTER COMPANY: REVIEW PROBLEM

In this chapter's Decision Point, we posed the following questions:

- How can Pente Computer Company manage its cash needs?
- How can the company reduce the level of uncollectible accounts and increase the likelihood that accounts receivable will be paid on time?
- How can the company evaluate the effectiveness of its credit policies and the level of its accounts receivable?

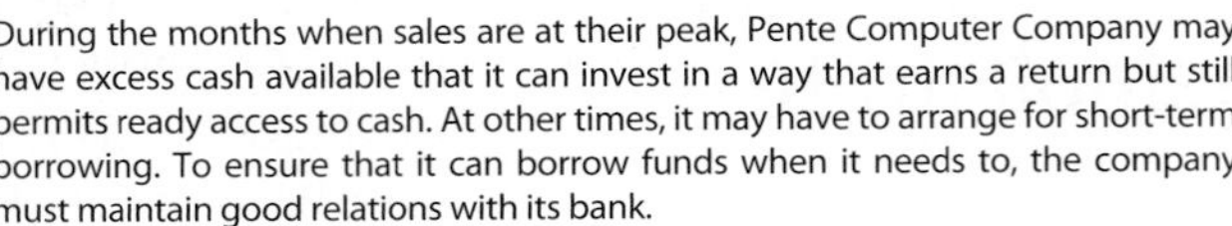

During the months when sales are at their peak, Pente Computer Company may have excess cash available that it can invest in a way that earns a return but still permits ready access to cash. At other times, it may have to arrange for short-term borrowing. To ensure that it can borrow funds when it needs to, the company must maintain good relations with its bank.

Use of Well-Known Public Companies

This textbook also offers examples from highly recognizable public companies, such as CVS Caremark, Southwest Airlines, Dell Computer, and Netflix, to relate basic accounting concepts and techniques to the real world. **Chapter 5, "Financial Reporting and Analysis,"** helps students interpret financial information. The latest available data is used in exhibits to incorporate the most recent FASB pronouncements. The authors illustrate current practices in financial reporting by referring to data from *Accounting Trends and Techniques* (AICPA) and integrate international topics wherever appropriate.

Consolidated means that data from all companies owned by CVS are combined. →

CVS Caremark Corporation
Consolidated Statements of Operations

CVS's fiscal year ends on the Saturday closest to December 31.

	Fiscal Year Ended		
(In millions, except per share amounts)	**Dec. 31, 2008 (52 weeks)**	**Dec. 29, 2007 (52 weeks)**	**Dec. 30, 2006 (53 weeks)**
Net revenues	$87,471.9	$76,329.5	$43,821.4
Cost of revenues	69,181.5	60,221.8	32,079.2
Gross profit	18,290.4	16,107.7	11,742.2
Total operating expenses	12,244.2	11,314.4	9,300.6
Operating profit[1]	6,046.2	4,793.3	2,441.6
Interest expense, net[2]	509.5	434.6	215.8
Earnings before income tax provision	5,536.7	4,358.7	2,225.8
Loss from discontinued operations, net of income tax benefit of $82.4	(132)	—	—
Income tax provision	2,192.6	1,721.7	856.9v
Net earnings[3]	3,212.1	2,637.0	1,368.9
Preference dividends, net of income tax benefit[4]	14.1	14.2	13.9
Net earnings available to common shareholders	$ 3,198.0	$ 2,622.8	$ 1,355.0
BASIC EARNINGS PER COMMON SHARE:[5]			
Net earnings	$ 2.23	$ 1.97	$ 1.65
Weighted average common shares outstanding	1,433.5	1,328.2	820.6
DILUTED EARNINGS PER COMMON SHARE:			
Net earnings	$ 2.18	$ 1.92	$ 1.60
Weighted average common shares outstanding	1,469.1	1,371.8	853.2

Revised and Expanded Assignments

Assignments have been carefully scrutinized for direct relevancy to the learning objectives in the chapters. Names and numbers for all Short Exercises, Exercises, and Problems have been changed except those used on videos. We have reversed the alternate and main problems from the previous edition. Most importantly, alternative problems have been expanded so that there are ample problems for any course.

All of the cases have been updated as appropriate and the number of cases in each chapter has been reduced in response to user preferences. The variety of cases in each chapter depends on their relevance to the chapter topics, but throughout the text there are cases involving conceptual understanding, ethical dilemmas, interpreting financial reports, group activities, business communication, and the Internet. Annual report cases based on CVS Caremark and Southwest Airlines can be found at the end of the chapter.

Specific Chapter Changes

The following chapter-specific changes have been made in this edition of *Principles of Accounting:*

Chapter 1: Uses of Accounting Information and the Financial Statements

- Discussion of performance measures revised using CVS and General Motors as examples of how these measures relate to profitability and liquidity
- Discussion of the statement of cash flows revised to relate the statement to business activities and goals
- Updated and enhanced coverage of the roles of the Financial Accounting Standards Board (FASB) and the International Accounting Standards Board (IASB)
- New Focus on Business Practice box on SEC's decision to let foreign companies registered in the United States use international financial reporting standards (IFRS)
- New study note on the role of the Public Company Accounting Oversight Board (PCAOB)

Chapter 2: Analyzing Business Transactions

- Learning Objective (LO) 3 revised to clarify and emphasize the role of T accounts, journal form, and their relationship to the general ledger
- New example of recognition violation
- Section on valuation revised to address fair value and IFRS
- New Focus on Business Practice box on fair value accounting in an international marketplace
- Cash flow discussion edited for clearer delineation of the sequence of transactions

Chapter 3: Measuring Business Income

- New example of earnings management focusing on Dell Computer
- New Focus on Business Practice box describing the FASB's rules for revenue recognition and the one broad principle (IFRS) that the IASB uses

Chapter 4: Completing the Accounting Cycle

- In-text examples focusing on Miller Design Studio simplified by using fewer accounts, thus clarifying the process of preparing closing entries and the worksheet

Chapter 5: Financial Reporting and Analysis

- Section on the objective of financial reporting revised to reflect FASB's emphasis on the needs of capital providers and other users of financial reports
- Coverage of qualitative characteristics simplified and shortened
- New Focus on Business Practice box on convergence of U.S. GAAP and IFRS and their effect on accounting standards
- New Focus on Business Practice box on how convergence of U.S. GAAP and IFRS can make financial analysis more difficult
- New Focus on Business Practice box on the use of ratios (performance measures) in executive compensation

Chapter 6: The Operating Cycle and Merchandising Transactions

- Discussion of the operating cycle revised for greater clarity
- T accounts and journal entries used to illustrate accounting for merchandising transactions under both the perpetual and periodic inventory systems
- Updated Focus on Business Practice box on the increased use of credit and debit cards
- Clearer differentiation between the cost of goods available for sale and the cost of goods sold in LO4
- New supplement on Special-Purpose Journals

Chapter 7: Internal Control

- New Focus on Business Practice box on the effectiveness of the Sarbanes-Oxley Act in preventing fraud
- New Focus on Business Practice box on methods of preventing shoplifting
- Material reformatted to clarify discussion of documents used in an internal control plan for purchases and cash disbursements

Chapter 8: Inventories

- Discussion of disclosure of inventory methods shortened for greater clarity
- New Focus on Business Practice box on the lower-of-cost-or-market rule
- New Focus on Business Practice box on the use of LIFO inside and outside the United States
- New Focus on Business Practice box on how IFRS and U.S. standards define fair value

Chapter 9: Cash and Receivables

- Concept of fair value introduced at various points throughout the chapter
- Revised Focus on Business Practice box on estimating cash collections
- New coverage of subprime loans

Chapter 10: Current Liabilities and Fair Value Accounting

- Chapter revised to include coverage of fair value accounting
- Discussion and assignments related to future value deleted to emphasize present value and fair value, which are more directly related to this course
- New study note on the disclosure of the fair value of short-term debt

Chapter 11: Long-Term Assets

- Coverage of tax laws revised to address the Economic Stimulus Act of 2008
- Coverage of intangible assets revised to reflect current standards
- Revised Focus on Business Practice box on customer lists

Chapter 12: Contributed Capital

- Revised Focus on Business Practice box on politics and accounting for stock options
- Section on cash flow information added to LO1
- Updated Focus on Business Practice box on share buybacks

Chapter 13: Long-Term Liabilities

- Bonds interest rates changed so that they are more realistic and less complicated than in previous edition
- Updated discussion of accounting for defined pension plans
- New Focus on Business Practice box on post-retirement liabilities
- Section on cash flow information added to LO1

Chapter 14: The Corporate Income Statement and the Statement of Stockholders' Equity

- Nonoperating items, which were covered in LO3 in previous edition, now discussed in LO1
- New Focus on Business Practice box on looking beyond the bottom line
- Revised Focus on Business Practice box on pro-forma earnings

Chapter 15: The Statement of Cash Flows

- Clarification of required disclosure of noncash investing and financing activities in LO1
- Sections on the risks of having too much cash and on interpreting the statement of cash flows added to LO2
- New Focus on Business Practice box on the IASB's support of the direct method

Chapter 16: Financial Performance Measurement

- Updated Focus on Business Practice box on pro-forma earnings
- Revised Focus on Business Practice box on performance measurement

Chapter 17: Partnerships

- New chapter added in response to users' requests

Chapter 18: The Changing Business Environment: A Manager's Perspective

- Updated definition of management accounting
- *Lean production* introduced as a key term
- Sections on total quality management and activity based management revised
- Updated Focus on Business Practice box on how to blow the whistle on fraud

Chapter 19: Cost Concepts and Cost Allocation

- Discussions of costs in LO2 in previous edition incorporated in LO1
- Section on document and cost flows through the inventory accounts in new LO3 revised
- Introduction to methods of product cost measurement added and section on computing service unit cost shortened in new LO4
- LO7 and LO8 streamlined and incorporated in new LO5

Chapter 20: Costing Systems: Job Order Costing

- Chapter 20 in previous edition separated into two chapters, with new Chapter 20 focusing on job order costing and new Chapter 21 focusing on process costing

- *Operations* costing system introduced as a key concept
- Discussions of manufacturer's job order cost card, computation of unit cost, and job order costing in a service organization included in new LO4
- New Focus on Business Practice box on the use of project costing

Chapter 21: Costing Systems: Process Costing

- New chapter (part of Chapter 20 in previous edition)

Chapter 22: Value-Based Systems: ABM and Lean

- LO1 and LO2 in last edition combined and revised
- Section on process value analysis included in LO1
- New listing of ABC's disadvantages in LO2
- New focus on lean operations in LO3

Chapter 23: Cost Behavior Analysis

- LO1 and LO2 in last edition combined and revised
- Discussions of variable, fixed, and mixed costs and discussions of step costs and linear relationships included in LO1
- Discussion of contribution margin income statement included in LO2
- LO5 revised to clarify concepts

Chapter 24: The Budgeting Process

- Section on advantages of budgeting and three key terms—*static budget, continuous budget,* and *zero-based budgeting*—added to revised LO1

Chapter 25: Performance Management and Evaluation

- LO1 and LO2 in last edition combined and revised

Chapter 26: Standard Costing and Variance Analysis

- LO1 and LO2 in last edition combined and revised

Chapter 27: Short-Run Decision Analysis

- Chapter revised to focus on short-run decisions and incremental analysis; capital investment analysis and time value of money now covered in Chapter 28

Chapter 28: Capital Investment Analysis

- New chapter

Online Solutions for Every Learning Style

South-Western, a division of Cengage Learning, offers a vast array of online solutions to suit your course and your students' learning styles. Choose the product that best meets your classroom needs and course goals. Please check with your sales representative for more details and ordering information.

CengageNOW™

CengageNOW for Needles/Powers *Principles of Accounting*, 11e is a powerful and fully integrated online teaching and learning system that provides you with flexibility and control. This complete digital solution offers a comprehensive set of digital tools to power your course. CengageNOW offers the following:

- Homework, including algorithmic variations
- Integrated e-book

- Personalized study plans, which include a variety of multimedia assets (from exercise demonstrations to videos to iPod content) for students as they master the chapter materials
- Assessment options, including the full test bank and algorithmic variations
- Reporting capability based on AACSB, AICPA, and IMA competencies and standards
- Course Management tools, including grade book
- WebCT and Blackboard Integration

Visit www.cengage.com/tlc for more information.

WebTutor™ on Blackboard® and WebCT™

WebTutor™ is available packaged with Needles/Powers *Principles of Accounting*, 11e or for individual student purchase. Jump-start your course and customize rich, text-specific content with your Course Management System.

- **Jump-start:** Simply load a WebTutor cartridge into your Course Management System.
- **Customize content:** Easily blend, add, edit, reorganize, or delete content. Content includes media assets, quizzing, test bank, web links, discussion topics, interactive games and exercises, and more.

Visit www.cengage.com/webtutor for more information.

Teaching Tools for Instructors

- **Instructor's Resource CD-ROM:** Included on this CD set are the key supplements designed to aid instructors, including the Solutions Manual, ExamView Test Bank, Word Test Bank, and Lecture PowerPoint slides.
- **Solutions Manual:** The Solutions Manual contains answers to all exercises, problems, and activities that appear in the text. As always, the solutions are author-written and verified multiple times for numerical accuracy and consistency with the core text.
- **ExamView® Pro Testing Software:** This intuitive software allows you to easily customize exams, practice tests, and tutorials and deliver them over a network, on the Internet, or in printed form. In addition, ExamView comes with searching capabilities that make sorting the wealth of questions from the printed test bank easy. The software and files are found on the IRCD.
- **Lecture PowerPoint® Slides:** Instructors will have access to PowerPoint slides online and on the IRCD. These slides are conveniently designed around learning objectives for partial chapter teaching and include art for dynamic presentations. There are also lecture outline slides for each chapter for those instructors who prefer them.
- **Instructor's Companion Website:** The instructor website contains a variety of resources for instructors, including the Instructor's Resource Manual (which has chapter planning matrices, chapter resource materials and outlines, chapter reviews, difficulty and time charts, etc.), and PowerPoint slides. www.cengage.com/accounting/needles

- **Klooster & Allen's General Ledger Software:** Prepared by Dale Klooster and Warren Allen, this best-selling, educational, general ledger package introduces students to the world of computerized accounting through a more intuitive, user-friendly system than the commercial software they will use in the future. In addition, students have access to general ledger files with information based on problems from the textbook and practice sets. This context allows them to see the difference between manual and computerized accounting systems firsthand. Also, the program is enhanced with a problem checker that enables students to determine if their entries are correct. Klooster & Allen emulates commercial general ledger packages more closely than other educational packages. Problems that can be used with Klooster/Allen are highlighted by an icon. The Inspector Files found on the IRCD allow instructors to grade students' work. A free Network Version is available to schools whose students purchase Klooster/Allen's General Ledger Software.

Learning Resources for Students

CengageNOW™

CengageNOW for Needles/Powers *Principles of Accounting*, 11e is a powerful and fully integrated online teaching and learning system that provides you with flexibility and control. This complete digital solution offers a comprehensive set of digital tools to power your course. CengageNOW offers the following:

- Homework, including algorithmic variations
- Integrated e-book
- Personalized study plans, which include a variety of multimedia assets (from exercise demonstrations to videos to iPod content) for students as they master the chapter materials
- Assessment options, including the full test bank and algorithmic variations
- Reporting capability based on AACSB, AICPA, and IMA competencies and standards
- Course Management tools, including grade book
- WebCT and Blackboard Integration

Visit www.cengage.com/tlc for more information.

WebTUTOR™

WebTutor™ on Blackboard® and WebCT™

- WebTutor™ is available packaged with Needles/Powers *Principles of Accounting*, 11e or for individual student purchase. Jump-start your course and customize rich, text-specific content with your Course Management System.
- **Jump-start:** Simply load a WebTutor cartridge into your Course Management System.
- **Customize content:** Easily blend, add, edit, reorganize, or delete content. Content includes media assets, quizzing, test bank, web links, discussion topics, interactive games and exercises, and more.

Visit www..cengage.com/webtutor for more information.

Klooster & Allen's General Ledger Software: This best-selling, educational, general ledger software package introduces you to the world of computerized accounting through a more intuitive, user-friendly system than the commercial software you'll use in the future. Also, the program is enhanced with a problem checker that provides feedback on selected activities and emulates commercial general ledger packages more closely than other educational packages. Problems that can be used with Klooster/Allen are highlighted by an icon.

Working Papers (Printed): A set of preformatted pages allow students to more easily work end-of-chapter problems and journal entries.

Student CD-ROM for Peachtree®: You will have access to Peachtree so you can familiarize yourself with computerized accounting systems used in the real world. You will gain experience from working with actual software, which will make you more desirable as a potential employee.

Electronic Working Papers in Excel® Passkey Access (for sale online): Students can now work end-of-chapter assignments electronically in Excel with easy-to-follow, preformatted worksheets. This option is available via an online download with a passkey.

Companion Website: The student website contains a variety of educational resources for students, including online quizzing, the Glossary, Flashcards, and Learning Objectives.

www.cengage.com/accounting/needles

ACKNOWLEDGEMENTS

A successful textbook is a collaborative effort. We are grateful to the many professors, other professional colleagues, and students who have taught and studied from our book, and we thank all of them for their constructive comments. In the space available, we cannot possibly mention everyone who has been helpful, but we do want to recognize those who made special contributions to our efforts in preparing the eleventh edition of *Principles of Accounting*.

We wish to express deep appreciation to colleagues at DePaul University, who have been extremely supportive and encouraging.

Very important to the quality of this book are our proofreaders, Margaret Kearney and Cathy Larson, to whom we give special thanks. We also appreciate the support of our Supervising Development Editor, Katie Yanos; Executive Editor, Sharon Oblinger; Senior Marketing Manager, Kristen Hurd; and Content Project Manager, Darrell Frye.

Others who have had a major impact on this book through their reviews, suggestions, and participation in surveys, interviews, and focus groups are listed below. We cannot begin to say how grateful we are for the feedback from the many instructors who have generously shared their responses and teaching experiences with us.

Daneen Adams, Santa Fe College
Sidney Askew, Borough of Manhattan Community College
Nancy Atwater, College of St. Scholastica
Algis Backaitis, Wayne County Community College
Abdul Baten, Northern Virginia Community College
Robert Beebe, Morrisville State College
Teri Bernstein, Santa Monica College
Martin Bertisch, York College
Tes Bireda, Hillsborough Community College
James Bryant, Catonsville Community College
Earl Butler, Broward Community College
Lloyd Carroll, Borough of Manhattan Community College
Stanley Carroll, New York City College of Technology
Roy Carson, Anne Arundel Community College
Janet Caruso, Nassau Community College
Sandra Cereola, Winthrop University
James J. Chimenti, Jamestown Community College
Carolyn Christesen, SUNY Westchester Community College
Stan Chu, Borough of Manhattan Community College
Jay Cohen, Oakton Community College
Sandra Cohen, Columbia College
Scott Collins, The Pennsylvania State University
Joan Cook, Milwaukee Area Tech College—Downtown
Barry Cooper, Borough of Manhattan Community College
Michael Cornick, Winthrop University
Robert Davis, Canisius College
Ron Deaton, Grays Harbor College
Jim Delisa, Highline Community College
Tim Dempsey, DeVry College of Technology
Vern Disney, University of South Carolina Sumter

Eileen Eichler, Farmingdale State College
Mary Ewanechko, Monroe Community College
Cliff Frederickson, Grays Harbor College
John Gabelman, Columbus State Community College
Lucille Genduso, Kaplan University
Nashwa George, Berkeley
Rom Gilbert, Santa Fe College
Janet Grange, Chicago State University
Tom Grant, Kutztown
Tim Griffin, Hillsborough Community College—Ybor City Campus
Sara Harris, Arapahoe Community College
Lori Hatchell, Aims Community College
Roger Hehman, Raymond Walters College/University of Cincinnati
Sueann Hely, West Kentucky Community & Technical College
Many Hernandez, Borough of Manhattan Community College
Michele Hill, Schoolcraft College
Cindy Hinz, Jamestown Community College
Jackie Holloway, National Park Community College
Phillip Imel, Southwest Virginia Community College
Jeff Jackson, San Jacinto College
Irene Joanette-Gallio, Western Nevada Community College
Vicki Jobst, Benedictine University
Doug Johnson, Southwest Community College
Jeff Kahn, Woodbury University
John Karayan, Woodbury University
Miriam Keller-Perkins, University of California-Berkeley
Randy Kidd, Longview Community College
David Knight, Borough of Manhattan Community College
Emil Koren, Saint Leo University
Bill Lasher, Jamestown Business College
Jennifer LeSure, Ivy Tech State College
Archish Maharaja, Point Park University
Harvey Man, Borough of Manhattan Community College
Robert Maxwell, College Of The Canyons
Stuart McCrary, Northwestern University
Noel McKeon, Florida Community College—Jacksonville
Terri Meta, Seminole Community College
Roger Moore, Arkansas State University—Beebe
Carol Murphy, Quinsigamond Community College
Carl Muzio, Saint John's University
Mary Beth Nelson, North Shore Community College
Andreas Nicolaou, Bowling Green State University
Patricia Diane Nipper, Southside Virginia Community College
Tim Nygaard, Madisonville Community College
Susan L. Pallas, Southeast Community College
Clarence Perkins, Bronx Community College
Janet Pitera, Broome Community College
Eric Platt, Saint John's University
Shirley Powell, Arkansas State University—Beebe
LaVonda Ramey, Schoolcraft College
Michelle Randall, Schoolcraft College
Eric Rothenburg, Kingsborough Community College
Rosemarie Ruiz, York College—CUNY
Michael Schaefer, Blinn College

Sarah Shepard, West Hills College Coalinga
Linda Sherman, Walla Walla Community College
Deborah Stephenson, Winston-Salem State University
Ira Stolzenberg, SUNY—Old Westbury
David Swarts, Clinton Community College
Linda Tarrago, Hillsborough Community College—Main Campus
Thomas Thompson, Savannah Technical College
Peter Vander Weyst, Edmonds Community College Lynnwood
Dale Walker, Arkansas State University—Beebe
Doris Warmflash, Westchester Community College
Wanda Watson, San Jacinto College—Central
Andy Williams, Edmonds Community College—Lynnwood
Josh Wolfson, Borough of Manhattan Community College
Paul Woodward, Santa Fe College
Allen Wright, Hillsborough Community College—Main Campus
Jian Zhou, SUNY at Binghamton

ABOUT THE AUTHORS

Belverd E. Needles, Jr., Ph.D., C.P.A., C.M.A.
DePaul University

Belverd Needles is an internationally recognized expert in accounting education. He has published in leading journals and is the author or editor of more than 20 books and monographs. His current research relates to international financial reporting, performance measurement, and corporate governance of high-performance companies in the United States, Europe, India, and Australia. His textbooks are used throughout the world and have received many awards, including the 2008 McGuffey Award from the Text and Academic Authors Association. Dr. Needles was named Educator of the Year by the American Institute of CPAs, Accountant of the Year for Education by the national honorary society Beta Alpha Psi, and Outstanding International Accounting Educator by the American Accounting Association. Among the numerous other awards he has received are the Excellence in Teaching Award from DePaul University and the Illinois CPA Society's Outstanding Educator Award and Life-Time Achievement Award. Active in many academic and professional organizations, he has served as the U.S. representative on several international accounting committees, including the Education Committee of the International Federation of Accountants (IFAC). He is currently vice president of education of the American Accounting Association.

Marian Powers, Ph.D.
Northwestern University

Internationally recognized as a dynamic teacher in executive education, Marian Powers specializes in teaching managers how to read and understand financial reports, including the impact that international financial reporting standards have on their companies. More than 1,000 executives per year from countries throughout the world, including France, the Czech Republic, Australia, India, China, and Brazil, attend her classes. She has taught at the Kellogg's Allen Center for Executive Education at Northwestern University since 1987 and at the Center for Corporate Financial Leadership since 2002. Dr. Powers's research on international financial reporting, performance measurement, and corporate governance has been published in leading journals, among them *The Accounting Review; The International Journal of Accounting; Issues in Accounting Education; The Journal of Accountancy; The Journal of Business, Finance and Accounting;* and *Financial Management*. She has also coauthored three interactive multimedia software products: Fingraph Financial Analyst™ (financial analysis software); Financial Analysis and Decision Making, a goal-based learning simulation focused on interpreting financial reports; and Introduction to Financial Accounting, a goal-based simulation that uses the Financial Consequences Model to introduce financial accounting and financial statements to those unfamiliar with accounting. Dr. Powers is a member of the American Accounting Association, European Accounting Association, International Association of Accounting Education and Research, and Illinois CPA Society. She currently serves on the board of directors of the Illinois CPA Society and the board of the CPA Endowment Fund of Illinois. She has served as vice president of Programs and secretary of the Educational Foundation.

Susan V. Crosson,
Santa Fe College

Susan V. Crosson is the accounting program coordinator and a professor of accounting at Santa Fe College, Gainesville, FL. Susan has also enjoyed teaching at the University of Florida, Washington University in St. Louis, University of Oklahoma, Johnson County Community College in Kansas, and Kansas City Kansas Community College. She is known for her innovative application of pedagogical strategies online and in the classroom. She is a recipient of the Outstanding Educator Award from the American Accounting Association's Two Year College Section, an Institute of Management Accountants' Faculty Development Grant to blend technology into the classroom, the Florida Association of Community Colleges Professor of the Year Award for Instructional Excellence, and the University of Oklahoma's Halliburton Education Award for Excellence. Susan is active in many academic and professional organizations. She served in the American Institute of CPA Pre-certification Education Executive Committee and is on the Florida Institute of CPAs Relations with Accounting Educators committee and the Florida Association of Accounting Educators Steering Committee. She has served as the American Accounting Association's Vice President for Sections and Regions and as a council member-at-large, chairperson of the Membership Committee, and was chairperson of the Two-Year Accounting Section. Previously she served as chairperson of the Florida Institute of CPAs Accounting Careers and Education Committee and was chair of the Florida Institute of CPAs Relations with Accounting Educators Committee. Susan was on the American Institute of CPAs' Core Competencies Best Practices Task Force also. Susan co-authors accounting textbooks for Cengage Learning: *Principles of Accounting*, *Financial and Managerial Accounting*, and *Managerial Accounting* with Bel Needles and Marian Powers. Susan holds a BBA in Economics and Accounting from Southern Methodist University and a MS in Accounting from Texas Tech University.

Principles of Accounting

Chapters 14–28

ELEVENTH EDITION

CHAPTER

14

The Corporate Income Statement and the Statement of Stockholders' Equity

Making a Statement

INCOME STATEMENT

Revenues

– Expenses

= Net Income

STATEMENT OF RETAINED EARNINGS

Beginning Balance

+ Net Income

– Dividends

= Ending Balance

BALANCE SHEET

Assets	**Liabilities**
	Stockholders' Equity

A = L + OE

STATEMENT OF CASH FLOWS

Operating activities
+ Investing activities
+ Financing activities
= Change in Cash
+ Beginning Balance
= Ending Cash Balance

The corporate income statement aids in the analysis of profitability and links to stockholders' equity, which in turn links to the stockholders' equity section of the balance sheet.

As we pointed out in an earlier chapter, earnings management—the practice of manipulating revenues and expenses to achieve a specific outcome—is unethical when companies use it to create misleading financial statements. Users of financial statements consider the possibility of earnings management by assessing the quality, or sustainability, of a company's earnings. To do so, they evaluate how the components of the company's income statement affect earnings. In this chapter, we focus on those components. We also cover earnings per share, the statement of stockholders' equity, stock dividends and stock splits, and book value per share.

LEARNING OBJECTIVES

LO1 Define *quality of earnings*, and identify the components of a corporate income statement. (pp. 616–621)

LO2 Show the relationships among income taxes expense, deferred income taxes, and net of taxes. (pp. 621–625)

LO3 Compute earnings per share. (pp. 625–627)

LO4 Define *comprehensive income*, and describe the statement of stockholders' equity. (pp. 627–630)

LO5 Account for stock dividends and stock splits. (pp. 630–635)

LO6 Calculate book value per share. (pp. 635–636)

DECISION POINT ▶ A USER'S FOCUS KOWALSKI, INC.

- ▶ Should Kowalski, Inc., declare a stock split?
- ▶ Should the company raise capital by issuing preferred stock?
- ▶ Should the company pay cash dividends or use cash to buy back its own stock?

Walter Kowalski is the chief executive officer of Kowalski, Inc., a manufacturing company that his father founded 25 years ago. The company's fiscal year just ended on June 30, 2010, and Walter is now considering what steps to take in the next fiscal year with regard to stockholders' equity. The current status of the company's stockholders' equity is as follows:

Contributed capital	
Common stock, no par value, $6 stated value, 500 shares authorized, 125 shares issued and outstanding	$ 750,000
Additional paid-in capital	410,000
Total contributed capital	$1,160,000
Retained earnings	485,000
Total stockholders' equity	$1,645,000

Among the questions Walter is wrestling with are whether the company should declare a stock split, whether it should issue preferred stock to raise capital, and whether it should pay cash dividends or use cash to buy back its own stock. In this chapter, you will learn about these issues, as well as about the structure and content of the corporate income statement and its interpretation.

Performance Measurement: Quality of Earnings Issues

LO1 Define *quality of earnings,* and identify the components of a corporate income statement.

Net income (net earnings) is the measure most commonly used to evaluate a company's performance. In fact, a survey of 2,000 members of the Association for Investment Management and Research indicated that the two most important economic measures in evaluating common stocks were expected changes in earnings per share and expected return on equity.[1] Net income is a key component of both measures.

Because of the importance of net income, or the "bottom line," in measuring a company's prospects, there is significant interest in evaluating the quality of the net income figure, or the **quality of earnings.** The quality of a company's earnings refers to the substance of earnings and their sustainability into future accounting periods. For example, if earnings increase because of a gain on the sale of an asset, this portion of earnings will not be sustained in the future.

The accounting estimates and methods that a company uses affect the quality of its earnings, as do these components of the income statement:

- Gains and losses on transactions
- Write-downs and restructurings
- Non-operating items

Because management has choices in the content and positioning of these income statement components, there is a potential for managing earnings to achieve specific income targets. It is therefore critical for users of income statements to understand these factors and take them into consideration when evaluating a company's performance.

Exhibit 14-1 shows the components of a typical corporate income statement. Net income or loss (the "bottom line" of the income statement) includes all revenues, expenses, gains, and losses over the accounting period. When a company has both continuing and discontinued operations, the operating income section is called **income from continuing operations.** Income from continuing operations before income taxes may include gains or losses on the sale of assets, write-downs, and restructurings. The income taxes expense section of the statement is subject to special accounting rules.

As you can see in Exhibit 14-1, the section of a corporate income statement that follows income taxes contains such nonoperating items as discontinued operations and extraordinary gains (or losses). Another item that may appear in this section is the write-off of goodwill when its value has been impaired. Earnings per share information appears at the bottom of the statement.

Study Note

It is important to know which items included in earnings are recurring and which are one-time items. Income from continuing operations before nonoperating items gives a clear signal about future results. In assessing a company's future earnings potential, nonoperating items are excluded because they are not expected to continue.

FOCUS ON BUSINESS PRACTICE

Why Do Investors Study Quality of Earnings?

Analysts for **Twentieth Century Mutual Funds**, a major investment company now merged with **American Century Investments Corporation**, make adjustments to a company's reported financial performance to create a more accurate picture of the company's ongoing operations. For example, suppose a paper manufacturer reports earnings of $1.30 per share. Further investigation, however, shows that the per share number includes a one-time gain on the sale of assets, which accounts for an increase of $0.25 per share. Twentieth Century would list the company as earning only $1.05 per share. "These kinds of adjustments help assure long-term decisions aren't based on one-time events."[2]

EXHIBIT 14-1 Corporate Income Statement

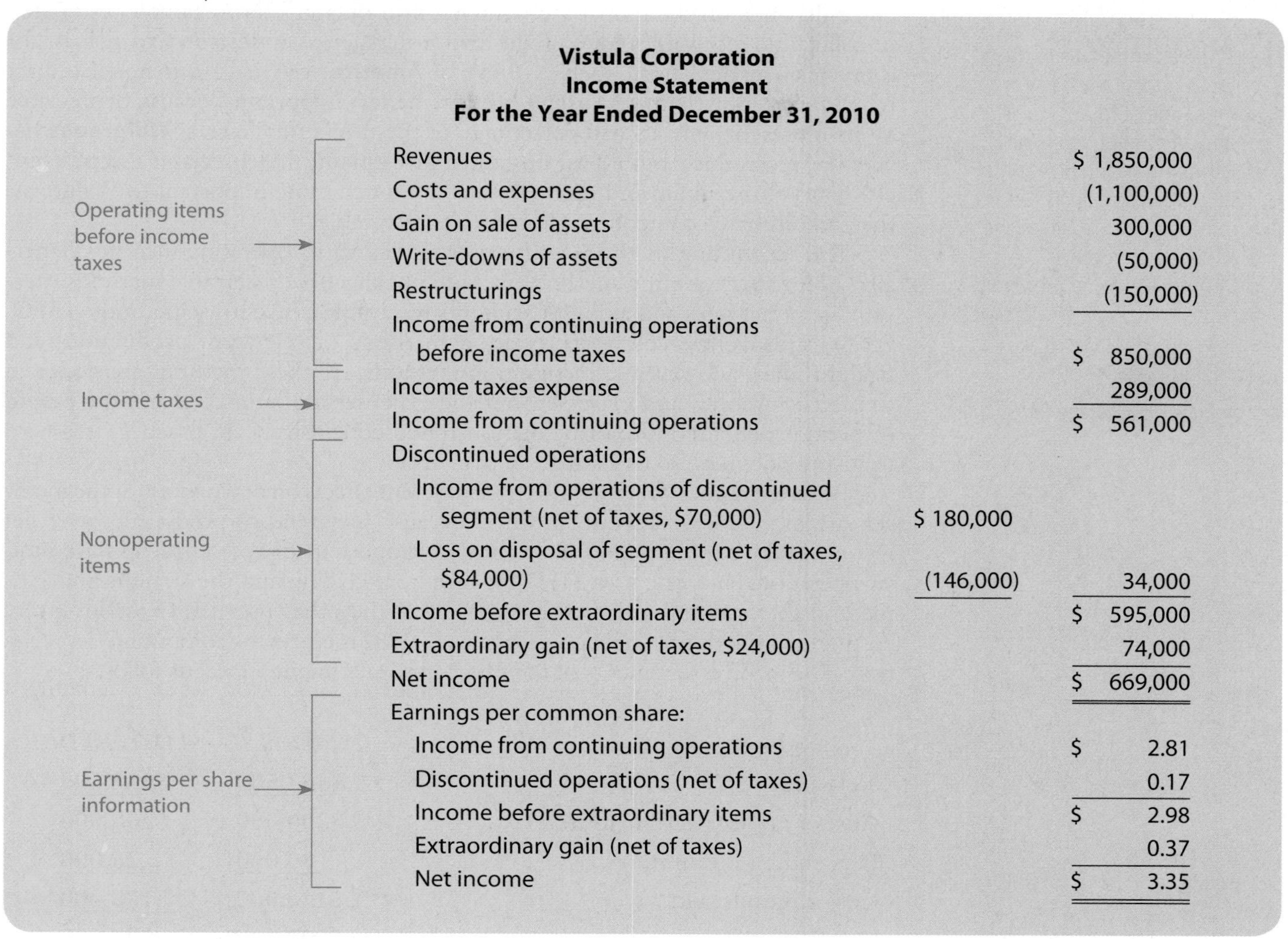

Vistula Corporation
Income Statement
For the Year Ended December 31, 2010

Operating items before income taxes	Revenues		$ 1,850,000
	Costs and expenses		(1,100,000)
	Gain on sale of assets		300,000
	Write-downs of assets		(50,000)
	Restructurings		(150,000)
	Income from continuing operations before income taxes		$ 850,000
Income taxes	Income taxes expense		289,000
	Income from continuing operations		$ 561,000
Nonoperating items	Discontinued operations		
	Income from operations of discontinued segment (net of taxes, $70,000)	$ 180,000	
	Loss on disposal of segment (net of taxes, $84,000)	(146,000)	34,000
	Income before extraordinary items		$ 595,000
	Extraordinary gain (net of taxes, $24,000)		74,000
	Net income		$ 669,000
Earnings per share information	Earnings per common share:		
	Income from continuing operations		$ 2.81
	Discontinued operations (net of taxes)		0.17
	Income before extraordinary items		$ 2.98
	Extraordinary gain (net of taxes)		0.37
	Net income		$ 3.35

The Effect of Accounting Estimates and Methods

Users of financial statements need to be aware of the impact that accounting estimates and methods have on the income that a firm reports. As you know, to comply with the matching rule, accountants must assign revenues and expenses to the periods in which they occur. If they cannot establish a direct relationship between revenues and expenses, they systematically allocate the expenses among the accounting periods that benefit from them, and in doing so, they must make estimates and exercise judgment. An accounting estimate should be based on realistic assumptions, but there is latitude in making the estimate, and the final judgment will affect the net income that appears on a company's income statement.

For example, when a company acquires an asset, the accountant must estimate the asset's useful life. Technological obsolescence could shorten the asset's expected useful life, and regular maintenance and repairs could lengthen it. Although the actual useful life cannot be known with certainty until some future date, the accountant's estimate of it affects both current and future operating income. Other areas that require accounting estimates include the residual value of assets, uncollectible accounts receivable, sales returns, total units of production, total recoverable units of natural resources, amortization periods, warranty claims, and environmental cleanup costs.

Study Note

Although companies in the same industry may have comparable earnings, their quality of earnings may not be comparable. To assess the quality of a company's reported earnings, you must know the estimates and methods it uses to compute income. Generally accepted accounting principles allow several methods, all yielding different results.

Accounting estimates are not equally important to all firms. Their importance depends on the industry in which a firm operates. For example, estimated uncollectible receivables for a credit card firm, such as **American Express**, or for a financial services firm, such as **Bank of America**, can have a material impact on earnings, but estimated useful life may be less important because depreciable assets represent only a small percentage of the firm's total assets. **Walgreens** has very few receivables, but it has substantial investments in depreciable assets. Thus, estimates of useful life and residual value are much more important to Walgreens than an estimate of uncollectible accounts receivable.

The accounting methods a firm uses also affect its operating income. Generally accepted accounting methods include uncollectible receivable methods (percentage of net sales and aging of accounts receivable), inventory methods (LIFO, FIFO, and average-cost), depreciation methods (accelerated, production, and straight-line), and revenue recognition methods. All these methods are designed to match revenues and expenses, but the expenses are estimates, and the period or periods benefited cannot be demonstrated conclusively. In practice, it is hard to justify one method of estimation over another.

Different accounting methods have different effects on net income. Some methods are more conservative than others because they tend to produce a lower net income in the current period. For example, suppose that two companies have similar operations, but one uses FIFO for inventory costing and the straight-line (SL) method for computing depreciation, whereas the other uses LIFO for inventory costing and the double-declining-balance (DDB) method for computing depreciation. The income statements of the two companies might appear as follows:

	FIFO and SL	*LIFO and DDB*
Net sales	$462,500	$462,500
Cost of goods available for sale	$200,000	$200,000
Less ending inventory	30,000	25,000
Cost of goods sold	$170,000	$175,000
Gross margin	$292,500	$287,500
Less depreciation expense	$ 20,000	$ 40,000
Less other expenses	85,000	85,000
Total operating expenses	$105,000	$125,000
Income from continuing operations before income taxes	$187,500	$162,500

The income from continuing operations before income taxes (operating income) for the firm that uses LIFO and DDB is lower because in periods of rising prices, the LIFO inventory costing method produces a higher cost of goods sold, and in the early years of an asset's useful life, accelerated depreciation yields a higher depreciation expense. The result is lower operating income. However, future operating income should be higher.

Although the choice of accounting method does not affect cash flows except for possible differences in income taxes, the $25,000 difference in operating income stems solely from the choice of accounting methods. Estimates of the useful lives and residual values of plant assets could lead to an even greater difference. In practice, of course, differences in net income occur for many reasons, but the user of financial statements must be aware of the discrepancies that can occur as a result of the accounting methods used in preparing the statements. In

FOCUS ON BUSINESS PRACTICE

Beware of the Bottom Line!

In the second quarter of 2007, **McDonald's** posted its second-ever loss: $711.7 million. Is this cause for concern? In fact, it is misleading: The company is actually in a period of rapidly growing revenues and profits. The loss resulted from a one-time, noncash impairment of $1.6 billion related to investments in Latin America. In another example, **Campbell Soup** showed unrealistically positive results in a recent year. Its income jumped by 31 percent due to a tax settlement and an accounting restatement. Without these items, its revenue and income would have been up less than 1 percent, and soup sales—its main product—actually dropped by 6 percent. The lesson to be learned is to look beyond the "bottom line" to the components of the income statement when evaluating a company's performance.[3]

general, an accounting method or estimate that results in lower current earnings produces a better quality of operating income.

The latitude that companies have in their choice of accounting methods and estimates could cause problems in the interpretation of financial statements were it not for the conventions of full disclosure and consistency. As noted in an earlier chapter, full disclosure requires management to explain the significant accounting policies used in preparing the financial statements in a note to the statements. Consistency requires that the same accounting procedures be followed from year to year. If a change in procedure is made, the nature of the change and its monetary effect must be explained in a note.

Gains and Losses

When a company sells or otherwise disposes of operating assets or marketable securities, a gain or loss generally results. Although these gains or losses appear in the operating section of the income statement, they usually represent one-time events. They are not sustainable, ongoing operations, and management often has some choice as to their timing. Thus, from an analyst's point of view, they should be ignored when considering operating income.

Write-Downs and Restructurings

Management has considerable latitude in deciding when an asset is no longer of value to the company. When management makes this judgment, a write-down or restructuring occurs.

- A **write-down**, also called a *write-off*, is a reduction in the value of an asset below its carrying value on the balance sheet.
- A **restructuring** is the estimated cost of a change in a company's operations. It usually involves the closing of facilities and the laying off of personnel.

Both write-downs and restructurings reduce current operating income and boost future income by shifting future costs to the current accounting period. They are often an indication of poor management decisions in the past, such as paying too much for the assets of another company or making operational changes that do not work out. Companies sometimes take all possible losses in the current year so that future years will be "clean" of these costs. Such "big baths," as they are called, commonly occur when a company is having a bad

FOCUS ON BUSINESS PRACTICE

Can You Believe "Pro Forma" Earnings?

Companies must report earnings in accordance with GAAP, but many also report "pro forma" earnings. Pro forma reporting of earnings, in the words of one analyst, means that they "have thrown out the bad stuff."[4] In other words, when companies report pro forma earnings, they are telling the investment community to ignore one-time losses and nonoperating items, which may reflect bad decisions in the past. In the late 1990s, technology firms with high growth rates and volatile or low earnings and firms that unexpectedly missed earnings targets widely relied on pro forma results. More recent research has shown that after the bubble burst in 2001–2002 and after the Enron collapse, the number of companies reporting pro forma earnings declined significantly.[5] The investment community learned that GAAP earnings are a better benchmark of a company's performance because they are based on recognized standards used by all companies, whereas there is no generally accepted way to report pro forma earnings. They are whatever the company wants you to see.

year. They also often occur in years when there is a change in management. The new management takes a "big bath" in the current year so it can show improved results in future years.

In a recent year, 35 percent of 600 large companies had write-downs of tangible assets, and 42 percent had restructurings. Another 12 percent had write-downs or charges related to intangible assets, often involving goodwill.[6]

Nonoperating Items

The nonoperating items that appear on the income statement include discontinued operations and extraordinary gains and losses, both of which can significantly affect net income. In Exhibit 14-1, earnings per common share for income from continuing operations is $2.81, but when all the nonoperating items are taken into consideration, net income per share is $3.35.

Discontinued operations are segments of a business, such as a separate major line of business or ones that serve a separate class of customer, that are no longer part of a company's operations. To make it easier to evaluate a company's ongoing operations, generally accepted accounting principles require that gains and losses from discontinued operations be reported separately on the income statement.

In Exhibit 14-1, the disclosure of discontinued operations has two parts. One part shows that after the decision to discontinue, the income from operations of the disposed segment was $180,000 (net of $70,000 taxes). The other part shows that the loss from the disposal of the segment was $146,000 (net of $84,000 tax savings). (The computation of the gains or losses involved in discontinued operations is covered in more advanced accounting courses.)

Extraordinary items are "events or transactions that are distinguished by their unusual nature *and* by the infrequency of their occurrence."[7] Items usually treated as extraordinary include the following:

1. An uninsured loss from flood, earthquake, fire, or theft
2. A gain or loss resulting from the passage of a new law
3. The expropriation (taking) of property by a foreign government

In Exhibit 14-1, the extraordinary gain was $74,000 after taxes of $24,000.

Assume the following data apply to Ace, Inc.: net sales, $180,000; cost of goods sold, $87,500; loss from discontinued operations (net of taxes of $17,500), $50,000; loss on disposal of discontinued operations (net of taxes of $4,000), $12,500; operating expenses, $32,500; income taxes expense on continuing operations, $25,000. From this information, prepare the company's income statement for the year ended December 31, 2011. (Ignore earnings per share information.)

SOLUTION

Ace, Inc.
Income Statement
For the Year Ended December 31, 2011

Net sales		$180,000
Cost of goods sold		87,500
Gross margin		$ 92,500
Operating expenses		32,500
Income from continuing operations before income taxes		$ 60,000
Income taxes expense		25,000
Income from continuing operations		$ 35,000
Discontinued operations		
Loss from discontinued operations (net of taxes, $17,500)	($50,000)	
Loss on disposal of discontinued operations (net of taxes, $4,000)	(12,500)	(62,500)
Net loss		($ 27,500)

Income Taxes

LO2 Show the relationships among income taxes expense, deferred income taxes, and net of taxes.

Corporations determine their taxable income (the amount on which they pay taxes) by deducting allowable expenses from taxable income. The federal tax laws determine which expenses corporations may deduct. (Rules for calculating and reporting taxable income in specialized industries, such as banking, insurance, mutual funds, and cooperatives, are highly technical and may vary significantly from the ones we discuss in this chapter.)

Table 14-1 shows the tax rates that apply to a corporation's taxable income. A corporation with taxable income of $70,000 would have a federal income tax liability of $12,500: $7,500 (the tax on the first $50,000 of taxable income) plus $5,000 (25 percent of the $20,000 earned in excess of $50,000).

Income taxes expense is recognized in the accounting records on an accrual basis. It may or may not equal the amount of taxes a corporation actually pays. The amount a corporation pays is determined by the rules of the income tax code. As we noted earlier in the text, small businesses often keep both their accounting records and tax records on a cash basis, so that the income taxes expense on their income statements equals their income taxes. This practice is accrual as long as the difference between the income calculated on an accrual basis and the income calculated for tax purposes is not material. However, the purpose of accounting is not to determine taxable income and tax liability, but to determine net income in accordance with GAAP.

Management has an incentive to use methods that minimize its firm's tax liability. But accountants, who are bound by accrual accounting and the materiality

> **Study Note**
> Many people think it is illegal to keep accounting records on a different basis from income tax records. However, the Internal Revenue Code and GAAP often do not agree. To work with two conflicting sets of guidelines, the accountant must keep two sets of records.

TABLE 14-1
Tax Rate Schedule for Corporations, 2008

Taxable Income		Tax Liability	
Over	But Not Over		Of the Amount Over
	$ 50,000	0 + 15%	—
$ 50,000	75,000	$ 7,500 + 25%	$ 50,000
75,000	100,000	13,750 + 34%	75,000
100,000	335,000	22,250 + 39%	100,000
335,000	10,000,000	113,900 + 34%	335,000
10,000,000	15,000,000	3,400,000 + 35%	10,000,000
15,000,000	18,333,333	5,150,000 + 38%	15,000,000
18,333,333	—	6,416,667 + 35%	18,333,333

Note: Tax rates are subject to change by Congress.

concept, cannot let tax procedures dictate their method of preparing financial statements if the result would be misleading. The difference between accounting income and taxable income, especially in large businesses, can be material. This discrepancy can result from differences in the timing of the recognition of revenues and expenses under accrual accounting and the tax method. The following table shows some possible variations:

	Accrual Accounting	*Tax Method*
Expense recognition	Accrual or deferral	At time of expenditure
Accounts receivable	Allowance	Direct charge-off
Inventories	Average-cost	FIFO
Depreciation	Straight-line	Accelerated cost recovery

Deferred Income Taxes

Study Note

The discrepancy between GAAP-based tax expense and Internal Revenue Code-based tax liability creates the need for the Deferred Income Taxes account.

Income tax allocation is the method used to accrue income taxes expense on the basis of accounting income when accounting income and taxable income differ. The account used to record the difference between income taxes expense and income taxes payable is called **Deferred Income Taxes**. For example, in the income statement in Exhibit 14-1, Vistula Corporation has income taxes expense of $289,000. Suppose, however, that Vistula's actual income taxes payable are $184,000. The following T account and entry show how income tax allocation would treat this situation:

A	=	L	+	SE
		−184,000		+289,000
		−105,000		

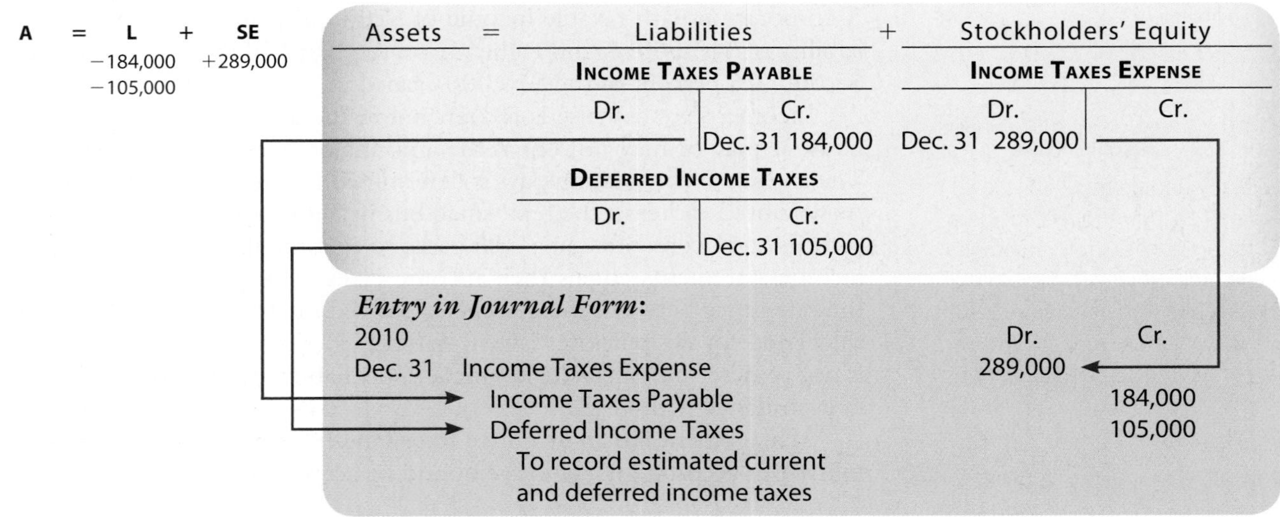

Study Note

Deferred Income Taxes is classified as a liability when it has a credit balance and as an asset when it has a debit balance. It is further classified as either current or long-term depending on when it is expected to reverse.

In other years, Vistula's Income Taxes Payable may exceed its Income Taxes Expense. In this case, the entry is the same except that Deferred Income Taxes is debited.

The Financial Accounting Standards Board has issued specific rules for recording, measuring, and classifying deferred income taxes.[8] Deferred income taxes are recognized for the estimated future tax effects resulting from temporary differences in the valuation of assets, liabilities, equity, revenues, expenses, gains, and losses for tax and financial reporting purposes. Temporary differences include revenues and expenses or gains and losses that are included in taxable income before or after they are included in financial income. In other words, the recognition point for revenues, expenses, gains, and losses is not the same for tax and financial reporting.

For example, advance payments for goods and services, such as magazine subscriptions, are not recognized as income until the products are shipped. However, for tax purposes, advance payments are usually recognized as revenue when cash is received. As a result, taxes paid exceed taxes expense, which creates a deferred income taxes asset (or prepaid taxes).

Classification of deferred income taxes as current or noncurrent depends on the classification of the asset or liability that created the temporary difference. For example, the deferred income taxes asset mentioned above would be classified as current if unearned subscription revenue were classified as a current liability. On the other hand, the temporary difference arising from depreciation is related to a long-term depreciable asset. Therefore, the resulting deferred income taxes would be classified as long-term. If a temporary difference is not related to an asset or liability, it is classified as current or noncurrent based on its expected date of reversal. (Temporary differences and the classification of deferred income taxes that results are covered in depth in more advanced courses.) Each year, the balance of the Deferred Income Taxes account is evaluated to determine whether it still accurately represents the expected asset or liability in light of legislated changes in income tax laws and regulations.

In any given year, the amount a company pays in income taxes is determined by subtracting (or adding) the deferred income taxes for that year from (or to) income taxes expense. In subsequent years, the amount of deferred income taxes can vary based on changes in tax laws and rates. A survey of the financial statements of 600 large companies indicates the importance of deferred income taxes to financial reporting. About 68 percent reported deferred income taxes with a credit balance in the long-term liability section of their balance sheets.[9]

Net of Taxes

The phrase **net of taxes** indicates that taxes (usually income taxes) have been taken into account in reporting an item in the financial statements. The phrase is used in a corporate income statement when a company has items that must be disclosed in a separate section. Each such item should be reported net of the applicable income taxes to avoid distorting the income taxes expense associated with ongoing operations and the resulting net operating income.

For example, assume that a corporation with operating income before income taxes of \$240,000 has a total tax expense of \$132,000 and that the total income includes a gain of \$200,000 on which a tax of \$60,000 is due. Also assume that the gain is not part of the corporation's normal operations and must be disclosed separately on the income statement as an extraordinary item. This is how the income taxes expense would be reported on the income statement:

Operating income before income taxes	$240,000
Income taxes expense	72,000
Income before extraordinary item	$168,000
Extraordinary gain (net of taxes, $60,000)	140,000
Net income	$308,000

If all the income taxes expense were deducted from operating income before income taxes, both the income before extraordinary item and the extraordinary gain would be distorted.

The procedure is the same in the case of an extraordinary loss. For example, given the same facts except that the income taxes expense is only $12,000 because of a $200,000 extraordinary loss, the result is a $60,000 tax savings:

Operating income before income taxes	$240,000
Income taxes expense	72,000
Income before extraordinary item	$168,000
Extraordinary loss (net of taxes, $60,000)	(140,000)
Net income	$ 28,000

In Exhibit 14-1, the total of the income tax items for Vistula Corporation is $299,000. That amount is allocated among five statement components, as follows:

Income taxes expense on income from continuing operations	$289,000
Income taxes on income from a discontinued segment	70,000
Income tax savings on the loss on the disposal of the segment	(84,000)
Income taxes on extraordinary gain	24,000
Total income taxes expense	$299,000

STOP & APPLY >

Jose Corporation reported the following accounting income before income taxes, income taxes expense, and net income for 2010 and 2011:

	2010	2011
Income before income taxes	$42,000	$42,000
Income taxes expense	13,245	13,245
Net income	$28,755	$28,755

On the balance sheet, deferred income taxes liability increased by $5,760 in 2010 and decreased by $2,820 in 2011.

1. How much was actually payable in income taxes for 2010 and 2011?
2. Prepare entries in journal form to record estimated current and deferred income taxes for 2010 and 2011.

SOLUTION

1. Income taxes calculated:

	2010	2011
Income taxes expense	$13,245	$13,245
Decrease (increase) in deferred income taxes	(5,760)	2,820
Income taxes payable	$ 7,485	$16,065

2. Entries prepared:

		Dr.	Cr.
2010	Income Taxes Expense	13,245	
	Deferred Income Taxes		5,760
	Income Taxes Payable		7,485
	To record estimated current and deferred income taxes for 2010		
2011	Income Taxes Expense	13,245	
	Deferred Income Taxes	2,820	
	Income Taxes Payable		16,065
	To record estimated current and deferred income taxes for 2011		

Earnings per Share

LO3 Compute earnings per share.

Study Note

Earnings per share is a measure of a corporation's profitability. It is one of the most closely watched financial ratios in the business world. Its disclosure on the income statement is required.

Readers of financial statements use earnings per share to judge a company's performance and to compare it with the performance of other companies. Because this information is so important, the Accounting Principles Board concluded that earnings per share of common stock should be presented on the face of the income statement.[10] As shown in Exhibit 14-1, this information is usually disclosed just below net income.

A corporate income statement always shows earnings per share for income from continuing operations and other major components of net income. For example, if a company has a gain or loss on discontinued operations or on extraordinary items, its income statement may present earnings per share amounts for the gain or loss.

Exhibit 14-2 shows how **Motorola**, the well-known manufacturer of telecommunications equipment, presents earnings per share on its income statement. As you can see, the statement covers three years, and discontinued operations had positive effects on earnings per share in two of the three years. However, the earnings per share for continuing operations is a better indicator of the company's future performance. The company is discontinuing some operations by

EXHIBIT 14-2 Motorola's Earnings per Share Presentation

	Years Ended December 31		
	2008	**2007**	**2006**
Earnings (loss) per common share:			
Basic:			
Continuing operations	($1.87)	($0.05)	$1.33
Discontinued operations	—	0.03	0.17
	($1.87)	($0.02)	$1.50
Diluted:			
Continuing operations	($1.87)	($0.05)	$1.30
Discontinued operations	—	0.03	0.16
	($1.87)	($0.02)	$1.46
Weighted averages common shares outstanding:			
Basic	2,265.40	2,312.70	2,446.30
Diluted	2,265.40	2,312.70	2,504.20

Source: Motorola, Inc., *Annual Report*, 2008.

selling or otherwise disposing of non-core divisions. Note that earnings per share are reported as basic and diluted.

Basic Earnings per Share

Basic earnings per share is the net income applicable to common stock divided by the weighted-average number of common shares outstanding. To compute this figure, one must determine if the number of common shares outstanding changed during the year and if the company paid dividends on preferred stock.

When a company has only common stock and the number of shares outstanding is the same throughout the year, the earnings per share computation is simple. Exhibit 14-1 shows that Vistula Corporation had net income of $669,000. If Vistula had 200,000 shares of common stock outstanding during the entire year, the earnings per share of common stock would be computed as follows:

$$\text{Earnings per Share} = \frac{\$669{,}000}{200{,}000\ \text{Shares}} = \$3.35^{*}\ \text{per Share}$$

If the number of shares outstanding changes during the year, it is necessary to figure the weighted-average number of shares outstanding for the year. Suppose that from January 1 to March 31, Vistula Corporation had 200,000 shares outstanding; from April 1 to September 30, it had 240,000 shares outstanding; and from October 31 to December 31, it had 260,000 shares outstanding. The weighted-average number of common shares outstanding and basic earnings per share would be determined this way:

200,000 shares × $^3/_{12}$ year	50,000
240,000 shares × $^6/_{12}$ year	120,000
260,000 shares × $^3/_{12}$ year	65,000
Weighted-average common shares outstanding	235,000

$$\text{Basic Earnings per Share} = \frac{\text{Net Income}}{\text{Weighted-Average Common Shares Outstanding}}$$

$$= \frac{\$669{,}000}{235{,}000\ \text{Shares}} = \$2.85\ \text{per Share}$$

If a company has nonconvertible preferred stock outstanding, the dividend for that stock must be subtracted from net income before earnings per share for common stock are computed. Suppose that Vistula Corporation has preferred stock on which it pays an annual dividend of $47,000. Earnings per share on common stock would be $2.65 [($669,000 − $47,000) ÷ 235,000 shares].

Diluted Earnings per Share

Companies can have a simple capital structure or a complex capital structure.

- A company has a **simple capital structure** if it has no preferred stocks, bonds, or stock options that can be converted to common stock. A company with a simple capital structure computes earnings per share as shown above.
- A company that has issued securities or stock options that can be converted to common stock has a **complex capital structure**. These securities and options have the potential of diluting the earnings per share of common stock.

*This number is rounded, as are some other results of computations that follow.

Potential dilution means that the conversion of stocks or bonds or the exercise of stock options can increase the total number of shares of common stock that a company has outstanding and thereby reduce a current stockholder's proportionate share of ownership in the company. For example, suppose that a person owns 10,000 shares of a company's common stock, which equals 2 percent of the outstanding shares of 500,000. Now suppose that holders of convertible bonds convert the bonds into 100,000 shares of stock. The person's 10,000 shares would then equal only 1.67 percent (10,000 ÷ 600,000) of the outstanding shares. In addition, the added shares outstanding would lower earnings per share and would most likely lower market price per share.

When a company has a complex capital structure, it must report two earnings per share figures: basic earnings per share and diluted earnings per share.[11] **Diluted earnings per share** are calculated by adding all potentially dilutive securities to the denominator of the basic earnings per share calculation. This figure shows stockholders the maximum potential effect of dilution on their ownership position. As you can see in Exhibit 14-2, the dilution effect for **Motorola** is not large, only 4 cents per share in 2006 ($1.50 − $1.46) and none in 2007 or 2008, because the company's only dilutive securities are a relatively few stock options.

STOP & APPLY >

During 2011, Sasha Corporation reported a net income of $1,529,500. On January 1, 2011, Sasha had 350,000 shares of common stock outstanding, and it issued an additional 210,000 shares of common stock on October 1. The company has a simple capital structure.

1. Determine the weighted-average number of common shares outstanding.
2. Compute earnings per share.

SOLUTION

1. Weighted-average number of common shares outstanding:

350,000 shares × $^{9}/_{12}$	262,500
560,000 shares × $^{3}/_{12}$	140,000
Weighted-average number of common shares outstanding	402,500

2. Earnings per share:
$1,529,500 ÷ 402,500 shares = $3.80

Comprehensive Income and the Statement of Stockholders' Equity

LO4 Define *comprehensive income*, and describe the statement of stockholders' equity.

The concept of comprehensive income and the statement of stockholders' equity provide further explanation of the income statement and the balance sheet and serve as links between those two statements.

Comprehensive Income

Some items that are not stock transactions affect stockholders' equity. These items, which come from sources other than stockholders and that account for the change in a company's equity during an accounting period, are called **comprehensive income**. Comprehensive income includes net income, changes in unrealized investment gains and losses, and other items affecting equity, such as foreign currency translation adjustments. The FASB takes the position that these changes in stockholders' equity should be summarized as income for a period.[12] Companies

EXHIBIT 14-3 eBay's Statement of Comprehensive Income

	Years Ended December 31		
(In thousands)	**2008**	**2007**	**2006**
Net income	$1,779,474	$ 348,251	$1,125,639
Other comprehensive income			
Foreign currency translation	(553,490)	645,202	588,150
Unrealized gains (losses) on investments, net	(464,171)	589,566	8,327
Unrealized gains (losses) on cash flow hedges	40,522	(175)	(194)
Estimated tax provision on above items	179,348	(229,514)	(3,216)
Net change in other comprehensive income	($ 797,791)	$1,005,079	$ 593,097
Comprehensive income	$ 981,683	$1,353,330	$1,718,706

Source: eBay Inc., *Annual Report*, 2008.

may report comprehensive income and its components in a separate financial statement, as **eBay** does in Exhibit 14-3, or as a part of another financial statement.

In a recent survey of 600 large companies, 579 reported comprehensive income. Of these, 83 percent reported comprehensive income in the statement of stockholders' equity, 13 percent reported it in a separate statement, and only 4 percent reported it in the income statement.[13] In Exhibit 14-4, we follow the most common practice and show it as a part of the statement of stockholders' equity.

EXHIBIT 14-4 Statement of Stockholders' Equity

Crisanti Corporation
Statement of Stockholders' Equity
For the Year Ended December 31, 2010

	Preferred Stock $100 Par Value 8% Convertible	Common Stock $10 Par Value	Additional Paid-in Capital	Retained Earnings	Treasury Stock	Accumulated Other Comprehensive Income	Total
Balance, December 31, 2009	$ 800,000	$600,000	$ 600,000	$1,200,000			$3,200,000
Net income				540,000			540,000
Foreign currency translation adjustment						($20,000)	(20,000)
Issuance of 10,000 shares of common stock		100,000	400,000				500,000
Conversion of 2,000 shares of preferred stock to 6,000 shares of common stock	(200,000)	60,000	140,000				—
10 percent stock dividend on common stock, 7,600 shares		76,000	304,000	(380,000)			—
Purchase of 1,000 shares of treasury stock					($48,000)		(48,000)
Cash dividends							
Preferred stock				(48,000)			(48,000)
Common stock				(95,200)			(95,200)
Balance, December 31, 2010	$ 600,000	$836,000	$1,444,000	$1,216,800	($48,000)	($20,000)	$4,028,800

The Statement of Stockholders' Equity

Study Note

The statement of stockholders' equity is a labeled calculation of the change in each stockholders' equity account over an accounting period.

The **statement of stockholders' equity**, also called the *statement of changes in stockholders' equity*, summarizes changes in the components of the stockholders' equity section of the balance sheet. Most companies use this statement in place of the statement of retained earnings because it reveals much more about the stockholders' equity transactions that took place during the accounting period.

For example, in Crisanti Corporation's statement of stockholders' equity in Exhibit 14-4, the first line shows the beginning balance of each account in the stockholders' equity section of the balance sheet. Each subsequent line discloses the effects of transactions on those accounts. Crisanti had a net income of $540,000 and a foreign currency translation loss of $20,000, which it reported as accumulated other comprehensive income. These two items together resulted in comprehensive income of $520,000.

Study Note

The ending balances on the statement of stockholders' equity are transferred to the stockholders' equity section of the balance sheet.

Crisanti's statement of stockholders' equity also shows that during 2010, the firm issued 10,000 shares of common stock for $500,000, had a conversion of $200,000 of preferred stock to common stock, declared and issued a 10 percent stock dividend on common stock, purchased treasury stock for $48,000, and paid cash dividends on both preferred and common stock. The ending balances of the accounts appear at the bottom of the statement. Those accounts and balances make up the stockholders' equity section of Crisanti's balance sheet on December 31, 2010, as shown in Exhibit 14-5.

Retained Earnings

The Retained Earnings column in Exhibit 14-4 has the same components as the statement of retained earnings. As we explained earlier in the text, **retained earnings** represent stockholders' claims to assets that arise from the earnings of the business. Retained earnings equal a company's profits since its inception, minus any losses, dividends to stockholders, or transfers to contributed capital.

It is important to remember that retained earnings are not the assets themselves. The existence of retained earnings means that assets generated by profitable

EXHIBIT 14-5 Stockholders' Equity Section of a Balance Sheet

Crisanti Corporation
Balance Sheet
December 31, 2010

Stockholders' Equity		
Contributed capital		
Preferred stock, $100 par value, 8 percent convertible, 20,000 shares authorized, 6,000 shares issued and outstanding		$ 600,000
Common stock, $10 par value, 200,000 shares authorized, 83,600 shares issued, 82,600 shares outstanding	$ 836,000	
Additional paid-in capital	1,444,000	2,280,000
Total contributed capital		$2,880,000
Retained earnings		1,216,800
Total contributed capital and retained earnings		$4,096,800
Less: Treasury stock, common (1,000 shares, at cost)	$ 48,000	
Foreign currency translation adjustment	20,000	68,000
Total stockholders' equity		$4,028,800

> **Study Note**
> A *deficit* is a negative (debit) balance in Retained Earnings. It is not the same as a net loss, which reflects a firm's performance in just one accounting period.

operations have been kept in the company to help it grow or meet other business needs. A credit balance in Retained Earnings is *not* directly associated with a specific amount of cash or designated assets. Rather, it means that assets as a whole have increased.

Retained Earnings can have a debit balance. Generally, this happens when a company's dividends and subsequent losses are greater than its accumulated profits from operations. In this case, the company is said to have a **deficit** (debit balance) in Retained Earnings. A deficit is shown in the stockholders' equity section of the balance sheet as a deduction from contributed capital.

STOP & APPLY >

Indicate which of the following items would appear on the statement of stockholders' equity:

a. Preferred stock cash dividends
b. Loss on disposal of segment
c. Issuance of common stock
d. Stock dividend
e. Income tax expense
f. Purchase of treasury stock
g. Income from continuing operations
h. Net income
i. Accumulated other comprehensive income

SOLUTION

a, c, d, f, h, i

Stock Dividends and Stock Splits

LO5 Account for stock dividends and stock splits.

Two transactions that commonly modify the content of stockholders' equity are stock dividends and stock splits. In the discussion that follows, we describe how to account for both kinds of transactions.

Stock Dividends

A **stock dividend** is a proportional distribution of shares among a corporation's stockholders. Unlike a cash dividend, a stock dividend involves no distribution of assets, and so it has no effect on a firm's assets or liabilities. A board of directors may declare a stock dividend for the following reasons:

1. It may want to give stockholders some evidence of the company's success without affecting working capital, which would be the case if it paid a cash dividend.
2. It may want to reduce the stock's market price by increasing the number of shares outstanding. (This goal is, however, more often met by a stock split.)
3. It may want to make a nontaxable distribution to stockholders. Stock dividends that meet certain conditions are not considered income and are therefore not taxed.
4. It may want to increase the company's permanent capital by transferring an amount from retained earnings to contributed capital.

> **Study Note**
> The declaration of a stock dividend results in a reshuffling of stockholders' equity—that is, a portion of retained earnings is converted to contributed capital. Total stockholders' equity is not affected.

> **Study Note**
>
> For a small stock dividend, the portion of retained earnings transferred is determined by multiplying the number of shares to be distributed by the stock's market price on the declaration date.

A stock dividend does not affect total stockholders' equity. Basically, it transfers a dollar amount from retained earnings to contributed capital. The amount transferred is the fair market value (usually, the market price) of the additional shares that the company issues. The laws of most states specify the minimum value of each share transferred, which is normally the minimum legal capital (par or stated value). When stock distributions are small—less than 20 to 25 percent of a company's outstanding common stock—generally accepted accounting principles hold that market value reflects their economic effect better than par or stated value. For this reason, market price should be used to account for small stock dividends.[14]

To illustrate how to account for a stock dividend, suppose that stockholders' equity in Rivera Corporation is as follows:

Contributed capital	
Common stock, $5 par value, 50,000 shares authorized, 15,000 shares issued and outstanding	$ 75,000
Additional paid-in capital	15,000
Total contributed capital	$ 90,000
Retained earnings	450,000
Total stockholders' equity	$540,000

Now suppose that on February 24, the market price of Rivera's stock is $20 per share, and on that date, its board of directors declares a 10 percent stock dividend to be distributed on March 31 to stockholders of record on March 15. No entry is needed for the date of record (March 15). The T accounts and entries for the declaration and distribution of the stock dividend are as follows:

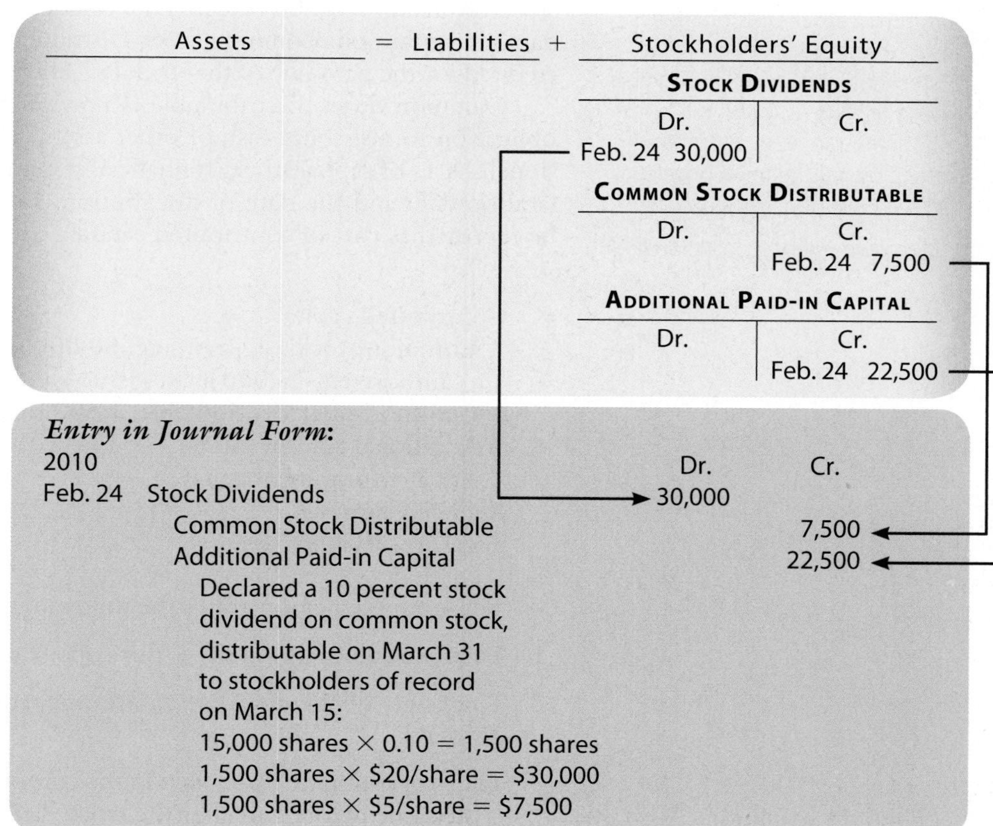

Entry in Journal Form:

2010		Dr.	Cr.
Feb. 24	Stock Dividends	30,000	
	Common Stock Distributable		7,500
	Additional Paid-in Capital		22,500
	Declared a 10 percent stock dividend on common stock, distributable on March 31 to stockholders of record on March 15: 15,000 shares × 0.10 = 1,500 shares; 1,500 shares × $20/share = $30,000; 1,500 shares × $5/share = $7,500		

Declaration Date

A	=	L	+	SE
				−30,000
				+ 7,500
				+22,500

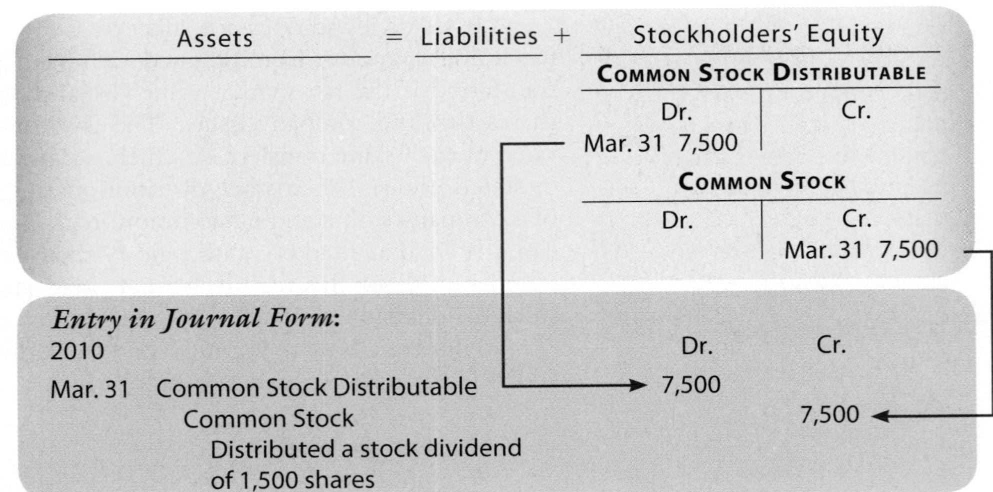

Distribution Date

A = L + SE
−7,500
+7,500

Entry in Journal Form:

2010		Dr.	Cr.
Mar. 31	Common Stock Distributable	7,500	
	Common Stock		7,500
	Distributed a stock dividend of 1,500 shares		

This stock dividend permanently transfers the market value of the stock, $30,000, from retained earnings to contributed capital and increases the number of shares outstanding by 1,500. The Stock Dividends account is used to record the total amount of the stock dividend. When the Stock Dividends account is closed to Retained Earnings at the end of the accounting period, Retained Earnings is reduced by the amount of the stock dividend. Common Stock Distributable is credited for the par value of the stock to be distributed (1,500 × $5 = $7,500).

In addition, when the market value is greater than the par value of the stock, the Additional Paid-in Capital account must be credited for the amount by which the market value exceeds the par value. In our example, the total market value of the stock dividend ($30,000) exceeds the total par value ($7,500) by $22,500. On the date of distribution, Common Stock Distributable is debited and Common Stock is credited for the par value of the stock ($7,500).

Study Note

Common Stock Distributable is a contributed capital (stockholders' equity) account, not a liability account. When the shares are issued, Common Stock Distributable is converted to the Common Stock account.

Common Stock Distributable is not a liability account because there is no obligation to distribute cash or other assets. The obligation is to distribute additional shares of capital stock. If financial statements are prepared between the declaration date and the date of distribution, Common Stock Distributable should be reported as part of contributed capital:

Contributed capital	
Common stock, $5 par value, 50,000 shares authorized, 15,000 shares issued and outstanding	$ 75,000
Common stock distributable, 1,500 shares	7,500
Additional paid-in capital	37,500
Total contributed capital	$120,000
Retained earnings	420,000
Total stockholders' equity	$540,000

This example demonstrates the following points:

1. Total stockholders' equity is the same before and after the stock dividend.
2. The assets of the corporation are not reduced, as they would be by a cash dividend.
3. The proportionate ownership in the corporation of any individual stockholder is the same before and after the stock dividend.

To illustrate these points, suppose a stockholder owns 500 shares before the stock dividend. After the 10 percent stock dividend is distributed, this stockholder would own 550 shares, as shown below:

	Stockholders' Equity	
	Before Dividend	**After Dividend**
Common stock	$ 75,000	$ 82,500
Additional paid-in capital	15,000	37,500
Total contributed capital	$ 90,000	$120,000
Retained earnings	450,000	420,000
Total stockholders' equity	$ 540,000	$540,000
Shares outstanding	15,000	16,500
Stockholders' equity per share	$ 36.00	$ 32.73

	Stockholders' Investment	
Shares owned	500	550
Shares outstanding	15,000	16,500
Percentage of ownership	3⅓%	3⅓%
Proportionate investment ($540,000 × 3⅓%)	$ 18,000	$ 8,000

Both before and after the stock dividend, stockholders' equity totals $540,000, and the stockholder owns 3⅓ percent of the company. The proportionate investment (stockholders' equity times percentage of ownership) remains at $18,000.

> **Study Note**
> When a stock dividend greater than 20 to 25 percent is declared, the transfer from retained earnings is based on the stock's par or stated value, not on its market value.

All stock dividends have an effect on the market price of a company's stock. But some stock dividends are so large that they have a material effect. For example, a 50 percent stock dividend would cause the market price of the stock to drop about 33 percent because the increase is now one-third of shares outstanding. The AICPA has decided that large stock dividends—those greater than 20 to 25 percent—should be accounted for by transferring the par or stated value of the stock on the declaration date from retained earnings to contributed capital.[15]

Stock Splits

> **Study Note**
> Stock splits and stock dividends reduce earnings per share because they increase the number of shares issued and outstanding. Cash dividends have no effect on earnings per share.

A **stock split** occurs when a corporation increases the number of shares of stock issued and outstanding, and reduces the par or stated value proportionally. A company may plan a stock split when it wants to lower its stock's market value per share and increase the demand for the stock at this lower price. It may do so if the market price has become so high that it hinders the trading of the stock or if it wants to signal to the market its success in achieving its operating goals.

Nike achieved these strategic objectives in a recent year by declaring a 2-for-1 stock split and increasing its cash dividend.[16] After the stock split, the number of the company's outstanding shares doubled, thereby cutting the share price from about $80 per share to $40 per share. The stock split left each stockholder's total wealth unchanged but increased the income stockholders received from dividends. The stock split was a sign that Nike has continued to do well.

To illustrate a stock split, suppose that MUI Corporation has 15,000 shares of $5.00 par value stock outstanding and the market value is $70.00 per share. The corporation plans a 2-for-1 split. This split will lower the par value to $2.50 and increase the number of shares outstanding to 30,000. A stockholder who previously owned 200 shares of the $5.00 par value stock would own 400 shares of the $2.50 par value stock after the split. When a stock split occurs,

FOCUS ON BUSINESS PRACTICE

Do Stock Splits Help Increase a Company's Market Price?

Stock splits tend to follow the market. When the market went up dramatically in 1998, 1999, and 2000, there were record numbers of stock splits—more than 1,000 per year. At the height of the market in early 2000, stock splitters included such diverse companies as **Alcoa, Apple Computer, Chase Manhattan, Intel, NVIDIA, Juniper Networks,** and **Tiffany & Co.** Some analysts liken stock splits to the air a chef whips into a mousse: It doesn't make it any sweeter, just frothier. There is no fundamental reason a stock should go up because of a stock split. When **Rambus Inc.**, a developer of high-speed memory technology, announced a 4-for-1 split on March 10, 2000, its stock rose more than 50 percent, to $471 per share.[17] But when the market deflated in 2001, its stock dropped to less than $10 per share. Research shows that stock splits have no long-term effect on stock prices.

the market value tends to fall in proportion to the increase in outstanding shares of stock. For example, MUI's 2-for-1 stock split would cause the price of its stock to drop by approximately 50 percent, to about $35.00. It would also halve earnings per share and cash dividends per share (unless the board increased the dividend). The lower price and increase in shares tend to promote the buying and selling of shares.

A stock split does not increase the number of shares authorized, nor does it change the balances in the stockholders' equity section of the balance sheet. It simply changes the par value and number of shares issued, both shares outstanding and treasury stock. Thus, an entry is unnecessary. However, it is appropriate to document the change with a memorandum entry in the general journal. For example:

July 15 The 15,000 shares of $5 par value common stock issued and outstanding were split 2 for 1, resulting in 30,000 shares of $2.50 par value common stock issued and outstanding.

The change for MUI Corporation is as follows:

Before Stock Split

Contributed capital	
Common stock, $5 par value, 50,000 shares authorized; 15,000 shares issued and outstanding	$ 75,000
Additional paid-in capital	15,000
Total contributed capital	$ 90,000
Retained earnings	450,000
Total stockholders' equity	$540,000

Study Note

A stock split affects only the calculation of common stock. In this case, there are twice as many shares after the split, but par value is half of what it was.

After Stock Split

Contributed capital	
Common stock, $2.50 par value, 50,000 shares authorized, 30,000 shares issued and outstanding	$ 75,000
Additional paid-in capital	15,000
Total contributed capital	$ 90,000
Retained earnings	450,000
Total stockholders' equity	$540,000

Although the per share amount of stockholders' equity is half as much after the split, the stockholder's proportionate interest in the company remains the same. Thus, a stockholder's wealth and ownership interest in the company are not materially affected by a stock split.

If the number of split shares will exceed the number of authorized shares, the corporation's board of directors must secure state and stockholders' approval before it can issue the additional shares.

STOP & APPLY >

Abbie Corporation's board of directors declared a 2 percent stock dividend applicable to the outstanding shares of its $10 par value common stock, of which 1,000,000 shares are authorized, 300,000 are issued, and 100,000 are held in the treasury. It then declared a 2-for-1 stock split on issued shares. How many authorized, issued, and treasury shares existed after each of these transactions? What is the par value per share?

SOLUTION

Stock dividend applies to outstanding shares:
(300,000 shares − 100,000 shares) × 0.02 = 4,000 shares

Stock split applies to all issued shares:
304,000 shares × 2 = 608,000 shares

Authorized shares are unchanged (1,000,000, but par value is now $5 per share); issued shares are 608,000; and outstanding shares are 408,000 (400,000 + 8,000)

Book Value

LO6 Calculate book value per share.

The word *value* is associated with shares of stock in several ways. Par value or stated value is set when the stock is authorized, and it establishes a company's legal capital. Neither par value nor stated value has any relationship to a stock's book value or market value. The **book value** of stock represents a company's total assets less its liabilities. It is simply the stockholders' equity in a company or, to put it another way, it represents a company's net assets. The **book value per share** is therefore the equity of the owner of one share of stock in the net assets of a company. That value, of course, generally does not equal the amount a stockholder receives if the company is sold or liquidated because in most cases, assets are recorded at historical cost, not at their current market value. Book value per share is often used as a guide for stock transactions by private companies for which there is no ready market for the company's stock.

If a company has only common stock outstanding, book value per share is calculated by dividing stockholders' equity by the number of common shares outstanding. Common stock distributable is included in the number of shares outstanding, but treasury stock is not. For example, if a firm has total stockholders' equity of $2,060,000 and 58,000 shares outstanding, the book value per share of its common stock would be $35.52 ($2,060,000 ÷ 58,000 shares).

If a company has both preferred and common stock, determining the book value per share is not so simple. Generally, the preferred stock's call value (or par value, if a call value is not specified) and any dividends in arrears are subtracted from stockholders' equity to determine the equity pertaining to common stock.

As an illustration, refer to the stockholders' equity section of Crisanti Corporation's balance sheet in Exhibit 14-5. If Crisanti has no dividends in arrears and its preferred stock is callable at $105, the equity pertaining to its common stock would be calculated as follows:

Total stockholders' equity	$4,028,800
Less equity allocated to preferred stockholders (6,000 shares × $105)	630,000
Equity pertaining to common stockholders	$3,398,800

As indicated in Exhibit 14-5, Crisanti has 82,600 shares of common stock outstanding (83,600 shares issued less 1,000 shares of treasury stock). Its book values per share are computed as follows:

Preferred stock: $630,000 ÷ 6,000 shares = $105 per share
Common stock: $3,398,800 ÷ 82,600 shares = $41.15 per share

If we assume the same facts except that Crisanti's preferred stock is 8 percent cumulative and that one year of dividends is in arrears, the stockholders' equity would be allocated as follows:

Total stockholders' equity		$4,028,800
Less call value of outstanding preferred shares	$630,000	
Dividends in arrears ($600,000 × 0.08)	48,000	
Equity allocated to preferred stockholders		678,000
Equity pertaining to common stockholders		$3,350,800

The book values per share would then be as follows:

Preferred stock: $678,000 ÷ 6,000 shares = $113 per share
Common stock: $3,350,800 ÷ 82,600 shares = $40.57 per share

STOP & APPLY >

Using the data from the stockholders' equity section of Park Corporation's balance sheet shown below, compute the book value per share for both the preferred and common stock.

Contributed capital	
Preferred stock, $100 par value, 6 percent cumulative, 20,000 shares authorized, 2,000 shares issued and outstanding*	$ 200,000
Common stock, $5 par value, 200,000 shares authorized, 100,000 shares issued and outstanding	500,000
Additional paid-in capital	300,000
Total contributed capital	$1,000,000
Retained earnings	500,000
Total stockholders' equity	$1,500,000

* The preferred stock is callable at $104 per share, and one year's dividends are in arrears.

SOLUTION

Preferred stock book value per share:
$104 + $6 = $110

Common stock book value per share:
[$1,500,000 − (2,000 preferred shares × $110)] ÷ 100,000 common shares = $12.80

▶ KOWALSKI, INC.: REVIEW PROBLEM

Stock Transactions and Stockholders' Equity
LO4 LO5 LO6

In the Decision Point at the beginning of this chapter, we noted that just after Kowalski, Inc.'s fiscal year ended on June 30, 2010, Walter Kowalski, the company's CEO, was deliberating about the following questions regarding stockholders' equity:

- Should Kowalski, Inc., declare a stock split?
- Should the company raise capital by issuing preferred stock?
- Should the company pay cash dividends or use cash to buy back its own stock?

The following transactions show how the company responded to these questions during the fiscal year that ended on June 30, 2011.

a. The board of directors declared a 2-for-1 stock split.

b. The board of directors obtained authorization to issue 25,000 shares of $100 par value, 6 percent noncumulative preferred stock, callable at $104.

c. The company issued 6,000 shares of common stock for a building appraised at $48,000.

d. It bought back 4,000 shares of its common stock for $32,000.

e. It issued 10,000 shares of preferred stock for $100 per share.

f. It sold 2,500 shares of treasury stock for $17,500.

g. It declared cash dividends of $6 per share on preferred stock and $0.20 per share on common stock.

h. It declared a 10 percent stock dividend on common stock to be distributed after the end of the fiscal year. The market value was $10 per share.

i. It closed net income for the year, $170,000.

j. It closed the Dividends and Stock Dividends accounts to Retained Earnings.

Required

1. Using the data presented in the Decision Point and the data in the list above, record the stockholders' equity components of the preceding transactions in T accounts. Indicate when there is no entry.
2. Using the data presented in the Decision Point and the data in the list above, prepare the stockholders' equity section of the company's balance sheet on June 30, 2011.
3. User insight: Compute the book values per share of common stock on June 30, 2010 and 2011, and of preferred stock on June 30, 2011, using the end-of-year shares outstanding. If Kowalski's stock is not traded in any market, how can the value of the stock be measured?

Answers to Review Problem

1. Entries in T accounts:

   a. No entry (memorandum in journal)

   b. No entry (memorandum in journal)

Preferred Stock

		e.	1,000,000

Common Stock

		Beg. Bal.	750,000
		c.	18,000
		End. Bal.	**768,000**

Common Stock Distributable

		h.	76,350

Additional Paid-in Capital

		Beg. Bal.	410,000
		c.	30,000
		h.	178,150
		End. Bal.	**618,150**

Retained Earnings

f.	2,500	Beg. Bal.	485,000
j.	365,400	i.	170,000
		End. Bal.	**287,100**

Treasury Stock

d.	32,000	f.	20,000
End. Bal.	**12,000**		

Cash Dividends

g.	110,900*	j.	110,900

Stock Dividends

h.	254,000**	j.	254,500

*10,000 × $6 = $ 60,000
254,500 × $0.20 = 50,900
$110,900

**254,500 shares × 0.10 × $10 = $254,500

2. Stockholders' equity section of the balance sheet:

Kowalski, Inc.
Balance Sheet
June 30, 2011

Stockholders' Equity

Contributed capital		
Preferred stock, $100 par value, 6 percent noncumulative, 25,000 shares authorized, 10,000 shares issued and outstanding		$1,000,000
Common stock, no par value, $3 stated value, 500,000 shares authorized, 256,000 shares issued, 254,500 shares outstanding	$768,000	
Common stock distributable, 25,450 shares	76,350	
Additional paid-in capital	618,150	1,462,500
Total contributed capital		$2,462,500
Retained earnings		287,100
Total contributed capital and retained earnings		$2,749,600
Less treasury stock (1,500 shares, at cost)		12,000
Total stockholders' equity		$2,737,600

3. Book values:

   June 30, 2010
   Common Stock: $1,645,000 ÷ 125,000 shares = $13.16 per share
   June 30, 2011
   Preferred Stock: Call price of $104 per share equals book value per share
   Common Stock:
   ($2,737,600 − $1,040,000) ÷ (254,500 shares + 25,450 shares)
   $1,697,600 ÷ 279,950 shares = $6.06 per share*

   *Rounded.

When there is no ready market for a company's common or preferred stock, book value per share is often used as a guide for determining the stock's value.

LO1 Define *quality of earnings,* and identify the components of a corporate income statement.

The quality of earnings refers to the substance of earnings and their sustainability into future accounting periods. The quality of a company's earnings may be affected by the accounting methods and estimates it uses and by the gains and losses, write-downs and restructurings, and nonoperating items that it reports on its income statement.

When a company has both continuing and discontinued operations, the operating income section of its income statement is called income from continuing operations. Income from continuing operations before income taxes is affected by choices of accounting methods and estimates and may contain gains and losses on the sale of assets, write-downs, and restructurings. The income taxes expense section of the statement is subject to special accounting rules. The lower part of the statement may contain such nonoperating items as discontinued operations and extraordinary gains and losses. Earnings per share information appears at the bottom of the statement.

LO2 Show the relationships among income taxes expense, deferred income taxes, and net of taxes.

Income taxes expense is the tax applicable to income from operations on an accrual basis. Income tax allocation is necessary when there is a material difference between accrual-based accounting income and taxable income—that is, between the income taxes expense reported on the income statement and actual income tax liability. The difference between income taxes expense and income taxes payable is debited or credited to an account called Deferred Income Taxes. The phrase *net of taxes* indicates that taxes have been taken into account in reporting an item in the financial statements.

LO3 Compute earnings per share.

Readers of financial statements use earnings per share to evaluate a company's performance and to compare it with the performance of other companies. Earnings per share of common stock are presented on the face of the income statement. The amounts are computed by dividing the income applicable to common stock by the number of common shares outstanding for the year. If the number of shares outstanding varied during the year, the weighted-average number of common shares outstanding is used in the computation. A company that has a complex capital structure must disclose both basic and diluted earnings per share on the face of its income statement.

LO4 Define *comprehensive income,* and describe the statement of stockholders' equity.

Comprehensive income includes all items from sources other than stockholders that account for changes in stockholders' equity during an accounting period. The statement of stockholders' equity summarizes changes over the period in each component of the stockholders' equity section of the balance sheet. This statement reveals much more than the statement of retained earnings does about the transactions that affect stockholders' equity.

LO5 Account for stock dividends and stock splits.

A stock dividend is a proportional distribution of shares among a corporation's stockholders. The following is a summary of the key dates and accounting treatments of stock dividends:

Key Date	Stock Dividend
Declaration date	Debit Stock Dividends for the market value of the stock to be distributed (if the stock dividend is small), and credit Common Stock Distributable for the stock's par value and Additional Paid-in Capital for the excess of the market value over the stock's par value.

Key Date	Stock Dividend
Record date	No entry is needed.
Date of distribution	Debit Common Stock Distributable and credit Common Stock for the par value of the stock.

A company usually declares a stock split to reduce the market value of its stock and thereby improve the demand for the stock. Because the par value of the stock normally decreases in proportion to the number of additional shares issued, a stock split has no effect on the dollar amount in stockholders' equity. A stock split does not require an entry, but a memorandum entry in the general journal is appropriate.

LO6 Calculate book value per share.

Book value per share is stockholders' equity per share. It is calculated by dividing stockholders' equity by the number of common shares outstanding. When a company has both preferred and common stock, the call or par value of the preferred stock and any dividends in arrears are deducted from stockholders' equity before dividing by the common shares outstanding.

REVIEW of Concepts and Terminology

The following concepts and terms were introduced in this chapter:

Book value 635 (LO6)

Complex capital structure 626 (LO3)

Comprehensive income 627 (LO4)

Deferred Income Taxes 622 (LO2)

Deficit 630 (LO4)

Discontinued operations 620 (LO1)

Extraordinary items 620 (LO1)

Income from continuing operations 616 (LO1)

Income tax allocation 622 (LO2)

Net of taxes 623 (LO2)

Quality of earnings 616 (LO1)

Restructuring 619 (LO1)

Retained earnings 629 (LO4)

Simple capital structure 626 (LO3)

Statement of stockholders' equity 629 (LO4)

Stock dividend 630 (LO5)

Stock split 633 (LO5)

Write-down 619 (LO1)

Key Ratios

Basic earnings per share 626 (LO3)

Book value per share 635 (LO6)

Diluted earnings per share 627 (LO3)

CHAPTER ASSIGNMENTS

BUILDING Your Basic Knowledge and Skills

Short Exercises

LO1 **Quality of Earnings**

SE 1. Each of the items listed below is a quality of earnings issue. Indicate whether the item is (a) an accounting method, (b) an accounting estimate, or (c) a non-operating item. For any item for which the answer is (a) or (b), indicate which alternative is usually the more conservative choice.

1. LIFO versus FIFO
2. Extraordinary loss
3. 10-year useful life versus 15-year useful life
4. Straight-line versus accelerated method
5. Discontinued operations
6. Immediate write-off versus amortization
7. Increase versus decrease in percentage of uncollectible accounts

LO1 **Corporate Income Statement**

SE 2. Assume that Jefferson Corporation's chief financial officer gave you the following information: net sales, $360,000; cost of goods sold, $175,000; loss from discontinued operations (net of income tax benefit of $35,000), $100,000; loss on disposal of discontinued operations (net of income tax benefit of $8,000), $25,000; operating expenses, $65,000; income taxes expense on continuing operations, $50,000. From this information, prepare the company's income statement for the year ended June 30, 2011. (Ignore earnings per share information.)

LO2 **Corporate Income Tax Rate Schedule**

SE 3. Using the corporate tax rate schedule in Table 14-1, compute the income tax liability for taxable income of (1) $800,000 and (2) $40,000,000.

LO3 **Earnings per Share**

SE 4. During 2010, Wells Corporation reported a net income of $1,338,400. On January 1, Wells had 720,000 shares of common stock outstanding. The company issued an additional 480,000 shares of common stock on August 1. In 2010, the company had a simple capital structure. During 2011, there were no transactions involving common stock, and the company reported net income of $1,740,000. Determine the weighted-average number of common shares outstanding for 2010 and 2011. Also compute earnings per share for 2010 and 2011.

LO4 **Statement of Stockholders' Equity**

SE 5. Refer to the statement of stockholders' equity for Crisanti Corporation in Exhibit 14-4 to answer the following questions: (1) At what price per share were the 10,000 shares of common stock sold? (2) What was the conversion price per share of the common stock? (3) At what price was the common stock selling on the date of the stock dividend? (4) At what price per share was the treasury stock purchased?

LO4 LO5 **Effects of Stockholders' Equity Actions**

SE 6. Tell whether each of the following actions will increase, decrease, or have no effect on total assets, total liabilities, and total stockholders' equity:

1. Declaration of a stock dividend
2. Declaration of a cash dividend
3. Stock split
4. Purchase of treasury stock

LO5 **Stock Dividends**

SE 7. On February 15, Asher Corporation's board of directors declared a 2 percent stock dividend applicable to the outstanding shares of its $10 par value common stock, of which 400,000 shares are authorized, 260,000 are issued, and 40,000 are held in the treasury. The stock dividend was distributed on March 15 to stockholders of record on March 1. On February 15, the market value of the common stock was $15 per share. On March 30, the board of directors declared a $0.50 per share cash dividend. No other stock transactions have occurred. Record, as necessary, the transactions of February 15, March 1, March 15, and March 30.

LO5 **Stock Split**

SE 8. On August 10, 2010, the board of directors of Karton, Inc. declared a 3-for-1 stock split of its $9 par value common stock, of which 200,000 shares were authorized and 62,500 were issued and outstanding. The market value on that date was $60 per share. On the same date, the balance of additional paid-in capital was $1,500,000, and the balance of retained earnings was $1,625,000. Prepare the stockholders' equity section of the company's balance sheet after the stock split. What entry, if any, is needed to record the stock split?

LO6 **Book Value for Preferred and Common Stock**

SE 9. Using data from the stockholders' equity section of Soong Corporation's balance sheet shown below, compute the book value per share for both the preferred and the common stock.

Contributed capital	
Preferred stock, $100 par value, 8 percent cumulative, 20,000 shares authorized, 1,000 shares issued and outstanding*	$ 100,000
Common stock, $10 par value, 200,000 shares authorized, 80,000 shares issued and outstanding	800,000
Additional paid-in capital	1,032,000
Total contributed capital	$1,932,000
Retained earnings	550,000
Total stockholders' equity	$2,482,000

*The preferred stock is callable at $108 per share, and one-year's dividends are in arrears.

Exercises

LO1 LO2 **Discussion Questions**

E 1. Develop brief answers to each of the following questions:

1. In what way is selling an investment for a gain potentially a negative in evaluating quality of earnings?
2. Is it unethical for new management to take an extra large write-off (a "big bath") in order to reduce future costs? Why or why not?
3. What is an argument against the recording of deferred income taxes?
4. Why is it useful to disclose discontinued operations separately on the income statement?

LO3 LO4 LO5 LO6 **Discussion Questions**

E 2. Develop brief answers to each of the following questions:

1. What is one way a company can improve its earnings per share without improving its earnings or net income?

2. Why is comprehensive income a part of stockholders' equity?
3. Upon receiving shares of stock from a stock dividend, why should the stockholder not consider the value of the stock as income?
4. What is the effect of a stock dividend or a stock split on book value per share?

LO1 **Effect of Alternative Accounting Methods**

E 3. At the end of its first year of operations, a company calculated its ending merchandise inventory according to three different accounting methods, as follows: FIFO, $95,000; average-cost, $90,000; LIFO, $86,000. If the company used the average-cost method, its net income for the year would be $34,000.

1. Determine net income if the company used the FIFO method.
2. Determine net income if the company used the LIFO method.
3. Which method is more conservative?
4. Will the consistency convention be violated if the company chooses to use the LIFO method? Why or why not?
5. Does the full-disclosure convention require disclosure of the inventory method used in the financial statements?

LO1 **Corporate Income Statement**

E 4. Assume that the Cetnar Corporation's chief financial officer gave you the following information: net sales, $1,900,000; cost of goods sold, $1,050,000; extraordinary gain (net of income taxes of $3,500), $12,500; loss from discontinued operations (net of income tax benefit of $30,000), $50,000; loss on disposal of discontinued operations (net of income tax benefit of $13,000), $35,000; selling expenses, $50,000; administrative expenses, $40,000; income taxes expense on continuing operations, $300,000. From this information, prepare the company's income statement for the year ended June 30, 2011. (Ignore earnings per share information.)

LO1 **Corporate Income Statement**

E 5. The items below are components of Patel Corporation's income statement for the year ended December 31, 2011. Recast the income statement in proper multistep form, including allocating income taxes to appropriate items (assume a 30 percent income tax rate) and showing earnings per share figures (100,000 shares outstanding).

Sales	$ 555,000
Cost of goods sold	(275,000)
Operating expenses	(112,500)
Restructuring	(55,000)
Total income taxes expense for period	(89,550)
Income from discontinued operations	80,000
Gain on disposal of discontinued operations	70,000
Extraordinary gain	36,000
Net income	$ 208,950
Earnings per share	$ 2.09

LO2 **Corporate Income Tax Rate Schedule**

E 6. Using the corporate tax rate schedule in Table 14-1, compute the income tax liability for the following situations:

Situation	Taxable Income
A	$ 70,000
B	85,000
C	320,000

LO2 **Income Tax Allocation**

E 7. The Danner Corporation reported the following accounting income before income taxes, income taxes expense, and net income for 2011 and 2012:

	2011	2012
Income before income taxes	$280,000	$280,000
Income taxes expense	88,300	88,300
Net income	$191,700	$191,700

On the balance sheet, deferred income taxes liability increased by $38,400 in 2011 and decreased by $18,800 in 2012.

1. How much did Danner actually pay in income taxes for 2011 and 2012?
2. Prepare entries in journal form to record income taxes expense for 2011 and 2012.

LO3 **Earnings per Share**

E 8. During 2011, Arthur Corporation reported a net income of $3,059,000. On January 1, Arthur had 2,800,000 shares of common stock outstanding. The company issued an additional 1,680,000 shares of common stock on October 1. In 2011, the company had a simple capital structure. During 2012, there were no transactions involving common stock, and the company reported net income of $4,032,000.

1. Determine the weighted-average number of common shares outstanding each year.
2. Compute earnings per share for each year.

LO4 **Statement of Stockholders' Equity**

E 9. The stockholders' equity section of Erich Corporation's balance sheet on December 31, 2010, follows.

Contributed capital	
Common stock, $2 par value, 500,000 shares authorized, 400,000 shares issued and outstanding	$ 800,000
Additional paid-in capital	1,200,000
Total contributed capital	$ 2,000,000
Retained earnings	4,200,000
Total stockholders' equity	$ 6,200,000

Prepare a statement of stockholders' equity for the year ended December 31, 2011, assuming these transactions occurred in sequence in 2011:

a. Issued 10,000 shares of $100 par value, 9 percent cumulative preferred stock at par after obtaining authorization from the state.
b. Issued 40,000 shares of common stock in connection with the conversion of bonds having a carrying value of $600,000.
c. Declared and issued a 2 percent common stock dividend. The market value on the date of declaration was $14 per share.
d. Purchased 10,000 shares of common stock for the treasury at a cost of $16 per share.
e. Earned net income of $460,000.
f. Declared and paid the full-year's dividend on preferred stock and a dividend of $0.40 per share on common stock outstanding at the end of the year.
g. Had foreign currency translation adjustment of negative $100,000.

LO5 **Journal Entries: Stock Dividends**

E 10. Snols Corporation has 30,000 shares of its $1 par value common stock outstanding. Record in journal form the following transactions as they relate to the company's common stock:

July	17	Declared a 10 percent stock dividend on common stock to be distributed on August 10 to stockholders of record on July 31. Market value of the stock was $5 per share on this date.
	31	Date of record.
Aug.	10	Distributed the stock dividend declared on July 17.
Sept.	1	Declared a $0.50 per share cash dividend on common stock to be paid on September 16 to stockholders of record on September 10.

LO5 **Stock Split**

E 11. Fernandez Corporation currently has 500,000 shares of $1 par value common stock authorized with 200,000 shares outstanding. The board of directors declared a 2-for-1 split on May 15, 2010, when the market value of the common stock was $2.50 per share. The retained earnings balance on May 15 was $700,000. Additional paid-in capital on this date was $20,000. Prepare the stockholders' equity section of the company's balance sheet before and after the stock split. What entry, if any, would be necessary to record the stock split?

LO5 **Stock Split**

E 12. On January 15, 2010, the board of directors of Tower International declared a 3-for-1 stock split of its $12 per value common stock, of which 3,200,000 shares were authorized and 800,000 were issued and outstanding. The market value on that date was $45 per share. On the same date, the balance of additional paid-in capital was $16,000,000, and the balance of retained earnings was $32,000,000. Prepare the stockholders' equity section of the company's balance sheet before and after the stock split. What entry, if any, is needed to record the stock split?

LO6 **Book Value for Preferred and Common Stock**

E 13. Below is the stockholders' equity section of Hegel Corporation's balance sheet. Determine the book value per share for both the preferred and the common stock.

Contributed capital	
Preferred stock, $100 per share, 6 percent cumulative, 10,000 shares authorized, 200 shares issued and outstanding*	$ 20,000
Common stock, $5 par value, 100,000 shares authorized, 10,000 shares issued, 9,000 shares outstanding	50,000
Additional paid-in capital	28,000
Total contributed capital	$ 98,000
Retained earnings	95,000
Total contributed capital and retained earnings	$193,000
Less treasury stock, common (1,000 shares at cost)	15,000
Total stockholders' equity	$178,000

*The preferred stock is callable at $105 per share, and one-year's dividends are in arrears.

Problems

LO1

Effect of Alternative Accounting Methods

P 1. Matka Corporation began operations in 2011. At the beginning of the year, the company purchased plant assets of $450,000, with an estimated useful life of 10 years and no residual value. During the year, the company had net sales of $650,000, salaries expense of $100,000, and other expenses of $40,000, excluding depreciation. In addition, Matka Corporation purchased inventory as follows:

Jan. 15	200 units at $400	$ 80,000
Mar. 20	100 units at $408	40,800
June 15	400 units at $416	166,400
Sept. 18	300 units at $412	123,600
Dec. 9	150 units at $420	63,000
Total	1,150 units	$473,800

At the end of the year, a physical inventory disclosed 250 units still on hand. The managers of Matka Corporation know they have a choice of accounting methods, but they are unsure how those methods will affect net income. They have heard of the FIFO and LIFO inventory methods and the straight-line and double-declining-balance depreciation methods.

Required

1. Prepare two income statements for Matka Corporation, one using the FIFO and straight-line methods and the other using the LIFO and double-declining-balance methods. Ignore income taxes.
2. Prepare a schedule accounting for the difference in the two net income figures obtained in requirement **1**.
3. User insight ▶ What effect does the choice of accounting method have on Matka's inventory turnover? What conclusions can you draw? Use the year-end balance to compute the ratio.
4. User insight ▶ How does the choice of accounting methods affect Matka's return on assets? Assume the company's only assets are cash of $40,000, inventory, and plant assets. Use year-end balances to compute the ratios. Is your evaluation of Matka's profitability affected by the choice of accounting methods?

LO1 LO2 LO3

Corporate Income Statement

P 2. Information concerning operations of Camping Gear Corporation during 2011 is as follows:

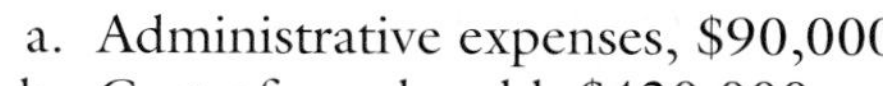

a. Administrative expenses, $90,000
b. Cost of goods sold, $420,000
c. Extraordinary loss from an earthquake (net of taxes, $36,000), $60,000
d. Sales (net), $900,000
e. Selling expenses, $80,000
f. Income taxes expense applicable to continuing operations, $105,000

Required

1. Prepare the corporation's income statement for the year ended December 31, 2011, including earnings per share information. Assume a weighted average of 50,000 common shares outstanding during the year.
2. User insight ▶ Which item in Camping Gear Corporation's income statement affects the company's quality of earnings? Why does it have an effect on quality of earnings?

LO1 LO2 LO3

Corporate Income Statement and Evaluation of Business Operations

P 3. During 2012, Vitos Corporation engaged in two complex transactions to improve the business—selling off a division and retiring bonds. The company has always issued a simple, single-step income statement, and the accountant has accordingly prepared the December 31 year-end income statements for 2011 and 2012, as shown below.

Vitos Corporation
Income Statements
For the Years Ended December 31, 2012 and 2011

	2012	2011
Net sales	$ 2,000,000	$ 2,400,000
Cost of goods sold	(1,100,000)	(1,200,000)
Operating expenses	(450,000)	(300,000)
Income taxes expense	(358,200)	(270,000)
Income from discontinued operations	320,000	
Gain on disposal of discontinued operations	280,000	
Extraordinary gain on retirement of bonds	144,000	
Net income	$ 835,800	$ 630,000
Earnings per share	$ 2.09	$ 1.58

Robert Vitos, the president of Vitos Corporation, is pleased to see that both net income and earnings per share increased by almost 33 percent from 2011 to 2012, and he intends to announce to the company's stockholders that the plan to improve the business has been successful.

Required

1. Recast the 2012 and 2011 income statements in proper multistep form, including allocating income taxes to appropriate items (assume a 30 percent income tax rate) and showing earnings per share figures (400,000 shares outstanding).

User insight ▶ 2. What is your assessment of Vitos Corporation's plan and business operations in 2012?

LO4 LO5

Dividends, Stock Splits, and Stockholders' Equity

P 4. The stockholders' equity section of the balance sheet of Lim Mills, Inc., as of December 31, 2010, was as follows:

Contributed capital	
Common stock, $3 par value, 1,000,000 shares authorized, 80,000 shares issued and outstanding	$240,000
Additional paid-in capital	75,000
Total contributed capital	$315,000
Retained earnings	240,000
Total stockholders' equity	$555,000

A review of the stockholders' equity records of Lim Mills, Inc., disclosed the following transactions during 2011:

Mar. 25 The board of directors declared a 5 percent stock dividend to stockholders of record on April 20 to be distributed on May 1. The market value of the common stock was $21 per share.

Apr.	20	Date of record for stock dividend.
May	1	Issued stock dividend.
Sept.	10	Declared a 3-for-1 stock split.
Dec.	15	Declared a 10 percent stock dividend to stockholders of record on January 15 to be distributed on February 15. The market price on this date is $9 per share.

Required

1. Record the stockholders' equity components of the transactions for Lim Mills, Inc., in T accounts.
2. Prepare the stockholders' equity section of the company's balance sheet as of December 31, 2011. Assume net income for 2011 is $494,000.

User insight ▶

3. If you owned 2,000 shares of Lim Mills stock on March 1, 2011, how many shares would you own on February 15, 2012? Would your proportionate share of the ownership of the company be different on the latter date from what it was on the former date? Explain your answer.

LO4 LO5

Dividends and Stock Split Transactions and Stockholders' Equity

P 5. The stockholders' equity section of Acerin Moving and Storage Corporation's balance sheet as of December 31, 2010, appears below.

Contributed capital	
Common stock, $2 par value, 6,000,000 shares authorized, 1,000,000 shares issued and outstanding	$2,000,000
Additional paid-in capital	800,000
Total contributed capital	$2,800,000
Retained earnings	2,160,000
Total stockholders' equity	$4,960,000

The company engaged in the following stockholders' equity transactions during 2011:

Mar.	5	Declared a $0.40 per share cash dividend to be paid on April 6 to stockholders of record on March 20.
	20	Date of record.
Apr.	6	Paid the cash dividend.
June	17	Declared a 10 percent stock dividend to be distributed August 17 to stockholders of record on August 5. The market value of the stock was $14 per share.
Aug.	5	Date of record for the stock dividend.
	17	Distributed the stock dividend.
Oct.	2	Split its stock 2 for 1.
Dec.	27	Declared a cash dividend of $0.20 payable January 27, 2012, to stockholders of record on January 14, 2012.

Required

1. Record the 2011 transactions in journal form.
2. Prepare the stockholders' equity section of the company's balance sheet as of December 31, 2011. Assume net income for the year is $800,000.

User insight ▶

3. If you owned some shares of Acerin, would you expect the total value of your shares to go up or down as a result of the stock dividends and stock split? What intangibles might affect the stock value?

Alternate Problems

LO4 LO5 LO6

Comprehensive Stockholders' Equity Transactions

P 6. On December 31, 2011, the stockholders' equity section of Koval Corporation's balance sheet appeared as follows:

Contributed capital	
Common stock, $8 par value, 400,000 shares authorized, 120,000 shares issued and outstanding	$ 960,000
Additional paid-in capital	2,560,000
Total contributed capital	$3,520,000
Retained earnings	1,648,000
Total stockholders' equity	$5,168,000

The following are selected transactions involving stockholders' equity in 2012:

Jan.	4	The board of directors obtained authorization for 40,000 shares of $40 par value noncumulative preferred stock that carried an indicated dividend rate of $4 per share and was callable at $42 per share.
	14	The company sold 24,000 shares of the preferred stock at $40 per share and issued another 4,000 in exchange for a building valued at $160,000.
Mar.	8	The board of directors declared a 2-for-1 stock split on the common stock.
Apr.	20	After the stock split, the company purchased 6,000 shares of common stock for the treasury at an average price of $12 per share.
May	4	The company sold 2,000 of the shares purchased on April 20, at an average price of $16 per share.
July	15	The board of directors declared a cash dividend of $4 per share on the preferred stock and $0.40 per share on the common stock.
	25	Date of record.
Aug.	15	Paid the cash dividend.
Nov.	28	The board of directors declared a 15 percent stock dividend when the common stock was selling for $20 per share to be distributed on January 5 to stockholders of record on December 15.
Dec.	15	Date of record for the stock dividend.

Required

1. Record the above transactions in journal form.
2. Prepare the stockholders' equity section of the company's balance sheet as of December 31, 2012. Net loss for 2012 was $436,000. (**Hint:** Use T accounts to keep track of transactions.)

User insight ▶

3. Compute the book value per share for preferred and common stock (including common stock distributable) on December 31, 2011 and 2012, using end-of-year shares outstanding. What effect would you expect the change in book value to have on the market price per share of the company's stock?

LO1 LO2 LO3

Corporate Income Statement

P 7. Income statement information for Nguyen Corporation in 2011 is as follows:

a. Administrative expenses, $110,000
b. Cost of goods sold, $440,000
c. Extraordinary loss from a storm (net of taxes, $10,000), $20,000
d. Income taxes expense, continuing operations, $42,000
e. Net sales, $890,000
f. Selling expenses, $190,000

Required

1. Prepare Nguyen Corporation's income statement for 2011, including earnings per share, assuming a weighted average of 100,000 shares of common stock outstanding for 2011.

User insight ▶

2. Which item in Nguyen Corporation's income statement affects the company's quality of earnings? Why does it have this effect?

LO4 LO5

Dividends, Stock Splits, and Stockholders' Equity

P 8. The stockholders' equity section of the balance sheet of Rago Corporation as of December 31, 2010, was as follows:

Contributed capital	
Common stock, $4 par value, 250,000 shares authorized, 100,000 shares issued and outstanding	$ 400,000
Additional paid-in capital	500,000
Total contributed capital	$ 900,000
Retained earnings	600,000
Total stockholders' equity	$1,500,000

Rago Corporation had the following transactions in 2011:

Feb.	28	The board of directors declared a 10 percent stock dividend to stockholders of record on March 25 to be distributed on April 5. The market value on this date is $16.
Mar.	25	Date of record for stock dividend.
Apr.	5	Issued stock dividend.
Aug.	3	Declared a 2-for-1 stock split.
Nov.	20	Purchased 9,000 shares of the company's common stock at $8 per share for the treasury.
Dec.	31	Declared a 5 percent stock dividend to stockholders of record on January 25 to be distributed on February 5. The market value per share was $9.

Required

1. Record the stockholders' equity components of the transactions for Rago Corporation in T accounts.
2. Prepare the stockholders' equity section of the company's balance sheet as of December 31, 2011. Assume net income for 2011 is $54,000.

User insight ▶

3. If you owned 500 shares of Rago stock on February 1, 2011, how many shares would you own on February 5, 2012? Would your proportionate share of the ownership of the company be different on the latter date from what it was on the former date? Explain your answer.

LO4 LO5 LO6

Comprehensive Stockholders' Equity Transactions

P 9. On December 31, 2010, the stockholders' equity section of Tsang Corporation's balance sheet appeared as follows:

Contributed capital	
Common stock, $8 par value, 200,000 shares authorized, 60,000 shares issued and outstanding	$ 480,000
Additional paid-in capital	1,280,000
Total contributed capital	$1,760,000
Retained earnings	824,000
Total stockholders' equity	$2,584,000

The following are selected transactions involving stockholders' equity in 2011. On January 4, the board of directors obtained authorization for 20,000 shares of $40 par value noncumulative preferred stock that carried an indicated dividend rate of $4 per share and was callable at $42 per share. On January 14, the company sold 12,000 shares of the preferred stock at $40 per share and issued another 2,000 in exchange for a building valued at $80,000. On March 8, the board of directors declared a 2-for-1 stock split on the common stock. On April 20, after the stock split, the company purchased 3,000 shares of common stock for the treasury at an average price of $12 per share; 1,000 of these shares subsequently were sold on May 4 at an average price of $16 per share. On July 15, the board of directors declared a cash dividend of $4 per share on the preferred stock and $0.40 per share on the common stock. The date of record was July 25. The dividends were paid on August 15. The board of directors declared a 15 percent stock dividend on November 28, when the common stock was selling for $20. The date of record for the stock dividend was December 15, and the dividend was to be distributed on January 5.

Required

1. Record the above transactions in journal form.
2. Prepare the stockholders' equity section of the company's balance sheet as of December 31, 2011. Net loss for 2011 was $218,000. (**Hint:** Use T accounts to keep track of transactions.)
3. Compute the book value per share for preferred and common stock (including common stock distributable) on December 31, 2010 and 2011, using end-of-year shares outstanding. What effect would you expect the change in book value to have on the market price per share of the company's stock?

User insight ▶ (item 3)

LO1

Effect of Alternative Accounting Methods

P 10. Zeigler Corporation began operations in 2010. At the beginning of the year, the company purchased plant assets of $900,000, with an estimated useful life of 10 years and no residual value. During the year, the company had net sales of $1,300,000, salaries expense of $200,000, and other expenses of $80,000, excluding depreciation. In addition, Zeigler Corporation purchased inventory as follows:

Jan. 15	400 units at $400	$160,000
Mar. 20	200 units at $408	81,600
June 15	800 units at $416	332,800
Sept. 18	600 units at $412	247,200
Dec. 9	300 units at $420	126,000
Total	2,300 units	$947,600

At the end of the year, a physical inventory disclosed 500 units still on hand. The managers of Zeigler Corporation know they have a choice of accounting methods, but they are unsure how those methods will affect net income. They have heard of the FIFO and LIFO inventory methods and the straight-line and double-declining-balance depreciation methods.

Required

1. Prepare two income statements for Zeigler Corporation, one using the FIFO and straight-line methods and the other using the LIFO and double-declining-balance methods. Ignore income taxes.
2. Prepare a schedule accounting for the difference in the two net income figures obtained in requirement **1**.
3. User insight ▶ What effect does the choice of accounting method have on Zeigler's inventory turnover? What conclusions can you draw? Use the year-end balance to compute the ratio.
4. User insight ▶ How does the choice of accounting methods affect Zeigler's return on assets? Assume the company's only assets are cash of $80,000, inventory, and plant assets. Use year-end balances to compute the ratios. Is your evaluation of Zeigler's profitability affected by the choice of accounting methods?

ENHANCING Your Knowledge, Skills, and Critical Thinking

LO5 Stock Split

C 1. When **Crocs**, the shoe company, reported in early 2007 that its first-quarter earnings had increased from the previous year, its stock price jumped to over $80 per share. At the same time, the company announced a 2-for-1 stock split.[18] What is a stock split and what effect does it have on the company's stockholders' equity? What effect will it likely have on the market value of the company's stock? In light of your answers, do you think the stock split is positive for the company and for its stockholders?

LO1 Classic Quality of Earnings Case

C 2. On Tuesday, January 19, 1988, **IBM** reported greatly increased earnings for the fourth quarter of 1987. Despite this reported gain in earnings, the price of IBM's stock on the New York Stock Exchange declined by $6 per share to $111.75. In sympathy with this move, most other technology stocks also declined.[19]

IBM's fourth-quarter net earnings rose from $1.39 billion, or $2.28 a share, to $2.08 billion, or $3.47 a share, an increase of 49.6 percent and 52.2 percent over the same period a year earlier. Management declared that these results demonstrated the effectiveness of IBM's efforts to become more competitive and that, despite the economic uncertainties of 1988, the company was planning for growth.

The apparent cause of the stock price decline was that the huge increase in income could be traced to nonrecurring gains. Investment analysts pointed out that IBM's high earnings stemmed primarily from such factors as a lower tax rate. Despite most analysts' expectations of a tax rate between 40 and 42 percent, IBM's was a low 36.4 percent, down from the previous year's 45.3 percent. Analysts were also disappointed in IBM's revenue growth. Revenues within the United States were down, and much of the company's growth in revenues came through favorable currency translations, increases that might not be repeated. In fact, some estimates of IBM's fourth-quarter earnings attributed $0.50 per share to currency translations and another $0.25 to tax-rate changes.

Other factors contributing to IBM's rise in earnings were one-time transactions, such as the sale of Intel Corporation stock and bond redemptions, along with a corporate stock buyback program that reduced the amount of stock outstanding in the fourth quarter by 7.4 million shares.

The analysts were concerned about the quality of IBM's earnings. Identify four quality of earnings issues reported in the case and the analysts' concern about each. In percentage terms, what is the impact of the currency changes on fourth-quarter earnings? Comment on management's assessment of IBM's performance. Do you agree with management? (Optional question: What has IBM's subsequent performance been?) Be prepared to discuss your answers in class.

Jackson Electronics, Inc.
Consolidated Statement of Stockholders' Equity
For the Year Ended September 30, 2011
(In thousands)

	Preferred Stock	Common Stock	Additional Paid-in Capital	Retained Earnings	Treasury Stock, Common	Accumulated Other Comprehensive Income	Total
Balance at September 30, 2010	$ 2,756	$3,902	$14,149	$119,312	($ 942)		$139,177
(1) Net income				18,753			18,753
(2) Unrealized gain on available for-sale securities						$12,000	12,000
(3) Redemption and retirement of preferred stock (27,560 shares)	(2,756)						(2,756)
(4) Stock options exercised (89,000 shares)		89	847				936
(5) Purchases of common stock for treasury (501,412 shares)					(12,552)		(12,552)
(6) Issuance of common stock (148,000 shares) in exchange for convertible subordinated debentures		148	3,635				3,783
(7) Issuance of common stock (715,000 shares) for cash		715	24,535				25,250
(8) Issuance of 500,000 shares of common stock in exchange for investment in Electrix Company shares		500	17,263				17,763
(9) Cash dividends—common stock ($0.80 per share)				(3,086)			(3,086)
Balance at September 30, 2011	$ 0	$5,354	$60,429	$134,979	($ 13,494)	$12,000	$199,268

LO1 LO4 **Interpretation of Statement of Stockholders' Equity**

C 3. The consolidated statement of stockholders' equity for Jackson Electronics, Inc., a manufacturer of a broad line of electrical components, is presented on the previous page. It has nine summary transactions.

1. Prepare an entry in journal form with an explanation for each transaction. In each case, if applicable, determine the average price per common share. At times, you will have to make assumptions about an offsetting part of the entry. For example, assume debentures (long-term bonds) are recorded at face value and that employees pay cash for stock purchased under company incentive plans.
2. Define comprehensive income and determine the amount for Jackson Electronics.

LO2 **Analysis of Income Taxes from Annual Report**

C 4. In its 2008 annual report, **Nike, Inc.**, the athletic sportswear company, provided the following data about its current and deferred income tax provisions (in millions):

	2008
Current income taxes due	$ 920.1
Deferred income taxes	(300.6)
Total provision for income taxes	$ 619.5

1. What were the 2008 income taxes on the income statement? Record in journal form the overall income tax liability for 2008, using income tax allocation procedures.
2. Nike's balance sheet contains both deferred income tax assets and deferred tax liabilities. How do such deferred income tax assets arise? How do such deferred income tax liabilities arise? Given the definition of liabilities, do you see a potential problem with the company's classifying deferred income taxes as a liability? Why or why not?

LO1 LO4 **Corporate Income Statement and Statement of Stockholders' Equity**

C 5. Refer to **CVS Corporation**'s annual report in the Supplement to Chapter 5 to answer the following questions:

1. Does CVS have discontinued operations or extraordinary items? Are there any items that would lead you to question the quality of CVS's earnings? Would you say the income statement for CVS is relatively simple or relatively complex? Why?
2. What transactions most often affect the stockholders' equity section of the CVS balance sheet? (**Hint:** Examine the statements of stockholders' equity.)

LO6 **Book Value and Market Value**

C 6. Refer to the annual report for **CVS Corporation** and the financial statements for **Southwest Airlines Co.** in the Supplement to Chapter 5. Compute the 2008 and 2007 book value per share for both companies and compare the results to the average stock price of each in the fourth quarter of 2008 as shown in the notes to the financial statements. Southwest's average price per share was $11.01 in 2008 and $13.59 in 2007. How do you explain the differences in book value per share, and how do you interpret their relationship to market prices?

CHAPTER

15 The Statement of Cash Flows

Making a Statement

INCOME STATEMENT

Revenues

– Expenses

= Net Income

STATEMENT OF RETAINED EARNINGS

Beginning Balance

+ Net Income

– Dividends

= Ending Balance

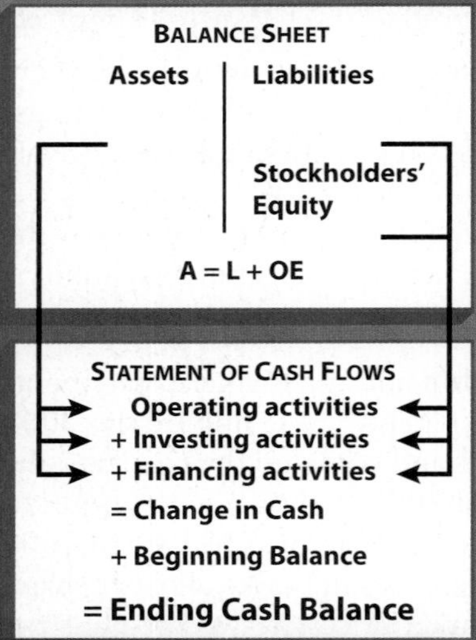

The statement of cash flows explains the changes in cash on the balance sheet.

Cash flows are the lifeblood of a business. They enable a company to pay expenses, debts, employees' wages, and taxes, and to invest in the assets it needs for its operations. Without sufficient cash flows, a company cannot grow and prosper. Because of the importance of cash flows, one must be alert to the possibility that items may be incorrectly classified in a statement of cash flows and that the statement may not fully disclose all pertinent information. This chapter identifies the classifications used in a statement of cash flows and explains how to analyze the statement.

LEARNING OBJECTIVES

LO1 Describe the principal purposes and uses of the statement of cash flows, and identify its components. (pp. 658–663)

LO2 Analyze the statement of cash flows. (pp. 663–667)

LO3 Use the indirect method to determine cash flows from operating activities. (pp. 668–674)

LO4 Determine cash flows from investing activities. (pp. 674–677)

LO5 Determine cash flows from financing activities. (pp. 678–681)

DECISION POINT ▶ A USER'S FOCUS LOPATA CORPORATION

Lopata Corporation is a distributor of accessories for cell phones, iPods, iPhones, and other small electronic devices. Lopata's managers have just finished preparing the company's financial statements for 2011. Although they are satisfied with net sales for the year—$825,000—they are concerned because cash flows from operating activities are less than net income ($58,300 vs. $82,200) and because cash and cash equivalents decreased by $8,000 during the year. They have also noted that the company has recently been having difficulty paying its bills on time.

Strong cash flows are critical to achieving and maintaining liquidity. If Lopata Corporation's cash flows are insufficient to maintain current operations or finance future growth, the company will have to sell investments, borrow funds, or issue stock. On the other hand, if its cash flows are strong, Lopata can use excess cash to reduce debt, thereby lowering its debt to equity ratio and improving its financial position. That, in turn, can increase the market value of its stock, which will increase stockholders' value.

Lopata's statement of cash flows will provide the company's managers, as well as its stockholders and potential investors, with information that is essential to evaluating the strength of the company's cash flows and liquidity.

- ▶ Why were Lopata Corporation's operating cash flows less than its net income, and why did its cash and cash equivalents decline during the year?
- ▶ What measures do managers, stockholders, and potential investors use to evaluate the strength of a company's cash flows and liquidity?

Overview of the Statement of Cash Flows

LO1 Describe the principal purposes and uses of the statement of cash flows, and identify its components.

CASH FLOW

The **statement of cash flows** shows how a company's operating, investing, and financing activities have affected cash during an accounting period. It explains the net increase (or decrease) in cash during the period. For purposes of preparing this statement, **cash** is defined as including both cash and cash equivalents. **Cash equivalents** are investments that can be quickly converted to cash; they have a maturity of 90 days or less when they are purchased. They include money market accounts, commercial paper, and U.S. Treasury bills. A company invests in cash equivalents to earn interest on cash that would otherwise be temporarily idle.

Suppose, for example, that a company has $1,000,000 that it will not need for 30 days. To earn a return on this amount, the company could place the cash in an account that earns interest (such as a money market account), lend the cash to another corporation by purchasing that corporation's short-term notes (commercial paper), or purchase a short-term obligation of the U.S. government (a Treasury bill).

Study Note

Money market accounts, commercial paper (short-term notes), and U.S. Treasury bills are considered cash equivalents because they are highly liquid, temporary (90 days or less) holding places for cash not currently needed to operate the business.

Because cash includes cash equivalents, transfers between the Cash account and cash equivalents are not treated as cash receipts or cash payments. On the statement of cash flows, cash equivalents are combined with the Cash account. Cash equivalents should not be confused with short-term investments, or marketable securities. These items are not combined with the Cash account on the statement of cash flows; rather, purchases of marketable securities are treated as cash outflows, and sales of marketable securities are treated as cash inflows.

Purposes of the Statement of Cash Flows

The primary purpose of the statement of cash flows is to provide information about a company's cash receipts and cash payments during an accounting period. A secondary purpose is to provide information about a company's operating, investing, and financing activities during the accounting period. Some information about those activities may be inferred from other financial statements, but the statement of cash flows summarizes *all* transactions that affect cash.

Uses of the Statement of Cash Flows

The statement of cash flows is useful to management, as well as to investors and creditors.

- Management uses the statement of cash flows to assess liquidity, to determine dividend policy, and to evaluate the effects of major policy decisions involving investments and financing. Examples include determining if short-term financing is needed to pay current liabilities, deciding whether to raise or lower dividends, and planning for investing and financing needs.
- Investors and creditors use the statement to assess a company's ability to manage cash flows, to generate positive future cash flows, to pay its liabilities, to pay dividends and interest, and to anticipate its need for additional financing.

Classification of Cash Flows

The statement of cash flows has three major classifications: operating, investing, and financing activities. The components of these activities are illustrated in Figure 15-1 and summarized below.

1. **Operating activities** involve the cash inflows and outflows from activities that enter into the determination of net income. Cash inflows in this

category include cash receipts from the sale of goods and services and from the sale of *trading securities*. Trading securities are a type of marketable security that a company buys and sells for the purpose of making a profit in the near term. Cash inflows also include interest and dividends received on loans and investments. Cash outflows include cash payments for wages, inventory, expenses, interest, taxes, and the purchase of trading securities. In effect, accrual-based income from the income statement is changed to reflect cash flows.

2. **Investing activities** involve the acquisition and sale of property, plant, and equipment and other long-term assets, including long-term investments. They also involve the acquisition and sale of short-term marketable

FIGURE 15-1 Classification of Cash Inflows and Cash Outflows

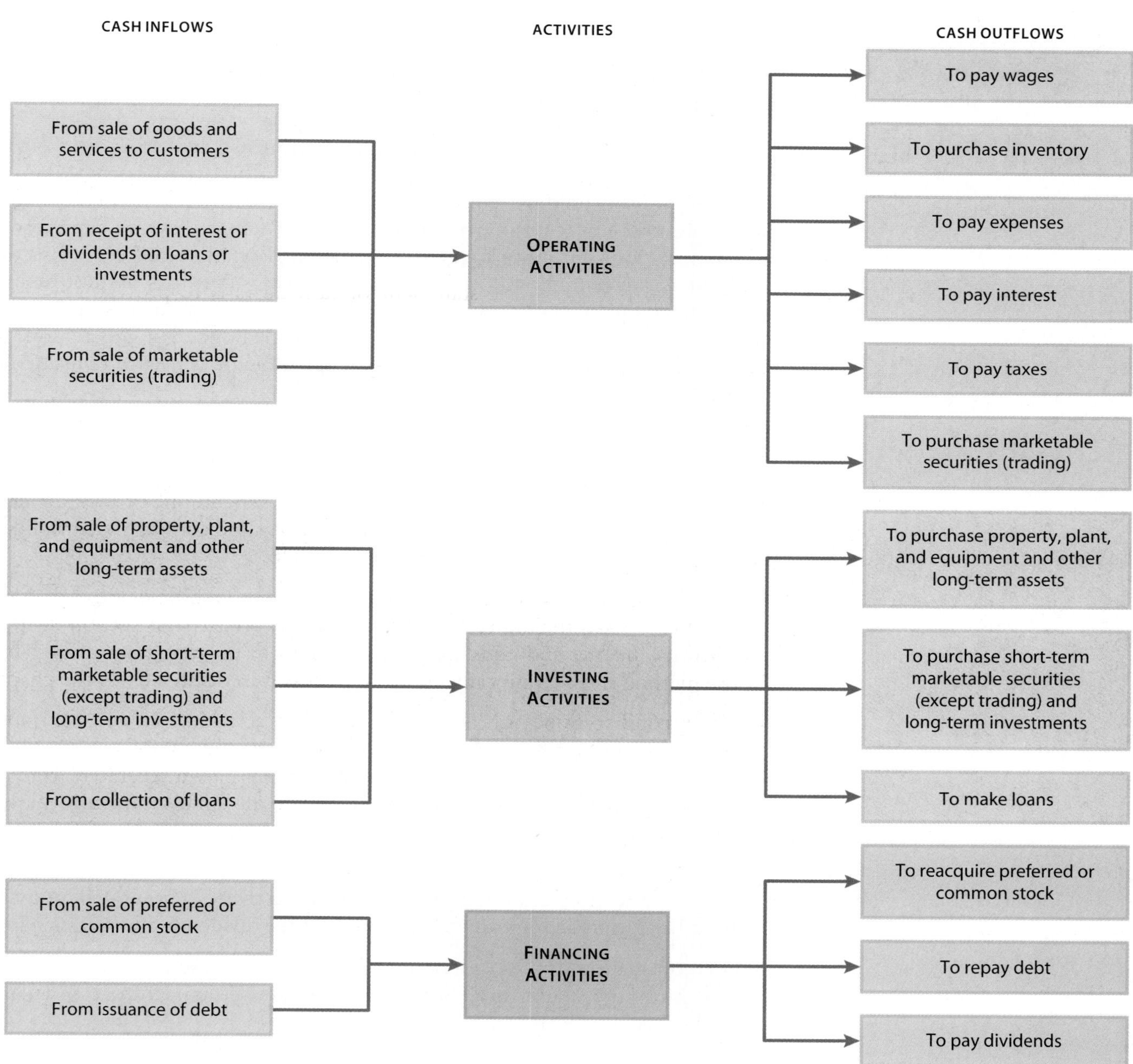

Study Note

Operating activities involve the day-to-day sale of goods and services, investing activities involve long-term assets and investments, and financing activities deal with stockholders' equity accounts and debt (borrowing).

securities, other than trading securities, and the making and collecting of loans. Cash inflows include the cash received from selling marketable securities and long-term assets and from collecting on loans. Cash outflows include the cash expended on purchasing these securities and assets and the cash lent to borrowers.

3. **Financing activities** involve obtaining resources from stockholders and providing them with a return on their investments and obtaining resources from creditors and repaying the amounts borrowed or otherwise settling the obligations. Cash inflows include the proceeds from stock issues and from short- and long-term borrowing. Cash outflows include the repayments of loans (excluding interest) and payments to owners, including cash dividends. Treasury stock transactions are also considered financing activities. Repayments of accounts payable or accrued liabilities are not considered repayments of loans; they are classified as cash outflows under operating activities.

Required Disclosure of Noncash Investing and Financing Transactions

Companies occasionally engage in significant **noncash investing and financing transactions**. These transactions involve only long-term assets, long-term liabilities, or stockholders' equity. For instance, a company might exchange a long-term asset for a long-term liability, settle a debt by issuing capital stock, or take out a long-term mortgage to purchase real estate. Noncash transactions represent significant investing and financing activities, but they are not reflected on the statement of cash flows because they do not affect current cash inflows or outflows. They will, however, affect future cash flows. For this reason, it is required that they be disclosed in a separate schedule or as part of the statement of cash flows.

Format of the Statement of Cash Flows

Amazon.com is the largest online retailer in the world and one of the 500 largest companies in the United States. Exhibit 15-1 shows the company's consolidated statements of cash flows for 2008, 2007, and 2006.

- The first section of the statement of cash flows is cash flows from operating activities. When the indirect method is used to prepare this section, it begins with net income and ends with cash flows from operating activities. This is the method most commonly used; we discuss it in detail later in the chapter.
- The second section, cash flows from investing activities, shows cash transactions involving capital expenditures (for property and equipment) and loans. Cash outflows for capital expenditures are usually shown separately from cash inflows from their disposal. However, when the inflows are not material, some companies combine these two lines to show the net amount of outflow as Amazon.com does.
- The third section, cash flows from financing activities, shows debt and common stock transactions, as well as payments for dividends and treasury stock.
- A reconciliation of the beginning and ending balances of cash appears at the bottom of the statement. These cash balances will tie into the cash balances of the balance sheets.

EXHIBIT 15-1 Consolidated Statement of Cash Flows

Amazon.com, Inc. Consolidated Statements of Cash Flows			
	For the Years Ended		
(In millions)	**2008**	**2007**	**2006**
Operating Activities			
Net income	$ 645	$ 476	$ 190
Adjustments to reconcile net income to net cash from operating activities:			
Depreciation and amortization	287	246	205
Stock-based compensation	275	185	101
Deferred income taxes	(5)	(99)	22
Excess tax benefits from stock-based compensation	(159)	(257)	(102)
Other	(60)	22	2
Changes in operating assets and liabilities:			
Inventories	(232)	(303)	(282)
Accounts receivable, net and other	(218)	(255)	(103)
Accounts payable	812	928	402
Accrued expenses and other	247	429	241
Additions to unearned revenue and other	105	33	26
Net cash provided by operating activities	$1,697	$ 1,405	$ 702
Investing Activities			
Purchases of fixed assets, including software and website development	$ (333)	$ (224)	($ 216)
Acquisitions, net of cash received and other	(494)	(75)	(32)
Sales and maturities of marketable securities and other investments	1,305	1,271	1,845
Purchases of marketable securities and other investments	(1,677)	(930)	(1,930)
Net cash provided by (used in) investing activities	($1,199)	$ 42	($ 333)
Financing Activities			
Proceeds from exercises of stock options	$ 11	$ 91	$ 35
Excess tax benefits from exercises of stock options	159	257	102
Common stock repurchased (Treasury stock)	(100)	(248)	(252)
Proceeds from long-term debt and other	87	24	98
Repayments of long-term debt and capital lease obligations	(355)	(74)	(383)
Net cash provided by (used in) financing activities	($ 198)	$ 50	($ 400)
Foreign-currency effect on cash and cash equivalents	$ (70)	$ 20	$ 40
Net (Decrease) Increase in Cash and Cash Equivalents	$ 230	$ 1,517	$ 9
Cash and Cash Equivalents, beginning of year	2,539	1,022	1,013
Cash and Cash Equivalents, end of year	$2,769	$ 2,539	$1,022

Source: Amazon.com, Inc., *Annual Report*, 2008 (adapted).

FOCUS ON BUSINESS PRACTICE IFRS

How Universal Is the Statement of Cash Flows?

Despite the importance of the statement of cash flows in assessing the liquidity of companies in the United States, there has been considerable variation in its use and format in other countries. For example, in many countries, the statement shows the change in working capital rather than the change in cash and cash equivalents. Although the European Union's principal directives for financial reporting do not address the statement of cash flows, international accounting standards require it, and international financial markets expect it to be presented. As a result, most multinational companies include the statement in their financial reports. Most European countries adopted the statement of cash flows when the European Union adopted international accounting standards.

Ethical Considerations and the Statement of Cash Flows

Although cash inflows and outflows are not as subject to manipulation as earnings are, managers are acutely aware of users' emphasis on cash flows from operations as an important measure of performance. Thus, an incentive exists to overstate these cash flows.

In earlier chapters, we cited an egregious example of earnings management. As you may recall, by treating operating expenses of about $10 billion over several years as purchases of equipment, **WorldCom** reduced reported expenses and improved reported earnings. In addition, by classifying payments of operating expenses as investments on the statement of cash flows, it was able to show an improvement in cash flows from operations. The inclusion of the expenditures in the investing activities section did not draw special attention because the company normally had large capital expenditures.

Another way a company can show an apparent improvement in its performance is through lack of transparency, or lack of full disclosure, in its financial statements. For instance, securitization—the sale of batches of accounts receivable—is clearly a means of financing, and the proceeds from it should be shown in the financing section of the statement of cash flows. However, because the accounting standards are somewhat vague about where these proceeds should go, some companies net the proceeds against the accounts receivable in the operating section of the statement and bury the explanation in the notes to the financial statements. By doing so, they make collections of receivables in the operating activities section look better than they actually were. It is not illegal to do this, but from an ethical standpoint, it obscures the company's true performance.

STOP & APPLY >

Filip Corporation engaged in the transactions listed below. Identify each transaction as (a) an operating activity, (b) an investing activity, (c) a financing activity, (d) a noncash transaction, or (e) not on the statement of cash flows. (Assume the indirect method is used.)

1. Purchased office equipment, a long-term investment.
2. Decreased accounts receivable.
3. Sold land at cost.
4. Issued long-term bonds for plant assets.
5. Increased inventory.

(continued)

6. Issued common stock.
7. Repurchased common stock.
8. Issued notes payable.
9. Increased income taxes payable.
10. Purchased a 60-day Treasury bill.
11. Purchased a long-term investment.
12. Declared and paid a cash dividend.

SOLUTION

1. b; 2. a; 3. b; 4. d; 5. a; 6. c; 7. c; 8. c; 9. a; 10. e (cash equivalent); 11. b; 12. c

Analyzing Cash Flows

LO2 Analyze the statement of cash flows.

Like the analysis of other financial statements, an analysis of the statement of cash flows can reveal significant relationships. Two areas on which analysts focus when examining a company's statement of cash flows are cash-generating efficiency and free cash flow.

Can a Company Have Too Much Cash?

Before the bull market ended in 2007, many companies had accumulated large amounts of cash. **Exxon Mobil**, **Microsoft**, and **Cisco Systems**, for example, had amassed more than $100 billion in cash. At that time, the average large company in the United States had 7 percent of its assets in cash.

Increased cash can be a benefit or a potential risk. Many companies put their cash to good use. Of course they are wise to have cash on hand for emergencies. They may also invest in productive assets, conduct research and development, pay off debt, buy back stock, or pay dividends. Sometimes, however, shareholders suffer when executives are too conservative and keep the money in low-paying money market accounts or make unwise acquisitions. For the user of financial statements, the lesson is that it is important to look closely at the components of the statement of cash flows to see how management is spending its cash.[1]

Cash-Generating Efficiency

Managers accustomed to evaluating income statements usually focus on the bottom-line result. While the level of cash at the bottom of the statement of cash flows is certainly an important consideration, such information can be obtained from the balance sheet. The focal point of cash flow analysis is on cash inflows and outflows from operating activities. These cash flows are used in ratios that measure **cash-generating efficiency,** which is a company's ability to generate cash from its current or continuing operations. The ratios that analysts use to compute cash-generating efficiency are cash flow yield, cash flows to sales, and cash flows to assets.

In this section, we compute these ratios for **Amazon.com** in 2008 using data for net income and net cash flows from Exhibit 15-1 and the following information from Amazon.com's 2008 annual report (all dollar amounts are in millions).

	2008	2007	2006
Net Sales	$19,166	$14,835	$10,711
Total Assets	8,314	6,485	4,363

Cash flow yield is the ratio of net cash flows from operating activities to net income:

K/R

$$\text{Cash Flow Yield} = \frac{\text{Net Cash Flows from Operating Activities}}{\text{Net Income}}$$

$$= \frac{\$1{,}697}{\$645}$$

$$= 2.6 \text{ Times*}$$

For most companies, the cash flow yield should exceed 1.0. In 2008, Amazon.com performed much better than this minimum. With a cash flow yield of 2.6 times, Amazon.com generated about $2.60 of cash for every dollar of net income.

The cash flow yield needs to be examined carefully. Keep in mind, for instance, that a firm with significant depreciable assets should have a cash flow yield greater than 1.0 because depreciation expense is added back to net income to arrive at cash flows from operating activities. If special items, such as discontinued operations, appear on the income statement and are material, income from continuing operations should be used as the denominator. Also, an artificially high cash flow yield may result if a firm has very low net income, which is the denominator in the ratio.

Cash flows to sales is the ratio of net cash flows from operating activities to sales:

K/R

$$\text{Cash Flows to Sales} = \frac{\text{Net Cash Flows from Operating Activities}}{\text{Sales}}$$

$$= \frac{\$1{,}697}{\$19{,}166}$$

$$= 8.9\%\text{*}$$

Thus, Amazon.com generated positive cash flows to sales of 8.9 percent in 2008. Another way to state this result is that every dollar of sales generates 8.9 cents in cash.

Cash flows to assets is the ratio of net cash flows from operating activities to average total assets:

K/R

$$\text{Cash Flows to Assets} = \frac{\text{Net Cash Flows from Operating Activities}}{\text{Average Total Assets}}$$

$$= \frac{\$1{,}697}{(\$8{,}314 + \$6{,}485) \div 2}$$

$$= 22.9\%\text{*}$$

At 22.9 percent, Amazon.com's cash flows to assets ratio indicates that for every dollar of assets, the company generates almost 23 cents. This excellent result is higher than its cash flows to sales ratio because of its good asset turnover ratio (sales ÷ average total assets) of 2.6 times (22.9% ÷ 8.9%). Cash flows to sales and cash flows to assets are closely related to the profitability measures of profit margin and return on assets. They exceed those measures by the amount of the cash flow yield ratio because cash flow yield is the ratio of net cash flows from operating activities to net income.

---

*Rounded.

Asking the Right Questions About the Statement of Cash Flows

Most readers of financial statements are accustomed to looking at the "bottom line" to get an overview of a company's financial status. They look at total assets on the balance sheet and net income on the income statement. However, the statement of cash flows requires a different approach because the bottom line of cash on hand does not tell the reader very much; changes in the components of the statement during the year are far more revealing.

In interpreting a statement of cash flows, it pays to know the right questions to ask. To illustrate, let's use **Amazon.com** as an example.

- In our discussion of cash flow yield, we saw that Amazon.com generated about $2.60 of cash from operating activities for every dollar of net income in 2007. What are the primary reasons that cash flows from operating activities differed from net income?

For Amazon.com, the largest positive items in 2008 were accounts payable and depreciation. They are added to net income for different reasons. Accounts payable represents an increase in the amount owed to creditors, whereas depreciation represents a noncash expense that is deducted in arriving at net income. Amazon.com's two largest negative items were increases in inventories and receivables. As a growing company, Amazon.com was managing its operating cycle by generating cash from creditors to pay for increases in inventories and receivables.

- Amazon.com had a use of almost $1.2 billion in cash in 2008 due to purchases of fixed assets, acquisitions. What were its most important investing activities other than capital expenditures?

The company managed its investing activities by purchasing fixed assets, making acquisitions, and making active use of investments in marketable securities and other investments. Due to the company's success in generating cash flows from operations, it was able to purchase more marketable securities and other investments than it sold during the year.

- Amazon.com's financing activities show a relatively small use of cash of about $200 million. How did the company manage its financing activities during that fiscal year?

Exercise of stock options and the tax effects of stock-based compensation provided funds to buy back treasury stock and pay off some long-term debt. Because of its good cash flow from operations, Amazon.com did not need long-term financing.

Free Cash Flow

As we noted in an earlier chapter, **free cash flow** is the amount of cash that remains after deducting the funds a company must commit to continue operating at its planned level. If free cash flow is positive, it means that the company has met all of its planned cash commitments and has cash available to reduce debt or to expand. A negative free cash flow means that the company will have to sell investments, borrow money, or issue stock in the short term to continue at its planned level; if a company's free cash flow remains negative for several years, it may not be able to raise cash by issuing stocks or bonds. On the statement of cash flows, cash commitments for current and continuing operations, interest, and income taxes are incorporated in cash flows from current operations.

FOCUS ON BUSINESS PRACTICE

Cash Flows Tell All

In early 2001, the telecommunications industry began one of the biggest market crashes in history. Could it have been predicted? The capital expenditures that telecommunications firms must make for equipment, such as cable lines and computers, are sizable. When the capital expenditures (a negative component of free cash flow) of 41 telecommunications companies are compared with their cash flows from sales over the six years preceding the crash, an interesting pattern emerges. In the first three years, both capital expenditures and cash flows from sales were about 20 percent of sales. In other words, operations were generating enough cash flows to cover capital expenditures. Although cash flows from sales in the next three years stayed at about 20 percent of sales, free cash flows turned very negative, and almost half of capital expenditures had to be financed by debt instead of operations, making these companies more vulnerable to the downturn in the economy that occurred in 2001[2] and especially in 2008. The predictive reliability of free cash flow was confirmed in a later study that showed that of 100 different measures, stock price to free cash flow was the best predictor of future increases in stock price.[3]

Study Note

The computation for free cash flow sometimes uses *net capital expenditures* in place of *purchases of plant assets + sales of plant assets.*

Amazon.com has a stated primary financial objective of "long-term sustainable growth in free cash flow."[4] The company definitely achieved this objective in 2008. Its free cash flow for this year is computed as follows (in millions):

$$\begin{aligned}\text{Free Cash Flow} &= \text{Net Cash Flows from Operating Activities} - \text{Dividends} - \\ &\quad\ \text{Purchases of Plant Assets} + \text{Sales of Plant Assets} \\ &= \$1{,}697 - \$0 - \$333 + \$0 \\ &= \$1{,}364\end{aligned}$$

Purchases of plant assets (capital expenditures) and sales (dispositions) of plant assets, if any, appear in the investing activities section of the statement of cash flows. Dividends, if any, appear in the financing activities section.

Construction firms must make large capital expenditures for plant assets, such as the equipment shown here. These expenditures are a negative component of free cash flow, which is the amount of cash that remains after deducting the funds a company needs to operate at its planned level. In 2007, negative free cash flows forced a number of construction firms to rely heavily on debt to finance their capital expenditures, thus increasing their vulnerability to the economic downturn of 2008.

Courtesy R, 2009/Used under license from Shutterstock.com.

FOCUS ON BUSINESS PRACTICE

What Do You Mean, "Free Cash Flow"?

Because the statement of cash flows has been around for less than 25 years, no generally accepted analyses have yet been developed. For example, the term *free cash flow* is commonly used in the business press, but there is no agreement on its definition. An article in *Forbes* defines *free cash flow* as "cash available after paying out capital expenditures and dividends, but *before taxes and interest*" [emphasis added].[5] An article in *The Wall Street Journal* defines it as "operating income less maintenance-level capital expenditures."[6] The definition with which we are most in agreement is the one used in *BusinessWeek:* free cash flow is net cash flows from operating activities less net capital expenditures and dividends. This "measures truly discretionary funds—company money that an owner could pocket without harming the business."[7]

Amazon.com is a growing company and does not have material sales of plant assets and does not pay dividends. The company's positive free cash flow of $1,364 million was due primarily to its strong operating cash flow of $1,697 million. Consequently, the company does not have to borrow money to expand.

Because cash flows can vary from year to year, analysts should look at trends in cash flow measures over several years. It is also important to consider the effect of seasonality on a company's sales. Because Amazon.com's sales peak toward the end of the year, the cash situation at that time may not be representative of the rest of the year. For example, Amazon.com's management states that

> Our cash, cash equivalents, and marketable securities balances typically reach their highest level [at the end of each year.] This operating cycle results in a corresponding increase in accounts payable at December 31. Our accounts payable balance generally declines during the first three months of the year, resulting in a corresponding decline in our cash . . ."[8]

& APPLY >

In 2011, Monfort Corporation had year-end assets of $2,400,000, sales of $2,000,000, net income of $400,000, net cash flows from operating activities of $360,000, dividends of $100,000, purchases of plant assets of $200,000, and sales of plant assets of $40,000. In 2010, year-end assets were $2,200,000. Calculate cash flow yield, cash flows to sales, cash flows to assets, and free cash flow.

SOLUTION

$$\text{Cash Flow Yield} = \frac{\$360{,}000}{\$400{,}000} = 0.9 \text{ Times}$$

$$\text{Cash Flows to Sales} = \frac{\$360{,}000}{\$2{,}000{,}000} = 0.18, \text{ or } 18\%$$

$$\text{Cash Flows to Assets} = \frac{\$360{,}000}{(\$2{,}400{,}000 + \$2{,}200{,}000) \div 2} = 0.16, \text{ or } 16\% \text{ (rounded)}$$

$$\text{Free Cash Flow} = \$360{,}000 - \$100{,}000 - \$200{,}000 + \$40{,}000 = \$100{,}000$$

Operating Activities

LO3 Use the indirect method to determine cash flows from operating activities.

CASH FLOW

To demonstrate the preparation of the statement of cash flows, we will work through an example step-by-step. The data for this example are presented in Exhibit 15-2, which shows Laguna Corporation's income statement for 2010, and in Exhibit 15-3, which shows Laguna's balance sheets for December 31, 2010 and 2009. Exhibit 15-3 shows the balance sheet accounts that we use for analysis and whether the change in each account is an increase or a decrease.

The first step in preparing the statement of cash flows is to determine cash flows from operating activities. The income statement indicates how successful a company has been in earning an income from its operating activities, but because that statement is prepared on an accrual basis, it does not reflect the inflow and outflow of cash related to operating activities. Revenues are recorded even though the company may not yet have received the cash, and expenses are recorded even though the company may not yet have expended the cash. Thus, to ascertain cash flows from operations, the figures on the income statement must be converted from an accrual basis to a cash basis.

There are two methods of accomplishing this:

- The **direct method** adjusts each item on the income statement from the accrual basis to the cash basis. The result is a statement that begins with cash receipts from sales and interest and deducts cash payments for purchases, operating expenses, interest payments, and income taxes to arrive at net cash flows from operating activities.
- The **indirect method** does not require the adjustment of each item on the income statement. It lists only the adjustments necessary to convert net income to cash flows from operations.

Study Note

The direct and indirect methods relate only to the operating activities section of the statement of cash flows. They are both acceptable for financial reporting purposes.

The direct and indirect methods always produce the same net figure. The average person finds the direct method easier to understand because its presentation of operating cash flows is more straightforward than that of the indirect method. However, the indirect method is the overwhelming choice of most companies and accountants. A survey of large companies shows that 99 percent use this method.[9]

EXHIBIT 15-2
Income Statement

Laguna Corporation
Income Statement
For the Year Ended December 31, 2010

Sales		$698,000
Cost of goods sold		520,000
Gross margin		$178,000
Operating expenses (including depreciation expense of $37,000)		147,000
Operating income		$ 31,000
Other income (expenses)		
Interest expense	($23,000)	
Interest income	6,000	
Gain on sale of investments	12,000	
Loss on sale of plant assets	(3,000)	(8,000)
Income before income taxes		$ 23,000
Income taxes expense		7,000
Net income		$ 16,000

EXHIBIT 15-3 Comparative Balance Sheets Showing Changes in Accounts

Laguna Corporation
Comparative Balance Sheets
December 31, 2010 and 2009

	2010	2009	Change	Increase or Decrease
Assets				
Current assets				
Cash	$ 46,000	$ 15,000	$ 31,000	Increase
Accounts receivable (net)	47,000	55,000	(8,000)	Decrease
Inventory	144,000	110,000	34,000	Increase
Prepaid expenses	1,000	5,000	(4,000)	Decrease
Total current assets	$ 238,000	$185,000	$ 53,000	
Investments	$ 115,000	$127,000	($ 12,000)	Decrease
Plant assets	$ 715,000	$505,000	$210,000	Increase
Less accumulated depreciation	(103,000)	(68,000)	(35,000)	Increase
Total plant assets	$ 612,000	$437,000	$175,000	
Total assets	$ 965,000	$749,000	$216,000	
Liabilities				
Current liabilities				
Accounts payable	$ 50,000	$ 43,000	$ 7,000	Increase
Accrued liabilities	12,000	9,000	3,000	Increase
Income taxes payable	3,000	5,000	(2,000)	Decrease
Total current liabilities	$ 65,000	$ 57,000	$ 8,000	
Long-term liabilities				
Bonds payable	295,000	245,000	50,000	Increase
Total liabilities	$ 360,000	$302,000	$ 58,000	
Stockholders' Equity				
Common stock, $5 par value	$ 276,000	$200,000	$ 76,000	Increase
Additional paid-in capital	214,000	115,000	99,000	Increase
Retained earnings	140,000	132,000	8,000	Increase
Treasury stock	(25,000)	0	(25,000)	Increase
Total stockholders' equity	$ 605,000	$447,000	$158,000	
Total liabilities and stockholders' equity	$ 965,000	$749,000	$216,000	

From an analyst's perspective, the indirect method is superior to the direct method because it begins with net income and derives cash flows from operations; the analyst can readily identify the factors that cause cash flows from operations. From a company's standpoint, the indirect method is easier and less expensive to prepare. For these reasons, we use the indirect method in our example.

As Figure 15-2 shows, the indirect method focuses on adjusting items on the income statement to reconcile net income to net cash flows from operating

FIGURE 15-2 Indirect Method of Determining Net Cash Flows from Operating Activities

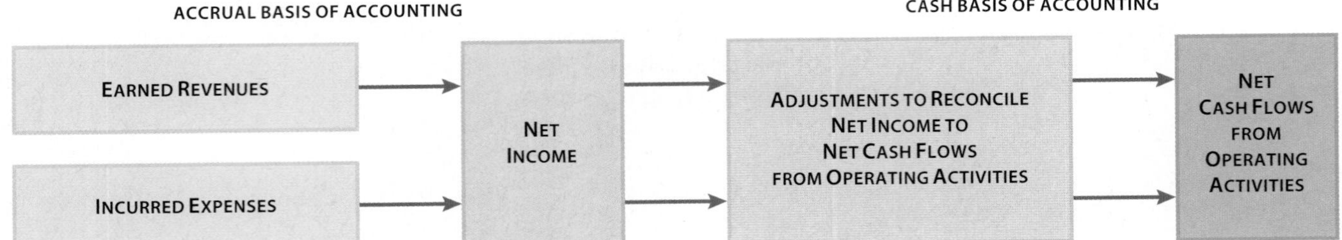

activities. These items include depreciation, amortization, and depletion; gains and losses; and changes in the balances of current asset and current liability accounts. The schedule in Exhibit 15-4 shows the reconciliation of Laguna Corporation's net income to net cash flows from operating activities. We discuss each adjustment in the sections that follow.

Depreciation

Study Note

Operating expenses on the income statement include depreciation expense, which does not require a cash outlay.

The investing activities section of the statement of cash flows shows the cash payments that the company made for plant assets, intangible assets, and natural resources during the accounting period. Depreciation expense, amortization expense, and depletion expense for these assets appear on the income statement as allocations of the costs of the original purchases to the current accounting period. The amount of these expenses can usually be found in the income statement or in a note to the financial statements. As you can see in Exhibit 15-2, Laguna Corporation's income statement discloses depreciation expense of $37,000, which would have been recorded as follows:

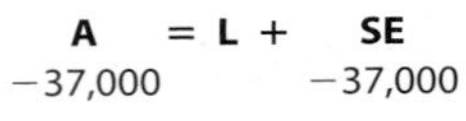

Entry in Journal Form:

	Dr.	Cr.
Depreciation Expense	37,000	
Accumulated Depreciation		37,000
To record annual depreciation on plant assets		

Even though depreciation expense appears on the income statement, it involves no outlay of cash and so does not affect cash flows in the current period. Thus, to arrive at cash flows from operations on the statement of cash flows,

FOCUS ON BUSINESS PRACTICE IFRS

The Direct Method May Become More Important

At present, the direct method of preparing the operating section of the statement of cash flows is not important, but this may change if the International Accounting Standards Board (IASB) has its way. As mentioned earlier in the text, 99 percent of public companies in the United States presently use the indirect method to show the operating activities section of the statement of cash flows. However, in the interest of converging U.S. GAAP with international financial reporting standards (IFRS), the IASB is promoting the use of the direct method, even though it is more costly for companies to prepare. IFRS will continue to require a reconciliation of net income and net cash flows from operating activities similar to what is now done in the indirect method. **CVS**'s statement of cash flows, as shown in the Supplement to Chapter 5, is one of the few U.S. companies to use the direct method with reconciliation. Thus, its approach is very similar to what all companies may do if IFRS are adopted in the United States.

EXHIBIT 15-4
Schedule of Cash Flows from Operating Activities: Indirect Method

Laguna Corporation Schedule of Cash Flows from Operating Activities For the Year Ended December 31, 2010		
Cash flows from operating activities		
Net income		$16,000
Adjustments to reconcile net income to net cash flows from operating activities		
Depreciation	$ 37,000	
Gain on sale of investments	(12,000)	
Loss on sale of plant assets	3,000	
Changes in current assets and current liabilities		
Decrease in accounts receivable	8,000	
Increase in inventory	(34,000)	
Decrease in prepaid expenses	4,000	
Increase in accounts payable	7,000	
Increase in accrued liabilities	3,000	
Decrease in income taxes payable	(2,000)	14,000
Net cash flows from operating activities		$30,000

an adjustment is needed to increase net income by the amount of depreciation expense shown on the income statement.

Gains and Losses

Study Note

Gains and losses by themselves do not represent cash flows; they are merely bookkeeping adjustments. For example, when a long-term asset is sold, it is the proceeds (cash received), not the gain or loss, that constitute cash flow.

Like depreciation expense, gains and losses that appear on the income statement do not affect cash flows from operating activities and need to be removed from this section of the statement of cash flows. The cash receipts generated by the disposal of the assets that resulted in the gains or losses are included in the investing activities section of the statement of cash flows. Thus, to reconcile net income to cash flows from operating activities (and prevent double counting), gains and losses must be removed from net income.

For example, on its income statement, Laguna Corporation shows a $12,000 gain on the sale of investments. This amount is subtracted from net income to reconcile net income to net cash flows from operating activities. The reason for doing this is that the $12,000 is included in the investing activities section of the statement of cash flows as part of the cash from the sale of the investment. Because the gain has already been included in the calculation of net income, the $12,000 gain must be subtracted to prevent double counting.

Laguna's income statement also shows a $3,000 loss on the sale of plant assets. This loss is already reflected in the sale of plant assets in the investing activities section of the statement of cash flows. Thus, the $3,000 is added to net income to reconcile net income to net cash flows from operating activities.

Changes in Current Assets

Decreases in current assets other than cash have positive effects on cash flows, and increases in current assets have negative effects on cash flows. A decrease in a current asset frees up invested cash, thereby increasing cash flow. An increase in a current asset consumes cash, thereby decreasing cash flow. For example, look at Laguna Corporation's income statement and balance sheets in Exhibits 15-2 and 15-3. Note that net sales in 2010 were $698,000 and that Accounts Receivable decreased by $8,000. Thus, collections were $8,000 more than sales recorded for the year, and the total cash received from sales was $706,000 ($698,000 + $8,000 = $706,000). The effect on Accounts Receivable can be illustrated as follows:

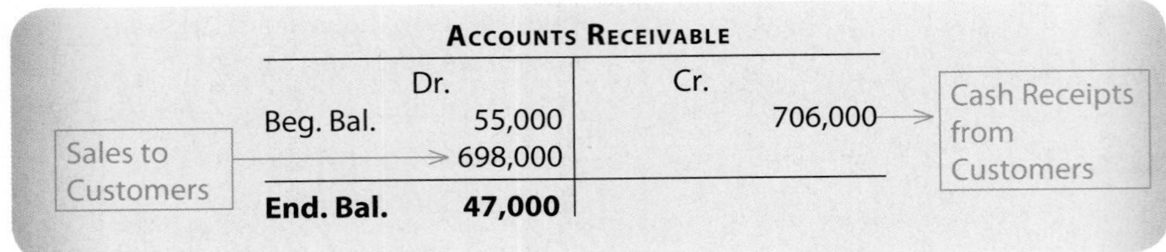

To reconcile net income to net cash flows from operating activities, the $8,000 decrease in accounts receivable is added to net income.

Inventory can be analyzed in the same way. For example, Exhibit 15-3 shows that Laguna's Inventory account increased by $34,000 between 2009 and 2010. This means that Laguna expended $34,000 more in cash for purchases than it included in cost of goods sold on its income statement. Because of this expenditure, net income is higher than net cash flows from operating activities, so $34,000 must be deducted from net income. By the same logic, the decrease of $4,000 in prepaid expenses shown on the balance sheets must be added to net income to reconcile net income to net cash flows from operating activities.

Changes in Current Liabilities

The effect that changes in current liabilities have on cash flows is the opposite of the effect of changes in current assets. An increase in a current liability represents a postponement of a cash payment, which frees up cash and increases cash flow in the current period. A decrease in a current liability consumes cash, which decreases cash flow. To reconcile net income to net cash flows from operating activities, increases in current liabilities are added to net income, and decreases are deducted. For example, Exhibit 15-3 shows that from 2009 to 2010, Laguna's accounts payable increased by $7,000. This means that Laguna paid $7,000 less to creditors than the amount indicated in the cost of goods sold on its income statement. The following T account illustrates this relationship:

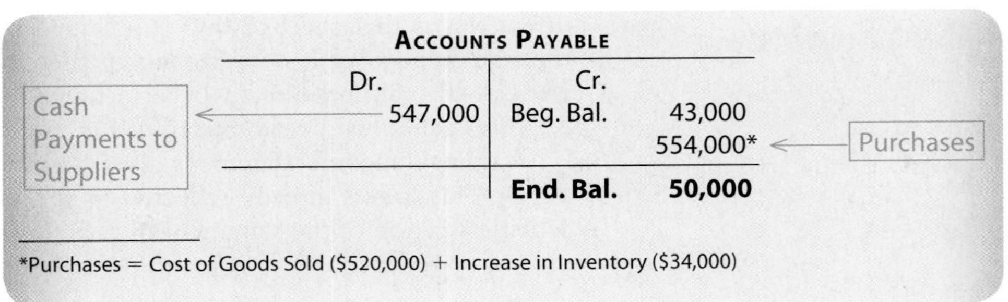

Thus, $7,000 must be added to net income to reconcile net income to net cash flows from operating activities. By the same logic, the increase of $3,000 in accrued liabilities shown on the balance sheets must be added to net income, and the decrease of $2,000 in income taxes payable must be deducted from net income.

Schedule of Cash Flows from Operating Activities

In summary, Exhibit 15-4 shows that by using the indirect method, net income of $16,000 has been adjusted by reconciling items totaling $14,000 to arrive at net cash flows from operating activities of $30,000. This means that although Laguna's net income was $16,000, the company actually had net cash flows of $30,000 available from operating activities to use for purchasing assets, reducing debts, and paying dividends.

The treatment of income statement items that do not affect cash flows can be summarized as follows:

	Add to or Deduct from Net Income
Depreciation expense	Add
Amortization expense	Add
Depletion expense	Add
Losses	Add
Gains	Deduct

The following summarizes the adjustments for increases and decreases in current assets and current liabilities:

	Add to Net Income	*Deduct from Net Income*
Current assets		
Accounts receivable (net)	Decrease	Increase
Inventory	Decrease	Increase
Prepaid expenses	Decrease	Increase
Current liabilities		
Accounts payable	Increase	Decrease
Accrued liabilities	Increase	Decrease
Income taxes payable	Increase	Decrease

FOCUS ON BUSINESS PRACTICE

What Is EBITDA, and Is It Any Good?

Some companies and analysts like to use EBITDA (an acronym for Earnings Before Interest, Taxes, Depreciation, and Amortization) as a short-cut measure of cash flows from operations. But recent events have caused many analysts to reconsider this measure of performance. For instance, when **WorldCom** transferred $3.8 billion from expenses to capital expenditures in one year, it touted its EBITDA; at the time, the firm was, in fact, nearly bankrupt. The demise of **Vivendi**, the big French company that imploded when it did not have enough cash to pay its debts and that also touted its EBITDA, is another reason that analysts have had second thoughts about relying on this measure of performance.

Some analysts are now saying that EBITDA is "to a great extent misleading" and that it "is a confusing metric. . . . Some take it for a proxy for profits and some take it for a proxy for cash flow, and it's neither."[10] Cash flows from operations and free cash flow, both of which take into account interest, taxes, and depreciation, are better and more comprehensive measures of a company's cash-generating efficiency.

For the year ended June 30, 2011, Hoffer Corporation's net income was $7,400. Its depreciation expense was $2,000. During the year, its Accounts Receivable increased by $4,400, Inventories increased by $7,000, Prepaid Rent decreased by $1,400, Accounts Payable increased by $14,000, Salaries Payable increased by $1,000, and Income Taxes Payable decreased by $600. The company also had a gain on the sale of investments of $1,800. Use the indirect method to prepare a schedule of cash flows from operating activities.

SOLUTION

Hoffer Corporation
Schedule of Cash Flows from Operating Activities
For the Year Ended June 30, 2011

Cash flows from operating activities		
Net income		$ 7,400
Adjustments to reconcile net income to net cash flows from operating activities		
Depreciation	$ 2,000	
Gain on sale of investments	(1,800)	
Changes in current assets and current liabilities		
Increase in accounts receivable	(4,400)	
Increase in inventories	(7,000)	
Decrease in prepaid rent	1,400	
Increase in accounts payable	14,000	
Increase in salaries payable	1,000	
Decrease in income taxes payable	(600)	4,600
Net cash flows from operating activities		$12,000

Investing Activities

LO4 Determine cash flows from investing activities.

To determine cash flows from investing activities, accounts involving cash receipts and cash payments from investing activities are examined individually. The objective is to explain the change in each account balance from one year to the next.

Although investing activities center on the long-term assets shown on the balance sheet, they also include any short-term investments shown under current assets on the balance sheet and any investment gains and losses on the income statement. The balance sheets in Exhibit 15-3 show that Laguna had no short-term investments and that its long-term assets consisted of investments and plant assets. The income statement in Exhibit 15-2 shows that Laguna had a gain on the sale of investments and a loss on the sale of plant assets.

The following transactions pertain to Laguna's investing activities in 2010:

1. Purchased investments in the amount of $78,000.
2. Sold for $102,000 investments that cost $90,000.
3. Purchased plant assets in the amount of $120,000.
4. Sold for $5,000 plant assets that cost $10,000 and that had accumulated depreciation of $2,000.
5. Issued $100,000 of bonds at face value in a noncash exchange for plant assets.

Study Note

Investing activities involve long-term assets and short- and long-term investments. Inflows and outflows of cash are shown in the investing activities section of the statement of cash flows.

In the following sections, we analyze the accounts related to investing activities to determine their effects on Laguna's cash flows.

Investments

Our objective in this section is to explain Laguna Corporation's $12,000 decrease in investments. We do this by analyzing the increases and decreases in Laguna's Investments account to determine their effects on the Cash account.

Item **1** in the list of Laguna's transactions states that its purchases of investments totaled $78,000 during 2010. This transaction, which caused a $78,000 decrease in cash flows, is recorded as follows:

A	=	L	+	SE
+78,000				
−78,000				

	Dr.	Cr.
Investments	78,000	
Cash		78,000
Purchase of investments		

Item **2** states that Laguna sold for $102,000 investments that cost $90,000. This transaction resulted in a gain of $12,000. It is recorded as follows:

A	=	L	+	SE
+102,000				+12,000
−90,000				

	Dr.	Cr.
Cash	102,000	
Investments		90,000
Gain on Sale of Investments		12,000
Sale of investments for a gain		

Study Note

The $102,000 price obtained, not the $12,000 gained, constitutes the cash flow.

The effect of this transaction is a $102,000 increase in cash flows. Note that the gain on the sale is included in the $102,000. This is the reason we excluded it in computing cash flows from operations. If it had been included in that section, it would have been counted twice. We have now explained the $12,000 decrease in the Investments account during 2010, as illustrated in the following T account:

Investments

Dr.		Cr.	
Beg. Bal.	127,000	Sales	90,000
Purchases	78,000		
End. Bal.	**115,000**		

The cash flow effects of these transactions are shown in the investing activities section of the statement of cash flows as follows:

Purchase of investments	($ 78,000)
Sale of investments	102,000

Notice that purchases and sales are listed separately as cash outflows and inflows to give readers of the statement a complete view of investing activity. However, some companies prefer to list them as a single net amount. If Laguna Corporation had short-term investments or marketable securities, the analysis of cash flows would be the same.

Plant Assets

For plant assets, we have to explain changes in both the Plant Assets account and the related Accumulated Depreciation account. Exhibit 15-3 shows that from 2009 to 2010, Laguna Corporation's plant assets increased by $210,000 and that accumulated depreciation increased by $35,000.

Item **3** in the list of Laguna's transactions in 2010 states that the company purchased plant assets totaling $120,000. The following entry records this cash outflow:

A	=	L	+	SE
+120,000				
−120,000				

	Dr.	Cr.
Plant Assets	120,000	
Cash		120,000
Purchase of plant assets		

Item **4** states that Laguna Corporation sold for $5,000 plant assets that cost $10,000 and that had accumulated depreciation of $2,000. Thus, this transaction resulted in a loss of $3,000. The entry to record it is as follows:

A	=	L	+	SE
+5,000				−3,000
+2,000				
−10,000				

	Dr.	Cr.
Cash	5,000	
Accumulated Depreciation	2,000	
Loss on Sale of Plant Assets	3,000	
Plant Assets		10,000
Sale of plant assets at a loss		

Study Note

Even though Laguna had a loss on the sale of plant assets, it realized a positive cash flow of $5,000, which will be reported in the investing activities section of its statement of cash flows. When the indirect method is used, the loss is eliminated with an "add-back" to net income.

Note that in this transaction, the positive cash flow is equal to the amount of cash received, $5,000. The loss on the sale of plant assets is included in the investing activities section of the statement of cash flows and excluded from the operating activities section by adjusting net income for the amount of the loss. The amount of a loss or gain on the sale of an asset is determined by the amount of cash received and does not represent a cash outflow or inflow.

The investing activities section of Laguna's statement of cash flows reports the firm's purchase and sale of plant assets as follows:

Purchase of plant assets	($120,000)
Sale of plant assets	5,000

Cash outflows and cash inflows are listed separately here, but companies sometimes combine them into a single net amount, as they do the purchase and sale of investments.

Item **5** in the list of Laguna's transactions is a noncash exchange that affects two long-term accounts, Plant Assets and Bonds Payable. It is recorded as follows:

A	=	L	+	SE
+100,000		+100,000		

	Dr.	Cr.
Plant Assets	100,000	
Bonds Payable		100,000
Issued bonds at face value for plant assets		

Although this transaction does not involve an inflow or outflow of cash, it is a significant transaction involving both an investing activity (the purchase of plant assets) and a financing activity (the issue of bonds payable). Because one purpose of the statement of cash flows is to show important investing and financing activities, the transaction is listed at the bottom of the statement of cash flows or in a separate schedule, as follows:

Schedule of Noncash Investing and Financing Transactions

Issue of bonds payable for plant assets	$100,000

We have now accounted for all the changes related to Laguna's plant asset accounts. The following T accounts summarize these changes:

PLANT ASSETS

Dr.		Cr.	
Beg. Bal.	505,000	Sales	10,000
Cash Purchase	120,000		
Noncash Purchase	100,000		
End. Bal.	**715,000**		

ACCUMULATED DEPRECIATION

Dr.		Cr.	
Sale	2,000	Beg. Bal.	68,000
		Dep. Exp.	37,000
		End. Bal.	**103,000**

Had the balance sheet included specific plant asset accounts (e.g., Equipment and the related accumulated depreciation account) or other long-term asset accounts (e.g., Intangibles), the analysis would have been the same.

STOP & APPLY >

The following T accounts show Matiz Company's plant assets and accumulated depreciation at the end of 2011:

PLANT ASSETS

Dr.		Cr.	
Beg. Bal.	65,000	Disposals	23,000
Purchases	33,600		
End. Bal.	**75,600**		

ACCUMULATED DEPRECIATION

Dr.		Cr.	
Disposals	14,700	Beg. Bal.	34,500
		Depreciation	10,200
		End. Bal.	**30,000**

Matiz's income statement shows a gain on the sale of plant assets of $4,400. Compute the amounts that should be shown as cash flows from investing activities, and show how they should appear on Matiz's 2011 statement of cash flows.

SOLUTION

Cash flows from investing activities:

Purchase of plant assets	($33,600)
Sale of plant assets	12,700

The T accounts show total purchases of plant assets of $33,600, which is an outflow of cash, and disposal of plant assets that cost $23,000 and that had accumulated depreciation of $14,700. The income statement shows a $4,400 gain on the sale of the plant assets. The cash inflow from the disposal was as follows:

Plant assets	$23,000
Less accumulated depreciation	14,700
Book value	$ 8,300
Add gain on sale	4,400
Cash inflow from sale of plant assets	$12,700

Because the gain on the sale is included in the $12,700 in the investing activities section of the statement of cash flows, it should be deducted from net income in the operating activities section.

Financing Activities

LO5 Determine cash flows from financing activities.

Determining cash flows from financing activities is very similar to determining cash flows from investing activities, but the accounts analyzed relate to short-term borrowings, long-term liabilities, and stockholders' equity. Because Laguna Corporation does not have short-term borrowings, we deal only with long-term liabilities and stockholders' equity accounts.

The following transactions pertain to Laguna's financing activities in 2010:

1. Issued $100,000 of bonds at face value in a noncash exchange for plant assets.
2. Repaid $50,000 of bonds at face value at maturity.
3. Issued 15,200 shares of $5 par value common stock for $175,000.
4. Paid cash dividends in the amount of $8,000.
5. Purchased treasury stock for $25,000.

Bonds Payable

Exhibit 15-3 shows that Laguna's Bonds Payable account increased by $50,000 in 2010. Both items **1** and **2** in the list above affect this account. We analyzed item **1** in connection with plant assets, but it also pertains to the Bonds Payable account. As we noted, this transaction is reported on the schedule of noncash investing and financing transactions. Item **2** results in a cash outflow, which is recorded as follows:

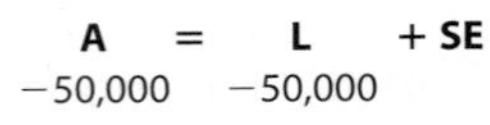

A	=	L	+ SE
−50,000		−50,000	

	Dr.	Cr.
Bonds Payable	50,000	
Cash		50,000
Repayment of bonds at face value at maturity		

This appears in the financing activities section of the statement of cash flows as follows:

Repayment of bonds	($50,000)

The following T account explains the change in Bonds Payable:

Bonds Payable

Dr.		Cr.	
Repayment	50,000	Beg. Bal.	245,000
		Noncash Issue	100,000
		End. Bal.	**295,000**

If Laguna Corporation had any notes payable, the analysis would be the same.

Common Stock

Like the Plant Assets account and its related account, accounts related to stockholders' equity should be analyzed together. For example, the Additional Paid-in Capital account should be examined along with the Common Stock account. In 2010, Laguna's Common Stock account increased by $76,000, and its Additional Paid-in Capital account increased by $99,000. Item **3** in the list of Laguna's transactions, which states that the company issued 15,200 shares of $5 par

FOCUS ON BUSINESS PRACTICE

How Much Cash Does a Company Need?

Some kinds of industries are more vulnerable to downturns in the economy than others. Historically, because of the amount of debt they carry and their large interest and loan payments, companies in the airline and automotive industries have been hard hit by economic downturns. But research has shown that high-tech companies with large amounts of intangible assets are also hard hit. Biotechnology, pharmaceutical, and computer hardware and software companies can lose up to 80 percent of their value in times of financial stress. In contrast, companies with large amounts of tangible assets, such as oil companies and railroads, can lose as little as 10 percent. To survive during economic downturns, it is very important for high-tech companies to use their cash-generating efficiency to build cash reserves. It makes sense for these companies to hoard cash and not pay dividends to the extent that companies in other industries do.[11]

value common stock for $175,000, explains these increases. The entry to record the cash inflow is as follows:

A	= L +	SE
+175,000		+76,000
		+99,000

	Dr.	Cr.
Cash	175,000	
Common Stock		76,000
Additional Paid-in Capital		99,000
Issued 15,200 shares of $5 par value common stock		

This appears in the financing activities section of the statement of cash flows as:

Issuance of common stock $175,000

The following analysis of this transaction is all that is needed to explain the changes in the two accounts during 2010:

Common Stock Dr.	Common Stock Cr.		Additional Paid-in Capital Dr.	Additional Paid-in Capital Cr.	
	Beg. Bal.	200,000		Beg. Bal.	115,000
	Issue	76,000		Issue	99,000
	End. Bal.	**276,000**		**End. Bal.**	**214,000**

Retained Earnings

At this point, we have dealt with several items that affect retained earnings. The only item affecting Laguna's retained earnings that we have not considered is the payment of $8,000 in cash dividends (item **4** in the list of Laguna's transactions). At the time it declared the dividend, Laguna would have debited its Cash Dividends account. After paying the dividend, it would have closed the Cash Dividends account to Retained Earnings and recorded the closing with the following entry:

A	= L +	SE
		−8,000
		+8,000

	Dr.	Cr.
Retained Earnings	8,000	
Cash Dividends		8,000
To close the Cash Dividends account		

Study Note

It is dividends paid, not dividends declared, that appear on the statement of cash flows.

Cash dividends would be displayed in the financing activities section of Laguna's statement of cash flows as follows:

Payment of dividends ($8,000)

The following T account shows the change in the Retained Earnings account:

Retained Earnings			
Dr.		Cr.	
Cash Dividends	8,000	Beg. Bal.	132,000
		Net Income	16,000
		End. Bal.	**140,000**

EXHIBIT 15-5
Statement of Cash Flows: Indirect Method

Laguna Corporation
Statement of Cash Flows
For the Year Ended December 31, 2010

Cash flows from operating activities		
Net income		$ 16,000
Adjustments to reconcile net income to net cash flows from operating activities		
Depreciation	$ 37,000	
Gain on sale of investments	(12,000)	
Loss on sale of plant assets	3,000	
Changes in current assets and current liabilities		
Decrease in accounts receivable	8,000	
Increase in inventory	(34,000)	
Decrease in prepaid expenses	4,000	
Increase in accounts payable	7,000	
Increase in accrued liabilities	3,000	
Decrease in income taxes payable	(2,000)	14,000
Net cash flows from operating activities		$ 30,000
Cash flows from investing activities		
Purchase of investments	($ 78,000)	
Sale of investments	102,000	
Purchase of plant assets	(120,000)	
Sale of plant assets	5,000	
Net cash flows from investing activities		(91,000)
Cash flows from financing activities		
Repayment of bonds	($ 50,000)	
Issuance of common stock	175,000	
Payment of dividends	(8,000)	
Purchase of treasury stock	(25,000)	
Net cash flows from financing activities		92,000
Net increase in cash		$ 31,000
Cash at beginning of year		15,000
Cash at end of year		$ 46,000

Schedule of Noncash Investing and Financing Transactions

Issue of bonds payable for plant assets	$100,000

Treasury Stock

As we noted in the chapter on contributed capital, many companies buy back their own stock on the open market. These buybacks use cash, as this entry shows:

A	=	L	+	SE
−25,000				−25,000

	Dr.	Cr.
Treasury Stock	25,000	
Cash		25,000
Purchased treasury stock		

Study Note

The purchase of treasury stock qualifies as a financing activity, but it is also a cash outflow.

This use of cash is classified in the statement of cash flows as a financing activity:

Purchase of treasury stock ($25,000)

The T account for this transaction is as follows:

Treasury Stock

	Dr.	Cr.
Purchase	25,000	

We have now analyzed all Laguna Corporation's income statement items, explained all balance sheet changes, and taken all additional information into account. Exhibit 15-5 shows how our data are assembled in Laguna's statement of cash flows.

STOP & APPLY >

During 2011, F & K Company issued $1,000,000 in long-term bonds at par, repaid $200,000 of notes payable at face value, issued notes payable of $40,000 for equipment, paid interest of $40,000, paid dividends of $25,000, and repurchased common stock in the amount of $50,000. Prepare the cash flows from financing activities section of the statement of cash flows.

SOLUTION

Cash flows from financing activities	
Issuance of long-term bonds	$1,000,000
Repayment of notes payable	(200,000)
Payment of dividends	(25,000)
Purchase of treasury stock	(50,000)
Net cash flows from financing activities	$ 725,000

Note: Interest is an operating activity. The exchange of the notes payable for equipment is a noncash investing and financing transaction.

▸ LOPATA CORPORATION: REVIEW PROBLEM

As we pointed out in this chapter's Decision Point, the managers of Lopata Corporation were concerned because in 2011, cash flows from operating activities were less than net income, cash and cash equivalents declined during the year, and the company was having trouble paying its bills on time. We asked the following questions:

- Why were Lopata Corporation's operating cash flows less than its net income, and why did its cash and cash equivalents decline during the year?
- What measures do managers, stockholders, and potential investors use to evaluate the strength of a company's cash flows and liquidity?

Statement of Cash Flows and Its Analysis
LO2 LO3
LO4 LO5
CASH FLOW

Lopata Corporation's income statement for 2011 appears below. Its comparative balance sheets for 2011 and 2010 follow. The company's records for 2011 provide this additional information:

a. Sold long-term investments that cost $35,000 for a gain of $6,250; made other long-term investments in the amount of $10,000.
b. Purchased 5 acres of land to build a parking lot for $12,500.
c. Sold equipment that cost $18,750 and that had accumulated depreciation of $12,650 at a loss of $1,150; purchased new equipment for $15,000.
d. Repaid notes payable in the amount of $50,000; borrowed $15,000 by signing new notes payable.
e. Converted $50,000 of bonds payable into 3,000 shares of common stock.
f. Reduced the Mortgage Payable account by $10,000.
g. Declared and paid cash dividends of $25,000.
h. Purchased treasury stock for $5,000.

	A	B	C
1	**Lopata Corporation**		
2	**Income Statement**		
3	**For the Year Ended December 31, 2011**		
4			
5	Net sales		$825,000
6	Cost of goods sold		460,000
7	Gross margin		$365,000
8	Operating expenses (including depreciation		
9	expense of $6,000 on buildings and		
10	$11,550 on equipment and amortization		
11	expense of $2,400)		235,000
12	Operating income		$130,000
13	Other income		
14	Interest expense	($27,500)	
15	Dividend income	1,700	
16	Gain on sale of investments	6,250	
17	Loss on disposal of equipment	(1,150)	(20,700)
18	Income before income taxes		$109,300
19	Income taxes expense		26,100
20	Net income		$ 83,200

	A	B	C	D	E
1	**Lopata Corporation**				
2	**Comparative Balance Sheets**				
3	**December 31, 2011 and 2010**				
4					
5		**2011**	**2010**	**Change**	**Increase or Decrease**
6		**Assets**			
7	Cash	$ 52,925	$ 60,925	($ 8,000)	Decrease
8	Accounts receivable (net)	148,000	157,250	(9,250)	Decrease
9	Inventory	161,000	150,500	10,500	Increase
10	Prepaid expenses	3,900	2,900	1,000	Increase
11	Long-term investments	18,000	43,000	(25,000)	Decrease
12	Land	75,000	62,500	12,500	Increase
13	Buildings	231,000	231,000	—	—
14	Accumulated depreciation–buildings	(45,500)	(39,500)	(6,000)	Increase
15	Equipment	79,865	83,615	(3,750)	Decrease
16	Accumulated depreciation–equipment	(21,700)	(22,800)	1,100	Decrease
17	Intangible assets	9,600	12,000	(2,400)	Decrease
18	Total assets	$712,090	$741,390	($29,300)	
19					
20	**Liabilities and Stockholders' Equity**				
21	Accounts payable	$ 66,875	$116,875	($50,000)	Decrease
22	Notes payable (current)	37,850	72,850	(35,000)	Decrease
23	Accrued liabilities	2,500	—	2,500	Increase
24	Income taxes payable	10,000	—	10,000	Increase
25	Bonds payable	105,000	155,000	(50,000)	Decrease
26	Mortgage payable	165,000	175,000	(10,000)	Decrease
27	Common stock, $10 par value	200,000	170,000	30,000	Increase
28	Additional paid-in capital	45,000	25,000	20,000	Increase
29	Retained earnings	104,865	46,665	58,200	Increase
30	Treasury stock	(25,000)	(20,000)	(5,000)	Increase
31	Total liabilities and stockholders' equity	$712,090	$741,390	($29,300)	

Required

1. Using the indirect method, prepare a statement of cash flows for Lopata Corporation for the year ended December 31, 2011.
2. User insight: Using data from Lopata's statement of cash flows, income statement, and comparative balance sheets, compute the company's cash flow yield, cash flows to sales, cash flows to assets, and free cash flow for 2011. What do your results indicate about the company's cash-generating efficiency? What do they indicate about Lopata's need to sell investments, issue stock, or borrow money to maintain current operations or finance future growth?
3. User insight: What is the apparent cause of Lopata's operating cash flow problem and the decline in its cash and cash equivalents?

Answers to Review Problem

1. Statement of cash flows using the indirect method:

	A	B	C
1	**Lopata Corporation**		
2	**Statement of Cash Flows**		
3	**For the Year Ended December 31, 2011**		
4			
5	**Cash flows from operating activities**		
6	Net income		$83,200
7	Adjustments to reconcile net income to net cash flows from operating activities		
8	Depreciation expense, buildings	$ 6,000	
9	Depreciation expense, equipment	11,550	
10	Amortization expense, intangible assets	2,400	
11	Gain on sale of investments	(6,250)	
12	Loss on disposal of equipment	1,150	
13	Changes in current assets and current liabilities		
14	Decrease in accounts receivable	9,250	
15	Increase in inventory	(10,500)	
16	Increase in prepaid expenses	(1,000)	
17	Decrease in accounts payable	(50,000)	
18	Increase in accrued liabilities	2,500	
19	Increase in income taxes payable	10,000	(24,900)
20	Net cash flows from operating activities		$58,300
21	**Cash flows from investing activities**		
22	Sale of long-term investments	$41,250 [a]	
23	Purchase of long-term investments	(10,000)	
24	Purchase of land	(12,500)	
25	Sale of equipment	4,950 [b]	
26	Purchase of equipment	(15,000)	
27	Net cash flows from investing activities		8,700
28	**Cash flows from financing activities**		
29	Repayment of notes payable	($50,000)	
30	Issuance of notes payable	15,000	
31	Reduction in mortgage	(10,000)	
32	Dividends paid	(25,000)	
33	Purchase of treasury stock	(5,000)	
34	Net cash flows from financing activities		(75,000)
35	Net (decrease) in cash		($ 8,000)
36	Cash at beginning of year		60,925
37	Cash at end of year		$52,925
38			
39	**Schedule of Noncash Investing and Financing Transactions**		
40	Conversion of bonds payable into common stock		$50,000
41			
42	[a] \$35,000 + \$6,250 (gain) = \$41,250		
43	[b] \$18,750 − \$12,650 = \$6,100 (book value) − \$1,150 (loss) = \$4,950		

2. Cash flow yield, cash flows to sales, cash flows to assets, and free cash flow for 2011:

$$\text{Cash Flow Yield} = \frac{\$58{,}300}{\$83{,}200} = 0.7 \text{ Times*}$$

$$\text{Cash Flows to Sales} = \frac{\$58{,}300}{\$825{,}000} = 7.1\%\text{*}$$

$$\text{Cash Flows to Assets} = \frac{\$58{,}300}{(\$712{,}090 + \$741{,}390) \div 2} = 8.0\%\text{*}$$

$$\text{Free Cash Flow} = \$58{,}300 - \$25{,}000 - \$12{,}500 - \$15{,}000 + \$4{,}950 = \$10{,}750$$

Lopata should generate at least $1 of net cash flows from operations for each $1 of net income. However, its cash flow yield shows that it generated only 70 cents for each $1 of net income. Judging from this result alone, Lopata's cash-generating efficiency is weak, and it seems likely that the company will have to sell investments, borrow money, or issue stock to maintain current operations or finance future growth.

3. The operating activities section of Lopata's statement of cash flows shows that the company reduced its accounts payable by $50,000. This one item more than offset the effects of all the other items and accounts for Lopata's operating cash flow problem and the decline in its cash and cash equivalents. Either Lopata unnecessarily paid its creditors a large amount, or its creditors have changed their terms. In the aftermath of the recession of the last few years, it has not been unusual for creditors to give less favorable terms as credit from banks has tightened.

---

*Rounded.

LO1 Describe the principal purposes and uses of the statement of cash flows, and identify its components.

The statement of cash flows shows how a company's operating, investing, and financing activities have affected cash during an accounting period. For the statement of cash flows, *cash* is defined as including both cash and cash equivalents. The primary purpose of the statement is to provide information about a firm's cash receipts and cash payments during an accounting period. A secondary purpose is to provide information about a firm's operating, investing, and financing activities. Management uses the statement to assess liquidity, determine dividend policy, and plan investing and financing activities. Investors and creditors use it to assess the company's cash-generating ability.

The statement of cash flows has three major classifications: (1) operating activities, which involve the cash effects of transactions and other events that enter into the determination of net income; (2) investing activities, which involve the acquisition and sale of marketable securities and long-term assets and the making and collecting of loans; and (3) financing activities, which involve obtaining resources from stockholders and creditors and providing the former with a return on their investments and the latter with repayment. Noncash investing and financing transactions are also important because they affect future cash flows; these exchanges of long-term assets or liabilities are of interest to potential investors and creditors.

LO2 Analyze the statement of cash flows.

In examining a firm's statement of cash flows, analysts tend to focus on cash-generating efficiency and free cash flow. Cash-generating efficiency is a firm's ability to generate cash from its current or continuing operations. The ratios used to measure cash-generating efficiency are cash flow yield, cash flows to sales, and cash flows to assets. Free cash flow is the cash that remains after deducting the funds a firm must commit to continue operating at its planned level. These commitments include current and continuing operations, interest, income taxes, dividends, and capital expenditures.

LO3 Use the indirect method to determine cash flows from operating activities.

The indirect method adjusts net income for all items in the income statement that do not have cash flow effects (such as depreciation, amortization, and gains and losses on sales of assets) and for changes in current assets and current liabilities that affect operating cash flows. Generally, increases in current assets have a negative effect on cash flows, and decreases have a positive effect. Conversely, increases in current liabilities have a positive effect on cash flows, and decreases have a negative effect.

LO4 Determine cash flows from investing activities.

Investing activities involve the acquisition and sale of property, plant, and equipment and other long-term assets, including long-term investments. They also involve the acquisition and sale of short-term marketable securities, other than trading securities, and the making and collecting of loans. Cash flows from investing activities are determined by analyzing the cash flow effects of changes in each account related to investing activities. The effects of gains and losses reported on the income statement must also be considered.

LO5 Determine cash flows from financing activities.

Determining cash flows from financing activities is almost identical to determining cash flows from investing activities. The difference is that the accounts analyzed relate to short-term borrowings, long-term liabilities, and stockholders' equity. After the changes in the balance sheet accounts from one accounting period to the next have been explained, all the cash flow effects should have been identified.

REVIEW of Concepts and Terminology

The following concepts and terms were introduced in this chapter:

Cash 658 (LO1)

Cash equivalents 658 (LO1)

Cash-generating efficiency 663 (LO2)

Direct method 668 (LO3)

Financing activities 660 (LO1)

Free cash flow 665 (LO2)

Indirect method 668 (LO3)

Investing activities 659 (LO1)

Noncash investing and financing transactions 660 (LO1)

Operating activities 658 (LO1)

Statement of cash flows 658 (LO1)

Key Ratios

Cash flows to assets 664 (LO2)

Cash flows to sales 664 (LO2)

Cash flow yield 664 (LO2)

CHAPTER ASSIGNMENTS

BUILDING Your Basic Knowledge and Skills

Short Exercises

LO1 **Classification of Cash Flow Transactions**

SE 1. The list that follows itemizes Furlong Corporation's transactions. Identify each as (a) an operating activity, (b) an investing activity, (c) a financing activity, (d) a noncash transaction, or (e) none of the above.

1. Sold land.
2. Declared and paid a cash dividend.
3. Paid interest.
4. Issued common stock for plant assets.
5. Issued preferred stock.
6. Borrowed cash on a bank loan.

LO2 **Cash-Generating Efficiency Ratios and Free Cash Flow**

SE 2. In 2011, Ross Corporation had year-end assets of \$550,000, sales of \$790,000, net income of \$90,000, net cash flows from operating activities of \$180,000, purchases of plant assets of \$120,000, and sales of plant assets of \$20,000, and it paid dividends of \$40,000. In 2010, year-end assets were \$500,000. Calculate the cash-generating efficiency ratios of cash flow yield, cash flows to sales, and cash flows to assets. Also calculate free cash flow.

LO2 **Cash-Generating Efficiency Ratios and Free Cash Flow**

SE 3. Examine the cash flow measures in requirement **2** of the review problem in this chapter. Discuss the meaning of these ratios.

LO3 **Computing Cash Flows from Operating Activities: Indirect Method**

SE 4. Wachowski Corporation had a net income of \$33,000 during 2010. During the year, the company had depreciation expense of \$14,000. Accounts Receivable increased by \$11,000, and Accounts Payable increased by \$5,000. Those were the company's only current assets and current liabilities. Use the indirect method to determine net cash flows from operating activities.

LO3 **Computing Cash Flows from Operating Activities: Indirect Method**

SE 5. During 2010, Minh Corporation had a net income of \$144,000. Included on its income statement were depreciation expense of \$16,000 and amortization expense of \$1,800. During the year, Accounts Receivable decreased by \$8,200, Inventories increased by \$5,400, Prepaid Expenses decreased by \$1,000, Accounts Payable decreased by \$14,000, and Accrued Liabilities decreased by \$1,700. Use the indirect method to determine net cash flows from operating activities.

LO4 **Cash Flows from Investing Activities and Noncash Transactions**

SE 6. During 2010, Howard Company purchased land for \$375,000. It paid \$125,000 in cash and signed a \$250,000 mortgage for the rest. The company also sold for \$95,000 cash a building that originally cost \$90,000, on which it had \$70,000 of accumulated depreciation, making a gain of \$75,000. Prepare the cash flows from investing activities section and the schedule of noncash investing and financing transactions of the statement of cash flows.

LO5 **Cash Flows from Financing Activities**

SE 7. During 2010, Arizona Company issued \$500,000 in long-term bonds at 96, repaid \$75,000 of bonds at face value, paid interest of \$40,000, and paid dividends of \$25,000. Prepare the cash flows from the financing activities section of the statement of cash flows.

LO1 LO3 LO4 LO5

Identifying Components of the Statement of Cash Flows

SE 8. Assuming the indirect method is used to prepare the statement of cash flows, tell whether each of the following items would appear (a) in cash flows from operating activities, (b) in cash flows from investing activities, (c) in cash flows from financing activities, (d) in the schedule of noncash investing and financing transactions, or (e) not on the statement of cash flows at all:

1. Dividends paid
2. Cash receipts from sales
3. Decrease in accounts receivable
4. Sale of plant assets
5. Gain on sale of investments
6. Issue of stock for plant assets
7. Issue of common stock
8. Net income

Exercises

LO1 LO2

Discussion Questions

E 1. Develop brief answers to each of the following questions:

1. Which statement is more useful—the income statement or the statement of cash flows?
2. How would you respond to someone who says that the most important item on the statement of cash flows is the change in the cash balance for the year?
3. If a company's cash flow yield is less than 1.0, would its cash flows to sales and cash flows to assets be greater or less than profit margin and return on assets, respectively?

LO3 LO4 LO5

Discussion Questions

E 2. Develop brief answers to each of the following questions:

1. If a company has positive earnings, can cash flows from operating activities ever be negative?
2. Which adjustments to net income in the operating activities section of the statement of cash flows are directly related to cash flows in other sections?
3. In computing free cash flow, what is an argument for treating the purchases of treasury stock like dividend payments?

LO1

Classification of Cash Flow Transactions

E 3. Koral Corporation engaged in the transactions listed below. Identify each transaction as (a) an operating activity, (b) an investing activity, (c) a financing activity, (d) a noncash transaction, or (e) not on the statement of cash flows. (Assume the indirect method is used.)

1. Declared and paid a cash dividend.
2. Purchased a long-term investment.
3. Increased accounts receivable.
4. Paid interest.
5. Sold equipment at a loss.
6. Issued long-term bonds for plant assets.
7. Increased dividends receivable.
8. Issued common stock.
9. Declared and issued a stock dividend.
10. Repaid notes payable.
11. Decreased wages payable.
12. Purchased a 60-day Treasury bill.
13. Purchased land.

LO2

Cash-Generating Efficiency Ratios and Free Cash Flow

E 4. In 2011, Heart Corporation had year-end assets of $1,200,000, sales of $1,650,000, net income of $140,000, net cash flows from operating activities of $195,000, dividends of $60,000, purchases of plant assets of $250,000, and sales of plant assets of $45,000. In 2010, year-end assets were $1,050,000. Calculate free cash flow and the cash-generating efficiency ratios of cash flow yield, cash flows to sales, and cash flows to assets.

LO3 Cash Flows from Operating Activities: Indirect Method

E 5. The condensed single-step income statement for the year ended December 31, 2012, of Sunderland Chemical Company, a distributor of farm fertilizers and herbicides, appears as follows:

Sales		$13,000,000
Less: Cost of goods sold	$7,600,000	
Operating expenses (including depreciation of $820,000.	3,800,000	
Income taxes expense	400,000	11,800,000
Net income		$ 1,200,000

Selected accounts from Sunderland Chemical Company's balance sheets for 2012 and 2011 are as follows:

	2012	2011
Accounts receivable	$2,400,000	$1,700,000
Inventory	840,000	1,020,000
Prepaid expenses	260,000	180,000
Accounts payable	960,000	720,000
Accrued liabilities	60,000	100,000
Income taxes payable	140,000	120,000

Present in good form a schedule of cash flows from operating activities using the indirect method.

LO3 Computing Cash Flows from Operating Activities: Indirect Method

E 6. During 2010, Diaz Corporation had net income of $41,000. Included on its income statement were depreciation expense of $2,300 and amortization expense of $300. During the year, Accounts Receivable increased by $3,400, Inventories decreased by $1,900, Prepaid Expenses decreased by $200, Accounts Payable increased by $5,000, and Accrued Liabilities decreased by $450. Determine net cash flows from operating activities using the indirect method.

LO3 Preparing a Schedule of Cash Flows from Operating Activities: Indirect Method

E 7. For the year ended June 30, 2011, net income for Silk Corporation was $7,400. Depreciation expense was $2,000. During the year, Accounts Receivable increased by $4,400, Inventories increased by $7,000, Prepaid Rent decreased by $1,400, Accounts Payable increased by $14,000, Salaries Payable increased by $1,000, and Income Taxes Payable decreased by $600. Use the indirect method to prepare a schedule of cash flows from operating activities.

LO4 Computing Cash Flows from Investing Activities: Investments

E 8. CUD Company's T account for long-term available-for-sale investments at the end of 2010 is as follows:

Investments			
Dr.		Cr.	
Beg. Bal.	152,000	Sales	156,000
Purchases	232,000		
End. Bal.	**228,000**		

In addition, CUD Company's income statement shows a loss on the sale of investments of $26,000. Compute the amounts to be shown as cash flows from investing activities, and show how they are to appear in the statement of cash flows.

LO4 Computing Cash Flows from Investing Activities: Plant Assets

E 9. The T accounts for plant assets and accumulated depreciation for CUD Company at the end of 2010 are as follows:

Plant Assets

Dr.		Cr.	
Beg. Bal.	260,000	Disposals	92,000
Purchases	134,400		
End. Bal.	**302,400**		

Accumulated Depreciation

Dr.		Cr.	
Disposals	58,800	Beg. Bal.	138,000
		Depreciation	40,800
		End. Bal.	**120,000**

In addition, CUD Company's income statement shows a gain on sale of plant assets of $17,600. Compute the amounts to be shown as cash flows from investing activities, and show how they are to appear on the statement of cash flows.

LO5 Determining Cash Flows from Financing Activities: Notes Payable

E 10. All transactions involving Notes Payable and related accounts of Pearl Company during 2010 are as follows:

	Dr.	Cr.
Cash	18,000	
Notes Payable		18,000
Bank loan		

	Dr.	Cr.
Patent	30,000	
Notes Payable		30,000
Purchase of patent by issuing note payable		

	Dr.	Cr.
Notes Payable	5,000	
Interest Expense	500	
Cash		5,500
Repayment of note payable at maturity		

Determine the amounts of the transactions affecting financing activities and show how they are to appear on the statement of cash flows for 2010.

LO3 LO4 LO5 Preparing the Statement of Cash Flows: Indirect Method

E 11. Olbrot Corporation's income statement for the year ended June 30, 2012, and its comparative balance sheets for June 30, 2012 and 2011 appear below and on the following page.

Olbrot Corporation
Income Statement
For the Year Ended June 30, 2012

Sales	$244,000
Cost of goods sold	148,100
Gross margin	$ 95,900
Operating expenses	45,000
Operating income	$ 50,900
Interest expense	2,800
Income before income taxes	$ 48,100
Income taxes expense	12,300
Net income	$ 35,800

Olbrot Corporation
Comparative Balance Sheets
June 30, 2012 and 2011

	2012	2011
Assets		
Cash	$139,800	$ 25,000
Accounts receivable (net)	42,000	52,000
Inventory	86,800	96,800
Prepaid expenses	6,400	5,200
Furniture	110,000	120,000
Accumulated depreciation–furniture	(18,000)	(10,000)
Total assets	$367,000	$289,000
Liabilities and Stockholders' Equity		
Accounts payable	$ 26,000	$ 28,000
Income taxes payable	2,400	3,600
Notes payable (long-term)	74,000	70,000
Common stock, $10 par value	230,000	180,000
Retained earnings	34,600	7,400
Total liabilities and stockholders' equity	$367,000	$289,000

Olbrot issued a $44,000 note payable for purchase of furniture; sold at carrying value furniture that cost $54,000 with accumulated depreciation of $30,600; recorded depreciation on the furniture for the year, $38,600; repaid a note in the amount of $40,000; issued $50,000 of common stock at par value; and paid dividends of $8,600. Prepare Olbrot's statement of cash flows for the year 2012 using the indirect method.

Problems

LO1 Classification of Cash Flow Transactions

P 1. Analyze each transaction listed in the table that follows and place X's in the appropriate columns to indicate the transaction's classification and its effect on cash flows using the indirect method.

	Cash Flow Classification				Effect on Cash Flows		
Transaction	**Operating Activity**	**Investing Activity**	**Financing Activity**	**Noncash Transaction**	**Increase**	**Decrease**	**No Effect**
1. Paid a cash dividend.							
2. Decreased accounts receivable.							
3. Increased inventory.							
4. Incurred a net loss.							
5. Declared and issued a stock dividend.							
6. Retired long-term debt with cash.							
7. Sold available-for-sale securities at a loss.							

(continued)

Transaction	Cash Flow Classification: Operating Activity	Investing Activity	Financing Activity	Noncash Transaction	Effect on Cash Flows: Increase	Decrease	No Effect
8. Issued stock for equipment.							
9. Decreased prepaid insurance.							
10. Purchased treasury stock with cash.							
11. Retired a fully depreciated truck (no gain or loss).							
12. Increased interest payable.							
13. Decreased dividends receivable on investment.							
14. Sold treasury stock.							
15. Increased income taxes payable.							
16. Transferred cash to money market account.							
17. Purchased land and building with a mortgage.							

LO1 LO2 **Interpreting and Analyzing the Statement of Cash Flows**

P 2. The comparative statements of cash flows for Executive Style Corporation, a manufacturer of high-quality suits for men, appear on the next page. To expand its markets and familiarity with its brand, the company attempted a new strategic diversification in 2011 by acquiring a chain of retail men's stores in outlet malls. Its plan was to expand in malls around the country, but department stores viewed the action as infringing on their territory.

Required

Evaluate the success of the company's strategy by answering the questions that follow.

1. What are the primary reasons cash flows from operating activities differ from net income? What is the effect on the acquisition in 2009? What conclusions can you draw from the changes in 2010?
2. Compute free cash flow for both years. What was the total cost of the acquisition? Was the company able to finance expansion in 2009 by generating internal cash flow? What was the situation in 2010?
3. User insight ▶ What are the most significant financing activities in 2009? How did the company finance the acquisition? Do you think this is a good strategy? What other issues might you question in financing activities?
4. User insight ▶ Based on results in 2010, what actions was the company forced to take and what is your overall assessment of the company's diversification strategy?

Executive Style Corporation
Statement of Cash Flows
For the Years Ended December 31, 2011 and 2010

(In thousands)	2011	2010
Cash flows from operating activities		
Net income (loss)	($ 21,545)	$ 38,015
Adjustments to reconcile net income to net cash flows from operating activities		
Depreciation	35,219	25,018
Loss on closure of retail outlets	35,000	
Changes in current assets and current liabilities		
Decrease (increase) in accounts receivable	50,000	(44,803)
Decrease (increase) in inventory	60,407	(51,145)
Decrease (increase) in prepaid expenses	1,367	2,246
Increase (decrease) in accounts payable	30,579	1,266
Increase (decrease) in accrued liabilities	1,500	(2,788)
Increase (decrease) in income taxes payable	(8,300)	(6,281)
	$205,772	($ 76,487)
Net cash flows from operating activities	$184,227	($ 38,472)
Cash flows from investing activities		
Capital expenditures, net	($ 16,145)	($ 33,112)
Purchase of Retail Division, cash portion	—	(201,000)
Net cash flows from investing activities	($ 16,145)	($234,112)
Cash flows from financing activities		
Increase (decrease) in notes payable to banks	($123,500)	$228,400
Reduction in long-term debt	(9,238)	(10,811)
Payment of dividends	(22,924)	(19,973)
Purchase of treasury stock	—	(12,500)
Net cash flows from financing activities	($155,662)	$185,116
Net increase (decrease) in cash	$ 12,420	($ 87,468)
Cash at beginning of year	16,032	103,500
Cash at end of year	$ 28,452	$ 16,032

Schedule of Noncash Investing and Financing Transactions

Issue of bonds payable for retail acquisition		$ 50,000

LO2 LO3 LO4 LO5

Statement of Cash Flows: Indirect Method

P 3. The comparative balance sheets for Alvin Arts, Inc., for December 31, 2011 and 2009 appear on the opposite page. Additional information about Alvin Arts's operations during 2010 is as follows: (a) net income, $28,000; (b) building and equipment depreciation expense amounts, $15,000 and $3,000, respectively; (c) equipment that cost $13,500 with accumulated depreciation of $12,500 sold at a gain of $5,300; (d) equipment purchases, $12,500; (e) patent amortization, $3,000; purchase of patent, $1,000; (f) funds borrowed by issuing notes payable, $25,000; notes payable repaid, $15,000; (g) land and building purchased for $162,000 by signing a mortgage for the total cost; (h) 1,500 shares of $20 par value common stock issued for a total of $50,000; and (i) paid cash dividends, $9,000.

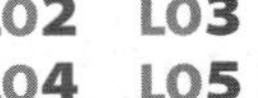

Alvin Arts, Inc.
Comparative Balance Sheets
December 31, 2010 and 2009

	2010	2009
Assets		
Cash	$ 94,560	$ 27,360
Accounts receivable (net)	102,430	75,430
Inventory	112,890	137,890
Prepaid expenses	—	20,000
Land	25,000	—
Building	137,000	—
Accumulated depreciation–building	(15,000)	—
Equipment	33,000	34,000
Accumulated depreciation–equipment	(14,500)	(24,000)
Patents	4,000	6,000
Total assets	$479,380	$276,680
Liabilities and Stockholders' Equity		
Accounts payable	$ 10,750	$ 36,750
Notes payable (current)	10,000	—
Accrued liabilities	—	12,300
Mortgage payable	162,000	—
Common stock, $10 par value	180,000	150,000
Additional paid-in capital	57,200	37,200
Retained earnings	59,430	40,430
Total liabilities and stockholders' equity	$479,380	$276,680

Required

1. Using the indirect method, prepare a statement of cash flows for Alvin Arts, Inc.
2. User insight ▶ Why did Alvin Arts have an increase in cash of $67,200 when it recorded net income of only $28,000? Discuss and interpret.
3. User insight ▶ Compute and assess cash flow yield and free cash flow for 2010. What is your assessment of Alvin's cash-generating ability?

LO2 LO3 LO4 LO5

Statement of Cash Flows: Indirect Method

P 4. The comparative balance sheets for Lopez Tools, Inc., for December 31, 2010 and 2009, are at the top of the next page. During 2010, the company had net income of $48,000 and building and equipment depreciation expenses of $40,000 and $30,000, respectively. It amortized intangible assets in the amount of $10,000; purchased investments for $58,000; sold investments for $75,000, on which it recorded a gain of $17,000; issued $120,000 of long-term bonds at face value; purchased land and a warehouse through a $160,000 mortgage; paid $20,000 to reduce the mortgage; borrowed $30,000 by issuing notes payable; repaid notes payable in the amount of $90,000; declared and paid cash dividends in the amount of $18,000; and purchased treasury stock in the amount of $10,000.

Lopez Tools, Inc.
Comparative Balance Sheets
December 31, 2010 and 2009

	2010	2009
Assets		
Cash	$ 128,800	$ 152,800
Accounts receivable (net)	369,400	379,400
Inventory	480,000	400,000
Prepaid expenses	7,400	13,400
Long-term investments	220,000	220,000
Land	180,600	160,600
Building	600,000	460,000
Accumulated depreciation–building	(120,000)	(80,000)
Equipment	240,000	240,000
Accumulated depreciation–equipment	(58,000)	(28,000)
Intangible assets	10,000	20,000
Total assets	$2,058,200	$1,938,200
Liabilities and Stockholders' Equity		
Accounts payable	$ 235,400	$ 330,400
Notes payable (current)	20,000	80,000
Accrued liabilities	5,400	10,400
Mortgage payable	540,000	400,000
Bonds payable	500,000	380,000
Common stock	650,000	650,000
Additional paid-in capital	40,000	40,000
Retained earnings	127,400	97,400
Treasury stock	(60,000)	(50,000)
Total liabilities and stockholders' equity	$2,058,200	$1,938,200

Required

1. Using the indirect method, prepare a statement of cash flows for Lopez Tools, Inc.

User insight ▶ 2. Why did Lopez Tools experience a decrease in cash in a year in which it had a net income of $48,000? Discuss and interpret.

User insight ▶ 3. Compute and assess cash flow yield and free cash flow for 2010. Why is each of these measures important in assessing cash-generating ability?

LO2 LO3 LO4 LO5

KA KLOOSTER & ALLEN

Statement of Cash Flows: Indirect Method

P 5. Wu Company's income statement for the year ended December 31, 2011, and its comparative balance sheets as of December 31, 2011 and 2010, are presented on the next page. During 2011, Wu Company engaged in these transactions:

a. Sold at a gain of $7,000 furniture and fixtures that cost $35,600, on which it had accumulated depreciation of $28,800.
b. Purchased furniture and fixtures in the amount of $39,600.
c. Paid a $20,000 note payable and borrowed $40,000 on a new note.
d. Converted bonds payable in the amount of $100,000 into 4,000 shares of common stock.
e. Declared and paid $6,000 in cash dividends.

Wu Company
Income Statement
For the Year Ended December 31, 2011

Sales		$1,609,000
Cost of goods sold		1,127,800
Gross margin		$ 481,200
Operating expenses (including depreciation expense of $46,800)		449,400
Income from operations		$ 31,800
Other income (expenses)		
Gain on sale of furniture and fixtures	$ 7,000	
Interest expense	(23,200)	(16,200)
Income before income taxes		$ 15,600
Income taxes expense		4,600
Net income		$ 11,000

Wu Company
Comparative Balance Sheets
December 31, 2011 and 2010

	2011	2010
Assets		
Cash	$164,800	$ 50,000
Accounts receivable (net)	165,200	200,000
Merchandise inventory	350,000	450,000
Prepaid rent	2,000	3,000
Furniture and fixtures	148,000	144,000
Accumulated depreciation–furniture and fixtures	(42,000)	(24,000)
Total assets	$788,000	$823,000
Liabilities and Stockholders' Equity		
Accounts payable	$143,400	$200,400
Income taxes payable	1,400	4,400
Notes payable (long-term)	40,000	20,000
Bonds payable	100,000	200,000
Common stock, $20 par value	240,000	200,000
Additional paid-in capital	181,440	121,440
Retained earnings	81,760	76,760
Total liabilities and stockholders' equity	$788,000	$823,000

Required

1. Using the indirect method, prepare a statement of cash flows for Wu Company. Include a supporting schedule of noncash investing transactions and financing transactions.

User insight ▶ 2. What are the primary reasons for Wu Company's large increase in cash from 2010 to 2011, despite its low net income?

User insight ▶ 3. Compute and assess cash flow yield and free cash flow for 2011. Compare and contrast what these two performance measures tell you about Wu Company's cash-generating ability.

Alternate Problems

LO1 Classification of Cash Flow Transactions

P 6. Analyze each transaction listed in the table that follows and place X's in the appropriate columns to indicate the transaction's classification and its effect on cash flows using the indirect method.

	Cash Flow Classification				Effect on Cash Flows		
Transaction	**Operating Activity**	**Investing Activity**	**Financing Activity**	**Noncash Transaction**	**Increase**	**Decrease**	**No Effect**
1. Increased accounts payable.							
2. Decreased inventory.							
3. Increased prepaid insurance.							
4. Earned a net income.							
5. Declared and paid a cash dividend.							
6. Issued stock for cash.							
7. Retired long-term debt by issuing stock.							
8. Purchased a long-term investment with cash.							
9. Sold trading securities at a gain.							
10. Sold a machine at a loss.							
11. Retired fully depreciated equipment.							
12. Decreased interest payable.							
13. Purchased available-for-sale securities (long-term).							
14. Decreased dividends receivable.							
15. Decreased accounts receivable.							
16. Converted bonds to common stock.							
17. Purchased 90-day Treasury bill.							

LO2 LO3 LO4 LO5 Statement of Cash Flows: Indirect Method

KLOOSTER & ALLEN

P 7. Ortega Corporation's income statement for the year ended June 30, 2011, and its comparative balance sheets as of June 30, 2011 and 2010, appear on the next page. During 2011, the corporation sold at a loss of $4,000 equipment that cost $24,000, on which it had accumulated depreciation of $17,000. It also purchased land and a building for $100,000 through an increase of $100,000 in Mortgage Payable; made a $20,000 payment on the mortgage; repaid $80,000 in notes but borrowed an additional $30,000 through the issuance of a new note payable; and declared and paid a $60,000 cash dividend.

Ortega Corporation
Income Statement
For the Year Ended June 30, 2011

Sales		$4,040,900
Cost of goods sold		3,656,300
Gross margin		$ 384,600
Operating expenses (including depreciation expense of $60,000)		189,200
Income from operations		$ 195,400
Other income (expenses)		
Loss on sale of equipment	($ 4,000)	
Interest expense	(37,600)	(41,600)
Income before income taxes		$ 153,800
Income taxes expense		34,200
Net income		$ 119,600

Ortega Corporation
Comparative Balance Sheets
June 30, 2011 and 2010

	2011	2010
Assets		
Cash	$ 167,000	$ 20,000
Accounts receivable (net)	100,000	120,000
Inventory	180,000	220,000
Prepaid expenses	600	1,000
Property, plant, and equipment	628,000	552,000
Accumulated depreciation–property, plant, and equipment	(183,000)	(140,000)
Total assets	$ 892,600	$ 773,000
Liabilities and Stockholders' Equity		
Accounts payable	$ 64,000	$ 42,000
Notes payable (due in 90 days)	30,000	80,000
Income taxes payable	26,000	18,000
Mortgage payable	360,000	280,000
Common stock, $5 par value	200,000	200,000
Retained earnings	212,600	153,000
Total liabilities and stockholders' equity	$ 892,600	$ 773,000

Required

1. Using the indirect method, prepare a statement of cash flows. Include a supporting schedule of noncash investing and financing transactions.

User insight ▶ 2. What are the primary reasons for Ortega Corporation's large increase in cash from 2010 to 2011?

User insight ▶ 3. Compute and assess cash flow yield and free cash flow for 2011. How would you assess the corporation's cash-generating ability?

LO2 LO3 LO4 LO5 K/R

Statement of Cash Flows: Indirect Method

P 8. The comparative balance sheets for Sharma Fabrics, Inc., for December 31, 2011 and 2010, appear on the next page. Additional information about Sharma Fabrics' operations during 2011 is as follows: (a) net income, $56,000; (b) building and equipment depreciation expense amounts, $30,000 and $6,000, respectively; (c) equipment that cost $27,000 with accumulated depreciation of $25,000 sold at a gain of $10,600; (d) equipment purchases, $25,000; (e) patent amortization, $6,000; purchase of patent, $2,000; (f) funds borrowed by issuing notes payable, $50,000; notes payable repaid, $30,000; (g) land and building purchased for $324,000 by signing a mortgage for the total cost; (h) 3,000 shares of $20 par value common stock issued for a total of $100,000; and (i) paid cash dividend, $18,000.

Sharma Fabrics, Inc.
Comparative Balance Sheets
December 31, 2011 and 2010

	2011	2010
Assets		
Cash	$189,120	$ 54,720
Accounts receivable (net)	204,860	150,860
Inventory	225,780	275,780
Prepaid expenses	—	40,000
Land	50,000	—
Building	274,000	—
Accumulated depreciation–building	(30,000)	—
Equipment	66,000	68,000
Accumulated depreciation–equipment	(29,000)	(48,000)
Patents	8,000	12,000
Total assets	$958,760	$553,360
Liabilities and Stockholders' Equity		
Accounts payable	$ 21,500	$ 73,500
Notes payable (current)	20,000	—
Accrued liabilities	—	24,600
Mortgage payable	324,000	—
Common stock, $10 par value	360,000	300,000
Additional paid-in capital	114,400	74,400
Retained earnings	118,860	80,860
Total liabilities and stockholders' equity	$958,760	$553,360

Required

1. Using the indirect method, prepare a statement of cash flows for Sharma Fabrics, Inc.

User insight ▶ 2. Why did Sharma Fabrics have an increase in cash of $134,400 when it recorded net income of only $56,000? Discuss and interpret.

User insight ▶ 3. Compute and assess cash flow yield and free cash flow for 2011. What is your assessment of Sharma's cash-generating ability?

LO2 LO3 LO4 LO5

Statement of Cash Flows: Indirect Method

K/R

P 9. The comparative balance sheets for Karidis Ceramics, Inc., for December 31, 2012 and 2011, are presented on the next page. During 2012, the company had net income of $96,000 and building and equipment depreciation expenses of $80,000 and $60,000, respectively. It amortized intangible assets in the amount of $20,000; purchased investments for $116,000; sold investments for $150,000, on which it recorded a gain of $34,000; issued $240,000 of long-term bonds at face value; purchased land and a warehouse through a $320,000 mortgage; paid $40,000 to reduce the mortgage; borrowed $60,000 by issuing notes payable; repaid notes payable in the amount of $180,000; declared and paid cash dividends in the amount of $36,000; and purchased treasury stock in the amount of $20,000.

Karidis Ceramics, Inc.
Comparative Balance Sheets
December 31, 2012 and 2011

	2012	2011
Assets		
Cash	$ 257,600	$ 305,600
Accounts receivable (net)	738,800	758,800
Inventory	960,000	800,000
Prepaid expenses	14,800	26,800
Long-term investments	440,000	440,000
Land	361,200	321,200
Building	1,200,000	920,000
Accumulated depreciation–building	(240,000)	(160,000)
Equipment	480,000	480,000
Accumulated depreciation–equipment	(116,000)	(56,000)
Intangible assets	20,000	40,000
Total assets	$4,116,400	$3,876,400
Liabilities and Stockholders' Equity		
Accounts payable	$ 470,800	$ 660,800
Notes payable (current)	40,000	160,000
Accrued liabilities	10,800	20,800
Mortgage payable	1,080,000	800,000
Bonds payable	1,000,000	760,000
Common stock	1,300,000	1,300,000
Additional paid-in capital	80,000	80,000
Retained earnings	254,800	194,800
Treasury stock	(120,000)	(100,000)
Total liabilities and stockholders' equity	$4,116,400	$3,876,400

Required

1. Using the indirect method, prepare a statement of cash flows for Karidis Ceramics, Inc.
2. User insight ▶ Why did Karidis Ceramics experience a decrease in cash in a year in which it had a net income of $96,000? Discuss and interpret.
3. User insight ▶ Compute and assess cash flow yield and free cash flow for 2012. Why is each of these measures important in assessing cash-generating ability?

LO2 LO3 LO4 LO5

Statement of Cash Flows: Indirect Method

P 10. O'Brien Corporation's income statement for the year ended December 31, 2012, and its comparative balance sheets as of December 31, 2012 and 2011, are presented on the next page. During 2012, O'Brien Corporation engaged in these transactions:

a. Sold at a gain of $3,500 furniture and fixtures that cost $17,800, on which it had accumulated depreciation of $14,400.
b. Purchased furniture and fixtures in the amount of $19,800.
c. Paid a $10,000 note payable and borrowed $20,000 on a new note.

d. Converted bonds payable in the amount of $50,000 into 2,000 shares of common stock.
e. Declared and paid $3,000 in cash dividends.

O'Brien Corporation
Income Statement
For the Year Ended December 31, 2012

Sales		$804,500
Cost of goods sold		563,900
Gross margin		$240,600
Operating expenses (including depreciation expense of $23,400)		224,700
Income from operations		$ 15,900
Other income (expenses)		
Gain on sale of furniture and fixtures	$ 3,500	
Interest expense	(11,600)	(8,100)
Income before income taxes		$ 7,800
Income taxes expense		2,300
Net income		$ 5,500

O'Brien Corporation
Comparative Balance Sheets
December 31, 2012 and 2011

	2012	2011
Assets		
Cash	$ 82,400	$ 25,000
Accounts receivable (net)	82,600	100,000
Merchandise inventory	175,000	225,000
Prepaid rent	1,000	1,500
Furniture and fixtures	74,000	72,000
Accumulated depreciation–furniture and fixtures	(21,000)	(12,000)
Total assets	$394,000	$411,500
Liabilities and Stockholders' Equity		
Accounts payable	$ 71,700	$100,200
Income taxes payable	700	2,200
Notes payable (long-term)	20,000	10,000
Bonds payable	50,000	100,000
Common stock, $20 par value	120,000	100,000
Additional paid-in capital	90,720	60,720
Retained earnings	40,880	38,380
Total liabilities and stockholders' equity	$394,000	$411,500

Required

1. Using the indirect method, prepare a statement of cash flows for O'Brien Corporation. Include a supporting schedule of noncash investing transactions and financing transactions.

User insight ▶ 2. What are the primary reasons for O'Brien Corporation's large increase in cash from 2011 to 2012, despite its low net income?

User insight ▶ 3. Compute and assess cash flow yield and free cash flow for 2012. Compare and contrast what these two performance measures tell you about O'Brien's cash-generating ability.

ENHANCING Your Knowledge, Skills, and Critical Thinking

LO1 LO3 **EBITDA and the Statement of Cash Flows**

C 1. When **Fleetwood Enterprises, Inc.**, a large producer of recreational vehicles and manufactured housing, warned that it might not be able to generate enough cash to satisfy debt requirements and could be in default of a loan agreement, its cash flow, defined in the financial press as "EBITDA" (earnings before interest, taxes, depreciation, and amortization), was a negative $2.7 million. The company would have had to generate $17.7 million in the next accounting period to comply with the loan terms.[12] To what section of the statement of cash flows does EBITDA most closely relate? Is EBITDA a good approximation for this section of the statement of cash flows? Explain your answer, which should include an identification of the major differences between EBITDA and the section of the statement of cash flows you chose.

LO2 **Anatomy of a Disaster**

C 2. On October 16, 2001, Kenneth Lay, chairman and CEO of **Enron Corporation**, announced the company's earnings for the first nine months of 2001 as follows:

> Our 26 percent increase in recurring earnings per diluted share shows the very strong results of our core wholesale and retail energy businesses and our natural gas pipelines. The continued excellent prospects in these businesses and Enron's leading market position make us very confident in our strong earnings outlook.[13]

Less than six months later, the company filed for the biggest bankruptcy in U.S. history. Its stock dropped to less than $1 per share, and a major financial scandal was underway.

Presented on the next page is Enron's statement of cash flows for the first nine months of 2001 and 2000 (restated to correct the previous accounting errors). Assume you report to an investment analyst who has asked you to analyze this statement for clues as to why the company went under.

1. For the two time periods shown, compute the cash-generating efficiency ratios of cash flow yield, cash flows to sales (Enron's revenues were $133,762 million in 2001 and $55,494 million in 2000), and cash flows to assets (use total assets of $61,783 million for 2001 and $64,926 million for 2000). Also compute free cash flows for the two years.
2. Prepare a memorandum to the investment analyst that assesses Enron's cash-generating efficiency in light of the chairman's remarks and that evaluates its available free cash flow, taking into account its financing activities. Identify significant changes in Enron's operating items and any special operating items that should be considered. Include your computations as an attachment.

LO2 **Ethics and Cash Flow Classifications**

C 3. Specialty Metals, Inc., a fast-growing company that makes metals for equipment manufacturers, has an $800,000 line of credit at its bank. One section in the credit agreement says that the ratio of cash flows from operations to interest expense must exceed 3.0. If this ratio falls below 3.0, the company must reduce the balance outstanding on its line of credit to one-half the total line if the funds borrowed against the line of credit exceed one-half of the total line.

After the end of the fiscal year, the company's controller informs the president: "We will not meet the ratio requirements on our line of credit in 2010

Enron Corporation
Statement of Cash Flows
For the Nine Months Ended September 30, 2001 and 2000

(In millions)	**2001**	**2000**
Cash Flows from Operating Activities		
Reconciliation of net income to net cash provided by operating activities		
Net income	$ 225	$ 797
Cumulative effect of accounting changes, net of tax	(19)	0
Depreciation, depletion and amortization	746	617
Deferred income taxes	(134)	8
Gains on sales of non-trading assets	(49)	(135)
Investment losses	768	0
Changes in components of working capital		
Receivables	987	(3,363)
Inventories	1	339
Payables	(1,764)	2,899
Other	464	(455)
Trading investments		
Net margin deposit activity	(2,349)	541
Other trading activities	173	(555)
Other, net	198	(566)
Net Cash Provided by (Used in) Operating Activities	$ (753)	$ 127
Cash Flows from Investing Activities		
Capital expenditures	$(1,584)	$(1,539)
Equity investments	(1,172)	(858)
Proceeds from sales of non-trading investments	1,711	222
Acquisition of subsidiary stock	0	(485)
Business acquisitions, net of cash acquired	(82)	(773)
Other investing activities	(239)	(147)
Net Cash Used in Investing Activities	$(1,366)	$(3,580)
Cash Flows from Financing Activities		
Issuance of long-term debt	$ 4,060	$ 2,725
Repayment of long-term debt	(3,903)	(579)
Net increase in short-term borrowings	2,365	1,694
Issuance of common stock	199	182
Net redemption of company-obligated preferred securities of subsidiaries	0	(95)
Dividends paid	(394)	(396)
Net (acquisition) disposition of treasury stock	(398)	354
Other financing activities	(49)	(12)
Net Cash Provided by Financing Activities	$ 1,880	$ 3,873
Increase (Decrease) in Cash and Cash Equivalents	$ (239)	$ 420
Cash and Cash Equivalents, Beginning of Period	1,240	333
Cash and Cash Equivalents, End of Period	$ 1,001	$ 753

Source: Adapted from Enron Corporation, SEC filings, 2001.

because interest expense was $1.2 million and cash flows from operations were $3.2 million. Also, we have borrowed 100 percent of our line of credit. We do not have the cash to reduce the credit line by $400,000."

The president says, "This is a serious situation. To pay our ongoing bills, we need our bank to increase our line of credit, not decrease it. What can we do?"

"Do you recall the $500,000 two-year note payable for equipment?" replied the controller. "It is now classified as 'Proceeds from Notes Payable' in cash flows provided from financing activities in the statement of cash flows. If we move it to cash flows from operations and call it 'Increase in Payables,' it would increase cash flows from operations to $3.7 million and put us over the limit."

"Well, do it," ordered the president. "It surely doesn't make any difference where it is on the statement. It is an increase in both places. It would be much worse for our company in the long term if we failed to meet this ratio requirement."

What is your opinion of the controller and president's reasoning? Is the president's order ethical? Who benefits and who is harmed if the controller follows the president's order? What are management's alternatives? What would you do?

LO1 LO2

Alternative Uses of Cash

C 4. Perhaps because of hard times in their start-up years, companies in the high-tech sector of American industry seem more prone than those in other sectors to building up cash reserves. For example, companies like **Cisco Systems**, **Intel**, **Dell**, and **Oracle** have amassed large cash balances.[14]

Assume you work for a company in the high-tech industry that has built up a substantial amount of cash. The company is still growing through development of new products, has some debt, and has never paid a dividend or bought treasury stock. The company is doing better than most companies in the current financial crisis but the company's stock price is lagging. Outline at least four strategies for using the company's cash to improve the company's financial outlook.

LO1

Analysis of the Statement of Cash Flows

C 5. Refer to the statement of cash flows in the **CVS Corporation** annual report in the Supplement to Chapter 5 to answer the following questions:

1. Does CVS use the indirect method of reporting cash flows from operating activities? Other than net earnings, what are the most important factors affecting the company's cash flows from operating activities? Explain the trend of each of these factors.
2. Based on the cash flows from investing activities, in 2007 and 2008, would you say that CVS is a contracting or an expanding company? Explain.
3. Has CVS used external financing during 2007 and 2008? If so, where did it come from?

LO1 LO2 LO3 LO4 LO5

Cash Flows Analysis

K/R

C 6. Refer to the annual report of **CVS Corporation** and the financial statements of **Southwest Airlines** in the Supplement to Chapter 5. Calculate for two years each company's cash flow yield, cash flows to sales, cash flows to assets, and free cash flow. At the end of 2006, Southwest's total assets were $13,460 million and CVS's total assets were $20,574.1 million.

Discuss and compare the trends of the cash-generating ability of CVS and Southwest. Comment on each company's change in cash and cash equivalents over the two-year period.

CHAPTER

16 Financial Performance Measurement

Making a Statement

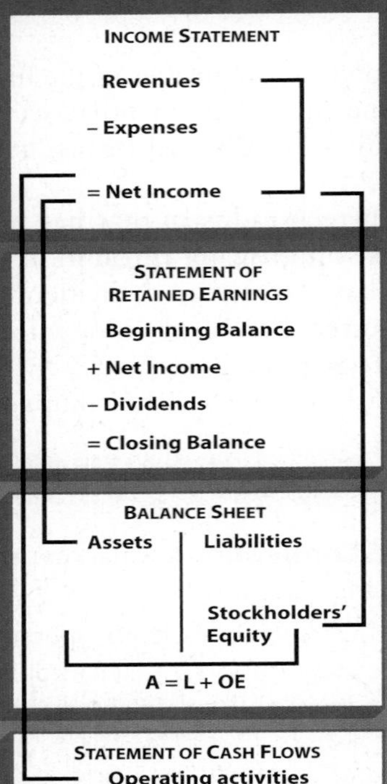

Comparisons within and across financial statements help the users of financial statements assess financial performance.

The ultimate purpose of financial reporting is to enable managers, creditors, investors, and other interested parties to evaluate a company's financial performance. In earlier chapters, we discussed the various measures used in assessing a company's financial performance; here, we provide a comprehensive summary of those measures. Because these measures play a key role in executive compensation, there is always the risk that they will be manipulated. Users of financial statements therefore need to be familiar with the analytical tools and techniques used in performance measurement and the assumptions that underlie them.

LEARNING OBJECTIVES

LO1 Describe the objectives, standards of comparison, sources of information, and compensation issues in measuring financial performance. (pp. 708–714)

LO2 Apply horizontal analysis, trend analysis, vertical analysis, and ratio analysis to financial statements. (pp. 715–722)

LO3 Apply ratio analysis to financial statements in a comprehensive evaluation of a company's financial performance. (pp. 722–730)

DECISION POINT ▸ A USER'S FOCUS WASHINGTON INVESTMENTS

Having studied the eating habits of Americans for several months, Maggie Washington, president of Washington Investments, has concluded that there is a trend toward eating out and that the trend will continue. She is therefore planning to invest in a fast-food restaurant chain, and she has narrowed her choice to two companies: Quik Burger and Big Steak. She is now thinking about how she should evaluate these companies and thus arrive at her final decision.

In this chapter, we discuss the various analytical tools and standards that Maggie can use to measure and compare the financial performance of the two companies.

- ▸ What analytical tools can Maggie Washington use to measure the financial performance of Quik Burger and Big Steak?
- ▸ What standards can she use to compare the performance of the two companies?

Foundations of Financial Performance Measurement

LO1 Describe the objectives, standards of comparison, sources of information, and compensation issues in measuring financial performance.

Financial performance measurement, also called *financial statement analysis*, uses all the techniques available to show how important items in a company's financial statements relate to the company's financial objectives. Persons with a strong interest in measuring a company's financial performance fall into two groups:

1. A company's top managers, who set and strive to achieve financial performance objectives; middle-level managers of business processes; and lower-level employees who own stock in the company
2. Creditors and investors, as well as customers who have cooperative agreements with the company

Financial Performance Measurement: Management's Objectives

All the strategic and operating plans that management formulates to achieve a company's goals must eventually be stated in terms of financial objectives. A primary objective is to increase the wealth of the company's stockholders, but this objective must be divided into categories. A complete financial plan should have financial objectives and related performance objectives in all the following categories:

Financial Objective	*Performance Objective*
Liquidity	The company must be able to pay bills when due and meet unexpected needs for cash.
Profitability	It must earn a satisfactory net income.
Long-term solvency	It must be able to survive for many years.
Cash flow adequacy	It must generate sufficient cash through operating, investing, and financing activities.
Market strength	It must be able to increase stockholders' wealth.

Management's main responsibility is to carry out its plan to achieve the company's financial objectives. This requires constant monitoring of key financial performance measures for each objective listed above, determining the cause of any deviations from the measures, and proposing ways of correcting the deviations. Management compares actual performance with the key performance measures in monthly, quarterly, and annual reports. The information in management's annual reports provides data for long-term trend analyses.

Financial Performance Measurement: Creditors' and Investors' Objectives

Creditors and investors use financial performance evaluation to judge a company's past performance and present position. They also use it to assess a company's future potential and the risk connected with acting on that potential. An investor focuses on a company's potential earnings ability because that ability will affect the market price of the company's stock and the amount of dividends the company will pay. A creditor focuses on the company's potential debt-paying ability.

Past performance is often a good indicator of future performance. To evaluate a company's past performance, creditors and investors look at trends in past sales, expenses, net income, cash flow, and return on investment. To evaluate its current position, they look at its assets, liabilities, cash position, debt in relation to equity, and levels of inventories and receivables. Knowing a company's past performance and current position can be important in judging its future potential and the related risk.

The risk involved in making an investment or loan depends on how easy it is to predict future profitability or liquidity. If an investor can predict with confidence that a company's earnings per share will be between $2.50 and $2.60 in the next year, the investment is less risky than if the earnings per share are expected to fall between $2.00 and $3.00. For example, the potential of an investment in an established electric utility company is relatively easy to predict on the basis of the company's past performance and current position. In contrast, the potential of an investment in a new Internet firm that has not yet established a record of earnings is very hard to predict. Investing in the Internet firm is therefore riskier than investing in the electric utility company.

In return for taking a greater risk, investors often look for a higher expected return (an increase in market price plus dividends). Creditors who take a greater risk by advancing funds to a company like the new Internet firm mentioned above may demand a higher interest rate and more assurance of repayment (a secured loan, for instance). The higher interest rate reimburses them for assuming the higher risk.

Standards of Comparison

When analyzing financial statements, decision makers must judge whether the relationships they find in the statements are favorable or unfavorable. Three standards of comparison that they commonly use are rule-of-thumb measures, a company's past performance, and industry norms.

> **Study Note**
> Rules of thumb evolve and change as the business environment changes. Not long ago, an acceptable current ratio was higher than today's 2:1.

Rule-of-Thumb Measures Many financial analysts, investors, and lenders apply general standards, or rule-of-thumb measures, to key financial ratios. For example, most analysts today agree that a current ratio (current assets divided by current liabilities) of 2:1 is acceptable.

In its *Industry Norms and Key Business Ratios,* the credit-rating firm of Dun & Bradstreet offers such rules of thumb as the following:

Current debt to tangible net worth: A business is usually in trouble when this relationship exceeds 80 percent.

Inventory to net working capital: Ordinarily, this relationship should not exceed 80 percent.

Although rule-of thumb measures may suggest areas that need further investigation, there is no proof that the levels they specify apply to all companies. A company with a current ratio higher than 2:1 may have a poor credit policy (causing accounts receivable to be too large), too much inventory, or poor cash management. Another company may have a ratio lower than 2:1 but still have excellent management in all three of those areas. Thus, rule-of-thumb measures must be used with caution.

Past Performance Comparing financial measures or ratios of the same company over time is an improvement over using rule-of-thumb measures. Such a comparison gives the analyst some basis for judging whether the measure or ratio is getting better or worse. Thus, it may be helpful in showing future trends. However, trends reverse at times, so such projections must be made with care.

Another problem with trend analysis is that past performance may not be enough to meet a company's present needs. For example, even though a company

FOCUS ON BUSINESS PRACTICE

Look Carefully at the Numbers

In recent years, companies have increasingly used pro forma statements—statements as they would appear without certain items—as a way of presenting a better picture of their operations than would be the case in reports prepared under GAAP. In one quarter, **Amazon.com** reported a "pro forma net" loss of $76 million; under GAAP, its net loss was $234 million. Pro forma statements, which are unaudited, have come to mean whatever a company's management wants them to mean. As a result, the SEC issued rules that prohibit companies from giving more prominence to non-GAAP measures and from using terms that are similar to GAAP measures.[1] Nevertheless, companies still report pro forma results. A common practice used by such companies as **Google**, **eBay**, and **Starbucks** is to provide in the notes to the financial statements income as it would be without the expense related to compensation for stock options.[2] Analysts should rely exclusively on financial statements that are prepared using GAAP and that are audited by an independent CPA.

improves its return on investment from 3 percent in one year to 4 percent the next year, the 4 percent return may not be adequate for the company's current needs. In addition, using a company's past performance as a standard of comparison is not helpful in judging its performance relative to that of other companies.

Industry Norms Using industry norms as a standard of comparison overcomes some of the limitations of comparing a company's measures or ratios over time. Industry norms show how a company compares with other companies in the same industry. For example, if companies in a particular industry have an average rate of return on investment of 8 percent, a 3 or 4 percent rate of return is probably not adequate.

Industry norms can also be used to judge trends. Suppose that because of a downturn in the economy, a company's profit margin dropped from 12 percent to 10 percent, while the average drop in profit margin of other companies in the same industry was from 12 to 4 percent. By this standard, the company would have done relatively well. Sometimes, instead of industry averages, data for the industry leader or a specific competitor are used for analysis.

Using industry norms as standards has three limitations:

1. Companies in the same industry may not be strictly comparable. Consider two companies in the oil industry. One purchases oil products and markets them through service stations. The other, an international company, discovers, produces, refines, and markets its own oil products. Because of the disparity in their operations, these two companies cannot be directly compared.

Study Note

Each segment of a diversified company represents an investment that the home office or parent company evaluates and reviews frequently.

2. Many large companies have multiple segments and operate in more than one industry. Some of these **diversified companies**, or *conglomerates*, operate in many unrelated industries. The individual segments of a diversified company generally have different rates of profitability and different degrees of risk. In analyzing a diversified company's consolidated financial statements, it is often impossible to use industry norms as a standard because there simply are no comparable companies.

   The FASB provides a partial solution to this problem. It requires diversified companies to report profit or loss, certain revenue and expense items, and assets for each of their segments. Segment information may be reported for operations in different industries or different geographical areas, or for

EXHIBIT 16-1
Selected Segment Information for Goodyear Tire & Rubber Company

(In millions)	2008	2007	2006
Sales			
North American Tire	$ 8,255	$ 8,862	$ 9,089
Europe, Middle East and Africa Tire	7,316	7,217	6,552
Latin American Tire	2,088	1,872	1,607
Asia Pacific Tire	1,829	1,693	1,503
Net Sales	**$19,488**	**$19,644**	**$18,751**
Segment Operating Income			
North American Tire	($ 156)	$ 139	($ 233)
Europe, Middle East and Africa Tire	425	582	513
Latin American Tire	367	359	326
Asia Pacific Tire	168	150	104
Total Segment Operating Income	**$ 804**	**$ 1,230**	**$ 710**
Assets*			
North American Tire	$ 5,514	$ 5,307	$ 4,798
Europe, Middle East and Africa Tire	5,707	6,020	5,758
Latin American Tire	1,278	1,265	986
Asia Pacific Tire	1,408	1,394	1,236
Total Segment Assets	**$13,907**	**$13,986**	**$12,778**
Corporate	1,319	3,205	—
Engineered Products	—	—	794
Total Assets	**$15,226**	**$17,191**	**$13,572**

*2006 assets estimated.
Source: Goodyear Tire & Rubber Company, *Annual Report,* 2008.

major customers.[3] Exhibit 16-1 shows how **Goodyear Tire & Rubber Company** reports data on sales, income, and assets for its four business segments. These data allow the analyst to compute important profitability performance measures, such as profit margin, asset turnover, and return on assets, for each segment and to compare them with the appropriate industry norms.

3. Another limitation of industry norms is that even when companies in the same industry have similar operations, they may use different acceptable accounting procedures. For example, they may use different methods of valuing inventories and different methods of depreciating assets.

Despite these limitations, if little information about a company's past performance is available, industry norms probably offer the best available standards for judging current performance—as long as they are used with care.

Sources of Information

The major sources of information about public corporations are reports published by the corporations themselves, reports filed with the SEC, business periodicals, and credit and investment advisory services.

Reports Published by the Corporation A public corporation's annual report is an important source of financial information. From a financial analyst's perspective, the main parts of an annual report are management's analysis of the past year's operations; the financial statements; the notes to the financial statements, which include a summary of significant accounting policies; the auditors' report; and financial highlights for a five- or ten-year period.

Most public corporations also publish **interim financial statements** each quarter and sometimes each month. These reports, which present limited information in the form of condensed financial statements, are not subject to a full audit by an independent auditor. The financial community watches interim statements closely for early signs of change in a company's earnings trend.

Reports Filed with the SEC Public corporations in the United States must file annual reports, quarterly reports, and current reports with the Securities and Exchange Commission (SEC). If they have more than $10 million in assets and more than 500 shareholders, they must file these reports electronically at www.sec.gov/edgar.shtml, where anyone can access them free of charge.

The SEC requires companies to file their annual reports on a standard form, called Form 10-K. Form 10-K contains more information than a company's annual report and is therefore a valuable source of information. Companies file their quarterly reports with the SEC on Form 10-Q. This report presents important facts about interim financial performance. The current report, filed on Form 8-K, must be submitted to the SEC within a few days of the date of certain significant events, such as the sale or purchase of a division or a change in auditors. The current report is often the first indicator of significant changes that will affect a company's financial performance in the future.

Business Periodicals and Credit and Investment Advisory Services Financial analysts must keep up with current events in the financial world. A leading source of financial news is *The Wall Street Journal*. It is the most complete financial newspaper in the United States and is published every business day. Useful periodicals that are published every week or every two weeks include *Forbes*, *Barron's*, *Fortune*, and the *Financial Times*.

Credit and investment advisory services also provide useful information. The publications of Moody's Investors Service and Standard & Poor's provide details about a company's financial history. Data on industry norms, average ratios, and credit ratings are available from agencies like Dun & Bradstreet. Dun & Bradstreet's *Industry Norms and Key Business Ratios* offers an annual analysis of 14 ratios for each of 125 industry groups, classified as retailing, wholesaling, manufacturing, and construction. *Annual Statement Studies*, published by Risk Management Association (formerly Robert Morris Associates), presents many facts and ratios for 223 different industries. The publications of a number of other agencies are also available for a yearly fee.

An example of specialized financial reporting readily available to the public is Mergent's *Handbook of Dividend Achievers*. It profiles companies that have increased their dividends consistently over the past ten years. A listing from that publication—for **PepsiCo Inc.**—is shown in Exhibit 16-2. As you can see, a wealth of information about the company, including the market action of its stock, its business operations, recent developments and prospects, and earnings and dividend data, is summarized on one page. We use the kind of data contained in Mergent's summaries in many of the analyses and ratios that we present later in this chapter.

Executive Compensation

As we noted earlier in the text, one intent of the Sarbanes-Oxley Act of 2002 was to strengthen the corporate governance of public corporations. Under this act, a public corporation's board of directors must establish a **compensation committee** made up of independent directors to determine how the company's top executives will be compensated. The company must disclose the components of

EXHIBIT 16-2 Listing from Mergent's Dividend Achievers

PEPSICO INC.

Exchange	Symbol	Price	52Wk Range	Yield	P/E
NYS	PEP	$68.03 (8/31/2007)	69.94-61.24	2.20	19.22

*7 Year Price Score 89.69 *NYSE Composite Index=100 *12 Month Price Score 99.39

Interim Earnings (Per Share)

Qtr.	Mar	Jun	Aug	Dec
2004	0.46	0.61	0.79	0.58
2005	0.53	0.70	0.51	0.65
2006	0.60	0.80	0.88	1.06
2007	0.65	0.94	...	...

Interim Dividends (Per Share)

Amt	Decl	Ex	Rec	Pay
0.30Q	11/17/2006	12/6/2006	12/8/2006	1/2/2007
0.30Q	2/2/2007	3/7/2007	3/9/2007	3/30/2007
0.375Q	5/2/2007	6/6/2007	6/8/2007	6/29/2007
0.375Q	7/19/2007	9/5/2007	9/7/2007	9/28/2007

Indicated Div: $1.50 (Div. Reinv. Plan)

Valuation Analysis

Forecast P/E	15.48 (1/10/2007)		
Market Cap	$110.3 Billion	Book Value	16.0 Billion
Price/Book	6.91	Price/Sales	3.03

Dividend Achiever Status

10 Year Growth Rate	10.00%
Total Years of Dividend Growth	35

Business Summary: Food (MIC: 4.1 SIC: 2086 NAIC: 312111)

PepsiCo is engaged in manufacturing, marketing and selling a range of salty, sweet and grain-based snacks, carbonated and non-carbonated beverages and foods. Co. is organized into four divisions: Frito-Lay North America (FLNA); PepsiCo Beverages North America (PBNA); PepsiCo International (PI); and Quaker Foods North America (QFNA). FLNA branded snacks include Lay's potato chips, Doritos tortilla chips and Rold Gold pretzels. PBNA's brands include Pepsi, Mountain Dew, Gatorade, Tropicana Pure Premium, and Lipton. PI's brands include Lay's, Walkers, Cheetos, Doritos, Ruffles, Gamesa and Sabritas. QFNA's brands include Quaker oatmeal, Rice-A-Roni and Near East side dishes.

Recent Developments: For the quarter ended June 16 2007, net income increased 13.2% to US$1.56 billion from US$1.38 billion in the year-earlier quarter. Revenues were US$9.61 billion, up 10.2% from US$8.71 billion the year before. Operating income was US$1.96 billion versus US$1.80 billion in the prior-year quarter, an increase of 8.8%. Direct operating expenses rose 12.4% to US$4.34 billion from US$3.86 billion in the comparable period the year before. Indirect operating expenses increased 8.3% to US$3.31 billion from US$3.05 billion in the equivalent prior-year period.

Prospects: Co. is seeing an increase in its net revenue, driven by robust snacks and beverage growth at its PepsiCo International division. Specifically, international snacks volume growth is being driven by double-digit growth in Russia and India, partially offset by low-single-digit declines at Sabritas in Mexico and Walkers in the U.K., while beverage volume growth is being fueled by double-digit growth in Pakistan, Russia, the Middle East and the U.K., partially offset by a mid-single-digit decline in Mexico and a double-digit decline in Thailand. Accordingly, Co. is raising its full year 2007 earnings guidance to at least $3.35 per share.

Financial Data

(US$ in Thousands)	6 Mos	3 Mos	12/30/2006	12/31/2005	12/25/2004	12/27/2003	12/28/2002	12/29/2001
Earnings Per Share	3.54	3.40	3.34	2.39	2.44	2.05	1.85	1.47
Cash Flow Per Share	3.86	3.95	3.70	3.45	2.99	2.53	2.65	2.39
Tang Book Value Per Share	5.71	5.51	5.50	5.20	4.84	3.82	4.93	2.17
Dividends Per Share	1.275	1.200	1.160	1.010	0.850	0.630	0.595	0.575
Dividend Payout %	36.02	35.32	34.73	42.26	34.84	30.73	32.16	39.12
Income Statement								
Total Revenue	16,957,000	7,350,000	35,137,000	32,562,000	29,261,000	26,971,000	25,112,000	26,935,000
EBITDA	4,233,000	1,769,000	8,399,000	7,732,000	6,848,000	6,269,000	6,077,000	5,189,000
Depn & Amortn	608,000	276,000	1,344,000	1,253,000	1,209,000	1,165,000	1,067,000	1,008,000
Income Before Taxes	3,590,000	1,473,000	6,989,000	6,382,000	5,546,000	4,992,000	4,868,000	4,029,000
Income Taxes	937,000	377,000	1,347,000	2,304,000	1,372,000	1,424,000	1,555,000	1,367,000
Net Income	2,653,000	1,096,000	5,642,000	4,078,000	4,212,000	3,568,000	3,313,000	2,662,000
Average Shares	1,665,000	1,673,000	1,687,000	1,706,000	1,729,000	1,739,000	1,789,000	1,807,000
Balance Sheet								
Total Assets	31,925,000	29,830,000	29,930,000	31,727,000	27,987,000	25,327,000	23,474,000	21,695,000
Current Liabilities	7,589,000	7,522,000	6,860,000	9,406,000	6,752,000	6,415,000	6,052,000	4,998,000
Long-Term Obligations	3,261,000	1,807,000	2,550,000	2,313,000	2,397,000	1,702,000	2,187,000	2,651,000
Total Liabilities	16,052,000	14,482,000	14,562,000	17,476,000	14,464,000	13,453,000	14,183,000	13,021,000
Stockholders' Equity	15,956,000	15,429,000	15,447,000	14,320,000	13,572,000	11,896,000	9,298,000	8,648,000
Shares Outstanding	1,621,000	1,631,000	1,638,000	1,656,000	1,679,000	1,705,000	1,722,000	1,756,000
Statistical Record								
Return on Assets %	18.73	18.84	18.35	13.44	15.84	14.66	14.71	13.34
Return on Equity %	37.96	37.90	38.01	28.77	33.17	33.76	37.02	33.58
EBITDA Margin %	24.96	24.07	23.90	23.75	23.40	23.24	24.20	19.26
Net Margin %	15.65	14.91	16.06	12.52	14.39	13.23	13.19	9.88
Asset Turnover	1.15	1.16	1.14	1.07	1.10	1.11	1.11	1.35
Current Ratio	1.29	1.16	1.33	1.11	1.28	1.08	1.06	1.17
Debt to Equity	0.20	0.12	0.17	0.16	0.18	0.14	0.24	0.31
Price Range	69.48-58.91	65.91-57.20	65.91-56.77	59.90-51.57	55.55-45.39	48.71-37.30	53.12-35.50	50.28-41.26
P/E Ratio	19.63-16.64	19.39-16.82	19.73-17.00	25.06-21.58	22.77-18.60	23.76-18.20	28.71-19.19	34.20-28.07
Average Yield %	1.99	1.93	1.90	1.82	1.66	1.43	1.29	1.25

Address: 700 Anderson Hill Road, Purchase, NY 10577-1444 **Telephone:** 914-253-2000 **Web Site:** www.pepsico.com	**Officers:** Steven S. Reinemund - Chmn., C.E.O. Indra K. Nooyi - Pres., C.F.O. **Transfer Agents:** The Bank of New York	**Investor Contact:** 914-253-3035 **No of Institutions:** 1292 **Shares:** 1,121,669,888 **% Held:** 68.49

Source: PepsiCo listing from *Mergent's Dividend Achievers Fall 2007: Featuring Second-Quarter Results for 2007*. Reprinted by permission of John Wiley & Sons Inc.

compensation and the criteria it uses to remunerate top executives in documents that it files with the SEC.

Formed in 1985, **Starbucks** is today a well-known specialty retailer. Starbucks provides its executives with incentives to improve the company's performance. Compensation and financial performance are thus linked to increasing shareholders' value. The components of **Starbucks'** compensation of executive officers are typical of those used by many companies:

- Annual base salary
- Incentive bonuses
- Stock option awards[4]

Incentive bonuses are based on financial performance measures that the compensation committee identifies as important to the company's long-term success. Many companies tie incentive bonuses to such measures as growth in revenues and return on assets, or return on equity. Starbucks bases 80 percent of its incentive bonus on an "earnings per share target approved by the compensation committee" and 20 percent on the executive's "specific individual performance."[5]

Stock option awards are usually based on how well the company is achieving its long-term strategic goals. In 2008, a challenging year for Starbucks, the company's CEO received a base salary of $1,190,000 and no incentive bonus. In November 2007, he received a stock option award of 687,113 shares of common stock.[6]

From one vantage point, earnings per share is a "bottom-line" number that encompasses all the other performance measures. However, using a single performance measure as the basis for determining compensation has the potential of leading to practices that are not in the best interests of the company or its stockholders. For instance, management could boost earnings per share by reducing the number of shares outstanding (the denominator in the earnings per share equation) while not improving earnings. It could accomplish this by using cash to repurchase shares of the company's stock (treasury stock), rather than investing the cash in more profitable operations.

As you study the comprehensive financial analysis of Starbucks in the coming pages, consider that knowledge of performance measurement not only is important for evaluating a company but also leads to an understanding of the criteria by which a board of directors evaluates and compensates management.

STOP & APPLY >

Identify each of the following as (a) an objective of financial statement analysis, (b) a standard for financial statement analysis, (c) a source of information for financial statement analysis, or (d) an executive compensation issue:

1. A company's past performance
2. Investment advisory services
3. Assessment of a company's future potential
4. Incentive bonuses
5. Industry norms
6. Annual report
7. Creating shareholder value
8. Form 10-K

SOLUTION

1. b; 2. c; 3. a; 4. d; 5. b; 6. c; 7. d; 8. c

Tools and Techniques of Financial Analysis

LO2 Apply horizontal analysis, trend analysis, vertical analysis, and ratio analysis to financial statements.

To gain insight into a company's financial performance, one must look beyond the individual numbers to the relationship between the numbers and their change from one period to another. The tools of financial analysis—horizontal analysis, trend analysis, vertical analysis, and ratio analysis—are intended to show these relationships and changes. To illustrate how these tools are used, we devote the rest of this chapter to a comprehensive financial analysis of **Starbucks Corporation**.

Horizontal Analysis

Study Note

It is important to ascertain the base amount used when a percentage describes an item. For example, inventory may be 50 percent of total current assets but only 10 percent of total assets.

Comparative financial statements provide financial information for the current year and the previous year. To gain insight into year-to-year changes, analysts use **horizontal analysis**, in which changes from the previous year to the current year are computed in both dollar amounts and percentages. The percentage change relates the size of the change to the size of the dollar amounts involved.

Exhibits 16-3 and 16-4 present **Starbuck Corporation**'s comparative balance sheets and income statements and show both the dollar and percentage changes. The percentage change is computed as follows:

$$\text{Percentage Change} = 100 \times \left(\frac{\text{Amount of Change}}{\text{Base Year Amount}}\right)$$

The **base year** is always the first year to be considered in any set of data. For example, when comparing data for 2007 and 2008, 2007 is the base year. As the balance sheets in Exhibit 16-3 show, between 2007 and 2008, Starbucks' total current assets increased by \$51.5 million, from \$1,696.5 million to \$1,748.0 million, or by 3.0 percent. This is computed as follows:

$$\text{Percentage Change} = \frac{\$51.5 \text{ million}}{\$1{,}696.5 \text{ million}} = 3.0\%$$

When examining such changes, it is important to consider the dollar amount of the change as well as the percentage change in each component. For example, the percentage increase in accounts receivable, net (14.4 percent) is slightly greater than the increase in prepaid and other current assets (13.7 percent). However, the dollar increase in accounts receivable is twice the dollar increase in prepaid and other current assets (\$41.6 million versus \$20.4 million). Thus, even though the percentage changes differ by only 0.7 percent, accounts receivable require much more investment.

Starbucks' balance sheets for this period, illustrated in Exhibit 16-3, also show an increase in total assets of \$328.7 million, or 6.2 percent. In addition, shareholders' equity increased by \$206.8 million, or 9.1 percent.

Starbucks' income statements in Exhibit 16-4 show that net revenues increased by \$971.5 million, or 10.3 percent, while gross margin increased by \$325.3 million, or 6.0 percent. This indicates that cost of sales grew faster than net revenues. In fact, cost of sales increased 16.2 percent compared with the 10.3 percent increase in net revenues.

Starbucks' total operating expenses increased by \$880.9, or 19.7 percent, also faster than the 10.3 percent increase in net revenues. As a result, operating income decreased by \$555.6 million, or 58.7 percent, and net income decreased by \$357.1, or 53.1 percent. The primary reason for the decreases in operating income and net income is that total cost of sales and operating expenses increased at a faster rate (16.2 and 19.7 percent, respectively) than net revenues (10.3 percent).

EXHIBIT 16-3 Comparative Balance Sheets with Horizontal Analysis

Starbucks Corporation
Consolidated Balance Sheets
September 28, 2008, and September 30, 2007

			Increase (Decrease)	
(Dollar amounts in millions)	**2008**	**2007**	**Amount**	**Percentage**
	Assets			
Current assets:				
Cash and cash equivalents	$ 269.8	$ 281.3	$ (11.5)	(4.1)
Short-term investments	52.5	157.4	(104.9)	(66.6)
Accounts receivable, net	329.5	287.9	41.6	14.4
Inventories	692.8	691.7	1.1	0.2
Prepaid and other current assets	169.2	148.8	20.4	13.7
Deferred income taxes, net	234.2	129.4	104.8	81.0
Total current assets	$1,748.0	$1,696.5	$ 51.5	3.0
Long-term investments	374.0	279.9	94.1	33.6
Property, plant, and equipment, net	2,956.4	2,890.4	66.0	2.3
Other assets	261.1	219.4	41.7	19.0
Other intangible assets	66.6	42.1	24.5	58.2
Goodwill	266.5	215.6	50.9	23.6
Total assets	$5,672.6	$5,343.9	$328.7	6.2
	Liabilities and Shareholders' Equity			
Current liabilities:				
Commercial paper and short-term borrowings	$ 713.0	$ 710.3	$ 2.7	0.4
Accounts payable	324.9	390.8	(65.9)	(16.9)
Accrued compensation and related costs	253.6	292.4	(38.8)	(13.3)
Accrued occupancy costs	136.1	74.6	61.5	82.4
Accrued taxes	76.1	92.5	(16.4)	(17.7)
Insurance reserves	152.5	137.0	15.5	11.3
Other accrued expenses	164.4	160.3	4.1	2.6
Deferred revenue	368.4	296.9	71.5	24.1
Current portion of long-term debt	0.7	0.8	(0.1)	(12.5)
Total current liabilities	$2,189.7	$2,155.6	$ 34.1	1.6
Long-term debt and other liabilities	992.0	904.2	87.8	9.7
Shareholders' equity	2,490.9	2,284.1	206.8	9.1
Total liabilities and shareholders' equity	$5,672.6	$5,343.9	$328.7	6.2

Source: Data from Starbucks Corporation, Form 10-K, 2008.

EXHIBIT 16-4 Comparative Income Statements with Horizontal Analysis

Starbucks Corporation
Consolidated Income Statements
For the Years Ended September 28, 2008, and September 30, 2007

(Dollar amounts in millions except per share amounts)	2008	2007	Increase (Decrease) Amount	Percentage
Net revenues	$10,383.0	$9,411.5	$ 971.5	10.3
Cost of sales, including occupancy costs	4,645.3	3,999.1	646.2	16.2
Gross margin	$ 5,737.7	$5,412.4	$ 325.3	6.0
Operating expenses				
Store operating expenses	$ 3,745.1	$3,215.9	$ 529.2	16.5
Other operating expenses	330.1	294.2	35.9	12.2
Depreciation and amortization expenses	549.3	467.2	82.1	17.6
General and administrative expenses	456.0	489.2	(33.2)	(6.8)
Restructuring charges	266.9	—	266.9	100.0
Total operating expenses	$ 5,347.4	$4,466.5	$ 880.9	19.7
Operating income	$ 390.3	$ 945.9	$(555.6)	(58.7)
Other income, net	122.6	148.4	(25.8)	(17.4)
Interest expense	(53.4)	(38.0)	(15.4)	40.5
Income before taxes	$ 459.5	$1,056.3	$(596.8)	(56.5)
Provision for income taxes	144.0	383.7	(239.7)	(62.5)
Income before cumulative change for FIN 47, net of taxes	$ 315.5	$ 672.6	$(357.1)	(53.1)
Cumulative effect of accounting change for FIN 47, net of taxes	—	—	—	0.0
Net income	$ 315.5	$ 672.6	$(357.1)	(53.1)
Per common share:				
Net income per common share before cumulative effect of change in accounting principle—basic	$ 0.43	$ 0.90	$ (0.47)	(52.2)
Cumulative effect of accounting change for FIN 47, net of taxes	—	—	—	0.0
Net income per common share—basic	$ 0.43	$ 0.90	$ (0.47)	(52.2)
Net income per common share before cumulative effect of change in accounting principle—diluted	$ 0.43	$ 0.87	$ (0.44)	(50.6)
Cumulative effect of accounting change for FIN 47, net of taxes	—	—	—	0.0
Net income per common share—diluted	$ 0.43	$ 0.87	$ (0.44)	(50.6)
Shares used in calculation of net income per common share—basic	731.5	749.8	(18.3)	(2.4)
Shares used in calculation of net income per common share—diluted	741.7	770.1	(28.4)	(3.7)

Source: Data from Starbucks Corporation, Form 10-K, 2008.

EXHIBIT 16-5
Trend Analysis

Starbucks Corporation
Net Revenues and Operating Income
Trend Analysis

	2008	2007	2006	2005	2004
Dollar values (In millions)					
Net revenues	$10,383.0	$9,411.5	$7,786.9	$6,369.3	$5,294.2
Operating income	390.3	945.9	800.0	703.9	549.5
Trend analysis (In percentages)					
Net revenues	196.1	177.8	147.1	120.3	100.0
Operating income	71.0	172.1	145.6	128.1	100.0

Source: Data from Starbucks Corporation, Form 10-K, 2008.

Trend Analysis

Trend analysis is a variation of horizontal analysis. With this tool, the analyst calculates percentage changes for several successive years instead of for just two years. Because of its long-term view, trend analysis can highlight basic changes in the nature of a business.

Study Note

To reflect the general five-year economic cycle of the U.S. economy, trend analysis usually covers a five-year period. Cycles of other lengths exist and are tracked by the National Bureau of Economic Research. Trend analysis needs to be of sufficient length to show a company's performance in both up and down markets.

In addition to presenting comparative financial statements, many companies present a summary of key data for five or more years in their annual reports. Exhibit 16-5 shows a trend analysis of **Starbucks**' five-year summary of net revenues and operating income.

Trend analysis uses an **index number** to show changes in related items over time. For an index number, the base year is set at 100 percent. Other years are measured in relation to that amount. For example, the 2008 index for Starbucks' net revenues is figured as follows (dollar amounts are in millions):

$$\text{Index} = 100 \times \left(\frac{\text{Index Year Amount}}{\text{Base Year Amount}}\right)$$

$$= 100 \times \left(\frac{\$10{,}383.0}{\$5{,}294.2}\right) = 196.1\%$$

The trend analysis in Exhibit 16-5 shows that Starbucks' net revenues increased over the five-year period. Overall, revenue grew 196.1 percent. However, operating income grew slower than net revenues in every year except for 2008 when the operating income declined. Figure 16-1 illustrates these trends.

Vertical Analysis

Vertical analysis shows how the different components of a financial statement relate to a total figure in the statement. The analyst sets the total figure at 100 percent and computes each component's percentage of that total. The resulting financial statement, which is expressed entirely in percentages, is called a **common-size statement**. Common-size balance sheets and common-size income statements for **Starbucks Corporation** are shown in pie-chart form in Figures 16-2 and 16-3 and in financial statement form in Exhibits 16-6 and 16-7. (On the balance sheet, the

FIGURE 16-1 Graph of Trend Analysis Shown in Exhibit 16-5

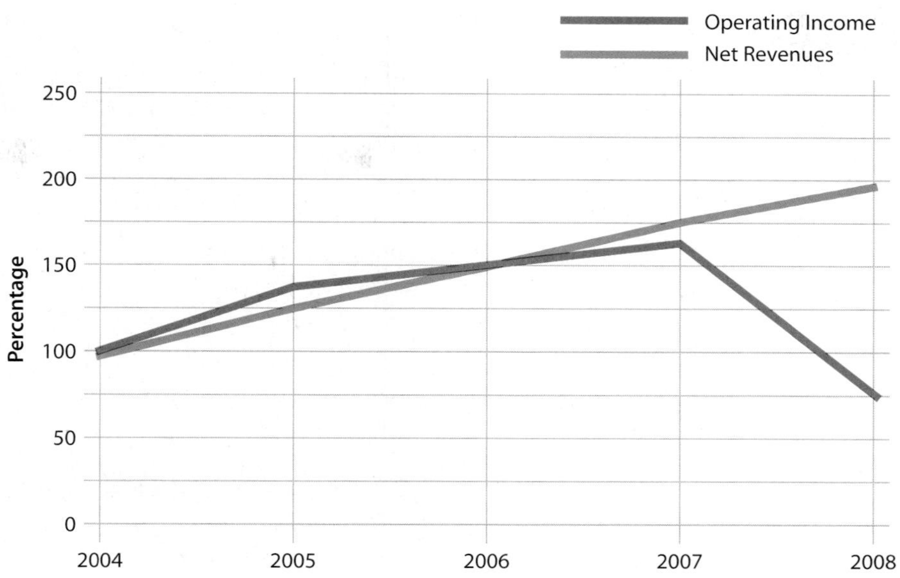

figure would be total assets or total liabilities and stockholders' equity, and on the income statement, it would be net revenues or net sales.)

Vertical analysis and common-size statements are useful in comparing the importance of specific components in the operation of a business and in identifying important changes in the components from one year to the next. The main conclusions to be drawn from our analysis of Starbucks are that the company's assets consist largely of current assets and property, plant, and equipment; that

FIGURE 16-2 Common-Size Balance Sheets Presented Graphically

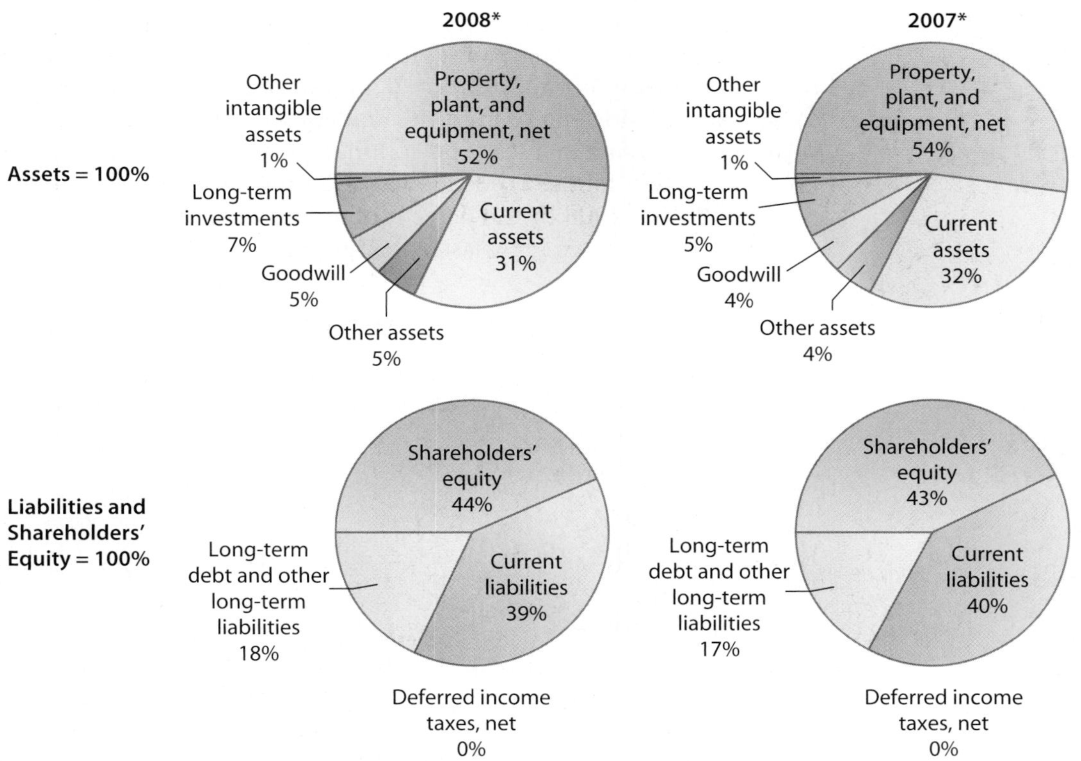

**Rounding causes some additions not to total precisely.*

EXHIBIT 16-6
Common-Size Balance Sheets

Starbucks Corporation
Common-Size Balance Sheets
September 28, 2008, and September 30, 2007

	2008	2007
Assets		
Current assets	30.8%	31.7%
Long-term investments	6.6	5.2
Property, plant, and equipment, net	52.1	54.1
Other assets	4.6	4.1
Other intangible assets	1.2	0.8
Goodwill	4.7	4.0
Total assets	100.0%	100.0%
Liabilities and Shareholders' Equity		
Current liabilities	38.6%	40.3%
Long-term debt and other liabilities	17.5	16.9
Shareholders' equity	43.9	42.7
Total liabilities and shareholders' equity	100.0%	100.0%

Note: Amounts do not precisely total 100 percent in all cases due to rounding.
Source: Data from Starbucks Corporation, Form 10-K, 2008.

the company finances assets primarily through equity and current liabilities; and that it has fewer long-term liabilities.

Looking at the pie charts in Figure 16-2 and the common-size balance sheets in Exhibit 16-6, you can see that Starbucks' is gradually shifting assets from current assets and long-term investments toward all other categories of long-term assets. At the same time, it is decreasing its proportion of current liabilities and increasing both long-term debt and shareholders' equity. You can also see that the relationship of liabilities and equity shifted slightly from stockholders' equity to current liabilities. The common-size income statements in Exhibit 16-7, illustrated in Figure 16-3, show that Starbucks increased its operating expenses from 2007 to 2008 by 4.0 percent of revenues (51.5% − 47.5%). In other words, operating expenses grew faster than revenues.

FIGURE 16-3
Common-Size Income Statements Presented Graphically

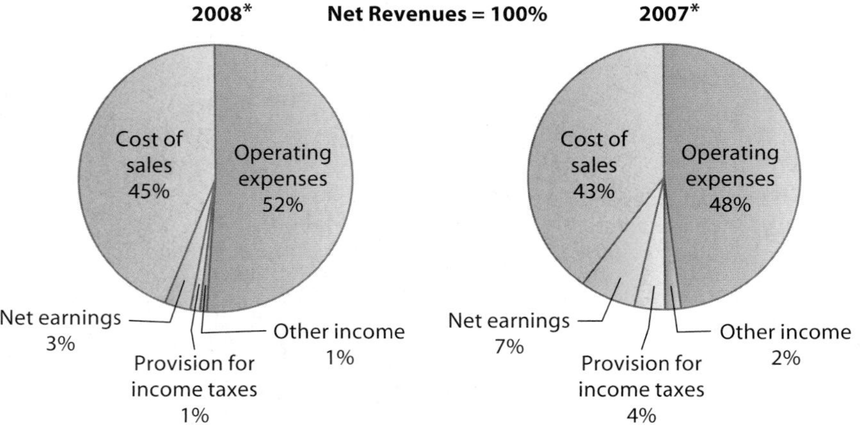

**Rounding causes some additions not to total precisely.*
Note: *Not all items are presented.*

EXHIBIT 16-7
Common-Size Income Statements

Starbucks Corporation
Common-Size Income Statements
For the Years Ended September 28, 2008 and September 30, 2007

	2008	2007
Net revenues	100.0%	100.0%
Cost of sales, including occupancy costs	44.7	42.5
Gross margin	55.3%	57.5%
Operating expenses:		
Store operating expenses	36.1%	34.2%
Other operating expenses	3.2	3.1
Depreciation and amortization expenses	5.3	5.0
General and administrative expenses	4.4	5.2
Restructuring charges	2.6	—
Total operating expenses	51.5%	47.5%
Operating income	3.8%	10.1%
Other income, net	1.2	1.6
Interest expense	(0.5)	(0.4)
Income before taxes	4.4%	11.2%
Provision for income taxes	1.4	4.1
Income before cumulative change for FIN 47, net of taxes	3.0%	7.1%
Cumulative effect of accounting change for FIN 47, net of taxes	—	—
Net income	3.0%	7.1%

Note: Amounts do not precisely total 100 percent in all cases due to rounding.
Source: Data from Starbucks Corporation, Form 10-K, 2008.

Common-size statements are often used to make comparisons between companies. They allow an analyst to compare the operating and financing characteristics of two companies of different size in the same industry. For example, the analyst might want to compare Starbucks with other specialty retailers in terms of percentage of total assets financed by debt or in terms of operating expenses as a percentage of net revenues. Common-size statements would show those and other relationships. These statements can also be used to compare the characteristics of companies that report in different currencies.

Ratio Analysis

Ratio analysis is an evaluation technique that identifies key relationships between the components of the financial statements. Ratios are useful tools for evaluating a company's financial position and operations and may reveal areas that need further investigation. To interpret ratios correctly, the analyst must have a general understanding of the company and its environment, financial data for several years or for several companies, and an understanding of the data underlying the numerator and denominator.

Ratios can be expressed in several ways. For example, a ratio of net income of \$100,000 to sales of \$1,000,000 can be stated as follows:

1. Net income is 1/10, or 10 percent, of sales.
2. The ratio of sales to net income is 10 to 1 (10:1), or sales are 10 times net income.
3. For every dollar of sales, the company has an average net income of 10 cents.

STOP & APPLY >

Different types of analysis achieve different objectives for the analyst. Match each of these types of analysis to their objective: (a) horizontal analysis, (b) trend analysis, (c) vertical analysis, and (d) ratio analysis.

1. Identifies key relationships among components of the financial statements
2. Provides a long-term view of key measures as to the direction of the company
3. Highlights the composition of assets, liabilities, and equity and changes in the components of the company from one year to the next
4. Provides insight into year-to-year changes

SOLUTION

1. d; 2. b; 3. c; 4. a

Comprehensive Illustration of Ratio Analysis

LO3 Apply ratio analysis to financial statements in a comprehensive evaluation of a company's financial performance.

In this section, to illustrate how analysts use ratio analysis in evaluating a company's financial performance, we perform a comprehensive ratio analysis of **Starbucks**' performance in 2007 and 2008. The following excerpt from the discussion and analysis section of Starbucks' 2008 annual report provides the context for our evaluation of the company's liquidity, profitability, long-term solvency, cash flow adequacy, and market strength:

> Throughout fiscal 2008, Starbucks continued to experience declining comparable store sales in its U.S. stores, primarily due to lower customer traffic. With the U.S. segment representing 76 percent of consolidated revenues, the impact of this decline on the company's financial results for fiscal 2008 was significant. For fiscal year 2008 comparable store sales declined 5 percent in the United States, with a declining trend over the course of the year, ending with a decline of 8 percent in the fourth quarter. The company also experienced declining comparable sales in Canada and the UK, its two largest company-operated international markets, primarily due to lower traffic. The company believes that the weaker traffic has been caused by a number of ongoing factors in the global economies that have negatively impacted consumers' discretionary spending, as well as factors within the company's control with respect to the pace of store openings in the United States and store level execution. In the United States, the economic factors included the higher cost of such basic consumer staples as gas and food, rising levels of unemployment and personal debt, reduced access to consumer credit, and lower home values as well as increased foreclosure activity in certain areas of the country (California and Florida) where Starbucks has a high concentration of company-operated stores. These developments, combined with recent and ongoing unprecedented shocks to the global financial system and capital markets, have all contributed to sharp declines in consumer confidence in the United States.

Evaluating Liquidity

As you know, liquidity is a company's ability to pay bills when they are due and to meet unexpected needs for cash. Because debts are paid out of working capital, all liquidity ratios involve working capital or some part of it. (Cash flow ratios are also closely related to liquidity.)

Study Note

When examining ratios in published sources, be aware that publishers often redefine the content of the ratios provided by the companies. While the general content is similar, variations occur. Be sure to ascertain and evaluate the information that a published source uses to calculate ratios.

Exhibit 16-8 presents **Starbucks**' liquidity ratios in 2007 and 2008. The **current ratio** and the **quick ratio** are measures of short-term debt-paying ability. The principal difference between the two ratios is that the numerator of the current ratio includes inventories and prepaid expenses. Inventories take longer to convert to cash than the current assets included in the numerator of the quick ratio. Starbucks' quick ratio was 0.3 times in both years 2007 and 2008. Its current ratio was 0.8 times in both years 2007 and 2008. From 2007 to 2008, its current assets grew at the same rate as current liabilities.

Starbucks' management of receivables and inventories worsened from 2007 to 2008. The **receivable turnover**, which measures the relative size of accounts receivable and the effectiveness of credit policies, fell from 36.7 times in 2007 to 33.6 times in 2008. The related ratio of **days' sales uncollected** increased by one day, from 9.9 days in 2007 to 10.9 days in 2008. The number of days is quite low because the majority of Starbucks' revenues are from cash sales.

The **inventory turnover**, which measures the relative size of inventories, increased from 6.0 times in 2007 to 6.7 times in 2008. This resulted in a favorable decrease in **days' inventory on hand**, from 60.8 days in 2007 to 54.5 days in 2008.

Starbucks' **operating cycle**, or the time it takes to sell products and collect for them, decreased from 70.7 days in 2007 (9.9 days + 60.8 days, or the days' sales uncollected plus the days' inventory on hand) to 65.4 days in 2008 (10.9 days + 54.5 days).

Related to the operating cycle is the number of days a company takes to pay its accounts payable. Starbucks' **payables turnover** increased from 11.1 times in 2007 to 13.0 times in 2008. This resulted in **days' payable** of 32.9 days in 2007 and 28.1 days in 2008. If the days' payable is subtracted from the operating cycle, Starbucks' financing period—the number of days of financing required—was 37.8 days in 2007 and 37.3 days in 2008 (Figure 16-4). Overall, Starbucks' liquidity declined.

Evaluating Profitability

Investors and creditors are interested in evaluating not only a company's liquidity but also its profitability—that is, its ability to earn a satisfactory income. Profitability is closely linked to liquidity because earnings ultimately produce the cash

FIGURE 16-4
Starbucks' Operating Cycle

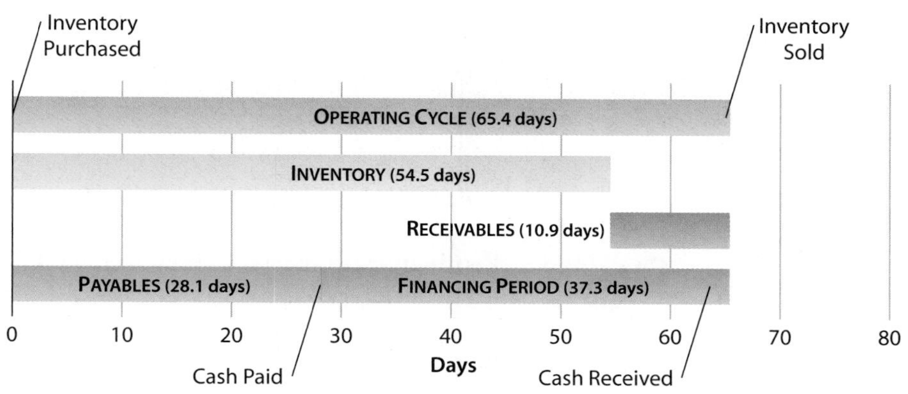

EXHIBIT 16-8 Liquidity Ratios of Starbucks Corporation

(Dollar amounts in millions)	2008	2007
Current ratio: Measure of short-term debt-paying ability		
$\frac{\text{Current Assets}}{\text{Current Liabilities}}$	$\frac{\$1,748.0}{\$2,189.7} = 0.8$ Times	$\frac{\$1,696.5}{\$2,155.6} = 0.8$ Times
Quick ratio: Measure of short-term debt-paying ability		
$\frac{\text{Cash + Marketable Securities + Receivables}}{\text{Current Liabilities}}$	$\frac{\$269.8 + \$52.5 + \$329.5}{\$2,189.7}$	$\frac{\$281.3 + \$157.4 + \$287.9}{\$2,155.6}$
	$= \frac{\$651.8}{\$2,189.7} = 0.3$ Times	$= \frac{\$726.6}{\$2,155.6} = 0.3$ Times
Receivable turnover: Measure of relative size of accounts receivable and effectiveness of credit policies		
$\frac{\text{Net Sales}}{\text{Average Accounts Receivable}}$	$\frac{\$10,383.0}{(\$329.5 + \$287.9) \div 2}$	$\frac{\$9,411.5}{(\$287.9 + \$224.3) \div 2}$
	$= \frac{\$10,383.0}{\$308.7} = 33.6$ Times	$= \frac{\$9,411.5}{\$256.1} = 36.7$ Times
Days' sales uncollected: Measure of average days taken to collect receivables		
$\frac{\text{Days in Accounting Period}}{\text{Receivable Turnover}}$	$\frac{365 \text{ Days}}{33.6 \text{ Times}} = 10.9$ Days	$\frac{365 \text{ Days}}{36.7 \text{ Times}} = 9.9$ Days
Inventory turnover: Measure of relative size of inventory		
$\frac{\text{Cost of Goods Sold}}{\text{Average Inventory}}$	$\frac{\$4,645.3}{(\$692.8 + \$691.7) \div 2}$	$\frac{\$3,999.1}{(\$691.7 + \$636.2) \div 2}$
	$= \frac{\$4,645.3}{\$692.3} = 6.7$ Times	$= \frac{\$3,999.1}{\$664.0} = 6.0$ Times
Days' inventory on hand: Measure of average days taken to sell inventory		
$\frac{\text{Days in Accounting Period}}{\text{Inventory Turnover}}$	$\frac{365 \text{ Days}}{6.7 \text{ Times}} = 54.5$ Days	$\frac{365 \text{ Days}}{6.0 \text{ Times}} = 60.8$ Days
Payables turnover: Measure of relative size of accounts payable		
$\frac{\text{Cost of Goods Sold +/− Change in Inventory}}{\text{Average Accounts Payable}}$	$\frac{\$4,645.3 + \$1.1}{(\$324.9 + \$390.8) \div 2}$	$\frac{\$3,999.1 + \$55.5^{*}}{(\$390.8 + \$340.9) \div 2}$
	$= \frac{\$4,646.4}{\$357.9} = 13.0$ Times	$= \frac{\$4,054.6}{\$365.9} = 11.1$ Times
Days' payable: Measure of average days taken to pay accounts payable		
$\frac{\text{Days in Accounting Period}}{\text{Payables Turnover}}$	$\frac{365 \text{ Days}}{13.0 \text{ Times}} = 28.1$ Days	$\frac{365 \text{ Days}}{11.1 \text{ Times}} = 32.9$ Days

*Figures for 2006 are from the balance sheet in Starbucks' Form 10-K, 2007.

Source: Data from Starbucks Corporation, Form 10-K, 2008; Form 10-K, 2007.

flow needed for liquidity. Exhibit 16-9 shows **Starbucks**' profitability ratios in 2007 and 2008.

Profit margin measures how well a company manages its costs per dollar of sales. Starbucks' profit margin decreased from 7.1 to 3.0 percent between 2007 and 2008. Its **asset turnover**, which measures how efficiently assets are used to produce sales (or net revenues), was stable at 1.9 times in 2007 and 2008. The result is a decrease in the company's earning power, or **return on assets**, from

EXHIBIT 16-9 Profitability Ratios of Starbucks Corporation

(Dollar amounts in millions)	**2008**	**2007**
Profit margin: Measure of net income produced by each dollar of sales		
$\frac{\text{Net Income}}{\text{Net Sales}}$	$\frac{\$315.5}{\$10{,}383.0} = 3.0\%$	$\frac{\$672.6}{\$9{,}411.5} = 7.1\%$
Asset turnover: Measure of how efficiently assets are used to produce sales		
$\frac{\text{Net Sales}}{\text{Average Total Assets}}$	$\frac{\$10{,}383.0}{(\$5{,}672.6 + \$5{,}343.9) \div 2}$	$\frac{\$9{,}411.5}{(\$5{,}343.9 + \$4{,}428.9^{*}) \div 2}$
	$= \frac{\$10{,}383.0}{\$5{,}508.3} = 1.9 \text{ Times}$	$= \frac{\$9{,}411.5}{\$4{,}886.4} = 1.9 \text{ Times}$
Return on assets: Measure of overall earning power or profitability		
$\frac{\text{Net Income}}{\text{Average Total Assets}}$	$\frac{\$315.5}{\$5{,}508.3} = 5.7\%$	$\frac{\$672.6}{\$4{,}886.4} = 13.8\%$
Return on equity: Measure of the profitability of stockholders' investments		
$\frac{\text{Net Income}}{\text{Average Stockholders' Equity}}$	$\frac{\$315.5}{(\$2{,}490.9 + \$2{,}284.1) \div 2}$	$\frac{\$672.6}{(\$2{,}284.1 + \$2{,}228.5^{*}) \div 2}$
	$= \frac{\$315.5}{\$2{,}387.5} = 13.2\%$	$= \frac{\$672.6}{\$2{,}256.3} = 29.8\%$

*Figures for 2006 are from the five-year selected financial data in Starbucks' Form 10-K, 2007.

Source: Data from Starbucks Corporation, Form 10-K, 2008; Form 10-K, 2007.

Study Note

In accounting literature, *profit* is expressed in different ways—for example, as income before income taxes, income after income taxes, or operating income. To draw appropriate conclusions from profitability ratios, analysts must be aware of the content of net income data.

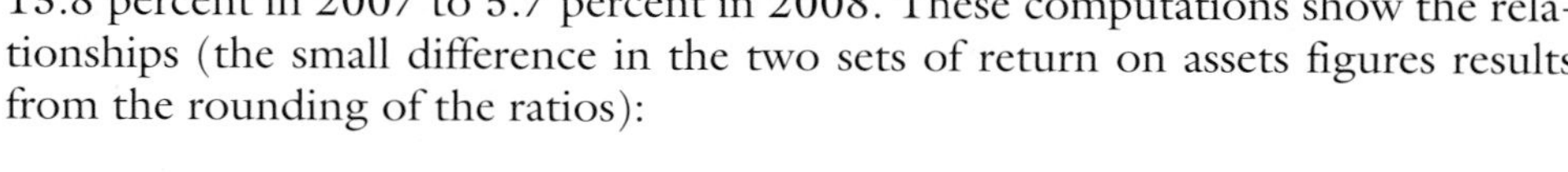

13.8 percent in 2007 to 5.7 percent in 2008. These computations show the relationships (the small difference in the two sets of return on assets figures results from the rounding of the ratios):

	Profit Margin		*Asset Turnover*		*Return on Assets*
	$\frac{\text{Net Income}}{\text{Net Sales}}$	×	$\frac{\text{Net Sales}}{\text{Average Total Assets}}$	=	$\frac{\text{Net Income}}{\text{Average Total Assets}}$
2007	7.1%	×	1.9	=	13.5%*
2008	3.0%	×	1.9	=	5.7%

Starbucks' **return on equity** also declined from 29.8 percent in 2007 to 13.2 percent in 2008.

Although we have used net income in computing profitability ratios for Starbucks, net income is not always a good indicator of a company's sustainable earnings. For instance, if a company has discontinued operations, income from continuing operations may be a better measure of sustainable earnings. For a company that has one-time items on its income statement—such as restructurings, gains, or losses—income from operations before these items may be a better measure. Some analysts like to use earnings before interest and taxes, or EBIT, for the earnings measure because it excludes the effects of the company's borrowings and the tax rates from the analysis. Whatever figure one uses for earnings, it is important to try to determine the effects of various components on future operations.

*Difference from 13.8% above is rounding.

FOCUS ON BUSINESS PRACTICE

What's the Best Way to Measure Performance for Management Compensation?

Efforts to link management compensation to performance measures and the creation of shareholder wealth are increasing. **Starbucks** uses earning per share (EPS) for this purpose. Some other companies, including **Walgreens**, use a better approach. This use of return on invested capital, which is closely related to return on assets, shows whether or not management is employing the assets profitably. Better still would be to compare the company's return on assets to its cost of debt and equity capital, as does **Target**.[7] Many analysts believe that this measure, which is called *economic value added (EVA)*, is superior to EPS. If the return on assets exceeds the cost of financing the assets with debt and equity, then management is indeed creating value for the shareholders.

Evaluating Long-Term Solvency

Study Note

Liquidity is a firm's ability to meet its current obligations; solvency is its ability to meet maturing obligations as they come due without losing the ability to continue operations.

Long-term solvency has to do with a company's ability to survive for many years. The aim of evaluating long-term solvency is to detect early signs that a company is headed for financial difficulty. Increasing amounts of debt in a company's capital structure mean that the company is becoming more heavily leveraged. This condition has a negative effect on long-term solvency because it represents increasing legal obligations to pay interest periodically and the principal at maturity. Failure to make those payments can result in bankruptcy.

Declining profitability and liquidity ratios are key indicators of possible failure. Two other ratios that analysts consider when assessing long-term solvency are debt to equity and interest coverage, which are shown in Exhibit 16-10. The **debt to equity ratio** measures capital structure and leverage by showing the amount of a company's assets provided by creditors in relation to the amount

In addition to using EVA® (Economic Value Added) to determine executive compensation, Target uses it to guide capital investment decisions. The company uses a benchmark of 9 percent for the estimated after-tax cost of capital invested in retail operations and a benchmark of 5 percent for capital invested in credit card operations. Target believes that a focus on EVA® fosters its objective of increasing average annual earnings per share by 15 percent or more over time.

Source: Courtesy of Justin Sullivan/Getty Images.

EXHIBIT 16-10 Long-term Solvency Ratios of Starbucks Corporation

(Dollar amounts in millions)	**2008**	**2007**
Debt to equity ratio: Measure of capital structure and leverage		
$\frac{\text{Total Liabilities}}{\text{Stockholders' Equity}}$	$\frac{\$3{,}181.7}{\$2{,}490.9} = 1.3$ Times	$\frac{\$3{,}059.8}{\$2{,}284.1} = 1.3$ Times
Interest coverage ratio: Measure of creditors' protection from default on interest payments		
$\frac{\text{Income Before Income Taxes + Interest Expense}}{\text{Interest Expense}}$	$\frac{\$459.5 + \$53.4}{\$53.4}$	$\frac{\$1{,}056.3 + \$38.0}{\$38.0}$
	$= \frac{\$512.9}{\$53.4} = 9.6$ Times	$= \frac{\$1{,}094.3}{\$38.0} = 28.8$ Times

Source: Data from Starbucks Corporation, Form 10-K, 2008.

Study Note

Because of innovative financing plans and other means of acquiring assets, lease payments and similar types of fixed obligations should be considered when evaluating long-term solvency.

provided by stockholders. **Starbucks**' debt to equity ratio was stable at 1.3 times in both 2007 and 2008. Recall from Exhibit 16-3 that the company increased both its liabilities and its stockholders' equity from 2007 to 2008. However, the company's current ratio is satisfactory and little changed. In sum, Starbucks' long-term solvency is not in danger.

If debt is risky, why have any? The answer is that the level of debt is a matter of balance. Despite its riskiness, debt is a flexible means of financing certain business operations. The interest paid on debt is tax-deductible, whereas dividends on stock are not. Because debt usually carries a fixed interest charge, the cost of financing can be limited, and leverage can be used to advantage. If a company can earn a return on assets greater than the cost of interest, it makes an overall profit. In addition, being a debtor in periods of inflation has advantages because the debt, which is a fixed dollar amount, can be repaid with cheaper dollars. However, the company runs the risk of not earning a return on assets equal to the cost of financing the assets, thereby incurring a loss.

The **interest coverage ratio** measures the degree of protection creditors have from default on interest payments. Starbucks' interest coverage declined from 28.8 times to 9.6 times due to almost twice as much interest. Nevertheless, interest coverage is still at a very safe level.

Evaluating the Adequacy of Cash Flows

Because cash flows are needed to pay debts when they are due, cash flow measures are closely related to liquidity and long-term solvency. Exhibit 16-11 presents **Starbucks**' cash flow adequacy ratios in 2007 and 2008.

Cash flow yield shows the cash-generating ability of a company's operations; it is measured by dividing cash flows from operating activities by net income. Starbucks' net cash flows from operating activities decreased from $1,331.2 million in 2007 to $1,258.7 million in 2008. Its cash flow yield actually increased from 2.0 to 4.0 times, revealing that net cash provided by operating activities increased faster than net income.

On the other hand, Starbucks' ratios for cash flows to sales and cash flows to assets declined. While the company's net sales and average total assets increased, the net cash flows from operating activities declined. **Cash flows to sales**, or the cash-generating ability of sales, decreased from 14.1 to 12.1 percent. **Cash flows to assets**, or the ability of assets to generate operating cash flows, decreased from 27.2 to 22.9 percent.

EXHIBIT 16-11 Cash Flow Adequacy Ratios of Starbucks Corporation

(Dollar amounts in millions)	**2008**	**2007**
Cash flow yield: Measure of the ability to generate operating cash flows in relation to net income		
Net Cash Flows from Operating Activities ÷ Net Income	$\frac{\$1{,}258.7^*}{\$315.5} = 4.0$ Times	$\frac{\$1{,}331.2^*}{\$672.6} = 2.0$ Times
Cash flows to sales: Measure of the ability of sales to generate operating cash flows		
Net Cash Flows from Operating Activities ÷ Net Sales	$\frac{\$1{,}258.7}{\$10{,}383.0} = 12.1\%$	$\frac{\$1{,}331.2}{\$9{,}411.5} = 14.1\%$
Cash flows to assets: Measure of the ability of assets to generate operating cash flows		
Net Cash Flows from Operating Activities ÷ Average Total Assets	$\frac{\$1{,}258.7}{(\$5{,}672.6 + \$5{,}343.9) \div 2}$	$\frac{\$1{,}331.2}{(\$5{,}343.9 + \$4{,}428.9) \div 2}$
	$= \frac{\$1{,}258.7}{\$5{,}508.3} = 22.9\%$	$= \frac{\$1{,}331.2}{\$4{,}886.4} = 27.2\%$
Free cash flow: Measure of cash remaining after providing for commitments		
Net Cash Flows from Operating Activities − Dividends − Net Capital Expenditures	$1,258.7 − $0 − $984.5*	$1,331.2* − $0 − $1,080.3
	= $274.2	= $250.9

*These figures are from the statement of cash flows in Starbucks' Form 10-K, 2008.

Source: Data from Starbucks Corporation, Form 10-K, 2008; Form 10-K, 2007.

> **Study Note**
>
> When the computation for free cash flow uses "net capital expenditures" in place of "purchases of plant assets minus sales of plant assets," it means that the company's sales of plant assets were too small or immaterial to be broken out.

However, Starbucks' **free cash flow**, the cash remaining after providing for commitments, increased. While the company's net capital expenditures decreased by $95.8 million, the net cash flows from operating activities decreased by only $72.5 million. Another factor in Starbucks' free cash flows is that the company pays no dividends. Management's comment with regard to liquidity and cash flows in the future is as follows:

> The Company's existing cash and liquid investments were $322.3 million and $438.7 million as of September 28, 2008 and September 30, 2007, respectively. The decrease in liquid investments was driven primarily by $59.8 million of auction rate securities, nearly all of which are held within the Company's wholly owned captive insurance company, that are not currently considered liquid and were reclassified to long-term investments in the second quarter of fiscal 2008. . . . The Company expects to use its cash and liquid investments, including any borrowings under its revolving credit facility and commercial paper program to invest in its core businesses, including new beverage innovations, as well as other new business opportunities related to its core businesses.[8]

EXHIBIT 16-12 Market Strength Ratios of Starbucks Corporation

	2008	2007
Price/earnings (P/E) ratio: Measure of investors' confidence in a company		
$\frac{\text{Market Price per Share}}{\text{Earnings per Share}}$	$\frac{\$15.25^*}{\$0.43}$ = 35.5 Times	$\frac{\$27.08^*}{\$0.90}$ = 30.1 Times
Dividends yield: Measure of a stock's current return to an investor		
$\frac{\text{Dividends per Share}}{\text{Market Price per Share}}$	Starbucks does not pay a dividend.	

*Market price is the average for the fourth quarter reported in Starbucks' Form 10-K.

Source: Data from Starbucks Corporation, Form 10-K, 2008.

Evaluating Market Strength

Market price is the price at which a company's stock is bought and sold. It indicates how investors view the potential return and risk connected with owning the stock. Market price by itself is not very informative, however, because companies have different numbers of shares outstanding, different earnings, and different dividend policies. Thus, market price must be related to earnings by considering the price/earnings (P/E) ratio and the dividends yield. Those ratios for **Starbucks** appear in Exhibit 16-12. We computed them by using the average market prices of Starbucks' stock during the fourth quarters of 2007 and 2008.

The **price/earnings (P/E) ratio**, which measures investors' confidence in a company, is the ratio of the market price per share to earnings per share. The P/E ratio is useful in comparing the earnings of different companies and the value of a company's shares in relation to values in the overall market. With a higher P/E ratio, the investor obtains less underlying earnings per dollar invested. Despite a decrease in earnings per share from $0.90 in 2007 to $0.43 in 2008, Starbucks' P/E ratio increased from 30.1 times in 2007 to 35.5 times in 2008 because the market value of its stock declined from about $27 to about $15. The implication is that investors are expecting Starbucks to grow faster in the future than it has in the past.

The **dividends yield** measures a stock's current return to an investor in the form of dividends. Because Starbucks pays no dividends, its stockholders must expect their return to come from increases in the stock's market value.

STOP & APPLY >

Sasah's, a retail firm, engaged in the transactions listed below. Opposite each transaction is a ratio and space to mark the transaction's effect on the ratio.

Transaction	Ratio	Effect		
		Increase	**Decrease**	**None**
a. Accrued salaries.	Current ratio			
b. Purchased inventory.	Quick ratio			
c. Increased allowance for uncollectible accounts.	Receivable turnover			
d. Purchased inventory on credit.	Payables turnover			
e. Sold treasury stock.	Profit margin			
f. Borrowed cash by issuing bond payable.	Asset turnover			
g. Paid wages expense.	Return on assets			
h. Repaid bond payable.	Debt to equity ratio			
i. Accrued interest expense.	Interest coverage ratio			
j. Sold merchandise on account.	Return on equity			
k. Recorded depreciation expense.	Cash flow yield			
l. Sold equipment.	Free cash flow			

Show that you understand the effect of business activities on performance measures by placing an *X* in the appropriate column to show whether the transaction increased, decreased, or had no effect on the ratio.

SOLUTION

Transaction	Ratio	Effect		
		Increase	**Decrease**	**None**
a. Accrued salaries.	Current ratio		X	
b. Purchased inventory.	Quick ratio		X	
c. Increased allowance for uncollectible accounts.	Receivable turnover	X		
d. Purchased inventory on credit.	Payables turnover		X	
e. Sold treasury stock.	Profit margin			X
f. Borrowed cash by issuing bond payable.	Asset turnover		X	
g. Paid wages expense.	Return on assets		X	
h. Repaid bond payable.	Debt to equity ratio	X		
i. Accrued interest expense.	Interest coverage ratio		X	
j. Sold merchandise on account.	Return on equity	X		
k. Recorded depreciation expense.	Cash flow yield	X		
l. Sold equipment.	Free cash flow	X		

▸ WASHINGTON INVESTMENTS: REVIEW PROBLEM

Comprehensive Ratio Analysis
LO1 LO3

In the Decision Point at the beginning of this chapter, we noted that Maggie Washington, President of Washington Investments, was planning to invest in either Quik Burger or Big Steak. We asked these questions:

- What analytical tools can Maggie Washington use to measure the financial performance of Quik Burger and Big Steak?
- What standards can she use to compare the performance of the two companies?

The 2010 income statements and balance sheets of the two companies appear below and on the next page. The following information pertaining to 2010 is also available to Maggie Washington:

- Quick Burger's statement of cash flows shows that it had net cash flows from operations of $2,200,000. Big Steak's statement of cash flows shows that its net cash flows from operations were $3,000,000.
- Net capital expenditures were $2,100,000 for Quik Burger and $1,800,000 for Big Steak.
- Quik Burger paid dividends of $500,000, and Big Steak paid dividends of $600,000.
- The market prices of the stocks of Quik Burger and Big Steak were $30 and $20, respectively.

Maggie Washington does not have financial information pertaining to prior years.

	A	B	C
1	**Income Statements**		
2	**For the Year Ended December 31, 2010**		
3	(In thousands, except per share amounts)		
4			
5		**Quik Burger**	**Big Steak**
6	Net sales	$53,000	$86,000
7	Costs and expenses		
8	Cost of goods sold	$37,000	$61,000
9	Selling expenses	7,000	10,000
10	Administrative expenses	4,000	5,000
11	Total costs and expenses	$48,000	$76,000
12	Income from operations	$ 5,000	$10,000
13	Interest expense	1,400	3,200
14	Income before income taxes	$ 3,600	$ 6,800
15	Income taxes	1,800	3,400
16	Net income	$ 1,800	$ 3,400
17	Earnings per share	$ 1.80	$ 1.13

	A	B	C
1	**Balance Sheets**		
2	**December 31, 2010**		
3	**(In thousands)**		
4		**Quik Burger**	**Big Steak**
5	**Assets**		
6			
7	Cash	$ 2,000	$ 4,500
8	Accounts receivable (net)	2,000	6,500
9	Inventory	2,000	5,000
10	Property, plant, and equipment (net)	20,000	35,000
11	Other assets	4,000	5,000
12	Total assets	$30,000	$56,000
13			
14	**Liabilities and Stockholders' Equity**		
15	Accounts payable	$ 2,500	$ 3,000
16	Notes payable	1,500	4,000
17	Bonds payable	10,000	30,000
18	Common stock, $1 par value	1,000	3,000
19	Additional paid-in capital	9,000	9,000
20	Retained earnings	6,000	7,000
21	Total liabilities and stockholders' equity	$30,000	$56,000

Required

Perform a comprehensive ratio analysis of both Quik Burger and Big Steak following the steps outlined below. Assume that all notes payable of these two companies are current liabilities and that all their bonds payable are long-term liabilities. Show dollar amounts in thousands, use end-of-year balances for averages, assume no change in inventory, and round all ratios and percentages to one decimal place.

1. Prepare an analysis of liquidity.
2. Prepare an analysis of profitability.
3. Prepare an analysis of long-term solvency.
4. Prepare an analysis of cash flow adequacy.
5. Prepare an analysis of market strength.
6. In each analysis, indicate the company that apparently had the more favorable ratio. (Consider differences of 0.1 or less to be neutral.)
7. User insight: In what ways would having access to prior years' information aid this analysis?
8. User insight: In addition to the results of your comprehensive ratio analysis, what other information would be helpful in making the investment decision?

Answers to Review Problem

1. Liquidity analysis:

	Ratio Name	Quik Burger		Big Steak		6. Company with More Favorable Ratio
a.	Current ratio	($2,000 + $2,000 + $2,000) / ($2,500 + $1,500)		($4,500 + $6,500 + $5,000) / ($3,000 + $4,000)		
		$6,000 / $4,000	= 1.5 times	$16,000 / $7,000	= 2.3 times	Big Steak
b.	Quick ratio	$4,000 / $4,000	= 1.0 times	($4,500 + $6,500) / ($3,000 + $4,000)		Big Steak
c.	Receivable turnover	$53,000 / $2,000	= 26.5 times	$86,000 / $6,500	= 13.2 times	Quik Burger
d.	Days' sales uncollected	365 days / 26.5 times	= 13.8 days	365 days / 13.2 times	= 27.7 days	Quik Burger
e.	Inventory turnover	$37,000 / $2,000	= 18.5 times	$61,000 / $5,000	= 12.2 times	Quik Burger
f.	Days' inventory on hand	365 days / 18.5 times	= 19.7 days	365 days / 12.2 times	= 29.9 days	Quik Burger
g.	Payables turnover	$37,000 / $2,000	= 18.5 times	$61,000 / $3,000	= 20.3 times	Big Steak
h.	Days' payable	365 days / 18.5 times	= 19.7 days	365 days / 20.3 times	= 18.0 days	Quik Burger

Note: This analysis indicates the company with the apparently more favorable ratio. Class discussion may focus on conditions under which different conclusions may be drawn.

2. Profitability analysis:

	Ratio Name	Quik Burger		Big Steak		6. Company with More Favorable Ratio
a.	Profit margin	$1,800 / $53,000	= 3.4%	$3,400 / $86,000	= 4.0%	Big Steak
b.	Asset turnover	$53,000 / $30,000	= 1.8 times	$86,000 / $56,000	= 1.5 times	Quik Burger
c.	Return on assets	$1,800 / $30,000	= 6.0%	$3,400 / $56,000	= 6.1%	Big Steak
d.	Return on equity	$1,800 / ($1,000 + $9,000 + $6,000)		$3,400 / ($3,000 + $9,000 + $7,000)		
		$1,800 / $16,000	= 11.3%	$3,400 / $19,000	= 17.9%	Big Steak

3. Long-term solvency analysis:

	Ratio Name	Quik Burger		Big Steak		6. Company with More Favorable Ratio
a.	Debt to equity ratio	($2,000 + $1,500 + $10,000) / ($1,000 + $9,000 + $6,000)		($3,000 + $4,000 + $30,000) / ($3,000 + $9,000 + $7,000)		
		= $13,500 / $16,000	= 0.8 times	$37,000 / $19,000	= 1.9 times	Quik Burger
b.	Interest coverage ratio	($3,600 + $1,400) / $1,400		($6,800 + $3,200) / $3,200		
		= $5,000 / $1,400	= 3.6 times	$10,000 / $3,200	= 3.1 times	Quik Burger

4. Cash flow adequacy analysis:

	Ratio Name	Quik Burger			Big Steak			6. Company with More Favorable Ratio
a.	Cash flow yield	$2,200 / $1,800	=	1.2 times	$3,000 / $3,400	=	0.9 times	Quik Burger
b.	Cash flows to sales	$2,200 / $53,000	=	4.2%	$3,000 / $86,000	=	3.5%	Quik Burger
c.	Cash flows to assets	$2,200 / $30,000	=	7.3%	$3,000 / $56,000	=	5.4%	Quik Burger
d.	Free cash flow	$2,200 - $500 -		= ($400)	$3,000 - $600 -		= $600	Big Steak

5. Market strength analysis:

	Ratio Name	Quik Burger			Big Steak			6. Company with More Favorable Ratio
a.	Price/earnings ratio	$ 30.00 / $ 1.80	=	16.7 times	$ 20.00 / $ 1.13	=	17.7 times	Big Steak
b.	Dividends yield	($500,000 ÷ 1,000,000 shares) / $30			($600,000 ÷ 3,000,000 shares) / $20			
		$ 0.50 / $ 30.00	=	1.7%	$ 0.20 / $ 20.00	=	1.0%	Quik Burger

7. Prior years' information would be helpful in two ways. First, turnover, return, and cash flows to assets ratios could be based on average amounts. Second, a trend analysis could be performed for each company.
8. Using information about industry norms provided by Dun & Bradstreet and other financial services would be helpful in comparing the performance of Big Steak and Quik Burger.

LO1 Describe the objectives, standards of comparison, sources of information, and compensation issues in measuring financial performance.

A primary objective in management's use of financial performance measurement is to increase the wealth of the company's stockholders. Creditors and investors use financial performance measurement to judge a company's past performance and current position, as well as its future potential and the risk associated with it. Creditors use the information gained from their analyses to make reliable loans that will be repaid with interest. Investors use the information to make investments that will provide a return that is worth the risk.

Three standards of comparison commonly used in evaluating financial performance are rule-of-thumb measures, a company's past performance, and industry norms. Rule-of-thumb measures are weak because of a lack of evidence that they can be widely applied. A company's past performance can offer a guideline for measuring improvement, but it is not helpful in judging performance relative to the performance of other companies. Although the use of industry norms overcomes this last problem, its disadvantage is that firms are not always comparable, even in the same industry.

The main sources of information about public corporations are reports that the corporations publish themselves, such as annual reports and interim financial statements; reports filed with the SEC; business periodicals; and credit and investment advisory services.

In public corporations, a committee made up of independent directors appointed by the board of directors determines the compensation of top executives. Although earnings per share can be regarded as a "bottom-line" number that encompasses all the other performance measures, using it as the sole basis for determining executive compensation may lead to management practices that are not in the best interests of the company or its stockholders.

LO2 Apply horizontal analysis, trend analysis, vertical analysis, and ratio analysis to financial statements.

Horizontal analysis involves the computation of changes in both dollar amounts and percentages from year to year.

Trend analysis is an extension of horizontal analysis in that it calculates percentage changes for several years. The analyst computes the changes by setting a base year equal to 100 and calculating the results for subsequent years as percentages of the base year.

Vertical analysis uses percentages to show the relationship of the component parts of a financial statement to a total figure in the statement. The resulting financial statements, which are expressed entirely in percentages, are called common-size statements.

Ratio analysis is a technique of financial performance evaluation that identifies key relationships between the components of the financial statements. To interpret ratios correctly, the analyst must have a general understanding of the company and its environment, financial data for several years or for several companies, and an understanding of the data underlying the numerators and denominators.

LO3 Apply ratio analysis to financial statements in a comprehensive evaluation of a company's financial performance.

A comprehensive ratio analysis includes the evaluation of a company's liquidity, profitability, long-term solvency, cash flow adequacy, and market strength. The ratios for measuring these characteristics are illustrated in Exhibits 16-8 through 16-12.

REVIEW of Concepts and Terminology

The following concepts and terms were introduced in this chapter:

Base year 715 (LO2)

Common-size statement 718 (LO2)

Compensation committee 712 (LO1)

Diversified companies 710 (LO1)

Financial performance measurement 708 (LO1)

Free cash flow 728 (LO3)

Horizontal analysis 715 (LO2)

Index number 718 (LO2)

Interim financial statements 712 (LO1)

Operating cycle 723 (LO3)

Ratio analysis 721 (LO2)

Trend analysis 718 (LO2)

Vertical analysis 718 (LO2)

Key Ratios

Asset turnover 724 (LO3)

Cash flows to assets 727 (LO3)

Cash flows to sales 727 (LO3)

Cash flow yield 727 (LO3)

Current ratio 723 (LO3)

Days' inventory on hand 723 (LO3)

Days' payable 723 (LO3)

Days' sales uncollected 723 (LO3)

Debt to equity ratio 726 (LO3)

Dividends yield 729 (LO3)

Interest coverage ratio 727 (LO3)

Inventory turnover 723 (LO3)

Payables turnover 723 (LO3)

Price/earnings (P/E) ratio 729 (LO3)

Profit margin 724 (LO3)

Quick ratio 723 (LO3)

Receivable turnover 723 (LO3)

Return on assets 724 (LO3)

Return on equity 725 (LO3)

CHAPTER ASSIGNMENTS

BUILDING Your Basic Knowledge and Skills

Short Exercises

LO1 **Objectives and Standards of Financial Performance Evaluation**

SE 1. Indicate whether each of the following items is (a) an objective or (b) a standard of comparison of financial statement analysis:

1. Industry norms
2. Assessment of a company's past performance
3. The company's past performance
4. Assessment of future potential and related risk
5. Rule-of-thumb measures

LO1 **Sources of Information**

SE 2. For each piece of information in the list that follows, indicate whether the best source would be (a) reports published by the company, (b) SEC reports, (c) business periodicals, or (d) credit and investment advisory services.

1. Current market value of a company's stock
2. Management's analysis of the past year's operations
3. Objective assessment of a company's financial performance
4. Most complete body of financial disclosures
5. Current events affecting the company

LO2 **Trend Analysis**

SE 3. Using 2010 as the base year, prepare a trend analysis for the following data, and tell whether the results suggest a favorable or unfavorable trend. (Round your answers to one decimal place.)

	2012	2011	2010
Net sales	$158,000	$136,000	$112,000
Accounts receivable (net)	43,000	32,000	21,000

LO2 **Horizontal Analysis**

SE 4. The comparative income statements and balance sheets of Sarot, Inc., appear on the next page. Compute the amount and percentage changes for the income statements, and comment on the changes from 2011 to 2012. (Round the percentage changes to one decimal place.)

LO2 **Vertical Analysis**

SE 5. Express the comparative balance sheets of Sarot, Inc., (shown on the next page) as common-size statements, and comment on the changes from 2011 to 2012. (Round computations to one decimal place.)

LO3 **Liquidity Analysis**

SE 6. Using the information for Sarot, Inc. (shown on the next page), in **SE 4** and **SE 5**, compute the current ratio, quick ratio, receivable turnover, days' sales uncollected, inventory turnover, days' inventory on hand, payables turnover, and days' payable for 2011 and 2012. Inventories were $16,000 in 2010, $20,000 in 2011, and $28,000 in 2012. Accounts receivable were $24,000 in 2010, $32,000 in 2011, and $40,000 in 2012. Accounts payable were $36,000 in 2010, $40,000 in 2011, and $48,000 in 2012. The company had no marketable securities or prepaid assets. Comment on the results. (Round computations to one decimal place.)

Sarot, Inc.
Comparative Income Statements
For the Years Ended December 31, 2012 and 2011

	2012	2011
Net sales	$720,000	$580,000
Cost of goods sold	448,000	352,000
Gross margin	$272,000	$228,000
Operating expenses	160,000	120,000
Operating income	$112,000	$108,000
Interest expense	28,000	20,000
Income before income taxes	$ 84,000	$ 88,000
Income taxes expense	28,000	32,000
Net income	$ 56,000	$ 56,000
Earnings per share	$ 2.80	$ 2.80

Sarot, Inc.
Comparative Balance Sheets
December 31, 2012 and 2011

	2012	2011
Assets		
Current assets	$ 96,000	$ 80,000
Property, plant, and equipment (net)	520,000	400,000
Total assets	$616,000	$480,000
Liabilities and Stockholders' Equity		
Current liabilities	$ 72,000	$ 88,000
Long-term liabilities	360,000	240,000
Stockholders' equity	184,000	152,000
Total liabilities and stockholders' equity	$616,000	$480,000

LO3 **Profitability Analysis**

SE 7. Using the information for Sarot, Inc., in **SE 4** and **SE 5**, compute the profit margin, asset turnover, return on assets, and return on equity for 2011 and 2012. In 2010, total assets were $400,000 and total stockholders' equity was $120,000. Comment on the results. (Round computations to one decimal place.)

LO3 **Long-term Solvency Analysis**

SE 8. Using the information for Sarot, Inc., in **SE** 4 and **SE 5**, compute the debt to equity ratio and the interest coverage ratio for 2011 and 2012. Comment on the results. (Round computations to one decimal place.)

LO3 **Cash Flow Adequacy Analysis**

SE 9. Using the information for Sarot, Inc., in **SE 4**, **SE 5**, and **SE** 7, compute the cash flow yield, cash flows to sales, cash flows to assets, and free cash flow for 2011 and 2012. Net cash flows from operating activities were $84,000 in 2011 and $64,000 in 2012. Net capital expenditures were $120,000 in 2011 and $160,000 in 2012. Cash dividends were $24,000 in both years. Comment on the results. (Round computations to one decimal place.)

LO3 **Market Strength Analysis**

SE 10. Using the information for Sarot, Inc., in **SE 4**, **SE 5**, and **SE 9**, compute the price/earnings (P/E) ratio and dividends yield for 2011 and 2012. The company had 20,000 shares of common stock outstanding in both years. The price of Sarot's common stock was $60 in 2011 and $40 in 2012. Comment on the results. (Round computations to one decimal place.)

Exercises

LO1 LO2 **Discussion Questions**

E 1. Develop brief answers to each of the following questions:

1. Why is it essential that management compensation, including bonuses, be linked to financial goals and strategies that achieve shareholder value?
2. How are past performance and industry norms useful in evaluating a company's performance? What are their limitations?
3. In a five-year trend analysis, why do the dollar values remain the same for their respective years while the percentages usually change when a new five-year period is chosen?

LO3 **Discussion Questions**

E 2. Develop brief answers to each of the following questions:

1. Why does a decrease in receivable turnover create the need for cash from operating activities?
2. Why would ratios that include one balance sheet account and one income statement account, such as receivable turnover or return on assets, be questionable if they came from quarterly or other interim financial reports?
3. Can you suggest a limitation of free cash flow in comparing one company to another?

LO1 **Issues in Financial Performance Evaluation: Objectives, Standards, Sources of Information, and Executive Compensation**

E 3. Identify each of the following as (a) an objective of financial statement analysis, (b) a standard for financial statement analysis, (c) a source of information for financial statement analysis, or (d) an executive compensation issue:

1. Average ratios of other companies in the same industry
2. Assessment of the future potential of an investment
3. Interim financial statements
4. Past ratios of the company
5. SEC Form 10-K
6. Assessment of risk
7. A company's annual report
8. Linking performance to shareholder value

LO2 **Trend Analysis**

E 4. Using 2008 as the base year, prepare a trend analysis of the following data, and tell whether the situation shown by the trends is favorable or unfavorable. (Round your answers to one decimal place.)

	2012	2011	2010	2009	2008
Net sales	$25,520	$23,980	$24,200	$22,880	$22,000
Cost of goods sold	17,220	15,400	15,540	14,700	14,000
General and administrative expenses	5,280	5,184	5,088	4,896	4,800
Operating income	3,020	3,396	3,572	3,284	3,200

LO2 **Horizontal Analysis**

E 5. Compute the amount and percentage changes for the comparative balance sheets for Davis Company below, and comment on the changes from 2010 to 2011. (Round the percentage changes to one decimal place.)

Davis Company
Comparative Balance Sheets
December 31, 2011 and 2010

	2011	2010
Assets		
Current assets	$ 18,600	$ 12,800
Property, plant, and equipment (net)	109,464	97,200
Total assets	$128,064	$110,000
Liabilities and Stockholders' Equity		
Current liabilities	$ 11,200	$ 3,200
Long-term liabilities	35,000	40,000
Stockholders' equity	81,864	66,800
Total liabilities and stockholders' equity	$128,064	$110,000

LO2 **Vertical Analysis**

E 6. Express the partial comparative income statements for Davis Company that follow as common-size statements, and comment on the changes from 2010 to 2011. (Round computations to one decimal place.)

Davis Company
Partial Comparative Income Statements
For the Years Ended December 31, 2011 and 2010

	2011	2010
Net sales	$212,000	$184,000
Cost of goods sold	127,200	119,600
Gross margin	$ 84,800	$ 64,400
Selling expenses	$ 53,000	$ 36,800
General expenses	25,440	18,400
Total operating expenses	$ 78,440	$ 55,200
Operating income	$ 6,360	$ 9,200

LO3 **Liquidity Analysis**

E 7. Partial comparative balance sheet and income statement information for Smith Company is as follows:

	2012	2011
Cash	$ 27,200	$ 20,800
Marketable securities	14,400	34,400
Accounts receivable (net)	89,600	71,200
Inventory	108,800	99,200
Total current assets	$240,000	$225,600
Accounts payable	$ 80,000	$ 56,400
Net sales	$645,120	$441,440
Cost of goods sold	435,200	406,720
Gross margin	$209,920	$ 34,720

In 2010, the year-end balances for Accounts Receivable and Inventory were $64,800 and $102,400, respectively. Accounts Payable was $61,200 in 2010 and is the only current liability. Compute the current ratio, quick ratio, receivable turnover, days' sales uncollected, inventory turnover, days' inventory on hand, payables turnover, and days' payable for each year. (Round computations to one decimal place.) Comment on the change in the company's liquidity position, including its operating cycle and required days of financing from 2011 to 2012.

LO3 **Turnover Analysis**

E 8. Modern Suits Rental has been in business for four years. Because the company has recently had a cash flow problem, management wonders whether there is a problem with receivables or inventories. Here are selected figures from the company's financial statements (in thousands):

	2011	2010	2009	2008
Net sales	$288.0	$224.0	$192.0	$160.0
Cost of goods sold	180.0	144.0	120.0	96.0
Accounts receivable (net)	48.0	40.0	32.0	24.0
Merchandise inventory	56.0	44.0	32.0	20.0
Accounts payable	26.0	20.0	16.0	10.0

Compute the receivable turnover, inventory turnover, and payables turnover for each of the four years, and comment on the results relative to the cash flow problem that the firm has been experiencing. Merchandise inventory was $22,000, accounts receivable were $22,000, and accounts payable were $8,000 in 2007. (Round computations to one decimal place.)

LO3 **Profitability Analysis**

E 9. Barr Company had total assets of $320,000 in 2010, $340,000 in 2011, and $380,000 in 2012. Its debt to equity ratio was 0.67 times in all three years. In 2011, Barr had net income of $38,556 on revenues of $612,000. In 2012, it had net income of $49,476 on revenues of $798,000. Compute the profit margin, asset turnover, return on assets, and return on equity for 2011 and 2012. Comment on the apparent cause of the increase or decrease in profitability. (Round the percentages and other ratios to one decimal place.)

LO3 **Long-term Solvency and Market Strength Ratios**

E 10. An investor is considering investing in the long-term bonds and common stock of Companies P and R. Both firms operate in the same industry. Both also pay a dividend per share of $8 and have a yield of 10 percent on their long-term bonds. Other data for the two firms are as follows:

	Company P	Company R
Total assets	$2,400,000	$1,080,000
Total liabilities	1,080,000	594,000
Income before income taxes	288,000	129,600
Interest expense	97,200	53,460
Earnings per share	3.20	5.00
Market price of common stock	40.00	47.50

Compute the debt to equity ratio, interest coverage ratio, and price/earnings (P/E) ratio, as well as the dividends yield, and comment on the results. (Round computations to one decimal place.)

LO3 **Cash Flow Adequacy Analysis**

E 11. Using the data below from the financial statements of Bali, Inc., compute the company's cash flow yield, cash flows to sales, cash flows to assets, and free cash flow. (Round computations to one decimal place.)

Net sales	$1,600,000
Net income	176,000
Net cash flows from operating activities	228,000
Total assets, beginning of year	1,445,000
Total assets, end of year	1,560,000
Cash dividends	60,000
Net capital expenditures	149,000

Problems

LO2 **Horizontal and Vertical Analysis**

P 1. Robert Corporation's condensed comparative income statements and comparative balance sheets for 2011 and 2010 follow.

Robert Corporation
Comparative Income Statements
For the Years Ended December 31, 2011 and 2010

	2011	2010
Net sales	$1,638,400	$1,573,200
Cost of goods sold	1,044,400	1,004,200
Gross margin	$ 594,000	$ 569,000
Operating expenses		
Selling expenses	$ 238,400	$ 259,000
Administrative expenses	223,600	211,600
Total operating expenses	$ 462,000	$ 470,600
Income from operations	$ 132,000	$ 98,400
Interest expense	32,800	19,600
Income before income taxes	$ 99,200	$ 78,800
Income taxes expense	31,200	28,400
Net income	$ 68,000	$ 50,400
Earnings per share	$ 3.40	$ 2.52

Robert Corporation Comparative Balance Sheets December 31, 2011 and 2010	2011	2010
Assets		
Cash	$ 40,600	$ 20,400
Accounts receivable (net)	117,800	114,600
Inventory	287,400	297,400
Property, plant, and equipment (net)	375,000	360,000
Total assets	$820,800	$792,400
Liabilities and Stockholders' Equity		
Accounts payable	$133,800	$238,600
Notes payable (short-term)	100,000	200,000
Bonds payable	200,000	—
Common stock, $10 par value	200,000	200,000
Retained earnings	187,000	153,800
Total liabilities and stockholders' equity	$820,800	$792,400

Required

1. Prepare schedules showing the amount and percentage changes from 2010 to 2011 for the comparative income statements and the balance sheets.
2. Prepare common-size income statements and balance sheets for 2010 and 2011.
3. User insight ▶ Comment on the results in requirements **1** and **2** by identifying favorable and unfavorable changes in the components and composition of the statements.

LO3 Effects of Transactions on Ratios

P 2. Sung Corporation, a clothing retailer, engaged in the transactions listed in the first column of the table below. Opposite each transaction is a ratio and space to mark the effect of each transaction on the ratio.

Transaction	Ratio	Effect: Increase	Effect: Decrease	Effect: None
a. Issued common stock for cash.	Asset turnover			
b. Declared cash dividend.	Current ratio			
c. Sold treasury stock.	Return on equity			
d. Borrowed cash by issuing note payable.	Debt to equity ratio			
e. Paid salaries expense.	Inventory turnover			
f. Purchased merchandise for cash.	Current ratio			
g. Sold equipment for cash.	Receivable turnover			
h. Sold merchandise on account.	Quick ratio			
i. Paid current portion of long-term debt.	Return on assets			
j. Gave sales discount.	Profit margin			
k. Purchased marketable securities for cash.	Quick ratio			
l. Declared 5% stock dividend.	Current ratio			
m. Purchased a building.	Free cash flow			

Required

User insight ▶ Show that you understand the effect of business activities on performance measures by placing an *X* in the appropriate column to show whether the transaction increased, decreased, or had no effect on the indicated ratio.

LO3 **Comprehensive Ratio Analysis**

P 3. The condensed comparative income statements and balance sheets of Tola Corporation appear below and on the next page. All figures are given in thousands of dollars, except earnings per share. Additional data for Tola Corporation in 2011 and 2010 are as follows:

	2011	2010
Net cash flows from operating activities	$32,000	$49,500
Net capital expenditures	$59,500	$19,000
Dividends paid	$15,700	$17,500
Number of common shares	15,000	15,000
Market price per share	$40	$60

Balances of selected accounts at the end of 2009 were accounts receivable (net), $26,350; inventory, $49,700; accounts payable, $32,400; total assets, $323,900; and stockholders' equity, $188,300. All of the bonds payable were long-term liabilities.

Tola Corporation
Comparative Income Statements
For the Years Ended December 31, 2011 and 2010

	2011	2010
Net sales	$400,200	$371,300
Cost of goods sold	227,050	198,100
Gross margin	$173,150	$173,200
Operating expenses		
Selling expenses	$ 65,050	$ 52,300
Administrative expenses	70,150	57,750
Total operating expenses	$135,200	$110,050
Income from operations	$ 37,950	$ 63,150
Interest expense	12,500	10,000
Income before income taxes	$ 25,450	$ 53,150
Income taxes expense	7,000	17,500
Net income	$ 18,450	$ 35,650
Earnings per share	$ 1.23	$ 2.38

Tola Corporation
Comparative Balance Sheets
December 31, 2011 and 2010

	2011	2010
Assets		
Cash	$ 15,550	$ 13,600
Accounts receivable (net)	36,250	21,350
Inventory	61,300	53,900
Property, plant, and equipment (net)	288,850	253,750
Total assets	$401,950	$342,600
Liabilities and Stockholders' Equity		
Accounts payable	$ 52,350	$ 36,150
Notes payable	25,000	25,000
Bonds payable	100,000	55,000
Common stock, $10 par value	150,000	150,000
Retained earnings	74,600	76,450
Total liabilities and stockholders' equity	$401,950	$342,600

Required

Perform the following analyses. Round percentages and ratios to one decimal place.

1. Prepare a liquidity analysis by calculating for each year the (a) current ratio, (b) quick ratio, (c) receivable turnover, (d) days' sales uncollected, (e) inventory turnover, (f) days' inventory on hand, (g) payables turnover, and (h) days' payable.
2. Prepare a profitability analysis by calculating for each year the (a) profit margin, (b) asset turnover, (c) return on assets, and (d) return on equity.
3. Prepare a long-term solvency analysis by calculating for each year the (a) debt to equity ratio and (b) interest coverage ratio.
4. Prepare a cash flow adequacy analysis by calculating for each year the (a) cash flow yield, (b) cash flows to sales, (c) cash flows to assets, and (d) free cash flow.
5. Prepare an analysis of market strength by calculating for each year the (a) price/earnings (P/E) ratio and (b) dividends yield.

User insight ▶

6. After making the calculations, indicate whether each ratio improved or deteriorated from 2010 to 2011 (use *F* for favorable and *U* for unfavorable and consider changes of 0.1 or less to be neutral).

LO3 **Comprehensive Ratio Analysis of Two Companies**

P 4. Agnes Ball is considering an investment in the common stock of a chain of retail department stores. She has narrowed her choice to two retail companies, Fast Corporation and Style Corporation, whose income statements and balance sheets are presented on the next page.

During the year, Fast Corporation paid a total of $50,000 in dividends. The market price per share of its stock is currently $60. In comparison, Style Corporation paid a total of $114,000 in dividends, and the current market price of its stock is $76 per share. Fast Corporation had net cash flows from operations of $271,500 and net capital expenditures of $625,000. Style Corporation had net cash flows from operations of $492,500 and net capital expenditures of $1,050,000. Information for prior years is not readily available. Assume that all notes payable are current liabilities and all bonds payable are long-term liabilities and that there is no change in inventory.

Income Statements

	Fast	Style
Net sales	$12,560,000	$25,210,000
Costs and expenses		
Cost of goods sold	$ 6,142,000	$14,834,000
Selling expenses	4,822,600	7,108,200
Administrative expenses	986,000	2,434,000
Total costs and expenses	$11,950,600	$24,376,200
Income from operations	$ 609,400	$ 833,800
Interest expense	194,000	228,000
Income before income taxes	$ 415,400	$ 605,800
Income taxes expense	200,000	300,000
Net income	$ 215,400	$ 305,800
Earnings per share	$ 4.31	$ 10.19

Balance Sheets

	Fast	Style
Assets		
Cash	$ 80,000	$ 192,400
Marketable securities (at cost)	203,400	84,600
Accounts receivable (net)	552,800	985,400
Inventory	629,800	1,253,400
Prepaid expenses	54,400	114,000
Property, plant, and equipment (net)	2,913,600	6,552,000
Intangibles and other assets	553,200	144,800
Total assets	$4,987,200	$9,326,600
Liabilities and Stockholders' Equity		
Accounts payable	$ 344,000	$ 572,600
Notes payable	150,000	400,000
Income taxes payable	50,200	73,400
Bonds payable	2,000,000	2,000,000
Common stock, $20 par value	1,000,000	600,000
Additional paid-in capital	609,800	3,568,600
Retained earnings	833,200	2,112,000
Total liabilities and stockholders' equity	$4,987,200	$9,326,600

Required

Conduct a comprehensive ratio analysis for each company, using the available information. Compare the results. Round percentages and ratios to one decimal place, and consider changes of 0.1 or less to be indeterminate.

1. Prepare a liquidity analysis by calculating for each company the (a) current ratio, (b) quick ratio, (c) receivable turnover, (d) days' sales uncollected, (e) inventory turnover, (f) days' inventory on hand, (g) payables turnover, and (h) days' payable.
2. Prepare a profitability analysis by calculating for each company the (a) profit margin, (b) asset turnover, (c) return on assets, and (d) return on equity.

3. Prepare a long-term solvency analysis by calculating for each company the (a) debt to equity ratio and (b) interest coverage ratio.
4. Prepare a cash flow adequacy analysis by calculating for each company the (a) cash flow yield, (b) cash flows to sales, (c) cash flows to assets, and (d) free cash flow.
5. Prepare an analysis of market strength by calculating for each company the (a) price/earnings (P/E) ratio and (b) dividends yield.

User insight ▶ 6. Compare the two companies by inserting the ratio calculations from 1 through 5 in a table with the following column headings: Ratio Name, Fast, Style, and Company with More Favorable Ratio. Indicate in the last column which company had the more favorable ratio in each case.

User insight ▶ 7. How could the analysis be improved if information about these companies' prior years were available?

Alternate Problems

LO3

Effects of Transactions on Ratios

P 5. Lim Corporation engaged in the transactions listed in the first column of the following table. Opposite each transaction is a ratio and space to indicate the effect of each transaction on the ratio.

Transaction	Ratio	Effect		
		Increase	Decrease	None
a. Sold merchandise on account.	Current ratio			
b. Sold merchandise on account.	Inventory turnover			
c. Collected on accounts receivable.	Quick ratio			
d. Wrote off an uncollectible account.	Receivable turnover			
e. Paid on accounts payable.	Current ratio			
f. Declared cash dividend.	Return on equity			
g. Incurred advertising expense.	Profit margin			
h. Issued stock dividend.	Debt to equity ratio			
i. Issued bonds payable.	Asset turnover			
j. Accrued interest expense.	Current ratio			
k. Paid previously declared cash dividend.	Dividends yield			
l. Purchased treasury stock.	Return on assets			
m. Recorded depreciation expense.	Cash flow yield			

Required

User insight ▶ Show that you understand the effect of business activities on performance measures by placing an *X* in the appropriate column to show whether the transaction increased, decreased, or had no effect on the indicated ratio.

LO3

Comprehensive Ratio Analysis

P 6. Data for Robert Company in 2011 and 2010 follow. These data should be used in conjunction with the data in **P 1**.

	2011	2010
Net cash flows from operating activities	($98,000)	$72,000
Net capital expenditures	$20,000	$32,500
Dividends paid	$22,000	$17,200
Number of common shares	20,000	20,000
Market price per share	$18	$30

Selected balances at the end of 2009 were accounts receivable (net), $103,400; inventory, $273,600; total assets, $732,800; accounts payable, $193,300; and stockholders' equity, $320,600. All Robert's notes payable were current liabilities; all its bonds payable were long-term liabilities.

Required

Perform a comprehensive ratio analysis following the steps outlined below. Round all answers to one decimal place.

1. Prepare a liquidity analysis by calculating for each year the (a) current ratio, (b) quick ratio, (c) receivable turnover, (d) days' sales uncollected, (e) inventory turnover, (f) days' inventory on hand, (g) payables turnover, and (h) days' payable.
2. Prepare a profitability analysis by calculating for each year the (a) profit margin, (b) asset turnover, (c) return on assets, and (d) return on equity.
3. Prepare a long-term solvency analysis by calculating for each year the (a) debt to equity ratio and (b) interest coverage ratio.
4. Prepare a cash flow adequacy analysis by calculating for each year the (a) cash flow yield, (b) cash flows to sales, (c) cash flows to assets, and (d) free cash flow.
5. Prepare a market strength analysis by calculating for each year the (a) price/earnings (P/E) ratio and (b) dividends yield.

User insight ▶ 6. After making the calculations, indicate whether each ratio improved or deteriorated from 2010 to 2011 (use *F* for favorable and *U* for unfavorable and consider changes of 0.1 or less to be neutral).

LO2 Horizontal and Vertical Analysis

P 7. Sanborn Corporation's condensed comparative income statements for 2012 and 2011 appear below. The corporation's condensed comparative balance sheets for 2012 and 2011 appear on the next page.

Sanborn Corporation
Comparative Income Statements
For the Years Ended December 31, 2012 and 2011

	2012	2011
Net sales	$3,276,800	$3,146,400
Cost of goods sold	2,088,800	2,008,400
Gross margin	$1,188,000	$1,138,000
Operating expenses		
Selling expenses	$ 476,800	$ 518,000
Administrative expenses	447,200	423,200
Total operating expenses	$ 924,000	$ 941,200
Income from operations	$ 264,000	$ 196,800
Interest expense	65,600	39,200
Income before income taxes	$ 198,400	$ 157,600
Income taxes expense	62,400	56,800
Net income	$ 136,000	$ 100,800
Earnings per share	$ 3.40	$ 2.52

Sanborn Corporation
Comparative Balance Sheets
December 31, 2012 and 2011

	2012	2011
Assets		
Cash	$ 81,200	$ 40,800
Accounts receivable (net)	235,600	229,200
Inventory	574,800	594,800
Property, plant, and equipment (net)	750,000	720,000
Total assets	$1,641,600	$1,584,800
Liabilities and Stockholders' Equity		
Accounts payable	$ 267,600	$ 477,200
Notes payable (short-term)	200,000	400,000
Bonds payable	400,000	—
Common stock, $10 par value	400,000	400,000
Retained earnings	374,000	307,600
Total liabilities and stockholders' equity	$1,641,600	$1,584,800

Required

1. Prepare schedules showing the amount and percentage changes from 2011 to 2012 for the comparative income statements and the balance sheets.
2. Prepare common-size income statements and balance sheets for 2011 and 2012.

User insight ▶ 3. Comment on the results in requirements **1** and **2** by identifying favorable and unfavorable changes in the components and composition of the statements.

LO3 Comprehensive Ratio Analysis of Two Companies

P 8. Ginger Adair is considering an investment in the common stock of a chain of retail department stores. She has narrowed her choice to two retail companies, Lewis Corporation and Ramsey Corporation, whose income statements and balance sheets are presented on the next page.

During the year, Lewis Corporation paid a total of $100,000 in dividends. The market price per share of its stock is currently $60. In comparison, Ramsey Corporation paid a total of $228,000 in dividends, and the current market price of its stock is $76 per share. Lewis Corporation had net cash flows from operations of $543,000 and net capital expenditures of $1,250,000. Ramsey Corporation had net cash flows from operations of $985,000 and net capital expenditures of $2,100,000. Information for prior years is not readily available. Assume that all notes payable are current liabilities and all bonds payable are long-term liabilities and that there is no change in inventory.

Income Statements

	Lewis	Ramsey
Net sales	$25,120,000	$50,420,000
Costs and expenses		
Cost of goods sold	$12,284,000	$29,668,000
Selling expenses	9,645,200	14,216,400
Administrative expenses	1,972,000	4,868,000
Total costs and expenses	$23,901,200	$48,752,400
Income from operations	$ 1,218,800	$ 1,667,600
Interest expense	388,000	456,000
Income before income taxes	$ 830,800	$ 1,211,600
Income taxes expense	400,000	600,000
Net income	$ 430,800	$ 611,600
Earnings per share	$ 4.31	$ 10.19

Balance Sheets

	Lewis	Ramsey
Assets		
Cash	$ 160,000	$ 384,800
Marketable securities (at cost)	406,800	169,200
Accounts receivable (net)	1,105,600	1,970,800
Inventory	1,259,600	2,506,800
Prepaid expenses	108,800	228,000
Property, plant, and equipment (net)	5,827,200	13,104,000
Intangibles and other assets	1,106,400	289,600
Total assets	$9,974,400	$18,653,200
Liabilities and Stockholders' Equity		
Accounts payable	$ 688,000	$ 1,145,200
Notes payable	300,000	800,000
Income taxes payable	100,400	146,800
Bonds payable	4,000,000	4,000,000
Common stock, $20 par value	2,000,000	1,200,000
Additional paid-in capital	1,219,600	7,137,200
Retained earnings	1,666,400	4,224,000
Total liabilities and stockholders' equity	$9,974,400	$18,653,200

Required

Conduct a comprehensive ratio analysis for each company, following the steps below. Compare the results. Round percentages and ratios to one decimal place, and consider changes of 0.1 or less to be indeterminate.

1. Prepare a liquidity analysis by calculating for each company the (a) current ratio, (b) quick ratio, (c) receivable turnover, (d) days' sales uncollected, (e) inventory turnover, (f) days' inventory on hand, (g) payables turnover, and (h) days' payable.
2. Prepare a profitability analysis by calculating for each company the (a) profit margin, (b) asset turnover, (c) return on assets, and (d) return on equity.

3. Prepare a long-term solvency analysis by calculating for each company the (a) debt to equity ratio and (b) interest coverage ratio.
4. Prepare a cash flow adequacy analysis by calculating for each company the (a) cash flow yield, (b) cash flows to sales, (c) cash flows to assets, and (d) free cash flow.
5. Prepare an analysis of market strength by calculating for each company the (a) price/earnings (P/E) ratio and (b) dividends yield.

User insight ▶

6. Compare the two companies by inserting the ratio calculations from 1 through 5 in a table with the following column headings: Ratio Name, Lewis, Ramsey, and Company with More Favorable Ratio. Indicate in the last column which company had the more favorable ratio in each case.

User insight ▶

7. How could the analysis be improved if information about these companies' prior years were available?

ENHANCING Your Knowledge, Skills, and Critical Thinking

LO1 LO3

Standards for Financial Performance Evaluation

C 1. In 2005, in a dramatic move, **Standard & Poor's Ratings Group**, the large financial company that evaluates the riskiness of companies' debt, downgraded its rating of **General Motors** and **Ford Motor Co**. debt to "junk" bond status because of concerns about the companies' profitability and cash flows. Despite aggressive cost cutting, both companies still face substantial future liabilities for health care and pension obligations. They are losing money or barely breaking even on auto operations that concentrate on slow-selling SUVs. High gas prices and competition force them to sell the cars at a discount.[9] What standards do you think Standard & Poor's would use to evaluate General Motors' progress? What performance measures would Standard & Poor's most likely use in making its evaluation? In light of the fortunes of these companies during the recent financial crisis, did Standard & Poor's deserve the criticism the company received?

LO1

Using Segment Information

C 2. Refer to Exhibit 16-1, which shows the segment information of **Goodyear Tire & Rubber Company**. In what business segments does Goodyear operate? What is the relative size of its business segments in terms of sales and income in the most recent year shown? Which segment is most profitable in terms of return on assets? Which segment is largest, and which segment is most profitable in terms of return on assets?

LO1

Using Investors' Services

C 3. Refer to Exhibit 16-2, which contains the **PepsiCo Inc**. listing from Mergent's *Handbook of Dividend Achievers*. Assume that an investor has asked you to assess PepsiCo's recent history and prospects. Write a memorandum to the investor that addresses the following points:

1. PepsiCo's earnings history. What has been the general relationship between PepsiCo's return on assets and its return on equity over the last seven years? What does this tell you about the way the company is financed? What figures back up your conclusion?
2. The trend of PepsiCo's stock price and price/earnings (P/E) ratio for the seven years shown.
3. PepsiCo's prospects, including developments likely to affect the company's future.

LO2 LO3 Effect of a One-Time Item on a Loan Decision

C 4. Apple a Day, Inc., and Unforgettable Edibles, Inc., are food catering businesses that operate in the same metropolitan area. Their customers include *Fortune* 500 companies, regional firms, and individuals. The two firms reported similar profit margins for the current year, and both base bonuses for managers on the achievement of a target profit margin and return on equity. Each firm has submitted a loan request to you, a loan officer for City National Bank. They have provided you with the following information:

	Apple a Day	Unforgettable Edibles
Net sales	$625,348	$717,900
Cost of goods sold	225,125	287,080
Gross margin	$400,223	$430,820
Operating expenses	281,300	371,565
Operating income	$118,923	$ 59,255
Gain on sale of real estate	—	81,923
Interest expense	(9,333)	(15,338)
Income before income taxes	$109,590	$125,840
Income taxes expense	25,990	29,525
Net income	$ 83,600	$ 96,315
Average stockholders' equity	$312,700	$390,560

1. Perform a vertical analysis and prepare a common-size income statement for each firm. Compute profit margin and return on equity.
2. Discuss these results, the bonus plan for management, and loan considerations. Identify the company that is the better loan risk.

LO3 Comprehensive Ratio Analysis

C 5. Using data from the **CVS Corporation** annual report in the Supplement to Chapter 5, conduct a comprehensive ratio analysis that compares the company's performance in 2008 and 2007. If you have computed ratios for CVS in previous chapters, you may prepare a table that summarizes the ratios and show calculations only for the ratios not previously calculated. If this is the first ratio analysis you have done for CVS, show all your computations. In either case, after each group of ratios, comment on the performance of CVS. Round your calculations to one decimal place. Prepare and comment on the following categories of ratios:

Liquidity analysis: current ratio, quick ratio, receivable turnover, days' sales uncollected, inventory turnover, days' inventory on hand, payables turnover, and days' payable. (Accounts Receivable, Inventories, and Accounts Payable were [in millions] $2,381.7, $7,108.9, and $2,521.5, respectively, in 2006.)

Profitability analysis: profit margin, asset turnover, return on assets, and return on equity. (Total assets and total shareholders' equity were [in millions] $20,574,1 and $9,917.6, respectively, in 2006.)

Long-term solvency analysis: debt to equity ratio and interest coverage ratio.

Cash flow adequacy analysis: cash flow yield, cash flows to sales, cash flows to assets, and free cash flow.

Market strength analysis: price/earnings (P/E) ratio and dividends yield.

LO3 Comparison of Key Financial Performance Measures

C 6. Refer to the annual report of **CVS Corporation** and the financial statements of **Southwest Airlines Co.** in the Supplement to Chapter 5. Prepare a table for the following key financial performance measures for the two most recent years for both companies. Use your computations in **C 5** or perform those analyses if you have not done so. Total assets for Southwest in 2006 were $13,460 million.

Profitability:	profit margin
	asset turnover
	return on assets
Long-term solvency:	debt to equity ratio
Cash flow adequacy:	cash flow yield
	free cash flow

Evaluate and comment on the relative performance of the two companies with respect to each of the above categories.

CHAPTER 17 Partnerships

Making a Statement

INCOME STATEMENT

Revenues

– Expenses

= Net Income

STATEMENT OF PARTNERS' EQUITY

Opening Balance

+ Net Income

– Withdrawals

= Partners' EQUITY

BALANCE SHEET

Assets	Liabilities
	Partners' Equity

STATEMENT OF CASH FLOWS

Operating activities
+ Investing activities
+ Financing activities
= Change in Cash
+ Starting Balance
= Ending Cash Balance

This chapter discusses the characteristics of the partnership form of business and examines accounting issues relating to the formation, dissolution, and liquidation of partnerships, as well as the division of income among partners.

LEARNING OBJECTIVES

LO1 **Identify the principal characteristics, advantages, and disadvantages of the partnership form of business.** (pp. 756–759)

LO2 **Record partners' investments of cash and other assets when a partnership is formed.** (pp. 759–760)

LO3 **Compute and record the income or losses that partners share, based on stated ratios, capital balance ratios, and partners' salaries and interest.** (pp. 761–766)

LO4 **Record a person's admission to or withdrawal from a partnership.** (pp. 767–772)

LO5 **Compute and record the distribution of assets to partners when they liquidate their partnership.** (pp. 772–778)

DECISION POINT ▸ A USER'S FOCUS HOLDER AND WILLIAMS PARTNERSHIP

Jack Holder and Dan Williams reached an agreement in 2010 to pool their resources and form a partnership to manufacture and sell university T-shirts. To form the partnership, Jack contributed $100,000, and Dan contributed $150,000. As they were preparing their partnership agreement, they had to make a number of important decisions, including how they would share the income or losses of the business and how they would handle both the admission of new partners and the withdrawal of partners. In this chapter, we discuss these issues, as well as several other accounting issues that partnerships entail.

- ▸ What details should be included in a partnership agreement?
- ▸ How would Jack Holder and Dan Williams share the income or losses of their business?
- ▸ How would they handle any changes in ownership that might occur?

Partnership Characteristics

LO1 Identify the principal characteristics, advantages, and disadvantages of the partnership form of business.

The Uniform Partnership Act, which has been adopted by most states, defines a **partnership** as "an association of two or more persons to carry on as co-owners of a business for profit." Partnerships are treated as separate entities in accounting, but legally there is no economic separation between them and their owners. They differ in many ways from the other forms of business. Here we describe some of their important characteristics.

Characteristics of Partnerships

A partnership is a voluntary association of individuals rather than a legal entity in itself. Therefore, a partner is responsible under the law for his or her partners' actions within the scope of the business. A partner also has unlimited liability for the debts of the partnership. Because of these potential liabilities, a partner must be allowed to choose the people who join the partnership. A person should select as partners individuals who share his or her business objectives.

Study Note

Partnerships and sole proprietorships are not legal entities; corporations are. All three, however, are considered accounting entities.

Partnership Agreement A partnership is easy to form. Two or more competent people simply agree to be partners in a common business purpose. Their agreement is known as a **partnership agreement.** The partnership agreement does not have to be in writing. However, good business practice calls for a written document that clearly states the details of the arrangement, including the name, location, and purpose of the business; the names of the partners and their respective duties; the investments of each partner; the method of distributing income and losses; and the procedures for the admission and withdrawal of partners, the withdrawal of assets allowed each partner, and the liquidation (termination) of the business.

Limited Life Because a partnership is formed by an agreement between partners, it has a **limited life.** It may be dissolved when a new partner is admitted; when a partner withdraws, goes bankrupt, is incapacitated (to the point that he or she cannot perform as obligated), retires, or dies; or when the terms of the partnership agreement are met (e.g., when the project for which the partnership was formed is completed). However, if the partners want the partnership to continue legally, the partnership agreement can be written to cover each of these situations. For example, the partnership agreement can state that if a partner dies, the remaining partner or partners must purchase the deceased partner's capital at book value from the heirs.

Mutual Agency Each partner is an agent of the partnership within the scope of the business. Because of this **mutual agency,** any partner can bind the partnership to a business agreement as long as he or she acts within the scope of the company's normal operations. For example, a partner in a used-car business can bind the partnership through the purchase or sale of used cars. But this partner cannot bind the partnership to a contract to buy men's clothing or any other goods that are not related to the used-car business. Because of mutual agency, it is very important for an individual to choose business partners who have integrity and who share his or her business objectives.

Unlimited Liability All partners have **unlimited liability** for their company's debt, which means that each partner is personally liable for all the debts of the partnership. If a partnership cannot pay its debts, creditors must first satisfy their claims from the assets of the business. If these assets are not enough to

Study Note

Unlimited liability means that potential responsibility for debts is not limited by one's investment, as it is in a corporation. Each person is personally liable for all debts of the partnership, including those arising from contingent liabilities such as lawsuits. Liability can be avoided only by filing for personal bankruptcy.

pay all debts, the creditors can seek payment from the personal assets of each partner. If one partner's personal assets are used up before the debts are paid, the creditors can claim additional assets from the remaining partners who are able to pay. Each partner, then, can be required by law to pay all the debts of the partnership.

Co-Ownership of Partnership Property When individuals invest property in a partnership, they give up the right to their separate use of the property. The property becomes an asset of the partnership and is owned jointly by the partners.

Participation in Partnership Income Each partner has the right to share in the company's income and the responsibility to share in its losses. The partnership agreement should state the method of distributing income and losses to each partner. If the agreement describes how income should be shared but does not mention losses, losses are distributed in the same way as income. If the agreement does not describe the method of income and loss distribution, the partners must by law share income and losses equally.

Study Note

There is no federal income tax on partnerships; partners are taxed at their personal rates. However, partnerships must file an informational return with the IRS, and some state and local governments levy a tax on them. An example of this is the Michigan Single Business Tax.

Advantages and Disadvantages of Partnerships

Partnerships have both advantages and disadvantages. One advantage is that a partnership is easy to form, change, and dissolve. Also, a partnership facilitates the pooling of capital resources and individual talents; it has no corporate tax burden (because a partnership is not a legal entity for tax purposes, it does not have to pay a federal income tax, as do corporations, but must file an informational return); and it gives the partners a certain amount of freedom and flexibility.

On the other hand, partnerships have the following disadvantages: the life of a partnership is limited; one partner can bind the partnership to a contract (mutual agency); the partners have unlimited personal liability; and it is more difficult for a partnership to raise large amounts of capital and to transfer ownership interests than it is for a corporation.

Limited Partnerships and Joint Ventures

Two other common forms of association that are a type of partnership or similar to a partnership are limited partnerships and joint ventures.

FOCUS ON BUSINESS PRACTICE

Why Are Limited Partnerships Used to Finance Big Projects?

Limited partnerships resemble corporations in that the liability of the partners is restricted to the amount of their investment in the business. Because limited partnerships curtail an investor's risk, they are sometimes used in place of corporations to raise funds from the public to finance large projects, such as the exploration and drilling of oil and gas wells, the manufacture of airplanes, and the development of real estate (including shopping centers, office buildings, and apartment complexes). For example, **Alliance Capital Management Limited Partnership**, a large investment advisor, manages more than $90 billion in assets for corporate and individual investors in various projects. The company's partnership units, or shares of ownership, sell on the New York Stock Exchange and can be purchased by the individual investor.

FOCUS ON BUSINESS PRACTICE

How Do Partnerships Facilitate International Investment?

When U.S. companies make investments abroad, they often find it wise to partner with a local company. Because many countries require that local investors own a substantial percentage of a newly formed business, partnering with a local company is often a necessary step. One way of accomplishing this is to form a joint venture, which matches a country's need for outside capital and operational know-how with investors' interest in business expansion and profitability. Joint ventures frequently take the form of partnerships among two or more corporations and other investors. Any income or losses from operations are divided among the participants according to a predetermined agreement.

Limited Partnerships A **limited partnership** is a special type of partnership that, like corporations, confines the limited partner's potential loss to the amount of his or her investment. Under this type of partnership the unlimited liability disadvantage of a partnership can be overcome. Usually, the limited partnership has a general partner who has unlimited liability but allows other partners to limit their potential loss. The potential loss of all partners in an ordinary partnership is limited only by personal bankruptcy laws.

Study Note

Many types of organizations have been created by law. They include S corporations and limited partnerships. Each provides legal (especially tax) advantages and disadvantages.

Joint Ventures In today's global environment, more companies are looking to form alliances similar to partnerships, called *joint ventures,* with other companies rather than to venture out on their own. A **joint venture** is an association of two or more entities for the purpose of achieving a specific goal, such as the manufacture of a product in a new market. Many joint ventures have an agreed-upon limited life. The entities forming joint ventures usually involve companies but can sometimes involve governments, especially in emerging economies. A joint venture brings together the resources, technical skills, political ties, and other assets of each of the parties for a common goal. Profits and losses are shared on an agreed-upon basis.

FOCUS ON BUSINESS PRACTICE

Corporations That Look Like Partnerships

Some types of corporations mimic the characteristics of partnerships. S corporations are corporations that U.S. tax laws treat as partnerships. Unlike normal corporations, S corporations do not pay federal income taxes. They have a limited number of stockholders, who report the income or losses on their investments in the business on their personal tax returns. This avoids the problem of double taxation.

In a limited liability corporation (LLC), the stockholders are partners, and their liability is limited to their investment in the business. LLCs are used mainly by accounting and consultancy firms.

Special-purpose entities (SPEs), which gained notoriety because of the **Enron** case, are firms with limited lives that a company creates to achieve a specific objective, such as raising money by selling receivables. By meeting certain conditions, a company that sets up an SPE can legitimately avoid including the debt of the SPE on its balance sheet. Enron used SPEs extensively and fraudulently to hide debt and other commitments.

Indicate whether each statement below is a reflection of (a) voluntary association, (b) a partnership agreement, (c) limited life, (d) mutual agency, or (e) unlimited liability.

1. When a partner is admitted, withdraws, retires, or dies, the partnership must be dissolved.
2. A partner may be required to pay the debts of the partnership out of personal assets.
3. A partner does not have to remain a partner if he or she does not want to.
4. A written contract specifies details of the arrangements among partners.
5. Any partner can bind the partnership to a business agreement.

SOLUTION

1. c; 2. e; 3. a; 4. b; 5. d

Accounting for Partners' Equity

LO2 Record partners' investments of cash and other assets when a partnership is formed.

Although accounting for a partnership is very similar to accounting for a sole proprietorship, there are differences. One is that the owner's equity in a partnership is called **partners' equity**. In accounting for partners' equity, it is necessary to maintain separate Capital and Withdrawals accounts for each partner and to divide the income and losses of the company among the partners.

The differences in the Capital accounts of a sole proprietorship and a partnership are as follows:

Sole Proprietorship		Partnership			
Blake, Capital		**Desmond, Capital**		**Frank, Capital**	
Dr.	Cr.	Dr.	Cr.	Dr.	Cr.
	50,000		30,000		40,000
Blake, Withdrawals		**Desmond, Withdrawals**		**Frank, Withdrawals**	
Dr.	Cr.	Dr.	Cr.	Dr.	Cr.
12,000		5,000		6,000	

In the partners' equity section of the balance sheet, the balance of each partner's Capital account is listed separately:

Liabilities and Partners' Equity	Dr.	Cr.
Total liabilities		$28,000
Partners' equity		
Desmond, capital	$25,000	
Frank, capital	34,000	
Total partners' equity		59,000
Total liabilities and partners' equity		$87,000

Each partner invests cash, other assets, or both in the partnership according to the partnership agreement. Noncash assets should be valued at their fair market value on the date they are transferred to the partnership. The assets invested by a partner are debited to the proper account, and the total amount is credited to the partner's Capital account.

To show how partners' investments are recorded, let's assume that Jerry Adcock and Rose Villa have agreed to combine their capital and equipment in a partnership to operate a jewelry store. According to their partnership agreement, Adcock will invest $28,000 in cash and $37,000 worth of furniture and displays, and Villa will invest $40,000 in cash and $30,000 worth of equipment. Related to the equipment is a note payable for $10,000, which the partnership assumes. The entries to record the partners' initial investments are as follows:

A	=	L	+	OE
+28,000				+65,000
+37,000				

Entry in Journal Form:

2010		Dr.	Cr.
July 1	Cash	28,000	
	Furniture and Displays	37,000	
	Jerry Adcock, Capital		65,000
	Initial investment of Jerry Adcock in Adcock and Villa		
1	Cash	40,000	
	Equipment	30,000	
	Notes Payable		10,000
	Rose Villa, Capital		60,000
	Initial investment of Rose Villa in Adcock and Villa		

A	=	L	+	OE
+30,000		+10,000		+60,000
+40,000				

Study Note

Villa's noncash contribution is equal to the fair market value of the equipment less the amount owed on the equipment.

The values assigned to the assets would be included in the partnership agreement. These values can differ from those carried on the partners' personal books. For example, the equipment that Rose Villa contributed had a value of only $22,000 on her books, but its market value had increased considerably after she purchased it. The book value of Villa's equipment is not important. The fair market value of the equipment at the time of transfer *is* important, however, because that value represents the amount of money Villa has invested in the partnership. Later investments are recorded in the same way.

STOP & APPLY >

On June 1, Sarah and Alma form a partnership to operate a fitness center. Sara contributes cash of $24,000, and Alma contributes exercise equipment that cost $20,000 but is valued at $16,000. Prepare the entry in journal form to record the partners' initial investments.

SOLUTION

		Dr.	Cr.
June 1	Cash	24,000	
	Exercise Equipment	16,000	
	Sara, Capital		24,000
	Alma, Capital		16,000
	Formation of partnership		

Distribution of Partnership Income and Losses

LO3 Compute and record the income or losses that partners share, based on stated ratios, capital balance ratios, and partners' salaries and interest.

A partnership's income and losses can be distributed according to whatever method the partners specify in the partnership agreement. Income in this form of business normally has three components: return to the partners for the use of their capital (called *interest on partners' capital*), compensation for services the partners have rendered (partners' salaries), and other income for any special contributions individual partners may make to the partnership or risks they may take. The breakdown of total income into its three components helps clarify how much each partner has contributed to the firm.

If all partners contribute equal capital, have similar talents, and spend the same amount of time in the business, then an equal distribution of income and losses would be fair. However, if one partner works full-time in the firm and another devotes only a fourth of his or her time, then the distribution of income or losses should reflect the difference. (This concept would apply to any situation in which the partners contribute unequally to the business.)

Distributing income and losses among partners can be accomplished by using stated ratios or capital balance ratios or by paying the partners' salaries and interest on their capital and sharing the remaining income according to stated ratios. *Salaries* and *interest* here are not *salaries expense* or *interest expense* in the ordinary sense of the terms. They do not affect the amount of reported net income. Instead, they refer to ways of determining each partner's share of net income or net loss on the basis of time spent and money invested in the partnership.

Study Note

The division of income is one area in which a partnership differs from a corporation. In corporations, each common share receives an equal dividend. Partners can use any method they agree on to divide partnership income.

Stated Ratios

One method of distributing income and losses is to give each partner a stated ratio of the total income or loss. If each partner is making an equal contribution to the firm, each can assume the same share of income and losses. It is important to understand that an equal contribution to the firm does not necessarily mean an equal capital investment in the firm. One partner may be devoting more time and talent to the firm, whereas another may have made a larger capital investment. And if the partners contribute unequally to the firm, unequal stated ratios can be appropriate.

Let's assume that Adcock and Villa had a net income last year of $140,000. Their partnership agreement states that the percentages of income and losses distributed to Jerry Adcock and Rose Villa should be 60 percent and 40 percent, respectively. The computation of each partner's share of the income and the entry to show the distribution are as follows:

Adcock ($140,000 × 0.60)	$ 84,000
Villa ($140,000 × 0.40)	56,000
Net income	$140,000

Study Note

The computations of each partner's share of net income are relevant to the closing entries in which the Income Summary account is closed to the partners' Capital accounts.

A	=	L	+	OE
				−140,000
				+84,000
				+56,000

Entry in Journal Form:

2011		Dr.	Cr.
June 30	Income Summary	140,000	
	Jerry Adcock, Capital		84,000
	Rose Villa, Capital		56,000
	Distribution of income for the year to the partners' Capital accounts		

Capital Balance Ratios

If invested capital produces the most income for the partnership, then income and losses may be distributed according to capital balances. The ratio used to distribute income and losses here may be based on each partner's capital balance at the beginning of the year or on the average capital balance of each partner during the year. The partnership agreement must describe the method to be used.

Ratios Based on Beginning Capital Balances To show how the first method works, let's look at the beginning capital balances of the partners in Adcock and Villa. At the start of the fiscal year, July 1, 2010, Jerry Adcock, Capital showed a $65,000 balance and Rose Villa, Capital showed a $60,000 balance. (Actually, these balances reflect the partners' initial investment; the partnership was formed on July 1, 2010.) The total partners' equity in the firm, then, was $125,000. Each partner's capital balance at the beginning of the year divided by the total partners' equity at the beginning of the year is that partner's beginning capital balance ratio:

	Beginning Capital Balance	*Beginning Capital Balance Ratio*
Jerry Adcock	$ 65,000	65,000 ÷ 125,000 = 0.52 = 52%
Rose Villa	60,000	60,000 ÷ 125,000 = 0.48 = 48%
	$125,000	

The income that each partner should receive when distribution is based on beginning capital balance ratios is determined by multiplying the total income by each partner's capital ratio. If we assume that income for the year was $140,000, Jerry Adcock's share of that income was $72,800, and Rose Villa's share was $67,200.

Jerry Adcock	$140,000 × 0.52 =	$ 72,800
Rose Villa	$140,000 × 0.48 =	67,200
		$140,000

Ratios Based on Average Capital Balances If Adcock and Villa use beginning capital balance ratios to determine the distribution of income, they do not consider any investments or withdrawals made during the year. But investments and withdrawals usually change the partners' capital ratios. If the partners believe their capital balances will change dramatically during the year, they can choose average capital balance ratios as a fairer means of distributing income and losses.

The following T accounts show the activity over the year in Adcock and Villa's partners' Capital and Withdrawals accounts:

JERRY ADCOCK, CAPITAL

Dr.	Cr.
	7/1/2010 65,000

JERRY ADCOCK, WITHDRAWALS

Dr.	Cr.
1/1/2011 10,000	

ROSE VILLA, CAPITAL

Dr.	Cr.
	7/1/2010 60,000
	2/1/2011 8,000

ROSE VILLA, WITHDRAWALS

Dr.	Cr.
11/1/2010 10,000	

Jerry Adcock withdrew $10,000 on January 1, 2011, and Rose Villa withdrew $10,000 on November 1, 2010, and invested an additional $8,000 of equipment on February 1, 2011. Again, the income for the year's operation (July 1, 2010, to June 30, 2011) was $140,000. The calculations for the average capital balances and the distribution of income are as follows:

Average Capital Balances

Partner	Date	Capital Balance ×	Months Unchanged =	Total		Average Capital Balance
Adcock	July–Dec.	$65,000 ×	6	= $390,000		
	Jan.–June	$55,000 ×	6	= 330,000		
			12	$720,000	÷ 12 =	$ 60,000
Villa	July–Oct.	$60,000 ×	4	= $240,000		
	Nov.–Jan.	$50,000 ×	3	= 150,000		
	Feb.–June	$58,000 ×	5	= 290,000		
			12	$680,000	÷ 12 =	56,667
				Total average capital		$116,667

Average Capital Balance Ratios

$$\text{Adcock} = \frac{\text{Adcock's Average Capital Balance}}{\text{Total Average Capital}} = \frac{\$60{,}000}{\$116{,}667} = 0.514 = 51.4\%$$

$$\text{Villa} = \frac{\text{Villa's Average Capital Balance}}{\text{Total Average Capital}} = \frac{\$56{,}667}{\$116{,}667} = 0.486 = 48.6\%$$

Distribution of Income

Partner	Income	×	Ratio	=	Share of Income
Adcock	$140,000	×	0.514	=	$ 71,960
Villa	$140,000	×	0.486	=	68,040
			Total income		$140,000

Notice that to determine the distribution of income (or loss), you must determine the average capital balances, the average capital balance ratios, and each partner's share of income or loss. To compute each partner's average capital balance, you must examine the changes that have occurred during the year in each partner's capital balance, changes that are the product of further investments and withdrawals. The partner's beginning capital is multiplied by the number of months the balance remains unchanged. After the balance changes, the new balance is multiplied by the number of months it remains unchanged. The process continues until the end of the year. The totals of these computations are added, and then they are divided by 12 to determine the average capital balances. Once the average capital balances are determined, the method of figuring capital balance ratios for sharing income and losses is the same as the method used for beginning capital balances.

Salaries, Interest, and Stated Ratios

Partners' contributions to a firm are usually not equal. To make up for the inequality, a partnership agreement can allow for partners' salaries, interest on partners' capital balances, or both in the distribution of income. Again, salaries and interest of this kind are not deducted as expenses before the partnership income is determined. They represent a method of arriving at an equitable distribution of income or losses.

Study Note

Partnership income or losses cannot be divided solely on the basis of salaries or interest. An additional component, such as stated ratios, is needed.

To illustrate an allowance for partners' salaries, we assume that Adcock and Villa agree to annual salaries of $8,000 and $7,000, respectively, and to divide any remaining income equally between them. Each salary is charged to the appropriate partner's Withdrawals account when paid. Assuming the same $140,000 income for the first year, the calculations for Adcock and Villa are as follows:

	Income of Partner		Income
	Adcock	Villa	Distributed
Total income for distribution			$140,000
Distribution of salaries			
Adcock	$ 8,000		
Villa		$ 7,000	(15,000)
Remaining income after salaries			$125,000
Equal distribution of remaining income			
Adcock ($125,000 × 0.50)	62,500		
Villa ($125,000 × 0.50)		62,500	(125,000)
Remaining income			—
Income of partners	$70,500	$69,500	$140,000

Salaries allow for differences in the services that partners provide the business. However, they do not take into account differences in invested capital. To allow for capital differences, each partner can receive, in addition to salary, a stated interest on his or her invested capital. Suppose that Jerry Adcock and Rose Villa agree to annual salaries of $8,000 and $7,000, respectively, as well as 10 percent interest on their beginning capital balances, and to share any remaining income equally. The calculations for Adcock and Villa, assuming income of $140,000, are as follows:

	Income of Partner		Income
	Adcock	Villa	Distributed
Total income for distribution			$140,000
Distribution of salaries			
Adcock	$ 8,000		
Villa		$ 7,000	(15,000)
Remaining income after salaries			$125,000
Distribution of interest			
Adcock ($65,000 × 0.10)	6,500		
Villa ($60,000 × 0.10)		6,000	(12,500)
Remaining income after salaries and interest			$112,500
Equal distribution of remaining income			
Adcock ($112,500 × 0.50)	56,250		
Villa ($112,500 × 0.50)		56,250	(112,500)
Remaining income			—
Income of partners	$70,750	$69,250	$140,000

Study Note

When negotiating a partnership agreement, be sure to look at (and negotiate) the impact of both profits (net income) and losses.

If the partnership agreement allows for the distribution of salaries or interest or both, the amounts must be allocated to the partners even if profits are not enough to cover the salaries and interest. In fact, even if the company has a loss, these allocations must still be made. The negative balance, or loss, after the allocation of salaries and interest must be distributed according to the stated ratio in the partnership agreement, or equally if the agreement does not mention a ratio.

FOCUS ON BUSINESS PRACTICE

What Are the Risks of Being a Partner in an Accounting Firm?

Partners in large accounting firms can make over $250,000 per year, with top partners drawing over $800,000. However, consideration of those incomes should take into account the risks that partners take and the fact that the incomes of partners in small accounting firms are often much lower.

Partners are not compensated in the same way as managers in corporations. Partners' income is not guaranteed, but rather is based on the performance of the partnership. Also, each partner is required to make a substantial investment of capital in the partnership. This capital remains at risk for as long as the partner chooses to stay in the partnership. For instance, in one notable case, when a large firm was convicted of destroying evidence in the **Enron** case, the partners lost their total investments as well as their income when their firm was subjected to lawsuits and other losses. The firm was eventually liquidated.

For example, let's assume that Adcock and Villa agreed to the following conditions, with much higher annual salaries, for the distribution of income and losses:

	Salaries	*Interest*	*Beginning Capital Balance*
Adcock	$70,000	10 percent of beginning capital balance	$65,000
Villa	$60,000		$60,000

The computations for the distribution of the income and losses, again assuming income of $140,000, are as follows:

	Income of Partner		Income
	Adcock	Villa	Distributed
Total income for distribution			$140,000
Distribution of salaries			
Adcock	$70,000		
Villa		$60,000	(130,000)
Remaining income after salaries			$ 10,000
Distribution of interest			
Adcock ($65,000 × 0.10)	6,500		
Villa ($60,000 × 0.10)		6,000	(12,500)
Negative balance after salaries and interest			($ 2,500)
Equal distribution of negative Balance*			
Adcock ($2,500 × 0.50)	(1,250)		
Villa ($2,500 × 0.50)		(1,250)	2,500
Remaining income			—
Income of partners	$75,250	$64,750	$140,000

*Notice that the negative balance is distributed equally because the agreement does not indicate how income and losses should be distributed after salaries and interest are paid.

EXHIBIT 17-1
Partial Income Statement for Adcock and Villa

Adcock and Villa
Partial Income Statement
For the Year Ended June 30, 2011

Net income		$140,000
Distribution to the partners		
Adcock		
Salary distribution	$70,000	
Interest on beginning capital balance	6,500	
Total	$76,500	
One-half of remaining negative amount	(1,250)	
Share of net income		$ 75,250
Villa		
Salary distribution	$60,000	
Interest on beginning capital balance	6,000	
Total	$66,000	
One-half of remaining negative amount	(1,250)	
Share of net income		64,750
Net income distributed		$140,000

Study Note

Using salaries and interest to divide income or losses among partners has no effect on the income statement. They are not expenses. Partners' salaries and interest are used only to allow the equitable division of the partnership's net income.

On the income statement for the partnership, the distribution of income or losses is shown below the net income figure. Exhibit 17-1 shows how this is done.

STOP & APPLY >

Kathy and Roger share income in their partnership in a 1:4 ratio. Kathy and Roger receive salaries of $16,000 and $10,000, respectively. How would they share a net income of $22,000 before salaries?

SOLUTION

	Income of Partner		Income
	Kathy	Roger	Distributed
Total income for distribution			$22,000
Distribution of salaries			
Kathy	$16,000		
Roger		$10,000	(26,000)
Negative balance after salaries			($ 4,000)
Distribution of negative balance			
Kathy ($4,000 × 0.20)	(800)		
Roger ($4,000 × 0.80)		(3,200)	4,000
Remaining income			—
Income of partners	$15,200	$ 6,800	$22,000

Dissolution of a Partnership

LO4 Record a person's admission to or withdrawal from a partnership.

Dissolution of a partnership occurs whenever there is a change in the original association of partners. When a partnership is dissolved, the partners lose their authority to continue the business as a going concern. The fact that the partners lose this authority does not necessarily mean that the business operation is ended or interrupted. However, it does mean—from a legal and accounting standpoint—that the separate entity ceases to exist. The remaining partners can act for the partnership in finishing the affairs of the business or in forming a new partnership that will be a new accounting entity. The dissolution of a partnership takes place through, among other events, the admission of a new partner, the withdrawal of a partner, or the death of a partner.

Admission of a New Partner

Study Note

Admission of a new partner never has an impact on net income. Regardless of the price a new partner pays, there are never any income statement accounts in the entry to admit a new partner.

The admission of a new partner dissolves the old partnership because a new association has been formed. Dissolving the old partnership and creating a new one requires the consent of all the original partners and the ratification of a new partnership agreement. When a new partner is admitted, a new partnership agreement should be in place.

An individual can be admitted to a partnership in one of two ways: by purchasing an interest in the partnership from one or more of the original partners or by investing assets in the partnership.

Purchasing an Interest from a Partner When a person purchases an interest in a partnership from an original partner, the transaction is a personal one between these two people. However, the interest purchased must be transferred from the Capital account of the selling partner to the Capital account of the new partner.

Suppose that Jerry Adcock decides to sell his interest of $70,000 in Adcock and Villa to Richard Davis for $100,000 on August 31, 2012, and that Rose Villa agrees to the sale. The entry to record the sale on the partnership books looks like this:

A	=	L	+	OE
				− 70,000
				+ 70,000

Entry in Journal Form:

2012		Dr.	Cr.
Aug. 31	Jerry Adcock, Capital	70,000	
	Richard Davis, Capital		70,000
	Transfer of Jerry Adcock's equity to Richard Davis		

Notice that the entry records the book value of the equity, not the amount Davis pays. The amount Davis pays is a personal matter between Adcock and him. Because the amount paid does not affect the assets or liabilities of the firm, it is not entered in the records.

Here's another example of a purchase. Assume that Richard Davis purchases half of Jerry Adcock's $70,000 interest in the partnership and half of Rose Villa's interest, assumed to be $80,000, by paying a total of $100,000 to the two partners on August 31, 2012. The entry to record this transaction on the partnership books would be as follows:

A	= L +	OE
		−35,000
		−40,000
		+75,000

Entry in Journal Form:

2012		Dr.	Cr.
Aug. 31	Jerry Adcock, Capital	35,000	
	Rose Villa, Capital	40,000	
	Richard Davis, Capital		75,000
	Transfer of half of Jerry Adcock's and Rose Villa's equity to Richard Davis		

Study Note

If the asset accounts did not reflect their current values, the asset accounts (and Capital accounts) would need to be adjusted before admitting the new partner.

Investing Assets in a Partnership When a new partner is admitted through an investment in the partnership, both the assets and the partners' equity in the firm increase. The increase occurs because the assets the new partner invests become partnership assets, and as partnership assets increase, partners' equity increases. For example, assume that Jerry Adcock and Rose Villa have agreed to allow Richard Davis to invest $75,000 in return for a one-third interest in their partnership. The Capital accounts of Jerry Adcock and Rose Villa are $70,000 and $80,000, respectively. Davis's $75,000 investment equals a one-third interest in the firm after the investment is added to the previously existing capital of the partnership.

Jerry Adcock, Capital	$ 70,000
Rose Villa, Capital	80,000
Davis's investment	75,000
Total capital after Davis's investment	$225,000
One-third interest = $225,000 ÷ 3 =	$ 75,000

The entry to record Davis's investment is as follows:

A	= L +	OE
+75,000		+75,000

Entry in Journal Form:

2012		Dr.	Cr.
Aug. 31	Cash	75,000	
	Richard Davis, Capital		75,000
	Admission of Richard Davis for a one-third interest in the company		

Study Note

The original partners receive a bonus because the entity is worth more as a going concern than the fair market value of the net assets would otherwise indicate. That is, the new partner is paying for unrecorded partnership value.

Bonus to the Old Partners A partnership is sometimes so profitable or otherwise advantageous that a new investor is willing to pay more than the actual dollar interest he or she receives in the partnership. For instance, suppose an individual pays $100,000 for an $80,000 interest in a partnership. The $20,000 excess of the payment over the interest purchased is a **bonus** to the original partners. The bonus must be distributed to the original partners according to the partnership agreement. When the agreement does not cover the distribution of bonuses, a bonus should be distributed to the original partners in accordance with the method for distributing income and losses.

Assume that the Adcock and Villa Company has operated for several years and that the partners' capital balances and the stated ratios for distribution of income and loss are as follows:

Partners	*Capital Balances*	*Stated Ratios*
Adcock	$160,000	55%
Villa	140,000	45
	$300,000	100%

Richard Davis wants to join the firm. He offers to invest $100,000 on December 1 for a one-fifth interest in the business and income. The original partners agree to the offer. This is the computation of the bonus to the original partners:

Partners' equity in the original partnership		$300,000
Cash investment by Richard Davis		100,000
Partners' equity in the new partnership		$400,000
Partners' equity assigned to Richard Davis ($400,000 × ⅕)		$ 80,000
Bonus to the original partners		
Investment by Richard Davis	$100,000	
Less equity assigned to Richard Davis	80,000	$ 20,000
Distribution of bonus to original partners		
Jerry Adcock ($20,000 × 0.55)	$ 11,000	
Rose Villa ($20,000 × 0.45)	9,000	$ 20,000

This is the entry that records Davis's admission to the partnership:

A	= L +	OE
+100,000		+11,000
		+9,000
		+80,000

Entry in Journal Form:

2012		Dr.	Cr.
Dec. 1	Cash	100,000	
	Jerry Adcock, Capital		11,000
	Rose Villa, Capital		9,000
	Richard Davis, Capital		80,000
	Investment by Richard Davis for a one-fifth interest in the firm, and the bonus distributed to the original partners		

Bonus to the New Partner There are several reasons that a partnership might want a new partner. A partnership in financial trouble might need additional cash. Or the partners might want to expand the firm's markets and need more capital for this purpose than they themselves can provide. Also, the partners might know a person who would bring a unique talent to the firm. Under these conditions, a new partner may be admitted to the partnership with the understanding that part of the original partners' capital will be transferred (credited) to the new partner's Capital account as a bonus.

For example, suppose that Jerry Adcock and Rose Villa have invited Richard Davis to join the firm. Davis is going to invest $60,000 on December 1 for a one-fourth interest in the company. The stated ratios for distribution of income or loss for Adcock and Villa are 55 percent and 45 percent, respectively. If Davis is to receive a one-fourth interest in the firm, the interest of the original partners represents a three-fourths interest in the business. The computation of Davis's bonus is as follows:

Total equity in partnership		
Jerry Adcock, Capital		$160,000
Rose Villa, Capital		140,000
Investment by Richard Davis		60,000
Partners' equity in the new partnership		$360,000
Partners' equity assigned to Richard Davis ($360,000 × ¼)		$ 90,000
Bonus to new partner		
Equity assigned to Richard Davis	$90,000	
Less cash investment by Richard Davis	60,000	$ 30,000
Distribution of bonus from original partners		
Jerry Adcock ($30,000 × 0.55)	$16,500	
Rose Villa ($30,000 × 0.45)	13,500	$ 30,000

The entry to record the admission of Richard Davis to the partnership is shown below:

A	= L +	OE
+60,000		−16,500
		−13,500
		+90,000

Entry in Journal Form:

2012		Dr.	Cr.
Dec. 1	Cash	60,000	
	Jerry Adcock, Capital	16,500	
	Rose Villa, Capital	13,500	
	Richard Davis, Capital		90,000
	To record the investment by Richard Davis of cash and a bonus from Adcock and Villa		

Withdrawal of a Partner

Since a partnership is a voluntary association, a partner usually has the right to withdraw at any time. However, to avoid disputes when a partner does decide to withdraw or retire, a partnership agreement should describe the procedures to be followed. The agreement should specify (1) whether an audit will be performed, (2) how the assets will be reappraised, (3) how a bonus will be determined, and (4) by what method the withdrawing partner will be paid.

Study Note

There is no impact on the income statement of a partnership when a partner withdraws. The only change is on the balance sheet.

A partner who wants to withdraw from a partnership can do so in one of several ways. The partner can sell his or her interest to another partner or to an outsider with the consent of the remaining partners, or the partner can withdraw assets equal to his or her capital balance, less than his or her capital balance (in this case, the remaining partners receive a bonus), or greater than his or her capital balance (in this case, the withdrawing partner receives a bonus). These alternatives are illustrated in Figure 17-1.

Study Note

Selling a partnership interest does not affect the assets and liabilities of the partnership. Therefore, total equity remains unchanged. The only effect of a partner's selling his or her interest to the existing partners or to a new partner is the change of names in the partners' equity section of the balance sheet.

Withdrawal by Selling Interest When a partner sells his or her interest to another partner or to an outsider with the consent of the other partners, the transaction is personal; it does not change the partnership assets or the partners' equity. For example, let's assume that the capital balances of Adcock, Villa, and Davis are $140,000, $100,000, and $60,000, respectively, for a total of $300,000.

Villa wants to withdraw from the partnership and is reviewing two offers for her interest. The offers are (1) to sell her interest to Davis for $110,000 or (2) to

Figure 17-1
Alternative Ways for a Partner to Withdraw

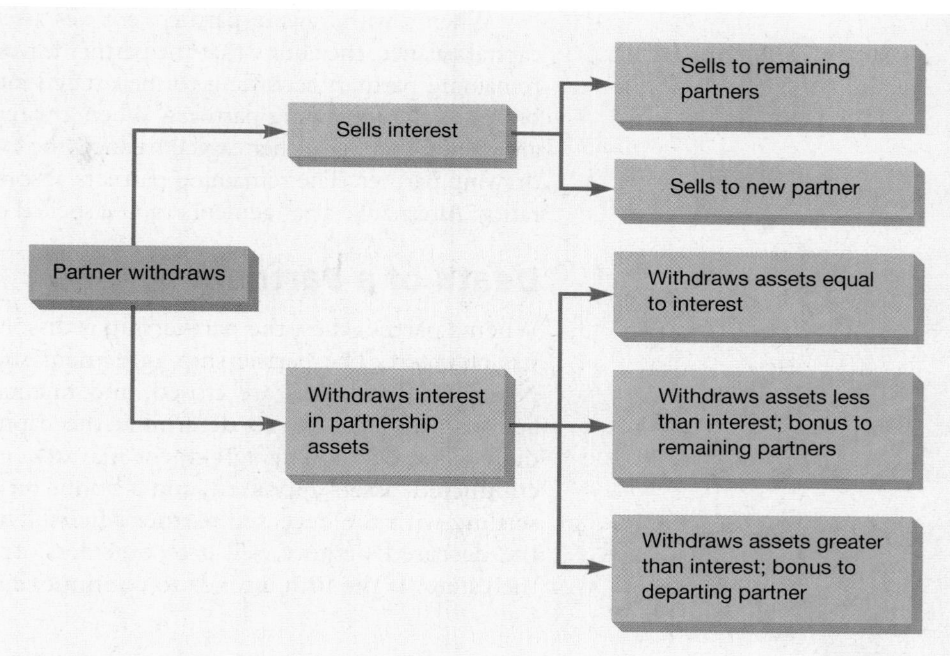

sell her interest to Judy Jones for $120,000. The remaining partners have agreed to either potential transaction. Because Davis and Jones would pay for Villa's interest from their personal assets, the partnership accounting records would show only the transfer of Villa's interest to Davis or Jones. The entries to record these possible transfers are as follows:

A	=	L	+	OE
				−100,000
				+100,000

1. If Villa's interest is purchased by Davis:

Rose Villa, Capital	100,000	
Richard Davis, Capital		100,000
Sale of Villa's partnership interest to Davis		

A	=	L	+	OE
				−100,000
				+100,000

2. If Villa's interest is purchased by Jones:

Rose Villa, Capital	100,000	
Judy Jones, Capital		100,000
Sale of Villa's partnership interest to Jones		

Withdrawal by Removing Assets A partnership agreement can allow a withdrawing partner to remove assets from the firm equal to his or her capital balance. Assume that Richard Davis decides to withdraw from Adcock, Villa, Davis & Company on January 21, 2012. Davis's capital balance is $60,000. The partnership agreement states that he can withdraw cash from the firm equal to his capital balance. If there is not enough cash, he must accept a promissory note from the new partnership for the balance. The remaining partners ask that Davis take only $50,000 in cash because of a cash shortage at the time of his withdrawal; he agrees to this request. The following entry records Davis's withdrawal:

A	=	L	+	OE
−50,000		+ 10,000		− 60,000

Entry in Journal Form:

		Dr.	Cr.
2013			
Jan. 21	Richard Davis, Capital	60,000	
	Cash		50,000
	Notes Payable, Richard Davis		10,000
	Withdrawal of Richard Davis from the partnership		

When a withdrawing partner removes assets that represent less than his or her capital balance, the equity that the partner leaves in the business is divided among the remaining partners according to their stated ratios. This distribution is considered a bonus to the remaining partners. When a withdrawing partner takes out assets that are greater than his or her capital balance, the excess is treated as a bonus to the withdrawing partner. The remaining partners absorb the bonus according to their stated ratios. Alternative arrangements can be spelled out in the partnership agreement.

Death of a Partner

When a partner dies, the partnership is dissolved because the original association has changed. The partnership agreement should state the actions to be taken. Normally, the books are closed, and financial statements are prepared. Those actions are necessary to determine the capital balance of each partner on the date of the death. The agreement may also indicate whether an audit should be conducted, assets appraised, and a bonus recorded, as well as the procedures for settling with the deceased partner's heirs. The remaining partners may purchase the deceased's equity, sell it to outsiders, or deliver specified business assets to the estate. If the firm intends to continue, a new partnership must be formed.

& APPLY >

Dan and Augie each own a $50,000 interest in a partnership. They agree to admit Bea as a partner by selling her a one-third interest for $80,000. How large a bonus will be distributed to Dan and Augie?

SOLUTION

Partners' equity in the original partnership		$100,000
Cash investment by Bea		80,000
Partners' equity in the new partnership		$180,000
Partners' equity assigned to Bea ($180,000 × 1/3)		$ 60,000
Bonus to the original partners		
Investment by Bea		$ 80,000
Less equity assigned to Bea		60,000
		$ 20,000
Distribution of bonus to original partners		
Dan ($20,000 × 0.50)	$10,000	
Augie ($20,000 × 0.50)	10,000	$ 20,000

Liquidation of a Partnership

LO5 Compute and record the distribution of assets to partners when they liquidate their partnership.

The **liquidation** of a partnership is the process of ending the business—of selling enough assets to pay the partnership's liabilities and distributing any remaining assets among the partners. Liquidation is a special form of dissolution. When a partnership is liquidated, the business will not continue.

The partnership agreement should indicate the procedures to be followed in the case of liquidation. Usually, the books are adjusted and closed, with the income or losses distributed to the partners. As the assets of the business are sold, any gain or losses should be distributed to the partners according to the stated ratios. As cash becomes available, it must be applied first to outside creditors, then to loans from partners, and finally to the partners' capital balances.

The process of liquidation can have a variety of financial outcomes. We look at two: (1) assets sold for a gain and (2) assets sold for a loss. For both alternatives, we make the assumptions that the books have been closed for Adcock, Villa, Davis & Company and that the following balance sheet exists before liquidation:

Adcock, Villa, Davis & Company
Balance Sheet
February 2, 2013

ASSETS		LIABILITIES	
Cash	$ 60,000	Accounts payable	$120,000
Accounts receivable	40,000		
Merchandise inventory	100,000	PARTNERS' EQUITY	
Plant assets (net)	200,000		
		Adcock, Capital	$ 85,000
		Villa, Capital	95,000
		Davis, Capital	100,000
		Total partners' equity	$280,000
		Total liabilities and	
Total assets	$400,000	partners' equity	$400,000

The stated ratios of Adcock, Villa, and Davis are 3:3:4, or 30, 30, and 40 percent, respectively.

Gain on Sale of Assets

Suppose that the following transactions took place in the liquidation of Adcock, Villa, Davis & Company:

1. The accounts receivable were collected for $35,000.
2. The inventory was sold for $110,000.
3. The plant assets were sold for $200,000.
4. The accounts payable of $120,000 were paid.
5. The gain of $5,000 from the realization of the assets was distributed according to the partners' stated ratios.
6. The partners received cash equivalent to the balances of their Capital accounts.

Study Note

Notice the proper use of the term *realization* in the February 13 and 14 entries. *Realization* means "conversion into cash."

These transactions are summarized in the statement of liquidation in Exhibit 17-2. The entries in journal form with their assumed transaction dates are as follows:

A	= L +	OE
+5,000		−35,000
−40,000		

A	= L +	OE
+110,000		+100,000
−10,000		

Entry in Journal Form:

2013		Dr.	Cr.	Explanation on Statement of Liquidation
Feb. 13	Cash	35,000		1.
	Gain or Loss from Realization	5,000		
	Accounts Receivable		40,000	
	Collection of accounts receivable			
14	Cash	110,000		2.
	Merchandise Inventory		100,000	
	Gain or Loss from Realization		10,000	
	Sale of inventory			

A = L + OE		Explanation on Statement of Liquidation	Dr.	Cr.	
A = L + OE +200,000 −200,000	Feb. 15	Cash	200,000		3.
		Plant Assets		200,000	
		Sale of plant assets			
A = L + OE −120,000 −120,000	16	Accounts Payable	120,000		4.
		Cash		120,000	
		Payment of accounts payable			
A = L + OE −5,000 +1,500 +1,500 +2,000	20	Gain or Loss from Realization	5,000		5.
		Jerry Adcock, Capital		1,500	
		Rose Villa, Capital		1,500	
		Richard Davis, Capital		2,000	
		Distribution of the net gain on assets ($10,000 gain minus $5,000 loss) to the partners			
A = L + OE −285,000 −86,500 −96,500 −102,000	20	Jerry Adcock, Capital	86,500		6.
		Rose Villa, Capital	96,500		
		Richard Davis, Capital	102,000		
		Cash		285,000	
		Distribution of cashto the partners			

EXHIBIT 17-2 Statement of Liquidation Showing Gain on Sale of Assets

Adcock, Villa, Davis & Company
Statement of Liquidation
February 2–20, 2013

Explanation	Cash	Other Assets	Accounts Payable	Adcock, Capital (30%)	Villa, Capital (30%)	Davis, Capital (40%)	Gain (or Loss) from Realization
Balance 2/2/13	$ 60,000	$340,000	$120,000	$85,000	$95,000	$100,000	
1. Collection of Accounts Receivable	35,000	(40,000)					($ 5,000)
	$ 95,000	$300,000	$120,000	$85,000	$95,000	$100,000	($ 5,000)
2. Sale of Inventory	110,000	(100,000)					10,000
	$205,000	$200,000	$120,000	$85,000	$95,000	$100,000	$ 5,000
3. Sale of Plant Assets	200,000	(200,000)					
	$405,000	—	$120,000	$85,000	$95,000	$100,000	$ 5,000
4. Payment of Liabilities	(120,000)		(120,000)				
	$285,000		—	$85,000	$95,000	$100,000	$ 5,000
5. Distribution of Gain (or Loss) from Realization				1,500	1,500	2,000	(5,000)
	$285,000			$86,500	$96,500	$102,000	—
6. Distribution of Cash to Partners	(285,000)			(86,500)	(96,500)	(102,000)	
	—			—	—	—	

Notice that the cash distributed to the partners is the balance in their respective Capital accounts. Cash is not distributed according to the partners' stated ratios.

Study Note

Because losses are allocated on the same basis as gains, the only difference in accounting for them is that debits and credits are switched.

Loss on Sale of Assets

We discuss two cases involving losses on the sale of a company's assets. In the first, the losses are small enough to be absorbed by the partners' capital balances. In the second, one partner's share of the losses is too large for his capital balance to absorb.

When a firm's assets are sold at a loss, the partners share the loss on liquidation according to their stated ratios. For example, assume that during the liquidation of Adcock, Villa, Davis & Company, the total cash received from the collection of accounts receivable and the sale of inventory and plant assets was $140,000. The statement of liquidation appears in Exhibit 17-3.

EXHIBIT 17-3 Statement of Liquidation Showing Loss on Sale of Assets

Adcock, Villa, Davis & Company
Statement of Liquidation
February 2–20, 2013

Explanation	Cash	Other Assets	Accounts Payable	Adcock, Capital (30%)	Villa, Capital (30%)	Davis, Capital (40%)	Gain (or Loss) from Realization
Balance 2/2/13	$ 60,000	$340,000	$120,000	$85,000	$95,000	$100,000	
1. Collection of Accounts Receivable and Sale of Inventory and Plant Assets	140,000	(340,000)					($200,000)
	$200,000	—	$120,000	$85,000	$95,000	$100,000	($200,000)
2. Payment of Liabilities	(120,000)		(120,000)				
	$ 80,000		—	$85,000	$95,000	$100,000	($200,000)
3. Distribution of Gain (or Loss) from Realization				(60,000)	(60,000)	(80,000)	200,000
	$ 80,000			$25,000	$35,000	$ 20,000	—
4. Distribution of Cash to Partners	(80,000)			(25,000)	(35,000)	(20,000)	
	—			—	—	—	

The entries in journal form for the transactions summarized in the statement of liquidation in Exhibit 17-3 are as follows:

Explanation on Statement of Liquidation

A	=	L	+	OE
+140,000				−200,000
−40,000				
−100,000				
−200,000				

Entry in Journal Form:

2013		Dr.	Cr.	
Feb. 15	Cash	140,000		1.
	Gain or Loss from Realization	200,000		
	Accounts Receivable		40,000	
	Merchandise Inventory		100,000	
	Plant Assets		200,000	
	Collection of accounts receivable and the sale of inventory and plant assets.			
16	Accounts Payable	120,000		2.
	Cash		120,000	
	Payment of accounts payable			
20	Jerry Adcock, Capital	60,000		3.
	Rose Villa, Capital	60,000		
	Richard Davis, Capital	80,000		
	Gain or Loss from Realization		200,000	
	Distribution of the loss on assets to the partners			
20	Jerry Adcock, Capital	25,000		4.
	Rose Villa, Capital	35,000		
	Richard Davis, Capital	20,000		
	Cash		80,000	
	Distribution of cash to the partners			

A	=	L	+	OE
−120,000		−120,000		

A	=	L	+	OE
				−60,000
				−60,000
				−80,000
				+200,000

A	=	L	+	OE
−80,000				−25,000
				−35,000
				−20,000

In some liquidations, a partner's share of the loss is greater than his or her capital balance. In such a situation, because partners are subject to unlimited liability, the partner must make up the deficit in his or her Capital account from personal assets. For example, suppose that after the sale of assets and the payment of liabilities, the remaining assets and partners' equity of Adcock, Villa, Davis & Company look like this:

Assets		
Cash		$ 30,000
Partners' equity		
Adcock, Capital	$ 25,000	
Villa, Capital	20,000	
Davis, Capital	(15,000)	$ 30,000

Richard Davis must pay $15,000 into the partnership from personal funds to cover his deficit. If he pays cash to the partnership, the following entry would record the cash contribution:

A	=	L	+	OE
+15,000				+15,000

Entry in Journal Form:

2013		Dr.	Cr.
Feb. 20	Cash	15,000	
	Richard Davis, Capital		15,000
	Additional investment of Richard Davis to cover the negative balance in his Capital account		

After Davis pays $15,000, there is enough cash to pay Adcock and Villa their capital balances and, thus, to complete the liquidation. The transaction is recorded in the following way:

A	=	L	+	OE
−45,000				−25,000
				−20,000

Entry in Journal Form:

2013		Dr.	Cr.
Feb. 20	Jerry Adcock, Capital	25,000	
	Rose Villa, Capital	20,000	
	Cash		45,000
	Distribution of cash to the partners		

If a partner does not have the cash to cover his or her obligations to the partnership, the remaining partners share the loss according to their established stated ratios. Remember that all partners have unlimited liability. As a result, if Richard Davis cannot pay the $15,000 deficit in his Capital account, Adcock and Villa must share the deficit according to their stated ratios. Each has a 30 percent stated ratio, so each must pay 50 percent of the losses that Davis cannot pay. The new stated ratios are computed as follows:

	Old Ratios	*New Ratios*	
Adcock	30%	30 ÷ 60 = 0.50 =	50%
Villa	30%	30 ÷ 60 = 0.50 =	50
	60%		100%

And the entries to record the transactions are as follows:

A	=	L	+	OE
				−7,500
				−7,500
				+15,000

Entry in Journal Form:

2013		Dr.	Cr.
Feb. 20	Jerry Adcock, Capital	7,500	
	Rose Villa, Capital	7,500	
	Richard Davis, Capital		15,000
	Transfer of Davis's deficit to Adcock and Villa		
20	Jerry Adcock, Capital	17,500	
	Rose Villa, Capital	12,500	
	Cash		30,000
	Distribution of cash to the partners		

A	=	L	+	OE
−30,000				−17,500
				−12,500

Davis's inability to meet his obligations at the time of liquidation does not relieve him of his liabilities to Adcock and Villa. If he is able to pay his liabilities at some time in the future, Adcock and Villa can collect the amount of Davis's deficit that they absorbed.

STOP & APPLY >

After the partnership between Joanna and Andrew has been operating for a year, their Capital accounts are $30,000 and $20,000, respectively. The firm has cash of $24,000 and inventory of $26,000. The partners decide to liquidate the partnership. The inventory is liquidated for only $8,000. Assuming the partners share income and losses in the ratio of one-third to Joanna and two-thirds to Andrew, how much cash will be distributed to each partner in liquidation?

SOLUTION

Loss on inventory computed:
$26,000 − $8,000 = $18,000

	Joanna	Andrew
Distribution of cash to partners:		
Capital balances	$30,000	$ 20,000
Distribution of loss		
Joanna ($18,000 × 1/3)	(6,000)	
Andrew ($18,000 × 2/3)		(12,000)
Cash to partners	$24,000	$ 8,000

▸ HOLDER AND WILLIAMS PARTNERSHIP: REVIEW PROBLEM

Distribution of Income and Admission of a Partner
LO3 LO4

In the Decision Point at the beginning of the chapter, we noted that when Jack Holder and Dan Williams were forming their partnership in 2010, they were faced with a number of important decisions. We asked these questions:

- What details should be included in a partnership agreement?
- How would Jack Holder and Dan Williams share the income or losses of their business?
- How would they handle any changes in ownership that might occur?

Jack and Dan drafted a written partnership agreement that clearly stated the details of the arrangement, including the name, location, and purpose of the business; their names and respective duties; the investments each of them had made; the method of distributing income and losses; and the procedures for the admission and withdrawal of partners, the withdrawal of assets allowed each partner, and the liquidation (termination) of the business. They decided that Jack, who had contributed $100,000 to the partnership, was to receive an annual salary of $6,000 and that Dan was to receive 3 percent interest annually on his original investment of $150,000. They were to share income and losses after salary and interest in a 2:3 ratio.

Required

1. In 2010, the partnership had an income of $27,000, and in 2011, it had a loss of $2,000 (before salaries and interest). Compute Jack Holder and Dan William's share of the income and loss, and prepare the required entries in journal form.
2. On January 1, 2012, Jean Ratcliffe offers Jack and Dan $60,000 for a 15 percent interest in the partnership. They agree to Ratcliffe's offer because they need her resources to expand the business. On January 1, 2012, the balance in Jack's Capital account is $113,600, and the balance in Dan's Capital account is $161,400. Record the admission of Jean Ratcliffe to the partnership, assuming that her investment represents a 15 percent interest in the total partners' capital and that a bonus will be distributed to Jack and Dan in the ratio of 2:3.

Answers to Review Problem

1. Income and loss shared by the partners:

	A	B	C	D	E
1			Income(Loss) of Partner		Income
2			Holder	Williams	Distributed
3	**2010**				
4	Total income for distribution				$27,000
5	Distribution of salary				
6	Holder		$ 6,000		(6,000)
7	Remaining income after salary				$21,000
8	Distribution of interest				
9	Williams ($150,000 × 0.03)			$ 4,500	(4,500)
10	Remaining income after salary and				
11	interest				$16,500
12	Distribution of remaining income				
13	Holder ($16,500 × $^2/_5$)		6,600		
14	Williams ($16,500 × $^3/_5$)			9,900	(16,500)
15	Remaining income				—
16	Income of partners		$12,600	$14,400	$27,000
17					
18					
19	**2011**				
20	Total loss for distribution				($ 2,000)
21	Distribution of salary				
22	Holder		$ 6,000		(6,000)
23	Negative balance after salary				($ 8,000)
24	Distribution of interest				
25	Williams ($150,000 × 0.03)			$ 4,500	(4,500)
26	Negative balance after salary				($12,500)
27	and interest				
28	Distribution of remaining income				
29	Holder ($16,500 × $^2/_5$)		(5,000)		
30	Williams ($16,500 × $^3/_5$)			(7,500)	12,500
31	Remaining income				—
32	Income and loss of partners		$ 1,000	($ 3,000)	($ 2,000)

Entry in Journal Form:

2010	Dr.	Cr.
Income Summary	27,000	
Jack Holder, Capital		12,600
Dan Williams, Capital		14,400
Distribution of income for the year to the partners' Capital accounts		

Entry in Journal Form:

2011	Dr.	Cr.
Dan Williams, Capital	3,000	
Income Summary		2,000
Jack Holder, Capital		1,000
Distribution of the loss for the year to the partners' Capital accounts		

2. Admission of the new partner:

Capital Balance and Bonus Computation

Ratcliffe, Capital = (Original Partners' Capital + New Partner's Investment) × 15%
= ($113,600 + $161,400 + $60,000) × 0.15 = $50,250
Bonus = New Partner's Investment − Ratcliffe, Capital
= $60,000 − $50,250
= $9,750

Distribution of Bonus

Holder	= $9,750 × $^2/_5$ =	$3,900
Williams	= $9,750 × $^3/_5$ =	5,850
	Total bonus	$9,750

Entry in Journal Form:

2012		Dr.	Cr.
Jan. 1	Cash	60,000	
	Jack Holder, Capital		3,900
	Dan Williams, Capital		5,850
	Jean Ratcliffe, Capital		50,250
	Sale of a 15 percent interest in the partnership to Jean Ratcliffe and the bonus paid to the original partners		

STOP & REVIEW >

LO1 Identify the principal characteristics, advantages, and disadvantages of the partnership form of business.

A partnership has several major characteristics that distinguish it from the other forms of business. It is a voluntary association of two or more people who combine their talents and resources to carry on a business. Their joint effort should be supported by a partnership agreement that spells out the venture's operating procedures. A partnership is dissolved by a partner's admission, withdrawal, or death and therefore has a limited life. Each partner acts as an agent of the partnership within the scope of normal operations and is personally liable for the partnership's debts. Property invested in the partnership becomes an asset of the partnership, owned jointly by all the partners. And, finally, each partner has the right to share in the company's income and the responsibility to share in its losses.

The advantages of a partnership are the ease of its formation and dissolution, the opportunity to pool several individuals' talents and resources, the lack of a corporate tax burden, and the freedom of action each partner enjoys. The disadvantages are the limited life of a partnership, mutual agency, the unlimited personal liability of the partners, and the difficulty of raising large amounts of capital and transferring partners' interest. Two other common forms of association that are a type of partnership or similar to a partnership are limited partnerships and joint ventures.

LO2 Record partners' investments of cash and other assets when a partnership is formed.

A partnership is formed when the partners contribute cash, other assets, or a combination of both to the business. The details are stated in the partnership agreement. Initial investments are recorded with a debit to Cash or another asset account and a credit to the investing partner's Capital account. The recorded amount of the other assets should be their fair market value on the date of transfer to the partnership. In addition, a partnership can assume an investing partner's liabilities. When this occurs, the partner's Capital account is credited with the difference between the assets invested and the liabilities assumed.

LO3 Compute and record the income or losses that partners share, based on stated ratios, capital balance ratios, and partners' salaries and interest.

The partners must share income and losses in accordance with the partnership agreement. If the agreement says nothing about the distribution of income and losses, the partners share them equally. Common methods used for distributing income and losses include stated ratios, capital balance ratios, and salaries and interest on capital investments. Each method tries to measure the individual partner's contribution to the operations of the business.

Stated ratios usually are based on the partners' relative contributions to the partnership. When capital balance ratios are used, income or losses are divided strictly on the basis of each partner's capital balance. The use of salaries and interest on capital investment takes into account both efforts (salary) and capital investment (interest) in dividing income or losses among the partners.

LO4 Record a person's admission to or withdrawal from a partnership.

An individual is admitted to a partnership by purchasing a partner's interest or by contributing additional assets. When an interest is purchased, the withdrawing partner's capital is transferred to the new partner. When the new partner contributes assets to the partnership, it may be necessary to recognize a bonus shared or borne by the original partners or by the new partner.

A person can withdraw from a partnership by selling his or her interest in the business to the remaining partners or a new partner or by withdrawing company assets. When assets are withdrawn, the amount can be equal to, less than, or greater than the partner's capital interest. When assets that have a value less than or greater than the partner's interest are withdrawn, a bonus is recognized and distributed among the remaining partners or to the departing partner.

LO5 Compute and record the distribution of assets to partners when they liquidate their partnership.

The liquidation of a partnership entails selling the assets necessary to pay the company's liabilities and then distributing any remaining assets to the partners. Any gain or loss on the sale of the assets is shared by the partners according to their stated ratios. When a partner has a deficit balance in a Capital account, that partner must contribute personal assets equal to the deficit. When a partner does not have personal assets to cover a capital deficit, the deficit must be absorbed by the solvent partners according to their stated ratios.

REVIEW of Concepts and Terminology

The following concepts and terms were introduced in this chapter:

Bonus 768 (LO4)

Dissolution 767 (LO4)

Joint venture 758 (LO1)

Limited life 756 (LO1)

Limited partnership 758 (LO1)

Liquidation 772 (LO5)

Mutual agency 756 (LO1)

Partners' equity 759 (LO2)

Partnership 756 (LO1)

Partnership agreement 756 (LO1)

Unlimited liability 756 (LO1)

CHAPTER ASSIGNMENTS

BUILDING Your Basic Knowledge and Skills

Short Exercises

LO1 **Partnership Characteristics**

SE 1. Indicate whether each statement below is a reflection of (a) voluntary association, (b) a partnership agreement, (c) limited life, (d) mutual agency, or (e) unlimited liability.

1. A partner may be required to pay the debts of the partnership out of personal assets.
2. A partnership must be dissolved when a partner is admitted, withdraws, retires, or dies.
3. Any partner can bind the partnership to a business agreement.
4. A partner does not have to remain a partner if he or she does not want to.
5. Details of the arrangements among partners are specified in a written contract.

LO2 **Partnership Formation**

SE 2. Bob contributes cash of $12,000, and Kim contributes office equipment that cost $10,000 but is valued at $8,000 to the formation of a new partnership. Prepare the entry in journal form to form the partnership.

LO3 **Distribution of Partnership Income**

SE 3. During the first year, the Bob and Kim partnership in **SE 2** earned an income of $5,000. Assume the partners agreed to share income and losses in the ratio of the beginning balances of their capital accounts. How much income should be transferred to each Capital account?

LO3 **Distribution of Partnership Income**

SE 4. During the first year, the Bob and Kim partnership in **SE 2** earned an income of $5,000. Assume the partners agreed to share income and losses by figuring interest on the beginning capital balances at 10 percent and dividing the remainder equally. How much income should be transferred to each Capital account?

LO3 **Distribution of Partnership Income**

SE 5. During the first year, the Bob and Kim partnership in **SE 2** earned an income of $5,000. Assume the partners agreed to share income and losses by figuring interest on the beginning capital balances at 10 percent, allowing a salary of $6,000 to Bob, and dividing the remainder equally. How much income (or loss) should be transferred to each Capital account?

LO4 **Withdrawal of a Partner**

SE 6. After the partnership has been operating for a year, the Capital accounts of Bob and Kim are $15,000 and $10,000, respectively. Kim withdraws from the partnership by selling her interest in the business to Sonia for $8,000. What will be the Capital account balances of the partners in the new Bob and Sonia partnership? Prepare the entry in journal form to record the transfer of ownership on the partnership books.

LO4 **Admission of a New Partner**

SE 7. After the partnership has been operating for a year, the Capital accounts of Bob and Kim are $15,000 and $10,000, respectively. Sonia buys a one-sixth interest in the partnership by investing cash of $11,000. What will be the Capital account balances of the partners in the new Bob, Kim, and Sonia partnership, assuming a bonus to the old partners, who share income and losses equally? Prepare the entry in journal form to record the transfer of ownership on the partnership books.

LO4 **Admission of a New Partner**

SE 8. After the partnership has been operating for a year, the Capital accounts of Bob and Kim are \$15,000 and \$10,000, respectively. Sonia buys a one-fourth interest in the partnership by investing cash of \$5,000. What will be the Capital account balances of the partners in the new Bob, Kim, and Sonia partnership, assuming that the new partner receives a bonus and that Bob and Kim share income and losses equally? Prepare the entry in journal form to record the transfer of ownership on the partnership books.

LO4 **Withdrawal of a New Partner**

SE 9. After the partnership has been operating for several years, the Capital accounts of Bob, Kim, and Sonia are \$25,000, \$16,000, and \$9,000, respectively. Sonia decides to leave the partnership and is allowed to withdraw \$9,000 in cash. Prepare the entry in journal form to record the withdrawal on the partnership books.

LO5 **Liquidation of a Partnership**

SE 10. After the partnership has been operating for a year, the Capital accounts of Bob and Kim are \$15,000 and \$10,000, respectively. The firm has cash of \$12,000 and office equipment of \$13,000. The partners decide to liquidate the partnership. The office equipment is sold for only \$4,000. Assuming the partners share income and losses in the ratio of one-third to Bob and two-thirds to Kim, how much cash will be distributed to each partner in liquidation?

Exercises

LO1 LO2 LO3 **Discussion Questions**

E 1. Develop brief answers to each of the following questions:

1. Why is it important for people to form partnerships with people they can trust?
2. When accounts receivable are transferred into a partnership, at what amount should they be recorded?
3. What is a disadvantage of receiving a large salary as part of a partner's distribution?

LO4 LO5 **Discussion Questions**

E 2. Develop brief answers to each of the following questions:

1. If the value of a partnership is worth far more than the book value of the assets on the balance sheet, would a new partner entering the partnership be more likely to pay a bonus to the old partners or receive a bonus from the old partners?
2. When a partnership is dissolved, what is an alternate approach to selling all the assets and distributing the proceeds, and what decisions will have to be made if this approach is taken?

LO2 **Partnership Formation**

E 3. Henri Mikels and Alex Jamison are watch repairmen who want to form a partnership and open a jewelry store. They have an attorney prepare their partnership agreement, which indicates that assets invested in the partnership will be recorded at their fair market value and that liabilities will be assumed at book value.

The assets contributed by each partner and the liabilities assumed by the partnership are as follows:

Assets	Henri Mikels	Alex Jamison	Total
Cash	$40,000	$30,000	$70,000
Accounts receivable	52,000	20,000	72,000
Allowance for uncollectible accounts	4,000	3,000	7,000
Supplies	1,000	500	1,500
Equipment	20,000	10,000	30,000
Liabilities			
Accounts payable	32,000	9,000	41,000

Prepare the entry in journal form necessary to record the original investments of Mikels and Jamison in the partnership.

LO3 **Distribution of Income**

E 4. Elijah Samuels and Tony Winslow agreed to form a partnership. Samuels contributed $200,000 in cash, and Winslow contributed assets with a fair market value of $400,000. The partnership, in its initial year, reported net income of $120,000. Calculate the distribution of the first year's income to the partners under each of the following conditions:

1. Samuels and Winslow failed to include stated ratios in the partnership agreement.
2. Samuels and Winslow agreed to share income and losses in a 3:2 ratio.
3. Samuels and Winslow agreed to share income and losses in the ratio of their original investments.
4. Samuels and Winslow agreed to share income and losses by allowing 10 percent interest on original investments and sharing any remainder equally.

LO3 **Distribution of Income or Losses: Salaries and Interest**

E 5. Assume that the partnership agreement of Samuels and Winslow in **E 4** states that Samuels and Winslow are to receive salaries of $20,000 and $24,000, respectively; that Samuels is to receive 6 percent interest on his capital balance at the beginning of the year; and that the remainder of income and losses are to be shared equally. Calculate the distribution of the income or losses under the following conditions:

1. Income totaled $120,000 before deductions for salaries and interest.
2. Income totaled $48,000 before deductions for salaries and interest.
3. There was a loss of $2,000.
4. There was a loss of $40,000.

LO3 **Distribution of Income: Average Capital Balance**

E 6. Barbara and Karen operate a furniture rental business. Their capital balances on January 1, 2010, were $160,000 and $240,000, respectively. Barbara withdrew cash of $32,000 from the business on April 1, 2010. Karen withdrew $60,000 cash on October 1, 2010. Barbara and Karen distribute partnership income based on their average capital balances each year. Income for 2010 was $160,000. Compute the income to be distributed to Barbara and Karen using their average capital balances in 2010.

LO4 **Admission of a New Partner: Recording a Bonus**

E 7. Ernie, Ron, and Denis have equity in a partnership of $40,000, $40,000, and $60,000, respectively, and they share income and losses in a ratio of 1:1:3. The partners have agreed to admit Henry to the partnership. Prepare entries in journal form to record the admission of Henry to the partnership under the following conditions:

1. Henry invests $60,000 for a 20 percent interest in the partnership, and a bonus is recorded for the original partners.
2. Henry invests $60,000 for a 40 percent interest in the partnership, and a bonus is recorded for Henry.

LO4 Withdrawal of a Partner

E 8. Danny, Steve, and Luis are partners. They share income and losses in the ratio of 3:2:1. Luis's Capital account has a $120,000 balance. Danny and Steve have agreed to let Luis take $160,000 of the company's cash when he retires from the business. What entry in journal form must be made on the partnership's books when Luis retires, assuming that a bonus to Luis is recognized and absorbed by the remaining partners?

LO5 Partnership Liquidation

E 9. Assume the following assets, liabilities, and partners' equity in the Ming and Demmick partnership on December 31, 2011:

Assets	=	Liabilities	+	Ming, Capital	+	Demmick, Capital
$160,000	=	$10,000	+	$90,000	+	$60,000

The partnership has no cash. When the partners agree to liquidate the business, the assets are sold for $120,000, and the liabilities are paid. Ming and Demmick share income and losses in a ratio of 3:1.

1. Prepare a statement of liquidation.
2. Prepare entries in journal form for the sale of assets, payment of liabilities, distribution of loss from realization, and final distribution of cash to Ming and Demmick.

LO5 Partnership Liquidation

E 10. Ariel, Mandy, and Tisha are partners in a tanning salon. The assets, liabilities, and capital balances as of July 1, 2010, are as follows:

Assets	$480,000
Liabilities	160,000
Ariel, Capital	140,000
Mandy, Capital	40,000
Tisha, Capital	140,000

Because competition is strong, business is declining, and the partnership has no cash, the partners have decided to sell the business. Ariel, Mandy, and Tisha share income and losses in a ratio of 3:1:1, respectively. The assets were sold for $260,000, and the liabilities were paid. Mandy has no other assets and will not be able to cover any deficits in her Capital account. How will the ending cash balance be distributed to the partners?

Problems

LO2 LO3 Partnership Formation and Distribution of Income

P 1. In January 2010, Edie Rivera and Babs Bacon agreed to produce and sell chocolate candies. Rivera contributed $240,000 in cash to the business. Bacon contributed the building and equipment, valued at $220,000 and $140,000, respectively. The partnership had an income of $84,000 during 2010 but was less successful during 2011, when income was only $40,000.

Required

1. Prepare the entry in journal form to record the investment of both partners in the partnership.
2. Determine the share of income for each partner in 2010 and 2011 under each of the following conditions:
   a. The partners agreed to share income equally.
   b. The partners failed to agree on an income-sharing arrangement.
   c. The partners agreed to share income according to the ratio of their original investments.
   d. The partners agreed to share income by allowing interest of 10 percent on their original investments and dividing the remainder equally.
   e. The partners agreed to share income by allowing salaries of $40,000 for Rivera and $28,000 for Bacon, and dividing the remainder equally.
   f. The partners agreed to share income by paying salaries of $40,000 to Rivera and $28,000 to Bacon, allowing interest of 9 percent on their original investments, and dividing the remainder equally.

User insight ▶

3. What are some of the factors that need to be considered in choosing the plan of partners' income sharing among the options shown in requirement 2?

LO3 **Distribution of Income: Salaries and Interest**

P 2. Naomi and Petri are partners in a tennis shop. They have agreed that Naomi will operate the store and receive a salary of $104,000 per year. Petri will receive 10 percent interest on his average capital balance during the year of $500,000. The remaining income or losses are to be shared by Naomi and Petri in a 2:3 ratio.

Required

Determine each partner's share of income and losses under each of the following conditions. In each case, the income or loss is stated before the distribution of salary and interest.

1. Income was $168,000.
2. Income was $88,000.
3. The loss was $25,600.

LO4 **Admission and Withdrawal of a Partner**

P 3. Marnie, Stacie, and Samantha are partners in Woodware Company. Their capital balances as of July 31, 2011, are as follows:

Marnie, Capital		Stacie, Capital		Samantha, Capital	
Dr.	Cr.	Dr.	Cr.	Dr.	Cr.
	45,000		15,000		30,000

Each partner has agreed to admit Connie to the partnership.

Required

1. Prepare the entries in journal form to record Connie's admission to or Marnie's withdrawal from the partnership under each of the following conditions:
   a. Connie pays Marnie $12,500 for 20 percent of Marnie's interest in the partnership.
   b. Connie invests $20,000 cash in the partnership and receives an interest equal to her investment.
   c. Connie invests $30,000 cash in the partnership for a 20 percent interest in the business. A bonus is to be recorded for the original partners on the basis of their capital balances.

d. Connie invests $30,000 cash in the partnership for a 40 percent interest in the business. The original partners give Connie a bonus according to the ratio of their capital balances on July 31, 2011.
e. Marnie withdraws from the partnership, taking $52,500. The excess of withdrawn assets over Marnie's partnership interest is distributed according to the balances of the Capital accounts.
f. Marnie withdraws by selling her interest directly to Connie for $60,000.

User insight ▶ 2. When a new partner enters a partnership, why would the new partner pay a bonus to the old partners, or why would the old partners pay a bonus to the new partner?

LO5 **Partnership Liquidation**

P 4. Caruso, Evans, and Weisman are partners in a retail lighting store. They share income and losses in the ratio of 2:2:1, respectively. The partners have agreed to liquidate the partnership. Here is the partnership balance sheet before the liquidation:

Caruso, Evans, and Weisman Partnership
Balance Sheet
August 31, 2010

Assets		Liabilities	
Cash	$ 280,000	Accounts payable	$ 360,000
Other assets	880,000	**Partners' Equity**	
		Caruso, Capital	$ 400,000
		Evans, Capital	240,000
		Weisman, Capital	160,000
		Total partners' equity	$ 800,000
		Total liabilities and	
Total assets	$1,160,000	partners' equity	$1,160,000

The other assets were sold on September 1, 2010, for $720,000. Accounts payable were paid on September 4, 2010. The remaining cash was distributed to the partners on September 11, 2010.

Required

1. Prepare a statement of liquidation.
2. Prepare the following entries in journal form:
   a. the sale of the other assets,
   b. payment of the accounts payable,
   c. the distribution of the loss from realization, and
   d. the distribution to the partners of the remaining cash.

Alternate Problems

LO3 **Distribution of Income: Salaries and Interest**

P 5. Jacob, Deric, and Jason are partners in the South Central Company. The partnership agreement states that Jacob is to receive 8 percent interest on his capital balance at the beginning of the year, Deric is to receive a salary of $100,000 a year, and Jason will be paid interest of 6 percent on his average capital balance during the year. Jacob, Deric, and Jason will share any income or loss after salary and interest in a 5:3:2 ratio. Jacob's capital balance at the beginning of the year was $600,000, and Jason's average capital balance for the year was $720,000.

Required

Determine each partner's share of income and losses under the following conditions. In each case, the income or loss is stated before the distribution of salary and interest.

1. Income was $545,200.
2. Income was $155,600.
3. The loss was $56,800.

LO4 Admission and Withdrawal of a Partner

P 6. Peter, Mara, and Vanessa are partners in the Image Gallery. As of November 30, 2011, the balance in Peter's Capital account was $50,000, the balance in Mara's was $60,000, and the balance in Vanessa's was $90,000. Peter, Mara, and Vanessa share income and losses in a ratio of 2:3:5.

Required

1. Prepare entries in journal form for each of the following independent conditions:
   a. Bob pays Vanessa $100,000 for four-fifths of Vanessa's interest.
   b. Bob is to be admitted to the partnership with a one-third interest for a $100,000 cash investment.
   c. Bob is to be admitted to the partnership with a one-third interest for a $160,000 cash investment. A bonus, based on the partners' ratio for income and losses, is to be distributed to the original partners when Bob is admitted.
   d. Bob is to be admitted to the partnership with a one-third interest for an $82,000 cash investment. A bonus is to be given to Bob on admission.
   e. Peter withdraws from the partnership, taking $66,000 in cash.
   f. Peter withdraws from the partnership by selling his interest directly to Bob for $70,000.

User insight ▶ 2. In general, when a new partner enters a partnership, why would the new partner pay a bonus to the old partners, or why would the old partners pay a bonus to the new partner?

LO5 Partnership Liquidation

P 7. The balance sheet of the Rose Partnership as of July 31, 2011, follows.

Rose Partnership
Balance Sheet
July 31, 2011

Assets		Liabilities	
Cash	$ 6,000	Accounts payable	$480,000
Accounts receivable	120,000	**Partners' Equity**	
Inventory	264,000		
Equipment (net)	462,000	Gerri, Capital	$ 72,000
		Susi, Capital	180,000
		Mari, Capital	120,000
		Total partners' equity	$372,000
		Total liabilities and	
Total assets	$852,000	partners' equity	$852,000

The partners—Gerri, Susi, and Mari—share income and losses in the ratio of 5:3:2. Because of a mutual disagreement, Gerri, Susi, and Mari have decided to liquidate the business.

Assume that Gerri cannot contribute any additional personal assets to the company during liquidation and that the following transactions occurred during liquidation: (a) Accounts receivable were sold for 60 percent of their book value. (b) Inventory was sold for $276,000. (c) Equipment was sold for $300,000. (d) Accounts payable were paid in full. (e) Gain or loss from realization was distributed to the partners' Capital accounts. (f) Gerri's deficit was transferred to the remaining partners in their new income and loss ratio. (g) The remaining cash was distributed to Susi and Mari.

Required

1. Prepare a statement of liquidation.
2. Prepare entries in journal form to liquidate the partnership and distribute any remaining cash.

LO2 LO3 LO4 LO5

Comprehensive Partnership Transactions

KA KLOOSTER & ALLEN

P 8. The following events pertain to a partnership formed by Mark Raymond and Stan Bryden to operate a floor-cleaning company:

2011

Feb. 14 The partnership was formed. Raymond transferred to the partnership $80,000 cash, land worth $80,000, a building worth $480,000, and a mortgage on the building of $240,000. Bryden transferred to the partnership $40,000 cash and equipment worth $160,000.

Dec. 31 During 2011, the partnership earned income of just $84,000. The partnership agreement specifies that income and losses are to be divided by paying salaries of $40,000 to Raymond and $60,000 to Bryden, allowing 8 percent interest on beginning capital investments, and dividing any remainder equally.

2012

Jan. 1 To improve the prospects for the company, the partners decided to take in a new partner, Chuck Menzer, who had experience in the floor-cleaning business. Menzer invested $156,000 for a 25 percent interest in the business. A bonus was transferred in equal amounts from the original partners' Capital accounts to Menzer's Capital account.

Dec. 31 During 2012, the company earned income of $87,200. The new partnership agreement specified that income and losses would be divided by paying salaries of $60,000 to Bryden and $80,000 to Menzer (no salary to Raymond), allowing 8 percent interest on beginning capital balances after Menzer's admission, and dividing the remainder equally.

2013

Jan. 1 Because it appeared that the business could not support the three partners, the partners decided to liquidate the partnership. The asset and liability accounts of the partnership were as follows: Cash, $407,200; Accounts Receivable (net), $68,000; Land, $80,000; Building (net), $448,000; Equipment (net), $236,000; Accounts Payable, $88,000; and Mortgage Payable, $224,000. The equipment was sold for $200,000. The accounts payable were paid. The loss was distributed equally to the partners' Capital accounts. A statement of liquidation was prepared, and the remaining assets and liabilities were distributed. Raymond agreed to accept cash plus the land and building at book value and the mortgage payable as payment for his share. Bryden accepted cash and the accounts receivable for his share. Menzer was paid in cash.

Required

Prepare entries in journal form to record all of the facts above. Support your computations with schedules, and prepare a statement of liquidation in connection with the January 1, 2013, entries.

ENHANCING Your Knowledge, Skills, and Critical Thinking

LO3 **Distribution of Partnership Income and Losses**

C 1. Landow, Donovan, and Hansa, who are forming a partnership to operate an antiques gallery, are discussing how income and losses should be distributed. Among the facts they are considering are the following:

a. Landow will contribute cash for operations of $100,000, Donovan will contribute a collection of antiques that is valued at $300,000, and Hansa will not contribute any assets.
b. Landow and Hansa will handle day-to-day business operations. Hansa will work full-time, and Landow will devote about half-time to the partnership. Donovan will not devote time to day-to-day operations. A full-time clerk in a retail store would make about $20,000 in a year, and a full-time manager would receive about $30,000.
c. The current interest rate on long-term bonds is 8 percent.

Landow, Donovan, and Hansa have just hired you as the partnership's accountant. Write a memorandum describing an equitable plan for distributing income and losses. Outline the reasons why you believe this plan is equitable. According to your plan, which partner will gain the most if the partnership is very profitable, and which will lose the most if the partnership has large losses?

LO1 **Partnership Agreement**

C 2. Form a partnership with one or two of your classmates. Assume that the two or three of you are forming a small service business. For example, you might form a company that hires college students to paint houses during the summer or to provide landscaping services.

Working together, draft a partnership agreement for your business. The agreement can be a simple one, with just a sentence or two for each provision. However, it should include the name, location, and purpose of the business; the names of the partners and their respective duties; the investments of each partner; methods for distributing profits and losses; and procedures for dealing with the admission or withdrawal of partners, the withdrawal of assets, the death of a partner, and liquidation of the business. Include a title, date, and signature lines.

LO1 LO2 LO4 **Death of a Partner**

C 3. South Shore Realty was started 20 years ago when T. S. Tyler, R. C. Strong, and A. J. Hibbert established a partnership to sell real estate near Galveston, Texas. The partnership has been extremely successful. In 2011, Tyler, the senior partner, who in recent years had not been very active in the partnership, died. Unfortunately, the partnership agreement is vague about how the partnership interest of a partner who dies should be valued. It simply states that "the estate of a deceased partner shall receive compensation for his or her interest in the partnership in a reasonable time after death." The attorney for Tyler's family believes that the estate should receive one-third of the assets of the partnership based on the fair market value of the net assets (total assets less total liabilities). The total assets of the partnership are $10 million in the accounting records, but the assets are worth at least $20 million. Because the firm's total liabilities are $4 million, the attorney is asking for $5.3 million (one-third of $16 million). Strong and Hibbert do not agree, but all parties want to avoid a protracted, expensive lawsuit. They have decided to put the question to an arbitrator, who will make a determination of the settlement.

Here are some other facts that may or may not be relevant. The current balances in the partners' Capital accounts are $1.5 million for Tyler, $2.5 million for Strong, and $2.0 million for Hibbert. Net income in 2011 is to be distributed to the Capital accounts in the ratio of 1:4:3. Before Tyler's semiretirement, the distribution ratio was 3:3:2. Assume you or your group is the arbitrator, and develop what you would consider a fair distribution of assets to Tyler's estate. Defend your solution.

LO1 LO3 Effects of a Lawsuit on Partnership

C 4. The Springfield Clinic is owned and operated by ten local doctors as a partnership. Recently, a paralyzed patient sued the clinic for malpractice, for a total of $20 million. The clinic carries malpractice liability insurance in the amount of $10 million. There is no provision for the possible loss from this type of lawsuit in the partnership's financial statements. The condensed balance sheet for 2011 is as follows:

Springfield Clinic
Condensed Balance Sheet
December 31, 2011

Assets		
Current assets	$246,000	
Property, plant, and equipment (net)	750,000	
Total assets		$996,000
Liabilities and Partners' Equity		
Current liabilities	$180,000	
Long-term debt	675,000	
Total liabilities		$855,000
Partners' equity		141,000
Total liabilities and partners' equity		$996,000

1. How should information about the lawsuit be disclosed in the December 31, 2011, financial statements of the partnership?
2. Assume that the clinic and its insurance company settle out of court by agreeing to pay a total of $10.1 million, of which $100,000 must be paid by the partnership. What effect will the payment have on the clinic's December 31, 2011, financial statements? Discuss the effect of the settlement on the Springfield Clinic doctors' personal financial situations.

LO1 **International Joint Ventures**

C 5. Nokia (www.nokia.com), the Finnish telecommunications company, has formed an equally owned joint venture with Capital Corporation, a state-owned Chinese company, to develop a center for the manufacture and development of telecommunications equipment in China, the world's fastest-growing market for this kind of equipment. The main aim of the development is to persuade Nokia's suppliers to move close to the company's main plant. The Chinese government looks favorably on companies that involve local suppliers.[1] What advantages does a joint venture have over a single company in entering a new market in another country? What are the potential disadvantages? Divide into groups. One-half of the groups will make a strong argument for the joint venture. The other half will make a strong case against the joint venture. Engage in a class debate over the joint venture.

LO1 **Comparison of Career Opportunities in Partnerships and Corporations**

C 6. Accounting firms are among the world's largest partnerships and provide a wide range of attractive careers for business and accounting majors. Through the Needles Website at http://www.cengage.com/accounting/needles, you can explore careers in public accounting by linking to the website of one of the Big Four accounting firms: **Deloitte & Touche**, **Ernst & Young**, **KPMG International**, and **PricewaterhouseCoopers**. Each firm's home page has a career opportunity section. For the firm you choose, compile a list of facts about the firm—size, locations, services, and career opportunities. Do you have the interest and background for a career in public accounting? Why or why not? How do you think working for a large partnership would differ from or be the same as working for a large corporation? Be prepared to discuss your findings in class.

CHAPTER

18

The Changing Business Environment: A Manager's Perspective

The Management Process

PLAN

- ▷ Formulate mission statement
- ▷ Set strategic, tactical, and operating performance objectives and measures

PERFORM

- ▷ Manage ethically
- ▷ Measure value chain and supply chain performance

EVALUATE

- ▷ Compare actual performance with performance levels established in planning stage
- ▷ Use tools of continuous improvement

COMMUNICATE

- ▷ Prepare business plan
- ▷ Prepare accurate financial statements
- ▷ Communicate information clearly and ethically

How managers plan, perform, evaluate, and report business can affect us all.

Management is expected to ensure that the organization uses its resources wisely, operates profitably, pays its debts, and abides by laws and regulations. To fulfill these expectations, managers establish the goals, objectives, and strategic plans that guide and control the organization's operating, investing, and financing activities. In this chapter, we describe the approaches that managers have developed to meet the challenges of today's changing business environment and the role that management accounting plays in meeting those challenges in an ethical manner.

LEARNING OBJECTIVES

LO1 **Distinguish management accounting from financial accounting and explain how management accounting supports the management process.** (pp. 796–803)

LO2 **Describe the value chain and its usefulness in analyzing a business.** (pp. 803–807)

LO3 **Identify the management tools used for continuous improvement.** (pp. 807–811)

LO4 **Explain the balanced scorecard and its relationship to performance measures.** (pp. 811–814)

LO5 **Identify the standards of ethical conduct for management accountants.** (pp. 814–816)

DECISION POINT ► A MANAGER'S FOCUS GOOD FOODS STORE

Vanna Lang is about to open a retail grocery store called Good Foods Store. She has assembled a team of store managers, and in a recent meeting, she and the managers discussed the factors they should concentrate on to ensure the store's success. They agreed that their company, like any other company, should aim to satisfy customer needs, develop efficient operating processes, foster career paths for employees, and become an innovative leader in marketing products and services. In this chapter, we follow Vanna Lang and her managers as they try to balance these factors while mapping out a strategic plan, performing their managerial duties, evaluating the results of their efforts, and communicating about the company's progress.

- ► What is Good Food Store's strategic plan?
- ► What management accounting tools does the company use to stay ahead of its competitors?
- ► What role does management accounting play in Good Foods Store's endeavors?

The Role of Management Accounting

LO1 Distinguish management accounting from financial accounting and explain how management accounting supports the management process.

To plan and control an organization's operations, to measure its performance, and to make decisions about products or services and many other internal control and governance matters, managers need accurate and timely accounting information. The role of management accounting is to provide an information system that enables managers and persons throughout an organization:

- to make informed decisions,
- to be more effective at their jobs, and
- to improve the organization's performance.

In 2008, the Institute of Management Accountants (IMA) updated the definition of **management accounting** as follows:

> Management accounting is a profession that involves partnering in management decision making, devising planning and performance management systems, and providing expertise in financial reporting and control to assist management in the formulation and implementation of an organization's strategy.[1]

This definition recognizes that regulation, globalization, and technology changes have redefined the management accountant's role from a traditional compliance, number-focused one to that of a strategic business partner within an organization. Thus, the importance of nonfinancial information has increased significantly. Today, management accounting information includes nonfinancial data as well as financial data in performance management, planning and budgeting, corporate governance, risk management, and internal controls.

Management Accounting and Financial Accounting: A Comparison

Study Note

Management accounting is *not* a subordinate activity to financial accounting. Rather, it is a process that includes financial accounting, tax accounting, information analysis, and other accounting activities.

Both management accounting and financial accounting assist decision makers by identifying, measuring, and processing relevant information and communicating this information through reports. Both provide managers with key measures of a company's performance and with cost information for valuing inventories on the balance sheet. Despite the overlap in their functions, management accounting and financial accounting differ in a number of ways. Table 18-1 summarizes these differences.

The primary users of management accounting information are people inside the organization, whereas financial accounting takes the actual results of management decisions about operating, investing, and financing activities and prepares financial statements for parties outside the organization—owners or stockholders, lenders, customers, and governmental agencies. Although these reports are prepared primarily for external use, managers also rely on them in evaluating an organization's performance.

Study Note

Financial accounting must adhere to the conventions of consistency and comparability to ensure the usefulness of information to parties outside the firm. Management accounting, on the other hand, can use innovative analyses and presentation techniques to enhance the usefulness of information to people within the firm.

Because management accounting reports are for internal use, their format can be flexible, driven by the user's needs. They may report either historical or future-oriented information without any formal guidelines or restrictions. In contrast, financial accounting reports, which focus on past performance, must follow generally accepted accounting principles as specified by the Securities and Exchange Commission (SEC).

The information in management accounting reports may be objective and verifiable, expressed in monetary terms or in physical measures of time or objects; the information may be based on estimates, and in such cases, it will be more subjective. In contrast, the statements that financial accounting provides must be based on objective and verifiable information, which is generally historical in nature and measured in monetary terms. Management accounting reports are

TABLE 18-1 Comparison of Management Accounting and Financial Accounting

Areas of Comparison	Management Accounting	Financial Accounting
Primary users	Managers, employees, supply-chain partners	Owners or stockholders, lenders, customers, governmental agencies
Report format	Flexible, driven by user's needs	Based on generally accepted accounting principles
Purpose of reports	Provide information for planning, control, performance measurement, and decision making	Report on past performance
Nature of information	Objective and verifiable for decision making; more subjective for planning (relies on estimates); confidential and private	Objective and verifiable; publicly available
Units of measure	Monetary at historical or current market or projected values; physical measures of time or number of objects	Monetary at historical and current market values
Frequency of reports	Prepared as needed; may or may not be on a periodic basis	Prepared on a periodic basis

prepared as often as needed—annually, quarterly, monthly, or even daily. Financial statements, on the other hand, are prepared and distributed periodically, usually on a quarterly and annual basis.

Management Accounting and the Management Process

Although management actions differ from organization to organization, they generally follow a four-stage management process. As illustrated at the beginning of this chapter and in the chapters that follow, the four stages of this process are:

- planning,
- performing,
- evaluating, and
- communicating.

Management accounting is essential in each stage of the process as managers make business decisions.

Planning Figure 18-1 shows the overall framework in which planning takes place. The overriding goal of a business is to increase the value of the stakeholders' interest in the business. The goal specifies the business's end point, or ideal state.

A company's **mission statement** describes the fundamental way in which the company will achieve its goal of increasing stakeholders' value. It also expresses the company's identity and unique character. For example, in its mission statement, **Wal-Mart**, the world's leading retailer and grocery chain, says that it wants "to give ordinary folk the chance to buy the same things as rich people."

The mission statement is essential to the planning process, which must consider how to add value through strategic objectives, tactical objectives, and operating objectives.

FIGURE 18-1
Overview of the Planning Framework

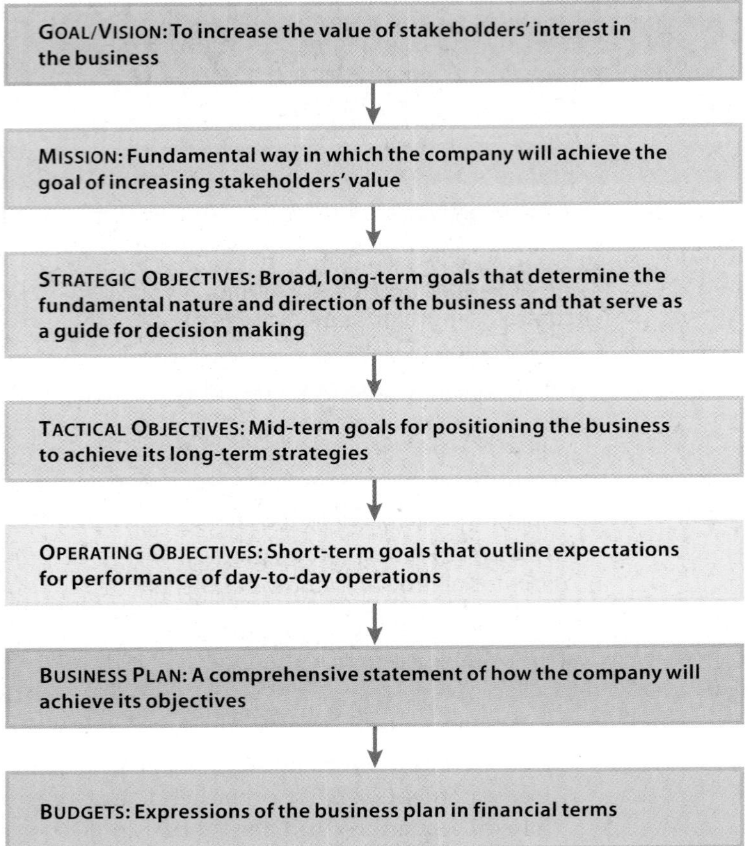

- **Strategic objectives** are broad, long-term goals that determine the fundamental nature and direction of a business and that serve as a guide for decision making. Strategic objectives involve such basic issues as what a company's main products or services will be, who its primary customers will be, and where it will operate. They stake out the strategic position that a company will occupy in the market—whether it will be a cost leader, quality leader, or niche satisfier.
- **Tactical objectives** are mid-term goals that position an organization to achieve its long-term strategies. These objectives, which usually cover a three- to five-year period, lay the groundwork for attaining the company's strategic objectives.
- **Operating objectives** are short-term goals that outline expectations for the performance of day-to-day operations. Operating objectives link to performance targets and specify how success will be measured.

To develop strategic, tactical, and operating objectives, managers must formulate a business plan. A **business plan** is a comprehensive statement of how a company will achieve its objectives. It is usually expressed in financial terms in the form of budgets, and it often includes performance goals for individuals, teams, products, or services.

EXAMPLE. As we noted in the Decision Point at the start of the chapter, Vanna Lang is about to open a retail grocery store called Good Foods Store. Lang's goal is to obtain an income from the business and to increase the value of her investment in it. After reading about how traditional grocers are being squeezed out by low-cost competitors like **Wal-Mart** and quality-focused stores like **Whole Foods Market**, Lang has made the following decisions about Good Foods Store:

- Good Foods Store's mission is to attract upscale customers and retain them by selling high-quality foods and providing excellent service in a pleasant atmosphere.
- Lang's strategic objectives call for buying high-quality fresh foods from local growers and international distributors and reselling these items to consumers.
- Her tactical objectives include implementing a stable supply chain of high-quality suppliers and a database to track customers' preferences.
- Her operating objectives call for courteous and efficient customer service. To measure performance in this area, she decides to keep a record of the number and type of complaints about poor customer service.

Before Lang can open her store, she needs to apply to a local bank for a start-up loan. To do so, she must have a business plan that provides a full description of the business, including a complete operating budget for the first two years of operations. The budget must include a forecasted income statement, a forecasted statement of cash flows, and a forecasted balance sheet for both years.

Because Lang does not have a financial background, she consults a local accounting firm for help in developing her business plan. To provide relevant input for the plan, she has to determine the types of products she wants to sell; the volume of sales she anticipates; the selling price for each product; the monthly costs of leasing or purchasing facilities, employing personnel, and maintaining the facilities; and the number of display counters, storage units, and cash registers that she will need.

Performing Planning alone does not guarantee satisfactory operating results. Management must implement the business plan in ways that make optimal use of available resources in an ethical manner. Smooth operations require one or more of the following:

- Hiring and training personnel
- Matching human and technical resources to the work that must be done
- Purchasing or leasing facilities
- Maintaining an inventory of products for sale
- Identifying operating activities, or tasks, that minimize waste and improve the quality of products or services

FOCUS ON BUSINESS PRACTICE

What's Going on in the Grocery Business?

Sales at large supermarket chains, such as **Kroger**, **Safeway**, and **Albertson's**, have been flat and profits weak because both ends of their customer market are being squeezed. Large-scale retailers like **Wal-Mart** and **Costco** are attracting cost-conscious grocery shoppers, and upscale grocery customers are being lured to specialty grocers like **Trader Joe's** and **Whole Foods Market**. Albertson's strategy to combat its flat sales and profits was to sell itself to other retailers, like **Supervalu** and **CVS**, to form larger businesses. Other grocery chains are reconsidering their company's mission and strategic options by adding new products and services, such as walk-in medical clinics, closing stores and downsizing, or entering new geographic markets.[2]

FIGURE 18-2 The Supply Chain

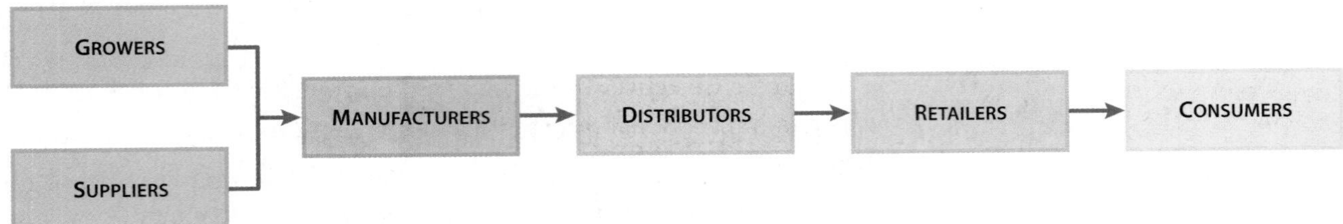

Managers execute the business plan by overseeing the company's daily operations. In small companies like Vanna Lang's, managers generally have frequent direct contact with their employees. They supervise them and interact with them to help them learn a task or improve their performance. In larger, more complex organizations, there is usually less direct contact between managers and employees. Instead of directly observing employees, managers in large companies like **Wal-Mart** monitor their employees' performance by measuring the time taken to complete an activity (such as how long it takes to process customer sales) or the frequency of an activity (such as the number of customers served per hour).

Critical to managing any retail business is a thorough understanding of their supply chain. As Figure 18-2 shows, the **supply chain** (also called the *supply network*) is the path that leads from the suppliers of the materials from which a product is made to the final consumer. In the supply chain for grocery stores, food and other items flow from growers and suppliers to manufacturers or distributors to retailers to consumers. The supply chain expresses the links between businesses—growers to vendors to the business to their customers.

EXAMPLE. Let's assume that Good Foods Store is now open for business. The budget prepared for the store's first two years of operation expresses in monetary terms how the business plan should be executed. Items that relate to the business plan appear in the budget and become authorizations for expenditures. They include such matters as spending on store fixtures, hiring employees, developing advertising campaigns, and pricing items for special sales. Lang's knowledge of her supply chain allows her to coordinate deliveries from local growers

The supply chain is the path that links producers to stores to the final consumer. In the supply chain for grocery stores, fruits and vegetables flow from growers and suppliers to manufacturers or distributors to retailers to consumers. The supply chain for this farmer's market is much shorter: grower to consumer.

Courtesy of Vasiliki/iStockphoto.

and international distributors so that she meets the demands of her customers without having too much or too little inventory on hand.

Evaluating When managers evaluate operating results, they compare the organization's actual performance with the performance levels they established in the planning stage. They earmark any significant variations for further analysis so that they can correct the problems. If the problems are the result of a change in the organization's operating environment, the managers may revise the original objectives. Ideally, the adjustments made in the evaluation stage will improve the company's performance.

EXAMPLE. To evaluate how well Good Foods Store is doing, Vanna Lang will compare the amounts estimated in the budget with actual results. If any differences appear, she will analyze why they have occurred. The reasons for these differences may lead Lang to change parts of her original business plan. In addition to reviewing employees' performance with regard to financial goals, such as avoiding waste, Lang will want to review how well her employees served customers. As noted earlier, she decided to monitor service quality by keeping a record of the number and type of complaints about poor customer service. Her review of this record may help her develop new and better strategies.

Communicating Whether accounting reports are prepared for internal or external use, they must provide accurate information and clearly communicate this information to the reader. Inaccurate or confusing internal reports can have a negative effect on a company's operations. Full disclosure and transparency in financial statements issued to external parties is a basic concept of generally accepted accounting principles, and violation of this principle can result in stiff penalties. After the reporting violations by **Enron**, **WorldCom**, and other companies, Congress passed legislation that requires the top management of companies that file financial statements with the Securities and Exchange Commission to certify that these statements are accurate. The penalty for issuing false public reports can be loss of compensation, fines, and jail time.

The key to producing accurate and useful internal and external reports whose meaning is transparent to the reader is to apply the four *w's*: why, who, what, and when.

- **Why?** Know the purpose of the report. Focus on it as you write.
- **Who?** Identify the audience for your report. Communicate at a level that matches your readers' understanding of the issue and their familiarity with accounting information. A detailed, informal report may be appropriate for

FOCUS ON BUSINESS PRACTICE

What Is Management's Responsibility for the Financial Statements?

Top-level managers have not only an ethical responsibility to ensure that the financial statements issued by their companies adhere to the principles of full disclosure and transparency; today, they have a legal responsibility as well. The Securities and Exchange Commission (SEC) requires the chief executive officers and chief financial officers of companies filing reports with the SEC to certify that those reports contain no untrue statements and include all facts needed to ensure that the reports are not misleading. In addition, the SEC requires managers to ensure that the information in reports filed with the SEC "is recorded, processed, summarized and reported on a timely basis."[3]

your manager, but a more concise summary may be necessary for other audiences, such as the president or board of directors of your organization.

- **What?** What information is needed, and what method of presentation is best? Select relevant information from reliable sources. You may draw information from pertinent documents or from interviews with knowledgeable managers and employees. The information should be not only relevant but also easy to read and understand. You may need to include visual aids, such as bar charts or graphs, to present the information clearly.
- **When?** Know the due date for the report. Strive to prepare an accurate report on a timely basis. If the report is urgently needed, you may have to sacrifice some accuracy in the interest of timeliness.

EXAMPLE. Assume that Vanna Lang has asked her company's accountant, Sal Chavez, to prepare financial statements and internal reports. In the financial statements that are prepared:

- The purpose—or *why*—is to report on the financial health of Good Foods Store.
- Lang, her bank and other creditors, and potential investors are the *who*.
- The *what* consists of disclosures about assets, liabilities, product costs, and sales.
- The required reporting deadline for the accounting period answers the question of *when*.

Lang will also want periodic internal reports on various aspects of her store's operations. For example, a monthly report may summarize the costs of ordering products from international distributors and the related shipping charges. If the costs in the monthly reports appear to be too high, she may ask for a special study. The results of such a study might result in a memorandum report like the one shown in Exhibit 18-1.

EXHIBIT 18-1 A Management Accounting Report

Memorandum

When: Today's Date

Who: To: V. Lang, Good Foods Store
From: Sal Chavez, Accountant

Why: Re: International Distributors Ordering and Shipping Costs—Analysis and Recommendations

What: As you requested, I have analyzed the ordering and shipping costs incurred when buying from international distributors. I found that during the past year, these costs were 9 percent of sales, or $36,000.

On average, we are placing about two orders per week, or eight orders per month. Placing each order requires about two and one-half hours of an employee's time. Further, the international distributors charge a service fee for each order, and shippers charge high rates for orders as small as ours.

My recommendations are (1) to reduce orders to four per month (the products' freshness will not be affected if we order at least once a week) and (2) to begin placing orders through the international distributors' websites (our international distributors do not charge a service fee for online orders). If we follow these recommendations, I project that the costs of receiving products will be reduced to 4 percent of sales, or $16,000, annually—a savings of $20,000.

In summary, management accounting can provide a constant stream of relevant information. Compare Lang's activities and information needs with the plan, perform, evaluate, and communicate steps of the management process. She started with a business plan, implemented the plan, and evaluated the results. Accounting information helped her develop her business plan, communicate that plan to her bank and employees, evaluate the performance of her employees, and report the results of operations. As you can see, accounting plays a critical role in managing the operations of any organization.

STOP & APPLY >

Indicate whether each of the following characteristics relates to management accounting (MA) or financial accounting (FA):

1. Focuses on various segments of the business entity
2. Demands objectivity
3. Relies on the criterion of usefulness rather than formal guidelines in reporting information
4. Measures units in historical dollars
5. Reports information on a regular basis
6. Uses only monetary measures for reports
7. Adheres to generally accepted accounting principles
8. Prepares reports whenever needed

SOLUTION

1. MA; 2. FA; 3. MA; 4. FA; 5. FA; 6. FA; 7. FA; 8. MA

Value Chain Analysis

LO2 Describe the value chain and its usefulness in analyzing a business.

Each step in the making of a product or the delivery of a service can be thought of as a link in a chain that adds value to the product or service. This concept of how a business fulfills its mission and objectives is known as the **value chain**. As shown in Figure 18-3, the steps that add value to a product or service—which range from research and development to customer service—are known as **primary processes**. The value chain also includes **support services**, such as legal services and management accounting. These services facilitate the primary processes but do not add value to the final product or service. Their roles are critical, however, to making the primary processes as efficient and effective as possible.

Primary Processes and Support Services

EXAMPLE. Let's assume that Good Foods Store has had some success, and Vanna Lang now wants to determine the feasibility of making and selling her own brand of candy. The primary processes that will add value to the new candy are as follows:

- ***Research and development:*** developing new and better products or services. Lang plans to add value by developing a candy that has less sugar content than similar confections.
- ***Design:*** creating improved and distinctive shapes, labels, or packages for products. For example, a package that is attractive and that describes the desirable features of Lang's new candy will add value to the product.

FIGURE 18-3 The Value Chain

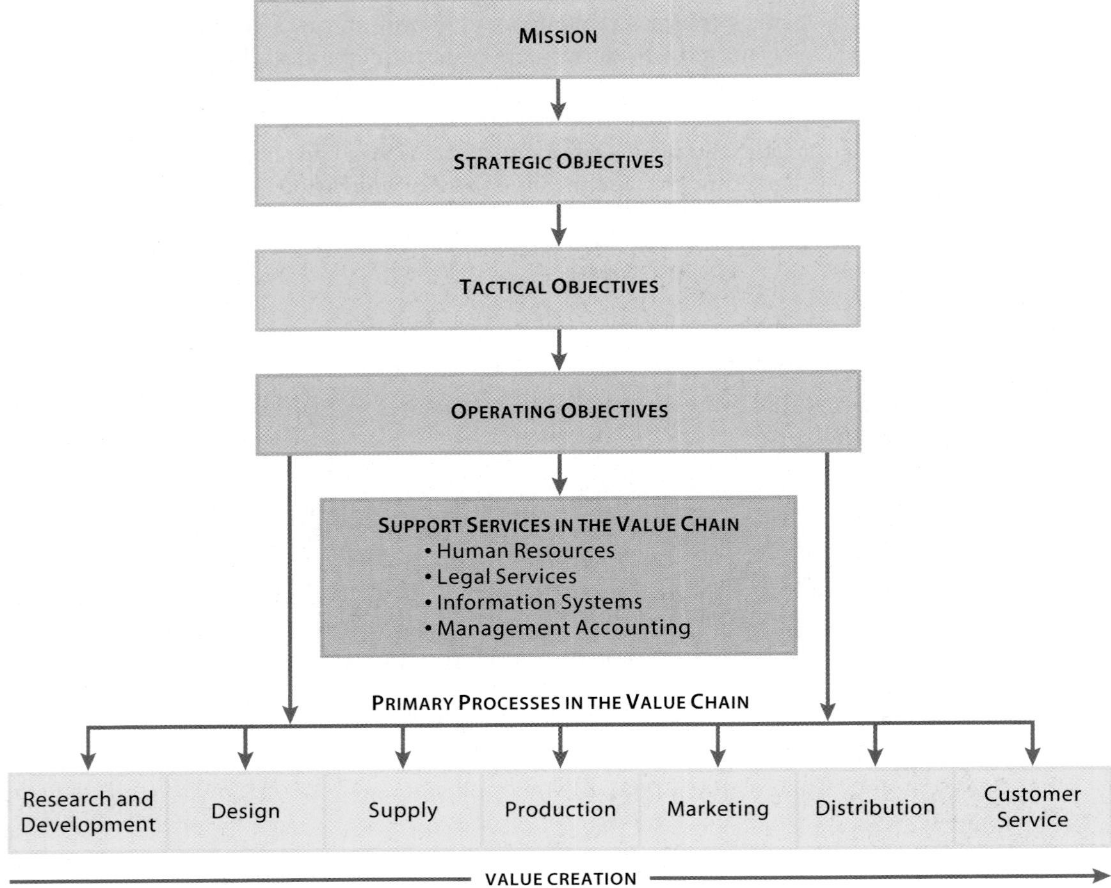

- ***Supply:*** purchasing materials for products or services. Lang will want to purchase high-quality sugar, chocolate, and other ingredients for the candy, as well as high-quality packaging.
- ***Production:*** manufacturing the product or service. To add value to the new candy, Lang will want to implement efficient manufacturing and packaging processes.
- ***Marketing:*** communicating information about the products or services and selling them. Attractive advertisements will facilitate sale of the new candy to customers.
- ***Distribution:*** delivering the product or service to the customer. Courteous and efficient service for in-store customers will add value to the product. Lang may also want to accommodate Internet customers by providing shipping.
- ***Customer service:*** following up with service after sales or providing warranty service. For example, Lang may offer free replacement of any candy that does not satisfy the customer. She could also use questionnaires to measure customer satisfaction.

The support services that provide the infrastructure for the primary processes are as follows:

- ***Human resources:*** hiring and training employees to carry out all the functions of the business. Lang will need to hire and train personnel to make the new candy.

- *Legal services:* maintaining and monitoring all contracts, agreements, obligations, and other relationships with outside parties. For example, Lang will want legal advice when applying for a trademark for the new candy's name and when signing contracts with suppliers.
- *Information systems:* establishing and maintaining technological means of controlling and communicating within the organization. Lang will want a computerized accounting system that keeps not only financial records but customer information as well.
- *Management accounting:* provides essential information in any business.

Advantages of Value Chain Analysis

Study Note

A company cannot succeed by trying to do everything at the highest level. It has to focus on its core competencies to give customers the best value.

An advantage of value chain analysis is that it allows a company to focus on its core competencies. A **core competency** is the thing that a company does best. It is what gives a company an advantage over its competitors. For example, **Wal-Mart** is known for having the lowest prices; that is its core competency.

A common result of value chain analysis is outsourcing, which can also be of benefit to a business. **Outsourcing** is the engagement of other companies to perform a process or service in the value chain that is not among an organization's core competencies. For instance, Wal-Mart outsources its inventory management to its vendors, who monitor and stock Wal-Mart's stores and warehouses.

Managers and Value Chain Analysis

In today's competitive global business environment, analysis of the value chain is critical to most companies' survival. Managers at Good Foods Store and other organizations must provide the highest value to customers at the lowest cost, and low cost often equates with the speed at which the primary processes of the value chain are executed. Time to market is very important.

Managers must also make the services that support the primary processes as efficient as possible. These services are essential and cannot be eliminated, but because they do not add value to the final product, they must be implemented as economically as possible. Businesses have been making progress in this area. For example, over the past ten years, the cost of the accounting function in many companies as a percentage of total revenue has declined from 6 percent to 2 percent. Technology has played a big role in making this economy possible.

EXAMPLE. To determine whether manufacturing and selling her own brand of candy will be profitable, Vanna Lang will need accurate information about the cost of the candy. She knows that if her candy is to be competitive, she cannot sell it for more than $10 per pound. Further, she has an idea of how much candy she can sell in the first year. Based on this information, her accountant, Sal Chavez, analyzes the value chain and projects the initial costs per pound shown in Exhibit 18-2. The total cost of $8 per pound worries Lang because with a selling price of $10, it leaves only $2, or 20 percent of revenue, to cover all the support services and provide a profit. Lang believes that if the enterprise is to be successful, this percentage, called the *margin,* must be at least 35 percent. Since the selling price is constrained by the competition, she must find a way to reduce costs.

- Option 1: Chavez tells her that the company could achieve a lower total cost per pound by selling a higher volume of candy, but that is not realistic for

EXHIBIT 18-2
Value Chain Analysis

Good Foods Store
Projected Costs of New Candy
June

Primary Process	Initial Costs per Pound	Revised Costs per Pound
Research and development	$0.25	$0.25
Design	0.10	0.10
Supply	1.10	0.60
Production	4.50	3.50
Marketing	0.50	0.50
Distribution	0.90	0.90
Customer service	0.65	0.65
Total cost	$8.00	$6.50

the new product. He also points out that the largest projected costs in the store's value chain are for supply and production. Because Lang plans to order ingredients from a number of suppliers, her orders would not be large enough to qualify for quantity discounts and savings on shipping. Using a single supplier could reduce the supply cost by $0.50 per unit.

- Option 2: Another way of reducing the cost of production would be to outsource this process to a candy manufacturer, whose high volume of products would allow it to produce the candy at a much lower cost than could be done at Good Foods Store. Outsourcing would reduce the production cost to $3.50 per unit. Thus, the total unit cost would be reduced to $6.50, as shown in Exhibit 18-2. This per unit cost would enable the company to sell the candy at a competitive $10 per pound and make the targeted margin of 35 percent ($3.50 ÷ $10.00).

This value chain analysis illustrates two important points. First, Good Food Store's mission is as a retailer. The company has no experience in making candy. Manufacturing candy would require a change in the company's mission and major changes in the way it does business.

Second, outsourcing portions of the value chain that are not part of a business's core competency is often the best business policy. Since Good Foods Store does not have a core competency in manufacturing candy, it would not be competitive in this field. Vanna Lang would be better off having an experienced candy manufacturer produce the candy according to her specifications and then selling the candy under her store's label. As Lang's business grows, increased volume may allow her to reconsider undertaking the manufacture of candy.

The following unit costs were determined by dividing the total costs of each component by the number of products produced. From these unit costs, determine the total cost per unit of primary processes and the total cost per unit of support services.

Research and development	$ 1.25
Human resources	1.35
Design	0.15
Supply	1.10
Legal services	0.40
Production	4.00
Marketing	0.80
Distribution	0.90
Customer service	0.65
Information systems	0.75
Management accounting	0.10
Total cost per unit	$11.45

SOLUTION

Primary Processes:	
Research and development	$1.25
Design	0.15
Supply	1.10
Production	4.00
Marketing	0.80
Distribution	0.90
Customer service	0.65
Total cost per unit	$8.85
Support Services:	
Human resources	$1.35
Legal services	0.40
Information systems	0.75
Management accounting	0.10
Total cost per unit	$2.60

Continuous Improvement

LO3 Identify the management tools used for continuous improvement.

Today managers in all parts of the world have ready access to international markets and to current information for informed decision making. As a result, global competition has increased significantly. One of the most valuable lessons gained from this increase in competition is that management cannot afford to become complacent. The concept of **continuous improvement** evolved to avoid such complacency. Organizations that adhere to continuous improvement are never satisfied with what is; they constantly seek improved quality and lower cost through better methods, products, services, processes, or resources. In response to this concept, several important management tools have emerged. These tools help companies remain competitive by focusing on continuous improvement of business methods.

Management Tools for Continuous Improvement

Among the management tools that companies use are the just-in-time operating philosophy, total quality management, activity-based management, and the theory of constraints.

Just-in-Time Operating Philosophy The **just-in-time (JIT) operating philosophy** requires that all resources—materials, personnel, and facilities—be acquired and used only when they are needed. Its objectives are to improve productivity and eliminate waste.

In a JIT environment, production processes are consolidated and workers are trained to be multiskilled so that they can operate several different machines. Materials and supplies are delivered just at the time they are needed in the production process, which significantly reduces inventories of materials. Production is usually started only when an order is received, and the ordered goods are shipped when completed, which reduces the inventories of finished goods.

When manufacturing companies adopt the JIT operating philosophy, the management system is called **lean production** since it reduces production time and costs, investment in materials inventory, and materials waste, and it results in higher-quality goods. Funds that are no longer invested in inventory can be redirected according to the goals of the company's business plan. JIT methods help retailers like **Wal-Mart** and manufacturers like **Harley-Davidson** assign more accurate costs to their products and identify the costs of waste and inefficient operation. Good Foods Store is considering following Wal-Mart's example, which requires vendors to restock inventory often and pays them only when the goods sell. This minimizes the funds invested in inventory and allows the retailer to focus on offering high-demand merchandise at attractive prices.

Total Quality Management **Total quality management (TQM)** requires that all parts of a business focus on quality. TQM's goal is the improved quality of products or services and the work environment. Workers are empowered to make operating decisions that improve quality in both areas. All employees are tasked to spot possible causes of poor quality, use resources efficiently and effectively to improve quality, and reduce the time needed to complete a task or provide a service.

TQM, like the JIT operating philosophy, focuses on improving product or service quality by identifying and reducing or eliminating the causes of waste. Like JIT, TQM results in reduced waste of materials, higher-quality goods, and lower production costs in manufacturing environments.

To determine the impact of poor quality on profits, TQM managers use accounting information about the **costs of quality**. The costs of quality include both the costs of achieving quality (such as training costs and inspection costs) and the costs of poor quality (such as the costs of rework and of handling customer complaints). Managers use information about the costs of quality:

- to relate their organization's business plan to its daily operating activities,
- to stimulate improvement by sharing this information with all employees,
- to identify opportunities for reducing costs and customer dissatisfaction, and
- to determine the costs of quality relative to net income.

For retailers like Wal-Mart and Good Foods Store, TQM results in a quality customer experience before, during, and after the sale.

Activity-Based Management **Activity-based management (ABM)** is an approach to managing an organization that identifies all major activities or tasks involved in making a product or service, determines the resources consumed by each of those activities and why the resources are used, and categorizes the activities as either adding value to a product or service or not adding value.

Activities that add value to a product or service, as perceived by the customer, are known as **value-adding activities**. All other activities are called

nonvalue-adding activities; they add cost to a product or service but do not increase its market value. ABM eliminates nonvalue-adding activities that do not support the organization; those that do support the organization are focal points for cost reduction. ABM results in reduced costs, reduced waste of resources, increased efficiency, and increased customer satisfaction.

ABM includes a management accounting practice called activity-based costing. **Activity-based costing (ABC)**:

- identifies all of an organization's major operating activities (both production and nonproduction),
- traces costs to those activities or cost pools, and
- assigns costs to the products or services that use the resources supplied by those activities.

The advantage to using ABC is that ABC produces more accurate costs than traditional cost allocation methods, which leads to improved decision making.

Theory of Constraints According to the **theory of constraints (TOC)**, limiting factors, or bottlenecks, occur during the production of any product or service, but once managers identify such a constraint, they can focus their attention and resources on it and achieve significant improvements. TOC thus helps managers set priorities for how they spend their time and resources. In identifying constraints, managers rely on the information that management accounting provides.

EXAMPLE. Suppose Vanna Lang wants to increase sales of store-roasted coffees. After reviewing management accounting reports, she concludes that the limited production capacity of her equipment—a roaster that can roast only 100 pounds of coffee beans per hour—limits the sales of the store's coffee. To overcome this constraint, she can rent or purchase a second roaster. The increase in production will enable her to increase coffee sales.

Achieving Continuous Improvement

JIT, TQM, ABM, and TOC all make a contribution to continuous improvement, as shown in Figure 18-4. In the just-in-time operating environment, management wages war on wasted time, wasted resources, and wasted space. All employees are encouraged to look for ways of improving processes and saving time. Total quality management focuses on improving the quality of the product or service and the work environment. It pursues continuous improvement by reducing the number of defective products and the time needed to complete a task or provide a service. Activity-based management seeks continuous improvement by emphasizing the ongoing reduction or elimination of nonvalue-adding activities. The theory of constraints helps managers focus resources on efforts that will produce the most effective improvements.

Each of these management tools can be used individually, or parts of them can be combined to create a new operating environment. They are applicable in service businesses, such as banking, as well as in manufacturing and retail businesses. By focusing attention on continuous improvement and fine-tuning of operations, they contribute to the same results in any organization:

- a reduction in product or service costs and delivery time,
- an improvement in the quality of the product or service, and
- an increase in customer satisfaction.

FIGURE 18-4 The Continuous Improvement Environment

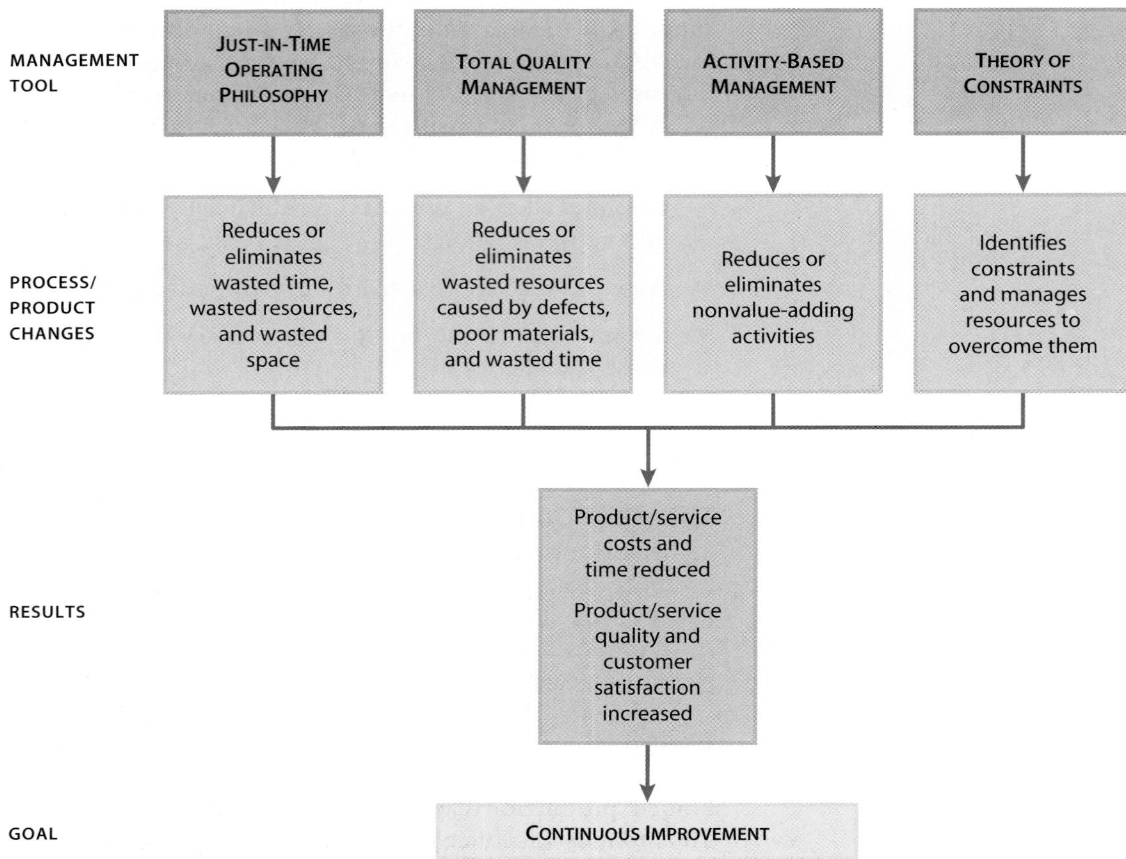

STOP & APPLY >

Recently, you dined with four chief financial officers (CFOs) who were attending a seminar on management tools and approaches to improving operations. During dinner, the CFOs shared information about their organizations' current operating environments. Excerpts from the dinner conversation appear below. Indicate whether each excerpt describes activity-based management (ABM), the just-in-time (JIT) operating philosophy, total quality management (TQM), or the theory of constraints (TOC).

CFO 1: We think quality can be achieved through carefully designed production processes. We focus on minimizing the time needed to move, store, queue, and inspect our materials and products. We've reduced inventories by purchasing and using materials only when they're needed.

CFO 2: Your approach is good. But we're more concerned with our total operating environment, so we have a strategy that asks all employees to contribute to the quality of both our products and our work environment. We focus on eliminating poor product quality by reducing waste and inefficiencies in our current operating methods.

CFO 3: Our organization has adopted a strategy for producing high-quality products that incorporates many of your approaches. We also want to manage our resources effectively, and we do it by monitoring operating activities. We analyze all activities to eliminate or reduce the ones that don't add value to products.

CFO 4: All of your approaches are good, but how do you set priorities for your management efforts? We find that we achieve the greatest improvements by focusing our time and resources on the bottlenecks in our production processes.

SOLUTION

CFO 1: JIT; CFO 2: TQM; CFO 3: ABM; CFO 4: TOC

Performance Measures: A Key to Achieving Organizational Objectives

LO4 Explain the balanced scorecard and its relationship to performance measures.

Performance measures are quantitative tools that gauge an organization's performance in relation to a specific goal or an expected outcome. Performance measures may be financial or nonfinancial.

- Financial performance measures include return on investment, net income as a percentage of sales, and the costs of poor quality as a percentage of sales. Such measures use monetary information to gauge the performance of a profit-generating organization or its segments—its divisions, departments, product lines, sales territories, or operating activities.
- Nonfinancial performance measures include the number of times an activity occurs or the time taken to perform a task. Examples are number of customer complaints, number of orders shipped the same day, and the time taken to fill an order. Such performance measures are useful in reducing or eliminating waste and inefficiencies in operating activities.

Using Performance Measures in the Management Process

Managers use performance measures in all stages of the management process.

- In the planning stage, they establish performance measures that will support the organization's mission and the objectives of its business plan, such as reducing costs and increasing quality, efficiency, timeliness, and customer satisfaction. As you will recall from earlier in the chapter, Vanna Lang selected the number of customer complaints as a performance measure to monitor the quality of service at Good Foods Store.
- As managers perform their duties, they use the performance measures they established in the planning stage to guide and motivate employees and to assign costs to products, departments, and operating activities. Vanna Lang will record the number of customer complaints during the year. She can group the information by type of complaint or by the employee involved in the service.
- When evaluating performance, managers use the information that performance measures have provided to analyze significant differences between actual and planned performance and to identify ways of improving performance. By comparing the actual and planned number of customer complaints, Lang can identify problem areas and develop solutions.

- When communicating with stakeholders, managers use information derived from performance measurement to report results and develop new budgets. If Lang needed formal reports, she could prepare performance evaluations based on this information.

The Balanced Scorecard

Study Note

The balanced scorecard focuses all perspectives of a business on accomplishing the business's mission.

If an organization is to achieve its mission and objectives, it must identify the areas in which it needs to excel and establish measures of performance in these critical areas. As we have indicated, effective performance measurement requires an approach that uses both financial and nonfinancial measures that are tied to a company's mission and objectives. One such approach that has gained wide acceptance is the balanced scorecard.

The **balanced scorecard** is a framework that links the perspectives of an organization's four stakeholder groups to the organization's mission, objectives, resources, and performance measures. The four stakeholder groups are as follows:

Study Note

The balanced scorecard provides a way of linking the lead performance indicators of employees, internal business processes, and customer needs to the lag performance indicator of external financial results. In other words, if managers can foster excellent performance for three of the stakeholder groups, good financial results will occur for the investor stakeholder group.

- Stakeholders with a financial perspective (owners, investors, and creditors) value improvements in financial measures, such as net income and return on investment.
- Stakeholders with a learning and growth perspective (employees) value high wages, job satisfaction, and opportunities to fulfill their potential.
- Stakeholders who focus on the business's internal processes value the safe and cost-effective production of high-quality products.
- Stakeholders with a customer perspective value high-quality products that are low in cost.

Although their perspectives differ, these stakeholder groups may be interested in the same measurable performance goals. For example, holders of both the customer and internal business processes perspectives are interested in performance that results in high-quality products.

EXAMPLE. Figure 18-5 applies the balanced scorecard to Good Foods Store. The company's mission is to be the food store of choice in the community. This mission is at the center of the company's balanced scorecard. Surrounding it are the four interrelated perspectives.

- ***Learning and Growth:*** At the base of the scorecard is the learning and growth perspective. Here, part of the objective, or performance goal, is to provide courteous service. Because training employees in customer service should result in courteous service, performance related to this objective can be measured in terms of how many employees have received training. The number of customer complaints is another measure of courteous service.
- ***Internal Business Processes:*** From the perspective of internal business processes, the objective is to help achieve the company's mission by managing the supply chain efficiently, which should contribute to customer satisfaction. Efficiency in the ordering process can be measured by recording the number of orders placed with distributors each month and the number of times per month that customers ask for items that are not in stock.
- ***Customer:*** If the objectives of the learning and growth and internal business processes perspectives are met, this should result in attracting customers and

FIGURE 18-5 The Balanced Scorecard for Good Foods Store

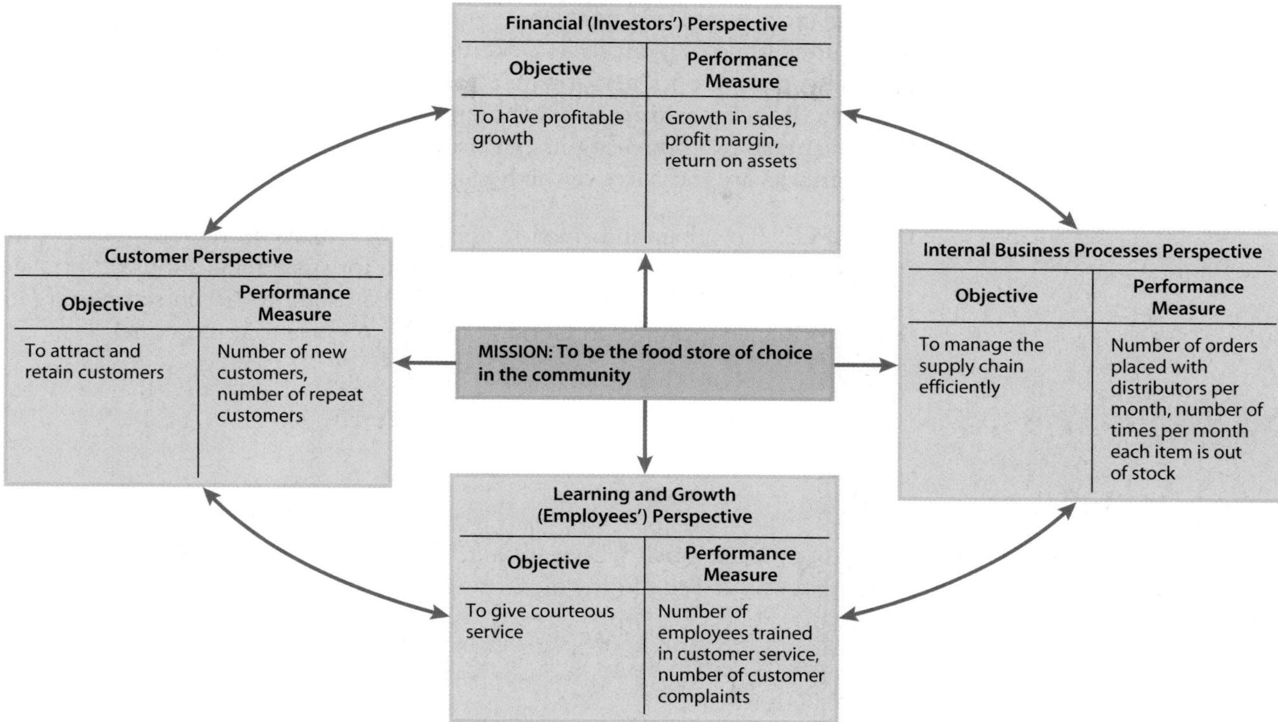

Source: Adapted from Robert S. Kaplan and David P. Norton, "The Balanced Scorecard: Measures That Drive Performance," Harvard Business Review, July–August 2005.

retaining them, which is the objective of the customer perspective. Performance related to this objective is measured by tracking the number of new customers and the number of repeat customers.

- ***Financial:*** Satisfied customers should help achieve the objective of the financial perspective, which is profitable growth. Profitable growth is measured by growth in sales, profit margin, and return on assets.

FOCUS ON BUSINESS PRACTICE

How Does the Balanced Scorecard Measure Success at Futura Industries?

Futura Industries is not a famous company, but it is one of the best. Based in Utah, it is rated as that state's top privately owned employer and serves a high-end niche in such diverse markets as floor coverings, electronics, transportation, and shower doors. In achieving its success, Futura uses the balanced scorecard. Futura has developed the following performance measures:

- Employee turnover is a measure of learning and growth.
- Percentage of sales from new products and total production cost per standard hour are measures of the company's internal processes.
- Number of customers' complaints and percentage of materials returned are the measures of customer satisfaction.
- Income and gross margin are among the measures of financial performance.[4]

Benchmarking

The balanced scorecard enables a company to determine whether it is making continuous improvement in its operations. But to ensure its success, a company must also compare its performance with that of similar companies in the same industry. **Benchmarking** is a technique for determining a company's competitive advantage by comparing its performance with that of its closest competitors. **Benchmarks** are measures of the best practices in an industry.

EXAMPLE. To obtain information about benchmarks in the retail grocery industry, Vanna Lang might join a trade association for small retail shops or food stores. Information about these benchmarks would be useful to her in setting targets for the performance measures in Good Foods Store's balanced scorecard.

STOP & APPLY >

Connie's Takeout caters to young professionals who want a good meal at home but do not have time to prepare it. Connie's has developed the following business objectives:

1. To provide fast, courteous service
2. To manage the inventory of food carefully
3. To have repeat customers
4. To be profitable and grow

Connie's has also developed the following performance measures:

5. Growth in revenues per quarter and net income
6. Average unsold food at the end of the business day as a percentage of the total food purchased that day
7. Average customer time at the counter before being waited on
8. Percentage of customers who have shopped in the store before

Match each of these objectives and performance measures with the four perspectives of the balanced scorecard: financial perspective, learning and growth perspective, internal business processes perspective, and customer perspective.

SOLUTION

Financial perspective: 4, 5; learning and growth perspective: 1, 7; internal business processes perspective: 2, 6; customer perspective: 3, 8

Standards of Ethical Conduct

LO5 Identify the standards of ethical conduct for management accountants.

Managers balance the interests of external parties (e.g., customers, owners, suppliers, governmental agencies, and the local community) when they make decisions about the proper use of organizational resources and the financial reporting of their actions. When ethical conflicts arise, management accountants have a responsibility to help managers balance those interests.

To be viewed credibly by the various parties who rely on the information they provide, management accountants must adhere to the highest standards of performance. To provide guidance, the Institute of Management Accountants has issued standards of ethical conduct for practitioners of management accounting and financial management. Those standards, presented in Exhibit 18-3, emphasize that management accountants have responsibilities in the areas of competence, confidentiality, integrity, and credibility.

EXHIBIT 18-3 Statement of Ethical Professional Practice

Members of IMA shall behave ethically. A commitment to ethical professional practice includes: overarching principles that express our values, and standards that guide our conduct.

PRINCIPLES

IMA's overarching ethical principles include: Honesty, Fairness, Objectivity, and Responsibility. Members shall act in accordance with these principles and shall encourage others within their organizations to adhere to them.

STANDARDS

A member's failure to comply with the following standards may result in disciplinary action.

I. COMPETENCE

Each member has a responsibility to:

1. Maintain an appropriate level of professional expertise by continually developing knowledge and skills.
2. Perform professional duties in accordance with relevant laws, regulations, and technical standards.
3. Provide decision support information and recommendations that are accurate, clear, concise, and timely.
4. Recognize and communicate professional limitations or other constraints that would preclude responsible judgment or successful performance of an activity.

II. CONFIDENTIALITY

Each member has a responsibility to:

1. Keep information confidential except when disclosure is authorized or legally required.
2. Inform all relevant parties regarding appropriate use of confidential information. Monitor subordinates' activities to ensure compliance.
3. Refrain from using confidential information for unethical or illegal advantage.

III. INTEGRITY

Each member has a responsibility to:

1. Mitigate actual conflicts of interest. Regularly communicate with business associates to avoid apparent conflicts of interest. Advise all parties of any potential conflicts.
2. Refrain from engaging in any conduct that would prejudice carrying out duties ethically.
3. Abstain from engaging in or supporting any activity that might discredit the profession.

IV. CREDIBILITY

Each member has a responsibility to:

1. Communicate information fairly and objectively.
2. Disclose all relevant information that could reasonably be expected to influence an intended user's understanding of the reports, analyses, or recommendations.
3. Disclose delays or deficiencies in information, timeliness, processing, or internal controls in conformance with organization policy and/or applicable law.

RESOLUTION OF ETHICAL CONFLICT

In applying the Standards of Ethical Professional Practice, you may encounter problems identifying unethical behavior or resolving an ethical conflict. When faced with ethical issues, you should follow your organization's established policies on the resolution of such conflict. If these policies do not resolve the ethical conflict, you should consider the following courses of action:

Discuss the issue with your immediate supervisor except when it appears that the supervisor is involved. In that case, present the issue to the next level. If you cannot achieve a satisfactory resolution, submit the issue to the next management level. If your immediate superior is the chief executive officer or equivalent, the acceptable reviewing authority may be a group such as the audit committee, executive committee, board of directors, board of trustees, or owners. Contact with levels above the immediate superior should be initiated only with your superior's knowledge, assuming he or she is not involved. Communication of such problems to authorities or individuals not employed or engaged by the organization is not considered appropriate, unless you believe there is a clear violation of the law.

Clarify relevant ethical issues by initiating a confidential discussion with an IMA Ethics Counselor or other impartial advisor to obtain a better understanding of possible courses of action.

Consult your own attorney as to legal obligations and rights concerning the ethical conflict.

Source: *IMA Statement of Ethical Professional Practice,* Institute of Management Accountants, www.imanet.org. Reprinted by permission.

FOCUS ON BUSINESS PRACTICE

How to Blow the Whistle on Fraud

According to **PricewaterhouseCoopers**'s fourth biennial survey of more than 5,400 companies in 40 countries, eradicating fraud is extremely difficult. Despite increased attention to fraud detection systems and stronger internal controls, half of the companies interviewed had fallen victim to some type of fraud in the previous two years. The average cost of the fraud was about $3.2 million per company. Fraud appeared most likely to happen in Africa, North America, and Central-Eastern Europe.

The Sarbanes-Oxley Act of 2002 requires that all publicly traded companies have an anonymous incident reporting system. Such a system can help prevent fraud, as can hotlines that provide guidance on ethical dilemmas involved in reporting fraud. An example of such an ethics hotline is the one that the Institute of Management Accountants instituted in 2002. However, PricewaterhouseCoopers's study found that the best fraud deterrents were a company-wide risk management system with a continuous proactive fraud-monitoring component and a strong ethical culture to which all employees subscribe.[5]

& APPLY >

Rank in order of importance the management accountant's four areas of responsibility: competence, confidentiality, integrity, and credibility. Explain the reasons for your ranking.

SOLUTION

Rankings will vary depending on the reasoning used concerning the four areas of responsibility. Ranking differences between individuals also reinforces the fact that we approach ethical behavior in a variety of ways and why a code of ethics is necessary.

▸ GOOD FOODS STORE: REVIEW PROBLEM

The Decision Point at the beginning of this chapter focused on Good Foods Store, a company whose mission is to attract upscale customers and retain them by selling high-quality foods and providing excellent service in a pleasant atmosphere. It posed these questions:

- What is Good Foods Store's strategic plan?
- What management accounting tools does the company use to stay ahead of its competitors?
- What role does management accounting play in Good Foods Store's endeavors?

Supply Chain and Value Chain Analysis
LO2

Good Foods Store's strategic plan focuses on achieving the company's objective of being the upscale retailer of choice for the foods and services it offers. This strategy drives the way Good Foods Store's managers address stakeholder perspectives, as well as how they formulate tactical and operating plans. To stay agile, flexible, and ahead of its competitors, Good Foods Store uses management tools like supply and value chains to standardize requirements and procedures to ensure a high-quality shopping experience.

Management accounting provides the information necessary for effective decision making. Good Foods Store's managers use management accounting information

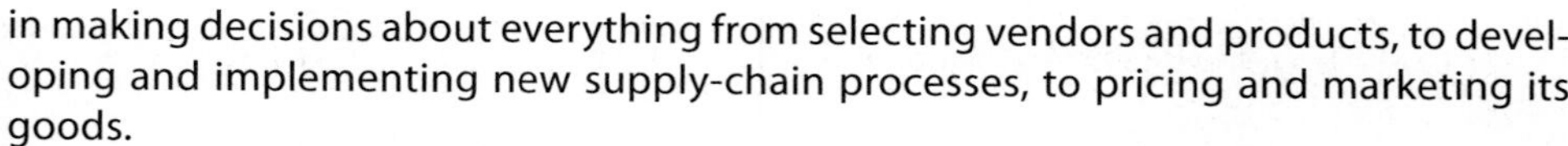

in making decisions about everything from selecting vendors and products, to developing and implementing new supply-chain processes, to pricing and marketing its goods.

Management accounting also provides Good Foods Store managers with objective data that they can use to measure the company's performance in terms of its key success factor—quality. Among the management accounting tools used are budgets, which set daily operating goals and provide targets for evaluating the store's performance. As Good Foods Store strives to improve its sales, earnings per share, and profitability, it will continue to rely on the information that management accounting provides.

As a convenience to customers, Good Foods Store wants to sell a variety of generic prescription drugs for $ 4.00 for a 30-day supply. To do so, Good Foods Store cannot pay its vendor, Medicine for All, more than $2.00 for a 30-day supply. Managers at Medicine for All and the Good Foods Store work together to analyze their value chains and supply chain to determine if the total cost of primary processes per 30-day supply can be reduced to less than $1.60. If it can, then the Good Foods Store deal is acceptable. A joint study by the management accountants has determined the following current per unit costs for primary processes:

Primary Process	**Cost per Unit**
Research and development	$0.50
Design	0.25
Supply	0.35
Production	0.50
Advertising and marketing	0.55
Distribution	0.20
Customer service	0.05
Total cost	$2.40

After analyzing operations, management at both companies believe the following proposals for cost reduction of primary processes are possible:

- Research and development and design are critical functions because the market and competition require constant development of new, safe packaging features and higher quality at lower cost. Nevertheless, management feels that the cost of these processes must be reduced by 20 percent.
- Five different suppliers currently provide the components for the generic medicines. Ordering these components from just two suppliers and negotiating lower prices could result in a savings of 30 percent.
- The generic drugs are currently manufactured in Mexico. By shifting production to China, the unit cost of production can be lowered by 40 percent.
- Management believes that by working with Good Foods Store they can cut their advertising and marketing budgets by 70 percent.
- Distribution costs are already very low, but management will set a target of reducing the cost by 10 percent.
- Customer support and service has been a weakness of the company and has resulted in lost sales. Management therefore proposes increasing the cost per unit of customer support to Good Foods Store by 50 percent.

Required

1. Prepare a table showing Medicine for All's current cost of primary processes and the projected cost per 30-days' supply based on management's proposals for cost reduction.

2. Will management's proposals for cost reduction achieve the targeted total cost of less than $1.60 per 30-day supply?

3. Manager insight: What are the company's support services? What role should these services play in the value chain analysis?

Answers to Review Problem

1.

	Current Cost per 30-Day Supply	Percentage (Decrease) Increase	Projected Cost per 30-Day Supply*
Research and development	$0.50	(20%)	$0.400
Design	0.25	(20%)	0.200
Supply	0.35	(30%)	0.245
Production	0.50	(40%)	0.300
Advertising and marketing	0.55	(70%)	0.165
Distribution	0.20	(10%)	0.180
Customer service	0.05	50%	0.075
Total	$2.40		$1.565

*Computations: $0.50 × (100% − 20%) = $0.40; $0.25 × (100% − 20%) = $0.20; $0.35 × (100% − 30%) = $0.245; $0.50 × (100% − 40%) = $0.30; $0.55 × (100% − 70%) = $0.165; $0.20 × (100% − 10%) = $0.18; and $0.05 × (100% + 50%) = $0.075.

2. Yes, $1.565 is lower than $1.60. Medicine for All and Good Foods Store have a mutually beneficial deal.

3. The support services are human resources, legal services, information systems, and management accounting. The analysis has not mentioned these services, which are necessary but do not provide direct value to the final product. Management should analyze these functions carefully to see if they can be reduced.

LO1 Distinguish management accounting from financial accounting and explain how management accounting supports the management process.

Management accounting involves partnering with management in decision making, devising planning and performance management systems, and providing expertise in financial reporting and control to assist management in the formulation and implementation of an organization's strategy.

Management accounting reports provide information for planning, control, performance measurement, and decision making to managers and employees when they need such information. These reports have a flexible format; they can present either historical or future-oriented information expressed in dollar amounts or physical measures. In contrast, financial accounting reports provide information about an organization's past performance to owners, lenders, customers, and governmental agencies on a periodic basis. Financial accounting reports follow strict guidelines defined by generally accepted accounting principles.

Management accounting supports each stage of the management process. When managers plan, they work with management accounting to establish strategic, tactical, and operating objectives that reflect their company's mission and to formulate a comprehensive business plan for achieving those objectives. The plan is usually expressed in financial terms in the form of budgets. When managers implement the plan, they use the information provided in the budgets to manage the business in the context of its supply chain. In evaluating performance, managers compare actual performance with planned performance and take steps to correct any problems. Reports reflect the results of planning, executing, and evaluating operations and may be prepared for external or internal use.

LO2 Describe the value chain and its usefulness in analyzing a business.

The value chain conceives of each step in the production of a product or the delivery of a service as a link in a chain that adds value to the product or service. These value-adding steps—research and development, design, supply, production, marketing, distribution, and customer service—are known as primary processes. The value chain also includes support services—human resources, legal services, information services, and management accounting. Support services facilitate the primary processes but do not add value to the final product. Value chain analysis enables a company to focus on its core competencies. Parts of the value chain that are not core competencies are frequently outsourced.

LO3 Identify the management tools used for continuous improvement.

Management tools for continuous improvement include the just-in-time (JIT) operating philosophy, total quality management (TQM), activity-based management (ABM), and the theory of constraints (TOC). These tools are designed to help businesses meet the demands of global competition by reducing resource waste and costs and by improving product or service quality, thereby increasing customer satisfaction.

Management accounting responds to a just-in-time operating environment by providing an information system that is sensitive to changes in production processes. In a total quality management environment, management accounting provides information about the costs of quality. Activity-based management's assignment of overhead costs to products or services relies on the accounting practice known as activity-based costing (ABC). In businesses that use the theory of constraints, management accounting identifies process or product constraints.

LO4 Explain the balanced scorecard and its relationship to performance measures. The balanced scorecard links the perspectives of an organization's stakeholder groups—financial (investors and owners), learning and growth (employees), internal business processes, and customers—to the organization's mission, objectives, resources, and performance measures. Performance measures are used to assess whether the objectives of each of the four perspectives are being met. Benchmarking is a technique for determining a company's competitive advantage by comparing its performance with that of its industry peers.

LO5 Identify the standards of ethical conduct for management accountants. The Statement of Ethical Professional Practice emphasizes the Institute of Management Accounting members' responsibilities in the areas of competence, confidentiality, integrity, and credibility. These standards of conduct help management accountants recognize and avoid situations that could compromise their ability to supply management with accurate and relevant information.

REVIEW of Concepts and Terminology

The following concepts and terms were introduced in this chapter:

Activity-based costing (ABC) 809 (LO3)

Activity-based management (ABM) 808 (LO3)

Balanced scorecard 812 (LO4)

Benchmarking 814 (LO4)

Benchmarks 814 (LO4)

Business plan 798 (LO1)

Continuous improvement 807 (LO3)

Core competency 805 (LO2)

Costs of quality 808 (LO3)

Just-in-time (JIT) operating philosophy 808 (LO3)

Lean production 808 (LO3)

Management accounting 796 (LO1)

Mission statement 797 (LO1)

Nonvalue-adding activities 809 (LO3)

Operating objectives 798 (LO1)

Outsourcing 805 (LO2)

Performance measures 811 (LO4)

Primary processes 803 (LO2)

Strategic objectives 798 (LO1)

Supply chain 800 (LO1)

Support services 803 (LO2)

Tactical objectives 798 (LO1)

Theory of constraints (TOC) 809 (LO3)

Total quality management (TQM) 808 (LO3)

Value-adding activities 808 (LO3)

Value chain 803 (LO2)

CHAPTER ASSIGNMENTS

BUILDING Your Basic Knowledge and Skills

Short Exercises

LO1 **Management Accounting Versus Financial Accounting**

SE 1. Management accounting differs from financial accounting in a number of ways. Indicate whether each of the following characteristics relates to management accounting (MA) or financial accounting (FA):

1. Publically reported
2. Forward looking
3. Usually confidential
4. Complies with accounting standards
5. Reports past performance
6. Uses physical measures as well as monetary ones for reports
7. Focus on business decision making
8. Driven by user needs

LO1 **Strategic Positioning**

SE 2. Organizations stake out different strategic positions to add value and achieve success. Some strive to be low-cost leaders like **Wal-Mart**, while others become the high-end quality leaders like **Whole Foods Market**. Identify which of the following organizations are low-cost leaders (C) and which are quality leaders (Q):

1. Tiffany & Co.
2. Yale University
3. Local community college
4. Lexus
5. Kia
6. Rent-a-Wreck
7. Hertz Rental Cars
8. Pepsi-Cola
9. Store-brand soda

LO1 **The Management Process**

SE 3. Indicate whether each of the following management activities in a department store is part of planning (PL), performing (PE), evaluating (E), or communicating (C):

1. Completing a balance sheet and income statement at the end of the year
2. Training a clerk to complete a cash sale
3. Meeting with department managers to develop performance measures for sales personnel
4. Renting a local warehouse to store excess inventory of clothing
5. Evaluating the performance of the shoe department by examining the significant differences between its actual and planned expenses for the month
6. Preparing an annual budget of anticipated sales for each department and the entire store

LO1 **Report Preparation**

SE 4. Molly Metz, president of Metz Industries, asked controller Rick Caputo to prepare a report on the use of electricity by each of the organization's five divisions. Increases in electricity costs in the divisions ranged from 20 to 35 percent over the past year. What questions should Rick ask before he begins his analysis?

LO1 LO2 **The Supply Chain and the Value Chain**

SE 5. Indicate whether each of the following is part of the supply chain (SC), a primary process (PP) in the value chain, or a support service (SS) in the value chain:

1. Human resources
2. Research and development
3. Supplier
4. Management accounting
5. Customer service
6. Retailer

LO2 **The Value Chain**

SE 6. The following unit costs were determined by dividing the total costs of each component by the number of products produced. From these unit costs, determine the total cost per unit of primary processes and the total cost per unit of support services.

Research and development	$ 1.40
Human resources	1.45
Design	0.15
Supply	1.10
Legal services	0.50
Production	4.00
Marketing	0.80
Distribution	0.90
Customer service	0.65
Information systems	0.85
Management accounting	0.20
Total cost per unit	$12.00

LO3 **JIT and Continuous Improvement**

SE 7. The just-in-time operating environment focuses on reducing or eliminating the waste of resources. Resources include physical assets such as machinery and buildings, labor time, and materials and parts used in the production process. Choose one of those resources and describe how it could be wasted. How can an organization prevent the waste of that resource? How can the concept of continuous improvement be implemented to reduce the waste of that resource?

LO3 **TQM and Value**

SE 8. DUDs Dry Cleaners recently adopted total quality management. Dee Mathias, the owner, has hired you as a consultant. Classify each of the following activities as either value-adding (V) or nonvalue-adding (NV):

1. Providing same-day service
2. Closing the store on weekends
3. Providing free delivery service
4. Having a seamstress on site
5. Making customers pay for parking

LO4 **The Balanced Scorecard: Stakeholder Values**

SE 9. In the balanced scorecard approach, stakeholder groups with different perspectives value different performance goals. Sometimes, however, they may be interested in the same goal. Indicate which stakeholder groups—financial (F), learning and growth (L), internal business processes (P), and customers (C)—value the following performance goals:

1. High wages
2. Safe products

3. Low-priced products
4. Improved return on investment
5. Job security
6. Cost-effective production processes

LO5 **Ethical Conduct**

SE 10. Topher Sones, a management accountant for Beauty Cosmetics Company, has lunch every day with his friend Joel Saikle, who is a management accountant for Glowy Cosmetics, Inc., a competitor of Beauty Cosmetics. Last week, Topher couldn't decide how to treat some information in a report he was preparing, so he discussed it with Joel. Is Topher adhering to the ethical standards of management accountants? Defend your answer.

Exercises

LO1 **Management Accounting Versus Financial Accounting**

E 1. Explain this statement: "It is impossible to distinguish the point at which financial accounting ends and management accounting begins."

LO1 **Management Accounting**

E 2. In 1982, the IMA defined management accounting as follows:

> The process of identification, measurement, accumulation, analysis, preparation, interpretation, and communication of financial information used by management to plan, evaluate, and control within the organization and to assure appropriate use of and accountability for its resources.[6]

Compare this definition with the updated one that appears in LO 1. How has the emphasis changed?

LO1 **The Management Process**

E 3. Indicate whether each of the following management activities in a community hospital is part of planning (PL), performing (PE), evaluating (E), or communicating (C):

1. Leasing five ambulances for the current year
2. Comparing the actual number with the planned number of patient days in the hospital for the year
3. Developing a strategic plan for a new pediatric wing
4. Preparing a report showing the past performance of the emergency room
5. Developing standards, or expectations, for performance in the hospital admittance area for next year
6. Preparing the hospital's balance sheet and income statement and distributing them to the board of directors
7. Maintaining an inventory of bed linens and bath towels
8. Formulating a corporate policy for the treatment and final disposition of hazardous waste materials
9. Preparing a report on the types and amounts of hazardous waste materials removed from the hospital in the last three months
10. Recording the time taken to deliver food trays to patients

LO1 **Report Preparation**

E 4. John Jefferson is the sales manager for Sunny Greeting Cards, Inc. At the beginning of the year, the organization introduced a new line of humorous birthday cards to the U.S. market. Management held a strategic planning meeting on August 31 to discuss next year's operating activities. One item on the agenda was to review the success of the new line of cards and decide if there was a need to change the selling price or to stimulate sales volume in the five sales territories. Jefferson was asked to prepare a report addressing those issues and to present it at the meeting. His report was to include the profits generated in each sales territory by the new card line only.

On August 31, Jefferson arrived at the meeting late and immediately distributed his report to the strategic planning team. The report consisted of comments made by seven of Jefferson's leading sales representatives. The comments were broad in scope and touched only lightly on the success of the new card line. Jefferson was pleased that he had met the deadline for distributing the report, but the other team members were disappointed in the information he provided.

Using the four *w's* for report presentation, comment on Jefferson's effectiveness in preparing his report.

LO1 The Supply Chain

E 5. In recent years, **United Parcel Service (UPS)** (www.ups-scs.com/solutions/casestudies.html) has been positioning itself as a solver of supply-chain issues. Visit its website and read one of the case studies related to its supply-chain solutions. Explain how UPS helped improve the supply chain of the business featured in the case.

LO1 The Planning Framework

E 6. Edward Ortez has just opened a company that imports fine ceramic gifts from Mexico and sells them over the Internet. In planning his business, Ortez did the following:

1. Listed his expected expenses and revenues for the first six months of operations
2. Decided that he wanted the company to provide him with income for a good lifestyle and funds for retirement
3. Determined that he would keep his expenses low and generate enough revenues during the first two months of operations so that he would have a positive cash flow by the third month
4. Decided to focus his business on providing customers with the finest Mexican ceramics at a favorable price
5. Developed a complete list of goals, objectives, procedures, and policies relating to how he would find, buy, store, sell, and ship goods and collect payment
6. Decided not to have a retail operation but to rely solely on the Internet to market the products
7. Decided to expand his website to include ceramics from other Central American countries over the next five years

Match each of Ortez's actions to the components of the planning framework: goal, mission, strategic objectives, tactical objectives, operating objectives, business plan, and budget.

LO2 The Value Chain

E 7. As mentioned in **E 6,** Edward Ortez recently opened his own company. He has been thinking of ways to improve the business. Here is a list of the actions that he will be undertaking:

1. Engaging an accountant to help analyze progress in meeting the objectives of the company
2. Hiring a company to handle payroll records and employee benefits
3. Developing a logo for labeling and packaging the ceramics
4. Making gift packages by placing gourmet food products in ceramic pots and wrapping them in plastic
5. Engaging an attorney to write contracts
6. Traveling to Mexico himself to arrange for the purchase of products and their shipment back to the company

7. Arranging new ways of taking orders over the Internet and shipping the products
8. Keeping track of the characteristics of customers and the number and types of products they buy
9. Following up with customers to see if they received the products and if they are happy with them
10. Arranging for an outside firm to keep the accounting records
11. Distributing brochures that display the ceramics and refer to the website

Classify each of Ortez's actions as one of the value chain's primary processes—research and development, design, supply, production, marketing, distribution, or customer service—or as a support service—human resources, legal services, information systems, or management accounting. Of the 11 actions, which are the most likely candidates for outsourcing? Why?

LO1 LO2 **The Supply Chain and Value Chain**

E 8. The items in the following list are associated with a hotel. Indicate which are part of the supply chain (S) and which are part of the value chain (V).

1. Travel agency
2. Housekeeping supplies
3. Special events and promotions
4. Customer service
5. Travel bureau website
6. Tour agencies

LO1 LO3 **Management Reports**

E 9. The reports that follow are from a grocery store. Which report would be used for financial purposes, and which would be used for activity-based decision making? Why?

Salaries	$ 1,000	Scan grocery purchases	$ 3,000
Equipment	2,200	Stock fruit	1,000
Freight	5,000	Bake rye bread	500
Supplies	800	Operate salad bar	2,500
Use and occupancy	1,000	Stock can goods	2,000
		Collapse cardboard boxes	1,000
Total	$10,000	Total	$10,000

LO2 **The Value Chain**

E 10. As shown in the data that follow, a producer of ceiling fans has determined the unit cost of its most popular model. From these unit costs, determine the total cost per unit of primary processes and the total cost per unit of support services.

Research and development	$ 5.00
Human resources	4.50
Design	1.50
Supply	1.00
Legal services	0.50
Production	4.50
Marketing	2.00
Distribution	2.50
Customer service	6.50
Information systems	1.80
Management accounting	0.20
Total cost per unit	$30.00

LO3 Comparison of ABM and JIT

E 11. The following are excerpts from a conversation between two managers about their companies' management systems. Identify the manager who works for a company that emphasizes ABM and the one who works for a company that emphasizes a JIT system.

Manager 1: We try to manage our resources effectively by monitoring operating activities. We analyze all major operating activities, and we focus on reducing or eliminating the ones that don't add value to our products.

Manager 2: We're very concerned with eliminating waste. We've designed our operations to reduce the time it takes to move, store, queue, and inspect materials. We've also reduced our inventories by buying and using materials only when we need them.

LO4 The Balanced Scorecard

E 12. Tim's Bargain Basement sells used goods at very low prices. Tim has developed the following business objectives:

1. To buy only the inventory that sells
2. To have repeat customers
3. To be profitable and grow
4. To keep employee turnover low

Tim also developed the following performance measures:

5. Growth in revenues and net income per quarter
6. Average unsold goods at the end of the business day as a percentage of the total goods purchased that day
7. Number of unemployment claims
8. Percentage of customers who have shopped in the store before

Match each of these objectives and performance measures with the four perspectives of the balanced scorecard: financial perspective, learning and growth perspective, internal business processes perspective, and customer perspective.

LO4 The Balanced Scorecard

E 13. Your college's overall goal is to add value to the communities it serves. In light of that goal, match each of the following stakeholders' perspectives with the appropriate objective:

Perspective	Objective
1. Financial (investors)	a. Adding value means that the faculty engages in meaningful teaching and research.
2. Learning and growth (employees)	b. Adding value means that students receive their degrees in four years.
3. Internal business processes	c. Adding value means that the college has winning sports teams.
4. Customers	d. Adding value means that fund-raising campaigns are successful.

LO5 Ethical Conduct

E 14. Katrina Storm went to work for NOLA Industries five years ago. She was recently promoted to cost accounting manager and now has a new boss, Vickery

Howe, the corporate controller. Last week, Storm and Howe went to a two-day professional development program on international accounting standards changes. During the first hour of the first day's program, Howe disappeared and Storm didn't see her again until the cocktail hour. The same thing happened on the second day. During the trip home, Storm asked Howe if she had enjoyed the conference. She replied: "Katrina, the golf course was excellent. You play golf. Why don't you join me during the next conference? I haven't sat in on one of those sessions in ten years. This is my R&R time. Those sessions are for the new people. My experience is enough to keep me current. Plus, I have excellent people to help me as we adjust our accounting system to the international changes being implemented."

Does Katrina Storm have an ethical dilemma? If so, what is it? What are her options? How would you solve her problem? Be prepared to defend your answer.

LO5 Corporate Ethics

E 15. To answer the following questions, conduct a search of several companies' websites: (1) Does the company have an ethics statement? (2) Does it express a commitment to environmental or social issues? (3) In your opinion, is the company ethically responsible? Select one of the companies you researched and write a brief description of your findings.

Problems

LO1 Report Preparation

P 1. Clothing Industries, Inc. is deciding whether to expand its line of women's clothing called Sami Pants. Sales in units of this product were 22,500, 28,900, and 36,200 in 2010, 2011, and 2012, respectively. The product has been very profitable, averaging 35 percent profit (above cost) over the three-year period. The company has 10 sales representatives covering seven states in the North. Production capacity at present is about 40,000 pants per year. There is adequate plant space for additional equipment, and the labor needed can be easily hired and trained.

The organization's management is made up of four vice presidents: the vice president of marketing, the vice president of production, the vice president of finance, and the vice president of management information systems. Each vice president is directly responsible to the president, Jefferson Henry.

Required

1. What types of information will Henry need before he can decide whether to expand the Sami Pants line?
2. Assume that one report needed to support Henry's decision is an analysis of sales, broken down by sales representative, over the past three years. How would each of the four *w's* pertain to this report?
3. Design a format for the report described in **2.**

LO2 The Value Chain

P 2. Reigle Electronics is a manufacturer of cell phones, a highly competitive business. Reigle's phones carry a price of $99, but competition forces the company to offer significant discounts and rebates. As a result, the average price of Reigle's cell phones has dropped to around $50, and the company is losing money. Management is applying value chain analysis to the company's operations in an effort to reduce costs and improve product quality. A study by the company's management accountant has determined the following per unit costs for primary processes:

Primary Process	Cost per Unit
Research and development	$ 2.50
Design	3.50
Supply	4.50
Production	6.70
Marketing	8.00
Distribution	1.90
Customer service	0.50
Total cost	$27.60

To generate a gross margin large enough for the company to cover its overhead costs and earn a profit, Reigle must lower its total cost per unit for primary processes to no more than $20. After analyzing operations, management reached the following conclusions about primary processes:

- Research and development and design are critical functions because the market and competition require constant development of new features with "cool" designs at lower cost. Nevertheless, management feels that the cost per unit of these processes must be reduced by 10 percent.
- Six different suppliers currently provide the components for the cell phones. Ordering these components from just two suppliers and negotiating lower prices could result in a savings of 15 percent.
- The cell phones are currently manufactured in Mexico. By shifting production to China, the unit cost of production can be lowered by 20 percent.
- Most cell phones are sold through wireless communication companies that are trying to attract new customers with low-priced cell phones. Management believes that these companies should bear more of the marketing costs and that it is feasible to renegotiate its marketing arrangements with them so that they will bear 35 percent of the current marketing costs.
- Distribution costs are already very low, but management will set a target of reducing the cost per unit by 10 percent.
- Customer service is a weakness of the company and has resulted in lost sales. Management therefore proposes increasing the cost per unit of customer service by 50 percent.

Required

1. Prepare a table showing the current cost per unit of primary processes and the projected cost per unit based on management's proposals for cost reduction.

Manager insight ▶

2. Will management's proposals for cost reduction achieve the targeted total cost per unit? What further steps should management take to reduce costs? Which steps that management is proposing do you believe will be the most difficult to accomplish?

Manager insight ▶

3. What are the company's support services? What role should these services play in the value chain analysis?

LO2 The Value Chain and Core Competency

P 3. Medic Products Company (MPC) is known for developing innovative and high-quality products for use in hospitals and medical and dental offices. Its latest product is a nonporous, tough, and very thin disposable glove that will not leak or split and molds tightly to the hand, making it ideal for use in medical and dental procedures. MPC buys the material it uses in making the gloves from another company, which manufactures it according to MPC's exact specifications and quality standards. MPC makes two models of the glove—one white and one transparent—in its own plant and sells them through independent agents who represent various manufacturers. When an agent informs MPC of a sale, MPC ships the order directly to the buyer. MPC advertises the gloves in professional journals and gives free samples to physicians and dentists. It provides a product warranty and periodically surveys users about the product's quality.

Required

1. Briefly explain how MPC accomplishes each of the primary processes in the value chain.
2. What is a core competency? Which one of the primary processes would you say is MPC's core competency? Explain your choice.

LO4 The Balanced Scorecard and Benchmarking

P 4. Howski Associates is an independent insurance agency that sells business, automobile, home, and life insurance. Maya Howski, senior partner of the agency, recently attended a workshop at the local university in which the balanced scorecard was presented as a way of focusing all of a company's functions on its mission. After the workshop, she met with her managers in a weekend brainstorming session. The group determined that Howski Associates' mission was to provide high-quality, innovative, risk-protection services to individuals and businesses. To ensure that the agency would fulfill this mission, the group established the following objectives:

- To provide a sufficient return on investment by increasing sales and maintaining the liquidity needed to support operations
- To add value to the agency's services by training employees to be knowledgeable and competent
- To retain customers and attract new customers
- To operate an efficient and cost-effective office support system for customer agents

To determine the agency's progress in meeting these objectives, the group established the following performance measures:

- Number of new ideas for customer insurance
- Percentage of customers who rate services as excellent
- Average time for processing insurance applications
- Number of dollars spent on training
- Growth in revenues for each type of insurance
- Average time for processing claims
- Percentage of employees who complete 40 hours of training during the year
- Percentage of new customer leads that result in sales
- Cash flow
- Number of customer complaints
- Return on assets
- Percentage of customers who renew policies
- Percentage of revenue devoted to office support system (information systems, accounting, orders, and claims processing)

Required

1. Prepare a balanced scorecard for Howski Associates by stating the agency's mission and matching its four objectives to the four stakeholder perspectives: the financial, learning and growth, internal business processes, and customer perspectives. Indicate which of the agency's performance measures would be appropriate for each objective.

Manager insight ▶ 2. Howski Associates is a member of an association of independent insurance agents that provides industry statistics about many aspects of operating an insurance agency. What is benchmarking, and in what ways would the industry statistics assist Howski Associates in further developing its balanced scorecard?

LO5 **Professional Ethics**

P 5. Taylor Zimmer is the controller for Value Corporation. He has been with the company for 17 years and is being considered for the job of chief financial officer. His boss, who is the current chief financial officer and former company controller, will be Value Corporation's new president. Zimmer has just discussed the year-end closing with his boss, who made the following statement during their conversation: "Taylor, why are you being so inflexible? I'm only asking you to postpone the $2,500,000 write-off of obsolete inventory for 10 days so that it won't appear on this year's financial statements. Ten days! Do it. Your promotion is coming up, you know. Make sure you keep all the possible outcomes in mind as you complete your year-end work. Oh, and keep this conversation confidential—just between you and me. Okay?"

Required

1. Identify the ethical issue or issues involved.
2. What do you believe is the appropriate solution to the problem? Be prepared to defend your answer.

Alternate Problems

LO1 **Report Preparation**

P 6. Daisy Flowers recently purchased Yardworks, Inc., a wholesale distributor of equipment and supplies for lawn and garden care. The organization, which is headquartered in Baltimore, has four distribution centers that service 14 eastern states. The centers are located in Boston, Massachusetts; Rye, New York; Reston, Virginia; and Lawrenceville, New Jersey. The company's profits for 2010, 2011, and 2012 were $225,400, $337,980, and $467,200, respectively.

Shortly after purchasing the organization, Flowers appointed people to the following positions: vice president, marketing; vice president, distribution; corporate controller; and vice president, research and development. Flowers called a meeting of this management group. She wants to create a deluxe retail lawn and garden center that would include a large, fully landscaped plant and tree nursery. The purposes of the retail center would be (1) to test equipment and supplies before selecting them for sales and distribution and (2) to showcase the effects of using the company's products. The retail center must also make a profit on sales.

Required

1. What types of information will Flowers need before deciding whether to create the retail lawn and garden center?
2. To support her decision, Flowers will need a report from the vice president of research and development analyzing all possible plants and trees that could be planted and their ability to grow in the places where the new retail center might be located. How would each of the four *w's* pertain to this report?
3. Design a format for the report in **2.**

LO2 **The Value Chain**

P 7. Soft Spot is a manufacturer of futon mattresses. Soft Spot's mattresses are priced at $60, but competition forces the company to offer significant discounts and rebates. As a result, the average price of the futon mattress has dropped to around $50, and the company is losing money. Management is applying value chain analysis to the company's operations in an effort to reduce costs and improve product quality. A study by the company's management accountant has determined the following per unit costs for primary processes and support services:

Primary Process	Cost per Unit
Research and development	$ 5.00
Design	3.00
Supply	4.00
Production	16.00
Marketing	6.00
Distribution	7.00
Customer service	1.00
Total cost per unit	$42.00
Support Service	
Human resources	$ 2.00
Information services	5.00
Management accounting	1.00
Total cost per unit	$ 8.00

To generate a gross margin large enough for the company to cover its overhead costs and earn a profit, Soft Spot must lower its total cost per unit for primary processes to no more than $32.00 and its support services to no more than $5.00. After analyzing operations, management reached the following conclusions about primary processes and support services:

- Research and development and design are critical functions because the market and competition require constant development of new features with "cool" designs at lower cost. Nevertheless, management feels that the cost per unit of these processes must be reduced by 20 percent.
- Ten different suppliers currently provide the components for the futons. Ordering these components from just two suppliers and negotiating lower prices could result in a savings of 15 percent.
- The futons are currently manufactured in Mali. By shifting production to China, the unit cost of production can be lowered by 40 percent.
- Management believes that by selling to large retailers like **Wal-Mart** it is feasible to lower current marketing costs by 25 percent.
- Distribution costs are already very low, but management will set a target of reducing the cost per unit by 10 percent.
- Customer service and support to large customers are key to keeping their business. Management therefore proposes increasing the cost per unit of customer service by 20 percent.
- By outsourcing its support services, management projects a 20 percent drop in these costs.

Required

1. Prepare a table showing the current cost per unit of primary processes and support services and the projected cost per unit based on management's proposals.

Manager insight ▶ 2. Will management's proposals achieve the targeted total cost per unit? What further steps should management take to reduce costs?

Manager insight ▶ 3. What role should the company's support services play in the value chain analysis?

LO2 The Value Chain and Core Competency

P 8. Sports Products Company (SPC) is known for developing innovative high-quality shoes for lacrosse. Its latest patented product is a tough, all-weather, and very flexible shoe. SPC buys the material it uses in making the shoes from another company, which manufactures it according to SPC's exact specifications and quality standards. SPC makes two models of the shoe—one white and one black—in its own plant. SPC sells them through independent distributors who represent various manufacturers. When a distributor informs SPC of a sale, SPC ships the order directly to the buyer. SPC advertises the shoes in sports magazines and gives free samples to well-known lacrosse players who endorse its products. It provides a product warranty and periodically surveys users about the product's quality.

Required

1. Briefly explain how SPC accomplishes each of the primary processes in the value chain.
2. What is a core competency? Which one of the primary processes would you say is SPC's core competency? Explain your choice.

LO4 The Balanced Scorecard and Benchmarking

P 9. Resource College is a liberal arts school that provides local residents the opportunity to take college courses and earn bachelor's degrees. Yolanda Howard, the school's provost, recently attended a workshop in which the balanced scorecard was presented as a way of focusing all of an organization's functions on its mission. After the workshop, she met with her administrative staff and college deans in a weekend brainstorming session. The group determined that the college's mission was to provide high-quality courses and degrees to individuals to add value to their lives. To ensure that the college would fulfill this mission, the group established the following objectives:

- To provide a sufficient return on investment by increasing tuition revenues and maintaining the liquidity needed to support operations
- To add value to the college's courses by encouraging faculty to be lifelong learners
- To retain students and attract new students
- To operate efficient and cost-effective student support systems

To determine the college's progress in meeting these objectives, the group established the following performance measures:

- Number of faculty publications
- Percentage of students who rate college as excellent
- Average time for processing student applications
- Number of dollars spent on professional development
- Growth in revenues for each department
- Average time for processing transcript requests
- Percentage of faculty who annually do 40 hours of professional development
- Percentage of new student leads that result in enrollment
- Cash flow
- Number of student complaints
- Return on assets
- Percentage of returning students
- Percentage of revenue devoted to student services systems (registrar, computer services, financial aid, and student health)

Required

1. Prepare a balanced scorecard for Resource College by stating the college's mission and matching its four objectives to the four stakeholder perspectives: the financial, learning and growth, internal business processes, and customer perspectives.
2. Indicate which of the college's performance measures would be appropriate for each objective.

LO3 LO5 Ethics and JIT Implementation

P 10. For almost a year, WEST Company has been changing its manufacturing process from a traditional to a JIT approach. Management has asked for employees' assistance in the transition and has offered bonuses for suggestions that cut time from the production operation. Don Hanley and Jerome Obbo each identified a time-saving opportunity and turned in their suggestions to their manager, Sam Knightly.

Knightly sent the suggestions to the committee charged with reviewing employees' suggestions, which inadvertently identified them as being Knightly's own. The committee decided that the two suggestions were worthy of reward and voted a large bonus for Knightly. When notified of this, Knightly could not bring himself to identify the true authors of the suggestions.

When Hanley and Obbo heard about Knightly's bonus, they confronted him with his fraudulent act and expressed their grievances. He told them that he needed the recognition to be eligible for an upcoming promotion and promised that if they kept quiet about the matter, he would make sure that they both received significant raises.

Required

1. Should Hanley and Obbo keep quiet? What other options are open to them?
2. How should Knightly have dealt with Hanley's and Obbo's complaints?

ENHANCING Your Knowledge, Skills, and Critical Thinking

LO1 Management Information

C 1. Obtain a copy of a recent annual report of a publicly held organization in which you have a particular interest. (Copies of annual reports are available at your campus library, at a local public library, on the Internet, or by direct request to an organization.) Assume that you have just been appointed to a middle-management position in a division of the organization you have chosen. You are interested in obtaining information that will help you better manage the activities of your division, and you have decided to study the contents of the annual report in an attempt to learn as much as possible.

You particularly want to know about the following: (1) size of inventory maintained; (2) ability to earn income; (3) reliance on debt financing; (4) types, volume, and prices of products or services sold; (5) type of production process used; (6) management's long-range strategies; (7) success (profitability) of the division's various product lines; (8) efficiency of operations; and (9) operating details of your division.

1. Write a brief description of the organization and its products or services and activities.
2. Based on a review of the financial statements and the accompanying disclosure notes, prepare a written summary of information pertaining to items 1 through 9 above.

3. Can you find any of the information in which you are interested in other sections of the annual report? If so, which information, and in which sections of the report is it?
4. The annual report also includes other types of information that you may find helpful in your new position. In outline form, summarize this additional information.

LO1 **Management Information Needs**

C 2. In **C 1**, you examined your new employer's annual report and found some useful information. However, you are interested in knowing whether your division's products or services are competitive, and you were unable to find the necessary information in the annual report.

1. What kinds of information about your competition do you want to find?
2. Why is this information relevant? (Link your response to a particular decision about your organization's products or services. For example, you might seek information to help you determine a new selling price.)
3. From what sources could you obtain the information you need?
4. When would you want to obtain this information?
5. Create a report that will communicate your findings to your superior.

LO1 **Report Preparation**

C 3. The registrar's office of Mainland College is responsible for maintaining a record of each student's grades and credits for use by students, instructors, and administrators.

1. Assume that you are a manager in the registrar's office and that you recently joined a team of managers to review the grade-reporting process. Explain how you would prepare a report of grades for students' use and the same report for instructors' use by answering the following questions:
   a. Who will read the grade report?
   b. Why is the grade report necessary?
   c. What information should the grade report contain?
   d. When is the grade report due?
2. Why does the information in a grade report for students' use and in a grade report for instructors' use differ?
3. Visit the registrar's office of your school in person or through your school's website. Obtain a copy of your grade report and a copy of the form that the registrar's office uses to report grades to instructors. Compare the information that these reports supply with the information you listed in requirement **1**. Explain any differences.
4. What can the registrar's office do to make sure that its grade reports are effective in communicating all necessary information to readers?

LO4 **Management Information Needs**

C 4. McDonald's is a leading competitor in the fast-food restaurant business. One component of McDonald's marketing strategy is to increase sales by expanding its foreign markets. At present, McDonald's restaurants operate in over 100 countries. In making decisions about opening restaurants in foreign markets, the company uses quantitative and qualitative financial and nonfinancial information. The following types of information would be important to such a decision: the cost of a new building (quantitative financial information), the estimated number of hamburgers to be sold in the first year (quantitative nonfinancial information), and site desirability (qualitative information).

Suppose you are a member of McDonald's management team that must decide whether to open a new restaurant in England. Identify at least two examples each of the (a) quantitative financial, (b) quantitative nonfinancial, and (c) qualitative information that you will need before you can make a decision.

LO1 LO4 Performance Measures and the Balanced Scorecard

C 5. Working in a group of four to six students, select a local business. The group should become familiar with the background of the business by interviewing its manager or accountant. Each group member should identify several performance objectives for the business and link each objective with a specific stakeholder's perspective from the balanced scorecard. (Select at least one performance objective for each perspective.) For each objective, ask yourself, "If I were the manager of the business, how would I set performance measures for each objective?" Then prepare an email stating the business's name, location, and activities and your linked performance objective and perspectives. Also list possible measures for each performance objective.

In class, members of the group should compare their individual emails and compile them into a group report by having each group member assume a different stakeholder perspective (add government and community if you want more than four perspectives). Each group should be ready to present all perspectives and the group's report on performance objectives and measures in class.

LO1 LO3 Cookie Company (Continuing Case)

C 6. Each of the rest of the chapters in this text includes a "cookie company" case that shows how you could operate your own cookie business. In this chapter, you will express your company's mission statement; set strategic, tactical, and operating objectives; decide on a name for your business; and identify management tools you might consider using to run your business.

1. In researching how to start and run a cookie business, you found the following three examples of cookie company mission statements:
   - To provide cheap cookies that taste great and fast courteous service!
   - Our mission is to make the best chocolate chip cookies that you have ever tasted.
   - Handmaking the best in custom cookie creations.

   a. Consider which of the mission statements most closely expresses what you want your company's identity and unique character to be. Why?
   b. Will your business focus on cost, quality, or satisfying a specific need?
   c. Write your company's mission statement.
2. Based on your mission statement, describe your broad long-term strategic objectives:
   - What will be your main products?
   - Who will be your primary customers?
   - Where will you operate your business?
3. You made the following decisions about your business:
   - To list expected expenses and revenues for the first six months of operations
   - To keep expenses low and generate enough revenues during the first two months of operations to have a positive cash flow by the third month
   - To develop a complete list of goals, objectives, procedures, and policies relating to how to find, buy, store, sell, and ship goods and collect payment
   - To rely solely on the Internet to market products
   - To expand the ecommerce website to include 20 varieties of cookies over the next five years

   Match each of the above to the following components of the planning framework: strategic objectives, tactical objectives, operating objectives, business plan, and budget.
4. What will be the name of your cookie company?
5. Which of the management tools listed in the chapter might you consider using to operate your business? Why?

CHAPTER

19

Cost Concepts and Cost Allocation

The Management Process

PLAN

- ▷ **Classify costs**
- ▷ **Compute predetermined overhead rates**

PERFORM

- ▷ **Flow service and product-related costs throught the inventory accounts**
- ▷ **Allocate overhead using either the traditional or ABC approach**
- ▷ **Compute the unit cost of a product or service**

EVALUATE

- ▷ **Compare actual and allocated overhead amounts**
- ▷ **Dispose of the under/over-applied overhead into Cost of Goods Sold account**

COMMUNICATE

- ▷ **Prepare external reports, i.e., service, retail, and manufacturing income statements**
- ▷ **Prepare internal management reports to monitor and manage costs**

How managers use cost information to solve, "How much does it cost?" can result in differing answers.

In this chapter, we describe how managers use information about costs, classify costs, compile product unit costs, and allocate overhead costs using the traditional method.

LEARNING OBJECTIVES

LO1 **Explain how managers classify costs and how they use these cost classifications.** (pp. 838–842)

LO2 **Compare how service, retail, and manufacturing organizations report costs on their financial statements and how they account for inventories.** (pp. 842–846)

LO3 **Describe the flow of costs through a manufacturer's inventory accounts.** (pp. 846–850)

LO4 **Define *product unit cost,* and compute the unit cost of a product or service.** (pp. 850–854)

LO5 **Define *cost allocation,* and explain how the traditional method of allocating overhead costs figure into calculating product or service unit cost.** (pp. 855–860)

DECISION POINT ► A MANAGER'S FOCUS THE CHOICE CANDY COMPANY

► How do managers at The Choice Candy Company determine the cost of a candy bar?

► How do they use cost information?

The Choice Candy Company's mission is to make the world's best-tasting chocolate candy bars. As in any other company, a primary goal for The Choice Candy Company is to make a profit and thereby increase the value of its stakeholders' interest in the business. Making top-quality products requires top-quality ingredients and skilled employees—both of which can be costly. If The Choice Candy Company is to achieve the goal of profitability and at the same time produce top-quality products, its managers have to be familiar with the cost concepts and cost allocation methods discussed in this chapter.

Cost Information

LO1 Explain how managers classify costs and how they use these cost classifications.

One of a company's primary goals is to be profitable. Because a company's owners expect to earn profits, managers have a responsibility to use the company's resources wisely and to generate revenues that will exceed the costs of the company's operating, investing, and financing activities. In this chapter, we focus on costs related to the operating activities of manufacturing, retail, and service organizations. We begin by looking at how managers in these different organizations use information about costs.

Managers' Use of Cost Information

Managers use information about operating costs to plan, perform, evaluate, and communicate the results of operating activities.

- Service organization managers find the estimated cost of services helpful in monitoring profitability and making decisions about such matters as bidding on future business, lowering or negotiating their fees, or dropping one of their services.
- In retail organizations, such as Good Foods Store, which we used as an example in the last chapter, managers work with the estimated cost of merchandise purchases to predict gross margin, operating income, and value of merchandise sold. They also use this information to make decisions about matters like reducing selling prices for clearance sales, lowering selling prices for bulk sales, or dropping a product line.
- Managers at manufacturing companies like **Hershey's** use estimated product costs to predict the gross margin and operating income on sales and to make decisions about such matters as dropping a product line, outsourcing the manufacture of a part to another company, bidding on a special order, or negotiating a selling price. In this chapter, we will use The Choice Candy Company, the hypothetical manufacturer of gourmet chocolate candy bars introduced in the Decision Point, to illustrate how managers of manufacturing companies use cost information.

Cost Information and Organizations

All organizations use cost information to determine profits and selling prices and to value inventories. Ultimately, a company is profitable only when its revenues from sales or services rendered exceed all its costs. But different types of organizations have different types of product or service costs.

- Service organizations like **Southwest Airlines** need information about the costs of providing services, which include the costs of labor and related overhead.
- Retail organizations like **Wal-Mart** and Good Foods Store need information about the costs of purchasing products for resale. These costs include adjustments for freight-in costs, purchase returns and allowances, and purchase discounts.
- Manufacturing organizations like **Hershey's** and The Choice Candy Company need information about the costs of manufacturing products. Product costs include the costs of direct materials, direct labor, and overhead.

Cost Classifications and Their Uses

A single cost can be classified and used in several ways, depending on the purpose of the analysis. Figure 19-1 provides an overview of commonly used cost classifications. These classifications enable managers to do the following:

1. Control costs by determining which are traceable to a particular cost object, such as a service or product.

FIGURE 19-1 Overview of Cost Classifications

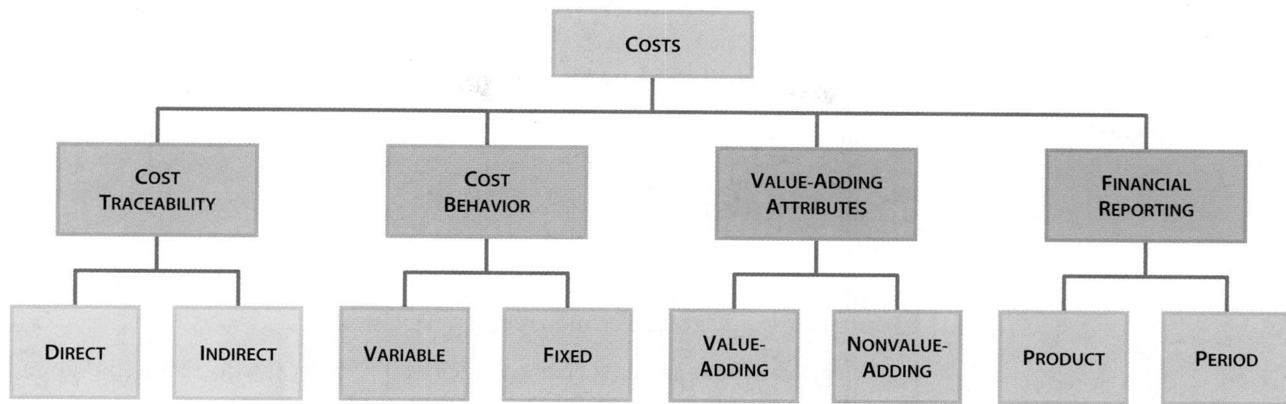

2. Calculate the number of units that must be sold to achieve a certain level of profit (cost behavior).
3. Identify the costs of activities that do and do not add value to a product or service.
4. Classify costs for the preparation of financial statements.

Cost Traceability

Managers trace costs to cost objects, such as products or services, sales territories, departments, or operating activities, to develop a fairly accurate measurement of costs.

- **Direct costs** are costs that can be conveniently and economically traced to a cost object. For example, the wages of workers who make candy bars can be conveniently traced to a particular batch because of time cards and payroll records. Similarly, the cost of chocolate's main ingredients—chocolate liquor, cocoa butter, sugar, and milk—can be easily traced.
- **Indirect costs** are costs that cannot be conveniently and economically traced to a cost object. Some examples include the nails used in furniture, the salt used in candy, and the rivets used in airplanes. For the sake of accuracy, however, these indirect costs must be included in the cost of a product or service. Because they are difficult to trace or an insignificant amount, management uses a formula to assign them to cost objects.

The following examples illustrate cost objects and their direct and indirect costs in service, retail, and manufacturing organizations:

- ***Service organization:*** In organizations such as an accounting firm, costs can be traced to a specific service, such as preparation of tax returns. Direct costs for such a service include the costs of government reporting forms, computer usage, and the accountant's labor. Indirect costs include the costs of supplies, office rental, utilities, secretarial labor, telephone usage, and depreciation of office furniture.
- ***Retail organization:*** Costs for organizations such as Good Foods Store can be traced to a department. For example, the direct costs of the produce department include the costs of fruits and vegetables and the wages of employees working in that department. Indirect costs include the costs of utilities to cool the produce displays and the storage and handling of the produce.

- ***Manufacturing organization:*** Costs for organizations such as The Choice Candy Company can be traced to the product. Direct costs include the costs of the materials and labor needed to make the candy. Indirect costs include the costs of utilities, depreciation of plant and equipment, insurance, property taxes, inspection, supervision, maintenance of machinery, storage, and handling.

Cost Behavior

Managers are also interested in the way costs respond to changes in volume or activity. By analyzing those variable and fixed patterns of behavior, they gain information to make better management decisions.

- A **variable cost** is a cost that changes in direct proportion to a change in productive output (or some other measure of volume).
- A **fixed cost** is a cost that remains constant within a defined range of activity or time period.

All types of organizations have variable and fixed costs. Here are a few examples:

Study Note

Notice in each of these examples that as more products or services are produced and sold, the variable costs increase proportionately. Fixed costs, however, remain the same for a specified period.

- Because the number of passengers drives the consumption of food and beverages on a flight, the cost of peanuts and beverages is a variable cost for **Southwest Airlines**. Fixed costs include the depreciation on the plane and the salaries and benefits of the flight and ground crews.
- The variable costs of Good Foods Store include the cost of groceries sold and any sales commissions. Fixed costs include the costs of building and lot rental, depreciation on store equipment, and the manager's salary.
- The variable costs of The Choice Candy Company include the costs of direct materials (e.g., sugar, cocoa), direct labor wages, indirect materials (e.g., salt), and indirect labor (e.g., inspection and maintenance labor). Fixed costs include the costs of supervisors' salaries and depreciation on buildings.

Value-Adding Versus Nonvalue-Adding Costs

Costs incurred to improve the quality of a product are value-adding costs if the customer is willing to pay more for the higher-quality product or service; otherwise, they are nonvalue-adding costs because they do not increase its market value.

- A **value-adding cost** is the cost of an activity that increases the market value of a product or service.
- A **nonvalue-adding cost** is the cost of an activity that adds cost to a product or service but does not increase its market value.

Managers examine the value-adding attributes of their company's operating activities and, wherever possible, reduce or eliminate activities that do not directly add value to the company's products or services. For example, the costs of administrative activities, such as accounting and human resource management, are nonvalue-adding costs. Because they are necessary for the operation of the business, they are monitored closely but cannot be eliminated.

TABLE 19-1 Examples of Cost Classifications for a Candy Manufacturer

Cost Examples	Traceability to Product	Cost Behavior	Value Attribute	Financial Reporting
Sugar for candy	Direct	Variable	Value-adding	Product (direct materials)
Labor for mixing	Direct	Variable	Value-adding	Product (direct labor)
Labor for supervision	Indirect	Fixed	Nonvalue-adding	Product (overhead)
Depreciation on mixing machine	Indirect	Fixed	Value-adding	Product (overhead)
Sales commission	—*	Variable	Value-adding†	Period
Accountant's salary	—*	Fixed	Nonvalue-adding	Period

*Sales commissions and accountants' salaries cannot be directly or indirectly traced to a cost object; they are not product costs.

†Sales commissions can be value-adding because customers' perceptions of the salesperson and the selling experience can strongly affect their perceptions of the product's market value.

Cost Classifications for Financial Reporting

> **Study Note**
> Product costs and period costs can be explained by using the matching rule. Product costs must be charged to the period in which the product generates revenue, and period costs are charged against the revenue of the current period.

For purposes of preparing financial statements, managers classify costs as product costs or period costs.

- **Product costs**, or *inventoriable* costs, are costs assigned to inventory; they include direct materials, direct labor, and overhead. Product costs appear on the income statement as cost of goods sold and on the balance sheet as inventory.
- **Period costs**, or *noninventoriable* costs, are costs of resources used during the accounting period that are not assigned to products. They appear as operating expenses on the income statement. For example, among the period costs listed on the income statement are selling, administrative, and general expenses.

Table 19-1 shows how some costs of a candy manufacturer can be classified in terms of traceability, behavior, value attribute, and financial reporting.

& APPLY >

Indicate whether each of the following costs for a gourmet chocolate candy maker is a product or a period cost, a variable or a fixed cost, a value-adding or a nonvalue-adding cost, and, if it is a product cost, a direct or an indirect cost of the candy:

Cost Classification

Product or Period	Variable or Fixed	Value-Adding or Nonvalue-Adding	Direct or Indirect
Product	Variable	Value-adding	Direct

1. Chocolate
2. Office rent
3. Candy chef wages
4. Dishwasher wages
5. Pinch of salt
6. Utilities to run mixer

(continued)

SOLUTION

	Cost Classification			
	Product or Period	**Variable or Fixed**	**Value-Adding or Nonvalue-Adding**	**Direct or Indirect**
Chocolate	Product	Variable	Value-adding	Direct
Office rent	Period	Fixed	Nonvalue-adding	—
Candy chef	Product	Variable	Value-adding	Direct
Dishwasher	Product	Variable	Value-adding	Indirect
Pinch of salt	Product	Variable	Value-adding	Indirect
Utilities to run mixer	Product	Variable	Value-adding	Indirect

Financial Statements and the Reporting of Costs

LO2 Compare how service, retail, and manufacturing organizations report costs on their financial statements and how they account for inventories.

Managers prepare financial statements at least once a year to communicate the results of their management activities for the period. The key to preparing an income statement or a balance sheet in any kind of organization is determining its cost of goods or services sold and the value of its inventories, if any.

Income Statement and Accounting for Inventories

Remember that all organizations—service, retail, and manufacturing—use the following income statement format:

$$\text{Sales} - \begin{matrix}\text{Cost of Sales}\\ \text{or}\\ \text{Cost of Goods Sold}\end{matrix} = \begin{matrix}\text{Gross}\\ \text{Margin}\end{matrix} - \begin{matrix}\text{Operating}\\ \text{Expenses}\end{matrix} = \text{Operating Income}$$

Figure 19-2 compares the financial statements of service, retail, and manufacturing organizations. Note in particular the differences in inventory accounts and cost of goods sold. As pointed out earlier, product costs, or inventoriable costs, appear as inventory on the balance sheet and as cost of goods sold on the income statement. Period costs, also called *noninventoriable costs* or *selling, administrative, and general expenses,* are reflected in the operating expenses on the income statement.

Because the operations of service and retail organizations differ from those of manufacturers, the accounts presented in their financial statements differ as well.

- Service organizations like **Southwest Airlines** and **United Parcel Service (UPS)** sell services and not products; they maintain no inventories for sale or resale. As a result, unlike manufacturing and retail organizations, they have no inventory accounts on their balance sheets.

Suppose that Good Foods Store, the retail shop that we used as an example in the last chapter, employs UPS to deliver its products. The cost of sales for UPS would include the wages and salaries of personnel plus the expense of the trucks, planes, supplies, and anything else that UPS uses to deliver packages for Good Foods Store.

- Retail organizations, such as **Wal-Mart** and Good Foods Store, which purchase products ready for resale, maintain just one inventory account on the balance sheet. Called the Merchandise Inventory account, it reflects the costs of goods held for resale.

FIGURE 19-2 Financial Statements of Service, Retail, and Manufacturing Organizations

	Service Company	Retail Company		Manufacturing Company	
Income Statement	Sales – Cost of sales = Gross margin – Operating expenses = Operating income	Sales – Cost of goods sold* = Gross margin – Operating expenses = Operating income		Sales – Cost of goods sold† = Gross margin – Operating expenses = Operating income	
		*Cost of goods sold: Beginning merchandise inventory + Net cost of purchases = Cost of goods available for sale – Ending merchandise inventory = Cost of goods sold		†Cost of goods sold: Beginning finished goods inventory + Cost of goods manufactured = Cost of goods available for sale – Ending finished goods inventory = Cost of goods sold	
Balance Sheet (current assets section)	No inventory accounts	One inventory account: Merchandise Inventory (finished product ready for sale)		Three inventory accounts: Materials Inventory (unused materials) Work in Process Inventory (unfinished product) Finished Goods Inventory (finished product ready for sale)	
Example with numbers		Income Statement:		Income Statement:	
		Beg. merchandise inventory	$ 3,000	Beg. finished goods inventory	$ 52,000
		+ Net cost of purchases	23,000	+ Cost of goods manufactured	144,000
		= Cost of goods available for sale	$26,000	= Cost of goods available for sale	$196,000
		– End. merchandise inventory	4,500	– End. finished goods inventory	78,000
		= Cost of goods sold	$21,500	= Cost of goods sold	$118,000
		Balance Sheet:		Balance Sheet:	
		Merchandise inventory, ending	$ 4,500	Finished goods inventory, ending	$ 78,000

Suppose that Good Foods Store had a balance of $3,000 in its Merchandise Inventory account at the beginning of the year. During the year, its purchases of food products totaled $23,000 (adjusted for purchase discounts, returns and allowances, and freight-in). At year-end, its Merchandise Inventory balance was $4,500. The cost of goods sold was thus $21,500.

▶ Manufacturing organizations like The Choice Candy Company, which make products for sale, maintain three inventory accounts on the balance sheet: the Materials Inventory, Work in Process Inventory, and Finished Goods Inventory accounts. The Materials Inventory account shows the cost of materials that have been purchased but not used in the production process. During the production process, the costs of manufacturing the product are accumulated in the Work in Process Inventory account; the balance of this account represents the costs of the unfinished product. Once the product is complete and ready for sale, its cost is transferred to the Finished Goods Inventory account; the balance in this account is the cost of the unsold completed product.

Suppose that The Choice Candy Company had a balance of $52,000 in its Finished Goods Inventory account at the beginning of the year. During the year, the cost of the products that the company manufactured totaled $144,000. At year end, its Finished Goods Inventory balance was $78,000. The cost of goods sold was thus $118,000.

Statement of Cost of Goods Manufactured

The key to preparing an income statement for a manufacturing organization is computing its cost of goods sold, which means that you must first determine the cost of goods manufactured. This dollar amount is calculated on the **statement of cost of goods manufactured**, a special report based on an analysis of the Work in Process Inventory account. At the end of an accounting period, the flow of all manufacturing costs incurred during the period is summarized in this statement. Exhibit 19-1 shows The Choice Candy Company's statement of cost of goods manufactured for the year.

It is helpful to think of the statement of cost of goods manufactured as being developed in three steps:

Step 1. ***Compute the cost of direct materials used during the accounting period.*** As shown in Exhibit 19-1, add the beginning balance in the Materials Inventory account to the direct materials purchased. The subtotal ($300,000) represents the cost of direct materials available for use during the accounting period. Next, subtract the ending balance of the Materials Inventory account from the cost of direct materials available for use. The difference is the cost of direct materials used during the period.

EXHIBIT 19-1
Statement of Cost of Goods Manufactured and Partial Income Statement for a Manufacturing Organization

The Choice Candy Company
Statement of Cost of Goods Manufactured
For the Year

Direct materials used		
Beginning materials inventory	$100,000	
Direct materials purchased	200,000	
Cost of direct materials available for use	$300,000	
Less ending materials inventory	50,000	
Step 1: Cost of direct materials used		$250,000
Direct labor		120,000
Overhead		60,000
Step 2: Total manufacturing costs		$430,000
Add beginning work in process inventory		20,000
Total cost of work in process during the year		$450,000
Less ending work in process Inventory		150,000
Step 3: Cost of goods manufactured		$300,000

The Choice Candy Company
Income Statement
For the Year

Sales		$500,000
Cost of goods sold		
Beginning finished goods inventory	$ 78,000	
Cost of goods manufactured	300,000	
Cost of goods available for sale	$378,000	
Less ending finished goods inventory	138,000	
Cost of goods sold		240,000
Gross margin		$260,000
Selling and administrative expenses		160,000
Operating income		$100,000

Step 2. ***Calculate total manufacturing costs for the period.*** As shown in Exhibit 19-1, the costs of direct materials used and direct labor are added to total overhead costs incurred during the period to arrive at total manufacturing costs.

Step 3. ***Determine total cost of goods manufactured for the period.*** As shown in Exhibit 19-1, add the beginning balance in the Work in Process Inventory account to total manufacturing costs to arrive at the total cost of work in process during the period. From this amount, subtract the ending balance in the Work in Process Inventory account to arrive at the cost of goods manufactured.

Study Note

An alternative to the cost of goods manufactured calculation uses the cost flow concept that is discussed in LO3.

Cost of Goods Sold and a Manufacturer's Income Statement

Exhibit 19-1 shows the relationship between The Choice Candy Company's income statement and its statement of cost of goods manufactured. The total amount of the cost of goods manufactured during the period is carried over to the income statement, where it is used to compute the cost of goods sold. The beginning balance of the Finished Goods Inventory account is added to the cost of goods manufactured to arrive at the total cost of goods available for sale during the period. The cost of goods sold is then computed by subtracting the ending balance in Finished Goods Inventory (what was not sold) from the total cost of goods available for sale (what was available for sale). The cost of goods sold is considered an expense in the period in which the goods are sold.

Study Note

It is important not to confuse the cost of goods manufactured with the cost of goods sold.

STOP & APPLY >

Given the following information, compute the ending balances of the Materials Inventory, Work in Process Inventory, and Finished Goods Inventory accounts:

Materials inventory, beginning balance	$ 230
Work in process inventory, beginning balance	250
Finished goods inventory, beginning balance	380
Direct materials purchased	850
Direct materials placed into production	740
Direct labor costs	970
Overhead costs	350
Cost of goods completed	1,230
Cost of goods sold	935

SOLUTION

Materials Inventory, ending balance:	
Materials Inventory, beginning balance	$ 230
Direct materials purchased	850
Direct materials placed into production	(740)
Materials Inventory, ending balance	$ 340
Work in Process Inventory, ending balance:	
Work in Process Inventory, beginning balance	$ 250
Direct materials placed into production	740
Direct labor costs	970

(continued)

Overhead costs	350
Cost of goods completed	(1,230)
Work in Process Inventory, ending balance	$1,080
Finished Goods Inventory, ending balance:	
Finished Goods Inventory, beginning balance	$ 380
Cost of goods completed	1,230
Cost of goods sold	(935)
Finished Goods Inventory, ending balance	$ 675

Inventory Accounts in Manufacturing Organizations

LO3 Describe the flow of costs through a manufacturer's inventory accounts.

Transforming materials into finished products ready for sale requires a number of production and production-related activities. A manufacturing organization's accounting system tracks these activities as product costs flowing through the Materials Inventory, Work in Process Inventory, and Finished Goods Inventory accounts.

- The **Materials Inventory account** shows the balance of the cost of unused materials.
- The **Work in Process Inventory account** shows the manufacturing costs that have been incurred and assigned to partially completed units of product.
- The **Finished Goods Inventory account** shows the costs assigned to all completed products that have not been sold.

Document Flows and Cost Flows Through the Inventory Accounts

Managers accumulate and report manufacturing costs based on documents pertaining to production and production-related activities. Figure 19-3 summarizes the typical relationships among the production activities, the documents for each of the three cost elements, and the inventory accounts affected by the activities. Looking at the relationship between activities and documents provides insight into how costs flow through the three inventory accounts and when an activity must be recorded in the accounting records.

To illustrate document flow and changes in inventory balances for production activities in Figure 19-3, we continue with our example of The Choice Candy Company, a typical manufacturing business.

Purchase of Materials

- The purchasing process starts with a *purchase request* prepared on a computer form which is submitted electronically for specific quantities of materials needed in the manufacturing process but not currently available in the materials storeroom. A qualified manager approves the request online. Based on the information in the purchase request, the Purchasing Department prepares a computer-generated *purchase order* and sends it to a supplier.
- When the materials arrive, an employee on the receiving dock examines the materials and enters the information into the company database as a *receiving report.* The system matches the information on the receiving report with the descriptions and quantities listed on the purchase order. A materials handler moves the newly arrived materials from the receiving area to the materials storeroom.

- The Choice Candy Company's accounting department receives a *vendor's invoice* from the supplier requesting payment for the purchased materials. The cost of those materials increases the balance of the Materials Inventory account and an account payable is recognized. If all documents match, payment is authorized to be made.

Production of Goods

- When candy bars are scheduled for production, the storeroom clerk receives a *materials request form*. In addition to showing authorization, it describes the types and quantities of materials that the storeroom clerk is to send to the production area, and it authorizes the release of those materials from the materials inventory into production.
- If all is in order, the storeroom clerk has the materials handler move the materials to the production floor.
  - The cost of the direct materials transferred will increase the balance of the Work in Process Inventory account and decrease the balance of the Materials Inventory account.
  - The cost of the indirect materials transferred will increase the balance of the Overhead account and decrease the balance of the Materials Inventory account. (We discuss overhead in more detail later in this chapter.)
- Each of the production employees who make the candy bars prepares a *time card* to record the number of hours he or she has worked on this and other orders each day.
  - The costs of the direct labor used to manufacture the candy bars increase the balance of the Work in Process Inventory account.
  - The costs of the indirect labor used to support the manufacture of the candy bars increase the balance of the Overhead account.
- A *job order cost card* can be used to record all direct material, direct labor, and overhead costs incurred as the products move through production.

Product Completion and Sale

- Employees place completed candy bars in cartons and then move the cartons to the finished goods storeroom, where they are kept until they are shipped to customers. The cost of the completed candy bars increases the balance of the Finished Goods Inventory account and decreases the balance of the Work in Process Inventory account.
- When candy bars are sold, a clerk prepares a *sales invoice*, and another employee fills the order by removing the candy bars from the storeroom, packaging them, and shipping them to the customer. A *shipping document* shows the quantity of the products that are shipped and gives a description of them. The cost of the candy bars sold increases the Cost of Goods Sold account and decreases the balance of the Finished Goods Inventory account.

The Manufacturing Cost Flow

Manufacturing cost flow is the flow of manufacturing costs (direct materials, direct labor, and overhead) through the Materials Inventory, Work in Process Inventory, and Finished Goods Inventory accounts into the Cost of Goods Sold account. A defined, structured manufacturing cost flow is the foundation for product costing, inventory valuation, and financial reporting. It supplies all the information necessary to prepare the statement of cost of goods manufactured and compute the cost of goods sold, as shown in Exhibit 19-1.

FIGURE 19-3 Activities, Documents, and Cost Flows Through the Inventory Accounts of a Manufacturing Organization

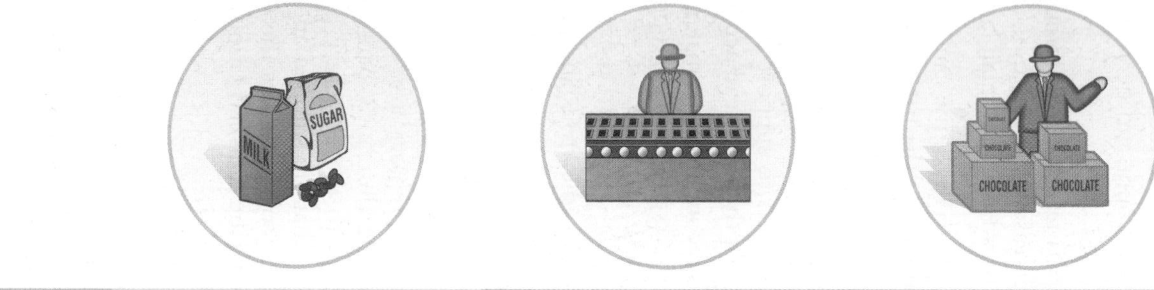

	PURCHASE OF MATERIALS	PRODUCTION OF GOODS	PRODUCT COMPLETION	PRODUCT SALE
ACTIVITIES	• Purchase, receive, inspect, and store materials. • Confirm receipt of materials. • Match documents.	• Move materials to production area. • Convert materials into finished product using direct labor and overhead.	• Move completed products to finished goods storage area and store until sold. • Move sold units to shipping.	• Ship products sold to customer.
DOCUMENTS	• Purchase request • Purchase order • Receiving report • Vendor's invoice	• Materials request form • Time card • Job order cost card	• Job order cost card	• Sales invoice • Shipping document • Job order cost card
INVENTORY ACCOUNTS (RELATED DOCUMENTS)	**MATERIALS INVENTORY** Debit: Cost of materials purchased (vendor's invoice) Credit: Cost of materials used in production (materials request form)	**WORK IN PROCESS INVENTORY** Debit: Cost of materials used in production (materials request form) Cost of direct labor (time card) Cost of overhead Credit: Cost of completed products (job order cost card)	**FINISHED GOODS INVENTORY** Debit: Cost of completed products (job order cost card) Credit: Cost of sold units (job order cost card)	**COST OF GOODS SOLD** Debit: Cost of sold units (job order cost card)

FIGURE 19-4 Manufacturing Cost Flow: An Example Using Actual Costing for The Choice Candy Company

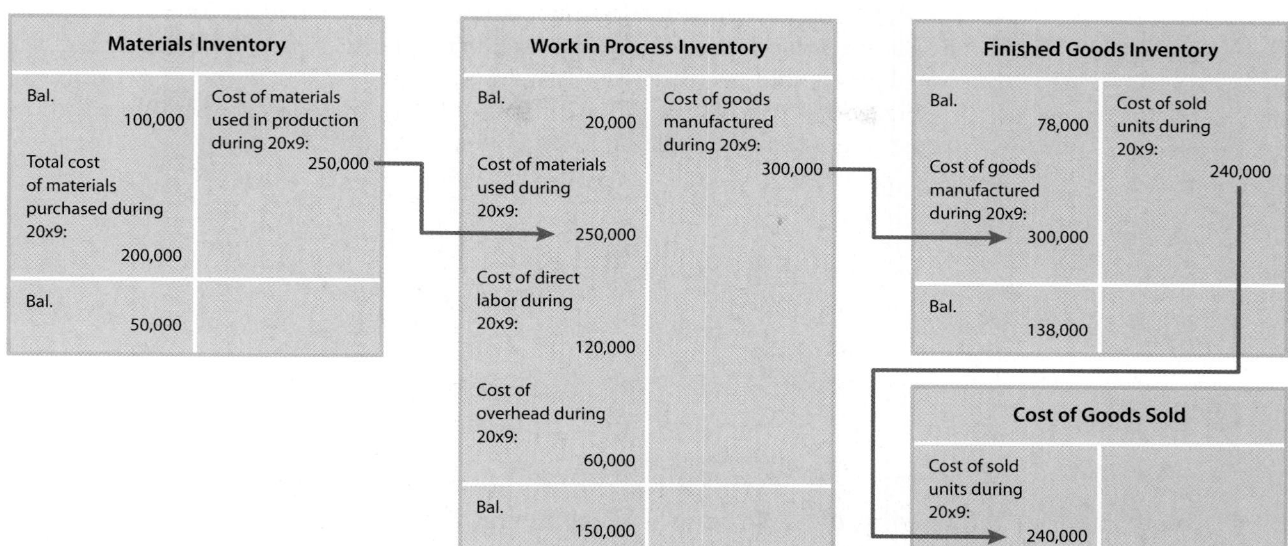

Figure 19-4 summarizes the manufacturing cost flow as it relates to the inventory accounts and production activity of The Choice Candy Company for the year ended December 31. To show the basic flows in this example, we assume that all materials can be traced directly to the candy bars. This means that there are no indirect materials in the Materials Inventory account. We also work with the actual amount of overhead, rather than an estimated amount.

Materials Inventory Because there are no indirect materials in this case, the Materials Inventory account shows the balance of unused direct materials. The cost of direct materials purchased increases the balance of the Materials Inventory account, and the cost of direct materials used by the Production Department decreases it.

Figure 19-4 shows the flows of material purchased and used through the Materials Inventory T account.

Work in Process Inventory The Work in Process Inventory account records the balance of partially completed units of the product.

- As direct materials and direct labor enter the production process, their costs are added to the Work in Process Inventory account. The cost of overhead for the current period is also added.
- The total costs of direct materials, direct labor, and overhead incurred and transferred to work in process inventory during an accounting period are called **total manufacturing costs** (also called *current manufacturing costs)*. These costs increase the balance of the Work in Process Inventory account.
- The cost of all units completed and moved to finished goods inventory during an accounting period is the **cost of goods manufactured**. The cost of goods manufactured for the period decreases the balance of the Work in Process Inventory account.

Figure 19-4 recaps the inflows of direct materials, direct labor, and overhead into the Work in Process Inventory T account and the resulting outflow of completed product costs.

Study Note

When costs are transferred from one inventory account to another in a manufacturing company, they remain assets. They are on the balance sheet and are not expensed on the income statement until the finished goods are sold.

Study Note

Materials Inventory and Work in Process Inventory support the production process, while Finished Goods Inventory supports the sales and distribution functions.

Finished Goods Inventory The Finished Goods Inventory account holds the balance of costs assigned to all completed products that a manufacturing company has not yet sold. The cost of goods manufactured increases the balance, and the cost of goods sold decreases the balance.

Figure 19-4 shows the inflow of cost of goods manufactured and the outflow of cost of goods sold to the Finished Goods Inventory T account.

STOP & APPLY >

Given the following information, use T accounts to compute the ending balances of the Materials Inventory, Work in Process Inventory, and Finished Goods Inventory accounts:

Materials Inventory, beginning balance	$ 230
Work in Process Inventory, beginning balance	250
Finished Goods Inventory, beginning balance	380
Direct materials purchased	850
Direct materials (DM) placed into production (used)	740
Direct labor (DL) costs	970
Overhead (OH) costs	350
Cost of goods completed (COGM)	1,230
Cost of goods sold (COGS)	935

SOLUTION

Material Inventory

Beg.	230	Used	740
Purchased	850		
End.	340		

Work in Process Inventory

Beg.	250	COGM	1,230
DM	740		
DL	970		
OH	350		
End.	1,080		

Finished Goods Inventory

Beg.	380	COGS	935
COGM	1,230		
End.	675		

Elements of Product Costs

LO4 Define *product unit cost,* and compute the unit cost of a product or service.

As noted above, product costs include all costs related to the manufacturing process. The three elements of product cost are direct materials costs, direct labor costs, and overhead costs.

- **Direct materials costs** are the costs of materials used in making a product that can be conveniently and economically traced to specific units of the product. Some examples of direct materials are the meat and bun in hamburgers, the oil and additives in a gallon of gasoline, and the sugar used in making candy. Direct materials may also include parts that a company purchases from another manufacturer, e.g., a battery and windshield for an automobile.
- **Direct labor costs** are the costs of the hands-on labor needed to make a product or service that can be traced to specific units. For example, the wages of production-line workers are direct labor costs.

- **Overhead costs** (also called *service overhead, factory overhead, factory burden, manufacturing overhead,* or *indirect production costs*) are production-related costs that cannot be practically or conveniently traced directly to an end product or service. They include **indirect materials costs**, such as the costs of nails, rivets, lubricants, and small tools, and **indirect labor costs**, such as the costs of labor for maintenance, inspection, engineering design, supervision, and materials handling. Other indirect manufacturing costs include the costs of building maintenance, property taxes, property insurance, depreciation on plant and equipment, rent, and utilities. As indirect costs, overhead costs are allocated to a product's cost using either traditional or activity-based costing methods, which we discuss later in the chapter.

To illustrate product costs and the manufacturing process, we'll refer again to The Choice Candy Company. Maggie Evans, the company's founder and president, has identified the following elements of the product cost of one candy bar:

- *Direct materials costs:* costs of sugar, chocolate, and wrapper
- *Direct labor costs:* costs of labor used in making the candy bar
- *Overhead costs:* indirect materials costs, including the costs of salt and flavorings; indirect labor costs, including the costs of labor to move materials to the production area and to inspect the candy bars during production; other indirect overhead costs, including depreciation on the building and equipment, utilities, property taxes, and insurance

Prime Costs and Conversion Costs

The three elements of manufacturing costs can be grouped into prime costs and conversion costs.

- **Prime costs** are the primary costs of production; they are the sum of the direct materials costs and direct labor costs.
- **Conversion costs** are the costs of converting direct materials into a finished product; they are the sum of direct labor costs and overhead costs.

These classifications are important for understanding the costing methods discussed in later chapters. Figure 19-5 summarizes the relationships among the product cost classifications presented so far.

FOCUS ON BUSINESS PRACTICE

Has Technology Shifted the Elements of Product Costs?

New technology and manufacturing processes have created new patterns of product costs. The three elements of product costs are still direct materials, direct labor, and overhead, but the percentage that each contributes to the total cost of a product has changed. From the 1950s through the 1970s, direct labor was the dominant element, making up over 40 percent of total product cost, while direct materials contributed 35 percent and overhead, around 25 percent. Thus, direct costs, traceable to the product, accounted for 75 percent of total product cost. Improved production technology caused a dramatic shift in the three product cost elements. Machines replaced people, significantly reducing direct labor costs. Today, only 50 percent of the cost of a product is directly traceable to the product; the other 50 percent is overhead, an indirect cost.

FIGURE 19-5
Relationships Among Product Cost Classifications

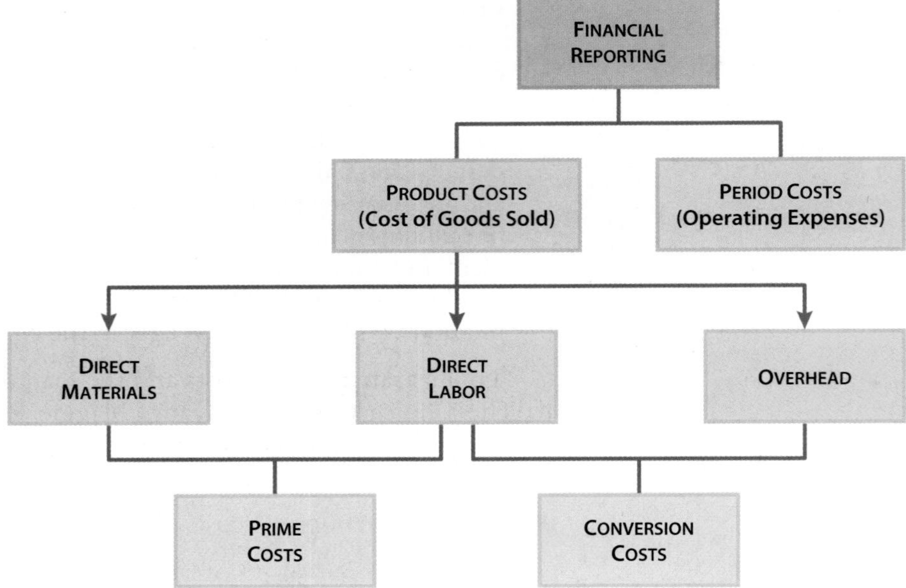

Computing Product Unit Cost

Product unit cost is the cost of manufacturing a single unit of a product. It is made up of the costs of direct materials, direct labor, and overhead. These three cost elements are accumulated as a batch or production run of products is being produced. When the batch or run has been completed, the product unit cost is computed by dividing the total cost of direct materials, direct labor, and overhead by the total number of units produced, or by determining the cost per unit for each element of the product cost and summing those per unit costs.

$$\text{Product Unit Cost} = \frac{\text{Direct Materials Cost} + \text{Direct Labor Cost} + \text{Overhead Cost}}{\text{Number of Units Produced}}$$

or

$$\text{Product Unit Cost} = \text{Direct Materials Cost per Unit} + \text{Direct Labor Cost per Unit} + \text{Overhead Cost per Unit}$$

Product Cost Measurement Methods

How products flow physically and how costs are incurred does not always match. For example, The Choice Candy Company physically produces candy bars 24 hours a day, 7 days a week, but the accounting department only does accounting 8 hours a day, 5 days a week. Because product cost data must be available 24/7, managers may use estimates or predetermined standards to compute product costs during the period. At the end of the period, these estimates are reconciled with the actual product costs so actual product costs appear in the financial statements. Here are the three methods managers and accountants can use to calculate product unit cost:

- Actual costing method,
- Normal costing method, or
- Standard costing method.

Table 19-2 summarizes how these three product cost-measurement methods use actual and estimated costs.

TABLE 19-2
Use of Actual and Estimated Costs in Three Cost-Measurement Methods

Product Cost Elements	Actual Costing	Normal Costing	Standard Costing
Direct materials	Actual costs	Actual costs	Estimated costs
Direct labor	Actual costs	Actual costs	Estimated costs
Overhead	Actual costs	Estimated costs	Estimated costs

Study Note

Many management decisions require estimates of future costs. Managers often use actual cost as a basis for estimating future cost.

Actual Costing Method The **actual costing** method uses the actual costs of direct materials, direct labor, and overhead when they become known to calculate the product unit cost. This means, many times, waiting until the end of the period when all the cost data are available. For most companies, this is not practical. Notice in the following example that product unit cost is computed after the job was completed and all cost information was known.

The Choice Candy Company produced 3,000 candy bars on December 28 for Good Foods Store. Sara Kearney, the company's accountant, calculated that the actual costs for the order were direct materials, \$540; direct labor, \$420; and overhead, \$210. The actual product unit cost for the order was \$0.39, calculated as follows:

Actual direct materials (\$540 ÷ 3,000 candy bars)	\$0.18
Actual direct labor (\$420 ÷ 3,000 candy bars)	0.14
Actual overhead (\$210 ÷ 3,000 candy bars)	0.07
Actual product cost per candy bar (\$1,170 ÷ 3,000 candy bars)	\$0.39

Study Note

The use of normal costing is widespread, since many overhead bills, such as utility bills, are not received until after products or services are produced and sold.

Normal Costing Method The **normal costing** method combines the easy-to-track actual direct costs of materials and labor with estimated overhead costs to determine a product unit cost.

- The normal costing method is simple and allows a smoother, more even assignment of overhead costs to production during an accounting period than is possible with the actual costing method.
- However, at the end of the accounting period, any difference between the estimated and actual costs must be identified and removed so that the financial statements show only the actual product costs.

Assume that Sara Kearney used normal costing to price the Good Foods Store order for 3,000 candy bars and that overhead was applied to the product's cost using an estimated rate of 60 percent of direct labor costs. In this case, the costs for the order would include the actual direct materials cost of \$540, the actual direct labor cost of \$420, and an estimated overhead cost of \$252 (\$420 × 60%). The product unit cost would be \$0.40:

Actual direct materials (\$540 ÷ 3,000 candy bars)	\$0.18
Actual direct labor (\$420 ÷ 3,000 candy bars)	0.14
Estimated overhead (\$252 ÷ 3,000 candy bars)	0.08
Normal product cost per candy bar (\$1,212 ÷ 3,000 candy bars)	\$0.40

Standard Costing Method The **standard costing** method uses estimated or standard costs of direct materials, direct labor, and overhead to calculate the product unit cost.

- Managers sometimes need product cost information before the accounting period begins so that they can control the cost of operating activities or price a proposed product for a customer. In such situations, product unit costs must be estimated, and the standard costing method can be helpful.
- Standard costing is very useful in performance management and evaluation because a manager can compare actual and standard costs to compute the variances. We cover standard costing in more detail in another chapter.

Assume that The Choice Candy Company is placing a bid to manufacture 2,000 candy bars for a new customer. From standard cost information developed at the beginning of the period, Kearney estimates the following costs: \$0.20 per unit for direct materials, \$0.15 per unit for direct labor, and \$0.09 per unit for overhead (assuming a standard overhead rate of 60 percent of direct labor cost). The standard cost per unit would be \$0.44:

Standard direct materials	\$0.20
Standard direct labor	0.15
Standard overhead (\$0.15 × 60%)	0.09
Standard product cost per candy bar	\$0.44

Computing Service Unit Cost

Delivering products, representing people in courts of law, selling insurance policies, and computing people's income taxes are typical of the services performed in many service organizations. Like other services, these are labor-intensive processes supported by indirect materials or supplies, indirect labor, and other overhead costs.

- The most important cost in a service organization is the direct cost of labor that can be traceable to the service rendered.
- The indirect costs incurred in performing a service are similar to those incurred in manufacturing a product. They are classified as overhead.
- These service costs appear on service organizations' income statements as cost of sales.

Study Note

Any material costs in a service organization would be for supplies used in providing services. Because these are indirect materials costs, they are included in overhead.

STOP & APPLY >

Fickle Picking Services provides inexpensive, high-quality labor for farmers growing vegetable and fruit crops. In September, Fickle Picking Services paid laborers \$4,000 to harvest 500 acres of apples. The company incurred overhead costs of \$2,400 for apple-picking services in September. This amount included the costs of transporting the laborers to the orchards; of providing facilities, food, and beverages for the laborers; and of scheduling, billing, and collecting from the farmers. Of this amount, 50 percent was related to picking apples. Compute the cost per acre to pick apples.

SOLUTION

Total cost to pick apples:	\$4,000 + (0.50 × \$2,400) = \$5,200
Cost per acre to pick apples:	\$5,200 ÷ 500 acres = \$10.40 per acre

Cost Allocation

LO5 Define *cost allocation,* and explain how the traditional method of allocating overhead costs figures into calculating product or service unit cost.

As noted earlier, the costs of direct materials and direct labor can be easily traced to a product or service, but overhead costs are indirect costs that must be collected and allocated in some manner.

- **Cost allocation** is the process of assigning a collection of indirect costs, such as overhead, to a specific **cost object**, such as a product or service, a department, or an operating activity, using an allocation base known as a cost driver.
- A **cost driver** might be direct labor hours, direct labor costs, units produced, or another activity base that has a cause-and-effect relationship with the cost.
- As the cost driver increases in volume, it causes the **cost pool**—the collection of indirect costs assigned to a cost object—to increase in amount.

Suppose The Choice Candy Company has a machine maintenance cost pool. The cost pool consists of overhead costs needed to maintain the machines, the cost object is the candy product, and the cost driver is machine hours. As more machine hours are used to maintain the machines, the amount of the cost pool increases, thus increasing the costs assigned to the candy product.

Allocating the Costs of Overhead

Allocating overhead costs to products or services is a four-step process that corresponds to the four stages of the management process:

1. *Planning.* In the first step, managers estimate overhead costs and calculate a rate at which they will assign those costs to products or services.
2. *Performing.* In the second step, this rate is applied to products or services as overhead costs are incurred and recorded during production.
3. *Evaluating.* In the third step, actual overhead costs are recorded as they are incurred, and managers calculate the difference between the estimated (or applied) and actual costs.
4. *Communicating.* In the fourth step, managers report on this difference.

Figure 19-6 summarizes these four steps in terms of their timing, the procedures involved, and the entries they require. It also shows how the cost flows in the various steps affect the accounting records.

Step 1. ***Planning the overhead rate.*** Before a period begins, managers determine cost pools and cost drivers and calculate a **predetermined overhead rate** by dividing the cost pool of total estimated overhead costs by the total estimated cost driver level.

- Grouping all estimated overhead costs into one cost pool and using direct labor hours or machine hours as the cost driver results in a single, plantwide overhead rate.
- This step requires no entry because no business activity has occurred.

Step 2. ***Applying the overhead rate.*** As units of the product or service are produced during the period, the estimated overhead costs are assigned to the product or service using the predetermined overhead rate.

- The predetermined overhead rate is multiplied by the actual cost driver level (e.g., the actual number of direct labor hours used to complete the product). The purpose of this calculation is to assign a consistent overhead cost to each unit produced during the period.
- An entry records the allocation of overhead. The entry to apply overhead to a product is recorded as a debit or increase to the Work in Process Inventory account and a credit or decrease to the Overhead account.

FIGURE 19-6
Allocating Overhead Costs: A Four-Step Process

Year 2010 — January 1 — Year 2011 → December 31

	Step 1: Planning the Overhead Rate	Step 2: Applying the Overhead Rate	Step 3: Recording Actual Overhead Costs	Step 4: Reconciling Applied and Actual Overhead Costs
Timing and Procedure	Before the accounting period begins, determine cost pools and cost drivers. Calculate the overhead rate by dividing the cost pool of total estimated overhead costs by the total estimated cost driver level.	During the accounting period, as units are produced, apply overhead costs to products by multiplying the predetermined overhead rate for each cost pool by the actual cost driver level for that pool. Record costs.	Record actual overhead costs as they are incurred during the accounting period.	At the end of the accounting period, calculate and reconcile the difference between applied and actual overhead costs.
Entry	None	Increase Work in Process Inventory account and decrease Overhead account: Dr. Work in Process Inventory XX Cr. Overhead XX	Increase Overhead account and decrease asset accounts or increase contra-asset or liability accounts: Dr. Overhead XX Cr. Various Accounts XX	Entry will vary depending on how costs have been applied. If overapplied, increase Overhead and decrease Cost of Goods Sold. If underapplied, increase Cost of Goods Sold and decrease Overhead.
Cost Flow Through the Accounts		Overhead Dr.: — Cr.: **Overhead applied using predetermined rate** Work in Process Inventory Dr.: **Overhead applied using predetermined rate** Cr.: —	Overhead Dr.: **Actual overhead costs recorded** Cr.: — Various Asset and Liability Accounts Dr.: — Cr.: **Actual overhead costs recorded**	**Overapplied:** Overhead Dr.: Actual overhead costs recorded; **Overapplied** Cr.: Overhead applied using predetermined rate Bal. $0 Cost of Goods Sold Dr.: Bal. Cr.: **Overapplied** Actual Bal. **Underapplied:** Overhead Dr.: Actual overhead costs recorded Cr.: Overhead applied using predetermined rate; **Underapplied** Bal. $0 Cost of Goods Sold Dr.: Bal.; **Underapplied** Cr.: — Actual Bal.

Step 3. ***Recording actual overhead costs.*** The actual overhead costs are recorded as they are incurred during the period.

- These costs include the actual costs of indirect materials, indirect labor, depreciation, property taxes, and other production costs.
- The entry made for the actual overhead costs records a debit in the Overhead account and a credit in the asset, contra-asset, or liability accounts affected.

Step 4. ***Reconciling the applied and actual overhead amounts.*** At the end of the period, the difference between the applied and actual overhead costs is calculated and reconciled.

Overapplied Overhead If the overhead costs applied to production during the period are greater than the actual overhead costs, the difference in the amounts represents **overapplied overhead costs**.

- If this difference is immaterial, the Overhead account is debited or increased and the Cost of Goods Sold or Cost of Sales account is credited or decreased by the difference.
- If the difference is material for the products produced, adjustments are made to the accounts affected—that is, the Work in Process Inventory, Finished Goods Inventory, and Cost of Goods Sold accounts.

Underapplied Overhead If the overhead costs applied to production during the period are less than the actual overhead costs, the difference represents **underapplied overhead costs**.

- If the difference is immaterial, the Cost of Goods Sold or Cost of Sales account is debited or increased and the Overhead account is credited or decreased by this difference.
- If the difference is material for the products produced, adjustments are made to the accounts affected—that is, the Work in Process Inventory, Finished Goods Inventory, and Cost of Goods Sold accounts.

Actual Cost of Goods Sold or Cost of Sales The adjustment for overapplied or underapplied overhead costs is necessary to reflect the actual overhead costs on the income statement.

Allocating Overhead: The Traditional Approach

The traditional approach to applying overhead costs to a product or service is to use a single plantwide overhead rate.

- This approach is especially useful when companies manufacture only one product or a few very similar products that require the same production processes and production-related activities, such as setup, inspection, and materials handling.
- The total overhead costs constitute one cost pool, and a traditional activity base—such as direct labor hours, direct labor costs, machine hours, or units of production—is the cost driver.

As we continue with our example of The Choice Candy Company, let's assume that the company will be selling two product lines in the coming year—plain candy bars and candy bars with nuts—and that Sara Kearney chooses direct labor hours as the cost driver. Kearney estimates that total overhead costs for the next year will be $20,000 and that total direct labor hours (DLH) worked will be 400,000 hours.

TABLE 19-3 Allocating Overhead Costs and Calculating Product Unit Cost: Traditional Approach

Step 1. Calculate overhead rate for cost pool:

$$\frac{\text{Estimated Total Overhead Costs}}{\text{Estimated Total Cost Driver Level}} = \frac{\$20{,}000}{400{,}000\ (\text{DLH})} = \$0.05 \text{ per DLH}$$

Step 2. Apply predetermined overhead rate to products:

	Plain Candy Bars	Candy Bars with Nuts
	Predetermined Overhead Rate × Actual Cost Driver Level = Cost Applied to Production	**Predetermined Overhead Rate × Actual Cost Driver Level = Cost Applied to Production**
Overhead applied: $0.05 per DLH	$0.05 × 250,000 DLH = $12,500	$0.05 × 150,000 DLH = $7,500
Overhead cost per unit:		
Cost Applied ÷ Number of Units	$12,500 ÷ 100,000 = $0.13	$7,500 ÷ 50,000 = $0.15

Product unit cost using normal costing:

	Plain Candy Bars	Candy Bars with Nuts
Product costs per unit:		
Direct materials	$0.18	$0.21
Direct labor	0.14	0.16
Applied overhead	0.13	0.15
Total product unit cost	$0.45	$0.52

Table 19-3 summarizes the first two steps in the traditional approach to allocating overhead costs.

Step 1. ***Planning the overhead rate.*** Kearney uses the following formula to compute the rate at which overhead costs will be applied:

$$\text{Predetermined Overhead Rate} = \frac{\$20{,}000}{400{,}000 \text{ DLH}} = \$0.05 \text{ per DLH}$$

Step 2. ***Applying the overhead rate.*** Kearney applies the predetermined overhead rate to the products. During the year, The Choice Candy Company actually uses 250,000 direct labor hours to produce 100,000 plain candy bars and 150,000 direct labor hours to produce 50,000 candy bars with nuts.

- The portion of the overhead cost applied to the plain candy bars totals $12,500 ($0.05 × 250,000 DLH), or $0.13 per unit ($12,500 ÷ 100,000 units).
- The portion of overhead applied to the candy bars with nuts totals $7,500 ($0.05 × 150,000 DLH), or $0.15 per unit ($7,500 ÷ 50,000 units).

Product Unit Cost Using the Normal Costing Approach Kearney also wants to calculate the product unit cost for the accounting period using normal costing. She gathers the following data for the two product lines:

	Plain Candy Bars	*Candy Bars with Nuts*
Actual direct materials cost per unit	$0.18	$0.21
Actual direct labor cost per unit	0.14	0.16
Prime cost per unit	$0.32	$0.37

At the bottom of Table 19-3 is Kearney's calculation of the normal product unit cost for each product line consisting of its prime costs plus applied overhead. The product unit cost of the candy bar with nuts ($0.52) is higher than the plain candy bar's cost ($0.45) because producing the candy bar with nuts required more expensive materials and more labor time.

Step 3. ***Recording actual overhead costs.*** Kearney records the actual overhead costs as they were incurred during the year. The actual overhead costs totaled $19,800. The entry she made records a debit in the Overhead account and a credit in the asset, contra-asset, or liability accounts affected.

Step 4. ***Reconciling the applied and actual overhead amounts.*** Kearney compares the actual and applied overhead costs to compute the amount of underapplied or overapplied overhead:

	Actual	*Applied*	*Overapplied*
Overhead Costs	$19,800	$20,000	$200

Study Note

Don't make the mistake of thinking that because a cost is not traced directly to a product, it is not a product cost. All manufacturing costs, both direct and indirect, are product costs.

Actual Cost of Goods Sold Cost of Goods Sold will be reduced by the $200 of overapplied overhead costs. The adjustment is necessary to reflect the actual overhead costs on the income statement.

Allocating Overhead: The ABC Approach

Activity-based costing (ABC) is a more accurate method of assigning overhead costs to products or services than the traditional approach. It categorizes all indirect costs by activity, traces the indirect costs to those activities, and assigns activity costs to products or services using a cost driver related to the cause of the cost.

- A company that uses ABC identifies production-related activities or tasks and the events and circumstances that cause, or drive, those activities, such as number of inspections or maintenance hours. As a result, many smaller activity pools are created from the single overhead cost pool used in the traditional method.
- This means that managers will calculate many rates. There will be an overhead rate, or activity cost rate, for each activity pool, which must be applied to products or services produced.
- Managers must select an appropriate number of activity pools instead of the traditional plantwide rate for overhead.

ABC will improve the accuracy of product or service cost estimates for organizations. More careful cost allocation means that managers will have better information for decision making. The ABC approach to allocating overhead will be covered in a later chapter.

& APPLY >

1. Compute the predetermined overhead rate for the Sample Service Company if its estimated overhead costs for the coming year will be $15,000 and 5,000 direct labor hours will be worked.
2. Calculate the amount of overhead costs applied by the Sample Service Company to one of its jobs if the job required 10 direct labor hours to complete.
3. Compute the total cost of the job if prime (direct material and direct labor) costs incurred by Sample Service Company to complete it were $60. If the job contained 5 units of service, what is the unit cost?
4. Using the traditional overhead rate computed in Step 1, determine the total amount of overhead applied to operations during the year if Sample Service Company compiles a total of 4,900 labor hours worked.
5. If Sample Company's actual overhead costs for the year are $14,800, compute the amount of under- or overapplied overhead for the year. Will the Cost of Goods Sold account be increased or decreased to correct the under- or overapplication of overhead?

SOLUTION

1. $$\text{Predetermined Overhead Rate} = \frac{\text{Estimated Overhead Costs}}{\text{Estimated Direct Labor Hours}} = \frac{\$15{,}000}{5{,}000\text{ DLH}} = \$3.00\text{ per DLH}$$

2. Overhead Costs Applied = Predetermined Overhead Rate × Actual Hours Worked

   $3 per DLH × 10 Actual Direct Labor Hours Worked = $30

3. Total Cost = Actual Direct Materials Cost + Actual Direct Labor Cost + Applied Overhead Cost

   = $60 + $30 = $90

   $$\text{Unit Cost} = \frac{\text{Total Cost of Job}}{\text{Units Produced}} = \frac{\$90}{5\text{ units}} = \$18\text{ per unit}$$

4. Overhead Costs Applied = Predetermined Overhead Rate × Actual Hours Worked During Year

   = $3 per DLH × 4,900 Actual Direct Labor Hours Worked

   = $14,700.00

5. | | | |
   |---|---|---|
   | Overhead Costs Applied | = | $14,700 |
   | Actual Overhead Costs | = | 14,800 |
   | Underapplied Overhead | = | $ 100, which will increase the Cost of Goods Sold account |

THE CHOICE CANDY COMPANY: REVIEW PROBLEM

In this chapter's Decision Point, we posed these questions:

- How do managers at The Choice Candy Company determine the cost of a candy bar?
- How do they use cost information?

To determine the cost of a candy bar, managers at The Choice Candy Company must conduct complex analyses of many product costs, as well as costs that are unrelated to products. They analyze both the traceable costs of direct labor and materials and the indirect costs needed to support candy production. They also consider any other relevant selling, administrative, or general operating costs that relate to the candy bars.

Classifying and analyzing costs helps managers make decisions that will sustain The Choice Candy Company's profitability. All costs must be analyzed in terms of their traceability and behavior and in terms of whether they add value and how they affect the financial statements. Because many costs cannot be directly traced to specific candy products, managers must use a method of allocation to assign them. Possibilities include the traditional allocation method and the activity-based costing method discussed in this chapter.

Calculating Cost of Goods Manufactured: Three Fundamental Steps

LO2 LO4

Assume that one of The Choice Candy Company's factories produces 50-pound blocks of dark chocolate and that it needs to prepare a year-end balance sheet and income statement, as well as a statement of cost of goods manufactured. During the year, the factory purchased $361,920 of direct materials. The factory's direct labor costs for the year were $99,085 (10,430 hours at $9.50 per hour); its indirect labor costs totaled $126,750 (20,280 hours at $6.25 per hour). Account balances for the year were as follows:

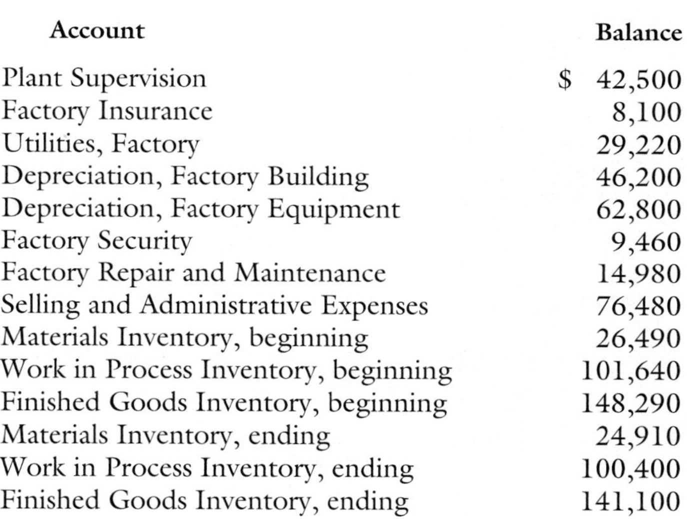

Account	Balance
Plant Supervision	$ 42,500
Factory Insurance	8,100
Utilities, Factory	29,220
Depreciation, Factory Building	46,200
Depreciation, Factory Equipment	62,800
Factory Security	9,460
Factory Repair and Maintenance	14,980
Selling and Administrative Expenses	76,480
Materials Inventory, beginning	26,490
Work in Process Inventory, beginning	101,640
Finished Goods Inventory, beginning	148,290
Materials Inventory, ending	24,910
Work in Process Inventory, ending	100,400
Finished Goods Inventory, ending	141,100

Required

1. Compute the cost of materials used during the year.
2. Given the cost of materials used, compute the total manufacturing costs for the year.

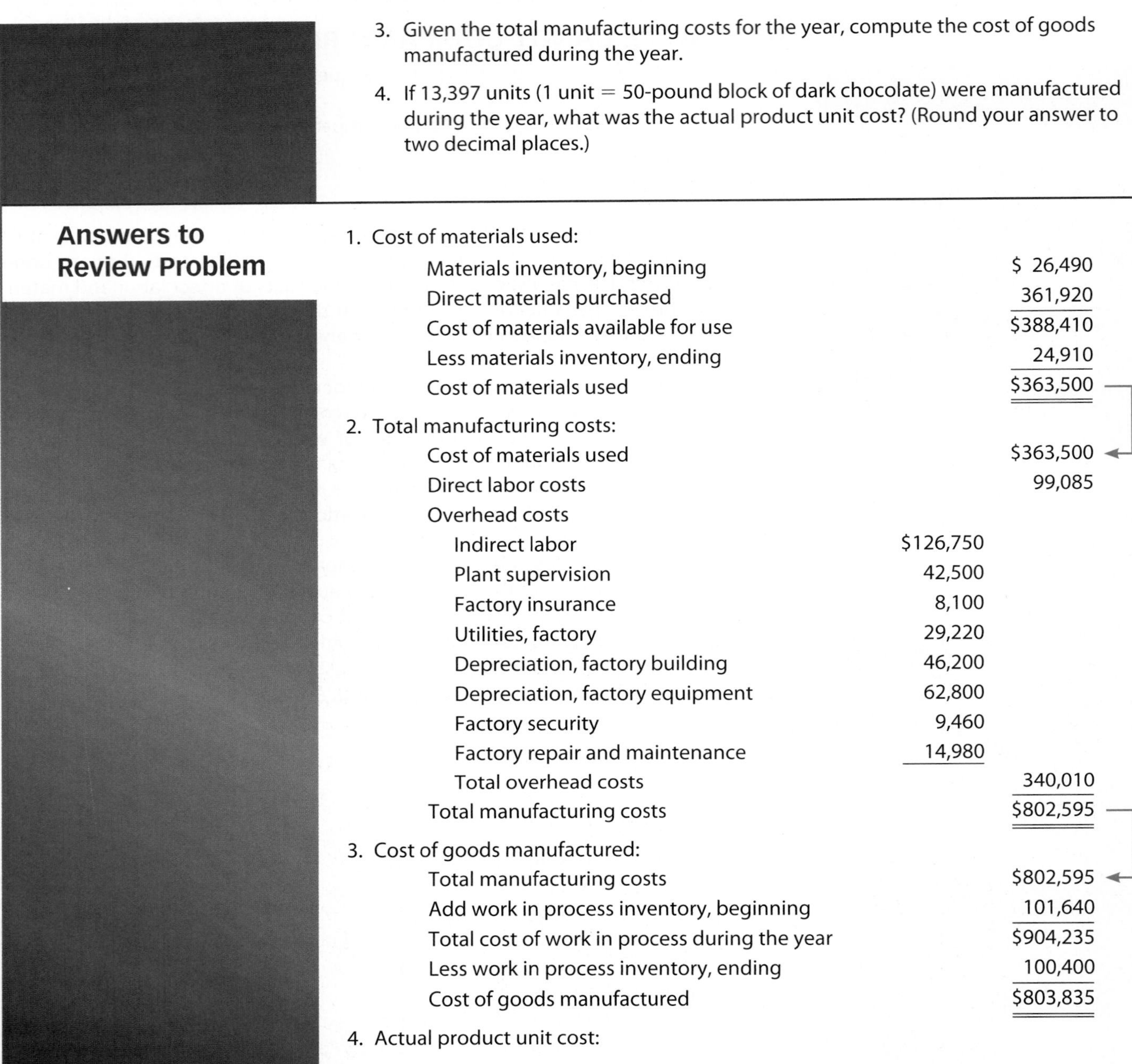

3. Given the total manufacturing costs for the year, compute the cost of goods manufactured during the year.
4. If 13,397 units (1 unit = 50-pound block of dark chocolate) were manufactured during the year, what was the actual product unit cost? (Round your answer to two decimal places.)

Answers to Review Problem

1. Cost of materials used:

Materials inventory, beginning	$ 26,490
Direct materials purchased	361,920
Cost of materials available for use	$388,410
Less materials inventory, ending	24,910
Cost of materials used	$363,500

2. Total manufacturing costs:

Cost of materials used		$363,500
Direct labor costs		99,085
Overhead costs		
Indirect labor	$126,750	
Plant supervision	42,500	
Factory insurance	8,100	
Utilities, factory	29,220	
Depreciation, factory building	46,200	
Depreciation, factory equipment	62,800	
Factory security	9,460	
Factory repair and maintenance	14,980	
Total overhead costs		340,010
Total manufacturing costs		$802,595

3. Cost of goods manufactured:

Total manufacturing costs	$802,595
Add work in process inventory, beginning	101,640
Total cost of work in process during the year	$904,235
Less work in process inventory, ending	100,400
Cost of goods manufactured	$803,835

4. Actual product unit cost:

$$\frac{\text{Cost of Goods Manufactured}}{\text{Number of Units Manufactured}} = \frac{\$803{,}835}{13{,}397 \text{ units}} = \$60.00^*$$

*Rounded.

LO1 Explain how managers classify costs and how they use these cost classifications.

Managers in manufacturing, retail, and service organizations use information about operating costs and product or service costs to prepare budgets, make pricing and other decisions, calculate variances between estimated and actual costs, and communicate results.

A single cost can be classified as a direct or an indirect cost, a variable or a fixed cost, a value-adding or a nonvalue-adding cost, and a product or a period cost. These cost classifications enable managers to control costs by tracing them to cost objects, to calculate the number of units that must be sold to obtain a certain level of profit, to identify the costs of activities that do and do not add value to a product or service, and to prepare financial statements for parties outside the organization.

LO2 Compare how service, retail, and manufacturing organizations report costs on their financial statements and how they account for inventories.

Because the operations of service, retail, and manufacturing organizations differ, their financial statements differ as well. A service organization maintains no inventory accounts on its balance sheet. The cost of sales on its income statement reflects the net cost of the services sold. A retail organization, which purchases products ready for resale, maintains only a Merchandise Inventory account, which is used to record and account for items in inventory. The cost of goods sold is simply the difference between the cost of goods available for sale and the ending merchandise inventory. A manufacturing organization, because it creates a product, maintains three inventory accounts: Materials Inventory, Work in Process Inventory, and Finished Goods Inventory. Manufacturing costs flow through all three inventory accounts. During the accounting period, the cost of completed products is transferred to the Finished Goods Inventory account, and the cost of units that have been manufactured and sold is transferred to the Cost of Goods Sold account.

LO3 Describe the flow of costs through a manufacturer's inventory accounts.

The flow of costs through the inventory accounts begins when costs for direct materials, direct labor, and overhead are incurred. Materials costs flow first into the Materials Inventory account, which is used to record the costs of materials when they are received and again when they are issued for use in a production process. All manufacturing-related costs—direct materials, direct labor, and overhead—are recorded in the Work in Process Inventory account as the production process begins. When products are completed, their costs are transferred from the Work in Process Inventory account to the Finished Goods Inventory account. Costs remain in the Finished Goods Inventory account until the products are sold, at which time they are transferred to the Cost of Goods Sold account.

LO4 Define *product unit cost,* and compute the unit cost of a product or service.

Direct materials costs are the costs of materials used in making a product that can be conveniently and economically traced to specific product units. Direct labor costs include all labor costs needed to make a product or service that can be traced to specific product units. All other production-related costs are classified and accounted for as overhead costs. Such costs cannot be easily traced to end products or services, so a cost allocation method is used to assign them to products or services.

When a batch of products has been completed, the product unit cost is computed by dividing the total cost of direct materials, direct labor, and overhead by the total number of units produced. The product unit cost can be calculated using the actual, normal, or standard costing method. Under actual costing, the actual costs of direct materials, direct labor, and overhead are used to compare the product unit cost. Under normal costing, the actual costs of direct materials and direct labor are combined with the estimated cost of overhead to determine the product unit cost. Under standard costing, the estimated costs of direct materials, direct labor, and overhead are used to calculate the product unit cost. The components of product cost may be classified as prime costs or conversion costs. Prime costs are the primary costs of production; they are the sum of direct materials costs and direct labor costs. Conversion costs are the costs of converting direct materials into finished product; they are the sum of direct labor costs and overhead costs.

Because no products are manufactured in the course of providing services, service organizations have no materials costs. They do, however, have both direct labor costs and overhead costs, which are similar to those in manufacturing organizations. To determine the cost of performing a service, professional labor and service-related overhead costs are included in the analysis.

LO5 Define *cost allocation,* and explain how the traditional method of allocating overhead costs figures into calculating product or service unit cost.

Cost allocation is the process of assigning collected indirect costs to a specific cost object using an allocation base known as a cost driver. The allocation of overhead costs requires the pooling of overhead costs that are affected by a common activity and the selection of a cost driver whose activity level causes a change in the cost pool. A cost pool is the collection of overhead costs assigned to a cost object. A cost driver is an activity base that causes the cost pool to increase in amount as the cost driver increases.

Allocating overhead is a four-step process that involves planning a rate at which overhead costs will be assigned to products or services, assigning overhead costs at this predetermined rate to products or services during production, recording actual overhead costs as they are incurred, and reconciling the difference between the actual and applied overhead costs. The Cost of Goods Sold or Cost of Sales account is corrected for an amount of over- or underapplied overhead costs assigned to the products or services. In manufacturing companies, if the difference is material, adjustments are made to the Work in Process Inventory, Finished Goods Inventory, and Cost of Goods Sold accounts.

The traditional method applies overhead costs to a product or service by estimating one predetermined overhead rate and multiplying that rate by the actual cost driver level. The product or service unit cost is computed either by dividing the total product or service cost (the sum of the total applied overhead cost and the actual costs of direct materials and direct labor) by the total number of units produced or by determining the cost per unit for each element of the product's or service's cost and summing those per unit costs.

REVIEW of Concepts and Terminology

The following concepts and terms were introduced in this chapter:

Activity-based costing (ABC) 859 (LO5)

Actual costing 853 (LO4)

Conversion costs 851 (LO4)

Cost allocation 855 (LO5)

Cost driver 855 (LO5)

Cost object 855 (LO5)

Cost of goods manufactured 849 (LO3)

Cost pool 855 (LO5)

Direct costs 839 (LO1)

Direct labor costs 850 (LO4)

Direct materials costs 850 (LO4)

Finished Goods Inventory account 846 (LO3)

Fixed cost 840 (LO1)

Indirect costs 839 (LO1)

Indirect labor costs 851 (LO4)

Indirect materials costs 851 (LO4)

Manufacturing cost flow 847 (LO3)

Materials Inventory account 846 (LO3)

Nonvalue-adding cost 840 (LO1)

Normal costing 853 (LO4)

Overapplied overhead costs 857 (LO5)

Overhead costs 851 (LO4)

Period costs 841 (LO1)

Predetermined overhead rate 855 (LO5)

Prime costs 851 (LO4)

Product costs 841 (LO1)

Product unit cost 852 (LO4)

Standard costing 853 (LO4)

Statement of cost of goods manufactured 844 (LO2)

Total manufacturing costs 849 (LO3)

Underapplied overhead costs 857 (LO5)

Value-adding cost 840 (LO1)

Variable cost 840 (LO1)

Work in Process Inventory account 846 (LO3)

CHAPTER ASSIGNMENTS

BUILDING Your Basic Knowledge and Skills

Short Exercises

LO1 **Cost Classifications**

SE 1. Indicate whether each of the following is a direct cost (D), an indirect cost (ID), or neither (N) and a variable (V) or a fixed (F) cost. Also indicate whether each adds value (VA) or does not add value (NVA) to the product and whether each is a product cost (PD) or a period cost (PER).

1. Production supervisor's salary
2. Sales commission
3. Wages of a production-line worker

LO2 **Income Statement for a Manufacturing Organization**

SE 2. Using the following information from Char Company, prepare an income statement through operating income for the year:

Sales	$900,000
Finished goods inventory, beginning	45,000
Cost of goods manufactured	585,000
Finished goods inventory, ending	60,000
Operating expenses	275,000

LO3 **Cost Flow in a Manufacturing Organization**

SE 3. Given the following information, compute the ending balances of the Materials Inventory, Work in Process Inventory, and Finished Goods Inventory accounts:

Materials Inventory, beginning balance	$ 23,000
Work in Process Inventory, beginning balance	25,750
Finished Goods Inventory, beginning balance	38,000
Direct materials purchased	85,000
Direct materials placed into production	74,000
Direct labor costs	97,000
Overhead costs	35,000
Cost of goods manufactured	123,000
Cost of goods sold	93,375

LO3 **Document Flows in a Manufacturing Organization**

SE 4. Identify the document needed to support each of the following activities in a manufacturing organization:

1. Placing an order for direct materials with a supplier
2. Recording direct labor time at the beginning and end of each work shift
3. Receiving direct materials at the shipping dock
4. Recording the costs of a specific job requiring direct materials, direct labor, and overhead
5. Issuing direct materials into production
6. Billing the customer for a completed order
7. Fulfilling a request from the Production Scheduling Department for the purchase of direct materials

LO4 **Elements of Manufacturing Costs**

E 5. Dalston Lui, the accountant at Brightlight, Inc., must group the costs of manufacturing candles. Indicate whether each of the following items should be classified as direct materials (DM), direct labor (DL), overhead (O), or none of these (N). Also indicate whether each is a prime cost (PC), a conversion cost (CC), or neither (N).

1. Depreciation of the cost of vats to hold melted wax
2. Cost of wax
3. Rent on the factory where candles are made
4. Cost of George's time to dip the wicks into the wax
5. Cost of coloring for candles
6. Cost of Ray's time to design candles for Halloween
7. Sam's commission to sell candles to Candles Plus

LO4 **Computation of Product Unit Cost**

E 6. What is the product unit cost for Job 14, which consists of 300 units and has total manufacturing costs of direct materials, $4,500; direct labor, $7,500; and overhead, $3,600? What are the prime costs and conversion costs per unit?

LO5 **Calculation of Underapplied or Overapplied Overhead**

SE 7. At year end, records show that actual overhead costs incurred were $25,870 and the amount of overhead costs applied to production was $27,000. Identify the amount of under- or overapplied overhead, and indicate whether the Cost of Goods Sold account should be increased or decreased to reflect actual overhead costs.

LO5 **Computation of Overhead Rate**

SE 8. Compute the overhead rate per service request for the Maintenance Department if estimated overhead costs are $18,290 and the number of estimated service requests is 3,100.

LO5 **Allocation of Overhead to Production**

SE 9. Calculate the amount of overhead costs applied to production if the predetermined overhead rate is $4 per direct labor hour and 1,200 direct labor hours were worked.

Exercises

LO1 **The Management Process and Operating Costs**

E 1. Indicate whether each of the following activities takes place during the planning (PL), performing (PE), evaluating (E), or communicating (C) stage of the management process:

1. Changing regular price to clearance price
2. Reporting results to appropriate personnel
3. Preparing budgets of operating costs
4. Comparing estimated and actual costs to determine variances

LO1 **Cost Classifications**

E 2. Indicate whether each of the following costs for a bicycle manufacturer is a product or a period cost, a variable or a fixed cost, a value-adding or a nonvalue-adding cost, and, if it is a product cost, a direct or an indirect cost of the bicycle:

	Cost Classification			
Example	Product or Period	Variable or Fixed	Value-Adding or Nonvalue-Adding	Direct or Indirect
Bicycle tire	Product	Variable	Value-adding	Direct

1. Depreciation on office computer
2. Labor to assemble bicycle
3. Labor to inspect bicycle
4. Internal auditor's salary
5. Lubricant for wheels

LO2 **Comparison of Income Statement Formats**

E 3. Indicate whether each of these equations applies to a service organization (SER), a retail organization (RET), or a manufacturing organization (MANF):

1. Cost of Goods Sold = Beginning Merchandise Inventory + Net Cost of Purchases − Ending Merchandise Inventory
2. Cost of Sales = Net Cost of Services Sold
3. Cost of Goods Sold = Beginning Finished Goods Inventory + Cost of Goods Manufactured − Ending Finished Goods Inventory

LO2 **Statement of Cost of Goods Manufactured**

E 4. During August, Radio Company's purchases of direct materials totaled $139,000; direct labor for the month was 3,400 hours at $8.75 per hour. Radio also incurred the following overhead costs: utilities, $5,870; supervision, $16,600; indirect materials, $6,750; depreciation, $6,200; insurance, $1,830; and miscellaneous, $1,100.

Beginning inventory accounts were as follows: Materials Inventory, $48,600; Work in Process Inventory, $54,250; and Finished Goods Inventory, $38,500. Ending inventory accounts were as follows: Materials Inventory, $50,100; Work in Process Inventory, $48,400; and Finished Goods Inventory, $37,450.

From the information given, prepare a statement of cost of goods manufactured.

LO2 **Statement of Cost of Goods Manufactured and Cost of Goods Sold**

E 5. Treetop Corp. makes irrigation sprinkler systems for tree nurseries. Ramsey Roe, Treetop's new controller, can find only the following partial information for the past year:

	Oak Division	Loblolly Division	Maple Division	Spruce Division
Direct materials used	$3	$ 7	$ g	$ 8
Total manufacturing costs	6	d	h	14
Overhead	1	3	2	j
Direct labor	a	6	4	4
Ending work in process inventory	b	3	2	5
Cost of goods manufactured	7	20	12	1
Beginning work in process inventory	2	e	3	k
Ending finished goods inventory	2	6	i	9
Beginning finished goods inventory	3	f	5	7
Cost of goods sold	c	18	13	9

Using the information given, compute the unknown values. List the accounts in the proper order, and show subtotals and totals as appropriate.

LO2 **Characteristics of Organizations**

E 6. Indicate whether each of the following is typical of a service organization (SER), a retail organization (RET), or a manufacturing organization (MANF):

1. Maintains only one balance sheet inventory account
2. Maintains no balance sheet inventory accounts
3. Maintains three balance sheet inventory accounts
4. Purchases products ready for resale
5. Designs and makes products for sale
6. Sells services
7. Determines the net cost of services sold
8. Includes the cost of goods manufactured in calculating cost of goods sold
9. Includes the net cost of purchases in calculating cost of goods sold

LO2 **Missing Amounts—Manufacturing**

E 7. Presented below are incomplete inventory and income statement data for Toliver Corporation. Determine the missing amounts.

	Cost of Goods Sold	Cost of Goods Manufactured	Beginning Finished Goods Inventory	Ending Finished Goods Inventory
1.	$ 10,000	$12,000	$ 1,000	?
2.	$140,000	?	$45,000	$60,000
3.	?	$89,000	$23,000	$20,000

LO2 **Inventories, Cost of Goods Sold, and Net Income**

E 8. The data presented below are for a retail organization and a manufacturing organization.

1. Fill in the missing data for the retail organization:

	First Quarter	Second Quarter	Third Quarter	Fourth Quarter
Sales	$ 9	$ e	$ 15	$ k
Gross margin	a	4	5	l
Ending merchandise inventory	5	f	5	m
Beginning merchandise inventory	4	g	h	5
Net cost of purchases	b	7	9	n
Operating income	3	2	i	2
Operating expenses	c	2	2	4
Cost of goods sold	5	6	j	11
Cost of goods available for sale	d	12	15	15

2. Fill in the missing data for the manufacturing organization:

	First Quarter	Second Quarter	Third Quarter	Fourth Quarter
Ending finished goods inventory	$a	$ 3	$ h	$ 6
Cost of goods sold	6	3	5	l
Operating income	1	3	1	m
Cost of goods available for sale	8	d	10	13
Cost of goods manufactured	5	e	i	8
Gross margin	4	f	j	7
Operating expenses	3	g	5	6
Beginning finished goods inventory	b	2	3	n
Sales	c	10	k	14

LO3 Documentation

E 9. Waltz Company manufactures music boxes. Seventy percent of its products are standard items produced in long production runs. The other 30 percent are special orders with specific requests for tunes. The latter cost from three to six times as much as the standard product because they require additional materials and labor.

Reza Seca, the controller, recently received a complaint memorandum from Iggy Paulo, the production supervisor, about the new network of source documents that has been added to the existing cost accounting system. The new documents include a purchase request, a purchase order, a receiving report, and a materials request. Paulo claims that the forms create extra work and interrupt the normal flow of production.

Prepare a written memorandum from Reza Seca to Iggy Paulo that fully explains the purpose of each type of document.

LO3 Cost Flows and Inventory Accounts

E 10. For each of the following activities, identify the inventory account (Materials Inventory, Work in Process Inventory, or Finished Goods Inventory), if any, that is affected. If an inventory account is affected, indicate whether the account balance will increase or decrease. (*Example:* Moved completed units to finished goods inventory. *Answer:* Increase Finished Goods Inventory; decrease Work in Process Inventory.) If no inventory account is affected, use "None of these" as your answer.

1. Moved materials requested by production
2. Sold units of product
3. Purchased and received direct materials for production
4. Used direct labor and overhead in the production process
5. Received payment from customer
6. Purchased office supplies and paid cash
7. Paid monthly office rent

LO4 Unit Cost Determination

E 11. The Pattia Winery is one of the finest wineries in the country. One of its famous products is a red wine called Old Vines. Recently, management has become concerned about the increasing cost of making Old Vines and needs to determine if the current selling price of $10 per bottle is adequate. The winery wants to achieve a 25 percent gross profit on the sale of each bottle. The following information is given to you for analysis:

Batch size		10,550 bottles
Costs		
Direct materials		
Olen Millot grapes	$22,155	
Chancellor grapes	9,495	
Bottles	5,275	
Total direct materials costs	$36,925	
Direct labor		
Pickers/loaders	$ 2,110	
Crusher	422	
Processors	8,440	
Bottler	13,293	
Total direct labor costs	$24,265	

Overhead	
Depreciation, equipment	$ 2,743
Depreciation, building	5,275
Utilities	1,055
Indirect labor	6,330
Supervision	7,385
Supplies	9,917
Repairs	1,477
Miscellaneous	633
Total overhead costs	$34,815
Total production costs	$96,005

1. Compute the unit cost per bottle for materials, labor, and overhead.
2. How would you advise management regarding the price per bottle of wine?
3. Compute the prime costs per unit and the conversion costs per unit.

LO4 Unit Costs in a Service Business

E 12. Walden Green provides custom farming services to owners of 5-acre wheat fields. In July, he earned $2,400 by cutting, turning, and baling 3,000 bales. In the same month, he incurred the following costs: gas, $150; tractor maintenance, $115; and labor, $600. His annual tractor depreciation is $1,500. What was Green's cost per bale? What was his revenue per bale? Should he increase the amount he charges for his services?

LO5 Computation of Overhead Rate

E 13. The overhead costs that Lucca Industries, Inc., used to compute its overhead rate for the past year are as follows:

Indirect materials and supplies	$ 79,200
Repairs and maintenance	14,900
Outside service contracts	17,300
Indirect labor	79,100
Factory supervision	42,900
Depreciation–machinery	85,000
Factory insurance	8,200
Property taxes	6,500
Heat, light, and power	7,700
Miscellaneous overhead	5,760
Total overhead costs	$346,560

The allocation base for the past year was 45,600 total machine hours. For the next year, all overhead costs except depreciation, property taxes, and miscellaneous overhead are expected to increase by 10 percent. Depreciation should increase by 12 percent, and property taxes and miscellaneous overhead are expected to increase by 20 percent. Plant capacity in terms of machine hours used will increase by 4,400 hours.

1. Compute the past year's overhead rate. (Carry your answer to three decimal places.)
2. Compute the overhead rate for next year. (Carry your answer to three decimal places.)

LO5 Computation and Application of Overhead Rate

E 14. Compumatics specializes in the analysis and reporting of complex inventory costing projects. Materials costs are minimal, consisting entirely of operating supplies (DVDs, inventory sheets, and other recording tools). Labor is the highest single expense, totaling $693,000 for 75,000 hours of work last year. Overhead costs for last year were $916,000 and were applied to specific jobs on the basis of labor hours worked. This year the company anticipates a 25 percent increase in overhead costs. Labor costs will increase by $130,000, and the number of hours worked is expected to increase by 20 percent.

1. Determine the total amount of overhead anticipated this year.
2. Compute the overhead rate for this year. (Round your answer to the nearest cent.)
3. During April of this year, 11,980 labor hours were worked. Calculate the overhead amount assigned to April production.

LO5 Disposition of Overapplied Overhead

E 15. At the end of this year, Compumatics had compiled a total of 89,920 labor hours worked. The actual overhead incurred was $1,143,400.

1. Using the overhead rate computed in **E 14,** determine the total amount of overhead applied to operations during the year.
2. Compute the amount of overapplied overhead for the year.
3. Will the Cost of Goods Sold account be increased or decreased to correct the overapplication of overhead?

Problems

LO2 A Manufacturing Organization's Balance Sheet

P 1. The following information is from the trial balance of Mills Manufacturing Company:

	Debit	Credit
Cash	$ 34,000	
Accounts receivable	27,000	
Materials inventory, ending	31,000	
Work in process inventory, ending	47,900	
Finished goods inventory, ending	54,800	
Production supplies	5,700	
Small tools	9,330	
Land	160,000	
Factory building	575,000	
Accumulated depreciation, factory building		$ 199,000
Factory equipment	310,000	
Accumulated depreciation, factory equipment		137,000
Patents	33,500	
Accounts payable		26,900
Insurance premiums payable		6,700
Income taxes payable		41,500
Mortgage payable		343,000
Common stock		200,000
Retained earnings		334,130
	$1,288,230	$1,288,230

Required

1. Manufacturing organizations use asset accounts that are not needed by retail organizations.
   a. List the titles of the asset accounts that are specifically related to manufacturing organizations.
   b. List the titles of the asset, liability, and equity accounts that you would see on the balance sheets of both manufacturing and retail organizations.

2. Assuming that the following information reflects the results of operations for the year, calculate the (a) gross margin, (b) cost of goods sold, (c) cost of goods available for sale, and (d) cost of goods manufactured:

Operating income	$138,130
Operating expenses	53,670
Sales	500,000
Finished goods inventory, beginning	50,900

Manager insight ▶ 3. Does Mills Manufacturing use the periodic or perpetual inventory system?

LO4 **Computation of Unit Cost**

P 2. Carola Industries, Inc., manufactures discs for several of the leading recording studios in the United States and Europe. Department 60 is responsible for the electronic circuitry within each disc. Department 61 applies the plastic-like surface to the discs and packages them for shipment. Carola recently produced 4,000 discs for the Milo Company. In fulfilling this order, the departments incurred the following costs:

	Department	
	60	61
Direct materials used	$29,440	$3,920
Direct labor	6,800	2,560
Overhead	7,360	4,800

1. Compute the unit cost for each department.
2. Compute the total unit cost for the Milo Company order.

Manager insight ▶ 3. The selling price for this order was $14 per unit. Was the selling price adequate? List the assumptions and/or computations upon which you based your answer. What suggestions would you make to Carola Industries' management about the pricing of future orders?

4. Compute the prime costs and conversion costs per unit for each department.

LO5 **Allocation of Overhead**

P 3. Natural Cosmetics Company applies overhead costs on the basis of machine hours. The overhead rate is computed by analyzing data from the previous year to determine the percentage change in costs. Thus, this year's overhead rate will be based on the percentage change multiplied by last year's costs.

	Last Year
Machine hours	57,360
Overhead costs	
Indirect labor	$ 23,530
Employee benefits	28,600
Manufacturing supervision	18,480
Utilities	14,490
Factory insurance	7,800
Janitorial services	12,100
Depreciation, factory and machinery	21,300
Miscellaneous overhead	7,475
Total overhead	$133,775

This year the cost of utilities is expected to increase by 40 percent over the previous year; the cost of indirect labor, employee benefits, and miscellaneous overhead is expected to increase by 30 percent over the previous year; the cost of insurance and depreciation is expected to increase by 20 percent over the previous year; and the cost of supervision and janitorial services is expected to increase by 10 percent over the previous year. Machine hours are expected to total 68,832.

Required

1. Compute the projected costs and the overhead rate for this year, using the information about expected cost increases. (Carry your answer to three decimal places.)
2. Jobs completed during this year and the machine hours used were as follows:

Job No.	Machine Hours
2214	12,300
2215	14,200
2216	9,800
2217	13,600
2218	11,300
2219	8,100

   Determine the amount of overhead to be applied to each job and to total production during this year. (Round answers to whole dollars.)
3. Actual overhead costs for this year were $165,845. Was overhead underapplied or overapplied? By how much? Should the Cost of Goods Sold account be increased or decreased to reflect actual overhead costs?

LO5 Allocation of Overhead

P 4. Byte Computer Company, a manufacturing organization, has just completed an order that Grater, Ltd., placed for 80 computers. Direct materials, purchased parts, and direct labor costs for the Grater order are as follows:

Cost of direct materials	$36,750.00	Direct labor hours	220
Cost of purchased parts	$21,300.00	Average direct labor pay rate	$15.25

Other operating costs are as follows:

Traditional costing data:

Overhead costs were applied at a single, plantwide overhead rate of 270 percent of direct labor dollars.

Required

Using the traditional costing method, compute the total cost of the Grater order.

Alternate Problems

LO2 Statement of Cost of Goods Manufactured

P 5. Dillo Vineyards, a large winery in Texas, produces a full line of varietal wines. The company, whose fiscal year begins on November 1, has just completed a record-breaking year. Its inventory account balances on October 31 of this year were Materials Inventory, $1,803,800; Work in Process Inventory, $2,764,500; and Finished Goods Inventory, $1,883,200. At the beginning of the year, the inventory account balances were Materials Inventory, $2,156,200; Work in Process Inventory, $3,371,000; and Finished Goods Inventory, $1,596,400.

During the fiscal year, the company's purchases of direct materials totaled $6,750,000. Direct labor hours totaled 142,500, and the average labor rate was $8.20 per hour. The following overhead costs were incurred during the year: depreciation–plant and equipment, $685,600; indirect labor, $207,300; property tax, plant and equipment, $94,200; plant maintenance, $83,700; small tools, $42,400; utilities, $96,500; and employee benefits, $76,100.

Required

Prepare a statement of cost of goods manufactured for the fiscal year ended October 31.

LO4 Unit Costs in a Service Business

P 6. Municipal Hospital relies heavily on cost data to keep its pricing structures in line with those of its competitors. The hospital provides a wide range of services, including intensive care, intermediate care, and a neonatal nursery. Joo Young, the hospital's controller, is concerned about the profits generated by the 30-bed intensive care unit (ICU), so she is reviewing current billing procedures for that unit. The focus of her analysis is the hospital's billing per ICU patient day. This billing equals the per diem cost of intensive care plus a 40 percent markup to cover other operating costs and generate a profit. ICU patient costs include the following:

Doctors' care	2 hours per day @ \$360 per hour (actual)
Special nursing care	4 hours per day @ \$85 per hour (actual)
Regular nursing care	24 hours per day @ \$28 per hour (average)
Medications	\$237 per day (average)
Medical supplies	\$134 per day (average)
Room rental	\$350 per day (average)
Food and services	\$140 per day (average)

One other significant ICU cost is equipment, which is about \$185,000 per room. Young has determined that the cost per patient day for the equipment is \$179.

Wiley Dix, the hospital director, has asked Young to compare the current billing procedure with another that uses industry averages to determine the billing per patient day.

Required

1. Compute the cost per patient per day.
2. Compute the billing per patient day using the hospital's existing markup rate. (Round answers to whole dollars.)
3. Industry averages for markup rates are as follows:

Equipment	30%	Medications	50%
Doctors' care	50	Medical supplies	50
Special nursing care	40	Room rental	30
Regular nursing care	50	Food and services	25

   Using these rates, compute the billing per patient day. (Round answers to the nearest whole dollars.)
4. Based on your findings in requirements **2** and **3**, which billing procedure would you recommend? Why?

LO5 Allocation of Overhead

P 7. Lund Products, Inc., uses a predetermined overhead rate in its production, assembly, and testing departments. One rate is used for the entire company; it is based on machine hours. The rate is determined by analyzing data from the previous year to determine the percentage change in costs. Thus this year's overhead rate will be based on the percentage change multiplied by last year's costs. Lise Jensen is about to compute the rate for this year using the following data:

	Last Year's Costs
Machine hours	41,800
Overhead costs	
Indirect materials	\$ 57,850
Indirect labor	25,440

(continued)

Supervision	$ 41,580
Utilities	11,280
Labor-related costs	9,020
Depreciation, factory	10,780
Depreciation, machinery	27,240
Property taxes	2,880
Insurance	1,920
Miscellaneous overhead	4,840
Total overhead	$192,830

This year the cost of indirect materials is expected to increase by 30 percent over the previous year. The cost of indirect labor, utilities, machinery depreciation, property taxes, and insurance is expected to increase by 20 percent over the previous year. All other expenses are expected to increase by 10 percent over the previous year. Machine hours for this year are estimated at 45,980.

Required

1. Compute the projected costs and the overhead rate for this year using the information about expected cost increases. (Round your answer to three decimal places.)
2. During this year, Lund Products completed the following jobs using the machine hours shown:

Job No.	Machine Hours	Job No.	Machine Hours
H–142	7,840	H–201	10,680
H–164	5,260	H–218	12,310
H–175	8,100	H–304	2,460

Determine the amount of overhead applied to each job. What was the total overhead applied during this year? (Round answers to the nearest dollar.)

3. Actual overhead costs for this year were $234,485. Was overhead underapplied or overapplied this year? By how much? Should the Cost of Goods Sold account be increased or decreased to reflect actual overhead costs?
4. At what point during this year was the overhead rate computed? When was it applied? Finally, when was underapplied or overapplied overhead determined and the Cost of Goods Sold account adjusted to reflect actual costs?

LO5 Allocation of Overhead

P 8. Fraser Products, Inc., which produces copy machines for wholesale distributors in the Pacific Northwest, has just completed packaging an order from Kent Company for 150 Model 14 machines. Direct materials, purchased parts, and direct labor costs for the Kent order are as follows:

Cost of direct materials	$17,450.00
Cost of purchased parts	$14,800.00
Direct labor hours	140
Average direct labor pay rate	$16.50

Other operating costs are as follows:

Traditional costing data:

Overhead costs were applied at a single, plantwide overhead rate of 240 percent of direct labor dollars.

Required

Using the traditional costing approach, compute the total cost of the Kent order.

ENHANCING Your Knowledge, Skills, and Critical Thinking

LO1 Cost Classifications

C 1. Visit a local fast-food restaurant. Observe all aspects of the operation and take notes on the entire process. Describe the procedures used to take, process, and fill an order and deliver the food to the customer. Based on your observations, make a list of the costs incurred by the restaurant. Then create a table similar to Table 19-1 in the text, in which you classify the costs you have identified by their traceability (direct or indirect), cost behavior (variable or fixed), value attribute (value-adding or nonvalue-adding), and implications for financial reporting (product or period costs). Bring your notes and your table to class and be prepared to discuss your findings.

LO1 Management Decision about a Supporting Service Function

C 2. As the manager of grounds maintenance for Latchey, a large insurance company in Missouri, you are responsible for maintaining the grounds surrounding the company's three buildings, the six entrances to the property, and the recreational facilities, which include a golf course, a soccer field, jogging and bike paths, and tennis, basketball, and volleyball courts. Maintenance includes gardening (watering, planting, mowing, trimming, removing debris, and so on) and land improvements (e.g., repairing or replacing damaged or worn concrete and gravel areas).

Early in January, you receive a memo from the president of Latchey requesting information about the cost of operating your department for the last 12 months. She has received a bid from Xeriscape Landscapes, Inc., to perform the gardening activities you now perform. You are to prepare a cost report that will help her decide whether to keep gardening activities within the company or to outsource the work.

1. Before preparing your report, answer the following questions:
   a. What kinds of information do you need about your department?
   b. Why is this information relevant?
   c. Where would you go to obtain this information (sources)?
   d. When would you want to obtain this information?
2. Draft a report showing only headings and line items that best communicate the costs of your department. How would you change your report if the president asked you to reduce the costs of operating your department?
3. One of your department's cost accounts is the Maintenance Expense–Garden Equipment account.
   a. Is this a direct or an indirect cost?
   b. Is it a product or a period cost?
   c. Is it a variable or a fixed cost?
   d. Does the activity add value to Latchey's provision of insurance services?
   e. Is it a budgeted or an actual cost in your report?

LO2 Financial Performance Measures

C 3. Tarbox Manufacturing Company makes sheet metal products for heating and air conditioning installations. For the past several years, the company's income has been declining. Its statements of cost of goods manufactured and income statements for the last two years are on the next two pages. You have been asked to comment on why the ratios for Tarbox's profitability have deteriorated.

Tarbox Manufacturing Company
Statements of Cost of Goods Manufactured
For the Years Ended December 31

	This Year		Last Year	
Direct materials used				
Materials inventory, beginning	$ 91,240		$ 93,560	
Direct materials purchased (net)	987,640		959,940	
Cost of direct materials available for use	$1,078,880		$1,053,500	
Less materials inventory, ending	95,020		91,240	
Cost of direct materials used		$ 983,860		$ 962,260
Direct labor		571,410		579,720
Overhead				
Indirect labor	$ 182,660		$ 171,980	
Power	34,990		32,550	
Insurance	22,430		18,530	
Supervision	125,330		120,050	
Depreciation	75,730		72,720	
Other overhead costs	41,740		36,280	
Total overhead		482,880		452,110
Total manufacturing costs		$2,038,150		$1,994,090
Add work in process inventory, beginning		148,875		152,275
Total cost of work in process during the period		$2,187,025		$2,146,365
Less work in process inventory, ending		146,750		148,875
Cost of goods manufactured		$2,040,275		$1,997,490

1. In preparing your comments, compute the following ratios for each year:
   a. Ratios of cost of direct materials used to total manufacturing costs, direct labor to total manufacturing costs, and total overhead to total manufacturing costs. (Round to one decimal place.)
   b. Ratios of sales salaries and commission expense, advertising expense, other selling expenses, administrative expenses, and total selling and administrative expenses to sales. (Round to one decimal place.)
   c. Ratios of gross margin to sales and net income to sales. (Round to one decimal place.)
2. From your evaluation of the ratios computed in **1**, state the probable causes of the decline in net income.
3. What other factors or ratios do you believe should be considered in determining the cause of the company's decreased income?

Tarbox Manufacturing Company
Income Statements
For the Years Ended December 31

	This Year		Last Year	
Sales		$2,942,960		$3,096,220
Cost of goods sold				
Finished goods inventory, beginning	$ 142,640		$ 184,820	
Cost of goods manufactured	2,040,275		1,997,490	
Cost of goods available for sale	$2,182,915		$ 2,182,310	
Less finished goods inventory, ending	186,630		142,640	
Total cost of goods sold		1,996,285		2,039,670
Gross margin		$ 946,675		$1,056,550
Selling and administrative expenses				
Sales salaries and commission expense	$ 394,840		$ 329,480	
Advertising expense	116,110		194,290	
Other selling expenses	82,680		72,930	
Administrative expenses	242,600		195,530	
Total selling and administrative expenses		836,230		792,230
Income from operations		$ 110,445		$ 264,320
Other revenues and expenses				
Interest expense		54,160		56,815
Income before income taxes		$ 56,285		$ 207,505
Income taxes expense		19,137		87,586
Net income		$ 37,148		$ 119,919

LO2 **Management Information Needs**

C 4. The H&W Pharmaceuticals Corporation manufactures most of its three pharmaceutical products in Indonesia. Inventory balances for March and April are as follows:

	March 31	April 30
Materials Inventory	$258,400	$228,100
Work in Process Inventory	138,800	127,200
Finished Goods Inventory	111,700	114,100

During April, purchases of direct materials, which include natural materials, basic organic compounds, catalysts, and suspension agents, totaled $612,600. Direct labor costs were $160,000, and actual overhead costs were $303,500. Sales of the company's three products for April totaled $2,188,400. General and administrative expenses were $362,000.

1. Prepare a statement of cost of goods manufactured and an income statement through operating income for the month ended April 30.
2. Why is it that the total manufacturing costs do not equal the cost of goods manufactured?
3. What additional information would you need to determine the profitability of each of the three product lines?
4. Indicate whether each of the following is a product cost or a period cost:
   a. Import duties for suspension agent materials
   b. Shipping expenses to deliver manufactured products to the United States
   c. Rent for manufacturing facilities in Jakarta
   d. Salary of the American production-line manager working at the Indonesian manufacturing facilities
   e. Training costs for an Indonesian accountant

LO4 Preventing Pollution and the Costs of Waste Disposal

C 5. Lake Weir Power Plant provides power to a metropolitan area of 4 million people. Sundeep Guliani, the plant's controller, has just returned from a conference on the Environmental Protection Agency's regulations concerning pollution prevention. She is meeting with Alton Guy, the president of the company, to discuss the impact of the EPA's regulations on the plant.

"Alton, I'm really concerned. We haven't been monitoring the disposal of the radioactive material we send to the Willis Disposal Plant. If Willis is disposing of our waste material improperly, we could be sued," said Guliani. "We also haven't been recording the costs of the waste as part of our product cost. Ignoring those costs will have a negative impact on our decision about the next rate hike."

"Sundeep, don't worry. I don't think we need to concern ourselves with the waste we send to Willis. We pay the company to dispose of it. The company takes it off our hands, and it's their responsibility to manage its disposal. As for the cost of waste disposal, I think we would have a hard time justifying a rate increase based on a requirement to record the full cost of waste as a cost of producing power. Let's just forget about waste and its disposal as a component of our power cost. We can get our rate increase without mentioning waste disposal," replied Guy.

What responsibility for monitoring the waste disposal practices at the Willis Disposal Plant does Lake Weir Power Plant have? Should Guliani take Guy's advice to ignore waste disposal costs in calculating the cost of power? Be prepared to discuss your response.

LO4 LO5 Cookie Company (Continuing Case)

C 6. In the "Cookie Company" case in the last chapter, you prepared a mission statement for your company. You also set its strategic, tactical, and operating objectives; decided on its name; and identified the tools you might use to run it. Here, you will form a company team and assign roles to team members, set cookie specifications, decide on a cookie recipe, and answer some questions about product costs.

1. Join with 4 or 5 other students in the class to form a company team. (Your instructor may assign groups or allow students to organize their own teams.)
   - Determine team members' tasks, and make team assignments (e.g., mixer, baker, quality controller, materials purchaser, accountant, marketing manager).

- Assign each task an hourly pay rate or monthly salary based on your team's perception of the job market for the task involved.
- Give the plan compiled thus far to your instructor and all team members in writing.

2. As a team, determine cookie specifications: quality, size, appearance, and special features (such as types of chips or nuts), as well as quantity and packaging.
3. As a team, select a cookie recipe that best fits the company's mission.
4. As a team, answer the following questions and submit the answers to your instructor:
   - Will your company use actual or normal costing when computing the cost per cookie? Explain your answer.
   - List the types of costs that your company will classify as overhead.

CHAPTER

20 Costing Systems: Job Order Costing

The Management Process

PLAN

- ▷ Select the costing system that's best for the business's products or services
- ▷ Estimate a job's costs, price, and profit
- ▷ Select the period's predetermined overhead rate(s)

PERFORM

- ▷ Track product cost flows using job order cost cards and inventory accounts
- ▷ Compute a job's actual revenue, costs, and profit
- ▷ Compute a job's cost per unit

EVALUATE

- ▷ Analyze performance by comparing job estimates with actual job costs

COMMUNICATE

- ▷ Prepare job estimates for potential customers
- ▷ Prepare internal management reports to manage and monitor jobs

Companies that produce made-to-order products or services use a job order costing system to account for costs and determine unit cost.

A product costing system is expected to provide unit cost information, to supply cost data for management decisions, and to furnish ending values for the Materials, Work in Process, and Finished Goods Inventory accounts. Managers will select a job order costing system, a process costing system, or a hybrid of the two systems. In this chapter, we describe job order costing, including how to prepare job order cost cards and how to compute product unit cost. We also describe how job order costing differs from process costing. Process costing will be covered in the next chapter.

LEARNING OBJECTIVES

LO1 **Explain why unit cost is important in the management process.** (pp. 884–885)

LO2 **Distinguish between the two basic types of product costing systems, and identify the information that each provides.** (pp. 885–887)

LO3 **Explain the cost flow in a manufacturer's job order costing system.** (pp. 887–893)

LO4 **Prepare a job order cost card, and compute a job order's product or service unit cost.** (pp. 893–896)

DECISION POINT ▶ A MANAGER'S FOCUS AUGUSTA CUSTOM GOLF CARTS, INC.

Augusta Custom Golf Cars, Inc., builds both general-purpose and customized golf carts. If Augusta's customers decide on a customized cart, they have a number of options. For example, they can choose the type of wheels and windshield the golf cart should have, the cart's interior and exterior trim, the upholstery fabric for its seat covers, and a dashboard with or without oversized cup holders for large water bottles. They can also specify whether they want the cart to have a music system, a global positioning system, and a propane heater. They can even specify the sound of the golf cart's horn.

In this chapter, we focus on the job order costing system—the type of system that makers of special-order products, such as Augusta's customized golf cart, use to account for the costs of their products and to provide unit cost information for management decisions.

- ▶ Is the product costing system that is used for custom-made items appropriate for mass-produced items?
- ▶ What performance measures would be most useful in evaluating the results of each type of product?

Product Unit Cost Information and the Management Process

LO1 Explain why unit cost is important in the management process.

Managers depend on relevant and reliable information about costs to manage their organizations. Although they vary in their approaches, managers share the same basic concerns as they move through the management process.

Planning

During the planning process, having knowledge of unit costs helps managers of both manufacturing and service companies set reasonable selling prices and estimate the cost of their products or services.

- Products: In manufacturing companies, such as Augusta Custom Golf Carts, **Toyota**, and **Levi Strauss & Co.**, managers use unit cost information to develop budgets, establish product prices, and plan production volumes.
- Services: In service organizations, such as **Century 21**, **H&R Block**, and **UPS**, managers use cost information to develop budgets, establish prices, set sales goals, and determine human resource needs.

Performing

Managers make decisions every day about controlling costs, managing the company's activity volume, ensuring quality, and negotiating prices. They use timely cost and volume information and actual unit costs to support their decisions.

- In manufacturing companies, managers use information about costs to decide whether to drop a product line, add a production shift, outsource the manufacture of a subassembly to another company, bid on a special order, or negotiate a selling price.
- In service organizations, managers use cost information to make decisions about bidding on jobs, dropping a current service, outsourcing a task to an independent contractor, adding staff, or negotiating a price.

Evaluating

When managers evaluate results, they watch for changes in cost and quality. They compare actual and targeted total and unit costs, assess relevant price and volume information, and then adjust their planning and decision-making strategies.

- For example, if a service business's unit cost has risen, managers may break the unit cost down into its many components to analyze where costs can be cut or how the service can be performed more efficiently.

Communicating

Internal and external users analyze the data in the performance evaluation reports prepared by managers to determine whether the business is achieving cost goals for their organization's products or services.

- When managers report to stakeholders, they prepare financial statements.
- In manufacturing companies, managers use product unit costs to determine inventory balances for the organization's balance sheet and the cost of goods sold for its income statement.
- In service organizations, managers use unit costs of services to determine cost of sales for the income statement.
- When managers prepare internal performance evaluation reports, they compare actual unit costs with targeted costs, as well as actual and targeted nonfinancial measures of performance.

Shelley's Kennel provides pet boarding. Shelley, the owner of the kennel, must make several business decisions soon. Write *yes* or *no* to indicate whether knowing the cost to board one animal for one day (i.e., the product unit cost) can help Shelley answer these questions:

1. Is the daily boarding fee high enough to cover the kennel's costs?
2. How much profit will the kennel make if it boards an average of 10 dogs per day for 50 weeks?
3. What costs can be reduced to make the kennel's boarding fee competitive with that of its competitor?

SOLUTION

1. Yes; 2. Yes; 3. Yes

Product Costing Systems

LO2 Distinguish between the two basic types of product costing systems, and identify the information that each provides.

To meet managers' needs for cost information, it is necessary to have a highly reliable product costing system specifically designed to record and report the organization's operations.

A **product costing system** is a set of procedures used to account for an organization's product costs and to provide timely and accurate unit cost information for pricing, cost planning and control, inventory valuation, and financial statement preparation.

- The product costing system enables managers to track costs throughout the management process.
- It provides a structure for recording the revenue earned from sales and the costs incurred for direct materials, direct labor, and overhead.

Two basic types of product costing systems have been developed: job order costing systems and process costing systems. Table 20-1 summarizes the characteristics of both costing systems.

TABLE 20-1
Characteristics of Job Order Costing and Process Costing Systems

Job Order Costing System	Process Costing System
Traces manufacturing costs to a specific job order	Traces manufacturing costs to processes, departments, or work cells and then assigns the costs to products manufactured
Measures the cost of each completed unit	Measures costs in terms of units completed during a specific period
Uses a single Work in Process Inventory account to summarize the cost of all job orders	Uses several Work in Process Inventory accounts, one for each process, department, or work cell
Typically used by companies that make unique or special-order products, such as customized publications, built-in cabinets, or made-to-order draperies	Typically used by companies that make large amounts of similar products or liquid products or that have long, continuous production runs of identical products, such as makers of paint, soft drinks, candy, bricks, and paper

Businesses that make special-order items, such as the kitchen cabinets shown here, use a job order costing system. With such a system, the costs of direct materials (e.g., the wood used in framing the cabinets), direct labor, and overhead (e.g., insurance and depreciation on tools and vehicles) are traced to a specific batch of products or job order. All costs are recorded on a job order cost card.

Courtesy of George Peters/ istockphoto.com.

A **job order costing system** is used by companies that make unique or special-order products, such as personalized ice cream creations, specially built cabinets, made-to-order draperies, or custom-tailored suits.

- It uses a single Work in Process Inventory account to record the costs of all job orders.
- It traces the costs of direct materials, direct labor, and overhead to a specific batch of products or a specific **job order** (i.e., a customer order for a specific number of specially designed, made-to-order products) by using a subsidiary ledger of job order cost cards.
- A **job order cost card** is usually an electronic or paper document on which all costs incurred in the production of a particular job order are recorded. The costs that a job order costing system gathers are used to measure the cost of each completed unit.

Study Note

In job order costing, costs are traced to jobs; in process costing, costs are traced to production processes.

A **process costing system** is used by companies that produce large amounts of similar products or liquid products or that have long, continuous production runs of identical products. Makers of paint, soft drinks, candy, bricks, paper, and gallon containers of ice cream would use such a system.

- It first traces the costs of direct materials, direct labor, and overhead to processes, departments or work cells and then assigns the costs to the products manufactured by those processes, departments, or work cells during a specific period.
- It uses several Work in Process Inventory accounts, one for each process, department, or work cell.

In reality, few production processes are a perfect match for either a job order costing system or a process costing system. The typical product costing system therefore combines parts of job order costing and process costing to create a hybrid system known as an **operations costing system** designed specifically for an organization's production process.

- For example, an automobile maker like **Toyota** may use process costing to track the costs of manufacturing a standard car and job order costing to track the costs of customized features, such as a convertible top or a stick shift.

FOCUS ON BUSINESS PRACTICE

Why Does Toyota Use a Hybrid Product Costing System?

Thanks to its virtual production line, **Toyota** can now manufacture custom vehicles in five days. Computer software allows Toyota to calculate the exact number of parts needed at each precise point on its production line for a certain mix of cars. The mix can be modified up to five days in advance of actual production, allowing Toyota to modify a production run to include custom orders. With its virtual production line and a hybrid product costing system, Toyota has gained an advantage over its competitors.[1]

& APPLY >

State whether a job order costing system or a process costing system would typically be used to account for the costs of the following:

1. Manufacturing golf tees
2. Manufacturing custom-designed fencing for a specific golf course
3. Providing pet grooming
4. Manufacturing golf balls
5. Manufacturing dog food
6. Providing private golf lessons

SOLUTION

1. Process; 2. Job; 3. Job; 4. Process; 5. Process; 6. Job

Job Order Costing in a Manufacturing Company

LO3 Explain the cost flow in a manufacturer's job order costing system.

A job order costing system is a system that traces the costs of a specific order or batch of products to provide timely, accurate cost information and to facilitate the smooth and continuous flow of that information. A basic part of a job order costing system is the set of procedures, electronic documents, and accounts that a company uses when it incurs costs for direct materials, direct labor, and overhead. Job order cost cards and cost flows through the inventory accounts form the core of a job order costing system.

Study Note

In a job order costing system, the specific job or batch of product, *not* a department or work cell, is the focus of cost accumulation.

To study the cost flows in a job order costing system, let's look at how Jonas Lytton, the owner of Augusta Custom Golf Carts, Inc., operates his business. As we noted in the Decision Point, Augusta builds both customized and general-purpose golf carts.

- The direct materials costs for a golf cart include the costs of a cart frame, wheels, upholstered seats, a windshield, a motor, and a rechargeable battery.
- Direct labor costs include the wages of the two production workers who assemble the golf carts.
- Overhead includes indirect materials costs for upholstery zippers, cloth straps to hold equipment in place, wheel lubricants, screws and fasteners, and silicon to attach the windshield. It also includes indirect labor costs for moving

materials to the production area and inspecting a golf cart during its construction; depreciation on the manufacturing plant and equipment used to make the golf carts; and utilities, insurance, and property taxes related to the manufacturing plant.

Exhibit 20-1 shows the flow of each of these costs. Notice that the beginning balance in the Materials Inventory account means that there are already direct and indirect materials in the materials storeroom. The beginning balance in Work in Process Inventory means that Job CC is in production (with specifics given in the job order cost card). The zero beginning balance in Finished Goods Inventory means that all previously completed golf carts have been shipped.

Materials

When Augusta receives or expects to receive a sales order, the purchasing process begins with a request for specific quantities of direct and indirect materials that are needed for the order but are not currently available in the materials storeroom. When the new materials arrive at Augusta, the Accounting Department records the materials purchased by making an entry that debits or increases the balance of the Materials Inventory account and credits either the Cash or Accounts Payable account (depending on whether the purchase was for cash or credit):

Study Note

It is often helpful to understand the process of tracking production costs as they flow through the three inventory accounts and the entries that are triggered by the organization's source documents. The entries that track product cost flows are provided as background.

	Dr.	Cr.
Materials Inventory	XX	
Cash or Accounts Payable		XX

During the month, Augusta made two purchases on credit. As shown in Exhibit 20-1, these purchases increase the debit balances in the Materials Inventory account and increase the credit balances in the Accounts Payable account.

- In transaction **1,** the company purchased cart frames costing \$572 and wheels costing \$340 for a total of \$912 from one of its vendors.
- In transaction **2,** the company purchased indirect materials costing \$82 from another vendor.

When golf carts are scheduled for production, requested materials are sent to the production area. To record the flow of direct materials requested from the Materials Inventory account into the Work in Process Inventory account, the entry is:

	Dr.	Cr.
Work in Process Inventory	XX	
Materials Inventory		XX

To record the flow of indirect materials requested from the Materials Inventory account into the Overhead account, the entry is:

	Dr.	Cr.
Overhead	XX	
Materials Inventory		XX

During the month, Augusta processes requests for direct and indirect materials. Notice that the direct materials requested appear as a debit in the Work in Process Inventory account, because that account records the costs of partially completed units of product, and as a credit in the Materials Inventory account.

EXHIBIT 20-1 The Job Order Costing System—Augusta, Inc.

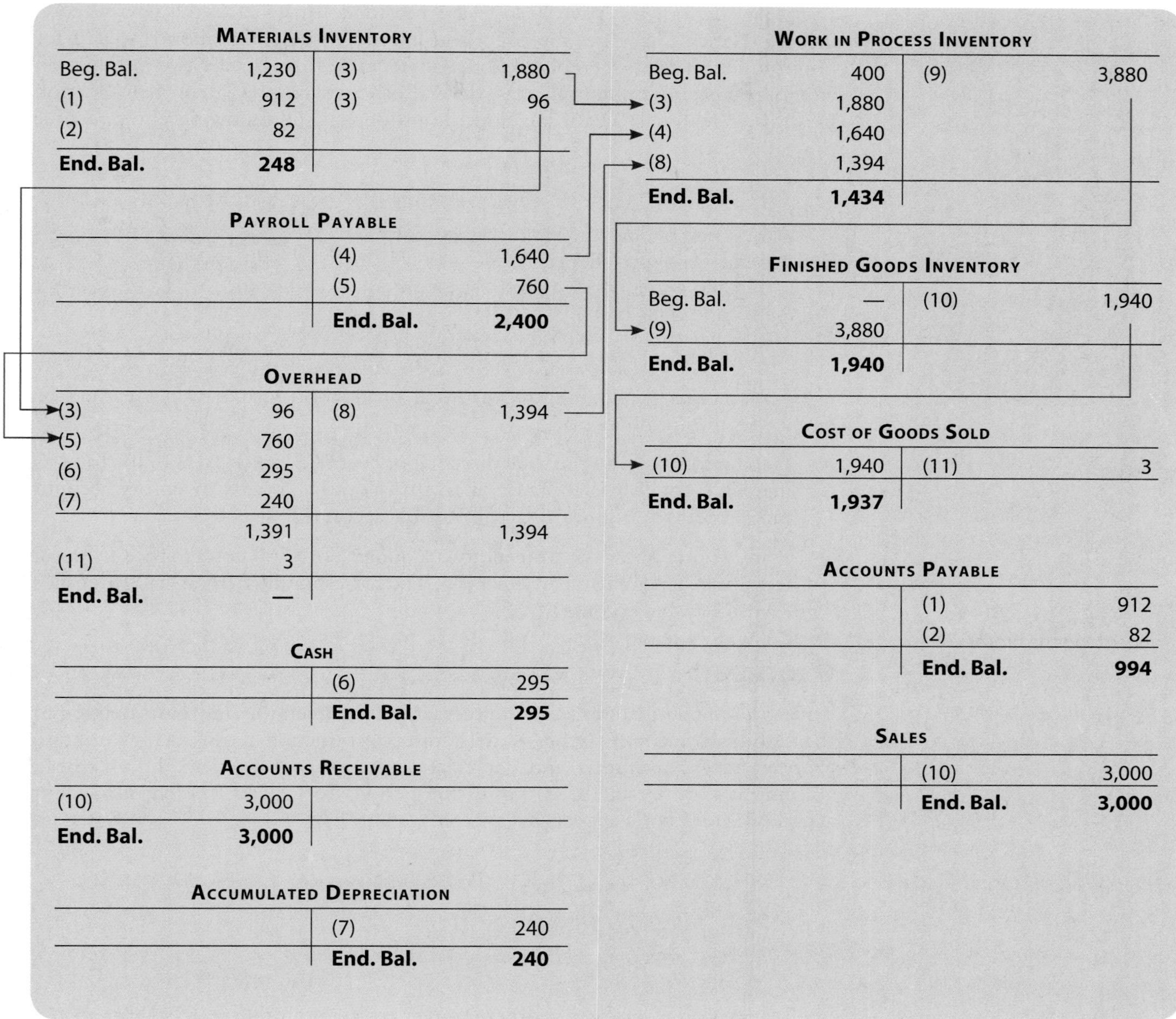

Notice that the indirect materials requested appear as a debit to the Overhead account instead of to a Work in Process Inventory account.

Transaction 3 shows the request for $1,880 of direct materials for the production of two jobs. These costs are also recorded on the corresponding job order cost cards.

- Job CC, a batch run of two general-purpose golf carts already in production, required $1,038 of the additional direct materials.
- Job JB, a customized golf cart made to the specifications of an individual customer, Alex Special, required $842 of the direct materials.

In addition, transaction 3 accounts for the $96 of indirect materials requested for production as a $96 debit to Overhead and a $96 credit to Materials Inventory.

Labor

Every pay period, the payroll costs are recorded. In general, the payroll costs include salaries and wages for direct and indirect production labor as well as for nonproduction-related employees. As noted earlier, Augusta's two production employees assemble the golf carts. Several other employees support production by moving materials and inspecting the products. The following entry records the payroll:

	Dr.	Cr.
Work in Process Inventory (direct labor costs)	XX	
Overhead (indirect labor costs)	XX	
Selling and Administrative Expenses (nonproduction-related salary and wage costs)	XX	
Payroll Payable		XX

Transactions 4 and 5 show the total production-related wages earned by employees during the period.

- Transaction 4 shows the total direct labor cost of $1,640 ($1,320 for Job CC and $320 for Job JB) as a debit to the Work in Process Inventory account and a credit to Augusta's Payroll Payable account.
- Transaction 5 shows that the indirect labor cost of $760 flows to the Overhead account instead of to a particular job. The corresponding credit is to Augusta's Payroll Payable account.

Overhead

Thus far, indirect materials and indirect labor have been the only costs debited to the Overhead account. Other actual indirect production costs, such as utilities, property taxes, insurance, and depreciation, are also charged to the Overhead account as they are incurred during the period. In general, the entry to incur actual overhead costs appears as:

	Dr.	Cr.
Overhead	XX	
Cash or Accounts Payable		XX
Accumulated Depreciation		XX

- Transaction 6 shows that other indirect costs amounting to $295 were paid.
- Transaction 7 records the $240 of production-related depreciation. The corresponding credit is to Augusta's Accumulated Depreciation account for $240.

During the period, to recognize all product-related costs for a job, an overhead cost estimate is applied to a job using a predetermined rate. Based on its budget and past experience, Augusta currently uses a predetermined overhead rate of 85 percent of direct labor costs. The entry to apply overhead using a predetermined rate is:

	Dr.	Cr.
Work in Process Inventory	XX	
Overhead		XX

In transaction 8, total overhead of $1,394 is applied, with $1,122 going to Job CC (85 percent of $1,320) and $272 going to Job JB (85 percent of $320).

- The Work in Process Inventory account is debited for $1,394 (85 percent of $1,640; see transaction 4), and the Overhead account is credited for the applied overhead of $1,394.

Completed Units

When a custom job or a batch of general-purpose golf carts is completed and ready for sale, the products are moved from the manufacturing area to the finished goods storeroom. To record the cost flow of completed products from the Work in Process Inventory account into the Finished Goods Inventory account, the entry is:

	Dr.	Cr.
Finished Goods Inventory	XX	
Work in Process Inventory		XX

As shown in transaction **9,** when Job CC is completed, its cost of $3,880 is transferred from the Work in Process Inventory account to the Finished Goods Inventory account by debiting Finished Goods Inventory for $3,880 and crediting Work in Process Inventory for $3,880.

- Its job order cost card is also completed and transferred to the finished goods file.

Sold Units

Study Note

In this example, the company uses a perpetual inventory system. In a periodic inventory system, the cost of goods sold is calculated at the end of the period.

When a company uses a perpetual inventory system, as Augusta does, two accounting entries are made when products are sold. One is prompted by the sales invoice and records the quantity and selling price of the products sold. The other entry, prompted by the delivery of products to a customer, records the quantity and cost of the products shipped. These two entries follow.

	Dr.	Cr.
Cash or Accounts Receivable (sales price 3 units sold)	XX	
Sales (sales price 3 units sold)		XX

	Dr.	Cr.
Cost of Goods Sold (unit cost 3 units sold)	XX	
Finished Goods Inventory (unit cost 3 units sold)		XX

In transaction **10,** the $1,940 cost of the one general-purpose golf cart that was sold during the period is transferred from the Finished Goods Inventory account to the Cost of Goods Sold account.

- The Finished Goods Inventory account has an ending balance of $1,940 for the one remaining unsold cart.
- The $3,000 sales price of the golf cart sold on account is also recorded.

Reconciliation of Overhead Costs

> **Study Note**
> Why do financial statements require the reconciliation of overhead costs? Financial statements report actual cost information; therefore, estimated overhead costs applied during the accounting period must be adjusted to reflect actual overhead costs.

To prepare financial statements at the end of the accounting period, the Cost of Goods Sold account must reflect actual product costs, including actual overhead. Thus, the Overhead account must be reconciled every period.

- ***Underapplied overhead:*** As you learned in a previous chapter, if at the end of the accounting period the actual overhead debit balance exceeds the applied overhead credit balance, then the Overhead account is said to be underapplied and the debit balance must be closed to the Cost of Goods Sold account. Here is the entry:

	Dr.	Cr.
Cost of Goods Sold	XX	
Overhead		XX

- ***Overapplied overhead:*** If the actual overhead cost for the period is less than the estimated overhead that was applied during the period, then the Overhead account is overapplied and the credit balance must be closed to the Cost of Goods Sold account. Here is the entry:

	Dr.	Cr.
Overhead	XX	
Cost of Goods Sold		XX

In transaction 11 since the actual overhead cost for the period ($1,391) is less than the overhead that was applied during the period ($1,394), the $3 credit balance must be closed to the Cost of Goods Sold account. The overapplied amount will reduce Cost of Goods Sold and it will then reflect the actual overhead costs incurred. Thus, $3 is deducted from the Cost of Goods Sold account, making the ending balance of that account $1,937.

STOP & APPLY >

Partial operating data for Sample Company are presented below. Sample Company's management has set the predetermined overhead rate for the current year at 60 percent of direct labor costs.

Account/Transaction	October
Beginning Materials Inventory	$ 4,000
Beginning Work in Process Inventory	6,000
Beginning Finished Goods Inventory	2,000
Direct materials used	16,000
Direct materials purchased	a
Direct labor costs	24,000
Overhead applied	b
Cost of units completed	c
Cost of Goods Sold	50,000
Ending Materials Inventory	3,000
Ending Work in Process Inventory	10,000
Ending Finished Goods Inventory	d

Using T accounts and the data provided, compute the unknown values. Show all your computations.

SOLUTION

Materials Inventory

Beg. Bal.	4,000	Used	16,000
(a) Purchases	15,000		
End. Bal.	**3,000**		

Work in Process Inventory

Beg. Bal.	6,000	(c) Completed during period	50,400
Direct materials used	16,000		
Direct labor	24,000		
(b) Overhead applied	14,400*		
End. Bal.	**10,000**		

Finished Goods Inventory

Beg. Bal.	2,000	Cost of goods sold	50,000
(c) Completed during period	50,400		
(d) **End. Bal.**	**2,400**		

*$24,000 × 60% = $14,400

A Job Order Cost Card and the Computation of Unit Cost

LO4 Prepare a job order cost card, and compute a job order's product or service unit cost.

As is evident from the preceding discussion, job order cost cards play a key role in a job order costing system. Each job being worked on has a job order cost card. As costs are incurred, they are classified by job and recorded on the appropriate card.

A Manufacturer's Job Order Cost Card and the Computation of Unit Cost

As you can see in Figure 20-1, a manufacturer's job order cost card has space for direct materials, direct labor, and overhead costs. It also includes the job order number, product specifications, the name of the customer, the date of the order, the projected completion date, and a cost summary. As a job incurs direct materials and direct labor costs, its job order cost card is updated. Overhead is also posted to the job order cost card at the predetermined rate.

- Job order cost cards for incomplete jobs make up the subsidiary ledger for the Work in Process Inventory account. To ensure correctness, the ending balance in the Work in Process Inventory account is compared with the total of the costs shown on the job order cost cards.

A job order costing system simplifies the calculation of product unit costs. When a job is finished, the costs of direct materials, direct labor, and overhead that have been recorded on its job order cost card are totaled.

- The product unit cost is computed by dividing the total costs for the job by the number of good (i.e., salable) units produced. The product unit cost is entered on the job order cost card and will be used to value items in

FIGURE 20-1
Job Order Cost Card for a Manufacturing Company

Job Order: CC

JOB ORDER COST CARD
Augusta, Inc.
Spring Hill, Florida

Customer: Stock **Batch:** X **Custom:**
Specifications: Two general-purpose golf carts
Date of Order: 2/26/11
Date of Completion: 3/6/11

Costs Charged to Job	Previous Months	Current Month	Cost Summary
Direct materials	$165	$1,038	$1,203
Direct labor	127	1,320	1,447
Overhead (85% of direct labor cost)	108	1,122	1,230
Totals	$400	$3,480	$3,880
Units completed			÷ 2
Product unit cost			$1,940

inventory. The job order cost card in Figure 20-1 shows the costs for completed Job CC. Two golf carts were produced at a total cost of $3,880, so the product unit cost was $1,940.

Job Order Costing in a Service Organization

Many service organizations use a job order costing system to compute the cost of rendering services. The most important cost for a service organization is labor, which is carefully accounted for through the use of time cards. The cost flow of services is similar to the cost flow of manufactured products. Job order cost cards are used to keep track of the costs incurred for each job. Job costs include labor, materials and supplies, and service overhead.

To cover these costs and earn a profit, many service organizations base jobs on **cost-plus contracts.** Such contracts require the customer to pay all costs incurred in performing the job plus a predetermined amount of profit, which is based on the amount of costs incurred. When the job is complete, the costs on the completed job order cost card become the cost of services. The cost of services is adjusted at the end of the accounting period for the difference between the applied service overhead costs and the actual service overhead costs.

To illustrate how a service organization uses a job order costing system, let's assume that a company called Dream Golf Retreats earns its revenue by designing and selling golf retreat packages to corporate clients. Figure 20-2 shows Dream Golf Retreats' job order cost card for the Work Corporation. Costs have been

FIGURE 20-2 Job Order Cost Card for a Service Organization

Job Order: 2011-A7

JOB ORDER COST CARD
Dream Golf Retreats

Customer: Work Corporation **Batch:** **Customer:** X
Specifications: Golf retreat for 45 executives
Date of Order: 3/24/11 **Date of Completion:** 4/8/11

Costs Charged to Job		**Previous Months**	**Current Month**	**Total Cost**
Planning				
Supplies		$ 100	$ —	$ 100
Labor		850		850
Overhead	(40% of planning labor costs)	340	—	340
Totals		$1,290		$1,290
Golf Activities				
Supplies		$ 970	$1,200	$2,170
Labor		400	620	1,020
Overhead	(50% of on site labor costs)	200	310	510
Totals		$1,570	$2,130	$3,700
Non-Golf Activities				
Cost of outsourcing		$ 90	$ 320	$ 410
Totals		$ 90	$ 320	$ 410

Cost Summary to Date		**Total Cost**
Planning		$1,290
Golf Activities		3,700
Non-Golf Activities		410
Total		$5,400
Profit Margin	(15% of total cost)	810
Job Revenue		$6,210

categorized into three separate activities: planning, golf activities, and nongolf activities.

Study Note

Job order cost cards for service businesses record costs by activities done for the job. The activity costs may include supplies, labor, and overhead.

- The service overhead cost for planning is 40 percent of planning labor cost, and the service overhead cost for golf activities is 50 percent of on-site labor cost.
- Total costs incurred for this job were $5,400.
- Dream Golf Retreats' cost-plus contract with Work Corporation has a 15 percent profit guarantee; therefore, $810 of profit margin is added to the total cost to arrive at the total contract revenue of $6,210, which is the amount billed to the Work Corporation.

STOP & APPLY >

Complete the following job order cost card for five custom-built cabinets:

Job Order 16

Job Order Cost Card
Unique Cupboards, LLP
Sample City, Oregon

Customer:	Brian Tofer	Batch: ___	Custom: X
Specifications:	5 custom cabinets		
Date of Order:	5/4/2011	Date of Completion:	6/8/2011

Costs Charged to Job	**Previous Months**	**Current Month**	**Cost Summary**
Direct materials	$3,500	$2,800	$?
Direct labor	2,300	1,600	?
Overhead applied	1,150	800	?
Totals	$?	$?	$?
Units completed			÷ ?
Product unit cost			$?

SOLUTION

Job Order 16

Job Order Cost Card
Unique Cupboards, LLP
Sample City, Oregon

Customer:	Brian Tofer	Batch: ___	Custom: X
Specifications:	5 custom cabinets		
Date of Order:	5/4/2011	Date of Completion:	6/8/2011

Costs Charged to Job	**Previous Months**	**Current Month**	**Cost Summary**
Direct materials	$3,500	$2,800	$ 6,300
Direct labor	2,300	1,600	3,900
Overhead applied	1,150	800	1,950
Totals	$6,950	$5,200	$12,150
Units completed			÷ 5
Product unit cost			$ 2,430

▶ AUGUSTA CUSTOM GOLF CARTS, INC.: REVIEW PROBLEM

The Decision Point at the beginning of this chapter focused on Augusta Custom Golf Carts, Inc., a company that makes both general-purpose and customized golf carts. It posed these questions:

- Is the product costing system that is used for custom-made items appropriate for mass-produced items?
- What performance measures would be most useful in evaluating the results of each type of product?

Whether a product costing system is appropriate depends on the nature of the production process. Because the production of custom-made items and the production of mass-produced items involve different processes, they generally require different costing systems.

Job Order Costing
LO4

- When a product is custom-made, it is possible to use a job order costing system, which collects the costs of each order.
- When a product is mass-produced, the costs of a specific unit cannot be collected because there is a continuous flow of similar products. In this case a process costing system is used, and costs are collected by process, department, or work cell.

With a job order costing system, Augusta's management can measure the profitability of each customized order by comparing the order's cost and price. If the company were to start mass-producing a line of gold carts for sale in retail establishments, it would have to adjust its costing system to determine the product cost of a unit. Management would then measure performance by comparing the budgeted and actual costs for a process, department, or work cell.

Suppose Augusta has begun catering golf cart reunion parties at its location. It uses job order cost cards to keep track of the costs of each party. Job costs (direct materials and supplies, direct labor, and service overhead) are categorized under three activities: planning and design, reunion, and cleanup. The service overhead charge for planning and design is 30 percent of the party planner's labor costs, and the service overhead charge for the reunion is 50 percent of the cost of the cake created for the party. Augusta has a cost-plus contact with a 25 percent profit guarantee for each reunion party.

One of Augusta's managers has tracked all costs of the Billy Cart reunion party, and now that the work is finished, it is time to complete the job order cost card. The costs for the Billy Cart job are as follows:

Costs During June	
Planning and design	
Supplies	$12.00
Party planner labor	25.00
Reunion	
Cake creation	21.50
Direct labor	16.00
Cleanup	
Janitorial service cost	35.25

Required

1. Create the job order cost card for the Billy Cart Reunion job.
2. What amount will the manager bill for the job?
3. Using the format of the Work in Process Inventory account in Exhibit 20-1, reconstruct the beginning balance and costs for the current month.

Answers to Review Problem

1. Job order cost card for the Billy Cart reunion party:

Job Order Cost Card
Augusta Custom Golf Carts, Inc.

Customer: Billy Cart Batch: ____ Custom: X
Specifications: Reunion party
Date of Order: 5/28/2011 Date of Completion: 6/5/2011

Costs Charged to Job	**Current Month**	**Total Cost**
Planning and design		
Supplies	$12.00	$12.00
Party planner labor	25.00	25.00
Overhead (30% of planning labor costs)	7.50	7.50
Totals	$44.50	$44.50
Reunion		
Cake creation	$21.50	$21.50
Direct labor	16.00	16.00
Overhead (50% of cake creation cost)	10.75	10.75
Totals	$48.25	$48.25
Cleanup		
Janitorial service costs	$35.25	$35.25
Totals	$35.25	$35.25
Cost Summary to Date		
Planning		
Reunion		
Cleanup		
Total		
Profit margin (25% of total cost)		
Job revenue		

2. The manager will bill $160.00 for this job.

3. Beginning balance and costs for the current month:

Work in Process Inventory

Beg. Bal.	0.00	Completed	128.00
Planning and design			
Supplies	12.00		
Party planner labor	25.00		
Overhead	7.50		
Party			
Cake creation	21.50		
Direct labor	16.00		
Overhead	10.75		
Cleanup			
Janitorial service costs	35.25		
End. Bal.	0.00		

LO1 Explain why unit cost is important in the management process.

When managers plan, information about costs helps them develop budgets, establish prices, set sales goals, plan production volumes, estimate product or service unit costs, and determine human resource needs. Daily, managers use cost information to make decisions about controlling costs, managing the company's volume of activity, ensuring quality, and negotiating prices. When managers evaluate results, they analyze actual and targeted information to evaluate performance and make any necessary adjustments to their planning and decision-making strategies. When managers communicate with stakeholders, they use unit costs to determine inventory balances and the cost of goods or services sold for the financial statements. They also analyze internal reports that compare the organization's measures of actual and targeted performance to determine whether cost goals for products or services are being achieved.

LO2 Distinguish between the two basic types of product costing systems, and identify the information that each provides.

A job order costing system is a product costing system used by companies that make unique, custom, or special-order products. Such a system traces the costs of direct materials, direct labor, and overhead to a specific batch of products or to a specific job order. A job order costing system measures the cost of each complete unit and summarizes the cost of all jobs in a single Work in Process Inventory account that is supported by job order cost cards.

A process costing system is a product costing system used by companies that produce large amounts of similar products or liquid products or that have long, continuous production runs of identical products. Such a system first traces the costs of direct materials, direct labor, and overhead to processes, departments, or work cells and then assigns the costs to the products manufactured by those processes, departments, or work cells. A process costing system uses several Work in Process Inventory accounts, one for each department, process, or work cell.

LO3 Explain the cost flow in a manufacturer's job order costing system.

In a manufacturer's job order costing system, the costs of materials are first charged to the Materials Inventory account. The various actual overhead costs are debited to the Overhead account. As products are manufactured, the costs of direct materials and direct labor are debited to the Work in Process Inventory account and are recorded on each job's job order cost card. Overhead costs are applied and debited to the Work in Process Inventory account and credited to the Overhead account using a predetermined overhead rate. They too are recorded on the job order cost card. When products and jobs are completed, the costs assigned to them are transferred to the Finished Goods Inventory account. Then, when the products are sold and shipped, their costs are transferred to the Cost of Goods Sold account.

LO4 Prepare a job order cost card, and compute a job order's product or service unit cost.

All costs of direct materials, direct labor, and overhead for a particular job are accumulated on a job order cost card. When the job has been completed, those costs are totaled. The total is then divided by the number of good units produced to find the product unit cost for that order. The product unit cost is entered on the job order cost card and will be used to value items in inventory.

Many service organizations use a job order costing system to track the costs of labor, materials and supplies, and service overhead to specific customer jobs. Labor is an important cost for service organizations, but their materials costs are usually negligible. To cover their costs and earn a profit, service organizations often base jobs on cost-plus contracts, which require the customer to pay all costs incurred plus a predetermined amount of profit.

REVIEW of Concepts and Terminology

The following concepts and terms were introduced in this chapter:

Cost-plus contracts 894 (LO4)

Job order 886 (LO2)

Job order cost card 886 (LO2)

Job order costing system 886 (LO2)

Operations costing system 886 (LO2)

Process costing system 886 (LO2)

Product costing system 885 (LO2)

CHAPTER ASSIGNMENTS

BUILDING Your Basic Knowledge and Skills

Short Exercises

LO1 Uses of Product Costing Information

SE 1. Silly Putter Miniature Golf provides 36 holes of miniature golf. Dan, the owner of the golf course, must make several business decisions soon. Write *yes* or *no* to indicate whether knowing the cost to play one golf game (i.e., the product unit cost) can help Dan answer these questions:

1. Is the fee for playing a golf game high enough to cover the related cost?
2. How much profit will Silly Putter make if it sells an average of 100 games per day for 50 weeks?
3. What costs can be reduced to make the fee competitive with that of its competitor?

LO2 Companies That Use Job Order Costing

SE 2. Write *yes* or *no* to indicate whether each of the following companies would typically use a job order costing system:

1. Soft-drink producer
2. Jeans manufacturer
3. Submarine contractor
4. Office building contractor
5. Stuffed-toy maker

LO2 Job Order Versus Process Costing Systems

SE 3. State whether a job order costing system or a process costing system would typically be used to account for the costs of the following:

1. Manufacturing bottles of water
2. Manufacturing custom-designed swimming pools
3. Providing babysitting
4. Manufacturing one-size-fits-all flip-flop shoes
5. Manufacturing canned food
6. Providing accounting services

LO3 Transactions in a Manufacturer's Job Order Costing System

SE 4. For each of the following transactions, state which account(s) would be debited and credited in a job order costing system:

1. Purchased materials on account, $12,890
2. Charged direct labor to production, $3,790
3. Requested direct materials for production, $6,800
4. Applied overhead to jobs in process, $3,570

LO3 Transactions in a Manufacturer's Job Order Costing System

SE 5. Enter the following transactions into T accounts:

1. Incurred $34,000 of direct labor and $18,000 of indirect labor
2. Applied overhead based on 12,680 labor hours @ $6.50 per labor hour

LO3 Accounts for Job Order Costing

SE 6. Identify the accounts in which each of the following transactions for Acorn Furniture, a custom manufacturer of oak tables and chairs, would be debited and credited:

1. Issued oak materials into production for Job ABC
2. Recorded direct labor time for the first week in February for Job ABC
3. Purchased indirect materials from a vendor on account
4. Received a production-related electricity bill
5. Applied overhead to Job ABC
6. Completed but did not yet sell Job ABC

LO4 **Product Unit Cost**

SE 7. Write *yes* or *no* to indicate whether each of the following costs is included in a product unit cost. Then explain your answers.

1. Direct materials costs
2. Fixed overhead costs
3. Variable selling costs
4. Fixed administrative costs
5. Direct labor costs
6. Variable overhead costs

LO4 **Computation of Product Unit Cost**

SE 8. Complete the following job order cost card for six custom-built computer systems:

Job Order 168

Job Order Cost Card
Keeper 3000
Apache City, North Dakota

Customer: Brian Patcher Batch: ____ Custom: X
Specifications: 6 Custom-Built Computer Systems
Date of Order: 4/4/2011 Date of Completion: 6/8/2011

Costs Charged to Job	Previous Months	Current Month	Cost Summary
Direct materials	$3,540	$2,820	$?
Direct labor	2,340	1,620	?
Overhead applied	2,880	2,550	?
Totals	$?	$?	$?
Units completed			÷ ?
Product unit cost			$?

LO4 **Job Order Costing in a Service Organization**

SE 9. For each of the following transactions, state which account(s) would be debited and credited in a job order costing system for a desert landscaping business:

1. Charged customer for landscape design
2. Purchased cactus plants and gravel on credit for one job
3. Paid three employees to prepare soil for gravel
4. Paid for rental equipment to move gravel to job site

LO4 **Job Order Costing with Cost-Plus Contracts**

SE 10. Complete the following job order cost card for an individual tax return:

Job Order 2011-A7

Job Order Cost Card
Doremus Tax Service
Puyallup, Washington

Customer: Arthur Farnsworth   Batch: ____   Custom: X
Specifications: Annual Individual Tax Return
Date of Order: 3/24/2011   Date of Completion: 4/8/2011

Costs Charged to Job	Previous Months	Current Month	Total Cost
Client interview			
Supplies	$10	$ —	$?
Labor	50	60	?
Overhead (40% of interview labor costs)	20	24	?
Totals	$?	$?	$?
Preparation of return			
Supplies	$—	$ 16	$?
Computer time	—	12	?
Labor	—	240	?
Overhead (50% of preparation labor costs)	—	120	?
Totals	$—	$?	$?
Delivery			
Postage	$—	$ 12	$?
Totals	$—	$?	$?

Cost Summary to Date	Total Cost
Client interview	$?
Preparation of return	?
Delivery	?
Total	$?
Profit margin (25% of total cost)	?
Job revenue	$?

Exercises

LO2 Product Costing

E 1. Bell Printing Company specializes in wedding invitations. Bell needs information to budget next year's activities. Write *yes* or *no* to indicate whether each of the following costs is likely to be available in the company's product costing system:

1. Cost of paper and envelopes
2. Printing machine setup costs
3. Depreciation of printing machinery
4. Advertising costs
5. Repair costs for printing machinery
6. Costs to deliver stationery to customers
7. Office supplies costs
8. Costs to design a wedding invitation
9. Cost of ink
10. Sales commissions

LO2 **Costing Systems: Industry Linkage**

E 2. Which of the following products would typically be accounted for using a job order costing system? Which would typically be accounted for using a process costing system? (a) Paint, (b) jelly beans, (c) jet aircraft, (d) bricks, (e) tailor-made suit, (f) liquid detergent, (g) helium gas canisters used to inflate balloons, and (h) aluminum compressed-gas cylinders with a special fiberglass wrap for a Mount Everest expedition.

LO2 **Costing Systems: Industry Linkage**

E 3. Which of the following products would typically be accounted for using a job order costing system? Which would typically be accounted for using a process costing system? (a) Standard nails, (b) television sets, (c) printed wedding invitations, (d) a limited edition of lithographs, (e) flea collars for pets, (f) personal marathon training program, (g) breakfast cereal, and (h) an original evening gown.

LO3 **Job Order Cost Flow**

E 4. The three product cost elements—direct materials, direct labor, and overhead—flow through a job order costing system in a structured, orderly fashion. Specific accounts and subsidiary ledgers are used to verify and record cost information. Write a paragraph describing the cost flow in a job order costing system.

LO3 **Work in Process Inventory: T Account Analysis**

E 5. On June 30, New Haven Company's Work in Process Inventory account showed a beginning balance of $29,400. The Materials Inventory account showed a beginning balance of $240,000. Production activity for July was as follows: Direct materials costing $238,820 were requested for production; total manufacturing payroll was $140,690, of which $52,490 was used to pay for indirect labor; indirect materials costing $28,400 were purchased and used; and overhead was applied at a rate of 150 percent of direct labor costs.

1. Record New Haven's materials, labor, and overhead costs for July in T accounts.
2. Compute the ending balance in the Work in Process Inventory account. Assume a transfer of $461,400 to the Finished Goods Inventory account during the period.

LO3 **T Account Analysis with Unknowns**

E 6. Partial operating data for Merton Company are presented below. Management has set the predetermined overhead rate for the current year at 120 percent of direct labor costs.

Account/Transaction	June	July
Beginning Materials Inventory	a	e
Beginning Work in Process Inventory	$ 89,605	f
Beginning Finished Goods Inventory	79,764	$ 67,660
Direct materials requested	59,025	g
Materials purchased	57,100	60,216
Direct labor costs	48,760	54,540
Overhead applied	b	h
Cost of units completed	c	231,861
Cost of Goods Sold	166,805	i
Ending Materials Inventory	32,014	27,628
Ending Work in Process Inventory	d	j
Ending Finished Goods Inventory	67,660	30,515

Using T accounts and the data provided, compute the unknown values. Show all your computations.

LO3 **T Account Analysis with Unknowns**

E 7. Partial operating data for Charing Cross Company are presented below. Charing Cross Company's management has set the predetermined overhead rate for the current year at 80 percent of direct labor costs.

Account/Transaction	December
Beginning Materials Inventory	$ 42,000
Beginning Work in Process Inventory	66,000
Beginning Finished Goods Inventory	29,000
Direct materials used	168,000
Direct materials purchased	a
Direct labor costs	382,000
Overhead applied	b
Cost of units completed	c
Cost of Goods Sold	808,000
Ending Materials Inventory	38,000
Ending Work in Process Inventory	138,600
Ending Finished Goods Inventory	d

Using T accounts and the data provided, compute the unknown values. Show all your computations.

LO4 **Job Order Cost Card and Computation of Product Unit Cost**

E 8. In January, the Cabinet Company worked on six job orders for specialty kitchen cabinets. It began Job A-62 for Zeke Cabinets, Inc., on January 10 and completed it on January 24. Partial data for Job A-62 are as follows:

	Costs	Machine Hours Used
Direct materials		
Cedar	$7,900	
Pine	6,320	
Hardware	2,930	
Assembly supplies	988	
Direct labor		
Sawing	2,840	120
Shaping	2,200	220
Finishing	2,250	180
Assembly	2,890	50

The Cabinet Company produced a total of 34 cabinets for Job A-62. Its current predetermined overhead rate is $21.60 per machine hour. From the information given, prepare a job order cost card and compute the job order's product unit cost. (Round to whole dollars.)

LO4 **Computation of Product Unit Cost**

E 9. Using job order costing, determine the product unit cost based on the following costs incurred during March: liability insurance, manufacturing, $2,500; rent, sales office, $2,900; depreciation, manufacturing equipment, $6,100; direct materials, $32,650; indirect labor, manufacturing, $3,480;

indirect materials, $1,080; heat, light, and power, manufacturing, $1,910; fire insurance, manufacturing, $2,600; depreciation, sales equipment, $4,250; rent, manufacturing, $3,850; direct labor, $18,420; manager's salary, manufacturing, $3,100; president's salary, $5,800; sales commissions, $8,250; and advertising expenses, $2,975. The Inspection Department reported that 48,800 good units were produced during March. Carry your answer to two decimal places.

LO4 **Computation of Product Unit Cost**

E 10. Wild Things, Inc., manufactures custom-made stuffed animals. Last month the company produced 4,540 stuffed bears with stethoscopes for the local children's hospital to sell at a fund-raising event. Using job order costing, determine the product unit cost of a stuffed bear based on the following costs incurred during the month: manufacturing utilities, $500; depreciation on manufacturing equipment, $450; indirect materials, $300; direct materials, $1,300; indirect labor, $800; direct labor, $2,400; sales commissions, $3,000; president's salary, $4,000; insurance on manufacturing plant, $600; advertising expense, $500; rent on manufacturing plant, $5,000; rent on sales office, $4,000; and legal expense, $250. Carry your answer to two decimal places.

LO4 **Computation of Product Unit Cost**

E 11. Arch Corporation manufactures specialty lines of women's apparel. During February, the company worked on three special orders: A-25, A-27, and B-14. Cost and production data for each order are as follows:

	Job A-25	Job A-27	Job B-14
Direct materials			
Fabric Q	$10,840	$12,980	$17,660
Fabric Z	11,400	12,200	13,440
Fabric YB	5,260	6,920	10,900
Direct labor			
Garment maker	8,900	10,400	16,200
Layout	6,450	7,425	9,210
Packaging	3,950	4,875	6,090
Overhead			
(120% of direct labor costs)	?	?	?
Number of units produced	700	775	1,482

1. Compute the total cost associated with each job. Show the subtotals for each cost category.
2. Compute the product unit cost for each job. (Round your computations to the nearest cent.)

LO4 **Job Order Costing in a Service Organization**

E 12. A job order cost card for Hal's Computer Services appears at the top of the next page. Complete the missing information. The profit factor in the organization's cost-plus contract is 30 percent of total cost.

Job Order Cost Card
Hal's Computer Services

Customer:	James Lowe
Job Order No.:	8-324
Contract Type:	Cost-Plus
Type of Service:	Software Installation and Internet Interfacing
Date of Completion:	October 6, 2011

Costs Charged to Job	**Total Cost**
Software installation services	
Installation labor	$300
Service overhead (?% of installation labor costs)	?
Total	$450
Internet services	
Internet labor	$200
Service overhead (20% of Internet labor costs)	40
Total	$?

Cost Summary to Date	**Total Cost**
Software installation services	$?
Internet services	?
Total	$?
Profit margin (30% of total cost)	?
Contract revenue	$?

LO4 **Job Order Costing in a Service Organization**

E 13. A job order cost card for Miniblinds by Jenny appears below. Complete the missing information. The profit factor in the company's cost-plus contract is 50 percent of total cost.

Job Order Cost Card
Miniblinds by Jenny

Customer:	Carmen Sawyer
Job Order No.:	8-482
Contract Type:	Cost-Plus
Type of Service:	Miniblind Installation and Design
Date of Completion:	June 12, 2011

Costs Charged to Job	**Total Cost**
Installation services	
Installation labor	$445
Service overhead (80% of installation labor costs)	?
Total	$?
Designer services	
Designer labor	$200
Service overhead (?% of designer labor costs)	?
Total	$400

Cost Summary to Date	**Total Cost**
Installation services	$?
Designer services	?
Total	$?
Profit margin (50% of total cost)	?
Contract revenue	$?

LO4 **Job Order Costing in a Service Organization**

E 14. Personal Shoppers, Inc., relieves busy women executives of the stress of shopping for clothes by taking an inventory of a client's current wardrobe and shopping for her needs for the next season or a special event. The company charges clients $30 per hour for the service plus the cost of the clothes purchased. It pays its employees various hourly wage rates.

During September, Personal Shoppers worked with three clients. It began Job 9-3, for Lucinda Mapley, on September 3 and completed the job on September 30. Using the partial data that follow, prepare the job order cost card. What amount of profit will Personal Shoppers make on this job?

Costs Charged to Job	Costs	Hours	Other
In-person consultation			
Supplies	$ 30		
Labor ($10 per hour)		4	
Overhead (10% of in-person labor costs)			
Shopping			
Purchases	$560		
Labor ($15 per hour)		8	
Overhead (25% of shopping labor costs)			
Telephone consultations			
Cell phone calls ($1 per call)			6 calls
Labor ($6 per hour)		2	
Overhead (50% of telephone labor costs)			

LO4 **Job Order Costing in a Service Organization**

E 15. A job order cost card for Personal Trainers, Inc., appears at the top of the next page. Fill in the missing information.

Problems

LO3 **T Account Analysis with Unknowns**

P 1. Flagstaff Enterprises makes flagpoles. Dan Dalripple, the company's new controller, can find only the following partial information for the past two months:

Account/Transaction	May	June
Beginning Materials Inventory	$ 36,240	$ e
Beginning Work in Process Inventory	56,480	f
Beginning Finished Goods Inventory	44,260	g
Materials purchased	a	96,120
Direct materials requested	82,320	h
Direct labor costs	b	72,250
Overhead applied	53,200	i
Cost of units completed	c	221,400
Cost of Goods Sold	209,050	j
Ending Materials Inventory	38,910	41,950
Ending Work in Process Inventory	d	k
Ending Finished Goods Inventory	47,940	51,180

The current year's predetermined overhead rate is 80 percent of direct labor cost.

Required

Using the data provided and T accounts, compute the unknown values.

Job Order H.W.

Job Order Cost Card
Personal Trainers, Inc.

Customer: Hillary White | Batch: ___ | Custom: X
Specifications: Marathon Training
Date of Order: 4/2/2011 | Date of Completion: 7/24/2011

Costs Charged to Job	Previous Months	Current Month	Total Cost
In-person consultation			
Training logbook	$ 20.00	$?	$20.00
Labor ($10 per hour)	20.00	?	50.00
Overhead (10% of in-person labor costs)	?	3.00	5.00
Total	$?	$?	$?
Training			
Bike rental	$ 30.00	$?	$60.00
Labor ($5 per hour)	150.00	300.00	?
Overhead (25% of training labor costs)	37.50	?	?
Total	$?	$?	$?
Telephone consultations			
Cell phone calls ($1 per call)	$ 30.00	$ 10.00	$?
Labor ($10 per hour)	10.00	10.00	?
Overhead (50% of telephone labor costs)	?	?	?
Total	$?	$?	$?
Total cost			$?

Job Revenue and Profit	
Logbook and bike rental	?
Service fee: 97 hours × $30	?
Job revenue	$2,990.00
Less total cost	?
Profit	$2,222.50

LO3 **Job Order Costing: T Account Analysis**

P 2. Par Carts, Inc., produces special-order golf carts, so Par Carts uses a job order costing system. Overhead is applied at the rate of 90 percent of direct labor cost. The following is a list of transactions for January:

Jan. 1 Purchased direct materials on account, $215,400.
2 Purchased indirect materials on account, $49,500.
4 Requested direct materials costing $193,200 (all used on Job X) and indirect materials costing $38,100 for production.
10 Paid the following overhead costs: utilities, $4,400; manufacturing rent, $3,800; and maintenance charges, $3,900.
15 Recorded the following gross wages and salaries for employees: direct labor, $120,000 (all for Job X); indirect labor, $60,620.
15 Applied overhead to production.
19 Purchased indirect materials costing $27,550 and direct materials costing $190,450 on account.
21 Requested direct materials costing $214,750 (Job X, $178,170; Job Y, $18,170; and Job Z, $18,410) and indirect materials costing $31,400 for production.

Jan. 31	Recorded the following gross wages and salaries for employees: direct labor, $132,000 (Job X, $118,500; Job Y, $7,000; Job Z, $6,500); indirect labor, $62,240.
31	Applied overhead to production.
31	Completed and transferred Job X (375 carts) and Job Y (10 carts) to finished goods inventory; total cost was $855,990.
31	Shipped Job X to the customer; total production cost was $824,520 and sales price was $996,800.
31	Recorded these overhead costs (adjusting entries): prepaid insurance expired, $3,700; property taxes (payable at year end), $3,400; and depreciation–machinery, $15,500.

Required

1. Record the entries for all transactions in January using T accounts for the following: Materials Inventory, Work in Process Inventory, Finished Goods Inventory, Overhead, Cash, Accounts Receivable, Prepaid Insurance, Accumulated Depreciation—Machinery, Accounts Payable, Payroll Payable, Property Taxes Payable, Sales, and Cost of Goods Sold. Use job order cost cards for Job X, Job Y, and Job Z. Determine the partial account balances. Assume no beginning inventory balances. Also assume that when the payroll was recorded, entries were made to the Payroll Payable account.
2. Compute the amount of underapplied or overapplied overhead as of January 31 and transfer it to the Cost of Goods Sold account.
3. Why should the Overhead account's underapplied or overapplied overhead be transferred to the Cost of Goods Sold account?

LO3 LO4 Job Order Cost Flow

P 3. On May 31, the inventory balances of Princess Designs, a manufacturer of high-quality children's clothing, were as follows: Materials Inventory, $21,360; Work in Process Inventory, $15,112; and Finished Goods Inventory, $17,120. Job order cost cards for jobs in process as of June 30 had these totals:

Job No.	Direct Materials	Direct Labor	Overhead
24-A	$1,596	$1,290	$1,677
24-B	1,492	1,380	1,794
24-C	1,984	1,760	2,288
24-D	1,608	1,540	2,002

The predetermined overhead rate is 130 percent of direct labor costs. Materials purchased and received in June were as follows:

June 4	$33,120
June 16	28,600
June 22	31,920

Direct labor costs for June were as follows:

June 15 payroll	$23,680
June 29 payroll	25,960

Direct materials requested by production during June were as follows:

June 6	$37,240
June 23	38,960

On June 30, Princess Designs sold on account finished goods with a 75 percent markup over cost for $320,000.

Required

1. Using T accounts for Materials Inventory, Work in Process Inventory, Finished Goods Inventory, Overhead, Accounts Receivable, Payroll Payable, Sales, and Cost of Goods Sold, reconstruct the transactions in June.
2. Compute the cost of units completed during the month.
3. What was the total cost of goods sold during June?
4. Determine the ending inventory balances.
5. Jobs 24-A and 24-C were completed during the first week of July. No additional materials costs were incurred, but Job 24-A required $960 more of direct labor, and Job 24-C needed an additional $1,610 of direct labor. Job 24-A was composed of 1,200 pairs of trousers; Job 24-C, of 950 shirts. Compute the product unit cost for each job. (Round your answers to two decimal places.)

LO4 **Job Order Costing in a Service Organization**

P 4. Riley & Associates is a CPA firm located in Clinton, Kansas. The firm deals primarily in tax and audit work. For billing of major audit engagements, it uses cost-plus contracts, and its profit factor is 25 percent of total job cost. Costs are accumulated for three primary activities: preliminary analysis, fieldwork, and report development. Current service overhead rates based on billable hours are preliminary analysis, $12 per hour; fieldwork, $20 per hour; and report development, $16 per hour. Supplies are treated as direct materials and are traceable to each engagement. Audits for three clients—Fulcrum, Inc., Rainy Day Bakeries, and Our Place Restaurants—are currently in process. During March, costs related to these projects were as follows:

	Fulcrum, Inc.	Rainy Day Bakeries	Our Place Restaurants
Beginning Balances			
Preliminary analysis	$1,160	$2,670	$2,150
Fieldwork	710	1,980	3,460
Report development	—	1,020	420
Costs During March			
Preliminary analysis			
Supplies	$ 710	$ 430	$ 200
Labor: hours	60	10	12
dollars	$1,200	$ 200	$ 240
Fieldwork			
Supplies	$ 450	$1,120	$ 890
Labor: hours	120	240	230
dollars	$4,800	$9,600	$9,200
Report development			
Supplies	$ 150	$ 430	$ 390
Labor: hours	30	160	140
dollars	$ 900	$4,800	$4,200

Required

1. Using the format shown in this chapter's Review Problem, create the job order cost card for each of the three audit engagements.
2. Riley & Associates will complete the audits of Rainy Day Bakeries and Our Place Restaurants by the end of March. What will the billing amount for each of those audit engagements be?
3. What is the March ending balance of Riley & Associates' Audit in Process account?

LO4 Job Order Costing in a Service Organization

P 5. Peruga Engineering Company specializes in designing automated characters and displays for theme parks. It uses cost-plus profit contracts, and its profit factor is 30 percent of total cost.

Peruga uses a job order costing system to track the costs of developing each job. Costs are accumulated for three primary activities: bid and proposal, design, and prototype development. Current service overhead rates based on engineering hours are as follows: bid and proposal, $18 per hour; design, $22 per hour; and prototype development, $20 per hour. Supplies are treated as direct materials, traceable to each job. Peruga worked on three jobs, P-12, P-15, and P-19, during January. The following table shows the costs for those jobs:

	P-12	P-15	P-19
Beginning Balances			
Bid and proposal	$2,460	$2,290	$ 940
Design	1,910	460	—
Prototype development	2,410	1,680	—
Costs During January			
Bid and proposal			
Supplies	$ —	$ 280	$2,300
Labor: hours	12	20	68
dollars	$ 192	$ 320	$1,088
Design			
Supplies	$ 400	$ 460	$ 290
Labor: hours	64	42	26
dollars	$1,280	$ 840	$ 520
Prototype development			
Supplies	$6,744	$7,216	$2,400
Labor: hours	120	130	25
dollars	$2,880	$3,120	$ 600

Required

1. Using the format shown in this chapter's Review Problem, create the job order cost card for each of the three jobs.
2. Peruga completed Jobs P-12 and P-15, and the customers approved the prototype products. Customer A plans to produce 12 special characters using the design and specifications created by Job P-12. Customer B plans to make 18 displays from the design developed by Job P-15. What dollar amount will each customer use as the cost of design for each of those products (i.e., what is the product unit cost for Jobs P-12 and P-15)? (Round to the nearest dollar.)

3. What is the January ending balance of Peruga's Contract in Process account for the three jobs?

Manager insight ▶ 4. Rank the jobs in order from most costly to least costly based on each job's total cost. From the rankings of cost, what observations can you make?

Manager insight ▶ 5. Speculate on the price that Peruga should charge for such jobs.

Alternate Problems

LO3 T Account Analysis with Unknowns

P 6. Hard Core Enterprises makes peripheral equipment for computers. Emily Vit, the company's new controller, can find only the following partial information for the past two months:

Account/Transaction	July	August
Beginning Materials Inventory	$ 52,000	$ e
Beginning Work in Process Inventory	24,000	f
Beginning Finished Goods Inventory	36,000	g
Materials purchased	a	31,000
Direct materials requested	77,000	h
Direct labor costs	b	44,000
Overhead applied	53,200	i
Cost of units completed	c	167,000
Cost of Goods Sold	188,000	j
Ending Materials Inventory	27,000	8,000
Ending Work in Process Inventory	d	k
Ending Finished Goods Inventory	12,000	19,000

The current year's predetermined overhead rate is 110 percent of direct labor cost.

Required

Using the data provided and T accounts, compute the unknown values.

LO3 Job Order Costing: T Account Analysis

P 7. Rhile Industries, Inc., produces colorful and stylish nursing uniforms. During September, Rhile Industries completed the following transactions:

Sept. 1 Purchased direct materials on account, $59,400.
3 Requested direct materials costing $26,850 for production (all for Job A).
4 Purchased indirect materials for cash, $22,830.
8 Issued checks for the following overhead costs: utilities, $4,310; manufacturing insurance, $1,925; and repairs, $4,640.
10 Requested direct materials costing $29,510 (all used on Job A) and indirect materials costing $6,480 for production.
15 Recorded the following gross wages and salaries for employees: direct labor, $62,900 (all for Job A); indirect labor, $31,610; manufacturing supervision, $26,900; and sales commissions, $32,980.
15 Applied overhead to production at a rate of 120 percent of direct labor cost.

Sept. 22 Paid the following overhead costs: utilities, $4,270; maintenance, $3,380; and rent, $3,250.

23 Recorded the purchase on account and receipt of $31,940 of direct materials and $9,260 of indirect materials.

27 Requested $28,870 of direct materials (Job A, $2,660; Job B, $8,400; Job C, $17,810) and $7,640 of indirect materials for production.

30 Recorded the following gross wages and salaries for employees: direct labor, $64,220 (Job A, $44,000; Job B, $9,000; Job C, $11,220); indirect labor, $30,290; manufacturing supervision, $28,520; and sales commissions, $36,200.

30 Applied overhead to production at a rate of 120 percent of direct labor cost.

30 Completed and transferred Job A (58,840 units) and Job B (3,525 units) to finished goods inventory; total cost was $322,400.

30 Shipped Job A to the customer; total production cost was $294,200, and sales price was $418,240.

30 Recorded the following adjusting entries: $2,680 for depreciation–manufacturing equipment; and $1,230 for property taxes, manufacturing, payable at month end.

Required

1. Record the entries for all Rhile's transactions in September using T accounts for the following: Materials Inventory, Work in Process Inventory, Finished Goods Inventory, Overhead, Cash, Accounts Receivable, Accumulated Depreciation—Manufacturing Equipment, Accounts Payable, Payroll Payable, Property Taxes Payable, Sales, Cost of Goods Sold, and Selling and Administrative Expenses. Use job order cost cards for Job A, Job B, and Job C. Determine the partial account balances. Assume no beginning inventory balances. Assume also that when payroll was recorded, entries were made to the Payroll Payable account. (Round your answers to the nearest whole dollar.)
2. Compute the amount of underapplied or overapplied overhead for September and transfer it to the Cost of Goods Sold account.
3. Why should the Overhead account's underapplied or overapplied overhead be transferred to the Cost of Goods Sold account?

LO3 LO4 Job Order Cost Flow

P 8. Laurence Norton is the chief financial officer of Rotham Industries, a company that makes special-order sound systems for home theaters. His records for February revealed the following information:

Beginning inventory balances	
Materials Inventory	$27,450
Work in Process Inventory	22,900
Finished Goods Inventory	19,200

Direct materials purchased and received	
February 6	$ 7,200
February 12	8,110
February 24	5,890
Direct labor costs	
February 14	$13,750
February 28	13,230
Direct materials requested for production	
February 4	$ 9,080
February 13	5,940
February 25	7,600

Job order cost cards for jobs in process on February 28 had the following totals:

Job No.	Direct Materials	Direct Labor	Overhead
AJ-10	$3,220	$1,810	$2,534
AJ-14	3,880	2,110	2,954
AJ-15	2,980	1,640	2,296
AJ-16	4,690	2,370	3,318

The predetermined overhead rate for the month was 140 percent of direct labor costs. Sales for February totaled $152,400, which represented a 70 percent markup over the cost of production.

Required

1. Using T accounts for Materials Inventory, Work in Process Inventory, Finished Goods Inventory, Overhead, Accounts Receivable, Payroll Payable, Sales, and Cost of Goods Sold, reconstruct the transactions in February.
2. Compute the cost of units completed during the month.
3. What was the total cost of goods sold during February?
4. Determine the ending balances in the inventory accounts.
5. During the first week of March, Jobs AJ-10 and AJ-14 were completed. No additional direct materials costs were incurred, but Job AJ-10 needed $720 more of direct labor, and Job AJ-14 needed an additional $1,140 of direct labor. Job AJ-10 was 40 units; Job AJ-14, 55 units. Compute the product unit cost for each completed job (round to two decimal places).

LO4 Job Order Costing in a Service Organization

P 9. Locust Lodge, a restored 1920s lodge located in Alabama, caters and serves special events for businesses and social occasions. The company earns 60 percent of its revenue from weekly luncheon meetings of local clubs like Rotary. The remainder of its business comes from bookings for weddings and receptions.

Locust Lodge uses job order cost cards to keep track of the costs incurred. Job costs are separated into three categories: food and beverage, labor, and facility overhead. The facility overhead cost for weekly events is 10 percent of food and beverage costs, the facility overhead cost for sit-down receptions is 40 percent of food and beverage costs, and the facility overhead cost for stand-up receptions is 20 percent of food and beverage costs. Accumulated costs for three Locust Lodge clients in the current quarter are as follows:

	Food and Beverage	Labor	Facility Overhead
Tuesday Club meetings	Last month: $2,000 This month: $2,500	Last month: $200 This month: $250	Last month: ? This month: ?
Doar-Turner engagement and wedding parties	Last month: $3,000 This month: $8,000 Both sit-down affairs	Last month: $1,000 This month: $2,000	Last month: ? This month: ?
Reception for the new president	This month: $5,000 A stand-up affair	This month: $1,000	This month: ?

The number of attendees served at Tuesday Club meetings is usually 200 per month. The Doar-Turner parties paid for 500 guests. The organizers of the reception for the new president paid for 1,000 invitees.

Required

1. Using the format shown in this chapter's Review Problem, create a job order cost card for each of the three clients.
2. Calculate the total cost of each of the three jobs on its job order cost card.
3. Calculate the cost per attendee for each job.

Manager insight ▶ 4. Rank the jobs in order from most costly to least costly based on each job's total cost and on the cost per attendee. From the rankings of cost, what observations are you able to make?

Manager insight ▶ 5. Speculate on the price that Locust Lodge should charge for such jobs.

LO4 Job Order Costing in a Service Organization

P 10. Refer to assignment **P 5** in this chapter. Peruga Engineering Company needs to analyze its jobs in process during the month of January.

Required

1. Using Excel's Chart Wizard and the job order cost cards that you created for Jobs P-12, P-15, and P-19, prepare a bar chart that compares the bid and proposal costs, design costs, and prototype development costs of the jobs. The suggested format to use for the information table necessary to complete the bar chart is as follows:

	A	B	C	D	E
1	1		P-12	P-15	P-19
2	2	Bid and proposal			
3	3	Design			
4	4	Prototype development			
5	5	Total job cost			
6					

2. Examine the chart you prepared in requirement **1.** List some reasons for the differences between the costs of the various jobs.

ENHANCING Your Knowledge, Skills, and Critical Thinking

LO1 Interpreting Nonfinancial Data

C 1. Eagle Manufacturing supplies engine parts to Cherokee Cycle Company, a major U.S. manufacturer of motorcycles. Like all of Cherokee's suppliers, Eagle has always added a healthy profit margin to its cost when quoting selling prices to Cherokee. Recently, however, several companies have offered to supply engine parts to Cherokee for lower prices than Eagle has been charging.

Because Eagle Manufacturing wants to keep Cherokee Cycle Company's business, a team of Eagle's managers analyzed their company's product costs and decided to make minor changes in the company's manufacturing process. No new equipment was purchased, and no additional labor was required. Instead, the machines were rearranged, and some of the work was reassigned.

To monitor the effectiveness of the changes, Eagle introduced three new performance measures to its information system: inventory levels, lead time (total time required for a part to move through the production process), and productivity (number of parts manufactured per person per day). Eagle's goal was to reduce the quantities of the first two performance measures and to increase the quantity of the third.

A section of a recent management report, shown below, summarizes the quantities for each performance measure before and after the changes in the manufacturing process were made.

Measure	Before	After	Improvement
Inventory in dollars	$21,444	$10,772	50%
Lead time in minutes	17	11	35%
Productivity (parts per person per day)	515	1,152	124%

1. Do you believe that Eagle improved the quality of its manufacturing process and the quality of its engine parts? Explain your answer.
2. Can Eagle lower its selling price to Cherokee? Explain your answer.
3. Did the introduction of the new measures affect the design of the product costing system? Explain your answer.
4. Do you believe that the new measures caused a change in Eagle's cost per engine part? If so, how did they cause the change?

LO1 LO2 Product Costing Systems and Nonfinancial Data

C 2. Refer to the information in **C1.** Jordan Smith, the president of Eagle Manufacturing, wants to improve the quality of the company's operations and products. She believes waste exists in the design and manufacture of standard engine parts. To begin the improvement process, she has asked you to (1) identify the sources of such waste, (2) develop performance measures to account for the waste, and (3) estimate the current costs associated with the waste. She has asked you to submit a memo of your findings within two weeks so that she can begin strategic planning to revise the price at which Eagle sells engine parts to Cherokee.

You have identified two sources of costly waste. The Production Department is redoing work that was not done correctly the first time, and the Engineering Design Department is redesigning products that were not initially designed to customer specifications. Having improper designs has caused the company to buy parts that are not used in production. You have also obtained the following information from the product costing system:

Direct labor costs	$673,402
Engineering design costs	124,709
Indirect labor costs	67,200
Depreciation on production equipment	84,300
Supervisors' salaries	98,340
Direct materials costs	432,223
Indirect materials costs	44,332

1. In preparation for writing your memo, answer the following questions:
   a. For whom are you preparing the memo? What is the appropriate length of the memo?
   b. Why are you preparing the memo?
   c. What information is needed for the memo? Where can you get this information? What performance measure would you suggest for each activity? Is the accounting information sufficient for your memo?
   d. When is the memo due? What can be done to provide accurate and timely information?
2. Prepare an outline of the sections you would want to include in your memo.

LO3 Job Order Costing

C 3. Many businesses accumulate costs for each job performed. Examples of businesses that use a job order costing system include print shops, car repair shops, health clinics, and kennels.

Visit a local business that uses job order costing, and interview the owner, manager, or accountant about the job order process and the documents the business uses to accumulate product costs. Write a paper that summarizes the information you obtained. Include the following in your summary:

1. The name of the business and the type of operations performed
2. The name and position of the individual you interviewed
3. A description of the process of starting and completing a job
4. A description of the accounting process and the documents used to track a job
5. Your responses to these questions:
   a. Did the person you interviewed know the actual amount of direct materials, direct labor, and overhead charged to a particular job? If the job includes some estimated costs, how are the estimates calculated? Do the costs affect the determination of the selling price of the product or service?
   b. Compare the documents discussed in this chapter with the documents used by the company you visited. How are they similar, and how are they different?
   c. In your opinion, does the business record and accumulate its product costs effectively? Explain.

LO4 Costing Procedures and Ethics

C 4. Kevin Rogers, the production manager of Stitts Metal Products Company, entered the office of controller Ed Harris and asked, "Ed, what gives here? I was charged for 330 direct labor hours on Job AD22, and my records show that we spent only 290 hours on that job. That 40-hour difference caused the total cost of direct labor and overhead for the job to increase by over $5,500. Are my records wrong, or was there an error in the direct labor assigned to the job?"

Harris replied, "Don't worry about it, Kevin. This job won't be used in your quarterly performance evaluation. Job AD22 was a federal government job, a cost-plus contract, so the more costs we assign to it, the more profit we make.

We decided to add a few hours to the job in case there is some follow-up work to do. You know how fussy the feds are." What should Kevin Rogers do? Discuss Ed Harris's costing procedure.

LO1 LO4 Role of Cost Information in Software Development

C 5. Software development companies frequently have a problem: When is "good enough" good enough? How many hours should be devoted to developing a new product? The industry's rule of thumb is that developing and shipping new software takes six to nine months. To be the first to market, a company must develop and ship products much more quickly than the industry norm. One performance measure that is used to answer the "good enough" question is a calculation based on the economic value (not cost) of what a company's developers create. The computation takes the estimated current market valuation of a firm and divides it by the number of product developers in the firm, to arrive at the market value created per developer. Some companies refine this calculation further to determine the value that each developer creates per workday. One company has estimated this value to be $10,000. Thus, for one software development company, "good enough" focuses on whether a new product's potential justifies an investment of time by someone who is worth $10,000 per day.

The salary cost of the company's developers is not used in the "good enough" calculation. Why is that cost not relevant?

LO4 Cookie Company (Continuing Case)

C 6. In the "Cookie Company" case in the last chapter, your team selected a cookie recipe for your company. In this chapter, your team will use that recipe to bake a batch of cookies, collect cost and time performance data related to the baking, create a marketing display for your company, and vote for the class's favorite cookie during an in-class cookie taste test. The goal of the taste test is to have your team's product voted the "best in class." One rule of the contest is that you may not vote for your own team's product.

1. Design a job measurement document that includes at least the following measures: cost per cookie; number of cookies produced (= number meeting specs + number rejected + number sampled for quality control + unexplained differences); size of cookies before baking; size of cookies after baking; and total throughput time (= mix time + [bake time for one cookie sheet × number of cookie sheets processed] + packaging time + downtime + cleanup time).
2. Design a job order cost card for your company that resembles one of those displayed in this chapter.
3. Using the recipe your team selected and assigning duties as described in the last chapter, bake a batch of cookies, and complete the job measurement document and job order cost card.
   - Assume an overhead rate of $2 for every $1 of direct material cost.
   - Assign direct labor cost for each production task based on the hourly rate or a monthly salary previously determined by your team.
4. Create a marketing display for your cookie product, and bring it to class on the day of the taste test. The marketing display should include 20 cookies on a plate or napkin and a poster that displays your company's name and mission statement, cookie recipe, job measurement document, and job order cost card.
5. During class, each student should look at all the marketing displays, taste 2 or 3 cookies and, on a ballot provided by your instructor, rank taste test results by giving 1 to the best cookie tasted, 2 to the next best, and so on. Students must sign their ballots before they turn them in to the instructor. (Remember, you cannot cast a vote for your own team's entry.) Your instructor will tabulate the ballots and announce the winning team.
6. Finally, write a review of your team members' efforts, and give it to your instructor.

CHAPTER

21 Costing Systems: Process Costing

The Management Process

PLAN

- **Select the costing system that's best for the business's products**
- **Prepare budgets for production departments where process costs will be tracked**

PERFORM

- **Track product cost flows through departments or processes**
- **Prepare process cost reports every period for each production department or process using either FIFO or the average costing approach**
- **Record the entries to transfer costs on to the next department or to finished goods inventory**

EVALUATE

- **Analyze performance by comparing budget and actual department costs**

COMMUNICATE

- **Prepare financial statements using the cost information provided by process costing**
- **Prepare internal management reports to manage and monitor processes and departments**

Long-term liability activities can impact all financial statements.

As we noted in the previous chapter, a product costing system is expected to provide unit cost information, to supply cost data for management decisions, and to furnish ending values for the Materials Inventory, Work in Process Inventory, and Finished Goods Inventory accounts. In this chapter, we focus on the process costing system, which is used by companies that make large amounts of similar products or liquid products. We also describe product flow patterns, equivalent production, and the preparation of process cost reports.

LEARNING OBJECTIVES

LO1 **Describe the process costing system, and identify the reasons for its use.** (pp. 922–923)

LO2 **Relate the patterns of product flows to the cost flow methods in a process costing environment, and explain the role of the Work in Process Inventory accounts.** (pp. 923–925)

LO3 **Define *equivalent production,* and compute equivalent units.** (pp. 925–928)

LO4 **Prepare a process cost report using the FIFO costing method.** (pp. 928–935)

LO5 **Prepare a process cost report using the average costing method.** (pp. 935–939)

DECISION POINT ▸ A MANAGER'S FOCUS MILK PRODUCTS COMPANY

- ▸ **Why is a process costing system appropriate for Milk Products Company?**
- ▸ **How does a process costing system facilitate management decisions?**

Milk Products Company processes raw milk into homogenized, pasteurized milk. The company's products, which it distributes within the local community, include whole milk, low-fat milk, skimmed milk, chocolate milk, ice cream, and yogurt. In this chapter, we explain why a company like Milk Products should use a process costing system and how this system provides the information that managers need to make sound product decisions.

The Process Costing System

LO1 Describe the process costing system, and identify the reasons for its use.

> **Study Note**
> In process costing, costs are traced to production processes, whereas in job order costing, costs are traced to jobs.

As we noted earlier, a **process costing system** is a product costing system used by companies that make large amounts of similar products or liquid products or that have long, continuous production runs of identical products.

- Companies that produce paint, beverages, chocolate syrup, computer chips, milk, paper, and gallon containers of ice cream are typical users of a process costing system.

Since one gallon of chocolate ice cream is identical to the next gallon, they should cost the same amount to produce. A process costing system first accumulates the costs of direct materials, direct labor, and overhead for each process, department, or work cell and then assigns those costs to the products produced during a particular period.

Managers use process costing in every stage of the management process:

- When managers plan, they use information about past and projected product costing and customer preferences to decide what a product should cost. After they have determined a target number of units to be sold, all product-related costs for that targeted number of units can be computed and used in the budget.
- During the period, managers track product and cost flows through their departments or processes and prepare process cost reports to assign production costs to the products manufactured.
- When managers evaluate performance, they compare targeted costs with actual costs. If costs have exceeded expectations, managers analyze why this has occurred and adjust their planning and decision-making strategies.
- When managers communicate with external stakeholders, they use actual units produced and costs incurred to value inventory on the balance sheet and cost of goods sold on the income statement. Managers are also interested in internal reports on whether goals for product costs are being achieved.

FOCUS ON BUSINESS PRACTICE

What Kinds of Companies Use Process Costing?

Process costing is appropriate for companies in many types of industries. The following list provides some examples:

Industry	*Company*	*Industry*	*Company*
Aluminum	**Alcoa, Inc.**	Machinery	**Caterpillar Inc.**
Beverages	**Coors**	Oil and gas	**ExxonMobil**
Building materials	**Owens Corning**	Chemicals	**Dow Chemicals**
Computers	**Apple Computer**	Plastic products	**Tupperware**
Foods	**Kellogg Company**	Soft drinks	**Coca-Cola**

STOP & APPLY >

Indicate whether the manufacturer of each of the following products should use a job order costing system or a process costing system to accumulate product costs:

a. Milk bottles

b. Chocolate milk

c. Nuclear submarines

d. Generic drugs

SOLUTION

a. Process; b. Process; c. Job order; d. Process

Patterns of Product Flows and Cost Flow Methods

LO2 Relate the patterns of product flows to the cost flow methods in a process costing environment, and explain the role of the Work in Process Inventory accounts.

During production in a process costing environment, products flow in a first-in, first-out (FIFO) fashion through several processes, departments, or work cells, and may undergo many different combinations of operations. Figure 21-1 illustrates the simple linear production flow of how milk is produced in a series of three processing steps, or departments. Each department has its own Work in Process Inventory account to accumulate the direct material, direct labor, and overhead costs associated with it.

- Homogenization department: Raw milk from the cow must be mixed to evenly distribute the butterfat. The homogenized milk and its associated cost then become the direct materials for the next department.
- Pasteurization department: The homogenized milk is heated to 145 degrees to kill the bacteria found in raw milk. The homogenized, pasteurized milk and all associated cost are then transferred on.

FIGURE 21-1 Product Flows in a Process Costing Environment

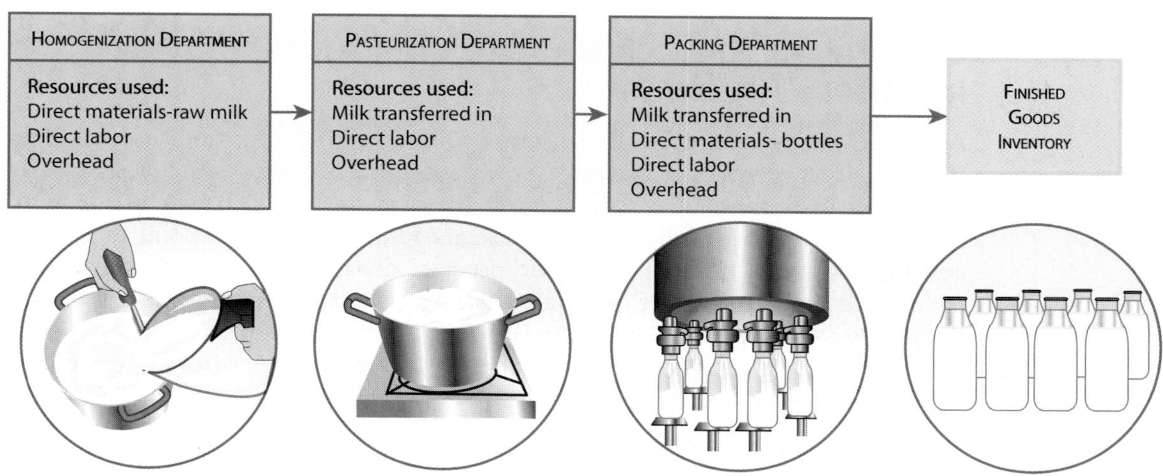

- Packaging department: The milk is put into bottles and transferred to Finished Goods Inventory since it is ready for sale.

The product unit cost of a bottle of milk is the sum of the cost elements in all three departments.

Process costing environments can be more or less complex than the one we have just described, but even in simple process costing environments, production generally involves a number of separate manufacturing processes, departments, or work cells.

- For example, the separate processes involved in manufacturing cookies include the mixing department, the baking department, and the packaging department.

As products pass through each manufacturing process, department, or work cell, the process costing system accumulates their costs and passes them on to the next process, department, or work cell. At the end of every accounting period, each manufacturing process, department, or work cell generates a report that assigns the costs that have accumulated during the period to the units that have transferred out of it and to the units that are still a part of its work in process. Managers use this report, called a **process cost report**, to assign costs by using a cost allocation method, such as the FIFO (first-in, first-out) costing method or the average costing method.

- In the **FIFO costing method**, the cost flow follows the logical physical flow of production—that is, the costs assigned to the first materials processed are the first costs transferred out when those materials flow to the next process, department, or work cell. Thus, in Figure 21-1, the costs assigned to the homogenized milk would be the first costs transferred to the pasteurization department.
- In contrast, the **average costing method** assigns an average cost to all products made during an accounting period; this method thus uses total cost averages and does not try to match cost flow with the physical flow of production.

We discuss process cost reports that use the FIFO and average costing methods later in this chapter.

Cost Flows Through the Work in Process Inventory Accounts

As we pointed out in the last chapter, a job order costing system uses a single Work in Process Inventory account, whereas a process costing system has a separate Work in Process Inventory account for each process, department, or work cell. As you can see in Figure 21-1, these accounts are the focal point of process costing. As products move from one process, department, or work cell to the next, the costs of the direct materials, direct labor, and overhead associated with them flow to the Work in Process Inventory account of that process, department, or work cell. The entry to record the transfer of product costs from one process, department, or work cell to another is:

	Dr.	Cr.
Work in Process Inventory (next department)	XX	
Work in Process Inventory (this department)		XX

Once the products are completed, packaged, and ready for sale, their costs are transferred to the Finished Goods Inventory account. The entry to record the transfer of the completed product costs out of Work in Process Inventory into Finished Goods Inventory is:

	Dr.	Cr.
Finished Goods Inventory	XX	
Work in Process Inventory (last department)		XX

As you will learn later in this chapter, the costs associated with these entries are calculated in a process cost report for the process, department, or work cell.

STOP & APPLY >

Milk Smoothies Inc. uses an automated mixing machine in its Mixing Department to combine three raw materials into a product called Strawberry Smoothie Mix. Total costs charged to the Mixing Department's Work in Process Inventory account during the month were $210,000. There were no units in beginning or ending work in process inventory. What is the entry in journal form to transfer the units completed to Finished Goods Inventory?

SOLUTION

Finished Goods Inventory	210,000	
Work in Process Inventory		210,000

Computing Equivalent Production

LO3 Define *equivalent production,* and compute equivalent units.

A process costing system makes no attempt to associate costs with particular job orders. Instead, it assigns the costs incurred in a process, department, or work cell to the units worked on during an accounting period by computing an average cost per unit of effort. To compute the unit cost, the total cost of direct materials, direct labor, and overhead is divided by the total number of units worked on during the period. Thus, exactly how many units were worked on during the period is a critical question. Do we count only units started and completed during the period? Or should we include partially completed units in the beginning work in process inventory? And what about incomplete products in the ending work in process inventory?

These questions relate to the concept of equivalent production. **Equivalent production** (also called *equivalent units*) is a measure that applies a percentage-of-completion factor to partially completed units to calculate the equivalent number of whole units produced during a period for each type of input (i.e., direct materials, direct labor, and overhead).

- The number of equivalent units produced is the sum of (1) total units started and completed during the period and (2) an amount representing the work done on partially completed products in both the beginning and the ending work in process inventories.

> **Study Note**
> Direct materials are sometimes added at stages of production other than the beginning (e.g., chocolate chips are added at the end of the mixing process).

Equivalent production must be computed separately for each type of input because of differences in the ways in which costs are incurred.

- Direct materials are usually added to production at the beginning of the process.
- The costs of direct labor and overhead are often incurred uniformly throughout the production process. Thus, it is convenient to combine direct labor and overhead when calculating equivalent units. These combined costs are called **conversion costs** (also called *processing costs*).

We will explain the computation of equivalent production by using a simplified example. One of the products Milk Products Company makes is a pint-sized, bottled milk drink. As illustrated in Figure 21-2, the company started Week 2 with one half-completed drink in process. During Week 2, it started and completed three drinks, and at the end of Week 2, it had one drink that was three-quarters completed.

Equivalent Production for Direct Materials

> **Study Note**
> The number of units started and completed is not the same as the total number of units completed during the period. Total units completed include both units in beginning work in process inventory that were completed and units started and completed.

At Milk Products, all direct materials, including liquids and bottles, are added at the beginning of production. Thus, the drink that was half-completed at the beginning of Week 2 had had all its direct materials added during the previous week.

- No direct materials costs for this drink are included in the computation of Week 2's equivalent units for the beginning inventory units.

During Week 2, work began on four new drinks—the three drinks that were completed and the drink that was three-quarters completed at week's end. Because all direct materials are added at the beginning of the production process, all four drinks were 100 percent complete with regard to direct materials at the end of Week 2.

- Thus, for Week 2, the equivalent production for direct materials was 4.0 units. This figure includes direct materials for both the 3.0 units that were started and completed and the 1.0 unit that was three-quarters completed.

FIGURE 21-2 Computation of Equivalent Production

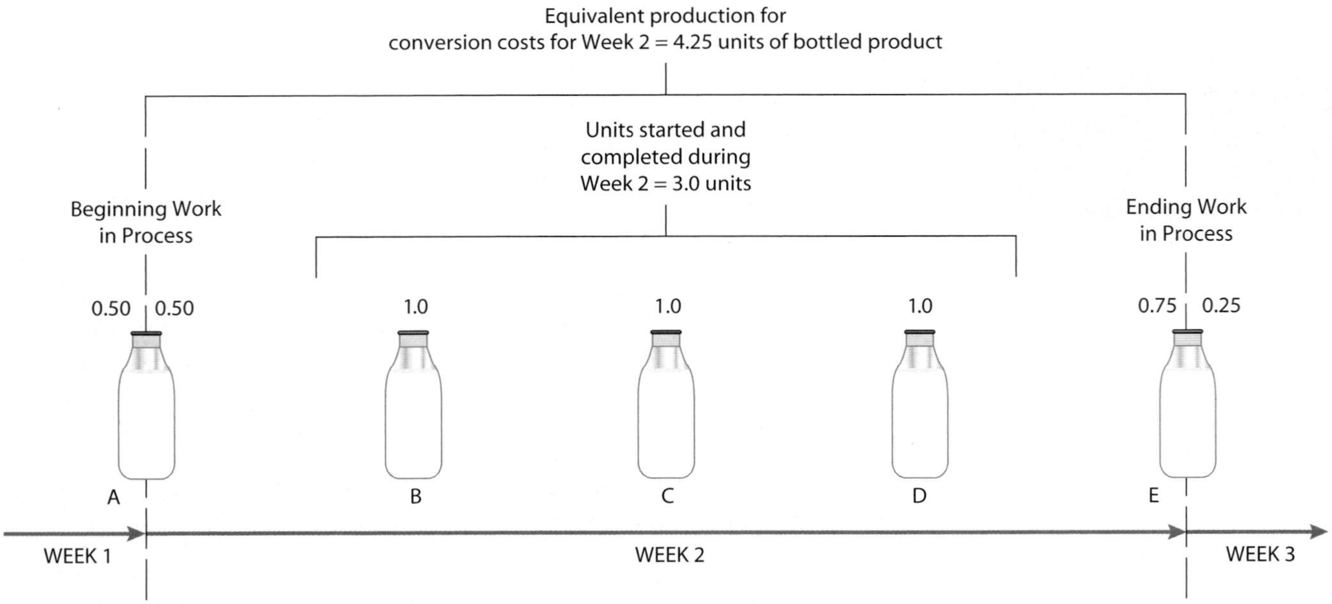

Note: Conversion costs (the cost of direct labor and overhead) are incurred uniformly as each physical unit of drink moves through production. Equivalent production for Week 2 is 4.25 units for conversion costs. But direct materials costs are all added to production at the beginning of the process. Because four physical units of drinks entered production in Week 2, equivalent production for the week is 4.0 units of effort for direct materials costs.

Equivalent Production for Conversion Costs

Study Note

Work in the current period is applied to three distinct product groups: units in beginning work in process inventory, which must be completed; goods started and completed during the period; and goods started but not completed by the end of the accounting period.

Because conversion costs at Milk Products are incurred uniformly throughout the production process, the equivalent production for conversion costs during Week 2 consists of three components: the cost to finish the half-completed unit in beginning work in process inventory (0.50), the cost to begin and finish three completed units (3.0), and the cost to begin work on the three-quarters-completed unit in ending work in process inventory (0.75).

► For Week 2, the total equivalent production for conversion costs was 4.25 units (0.50 of beginning inventory + 3.0 of units started and completed + 0.75 of ending inventory).

In reality, Milk Products would make many more drinks during an accounting period and would have many more partially completed drinks in its beginning and ending work in process inventories. The number of partially completed drinks would be so great that it would be impractical to take a physical count of them. So, instead of taking a physical count, Milk Products would estimate an average percentage of completion for all drinks in process.

Summary of Equivalent Production

The following is a recap of the current equivalent production for direct materials and conversion costs for the period for Milk Products:

	Physical Units	Equivalent Units of Effort			
		Direct Materials		Conversion Costs	
Beginning inventory	1.00				
Units started this period	4.00				
Units to be accounted for	5.00				
Beginning inventory	1.00	—	0%	0.50	50%
Units started and completed	3.00	3.00	100%	3.00	100%
Ending inventory	1.00	1.00	100%	0.75	75%
Units accounted for	5.00	4.00		4.25	

STOP & APPLY >

Milk Smoothies, Inc., adds direct materials when it starts its drink mix production process and adds conversion costs uniformly throughout this process. Given the following information from Milk Smoothie's records for July, compute the current period's equivalent units of production:

Units in beginning inventory: 2,000
Units started during the period: 13,000
Units partially completed: 500
Percentage of completion of beginning inventory: 100% for direct materials; 40% for conversion costs
Percentage of completion of ending work in process inventory: 100% for direct materials; 70% for conversion costs.

(continued)

SOLUTION

Milk Smoothies, Inc.
For the Month Ended July 31

	Physical Units	Equivalent Units of Effort			
		Direct Materials		Conversion Costs	
Beginning inventory	2,000				
Units started this period	13,000				
Units to be accounted for	15,000				
Beginning inventory	2,000	—	0%	1,200	60%
Units started and completed	12,500	12,500	100%	12,500	100%
Ending inventory	500	500	100%	350	70%
Units accounted for	15,000	13,000		14,050	

Preparing a Process Cost Report Using the FIFO Costing Method

LO4 Prepare a process cost report using the FIFO costing method.

Study Note

The FIFO method focuses on the work done in the current period only.

As we mentioned earlier, a process cost report, such as the one shown in Exhibit 21-1, is a report that managers use to track and analyze costs for a process, department, or work cell in a process costing system. In a process cost report that uses the FIFO costing method, the cost flow follows the logical physical flow of production—that is, the costs assigned to the first products processed are the first costs transferred out when those products flow to the next process, department, or work cell.

As illustrated in Exhibit 21-1, the preparation of a process cost report involves five steps. The first two steps account for the units of product being processed:

- **Step 1.** ***Account for physical units.***
- **Step 2.** ***Account for equivalent units of effort.***

The next two steps account for the costs of the direct materials, direct labor, and overhead being incurred:

- **Step 3.** ***Account for the costs incurred.***
- **Step 4.** ***Compute the cost per equivalent unit.***

The final step assigns costs to products being transferred out of the area and to those remaining behind in ending work in process inventory:

- **Step 5.** ***Assign costs to products transferred out or in ending inventory.***

Accounting for Units

Managers must account for the physical flow of products through their areas (Step 1) before they can compute equivalent production for the accounting period (Step 2). To continue with the Milk Products example, assume the following facts for the accounting period of February:

- The beginning work in process inventory consists of 6,200 partially completed units (60 percent processed in the previous period).
- During the period, the 6,200 units in beginning inventory were completed, and 57,500 units were started into production.

EXHIBIT 21-1 Process Cost Report: FIFO Costing Method

Step 1: *Account for physical units.*

Beginning inventory (units started last period)	6,200
Units started this period	57,500
Units to be accounted for	63,700

Step 2: *Account for equivalent units.*

	Physical Units	Direct Materials	% Incurred During Period	Conversion Costs	% Incurred During Period
		Current Equivalent Units of Effort			
Beginning inventory (units completed this period)	6,200	0	0%	2,480	40%
Units started and completed this period	52,500	52,500	100%	52,500	100%
Ending inventory (units started but not completed this period)	5,000	5,000	100%	2,250	45%
Units accounted for	63,700	57,500		57,230	

Step 3: *Account for costs.*

	Total Costs		Direct Materials		Conversion Costs
Beginning inventory	$ 41,540	=	$ 20,150	+	$ 21,390
Current costs	510,238	=	189,750	+	320,488
Total costs	$551,778				

Step 4: *Compute cost per equivalent unit.*

			Direct Materials		Conversion Costs
Current Costs / Equivalent Units			$189,750 / 57,500		$320,488 / 57,230
Cost per equivalent unit	$8.90	=	$3.30	+	$5.60

Step 5: *Assign costs to cost of goods manufactured and ending inventory.*

Cost of goods manufactured and transferred out:					
From beginning inventory	$ 41,540				
Current costs to complete	13,888	=	$0	+	(2,480 × $5.60)
Units started and completed this period	467,250	=	(52,500 × $3.30) +		(52,500 × $5.60)
Cost of goods manufactured	$522,678		*(No rounding necessary)*		
Ending inventory	29,100	=	(5,000 × $3.30) +		(2,250 × $5.60)
Total costs	$551,778				

Work in Process Inventory Account: Cost Recap

Beg. Bal.	41,540	(Cost of goods manufactured and transferred out)	522,678
Direct materials	189,750		
Conversion costs	320,488		
End. Bal.	**29,100**		

Work in Process Inventory Account: Unit Recap

Beg. Bal.	6,200	(FIFO units transferred out from the 6,200 in beginning inventory plus the 52,500 started and completed)	58,700
Units started	57,500		
End. Bal.	**5,000**		

- Of the 57,500 units started during the period, 52,500 units were completed. The other 5,000 units remain in ending work in process inventory and are 45 percent complete.

Step 1. In Step 1 Exhibit 21-1, Milk Products' department manager computes the total units to be accounted for by adding the 6,200 units in beginning inventory to the 57,500 units started into production during this period. These 63,700 units are the actual physical units that the manager is responsible for during the period.

Step 1 continues accounting for physical units. As shown in Exhibit 21-1, the 6,200 units in beginning inventory that were completed during the period, the 52,500 units that were started and finished in the period, and the 5,000 units remaining in the department at the end of the period are summed, and the total is listed as "units accounted for." (Note that the "units accounted for" must equal the "units to be accounted for" in Step 1.)

Study Note

The percentage of completion for beginning work in process inventory is the amount of work completed during the previous period. Under FIFO, the amount of effort required to complete beginning work in process inventory is the relevant percentage.

Step 2. The units accounted for in Step 1 are used to compute equivalent production for the department's direct materials and conversion costs for the month, as described below.

- ***Beginning Inventory*** Because all direct materials are added at the beginning of the production process, the 6,200 partially completed units that began February as work in process were already 100 percent complete in regard to direct materials. They were 60 percent complete in regard to conversion costs on February 1. The remaining 40 percent of their conversion costs were incurred as they were completed during the month. Thus, as shown in the "Conversion Costs" column of Exhibit 21-1, the equivalent production for their conversion costs is 2,480 units (6,200 × 40%).

Study Note

Units in beginning work in process inventory represent work accomplished in the previous accounting period that has already been assigned a certain portion of its total cost. Those units must be completed in the current period, incurring additional costs.

- ***Units Started and Completed During the Period*** All the costs of the 52,500 units started and completed during February were incurred during this accounting period. Thus, the full amount of 52,500 is entered as the equivalent units for both direct materials costs and conversion costs.

- ***Ending Inventory*** Because the materials for the 5,000 drinks still in process at the end of February were added when the drinks went into production during the month, the full amount of 5,000 is entered as the equivalent units for direct materials costs. However, these drinks are only 45 percent complete in terms of conversion costs. Thus, as shown in the "Conversion Costs" column of Exhibit 21-1, the equivalent production for their conversion costs is 2,250 units (5,000 × 45%).

- ***Totals*** Step 2 is completed by summing all the physical units to be accounted for, all equivalent units for direct materials costs, and all equivalent units for conversion costs. Exhibit 21-1 shows that for February, Milk Products accounted for 63,700 units. Equivalent units for direct materials costs totaled 57,500, and equivalent units for conversion costs totaled 57,230. Once Milk Products knows February's equivalent unit amounts, it can complete the remaining three steps in the preparation of a process cost report.

Accounting for Costs

Thus far, we have focused on accounting for units of productive output—in our example, bottled milk drinks. We now turn our focus to cost information.

- Step 3 in preparing a process cost report involves accumulating and analyzing all costs charged to the Work in Process Inventory account of each production process, department, or work cell.
- In Step 4, the cost per equivalent unit for direct materials costs and conversion costs is computed.

The following information about Milk Products' manufacture of drinks during February enables us to complete Steps 3 and 4:

Work in Process Inventory		
Costs from beginning inventory:		
Direct materials costs	20,150	
Conversion costs	21,390	
Current period costs:		
Direct materials costs	189,750	
Conversion costs	320,488	

Step 3. As shown in Exhibit 21-1, all costs for the period are accumulated in the Total Costs column. Beginning inventory's direct materials costs of \$20,150 are added to its conversion costs of \$21,390 to determine the total cost of beginning inventory (\$41,540). Current period costs for direct materials (\$189,750) are added to conversion costs (\$320,488) to determine the total current manufacturing costs (\$510,238). The grand total of \$551,778 is the sum of beginning inventory costs (\$41,540) and current period costs (\$510,238). Notice that only the Total Costs column is totaled. Because only the current period costs for direct materials and conversion are used in Step 4, there is no need to find the total costs of the direct materials and conversion costs columns in Step 3.

> **Study Note**
> The cost per equivalent unit using the FIFO method measures the current cost divided by current effort. Notice in Exhibit 21-1 that the cost of beginning work in process inventory is omitted.

Step 4. The direct materials costs and conversion costs for the current period are divided by their respective units of equivalent production to arrive at the cost per equivalent unit. Prior period costs attached to units in beginning inventory are not included in these computations because the FIFO costing method uses a separate costing analysis for each accounting period. (The FIFO method treats the costs of beginning inventory separately, in Step 5.) Exhibit 21-1 shows that the total current cost of \$8.90 per equivalent unit consists of \$3.30 per equivalent unit for direct materials costs (\$189,750 ÷ 57,500 equivalent units) plus \$5.60 per equivalent unit for conversion costs (\$320,488 ÷ 57,230 equivalent units). (Note that the equivalent units are taken from Step 2 of Exhibit 21-1.)

Assigning Costs

Step 5. Step 5 in the preparation of a process costing report uses information from Steps 2 and 4 to assign costs, as shown in Exhibit 21-1. This final step determines the costs that are transferred out either to the next production process, department, or work cell or to the Finished Goods Inventory account (i.e., the cost of goods manufactured), as well as the costs that remain in the ending balance in the Work in Process Inventory account. The total costs assigned to units completed and transferred out and to ending inventory must equal the total costs in Step 3.

> **Study Note**
> The process cost report is developed for the purpose of assigning a value to one transaction: the transfer of goods from one department to another or to finished goods inventory. The ending balance in the Work in Process Inventory account represents the costs that remain after this transfer.

- ***Cost of Goods Manufactured and Transferred Out*** Step 5 in Exhibit 21-1 shows that the costs transferred to the Finished Goods Inventory account include the $41,540 in direct materials and conversion costs for completing the 6,200 units in beginning inventory. Step 2 in the exhibit shows that 2,480 equivalent units of conversion costs were required to complete these 6,200 units. Because the equivalent unit conversion cost for February is $5.60, the cost to complete the units carried over from January is $13,888 (2,480 units × $5.60).

Each of the 52,500 units started and completed in February cost $8.90 to produce. Their combined cost of $467,250 is added to the $41,540 and $13,888 of costs required to produce the 6,200 units from beginning inventory to arrive at the total of $522,678 that is transferred to the Finished Goods Inventory account. The entry resulting from doing the process cost report for February is:

	Dr.	Cr.
Finished Goods Inventory	522,678	
Work in Process Inventory		522,678

> **Study Note**
> All costs must be accounted for, including both costs from beginning inventory and costs incurred during the current period. All costs must be assigned to either ending inventory or the goods transferred out.

- ***Ending Inventory*** All costs remaining in Milk Products Company's Work in Process Inventory account after the cost of goods manufactured has been transferred out represent the costs of the drinks still in production at the end of February. As shown in Step 5 of Exhibit 21-1, the balance of $29,100 in the ending Work in Process Inventory is made up of $16,500 of direct materials costs (5,000 units × $3.30 per unit) and $12,600 of conversion costs (2,250 × $5.60 per unit).

> **Study Note**
> Rounding product unit costs to even dollars may lead to a significant difference in total costs, giving the impression that costs have been miscalculated. Carry product unit costs to two decimal places where appropriate.

Rounding Differences As you perform Step 5 in any process cost report, remember that the total costs in Steps 3 and 5 must always be the same number. In Exhibit 21-1, for example, they are both $551,778.

- If the total costs in Steps 3 and 5 are not the same, first check for omission of any costs and for calculation errors.
- If that does not solve the problem, check whether any rounding was necessary in computing the costs per equivalent unit in Step 4. If rounding was done in Step 4, rounding differences will occur when assigning costs in Step 5. In that case, adjust the total costs transferred out for any rounding difference so that the total costs in Step 5 equal the total costs in Step 3.

Recap of Work in Process Inventory Account When the process cost report is complete, an account recap may be prepared to show the effects of the report on the Work in Process Inventory account for the period. Two recaps of Milk Products' Work in Process Inventory account for February—one for costs and one for units—appear at the end of Exhibit 21-1.

Process Costing for Two or More Production Departments

In this example, Milk Products Company has only one production department for making milk drinks, so it needs only one Work in Process Inventory account. However, a company that has more than one production process or department to make various products must have a Work in Process Inventory account for each process or department.

For instance, when processing raw milk, a milk producer like Milk Products Company has a production department for homogenization, another for pasteurization, and another for packaging needs—three Work in Process Inventory accounts.

- When products flow from the Homogenization Department to the Pasteurization Department, their costs flow from the Homogenization Department's Work in Process Inventory account to the Pasteurization Department's Work in Process Inventory account.
- The costs transferred into the Pasteurization Department's Work in Process Inventory account are treated in the same way as the cost of direct materials added at the beginning of the production process.
- When production flows to the Packaging Department, the accumulated costs (incurred in the two previous departments) are transferred to that department's Work in Process Inventory account.
- At the end of the accounting period, a separate process cost report is prepared for each department.

Pop Chewing Gum Company produces bubble gum. Direct materials are blended at the beginning of the manufacturing process. No materials are lost in the process, so one kilogram of materials input produces one kilogram of bubble gum. Direct labor and overhead costs are incurred uniformly throughout the blending process.

- On June 30, 16,000 units were in process. All direct materials had been added, but the units were only 70 percent complete in regard to conversion costs. Direct materials costs of $8,100 and conversion costs of $11,800 were attached to the beginning inventory.
- During July, 405,000 kilograms of materials were used at a cost of $202,500. Direct labor charges were $299,200, and overhead costs applied during July were $284,000.
- The ending work in process inventory was 21,600 kilograms. All direct materials have been added to those units, and 25 percent of the conversion costs have been assigned. Output from the Blending Department is transferred to the Packaging Department.

Required

1. Prepare a process cost report using the FIFO costing method for the Blending Department for July.
2. Identify the amount that should be transferred out of the Work in Process Inventory account, and state where those dollars should be transferred. What is the entry in journal form?

(continued)

SOLUTION

1. FIFO Process Cost Report—Blending Department for July:

Pop Chewing Gum Company
Blending Department
Process Cost Report: FIFO Method
For the Month Ended July 31

		Physical Units	Direct Materials	% Incurred During Period	Conversion Costs	% Incurred During Period
Step 1: *Account for physical units.*	Beginning inventory (units started last period)	16,000				
	Units started this period	405,000				
	Units to be accounted for	421,000	**Current Equivalent Units of Effort**			
Step 2: *Account for equivalent units.*	Beginning inventory (units completed this period)	16,000	0	0%	4,800	30%
	Units started and completed this period	383,400	383,400	100%	383,400	100%
	Ending inventory (units started but not completed this period)	21,600	21,600	100%	5,400	25%
	Units accounted for	421,000	405,000		393,600	
Step 3: *Account for costs.*		**Total Costs**				
	Beginning inventory	$ 19,900	= $ 8,100	+	$ 11,800	
	Current costs	785,700	= 202,500	+	583,200	
	Total costs	$805,600				
Step 4: *Compute cost per equivalent unit.*	Current Costs / Equivalent Units		$202,500 / 405,000		$583,200 / 393,600	
	Cost per equivalent unit	$1.98	= $0.50	+	$1.48*	

**Rounded to nearest cent*

Step 5: *Assign costs to cost of goods manufactured and ending inventory.*	Cost of goods manufactured and transferred out:			
	From beginning inventory	$ 19,900		
	Current costs to complete	7,104	= $0	+ (4,800 × $1.48)
	Units started and completed this period	759,132	= (383,400 × $0.50)	+ (383,400 × $1.48)
	Cost of goods manufactured	$786,808	*[Cost of goods manufactured must be $786,808 (add rounding of $672) since Total costs = Ending inventory + Cost of goods manufactured]*	
	Ending inventory	18,792	= (21,600 × $0.50)	+ (5,400 × $1.48)
	Total costs	$805,600		

WORK IN PROCESS INVENTORY ACCOUNT: COST RECAP

Beg. Bal.	19,900	(Cost of goods manufactured and transferred out)	786,808
Direct materials	202,500		
Conversion costs	583,200		
End. Bal.	**18,792**		

WORK IN PROCESS INVENTORY ACCOUNT: UNIT RECAP

Beg. Bal.	16,000	(FIFO units transferred out from the 16,000 in beginning inventory plus the 383,400 started and completed)	399,400
Units started	405,000		
End. Bal.	**21,600**		

(continued)

2. The amount of $786,808 should be transferred to the Work in Process Inventory account of the Packaging Department. The entry is:

Work in Process Inventory (Packaging Department)	786,808	
Work in Process Inventory (Blending Department)		786,808

Preparing a Process Cost Report Using the Average Costing Method

LO5 Prepare a process cost report using the average costing method.

When a process cost report uses the average costing method, cost flows do not follow the logical physical flow of production as they do when the FIFO method is used. Instead, the costs in beginning inventory are combined with current period costs to compute an average product unit cost.

- Preparing a process cost report using the average costing method involves the same five steps as preparing one using the FIFO method, but the procedures for completing the steps differ.

We now return to the example of Milk Products Company making milk drinks, but this time we assume that Milk Products uses the average costing method of process costing.

Accounting for Units

Step 1. Step 1 of a process cost report, which accounts for the physical units in a production process, department, or work cell during an accounting period, is identical for the average costing and FIFO costing methods. The physical units in beginning inventory are added to the physical units started during the period to arrive at "units to be accounted for." In Step 1 of Exhibit 21-2, Milk Products' department manager computes the 63,700 total units to be accounted for by adding the 6,200 units in beginning inventory to the 57,500 units started into production in this period.

Step 2. Step 2 also accounts for production during the period in terms of units. After the number of units completed and transferred to finished goods inventory and the number of units in ending inventory have been added to arrive at "units accounted for," the equivalent units in terms of direct materials costs and conversion costs are computed, as described below.

- ***Units Completed and Transferred Out*** As you can see in Exhibit 21-2, the average costing method treats both the direct materials costs and the conversion costs of the 58,700 units completed in February (6,200 units from beginning inventory + 52,500 started this period) as if they were incurred in the current period. Thus, the full amount of 58,700 is entered as the equivalent units for these costs. In contrast, as shown in Exhibit 21-1, the FIFO costing method disregards the previous period costs of units started in the last period and calculates only the equivalent units required in the current period to complete the units in beginning inventory.

- ***Ending Inventory*** The average costing method treats ending inventory in exactly the same way as the FIFO costing method. Because all direct materials are added at the beginning of the production process, the full amount of 5,000 is entered as the equivalent units for direct materials cost. Because the 5,000 units in ending inventory are

EXHIBIT 21-2 Process Cost Report: Average Costing Method

Step 1: *Account for physical units.*

Beginning inventory (units started last period)	6,200
Units started this period	57,500
Units to be accounted for	63,700

Step 2: *Account for equivalent units.*

	Physical Units	Direct Materials	% Incurred During Period	Conversion Costs	% Incurred During Period
		Total Equivalent Units of Effort			
Units completed and transferred out	58,700	58,700	100%	58,700	100%
Ending inventory (units started but not completed this period)	5,000	5,000	100%	2,250	45%
Units accounted for	63,700	63,700		60,950	

Step 3: *Account for costs.*

	Total Costs		Direct Materials		Conversion Costs
Beginning inventory	$ 41,540	=	$ 20,150	+	$ 21,390
Current costs	510,238	=	189,750	+	320,488
Total costs	$551,778		$209,900		$341,878

Step 4: *Compute cost per equivalent unit.*

	Total Costs		Direct Materials		Conversion Costs
Total Costs / Equivalent Units			$209,900 / 63,700		$341,878 / 60,950
Cost per equivalent unit	$8.91	=	$3.30*	+	$5.61*

Rounded to nearest cent

Step 5: *Assign costs to cost of goods manufactured and ending inventory.*

Cost of goods manufactured and transferred out: $522,655 = (58,700 × $3.30) + (58,700 × $5.61)
(Cost of goods manufactured must be $522,655 (less rounding of $362) since Total costs = Ending inventory + Cost of goods manufactured)

Ending inventory: 29,123* = (5,000 × $3.30) + (2,250 × $5.61)
*Rounded.

Total costs: $551,778

Work in Process Inventory Account: Cost Recap

Beg. Bal.	41,540	(Cost of goods manufactured and transferred out)	522,655
Direct materials	189,750		
Conversion costs	320,488		
End. Bal.	**29,123**		

Work in Process Inventory Account: Unit Cost Recap

Beg. Bal.	6,200	(Units transferred out)	58,700
Units started	57,500		
End. Bal.	**5,000**		

only 45 percent complete in terms of conversion costs, the amount of equivalent units is 2,250 (5,000 × 45%).

- ***Totals*** Whether the FIFO costing method or the average costing method is used, Step 2 in a process cost report is completed by summing all the physical units to be accounted for, all equivalent units for direct materials costs, and all equivalent units for conversion costs. Exhibit 21-2 shows that for the month of February, Milk Products accounted for 63,700 physical units. Equivalent units for direct materials costs totaled 63,700, and equivalent units for conversion costs totaled 60,950.

Accounting for Costs

As we noted in our discussion of process cost reports that use the FIFO method, Step 3 of the report accumulates and analyzes all costs in the Work in Process Inventory account, and Step 4 computes the cost per equivalent unit for direct materials costs and conversion costs. You may recall from the discussion that the costs of Milk Products' beginning inventory were $20,150 for direct materials and $21,390 for conversion. Current period costs were $189,750 for direct materials and $320,488 for conversion.

Step 3. If you compare Exhibit 21-2 with Exhibit 21-1, you will see that the average costing and FIFO costing methods deal with Step 3 in the same manner. All direct materials costs and conversion costs for beginning inventory and the current period are accumulated in the Total Costs column. The total of $551,778 consists of $209,900 in direct materials costs and $341,878 in conversion costs.

Step 4. Step 4 computes the cost per equivalent unit for direct materials costs and conversion costs by dividing the total of these costs by their respective equivalent units. The $8.91 total cost per equivalent unit consists of $3.30 per equivalent unit for direct materials ($209,900 ÷ 63,700 equivalent units) plus $5.61 per equivalent unit for conversion ($341,878 ÷ 60,950 equivalent units).

- Notice that the cost per equivalent unit for both direct materials and conversion costs has been rounded to the nearest cent. In this text, any rounding differences are assigned to the units transferred out in Step 5.

- Notice also that the average costing and FIFO costing methods use different numerators and denominators in Step 4. Average costing divides *total* cost by *total* equivalent units, whereas FIFO divides *current* costs by *current* equivalent units.

Assigning Costs

Step 5. Using information from Steps 2 and 4, Step 5 of a process cost report assigns direct materials and conversion costs to the units transferred out and to the units still in process at the end of the period. As noted above, any rounding issues that arise in completing Step 5 are included in units completed and transferred out. Milk Products completes Step 5 as described next.

- ***Cost of Goods Manufactured and Transferred Out*** As shown in Exhibit 21-2, the costs of the units completed and transferred out are assigned by multiplying the equivalent units for direct materials and conversion costs (accounted for in Step 2) by their respective cost per equivalent unit (computed in Step 4) and then totaling these assigned values. Thus, the $522,655 assigned to cost of goods manufactured and transferred out includes $193,710 of direct materials costs (58,700 equivalent units × $3.30 cost per equivalent unit) plus $329,307 of conversion costs (58,700 equivalent units × $5.61 cost per equivalent unit). In this case, because the costs per equivalent unit were rounded in Step 4, a rounding difference of $362 has been deducted from the total cost. The $522,655 of transferred costs will go to the Finished Goods Inventory account, since the goods are ready for sale. The entry resulting from doing the process cost report for February is:

	Dr.	Cr.
Finished Goods Inventory	522,655	
Work in Process Inventory		522,655

- ***Ending Inventory*** The costs of the units in ending work in process inventory are assigned in the same way as the costs of cost of goods manufactured and transferred out. As you can see in Exhibit 21-2, the total of $29,123 assigned to ending inventory includes $16,500 of direct materials costs (5,000 equivalent units × $3.30 cost per equivalent unit) plus $12,623 of conversion costs (2,250 equivalent units × $5.61 cost per equivalent unit). The $29,123 (rounded) will appear as the ending balance in this department's Work in Process Inventory account.

Recap of Work in Process Inventory Account As we noted earlier, when a process cost report is complete, an account recap may be prepared to show the effects of the report on the Work in Process Inventory account for the period. Exhibit 21-2 includes a cost recap and a unit recap of Milk Products' Work in Process Inventory account for February.

& APPLY >

Pop Chewing Gum Company produces several flavors of bubble gum. Direct materials are blended at the beginning of the manufacturing process. No materials are lost in the process, so one kilogram of materials input produces one kilogram of bubble gum. Direct labor and overhead costs are incurred uniformly throughout the blending process.

- On June 30, 16,000 units were in process. All direct materials had been added, but the units were only 70 percent complete in regard to conversion costs. Direct materials costs of $8,100 and conversion costs of $11,800 were attached to the beginning inventory.
- During July, 405,000 kilograms of materials were used at a cost of $202,500. Direct labor charges were $299,200, and overhead costs applied during July were $284,000.
- The ending work in process inventory was 21,600 kilograms. All direct materials have been added to those units, and 25 percent of the conversion costs have been assigned. Output from the Blending Department is transferred to the Packaging Department.

Required

1. Prepare a process cost report using the average costing method for the Blending Department for July.
2. Identify the amount that should be transferred out of the Work in Process Inventory account, and state where those dollars should be transferred. What is the entry in journal form?

(continued)

SOLUTION

1. Average Costing Process Cost Report–Blending Department for July:

Pop Chewing Gum Company
Blending Department
Process Cost Report: Average Costing Method
For the Month Ended July 31

				Total Equivalent Units of Effort				
		Physical Units		**Direct Materials Costs**	**% Incurred During Period**		**Conversion Costs**	**% Incurred During Period**
Step 1: *Account for physical units.*	Beginning inventory (units started last period)	16,000						
	Units started this period	405,000						
	Units to be accounted for	421,000						
Step 2: *Account for equivalent units.*	Units completed and transferred out	399,400		399,400	100%		399,400	100%
	Ending inventory (units started but not completed this period)	21,600		21,600	100%		5,400	25%
	Units accounted for	421,000		421,000			404,800	
Step 3:		**Total Costs**						
Account for costs.	Beginning inventory	$ 19,900	=	$ 8,100		+	$ 11,800	
	Current costs	785,700	=	202,500		+	583,200	
	Total costs	$805,600		$210,600			$595,000	
Step 4: *Compute cost per equivalent unit.*	Total Costs / Equivalent Units			$210,600 / 421,000			$595,000 / 404,800	
	Cost per equivalent unit	$1.97	=	$0.50*		+	$1.47*	
				Rounded to nearest cent				
Step 5: *Assign costs to cost of goods manufactured inventory.*	Cost of goods manufactured and transferred out	$786,862 (Add rounding $44)	=	(399,400 × $0.50)		+	(399,400 × $1.47)	
	Ending inventory	18,738	=	(21,600 × $0.50)		+	(5,400 × $1.47)	
	Total costs	$805,600						

WORK IN PROCESS INVENTORY ACCOUNT: COST RECAP

Beg. Bal.	19,900	(Cost of goods manufactured and transferred out)	786,862
Direct materials	202,500		
Conversion costs	583,200		
End. Bal.	**18,738**		

WORK IN PROCESS INVENTORY ACCOUNT: UNIT RECAP

Beg. Bal.	16,000	(Units transferred out)	399,400
Units started	405,000		
End. Bal.	**21,600**		

2. The amount of $786,862 should be transferred to the Work in Process Inventory account of the Packaging Department. The entry is:

Work in Process Inventory (Packaging Department)	786,862	
Work in Process Inventory (Blending Department)		786,862

▸ MILK PRODUCTS COMPANY: REVIEW PROBLEM

Process Costing Using the FIFO Costing and Average Costing Methods

LO4 LO5

The Decision Point at the beginning of this chapter focused on Milk Products Company, a company that provides its local community with milk and other dairy products. It posed these questions:

- Why is a process costing system appropriate for Milk Products Company?
- How does a process costing system facilitate management decisions?

Because the processing of milk and the production of dairy products involve a continuous flow of similar products, the most appropriate costing system for Milk Products Company is the process costing system. Such a system accumulates costs by process, department, or work cell and assigns them to the products as they pass through the production system.

Managers use the cost information that a process costing system provides at each stage of the management process. They use this information in making decisions about everything from setting selling prices to controlling costs, ensuring quality, and evaluating performance. The process cost report prepared at the end of each accounting period, which tracks and analyzes costs for a process, department, or work cell, is a very valuable source of cost information.

As noted in the Decision Point, Milk Products Company makes and distributes chocolate milk. To produce chocolate milk, the Mixing Department uses two basic direct materials: milk and chocolate syrup. No materials are lost in the process, so one gallon of material input produces one gallon of chocolate milk. Direct labor and overhead costs are incurred uniformly throughout the mixing process.

Assume that 15,000 units of chocolate milk were in process at the beginning of the month. All direct materials had been added, but the units were only two-thirds complete in regard to conversion costs. Direct materials costs of $19,200 and conversion costs of $14,400 were attached to the beginning inventory.

During the month, 435,000 gallons of materials were used at a cost of $426,300. Direct labor charges were $100,000, and overhead costs applied during the month were $300,000. The ending work in process inventory was 50,000 gallons. All direct materials have now been added to those units, and 20 percent of the conversion costs have been assigned. Output from the Mixing Department has been transferred to the Packaging Department.

Required

1. Using the FIFO costing methods, prepare a process cost report for the Mixing Department for the month.
2. What amount should be transferred out of the Work in Process Inventory account, and where should those dollars be transferred? What is the entry in journal form?
3. Using the average costing methods, repeat requirement **1**.
4. Answer the questions in requirement **2** as they apply to the process cost report that you prepared in requirement **3**.

Answers to Review Problem

1. Process cost report prepared using the FIFO costing method:

Mixing Department
Process Cost Report—FIFO Costing Method
For the Month

Beginning inventory	15,000					
Units started this period	435,000					
Units to be accounted for	450,000					
		Current Equivalent Units of Effort				
	Physical Units	**Direct Materials Costs**	**% Incurred During Period**	**Conversion Costs**	**% Incurred During Period**	
Beginning inventory	15,000	—	0%	5,000	33%	
Units started and completed	385,000	385,000	100%	385,000	100%	
Ending inventory	50,000	50,000	100%	10,000	20%	
Units accounted for	450,000	435,000		400,000		
	Total Costs					
Beginning inventory	$ 33,600	= $ 19,200	+	$ 14,400		
Current costs	838,300	= 426,300	+	412,000		
Total costs	$871,900					
Current Costs / Equivalent Units		$426,300 / 435,000		$412,000 / 400,000		
Cost per equivalent unit	$2.01	= $0.98	+	$1.03		
Cost of goods manufactured and transferred out:						
From beginning inventory	$ 33,600					
Current costs to complete	5,150	= $0		(5,000 × $1.03)		
Units started and completed	773,850	= (385,000 × $0.98)	+	(385,000 × $1.03)		
Cost of goods manufactured	$812,600					
Ending inventory	59,300	= (50,000 × $0.98)	+	(10,000 × $1.03)		
Total costs	$871,900					

2. The amount of $812,600 should be transferred to the Work in Process Inventory account of the Packaging Department. The entry is:

Work in Process (Packaging Inventory Department)	812,600	
Work in Process (Mixing Inventory Department)		812,600

3. Process cost report using the average costing method:

Mixing Department
Process Cost Report—Average Costing Method
For the Month

Beginning inventory	15,000				
Units started this period	435,000				
Units to be accounted for	450,000				
		Total Equivalent Units of Effort			
	Physical Units	**Direct Materials Costs**	**% Incurred During Period**	**Conversion Costs**	**% Incurred During Period**
Units completed and transferred out	400,000	400,000	100%	400,000	100%
Ending inventory	50,000	50,000	100%	10,000	20%
Units accounted for	450,000	450,000		410,000	
	Total Costs				
Beginning inventory	$ 33,600 =	$ 19,200	+	$ 14,400	
Current costs	838,300 =	426,300	+	412,000	
Total costs	$871,900	$445,500		$426,400	
Total Costs / Equivalent Units		$445,500 / 450,000		$426,400 / 410,000	
Cost per equivalent unit	$2.03 =	$0.99	+	$1.04	
Cost of goods manufactured and transferred out	$812,000 =	(400,000 × $0.99)	+	(400,000 × $1.04)	
Ending inventory	59,900 =	(50,000 × $0.99)	+	(10,000 × $1.04)	
Total costs	$871,900				

4. The amount of $812,000 should be transferred to the Work in Process Inventory account of the Packaging Department. The entry is:

Work in Process (Packaging Inventory Department)	812,000	
Work in Process (Mixing Inventory Department)		812,000

STOP & REVIEW >

LO1 Describe the process costing system, and identify the reasons for its use.

A process costing system is a product costing system used by companies that produce large amounts of similar products or liquid products or that have long, continuous production runs of identical products. Because these companies have a continuous production flow, it would be impractical for them to use a job order costing system, which tracks costs to a specific batch of products or a specific job order. In contrast to a job order costing system, a process costing system accumulates the costs of direct materials, direct labor, and overhead for each process, department, or work cell and assigns those costs to the products as they are produced during a particular period.

The product costs provided by a process costing system play a key role in the management process. When managers plan, they use past and projected information about product costs to set selling prices and prepare budgets. Each day, managers use cost information to make decisions about controlling costs, managing the company's volume of activity, ensuring quality, and negotiating prices. Actual costs are incurred as units are produced, so actual unit costs can be computed. When managers evaluate performance results, they compare targeted costs with actual costs. When managers communicate with external stakeholders, they use actual units produced and costs incurred to value inventory on the balance sheet and cost of goods sold on the income statement. They also analyze internal reports that compare the organization's measures of actual and targeted performance to determine whether cost goals for products or services are being achieved.

LO2 Relate the patterns of product flows to the cost flow methods in a process costing environment, and explain the role of the Work in Process Inventory accounts.

During production in a process costing environment, products flow in a first-in, first-out (FIFO) fashion through several processes, departments, or work cells. As they do, the process costing system accumulates their costs and passes them on to the next process, department, or work cell. At the end of every accounting period, the system generates a report that assigns the costs that have accumulated during the period to the units that have transferred out of the process, department, or work cell and to the units that are still work in process. The process cost report may assign costs by using the FIFO costing method, in which the costs assigned to the first products processed are the first costs transferred out when those products flow to the next process, department, or work cell, or the average costing method, which assigns an average cost to all products made during an accounting period.

The Work in Process Inventory accounts are the focal point of a process costing system. Each production process, department, or work cell has its own Work in Process Inventory account. All costs charged to that process, department, or work cell flow into its Work in Process Inventory account. A process cost report prepared at the end of every accounting period assigns the costs that have accumulated during the period to the units that have flowed out of the process, department, or work cell (the cost of goods transferred out) and to the units that are still in process (the cost of ending inventory).

LO3 Define *equivalent production,* and compute equivalent units.

Equivalent production is a measure that applies a percentage-of-completion factor to partially completed units to compute the equivalent number of whole units produced in an accounting period for each type of input. Equivalent units are computed from (1) units in the beginning work in process inventory and their percentage of completion, (2) units started and completed during the period, and (3) units in the ending work in process inventory and their percentage of completion. The computation of equivalent units differs depending on whether the FIFO method or the average costing method is used.

LO4 Prepare a process cost report using the FIFO costing method.

In a process cost report that uses the FIFO costing method, the cost flow follows the logical physical flow of production—that is, the costs assigned to the first products processed are the first costs transferred when those products flow to the next process, department, or work cell. Preparation of a process cost report involves five steps. Steps 1 and 2 account for the physical flow of products and compute the equivalent units of production. Once equivalent production has been determined, the focus of the report shifts to accounting for costs. In Step 3, all direct materials costs and conversion costs for the current period are added to arrive at total costs. In Step 4, the cost per equivalent unit for both direct materials costs and conversion costs is found by dividing those costs by their respective equivalent units. In Step 5, costs are assigned to the units completed and transferred out during the period, as well as to the ending work in process inventory. The costs assigned to units completed and transferred out include the costs incurred in the preceding period and the conversion costs that were needed to complete those units during the current period. That amount is added to the total cost of producing all units started and completed during the period. The result is the total cost transferred out for the units completed during the period. Step 5 also assigns costs to units still in process at the end of the period by multiplying their direct materials costs and conversion costs by their respective equivalent units. The total equals the balance in the Work in Process Inventory account at the end of the period.

LO5 Prepare a process cost report using the average costing method.

The average costing method is an alternative method of accounting for production costs in a manufacturing environment characterized by a continuous production flow. The difference between a process costing report that uses the FIFO method and one that uses the average costing method is that the latter does not differentiate when work was done on inventory. When the average costing method is used, the costs in beginning inventory are averaged with the current period costs to compute the product unit costs. These costs are used to value the ending balance in Work in Process Inventory and the goods completed and transferred out of the process, department, or work cell.

REVIEW of Concepts and Terminology

The following concepts and terms were introduced in this chapter:

Average costing method 924 (LO2)

Conversion costs 926 (LO3)

Equivalent production 925 (LO3)

FIFO costing method 924 (LO2)

Process cost report 924 (LO2)

Process costing system 922 (LO1)

CHAPTER ASSIGNMENTS

BUILDING Your Basic Knowledge and Skills

Short Exercises

LO1 **Process Costing Versus Job Order Costing**

SE 1. Indicate whether the manufacturer of each of the following products should use a job order costing system or a process costing system to accumulate product costs:

1. Plastics
2. Ocean cruise ships
3. Cereal
4. Medical drugs for veterinary practices

LO1 **Process Costing Versus Job Order Costing**

SE 2. Indicate whether each of the following is a characteristic of job order costing or of process costing:

1. Several Work in Process Inventory accounts are used, one for each department or work cell in the process.
2. Costs are grouped by process, department, or work cell.
3. Costs are measured for each completed job.
4. Only one Work in Process Inventory account is used.
5. Costs are measured in terms of units completed in specific time periods.
6. Costs are assigned to specific jobs or batches of product.

LO2 **Process Costing and a Work in Process Inventory Account**

SE 3. Chemical Pro uses an automated mixing machine in its Mixing Department to combine three raw materials into a product called Triogo. On average, each unit of Triogo contains \$3 of Material X, \$6 of Material Y, \$9 of Material Z, \$2 of direct labor, and \$12 of overhead. Total costs charged to the Mixing Department's Work in Process Inventory account during the month were \$208,000. There were no units in beginning or ending work in process inventory. How many units were completed and transferred to Finished Goods Inventory during the month?

LO3 **Equivalent Production: FIFO Costing Method**

SE 4. Blue Blaze adds direct materials at the beginning of its production process and adds conversion costs uniformly throughout the process. Given the following information from Blue Blaze's records for July and using Steps 1 and 2 of the FIFO costing method, compute the equivalent units of production:

Units in beginning inventory	3,000
Units started during the period	17,000
Units partially completed	2,500
Percentage of completion of ending work in process inventory	100% for direct materials; 70% for conversion costs
Percentage of completion of beginning inventory	100% for direct materials; 40% for conversion costs

LO4 **Determining Unit Cost: FIFO Costing Method**

SE 5. Using the information from **SE 4** and the following data, compute the total cost per equivalent unit:

	Beginning Work in Process	Costs for the Period
Direct materials	\$20,400	\$7,600
Conversion costs	32,490	2,545

LO4 **Assigning Costs: FIFO Costing Method**

SE 6. Using the data in **SE 4** and **SE 5**, assign costs to the units transferred out and to the units in ending inventory for July.

LO5 **Equivalent Production: Average Costing Method**

SE 7. Using the same data as in **SE 4** but Steps 1 and 2 of the average costing method, compute the equivalent units of production for the month.

LO5 **Determining Unit Cost: Average Costing Method**

SE 8. Using the average costing method and the information from **SE 4, SE 5,** and **SE 7,** compute the total cost per equivalent unit.

LO5 **Assigning Costs: Average Costing Method**

SE 9. Using the data in **SE 4, SE 5, SE 7,** and **SE 8** and assuming that Blue Blaze uses the average costing method, assign costs to the units completed and transferred out and to the units in ending inventory for July.

LO5 **Equivalent Production: Average Costing Method**

SE 10. Red Company adds direct materials at the beginning of its production process and adds conversion costs uniformly throughout the process. Given the following information from Red Company's records for July, compute the current period's equivalent units of production for direct materials and conversion costs:

Units in beginning inventory: 2,000

Units started during the period: 13,000

Units partially completed: 500

Percentage of completion of beginning inventory: 100% for direct materials; 40% for conversion costs

Percentage of completion of ending work in process inventory: 100% for direct materials; 70% for conversion costs

Exercises

LO1 **Process Costing Versus Job Order Costing**

E 1. Indicate whether the manufacturer of each of the following products should use a job order costing system or a process costing system to accumulate product costs:

1. Paint
2. Fruit juices
3. Tailor-made suits
4. Milk
5. Coffee cups printed with your school insignia
6. Paper
7. Roller coaster for a theme park
8. Posters for a fund-raising event

LO2 **Use of Process Costing Information**

E 2. Tom's Bakery makes a variety of cakes, cookies, and pies for distribution to five major chains of grocery stores in the area. The company uses a standard manufacturing process for all items except special-order cakes. It currently uses a process costing system. Tom, the owner of the company, has some urgent questions, which are listed at the top of the next page. Which of these questions can be answered using information from a process costing system? Which can be best answered using information from a job order costing system? Explain your answers.

1. How much does it cost to make one chocolate cheesecake?
2. Did the cost of making special-order cakes exceed the cost budgeted for this month?
3. What is the value of the pie inventory at the end of June?
4. What were the costs of the cookies sold during June?
5. At what price should Tom's Bakery sell its famous brownies to the grocery store chains?
6. Were the planned production costs of $3,000 for making pies in June exceeded?

LO2 Work in Process Inventory Accounts in Process Costing Systems

E 3. Gilbert, Inc., which uses a process costing system, makes a chemical used as a food preservative. The manufacturing process involves Departments A and B. The company had the following total costs and unit costs for completed production last month, when it manufactured 10,000 pounds of the chemical. Neither Department A nor Department B had any beginning or ending work in process inventories.

	Total Cost	Unit Cost
Department A		
Direct materials	$10,000	$1.00
Direct labor	2,600	0.26
Overhead	1.300	0.13
Total costs	$13,900	$1.39
Department B		
Direct materials	$ 3,000	$0.30
Direct labor	700	0.07
Overhead	1,000	0.10
Total costs	$ 4,700	$0.47
Totals	$18,600	$1.86

1. How many Work in Process Inventory accounts would Gilbert use?
2. What dollar amount of the chemical's production cost was transferred from Department A to Department B last month?
3. What dollar amount was transferred from Department B to the Finished Goods Inventory account?
4. What dollar amount is useful in determining a selling price for 1 pound of the chemical?

LO3 Equivalent Production: FIFO Costing Method

E 4. McQuary Stone Company produces bricks. Although the company has been in operation for only 12 months, it already enjoys a good reputation. During its first 12 months, it put 600,000 bricks into production and completed and transferred 586,000 bricks to finished goods inventory. The remaining bricks were still in process at the end of the year and were 60 percent complete.

The company's process costing system adds all direct materials costs at the beginning of the production process; conversion costs are incurred uniformly throughout the process. From this information, compute the equivalent units of production for direct materials and conversion costs for the company's first year, which ended December 31. Use the FIFO costing method.

LO3 Equivalent Production: FIFO Costing Method

E 5. O'Leon Enterprises makes Perfect Shampoo for professional hair stylists. On July 31, it had 5,200 liters of shampoo in process that were 80 percent complete in regard to conversion costs and 100 percent complete in regard to direct materials costs. During August, it put 212,500 liters of direct materials into production. Data for Work in Process Inventory on August 31 were as follows: shampoo, 4,500 liters; stage of completion, 60 percent for conversion costs and 100 percent for direct materials. From this information, compute the equivalent units of production for direct materials and conversion costs for the month. Use the FIFO costing method.

LO3 Equivalent Production: FIFO Costing Method

E 6. Paper Savers Corporation produces wood pulp that is used in making paper. The following data pertain to the company's production of pulp during September:

		Percentage Complete	
	Tons	Direct Materials	Conversion Costs
Work in process, Aug. 31	40,000	100%	60%
Placed into production	250,000	—	—
Work in process, Sept. 30	80,000	100%	40%

Compute the equivalent units of production for direct materials and conversion costs for September using the FIFO costing method.

LO4 Work in Process Inventory Accounts: Total Unit Cost

E 7. Scientists at Anschultz Laboratories, Inc., have just perfected Dentalite, a liquid substance that dissolves tooth decay. The substance, which is generated by a complex process involving five departments, is very expensive. Cost and equivalent unit data for the latest week are as follows (units are in ounces):

	Direct Materials		Conversion Costs	
Dept.	Dollars	Equivalent Units	Dollars	Equivalent Units
A	$12,000	1,000	$33,825	2,050
B	21,835	1,985	13,065	1,005
C	23,896	1,030	20,972	2,140
D	—	—	22,086	2,045
E	—	—	15,171	1,945

From these data, compute the unit cost for each department and the total unit cost of producing 1 ounce of Dentalite.

LO4 Determining Unit Cost: FIFO Costing Method

E 8. Reuse Cookware, Inc., manufactures sets of heavy-duty pots. It has just completed production for August. At the beginning of August, its Work in Process Inventory account showed direct materials costs of $31,700 and conversion costs of $29,400. The cost of direct materials used in August was $275,373; conversion costs were $175,068. During the month, the company started and completed 15,190 sets. For August, a total of 16,450 equivalent sets for direct materials and 16,210 equivalent sets for conversion costs have been computed.

From this information, determine the cost per equivalent set for August. Use the FIFO costing method.

LO4 Assigning Costs: FIFO Costing Method

E 9. The Bakery produces tea cakes. It uses a process costing system. In March, its beginning inventory was 450 units, which were 100 percent complete for direct materials costs and 10 percent complete for conversion costs. The cost of beginning inventory was $655. Units started and completed during the month totaled 14,200. Ending inventory was 410 units, which were 100 percent complete for direct materials costs and 70 percent complete for conversion costs. Costs per equivalent unit for March were $1.40 for direct materials costs and $0.80 for conversion costs.

From this information, compute the cost of goods transferred to the Finished Goods Inventory account, the cost remaining in the Work in Process Inventory account, and the total costs to be accounted for. Use the FIFO costing method.

LO4 **Process Cost Report: FIFO Costing Method**

E 10. Toy Country Corporation produces children's toys using a liquid plastic formula and a continuous production process. In the company's toy truck work cell, the plastic is heated and fed into a molding machine. The molded toys are then cooled and trimmed and sent to the packaging work cell. All direct materials are added at the beginning of the process. In November, the beginning work in process inventory was 420 units, which were 40 percent complete; the ending balance was 400 units, which were 70 percent complete.

During November, 15,000 units were started into production. The Work in Process Inventory account had a beginning balance of $937 for direct materials costs and $370 for conversion costs. In the course of the month, $35,300 of direct materials were added to the process, and $31,760 of conversion costs were assigned to the work cell. Using the FIFO costing method, prepare a process cost report that computes the equivalent units for November, the product unit cost for the toys, and the ending balance in the Work in Process Inventory account.

LO5 **Equivalent Production: Average Costing Method**

E 11. Using the data in **E 4** and assuming that the company uses the average costing method, compute the equivalent units of production for direct materials and conversion costs for the year ended December 31.

LO5 **Equivalent Production: Average Costing Method**

E 12. Using the data in **E 5** and assuming that the company uses the average costing method, compute the equivalent units of production for direct materials and conversion for August.

LO5 **Equivalent Production: Average Costing Method**

E 13. Using the data in **E 6** and assuming that the company uses the average costing method, compute the equivalent units of production for direct materials and conversion for September.

LO5 **Determining Unit Cost: Average Costing Method**

E 14. Using the data in **E 8** and the average costing method, determine the cost per equivalent set for August. Assume equivalent sets are 16,900 for direct materials costs and 17,039 for conversion costs.

LO5 **Process Cost Report: Average Costing Method**

E 15. Using the data in **E 10** and the average costing method, prepare a process cost report that computes the equivalent units for November, the product unit cost for the toys, and the ending balance in the Work in Process Inventory account.

Problems

LO4 LO5 **Process Costing: FIFO Costing and Average Costing Methods**

P 1. Lightning Industries specializes in making Flash, a high-moisture, low-alkaline wax used to protect and preserve skis. The company began producing a new, improved brand of Flash on January 1. Materials are introduced at the beginning of the production process. During January, 15,300 pounds were used at a cost of $46,665. Direct labor of $17,136 and overhead costs of $25,704 were incurred uniformly throughout the month. By January 31, 13,600 pounds of Flash had been completed and transferred to the finished goods inventory (1 pound of input equals 1 pound of output). Since no spoilage occurred, the leftover materials remained in production and were 40 percent complete on average.

Required

1. Using the FIFO costing method, prepare a process cost report for January.
2. From the information in the process cost report, identify the amount that should be transferred out of the Work in Process Inventory account, and state where those dollars should be transferred.
3. Repeat **1** and **2** using the average costing method.

LO4 **Process Costing: FIFO Costing Method**

P 2. Liquid Extracts Company produces a line of fruit extracts for home use in making wine, jams and jellies, pies, and meat sauces. Fruits enter the production process in pounds; the product emerges in quarts (1 pound of input equals 1 quart of output). On May 31, 4,250 units were in process. All direct materials had been added, and the units were 70 percent complete for conversion costs. Direct materials costs of $4,607 and conversion costs of $3,535 were attached to the units in beginning work in process inventory. During June, 61,300 pounds of fruit were added at a cost of $71,108. Direct labor for the month totaled $19,760, and overhead costs applied were $31,375. On June 30, 3,400 units remained in process. All direct materials for these units had been added, and 50 percent of conversion costs had been incurred.

Required

1. Using the FIFO costing method, prepare a process cost report for June.
2. From the information in the process cost report, identify the amount that should be transferred out of the Work in Process Inventory account, and state where those dollars should be transferred.

LO4 **Process Costing: One Process and Two Time Periods—FIFO Costing Method**

P 3. Wash Clean Laboratories produces biodegradable liquid detergents that leave no soap film. The production process has been automated, so the product can now be produced in one operation instead of in a series of heating, mixing, and cooling operations. All direct materials are added at the beginning of the process, and conversion costs are incurred uniformly throughout the process. Operating data for July and August are as follows:

	July	August
Beginning work in process inventory		
Units (pounds)	2,300	3,050
Direct materials	$4,699	?*
Conversion costs	$1,219	?*
Production during the period		
Units started (pounds)	31,500	32,800
Direct materials	$65,520	$66,912
Conversion costs	$54,213	$54,774
Ending work in process inventory		
Units (pounds)	3,050	3,600

*From calculations at end of July.

The beginning work in process inventory was 30 percent complete for conversion costs. The ending work in process inventory for July was 60 percent complete; for August, it was 50 percent complete. Assume that the loss from spoilage and evaporation was negligible.

Required

1. Using the FIFO costing method, prepare a process cost report for July.
2. From the information in the process cost report, identify the amount that should be transferred out of the Work in Process Inventory account, and state where those dollars should be transferred.
3. Repeat **1** and **2** for August.

LO5 **Process Costing: Average Costing Method and Two Time Periods**

P 4. Lid Corporation produces a line of beverage lids. The production process has been automated, so the product can now be produced in one operation rather than in the three operations that were needed before the company purchased the automated machinery. All direct materials are added at the beginning of the process, and conversion costs are incurred uniformly throughout the process. Operating data for May and June are as follows:

	May	June
Beginning work in process inventory		
Units (May: 40% complete)	220,000	?
Direct materials	$3,440	$400
Conversion costs	$6,480	$420
Production during the month		
Units started	24,000,000	31,000,000
Direct materials	$45,000	$93,200
Conversion costs	$66,000	$92,796
Ending work in process inventory		
Units (May: 70% complete; June: 60% complete)	200,000	320,000

1. Using the average costing method, prepare process cost reports for May and June. (Round unit costs to three decimal places; round all other costs to the nearest dollar.)
2. From the information in the process cost report for May, identify the amount that should be transferred out of the Work in Process Inventory account, and state where those dollars should be transferred.
3. Compare the product costing results for June with the results for May. What is the most significant change? What are some of the possible causes of this change?

LO5 **Process Costing: Average Costing Method**

P 5. Hurricane Products, Inc., makes high-vitamin, calorie-packed wafers that are popular among professional athletes because they supply quick energy. The company produces the wafers in a continuous flow, and it uses a process costing system based on the average costing method. It recently purchased several automated machines so that the wafers can be produced in a single department. All direct materials are added at the beginning of the process. The costs for the machine operators' labor and production-related overhead are incurred uniformly throughout the process.

In February, the company put a total of 231,200 liters of direct materials into production at a cost of $294,780. Two liters of direct materials were used to produce one unit of output (one unit = 144 wafers). Direct labor costs for February were $60,530, and overhead was $181,590. The beginning work in process inventory for February was 14,000 units, which were 100 percent complete for direct materials and 20 percent complete for conversion costs. The total cost of those units was $55,000, $48,660 of which was assigned to the cost of direct materials. The ending work in process inventory of 12,000 units was fully complete for direct materials but only 30 percent complete for conversion costs.

Required

1. Using the average costing method and assuming no loss due to spoilage, prepare a process cost report for February.
2. From the information in the process cost report, identify the amount that should be transferred out of the Work in Process Inventory account, and state where those dollars should be transferred.

Alternate Problems

LO4 LO5 Process Costing: FIFO Costing and Average Costing Methods

P 6. Sunshine Soda Company manufactures and sells several different kinds of soft drinks. Direct materials (sugar syrup and artificial flavor) are added at the beginning of production in the Mixing Department. Direct labor and overhead costs are applied to products throughout the process. For August, beginning inventory for the citrus flavor was 2,400 gallons, 80 percent complete. Ending inventory was 3,600 gallons, 50 percent complete. Production data show 240,000 gallons started during August. A total of 238,800 gallons was completed and transferred to the Bottling Department. Beginning inventory costs were $600 for direct materials and $676 for conversion costs. Current period costs were $57,600 for direct materials and $83,538 for conversion costs.

Required

1. Using the FIFO costing method, prepare a process cost report for the Mixing Department for August.
2. From the information in the process cost report, identify the amount that should be transferred out of the Work in Process Inventory account, and state where those dollars should be transferred.
3. Repeat **1** and **2** using the average costing method.

LO4 Process Costing: FIFO Costing Method

P 7. Canned fruits and vegetables are the main products made by Good Foods, Inc. All direct materials are added at the beginning of the Mixing Department's process. When the ingredients have been mixed, they go to the Cooking Department. There the mixture is heated to 100° Celsius and simmered for 20 minutes. When cooled, the mixture goes to the Canning Department for final processing. Throughout the operations, direct labor and overhead costs are incurred uniformly. No direct materials are added in the Cooking Department. Cost data and other information for the Mixing Department for January are as follows:

Production Cost Data	Direct Materials	Conversion Costs
Mixing Department		
Beginning inventory	$ 28,560	$ 5,230
Current period costs	450,000	181,200
Work in process inventory		
Beginning inventory		
Mixing Department (40% complete)	5,000 liters	
Ending inventory		
Mixing Department (60% complete)	6,000 liters	
Unit production data		
Units started during January	90,000 liters	
Units transferred out during January	89,000 liters	

Assume that no spoilage or evaporation loss took place during January.

Required

1. Using the FIFO costing method, prepare a process cost report for the Mixing Department for January.

Manager insight ▶

2. Explain how the analysis for the Cooking Department will differ from the analysis for the Mixing Department.

LO4 **Process Costing: One Process and Two Time Periods—FIFO Costing Method**

P 8. Honey Dews Company produces organic honey, which it sells to health food stores and restaurants. The company owns thousands of beehives. No direct materials other than honey are used. The production operation is a simple one. Impure honey is added at the beginning of the process and flows through a series of filterings, leading to a pure finished product. Costs of labor and overhead are incurred uniformly throughout the filtering process. Production data for April and May are as follows:

	April	May
Beginning work in process inventory		
Units (liters)	7,100	12,400
Direct materials	$2,480	?*
Conversion costs	$5,110	?*
Production during the period		
Units started (liters)	288,000	310,000
Direct materials	$100,800	$117,800
Conversion costs	$251,550	$277,281
Ending work in process inventory		
Units (liters)	12,400	16,900

*From calculations at end of April.

The beginning work in process inventory for April was 80 percent complete for conversion costs, and ending work in process inventory was 20 percent complete. The ending work in process inventory for May was 30 percent complete for conversion costs. Assume that there was no loss from spoilage or evaporation.

Required

1. Using the FIFO method, prepare a process cost report for April.
2. From the information in the process cost report, identify the amount that should be transferred out of the Work in Process Inventory account, and state where those dollars should be transferred.
3. Repeat **1** and **2** for May.

LO5 **Process Costing: Average Costing Method and Two Time Periods**

P 9. Carton Corporation produces a line of beverage cartons. The production process has been automated, so the product can now be produced in one operation rather than in the three operations that were needed before the company purchased the automated machinery. All direct materials are added at the beginning of the process, and conversion costs are incurred uniformly throughout the process. Operating data for July and August are as follows:

	July	August
Beginning work in process inventory		
Units (July: 20% complete)	20,000	?
Direct materials	$20,000	$6,000
Conversion costs	$30,000	$6,000
Production during the month		
Units started	70,000	90,000
Direct materials	$34,000	$59,000
Conversion costs	$96,000	$130,800

(continued)

Ending work in process inventory		
Units (July: 40% complete; August: 60% complete)	10,000	25,000

1. Using the average costing method, prepare process cost reports for July and August. (Round unit costs to two decimal places; round all other costs to the nearest dollar.)
2. From the information in the process cost report for July, identify the amount that should be transferred out of the Work in Process Inventory account, and state where those dollars should be transferred.
3. Compare the product costing results for August with the results for July. What is the most significant change? What are some of the possible causes of this change?

LO5 Process Costing: Average Costing Method

P 10. Many of the products made by Wireless Plastics Company are standard telephone replacement parts that require long production runs and are produced continuously. A unit for Wireless Plastics is a box of parts. During April, direct materials for 25,250 units were put into production. Total cost of direct materials used during April was $2,273,000. Direct labor costs totaled $1,135,000, and overhead was $2,043,000. The beginning work in process inventory contained 1,600 units, which were 100 percent complete for direct materials costs and 60 percent complete for conversion costs. Costs attached to the units in beginning inventory totaled $232,515, which included $143,500 of direct materials costs. At the end of the month, 1,250 units were in ending inventory; all direct materials had been added, and the units were 70 percent complete for conversion costs.

Required

1. Using the average costing method and assuming no loss due to spoilage, prepare a process cost report for April.
2. From the information in the process cost report, identify the amount that should be transferred out of the Work in Process Inventory account, and state where those dollars should be transferred.

ENHANCING Your Knowledge, Skills, and Critical Thinking

LO1 Concept of Process Costing Systems

C 1. For more than 60 years, **Dow Chemical Company** has made and sold a tasteless, odorless, and calorie-free substance called Methocel. When heated, this liquid plastic (methyl cellulose) has the unusual characteristic (for plastics) of becoming a gel that resembles cooked egg whites. It is used in over 400 food products, including gravies, soups, and puddings. It was also used as wampa drool in *The Empire Strikes Back* and dinosaur sneeze in *Jurassic Park*. What kind of costing system is most appropriate for the manufacture of Methocel? Why is that system most appropriate? Describe the system, and include in the description a general explanation of how costs are determined.

LO1 LO2 Continuing Professional Education

C 2. Paula Woodward is the head of the Information Systems Department at Moreno Manufacturing Company. Roland Randolph, the company's controller, is meeting with her to discuss changes in data gathering that relate to the company's new flexible manufacturing system. Woodward opens the conversation by saying,

"Roland, the old job order costing methods just will not work with the new flexible manufacturing system. The new system is based on continuous product flow, not batch processing. We need to change to a process costing system for both data gathering and product costing. Otherwise, our product costs will be way off, and it will affect our pricing decisions. I found out about the need for this change at a professional seminar I attended last month. You should have been there with me."

Randolph responds, "Paula, who is the accounting expert here? I know what product costing approach is best for this situation. Job order costing has provided accurate information for this product line for more than 15 years. Why should we change just because we've purchased a new machine? We've purchased several machines for this line over the years. And as for your seminar, I don't need to learn about costing methods. I was exposed to them all when I studied management accounting back in the late 1970s."

Is Randolph's behavior ethical? If not, what has he done wrong? What can Woodward do if Randolph continues to refuse to update the product costing system?

LO3 LO4 Analysis of Product Cost

C 3. Ready Tire Corporation makes several lines of automobile and truck tires. The company operates in a competitive marketplace, so it relies heavily on cost data from its FIFO-based process costing system. It uses that information to set prices for its most competitive tires. The company's radial line has lost some of its market share during each of the past four years. Management believes that price breaks allowed by the company's three biggest competitors are the main reason for the decline in sales.

The company controller, Sara Birdsong, has been asked to review the product costing information that supports pricing decisions on the radial line. In preparing her report, she collected the following data for last year, the most recent full year of operations:

		Units	Dollars
Equivalent units	Direct materials	84,200	
	Conversion costs	82,800	
Manufacturing costs:	Direct materials		$1,978,700
	Direct labor		800,400
	Overhead		1,600,800
Unit cost data:	Direct materials		23.50
	Conversion costs		29.00
Work in process inventory:			
Beginning (70% complete)		4,200	
Ending (30% complete)		3,800	

Units started and completed last year totaled 80,400. Attached to the beginning Work in Process Inventory account were direct materials costs of $123,660 and conversion costs of $57,010. Birdsong found that little spoilage had occurred. The proper cost allowance for spoilage was included in the predetermined overhead rate of $2 per direct labor dollar. The review of direct labor cost revealed, however, that $90,500 had been charged twice to the production account, the second time in error. This resulted in overly high overhead costs being charged to the production account.

The radial has been selling for $92 per tire. This price was based on last year's unit data plus a 75 percent markup to cover operating costs and profit. The company's three main competitors have been charging about $87 for a tire of comparable quality. The company's process costing system adds all direct materials at the beginning of the process, and conversion costs are incurred uniformly throughout the process.

1. Identify what inaccuracies in costs, inventories, and selling prices result from the company's cost-charging error.
2. Prepare a revised process cost report for last year. Round unit costs to two decimal places. Round total costs to whole dollars.
3. What should have been the minimum selling price per tire this year?
4. Suggest ways of preventing such errors in the future.

LO4 **Setting a Selling Price**

C 4. For the past four years, three companies have dominated the soft drink industry, holding a combined 85 percent of market share. Wonder Cola, Inc., ranks second nationally in soft drink sales. Its management is thinking about introducing a new low-calorie drink called Null Cola.

Wonder soft drinks are processed in a single department. All ingredients are added at the beginning of the process. At the end of the process, the beverage is poured into bottles that cost $0.24 per case produced. Direct labor and overhead costs are applied uniformly throughout the process.

Corporate controller Adam Daneen believes that costs for the new cola will be very much like those for the company's Cola Plus drink. Last year, he collected the following data about Cola Plus:

	Units*	Costs
Work in process inventory		
January 1†	2,200	
Direct materials costs		$ 2,080
Conversion costs		620
December 31‡	2,000	
Direct materials costs		1,880
Conversion costs		600
Units started during year	458,500	
Costs for year		
Liquid materials added		430,990
Direct labor and overhead		229,400
Bottles		110,068

*Each unit is a 24-bottle case.

†50% complete.

‡60% complete.

The company's variable general administrative and selling costs are $1.10 per unit. Fixed administrative and selling costs are assigned to products at the rate of $0.50 per unit. Each of Wonder Cola's two main competitors is already marketing a diet cola. Company A's product sells for $4.10 per unit; Company B's, for $4.05. All costs are expected to increase by 10 percent in the next three years. Wonder Cola tries to earn a profit of at least 15 percent on the total unit cost.

1. What factors should Wonder Cola, Inc., consider in setting a unit selling price for a case of Null Cola?
2. Using the FIFO costing method, compute (a) equivalent units for direct materials, cases of bottles, and conversion costs; (b) the total production cost per unit; and (c) the total cost per unit of Cola Plus for the year.
3. What is the expected unit cost of Null Cola for the year?
4. Recommend a unit selling price range for Null Cola, and give the reason(s) for your choice.

LO2 LO3 LO4

Using the Process Costing System

C 5. You are the production manager for Great Grain Corporation, a manufacturer of four cereal products. The company's best-selling product is Smackaroos, a sugar-coated puffed rice cereal. Yesterday, Clark Winslow, the controller, reported that the production cost for each box of Smackaroos has increased approximately 22 percent in the last four months. Because the company is unable to increase the selling price for a box of Smackaroos, the increased production costs will reduce profits significantly.

Today, you received a memo from Gilbert Rom, the company president, asking you to review your production process to identify inefficiencies or waste that can be eliminated. Once you have completed your analysis, you are to write a memo presenting your findings and suggesting ways to reduce or eliminate the problems. The president will use your information during a meeting with the top management team in ten days.

You are aware of previous problems in the Baking Department and the Packaging Department. Winslow has provided you with process cost reports for the two departments. He has also given you the following detailed summary of the cost per equivalent unit for a box of Smackaroos cereal:

	April	May	June	July
Baking Department				
Direct materials	$1.25	$1.26	$1.24	$1.25
Direct labor	0.50	0.61	0.85	0.90
Overhead	0.25	0.31	0.34	0.40
Department totals	$2.00	$2.18	$2.43	$2.55
Packaging Department				
Direct materials	$0.35	$0.34	$0.33	$0.33
Direct labor	0.05	0.05	0.04	0.06
Overhead	0.10	0.16	0.15	0.12
Department totals	$0.50	$0.55	$0.52	$0.51
Total cost per equivalent unit	$2.50	$2.73	$2.95	$3.06

1. In preparation for writing your memo, answer the following questions:
   a. For whom are you preparing the memo? Does this affect the length of the memo? Explain.
   b. Why are you preparing the memo?
   c. What actions should you take to gather information for the memo? What information is needed? Is the information that Winslow provided sufficient for analysis and reporting?
   d. When is the memo due? What can be done to provide accurate, reliable, and timely information?
2. Based on your analysis of the information that Winslow provided, where is the main problem in the production process?
3. Prepare an outline of the sections you would want in your memo.

LO1

Cookie Company (Continuing Case)

C 6. In this segment of our continuing case, you are considering whether process costing is more appropriate for your cookie company than job order costing. List reasons why your company may choose to use process costing instead of job order costing.

CHAPTER 22

Value-Based Systems: ABM and Lean

The Management Process

PLAN

- ▷ **Identify activities that add value to products and services**
- ▷ **Identify the resources necessary to perform value-adding activities**
- ▷ **Conduct process value analysis of current business to identify improvement opportunities**
- ▷ **Develop a business plan focused on value-enhanced products and services where waste is eliminated**
- ▷ **Set value and waste goals and select key performance indicators of success**

PERFORM

- ▷ **Implement plan to achieve goals**
- ▷ **Measure value chain and supply-chain performance**
- ▷ **Eliminate waste in products and business processes**

EVALUATE

- ▷ **Assess if value enhancement and waste elimination goals are being met**
- ▷ **Revise business plan as a result of management analysis**

COMMUNICATE

- ▷ **Prepare external reports that summarize performance**
- ▷ **Prepare internal planning, performance, and analysis reports**

Managers can use ABM and/or a lean approach to add value for their customers.

To remain competitive in today's challenging business environment, companies have had to rethink their organizational processes and basic operating methods. Managers focus on creating value for their customers. They design their internal value chain and external supply chain to provide customer-related, activity-based information; to track costs; and to eliminate waste and inefficiencies. In this chapter, we describe two systems that help managers improve operating processes and make better decisions: activity-based management and the lean operating philosophy.

LEARNING OBJECTIVES

LO1 **Explain why managers use *value-based systems* and discuss their relationship to the supply chain and the value chain.** (pp. 960–964)

LO2 **Define *activity-based costing* and explain how a cost hierarchy and a bill of activities are used.** (pp. 964–968)

LO3 **Define the elements of a lean operation and identify the changes in inventory management that result when a firm adopts its just-in-time operating philosophy.** (pp. 968–972)

LO4 **Define and apply *backflush costing*, and compare the cost flows in traditional and backflush costing.** (pp. 972–975)

LO5 **Compare ABM and lean operations as value-based systems.** (p. 976)

DECISION POINT ► A MANAGER'S FOCUS BEAN BAG CONVERTIBLES, INC.

Bean Bag Convertibles, Inc., produces comfortable sofas that can be easily converted to beds, which makes them ideal for college dorm rooms and studio apartments. Each month, the company assembles thousands of these built-to-order sofas by filling durable mattress-shaped bags with shredded foam and inserting them into different-shaped slipcovers in a variety of fabrics, and it generally delivers them in less than a week after customers have placed their orders. Because of the efficiency with which it assembles and delivers its products, Bean Bag Convertibles has an advantage over its competitors. The company's use of activity-based systems and the speed of its supply chain are critical factors in maintaining this competitive edge.

- ► How have activity-based systems helped Bean Bag Convertibles, Inc., improve its production processes and reduce delivery time?
- ► How do the managers of Bean Bag Convertibles, Inc., plan to remain competitive in a challenging business environment?

Value-Based Systems and Management

LO1 Explain why managers use *value-based systems* and discuss their relationship to the supply chain and the value chain.

Many companies, including Bean Bag Convertibles, Inc., are rethinking how to operate in volatile business environments that are strongly influenced by customer demands. Managers realize value-based systems, instead of traditional cost-based systems like those studied previously, provide the information they need. **Value-based systems** are information systems that provide customer-related, activity-based information. Value-based systems focus on eliminating waste as companies produce and deliver quality products and services demanded by customers. Managers can use value-based information to compare the value created by products or services with the **full product cost**, which includes not only the costs of direct materials and direct labor, but also the costs of all production and nonproduction activities required to satisfy the customer. For example, the full product cost of a Bean Bag sofa includes the cost of the shredded foam and upholstery, as well as the costs of taking the sales order, processing the order, packaging and shipping the sofa, and providing subsequent customer service for warranty work.

Creating value by satisfying customers' needs for quality, reasonable price, and timely delivery requires that managers do the following:

- Work with suppliers and customers.
- View the organization as a collection of value-adding activities.
- Use resources for value-adding activities.
- Reduce or eliminate non-value-adding activities.
- Know the total cost of creating value for a customer.

Each company in a supply chain is a customer of an earlier supplier. The furniture maker shown here would be a customer of a supplier of high-quality wood and perhaps of a metal manufacturer, caning supplier, and leather manufacturer. His customer might be a furniture wholesaler or retail store. The retail store, which sells the furniture to customers, is the final link in the supply chain.

Courtesy of PhotostoGO.com.

If an organization's business plan focuses on providing products or services that customers esteem, then managers will work both externally and internally to manage their supply chain and value chains, respectively.

- Externally, with suppliers and customers, managers will find ways of improving quality, reducing costs, and shortening delivery time.
- Internally, managers will find the best ways of using resources to create and maintain the value of their products or services. This requires matching resources to the operating activities that add value to a product or service. Managers will examine all business activities involved in value creation for waste, including research and development, design, supply, production, storage, sales and marketing, distribution, and customer service.

Value Chains and Supply Chains

A **value chain** is a sequence of activities inside the organization, also known as *primary processes,* that add value to a company's product or service; the value chain also includes support services, such as management accounting, that facilitate the primary processes. Managers see their organization's internal value chain as part of a larger system that includes the value chains of suppliers and customers. This larger system is the **supply chain**—the path that leads from the suppliers of the materials from which a product is made to the final customer. The supply chain (also called the *supply network*) includes both suppliers and suppliers' suppliers, and customers and customers' customers. It links businesses together in a relationship chain of business to business to business.

As Figure 22-1 shows, in the supply chain for a furniture company like Bean Bag Convertibles, Inc., a cotton farmer supplies cotton to the upholstery manufacturer, which supplies upholstery to the furniture manufacturer. The furniture manufacturer supplies furniture to furniture stores, which in turn supply furniture

FIGURE 22-1 The Supply Chain and Value Chain in a Furniture Company

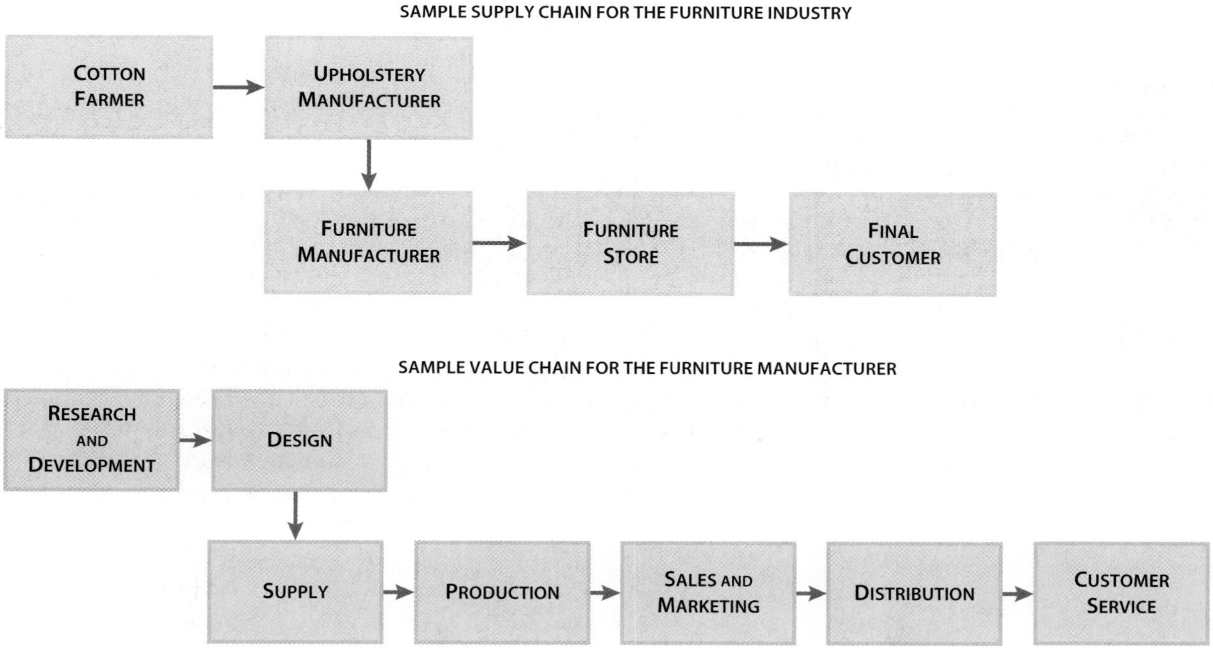

SAMPLE SUPPLY CHAIN FOR THE FURNITURE INDUSTRY

Cotton Farmer → Upholstery Manufacturer → Furniture Manufacturer → Furniture Store → Final Customer

SAMPLE VALUE CHAIN FOR THE FURNITURE MANUFACTURER

Research and Development → Design → Supply → Production → Sales and Marketing → Distribution → Customer Service to the final customers. Each organization in this supply chain is a customer of an earlier supplier, and each has its own value chain.

The sequence of primary processes in the value chain varies from company to company depending on a number of factors, including the size of the company and the types of products or services that it sells. Figure 22-1 also shows the primary processes that add value for a furniture manufacturer—research and development, design, supply, production, sales and marketing, distribution, and customer service.

Understanding value chains and supply chains gives managers a better grasp of their company's internal and external operations. Managers who understand the supply chain and how their company's value-adding activities fit into their suppliers' and customers' value chains can see their company's role in the overall process of creating and delivering products or services. When organizations work cooperatively with others in their supply chain, they can develop new processes that reduce the total costs of their products or services.

- For example, Bean Bag Convertibles, Inc., places computers for online order entry in its sofa kiosks located in indoor shopping malls. The computers streamline the processing of orders and make the orders more accurate. In this case, even though Bean Bag incurs the cost of the computers, the total cost of making and delivering furniture decreases because the cost of order processing decreases.

Process Value Analysis

Process value analysis (PVA) is a technique that managers use to identify and link all the activities involved in the value chain. It analyzes business processes by relating activities to the events that prompt those activities and to the resources that the activities consume. PVA forces managers to look critically at all phases of their operations. PVA improves cost traceability and results in significantly more accurate product costs, which in turn improves management decisions and increases profitability. By using PVA to identify non-value-adding activities, companies can reduce their costs and redirect their resources to value-adding activities.

FOCUS ON BUSINESS PRACTICE

What Is VBM?

Value-based management (VBM) is a long-term strategy that many businesses use to reward managers who create and sustain shareholder wealth and value. In other words, VBM encourages managers to think like business owners. Three elements are essential for a successful VBM program. First, VBM must have the full support of top management. Second, performance and compensation must be linked, because "what gets measured and rewarded gets done." Finally, everyone involved must understand the what, why, and how of the program. Since a variety of VBM approaches exist, each company can tailor its VBM performance metrics and implementation strategy to meet its particular needs.[1]

Value-Adding and Non-Value-Adding Activities

Study Note

The customer's perspective governs whether an activity adds value to a product or service. To minimize costs, managers continuously seek to improve processes and activities. To manage the cost of an activity, they can reduce the activity's frequency or eliminate it entirely.

A **value-adding activity** is one that adds value to a product or service as perceived by the customer. In other words, if customers are willing to pay for the activity, it adds value to the product or service. Examples include designing the components of a new recliner, assembling the recliner, and upholstering it.

A **non-value-adding activity** is one that adds cost to a product or service but does not increase its market value. Managers eliminate non-value-adding activities that are not essential to an organization and reduce the costs of those that are essential, such as legal services, management accounting, machine repair, materials handling, and building maintenance. For example, inspection costs can be reduced if an inspector samples one of every three reclining mechanisms received from a supplier rather than inspecting every mechanism. If the supplier is a reliable source of high-quality mechanisms, such a reduction in inspection activity is appropriate.

Another way managers can reduce costs is to outsource an activity—that is, to have it done by another company that is more competent at the work and can perform it at a lower cost. For example, many companies outsource purchasing, accounting, and the maintenance of their information systems.

Some activities can be eliminated completely if business processes are changed.

Value-Based Systems

In this chapter, we explore two types of value-based systems—activity-based management (ABM) and lean operations. Both can be used together or separately to eliminate waste and manage activities.

Study Note

ABM and lean operations focus on value-adding activities—not costs—to increase income.

- They create opportunities to improve the nonfinancial performance measures as well as cost information supplied to managers.
- They help managers view their organization as a collection of activities. Value-based cost information helps managers improve operating processes and make better pricing decisions.

Activity-Based Management

As you may recall from an earlier chapter, **activity-based management (ABM)** is an approach to managing an organization that identifies all major operating activities, determines the resources consumed by each activity and the cause of the resource usage, and categorizes the activities as either adding value to a product or service or not adding value. ABM focuses on reducing or eliminating non-value-adding activities.

- Because it provides financial and performance information at the activity level, ABM is useful both for strategic planning and for making tactical and operational decisions about business segments, such as product lines, market segments, and customers.
- It also helps managers eliminate waste and inefficiencies and redirect resources to activities that add value to the product or service.

Activity-based costing (ABC) is the tool used in an ABM environment to assign activity costs to cost objects. ABC helps managers make better pricing decisions, inventory valuations, and profitability decisions.

Managing Lean Operations

A **lean operation** focuses on eliminating waste in an organization. In other words, business processes should focus on what a customer is willing to pay for. Lean operations emphasize the elimination of three kinds of waste:

- Waste that can be eliminated proactively through good planning and design of the product or service and the production processes for making it.
- Waste that can be eliminated during production by smart production scheduling and consistently following standardized product and processing plans to assure quality.
- Waste that can be eliminated by management analysis of the actions of workers and machines in the process of making products and services.

Just-in-time (JIT) is one of the key strategies of a lean operation to reorganize production activities and manage inventory.

STOP & APPLY >

The reports that follow are from a Bean Bag Convertibles, Inc., kiosk location. Which report would be used for financial purposes, and which would be used for activity-based decision making? Why?

Salaries/Commissions	$1,400	Enter sales orders	$1,000
Equipment	1,200	Attend sales training	1,000
Office Supplies	300	Create ad campaign	1,500
Rent	1,000	Maintain website	500
Insurance	1,000	Resolve problems	900
Total	$4,900	Total	$4,900

SOLUTION

The report on the left is the financial report because it is organized by costs. The report on the right is the ABM report because it is organized by activities or tasks. Even though the total costs are the same in both reports, the ABM report focuses on reducing non-value-adding activities rather than minimizing costs.

Activity-Based Costing

LO2 Define *activity-based costing* and explain how a cost hierarchy and a bill of activities are used.

As access to value chain data has improved, managers have refined the issue of how to assign costs fairly to products or services to determine unit costs. You may recall from an earlier chapter that traditional methods of allocating overhead costs to products use such cost drivers as direct labor hours, direct labor costs, or machine hours and one overhead rate. More than 20 years ago, organizations began realizing that these methods did not assign overhead costs to their product lines accurately and that the resulting inaccuracy in product unit costs was causing poor pricing decisions and poor control of overhead costs. In their search for more accurate product costing, many organizations embraced activity-based costing.

Study Note

ABC can be used to allocate all the various costs that make up overhead and nonmanufacturing activity costs as well.

Activity-based costing (ABC) is a method of assigning costs that calculates a more accurate product cost than traditional methods. It does so by categorizing all indirect costs by activity, tracing the indirect costs to those activities, and assigning those costs to products or services using a cost driver related to the cause of the cost.

Activity-based costing is an important tool of activity-based management because it improves the accuracy in allocating activity-driven costs to cost objects (i.e., products or services). To implement activity-based costing, managers:

1. Identify and classify each activity.
2. Estimate the cost of resources for each activity.
3. Identify a cost driver for each activity and estimate the quantity of each cost driver.
4. Calculate an activity cost rate for each activity.
5. Assign costs to cost objects based on the level of activity required to make the product or provide the service.

Study Note

ABC reflects the cause-and-effect relationships between costs and individual processes, products, services, or customers.

While ABC does increase the accuracy of cost information and gives managers greater control over the costs they manage, it does have its limitations, including the following:

- High measurement costs necessary to collect accurate data from many activities instead of just one overhead account may make ABC too costly.
- Some costs are difficult to assign to a specific activity or cost object since they benefit the business in general (e.g., the president's salary) and should not be arbitrarily allocated.
- ABC allocations may add undue complexity and complications to controlling costs.

The Cost Hierarchy and the Bill of Activities

Two tools used in implementing ABC are a cost hierarchy and a bill of activities.

Cost Hierarchy A **cost hierarchy** is a framework for classifying activities according to the level at which their costs are incurred. Many companies use this framework to allocate activity-based costs to products or services. In a manufacturing company, the cost hierarchy typically has four levels: the unit level, the batch level, the product level, and the facility level.

- **Unit-level activities** are performed each time a unit is produced and are generally considered variable costs. For example, when a furniture manufacturer like **La-Z-Boy** installs a recliner mechanism in a chair, unit-level activities include the direct material cost of the recliner mechanism and direct labor connecting the mechanism to the chair frame. Because each chair contains only one mechanism, these activities have a direct correlation to the number of chairs produced.
- **Batch-level activities** are performed each time a batch or production run of goods is produced. Examples of batch-level activities include setup and materials handling for the production run of a certain style of recliner. These activities vary with the number of batches prepared or production runs completed.

TABLE 22-1
Sample Activities in Cost Hierarchies

Activity Level	Furniture Manufacturer: Recliner Mechanism Installation
Unit level	Install mechanism
	Test mechanism
Batch level	Set up installation process
	Move mechanisms
	Inspect mechanisms
Product level	Redesign installation process
Facility level	Provide facility maintenance, lighting, and security

- **Product-level activities** are performed to support a particular product line. Examples of product-level activities include implementing design, engineering, or marketing changes for a particular brand of product. These activities vary with the number of brands or product designs a company has.
- **Facility-level activities** are performed to support a facility's general manufacturing process and are generally fixed costs. Examples for a furniture manufacturer include maintaining, lighting, securing, and insuring the factory. These activities are generally a fixed amount for a certain time period.

Note that the frequency of activities varies across levels and that the cost hierarchy includes both value-adding and non-value-adding activities. Service organizations can also use a cost hierarchy to group their activities; the four levels typically are the unit level, the batch level, the service level, and the operations level. Table 22-1 lists examples of activities in the cost hierarchies of a manufacturing company.

Study Note
A bill of activities summarizes costs relating to a product or service and supports the calculation of the product or service unit cost.

Bill of Activities Once managers have created the cost hierarchy, they group the activities into the specified levels and prepare a summary of the activity costs assigned to the selected cost objects. A **bill of activities** is a list of activities and related costs that is used to compute the costs assigned to activities and the product unit cost. More complex bills of activities group activities into activity pools and include activity cost rates and the cost driver levels used to assign costs to cost objects.

- A bill of activities may be used as the primary document or as a supporting schedule to calculate the product unit cost in both job order and process costing systems and in both manufacturing and service businesses.

STOP & APPLY >

Bean Bag Convertibles, Inc. has received an order for 100 bean bag sofa convertibles from FurnitureTown, LLC. A partially complete bill of activities for that order appears on the next page. Fill in the missing data.

(continued)

Bill of Activities for FurnitureTown, LLC, Order

Activity	Activity Cost Rate	Cost Driver Level	Activity Cost
Unit level			
Parts production	$50 per machine hour	5 machine hours	$?
Assembly	$30 per direct labor hour	10 direct labor hours	?
Packing	$3.50 per unit	100 units	?
Batch level			
Work setup	$25 per setup	4 setups	?
Product level			
Product design	$160 per design hour	20 design hours	?
Facility level			
Building occupancy	200% of assembly labor cost	?	?
Total activity costs assigned to job			$?
Total job units			÷ 100
Activity costs per unit (total activity costs ÷ total units)			$?
Job cost summary:			
Direct materials			$1,000
Purchased parts			500
Activity costs			?
Total cost of order			$?
Product unit cost (total cost/100 units)			**$?**

SOLUTION

Bill of Activities for FurnitureTown, LLC Order

Activity	Activity Cost Rate	Cost Driver Level	Activity Cost
Unit level			
Parts production	$50 per machine hour	5 machine hours	$ 250
Assembly	$30 per direct labor hour	10 direct labor hours	300
Packing	$3.50 per unit	100 units	350
Batch level			
Work setup	$25 per setup	4 setups	100
Product level			
Product design	$160 per design hour	2 design hours	320
Facility level			
Building occupancy	200% of assembly labor cost	$300	600
Total activity costs assigned to job			$ 1,920
Total job units			÷ 100
Activity costs per unit (total activity costs ÷ total units)			$ 19.20
Job cost summary:			
Direct materials			$ 1,000
Purchased parts			500
Activity costs			1,920
Total cost of order			$ 3,420
Product unit cost (total cost/100 units)			**$34.20**

FOCUS ON BUSINESS PRACTICE

The Evolution to Lean Operations

- Eli Whitney perfected the concept of interchangeable parts in 1799, when he produced 10,000 muskets for the U.S. Army for the low price of $13.40 per musket.
- In the late 1890s, Frederick W. Taylor used his ideas of scientific management to standardize work through time studies.
- In the early twentieth century, Frank and Lillian Galbraith (parents of the authors of *Cheaper by the Dozen*) focused on eliminating waste by studying worker motivation and using motion studies and process charting.
- Starting in 1910, Henry Ford and Charles E. Sorensen arranged all the elements of manufacturing into a continuous system called the *production line*.
- After World War II, Taichii Ohno and Shigeo Shingo recognized the importance of inventory management, and they perfected the Toyota production system, from which lean production developed.[2]

The New Operating Environment and Lean Operations

LO3 Define the elements of a lean operation and identify the changes in inventory management that result when a firm adopts its just-in-time operating philosophy.

Study Note

Traditional environments emphasize *functional* departments that tend to group similar activities together (e.g., repairs and maintenance).

To achieve lean operations, managers focus on the elimination of waste. A company must redesign its operating systems, plant layout, and basic management methods to conform to several basic concepts:

- Simple is better.
- The quality of the product or service is critical from product design to customer satisfaction.
- The work environment must emphasize continuous improvement.
- Maintaining large inventories wastes resources and may hide poor work.
- Activities or functions that do not add value to a product or service should be eliminated or reduced.
- Goods should be produced only when needed.
- Workers must be multiskilled and must participate in eliminating waste.
- Building and maintaining long-term relationships with suppliers is important.

Application of these lean elements creates a lean operation throughout the company's value chain and guides all employees' work. Piecemeal attempts at lean operations have proved disastrous when the implementation focused on a few lean tools and methodologies instead of understanding how to think lean throughout the organization.

Just-in-Time (JIT)

Traditionally, a company operated with large amounts of inventory, including finished goods stored in anticipation of customers' orders; purchased materials infrequently but in large amounts; had long production runs with infrequent setups; manufactured large batches of products; and trained each member of its work force to perform a limited number of tasks. Managers determined that changes in how inventory was processed were necessary because

- Large amounts of an organization's space and money were tied up in inventory.
- The source of poor-quality materials, products, or services was hard to pinpoint.

- The number of non-value-adding activities was growing.
- Accounting for the manufacturing process was becoming ever more complex.

In a lean operation, the **just-in-time (JIT) operating philosophy** requires that all resources—materials, personnel, and facilities—be acquired and used only as needed to create value for customers. A JIT environment reveals waste and eliminates it by the following principles:

> **Study Note**
> Pull-through production represents a change in concept. Instead of producing goods in anticipation of customers' needs, customers' orders trigger the production process.

Minimum Inventory Levels In the traditional manufacturing environment, parts, materials, and supplies are purchased far in advance and stored until the production department needs them. In contrast, in a JIT environment, materials and parts are purchased and received only when they are needed. The JIT approach lowers costs by reducing the space needed for inventory storage, the amount of materials handling, and the amount of inventory obsolescence. It also reduces the need for inventory control facilities, personnel, and recordkeeping. In addition, it significantly decreases the amount of work in process inventory and the amount of working capital tied up in all inventories.

Pull-Through Production The JIT operating philosophy requires **pull-through production**, a system in which a customer's order triggers the purchase of materials and the scheduling of production for the products that have been ordered. In contrast, with the **push-through method** used in traditional manufacturing operations, products are manufactured in long production runs and stored in anticipation of customers' orders. With pull-through production, the size of a customer's order determines the size of a production run, and the company purchases materials and parts as needed. Inventory levels are kept low, and machines must be set up more frequently as different job are worked on.

> **Study Note**
> In the JIT environment, normal operating activities—setup, production, and maintenance—still take place. But the timing of those activities is altered to promote smoother operations and to minimize downtime.

Quick Setup and Flexible Work Cells In the past, managers felt that it was more cost-effective to produce large batches of goods because producing small batches increases the number of machine setups. The success of JIT has disproved this. By placing machines in more efficient locations and standardizing setups, setup time can be minimized.

In a traditional factory layout, similar machines are grouped together, forming functional departments. Products are routed through these departments in sequence, so that all necessary operations are completed in order. This process can take several days or weeks, depending on the size and complexity of the job. By changing the factory layout so that all the machines needed for sequential processing are placed together, the JIT operating philosophy may cut the manufacturing time of a product from days to hours, or from weeks to days. The new cluster of machinery forms a flexible **work cell**, an autonomous production line that can perform all required operations efficiently and continuously. The flexible work cell handles a "family of products"—that is, products of similar shape or size. Product families require minimal setup changes as workers move from one job to the next. The more flexible the work cell is, the greater its potential to minimize total production time.

A Multiskilled Work Force In the flexible work cells of a JIT environment, one worker may be required to operate several types of machines simultaneously. The worker may have to set up and retool the machines and even perform routine maintenance on them. A JIT operating philosophy thus requires a multiskilled work force, and multiskilled workers have been very effective in contributing to high levels of productivity.

High Levels of Product Quality A JIT environment results in high-quality products since high-quality direct materials are used and because inspections are made throughout the production process. In a JIT environment, inspection as a separate step does not add value to a product, so inspection is incorporated into ongoing operations. A JIT machine operator inspects the products as they pass through the manufacturing process. If the operator detects a flaw, he or she shuts down the work cell to prevent the production of similarly flawed products while the cause of the problem is being determined. The operator either fixes the problem or helps others find a way to correct it. This integrated inspection procedure, combined with high-quality materials, produces high-quality finished goods.

Study Note

That inspections are necessary is an admission that problems with quality do occur. Continuous inspection throughout production as opposed to inspection only at the end creates awareness of a problem at the point where it occurs.

Effective Preventive Maintenance When a company rearranges its machinery into flexible work cells, each machine becomes an integral part of its cell. If one machine breaks down, the entire work cell stops functioning, and the product cannot easily be routed to another machine while the malfunctioning machine is being repaired. Continuous JIT operations therefore require an effective system of preventive maintenance. Preventing machine breakdowns is considered more important and more cost-effective than keeping machines running continuously. Machine operators are trained to perform minor repairs when they detect problems. Machines are serviced regularly—much as an automobile is—to help guarantee continued operation. The machine operator conducts routine maintenance during periods of downtime between orders. (Remember that in a JIT setting, the work cell does not operate unless there is a customer order for the product. Machine operators take advantage of such downtime to perform routine maintenance.)

Study Note

Although separate inspection costs are reduced in a JIT operating environment, some additional time is added to production because the machine operator is now performing the inspection function. The objectives are to reduce total costs and to increase quality.

Continuous Improvement of the Work Environment

A JIT operating philosophy fosters loyalty among workers, who are likely to see themselves as part of a team because they are so deeply involved in the production process. Machine operators must have the skills to run several types of machines, detect defective products, suggest measures to correct problems, and maintain the machinery within their work cells. In addition, each worker is encouraged to suggest improvements to the production process. In Japanese, this is called *kaizen,* meaning "good change." Companies with a JIT operating philosophy receive thousands of employee suggestions and implement a high percentage of them, and they reward workers for suggestions that improve the process. Such an environment fosters workers' initiative and benefits the company.

Study Note

The JIT operating philosophy must be adopted by everyone in a company before its total benefits can be realized.

Accounting for Product Costs in a JIT Operating Environment

When a firm like Bean Bag Convertibles, Inc., shifts to lean operations and adopts a JIT operating philosophy, managers must take a new approach to evaluating costs and controlling operations. The changes in the operations will affect how costs are determined and what measures are used to monitor performance.

When a company adopts a JIT operating philosophy, the work cells and the goal of reducing or eliminating non-value-adding activities change the way costs are classified and assigned. In this section, we examine those changes.

Classifying Costs The traditional production process can be divided into five time frames:

Processing time	The actual amount of time spent working on a product
Inspection time	The time spent looking for product flaws or reworking defective units

Moving time The time spent moving a product from one operation or department to another

Queue time The time a product spends waiting to be worked on once it arrives at the next operation or department

Storage time The time a product spends in materials inventory, work in process inventory, or finished goods inventory

In product costing under JIT, costs associated with processing time are classified as either direct materials costs or conversion costs. **Conversion costs** are the sum of the direct labor costs and overhead costs incurred by a production department, work cell, or other work center. According to JIT, costs associated with inspection, moving, queue, and storage time should be reduced or eliminated because they do not add value to the product.

Assigning Costs In a JIT operating environment, managers focus on **throughput time**, the time it takes to move a product through the entire production process. Measures of product movement, such as machine time, are used to apply conversion costs to products.

Sophisticated computer monitoring of the work cells allows many costs to be traced directly to the cells in which products are manufactured. As Table 22-2 shows, several costs that in a traditional environment are treated as indirect costs and applied to products using an overhead rate are treated as the direct costs of a JIT work cell. Because the products that a work cell manufactures are similar in nature, direct materials and conversion costs should be nearly uniform for each product in a cell.

- The costs of repairs and maintenance, materials handling, operating supplies, utilities, and supervision can be traced directly to work cells as they are incurred.
- Depreciation charges are based on units of output, not on time, so depreciation can be charged directly to work cells based on the number of units produced.
- Building occupancy costs, insurance premiums, and property taxes remain indirect costs and must be assigned to the work cells for inclusion in the conversion cost.

TABLE 22-2
Direct and Indirect Costs in Traditional and JIT Environments

	Costs in a Traditional Environment	Costs in a JIT Environment
Direct materials	Direct	Direct
Direct labor	Direct	Direct
Repairs and maintenance	Indirect	Direct to work cell
Materials handling	Indirect	Direct to work cell
Operating supplies	Indirect	Direct to work cell
Utilities costs	Indirect	Direct to work cell
Supervision	Indirect	Direct to work cell
Depreciation	Indirect	Direct to work cell
Supporting service functions	Indirect	Mostly direct to work cell
Building occupancy	Indirect	Indirect
Insurance and taxes	Indirect	Indirect

STOP & APPLY >

The cost categories in the following list are typical of a furniture manufacturer like Bean Bag Convertibles, Inc. Identify each cost as direct or indirect, assuming that it was incurred in (1) a traditional manufacturing setting and (2) a JIT environment. State the reasons for changes in classification.

	Traditional Setting	JIT Setting	Reason for Change
Direct materials			
Direct labor			
Supervisory salaries			
Electrical power			
Operating supplies			
Purchased parts			
Employee benefits			
Indirect labor			
Insurance and taxes, plant			

SOLUTION

	Traditional Setting	JIT Setting	Reason for Change
Direct materials	Direct	Direct	
Direct labor	Direct	Direct	
Supervisory salaries	Indirect	Direct	Traceable to work cell
Electrical power	Indirect	Direct	Traceable to work cell
Operating supplies	Indirect	Direct	Traceable to work cell
Purchased parts	Direct	Direct	
Employee benefits	Indirect	Direct	Traceable to work cell
Indirect labor	Indirect	Direct	Traceable to work cell
Insurance and taxes, plant	Indirect	Indirect	

Backflush Costing

LO4 Define and apply *backflush costing,* and compare the cost flows in traditional and backflush costing.

Managers in a lean operating environment are continuously seeking ways of reducing wasted resources and wasted time. So far, we have focused on how they can trim waste from operations, but they can reduce waste in other areas as well, including the accounting process. Because a lean operation reduces labor costs, the accounting system can combine the costs of direct labor and overhead into the single category of conversion costs, and because in JIT, materials arrive just in time to be used in the production process, there is little reason to maintain a separate Materials Inventory account. Thus, by simplifying cost flows through the accounting records, it is possible to reduce the time it takes to record and account for the costs of the manufacturing process.

A lean organization can also streamline its accounting process by using backflush costing. In **backflush costing**, all product costs are first accumulated in the Cost of Goods Sold account; at the end of the accounting period, they are "flushed back," or worked backward, into the appropriate inventory accounts. By having all product costs flow straight to a final destination and working back to determine the proper balances for the inventory accounts at the end of the period, this method saves recording time. As illustrated in Figure 22-2, it eliminates the need to record several transactions that must be recorded in traditional operating environments.

Study Note

Backflush costing eliminates the need to make journal entries during the period to track cost flows through the production process as the product is made.

FIGURE 22-2 Comparison of Cost Flows in Traditional and Backflush Costing

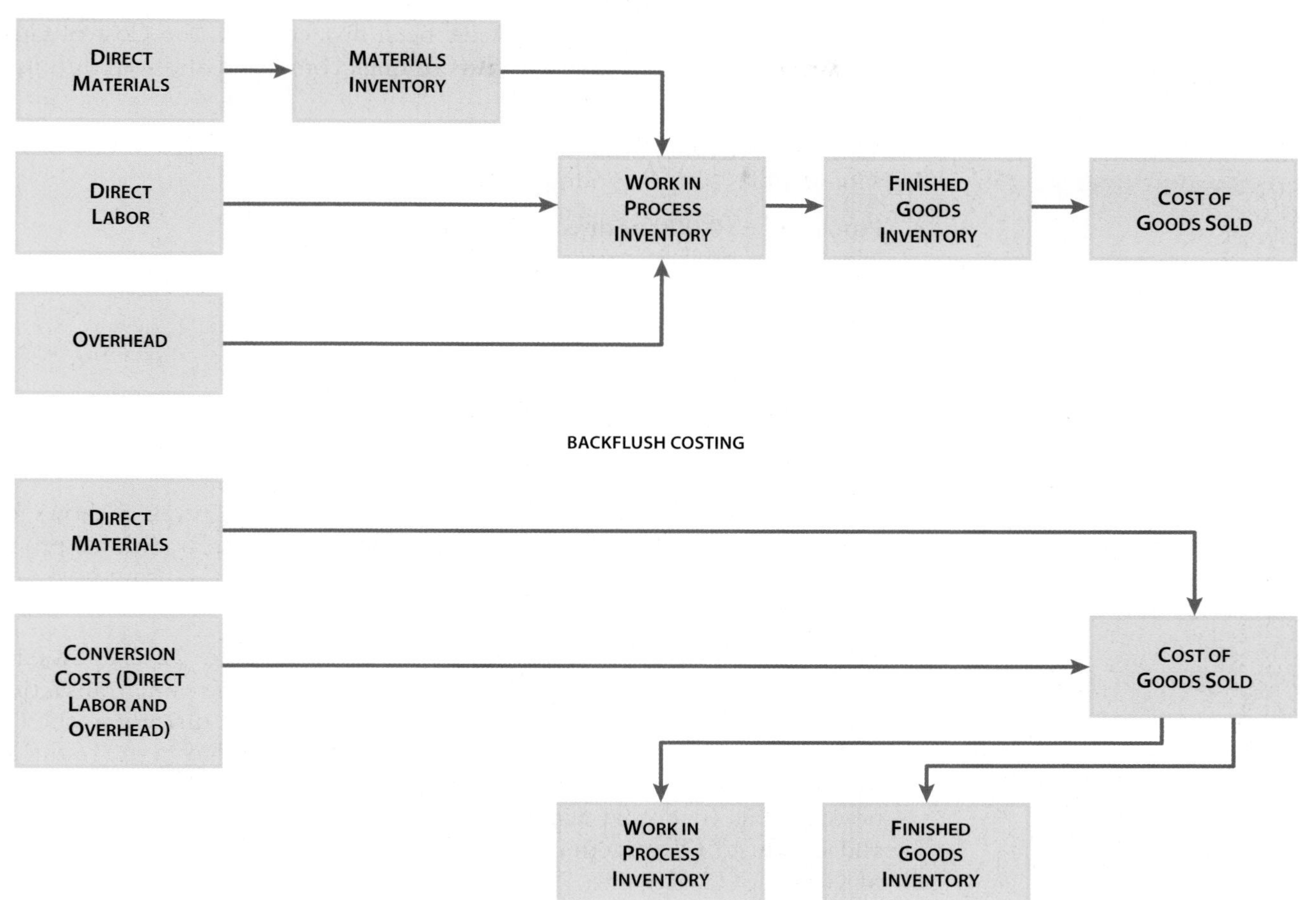

In a traditional environment, costs are tracked through the various production departments as products or services move through the production process.

Traditional costing methods:

- When direct materials arrive at a factory, their costs flow into the Materials Inventory account.
- When the direct materials are requisitioned into production, their costs flow into the Work in Process Inventory account. When direct labor is used, its costs are added to the Work in Process Inventory account. Overhead is applied to production using a base like direct labor hours, machine hours, or number of units produced and is added to the other costs in the Work in Process Inventory account.
- At the end of the manufacturing process, the costs of the finished units are transferred to the Finished Goods Inventory account, and when the units are sold, their costs are transferred to the Cost of Goods Sold account.

JIT costing method:

- In a JIT setting, direct materials arrive just in time to be placed into production. As you can see in Figure 22-2, when backflush costing is used, the direct materials costs and the conversion costs (direct labor and overhead) are immediately charged to the Cost of Goods Sold account.

Study Note

In backflush costing, entries to the Work in Process Inventory and Finished Goods Inventory accounts are made at the end of the period.

- At the end of the period, the costs of goods in work in process inventory and in finished goods inventory are determined, and those costs are flushed back to the Work in Process Inventory account and the Finished Goods Inventory account. Once those costs have been flushed back, the Cost of Goods Sold account contains only the costs of units completed and sold during the period.

To illustrate, assume that the following transactions occurred at one of Bean Bag Convertibles , Inc.'s production facilities last month:

1. Purchased $20,000 of direct materials on account.
2. Used all of the direct materials in production during the month.
3. Incurred direct labor costs of $8,000.
4. Applied $24,000 of overhead to production.
5. Completed units costing $51,600 during the month.
6. Sold units costing $51,500 during the month.

- ***Traditional costing methods:*** The top diagram in Figure 22-3 shows how these transactions would be entered in T accounts when traditional product costing is used. You can trace the flow of each cost by following its transaction number.
- ***JIT costing method:*** The bottom diagram in Figure 22-3 shows how backflush costing in a JIT environment would treat the same transactions. The cost of direct materials (Transaction 1) is charged directly to the Cost of Goods Sold account. Transaction 2, which is included in the traditional method, is not included when backflush costing is used because there is no Materials Inventory account. The costs of direct labor (Transaction 3) and overhead (Transaction 4) are combined and transferred to the Cost of Goods Sold account. The total in the Cost of Goods Sold account is then $52,000 ($20,000 for direct materials and $32,000 for conversion costs).

Once all product costs for the period have been entered in the Cost of Goods Sold account, the amounts to be transferred back to the inventory accounts are calculated.

- The amount transferred to the Finished Goods Inventory account is the difference between the cost of units sold (Transaction 6) and the cost of completed units (Transaction 5) ($51,600 − $51,500 = $100).
- The remaining difference in the Cost of Goods Sold account represents the cost of the work that is still in production at the end of the period. It is the amount charged to the Cost of Goods Sold account during the period less the actual cost of goods finished during the period (Transaction 5) [($20,000 + $8,000 + $24,000) − $51,600 = $400]; this amount is transferred to the Work in Process Inventory account.
- Notice that the ending balance in the Cost of Goods Sold account, $51,500, is the same as the ending balance when traditional costing is used. The difference is that backflush costing enabled us to use fewer accounts and to avoid recording several transactions.

FIGURE 22-3 Cost Flows Through T Accounts in Traditional and Backflush Costing

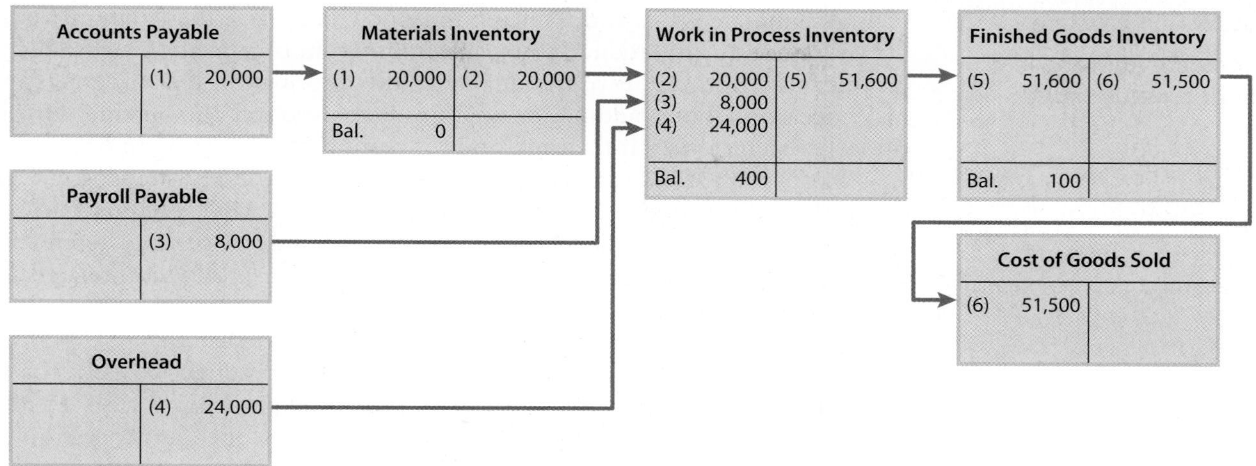

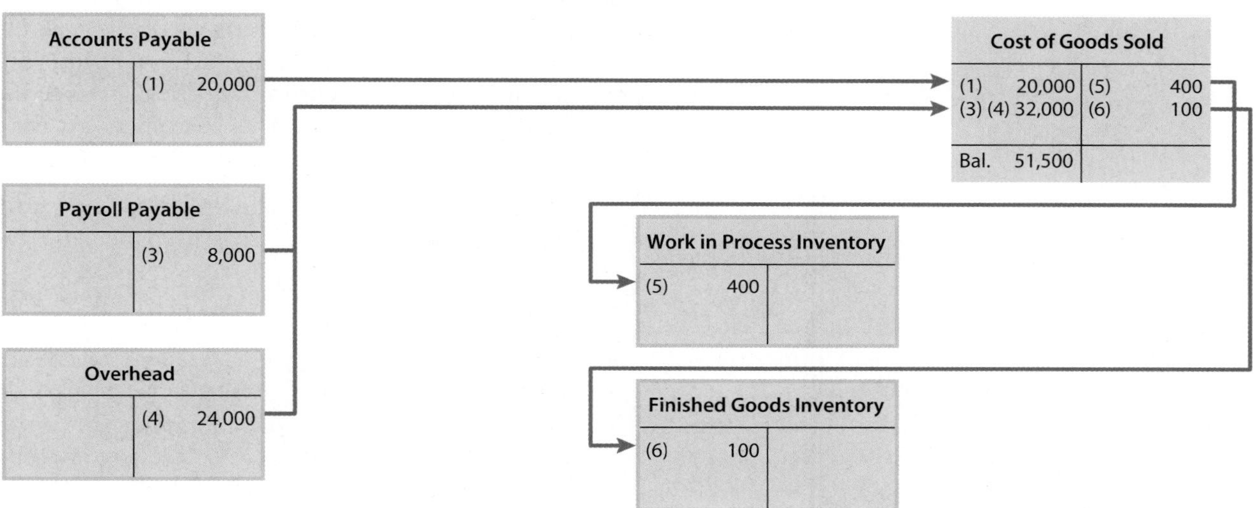

STOP & APPLY >

For work done during August, Bean Bag Convertibles, Inc., incurred direct materials costs of $123,450 and conversion costs of $265,200. The company employs a just-in-time operating environment and backflush costing.

At the end of August, it was determined that the Work in Process Inventory account had been assigned $980 of costs, and the ending balance of the Finished Goods Inventory account was $1,290. There were no beginning inventory balances. How much was charged to the Cost of Goods Sold account during August? What was the ending balance of the Cost of Goods Sold account?

SOLUTION

A total of $388,650 ($123,450 + $265,200) was charged to the Cost of Goods Sold account during August. The ending balance of Cost of Goods Sold was $386,380 ($388,650 − $980 − $1,290).

Comparison of ABM and Lean

LO5 Compare ABM and lean operations as value-based systems.

> **Study Note**
> ABM's primary goal is to calculate product or service cost accurately. Lean's primary goal is to eliminate waste in business processes.

ABM and lean have several things in common. As value-based systems, both analyze processes and identify value-adding and non-value-adding activities. Both seek to eliminate waste and reduce non-value-adding activities to improve product or service quality, reduce costs, and improve an organization's efficiency and productivity. Both improve the quality of the information that managers use to make decisions about bidding, pricing, product lines, and outsourcing. However, the two systems differ in their methods of costing and cost assignment.

ABM's tool, ABC, calculates product or service cost by using cost drivers to assign the indirect costs of production to cost objects. ABC is often a fairly complex accounting method used with job order and process costing systems. Note that the ABC method can also be used to examine non-production-related activities, such as marketing and shipping.

Lean uses JIT and reorganizes many activities so that they are performed within work cells. The costs of those activities become direct costs of the work cell and of the products made in that cell. The total production costs within the cell can then be assigned by using simple cost drivers, such as process hours or direct materials cost. Companies that have implemented lean operations may use backflush costing rather than job order costing or process costing. This approach focuses on the output at the end of the production process and simplifies the accounting system. Table 22-3 summarizes the characteristics of ABM and lean.

A company can use both ABM and lean. ABM and ABC will improve the accuracy of the company's product or service costing and help it to reduce or eliminate business activities that do not add value for its customers. At the same time, the company can apply lean thinking to simplify processes, use resources effectively, and eliminate waste.

TABLE 22-3 Comparison of ABM and Lean Activity-Based Systems

	ABM	Lean
Primary purpose	To eliminate or reduce non-value-adding activities	To eliminate or reduce waste in all aspects of a business, including its processes and products or services
Cost assignment	Uses ABC to assign overhead costs to the product by using appropriate cost drivers	Uses JIT and reorganizes production activities into work cells; overhead costs incurred in the work cell become direct costs of the cell's products
Costing method	Integrates ABC with job order or process costing to calculate product costs	May use backflush costing to calculate product costs
Limitation	ABC can involve costly data collection and complex allocations	Requires management to think differently and use different performance measures

& APPLY >

Couch Potato Inc., produces futon mattresses. The company recently changed from a traditional production environment to just-in-time work cells. Would you recommend the use of ABM/ABC or backflush costing for tracking product costs? Explain your choice.

SOLUTION

Since the company produces similar products, it lends itself well to backflush costing for the calculation of product costs. A company that makes a variety of products with differing activity choices in a job order setting is better served by the more accurate and more complex procedures of ABM/ABC product costing.

▶ BEAN BAG CONVERTIBLES, INC.: REVIEW PROBLEM

In this chapter's Decision Point, we asked the following questions:

- How have activity-based systems helped Bean Bag Convertibles, Inc., improve its production processes and reduce delivery time?
- How do the managers of Bean Bag Convertibles, Inc., plan to remain competitive in a challenging business environment?

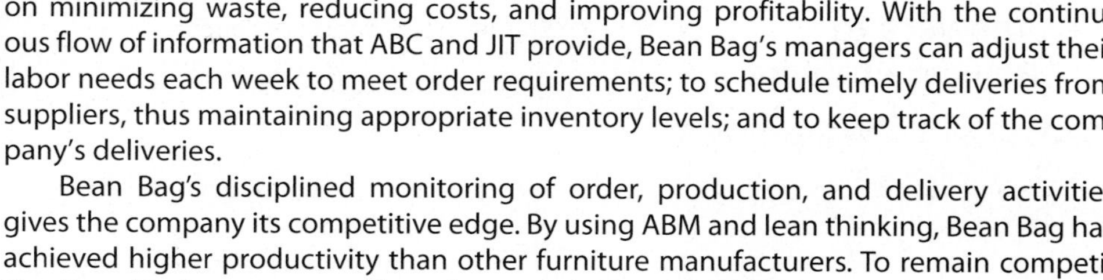

Bean Bag Convertibles, Inc.'s managers use activity-based management (ABM) and a lean operation to identify and reduce or eliminate activities that do not add value to the company's products and to improve production processes. These systems focus on minimizing waste, reducing costs, and improving profitability. With the continuous flow of information that ABC and JIT provide, Bean Bag's managers can adjust their labor needs each week to meet order requirements; to schedule timely deliveries from suppliers, thus maintaining appropriate inventory levels; and to keep track of the company's deliveries.

Activity-Based Costing
LO2

Bean Bag's disciplined monitoring of order, production, and delivery activities gives the company its competitive edge. By using ABM and lean thinking, Bean Bag has achieved higher productivity than other furniture manufacturers. To remain competitive, Bean Bag's managers will continue to rely on ABM and lean.

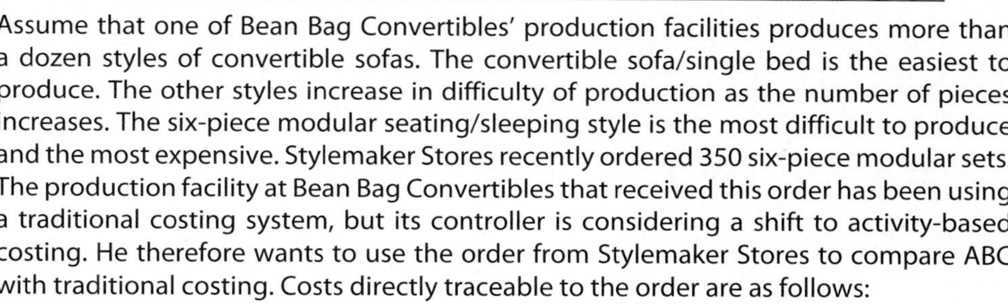

Assume that one of Bean Bag Convertibles' production facilities produces more than a dozen styles of convertible sofas. The convertible sofa/single bed is the easiest to produce. The other styles increase in difficulty of production as the number of pieces increases. The six-piece modular seating/sleeping style is the most difficult to produce and the most expensive. Stylemaker Stores recently ordered 350 six-piece modular sets. The production facility at Bean Bag Convertibles that received this order has been using a traditional costing system, but its controller is considering a shift to activity-based costing. He therefore wants to use the order from Stylemaker Stores to compare ABC with traditional costing. Costs directly traceable to the order are as follows:

Direct materials	$57,290
Purchased parts	$76,410
Direct labor hours	1,320
Average direct labor pay rate per hour	$14.00

With the traditional costing approach, the controller applies overhead costs at a rate of 320 percent of direct labor costs.

For activity-based costing of the Stylemaker Stores order, the controller uses the following data:

Activity	Cost Driver	Activity Cost Rate	Activity Usage
Product design	Engineering hours	$62 per engineering hour	76 engineering hours
Work cell setup	Number of setups	$90 per setup	16 setups
Parts production	Machine hours	$38 per machine hour	380 machine hours
Assembly	Assembly labor hours	$40 per assembly labor hour	500 assembly labor hours
Product simulation	Testing hours	$90 per testing hour	28 testing hours
Packaging and shipping	Product units	$13 per unit	350 units
Building occupancy	Direct labor cost	125% of direct labor cost	$18,480 direct labor cost

Required

1. Use the traditional costing approach to compute the total cost and product unit cost of the Stylemaker Stores order.
2. Using the cost hierarchy for manufacturing companies, classify each activity of the Stylemaker Stores order according to the level at which it occurs.
3. Prepare a bill of activities for the operating costs.
4. Use ABC to compute the total cost and product unit cost.
5. What is the difference between the product unit cost you computed using the traditional approach and the one you computed using ABC? Does the use of ABC guarantee cost reduction for every order?

Answers to Review Problem

1. Traditional costing approach:

Direct materials	$ 57,290
Purchased parts	76,410
Direct labor	18,480
Overhead (320% of direct labor cost)	59,136
Total cost of order	$211,316
Product unit cost (total costs ÷ 350 units)	$ 603.76

2. Activities classified by level of the manufacturing cost hierarchy:

Unit level:	Parts production
	Assembly
	Packaging and shipping
Batch level:	Work cell setup
Product level:	Product design
	Product simulation
Facility level:	Building occupancy

3, 4. Bill of activities and total cost and product unit cost computed with ABC:

Bill of Activities
Stylemaker Stores Order

Activity	Activity Cost Rate	Cost Driver Level	Activity Cost
Unit level			
Parts production	$38 per machine hour	380 machine hours	$ 14,440
Assembly	$40 per assembly labor hour	500 assembly labor hours	20,000
Packaging and shipping	$13 per unit	350 units	4,550
Batch level			
Work cell setup	$90 per setup	16 setups	1,440
Product level			
Product design	$62 per engineering hour	76 engineering hours	4,712
Product simulation	$90 per testing hour	28 testing hours	2,520
Facility level			
Building occupancy	125% of direct labor cost	$18,480 direct labor cost	23,100
Total activity costs assigned to job			$ 70,762
Total job units			÷ 350
Activity costs per unit (total activity costs ÷ total units)			$ 202.18*
Cost summary			
Direct materials			$ 57,290
Purchased parts			76,410
Activity costs (includes labor and overhead)			70,762
Total cost of order			$204,462
Product unit cost (total cost of order ÷ 350 units)			$ 584.18*

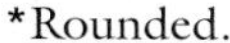

*Rounded.

5.

Product unit cost using traditional costing approach:	$603.76
Product unit cost using activity-based costing approach:	584.18*
Difference:	$ 19.58

Although the product unit cost computed using ABC is lower than the one computed using the traditional costing approach, ABC does not guarantee cost reduction for every product. It does improve cost traceability, which often identifies products that are "undercosted" or "overcosted" by a traditional product costing system.

STOP & REVIEW >

LO1 Explain why managers use *value-based systems* and discuss their relationship to the supply chain and the value chain.

Value-based systems categorize activities as either adding value to a product or service or not adding value. It enables managers to see their organization as a collection of value-creating activities (a value chain) that operates as part of a larger system that includes suppliers' and customers' value chains (a supply chain). This perspective helps managers work cooperatively both inside and outside their organizations to reduce costs by eliminating waste and inefficiencies and by redirecting resources toward value-adding activities. PVA is a technique that managers use to identify and link all the activities involved in the value chain. It analyzes business processes by relating activities to the events that prompt the activities and to the resources that the activities consume. A value-adding activity adds value to a product or service as perceived by the customer. A non-value-adding activity adds cost to a product or service but does not increase its market value.

LO2 Define *activity-based costing* and explain how a cost hierarchy and a bill of activities are used.

Activity-based costing (ABC) is a method of assigning costs that calculates a more accurate product cost than traditional methods do. It does so by categorizing all indirect costs by activity, tracing the indirect costs to those activities, and assigning those costs to products using a cost driver related to the cause of the cost. To implement ABC, managers (1) identify and classify each activity, (2) estimate the cost of resources for each activity, (3) identify a cost driver for each activity and estimate the quantity of each cost driver, (4) calculate an activity cost rate for each activity, and (5) assign costs to cost objects based on the level of activity required to make the product or provide the service. ABC's primary disadvantage is that it is costly to implement.

Two tools—a cost hierarchy and a bill of activities—help in the implementation of ABC. To create a cost hierarchy, managers classify activities into four levels. Unit-level activities are performed each time a unit is produced. Batch-level activities are performed each time a batch of goods is produced. Product-level activities are performed to support a particular product line or brand. Facility-level activities are performed to support a facility's general manufacturing process. A bill of activities is then used to compute the costs assigned to activities and the product or service unit cost.

LO3 Define the elements of a lean operation and identify the changes in inventory management that result when a firm adopts its just-in-time operating philosophy.

Lean operation's objective is to eliminate waste. One of the primary elements is to operate production on a just-in-time (JIT) basis. The elements of a JIT environment are minimum inventory levels, pull-through production, quick setup and flexible work cells, a multiskilled work force, high levels of product quality, effective preventive maintenance, and continuous improvement of the work environment.

In product costing under JIT, processing costs are classified as either direct materials costs or conversion costs. The costs associated with inspection time, moving time, queue time, and storage time are reduced or eliminated. With computerized monitoring of the work cells, many costs that are treated as indirect or overhead costs in traditional manufacturing settings become direct costs since they can be traced directly to work cells. The only costs that remain indirect costs and must be assigned to the work cells are those that cannot be linked to a specific work cell. In other words, those associated with building occupancy, insurance, and property taxes.

LO4 Define and apply *backflush costing,* and compare the cost flows in traditional and backflush costing.

In backflush costing, all product costs are first accumulated in the Cost of Goods Sold account; at the end of the accounting period, they are "flushed back," or worked backward, into the appropriate inventory accounts. Backflush costing is commonly used to account for product costs in a JIT operating environment. It differs from the traditional costing approach, which records the costs of materials purchased in the Materials Inventory account and uses the Work in Process Inventory account to record the costs of direct materials, direct labor, and overhead during the production process. The objective of backflush costing is to save recording time, which cuts costs.

LO5 Compare ABM and lean operations as value-based systems.

As value-based systems, both ABM and lean seek to eliminate waste and reduce non-value-adding activities. However, they differ in their approaches to cost assignment and calculation of product cost. ABM uses ABC to assign indirect costs to products using cost drivers; lean uses JIT to reorganize activities so that they are performed within work cells, and the overhead costs incurred in a work cell become direct costs of the products made in that cell. ABM uses job order or process costing to calculate product costs, whereas lean may use backflush costing.

REVIEW of Concepts and Terminology

The following concepts and terms were introduced in this chapter:

Activity-based costing (ABC) 965 (LO2)

Activity-based management (ABM) 963 (LO1)

Backflush costing 972 (LO4)

Batch-level activities 965 (LO2)

Bill of activities 966 (LO2)

Conversion costs 971 (LO3)

Cost hierarchy 965 (LO2)

Facility-level activities 966 (LO2)

Full product cost 960 (LO1)

Inspection time 970 (LO3)

Just-in-time (JIT) operating philosophy 969 (LO3)

Lean operations 964 (LO1)

Moving time 971 (LO3)

Non-value-adding activity 963 (LO1)

Processing time 970 (LO3)

Process value analysis (PVA) 962 (LO1)

Product-level activities 966 (LO2)

Pull-through production 969 (LO3)

Push-through method 969 (LO3)

Queue time 971 (LO3)

Storage time 971 (LO3)

Supply chain 961 (LO1)

Throughput time 971 (LO3)

Unit-level activities 965 (LO2)

Value-adding activity 963 (LO1)

Value-based systems 960 (LO1)

Value chain 961 (LO1)

Work cell 969 (LO3)

CHAPTER ASSIGNMENTS

BUILDING Your Basic Knowledge and Skills

Short Exercises

LO1 Activity-Based Systems

SE 1. Thom Lutz started a retail clothing business two years ago. Lutz's first year was very successful, but sales dropped 50 percent in the second year. A friend who is a business consultant analyzed Lutz's business and came up with two basic reasons for the decline in sales: (1) Lutz has been placing orders late in each season, and (2) shipments of clothing have been arriving late and in poor condition. What measures can Lutz take to improve his business and persuade customers to return?

LO1 The Value Chain

SE 2. Which of the following activities would be part of the value chain of a manufacturing company? Which activities do not add value?

1. Product marketing
2. Machine drilling
3. Materials storage
4. Product design
5. Product packing
6. Cost accounting
7. Moving work in process
8. Inventory control

LO1 The Supply Chain

SE 3. Jack DuBois is developing plans to open a restaurant called Ribs 'n Slaw. He has located a building and will lease all the furniture and equipment he needs for the restaurant. Food Servers, Inc. will supply all the restaurant's personnel. Identify the components of Ribs 'n Slaw's supply chain.

LO1 Value-Adding and Non-Value-Adding Activities

SE 4. Indicate whether the following activities of a submarine sandwich shop are value-adding (V) or non-value-adding (NV):

1. Purchasing sandwich ingredients
2. Storing condiments
3. Making sandwiches
4. Cleaning up the shop
5. Making home deliveries
6. Accounting for sales and costs

LO2 The Cost Hierarchy

SE 5. Engineering design is an activity that is vital to the success of any motor vehicle manufacturer. Identify the level at which engineering design would be classified in the cost hierarchy used with ABC for each of the following:

1. A maker of unique editions of luxury automobiles
2. A maker of built-to-order city and county emergency vehicles (orders are usually placed for 10 to 12 identical vehicles)
3. A maker of a line of automobiles sold throughout the world

LO2 The Cost Hierarchy

SE 6. Match the four levels of the cost hierarchy to the following activities of a blue jeans manufacturer that uses activity-based management:

1. Routine maintenance of sewing machines
2. Designing a pattern for a new style
3. Sewing seams on a garment
4. Producing 100 jeans of a certain style in a certain size

LO3 **Elements of a JIT Operating Environment**

SE 7. Maintaining minimum inventory levels and using pull-through production are important elements of a just-in-time operating environment. How does pull-through production help minimize inventories?

LO3 **Product Costing Changes in a JIT Environment**

SE 8. Aromatherapy Products Company is in the process of adopting the just-in-time operating environment for its lotion-making operations. Indicate which of the following overhead costs are non-value-adding costs (NVA) and which can be traced directly to the new lotion-making work cell (D):

1. Storage containers for work in process inventory
2. Insurance on the storage warehouse
3. Machine electricity
4. Machine repairs
5. Depreciation of the storage container moving equipment
6. Machine setup labor

LO4 **Backflush Costing**

SE 9. For work done during August, Pansey Company incurred direct materials costs of $120,000 and conversion costs of $260,000. The company employs a just-in-time operating philosophy and backflush costing. At the end of August, it was determined that the Work in Process Inventory account had been assigned $900 of costs, and the ending balance of the Finished Goods Inventory account was $1,300. There were no beginning inventory balances. How much was charged to the Cost of Goods Sold account during August? What was the ending balance of that account?

LO5 **Comparison of ABM and Lean**

SE 10. Hwang Corp. recently installed three just-in-time work cells in its screen-making division. The work cells will make large quantities of similar products for major window and door manufacturers. Should Hwang use lean with JIT and backflush costing or ABM and ABC to account for product costs? Defend your choice of activity-based system.

Exercises

LO1 **Management Reports**

E 1. The reports that follow are from a department in an insurance company. Which report would be used for financial purposes, and which would be used for activity-based decision making? Why?

Salaries	$ 1,400	Enter claims into system	$ 2,000
Equipment	1,200	Analyze claims	1,000
Travel expenses	8,000	Suspend claims	1,500
Supplies	300	Receive inquiries	1,500
Use and occupancy	3,000	Resolve problems	400
		Process batches	3,000
		Determine eligibility	4,000
		Make copies	200
		Write correspondence	100
		Attend training	200
Total	$13,900	Total	$13,900

LO1 **The Supply Chain and Value Chain**

E 2. Indicate which of the following persons and activities associated with a lawn and garden nursery are part of the supply chain (S) and which are part of the value chain (V):

1. Plant and tree vendor
2. Purchasing potted trees
3. Computer and software company
4. Creating marketing plans
5. Advertising company
6. Scheduling delivery trucks
7. Customer service

LO1 **The Supply Chain and Value Chain**

E 3. The items in the following list are associated with a bank. Indicate which are part of the supply chain (S) and which are part of the value chain (V).

1. Federal Reserve Bank
2. Student loan processing
3. Investment services
4. ATM
5. Customer

LO1 **Value Analysis**

E 4. Libbel Enterprises has been in business for 30 years. Last year, the company purchased Chemcraft Laboratory and entered the chemical processing business. Libbel's controller prepared a process value analysis of the new operation and identified the following activities:

New product research
Design testing
Materials storage
Product curing process
Product scheduling
Product spoilage
Customer follow-up
Product sales
Packaging process
Materials inspection
New product marketing
Product inspection
Product delivery
Materials delivery
Product bottling process
Product warranty work
Product engineering
Purchasing of direct materials
Finished goods storage
Cleanup of processing areas
Product mixing process

Identify the value-adding activities in this list, and classify them into the activity areas of the value chain illustrated in Figure 22-1 in this chapter. Prepare a separate list of the non-value-adding activities.

LO1 **Value-Adding Activities**

E 5. When Courtney Tybee prepared a process value analysis for her company, she identified the following primary activities. Identify the value-adding activities (VA) and the non-value-adding activities (NVA).

1. Production scheduling
2. Customer follow-up
3. Materials moving
4. Product inspection
5. Engineering design
6. Product marketing
7. Product sales
8. Materials storage

LO2 **The Cost Hierarchy**

E 6. Copia Electronics makes speaker systems. Its customers range from new hotels and restaurants that need specifically designed sound systems to nationwide retail outlets that order large quantities of similar products. The following activities are part of the company's operating process:

New retail product design
Retail product marketing
Unique system design
Unique system packaging
Purchasing of materials
Building repair
Retail sales commissions
Bulk packing of orders
Assembly labor
Assembly line setup
Building security
Facility supervision

Classify each activity as unit level (UL), batch level (BL), product level (PL), or facility level (FL).

LO2 **Bill of Activities**

E 7. Lake Corporation has received an order for handheld computers from Union, LLC. A partially complete bill of activities for that order appears below. Fill in the missing data.

Lake Corporation
Bill of Activities for Union, LLC
Order Form

Activity	Activity Cost Rate	Cost Driver Level	Activity Cost
Unit level			
Parts production	$50 per machine hour	200 machine hours	$?
Assembly	$20 per direct labor hour	100 direct labor hours	?
Packaging and shipping	$12.50 per unit	400 units	?
Batch level			
Work cell setup	$100 per setup	16 setups	?
Product level			
Product design	$60 per engineering hour	80 engineering hours	?
Product simulation	$80 per testing hour	30 testing hours	?
Facility level			
Building occupancy	200% of assembly labor cost	?	?
Total activity costs assigned to job			$?
Total job units			400
Activity costs per unit (total activity costs ÷ total units)			$?
Cost summary			
Direct materials			$60,000
Purchased parts			80,000
Activity costs			?
Total cost of order			$?
Product unit cost (total cost ÷ 400 units)			$?

LO2 **Activity Cost Rates**

E 8. Compute the activity cost rates for materials handling, assembly, and design based on these data:

Materials	
Cloth	$26,000
Fasteners	4,000
Purchased parts	40,000
Materials handling	
Labor	8,000
Equipment depreciation	5,000
Electrical power	2,000
Maintenance	6,000
Assembly	
Machine operators	5,000

Design	
Labor	5,000
Electrical power	1,000
Overhead	8,000

Output totaled 40,000 units. Each unit requires three machine hours of effort. Materials handling costs are allocated to the products based on direct materials cost. Design costs are allocated based on units produced. Assembly costs are allocated based on 500 machine operator hours. [**Hint:** Activity cost rate = (Total activity costs ÷ Total allocation base). Examples of an allocation base include total dollars of materials, total machine operator hours, or total units of output.]

LO3 **Elements of a Lean Operating Environment**

E 9. The following numbered items are concepts that underlie value-based systems, such as ABM and lean. Match each concept to the related lettered element(s) of a lean operating environment.

1. Business processes are simplified.
2. The quality of the product or service is critical.
3. Employees are cross-trained.
4. Large inventories waste resources and may hide bad work.
5. Goods should be produced only when needed.
6. Equipment downtime is minimized.

a. Minimum inventory levels
b. Pull-through production
c. Quick machine setups and flexible work cells
d. A multiskilled work force
e. High levels of product quality
f. Effective preventive maintenance

LO3 **Comparison of Traditional Manufacturing Environments and JIT**

E 10. Identify which of the following exist in a traditional manufacturing environment and which exist in a JIT environment:

1. Large amounts of inventory
2. Complex manufacturing processes
3. A multiskilled labor force
4. Flexible work cells
5. Push-through production methods
6. Materials purchased infrequently but in large lot sizes
7. Infrequent setups

LO3 **Direct and Indirect Costs in JIT and Traditional Manufacturing Environments**

E 11. The cost categories in this list are typical of many manufacturing operations:

Direct materials:	Direct labor	Depreciation–machinery
Sheet steel	Engineering labor	Supervisory salaries
Iron castings	Indirect labor	Electrical power
Assembly parts:	Operating supplies	Insurance and taxes–plant
Part 24RE6	Small tools	President's salary
Part 15RF8	Depreciation–plant	Employee benefits

Identify each cost as direct or indirect, assuming that it was incurred in (1) a traditional manufacturing setting and (2) a JIT environment. State the reasons for changes in classification.

LO4 **Backflush Costing**

E 12. Conda Products Company implemented a JIT work environment in its trowel division eight months ago, and the division has been operating at near capacity since then. At the beginning of May, Work in Process Inventory and Finished Goods Inventory had zero balances. The following transactions took place last week:

May 28	Ordered, received, and used handles and sheet metal costing \$11,340.
29	Direct labor costs incurred, \$5,400.
29	Overhead costs incurred, \$8,100.
30	Completed trowels costing \$24,800.
31	Sold trowels costing \$24,000.

Using backflush costing, calculate the ending balance in the Work in Process Inventory and Finished Goods Inventory accounts.

LO4 **Backflush Costing**

E 13. Good Morning Enterprises produces digital alarm clocks. It has a just-in-time assembly process and uses backflush costing to record production costs. Overhead is assigned at a rate of \$17 per assembly labor hour. There were no beginning inventories in March. During March, the following operating data were generated:

Cost of direct materials purchased and used	\$53,200
Direct labor costs incurred	\$27,300
Overhead costs assigned	?
Assembly hours worked	3,840 hours
Ending work in process inventory	\$1,050
Ending finished goods inventory	\$960

Using T accounts, show the flow of costs through the backflush costing system. What is the total cost of goods sold in March?

LO5 **Comparison of ABM and Lean**

E 14. Identify each of the following as a characteristic of ABM or lean:

1. Backflush costing
2. ABC used to assign overhead costs to the product cost
3. ABC integrated with job order or process costing systems
4. Complexity reduced by using work cells, minimizing inventories, and reducing or eliminating non-value-adding activities
5. Activities reorganized so that they are performed within work cells

LO5 **Comparison of ABM and Lean**

E 15. The following are excerpts from a conversation between two managers about their companies' activity-based systems. Identify the manager who works for a company that emphasizes ABM and the one who works for a company that emphasizes a lean system.

Manager 1: We try to manage our resources effectively by monitoring operating activities. We analyze all major operating activities, and we focus on reducing or eliminating the ones that don't add value to our products. Our product costs are more accurate since we allocate activity costs to products and services.

Manager 2: We're very concerned with eliminating waste to reduce costs. We've designed our operations in flexible work cells to reduce the time it takes to move, store, queue, and inspect materials. We've also reduced our inventories by buying and using materials only when we need them.

Problems

LO1 **The Value Chain and Process Value Analysis**

P 1. Lindstrom Industries, Inc. produces chain saws, weed whackers, and lawn mowers for major retail chains. Lindstrom makes these products to order in large quantities for each customer. It has adopted activity-based management, and its controller is in the process of developing an ABC system. The controller has identified the following primary activities of the company:

Product delivery	Production–assembly
Customer follow-up	Engineering design
Materials and parts purchasing	Product inspection
Materials storage	Processing areas cleanup
Materials inspection	Product marketing
Production–drilling	Building maintenance
Product packaging	Product sales
Product research	Product rework
Finished goods storage	Production–grinding
Production–machine setup	Personnel services
Materials moving	Production scheduling

Required

1. Identify the activities that do not add value to Lindstrom's products.
2. Assist the controller's analysis by grouping the value-adding activities into the activity areas of the value chain shown in Figure 22-1.

Manager insight ▶ 3. State whether each non-value-adding activity is necessary or unnecessary. Suggest how each unnecessary activity could be reduced or eliminated.

LO2 **Activity-Based Costing**

P 2. Boulware Products, Inc. produces printers for wholesale distributors. It has just completed packaging an order from Shawl Company for 450 printers. Before the order is shipped, the controller wants to compare the unit costs computed under the company's new activity-based costing system with the unit costs computed under its traditional costing system. Boulware's traditional costing system assigned overhead costs at a rate of 240 percent of direct labor cost.

Data for the Shawl order are as follows: direct materials, $17,552; purchased parts, $14,856; direct labor hours, 140; and average direct labor pay rate per hour, $17.

Data for activity-based costing related to processing direct materials and purchased parts for the Shawl order are as follows:

Activity	Cost Driver	Activity Cost Rate	Activity Usage
Engineering systems design	Engineering hours	$28 per engineering hour	18 engineering hours
Setup	Number of setups	$36 per setup	12 setups
Parts production	Machine hours	$37 per machine hour	82 machine hours
Product assembly	Assembly hours	$42 per assembly hour	96 assembly hours
Packaging	Number of packages	$5.60 per package	150 packages
Building occupancy	Machine hours	$10 per machine hour	82 machine hours

Required

1. Use the traditional costing approach to compute the total cost and the product unit cost of the Shawl order.
2. Using the cost hierarchy, identify each activity as unit level, batch level, product level, or facility level.
3. Prepare a bill of activities for the activity costs.
4. Use ABC to compute the total cost and product unit cost of the Shawl order.

Manager insight ▶
5. What is the difference between the product unit cost you computed using the traditional approach and the one you computed using ABC? Does the use of ABC guarantee cost reduction for every order?

LO2 Activity Cost Rates

P 3. Noir Company produces four versions of its model J17-21 bicycle seat. The four versions have different shapes, but their processing operations and production costs are identical. During July, these costs were incurred:

Direct materials	
Leather	$25,430
Metal frame	39,180
Bolts	3,010
Materials handling	
Labor	8,232
Equipment depreciation	4,410
Electrical power	2,460
Maintenance	5,184
Assembly	
Direct labor	13,230
Engineering design	
Labor	4,116
Electrical power	1,176
Engineering overhead	7,644
Overhead	
Equipment depreciation	7,056
Indirect labor	30,870
Supervision	17,640
Operating supplies	4,410
Electrical power	10,584
Repairs and maintenance	21,168
Building occupancy overhead	52,920

July's output totaled 29,400 units. Each unit requires three machine hours of effort. Materials handling costs are allocated to the products based on direct materials cost, engineering design costs are allocated based on units produced, and overhead is allocated based on machine hours. Assembly costs are allocated based on direct labor hours, which are estimated at 882 for July.

During July, Noir Company completed 520 bicycle seats for Job 142. The activity usage for Job 142 was as follows: direct materials, $1,150; direct labor hours, 15.

Required

1. Compute the following activity cost rates: (a) materials handling cost rate; (b) assembly cost rate, (c) engineering design cost rate, and (d) overhead rate.

2. Prepare a bill of activities for Job 142.
3. Use activity-based costing to compute the job's total cost and product unit cost.

LO3 Direct and Indirect Costs in Lean and Traditional Manufacturing Environments

P 4. Funz Company, which produces wooden toys, is about to adopt a lean operating environment. In anticipation of the change, Letty Hernandez, Funz's controller, prepared the following list of costs for December:

Wood	$1,200	Insurance–plant	$ 324
Bolts	32	President's salary	4,000
Small tools	54	Engineering labor	2,700
Depreciation–plant	450	Utilities	1,250
Depreciation–machinery	275	Building occupancy	1,740
Direct labor	2,675	Supervision	2,686
Indirect labor	890	Operating supplies	254
Purchased parts	58	Repairs and maintenance	198
Materials handling	74	Employee benefits	2,654

Required

1. Identify each cost as direct or indirect, assuming that it was incurred in a traditional manufacturing setting.
2. Identify each cost as direct or indirect, assuming that it was incurred in a lean environment.
3. Assume that the costs incurred in the lean environment are for a work cell that completed 1,250 toy cars in December. Compute the total direct cost and the direct cost per unit for the cars produced.

LO4 Backflush Costing

P 5. Automotive Parts Company produces 12 parts for car bodies and sells them to three automobile assembly companies in the United States. The company implemented lean operating and costing procedures three years ago. Overhead is applied at a rate of $26 per work cell hour used. All direct materials and purchased parts are used as they are received.

One of the company's work cells produces automotive fenders that are completely detailed and ready to install when received by the customer. The cell is operated by four employees and involves a flexible manufacturing system with 14 workstations. Operating details for February for this cell are as follows:

Beginning work in process inventory	—
Beginning finished goods inventory	$420
Cost of direct materials purchased on account and used	$213,400
Cost of parts purchased on account and used	$111,250
Direct labor costs incurred	$26,450
Overhead costs assigned	?
Work cell hours used	8,260
Costs of goods completed during February	$564,650
Ending work in process inventory	$1,210
Ending finished goods inventory	$670

Required

1. Using T accounts, show the cost flows through a backflush costing system.
2. Using T accounts, show the cost flows through a traditional costing system.
3. What is the total cost of goods sold for the month?

Alternate Problems

LO1 LO2 **The Value Chain and Process Value Analysis**

P 6. Direct Marketing Inc. (DMI) offers database marketing strategies to help companies increase their sales. DMI's basic package of services includes the design of a mailing piece (either a Direct Mailer or a Store Mailer), creation and maintenance of marketing databases containing information about the client's target group, and a production process that prints a promotional piece and prepares it for mailing. In its marketing strategies, DMI targets working women ages 25 to 54 who are married with children and who have an annual household income in excess of $50,000. DMI has adopted activity-based management, and its controller is in the process of developing an ABC system. The controller has identified the following primary activities of the company:

Use database of customers	Accounting
Service sales	Mailer assembly
Deliver mailers to post office	Process orders
Supplies storage	Purchase supplies
Client follow-up	Design mailer
Database research trends	Building maintenance
Schedule order processing	Processing cleanup
Personnel	Mailer rework

Required

1. Identify the activities that do not add value to DMI's services.
2. Assist the controller's analysis by grouping the value-adding activities into the activity areas of the value chain shown in Figure 22-1.
3. State whether each non-value-adding activity is necessary or unnecessary. Suggest how each unnecessary activity could be reduced or eliminated. (Manager insight ▶)

LO2 **Activity-Based Costing**

P 7. Kauli Company produces cellular phones. It has just completed an order for 10,000 phones placed by Stay Connect, Ltd. Kauli recently shifted to an activity-based costing system, and its controller is interested in the impact that the ABC system had on the Stay Connect order. Data for that order are as follows: direct materials, $36,950; purchased parts, $21,100; direct labor hours, 220; average direct labor pay rate per hour, $15.

Under Kauli's traditional costing system, overhead costs were assigned at a rate of 270 percent of direct labor cost.

Data for activity-based costing for the Stay Connect order are as follows:

Activity	Cost Driver	Activity Cost Rate	Activity Usage
Electrical engineering design	Engineering hours	$19 per engineering hour	32 engineering hours
Setup	Number of setups	$29 per setup	11 setups
Parts production	Machine hours	$26 per machine hour	134 machine hours
Product testing	Number of tests	$32 per test	52 tests
Packaging	Number of packages	$0.0374 per package	10,000 packages
Building occupancy	Machine hours	$9.80 per machine hour	134 machine hours
Assembly	Direct labor hours	$15 per direct labor hour	220 direct labor hours

Required

1. Use the traditional costing approach to compute the total cost and the product unit cost of the Stay Connect order.
2. Using the cost hierarchy, identify each activity as unit level, batch level, product level, or facility level.
3. Prepare a bill of activities for the activity costs.
4. Use ABC to compute the total cost and product unit cost of the Stay Connect order.
5. What is the difference between the product unit cost you computed using the traditional approach and the one you computed using ABC? Does the use of ABC guarantee cost reduction for every order?

Manager insight ▶

LO2 **Activity Cost Rates**

P 8. Meanwhile Company produces three models of aluminum skateboards. The models have minor differences, but their processing operations and production costs are identical. During June, these costs were incurred:

Direct materials	
Aluminum frame	$162,524
Bolts	3,876
Purchased parts	
Wheels	74,934
Decals	5,066
Materials handling *(assigned based on direct materials cost)*	
Labor	17,068
Utilities	4,438
Maintenance	914
Depreciation	876
Assembly line *(assigned based on labor hours)*	
Labor	46,080
Setup *(assigned based on number of setups)*	
Labor	6,385
Supplies	762
Overhead	3,953
Product testing *(assigned based on number of tests)*	
Labor	2,765
Supplies	435
Building occupancy *(assigned based on machine hours)*	
Insurance	5,767
Depreciation	2,452
Repairs and maintenance	3,781

For June, output totaled 32,000 skateboards. Each board required 1.5 machine hours of effort. During June, Meanwhile's assembly line worked 2,304 hours, performed 370 setups and 64,000 product tests, and completed an order for 1,000 skateboards placed by Whatever Toys Company. The job incurred costs of $5,200 for direct materials and $2,500 for purchased parts. It required 3 setups, 2,000 tests, and 72 assembly line hours.

Required

1. Compute the following activity cost rates:
   a. Materials handling cost rate
   b. Assembly line cost rate

c. Setup cost rate
d. Product testing cost rate
e. Building occupancy cost rate
2. Prepare a bill of activities for the Whatever Toys job.
3. Use activity-based costing to compute the job's total cost and product unit cost. (Round your answer to two decimal places.)

LO3 Direct and Indirect Costs in JIT and Traditional Manufacturing Environments

P 9. Caffene Company, which processes coffee beans into ground coffee, is about to adopt a JIT operating environment. In anticipation of the change, Hattie Peralto, Caffene's controller, prepared the following list of costs for the month:

Coffee beans	$5,000	Insurance–plant	$ 300
Bags	100	President's salary	4,000
Small tools	80	Engineering labor	1,700
Depreciation–plant	400	Utilities	1,250
Depreciation–grinder	200	Building occupancy	1,940
Direct labor	1,000	Supervision	400
Indirect labor	300	Operating supplies	205
Labels	20	Repairs and maintenance	120
Materials handling	75	Employee benefits	500

Required

1. Identify each cost as direct or indirect, assuming that it was incurred in a traditional manufacturing setting.
2. Identify each cost as direct or indirect, assuming that it was incurred in a just-in-time (JIT) environment.
3. Assume that the costs incurred in the JIT environment are for a work cell that completed 5,000 1-pound bags of coffee during the month. Compute the total direct cost and the direct cost per unit for the bags produced.

LO4 Backflush Costing

P10. Reilly Corporation produces metal fasteners using six work cells, one for each of its product lines. It implemented just-in-time operations and costing methods two years ago. Overhead is assigned using a rate of $14 per machine hour for the Machine Snap Work Cell. There were no beginning inventories on April 1. All direct materials and purchased parts are used as they are received. Operating details for April for the Machine Snap Work Cell are as follows:

Cost of direct materials purchased on account and used	$104,500
Cost of parts purchased on account and used	$78,900
Direct labor costs incurred	$39,000
Overhead costs assigned	?
Machine hours used	12,220
Costs of goods completed during April	$392,540
Ending work in process inventory	$940
Ending finished goods inventory	$1,020

Required

1. Using T accounts, show the flow of costs through a backflush costing system.
2. Using T accounts, show the flow of costs through a traditional costing system.
3. What is the total cost of goods sold for April using a traditional costing system?

ENHANCING Your Knowledge, Skills, and Critical Thinking

LO1 LO2 **ABM and ABC in a Service Business**

C 1. MUF, a CPA firm, has provided audit and tax services to businesses in the London area for over 50 years. Recently, the firm decided to use ABM and activity-based costing to assign its overhead costs to those service functions. Gemma Fior is interested in seeing how the change from the traditional to the activity-based costing approach affects the average cost per audit job. The following information has been provided to assist in the comparison:

Total direct labor costs	£400,000
Other direct costs	120,000
Total direct costs	£520,000

The traditional costing approach assigned overhead costs at a rate of 120 percent of direct labor costs.

Data for activity-based costing of the audit function are as follows:

Activity	Cost Driver	Activity Cost Rate	Activity Usage
Professional development	Number of employees	£2,000 per employee	50 employees
Administration	Number of jobs	£1,000 per job	50 jobs
Client development	Number of new clients	£5,000 per new client	29 new clients

1. Using direct labor cost as the cost driver, calculate the total costs for the audit function. What is the average cost per job?
2. Using activity-based costing to assign overhead, calculate the total costs for the audit function. What is the average cost per job?
3. Calculate the difference in total costs between the two approaches. Why would activity-based costing be the better approach for assigning overhead to the audit function?
4. Your instructor will divide the class into groups to work through the case. One student from each group should present the group's findings to the class.

LO2 **ABC and Selling and Administrative Expenses**

C 2. Sandee Star, the owner of Star Bakery, wants to know the profitability of each of her bakery's customer groups. She is especially interested in the State Institutions customer group, which is one of the company's largest. Currently, the bakery is selling doughnuts and snack foods to ten state institutions in three states. The controller has prepared the following income statement for the State Institutions customer group:

Star Bakery
Income Statement for State Institutions Customer Group
For the Year Ended December 31

Sales ($5 per case × 50,000 cases)	$250,000
Cost of goods sold ($3.50 per case × 50,000 cases)	175,000
Gross margin	$ 75,000
Less: Selling and administrative activity costs	94,750
Operating income (loss) contributed by State Institutions customer group	($ 19,750)

Activity	Activity Cost Rate	Actual Cost Driver Level	Activity Cost
Make sales calls	$60 per sales call	60 sales calls	$ 3,600
Prepare sales orders	10 per sales order	900 sales orders	9,000
Handle inquiries	5 per minute	1,000 minutes	5,000
Ship products	1 per case sold	50,000 cases	50,000
Process invoices	20 per invoice	950 invoices	19,000
Process credits	20 per notice	40 notices	800
Process billings and collections	7 per billing	1,050 billings	7,350
Total selling and administrative activity costs			$94,750

The controller has also provided budgeted information about selling and administrative activities for the State Institutions customer group. For this year, the planned activity cost rates and the annual cost driver levels for each selling and administrative activity are as follows:

Activity	Planned Activity Cost Rate	Planned Annual Cost Driver Level
Make sales calls	$60 per sales call	59 sales calls
Prepare sales orders	10 per sales order	850 sales orders
Handle inquiries	5.10 per minute	1,000 minutes
Ship products	0.60 per case sold	50,000 cases
Process invoices	1 per invoice	500 invoices
Process credits	10 per notice	5 notices
Process billings and collections	4 per billing	600 billings

You have been called in as a consultant on the State Institutions customer group.

1. Calculate the planned activity cost for each activity.
2. Calculate the differences between the planned activity cost and the State Institutions customer group's activity costs for this year.
3. From your evaluation of the differences calculated in **2** and your review of the income statement, identify the non-value-adding activities and state which selling and administrative activities should be examined.
4. What actions might the company take to reduce the costs of non-value-adding selling and administrative activities?

LO2 **ABC in Planning and Control**

C 3. Refer to the income statement in **C 2** for the State Institutions customer group for the year ended December 31, this year. Sandee Star, the owner of Star Bakery, is in the process of budgeting income for next year. She has asked the controller to prepare a budgeted income statement for the State Institutions customer group. She estimates that the selling price per case, the number of cases sold, the cost of goods sold per case, and the activity costs for making sales calls, preparing sales orders, and handling inquiries will remain the same for next year. She has contracted with a new freight company to ship the 50,000 cases at $0.60 per case sold. She has also analyzed the procedures for invoicing, processing credits, billing, and collecting and has decided that it would be less expensive for a customer service agency to do the work. The agency will charge the bakery 1.5 percent of the total sales revenue.

1. Prepare a budgeted income statement for the State Institutions customer group for next year; the year ends December 31.
2. Refer to the information in **C 2.** Assuming that the planned activity cost rate and planned annual cost driver level for each selling and administrative activity remain the same next year, calculate the planned activity cost for each activity.
3. Calculate the differences between the planned activity costs (determined in **2**) and the State Institutions customer group's budgeted activity costs for next year (determined in **1**).
4. Evaluate the results of changing freight companies and outsourcing the customer service activities.

LO3 **Lean in a Service Business**

C 4. The initiation banquet for new members of your business club is being held at an excellent restaurant. You are sitting next to two college students who are majoring in marketing. In discussing the accounting course they are taking, they mention that they are having difficulty understanding the lean philosophy. They have read that the elements of a company's operating system support the concepts of simplicity, continuous improvement, waste reduction, timeliness, and efficiency. They realize that to understand lean thinking in a complex manufacturing environment, they must first understand lean in a simpler context. They ask you to explain the philosophy and provide an example.

Briefly explain the lean philosophy. Apply the elements of a JIT operating system to the restaurant where the banquet is being held. Do you believe the lean philosophy applies in all restaurant operations? Explain your answer.

LO3 **Activities, Cost Drivers, and JIT**

C 5. Fifteen years ago, Bruce Sable, together with 10 financial supporters, founded Sable Corporation. Located in Atlanta, the company originally manufactured roller skates, but 12 years ago, on the advice of its marketing department, it switched to making skateboards. More than 4 million skateboards later, Sable Corporation finds itself an industry leader in both volume and quality. To retain market share, it has decided to automate its manufacturing process. It has ordered flexible manufacturing systems for wheel assembly and board shaping. Manual operations will be retained for board decorating because some hand painting is involved. All operations will be converted to a just-in-time environment.

Bruce Sable wants to know how the JIT approach will affect the company's product costing practices and has called you in as a consultant.

1. Summarize the elements of a JIT environment.
2. How will the automated systems change product costing?
3. What are some cost drivers that the company should employ? In what situations should it employ them?

LO1 LO2 LO3 LO5

Cookie Company (Continuing Case)

C 6. As we continue with this case, assume that your company has been using a continuous manufacturing process to make chocolate chip cookies. Demand has been so great that the company has built a special plant that makes only custom-ordered cookies. The cookies are shaped by machines but vary according to the customer's specific instructions. Ten basic sizes of cookies are produced and then customized. Slight variations in machine setup produce the different sizes.

In the past six months, several problems have developed. Even though a computer-controlled machine is used in the manufacturing process, the company's backlog is growing rapidly, and customers are complaining that delivery is too slow. Quality is declining because cookies are being pushed through production without proper inspection. Working capital is tied up in excessive amounts of inventory and storage space. Workers are complaining about the pressure to produce the backlogged orders. Machine breakdowns are increasing. Production control reports are not useful because they are not timely and contain irrelevant information. The company's profitability and cash flow are suffering.

Assume that you have been appointed CEO and that the company has asked you to analyze its problems. The board of directors asks that you complete your preliminary analysis quickly so that you can present it to the board at its midyear meeting.

1. In memo form, prepare a preliminary report recommending specific changes in the manufacturing processes.
2. In preparing the report, answer the following questions:
   a. Why are you preparing the report? What is its purpose?
   b. Who is the audience for this report?
   c. What kinds of information do you need to prepare the report, and where will you find it (i.e., what sources will you use)?
   d. When do you need to obtain the information?

CHAPTER

23 Cost Behavior Analysis

The Management Process

PLAN

- ▷ **Identify cost behavior as either a variable, fixed, or mixed cost**
- ▷ **Use cost formulas to develop business plans and budgets**

PERFORM

- ▷ **Record actual cost and sales data**
- ▷ **Prepare scattergraphs to verify cost behavior classifications**
- ▷ **Develop cost formulas based on actual cost data using one or more methods**
- ▷ **Determine the relevant range of the cost formula**
- ▷ **Compute breakeven for single products or a mix of products**

EVALUATE

- ▷ **Assess what-ifs and profit projections using C-V-P analysis**
- ▷ **Determine if C-V-P assumptions are true**

COMMUNICATE

- ▷ **Prepare external reports that summarize performance**
- ▷ **Prepare contribution margin income statements for internal use**

Analysis of cost behavior is important not only in achieving profitability but also in using resources wisely.

Knowing how costs will behave is essential for managers as they chart their organization's course. Managers commonly analyze alternative courses of action using cost behavior information so they can select the course that will best generate income for an organization's owners, maintain liquidity for its creditors, and use the organization's resources responsibly.

LEARNING OBJECTIVES

LO1 Define *cost behavior*, and identify variable, fixed, and mixed costs. (pp. 1000–1005)

LO2 Separate mixed costs into their variable and fixed components, and prepare a contribution margin income statement. (pp. 1006–1010)

LO3 Define *cost-volume-profit (C-V-P) analysis*, and discuss how managers use it as a tool for planning and control. (pp. 1010–1012)

LO4 Define *breakeven point*, and use contribution margin to determine a company's breakeven point for multiple products. (pp. 1012–1016)

LO5 Use C-V-P analysis to project the profitability of products and services. (pp. 1017–1020)

DECISION POINT ▸ A MANAGER'S FOCUS MY MEDIA PLACE

My Media Place designs and sells websites to small businesses and individuals. It also provides a number of services, including website setups, and sells related networking products. Although relatively new, the company has been successful, and it is now thinking about expanding the range of products and services that it offers. In deciding whether to expand the company's offerings, the managers of My Media Place have to evaluate the mix of products and services that would appeal to customers and that would allow the company to optimize its resources and profits. In this chapter, we describe how managers in any company make such an evaluation.

- ▸ How will My Media Place's managers decide which products and services to offer?
- ▸ Why do managers analyze cost behavior?

Cost Behavior and Management

LO1 Define *cost behavior*, and identify variable, fixed, and mixed costs.

Cost behavior—the way costs respond to changes in volume or activity—is a factor in almost every decision managers make. Managers commonly use it to analyze alternative courses of action so they can select the course that will best generate income for an organization's owners, use resources wisely, and maintain liquidity for its creditors. The management process described on the first page of this chapter explains how managers use cost behavior when they plan, perform, evaluate, and communicate.

Service businesses like **Flickr**, **Facebook**, and **Google** find cost behavior analyses useful when planning the optimal mix of services to offer. For example, Google's managers analyze cost behavior of new features for products like Gmail in their online Google Labs to gather user data and feedback before officially deciding to add a new feature.

During the year, managers collect cost behavior data and use it in decision making. Managers must understand and anticipate cost behavior to determine the impact of their actions on operating income and resource optimization. For example, Google's managers must understand the changes in income that can result from buying new, more productive servers or launching an online advertising product like AdWords or AdSense.

When evaluating operations and preparing reports for various product or service lines or geographic regions, managers in all types of organizations use reports to analyze how changes in cost and sales affect the profitability of product lines, sales territories, customers, departments, and other segments.

Although our focus in this chapter is on cost behavior as it relates to products and services, cost behavior can also be observed in selling, administrative, and general activities. For example, increases in the number of shipments affect shipping costs; the number of units sold or total sales revenue affects the cost of sales commissions; and the number of customers billed affects total billing costs. If managers can predict how costs behave, whether they are product- or service-related or are for selling, administrative, or general activities, then costs become manageable.

FOCUS ON BUSINESS PRACTICE

A Different Kind of Company

Google's informal motto is simple: "Don't be evil." In the preface to its Code of Conduct, Google states that "being a different kind of company" depends on employees' applying the company's core values "in all aspects of [their] lives as Google employees."[1]

The company's Code of Conduct provides ethical guidelines in the following areas:

- Serving users
- Respecting each other
- Avoiding conflicts of interest
- Preserving confidentiality
- Maintaining books and records
- Protecting Google's assets
- Obeying the law

The Behavior of Costs

Some costs vary with volume or operating activity (variable costs). Others remain fixed as volume changes (fixed costs). Between those two extremes are costs that exhibit characteristics of each type (mixed costs).

> **Study Note**
> Variable costs change in *direct proportion* to changes in activity; that is, they increase *in total* with an increase in volume and decrease *in total* with a decrease in volume, but they remain the same on a *per unit* basis.

Variable Costs Total costs that change in direct proportion to changes in productive output (or any other measure of volume) are called **variable costs**. In a previous chapter we referred to them as unit-level activities since the cost is incurred each time a unit is produced or a service is delivered. For example, direct materials, direct labor, operating supplies, and gasoline are variable costs.

Total variable cost costs go up or down as volume increases or decreases, but the cost per unit remains unchanged, as demonstrated by the linear relationship between direct labor and units produced in Figure 23-1. Notice the relationship graphs as a straight line. In the figure, each unit of output requires $2.50 of labor cost. Total labor costs grow in direct proportion to the increase in units of output. For two units, total labor costs are $5.00; for six units, the organization incurs $15.00 in labor costs.

The **variable cost formula** for variable cost behavior is that of a straight line: $Y = a(X)$, where Y is total variable cost, a is the variable rate per unit, and X is the units produced. The cost formula for direct labor in Figure 23-1 is:

Total Direct Labor Costs = $2.50 × Units Produced

Figure 23-2 illustrates other examples of variable costs. All those costs—whether incurred by a manufacturer like **La-Z-Boy** or **Intel**, a service business like **Flickr**, **Facebook**, or **Google**, or a merchandiser like **Wal-Mart**—are variable based on either productive output or total sales.

Because variable costs increase or decrease in direct proportion to volume or output, it is important to know an organization's operating capacity. **Operating capacity** is the upper limit of an organization's productive output capability, given its existing resources. It describes just what an organization can accomplish in a given period. In our discussions, we assume that operating capacity is constant and that all activity occurs within the limits of current operating capacity.

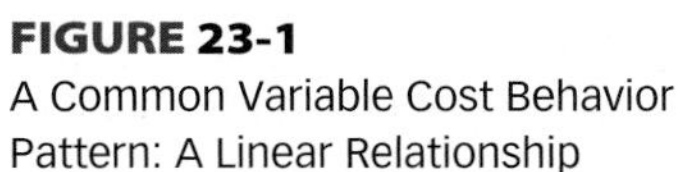

FIGURE 23-1
A Common Variable Cost Behavior Pattern: A Linear Relationship

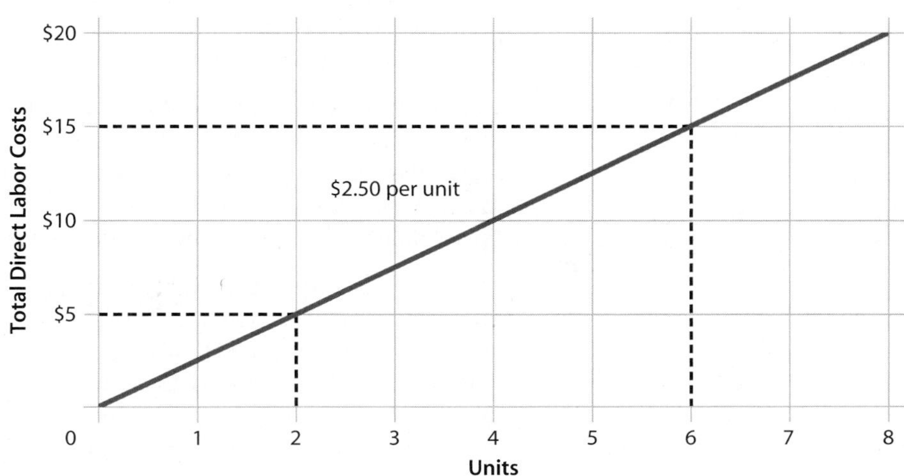

FIGURE 23-2 Examples of Variable, Fixed, and Mixed Costs

Costs	Manufacturing Company—Tire Manufacturer	Merchandising Company—Department Store	Service Company—Bank
VARIABLE	Direct materials Direct labor (hourly) Indirect labor (hourly) Operating supplies Small tools	Merchandise to sell Sales commissions Shelf stockers (hourly)	Computer equipment leasing (based on usage) Computer operators (hourly) Operating supplies Data storage disks
FIXED	Depreciation, machinery and building Insurance premiums Labor (salaried) Supervisory salaries Property taxes (on machinery and building)	Depreciation, equipment and building Insurance premiums Buyers (salaried) Supervisory salaries Property taxes (on equipment and building)	Depreciation, furniture and fixtures Insurance premiums Salaries: Programmers Systems designers Bank administrators Rent, buildings
MIXED	Electrical power Telephone Heat	Electrical power Telephone Heat	Electrical power Telephone Heat

There are three common measures, or types, of operating capacity: theoretical, or ideal, capacity; practical capacity; and normal capacity.

- **Theoretical (ideal) capacity** is the maximum productive output for a given period in which all machinery and equipment are operating at optimum speed, without interruption. No company ever actually operates at such an ideal level.
- **Practical capacity** is theoretical capacity reduced by normal and expected work stoppages, such as machine breakdowns; downtime for retooling, repairs, and maintenance; and employees' breaks. Practical capacity is sometimes called *engineering capacity* and is used primarily as a planning goal of what could be produced if all went well, but no company ever actually operates at such a level.
- **Normal capacity** is the average annual level of operating capacity needed to meet expected sales demand. Normal capacity is the realistic measure of what an organization is *likely* to produce, not what it *can* produce. Thus, each variable cost should be related to an appropriate measure of normal capacity. For example, operating costs can be related to machine hours used or total units produced and sales commissions usually vary in direct proportion to total sales dollars.

Study Note

An activity base is often called *denominator activity or cost driver*; it is the activity for which relationships are established. The basic relationships should not change greatly if activity fluctuates around the level of denominator activity.

The basis for measuring the activity of variable costs should be carefully selected for two reasons:

- First, an appropriate activity base simplifies cost planning and control.
- Second, managers must combine (aggregate) many variable costs with the same activity base so that the costs can be analyzed in a reasonable way. Such aggregation also provides information that allows management to predict future costs.

The general guide for selecting an activity base is to relate costs to their most logical or causal factor. For example, direct material and direct labor costs should be considered variable in relation to the number of units produced.

Study Note

Because fixed costs are expected to hold relatively constant over the entire relevant range of activity, they can be described as the costs of providing capacity.

Fixed Costs **Fixed costs** behave very differently from variable costs. Fixed costs are total costs that remain constant within a relevant range of volume or activity. **Relevant range** is the span of activity in which a company expects to operate. Within the relevant range, it is assumed that both total fixed costs and per unit variable costs are constant. In a previous chapter we referred to fixed costs as facility-level activities. Look back at Figure 23-2 for examples of fixed costs. The manufacturer, the department store, and the bank all incur depreciation costs and fixed annual insurance premiums. In addition, all salaried personnel have fixed earnings for a particular period. The manufacturer and the department store own their buildings and pay annual property taxes, and the bank pays an annual fixed rental charge for the use of its building.

Study Note

Cost behavior is closely linked to the concept of cost control. In the short run, it is generally easier to control variable costs than fixed costs.

According to economic theory, all costs tend to be variable in the long run; thus, as the examples in Figure 23-2 suggest, a cost is fixed only within a limited period. A change in plant capacity, labor needs, or other production factors causes fixed costs to increase or decrease. Management usually considers a one-year period when planning and controlling costs; thus fixed costs are expected to be constant within that period.

Of course, fixed costs change when activity exceeds the relevant range. These costs are called *step costs* or *step-variable*, *step-fixed*, or *semifixed costs*. A **step cost** remains constant in a relevant range of activity and increases or decreases in a step-like manner when activity is outside the relevant range.

For example, assume that one Customer Support Team at My Media Place, the company discussed in the Decision Point, has the capacity to handle up to 500,000 customer incidents per 8-hour shift. The relevant range, then, is from 0 to 500,000 units. Unfortunately, volume has increased to more than 500,000 incidents per 8-hour shift, taxing current equipment capacity and the quality of customer care. My Media Place must add another Customer Support Team to handle the additional volume. Figure 23-3 shows this behavior pattern. The fixed costs for the first 500,000 units of production are $4,000. Those costs hold steady at $4,000 for any level of output within the relevant range. But if output goes above 500,000 units, another team must be added, pushing fixed costs to $8,000.

Fixed cost behavior expressed mathematically in the **fixed cost formula** is a horizontal line in the relevant range: $Y = b$, where Y is total fixed cost and b is the fixed cost in the relevant range. The fixed cost formula for up to 500,000 units in Figure 23-3 is:

Total Fixed Costs = $4,000

On a per unit basis, fixed costs go down as volume goes up, as long as a firm is operating within the relevant range of activity. Look at how the Customer

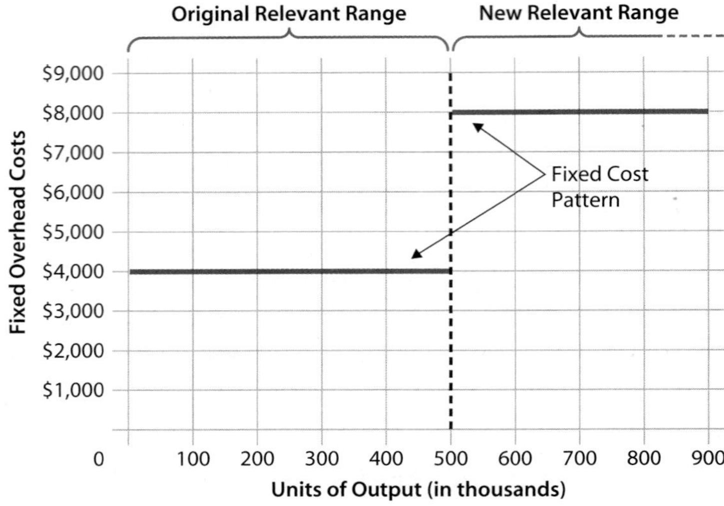

FIGURE 23-3
A Common Step-Like Fixed Cost Behavior Pattern

Support Team costs per unit fall as the volume of activity increases within the relevant range:

Volume of Activity	*Support Team Cost per Unit*
100,000 units	$4,000 ÷ 100,000 = $0.0400
300,000 units	$4,000 ÷ 300,000 = $0.0133*
500,000 units	$4,000 ÷ 500,000 = $0.0080
600,000 units	$8,000 ÷ 600,000 = $0.0133*

*Rounded.

At 600,000 units, the activity level is above the relevant range, which means another team must be added; thus, the per unit cost changes to $0.0133.

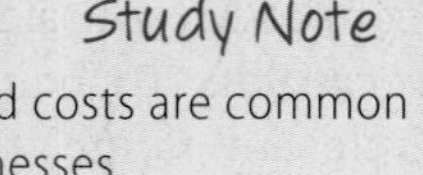

Study Note
Mixed costs are common in businesses.

Mixed Costs **Mixed costs** have both variable and fixed cost components. Part of a mixed cost changes with volume or usage, and part is fixed over a particular period.

- Look back at Figure 23-2 for examples of mixed costs. The manufacturer, the department store, and the bank all incur electric, telephone, and heat costs that have both variable and fixed cost components. For example, electric costs include charges per kilowatt-hour used plus a basic monthly service charge. The kilowatt-hour charges are variable because they depend on the amount of use; the monthly service charge is a fixed cost.

Figure 23-4 depicts an organization's total electricity costs. The monthly bill begins with a fixed service charge and increases as kilowatt-hours are consumed.

FIGURE 23-4
Behavior Patterns of Mixed Costs

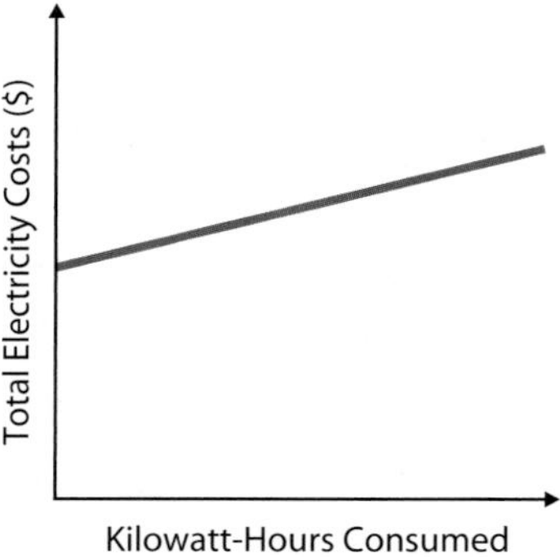

FIGURE 23-5
The Relevant Range and Linear Approximation

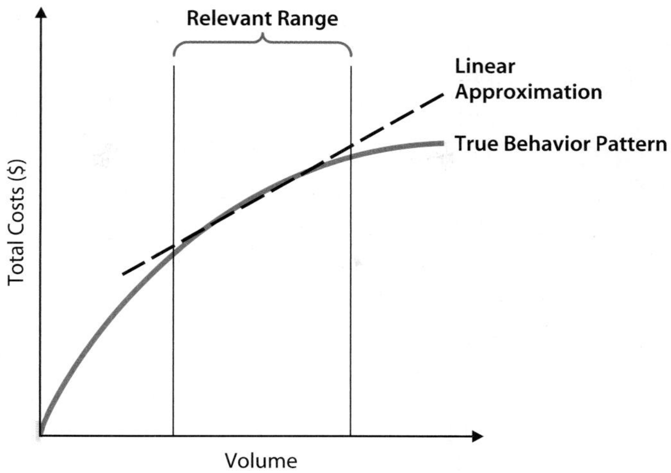

Mixed cost behavior is expressed mathematically in the **mixed cost formula**, which is the linear equation $Y = a(X) + b$, where Y is total mixed cost, a the variable rate per unit, X the units produced, and b the fixed cost for the period.

Study Note

Nonlinear costs can be roughly estimated by treating them as if they were linear (variable) costs within set limits of volume.

Many mixed costs vary with operating activity in a nonlinear fashion. To simplify cost analysis procedures and make mixed costs easier to use, accountants have developed a method of converting nonlinear costs into linear ones. Called *linear approximation*, this method relies on the concept of relevant range. Under that concept, many nonlinear costs can be estimated using the linear approximation approach illustrated in Figure 23-5. Those estimated costs can then be treated as part of the other variable and fixed costs.

A linear approximation of a nonlinear cost is not a precise measure, but it allows the inclusion of nonlinear costs in cost behavior analysis, and the loss of accuracy is usually not significant. The goal is to help management estimate costs and prepare budgets, and linear approximation helps accomplish that goal.

STOP & APPLY >

Indicate whether each of the following costs is usually variable (V) or fixed (F):

1. Operating supplies
2. Real estate taxes
3. Gasoline for a delivery truck
4. Property insurance
5. Depreciation expense of computers (calculated with the straight-line method)
6. Depreciation expense of machinery (calculated with the units-of-production method)

SOLUTION

1. V; 2. F; 3. V; 4. F; 5. F; 6. V

Mixed Costs and the Contribution Margin Income Statement

LO2 Separate mixed costs into their variable and fixed components, and prepare a contribution margin income statement.

For cost planning and control purposes, mixed costs must be divided into their variable and fixed components. The separate components can then be grouped with other variable and fixed costs for analysis. Four methods are commonly used to separate mixed cost components: the engineering, scatter diagram, high-low, and statistical methods.

- Because the results yielded by each of these four methods are likely to differ, managers often use multiple approaches to find the best possible estimate for a mixed cost.

The Engineering Method

The **engineering method** is used to separate costs into their fixed and variable components by performing a step-by-step analysis of the tasks, costs, and processes involved. This type of analysis is sometimes called a *time and motion study*. The engineering method is expensive because it is so detailed, and it is generally used to estimate the cost of activities or new products. For example, the U.S. Postal Service conducts periodic audits of how many letters a postal worker should be able to deliver on a particular mail route within a certain period.

The Scatter Diagram Method

Study Note

A scatter diagram shows how closely volume and costs are correlated. A tight, closely associated group of data is better suited to linear approximation than a random or circular pattern of data points.

When there is doubt about the behavior pattern of a particular cost, especially a mixed cost, it helps to plot past costs and related measures of volume in a scatter diagram. A **scatter diagram** is a chart of plotted points that helps determine whether a linear relationship exists between a cost item and its related activity measure. It is a form of linear approximation. If the diagram suggests a linear relationship, a cost line can be imposed on the data by either visual means or statistical analysis. For example, suppose that My Media Place incurred the following machine hours and electricity costs last year:

Month	*Machine Hours*	*Electricity Costs*
January	6,250	$ 24,000
February	6,300	24,200
March	6,350	24,350
April	6,400	24,600
May	6,300	24,400
June	6,200	24,300
July	6,100	23,900
August	6,050	23,600
September	6,150	23,950
October	6,250	24,100
November	6,350	24,400
December	6,450	24,700
Totals	75,150	$290,500

Figure 23-6 shows a scatter diagram of these data. The diagram suggests a linear relationship between machine hours and the cost of electricity. If we were to add a line to the diagram to represent the linear relationship, the estimated fixed electricity cost would occur at the point at which the line intersects the vertical axis, or $23,200 of fixed monthly electric costs. The variable cost per machine hour can be estimated by determining the slope of the line, much as is done in Step 1 of the high-low method.

Like most businesses, the U.S. Postal Service is concerned about delivery time. To determine how many deliveries a postal worker should be able to make within a certain period, it conducts periodic audits using the engineering method (a type of analysis that is also known as a time and motion study).

Courtesy of Michelle Malven/ istockphoto.com.

The High-Low Method

The **high-low method** is a common, three-step approach to determining the variable and fixed components of a mixed cost. It is based on the premise that only two data points are necessary to define a linear cost-volume relationship, $Y = a(X) + b$, where Y is total mixed cost, a is the variable rate per unit, X is the volume level, and b is the total fixed cost for the period. It is a relatively crude method since it uses only the high and low data observations to predict cost behavior.

- The disadvantage of this method is that if one or both data points are not representative of the remaining data set, the estimate of variable and fixed costs may not be accurate.
- Its advantage is that it can be used when only limited data are available.

FIGURE 23-6
Scatter Diagram of Machine Hours and Electricity Costs

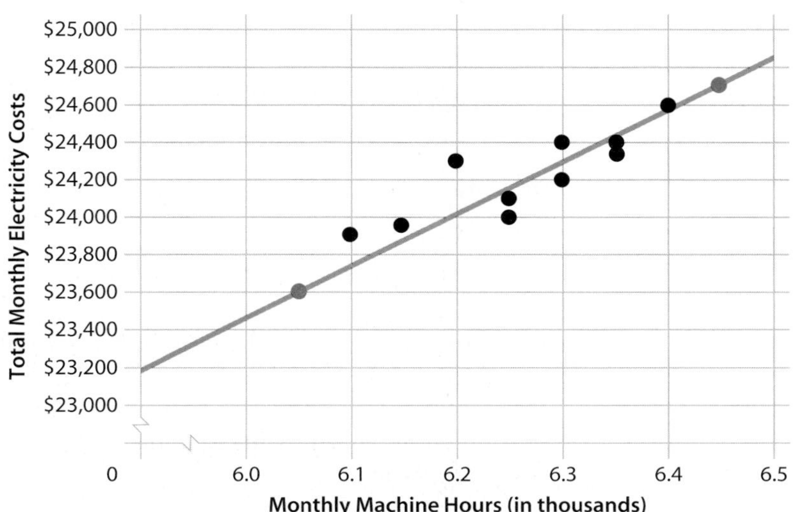

The method involves three steps:

1. Find the variable rate—that is, the *a* in $Y = a(X) + b$.
2. Find the total fixed costs—that is, the *b* in $Y = a(X) + b$.
3. Express the cost formula to estimate total costs within the relevant range:

$$Y = a(X) + b, \text{ or Total Cost} = \text{Variable Rate(Volume Level)} + \text{Fixed Costs}$$

Using My Media Place's last 12 months of machine usage and electric cost data, here is a step-by-step example of how to use the high-low method:

Step 1. *Find the variable rate.*

Study Note

Step 1 is also how you compute the slope of a line, that is, Change in *Y*/Change in *X*.

- Select the periods of highest and lowest activity within the accounting period. In our example, the highest-volume machine-hour month was in December and the lowest was in August.
- Find the difference between the highest and lowest amounts for both the machine hours and their related electricity costs.
- Compute the variable rate, that is, the variable cost per machine hour, by dividing the difference in cost by the difference in machine hours.

Volume	*Month*	*Activity Level (X)*	*Cost (Y)*
High	December	6,450 hours	$24,700
Low	August	6,050 hours	23,600
Difference		400 hours	$ 1,100

$$\begin{aligned}\text{Variable Cost per Machine Hour} &= \$1{,}100 \div 400 \text{ Machine Hours}\\ &= \$2.75 \text{ per Machine Hour}\end{aligned}$$

Step 2. *Find the total fixed costs.* Compute total fixed costs for a month by putting the known variable rate and the information from the month with the highest volume into the cost formula and solve for the total fixed costs:

$$\begin{aligned}\text{Total Fixed Costs} &= \text{Total Costs} - \text{Total Variable Costs}\\ \text{Total Fixed Costs for December} &= \$24{,}700.00 - (6{,}450 \text{ Hours} \times \$2.75)\\ &= \$6{,}962.50\end{aligned}$$

You can check your answer by recalculating total fixed costs using the month with the lowest activity. Total fixed costs will be the same:

$$\begin{aligned}\text{Total Fixed Costs for August} &= \$23{,}600.00 - (6{,}050 \text{ Hours} \times \$2.75)\\ &= \$6{,}962.50\end{aligned}$$

Step 3. *Express the cost formula to estimate the total costs within the relevant range.*

$$\text{Total Electricity Costs per Month} = \$2.75 \text{ per Machine Hour} + \$6{,}962.50$$

Remember that the cost formula will work only within the relevant range. In this example, the formula would work for amounts between 6,050 machine hours and 6,450 machine hours. To estimate the electricity costs for machine hours outside the relevant range (in this case, below 6,050 machine hours or above 6,450 machine hours), a new cost formula must be calculated.

Statistical Methods

Statistical methods, such as **regression analysis**, mathematically describe the relationship between costs and activities and are used to separate mixed costs into variable and fixed components. Because all data observations are used, the resulting linear equation is more representative of cost behavior than either the high-low or scatter diagram methods. Regression analysis can be performed using one or more activities to predict costs. For example, overhead costs can be predicted using only machine hours (a simple regression analysis), or they can be predicted using both machine hours and labor hours (a multiple regression analysis) because both activities affect overhead.

We leave further description of regression analysis to statistics courses, which provide detailed coverage of this method.

Contribution Margin Income Statements

Once an organization's costs are classified as being either variable or fixed, the traditional income statement can be reorganized into a more useful format for internal operations and decision making. Table 23-1 compares the structure of a traditional and a contribution margin income statement (sometimes referred to as a *variable costing income statement*). A **contribution margin income statement** is formatted to emphasize cost behavior rather than organizational functions. **Contribution margin (CM)** is the amount that remains after all variable costs are subtracted from sales. All variable costs related to production, selling, and administration are subtracted from sales to determine the total contribution margin. All fixed costs related to production, selling, and administration are subtracted from the total contribution margin to determine operating income.

▶ Although both statements arrive at the same operating income, the traditional approach divides costs into product and period costs, whereas the contribution margin approach divides costs into variable and fixed costs.

The contribution margin income statement enables managers to view revenue and cost relationships on a per unit basis or as a percentage of sales. If managers understand these relationships as expressed by the contribution margin income statement, then they can determine how many units they must sell to avoid losing money, or what the sales price per unit must be to cover costs, or what their profits will be for a certain dollar amount of sales revenue. In the next section, you will learn about cost-volume-profit analysis as a tool for planning and control. Table 23-2 shows the two ways a contribution margin income statement can be presented.

Table 23-1
Comparison of Income Statements

Traditional Income Statement	Contribution Margin Income Statement
Sales revenue	Sales revenue
– Cost of goods sold, variable	– Cost of goods sold, variable
– Cost of goods sold, fixed	– Operating expenses, variable
= Gross margin	= Contribution margin
– Operating expenses, variable	– Cost of goods sold, fixed
– Operating expenses, fixed	– Operating expenses, fixed
= Operating income	= Operating income

Table 23-2 Contribution Margin Income Statement

	Per unit Relationships	As a Percentage of Sales
Sales revenue	Sales price per unit × Units sold	Sales revenue ÷ Sales revenue
Less variable costs	– Variable rate per unit × Units sold	– Variable costs ÷ Sales revenue
Contribution margin	= Contribution margin per unit × Units sold	= Contribution margin ÷ Sales revenue
Less fixed costs	– Total fixed costs	– Fixed costs
Operating income	= $XXXXX	= Operating income

STOP & APPLY >

Using the high-low method and the following information, compute the monthly variable cost per kilowatt-hour and the monthly fixed electricity cost for a local business. Finally, express the monthly electricity cost formula and its relevant range.

Month	Kilowatt-Hours Used	Electricity Costs
April	90	$450
May	80	430
June	70	420

SOLUTION

Volume	Month	Activity Level	Cost
High	April	90 hours	$450
Low	June	70 hours	420
Difference		20 hours	$ 30

Variable cost per kilowatt-hour = $30 ÷ 20 hours
= $1.50 per hour

Fixed costs for April: $450 − (90 × $1.50) = $315
Fixed costs for June: $420 − (70 × $1.50) = $315

Monthly electricity costs = ($1.50 × Hours) + $315. The cost formula can be used for hourly activity between 70 and 90 hours per month.

Cost-Volume-Profit Analysis

LO3 Define *cost-volume-profit (C-V-P) analysis*, and discuss how managers use it as a tool for planning and control.

Cost-volume-profit (C-V-P) analysis is an examination of the cost behavior patterns that underlie the relationships among cost, volume of output, and profit. C-V-P analysis usually applies to a single product, product line, or division of a company. For that reason, *profit*, which is only part of an entire company's operating income, is the term used in the C-V-P equation. The equation is expressed as

$$\text{Sales Revenue} - \text{Variable Costs} - \text{Fixed Costs} = \text{Profit}$$
$$S - VC - FC = P$$

Study Note

One of the important benefits of C-V-P analysis is that it allows managers to adjust different variables and to evaluate how these changes affect profit.

or as

$$\text{Sales Price(Units Sold)} - \text{Variable Rate(Units Sold)} - \text{Fixed Costs} = \text{Profit}$$
$$\text{SP}(X) - \text{VR}(X) - \text{FC} = \text{P}$$

For example, suppose My Media Place wants to make a profit of \$50,000 on one of its services. The service sells for \$95.50 per unit and has variable costs of \$80 per unit. If 4,000 units are sold during the period, what were the fixed costs? Use the equation $\text{SP}(X) - \text{VR}(X) - \text{FC} = \text{P}$ to solve for the unknown fixed costs.

$$\$95.50(4{,}000) - \$80(4{,}000) - \text{FC} = \$50{,}000$$
$$\$382{,}000 - \$320{,}000 - \text{FC} = \$50{,}000$$
$$\text{FC} = \$12{,}000$$

In cases involving the income statement of an entire company, the term *operating income* is more appropriate than *profit*. In the context of C-V-P analysis, however, *profit* and *operating income* mean the same thing.

C-V-P analysis is a tool for both planning and control. The techniques and the problem-solving procedures involved in the process express relationships among revenue, sales mix, cost, volume, and profit. Those relationships provide a general model of financial activity that managers can use for short-range planning and for evaluating performance and analyzing alternative courses of action.

For planning, managers can use C-V-P analysis to calculate net income when sales volume is known, or they can determine the level of sales needed to reach a targeted amount of net income. C-V-P analysis is used extensively in budgeting as well, and is also a way of measuring how well an organization's departments are performing. At the end of a period, sales volume and related actual costs are analyzed to find actual net income. A department's performance is measured by comparing actual costs with expected costs—costs that have been computed by applying C-V-P analysis to actual sales volume. The result is a performance report on which managers can base the control of operations.

In addition, managers use C-V-P analysis to measure the effects of alternative courses of action, such as changing variable or fixed costs, expanding or contracting sales volume, and increasing or decreasing selling prices. C-V-P analysis is useful in making decisions about product pricing, product mix (when an organization makes more than one product or offers more than one service), adding or dropping a product line, and accepting special orders.

C-V-P analysis has many applications, all of which managers use to plan and control operations effectively. However, it is useful only under certain conditions and only when certain assumptions hold true. Those conditions and assumptions are as follows:

1. The behavior of variable and fixed costs can be measured accurately.
2. Costs and revenues have a close linear approximation throughout the relevant range. For example, if costs rise, revenues rise proportionately.
3. Efficiency and productivity hold steady within the relevant range of activity.
4. Cost and price variables also hold steady during the period being planned.
5. The sales mix does not change during the period being planned.
6. Production and sales volume are roughly equal.

If one or more of these conditions and assumptions are absent, the C-V-P analysis may be misleading.

STOP & APPLY >

A local business wants to make a profit of $10,000 each month. It has variable costs of $5 per unit and fixed costs of $20,000 per month. How much must it charge per unit if 6,000 units are sold?

SOLUTION

Using the equation SP(X) − VR(X) − FC = P to set up and solve for the unknown sales price:

$$\text{SP}(6{,}000) - \$5(6{,}000) - \$20{,}000 = \$10{,}000$$

$$\text{SP} = \frac{\$5(6{,}000) + \$20{,}000 + \$10{,}000}{6{,}000 \text{ Units}} = \frac{\$60{,}000}{6{,}000} = \$10 \text{ per Unit}$$

Breakeven Analysis

LO4 Define *breakeven point,* and use contribution margin to determine a company's breakeven point for multiple products.

Breakeven analysis uses the basic elements of cost-volume-profit relationships. The **breakeven point** is the point at which total revenues equal total costs. It is thus the point at which an organization can begin to earn a profit. When a new venture or product line is being planned, the likelihood of the project's success can be quickly measured by finding its breakeven point. If, for instance, the breakeven point is 24,000 units and the total market is only 25,000 units, the margin of safety would be very low, and the idea should be considered carefully. The **margin of safety** is the number of sales units or amount of sales dollars by which actual sales can fall below planned sales without resulting in a loss—in this example, 1,000 units.

Sales (S), variable costs (VC), and fixed costs (FC) are used to compute the breakeven point, which can be stated in terms of sales units or sales dollars. The general equation for finding the breakeven point is as follows:

$$\text{S} - \text{VC} - \text{FC} = \$0$$

Or as

$$\text{SP}(X) - \text{VR}(X) - \text{FC} = \$0$$

Suppose, for example, that one of the services My Media Place sells is website setups. Variable costs are $50 per unit, and fixed costs average $20,000 per year. A unit is a basic website setup which sells for $90.

- ***Breakeven in sales units:*** Given this information, we can compute the breakeven point for website setup services in sales units (X equals sales units):

$$\begin{aligned} \text{S} - \text{VC} - \text{FC} &= \$0 \\ \$90X - \$50X - \$20{,}000 &= \$0 \\ \$40X &= \$20{,}000 \\ X &= 500 \text{ Units} \end{aligned}$$

- ***Breakeven in sales dollars:*** We can also compute breakeven in sales dollars since sales price multiplied by breakeven in sales units equals breakeven in sales dollars:

$$\$90 \times 500 \text{ Units} = \$45{,}000$$

- ***Breakeven by scatter diagram:*** In addition, we can make a rough estimate of the breakeven point using a scatter diagram. This method is less exact, but it does yield meaningful data. Figure 23-7 shows a breakeven graph for My Media Place. As you can see there, the graph has five parts:

  1. A horizontal axis for units of output
  2. A vertical axis for dollars
  3. A line running horizontally from the vertical axis at the level of fixed costs
  4. A total cost line that begins at the point where the fixed cost line crosses the vertical axis and slopes upward to the right (The slope of the line depends on the variable cost per unit.)
  5. A total revenue line that begins at the origin of the vertical and horizontal axes and slopes upward to the right (The slope depends on the selling price per unit.)

At the point at which the total revenue line crosses the total cost line, revenues equal total costs. The breakeven point, stated in either sales units or dollars of sales, is found by extending broken lines from this point to the axes. As Figure 23-7 shows, My Media Place will break even when it has sold 500 website setups for $45,000.

Study Note

Contribution margin equals sales minus variable costs, whereas gross margin equals sales minus the cost of goods sold.

Using an Equation to Determine the Breakeven Point

A simpler method of determining the breakeven point uses contribution margin in an equation. You will recall from the contribution margin income statement that the contribution margin (CM) is the amount that remains after all variable costs are subtracted from sales:

$$S - VC = CM$$

FIGURE 23-7
Graphic Breakeven Analysis for My Media Place

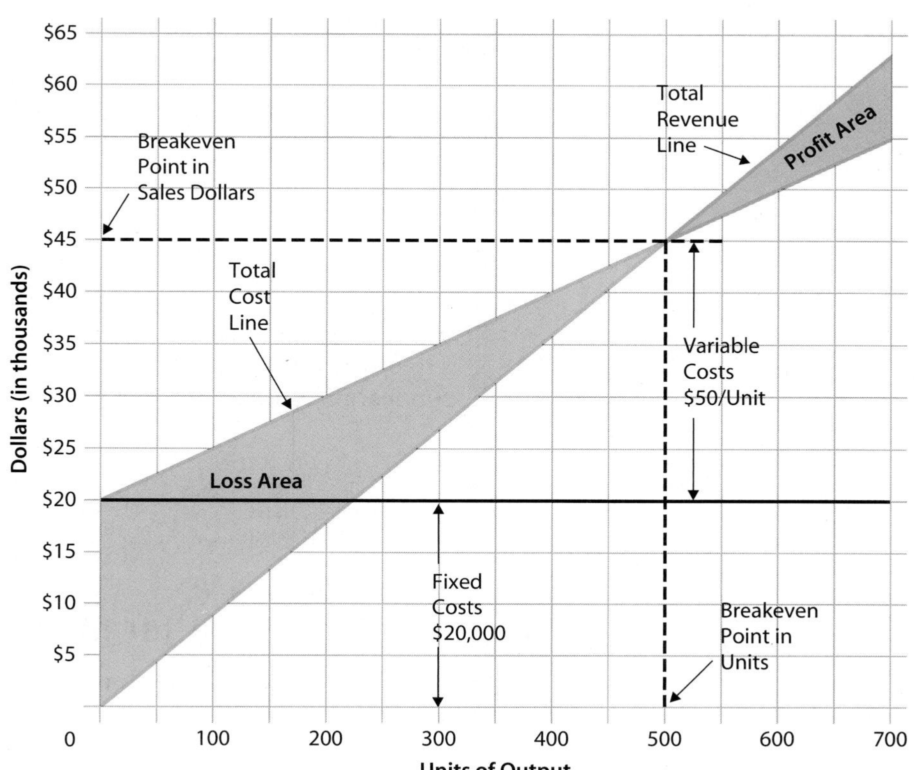

Study Note

The maximum contribution a unit of product or service can make is its selling price. After paying for itself (variable costs), a product or service provides a contribution margin to help pay total fixed costs and then earn a profit.

A product line's contribution margin represents its net contribution to paying off fixed costs and earning a profit. Profit (P) is what remains after fixed costs are paid and subtracted from the contribution margin:

$$\text{CM} - \text{FC} = \text{P}$$

The example that follows uses the contribution margin income statement approach to organize the facts and to determine the profitability of one of My Media Place's products.

		Units Produced and Sold		
Symbols		**250**	**500**	**750**
S	Sales revenue ($90 per unit)	$22,500	$45,000	$67,500
VC	Less variable costs ($50 per unit)	12,500	25,000	37,500
CM	Contribution margin ($40 per unit)	$10,000	$20,000	$30,000
FC	Less fixed costs	20,000	20,000	20,000
P	Profit (loss)	($10,000)	$ 0	$10,000

The breakeven point (BE) can be expressed as the point at which contribution margin minus total fixed costs equals zero (or the point at which contribution margin equals total fixed costs).

- ***Breakeven in sales units:*** In terms of units of product, the equation for the breakeven point looks like this:

$$(\text{CM per Unit} \times \text{BE Units}) - \text{FC} = \$0$$

It can also be expressed like this:

$$\text{BE Units} = \frac{\text{FC}}{\text{CM per unit}}$$

To show how the formula works, we use the data for My Media Place:

$$\text{BE Units} = \frac{\text{FC}}{\text{CM per unit}} = \frac{\$20{,}000}{\$90 - \$50} = \frac{\$20{,}000}{\$40} = 500 \text{ Units}$$

- ***Breakeven in sales dollars:*** The breakeven point in total sales dollars may be determined by multiplying the breakeven point in units by the selling price (SP) per unit:

$$\text{BE Dollars} = \text{SP} \times \text{BE Units} = \$90 \times 500 \text{ Units} = \$45{,}000$$

  - An alternative way of determining the breakeven point in total sales dollars is to divide the fixed costs by the contribution margin ratio. The contribution margin ratio is the contribution margin divided by the selling price:

$$\text{CM Ratio} = \frac{\text{CM}}{\text{SP}} = \frac{\$40}{\$90} = 0.444^*, \text{ or } 4/9$$

$$\text{BE Dollars} = \frac{\text{FC}}{\text{CM Ratio}} = \frac{\$20{,}000}{0.444} = \$45{,}045^*$$

The Breakeven Point for Multiple Products

To satisfy the needs of different customers, most companies sell a variety of products or services that often have different variable and fixed costs and different

*Rounded.

Study Note

A company's sales mix can be very dynamic. If the mix is constantly changing, an assumption of stability may undermine the C-V-P analysis.

selling prices. To calculate the breakeven point for each product, its unit contribution margin must be weighted by the sales mix. The **sales mix** is the proportion of each product's unit sales relative to the company's total unit sales.

Let's assume that My Media Place sells two types of websites: standard and express. If the company sells 500 units, of which 300 units are standard and 200 are express, the sales mix would be 3:2. For every three standard websites sold, two express websites are sold. The sales mix can also be stated in percentages. Of the 500 units sold, 60 percent (300 ÷ 500) are standard sales, and 40 percent (200 ÷ 500) are express sales (see Figure 23-8).

The breakeven point for multiple products can be computed in three steps:

1. Compute the weighted-average contribution margin.
2. Calculate the weighted-average breakeven point.
3. Calculate the breakeven point for each product.

To illustrate, we will use My Media Place's sales mix of 60 percent standard websites to 40 percent express websites and total fixed costs of $32,000; the selling price, variable cost, and contribution margin per unit for each product line are shown in Step 1 below.

Step 1. *Compute the weighted-average contribution margin.* To do so, multiply the contribution margin for each product by its percentage of the sales mix, as follows:

	Selling Price		*Variable Costs*		*Contribution Margin (CM)*		*Percentage of Sales Mix*		*Weighted-Average CM*
Standard	$90	−	$50	=	$40	×	60%	=	$24
Express	$40	−	$20	=	$20	×	40%	=	8
Weighted-average contribution margin									$32

Step 2. *Calculate the weighted-average breakeven point.* Divide total fixed costs by the weighted-average contribution margin:

Weighted-Average Breakeven Point = Total Fixed Costs ÷ Weighted-Average Contribution Margin
= $32,000 ÷ $32
= 1,000 Units

FIGURE 23-8
Sales Mix for My Media Place

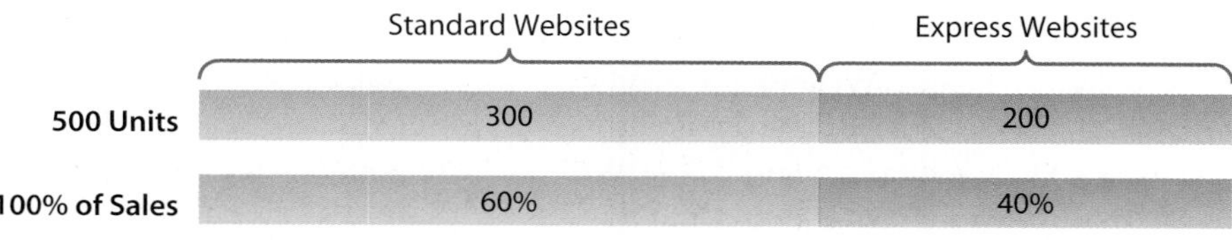

or

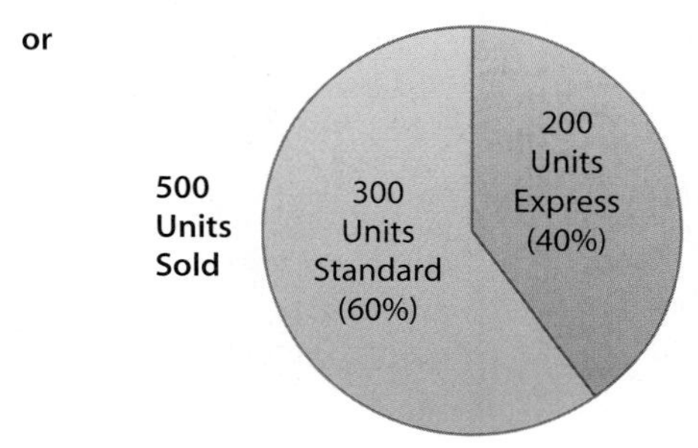

Step 3. *Calculate the breakeven point for each product.* Multiply the weighted-average breakeven point by each product's percentage of the sales mix:

	Weighted-Average Breakeven Point		*Sales Mix*		*Breakeven Point*
Standard	1,000 units	×	60%	=	600 units
Express	1,000 units	×	40%	=	400 units

To verify, determine the contribution margin of each product and subtract the total fixed costs:

Contribution Margin		
Standard	600 × $40 =	$24,000
Express	400 × $20 =	8,000
Total contribution margin		$32,000
Less fixed costs		32,000
Profit		$ 0

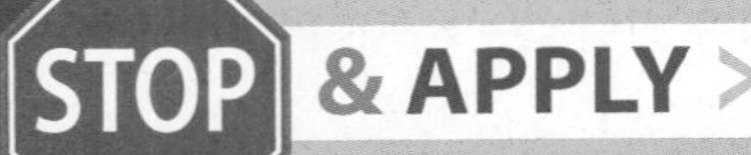

Using the contribution margin approach, find the breakeven point in units for a local business's two products. Product M's selling price per unit is $20, and its variable cost per unit is $11. Product N's selling price per unit is $12, and its variable cost per unit is $6. Fixed costs are $24,000, and the sales mix of Product M to Product N is 2:1.

SOLUTION

Step 1.

	Selling Price		Variable Costs		Contribution Margin (CM)		Percentage of Sales Mix		Weighted-Average CM
M	$20	–	$11	=	$9	×	66.7%	=	$6
N	$12	–	$ 6	=	$6	×	33.3%	=	2
Weighted-average contribution margin									$8

Step 2.

Weighted-Average Breakeven Point = $24,000 ÷ $8.00 = 3,000 Units

Step 3. Breakeven point for each product line:

		Weighted-Average Breakeven Point	×	Sales Mix	=	Breakeven Point
M	=	3,000 Units	×	0.667	=	2,000 Units
N	=	3,000 Units	×	0.333	=	1,000 Units

Check: Contribution Margin

Product M	=	2,000	×	$9	=	$18,000
Product N	=	1,000	×	$6	=	6,000
Total contribution margin						$24,000
Less fixed costs						24,000
Profit						$ 0

Using C-V-P Analysis to Plan Future Sales, Costs, and Profits

LO5 Use C-V-P analysis to project the profitability of products and services.

The primary goal of a business venture is not to break even; it is to generate profits. C-V-P analysis adjusted for targeted profit can be used to estimate the profitability of a venture. This approach is excellent for "what-if" analysis, in which managers select several scenarios and compute the profit that may be anticipated from each. Each scenario generates a different amount of profit or loss.

- For instance, what if sales increase by 17,000 units? What effect will the increase have on profit? What if sales increase by only 6,000 units? What if fixed costs are reduced by $14,500? What if the variable unit cost increases by $1.40?

Applying C-V-P to Target Profits

To illustrate two ways a business can apply C-V-P analysis to target profits, assume that My Media Place has set $4,000 in profit as this year's goal. If all the data in our earlier example remain the same, how many websites must My Media Place sell to reach the targeted profit?

- ***Contribution margin approach:***

$$
\begin{aligned}
S &= VC + FC + P \\
\$90X &= \$50X + \$20{,}000 + \$4{,}000 \\
\$40X &= \$24{,}000 \\
X &= 600 \text{ Units}
\end{aligned}
$$

- ***Equation approach:*** Add the targeted profit to the numerator of the contribution margin breakeven equation and solve for targeted sales in units:

$$\text{Targeted Sales Units} = \frac{FC + P}{\text{CM per Unit}}$$

The number of sales units My Media Place needs to generate $4,000 in profit is computed this way:

$$\text{Targeted Sales Units} = \frac{FC + P}{\text{CM per Unit}} = \frac{\$20{,}000 + \$4{,}000}{\$40} = \frac{\$24{,}000}{\$40}$$

$$= 600 \text{ Units}$$

To summarize My Media Place's plans for the coming year, a contribution income statement can be used. As you can see in the contribution income statement for My Media Place shown below, the focus of such a statement is on cost behavior, *not* cost function. (As we noted earlier, in income statements, the term *operating income* is more appropriate than *profit*.)

My Media Place's planning team wants to consider three alternatives to the original plan shown in the statement. In the following sections, we examine each

Contribution Income Statement
For the Year Ended December 31

	Per Unit	*Total for 600 Units*
Sales revenue	$90	$54,000
Less variable costs	50	30,000
Contribution margin	$40	$24,000
Less fixed costs		20,000
Operating income		$ 4,000

of these alternatives and its impact on projected operating income. In the summary, we review our work from a strategic management perspective and analyze the different breakeven points of the three alternatives.

What-If Alternative 1: Decrease Variable Costs, Increase Sales Volume What if website design labor were outsourced? Based on the planning team's research, the direct labor cost of a website would decrease by $3 to $47 and sales volume would increase by 10 percent to 660 units. How does this alternative affect operating income?

	Per Unit	*Total for 660 Units*
Sales revenue	$90	$59,400
Less variable costs	47	31,020
Contribution margin	$43	$28,380
Less fixed costs		20,000
Operating income		$ 8,380
Alternative 1:		
Increase in operating income ($8,380 − $4,000)		$ 4,380

What-If Alternative 2: Increase Fixed Costs, Increase Sales Volume What if the Marketing Department suggests that a $500 increase in advertising costs would increase sales volume by 5 percent to 630 units? How does this alternative affect operating income?

	Per Unit	*Total for 630 Units*
Sales revenue	$90	$56,700
Less variable costs	50	31,500
Contribution margin	$40	$25,200
Less fixed costs		20,500
Operating income		$ 4,700
Alternative 2:		
Increase in operating income ($4,700 − $4,000)		$ 700

What-If Alternative 3: Increase Selling Price, Decrease Sales Volume What is the impact of a $10 increase in selling price on the company's operating income? If the selling price is increased, the planning team estimates that the sales volume will decrease by 15 percent to 510 units. How does this alternative affect operating income?

	Per Unit	*Total for 510 Units*
Sales revenue	$100	$51,000
Less variable costs	50	25,500
Contribution margin	$ 50	$25,500
Less fixed costs		20,000
Operating income		$ 5,500
Alternative 3:		
Increase in operating income ($5,500 − $4,000)		$ 1,500

Study Note

Remember that the breakeven point provides a rough estimate of the number of units that must be sold to cover the total costs.

Comparative Summary In preparation for a meeting, the planning team at My Media Place compiled the summary presented in Exhibit 23-1. It compares the three alternatives with the original plan and shows how changes in variable and fixed costs, selling price, and sales volume affect the breakeven point.

- Note that the decrease in variable costs (direct materials) proposed in Alternative 1 increases the contribution margin per unit (from $40 to $43), which reduces the breakeven point. Because fewer sales dollars are required to cover variable costs, the breakeven point is reached sooner than in the original plan—at a sales volume of 466 units rather than at 500 units.
- In Alternative 2, the increase in fixed costs has no effect on the contribution margin per unit, but it does require the total contribution margin to cover more fixed costs before reaching the breakeven point. Thus, the breakeven point is higher than in the original plan—513 units as opposed to 500.
- The increase in selling price in Alternative 3 increases the contribution margin per unit, which reduces the breakeven point. Because more sales dollars are available to cover fixed costs, the breakeven point of 400 units is lower than the breakeven point in the original plan.

From a strategic standpoint, which plan should the planning team choose? If they want the highest operating income, they will choose Alternative 1. If, however, they want the company to begin generating operating income more quickly, they will choose the plan with the lowest breakeven point, Alternative 3.

Additional qualitative information may help the planning team make a better decision. Will customers perceive that the quality of the website is lower if the company outsources the web work, as proposed in Alternative 1? Will increased expenditures on advertising yield a 5 percent increase in sales volume, as Alternative 2 suggests? Will the increase in selling price suggested in Alternative 3 create more than a 15 percent decline in unit sales?

Quantitative information is essential for planning, but managers must also be sensitive to qualitative factors, such as product quality, reliability and quality of suppliers, and availability of human and technical resources.

EXHIBIT 23-1
Comparative Summary of Alternatives at My Media Place

	Original Plan	Alternative 1	Alternative 2	Alternative 3
	Totals for 600 Units	Decrease Direct Materials Costs for 660 Units	Increase Advertising Costs for 630 Units	Increase Selling Price for 510 Units
Sales revenue	$54,000	$59,400	$56,700	$51,000
Less variable costs	30,000	31,020	31,500	25,500
Contribution margin	$24,000	$28,380	$25,200	$25,500
Less fixed costs	20,000	20,000	20,500	20,000
Operating income	$ 4,000	$ 8,380	$ 4,700	$ 5,500
Breakeven point in whole units (FC ÷ CM)				
$20,000 ÷ $40 =	500			
$20,000 ÷ $43 =		466*		
$20,500 ÷ $40 =			513*	
$20,000 ÷ $50 =				400

*Rounded up to next whole unit.

& APPLY >

Assume a local real estate appraisal business is planning its home appraisal activities for the coming year. The manager estimates that her variable costs per appraisal will be $220, monthly fixed costs are $16,200, and service fee revenue will be $400 per appraisal. How many appraisals will the business have to perform each month to achieve a targeted profit of $18,000 per month?

SOLUTION

$$\begin{aligned} \text{Let } X &= \text{Targeted Sales in Units} \\ \text{S} - \text{VC} - \text{FC} &= \text{P} \\ \$400X - \$220X - \$16{,}200 &= \$18{,}000 \\ \$180X &= \$34{,}200 \\ X &= 190 \text{ Appraisals per Month} \end{aligned}$$

▶ MY MEDIA PLACE: REVIEW PROBLEM

Breakeven Analysis and Profitability Planning
LO4 LO5

The Decision Point at the beginning of this chapter focused on My Media Place, a company that is considering expanding the range of products and services that it offers. It posed these questions:

- How will My Media Place's managers decide which products and services to offer?
- Why do managers analyze cost behavior?

To decide on a sales mix for My Media Place, its managers will have to consider the variable and fixed costs of producing the products and services in the mix and the effect that the mix would have on resource usage and profitability.

Analyzing cost behavior is essential in making decisions that will profit the company and make the best use of its resources. Managers use a variety of methods and formulas to separate mixed costs into their variable and fixed components. With an understanding of cost behavior patterns, managers can use cost-volume-profit analysis to evaluate "what-if" scenarios and to determine selling prices that cover both fixed and variable costs and that take into account the variability of demand for their company's products or services.

Suppose My Media Place is considering entering the online digital lockbox business by renting server space to customers to store their movies, music, photos, and other computer files. Its managers believe this business has a large potential market as more individuals and small businesses are starting to move their backup files to secure online servers that can be accessed around the clock. Here is a summary of data projections for this business:

Selling price per year per customer account:	$95
Direct supplies	$23
Direct labor	8
Overhead	6
Selling expense	5
Variable costs per unit	$42
Overhead	$195,000
Advertising	55,000
Administrative expense	68,000
Total annual fixed costs	$318,000

Required

1. Compute the annual breakeven point in customer accounts.
2. My Media Place projects sales to 6,500 customer accounts next year. If that projection is accurate, how much profit will it realize?
3. To improve profitability, management is considering the following four alternative courses of action. (In performing the required steps, use the figures from items **1** and **2**, and treat each alternative independently.)
   a. Calculate the number of accounts My Media Place must sell to generate a targeted profit of $95,400. Assume that costs and selling price remain constant.
   b. Calculate the operating income if the company increases the number of accounts sold by 20 percent and cuts the selling price by $5 per account.
   c. Determine the number of accounts that must be sold to break even if advertising costs (fixed costs) increase by $47,700.
   d. Find the number of accounts that must be sold to generate a targeted profit of $120,000 if variable costs decrease by 10 percent.

Answers to Review Problem

1. Annual breakeven point in customer accounts:

$$\text{Breakeven Units} = \frac{\text{FC}}{\text{CM per Unit}} = \frac{\$318{,}000}{\$95 - \$42} = \frac{\$318{,}000}{\$53} = 6{,}000 \text{ Units}$$

2. Profit from sale of 6,500 accounts:

Units sold	6,500
Units required to break even	6,000
Units over breakeven	500

$$\text{Profit} = \$53 \text{ per unit} \times 500 = \$26{,}500$$

Contribution margin equals sales minus all variable costs. Contribution margin per account equals the amount left to cover fixed costs and earn a profit after variable costs have been subtracted from sales dollars. If all fixed costs have been absorbed by the time breakeven is reached, the entire contribution margin of each unit sold in excess of breakeven represents profit.

3. a. Number of accounts that must be sold to generate a targeted profit of $95,400:

$$\text{Targeted Sales Units} = \frac{\text{FC} + \text{P}}{\text{CM per Unit}}$$

$$\frac{\$318{,}000 + \$95{,}400}{\$53} = \frac{\$413{,}400}{\$53} = 7{,}800 \text{ Units}$$

   b. Operating income if account sales increase 20 percent and selling price per account decreases by $5:

Sales revenue [7,800 (6,500 × 1.20) accounts at $90 per account]	$702,000
Less variable costs (7,800 units × $42)	327,600
Contribution margin	$374,400
Less fixed costs	318,000
Operating income	$ 56,400

c. Number of accounts needed to break even if advertising costs (fixed costs) increase by $47,700:

$$\text{BE Units} = \frac{\text{FC}}{\text{CM per Unit}}$$

$$\frac{\$318{,}000 + \$47{,}700}{\$53} = \frac{\$365{,}700}{\$53} = 6{,}900 \text{ Units}$$

d. Number of accounts that must be sold to generate a targeted profit of $120,000 if variable costs decrease by 10 percent:

$$\text{CM per Account} = \$95.00 - (\$42.00 \times 0.90) = \$95.00 - \$37.80 = \$57.20$$

$$\text{Targeted Sales Units} = \frac{\text{FC} + \text{P}}{\text{CM per Unit}}$$

$$\frac{\$318{,}000 + \$120{,}000}{\$57.20} = \frac{\$438{,}000}{\$57.20} = 7{,}658 \text{ Units*}$$

*Note that the answer is rounded up to the next whole unit.

STOP & REVIEW >

LO1 Define *cost behavior*, and identify variable, fixed, and mixed costs.

Cost behavior is the way costs respond to changes in volume or activity. Some costs vary in relation to volume or operating activity; other costs remain fixed as volume changes. Cost behavior depends on whether the focus is total costs or cost per unit. Total costs that change in direct proportion to changes in productive output (or any other volume measure) are called *variable costs*. They include hourly wages, the cost of operating supplies, direct materials costs, and the cost of merchandise. Total *fixed costs* remain constant within a relevant range of volume or activity. They change only when volume or activity exceeds the relevant range—for example, when new equipment or new buildings must be purchased, higher insurance premiums and property taxes must be paid, or additional supervisory personnel must be hired to accommodate increased activity. A *mixed cost*, such as the cost of electricity, has both variable and fixed cost components.

LO2 Separate mixed costs into their variable and fixed components, and prepare a contribution margin income statement.

For cost planning and control, mixed costs must be separated into their variable and fixed components. To separate them, managers use a variety of methods, including the engineering, scatter diagram, high-low, and statistical methods. When preparing a contribution margin income statement, all variable costs related to production, selling, and administration are subtracted from sales to determine the total contribution margin; then, all fixed costs are subtracted from the total contribution margin to determine operating income.

LO3 Define *cost-volume-profit (C-V-P) analysis*, and discuss how managers use it as a tool for planning and control.

Cost-volume-profit analysis is an examination of the cost behavior patterns that underlie the relationships among cost, volume of output, and profit. It is a tool for both planning and control. The techniques and problem-solving procedures involved in C-V-P analysis express relationships among revenue, sales mix, cost, volume, and profit. Those relationships provide a general model of financial activity that management can use for short-range planning and for evaluating performance and analyzing alternatives.

LO4 Define *breakeven point*, and use contribution margin to determine a company's breakeven point for multiple products.

The *breakeven point* is the point at which total revenues equal total costs—in other words, the point at which net sales equal variable costs plus fixed costs. Once the number of units needed to break even is known, the number can be multiplied by the product's selling price to determine the breakeven point in sales dollars. *Contribution margin* is the amount that remains after all variable costs have been subtracted from sales. A product's contribution margin represents its net contribution to paying off fixed costs and earning a profit. The breakeven point in units can be computed by using the following formula:

$$\text{BE Units} = \frac{\text{FC}}{\text{CM per Unit}}$$

Sales mix is used to calculate the breakeven point for each product when a company sells more than one product.

LO5 Use C-V-P analysis to project the profitability of products and services.

The addition of targeted profit to the breakeven equation makes it possible to plan levels of operation that yield the targeted profit. The formula in terms of contribution margin is

$$\text{Targeted Sales Units} = \frac{\text{FC} + \text{P}}{\text{CM per Unit}}$$

C-V-P analysis, whether used by a manufacturing company or a service organization, enables managers to select several "what-if" scenarios and evaluate the outcome of each to determine which will generate the desired amount of profit.

REVIEW of Concepts and Terminology

The following concepts and terms were introduced in this chapter:

Breakeven point 1012 (LO4)

Contribution margin (CM) 1009 (LO2)

Contribution margin income statement 1009 (LO2)

Cost behavior 1000 (LO1)

Cost-volume-profit (C-V-P) analysis 1010 (LO3)

Engineering method 1006 (LO2)

Fixed cost formula 1003 (LO1)

Fixed costs 1003 (LO1)

High-low method 1007 (LO2)

Margin of safety 1012 (LO4)

Mixed cost formula 1005 (LO1)

Mixed costs 1004 (LO1)

Normal capacity 1002 (LO1)

Operating capacity 1001 (LO1)

Practical capacity 1002 (LO1)

Regression analysis 1009 (LO2)

Relevant range 1003 (LO1)

Sales mix 1015 (LO4)

Scatter diagram 1006 (LO2)

Step cost 1003 (LO1)

Theoretical (ideal) capacity 1002 (LO1)

Variable cost formula 1001 (LO1)

Variable costs 1001 (LO1)

CHAPTER ASSIGNMENTS

BUILDING Your Basic Knowledge and Skills

Short Exercises

LO1 **Concept of Cost Behavior**

SE 1. Dapper Hat Makers is in the business of designing and producing specialty hats. The material used for derbies costs $4.50 per unit, and Dapper pays each of its two full-time employees $360 per week. If Employee A makes 15 derbies in one week, what is the variable cost per derby, and what is this worker's fixed cost per derby? If Employee B makes only 12 derbies in one week, what are this worker's variable and fixed costs per derby?

LO1 **Identification of Variable, Fixed, and Mixed Costs**

SE 2. Identify the following as (a) fixed costs, (b) variable costs, or (c) mixed costs:

1. Direct materials
2. Electricity
3. Operating supplies
4. Personnel manager's salary
5. Factory building rent

LO2 **Mixed Costs: High-Low Method**

SE 3. Using the high-low method and the following information, compute the monthly variable cost per telephone hour and total fixed costs for Sadiko Corporation.

Month	Telephone Hours Used	Telephone Costs
April	96	$4,350
May	93	4,230
June	105	4,710

LO2 **Contribution Margin Income Statement**

SE 4. Prepare a contribution margin income statement if DeLuca, Inc., wants to make a profit of $20,000. It has variable costs of $8 per unit and fixed costs of $12,000. How much must it charge per unit if 4,000 units are sold?

LO4 **Breakeven Analysis in Units and Dollars**

SE 5. How many units must Braxton Company sell to break even if the selling price per unit is $8.50, variable costs are $4.30 per unit, and fixed costs are $3,780? What is the breakeven point in total dollars of sales?

LO4 **Contribution Margin in Units**

SE 6. Using the contribution margin approach, find the breakeven point in units for Norcia Consumer Products if the selling price per unit is $11, the variable cost per unit is $6, and the fixed costs are $5,500.

LO4 **Contribution Margin Ratio**

SE 7. Compute the contribution margin ratio and the breakeven point in total sales dollars for Wailley Products if the selling price per unit is $16, the variable cost per unit is $6, and the fixed costs are $6,250.

LO4 **Breakeven Analysis for Multiple Products**

SE 8. Using the contribution margin approach, find the breakeven point in units for Sardinia Company's two products. Product A's selling price per unit is $10, and its variable cost per unit is $4. Product B's selling price per unit is $8, and its variable cost per unit is $5. Fixed costs are $15,000, and the sales mix of Product A to Product B is 2:1.

LO4 LO5 **Contribution Margin and Projected Profit**

SE 9. If Oui Watches sells 300 watches at $48 per watch and has variable costs of $18 per watch and fixed costs of $4,000, what is the projected profit?

LO2 **Monthly Costs and the High-Low Method**

SE 10. Guy Spy, a private investigation firm, investigated 91 cases in December and had the following costs: direct labor, $190 per case; and service overhead of $20,840. Service overhead for October was $21,150; for November, it was $21,350. The number of cases investigated during October and November was 93 and 97, respectively. Compute the variable and fixed cost components of service overhead using the high-low method. Then determine the variable and fixed costs per case for December. (Round to nearest dollar where necessary.)

Exercises

LO1 **Identification of Variable and Fixed Costs**

E 1. Indicate whether each of the following costs of productive output is usually (a) variable or (b) fixed:

1. Packing materials for stereo components
2. Real estate taxes
3. Gasoline for a delivery truck
4. Property insurance
5. Depreciation expense of buildings (calculated with the straight-line method)
6. Supplies
7. Indirect materials
8. Bottles used to package liquids
9. License fees for company cars
10. Wiring used in radios
11. Machine helper's wages
12. Wood used in bookcases
13. City operating license
14. Machine depreciation based on machine hours used
15. Machine operator's hourly wages
16. Cost of required outside inspection of each unit produced

LO1 **Variable Cost Analysis**

E 2. Zero Time Oil Change has been in business for six months. The company pays $0.50 per quart for the oil it uses in servicing cars. Each job requires an average of 4 quarts of oil. The company estimates that in the next three months, it will service 240, 288, and 360 cars.

1. Compute the cost of oil for each of the three months and the total cost for all three months.

Month	Cars to Be Serviced	Required Quarts/Car	Cost/Quart	Total Cost/Month
1	240	4	$0.50	______
2	288	4	0.50	______
3	360	4	0.50	______
Three-month total	888			______

2. Complete the following sentences by choosing the words that best describe the cost behavior at Zero Time Oil Change:
   a. Cost per unit (increased, decreased, remained constant).
   b. Total variable cost per month (increased, decreased) as the quantity of oil used (increased, decreased).

LO2 Mixed Costs: High-Low Method

E 3. Whitehouse Company manufactures major appliances. Because of growing interest in its products, it has just had its most successful year. In preparing the budget for next year, its controller compiled these data:

Month	Volume in Machine Hours	Electricity Cost
July	6,000	$ 60,000
August	5,000	53,000
September	4,500	49,500
October	4,000	46,000
November	3,500	42,500
December	3,000	39,000
Six-month total	26,000	$290,000

Using the high-low method, determine the variable electricity cost per machine hour and the monthly fixed electricity cost. Estimate the total variable electricity costs and fixed electricity costs if 4,800 machine hours are projected to be used next month.

LO2 Mixed Costs: High-Low Method

E 4. When Jerome Company's monthly costs were $75,000, sales were $80,000; when its monthly costs were $60,000, sales were $50,000. Use the high-low method to develop a monthly cost formula for Jerome's coming year.

LO2 LO4 Contribution Margin Income Statement and Ratio

E 5. Senora Company manufactures a single product that sells for $110 per unit. The company projects sales of 500 units per month. Projected costs are as follows:

Type of Cost	Manufacturing	Nonmanufacturing
Variable	$10,000	$5,000
Nonvariable	$12,500	$7,500

1. Prepare a contribution margin income statement for the month.
2. What is the contribution margin ratio?
3. What volume, in terms of units, must the company sell to break even?

LO4 LO5 Contribution Margin Income Statement and C-V-P Analysis

E 6. Using the data in the contribution margin income statement for Sedona, Inc., that appears at the top of the next page, calculate (1) selling price per unit, (2) variable costs per unit, and (3) breakeven point in units and in sales dollars.

Sedona, Inc.
Contribution Margin Income Statement
For the Year Ended December 31

Sales (10,000 units)		$16,000,000
Less variable costs		
Cost of goods sold	$8,000,000	
Selling, administrative, and general	4,000,000	
Total variable costs		12,000,000
Contribution margin		$ 4,000,000
Less fixed costs		
Overhead	$1,200,000	
Selling, administrative, and general	800,000	
Total fixed costs		2,000,000
Operating income		$ 2,000,000

LO4 **Graphic Breakeven Analysis**

E 7. Identify the letter of the point, line segment, or area of the breakeven graph shown below that correctly completes each of the following statements:

1. The maximum possible operating loss is
   a. A c. B
   b. D d. F
2. The breakeven point in sales dollars is
   a. C c. A
   b. D d. G
3. At volume F, total contribution margin is
   a. C c. E
   b. D d. G
4. Operating income is represented by area
   a. KDL c. BDC
   b. KCJ d. GCJ
5. At volume J, total fixed costs are represented by
   a. H c. I
   b. G d. J
6. If volume increases from F to J, the change in total costs is
   a. HI minus DE c. BC minus DF
   b. DF minus HJ d. AB minus DE

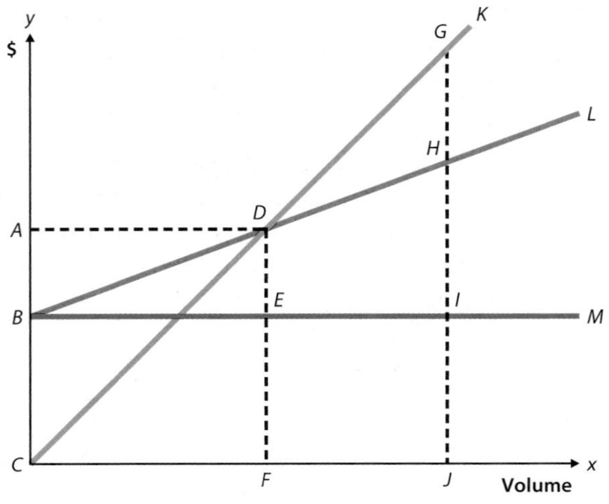

LO4 **Breakeven Analysis**

E 8. Techno Designs produces head covers for golf clubs. The company expects to generate a profit next year. It anticipates fixed manufacturing costs of $126,500 and fixed general and administrative expenses of $82,030 for the year. Variable manufacturing and selling costs per set of head covers will be $4.65 and $2.75, respectively. Each set will sell for $13.40.

1. Compute the breakeven point in sales units.
2. Compute the breakeven point in sales dollars.
3. If the selling price is increased to $14 per unit and fixed general and administrative expenses are cut by $33,465, what will the new breakeven point be in units?
4. Prepare a graph to illustrate the breakeven point computed in **2**.

LO4 LO5 **Breakeven Analysis and Pricing**

E 9. McLennon Company has a plant capacity of 100,000 units per year, but its budget for this year indicates that only 60,000 units will be produced and sold. The entire budget for this year is as follows:

Sales (60,000 units at $4)		$240,000
Less cost of goods produced (based on production of 60,000 units)		
Direct materials (variable)	$60,000	
Direct labor (variable)	30,000	
Variable ovesrhead costs	45,000	
Fixed overhead costs	75,000	
Total cost of goods produced		210,000
Gross margin		$ 30,000
Less selling and administrative expenses		
Selling (fixed)	$24,000	
Administrative (fixed)	36,000	
Total selling and administrative expenses		60,000
Operating income (loss)		($ 30,000)

1. Given the budgeted selling price and cost data, how many units would McLennon have to sell to break even? (**Hint:** Be sure to consider selling and administrative expenses.)
2. Market research indicates that if McLennon were to drop its selling price to $3.80 per unit, it could sell 100,000 units. Would you recommend the drop in price? What would the new operating income or loss be?

LO4 **Breakeven Point for Multiple Products**

E 10. Saline Aquarium, Inc., manufactures and sells aquariums, water pumps, and air filters. The sales mix is 1:2:2 (i.e., for every one aquarium sold, two water pumps and two air filters are sold). Using the contribution margin approach, find the breakeven point in units for each product. The company's fixed costs are $26,000. Other information is as follows:

	Selling Price per Unit	Variable Costs per Unit
Aquariums	$60	$25
Water pumps	20	12
Air filters	10	3

LO4 Breakeven Point for Multiple Products

E 11. Hamburgers and More, Inc., sells hamburgers, drinks, and fries. The sales mix is 1:3:2 (i.e., for every one hamburger sold, three drinks and two fries are sold). Using the contribution margin approach, find the breakeven point in units for each product. The company's fixed costs are $2,040. Other information is as follows:

	Selling Price per Unit	Variable Costs per Unit
Hamburgers	$0.99	$0.27
Drinks	0.99	0.09
Fries	0.99	0.15

LO4 Sales Mix Analysis

E 12. Ella Mae Simpson is the owner of a hairdressing salon in Palm Coast, Florida. Her salon provides three basic services: shampoo and set, permanents, and cut and blow dry. The following are its operating results from the past quarter:

Type of Service	Number of Customers	Total Sales	Contribution Margin in Dollars
Shampoo and set	1,200	$24,000	$14,700
Permanents	420	21,000	15,120
Cut and blow dry	1,000	15,000	10,000
	2,620	$60,000	$39,820
Total fixed costs			30,000
Profit			$ 9,820

Compute the breakeven point in units based on the weighted-average contribution margin for the sales mix.

LO4 LO5 Contribution Margin and Profit Planning

E 13. Target Systems, Inc., makes heat-seeking missiles. It has recently been offered a government contract from which it may realize a profit. The contract purchase price is $130,000 per missile, but the number of units to be purchased has not yet been decided. The company's fixed costs are budgeted at $3,973,500, and variable costs are $68,500 per unit.

1. Compute the number of units the company should agree to make at the stated contract price to earn a profit of $1,500,000.
2. Using a lighter material, the variable unit cost can be reduced by $1,730, but total fixed overhead will increase by $27,500. How many units must be produced to make $1,500,000 in profit?
3. Given the figures in **2**, how many additional units must be produced to increase profit by $1,264,600?

LO5 Planning Future Sales

E 14. Short-term automobile rentals are the specialty of ASAP Auto Rentals, Inc. Average variable operating costs have been $12.50 per day per automobile. The company owns 60 automobiles. Fixed operating costs for the next year are expected to be $145,500. Average daily rental revenue per automobile is expected to be $34.50. Management would like to earn a profit of $47,000 during the year.

1. Calculate the total number of daily rentals the company must have during the year to earn the targeted profit.
2. On the basis of your answer to **1**, determine the average number of days each automobile must be rented.

3. Determine the total revenue needed to achieve the targeted profit of $47,000.
4. What would the total rental revenue be if fixed operating costs could be lowered by $5,180 and the targeted profit increased to $70,000?

LO2 LO5 **Cost Behavior in a Service Business**

E 15. Luke Ricci, CPA, is the owner of a firm that provides tax services. The firm charges $50 per return for the direct professional labor involved in preparing standard short-form tax returns. In January, the firm prepared 850 such returns; in February, 1,000; and in March, 700. Service overhead (telephone and utilities, depreciation on equipment and building, tax forms, office supplies, and wages of clerical personnel) for January was $18,500; for February, $20,000; and for March, $17,000.

1. Determine the variable and fixed cost components of the firm's Service Overhead account.
2. What would the estimated total cost per tax return be if the firm prepares 825 standard short-form tax returns in April?

LO5 **C-V-P Analysis in a Service Business**

E 16. Flossmoor Inspection Service specializes in inspecting cars that have been returned to automobile leasing companies at the end of their leases. Flossmoor's charge for each inspection is $50; its average cost per inspection is $15. Tony Lomangeno, Flossmoor's owner, wants to expand his business by hiring another employee and purchasing an automobile. The fixed costs of the new employee and automobile would be $3,000 per month. How many inspections per month would the new employee have to perform to earn Lomangeno a profit of $1,200?

Problems

LO1 LO2 LO5 **Cost Behavior and Projection for a Service Business**

P 1. Power Brite Painting Company specializes in refurbishing exterior painted surfaces that have been hard hit by humidity and insect debris. It uses a special technique, called pressure cleaning, before priming and painting the surface. The refurbishing process involves the following steps:

1. Unskilled laborers trim all trees and bushes within two feet of the structure.
2. Skilled laborers clean the building with a high-pressure cleaning machine, using about 6 gallons of chlorine per job.
3. Unskilled laborers apply a coat of primer.
4. Skilled laborers apply oil-based exterior paint to the entire surface.

On average, skilled laborers work 12 hours per job, and unskilled laborers work 8 hours. The refurbishing process generated the following operating results during the year on 628 jobs:

Skilled labor	$20 per hour
Unskilled labor	$8 per hour
Gallons of chlorine used	3,768 gallons at $5.50 per gallon
Paint primer	7,536 gallons at $15.50 per gallon
Paint	6,280 gallons at $16 per gallon
Depreciation of paint-spraying equipment	$600 per month depreciation
Lease of two vans	$800 per month total
Rent on storage building	$450 per month

Data on utilities for the year are as follows:

Month	Number of Jobs	Cost	Hours Worked
January	42	$ 3,950	840
February	37	3,550	740
March	44	4,090	880
April	49	4,410	980
May	54	4,720	1,080
June	62	5,240	1,240
July	71	5,820	1,420
August	73	5,890	1,460
September	63	5,370	1,260
October	48	4,340	960
November	45	4,210	900
December	40	3,830	800
Totals	628	$55,420	12,560

Required

1. Classify the costs as variable, fixed, or mixed.
2. Using the high-low method, separate mixed costs into their variable and fixed components. Use total hours worked as the basis.
3. Compute the average cost per job for the year. (**Hint:** Divide the total of all costs for the year by the number of jobs completed.)
4. Project the average cost per job for next year if variable costs per job increase 20 percent.

Manager insight ▶

5. Why can actual utilities costs vary from the amount computed using the utilities cost formula?

LO4 LO5

Breakeven Analysis

P 2. Luce & Morgan, a law firm in downtown Jefferson City, is considering opening a legal clinic for middle- and low-income clients. The clinic would bill at a rate of $18 per hour. It would employ law students as paraprofessional help and pay them $9 per hour. Other variable costs are anticipated to be $5.40 per hour, and annual fixed costs are expected to total $27,000.

Required

1. Compute the breakeven point in billable hours.
2. Compute the breakeven point in total billings.
3. Find the new breakeven point in total billings if fixed costs should go up by $2,340.
4. Using the original figures, compute the breakeven point in total billings if the billing rate decreases by $1 per hour, variable costs decrease by $0.40 per hour, and fixed costs go down by $3,600.

LO4 LO5

Planning Future Sales: Contribution Margin Approach

P 3. Icon Industries is considering a new product for its Trophy Division. The product, which would feature an alligator, is expected to have global market appeal and to become the mascot for many high school and university athletic teams. Expected variable unit costs are as follows: direct materials, $18.50; direct labor, $4.25; production supplies, $1.10; selling costs, $2.80; and other, $1.95. Annual fixed costs are depreciation, building, and equipment, $36,000; advertising, $45,000; and other, $11,400. Icon Industries plans to sell the product for $55.00.

Required

1. Using the contribution margin approach, compute the number of units the company must sell to (a) break even and (b) earn a profit of $70,224.

2. Using the same data, compute the number of units that must be sold to earn a profit of $139,520 if advertising costs rise by $40,000.
3. Using the original information and sales of 10,000 units, compute the selling price the company must use to make a profit of $131,600. (**Hint:** Calculate contribution margin per unit first.)

Manager insight ▶

4. According to the vice president of marketing, Albert Flora, the most optimistic annual sales estimate for the product would be 15,000 units, and the highest competitive selling price the company can charge is $52 per unit. How much more can be spent on fixed advertising costs if the selling price is $52, if the variable costs cannot be reduced, and if the targeted profit for 15,000 unit sales is $251,000?

LO4 LO5 **Breakeven Analysis and Planning Future Sales**

P 4. Write Company has a maximum capacity of 200,000 units per year. Variable manufacturing costs are $12 per unit. Fixed overhead is $600,000 per year. Variable selling and administrative costs are $5 per unit, and fixed selling and administrative costs are $300,000 per year. The current sales price is $23 per unit.

Required

1. What is the breakeven point in (a) sales units and (b) sales dollars?
2. How many units must Write Company sell to earn a profit of $240,000 per year?
3. A strike at one of the company's major suppliers has caused a shortage of materials, so the current year's production and sales are limited to 160,000 units. To partially offset the effect of the reduced sales on profit, management is planning to reduce fixed costs to $841,000. Variable cost per unit is the same as last year. The company has already sold 30,000 units at the regular selling price of $23 per unit.
   a. What amount of fixed costs was covered by the total contribution margin of the first 30,000 units sold?
   b. What contribution margin per unit will be needed on the remaining 130,000 units to cover the remaining fixed costs and to earn a profit of $210,000 this year?

LO4 LO5 **Planning Future Sales for a Service Business**

P 5. Lending Hand Financial Corporation is a subsidiary of Gracey Enterprises. Its main business is processing loan applications. Last year, Bettina Brent, the manager of the corporation's loan department, established a policy of charging a $250 fee for every loan application processed. Next year's variable costs have been projected as follows: loan consultant's wages, $15.50 per hour (a loan application takes 5 hours to process); supplies, $2.40 per application; and other variable costs, $5.60 per application. Annual fixed costs include depreciation of equipment, $8,500; building rental, $14,000; promotional costs, $12,500; and other fixed costs, $8,099.

Required

1. Using the contribution margin approach, compute the number of loan applications the company must process to (a) break even and (b) earn a profit of $14,476.
2. Using the same approach and assuming promotional costs increase by $5,662, compute the number of applications the company must process to earn a profit of $20,000.
3. Assuming the original information and the processing of 500 applications, compute the loan application fee the company must charge if the targeted profit is $41,651.

Manager insight ▶ 4. Brent's staff can handle a maximum of 750 loan applications. How much more can be spent on promotional costs if the highest fee tolerable to the customer is $280, if variable costs cannot be reduced, and if the targeted profit for the loan applications is $50,000?

Alternate Problems

LO1 LO2 LO5

Mixed Costs

P 6. Officials of the Hidden Hills Golf and Tennis Club are in the process of preparing a budget for the year ending December 31. Because Ramon Saud, the club treasurer, has had difficulty with two expense items, the process has been delayed by more than four weeks. The two items are mixed costs—expenses for electricity and for repairs and maintenance—and Saud has been having trouble breaking them down into their variable and fixed components.

An accountant friend has suggested that he use the high-low method to divide the costs into their variable and fixed parts. The spending patterns and activity measures related to each cost during the past year are as follows:

	Electricity Expense		Repairs and Maintenance	
Month	Amount	Kilowatt-Hours	Amount	Labor Hours
January	$ 7,500	210,000	$ 7,578	220
February	8,255	240,200	7,852	230
March	8,165	236,600	7,304	210
April	8,960	268,400	7,030	200
May	7,520	210,800	7,852	230
June	7,025	191,000	8,126	240
July	6,970	188,800	8,400	250
August	6,990	189,600	8,674	260
September	7,055	192,200	8,948	270
October	7,135	195,400	8,674	260
November	8,560	252,400	8,126	240
December	8,415	246,600	7,852	230
Totals	$92,550	2,622,000	$96,416	2,840

Required

1. Using the high-low method, compute the variable cost rates used last year for each expense. What was the monthly fixed cost for electricity and for repairs and maintenance?
2. Compute the total variable cost and total fixed cost for each expense category for last year.
3. Saud believes that in the coming year, the electricity rate will increase by $0.005 and the repairs rate, by $1.20. Usage of all items and their fixed cost amounts will remain constant. Compute the projected total cost for each category. How will the cost increases affect the club's profits and cash flow?

LO4 LO5

Breakeven Analysis

P 7. At the beginning of each year, the Accounting Department at Moon Glow Lighting, Ltd., must find the point at which projected sales revenue will equal total budgeted variable and fixed costs. The company produces custom-made, low-voltage outdoor lighting systems. Each system sells for an average of $435. Variable costs per unit are $210. Total fixed costs for the year are estimated to be $166,500.

Required

1. Compute the breakeven point in sales units.
2. Compute the breakeven point in sales dollars.
3. Find the new breakeven point in sales units if the fixed costs go up by $10,125.
4. Using the original figures, compute the breakeven point in sales units if the selling price decreases to $425 per unit, fixed costs go up by $15,200, and variable costs decrease by $15 per unit.

LO4 LO5 Planning Future Sales: Contribution Margin Approach

P 8. Garden Marbles manufactures birdbaths, statues, and other decorative items, which it sells to florists and retail home and garden centers. Its design department has proposed a new product, a statue of a frog, that it believes will be popular with home gardeners. Expected variable unit costs are direct materials, $9.25; direct labor, $4.00; production supplies, $0.55; selling costs, $2.40; and other, $3.05. The following are fixed costs: depreciation, building, and equipment, $33,000; advertising, $40,000; and other, $6,000. Management plans to sell the product for $29.25.

Required

1. Using the contribution margin approach, compute the number of statues the company must sell to (a) break even and (b) earn a profit of $50,000.
2. Using the same data, compute the number of statues that must be sold to earn a profit of $70,000 if advertising costs rise by $20,000.
3. Using the original data and sales of 15,000 units, compute the selling price the company must charge to make a profit of $100,000.

Manager insight ▶

4. According to the vice president of marketing, Yvonne Palmer, if the price of the statues is reduced and advertising is increased, the most optimistic annual sales estimate is 25,000 units. How much more can be spent on fixed advertising costs if the selling price is reduced to $28.00 per statue, if the variable costs cannot be reduced, and if the targeted profit for sales of 25,000 statues is $120,000?

LO4 LO5 Breakeven Analysis and Planning Future Sales

P 9. Peerless Company has a maximum capacity of 500,000 units per year. Variable manufacturing costs are $25 per unit. Fixed overhead is $900,000 per year. Variable selling and administrative costs are $5 per unit, and fixed selling and administrative costs are $300,000 per year. The current sales price is $36 per unit.

Required

1. What is the breakeven point in (a) sales units and (b) sales dollars?
2. How many units must Peerless Company sell to earn a profit of $600,000 per year?
3. A strike at one of the company's major suppliers has caused a shortage of materials, so the current year's production and sales are limited to 400,000 units. To partially offset the effect of the reduced sales on profit, management is planning to reduce fixed costs to $1,000,000. Variable cost per unit is the same as last year. The company has already sold 30,000 units at the regular selling price of $36 per unit.
   a. What amount of fixed costs was covered by the total contribution margin of the first 30,000 units sold?
   b. What contribution margin per unit will be needed on the remaining 370,000 units to cover the remaining fixed costs and to earn a profit of $300,000 this year?

LO5 Planning Future Sales for a Service Business

P 10. Home Mortgage Inc.'s primary business is processing mortgage loan applications. Last year, Jenna Jason, the manager of the mortgage application department, established a policy of charging a $500 fee for every loan application processed. Next year's variable costs have been projected as follows: mortgage processor wages, $30 per hour (a mortgage application takes 3 hours to process); supplies, $10 per application; and other variable costs, $15 per application. Annual fixed costs include depreciation of equipment, $5,000; building rental, $34,000; promotional costs, $45,000; and other fixed costs, $20,000.

Required

1. Using the contribution margin approach, compute the number of loan applications the company must process to (a) break even and (b) earn a profit of $50,000.
2. Using the same approach and assuming promotional costs increase by $5,400, compute the number of applications the company must process to earn a profit of $60,000.
3. Assuming the original information and the processing of 500 applications, compute the loan application fee the company must charge if the targeted profit is $40,000.
4. Manager insight ▶ Jason's staff can handle a maximum of 750 loan applications. How much more can be spent on promotional costs if the highest fee tolerable to the customer is $400, if variable costs cannot be reduced, and if the targeted profit for the loan applications is $50,000?

ENHANCING Your Knowledge, Skills, and Critical Thinking

LO4 Breaking Even and Ethics

C 1. Lesley Chomski is the supervisor of the New Product Division of MCO Corporation. Her annual bonus is based on the success of new products and is computed on the number of sales that exceed each new product's projected breakeven point. In reviewing the computations supporting her most recent bonus, Chomski found that although an order for 7,500 units of a new product called R56 had been refused by a customer and returned to the company, the order had been included in the bonus calculations. She later discovered that the company's accountant had labeled the return an overhead expense and had charged the entire cost of the returned order to the plantwide Overhead account. The result was that product R56 appeared to exceed breakeven by more than 5,000 units and Chomski's bonus from this product amounted to over $1,000. What actions should Chomski take? Be prepared to discuss your response in class.

LO1 LO4 Cost Behavior and Contribution Margin

C 2. Visit a local fast-food restaurant. Observe all aspects of the operation and take notes on the entire process. Describe the procedures used to take, process, and fill an order and deliver the order to the customer. Based on your observations, make a list of the costs incurred by the operation. Identify at least three variable costs and three fixed costs. Can you identify any potential mixed costs? Why is the restaurant willing to sell a large drink for only a few cents more than a medium drink? How is the restaurant able to offer a "value meal" (e.g., sandwich, drink, and fries) for considerably less than those items would cost if they were bought separately? Bring your notes to class and be prepared to discuss your findings.

Your instructor will divide the class into groups to discuss the case. Summarize your group's discussion, and ask one member of the group to present the summary to the rest of the class.

LO3 LO4 **C-V-P Analysis**

C 3. Based in Italy, Datura, Ltd., is an international importer-exporter of pottery with distribution centers in the United States, Europe, and Australia. The company was very successful in its early years, but its profitability has since declined. As a member of a management team selected to gather information for Datura's next strategic planning meeting, you have been asked to review its most recent contribution margin income statement for the year ended December 31, 2010, which appears below.

Datura, Ltd.
Contribution Margin Income Statement
For the Year Ended December 31, 2010

Sales revenue		€13,500,000
Less variable costs		
Purchases	€6,000,000	
Distribution	2,115,000	
Sales commissions	1,410,000	
Total variable costs		9,525,000
Contribution margin		€ 3,975,000
Less fixed costs		
Distribution	€ 985,000	
Selling	1,184,000	
General and administrative	871,875	
Total fixed costs		3,040,875
Operating income		€ 934,125

In 2010, Datura sold 15,000 sets of pottery.

1. For each set of pottery sold in 2010, calculate the (a) selling price, (b) variable purchases cost, (c) variable distribution cost, (d) variable sales commission, and (e) contribution margin.
2. Calculate the breakeven point in units and in sales euros.
3. Historically, Datura's variable costs have been about 60 percent of sales. What was the ratio of variable costs to sales in 2010? List three actions Datura could take to correct the difference.
4. How would fixed costs have been affected if Datura had sold only 14,000 sets of pottery in 2010?

LO5 **C-V-P Analysis Applied**

C 4. Refer to the information in **C 3**. In January 2011, Sophia Callas, the president of Datura, Ltd., conducted a strategic planning meeting. During the meeting, Phillipe Mazzeo, vice president of distribution, noted that because of a new contract with an international shipping line, the company's fixed distribution costs for 2011 would be reduced by 10 percent and its variable distribution costs by 4 percent. Gino Roma, vice president of sales, offered the following information:

> We plan to sell 15,000 sets of pottery again in 2011, but based on review of the competition, we are going to lower the selling price to €890 per set. To encourage increased sales, we will raise sales commissions to 12 percent of the selling price.

Sophia Callas is concerned that the changes described by Roma and Mazzeo may not improve operating income sufficiently in 2011. If operating income does not increase by at least 10 percent, she will want to find other ways to reduce the company's costs. She asks you to evaluate the situation in a written report. Because it is already January of 2011 and changes need to be made quickly, she requests your report within five days.

1. Prepare a budgeted contribution margin income statement for 2011. Your report should show the budgeted (estimated) operating income based on the information provided above and in **C 3**. Will the changes improve operating income sufficiently? Explain.
2. In preparation for writing your report, answer the following questions:
   a. Why are you preparing the report?
   b. Who needs the report?
   c. What sources of information will you use?
   d. When is the report due?

LO5 Planning Future Sales

C 5. As noted in **C 3 and 4**, Datura, Ltd., sold 15,000 sets of pottery in 2010. For the next year, 2011, Datura's strategic planning team targeted sales of 15,000 sets of pottery, reduced the selling price to €890 per set, increased sales commissions to 12 percent of the selling price, and decreased fixed distribution costs by 10 percent and variable distribution costs by 4 percent. It was assumed that all other costs would stay the same.

Based on an analysis of these changes, Sophia Callas, Datura's president, is concerned that the proposed strategic plan will not meet her goal of increasing Datura's operating income by 10 percent over last year's income and that the operating income will be less than last year's income. She has come to you for spreadsheet analysis of the proposed strategic plan and for analysis of a special order she just received from an Australian distributor for 4,500 sets of pottery. The order's selling price, variable purchases cost per unit, sales commission, and total fixed costs will be the same as for the rest of the business, but the variable distribution costs will be €160 per unit.

Using an Excel spreadsheet, complete the following tasks:

1. Calculate the targeted operating income for 2011 using just the proposed strategic plan.
2. Prepare a budgeted contribution margin income statement for 2011 based on just the strategic plan. Do you agree with Datura's president that the company's projected operating income for 2011 will be less than the operating income for 2010? Explain your answer.
3. Calculate the total contribution margin from the Australian sales.
4. Prepare a revised budgeted contribution margin income statement for 2011 that includes the Australian order. (**Hint:** Combine the information from **2** and **3** above.)
5. Does Datura need the Australian sales to achieve its targeted operating income for 2011?

LO1 LO2 Cookie Company (Continuing Case)

C 6. In this segment of our continuing "cookie company" case, you will classify the costs of the business as variable, fixed, or mixed; use the high-low method to evaluate utility costs; and prepare a contribution margin income statement.

1. Review your cookie recipe and the overhead costs you identified in Chapter 19, and classify the costs as variable, fixed, or mixed costs.

2. Obtain your electric bills for three months, and use the high-low method's cost formula to determine the monthly cost of electricity—that is, monthly electric cost = variable rate per kilowatt-hour + monthly fixed cost. If you do not receive an electric bill, use the following information:

Month	Kilowatt-Hours Used	Electric Costs
August	1,439	$202
September	1,866	230
October	1,146	158

3. Prepare a daily contribution margin income statement based on the following assumptions:

   My Cookie Company makes only one kind of cookie and sells it for $1.00 per unit. The company projects sales of 500 units per day. Projected daily costs are as follows:

Type of Cost	Manufacturing	Nonmanufacturing
Variable	$100	$50
Nonvariable	120	60

   a. What is the contribution margin ratio?
   b. What volume, in terms of units, must the company sell to break even each day?

CHAPTER

24 The Budgeting Process

The Management Process

PLAN

- ▷ **Review strategic, tactical, and operating objectives**
- ▷ **Analyze and forecast sales**
- ▷ **Analyze costs and determine cost formulas**
- ▷ **Prepare operating budgets**
- ▷ **Prepare financial budgets**

PERFORM

- ▷ **Implement budgets to grant authority and responsibility for operating objectives**

EVALUATE

- ▷ **Compare actual results with budgets; revise budgets if needed**

COMMUNICATE

- ▷ **Prepare internal budget reports that summarize and analyze performance**
- ▷ **Prepare pro forma financial statements for external use**

Budgeting is not only an essential part of planning; it also helps managers control, evaluate, and report on operations.

When managers develop budgets, they match their organizational goals with the resources necessary to accomplish those goals. During the budgeting process, they evaluate operational, tactical, value chain, and capacity issues; assess how resources can be used efficiently; and develop contingency budgets as business conditions change. In this chapter, we describe the budgeting process, identify the elements of a master budget, and demonstrate how managers prepare operating budgets and financial budgets.

LEARNING OBJECTIVES

LO1 **Define *budgeting,* and explain budget basics.** (pp. 1042–1045)

LO2 **Identify the elements of a master budget in different types of organizations and the guidelines for preparing budgets.** (pp. 1045–1049)

LO3 **Prepare the operating budgets that support the financial budgets.** (pp. 1049–1056)

LO4 **Prepare a budgeted income statement, a cash budget, and a budgeted balance sheet.** (pp. 1057–1063)

DECISION POINT ▸ A MANAGER'S FOCUS FRAMECRAFT COMPANY

Framecraft Company is a local manufacturer specializing in high-quality plastic picture frames. Because the company believes its work force is its most valuable asset, one of its priorities is to help employees attain their personal goals. To achieve congruence between its goals and objectives and its employees' personal aspirations, Framecraft has adopted a participatory budgeting process—an ongoing dialogue that involves personnel at all levels of a company in making budgeting decisions. This dialogue provides both managers and lower-level employees with insight into the company's current activities and future direction and motivates them to improve their performance, which, in turn, improves the company's performance.

- ▸ How does Framecraft Company translate long-term goals into operating objectives?
- ▸ What is the effect of Framecraft's budgeting process?

The Budgeting Process

LO1 Define *budgeting,* and explain budget basics.

> **Study Note**
> For-profit organizations often use the term *profit planning* rather than *budgeting.*

Budgeting is the process of identifying, gathering, summarizing, and communicating financial and nonfinancial information about an organization's future activities. It is an essential part of the continuous planning that an organization must do to accomplish its long-term goals. The budgeting process provides managers of all types of organizations—including for-profit organizations and not-for-profit organizations—the opportunity to match their organizational goals with the resources necessary to accomplish those goals.

Budgets—plans of action based on forecasted transactions, activities, and events—are synonymous with managing an organization. They are essential to accomplishing the goals articulated in an organization's strategic plan. They are used to communicate information, coordinate activities and resource usage, motivate employees, and evaluate performance. For example, a board of directors may use budgets to determine managers' areas of responsibility and to measure managers' performance in those areas.

Budgets are, of course, also used to manage and account for cash. Such budgets establish targeted levels of cash receipts and limits on the spending of cash for particular purposes.

Advantages of Budgeting

Budgeting is advantageous for organizations, because:

1. Budgets foster organizational communication.
2. Budgets ensure a focus both on future events and on resolving day-to-day issues.
3. Budgets assign resources and the responsibility to use them wisely to managers who are held accountable for their results.
4. Budgets can identify potential constraints before they become problems.
5. Budgets facilitate congruence between organizational and personal goals.
6. Budgets define organizational goals and objectives numerically, against which actual performance results can be evaluated.

FOCUS ON BUSINESS PRACTICE

What Can Cause the Planning Process to Fail?

When chief financial officers were asked what caused their planning process to fail, these were the six factors they most commonly cited:[1]

- An inadequately defined strategy
- No clear link between strategy and the operational budget
- Lack of individual accountability for results
- Lack of meaningful performance measures
- Inadequate pay for performance
- Lack of appropriate data

Budgeting and Goals

Long-Term Goals **Strategic planning** is the process by which management establishes an organization's long-term goals. These goals define the strategic direction that an organization will take over a ten-year period and are the basis for making annual operating plans and preparing budgets. Long-term goals cannot be vague; they must set specific tactical targets and timetables and assign operating responsibility for achieving the goals to specific personnel. For example, a long-term goal for a company that currently holds only 4 percent of its product's market share might specify that the vice president of marketing is to develop strategies to ensure that the company controls 10 percent of the market in five years and 15 percent by the end of ten years.

> **Study Note**
> As plans are formulated for time periods closer to the current date, they become more specific and quantified. The annual budget is a very specific plan of action.

Short-Term Goals Annual operating plans involve every part of an enterprise and are much more detailed than long-term strategic plans. To formulate an annual operating plan, an organization must restate its long-term goals in terms of what it needs to accomplish during the next year. The process entails making decisions about sales and profit targets, human resource needs, and the introduction of new products or services. The short-term goals identified in an annual operating plan are the basis of an organization's operating budgets for the year.

Budgeting Basics

Once long- and short-term goals have been decided, the organization's management play a central role in coordinating the budgeting process. Together, they set the basics of the budgeting process, including assigning budget authority, inviting employee participation, selecting the budget period, and implementing the budget.

Budget Authority Every budget and budget line item is associated with a specific role or job in an organization. For example, a department manager is responsible for the department's budget, and the marketing vice president is responsible for what is spent on advertising.

Since manager responsibilities and budget authority are linked, managers must explain or take corrective action for any deviations between budget and actual results. Responsibility accounting, which will be discussed in greater detail in the next chapter, authorizes managers to take control of and be held accountable for the revenues and expenses in their budgets. It assigns resources and the responsibility to use them wisely to managers. If managers do not have budget authority over what they need to accomplish their job responsibilities, they lack the control necessary to accomplish their duties and cannot be held accountable for results. The concept of responsibility accounting holds managers accountable for only those budget items that they actually control.

Participation Because an organization's main activities—such as production, sales, and employee training—take place at its lower levels, the information necessary for establishing a budget flows from the employees and supervisors of those activities through middle managers to senior executives. Each person in this chain of communication thus plays a role in developing a budget, as well as in implementing it. If these individuals feel that they have a voice in setting the budget targets, they will be motivated to ensure that their departments attain those targets and stay within the budget. If they do not feel that they have a role in the budgeting process, motivation will suffer. The key to a successful budget is therefore **participative budgeting**, a process in which personnel at all levels of an organization actively engage in making decisions about the budget. Participative budgeting depends on joint decision making; without it the budgeting process will be authoritative rather than participative. Without input from personnel at all operational levels, the budget targets may be unrealistic and impossible to attain.

Budget Period Budgets, like the company's fiscal period, generally cover a one-year period of time. An annual operating budget may be divided further by an organization into monthly or quarterly periods depending on how detailed the information needs are. In this chapter, you will be working with both monthly and quarterly budgets.

The organization's management will decide if they will use a static or continuous budgeting process. **Static budgets** are prepared once a year and do not change during the annual budget period. To ensure that its managers have continuously updated operating data against which to measure performance, an organization may select an ongoing budgeting process, called a continuous budget. A **continuous budget** is a 12-month forward rolling budget that summarizes budgets for the next 12 months. Each month managers prepare a budget for that month, 12 months hence. Thus the budget is continuously reviewed and revised during the year.

Budget Approach Traditional budgeting approaches require managers to justify only budget changes over the past year. An alternative to traditional budgeting is zero-based budgeting. **Zero-based budgeting** requires that every budget item be justified annually, not just the changes. So each year the budget is built from scratch.

Budget Implementation The **budget committee**, which includes many of the organization's management, and the controller have overall responsibility for budget implementation. The budget committee oversees each stage in the preparation of the organization's overall budget, mediates any departmental disputes that may arise in the process, and gives final approval to the budget. The makeup of the committee ensures that the budgeting process has a company wide perspective.

A budget may have to go through many revisions before it includes all planning decisions and has the approval of the budget committee. Once the committee approves the budget, periodic reports from department managers allow the committee to monitor the company's progress in attaining budget targets.

Successful budget implementation depends on two factors—clear communication and the support of top management. To ensure their cooperation in implementing the budget, all key persons involved must know what roles they are expected to play and must have specific directions on how to achieve their performance goals. Thus, the controller and other members of the budget committee must be very clear in communicating performance expectations and budget targets. Equally important, top management must show support for the budget and encourage its implementation. The process will succeed only if middle- and lower-level managers are confident that top management is truly interested in the outcome and is willing to reward personnel for meeting the budget targets. Today, many organizations have employee incentive plans that tie the achievement of budget targets to bonuses or other types of compensation.

Study Note

Because good communication can eliminate many of the problems that typically arise in the budgeting process, company-wide dialogue is extremely important.

Randi Quelle is the manager of the electronics department in a large discount store. During a recent meeting, Quelle and her supervisor agreed that Quelle's goal for the next year would be to increase by 20 percent the number of flat-screen televisions sold. The department sold 500 TV sets last year. Two sales persons currently work for Quelle. What types of budgets should Quelle use to help her achieve her sales goal? What kinds of information should those budgets provide?

SOLUTION

Budgets and information that might be useful include:

1. Breakdown by month of last year's sales to use as a guide to build this year's monthly targets. This would include seasonal sales information.
2. Budgets by sales person, which may indicate a need for a third sales person.
3. Inventory and purchasing information.
4. Budgets of sales promotion and advertising.
5. Information on customer flow and the best times to sell.

The Master Budget

LO2 Identify the elements of a master budget in different types of organizations and the guidelines for preparing budgets.

A **master budget** consists of a set of operating budgets and a set of financial budgets that detail an organization's financial plans for a specific accounting period, generally a year. When a master budget covers an entire year, some of the operating and financial budgets may show planned results by month or by quarter.

- As the term implies, **operating budgets** are plans used in daily operations. They are also the basis for preparing the **financial budgets**, which are projections of financial results for the accounting period.
- Financial budgets include a budgeted income statement, a capital expenditures budget, a cash budget, and a budgeted balance sheet.

The budgeted financial statements—that is, the budgeted income statement and budgeted balance sheet—are also called **pro forma financial statements**, meaning that they show projections rather than actual results. Pro forma financial statements are often used to communicate business plans to external parties.

If, for example, you wanted to obtain a bank loan so that you could start a new business, you would have to present the bank with a pro forma, or budgeted, income statement and balance sheet showing that you could repay the loan with cash generated by profitable operations.

Study Note

Budgeted financial statements are often referred to as *forecasted financial statements, pro forma financial statements,* or *forward-looking financial statements.*

Preparation of a Master Budget

Suppose you have started your own business. Whether it is a manufacturing, retail, or service organization, to manage it effectively, you would prepare a master budget each period. A master budget provides the information needed to match long-term goals to short-term activities and to plan the resources needed to ensure an organization's profitability and liquidity.

Figures 24-1, 24-2, and 24-3 display the elements of a master budget for a manufacturing organization, a retail organization, and a service organization, respectively. As these illustrations indicate, the process of preparing a master budget is similar in all three types of organizations in that each prepares a set of

FIGURE 24-1 Preparation of a Master Budget for a Manufacturing Organization

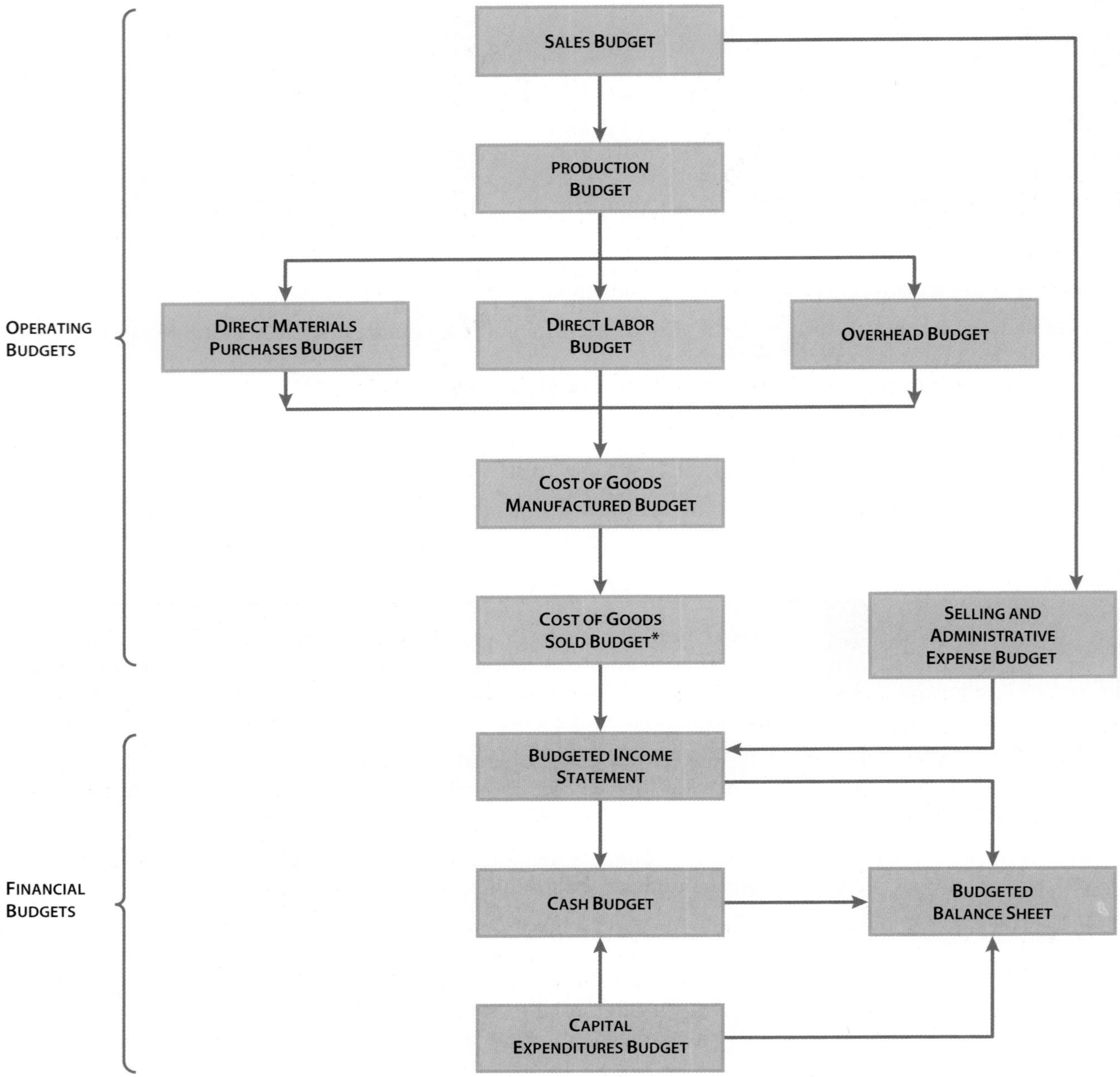

*Some organizations choose to include the cost of goods sold budget in the budgeted income statement.

operating budgets that serve as the basis for preparing the financial budgets. The process differs mainly in the kinds of operating budgets that each type of organization prepares.

- The operating budgets of manufacturing organizations, such as Framecraft, include budgets for sales, production, direct materials, direct labor, overhead, selling and administrative expenses, and cost of goods manufactured.
- Retail organizations, such as **Michaels**, **Talbots**, and **Lowe's**, prepare a sales budget, a purchases budget, a selling and administrative expense budget, and a cost of goods sold budget.

FIGURE 24-2
Preparation of a Master Budget for a Retail Organization

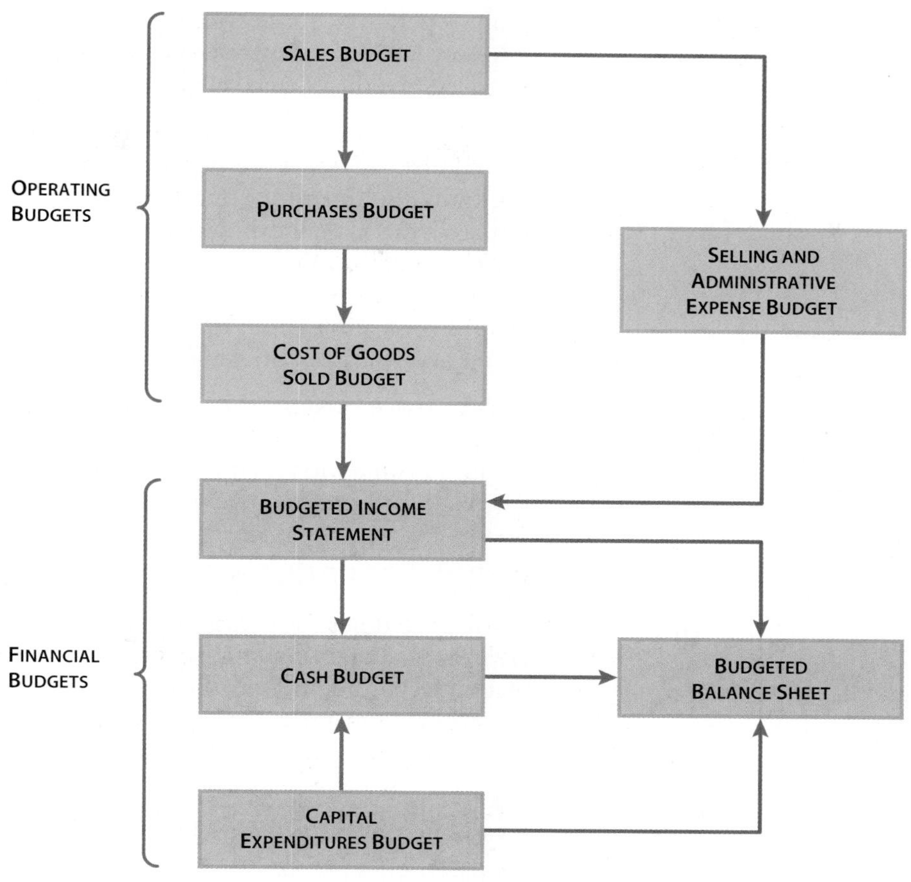

FIGURE 24-3 Preparation of a Master Budget for a Service Organization

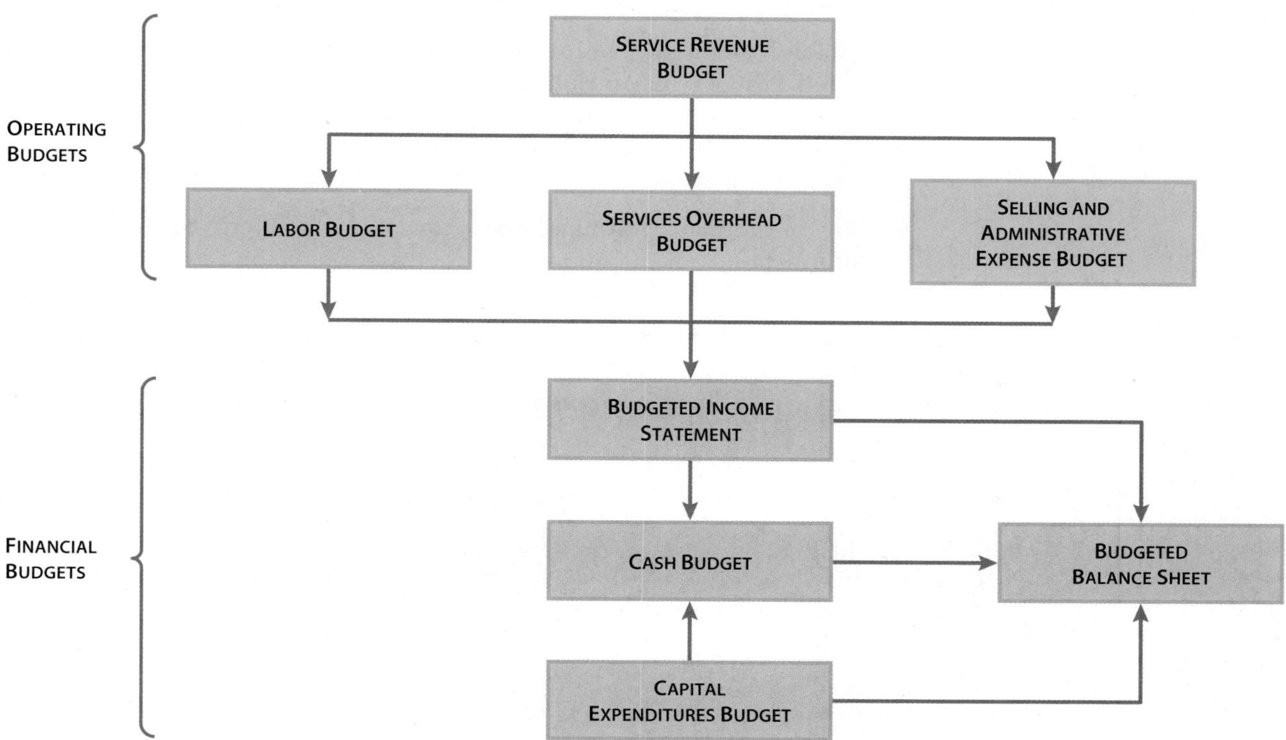

- The operating budgets of service organizations, such as **Enterprise Rent-A-Car**, **UPS**, and **Amtrak**, include budgets for service revenue (sales), labor, services overhead, and selling and administrative expenses.

The sales budget (or, in service organizations, the service revenue budget) is prepared first because it is used to estimate sales volume and revenues. Once managers know the quantity of products or services to be sold and how many sales dollars to expect, they can develop other budgets that will enable them to manage their organization's resources so that they generate profits on those sales.

For example, in a retail organization, the purchases budget provides managers with information about the quantity of merchandise needed to meet the sales demand and yet maintain a minimum level of inventory.

- In a service organization, the labor budget provides information about the labor hours and labor rates needed to provide services and generate the revenues planned for each period; managers use this information in scheduling services and setting prices.

Budget Procedures

Because procedures for preparing budgets vary from organization to organization, there is no standard format for budget preparation. The only universal requirement is that budgets communicate the appropriate information to the reader in a clear and understandable manner. By keeping that in mind and using the following guidelines, managers can improve the quality of budgets in any type of organization:

1. Know the purpose of the budget, and clearly identify who is responsible for carrying out the activities in the budget.
2. Identify the user group and its information needs.
3. Identify sources of accurate, meaningful budget information. Such information may be gathered from documents or from interviews with employees, suppliers, or managers who work in the related areas.
4. Establish a clear format for the budget. A budget should begin with a clearly stated heading that includes the organization's name, the type of budget, and the accounting period under consideration. The budget's components should be clearly labeled, and the unit and financial data should be listed in an orderly manner.
5. Use appropriate formulas and calculations in deriving the quantitative information.
6. Revise the budget until it includes all planning decisions. Several revisions may be required before the final version is ready for distribution.

STOP & APPLY >

Identify the order in which the following budgets are prepared:

1. Overhead budget
2. Production budget
3. Direct labor budget
4. Direct materials purchases budget
5. Sales budget
6. Budgeted balance sheet
7. Cash budget
8. Budgeted income statement

SOLUTION

1. Sales budget
2. Production budget
3. Direct materials purchases budget, direct labor budget, and overhead budget
4. Budgeted income statement
5. Cash budget
6. Budgeted balance sheet

Operating Budgets

LO3 Prepare the operating budgets that support the financial budgets.

Although procedures for preparing operating budgets vary, the tools used in the process do not. In this section, we use Framecraft Company to illustrate how a manufacturing organization prepares its operating budgets. Because Framecraft makes only one product—a plastic picture frame—it prepares only one of each type of operating budget. Organizations that manufacture a variety of products or provide many types of services may prepare either separate operating budgets or one comprehensive budget for each product or service.

The Sales Budget

Study Note

The sales budget is the only budget based on an estimate of customer demand. Other budgets for the period are prepared from it and are based on the numbers it provides.

As we indicated earlier, the first step in preparing a master budget is to prepare a sales budget. A **sales budget** is a detailed plan, expressed in both units and dollars, that identifies the sales expected during an accounting period. Sales managers use this information to plan sales- and marketing-related activities and to determine their human, physical, and technical resource needs. Accountants use the information to determine estimated cash receipts for the cash budget.

The following equation is used to determine the total budgeted sales:

$$\begin{matrix}\text{Total} \\ \text{Budgeted} \\ \text{Sales}\end{matrix} = \begin{matrix}\text{Estimated} \\ \text{Selling Price} \\ \text{per Unit}\end{matrix} \times \begin{matrix}\text{Estimated} \\ \text{Sales in} \\ \text{Units}\end{matrix}$$

Although the calculation is easy, selecting the best estimates for the selling price per unit and the sales demand in units can be difficult.

- An estimated selling price below the current selling price may be needed if competitors are currently selling the same product or service at lower prices or if the organization wants to increase its share of the market.
- On the other hand, if the organization has improved the quality of its product or service by using more expensive materials or processes, the estimated selling price may have to be higher than the current price.

The estimated sales volume is very important because it will affect the level of operating activities and the amount of resources needed for operations. To help estimate sales volume, managers often use a **sales forecast**, which is a projection of sales demand (the estimated sales in units) based on an analysis of external and internal factors. The external factors include:

1. The state of the local and national economies
2. The state of the industry's economy
3. The nature of the competition and its sales volume and selling price

EXHIBIT 24-1
Sales Budget

Framecraft Company
Sales Budget
For the Year Ended December 31

	Quarter 1	Quarter 2	Quarter 3	Quarter 4	Year
Sales in units	10,000	30,000	10,000	40,000	90,000
× Selling price per unit	× $5	× $5	× $5	× $5	× $5
Total sales	$50,000	$150,000	$50,000	$200,000	$450,000

Internal factors taken into consideration in a sales forecast include:

1. The number of units sold in prior periods
2. The organization's credit policies
3. The organization's collection policies
4. The organization's pricing policies
5. Any new products that the organization plans to introduce to the market
6. The capacity of the organization's manufacturing facilities

Exhibit 24-1 illustrates Framecraft Company's sales budget for the year. The budget shows the estimated number of unit sales and dollar revenue amounts for each quarter and for the entire year. Because a sales forecast indicated a highly competitive marketplace, Framecraft's managers have estimated a selling price of $5 per unit. The sales forecast also indicated highly seasonal sales activity; the estimated sales volume therefore varies from 10,000 to 40,000 per quarter.

The Production Budget

A **production budget** is a detailed plan showing the number of units that a company must produce to meet budgeted sales and inventory needs. Production managers use this information to plan for the materials and human resources that production-related activities will require. To prepare a production budget, managers must know the budgeted number of unit sales (which is specified in the sales budget) and the desired level of ending finished goods inventory for each period in the budget year. That level is often stated as a percentage of the next period's budgeted unit sales.

For example, Framecraft Company's desired level of ending finished goods inventory is 10 percent of the next quarter's budgeted unit sales. (Its desired level of beginning finished goods inventory is 10 percent of the current quarter's budgeted unit sales.)

The following formula identifies the production needs for each accounting period:

$$\text{Total Production Units} = \text{Budgeted Sales in Units} + \text{Desired Units of Ending Finished Goods Inventory} - \text{Desired Units of Beginning Finished Goods Inventory}$$

Exhibit 24-2 shows Framecraft Company's production budget for the year. Notice that each quarter's desired total units of ending finished goods inventory become the next quarter's desired total units of beginning finished goods inventory.

EXHIBIT 24-2
Production Budget

Framecraft Company
Production Budget
For the Year Ended December 31

	Quarter				
	1	**2**	**3**	**4**	**Year**
Sales in units	10,000	30,000	10,000	40,000	90,000
Plus desired units of ending finished goods inventory	3,000	1,000	4,000	1,500	1,500
Desired total units	13,000	31,000	14,000	41,500	91,500
Less desired units of beginning finished goods inventory	1,000	3,000	1,000	4,000	1,000
Total production units	12,000	28,000	13,000	37,500	90,500

- Because unit sales of 15,000 are budgeted for the first quarter of next year, the ending finished goods inventory for the fourth quarter of the year is 1,500 units (0.10 × 15,000 units), which is the same as the desired number of units of ending finished goods inventory for the entire year.
- Similarly, the number of desired units for the first quarter's beginning finished goods inventory—1,000—is the same as the desired number of units of beginning finished goods inventory for the entire year.

The Direct Materials Purchases Budget

A **direct materials purchases budget** is a detailed plan that identifies the quantity of purchases required to meet budgeted production and inventory needs and the costs associated with those purchases. A purchasing department uses this information to plan purchases of direct materials. Accountants use the same information to estimate cash payments to suppliers.

To prepare a direct materials purchases budget, managers must know what production needs will be in each accounting period in the budget; this information is provided by the production budget. They must also know the desired level of the direct materials inventory for each period and the per unit cost of direct materials. The desired level of ending direct materials inventory is usually stated as a percentage of the next period's production needs.

For example, Framecraft's desired level of ending direct materials inventory is 20 percent of the next quarter's budgeted production needs. (Its desired level of beginning direct materials inventory is 20 percent of the current quarter's budgeted production needs.)

The following three steps are involved in preparing a direct materials purchases budget:

Step 1. Calculate each period's total production needs in units of direct materials. Plastic is the only direct material used in Framecraft Company's picture frames; each frame requires 10 ounces. Framecraft's managers therefore calculate units of production needs in ounces; they multiply the number of frames budgeted for production in a quarter by the 10 ounces of plastic that each frame requires.

Step 2. Determine the quantity of direct materials to be purchased during each accounting period in the budget using the following formula:

Total Units of Direct Materials to Be Purchased	=	Total Production Needs in Units of Direct Materials	+	Desired Units of Ending Direct Materials Inventory	−	Desired Units of Beginning Direct Materials Inventory

Step 3. Calculate the cost of the direct materials purchases by multiplying the total number of unit purchases by the direct materials cost. Framecraft's Purchasing Department has estimated the cost of the plastic used in the picture frames at $0.05 per ounce.

Exhibit 24-3 shows Framecraft's direct materials purchases budget for the year. Notice that each quarter's desired units of ending direct materials inventory become the next quarter's desired units of beginning direct materials inventory.

- The company's budgeted number of units for the first quarter of the following year is 150,000 ounces; its ending direct materials inventory for the fourth quarter of this year is therefore 30,000 ounces (0.20 × 150,000 ounces), which is the same as the number of desired units of ending direct materials inventory for the entire year.
- Similarly, the number of desired units for the first quarter's beginning direct materials inventory—24,000 ounces—is the same as the beginning amount for the entire year.

EXHIBIT 24-3
Direct Materials Purchases Budget

Framecraft Company
Direct Materials Purchases Budget
For the Year Ended December 31

	Quarter				
	1	**2**	**3**	**4**	**Year**
Total production units	12,000	28,000	13,000	37,500	90,500
× 10 ounces per unit	× 10	× 10	× 10	× 10	× 10
Total production needs in ounces	120,000	280,000	130,000	375,000	905,000
Plus desired ounces of ending direct materials inventory	56,000	26,000	75,000	30,000	30,000
	176,000	306,000	205,000	405,000	935,000
Less desired ounces of beginning direct materials inventory	24,000	56,000	26,000	75,000	24,000
Total ounces of direct materials to be purchased	152,000	250,000	179,000	330,000	911,000
× Cost per ounce	× $0.05	× $0.05	× $0.05	× $0.05	× $0.05
Total cost of direct materials purchases	$ 7,600	$ 12,500	$ 8,950	$ 16,500	$ 45,550

The Direct Labor Budget

A **direct labor budget** is a detailed plan that estimates the direct labor hours needed during an accounting period and the associated costs. Production managers use estimated direct labor hours to plan how many employees will be required during the period and the hours that each will work, and accountants use estimated direct labor costs to plan for cash payments to the workers. Managers of human resources use the information in a direct labor budget in deciding whether to hire new employees or reduce the existing work force and also as a guide in training employees and preparing schedules of employee fringe benefits.

The following two steps are used to prepare a direct labor budget:

Step 1. Estimate the total direct labor hours by multiplying the estimated direct labor hours per unit by the anticipated units of production (see Exhibit 24-2).

Step 2. Calculate the total budgeted direct labor cost by multiplying the estimated total direct labor hours by the estimated direct labor cost per hour. A company's human resources department provides an estimate of the hourly labor wage.

$$\text{Total Budgeted Direct Labor Costs} = \text{Estimated Total Direct Labor Hours} \times \text{Estimated Direct Labor Cost per Hour}$$

Exhibit 24-4 shows how Framecraft Company uses these formulas to estimate the total direct labor cost. Framecraft's Production Department needs an estimated one-tenth (0.10) of a direct labor hour to complete one unit. Its Human Resources Department estimates a direct labor cost of $6 per hour.

The Overhead Budget

An **overhead budget** is a detailed plan of anticipated manufacturing costs, other than direct materials and direct labor costs, that must be incurred to meet budgeted production needs. It has two purposes: to integrate the overhead cost budgets developed by the managers of production and production-related departments and to group information for the calculation of overhead rates for the next accounting period. The format for presenting information in an overhead budget is flexible. Grouping information by activities is useful for organizations that use activity-based costing. This approach makes it easier for accountants to determine the application rates for each cost pool.

EXHIBIT 24-4
Direct Labor Budget

Framecraft Company
Direct Labor Budget
For the Year Ended December 31

	Quarter				
	1	**2**	**3**	**4**	**Year**
Total production units	12,000	28,000	13,000	37,500	90,500
× Direct labor hours per unit	× 0.10	× 0.10	× 0.10	× 0.10	× 0.10
Total direct labor hours	1,200	2,800	1,300	3,750	9,050
× Direct labor cost per hour	× $6	× $6	× $6	× $6	× $6
Total direct labor cost	$ 7,200	$16,800	$ 7,800	$22,500	$54,300

EXHIBIT 24-5
Overhead Budget

Framecraft Company
Overhead Budget
For the Year Ended December 31

	Quarter 1	2	3	4	Year
Variable overhead costs					
Factory supplies	$ 2,160	$ 5,040	$ 2,340	$ 6,750	$ 16,290
Employee benefits	2,880	6,720	3,120	9,000	21,720
Inspection	1,080	2,520	1,170	3,375	8,145
Maintenance and repairs	1,920	4,480	2,080	6,000	14,480
Utilities	3,600	8,400	3,900	11,250	27,150
Total variable overhead costs	$11,640	$27,160	$12,610	$36,375	$ 87,785
Fixed overhead costs					
Depreciation–machinery	$ 2,810	$ 2,810	$ 2,810	$ 2,810	$ 11,240
Depreciation–building	3,225	3,225	3,225	3,225	12,900
Supervision	9,000	9,000	9,000	9,000	36,000
Maintenance and repairs	2,150	2,150	2,150	2,150	8,600
Other overhead expenses	3,175	3,175	3,175	3,175	12,700
Total fixed overhead costs	$20,360	$20,360	$20,360	$20,360	$ 81,440
Total overhead costs	$32,000	$47,520	$32,970	$56,735	$169,225

As Exhibit 24-5 shows, Framecraft Company prefers to group overhead information into variable and fixed costs to facilitate C-V-P analysis. The single overhead rate is the estimated total overhead costs divided by the estimated total direct labor hours.

For example, Framecraft's predetermined overhead rate is $18.70* per direct labor hour ($169,225 ÷ 9,050 direct labor hours), or $1.87 per unit produced ($18.70 per direct labor hour × 0.10 direct labor hour per unit). The variable portion of the overhead rate is $9.70 per direct labor hour ($87,785 ÷ 9,050 direct labor hours), which includes factory supplies, $1.80; employee benefits, $2.40; inspection, $0.90; maintenance and repairs, $1.60; and utilities, $3.00.

The Selling and Administrative Expense Budget

A **selling and administrative expense budget** is a detailed plan of operating expenses, other than those related to production, that are needed to support sales and overall operations during an accounting period. Accountants use this budget to estimate cash payments for products or services not used in production-related activities.

Framecraft Company's selling and administrative expense budget appears in Exhibit 24-6. The company groups its selling and administrative expenses into variable and fixed components for purposes of cost behavior analysis, C-V-P analysis, and profit planning.

*Rounded.

EXHIBIT 24-6
Selling and Administrative Expense Budget

Framecraft Company
Selling and Administrative Expense Budget
For the Year Ended December 31

	Quarter				
	1	**2**	**3**	**4**	**Year**
Variable selling and administrative expenses					
Delivery expenses	$ 800	$ 2,400	$ 800	$ 3,200	$ 7,200
Sales commissions	1,000	3,000	1,000	4,000	9,000
Accounting	700	2,100	700	2,800	6,300
Other administrative expenses	400	1,200	400	1,600	3,600
Total variable selling and administrative expenses	$ 2,900	$ 8,700	$ 2,900	$11,600	$ 26,100
Fixed selling and administrative expenses					
Sales salaries	$ 4,500	$ 4,500	$ 4,500	$ 4,500	$ 18,000
Executive salaries	12,750	12,750	12,750	12,750	51,000
Depreciation–office equipment	925	925	925	925	3,700
Taxes and insurance	1,700	1,700	1,700	1,700	6,800
Total fixed selling and administrative expenses	$19,875	$19,875	$19,875	$19,875	$ 79,500
Total selling and administrative expenses	$22,775	$28,575	$22,775	$31,475	$105,600

Study Note

Remember that selling and administrative expenses are period costs, not product costs.

For example, Framecraft Company's estimated variable selling and administrative expense rate is $0.29 per unit sold, which includes delivery expenses, $0.08; sales commissions, $0.10; accounting, $0.07; and other administrative expenses, $0.04.

The Cost of Goods Manufactured Budget

A **cost of goods manufactured budget** is a detailed plan that summarizes the estimated costs of production during an accounting period. The sources of information for total manufacturing costs are the direct materials, direct labor, and overhead budgets. Most manufacturing organizations anticipate some work in process at the beginning or end of the period covered by a budget. However, Framecraft Company has a policy of no work in process on December 31 of any year. Exhibit 24-7 summarizes the company's estimated costs of production for the year. (The right-hand column of the exhibit shows the sources of key data.)

The budgeted, or standard, product unit cost for one picture frame is rounded to $2.97 ($268,775 ÷ 90,500 units).

EXHIBIT 24-7
Cost of Goods Manufactured Budget

Framecraft Company
Cost of Goods Manufactured Budget
For the Year Ended December 31

			Source of Data
Direct materials used			
Direct materials inventory, beginning	$ 1,200*		**Exhibit 24-3**
Purchases	45,550		**Exhibit 24-3**
Cost of direct materials available for use	$46,750		
Less direct materials inventory, ending	1,500*		**Exhibit 24-3**
Cost of direct materials used		$ 45,250	
Direct labor costs		54,300	**Exhibit 24-4**
Overhead costs		169,225	**Exhibit 24-5**
Total manufacturing costs		$268,775	
Work in process inventory, beginning		—†	
Less work in process inventory, ending		—†	
Cost of goods manufactured		$268,775	

*The desired direct materials inventory balance at the beginning of the year is $1,200 (24,000 ounces × $0.05 per ounce); at year end, it is $1,500 (30,000 ounces × $0.05 per ounce).
† It is the company's policy to have no units in process at the beginning or end of the year.

STOP & APPLY >

Sample Company is preparing a production budget for the year. The company's policy is to maintain a finished goods inventory equal to one-half of the next month's sales. Sales of 4,000 units are budgeted for April. Use the following monthly production budget for the first quarter to determine how many units should be produced in January, February, and March:

	January	February	March
Sales in units	3,000	2,400	6,000
Add desired units of ending finished goods inventory	?	?	?
Desired total units			
Less desired units of beginning finished goods inventory	?	?	?
Total production units	?	?	?

SOLUTION

	January	February	March
Sales in units	3,000	2,400	6,000
Add desired units of ending finished goods inventory	1,200	3,000	2,000
Desired total units	4,200	5,400	8,000
Less desired units of beginning finished goods inventory	1,500	1,200	3,000
Total production units	2,700	4,200	5,000

Financial Budgets

LO4 Prepare a budgeted income statement, a cash budget, and a budgeted balance sheet.

With revenues and expenses itemized in the operating budgets, an organization's controller is able to prepare the financial budgets, which, as we noted earlier, are projections of financial results for the accounting period. Financial budgets include a budgeted income statement, a capital expenditures budget, a cash budget, and a budgeted balance sheet.

The Budgeted Income Statement

A **budgeted income statement** projects an organization's net income for an accounting period based on the revenues and expenses estimated for that period. Exhibit 24-8 shows Framecraft Company's budgeted income statement for the year. The company's expenses include 8 percent interest paid on a $70,000 note payable and income taxes paid at a rate of 30 percent.

Information about projected sales and costs comes from several operating budgets, as indicated by the right-hand column of Exhibit 24-8, which identifies the sources of key data and makes it possible to trace how Framecraft Company's budgeted income statement was developed.

At this point, you can review the overall preparation of the operating budgets and the budgeted income statement by comparing the preparation flow in Figure 24-2 with the budgets in Exhibits 24-1 through 24-8. You will notice that Framecraft Company has no budget for cost of goods sold; that information is included in its budgeted income statement.

EXHIBIT 24-8
Budgeted Income Statement

Framecraft Company
Budgeted Income Statement
For the Year Ended December 31

			Source of Data
Sales		$450,000	**Exhibit 24-1**
Cost of goods sold			
Finished goods inventory, beginning	$ 2,970*		**Exhibit 24-2**
Cost of goods manufactured	268,775		**Exhibit 24-7**
Cost of goods available for sale	$271,745		
Less finished goods inventory, ending	4,455*		**Exhibit 24-2**
Cost of goods sold		267,290	
Gross margin		$182,710	
Selling and administrative expenses		105,600	**Exhibit 24-6**
Income from operations		$ 77,110	
Interest expense (8% × $70,000)		5,600	
Income before income taxes		$ 71,510	
Income taxes expense (30%)		21,453	
Net income		$ 50,057	

Note: Finished goods inventory balances assume that product unit costs were the same in both years:

*Beginning	Ending
1,000 units (Exhibit 24-2)	1,500 units (Exhibit 24-2)
× $2.97*	× $2.97*
$2,970	$4,455

*$268,775 ÷ 90,500 units (Exhibits 24-7 and 24-2) = $2.97 (Rounded)

The Capital Expenditures Budget

A **capital expenditures budget** is a detailed plan outlining the anticipated amount and timing of capital outlays for long-term assets during an accounting period. Managers rely on the information in a capital expenditures budget when making decisions about such matters as buying equipment, building a new plant, purchasing and installing a materials handling system, or acquiring another business. Framecraft Company's capital expenditures budget for the year includes $30,000 for the purchase of a new frame making machine. The company plans to pay $15,000 in the first quarter of the year, when the order is placed, and $15,000 in the second quarter of the year, when it receives the extrusion machine. This information is necessary for preparing the company's cash budget. We discuss capital expenditures in more detail in a later chapter.

The Cash Budget

A **cash budget** is a projection of the cash that an organization will receive and the cash that it will pay out during an accounting period. It summarizes the cash flow prospects of all transactions considered in the master budget. The information that the cash budget provides enables managers to plan for short-term loans when the cash balance is low and for short-term investments when the cash balance is high. Table 24-1 shows how the elements of a cash budget relate to operating, investing, and financing activities.

A cash budget excludes planned noncash transactions, such as depreciation expense, amortization expense, issuance and receipt of stock dividends, uncollectible accounts expense, and gains and losses on sales of assets. Some organizations also exclude deferred taxes and accrued interest from the cash budget.

The following formula is useful in preparing a cash budget:

$$\text{Estimated Ending Cash Balance} = \text{Total Estimated Cash Receipts} - \text{Total Estimated Cash Payments} + \text{Estimated Beginning Cash Balance}$$

Estimates of cash receipts are based on information from several sources. Among these sources are the sales budget, the budgeted income statement, cash budgets from previous periods, cash collection records and analyses of collection trends, and records pertaining to notes, stocks, and bonds. Information used in estimating cash payments

TABLE 24-1
Elements of a Cash Budget

Activities	Cash Receipts From	Cash Payments For
Operating	Cash sales	Purchases of materials
	Cash collections on credit sales	Direct labor
	Interest income from investments	Overhead expenses
	Cash dividends from investments	Selling and administrative expenses
		Interest expense
		Income taxes
Investing	Sale of investments	Purchases of investments
	Sale of long-term assets	Purchases of long-term assets
Financing	Proceeds from loans	Loan repayments
	Proceeds from issue of stock	Cash dividends to stockholders
	Proceeds from issue of bonds	Retirement of bonds
		Purchases of treasury stock

Note: Classifications of cash receipts and cash payments correspond to those in a statement of cash flows.

comes from the operating budgets, the budgeted income statement, the capital expenditures budget, the previous year's financial statements, and loan records.

In estimating cash receipts and cash payments for the cash budget, many organizations prepare supporting schedules.

For example, Framecraft Company's controller converts credit sales to cash inflows and purchases made on credit to cash outflows and then discloses those conversions on schedules that support the cash budget. The schedule in Exhibit 24-9 shows the cash that Framecraft Company expects to collect from customers during the year.

- Cash sales represent 20 percent of the company's expected sales; the other 80 percent are credit sales.
- Experience has shown that Framecraft collects payments for 60 percent of all credit sales in the quarter of sale, 30 percent in the quarter following sale, and 10 percent in the second quarter following sale.

As you can see in Exhibit 24-9, Framecraft's balance of accounts receivable was $48,000 at the beginning of the budget year. The company expects to collect $38,000 of that amount in the first quarter and the remaining $10,000 in the second quarter. At the end of the budget year, the estimated ending balance of accounts receivable is $68,000—that is, $4,000 from the third quarter's credit sales [($50,000 × 0.80) × 0.10] plus $64,000 from the fourth quarter's sales [($200,000 × 0.80) × 0.40]. The expected cash collections for each quarter and for the year appear in the total cash receipts section of the cash budget.

Exhibit 24-10 shows Framecraft's schedule of expected cash payments for direct materials during the year. This information is summarized in the first line of the cash payments section of the company's cash budget. Framecraft pays 50 percent of the invoices it receives in the quarter of purchase and the other 50 percent in the following quarter.

The beginning balance of accounts payable for the first quarter is given at $4,200. At the end of the budget year, the estimated ending balance of accounts payable is $8,250 (50 percent of the $16,500 of direct materials purchases in the fourth quarter).

EXHIBIT 24-9
Schedule of Expected Cash Collections from Customers

Framecraft Company
Schedule of Expected Cash Collections from Customers
For the Year Ended December 31

	Quarter 1	Quarter 2	Quarter 3	Quarter 4	Year
Accounts receivable, beginning	$38,000	$ 10,000	$ —	$ —	$ 48,000
Cash sales	10,000	30,000	10,000	40,000	90,000
Collections of credit sales					
First quarter ($40,000)	24,000	12,000	4,000		40,000
Second quarter ($120,000)		72,000	36,000	12,000	120,000
Third quarter ($40,000)			24,000	12,000	36,000
Fourth quarter ($160,000)				96,000	96,000
Total cash to be collected from customers	$72,000	$124,000	$74,000	$160,000	$430,000

EXHIBIT 24-10
Schedule of Expected Cash Payments for Direct Materials

Framecraft Company
Schedule of Expected Cash Payments for Direct Materials
For the Year Ended December 31

	Quarter				
	1	**2**	**3**	**4**	**Year**
Accounts payable, beginning	$4,200	$ —	$ —	$ —	$ 4,200
First quarter ($7,600)	3,800	3,800			7,600
Second quarter ($12,500)		6,250	6,250		12,500
Third quarter ($8,950)			4,475	4,475	8,950
Fourth quarter ($16,500)				8,250	8,250
Total cash payments for direct materials	$8,000	$10,050	$10,725	$12,725	$41,500

Framecraft's cash budget for the year appears in Exhibit 24-11. It shows the estimated cash receipts and cash payments for the period, as well as the cash increase or decrease. The cash increase or decrease plus the period's beginning cash balance equals the ending cash balance anticipated for the period. As you can see in Exhibit 24-11, the beginning cash balance for the first quarter is $20,000. This amount is also the beginning cash balance for the year.

Note that each quarter's budgeted ending cash balance becomes the next quarter's beginning cash balance. Also note that equal income tax payments are made quarterly. You can trace the development of this budget by referring to the data sources listed in the exhibit.

Many organizations maintain a minimum cash balance to provide a margin of safety against uncertainty. If the ending cash balance on the cash budget falls below the minimum level required, short-term borrowing may be necessary to cover planned cash payments during the year. If the ending cash balance is significantly larger than the organization needs, it may invest the excess cash in short-term securities to generate additional income.

For example, if Framecraft Company wants a minimum of $10,000 cash available at the end of each quarter, its balance of $7,222 at the end of the first quarter indicates that there is a problem.

Framecraft's management has several options for handling this problem. It can borrow cash to cover the first quarter's cash needs, delay purchasing the new extrusion machine until the second quarter, or reduce some of the operating expenses. On the other hand, the balance at the end of the fourth quarter may be higher than the company wants, in which case management might invest a portion of the idle cash in short-term securities.

FOCUS ON BUSINESS PRACTICE

Can Budgeting Lead to a Breakdown in Corporate Ethics?

When budgets are used to force performance results, as they were at **WorldCom**, breaches in corporate ethics can occur. One former WorldCom employee described the situation at that company as follows: "You would have a budget, and he [WorldCom CEO Bernard Ebbers] would mandate that you had to be 2% under budget. Nothing else was acceptable."[2] This type of restrictive budget policy appears to have been a factor in many of the recent corporate scandals.

EXHIBIT 24-11 Cash Budget

Framecraft Company
Cash Budget
For the Year Ended December 31

	Quarter 1	Quarter 2	Quarter 3	Quarter 4	Year	Source of Data
Cash receipts						
Cash collections from customers	$ 72,000	$124,000	$74,000	$160,000	$430,000	Exhibit 24-9
Total cash receipts	$ 72,000	$124,000	$74,000	$160,000	$430,000	
Cash payments						
Direct materials	$ 8,000	$ 10,050	$10,725	$ 12,725	$ 41,500	Exhibit 24-10
Direct labor	7,200	16,800	7,800	22,500	54,300	Exhibit 24-4
Factory supplies	2,160	5,040	2,340	6,750	16,290	Exhibit 24-5
Employee benefits	2,880	6,720	3,120	9,000	21,720	Exhibit 24-5
Inspection	1,080	2,520	1,170	3,375	8,145	Exhibit 24-5
Variable maintenance and repairs	1,920	4,480	2,080	6,000	14,480	Exhibit 24-5
Utilities	3,600	8,400	3,900	11,250	27,150	Exhibit 24-5
Supervision	9,000	9,000	9,000	9,000	36,000	Exhibit 24-5
Fixed maintenance and repairs	2,150	2,150	2,150	2,150	8,600	Exhibit 24-5
Other overhead expenses	3,175	3,175	3,175	3,175	12,700	Exhibit 24-5
Delivery expenses	800	2,400	800	3,200	7,200	Exhibit 24-6
Sales commissions	1,000	3,000	1,000	4,000	9,000	Exhibit 24-6
Accounting	700	2,100	700	2,800	6,300	Exhibit 24-6
Other administrative expenses	400	1,200	400	1,600	3,600	Exhibit 24-6
Sales salaries	4,500	4,500	4,500	4,500	18,000	Exhibit 24-6
Executive salaries	12,750	12,750	12,750	12,750	51,000	Exhibit 24-6
Taxes and insurance	1,700	1,700	1,700	1,700	6,800	Exhibit 24-6
Capital expenditures*	15,000	15,000			30,000	Exhibit 24-6
Interest expense	1,400	1,400	1,400	1,400	5,600	Exhibit 24-8
Income taxes	5,363	5,363	5,363	5,364	21,453	Exhibit 24-8
Total cash payments	$ 84,778	$117,748	$74,073	$123,239	$399,838	
Cash increase (decrease)	$(12,778)	$ 6,252	$ (73)	$ 36,761	$ 30,162	
Beginning cash balance	20,000	7,222	13,474	13,401	20,000	
Ending cash balance	$ 7,222	$ 13,474	$13,401	$ 50,162	$ 50,162	

*The company plans to purchase an extrusion machine costing $30,000 and to pay for it in two installments of $15,000 each in the first and second quarters of the year.

The Budgeted Balance Sheet

A **budgeted balance sheet** projects an organization's financial position at the end of an accounting period. It uses all estimated data compiled in the course of preparing a master budget and is the final step in that process. Exhibit 24-12 presents Framecraft Company's budgeted balance sheet at the end of the budget year. Again, the data sources are listed in the exhibit. The beginning balances for Land, Notes Payable, Common Stock, and Retained Earnings were $50,000, $70,000, $150,000, and $50,810, respectively.

EXHIBIT 24-12
Budgeted Balance Sheet

Framecraft Company Budgeted Balance Sheet December 31				Source of Data
Assets				
Current assets				
Cash		$ 50,162		Exhibit 24-11
Accounts receivable		68,000[a]		Exhibit 24-9
Direct materials inventory		1,500		Exhibit 24-7
Work in process inventory		—		Exhibit 24-7, Note
Finished goods inventory		4,455		Exhibit 24-8, Note
Total current assets			$124,117	
Property, plant, and equipment				
Land		$ 50,000		
Plant and equipment[b]	$200,000			
Less accumulated depreciation[c]	45,000	155,000		
Total property, plant, and equipment			205,000	
Total assets			$329,117	
Liabilities				
Current liabilities				
Accounts payable			$ 8,250[d]	Exhibit 24-10, Note
Total current liabilities			$ 8,250	
Long-term liabilities				
Notes payable			70,000	
Total liabilities			$ 78,250	
Stockholders' Equity				
Common stock		$150,000		
Retained earnings[e]		100,867		
Total stockholders' equity			250,867	
Total liabilities and stockholders' equity			$329,117	

[a]The accounts receivable balance at year end is $68,000: $4,000 from the third quarter's sales [($50,000 × 0.80) × 0.10] plus $64,000 from the fourth quarter's sales [($200,000 × 0.80) × 0.40].
[b]The plant and equipment balance includes the $30,000 purchase of an extrusion machine.
[c]The accumulated depreciation balance includes depreciation expense of $27,840 for machinery, building, and office equipment ($11,240, $12,900, and $3,700, respectively).
[d]At year end, the estimated ending balance of accounts payable is $8,250 (50 percent of the $16,500 of direct materials purchases in the fourth quarter).
[e]The retained earnings balance at December 31 equals the beginning retained earnings balance plus the net income projected for the year ($50,810 and $50,057, respectively).

STOP & APPLY >

Sample Corporation's budgeted balance sheet for the beginning of the coming year shows total assets of $5,000,000 and total liabilities of $2,000,000. Common stock and retained earnings make up the entire stockholders' equity section of the balance sheet. Common stock remains at its beginning balance of $1,500,000. The projected net income for the year is $350,000. The company plans to pay no cash dividends. What is the balance of retained earnings at the beginning and end of the year?

SOLUTION

Using the accounting equation A = L + OE knowing that common stock + retained earnings makes up the entire OE and the information given:

Beginning retained earnings:

$5,000,000 = $2,000,000 + $1,500,000 + Beginning RE

Thus, the beginning balance of retained earnings is $1,500,000.

Ending retained earnings:

Beginning retained earnings	$1,500,000
+ Net income	350,000
− Dividends	0
Ending retained earnings	$1,850,000

▸ FRAMECRAFT COMPANY: REVIEW PROBLEM

Preparing a Cash Budget
LO4

The budgeting process can be a highly effective way of linking strategic planning to operations, especially when it is participatory—that is, when it involves all employees in an ongoing dialogue about a company's activities and direction and engages them in making budgeting decisions. In this chapter's Decision Point, we noted that a participatory budgeting process is the basis for Framecraft's budgeting decisions. We also asked these questions:

- How does Framecraft Company translate long-term goals into operating objectives?
- What is the effect of Framecraft's budgeting process?

As you know after reading this chapter, Framecraft uses its budgets to translate its long-term goals into annual operating objectives. Because the budgets express these goals and objectives in concrete terms, managers and employees are able to act in ways that will achieve them. Budgets also give managers and employees a means of monitoring the results of their actions. At Framecraft, the ongoing dialogue about strategy that is part of the participative budgeting process fosters rapid improvements in productivity and customer service, as well as innovation in product and market development.

Suppose Framecraft Company has an Info Processing Division that provides database management services for the professional photographers who buy its frames. The division uses state-of-the-art equipment and employs five information specialists. Each specialist works an average of 160 hours a month. The division's controller has compiled the following information:

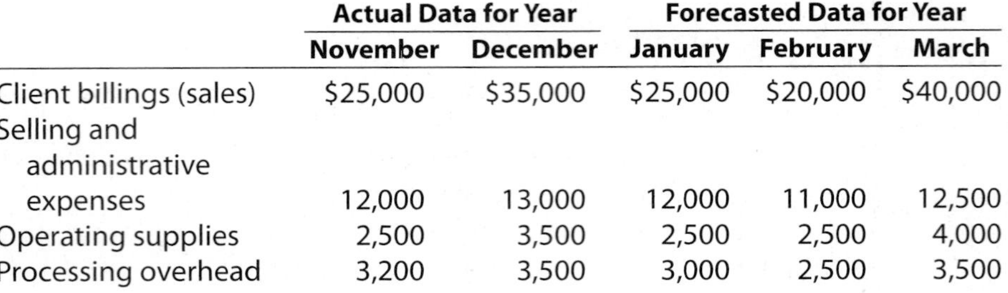

	Actual Data for Year		Forecasted Data for Year		
	November	December	January	February	March
Client billings (sales)	$25,000	$35,000	$25,000	$20,000	$40,000
Selling and administrative expenses	12,000	13,000	12,000	11,000	12,500
Operating supplies	2,500	3,500	2,500	2,500	4,000
Processing overhead	3,200	3,500	3,000	2,500	3,500

Of the client billings, 60 percent are cash sales collected during the month of sale, 30 percent are collected in the first month following the sale, and 10 percent are collected in the second month following the sale. Operating supplies are paid for in the month of purchase. Selling and administrative expenses and processing overhead are paid in the month following the cost's incurrence.

The division has a bank loan of $12,000 at a 12 percent annual interest rate. Interest is paid monthly, and $2,000 of the loan principal is due on February 28 of next year. Income taxes of $4,550 for this calendar year are due and payable on March 15 of next year. The information specialists earn $8.50 an hour, and all payroll-related employee benefit costs are included in processing overhead. The division anticipates no capital expenditures for the first quarter of the coming year. It expects its cash balance on December 31 of this year to be $13,840.

Required

Prepare a monthly cash budget for the Info Processing Division for the three-month period ending March 31 of next year. Comment on whether the ending cash balances are adequate for the division's cash needs.

Answers to Review Problem

Info Processing Division
Monthly Cash Budgets
For the Quarter Ended March 31

	January	February	March	Quarter
Total cash receipts	$28,000	$23,000	$32,500	$83,500
Cash payments				
Operating supplies	$ 2,500	$ 2,500	$ 4,000	$ 9,000
Direct labor	6,800	6,800	6,800	20,400
Selling & admin. expenses	13,000	12,000	11,000	36,000
Processing overhead	3,500	3,000	2,500	9,000
Interest expense	120	120	100	340
Loan payment	—	2,000	—	2,000
Income tax payment	—	—	4,550	4,550
Total cash payments	$25,920	$26,420	$28,950	$81,290
Cash increase (decrease)	$ 2,080	($ 3,420)	$ 3,550	$ 2,210
Beginning cash balance	13,840	15,920	12,500	13,840
Ending cash balance	$15,920	$12,500	$16,050	$16,050

The details supporting the individual computations in this cash budget are as follows:

	January	February	March
Client billings			
November	$ 2,500	—	—
December	10,500	$ 3,500	—
January	15,000	7,500	$ 2,500
February	—	12,000	6,000
March	—	—	24,000
	$28,000	$23,000	$32,500
Operating supplies			
Paid for in the month purchased	$ 2,500	$ 2,500	$ 4,000
Direct labor			
5 employees × 160 hours a month × $8.50 an hour	6,800	6,800	6,800
Selling and administrative expenses			
Paid in the month following incurrence	13,000	12,000	11,000
Processing overhead			
Paid in the month following incurrence	3,500	3,000	2,500
Interest expense			
January and February = 1% of $12,000	120	120	—
March = 1% of $10,000	—	—	100
Loan payment	—	2,000	—
Income tax payment	—	—	4,550

The ending cash balances of $15,920, $12,500, and $16,050 for January, February, and March, respectively, appear to be comfortable but not too large for the Info Processing Division.

& REVIEW >

LO1 Define *budgeting,* and explain budget basics.

Budgeting is the process of identifying, gathering, summarizing, and communicating financial and nonfinancial information about an organization's future activities. Budgeting is not only an essential part of planning; it also helps managers control, evaluate, and report on operations. When managers develop budgets, they match their organizational goals with the resources necessary to accomplish those goals. During the budgeting process, they evaluate operational, tactical, value chain, and capacity issues; assess how resources can be efficiently used; and develop contingency budgets as business conditions change. During the budget period, budgets authorize managers to use resources and provide guidelines to control costs. When managers assess performance, they can compare actual operating results to budget plans and evaluate the variances. Participative budgeting, a process in which personnel at all levels actively engage in making decisions about the budget, is key to a successful budget.

Budgets can be static, meaning they do not change during the annual budget period, or continuous, meaning they are a forward-moving budget for the next 12 months. Traditional budgeting approaches require managers to justify only budget changes over the past year. An alternative to traditional budgeting is a zero-based budgeting approach, which requires every budget item to be justified, not just the changes.

A budget committee made up of top management has overall responsibility for budget implementation. The company's controller and the budget committee oversee each stage in the preparation of the master budget, mediate any departmental disputes that may arise during the process, and give final approval to the budget. After the master budget is approved, periodic reports from department managers enable the committee to monitor the progress the company is making in attaining budget targets.

LO2 Identify the elements of a master budget in different types of organizations and the guidelines for preparing budgets.

A master budget consists of a set of operating budgets and a set of financial budgets that detail an organization's financial plans for a specific accounting period. The operating budgets serve as the basis for preparing the financial budgets, which include a budgeted income statement, a capital expenditures budget, a cash budget, and a budgeted balance sheet.

The operating budgets of a manufacturing organization include budgets for sales, production, direct materials purchases, direct labor, overhead, selling and administrative expenses, and cost of goods manufactured. The operating budgets of a retail organization include budgets for sales, purchases, selling and administrative expenses, and cost of goods sold. The operating budgets of a service organization include budgets for service revenue, labor, services overhead, and selling and administrative expenses.

The guidelines for preparing budgets include identifying the purpose of the budget, the user group and its information needs, and the sources of budget information; establishing a clear format for the budget; and using appropriate formulas and calculations to derive the quantitative information.

LO3 Prepare the operating budgets that support the financial budgets.

The initial step in preparing a master budget in any type of organization is to prepare a sales budget. Once sales have been estimated, the manager of a manufacturing organization's production department is able to prepare a budget that shows how many units of products must be manufactured to meet the projected sales volume. With that information in hand, other managers are able to prepare budgets for direct materials purchases, direct labor, overhead, selling and administrative expenses, and cost of goods manufactured. A cost of goods sold budget may be prepared separately, or it may be included in the cost of goods manufactured budget for a manufacturing organization. The operating budgets supply the information needed to prepare the financial budgets.

LO4 Prepare a budgeted income statement, a cash budget, and a budgeted balance sheet.

With estimated revenues and expenses itemized in the operating budgets, a controller is able to prepare the financial budgets. A budgeted income statement projects an organization's net income for a specific accounting period. A capital expenditures budget estimates the amount and timing of the organization's capital outlays during the period. A cash budget projects its cash receipts and cash payments for the period. Estimates of cash receipts and payments are needed to prepare a cash budget. Information about cash receipts comes from several sources, including the sales budget, the budgeted income statement, and various financial records. Sources of information about cash payments include the operating budgets, the budgeted income statement, and the capital expenditures budget. The difference between the total estimated cash receipts and total estimated cash payments is the cash increase or decrease anticipated for the period. That total plus the period's beginning cash balance equals the ending cash balance. The final step in developing a master budget is to prepare a budgeted balance sheet, which projects the organization's financial position at the end of the accounting period. All budgeted data are used in preparing this statement.

REVIEW of Concepts and Terminology

The following concepts and terms were introduced in this chapter:

Budget committee 1044 (LO1)

Budgeted balance sheet 1061 (LO4)

Budgeted income statement 1057 (LO4)

Budgeting 1042 (LO1)

Budgets 1042 (LO1)

Capital expenditures budget 1058 (LO4)

Cash budget 1058 (LO4)

Continuous budget 1044 (LO1)

Cost of goods manufactured budget 1055 (LO3)

Direct labor budget 1053 (LO3)

Direct materials purchases budget 1051 (LO3)

Financial budgets 1045 (LO2)

Master budget 1045 (LO2)

Operating budgets 1045 (LO2)

Overhead budget 1053 (LO3)

Participative budgeting 1043 (LO1)

Production budget 1050 (LO3)

Pro forma financial statements 1045 (LO2)

Sales budget 1049 (LO3)

Sales forecast 1049 (LO3)

Selling and administrative expense budget 1054 (LO3)

Static budgets 1044 (LO1)

Strategic planning 1043 (LO1)

Zero-based budgeting 1044 (LO1)

CHAPTER ASSIGNMENTS

BUILDING Your Basic Knowledge and Skills

Short Exercises

LO1 **Budgeting in a Retail Organization**

SE 1. Sam Zubac is the manager of the shoe department in a discount department store. During a recent meeting, Zubac and his supervisor agreed that Zubac's goal for the next year would be to increase the number of pairs of shoes sold by 20 percent. The department sold 8,000 pairs of shoes last year. Two sales people currently work for Zubac. What types of budgets should Zubac use to help him achieve his sales goal? What kinds of information should those budgets provide?

LO1 **Budgetary Control**

SE 2. Andi Kures owns a tree nursery. She analyzes her business's results by comparing actual operating results with figures budgeted at the beginning of the year. When the business generates large profits, she often overlooks the differences between actual and budgeted data. But when profits are low, she spends many hours analyzing the differences. If you owned Kures's business, would you use her approach to budgetary control? If not, what changes would you make?

LO2 LO3 **Components of a Master Budget**

SE 3. A master budget is a compilation of forecasts for the coming year or operating cycle made by various departments or functions within an organization. What is the most important forecast made in a master budget? List the reasons for your answer. Which budgets must managers prepare before they can prepare a direct materials purchases budget?

LO3 **Production Budget**

SE 4. Isobel Law, the controller for Aberdeen Lock Company, is preparing a production budget for the year. The company's policy is to maintain a finished goods inventory equal to one-half of the following month's sales. Sales of 7,000 locks are budgeted for April. Complete the monthly production budget for the first quarter:

	January	February	March
Sales in units	5,000	4,000	6,000
Add desired units of ending finished goods inventory	2,000	?	?
Desired total units	7,000		
Less desired units of beginning finished goods inventory	?	?	?
Total production units	4,500	?	?

LO3 **Preparing an Operating Budget**

SE 5. Ulster Company expects to sell 50,000 units of its product in the coming year. Each unit sells for $45. Sales brochures and supplies for the year are expected to cost $9,000. Two sales representatives cover the southeast region. Each representative's base salary is $20,000, and each earns a sales commission of 5 percent of the selling price of the units he or she sells. The sales representatives supply their own transportation; they are reimbursed for travel at a rate of

$0.60 per mile. The company estimates that the sales representatives will drive a total of 75,000 miles next year. From the information provided, calculate Ulster Company's budgeted selling expenses for the coming year.

LO3 LO4 **Budgeted Gross Margin**

SE 6. Operating budgets for the Paolo Company reveal the following information: net sales, $450,000; beginning materials inventory, $23,000; materials purchased, $185,000; beginning work in process inventory, $64,700; beginning finished goods inventory, $21,600; direct labor costs, $34,000; overhead applied, $67,000; ending work in process inventory, $61,200; ending materials inventory, $18,700; and ending finished goods inventory, $16,300. Compute Paolo Company's budgeted gross margin.

LO4 **Estimating Cash Collections**

SE 7. KDP Insurance Company specializes in term life insurance contracts. Cash collection experience shows that 30 percent of billed premiums are collected in the month before they are due, 60 percent are paid in the month in which they are due, and 6 percent are paid in the month following their due date. Four percent of the billed premiums are paid late (in the second month following their due date) and include a 10 percent penalty payment. Total billing notices in January were $58,000; in February, $62,000; in March, $66,000; in April, $65,000; in May, $60,000; and in June, $62,000. How much cash does the company expect to collect in May?

LO4 **Cash Budget**

SE 8. The projections of direct materials purchases that follow are for the Stromboli Corporation.

	Purchases on Account	Cash Purchases
December, 2010	$40,000	$20,000
January, 2011	60,000	30,000
February, 2011	50,000	25,000
March, 2011	70,000	35,000

The company pays for 60 percent of purchases on account in the month of purchase and 40 percent in the month following the purchase. Prepare a monthly schedule of expected cash payments for direct materials for the first quarter of 2011.

LO4 **Cash Budget**

SE 9. Alberta Limited needs a cash budget for the month of November. The following information is available:

a. The cash balance on November 1 is $6,000.
b. Sales for October and November are $80,000 and $60,000, respectively. Cash collections on sales are 30 percent in the month of sale and 65 percent in the month after the sale; 5 percent of sales are uncollectible.
c. General expenses budgeted for November are $25,000 (depreciation represents $2,000 of this amount).
d. Inventory purchases will total $30,000 in October and $40,000 in November. The company pays for half of its inventory purchases in the month of purchase and for the other half the month after purchase.
e. The company will pay $4,000 in cash for office furniture in November. Sales commissions for November are budgeted at $12,000.
f. The company maintains a minimum ending cash balance of $4,000 and can borrow from the bank in multiples of $100. All loans are repaid after 60 days.

Prepare a cash budget for Alberta Limited for the month of November.

LO4 **Budgeted Balance Sheet**

SE 10. Wellman Corporation's budgeted balance sheet for the coming year shows total assets of $4,650,000 and total liabilities of $1,900,000. Common stock and retained earnings make up the entire stockholders' equity section of the balance sheet. Common stock remains at its beginning balance of $1,500,000. The projected net income for the year is $349,600. The company pays no cash dividends. What is the balance of retained earnings at the beginning of the budget period?

Exercises

LO1 **Characteristics of Budgets**

E 1. You recently attended a workshop on budgeting and overheard the following comments as you walked to the refreshment table:

1. "Budgets are the same regardless of the size of an organization or management's role in the budgeting process."
2. "Budgets can include financial or nonfinancial data. In our organization, we plan the number of hours to be worked and the number of customer contacts we want our sales people to make."
3. "All budgets are complicated. You have to be an expert to prepare one."
4. "Budgets don't need to be highly accurate. No one in our company stays within a budget anyway."

Do you agree or disagree with each comment? Explain your answers.

LO1 **Budgeting and Goals**

E 2. Effective planning of long- and short-term goals has contributed to the success of Multitasker Calendars, Inc. Described below are the actions that the company's management team took during a recent planning meeting. Indicate whether the goals related to those actions are short-term or long-term.

1. In forecasting the next 10-year period, the management team considered economic and industry forecasts, employee–management relationships, and the structure and role of management.
2. Based on the 10-year forecast, the team made decisions about next year's sales and profit targets.

LO1 **Budgeting and Goals**

E 3. Assume that you work in the accounting department of a small wholesale warehousing company. Inspired by a recent seminar on budgeting, the company's president wants to develop a budgeting system and has asked you to direct it. Identify the points concerning the initial steps in the budgeting process that you should communicate to the president. Concentrate on principles related to long-term goals and short-term goals.

LO2 LO3 LO4 **Components of a Master Budget**

E 4. Identify the order in which the following budgets are prepared. Use the letter *a* to indicate the first budget to be prepared, *b* for the second, and so on.

1. Production budget
2. Direct labor budget
3. Direct materials purchases budget
4. Sales budget
5. Budgeted balance sheet
6. Cash budget
7. Budgeted income statement

LO3 **Sales Budget**

E 5. Quarterly and annual sales for this year for Steen Manufacturing Company follow. Prepare a sales budget for next year for the company based on the estimated percentage increases shown by product class. Show both quarterly and annual totals for each product class.

Steen Manufacturing Company
Actual Sales Revenue
For the Year Ended December 31

Product Class	January–March	April–June	July–September	October–December	Annual Totals	Estimated Percent Increases by Product Class
Marine products	$ 44,500	$ 45,500	$ 48,200	$ 47,900	$ 186,100	10%
Mountain products	36,900	32,600	34,100	37,200	140,800	5%
River products	29,800	29,700	29,100	27,500	116,100	30%
Hiking products	38,800	37,600	36,900	39,700	153,000	15%
Running products	47,700	48,200	49,400	49,900	195,200	25%
Biking products	65,400	65,900	66,600	67,300	265,200	20%
Totals	$263,100	$259,500	$264,300	$269,500	$1,056,400	

LO3 **Production Budget**

E 6. Santa Fe Corporation produces and sells a single product. Expected sales for September are 12,000 units; for October, 15,000 units; for November, 9,000 units; for December, 10,000 units; and for January, 14,000 units. The company's desired level of ending finished goods inventory at the end of a month is 10 percent of the following month's sales in units. At the end of August, 1,200 units were on hand. How many units need to be produced in the fourth quarter?

LO3 **Direct Materials Purchases Budget**

E 7. The U-Z Door Company manufactures garage door units. The units include hinges, door panels, and other hardware. Prepare a direct materials purchases budget for the first quarter of the year based on budgeted production of 16,000 garage door units. Sandee Morton, the controller, has provided the information that follows.

Hinges	4 sets per door	$11.00 per set
Door panels	4 panels per door	$27.00 per panel
Other hardware	1 lock per door	$31.00 per lock
	1 handle per door	$22.50 per handle
	2 roller tracks per door	$16.00 per set of 2 roller tracks
	8 rollers per door	$ 4.00 per roller

Assume no beginning or ending quantities of direct materials inventory.

LO3 **Direct Materials Purchases Budget**

E 8. Hard Corporation projects sales of $230,000 in May, $250,000 in June, $260,000 in July, and $240,000 in August. Since the dollar value of the company's cost of goods sold is generally 65 percent of total sales, cost of goods sold is $149,500 in May, $162,500 in June, $169,000 in July, and $156,000 in August. The dollar value of its desired ending inventory is 25 percent of the following month's cost of goods sold.

Compute the total purchases in dollars budgeted for June and the total purchases in dollars budgeted for July.

LO3 **Direct Labor Budget**

E 9. Paige Metals Company has two departments—Cutting and Grinding—and manufactures three products. Budgeted unit production for the coming year is 21,000 of Product T, 36,000 of Product M, and 30,000 of Product B. The company is currently analyzing direct labor hour requirements for the coming year. Data for each department are as follows:

	Cutting	Grinding
Estimated hours per unit		
Product T	1.1	0.5
Product M	0.6	2.9
Product B	3.2	1.0
Hourly labor rate	$9	$7

Prepare a direct labor budget for the coming year that shows the budgeted direct labor costs for each department and for the company as a whole.

LO3 **Overhead Budget**

E 10. Carole Dahl is chief financial officer of the Phoenix Division of Dahl Corporation, a multinational company with three operating divisions. As part of the budgeting process, Dahl's staff is developing the overhead budget for next year. The division estimates that it will manufacture 50,000 units during the year. The budgeted cost information is as follows:

	Variable Rate per Unit	Total Fixed Costs
Indirect materials	$1.00	
Indirect labor	4.00	
Supplies	0.40	
Repairs and maintenance	3.00	$ 40,000
Electricity	0.10	20,000
Factory supervision		180,000
Insurance		25,000
Property taxes		35,000
Depreciation–machinery		82,000
Depreciation–building		72,000

Using these data, prepare the division's overhead budget for next year.

LO4 **Cash Collections**

E 11. Dacahr Bros., Inc., is an automobile maintenance and repair company with outlets throughout the western United States. Henley Turlington, the company controller, is starting to assemble the cash budget for the fourth quarter. Projected sales for the quarter are as follows:

	On Account	Cash
October	$452,000	$196,800
November	590,000	214,000
December	720,500	218,400

Cash collection records pertaining to sales on account indicate the following collection pattern:

Month of sale	40%
First month following sale	30%
Second month following sale	28%
Uncollectible	2%

Sales on account during August were $346,000. During September, sales on account were $395,000.

Compute the amount of cash to be collected from customers during each month of the fourth quarter.

LO4 **Cash Collections**

E 12. XYZ Company collects payment on 50 percent of credit sales in the month of sale, 40 percent in the month following sale, and 5 percent in the second month following the sale. Its sales budget is as follows:

Month	Cash Sales	Credit Sales
May	$20,000	$ 40,000
June	40,000	60,000
July	60,000	80,000
August	80,000	100,000

Compute XYZ Company's total cash collections in July and its total cash collections in August.

LO4 **Cash Budget**

E 13. SABA Enterprises needs a cash budget for the month of June. The following information is available:

a. The cash balance on June 1 is $4,000.
b. Sales for May and June are $50,000 and $40,000, respectively. Cash collections on sales are 40 percent in the month of sale and 50 percent in the month after the sale; 10 percent of sales are uncollectible.
c. General expenses budgeted for June are $20,000 (depreciation represents $1,000 of this amount).
d. Inventory purchases will total $40,000 in May and $30,000 in June. The company pays for half of its inventory purchases in the month of purchase and for the other half the month after purchase.
e. The company will pay $5,000 in cash for office furniture in June. Sales commissions for June are budgeted at $6,000.
f. The company maintains a minimum ending cash balance of $4,000 and can borrow from the bank in multiples of $100. All loans are repaid after 60 days.

Prepare a cash budget for SABA Enterprises for the month of June.

LO4 **Cash Budget**

E 14. Tex Kinkaid's dream was to develop the biggest produce operation with the widest selection of fresh fruits and vegetables in northern Texas. Within three years of opening Minigarden Produce, Inc., Kincaid accomplished his objective. Kinkaid has asked you to prepare monthly cash budgets for Minigarden Produce for the quarter ended September 30.

Credit sales to retailers in the area constitute 80 percent of Minigarden Produce's business; cash sales to customers at the company's retail outlet make up the other 20 percent. Collection records indicate that Minigarden Produce collects payment on 50 percent of all credit sales during the month of sale, 30 percent in the month after the sale, and 20 percent in the second month after the sale.

The company's total sales in May were $66,000; in June, they were $67,500. Anticipated sales in July are $69,500; in August, $76,250; and in September, $84,250. The company's purchases are expected to total $43,700 in July, $48,925 in August, and $55,725 in September. The company pays for all purchases in cash.

Projected monthly costs for the quarter include $1,040 for heat, light, and power; $375 for bank fees; $1,925 for rent; $1,120 for supplies; $1,705 for depreciation of equipment; $1,285 for equipment repairs; and $475 for miscellaneous expenses. Other projected costs for the quarter are salaries and wages of $18,370 in July, $19,200 in August, and $20,300 in September.

The company's cash balance at June 30 was $2,745. It has a policy of maintaining a minimum monthly cash balance of $1,500.

1. Prepare a monthly cash budget for Minigarden Produce, Inc., for the quarter ended September 30.
2. Should Minigarden Produce anticipate taking out a loan during the quarter? If so, how much should it borrow, and when?

LO4 **Budgeted Income Statement**

E 15. Delft House, Inc., a multinational company based in Amsterdam, organizes and coordinates art shows and auctions throughout the world. Its budgeted and actual costs for last year are as follows:

	Budgeted Cost	Actual Cost
Salaries expense, staging	€ 480,000	€ 512,800
Salaries expense, executive	380,000	447,200
Travel costs	640,000	652,020
Auctioneer services	540,000	449,820
Space rental costs	251,000	246,580
Printing costs	192,000	182,500
Advertising expense	169,000	183,280
Insurance, merchandise	84,800	77,300
Insurance, liability	64,000	67,100
Home office costs	209,200	219,880
Shipping costs	105,000	112,560
Miscellaneous	25,000	25,828
Total operating expenses	€3,140,000	€3,176,868
Net receipts	€6,200,000	€6,369,200

Delft House, Inc., has budgeted the following fixed costs for the coming year: executive salaries, €440,000; advertising expense, €190,000; merchandise insurance, €80,000; and liability insurance, €68,000. Additional information pertaining to the operations of Delft House, Inc., in the coming years is as follows:

a. Net receipts are estimated at €6,400,000.
b. Salaries expense for staging will increase 20 percent over the actual figures for the last year.

c. Travel costs are expected to be 11 percent of net receipts.
d. Auctioneer services will be billed at 9.5 percent of net receipts.
e. Space rental costs will be 20 percent higher than the amount budgeted in the last year.
f. Printing costs are expected to be €190,000.
g. Home office costs are budgeted for €230,000.
h. Shipping costs are expected to be 20 percent higher than the amount budgeted in the last year.
i. Miscellaneous expenses for the coming year will be budgeted at €28,000.

Because the company sells only services, it has expenses only and no cost of sales. (Net receipts equal gross margin.)

1. Using a 40 percent income tax rate, prepare the company's budgeted income statement for the coming year.
2. Should the budget committee be worried about the trend in the company's operations? Explain your answer.

Problems

LO3 Preparing Operating Budgets

P 1. The principal product of Yangsoo Enterprises, Inc., is a multipurpose hammer that carries a lifetime guarantee. Listed next are cost and production data for the Yangsoo hammer.

Direct materials
- Anodized steel: 2 kilograms per hammer at $1.60 per kilogram
- Leather strapping for the handle: 0.5 square meter per hammer at $4.40 per square meter

Direct labor
- Forging operation: $12.50 per labor hour; 6 minutes per hammer
- Leather-wrapping operation: $12.00 per direct labor hour; 12 minutes per hammer

Overhead
- Forging operation: rate equals 70 percent of department's direct labor dollars
- Leather-wrapping operation: rate equals 50 percent of department's direct labor dollars

In October, November, and December, Yangsoo Enterprises expects to produce 108,000, 104,000, and 100,000 hammers, respectively. The company has no beginning or ending balances of direct materials inventory or work in process inventory for the year.

Required

1. For the three-month period ending December 31, prepare monthly production cost information for the Yangsoo hammer. Classify the costs as direct materials, direct labor, or overhead, and show your computations.
2. Prepare a cost of goods manufactured budget for the hammer. Show monthly cost data and combined totals for the quarter for each cost category.

LO3 LO4 **Preparing a Comprehensive Budget**

P 2. Bertha's Bathworks produces hair and bath products. Its biggest customer is a national retail chain that specializes in such products. Bertha Jackson, the owner of Bertha's Bathworks, would like to have an estimate of the company's net income in the coming year.

Required

Project Bertha's Bathworks' net income next year by completing the operating budgets and budgeted income statement that follow.

1. Sales Budget:

Bertha's Bathworks
Sales Budget
For the Year Ended December 31

	Quarter				
	1	**2**	**3**	**4**	**Year**
Sales in units	4,000	3,000	5,000	5,000	17,000
× Selling price per unit	× $5	× ?	× ?	× ?	× ?
Total sales	$20,000	?	?	?	?

2. Production Budget:

Bertha's Bathworks
Production Budget
For the Year Ended December 31

	Quarter				
	1	**2**	**3**	**4**	**Year**
Sales in units	4,000	?	?	?	?
Plus desired units of ending finished goods inventory*	**300**	?	?	**600**	**600**
Desired total units	4,300				
Less desired units of beginning finished goods inventory†	**400**	?	?	?	**400**
Total production units	3,900	?	?	?	?

*Desired units of ending finished goods inventory = 10% of next quarter's budgeted sales.
†Desired units of beginning finished goods inventory = 10% of current quarter's budgeted sales.

3. Direct Materials Purchases Budget:

Bertha's Bathworks
Direct Materials Purchases Budget
For the Year Ended December 31

	Quarter				
	1	**2**	**3**	**4**	**Year**
Total production units	3,900	3,200	5,000	5,100	17,200
× 3 ounces per unit	× 3	× ?	× ?	× ?	× ?
Total production needs in ounces	11,700	?	?	?	?
Plus desired ounces of ending direct materials inventory*	**1,920**	?	?	**3,600**	**3,600**
	13,620	?	?	?	?
Less desired ounces of beginning direct materials inventory†	**2,340**	?	?	?	**2,340**
Total ounces of direct materials to be purchased	11,280	?	?	?	?
× Cost per ounce	×$0.10	× ?	× ?	× ?	× ?
Total cost of direct materials purchases	$1,128	?	?	?	?

*Desired ounces of ending direct materials inventory = 20% of next quarter's budgeted production needs in ounces.
†Desired ounces of beginning direct materials inventory = 20% of current quarter's budgeted production needs in ounces.

4. Direct Labor Budget:

Bertha's Bathworks
Direct Labor Budget
For the Year Ended December 31

	Quarter				
	1	**2**	**3**	**4**	**Year**
Total production units	3,900	?	?	?	?
× Direct labor hours per unit	×0.10	× ?	× ?	× ?	× ?
Total direct labor hours	390	?	?	?	?
× Direct labor cost per hour	× $7	× ?	× ?	× ?	× ?
Total direct labor cost	$2,730	?	?	?	?

5. Overhead Budget:

Bertha's Bathworks
Overhead Budget
For the Year Ended December 31

	Quarter				
	1	**2**	**3**	**4**	**Year**
Variable overhead costs					
Factory supplies ($0.05)	$ 195	?	?	?	?
Employee benefits ($0.25)	975	?	?	?	?
Inspection ($0.10)	390	?	?	?	?
Maintenance and repairs ($0.15)	585	?	?	?	?
Utilities ($0.05)	195	?	?	?	?
Total variable overhead costs	$2,340	?	?	?	?
Fixed overhead costs					
Depreciation–machinery	$ 500	?	?	?	?
Depreciation–building	700	?	?	?	?
Supervision	1,800	?	?	?	?
Maintenance and repairs	400	?	?	?	?
Other overhead expenses	600	?	?	?	?
Total fixed overhead costs	$4,000	?	?	?	?
Total overhead costs	$6,340	?	?	?	?

Note: The figures in parentheses are variable costs per unit.

6. Selling and Administrative Expense Budget:

Bertha's Bathworks
Selling and Administrative Expense Budget
For the Year Ended December 31

	Quarter				
	1	**2**	**3**	**4**	**Year**
Variable selling and administrative expenses					
Delivery expenses ($0.10)	$ 400	?	?	?	?
Sales commissions ($0.15)	600	?	?	?	?
Accounting ($0.05)	200	?	?	?	?
Other administrative expenses ($0.20)	800	?	?	?	?
Total variable selling and administrative expenses	$2,000	?	?	?	?
Fixed selling and administrative expenses					
Sales salaries	$5,000	?	?	?	?
Depreciation, office equipment	900	?	?	?	?
Taxes and insurance	1,700	?	?	?	?
Total fixed selling and administrative expenses	$7,600	?	?	?	?
Total selling and administrative expenses	$9,600	?	?	?	?

Note: The figures in parentheses are variable costs per unit.

7. Cost of Goods Manufactured Budget:

Bertha's Bathworks
Cost of Goods Manufactured Budget
For the Year Ended December 31

Direct materials used		
Direct materials inventory, beginning	?	
Purchases	?	
Cost of direct materials available for use	?	
Less direct materials inventory, ending	?	
Cost of direct materials used		?
Direct labor costs		?
Overhead costs		?
Total manufacturing costs		?
Work in process inventory, beginning		?
Less work in process inventory, ending*		?
Cost of goods manufactured		?
Manufactured Cost per Unit = Cost of Goods Manufactured ÷ Units Produced		?

*It is the company's policy to have no units in process at the end of the year.

8. Budgeted Income Statement:

Bertha's Bathworks
Budgeted Income Statement
For the Year Ended December 31

Sales		?
Cost of goods sold		
Finished goods inventory, beginning	?	
Cost of goods manufactured	?	
Cost of goods available for sale	?	
Less finished goods inventory, ending	?	
Cost of goods sold		?
Gross margin		?
Selling and administrative expenses		?
Income from operations		?
Income taxes expense (30%)*		?
Net income		?

*The figure in parentheses is the company's income tax rate.

LO4 **Basic Cash Budget**

P 3. Felasco Nurseries, Inc., has been in business for six years and has four divisions. Ethan Poulis, the corporation's controller, has been asked to prepare a cash budget for the Southern Division for the first quarter. Projected data supporting this budget follow.

Sales (60% on credit)		Purchases	
November	$160,000	December	$ 86,800
December	200,000	January	124,700
January	120,000	February	99,440
February	160,000	March	104,800
March	140,000		

Collection records of accounts receivable have shown that 30 percent of all credit sales are collected in the month of sale, 60 percent in the month following the sale, and 8 percent in the second month following the sale; 2 percent of the sales are uncollectible. All purchases are paid for in the month after the purchase. Salaries and wages are projected to be $25,200 in January, $33,200 in February, and $21,200 in March. Estimated monthly costs are utilities, $4,220; collection fees, $1,700; rent, $5,300; equipment depreciation, $5,440; supplies, $2,480; small tools, $3,140; and miscellaneous, $1,900.

Each of the corporation's divisions maintains a $6,000 minimum cash balance. As of December 31, the Southern Division had a cash balance of $9,600.

Required

1. Prepare a monthly cash budget for Felasco Nurseries' Southern Division for the first quarter.
2. Should Felasco Nurseries anticipate taking out a loan for the Southern Division during the quarter? If so, how much should it borrow, and when? (Manager insight ▶)

LO4 **Cash Budget**

P 4. Security Services Company provides security monitoring services. It employs five security specialists. Each specialist works an average of 160 hours a month. The company's controller has compiled the following information:

	Actual Data for Last Year		Forecasted Data for Next Year		
	November	December	January	February	March
Security billings (sales)	$30,000	$35,000	$25,000	$20,000	$30,000
Selling and administrative expenses	10,000	11,000	9,000	8,000	10,500
Operating supplies	2,500	3,500	2,500	2,000	3,000
Service overhead	3,000	3,500	3,000	2,500	3,000

Sixty percent of the client billings are cash sales collected during the month of sale; 30 percent are collected in the first month following the sale; and 10 percent are collected in the second month following the sale. Operating supplies are paid for in the month of purchase. Selling and administrative expenses and service overhead are paid in the month following the cost's incurrence.

The company has a bank loan of $12,000 at a 12 percent annual interest rate. Interest is paid monthly, and $2,000 of the loan principal is due on February 28. Income taxes of $4,500 for the last calendar year are due and payable on March 15. The five security specialists each earn $8.50 an hour, and all payroll-related employee benefit costs are included in service overhead. The company anticipates no capital expenditures for the first quarter of the coming year. It expects its cash balance on December 31 to be $13,000.

Required

Prepare a monthly cash budget for Security Services Company for the three-month period ended March 31.

LO4 Budgeted Income Statement and Budgeted Balance Sheet

P 5. Moontrust Bank has asked the president of Wishware Products, Inc., for a budgeted income statement and budgeted balance sheet for the quarter ended June 30. These pro forma financial statements are needed to support Wishware Products' request for a loan.

Wishware Products routinely prepares a quarterly master budget. The operating budgets prepared for the quarter ending June 30 have provided the following information: Projected sales for April are $220,400; for May, $164,220; and for June, $165,980. Direct materials purchases for the period are estimated at $96,840; direct materials usage, at $102,710; direct labor expenses, at $71,460; overhead, at $79,940; selling and administrative expenses, at $143,740; capital expenditures, at $125,000 (to be spent on June 29); cost of goods manufactured, at $252,880; and cost of goods sold, at $251,700.

Balance sheet account balances at March 31 were as follows: Accounts Receivable, $26,500; Materials Inventory, $23,910; Work in Process Inventory, $31,620; Finished Goods Inventory, $36,220; Prepaid Expenses, $7,200; Plant, Furniture, and Fixtures, $498,600; Accumulated Depreciation–Plant, Furniture, and Fixtures, $141,162; Patents, $90,600; Accounts Payable, $39,600; Notes Payable, $105,500; Common Stock, $250,000; and Retained Earnings, $207,158.

Projected monthly cash balances for the second quarter are as follows: April 30, $20,490; May 31, $35,610; and June 30, $45,400. During the quarter, accounts receivable are expected to increase by 30 percent, patents to go up by $6,500, prepaid expenses to remain constant, and accounts payable to go down by 10 percent (Wishware Products will make a $5,000 payment on a note payable, $4,100 of which is principal reduction). The federal income tax rate is 34 percent, and the second quarter's tax is paid in July. Depreciation for the quarter will be $6,420, which is included in the overhead budget. The company will pay no dividends.

Required

1. Prepare a budgeted income statement for the quarter ended June 30. Round answers to the nearest dollar.
2. Prepare a budgeted balance sheet as of June 30.

Alternate Problems

LO3 Preparing Operating Budgets

P 6. The principal product of Waterworks, Inc., is a metal water bottle that carries a lifetime guarantee. Listed here are cost and production data for the water bottle.

Direct materials
Stainless steel: 0.25 kilogram per bottle at $8.00 per kilogram
Clip for the handle: 1 per bottle at $0.10 each

Direct labor
Stamping operation: $30 per labor hour; 2 minutes per bottle

Overhead
Stamping operation: rate equals 70 percent of department's direct labor dollars

In January, February, and March, Waterworks expects to produce 200,000, 225,000, and 150,000 bottles, respectively. The company has no beginning or ending balances of direct materials inventory or work in process inventory for the year.

Required

1. For the three-month period ending March 31, prepare monthly production cost information for the metal water bottle. Classify the costs as direct materials, direct labor, or overhead, and show your computations.
2. Prepare a cost of goods manufactured budget for the water bottle. Show monthly cost data and combined totals for the quarter for each cost category.

LO3 LO4 **Preparing a Comprehensive Budget**

P 7. The Bottled Water Company has been bottling and selling water since 1940. Ginnie Adams, the current owner of The Bottled Water Company, would like to know how a new product would affect the company's net income in the coming year.

Required

Calculate The Bottled Water Company's net income for the new product in the coming year by completing the operating budgets and budgeted income statement that follow.

1. Sales Budget:

The Bottled Water Company
Sales Budget
For the Year Ended December 31

	Quarter				
	1	**2**	**3**	**4**	**Year**
Sales in units	40,000	30,000	50,000	55,000	175,000
× Selling price per unit	× $1	× ?	× ?	× ?	× ?
Total sales	$40,000	?	?	?	?

2. Production Budget:

The Bottled Water Company
Production Budget
For the Year Ended December 31

	Quarter				
	1	**2**	**3**	**4**	**Year**
Sales in units	40,000	?	?	?	?
Plus desired units of ending finished goods inventory*	3,000	?	?	6,000	6,000
Desired total units	43,000				
Less desired units of beginning finished goods inventory†	4,000	?	?	?	4,000
Total production units	39,000	?	?	?	?

*Desired units of ending finished goods inventory = 10% of next quarter's budgeted sales.
†Desired units of beginning finished goods inventory = 10% of current quarter's budgeted sales.

3. Direct Materials Purchases Budget:

The Bottled Water Company
Direct Materials Purchases Budget
For the Year Ended December 31

	Quarter 1	2	3	4	Year
Total production units	39,000	32,000	50,500	55,500	?
× 20 ounces per unit	× 20	× ?	× ?	× ?	× ?
Total production needs in ounces	780,000	?	?	?	?
Plus desired ounces of ending direct materials inventory*	128,000	?	?	240,000	240,000
	908,000	?	?	?	?
Less desired ounces of beginning direct materials inventory†	156,000	?	?	?	156,000
Total ounces of direct materials to be purchased	752,000	?	?	?	?
× Cost per ounce	× $0.01	× ?	× ?	× ?	× ?
Total cost of direct materials purchases	$ 7,520	?	?	?	?

*Desired ounces of ending direct materials inventory = 20% of next quarter's budgeted production needs in ounces.
†Desired ounces of beginning direct materials inventory = 20% of current quarter's budgeted production needs in ounces.

4. Direct Labor Budget:

The Bottled Water Company
Direct Labor Budget
For the Year Ended December 31

	Quarter 1	2	3	4	Year
Total production units	39,000	?	?	?	?
× Direct labor hours per unit	× 0.001	× ?	× ?	× ?	× ?
Total direct labor hours	39.0	?	?	?	?
× Direct labor cost per hour	× $8	× ?	× ?	× ?	× ?
Total direct labor cost	$312	?	?	?	?

5. Overhead Budget:

The Bottled Water Company
Overhead Budget
For the Year Ended December 31

	Quarter 1	2	3	4	Year
Variable overhead costs					
Factory supplies ($0.01)	$ 390	?	?	?	?
Employee benefits ($0.05)	1,950	?	?	?	?
Inspection ($0.01)	390	?	?	?	?
Maintenance and repairs ($0.02)	780	?	?	?	?
Utilities ($0.01)	390	?	?	?	?
Total variable overhead costs	$3,900	?	?	?	?
Total fixed overhead costs	1,500	?	?	?	?
Total overhead costs	$5,400	?	?	?	?

Note: The figures in parentheses are variable costs per unit.

6. Selling and Administrative Expense Budget:

The Bottled Water Company
Selling and Administrative Expense Budget
For the Year Ended December 31

	Quarter 1	2	3	4	Year
Variable selling and administrative expenses					
Delivery expenses ($0.01)	$ 400	?	?	?	?
Sales commissions ($0.02)	800	?	?	?	?
Accounting ($0.01)	400	?	?	?	?
Other administrative expenses ($0.01)	400	?	?	?	?
Total variable selling and administrative expenses	$2,000	?	?	?	?
Total fixed selling and administrative expenses	5,000	?	?	?	?
Total selling and administrative expenses	$7,000	?	?	?	?

Note: The figures in parentheses are variable costs per unit.

7. Cost of Goods Manufactured Budget:

The Bottled Water Company
Cost of Goods Manufactured Budget
For the Year Ended December 31

Direct materials used		
Direct materials inventory, beginning	?	
Purchases during the year	?	
Cost of direct materials available for use	?	
Less direct materials inventory, ending		?
Cost of direct materials used		?
Direct labor costs		?
Overhead costs		?
Total manufacturing costs		?
Work in process inventory, beginning*		0
Less work in process inventory, ending*		0
Cost of goods manufactured		?
Manufactured Cost per Unit = Cost of Goods Manufactured ÷ Units Produced		?

*It is the company's policy to have no units in process at the end of the year.

8. Budgeted Income Statement:

The Bottled Water Company
Budgeted Income Statement
For the Year Ended December 31

Sales		?
Cost of goods sold		
Finished goods inventory, beginning	?	
Cost of goods manufactured	?	
Cost of goods available for sale	?	
Less finished goods inventory, ending	?	
Cost of goods sold		?
Gross margin		?
Selling and administrative expenses		?
Income from operations		?
Income taxes expense (30%)*		?
Net income		?

*The figure in parentheses is the company's income tax rate.

LO4 Comprehensive Cash Budget

P 8. Located in Telluride, Colorado, Wellness Centers, Inc., emphasizes the benefits of regular workouts and the importance of physical examinations. The corporation operates three fully equipped fitness centers, as well as a medical center that specializes in preventive medicine. The data that follow pertain to the corporation's first quarter.

Cash Receipts
Memberships: December, 870; January, 880; February, 910; March, 1,030
Membership dues: $90 per month, payable on the 10th of the month
(80 percent collected on time; 20 percent collected one month late)
Medical examinations: January, $35,610; February, $41,840; March, $45,610
Special aerobics classes: January, $4,020; February, $5,130; March, $7,130
High-protein food sales: January, $4,890; February, $5,130; March, $6,280

Cash Payments
Salaries and wages:
Corporate officers: 2 at $12,000 per month
Physicians: 2 at $7,000 per month
Nurses: 3 at $2,900 per month
Clerical staff: 2 at $1,500 per month
Aerobics instructors: 3 at $1,100 per month
Clinic staff: 6 at $1,700 per month
Maintenance staff: 3 at $900 per month
Health-food servers: 3 at $750 per month

Purchases:
Muscle-toning machines: January, $14,400; February, $13,800 (no purchases in March)
Pool supplies: $520 per month
Health food: January, $3,290; February, $3,460; March, $3,720
Medical supplies: January, $10,400; February, $11,250; March, $12,640
Medical uniforms and disposable garments: January, $7,410; February, $3,900; March, $3,450
Medical equipment: January, $11,200; February, $3,400; March $5,900
Advertising: January, $2,250; February, $1,190; March, $2,450
Utilities expense: January, $5,450; February, $5,890; March, $6,090

Insurance:
Fire: January, $3,470
Liability: March, $3,980

Property taxes: $3,760 due in January
Federal income taxes: Last year's taxes of $21,000 due in March
Miscellaneous: January, $2,625; February, $2,800; March, $1,150

Wellness Centers' controller anticipates that the beginning cash balance on January 1 will be $9,840.

Required

Prepare a cash budget for Wellness Centers, Inc., for the first quarter of the year. Use January, February, March, and Quarter as the column headings.

LO4 Cash Budget

P 9. FM Company provides fraud monitoring services. It employs four fraud specialists. Each specialist works an average of 200 hours a month. The company's controller has compiled the following information:

	Actual Data for Last Year		Forecasted Data for Next Year		
	November	December	January	February	March
Billings (sales)	$100,000	$80,000	$60,000	$50,000	$70,000
Selling and administrative expenses	15,000	12,000	8,000	7,000	10,000
Operating supplies	2,500	3,500	2,500	2,000	3,000
Service overhead	14,000	13,500	13,000	12,500	13,000

Seventy percent of the client billings are cash sales collected during the month of sale; 20 percent are collected in the first month following the sale; and 10 percent are collected in the second month following the sale. Operating supplies are paid in the month of purchase. Selling and administrative expenses and service overhead are paid in the month the cost is incurred.

The company has a bank loan of $12,000 at a 6 percent annual interest rate. Interest is paid monthly, and $2,000 of the loan principal is due on February 28. Income taxes of $6,500 for last calendar year are due and payable on March 15. The four security specialists each earn $48.00 an hour, and all payroll-related employee benefit costs are included in service overhead. The company anticipates no capital expenditures for the first quarter of the coming year. It expects its cash balance on December 31 to be $10,000.

Required

Prepare a monthly cash budget for FM Company for the three-month period ended March 31.

LO4 Budgeted Income Statement and Budgeted Balance Sheet

P 10. Stillwater Video Company, Inc., produces and markets two popular video games, *High Range* and *Star Boundary*. The closing account balances on the company's balance sheet for last year are as follows: Cash, $18,735; Accounts Receivable, $19,900; Materials Inventory, $18,510; Work in Process Inventory, $24,680; Finished Goods Inventory, $21,940; Prepaid Expenses, $3,420; Plant and Equipment, $262,800; Accumulated Depreciation–Plant and Equipment, $55,845; Other Assets, $9,480; Accounts Payable, $52,640; Mortgage Payable, $70,000; Common Stock, $90,000; and Retained Earnings, $110,980.

Operating budgets for the first quarter of the coming year show the following estimated costs: direct materials purchases, $58,100; direct materials usage, $62,400; direct labor expense, $42,880; overhead, $51,910; selling expenses, $35,820; general and administrative expenses, $60,240; cost of goods manufactured, $163,990; and cost of goods sold, $165,440. Estimated ending cash balances are as follows: January, $34,610; February, $60,190; and March, $54,802. The company will have no capital expenditures during the quarter.

Sales are projected to be $125,200 in January, $105,100 in February, and $112,600 in March. Accounts receivable are expected to double during the quarter, and accounts payable are expected to decrease by 20 percent. Mortgage payments for the quarter will total $6,000, of which $2,000 will be interest expense. Prepaid expenses are expected to go up by $20,000, and other assets are projected to increase by 50 percent over the budget period. Depreciation for plant and equipment (already included in the overhead budget) averages 5 percent of total plant and equipment per year. Federal income taxes (34 percent of profits) are payable in April. The company pays no dividends.

Required

1. Prepare a budgeted income statement for the quarter ended March 31.
2. Prepare a budgeted balance sheet as of March 31.

ENHANCING Your Knowledge, Skills, and Critical Thinking

LO1 LO2 **Policies for Budget Development**

C 1. Hector Corporation is a manufacturing company with annual sales of $25 million. Its budget committee has created the following policy that the company uses each year in developing its master budget for the following calendar year:

May	The company's controller and other members of the budget committee meet to discuss plans and objectives for next year. The controller conveys all relevant information from this meeting to division managers and department heads.
June	Division managers, department heads, and the controller meet to discuss the corporate plans and objectives for next year. They develop a timetable for developing next year's budget data.
July	Division managers and department heads develop budget data. The vice president of sales provides them with final sales estimates, and they complete monthly sales estimates for each product line.
August	Estimates of next year's monthly production activity and inventory levels are completed. Division managers and department heads communicate these estimates to the controller, who distributes them to other operating areas.
September	All operating areas submit their revised budget data. The controller integrates their labor requirements, direct materials requirements, unit cost estimates, cash requirements, and profit estimates into a preliminary master budget.
October	The budget committee meets to discuss the preliminary master budget and to make any necessary corrections, additions, or deletions. The controller incorporates all authorized changes into a final draft of the master budget.
November	The controller submits the final draft to the budget committee for approval. If the committee approves it, it is distributed to all corporate officers, division managers, and department heads.

1. Comment on this policy.
2. What changes would you recommend?

LO1 LO3 **Ethical Considerations in Budgeting**

C 2. Javier Gonzales is the manager of the Repairs and Maintenance Department of JG Industries. He is responsible for preparing his department's annual budget. Most managers in the company inflate their budget numbers by at least 10 percent because their bonuses depend upon how much below budget their departments operate. Gonzales turned in the following information for his department's budget for next year to the company's budget committee:

	Budget This Year	Actual This Year	Budget Next Year
Supplies	$ 20,000	$ 16,000	$ 24,000
Labor	80,000	82,000	96,000
Utilities	8,500	8,000	10,200
Tools	12,500	9,000	15,000
Hand-carried equipment	25,000	16,400	30,000
Cleaning materials	4,600	4,200	5,520
Miscellaneous	2,000	2,100	2,400
Totals	$152,600	$137,700	$183,120

Because the figures for next year are 20 percent above those in this year's budget, the budget committee questioned them. Gonzales defended them by saying that he expects a significant increase in activity in his department next year.

What do you think are the real reasons for the increase in the budgeted amounts? What ethical considerations enter into this situation?

LO4 Budgeting for Cash Flows

C 3. The nature of a company's business affects its need to budget for cash flows. **H&R Block** is a service company whose main business is preparing tax returns. Most tax returns are prepared after January 31 and before April 15. For a fee and interest, the company will advance cash to clients who are due refunds. The clients are expected to repay the cash advances when they receive their refunds. Although H&R Block has some revenues throughout the year, it devotes most of the nontax season to training potential employees in tax preparation procedures and to laying the groundwork for the next tax season.

Toys "R" Us is a toy retailer whose sales are concentrated in October, November, and December of one year and January of the next year. Sales continue at a steady but low level during the rest of the year. The company purchases most of its inventory between July and September.

Johnson & Johnson sells the many health care products that it manufactures to retailers, and the retailers sell them to the final customer. Johnson & Johnson offers retailers credit terms.

Discuss the nature of cash receipts and cash disbursements over a calendar year in the three companies we have just described. What are some key estimates that the management of these companies must make when preparing a cash budget?

LO1 LO4 Budgeting Procedures

C 4. Since Rood Enterprises inaugurated participative budgeting 10 years ago, everyone in the organization—from maintenance personnel to the president's staff—has had a voice in the budgeting process. Until recently, participative budgeting has worked in the best interests of the company as a whole. Now, however, it is becoming evident that some managers are using the practice solely to benefit their own divisions. The budget committee has therefore asked you, the company's controller, to analyze this year's divisional budgets carefully before incorporating them into the company's master budget.

The Motor Division was the first of the company's six divisions to submit its budget request for next year. The division's budgeted income statement follows.

Rood Enterprises
Motor Division
Budgeted Income Statement
For the Years Ended December 31

	Budget for This Year	Budget for Next Year	Increase (Decrease)
Net sales			
Radios	$ 850,000	$ 910,000	$ 60,000
Appliances	680,000	740,000	60,000
Telephones	270,000	305,000	35,000
Miscellaneous	84,400	90,000	5,600
Net sales	$1,884,400	$2,045,000	$160,600
Less cost of goods sold	750,960	717,500*	(33,460)
Gross margin	$1,133,440	$1,327,500	$194,060
Operating expenses			
Wages			
Warehouse	$ 94,500	$ 102,250	$ 7,750
Purchasing	77,800	84,000	6,200
Delivery/shipping	69,400	74,780	5,380
Maintenance	42,650	45,670	3,020
Salaries			
Supervisory	60,000	92,250	32,250
Executive	130,000	164,000	34,000
Purchases, supplies	17,400	20,500	3,100
Maintenance	72,400	82,000	9,600
Depreciation	62,000	74,750†	12,750
Building rent	96,000	102,500	6,500
Sales commissions	188,440	204,500	16,060
Insurance			
Fire	12,670	20,500	7,830
Liability	18,200	20,500	2,300
Utilities	14,100	15,375	1,275
Taxes			
Property	16,600	18,450	1,850
Payroll	26,520	41,000	14,480
Miscellaneous	4,610	10,250	5,640
Total operating expenses	$1,003,290	$1,173,275	$169,985
Income from operations	$ 130,150	$ 154,225	$ 24,075

*Less expensive merchandise will be purchased in the next year to boost profits.
†Depreciation is increased because additional equipment must be bought to handle increased sales.

1. Recast the Motor Division's budgeted income statement in the following format (round percentages to two places):

	Budget for This Year		Budget for Next Year	
Account	**Amount**	**Percentage of Net Sales**	**Amount**	**Percentage of Net Sales**

2. Actual results for this year revealed the following information about revenues and cost of goods sold:

	Amount	Percentage of Net Sales
Net sales		
Radios	$ 780,000	43.94
Appliances	640,000	36.06
Telephones	280,000	15.77
Miscellaneous	75,000	4.23
Net sales	$1,775,000	100.00
Less cost of goods sold	763,425	43.01
Gross margin	$1,011,575	56.99

On the basis of this information and your analysis in **1**, what do you think the budget committee should say to the managers of the Motor Division? Identify any specific areas of the budget that may need to be revised, and explain why the revision is needed.

LO3 LO4 The Budgeting Process

C 5. Refer to our development of Framecraft Company's master budget in this chapter. Suppose that because of a new customer in Canada, the company or management has decided to increase budgeted sales in the first quarter by 5,000 units. The expenses for this sale will include direct materials, direct labor, variable overhead, and variable selling and administrative expenses. The delivery expense for the Canadian customer will be $0.18 per unit rather than the regular $0.08 per unit. The desired units of beginning finished goods inventory will remain at 1,000 units.

1. Using an Excel spreadsheet, revise Framecraft Company's budgeted income statement and the operating budgets that support it to reflect the changes described above. (Round manufactured cost per unit to three decimals.)
2. What was the change in income from operations? Would you recommend accepting the order from the Canadian customer? If so, why?

LO1 LO2 LO4 Cookie Company (Continuing Case)

C 6. In this segment of our continuing case, you have decided to open a store where you will sell your company's cookies, as well as coffee, tea, and other beverages. You believe that the store will be able to provide excellent service and undersell the local competition. To fund operations, you are applying for a loan from the Small Business Administration. The loan application requires you to submit two financial budgets—a pro forma income statement and a pro forma balance sheet—within six weeks.

How do the four *w*'s of preparing an accounting report apply in this situation—that is, *why* are you preparing these financial budgets, *who* needs them, *what* information do you need to prepare them, and *when* are they due?

CHAPTER 25

Performance Management and Evaluation

The Management Process

PLAN

- **Translate the organization's mission and vision into operational objectives from multiple stakeholders' perspectives**
- **Select performance measures for objectives**
- **Establish targets for each performance objective**

PERFORM

- **Balance the needs of all stakeholders when making decisions**
- **Improve performance by tracking causal relationships among objectives, measures, and targets**

EVALUATE

- **Compare financial and nonfinancial results with performance targets**
- **Analyze results and take corrective actions**

COMMUNICATE

- **Prepare reports of interest to stakeholder groups**

If managers want satisfactory results, they must understand the cause-and-effect relationships between their actions and their organization's overall performance. By measuring and tracking the relationships that they are responsible for, managers can improve performance and thereby add value for all of their organization's stakeholders. In this chapter, we describe the role of the balanced scorecard, responsibility accounting, and economic value added as they relate to performance management and evaluation. We also point out how managers can use a wide range of financial and nonfinancial data to manage and evaluate performance more effectively.

LEARNING OBJECTIVES

LO1 **Define a *performance management and evaluation system*, and describe how the balanced scorecard aligns performance with organizational goals.** (pp. 1094–1097)

LO2 **Define *responsibility accounting*, and describe the role that responsibility centers play in performance management and evaluation.** (pp. 1097–1101)

LO3 **Prepare performance reports for cost centers using flexible budgets and for profit centers using variable costing.** (pp. 1102–1105)

LO4 **Prepare performance reports for investment centers using the traditional measures of return on investment and residual income and the newer measure of economic value added.** (pp. 1105–1111)

LO5 **Explain how properly linked performance incentives and measures add value for all stakeholders in performance management and evaluation.** (pp. 1111–1114)

DECISION POINT ► A MANAGER'S FOCUS WINTER WONDERLAND RESORT

- ► How do managers at Winter Wonderland Resort link performance measures and set performance targets to achieve performance objectives?
- ► How do they use the resort's all-in-one card system and its integrated database to improve performance management and evaluation?

Winter Wonderland Resort is a full-service resort and spa. When guests first check in, they are issued an "all-in-one" charge card, which they can use to pay for anything they might buy at the resort—for example, meals or snacks, skiing or snowboarding lessons, lift tickets, treatments at the spa, or merchandise from one of the resort's retail shops.

Guests like the all-in-one card because of its convenience and because each time they use it, they earn points toward free lodging, meals, or lift tickets. The resort's managers like the card system because it is a simple way of collecting vast amounts of both financial and nonfinancial information. Each time a guest makes a purchase, the all-in-one card is electronically scanned; the new data then becomes part of an integrated management information system, which managers use in a variety of ways to measure and evaluate the resort's performance.

Performance Measurement

LO1 Define a *performance management and evaluation system*, and describe how the balanced scorecard aligns performance with organizational goals.

A **performance management and evaluation system** is a set of procedures that account for and report on both financial and nonfinancial performance so that a company can identify how well it is doing, where it is going, and what improvements will make it more profitable.

What to Measure, How to Measure

Performance measurement is the use of quantitative tools to gauge an organization's performance in relation to a specific goal or an expected outcome. For performance measurement to succeed, managers must be able to distinguish between what is being measured and the actual measures used to monitor performance. For instance, product or service quality is not a performance measure. It is part of a management strategy: Management wants to produce the highest-quality product or service possible, given the resources available. Product or service quality thus is what management wants to measure.

> **Study Note**
>
> What a manager is measuring—for example, quality—is not the same thing as the actual measures used to monitor performance—for example, the number of defective units per hour.

To measure product or service quality, managers must collaborate with other managers to develop a group of measures, such as the balanced scorecard, that will identify changes in product or service quality and help employees determine what needs to be done to improve quality.

Other Measurement Issues

Each organization must develop a set of performance measures that is appropriate to its situation. In addition to answering the basic questions of what to measure and how to measure, management must consider a variety of other issues, including the following:

- What performance measures can be used?
- How can managers monitor the level of product or service quality?
- How can managers monitor production and other business processes to identify areas that need improvement?
- How can managers measure customer satisfaction?
- How can managers monitor financial performance?
- Are there other stakeholders to whom a manager is accountable?
- What performance measures do government entities impose on the company?
- How can a manager measure the company's effect on the environment?

FOCUS ON BUSINESS PRACTICE

"Old" Doesn't Mean "Out-of-Date"

The *tableau de bord*, or "dashboard," was developed by French engineers around 1900 as a concise performance measurement system that helped managers understand the cause-and-effect relationships between their decisions and the resulting performance. The indicators, both financial and nonfinancial, allowed managers at all levels to monitor their progress in terms of the mission and objectives of their unit and of their company overall. Like a set of nested Russian dolls, each unit's key success factors and key performance indicators were integrated with those of other units. The dashboard continues to encourage a performance measurement system that focuses on and supports an organization's strategic plan.[1]

Organizational Goals and the Balanced Scorecard

The **balanced scorecard**, developed by Robert S. Kaplan and David R Norton, is a framework that links the perspectives of an organization's four basic stakeholder groups—financial (investors), learning and growth (employees), internal business processes, and customers—with the organization's mission and vision, performance measures, strategic and tactical plans, and resources. To succeed, an organization must add value for all groups in both the short and the long term. Thus, an organization will determine each group's objectives and translate them into performance measures that have specific, quantifiable performance targets. Ideally, managers should be able to see how their actions contribute to the achievement of organizational goals and understand how their compensation is related to their actions. The balanced scorecard assumes that an organization will get only what it measures.

The Balanced Scorecard and Management

To illustrate how managers use the balanced scorecard, we will refer to Winter Wonderland Resort's all-in-one card system, which we described in the Decision Point.

Planning During the planning stage, the balanced scorecard provides a framework that enables managers to translate their organization's vision and strategy into operational terms. Managers evaluate the company's vision from the perspective of each stakeholder group and seek to answer one key question for each group:

- ***Financial (investors):*** To achieve our organization's vision, how should we appear to our shareholders?
- ***Learning and growth (employees):*** To achieve our organization's vision, how should we sustain our ability to improve and change?
- ***Internal business processes:*** To succeed, in which business processes must our organization excel?
- ***Customers:*** To achieve our organization's vision, how should we appeal to our customers?

> **Study Note**
> The alignment of an organization's strategy with all the perspectives of the balanced scorecard results in performance objectives that benefit all stakeholders.

These key questions align the organization's strategy from all perspectives. The answers to the questions result in performance objectives that are mutually beneficial to all stakeholders. Once the organization's objectives are set, managers can select performance measures and set performance targets to translate the objectives into an action plan. For example, if Winter Wonderland Resorts' collective vision and strategy is to please guests, its managers might establish the following overall objectives:

Perspective	*Objective*
Financial (investors)	Increase guests' spending at the resort.
Learning and growth (employees)	Continually cross-train employees in each other's duties to sustain premium-quality service for guests.
Internal business processes	Leverage market position by introducing and improving innovative marketing and technology-driven advances that clearly benefit guests.
Customers	Create new premium-price experiences and facilities for vacations in all seasons.

These overall objectives are then translated into specific performance objectives and measures for specific managers. Figure 25-1 summarizes how Winter

Wonderland Resort's managers might link their organization's vision and strategy to objectives, then link the objectives to logical performance measures, and, finally, set performance targets for a ski lift manager. As a result, a ski lift manager will have a variety of performance measures that balance the perspectives and needs of all stakeholders.

Performing Managers use the mutually agreed-upon strategic and tactical objectives for the entire organization as the basis for decision making within their individual areas of responsibility. This practice ensures that they consider the needs of all stakeholder groups and shows how measuring and managing performance for some stakeholder groups can lead to improved performance for another stakeholder group. Specifically, improving the performance of leading indicators like internal business processes and learning and growth will create improvements for customers, which in turn will result in improved financial performance (a lagging indicator). For example, when making decisions about available ski lift capacity, the ski lift manager will balance such factors as lift ticket sales, snow conditions, equipment reliability, trained staff availability, and length of wait for ski lifts.

When managers understand the causal and linked relationship between their actions and their company's overall performance, they can see new ways to be more effective. For example, a ski lift manager may hypothesize that shorter waiting lines for the ski lifts would improve customer satisfaction and lead to more visits to the ski lift. The manager could test this possible cause-and-effect relationship by measuring and tracking the length of ski lift waiting lines and the number of visits to the ski lift. If a causal relationship exists, the manager can improve the performance of the ski lift operation by doing everything possible to ensure that

FIGURE 25-1 Sample Balanced Scorecard of Linked Objectives, Performance Measures, and Targets

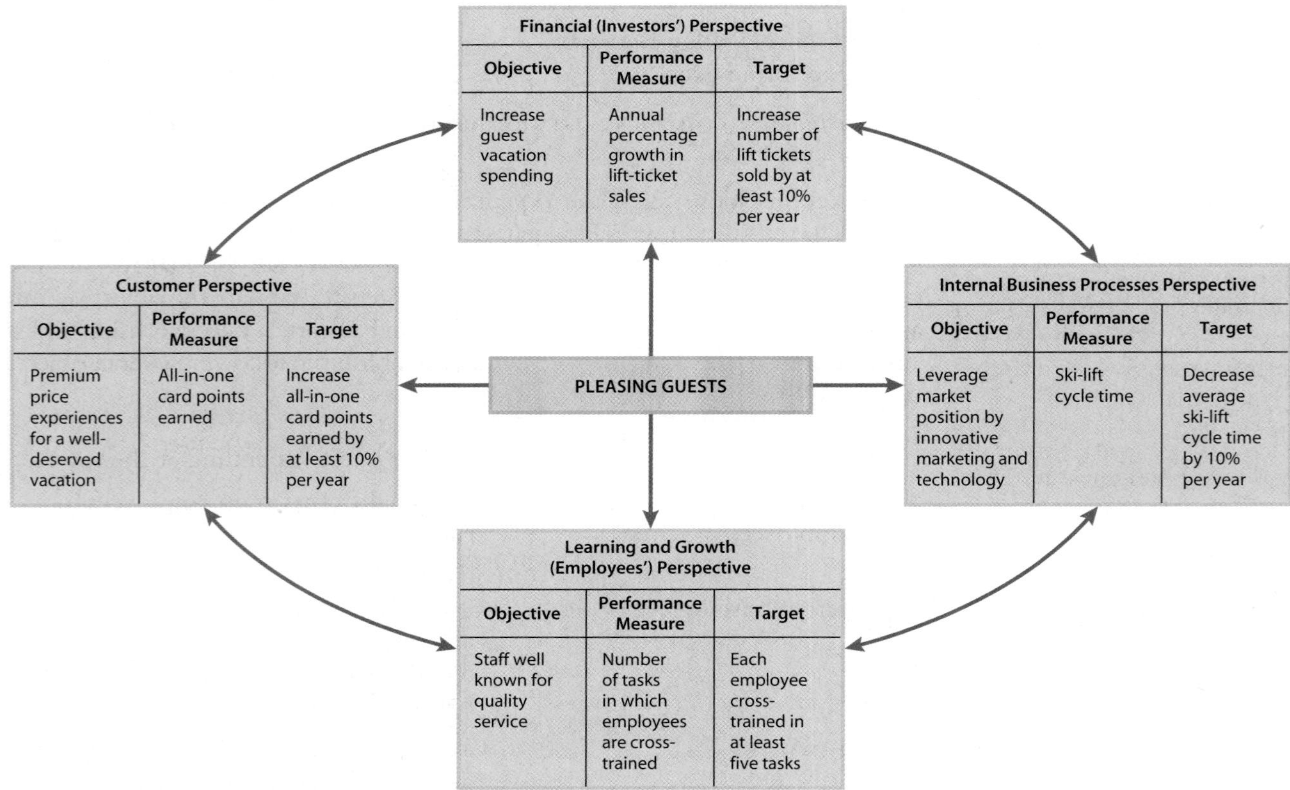

Source: Adapted from Robert S. Kaplan and David P. Norton, "Using the Balanced Scorecard as a Strategic Management System," *Harvard Business Review*, January–February 1996.

waiting lines are short because a quicker ride to the top will result in improved results for the operation and for other perspectives as well.

Evaluating Managers compare performance objectives and targets with actual results to determine if the targets were met, what measures need to be changed, and what strategies or objectives need revision. For example, the ski lift manager would analyze the reasons for performance gaps and make recommendations to improve the performance of the ski lift area.

Communicating A variety of reports enable managers to monitor and evaluate performance measures that add value for stakeholder groups. For example, the database makes it possible to prepare financial performance reports, customer statements, internal business process reports for targeted performance measures and results, and performance appraisals of individual employees.

The balanced scorecard adds dimension to the management process. Managers plan, perform, evaluate, and communicate the organization's performance from multiple perspectives. By balancing the needs of all stakeholders, managers are more likely to achieve their objectives in both the short and the long term.

STOP & APPLY >

Molly Sams wants to measure customer satisfaction within her sales region. Link an appropriate performance measure with each balanced scorecard perspective.

Customer Satisfaction	Possible Performance Measures
1. Financial (investors)	a. Number of cross-trained staff
2. Learning and growth (employees)	b. Customer satisfaction rating
3. Internal business processes	c. Time lapse from order to delivery
4. Customers	d. Dollar sales to repeat customers

SOLUTION

1. d; 2. a; 3. c; 4. b

Responsibility Accounting

LO2 Define *responsibility accounting*, and describe the role that responsibility centers play in performance management and evaluation.

As part of their performance management systems, many organizations assign resources to specific areas of responsibility and track how the managers of those areas use those resources. For example, Winter Wonderland Resort assigns resources to its Lodging, Dining, Retail and Rental, Ski School, and Real Estate divisions and holds the managers of those divisions responsible for generating revenue and managing costs. Within each division, other managers are assigned responsibility for such areas as Children and Adult Ski School, Snowboard School, or Private Lessons.

All managers at all levels are then evaluated in terms of their ability to manage their areas of responsibility in keeping with the organization's goals.

To assist in performance management and evaluation, many organizations use responsibility accounting. **Responsibility accounting** is an information system that classifies data according to areas of responsibility and reports each area's activities by including only the revenue, cost, and resource categories that the

Research and development units are a type of discretionary cost center in which a manager is accountable for costs only and the relationship between resources and products or services produced is not well defined. A common performance measure used to evaluate research and development activities is the number of patents obtained.

Courtesy of Image Source/Getty Images.

assigned manager can control. A **responsibility center** is an organizational unit whose manager has been assigned the responsibility of managing a portion of the organization's resources. The activities of a responsibility center dictate the extent of a manager's responsibility.

A report for a responsibility center should contain only the costs, revenues, and resources that the manager of that center can control. Such costs and revenues are called **controllable costs and revenues** because they are the result of a manager's actions, influence, or decisions. A responsibility accounting system ensures that managers will not be held responsible for items that they cannot change.

Types of Responsibility Centers

There are five types of responsibility centers: (1) cost centers, (2) discretionary cost centers, (3) revenue centers, (4) profit centers, and (5) investment centers. The key characteristics of the five types of responsibility centers are summarized in Table 25-1.

Cost Centers A responsibility center whose manager is accountable only for controllable costs that have well-defined relationships between the center's resources and certain products or services is called a **cost center**.

> Manufacturing companies like **Apple Computer** use cost centers to manage assembly plants, where the relationship between the costs of resources (direct material, direct labor) and the resulting products is well defined.

Service organizations use cost centers to manage activities in which resources are clearly linked with a service that is provided at no additional charge. For example,

TABLE 25-1
Types of Responsibility Centers

Responsibility Center	Manager Accountable For	How Performance Is Measured	Examples
Cost center	Only controllable costs, where there are well-defined links between the costs of resources and the resulting products or services	Compare actual costs with flexible and master budget costs Analyze resulting variances	Product: Manufacturing assembly plants Service: Food service for hospital patients
Discretionary cost center	Only controllable costs; the links between the costs of resources and the resulting products or services are *not* well defined	Compare actual noncost-based measures with targets Determine compliance with preapproved budgeted spending limits	Product or service: Administrative activities such as accounting, human resources, and research and development
Revenue center	Revenue generation	Compare actual revenue with budgeted revenue Analyze resulting variances	Product: Phone or e-commerce sales for pizza delivery Service: Reservation center on Internet
Profit center	Operating income resulting from controllable revenues and costs	Compare actual variable costing income statement with the budgeted income statement	Product or service: Local store of a national chain
Investment center	Controllable revenues, costs, and the investment of resources to achieve organizational goals	Return on investment Residual income Economic value added	Product: A division of a multinational corporation Service: A national office of a multinational consulting firm

in nursing homes and hospitals, there is a clear relationship between the costs of food and direct labor and the number of inpatient meals served.

The performance of a cost center is usually evaluated by comparing an activity's actual cost with its budgeted cost and analyzing the resulting variances. You will learn more about this performance evaluation process in the chapter on standard costing.

Discretionary Cost Centers A responsibility center whose manager is accountable for costs only and in which the relationship between resources and the products or services produced is not well defined is called a **discretionary cost center**.

Departments that perform administrative activities, such as accounting, human resources, and legal services, are typical examples of discretionary cost centers. These centers, like cost centers, have approved budgets that set spending limits.

Because the spending and use of resources in discretionary cost centers are not clearly linked to the production of a product or service, cost-based measures usually cannot be used to evaluate performance (although such centers are penalized if they exceed their approved budgets). For example, among the performance measures used to evaluate the research and development activities are the number of patents obtained and the number of cost-saving innovations that are developed.

At service organizations, such as the **United Way**, a common measure of administrative activities is how low their costs are as a percentage of total contributions.

Revenue Center A responsibility center whose manager is accountable primarily for revenue and whose success is based on its ability to generate revenue is called a **revenue center**. Examples of revenue centers are **Hertz**'s national car reservation center and the clothing retailer **Nordstrom**'s ecommerce order department.

A revenue center's performance is usually evaluated by comparing its actual revenue with its budgeted revenue and analyzing the resulting variances. Performance measures at both manufacturing and service organizations may include sales dollars, number of customer sales, or sales revenue per minute.

Profit Centers A responsibility center whose manager is accountable for both revenue and costs and for the resulting operating income is called a **profit center**.

A good example is a local store of a national chain, such as **Wal-Mart** or **Jiffy Lube**.

The performance of a profit center is usually evaluated by comparing the figures on its actual income statement with the figures on its master or flexible budget income statement.

Investment Centers A responsibility center whose manager is accountable for profit generation and can also make significant decisions about the resources that the center uses is called an **investment center**. For example, the president of **Harley-Davidson**'s Buell subsidiary and the president of **Brinker International**'s Chili's Grill and Bar can control revenues, costs, and the investment of assets to achieve organizational goals.

The performance of these centers is evaluated using such measures as return on investment, residual income, and economic value added. These measures are used in all types of organizations, both manufacturing and nonmanufacturing, and are discussed later in this chapter.

Organizational Structure and Performance Management

Much can be learned about an organization by examining how its managers organize activities and resources. A company's organizational structure formalizes its lines of managerial authority and control. An **organization chart** is a visual representation of an organization's hierarchy of responsibility for the purposes of management control. Within an organization chart, the five types of responsibility centers are arranged by level of management authority and control.

FIGURE 25-2 Partial Organization Chart of a Restaurant Division

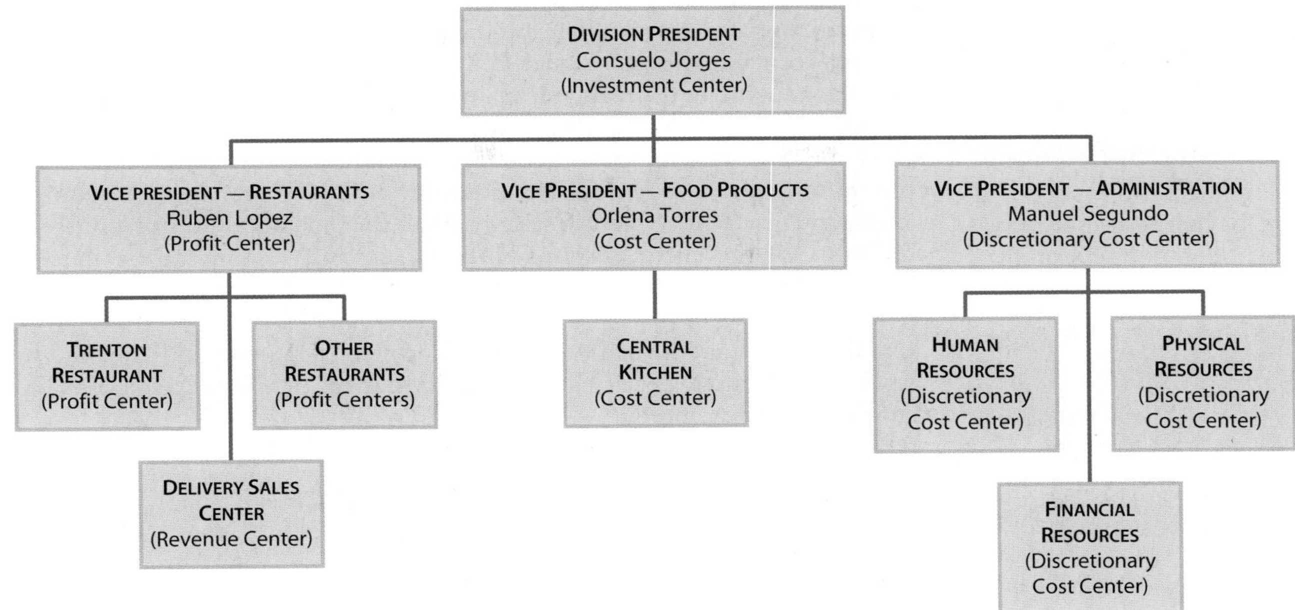

By examining a typical corporate organization chart, you can see how a responsibility accounting system works. Figure 25-2 shows part of the management structure for the Restaurant Division of a major hospitality corporation. Notice that the figure shows examples of all five types of responsibility centers.

In a responsibility accounting system, the performance reports for each level of management are tailored to each manager's individual needs for information. As information moves up the organizational chart, it is usually condensed. Performance reporting by responsibility level enables an organization to trace the source of a cost, revenue, or resource to the manager who controls it and to evaluate that manager's performance accordingly.

STOP & APPLY >

Identify the most appropriate type of responsibility center for each of the following organizational units:

1. A pizza store in a pizza chain
2. The ticket sales center of a major airline
3. The food service function at a nursing home
4. A subsidiary of a business conglomerate
5. The information technology area of a company

SOLUTION

1. Profit center
2. Revenue center
3. Cost center
4. Investment center
5. Discretionary cost center

Performance Evaluation of Cost Centers and Profit Centers

LO3 Prepare performance reports for cost centers using flexible budgets and for profit centers using variable costing.

Study Note

Only controllable items should be included on a manager's performance report.

Because performance reports contain information about costs, revenues, and resources that are controllable by individual managers, they allow comparisons between actual performance and budget expectations. Such comparisons allow management to evaluate an individual's performance with respect to responsibility center objectives and companywide objectives and to recommend changes. It is important to emphasize that performance reports should contain only costs, revenues, and resources that the manager can control. If a performance report includes items that the manager cannot control, the credibility of the entire responsibility accounting system can be called into question. It is up to management to structure and interpret the performance results fairly.

The content and format of a performance report depend on the nature of the responsibility center. Let us take a closer look at the performance reports for cost centers and profit centers.

Evaluating Cost Center Performance Using Flexible Budgeting

In the Restaurant Division of a major hospitality company, the Central Kitchen is where the food products that the restaurants sell are prepared. It is a cost center because its costs have well-defined relationships with the resulting products, which are then transferred to the restaurants for further processing and sale. To ensure that the central kitchen is meeting its performance goals, the manager will evaluate the performance of each food item produced. A separate report on each product will compare its actual costs with the corresponding amounts from the budget.

The performance report on House Dressing is presented in Exhibit 25-1. It compares data from the master budget (prepared at the beginning of the period) with the actual results for the period. As you can see, actual costs exceeded budgeted costs. Most managers would consider such a cost overrun significant. But was there really a cost overrun?

> The amounts budgeted in the master budget are based on an output of 1,000 units of dressing; however, the actual output was 1,200 units of dressing.

To judge the central kitchen's performance accurately, the company's managers must change the budgeted data in the master budget to reflect an output of 1,200 units. They can do this by using a flexible budget.

A **flexible budget** (also called a *variable budget*) is a summary of expected costs for a range of activity levels. Unlike a static budget, a flexible budget provides forecasted data that can be adjusted for changes in the level of output.

> A flexible budget is derived by multiplying actual unit output by predetermined unit costs for each cost item in the report.

The flexible budget is used primarily as a cost control tool in evaluating performance at the end of a period, as in Exhibit 25-1.

You will learn that favorable (positive, or F) and unfavorable (negative, or U) variances between actual costs and the flexible budget can be further examined by using standard costing to compute specific variances for direct materials, direct labor, and variable and fixed overhead. Also, you will use the flexible budget as a cost control tool to evaluate performance. Refer to the chapter on standard costing for further information on performance evaluation using variances or the flexible budget.

EXHIBIT 25-1
Central Kitchen's Performance Report on House Dressing

	Actual Results	Variance	Flexible Budget	Variance	Master Budget
Gallons produced	**1,200**	**0**	**1,200**	**200 (F)**	**1,000**
Center costs					
Direct materials ($0.25 per gallon)	$312	$12 (U)	$300	$50 (U)	$250
Direct labor ($0.05 per gallon)	72	12 (U)	60	10 (U)	50
Variable overhead ($0.03 per gallon)	33	3 (F)	36	6 (U)	30
Fixed overhead	2	3 (F)	5	0	5
Total cost	$419	$18 (U)	$401	$66 (U)	$335
Performance measures					
Defect-free gallons to total produced	0.98	0.01 (U)	N/A	N/A	0.99
Average throughput time per gallon	11 minutes	1 minute (F)	N/A	N/A	12 minutes

Note: In this exhibit and others that appear later in this chapter, (F) indicates a favorable variance, and (U) indicates an unfavorable variance.

Evaluating Profit Center Performance Using Variable Costing

Restaurants are profit centers since each is accountable for its own revenues and costs and for the resulting operating income. A profit center's performance is usually evaluated by comparing its actual income statement results to its budgeted income statement.

Variable costing is a method of preparing profit center performance reports that classifies a manager's controllable costs as either variable or fixed. Variable costing produces a variable costing income statement instead of a traditional income statement (also called a *full costing* or *absorption costing* or *traditional income statement*), which is used for external reporting purposes.

A variable costing income statement is the same as a contribution margin income statement, the format of which you may recall from its use in cost-volume-profit analysis.

Such an income statement is useful in performance management and evaluation because it focuses on cost variability and the profit center's contribution to operating income.

The variable costing income statement differs from the traditional income statement prepared for financial reporting, as shown by the two income statements in Exhibit 25-2 for Trenton Restaurant, which is part of the Restaurant Divison. In the traditional income statement, all manufacturing costs are assigned to cost of goods sold; in the variable costing income statement, only the variable manufacturing costs are included.

- Under variable costing, direct materials costs, direct labor costs, and variable overhead costs are the only cost elements used to compute variable cost of goods sold.

EXHIBIT 25-2
Variable Costing Income Statement Versus Traditional Income Statement for Trenton Restaurant

Variable Costing Income Statement		Traditional Income Statement	
Sales	$2,500	Sales	$2,500
Variable cost of goods sold	1,575	Cost of goods sold	1,745
Variable selling expenses	325	($1,575 + $170 = $1,745)	
Contribution margin	$ 600	Gross margin	$ 755
Fixed manufacturing costs	170	Variable selling expenses	325
Fixed selling expenses	230	Fixed selling expenses	230
Profit center operating income	$ 200	Profit center operating income	$ 200

- Fixed manufacturing costs are considered costs of the current accounting period. Notice that fixed manufacturing costs are listed with fixed selling expenses after the contribution margin has been computed.

In addition to tracking financial performance measures, a manager of a profit center may also want to measure and evaluate nonfinancial information. For example, the number of food orders processed and the average amount of a sales order at the Trenton Restaurant. The resulting report, based on variable costing and flexible budgeting, is shown in Exhibit 25-3.

Although performance reports vary in format depending on the type of responsibility center, they have some common themes:

- All responsibility center reports compare actual results to budgeted figures and focus on the differences.
- Often, comparisons are made to a flexible budget as well as to the master budget.
- Only the items that the manager can control are included in the performance report.
- Nonfinancial measures are also examined to achieve a more balanced view of the manager's responsibilities.

EXHIBIT 25-3 Performance Report Based on Variable Costing and Flexible Budgeting for the Trenton Restaurant

	Actual Results	Variance	Flexible Budget	Variance	Master Budget
Meals served	**750**	**0**	**750**	**250 (U)**	**1,000**
Sales (average meal $2.85)	$2,500.00	$362.50 (F)	$2,137.50	$712.50 (U)	$2,850.00
Controllable variable costs					
Variable cost of goods sold ($1.50)	1,575.00	450.00 (U)	1,125.00	375.00 (F)	1,500.00
Variable selling expenses ($0.40)	325.00	25.00 (U)	300.00	100.00 (F)	400.00
Contribution margin	$ 600.00	$112.50 (U)	$ 712.50	$237.50 (U)	$ 950.00
Controllable fixed costs					
Fixed manufacturing expenses	170.00	30.00 (F)	200.00	0.00	200.00
Fixed selling expenses	230.00	20.00 (F)	250.00	0.00	250.00
Profit center operating income	$ 200.00	$ 62.50 (U)	$ 262.50	$237.50 (U)	$ 500.00
Other nonfinancial performance measures					
Number of orders processed	300	50 (F)	N/A	N/A	250
Average sales order	$8.34	$3.06 (U)	N/A	N/A	$11.40

Complete the following performance report for a profit center for the month ended December 31:

	Actual Results	Variance	Master Budget
Sales	$?	$ 20 (F)	$ 120
Controllable variable costs			
Variable cost of goods sold	25	10 (U)	?
Variable selling and administrative expenses	15	?	5
Contribution margin	$100	?	$ 100
Controllable fixed costs	?	10 (F)	60
Profit center income	$ 50	$ 10 (F)	$?
Performance measures			
Number of orders processed	50	20 (F)	?
Average daily sales	$?	$0.66 (F)	$4.00
Number of units sold	100	40 (F)	?

SOLUTION

Profit Center
For the Month Ended December 31

	Actual Results	Variance	Master Budget
Sales	$ 140	$ 20 (F)	$ 120
Controllable variable costs			
Variable cost of goods sold	25	10 (U)	15
Variable selling and administrative expenses	15	10 (U)	5
Contribution margin	$ 100	$ 0	$ 100
Controllable fixed costs	50	10 (F)	60
Profit center operating income	$ 50	$ 10 (F)	$ 40
Performance measures			
Number of orders processed	50	20 (F)	30
Average daily sales	$4.66	$0.66 (F)	$4.00
Number of units sold	100	40 (F)	60

Performance Evaluation of Investment Centers

LO4 Prepare performance reports for investment centers using the traditional measures of return on investment and residual income and the newer measure of economic value added.

The evaluation of an investment center's performance requires more than a comparison of controllable revenues and costs with budgeted amounts. Because the managers of investment centers also control resources and invest in assets, other performance measures must be used to hold them accountable for revenues, costs, and the capital investments that they control. In this section, we focus on the traditional performance evaluation measures of return on investment and residual income and the relatively new performance measure of economic value added.

Return on Investment

Traditionally, the most common performance measure that takes into account both operating income and the assets invested to earn that income is **return on investment (ROI)**. Return on investment is computed as follows:

EXHIBIT 25-4
Performance Report Based on Return on Investment for the Restaurant Division

	Actual Results	Variance	Master Budget
Operating income	$610	$280 (U)	$ 890
Assets invested	$800	$200 (F)	$1,000
Performance measure			
ROI	76%	13% (U)	89%

ROI = Operating Income ÷ Assets Invested

$890 ÷ $1,000 = 0.89 = 89%

$610 ÷ $800 = 0.76 = 76%*

*Rounded.

$$\text{Return on Investment (ROI)} = \frac{\text{Operating Income}}{\text{Assets Invested}}$$

In this formula, *assets invested* is the average of the beginning and ending asset balances for the period.

Properly measuring the income and the assets specifically controlled by a manager is critical to the quality of this performance measure. Using ROI, it is possible to evaluate the manager of any investment center, whether it is an entire company or a unit within a company such as a subsidiary, division, or other business segment. For example, assume that the Restaurant Division of a major hospitality corporation had actual operating income of $610 and that the average assets invested were $800. The master budget called for $890 in operating income and $1,000 in invested assets. As shown in Exhibit 25-4, the budgeted ROI for the division would be 89 percent, and the actual ROI would be 76 percent. The actual ROI was lower than the budgeted ROI because the division's actual operating income was lower than expected relative to the actual assets invested.

For investment centers, the ROI computation is really the aggregate measure of many interrelationships. The basic ROI equation, Operating Income ÷ Assets Invested, can be rewritten to show the many elements within the aggregate ROI number that a manager can influence. Two important indicators of performance are profit margin and asset turnover. **Profit margin** is the ratio of operating income to sales; it represents the percentage of each sales dollar that results in profit. **Asset turnover** is the ratio of sales to average assets invested; it indicates the productivity of assets, or the number of sales dollars generated by each dollar invested in assets.

> **Study Note**
> Profit margin focuses on the income statement, and asset turnover focuses on the balance sheet aspects of ROI.

Return on investment is equal to profit margin multiplied by asset turnover:

$$\text{ROI} = \text{Profit Margin} \times \text{Asset Turnover}$$

$$\text{ROI} = \frac{\text{Operating Income}}{\text{Sales}} \times \frac{\text{Sales}}{\text{Assets Invested}} = \frac{\text{Operating Income}}{\text{Assets Invested}}$$

Profit margin and asset turnover help explain changes in return on investment for a single investment center or differences in return or investment among investment centers. Therefore, the formula ROI = Profit Margin × Asset Turnover is useful for analyzing and interpreting the elements that make up a business's overall return on investment.

Du Pont, one of the first organizations to recognize the many interrelationships that affect ROI, designed a formula similar to the one diagrammed in Figure 25-3. You can see that ROI is affected by a manager's decisions about pricing, product

FIGURE 25-3 Factors Affecting the Computation of Return on Investment

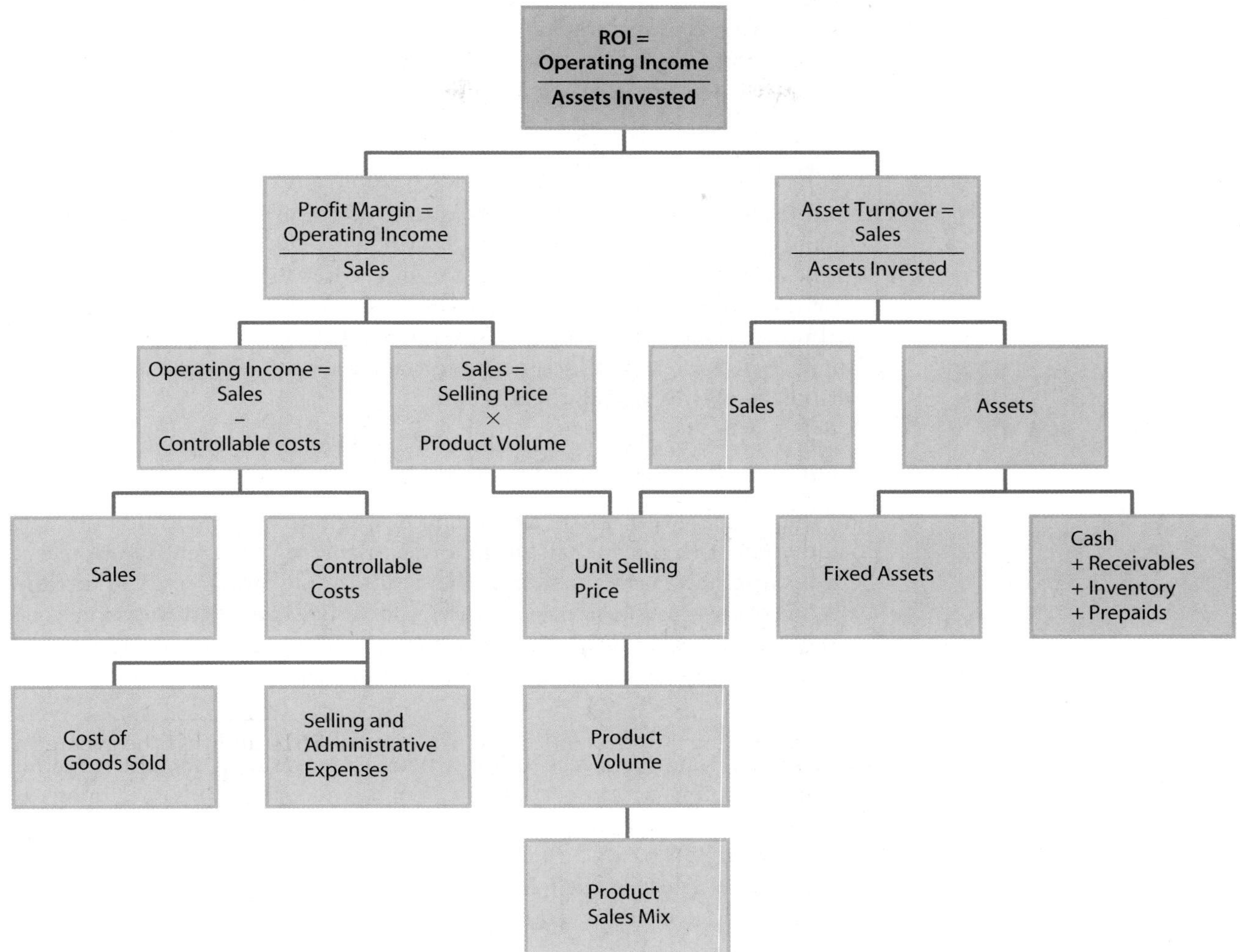

sales mix, capital budgeting for new facilities, product sales volume, and other financial matters. In essence, a single ROI number is a composite index of many cause-and-effect relationships and interdependent financial elements. A manager can improve ROI by increasing sales, decreasing costs, or decreasing assets.

Drawbacks Because of the many factors that affect ROI, management should use this measure cautiously in evaluating performance. If ROI is overemphasized, investment center managers may react by making business decisions that favor their personal ROI performance at the expense of companywide profits or the long-term success of other investment centers. To avoid such problems, other performance measures should always be used in conjunction with ROI—for example, comparisons of revenues, costs, and operating income with budget amounts or past trends; sales growth percentages; market share percentages; or other key variables in the organization's activity. ROI should also be compared with budgeted goals and with past ROI trends because changes in this ratio over time can be more revealing than any single number.

> **Study Note**
> ROI is expressed as a percentage, and residual income is expressed in dollars.

Residual Income

Because of the pitfalls of using return on investment as a performance measure, other approaches to evaluating investment centers have evolved. Residual income is one of those performance measures. **Residual income (RI)** is the operating income that an investment center earns above a minimum desired return on invested assets. Residual income is not a ratio but a dollar amount: the amount of profit left after subtracting a predetermined desired income target for an investment center. The formula for computing the residual income of an investment center is

$$\text{Residual Income} = \text{Operating Income} - (\text{Desired ROI} \times \text{Assets Invested})$$

As in the computation of ROI, assets invested is the average of the center's beginning and ending asset balances for the period.

The desired RI will vary from investment center to investment center depending on the type of business and the level of risk assumed. The performance report based on residual income for the Restaurant Division is shown in Exhibit 25-5. Assume that the residual income performance target is to exceed a 20 percent return on assets invested in the division.

Note that the division's residual income is $450, which was lower than the $690 that was projected in the master budget.

Comparisons with other residual income figures will strengthen the analysis. To add context to the analysis of the division and its manager, questions such as the following need to be answered: How did the division's residual income this year compare with its residual income in previous years? Did the actual residual income exceed the budgeted residual income? How did this division's residual income compare with the amounts generated by other investment centers of the company?

Drawbacks Caution is called for when using residual income to compare investment centers within a company. For their residual income figures to be comparable, all investment centers must have equal access to resources and similar asset investment bases. Some managers may be able to produce larger residual incomes simply because their investment centers are larger rather than because their performance is better. Like ROI, RI has some flaws.

Economic Value Added

More and more businesses are using the shareholder wealth created by an investment center, or the **economic value added (EVA)**, as an indicator of performance. The calculation of EVA, a registered trademark of the consulting

EXHIBIT 25-5
Performance Report Based on Residual Income for the Restaurant Division

	Actual Results	Variance	Master Budget
Operating income	$610	$280 (U)	$ 890
Assets invested	$800	$200 (F)	$1,000
Desired ROI			20%
Performance measures			
ROI	76%	13% (U)	89%
Residual income	$450	$240 (U)	$ 690

Residual Income = Operating Income − (Desired ROI × Assets Invested)

$\$890 - 20\%(\$1{,}000) = \$690$

$\$610 - 20\%(\$800) = \$450$

EXHIBIT 25-6
Performance Report Based on Economic Value Added for the Restaurant Division

	Actual Results	Variance	Master Budget
Performance measures			
ROI	76%	13% (U)	89%
Residual income	$450	$240 (U)	$690
Economic value added	$334		

Economic Value Added = After-Tax Operating Income − [Cost of Capital × (Total Assets − Current Liabilities)]
$400 − 12% ($800 − $250) = $334

firm **Stern Stewart & Company**, can be quite complex because it makes various cost of capital and accounting principles adjustments. You will learn more about the cost of capital in the chapter that discusses capital investment decisions. However, for the purposes of computing EVA, the **cost of capital** is the minimum desired rate of return on an investment, such as the assets invested in an investment center.

Basically, the computation of EVA is similar to the computation of residual income, except that after-tax operating income is used instead of pretax operating income, and a cost of capital percentage is multiplied by the center's invested assets less current liabilities instead of a desired ROI percentage being multiplied by invested assets. Also, like residual income, the economic value added is expressed in dollars. The formula is

EVA = After-Tax Operating Income − [Cost of Capital × (Total Assets − Current Liabilities)]

A very basic computation of economic value added for the Restaurant Division is shown in Exhibit 25-6. The report assumes that the division's after-tax operating income is $400, its cost of capital is 12 percent, its total assets are $800, and its current liabilities are $250.

- The report shows that the division has added $334 to its economic value after taxes and cost of capital.
- In other words, the division produced after-tax profits of $334 in excess of the cost of capital required to generate those profits.

The factors that affect the computation of economic value added are illustrated in Figure 25-4. An investment center's economic value is affected by managers' decisions on pricing, product sales volume, taxes, cost of capital, capital investments, and other financial matters.

- In essence, the EVA number is a composite index drawn from many cause-and-effect relationships and interdependent financial elements.
- A manager can improve the economic value of an investment center by increasing sales, decreasing costs, decreasing assets, or lowering the cost of capital.

Drawbacks Because many factors affect the economic value of an investment center and its cost of capital, management should be cautious when drawing conclusions about performance. The evaluation will be more meaningful if the current economic value added is compared to EVAs from previous periods, target EVAs, and EVAs from other investment centers.

FIGURE 25-4 Factors Affecting the Computation of Economic Value Added

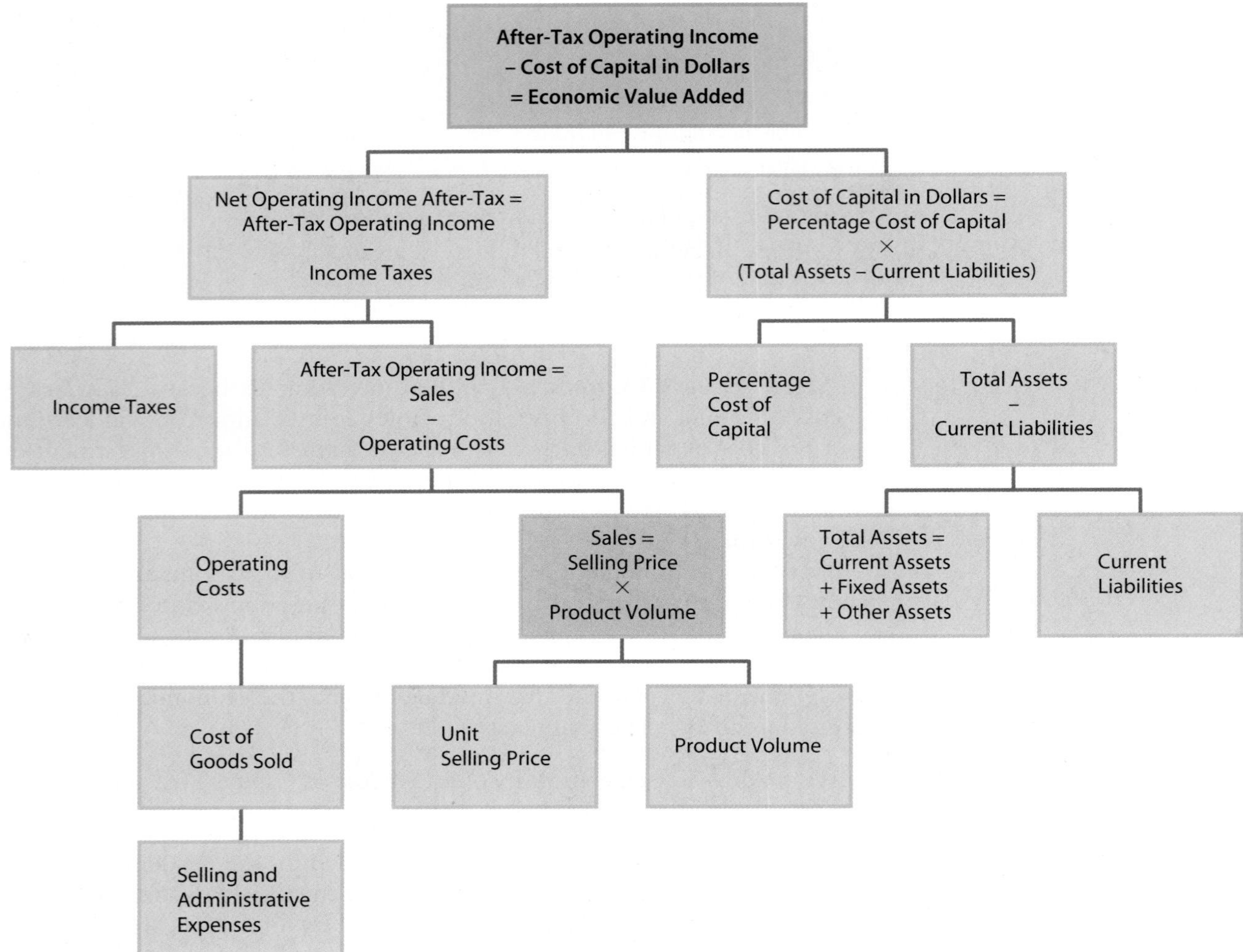

The Importance of Multiple Performance Measures

In summary, to be effective, a performance management system must consider both operating results and multiple performance measures, such as return on investment, residual income, and economic value added. Comparing actual results to budgeted figures adds meaning to the evaluation. Performance measures such as ROI, RI, and EVA indicate whether an investment center is effective in coordinating its own goals with companywide goals because these measures take into account both operating income and the assets used to produce that income. However, all three measures are limited by their focus on short-term financial performance.

- To obtain a fuller picture, management needs to break these three measures down into their components, analyze such information as responsibility center income over time, and compare current results to the targeted amounts in the flexible or master budget.
- In addition, the analysis of such nonfinancial performance indicators as average throughput time, employee turnover, and number of orders processed will ensure a more balanced view of a business's well-being and how to improve it.

Brew Mountain Company sells coffee and hot beverages. Its Coffee Cart Division sells to skiers as they come off the mountain. The balance sheet for the Coffee Cart Division showed that the company had invested assets of $30,000 at the beginning of the year and $50,000 at the end of the year. During the year, the division's operating income was $80,000 on sales of $120,000.

a. Compute the division's residual income if the desired ROI is 20 percent.

b. Compute the return on investment for the division.

c. Compute the economic value added for Brew Mountain Company if total corporate assets are $600,000, current liabilities are $80,000, after-tax operating income is $70,000, and the cost of capital is 12 percent.

SOLUTION

a. $80,000 – [20% × ($30,000 + $50,000) ÷ 2] = $72,000

b. $80,000 ÷ [($30,000 + $50,000) ÷ 2] = 200%

c. $70,000 – [12% × ($600,000 – $80,000)] = $7,600

Performance Incentives and Goals

LO5 Explain how properly linked performance incentives and measures add value for all stakeholders in performance management and evaluation.

The effectiveness of a performance management and evaluation system depends on how well it coordinates the goals of responsibility centers, managers, and the entire company. Two factors are key to the successful coordination of goals:

- The logical linking of goals to measurable objectives and targets
- The tying of appropriate compensation incentives to the achievement of the targets—that is, performance-based pay

Linking Goals, Performance Objectives, Measures, and Performance Targets

The causal links among an organization's goals, performance objectives, measures, and targets must be apparent. For example, if a company seeks to be an environmental steward, as Winter Wonderland Resort does, it may choose the following linked goal, objective, measure, and performance target:

Goal	*Objective*	*Measure*	*Performance Target*
To be an environmental steward	To reduce, reuse, and recycle	Number of tons recycled per year	To recycle at least one pound per guest

You may recall that the balanced scorecard also links objectives, measures, and targets, as shown in Figure 25-1 earlier in this chapter.

FOCUS ON BUSINESS PRACTICE

Pay-for-Performance Reality Check

Many service businesses, such as the CPA firm **Meyners + Company**, assume that aligning staff performance and compensation with the business's core values and competencies is a simple matter. But for Meyners, it turned out that administering a pay-for-performance program was time-consuming and data-intensive. Based on a survey of the entire firm four years after the program was inaugurated, the pay-for-performance structure was simplified, and employees were offered other types of incentives.[2]

Performance-Based Pay

The tying of appropriate compensation incentives to performance targets increases the likelihood that the goals of responsibility centers, managers, and the entire organization will be well coordinated. Unfortunately, this linkage does not always happen. Responsibility center managers are more likely to achieve their performance targets if their compensation depends on it. **Performance-based pay** is the linking of employee compensation to the achievement of measurable business targets.

Cash bonuses, awards, profit-sharing plans, and stock options are common types of incentive compensation.

- Cash bonuses are usually given to reward an individual's short-term performance. A bonus may be stated as a fixed dollar amount or as a percentage of a target figure, such as 5 percent of operating income or 10 percent of the dollar increase in operating income.
- An award may be a trip or some other form of recognition for desirable individual or group performance. For example, many companies sponsor a trip for all managers who have met their performance targets during a specified period. Other companies award incentive points that employees may redeem for goods or services. (Notice that awards can be used to encourage both short-term and long-term performance.)
- Profit-sharing plans reward employees with a share of the company's profits.
- Employees often receive company stock as recognition of their contribution to a profitable period. Using stock as a reward encourages employees to think and act as both investors and employees and encourages a stable work force. In terms of the balanced scorecard, employees assume two stakeholder perspectives and take both a short- and a long-term viewpoint. Companies use stock to motivate employees to achieve financial targets that increase the company's stock price.

The Coordination of Goals

What performance incentives and measures should a company use to manage and evaluate performance? What actions and behaviors should an organization reward? Which incentive compensation plans work best? The answers to such questions depend on the facts and circumstances of each organization. To determine

FOCUS ON BUSINESS PRACTICE

Aligning Incentives Among Supply-Chain Partners

A study of more than 50 supply networks found that misaligned performance incentives are often the cause of inventory buildups or shortages, misguided sales efforts, and poor customer relations. A supply chain works only if the partners work together effectively by adopting revenue-sharing contracts, using technology to track shared information, and/or working with intermediaries to build trust. Such incentives among supply-chain partners must be reassessed periodically as business conditions change.[3]

the right performance incentives for their organization, employees and managers must answer several questions:

- When should the reward be given—now or sometime in the future?
- Whose performance should be rewarded—that of responsibility centers, individual managers, or the entire company?
- How should the reward be computed?
- On what should the reward be based?
- What performance criteria should be used?
- Does our performance incentive plan address the interests of all stakeholders?

The effectiveness of a performance management and evaluation system relies on the coordination of responsibility center, managerial, and company goals. Performance can be optimized by linking goals to measurable objectives and targets and by tying appropriate compensation incentives to the achievement of the targets. Common types of incentive compensation are cash bonuses, awards, profit-sharing plans, and stock options. Each organization's unique circumstances will determine the correct mix of measures and compensation incentives for that organization. If management values the perspectives of all of its stakeholder groups, its performance management and evaluation system will balance and benefit all interests.

& APPLY >

Necessary Toys, Inc., has adopted the balanced scorecard to motivate its managers to work toward the companywide goal of leading its industry in innovation. Identify the four stakeholder perspectives that would link to the following objectives, measures, and targets:

Perspective	Objective	Measure	Target
	Profitable new products	New-product ROI	New-product ROI of at least 75 percent
	Work force with cutting-edge skills	Percentage of employees cross-trained on work-group tasks	100 percent of work group cross-trained on new tasks within 30 days
	Agile product design and production processes	Time to market (the time between a product idea and its first sales)	Time to market less than one year for 80 percent of product introductions
	Successful product introductions	New-product market share	Capture 80 percent of new-product market within one year

SOLUTION

Goal: Company leads its industry in innovation

Perspective	Objective	Measure	Target
Financial (investors)	Profitable new products	New-product ROI	New-product ROI of at least 75 percent
Learning and growth (employees)	Work force with cutting-edge skills	Percentage of employees cross-trained on work-group tasks	100 percent of work group cross-trained on new tasks within 30 days
Internal business processes	Agile product design and production processes	Time to market (the time between a product idea and its first sales)	Time to market less than one year for 80 percent of product introductions
Customers	Successful product introductions	New-product market share	Capture 80 percent of new-product market within one year

▶ WINTER WONDERLAND RESORT: REVIEW PROBLEM

In this chapter's Decision Point, we asked these questions:

- How do managers at Winter Wonderland Resort link performance measures and set performance targets to achieve performance objectives?
- How do they use the resort's all-in-one card system and its integrated database to improve performance management and evaluation?

Managers at Winter Wonderland Resort link their organization's vision and strategy to their performance objectives; they then link the objectives to logical performance measures; and, finally, they set performance targets. A balanced scorecard approach enables them to consider the perspectives of all the organization's stakeholders: financial (investors), learning and growth (employees), internal business processes, and customers.

As we indicated in the Decision Point, Winter Wonderland Resort's managers like the all-in-one-card system because it is a quick and easy way of collecting huge amounts of valuable and versatile information. Whenever a guest's card is scanned, new data enter the system and become part of an integrated management information system that allows managers to measure and control costs, quality, and performance in all of the resort's areas. The system's ability to store both financial and nonfinancial data about all aspects of the resort enables managers to learn about and balance the interests of all the organization's stakeholders. The managers can then use the information to answer traditional financial questions about such matters as the cost of sales and the value of inventory (e.g., food ingredients in the resort's restaurants and the merchandise in its shops) and to obtain performance data about the resort's activities, products, services, and customers. In addition, the system provides managers with timely feedback about their performance, which encourages continuous improvement.

Evaluating Profit Center and Investment Center Performance

LO3 LO4 LO5

Mary Fortenberry, Winter Wonderland Resort's general manager, is responsible for guest activities, administration, and food and lodging. She is also solely responsible for Winter Wonderland Resort's capital investments. The organization chart that follows shows the resort's various activities and the levels of authority that Fortenberry has established:

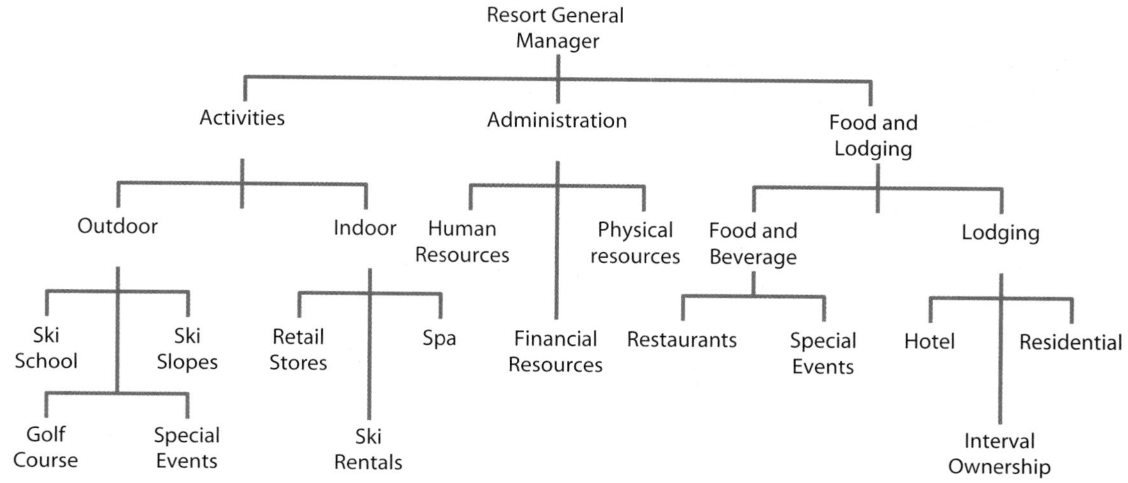

Three divisional managers receive compensation based on their division's performance and have the authority to make employee compensation decisions for their division. Alexandra Patel manages the Food and Lodging Division. The Food and Lodging Division's master budget and actual results for the year ended June 30 follow.

Winter Wonderland Resort Food and Lodging Division For the Year Ended June 30 (Dollar amounts in thousands)	Master Budget	Actual Results
Guest days	4,000	4,100
Sales	$38,000	$40,000
Variable cost of sales	24,000	25,000
Variable selling and administrative expenses	4,000	4,250
Fixed cost of sales	2,000	1,800
Fixed selling and administrative expenses	2,500	2,500

Required

1. What types of responsibility centers are Administration, Food and Lodging, and Resort General Manager?
2. Assume that Food and Lodging is a profit center. Prepare a performance report using variable costing and flexible budgeting. Determine the variances between actual results and the corresponding figures in the flexible budget and the master budget.
3. Assume that the divisional managers have been assigned responsibility for capital expenditures and that their divisions are thus investment centers. Food and Lodging is expected to generate a desired ROI of at least 30 percent on average assets invested of $10,000,000.
   a. Compute the division's return on investment and residual income using the average assets invested in both the actual and budget calculations.
   b. Using the ROI and residual income, evaluate Alexandra Patel's performance as divisional manager.
4. Compute the division's actual economic value added if the division's assets are $12,000,000, current liabilities are $3,000,000, after-tax operating income is $4,500,000, and the cost of capital is 20 percent.

Answers to Review Problem

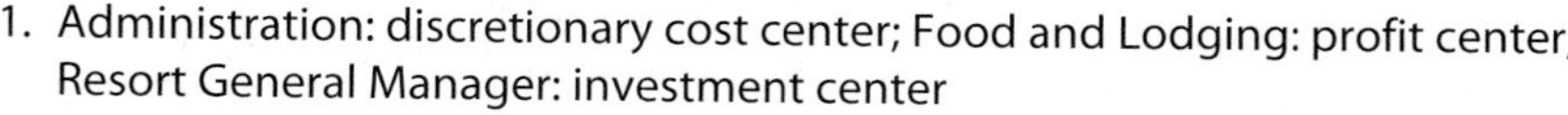

1. Administration: discretionary cost center; Food and Lodging: profit center; Resort General Manager: investment center

2. Performance report:

Winter Wonderland Resort Food and Lodging Division For the Year Ended June 30 (Dollar amounts in thousands)							
	Actual Results	Variance		Flexible Budget	Variance		Master Budget
Guest days	4,100	—		4,100	100	(F)	4,000
Sales	$40,000	$1,050	(F)	$38,950	$950	(F)	$38,000
Controllable variable costs							
Variable cost of sales	25,000	400	(U)	24,600	600	(U)	24,000
Variable selling and administrative expenses	4,250	150	(U)	4,100	100	(U)	4,000
Contribution margin	$10,750	$ 500	(F)	$10,250	$250	(F)	$10,000
Controllable fixed costs							
Fixed cost of sales	1,800	200	(F)	2,000	—		2,000
Fixed selling and administrative expenses	2,500	—		2,500	—		2,500
Division operating income	$ 6,450	$ 700	(F)	$ 5,750	$250	(F)	$ 5,500

3. a. **Return on investment**

   Actual results: $6,450,000 ÷ $10,000,000 = 64.50%

   Flexible budget: $5,750,000 ÷ $10,000,000 = 57.50%

   Master budget: $5,500,000 ÷ $10,000,000 = 55.00%

   Residual income

   Actual results: $6,450,000 − 30%($10,000,000) = $3,450,000

   Flexible budget: $5,750,000 − 30%($10,000,000) = $2,750,000

   Master budget: $5,500,000 − 30%($10,000,000) = $2,500,000

   b. Alexandra Patel's performance as the divisional manager of Food and Lodging exceeds company performance expectations. Actual ROI was 64.5 percent, whereas the company expected an ROI of 30 percent and the flexible budget and the master budget showed projections of 57.5 percent and 55.0 percent, respectively. Residual income also exceeded expectations. The Food and Lodging Division generated $3,450,000 in residual income when the flexible budget and master budget had projected RIs of $2,750,000 and $2,500,000, respectively. The performance report for the division shows 100 more guest days than had been anticipated and a favorable controllable fixed cost variance. As a manager, Patel will investigate the unfavorable variances associated with her controllable variable costs.

4. Economic value added:

   $4,500,000 − 20%($12,000,000 − $3,000,000) = $2,700,000

STOP & REVIEW >

LO1 Define *a performance management and evaluation system,* and describe how the balanced scorecard aligns performance with organizational goals.

An effective performance management and evaluation system accounts for and reports on both financial and nonfinancial performance so that an organization can ascertain how well it is doing, where it is going, and what improvements will make it more profitable. Each organization must develop a unique set of performance measures that are appropriate to its specific situation. Besides answering basic questions about what to measure and how to measure, management must consider a variety of other issues. Managers must collaborate to develop a group of measures, such as the balanced scorecard, that will help them determine how to improve performance.

The balanced scorecard is a framework that links the perspectives of an organization's four basic stakeholder groups—financial, learning and growth, internal business processes, and customers—with its mission and vision, performance measures, strategic and tactical plans, and resources. Ideally, managers should see how their actions help to achieve organizational goals and understand how their compensation is linked to their actions. The balanced scorecard assumes that an organization will get what it measures.

LO2 Define *responsibility accounting,* and describe the role that responsibility centers play in performance management and evaluation.

Responsibility accounting classifies data according to areas of responsibility and reports each area's activities by including only the revenue, cost, and resource categories that the assigned manager can control. There are five types of responsibility centers: cost, discretionary cost, revenue, profit, and investment. Performance reporting by responsibility center allows the source of a cost, revenue, or resource to be traced to the manager who controls it and thus makes it easier to evaluate a manager's performance.

LO3 Prepare performance reports for cost centers using flexible budgets and for profit centers using variable costing.

Performance reports contain information about the costs, revenues, and resources that individual managers can control. The content and format of a performance report depend on the nature of the responsibility center.

The performance of a cost center can be evaluated by comparing its actual costs with the corresponding amounts in the flexible and master budgets. A flexible budget is a summary of anticipated costs for a range of activity levels. It provides forecasted cost data that can be adjusted for changes in the level of output. A flexible budget is derived by multiplying actual unit output by predetermined standard unit costs for each cost item in the report. As you will learn in another chapter, the resulting variances between actual costs and the flexible budget can be examined further by using standard costing to compute specific variances for direct materials, direct labor, and overhead.

The performance of a profit center is usually evaluated by comparing the profit center's actual income statement results with its budgeted income statement. When variable costing is used, the controllable costs of the profit center's manager are classified as variable or fixed. The resulting performance report takes the form of a contribution margin income statement instead of a traditional income statement. The variable costing income statement is useful because it focuses on cost variability and the profit center's contribution to operating income.

LO4 Prepare performance reports for investment centers using the

Traditionally, the most common performance measure has been return on investment (ROI). The basic formula is ROI = Operating Income ÷ Assets Invested. Return on investment can also be examined in terms of profit margin and asset

traditional measures of return on investment and residual income and the newer measure of economic value added.

turnover. In this case, ROI = Profit Margin × Asset Turnover, where Profit Margin = Operating Income ÷ Sales, and Asset Turnover = Sales ÷ Assets Invested. Residual income (RI) is the operating income that an investment center earns above a minimum desired return on invested assets. It is expressed as a dollar amount: Residual Income = Operating Income − (Desired ROI × Assets Invested). It is the amount of profit left after subtracting a predetermined desired income target for an investment. Today, businesses are increasingly using the shareholder wealth created by an investment center, or economic value added (EVA), as a performance measure. The calculation of economic value added can be quite complex because of the various adjustments it involves. Basically, it is similar to the calculation of residual income: EVA = After-Tax Operating Income − Cost of Capital in Dollars. A manager can improve the economic value of an investment center by increasing sales, decreasing costs, decreasing assets, or lowering the cost of capital.

LO5 Explain how properly linked performance incentives and measures add value for all stakeholders in performance management and evaluation.

The effectiveness of a performance management and evaluation system depends on how well it coordinates the goals of responsibility centers, managers, and the entire company. Performance can be optimized by linking goals to measurable objectives and targets and tying appropriate compensation incentives to the achievement of those targets. Common types of incentive compensation are cash bonuses, awards, profit-sharing plans, and stock options. If management values the perspectives of all of its stakeholder groups, its performance management and evaluation system will balance and benefit all interests.

REVIEW of Concepts and Terminology

The following concepts and terms were introduced in this chapter:

Balanced scorecard 1095 (LO1)

Controllable costs and revenues 1098 (LO2)

Cost center 1098 (LO2)

Cost of capital 1109 (LO4)

Discretionary cost center 1099 (LO2)

Economic value added (EVA) 1108 (LO4)

Flexible budget 1102 (LO3)

Investment center 1100 (LO2)

Organization chart 1100 (LO2)

Performance-based pay 1112 (LO5)

Performance management and evaluation system 1094 (LO1)

Performance measurement 1094 (LO1)

Profit center 1100 (LO2)

Residual income (RI) 1108 (LO4)

Responsibility accounting 1097 (LO2)

Responsibility center 1098 (LO2)

Revenue center 1100 (LO2)

Variable costing 1103 (LO3)

Key Ratio

Asset turnover 1106 (LO4)

Profit margin 1106 (LO4)

Return on investment (ROI) 1105 (LO4)

CHAPTER ASSIGNMENTS

BUILDING Your Basic Knowledge and Skills

Short Exercises

LO1 Balanced Scorecard

SE 1. One of your college's overall goals is customer satisfaction. In light of that goal, match each of the following stakeholders' perspectives with the appropriate objective:

Perspective	Objective
1. Financial (investors)	a. Customer satisfaction means that the faculty (employees) engages in cutting-edge research.
2. Learning and growth	b. Customer satisfaction means that students receive their degrees in four years.
3. Internal business processes	c. Customer satisfaction means that the college has a winning athletics program.
4. Customers	d. Customer satisfaction means that fund-raising campaigns are successful.

LO2 Responsibility Centers

SE 2. Identify each of the following as a cost center, a discretionary cost center, a revenue center, a profit center, or an investment center:

1. The manager of center A is responsible for generating cash inflows and incurring costs with the goal of making money for the company. The manager has no responsibility for assets.
2. Center B produces a product that is not sold to an external party but transferred to another center for further processing.
3. The manager of center C is responsible for the telephone order operations of a large retailer.
4. Center D designs, produces, and sells products to external parties. The manager makes both long-term and short-term decisions.
5. Center E provides human resource support for the other centers in the company.

LO2 Controllable Costs

SE 3. Ha Kim is the manager of the Paper Cutting Department in the Northwest Division of Striking Paper Products. Identify each of the following costs as either controllable or not controllable by Kim:

1. Lumber Department hauling costs
2. Salaries of cutting machine workers
3. Cost of cutting machine parts
4. Cost of electricity for the Northwest Division
5. Vice president's salary

LO3 Cost Center Performance Report

SE 4. Complete the following performance report for cost center C for the month ended December 31:

	Actual Results	Variance	Flexible Budget	Variance	Master Budget
Units produced	80	0	?	(20) U	100
Center costs					
Direct materials	$ 84	$?	$ 80	$?	$100
Direct labor	150	?	?	40(F)	200
Variable overhead	?	20(U)	240	?	300
Fixed overhead	270	?	250	?	250
Total cost	$?	$34(U)	$?	$120(F)	$850
Performance measures					
Defect-free units to total produced	80%	?	N/A	N/A	90%
Average throughput time per unit	11 minutes	?	N/A	N/A	10 minutes

LO3 **Profit Center Performance Report**

SE 5. Complete the following performance report for profit center P for the month ended December 31:

	Actual Results	Variance	Master Budget
Sales	$?	$ 20 (F)	$ 120
Controllable variable costs			
Variable cost of goods sold	25	10 (U)	?
Variable selling and administrative expenses	15	?	5
Contribution margin	$100	$?	$ 100
Controllable fixed costs	?	20 (F)	60
Profit center operating income	$ 60	$ 20 (F)	$?
Performance measures			
Number of orders processed	50	20 (F)	?
Average daily sales	$?	$0.68 (F)	$4.00
Number of units sold	100	40 (F)	?

LO4 **Return on Investment**

SE 6. Complete the profit margin, asset turnover, and return on investment calculations for investment centers D and V

	Subsidiary D	Subsidiary V
Sales	$1,650	$2,840
Operating income	$ 180	$ 210
Average assets invested	$ 940	$1,250
Profit margin	?	7.39%
Asset turnover	1.76 times	?
ROI	?	?

LO4 **Return on Investment**

SE 7. Complete the average assets invested, profit margin, asset turnover, and return on investment calculations for investment centers J and K on the next page.

	Subsidiary J	Subsidiary K
Sales	$2,000	$2,000
Operating income	$500	$800
Beginning assets invested	$4,000	$500
Ending assets invested	$6,000	$1,500
Average assets invested	$?	$?
Profit margin	25%	?
Asset turnover	?	2 times
ROI	?	?

LO4 **Residual Income**

SE 8. Complete the operating income, ending assets invested, average assets invested, and residual income calculations for investment centers H and F:

	Subsidiary H	Subsidiary F
Sales	$20,000	$25,000
Operating income	$1,500	$?
Beginning assets invested	$4,000	$500
Ending assets invested	$6,000	$?
Average assets invested	$?	$1,000
Desired ROI	20%	20%
Residual income	$?	$600

LO4 **Economic Value Added**

SE 9. Complete the current liabilities, total assets−current liabilities, and economic value added calculations for investment centers M and N:

	Subsidiary M	Subsidiary N
Sales	$15,000	$18,000
After-tax operating income	$1,000	$1,100
Total assets	$4,000	$5,000
Current liabilities	$1,000	$?
Total assets − current liabilities	$?	$3,500
Cost of capital	15%	15%
Economic value added	$?	$?

LO5 **Coordination of Goals**

SE 10. One of your college's goals is customer satisfaction. In view of that goal, identify each of the following as a linked objective, a measure, or a performance target:

1. To have successful fund-raising campaigns
2. Number of publications per year per tenure-track faculty
3. To increase the average donation by 10 percent
4. Average number of dollars raised per donor
5. To have faculty engage in cutting-edge research
6. To increase the number of publications per faculty member by at least one per year

Exercises

LO1 **Balanced Scorecard**

E 1. Biggs Industries is considering adopting the balanced scorecard and has compiled the following list of possible performance measures. Select the balanced scorecard perspective that best matches each performance measure.

Performance Measure	Balanced Scorecard Perspective
1. Residual income	a. Financial (investors)
2. Customer satisfaction rating	b. Learning and growth (employees)
3. Employee absentee rate	c. Internal business processes
4. Growth in profits	d. Customers
5. On-time deliveries	
6. Manufacturing processing time	

LO1 **Balanced Scorecard**

E 2. Valient Online Products is considering adopting the balanced scorecard and has compiled the following list of possible performance measures. Select the balanced scorecard perspective that best matches each performance measure.

Performance Measure	Balanced Scorecard Perspective
1. Economic value added	a. Financial (investors)
2. Employee turnover	b. Learning and growth (employees)
3. Average daily sales	c. Internal business processes
4. Defect-free units	d. Customers
5. Number of repeat customer visits	
6. Employee training hours	

LO1 **Performance Measures**

E 3. Beva Washington wants to measure her division's product quality. Link an appropriate performance measure with each balanced scorecard perspective.

Product Quality	Possible Performance Measures
1. Financial (investors)	a. Number of defective products returned
2. Learning and growth (employees)	b. Number of products failing inspection
3. Internal business processes	c. Increased market share
4. Customers	d. Savings from employee suggestions

LO1 **Performance Measures**

E 4. Sam Yu wants to measure customer satisfaction within his region. Link an appropriate performance measure with each balanced scorecard perspective.

Customer Satisfaction	Possible Performance Measures
1. Financial (investors)	a. Number of staff promotions
2. Learning and growth (employees)	b. Number of repeat customers
3. Internal business processes	c. Number of process improvements
4. Customers	d. Percentage sales increase over last period

LO2 **Responsibility Centers**

E 5. Identify the most appropriate type of responsibility center for each of the following organizational units:

1. A manufacturing department of a large corporation
2. An eye clinic in a community hospital
3. The South American division of a multinational company
4. The food preparation plant of a large restaurant chain
5. The catalog order department of a retailer

LO2 **Controllable Costs**

E 6. Angel Sweets produces pies. The company has the following three-tiered manufacturing structure:

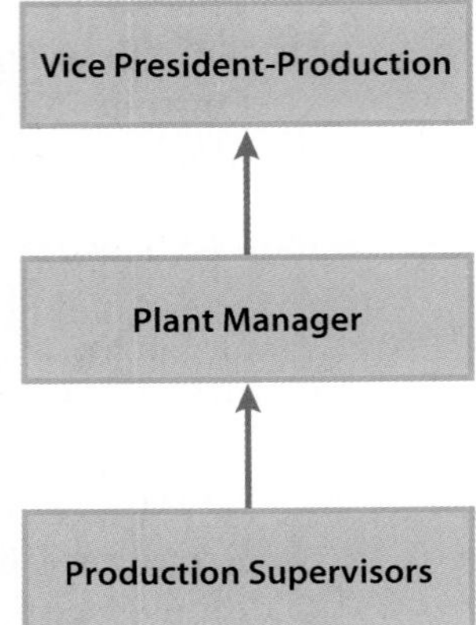

Identify the manager responsible for each of the following costs:

1. Repair and maintenance costs
2. Materials handling costs
3. Direct labor
4. Supervisors' salaries
5. Maintenance of plant grounds
6. Depreciation–equipment
7. Plant manager's salary
8. Cost of materials used
9. Storage of finished goods
10. Property taxes–plant
11. Depreciation–plant

LO2 **Organization Chart**

E 7. Happy Industries wants to formalize its management structure by designing an organization chart. The company has a president, a board of directors, and two vice presidents. Four discretionary cost centers—Financial Resources, Human Resources, Information Resources, and Physical Resources—report to one of the vice presidents. The other vice president has one manufacturing plant with three subassembly areas reporting to her. Draw the company's organization chart.

LO3 **Performance Reports**

E 8. Jackie Jefferson, a new employee at Handown, Inc., is learning about the various types of performance reports. Describe the typical contents of a performance report for each type of responsibility center.

LO3 **Variable Costing Income Statement**

E 9. Vegan, LLC, owns a chain of gourmet vegetarian take-out markets. Last month, Store Q generated the following information: sales, $890,000; direct materials, $220,000; direct labor, $97,000; variable overhead, $150,000; fixed overhead, $130,000; variable selling and administrative expenses, $44,500; and fixed selling expenses, $82,300. There were no beginning or ending inventories. Average daily sales (25 business days) were $35,600. Customer orders processed totaled 15,000.

Vegan had budgeted monthly sales of $900,000; direct materials, $210,000; direct labor, $100,000; variable overhead, $140,000; fixed overhead, $140,000; variable selling and administrative expenses, $45,000; and fixed selling expenses, $60,000. Store Q had been projected to do $36,000 in daily sales and process 16,000 customer orders. Using this information, prepare a performance report for Store Q.

LO3 **Variable Costing Income Statement**

E 10. The income statement in the traditional reporting format for Green Products, Inc., for the year ended December 31, is as follows:

Green Products, Inc. Income Statement For the Year Ended December 31	
Sales	$296,400
Cost of goods sold	112,750
Gross margin	$183,650
Selling expenses	
Variable	69,820
Fixed	36,980
Administrative expenses	27,410
Operating income	$ 49,440

Total fixed manufacturing costs for the year were $16,750. All administrative expenses are considered to be fixed.

Using this information, prepare an income statement for Green Products, Inc., for the year ended December 31, using the variable costing format.

LO3 Performance Report for a Cost Center

E 11. Archer, LLC, owns a blueberry processing plant. Last month, the plant generated the following information: blueberries processed, 50,000 pounds; direct materials, $50,000; direct labor, $10,000; variable overhead, $12,000; and fixed overhead, $13,000. There were no beginning or ending inventories. Average daily pounds processed (25 business days) were 2,000. Average rate of processing was 250 pounds per hour.

At the beginning of the month, Archer had budgeted costs of blueberries, $45,000; direct labor, $10,000; variable overhead, $14,000; and fixed overhead, $14,000. The monthly master budget was based on producing 50,000 pounds of blueberries each month. This means that the plant had been projected to process 2,000 pounds daily at the rate of 240 pounds per hour.

Using this information, prepare a performance report for the month for the blueberry processing plant. Include a flexible budget and a computation of variances in your report. Indicate whether the variances are favorable (F) or unfavorable (U) to the performance of the plant.

LO4 Investment Center Performance

E 12. Momence Associates is evaluating the performance of three divisions: Maple, Oaks, and Juniper. Using the following data, compute the return on investment and residual income for each division, compare the divisions' performance, and comment on the factors that influenced performance:

	Maple	Oaks	Juniper
Sales	$100,000	$100,000	$100,000
Operating income	$10,000	$10,000	$20,000
Assets invested	$25,000	$12,500	$25,000
Desired ROI	40%	40%	40%

LO4 Economic Value Added

E 13. Leesburg, LLP, is evaluating the performance of three divisions: Lake, Sumter, and Poe. Using the data that appear on the next page, compute the economic value added by each division, and comment on each division's performance.

	Lake	Sumter	Poe
Sales	$100,000	$100,000	$100,000
After-tax operating income	$10,000	$10,000	$20,000
Total assets	$25,000	$12,500	$25,000
Current liabilities	$5,000	$5,000	$5,000
Cost of capital	15%	15%	15%

LO5 **Performance Incentives**

E 14. Dynamic Consulting is advising Solid Industries on the short-term and long-term effectiveness of cash bonuses, awards, profit sharing, and stock as performance incentives. Prepare a chart identifying the effectiveness of each incentive as either long-term or short-term or both.

LO5 **Goal Congruence**

E 15. Serious Toys, Inc., has adopted the balanced scorecard to motivate its managers to work toward the companywide goal of leading its industry in innovation. Identify the four stakeholder perspectives that would link to the following objectives, measures, and targets:

Perspective	Objective	Measure	Target
	Profitable new products	New product RI	New-product RI of at least $100,000
	Work force with cutting-edge skills	Percentage of employees cross-trained on work-group tasks	90 percent of work-group cross-trained on new tasks within 10 days
	Agile production processes	Time to market (the time between a product idea and its first sales)	Time to market less than 6 months for 80% of product introductions
	Successful product introductions	New-product market share	Capture 75% of new product market within 6 months

Problems

LO2 LO3 **Evaluating Cost Center Performance**

P 1. Beverage Products, LLC, manufactures metal beverage containers. The division that manufactures soft-drink beverage cans for the North American market has two plants that operate 24 hours a day, 365 days a year. The plants are evaluated as cost centers. Small tools and supplies are considered variable overhead. Depreciation and rent are considered fixed overhead. The master budget for a plant and the operating results of the two North American plants, East Coast and West Coast, are as follows:

	Master Budget	East Coast	West Coast
Center costs			
Rolled aluminum ($0.01)	$4,000,000	$3,492,000	$5,040,000
Lids ($0.005)	2,000,000	1,980,000	2,016,000
Direct labor ($0.0025)	1,000,000	864,000	1,260,000
Small tools and supplies ($0.0013)	520,000	432,000	588,000
Depreciation and rent	480,000	480,000	480,000
Total cost	$8,000,000	$7,248,000	$9,384,000

Performance measures			
Cans processed per hour	45,662	41,096	47,945
Average daily pounds of scrap metal	5	6	7
Cans processed (in millions)	400	360	420

Required

1. Prepare a performance report for the East Coast plant. Include a flexible budget and variance analysis.
2. Prepare a performance report for the West Coast plant. Include a flexible budget and variance analysis.
3. Compare the two plants, and comment on their performance.

Manager insight ▶ 4. Explain why a flexible budget should be prepared.

LO3 **Traditional and Variable Costing Income Statements**

P 2. Roofing tile is the major product of the Tops Corporation. The company had a particularly good year, as shown by its operating data. It sold 88,400 cases of tile. Variable cost of goods sold was $848,640; variable selling expenses were $132,600; fixed overhead was $166,680; fixed selling expenses were $152,048; and fixed administrative expenses were $96,450. Selling price was $18 per case. There were no partially completed jobs in process at the beginning or the end of the year. Finished goods inventory had been used up at the end of the previous year.

Required

1. Prepare the calendar year-end income statement for the Tops Corporation using the traditional reporting format.
2. Prepare the calendar year-end income statement for the Tops Corporation using the variable costing format.

LO2 LO3 LO4 **Evaluating Profit and Investment Center Performance**

P 3. Bobbie Howell, the managing partner of the law firm Howell, Bagan, and Clark, LLP, makes asset acquisition and disposal decisions for the firm. As managing partner, she supervises the partners in charge of the firm's three branch offices. Those partners have the authority to make employee compensation decisions. The partners' compensation depends on the profitability of their branch office. Victoria Smith manages the City Branch, which has the following master budget and actual results for the year:

	Master Budget	Actual Results
Billed hours	5,000	4,900
Revenue	$250,000	$254,800
Controllable variable costs		
Direct labor	120,000	137,200
Variable overhead	40,000	34,300
Contribution margin	$ 90,000	$ 83,300
Controllable fixed costs		
Rent	30,000	30,000
Other administrative expenses	45,000	42,000
Branch operating income	$ 15,000	$ 11,300

Required

1. Assume that the City Branch is a profit center. Prepare a performance report that includes a flexible budget. Determine the variances between actual results, the flexible budget, and the master budget.

2. Evaluate Victoria Smith's performance as manager of the City Branch.
3. Assume that the branch managers are assigned responsibility for capital expenditures and that the branches are thus investment centers. City Branch is expected to generate a desired ROI of at least 30 percent on average invested assets of $40,000.
   a. Compute the branch's return on investment and residual income.
   b. Using the ROI and residual income, evaluate Victoria Smith's performance as branch manager. (Manager insight ▶)

LO4 **Return on Investment and Residual Income**

P 4. The financial results for the past two years for Ornamental Iron, a division of Iron Foundry Company, follow:

Iron Foundry Company
Ornamental Iron Division
Balance Sheet
December 31

	This Year	Last Year
Assets		
Cash	$ 5,000	$ 3,000
Accounts receivable	10,000	8,000
Inventory	30,000	32,000
Other current assets	600	600
Plant assets	128,300	120,300
Total assets	$173,900	$163,900
Liabilities and Stockholders' Equity		
Current liabilities	$ 13,900	$ 10,000
Long-term liabilities	90,000	93,900
Stockholders' equity	70,000	60,000
Total liabilities and stockholders' equity	$173,900	$163,900

Iron Foundry Company
Ornamental Iron Division
Income Statement
For the Years Ended December 31

	This Year	Last Year
Sales	$180,000	$160,000
Cost of goods sold	100,000	90,000
Selling and administrative expenses	27,500	26,500
Operating income	$ 52,500	$ 43,500
Income taxes	17,850	14,790
After-tax operating income	$ 34,650	$ 28,710

Required

1. Compute the division's profit margin, asset turnover, and return on investment for this year and last year. Beginning total assets for last year were $157,900. Round to two decimal places.
2. The desired return on investment for the division has been set at 12 percent. Compute Ornamental Iron's residual income for this year and last year.
3. The cost of capital for the division is 8 percent. Compute the division's economic value added for this year and last year.

Manager insight ▶

4. Before drawing conclusions about this division's performance, what additional information would you want?

LO4

Return on Investment and Economic Value Added

P 5. The balance sheet for the New Products Division of NuBone Corporation showed invested assets of $200,000 at the beginning of the year and $300,000 at the end of the year. During the year, the division's operating income was $12,500 on sales of $500,000.

Required

1. Compute the division's residual income if the desired ROI is 6 percent.
2. Compute the following performance measures for the division: (a) profit margin, (b) asset turnover, and (c) return on investment
3. Recompute the division's ROI under each of the following independent assumptions:
   a. Sales increase from $500,000 to $600,000, causing operating income to rise from $12,500 to $30,000.
   b. Invested assets at the beginning of the year are reduced from $200,000 to $100,000.
   c. Operating expenses are reduced, causing operating income to rise from $12,500 to $20,000.
4. Compute NuBone's EVA if total corporate assets are $500,000, current liabilities are $80,000, after-tax operating income is $50,000, and the cost of capital is 8 percent.

Alternate Problems

LO2 LO3

Evaluating Cost Center Performance

P 6. Plastic Products, LLC, manufactures plastic beverage bottles. The division that manufactures water bottles for the North American market has two plants that operate 24 hours a day, 365 days a year. The plants are evaluated as cost centers. Small tools and supplies are considered variable overhead. Depreciation and rent are considered fixed overhead. The master budget for a plant and the operating results of the two North American plants, North and South, are as follows:

	Master Budget	North Actual	South Actual
Center costs			
Plastic pellets ($0.009)	$4,500,000	$3,880,000	$5,500,000
Caps ($0.004)	2,000,000	1,990,000	2,000,000
Direct labor ($0.002)	1,000,000	865,000	1,240,000
Small tools and supplies ($0.0005)	250,000	198,000	280,000
Depreciation and rent	450,000	440,000	480,000
Total cost	$8,200,000	$7,373,000	$9,500,000

Performance measures			
Bottles processed per hour	69,450	62,000	70,250
Average daily pounds of scrap	5	6	7
Bottles processed (in millions)	500	450	520

Required

1. Prepare a performance report for the North plant. Include a flexible budget and variance analysis.
2. Prepare a performance report for the South plant. Include a flexible budget and variance analysis.
3. Compare the two plants, and comment on their performance.

Manager insight ▶ 4. Explain why a flexible budget should be prepared.

LO3 **Traditional and Variable Costing Income Statements**

P 7. Interior designers often use the deluxe carpet products of Lux Mills, Inc. The Maricopa blend is the company's top product line. In March, Lux produced and sold 174,900 square yards of Maricopa blend. Factory operating data for the month included variable cost of goods sold of $2,623,500 and fixed overhead of $346,875. Other expenses were variable selling expenses, $166,155; fixed selling expenses, $148,665; and fixed general and administrative expenses, $231,500. Total sales revenue equaled $3,935,250. All production took place in March, and there was no work in process at month end. Goods are usually shipped when completed.

Required

1. Prepare the March income statement for Lux Mills, Inc., using the traditional reporting format.
2. Prepare the March income statement for Lux Mills, Inc., using the variable costing format.

LO2 LO3 LO4 **Return on Investment and Residual Income**

P 8. Portia Carter is the president of a company that owns six multiplex movie theaters. Carter has delegated decision-making authority to the theater managers for all decisions except those relating to capital expenditures and film selection. The theater managers' compensation depends on the profitability of their theaters. Max Burgman, the manager of the Park Theater, had the following master budget and actual results for the month:

	Master Budget	Actual Results
Tickets sold	120,000	110,000
Revenue–tickets	$ 840,000	$ 880,000
Revenue–concessions	480,000	330,000
Total revenue	$1,320,000	$1,210,000
Controllable variable costs		
Concessions	120,000	99,000
Direct labor	420,000	330,000
Variable overhead	540,000	550,000
Contribution margin	$ 240,000	$ 231,000
Controllable fixed costs		
Rent	55,000	55,000
Other administrative expenses	45,000	50,000
Theater operating income	$ 140,000	$ 126,000

Required

1. Assuming that the theaters are profit centers, prepare a performance report for the Park Theater. Include a flexible budget. Determine the variances between actual results, the flexible budget, and the master budget.
2. Evaluate Burgman's performance as manager of the Park Theater.
3. Assume that the managers are assigned responsibility for capital expenditures and that the theaters are thus investment centers. Park Theater is expected to generate a desired ROI of at least 6 percent on average invested assets of $2,000,000.
   a. Compute the theater's return on investment and residual income.
   b. Using the ROI and residual income, evaluate Burgman's performance as manager. (Manager insight ▶)

LO4 **Return on Investment and Residual Income**

P 9. The financial results for the past two years for ABB Company, follow.

ABB Company
Balance Sheet
December 31

	This Year	Last Year
Assets		
Cash	$ 9,000	$ 4,000
Accounts receivable	40,000	50,000
Inventory	30,000	25,000
Other current assets	1,000	1,000
Plant assets	120,000	100,000
Total assets	$200,000	$180,000
Liabilities and Stockholders' Equity		
Current liabilities	$ 10,000	$ 10,000
Long-term Liabilities	20,000	10,000
Stockholders' equity	170,000	160,000
Total liabilities and stockholders' equity	$200,000	$180,000

ABB Company
Income Statement
For the Years Ended
December 31

	This Year	Last Year
Sales	$250,000	$200,000
Cost of goods sold	150,000	115,000
Selling and administrative expenses	30,000	25,000
Operating income	$ 70,000	$ 60,000
Income taxes	21,000	18,000
After-tax operating income	$ 49,000	$ 42,000

Required

1. Compute the company's profit margin, asset turnover, and return on investment for this year and last year. Beginning total assets for last year were $160,000. Round to two decimal places.

2. The desired return on investment for the company has been set at 10 percent. Compute ABB's residual income for this year and last year.
3. The cost of capital for the company is 5 percent. Compute the company's economic value added for this year and last year.

Manager insight ▶ 4. Before drawing conclusions about this company's performance, what additional information would you want?

LO4 **Return on Investment and Economic Value Added**

P 10. Micanopy Company makes replicas of Indian artifacts. The balance sheet for the Arrowhead Division showed that the company had invested assets of $300,000 at the beginning of the year and $500,000 at the end of the year. During the year, Arrowhead Division's operating income was $80,000 on sales of $1,200,000.

Required

1. Compute Arrowhead Division's residual income if the desired ROI is 20 percent.
2. Compute the following performance measures for the division: (a) profit margin, (b) asset turnover, and (c) return on investment.
3. Compute Micanopy Company's economic value added if total corporate assets are $6,000,000, current liabilities are $800,000, after-tax operating income is $750,000, and the cost of capital is 12 percent.

ENHANCING Your Knowledge, Skills, and Critical Thinking

LO1 **Balanced Scorecard Results**

C 1. IT, Inc., has adopted the balanced scorecard approach to motivate the managers of its product divisions to work toward the companywide goal of leading its industry in innovation. The corporation's selected performance measures and scorecard results are as follows:

	Division			Performance
Measure	A	B	C	Target
New product ROI	80%	75%	70%	75%
Employees cross-trained in new tasks within 30 days	95	96	94	100
New product's time to market less than one year	85	90	86	80
New product's market share one year after introduction	50	100	80	80

Can you effectively compare the performance of the three divisions against the targets? What other measures mentioned in this chapter are needed to evaluate performance effectively?

LO1 LO2 **Responsibility Centers**

C 2. Wood4Fun makes wooden playground equipment for the institutional and consumer markets. The company strives for low-cost, high-quality production because it operates in a highly competitive market in which product price is set by the marketplace and is not based on production costs. The company is organized into responsibility centers. The vice president of manufacturing is responsible for three manufacturing plants. The vice president of sales is responsible for four sales regions. Recently, these two vice presidents began to disagree about whether the manufacturing plants are cost centers or profit centers. The vice president of manufacturing views the plants as cost centers because the managers of the plants control only product-related costs. The vice president of sales believes the plants are profit centers because product quality and product cost strongly affect company profits.

1. Identify the controllable performance that Wood4Fun values and wants to measure. Give at least three examples of performance measures that Wood4-Fun could use to monitor such performance.
2. For the manufacturing plants, what type of responsibility center is most consistent with the controllable performance Wood4Fun wants to measure?
3. For the sales regions, what type of responsibility center is most appropriate?

LO1 LO2 LO3 LO5

Types of Responsibility Centers

C 3. Yuma Foods acquired Aldo's Tortillas several years ago. Aldo's has continued to operate as an independent company, except that Yuma Foods has exclusive authority over capital investments, production quantity, and pricing decisions because Yuma has been Aldo's only customer since the acquisition. Yuma uses return on investment to evaluate the performance of Aldo's manager. The most recent performance report is as follows:

Yuma Foods
Performance Report for Aldo's Tortillas
For the Year Ended June 30

Sales	$6,000
Variable cost of goods sold	3,000
Variable administrative expenses	1,000
Variable corporate expenses (% of sales)	600
Contribution margin	$1,400
Fixed overhead (includes depreciation of $100)	400
Fixed administrative expenses	500
Operating income	$ 500
Average assets invested	$5,500
Return on investment	9.09%*

*Rounded.

1. Analyze the items listed in the performance report, and identify the items that Aldo controls and those that Yuma controls. In your opinion, what type of responsibility center is Aldo's Tortillas? Explain your response.
2. Prepare a revised performance report for Aldo's Tortillas and an accompanying memo to the president of Yuma Foods that explains why it is important to change the content of the report. Cite some basic principles of responsibility accounting to support your recommendation.

LO1 LO4 LO5

Economic Value Added and Performance

C 4. Sevilla Consulting offers environmental consulting services worldwide. The managers of branch offices are rewarded for superior performance with bonuses based on the economic value that the office adds to the company. Last year's operating results for the entire company and for its three offices, expressed in millions of U.S. dollars, are as follows:

	Worldwide	Europe	Americas	Asia
Cost of capital	9%	10%	8%	12%
Total assets	$210	$70	$70	$70
Current liabilities	80	10	40	30
After-tax operating income	15	5	5	5

1. Compute the economic value added for each office worldwide. What factors affect each office's economic value added? How can an office improve its economic value added?
2. If managers' bonuses are based on economic value added to office performance, what specific actions will managers be motivated to take?
3. Is economic value added the only performance measure needed to evaluate investment centers adequately? Explain your response.

LO4 Return on Investment and Residual Income

C 5. Suppose Alexandra Patel, the manager of the Food and Lodging Division at Winter Wonderland Resort, has hired you as a consultant to help her examine her division's performance under several different circumstances.

1. Type the data that follow into an Excel spreadsheet to compute the division's actual return on investment and residual income. (Data are from parts **3** and **4** of this chapter's Review Problem.) Match your data entries to the rows and columns shown below. (**Hint:** Remember to format each cell for the type of numbers it holds, such as percentage, currency, or general.)

	A	B	C	D
1				**Investment Center**
2				**Food and Lodging Division**
3				**Actual Results**
4	Sales			$40,000,000
5	Operating income			$ 6,450,000
6	Average assets invested			$10,000,000
7	Desired ROI			30%
8	Return on Investment			=(D5/D6)
9	Profit Margin			=(D5/D4)
10	Asset Turnover			=(D4/D6)
11	Residual Income			=(D5-(D7*D6))
12				

2. Patel would like to know how the figures would change if Food and Lodging had a desired ROI of 40 percent and average assets invested of $10,000,000. Revise your spreadsheet from **1** to compute the division's return on investment and residual income under those conditions.
3. Patel also wants to know how the figures would change if Food and Lodging had a desired ROI of 30 percent and average assets invested of $12,000,000. Revise your spreadsheet from **1** to compute the division's return on investment and residual income under those conditions.
4. Does the use of formatted spreadsheets simplify the computation of ROI and residual income? Do such spreadsheets make it easier to perform "what-if" analyses?

LO4 Cookie Company (Continuing Case)

C 6. As we continue with this case, assume that your cookie store is now part of a national chain. The store has been consistently profitable, and sales remain satisfactory despite a temporary economic downturn in your area.

At the first of the year, corporate headquarters set a targeted return on investment of 20 percent for your store. The store currently averages $140,000 in invested assets (beginning invested assets, $130,000; ending invested assets, $150,000) and is projected to have an operating income of $30,800. You are considering whether to take one or both of the following actions before the end of the year:

- Hold off recording and paying $5,000 in bills owed until the start of the next fiscal year.
- Write down to zero value $3,000 in store inventory (nonperishable containers) that you have been unable to sell.

Currently, your bonus is based on store profits. Next year, corporate headquarters is changing its performance incentive program so that bonuses will be based on a store's actual return on investment.

1. What effect would each of the actions that you are considering have on the store's operating income this year? (**Hint:** Use Figure 25-3 to trace the effects.) In your opinion, is either action unethical?
2. Independent of question 1, how would the inventory write-down affect next year's income and return on investment if the inventory is sold for $4,000 next year, when corporate headquarters changes its performance incentive plan for store managers? In your opinion, do you have an ethical dilemma?

CHAPTER

26

Standard Costing and Variance Analysis

The Management Process

PLAN

- ▷ Prepare the operating budgets, and determine standard costs
- ▷ Establish cost-based goals for products and services

PERFORM

- ▷ Apply cost standards as work is performed in cost centers
- ▷ Collect actual cost data

EVALUATE

- ▷ Use flexible budgets to evaluate manager performance
- ▷ Calculate variances between standard and actual costs for direct materials, direct labor, variable overhead, and fixed overhead
- ▷ Determine their causes and take corrective action

COMMUNICATE

- ▷ Prepare cost center performance reports using standard costing
- ▷ Prepare comparative analyses of flexible budgets to actual results for materials, labor, and overhead

Standard costs are useful tools for management because they are based on realistic estimates of operating costs. Managers use them to develop budgets, to control costs, and to prepare reports. Because of their usefulness in comparing planned and actual costs, standard costs have usually been most closely associated with the performance evaluation of cost centers. In this chapter, we describe how standard costs are computed and how managers use the variances between standard and actual costs to evaluate performance and control costs.

LEARNING OBJECTIVES

LO1 **Define *standard costs*, explain how standard costs are developed, and compute a standard unit cost.** (pp. 1138–1142)

LO2 **Prepare a flexible budget, and describe how managers use variance analysis to control costs.** (pp. 1142–1147)

LO3 **Compute and analyze direct materials variances.** (pp. 1147–1150)

LO4 **Compute and analyze direct labor variances.** (pp. 1150–1153)

LO5 **Compute and analyze overhead variances.** (pp. 1154–1161)

LO6 **Explain how variances are used to evaluate managers' performance.** (pp. 1161–1163)

DECISION POINT ▶ A MANAGER'S FOCUS ICU, INC.

ICU, Inc., is known for its innovative use of robotic technology. One of the company's products is the Watch Dog, a mobile robot designed for home surveillance. The Watch Dog is equipped with a built-in video camera and audio component, and it connects wirelessly to any computer. While owners are away from home, they can use a computer or cell phone with an online connection to monitor the Watch Dog as it patrols their home and observe and listen to anything that is happening there.

ICU, Inc., is highly profitable. A key factor in its success is its managers' establishment of standard costs for each of the company's product lines. Managers use these standard costs as performance targets and as benchmarks against which they measure actual spending trends. As a result, the company is able to keep its operating costs low and to sell its products at affordable prices. With its relatively inexpensive price tag, the Watch Dog has become a popular alternative to other home security systems.

- ▶ How does setting performance standards help managers control costs?
- ▶ How do managers use standard costs to evaluate the performance of cost centers?

Standard Costing

LO1 Define *standard costs,* explain how standard costs are developed, and compute a standard unit cost.

Standard costs are realistic estimates of costs based on analyses of both past and projected operating costs and conditions. They are usually stated in terms of cost per unit. They provide a standard, or predetermined, performance level for use in **standard costing,** a method of cost control that also includes a measure of actual performance and a measure of the difference, or **variance,** between standard and actual performance. This method of measuring and controlling costs differs from the actual and normal costing methods in that it uses estimated costs exclusively to compute all three elements of product cost—direct materials, direct labor, and overhead.

Standard costing is especially effective for managing cost centers. You may recall that a cost center is a responsibility center in which there are well-defined links between the cost of the resources (direct materials, direct labor, and overhead) and the resulting products or services.

A disadvantage to using standard costing is that it can be expensive because the estimated costs are based not just on past costs, but also on engineering estimates, forecasted demand, worker input, time and motion studies, and type and quality of direct materials. However, this method can be used in any type of business. Both manufacturers and service businesses can use standard costing in conjunction with a job order costing, process costing, or activity-based costing system.

Standard Costs and Managers

Study Note

Standard costs are necessary for planning and control. Budgets are developed from standard costs, and performance is measured against them.

As we noted in the introduction to this chapter, standard costs are useful tools for management. Managers use them to develop budgets, to control costs, and to prepare reports. Because of their usefulness in comparing planned and actual costs, standard costs have usually been most closely associated with the performance evaluation of cost centers.

In recent years, the increasing automation of manufacturing processes has caused a significant decrease in direct labor costs and a corresponding decline in the importance of labor-related standard costs and variances. As a result, managers at manufacturing companies, which once used standard costing for all three elements of product cost, may now apply this method only to direct materials and overhead.

Today, many service organizations' managers also use standard costing. Although a service organization has no direct materials costs, labor and overhead costs are very much a part of providing services, and standard costing is an effective way of planning and controlling them.

FOCUS ON BUSINESS PRACTICE

Why Go on a Factory Tour?

If you've had some manufacturing experience, you probably understand the importance of standard costing and variance analysis. If you haven't had any manufacturing experience, you can gain insight into the importance of cost planning and control by visiting a factory. Consult your local chamber of commerce for factory tours near you. You can also tour factories online. Check out the virtual production tour of jelly beans at www.jellybelly.com or see how chocolate is made at www.hersheys.com.

Computing Standard Costs

A fully integrated standard costing system uses standard costs for all the elements of product cost: direct materials, direct labor, and overhead. Inventory accounts for materials, work in process, and finished goods, as well as the Cost of Goods Sold account, are maintained and reported in terms of standard costs, and standard unit costs are used to compute account balances. Actual costs are recorded separately so that managers can compare what should have been spent (the standard costs) with the actual costs incurred in the cost center.

A standard unit cost for a manufactured product has the following six elements:

- Price standard for direct materials
- Quantity standard for direct materials
- Standard for direct labor rate
- Standard for direct labor time
- Standard for variable overhead rate
- Standard for fixed overhead rate

To compute a standard unit cost, it is necessary to identify and analyze each of these elements. (A standard unit cost for a service includes only the elements that relate to direct labor and overhead.)

Standard Direct Materials Cost

The **standard direct materials cost** is found by multiplying the price standard for direct materials by the quantity standard for direct materials. For example, if the price standard for a certain item is \$2.75 and a specific job calls for a quantity standard of eight of the items, the standard direct materials cost for that job is computed as follows:

Standard Direct Materials Cost	=	Direct Materials Price Standard	×	Direct Materials Quantity Standard
\$22.00	=	\$2.75	×	8

The **direct materials price standard** is a careful estimate of the cost of a specific direct material in the next accounting period. An organization's purchasing agent or its purchasing department is responsible for developing price standards for all direct materials and for making the actual purchases. When estimating a direct materials price standard, the purchasing agent or department must take into account all possible price increases, changes in available quantities, and new sources of supply.

The **direct materials quantity standard** is an estimate of the amount of direct materials, including scrap and waste, that will be used in an accounting period. It is influenced by product engineering specifications, the quality of direct materials, the age and productivity of machinery, and the quality and experience of the work force. Production managers or management accountants usually establish and monitor standards for direct materials quantity, but engineers, purchasing agents, and machine operators may also contribute to the development of these standards.

Standard Direct Labor Cost

The **standard direct labor cost** for a product, task, or job order is calculated by multiplying the standard wage for direct labor by the standard hours of direct labor. For example, if the standard direct labor rate is \$8.40 per hour and a product takes 1.5 standard direct labor hours to produce, the product's standard direct labor cost is computed as follows:

$$\text{Standard Direct Labor Cost} = \text{Direct Labor Rate Standard} \times \text{Direct Labor Time Standard}$$

$$\$12.60 = \$8.40 \times 1.5 \text{ hours}$$

Study Note

Both the direct labor rate standard and the direct labor time standard are based on an average of the different levels of skilled workers, and both are related to the production of one unit or batch.

The **direct labor rate standard** is the hourly direct labor rate that is expected to prevail during the next accounting period for each function or job classification. Although rate ranges are established for each type of worker and rates vary within those ranges according to each worker's experience and length of service, an average standard rate is developed for each task. Even if the person making the product is paid more or less than the standard rate, the standard rate is used to calculate the standard direct labor cost. Standard labor rates are fairly easy to develop because labor rates are either set by a labor union contract or defined by the company.

The **direct labor time standard** is the expected labor time required for each department, machine, or process to complete the production of one unit or one batch of output. In many cases, standard time per unit is a small fraction of an hour. Current time and motion studies of workers and machines, as well as records of their past performance, provide the data for developing this standard. The direct labor time standard should be revised whenever a machine is replaced or the quality of the labor force changes.

Standard Overhead Cost

The **standard overhead cost** is the sum of the estimates of variable and fixed overhead costs in the next accounting period. It is based on standard overhead rates that are computed in much the same way as the predetermined overhead rate that we discussed in an earlier chapter. Unlike that rate, however, the standard overhead rate has two parts, one for variable costs and one for fixed costs. The reason for computing the standard variable and fixed overhead rates separately is that their cost behavior differs.

The **standard variable overhead rate** is computed by dividing the total budgeted variable overhead costs by an expression of capacity, such as the number of standard machine hours or standard direct labor hours. (Other bases may be used if machine hours or direct labor hours are not good predictors, or drivers, of variable overhead costs.) For example, using standard machine hours as the base, the formula is as follows:

$$\text{Standard Variable Overhead Rate} = \frac{\text{Total Budgeted Variable Overhead Costs}}{\text{Expected Number of Standard Machine Hours}}$$

The **standard fixed overhead rate** is computed by dividing the total budgeted fixed overhead costs by an expression of capacity, usually normal capacity in terms of standard hours or units. The denominator is expressed in the same terms as the variable overhead rate. For example, using normal capacity in terms of standard machine hours as the denominator, the formula is as follows:

$$\text{Standard Fixed Overhead Rate} = \frac{\text{Total Budgeted Fixed Overhead Costs}}{\text{Normal Capacity in Terms of Standard Machine Hours}}$$

Recall that normal capacity is the level of operating capacity needed to meet expected sales demand. Using it as the application base ensures that all fixed overhead costs have been applied to units produced by the time normal capacity is reached.

Total Standard Unit Cost

Using standard costs eliminates the need to calculate unit costs from actual cost data every week or month or for each batch of goods produced. Once standard costs for direct materials, direct labor, and variable and fixed overhead have been developed, a total standard unit cost can be computed at any time.

To illustrate how standard costs are used to compute total unit cost, let's suppose that ICU, Inc., the company discussed in the Decision Point, has recently updated the standards for its line of surveillance robots called Watch Dog. Direct materials price standards are now $9.20 per square foot for casing materials and $20.17 for each mechanism. Direct materials quantity standards are 0.025 square foot of casing materials per robot and one mechanism per robot. Direct labor time standards are 0.01 hour per robot for the Case Stamping Department and 0.05 hour per robot for the Assembly Department. Direct labor rate standards are $8.00 per hour for the Case Stamping Department and $10.20 per hour for the Assembly Department. Standard manufacturing overhead rates are $12.00 per direct labor hour for the standard variable overhead rate and $9.00 per direct labor hour for the standard fixed overhead rate. The standard cost of making one robot would be computed in the following manner:

Direct materials costs:	
Casing ($9.20 per sq. ft. × 0.025 sq. ft.)	$ 0.23
One mechanism	20.17
Direct labor costs:	
Case Stamping Department ($8.00 per hour × 0.01 hour per robot)	0.08
Assembly Department ($10.20 per hour × 0.05 hour per robot)	0.51
Variable overhead ($12.00 per hour × 0.06 hour per robot)	0.72
Total standard variable cost of one robot	$21.71
Fixed overhead ($9.00 per hour × 0.06 hour per robot)	0.54
Total standard cost of one robot	$22.25

Study Note

The total standard cost of $22.25 represents the *desired* cost of producing one robot.

The total standard cost of producing a watch like this or a robot like the Watch Dog, represents the desired production cost. It is based on the standards established for direct materials costs, direct labor costs, and variable and fixed overhead.

Courtesy of Timothy Goodwin/ istockphoto.com.

STOP & APPLY >

Using the following information, compute the standard unit cost of a 5-pound bag of sugar:

Direct materials quantity standard	5 pounds per unit
Direct materials price standard	\$0.05 per pound
Direct labor time standard	0.01 hour per unit
Direct labor rate standard	\$10.00 per hour
Variable overhead rate standard	\$0.15 per machine hour
Fixed overhead rate standard	\$0.10 per machine hour
Machine hour standard	0.5 hour per unit

SOLUTION

Direct materials cost (\$0.05 × 5 pounds)	\$0.25
Direct labor cost (\$10.00 × 0.01 hour)	0.10
Variable overhead (\$0.15 × 0.5 machine hour)	0.08
Fixed overhead (\$0.10 × 0.5 machine hour)	0.05
Total standard unit cost	\$0.48

Variance Analysis

LO2 Prepare a flexible budget, and describe how managers use variance analysis to control costs.

Managers in all types of organizations constantly compare the costs of what was expected to happen with the costs of what actually did happen. By examining the differences, or variances, between standard and actual costs, they can gather much valuable information. **Variance analysis** is the process of computing the differences between standard costs and actual costs and identifying the causes of those differences. In this section, we look at how managers use flexible budgets to improve the accuracy of variance analysis and how they use variance analysis to control costs.

The Role of Flexible Budgets in Variance Analysis

The accuracy of variance analysis depends to a large extent on the type of budget that managers use when comparing variances. Static, or fixed, budgets forecast revenues and expenses for just one level of sales and just one level of output. The budgets that make up a master budget are usually based on a single level of output, but many things can happen over an accounting period that will cause actual output to differ from the estimated output. If a company produces more products than predicted, total production costs will almost always be greater than predicted. When that is the case, a comparison of actual production costs with fixed budgeted costs will inevitably show variances.

The performance report in Exhibit 26-1 compares data from the static master budget of ICU, Inc., with the actual costs of the company's Watch Division, the division responsible for manufacturing the surveillance robot called the Watch Dog. As you can see, actual costs exceeded budgeted costs by \$5,539. On the face of it, most managers would consider such a cost overrun significant. But was there really a cost overrun? The budgeted amounts are based on an output of 17,500 units; however, the actual output was 19,100 units.

EXHIBIT 26-1
Performance Report Using Data from a Static Budget

ICU, Inc.
Performance Report—Watch Division
For the Year Ended December 31

Cost Category	Budgeted Costs*	Actual Costs†	Difference Under (Over) Budget
Direct materials	$357,000	$361,000	($4,000)
Direct labor	10,325	11,779	(1,454)
Variable overhead			
Indirect materials	3,500	3,600	(100)
Indirect labor	5,250	5,375	(125)
Utilities	1,750	1,810	(60)
Other	2,100	2,200	(100)
Fixed overhead			
Supervisory salaries	4,000	3,500	500
Depreciation	2,000	2,000	—
Utilities	450	450	—
Other	3,000	3,200	(200)
Totals	$389,375	$394,914	($5,539)

*Budgeted costs are based on an output of 17,500 units.
†Actual output was 19,100 units.

To judge the division's performance accurately, the company's managers must change the budgeted data to reflect an output of 19,100 units. They can do this by using a flexible budget. A **flexible budget** (also called a *variable budget*) is a summary of expected costs for a range of activity levels. Unlike a static budget, a flexible budget provides forecasted data that can be adjusted for changes in the level of output.

The flexible budget is used primarily as a cost control tool in evaluating performance at the end of a period.

A flexible budget for ICU's Watch Division appears in Exhibit 26-2. It shows the estimated costs for 15,000, 17,500, and 20,000 units of output. The total cost of a variable cost item is found by multiplying the number of units produced

FOCUS ON BUSINESS PRACTICE

Why Complicate the Flexible Budget?

Because of the database capabilities of enterprise resource management (ERM) systems and the principles of resource consumption accounting (RCA), the flexible budget has become more complicated. This new and more complex version of a flexible budget is called *authorized reporting*. Authorized reporting is like a flexible budget in that it restates an accounting period's costs in terms of different levels of output, but it enhances cost restatement by taking into account all the factors that can influence a cost's behavior. With its sophisticated cost analyses, authorized reporting is a more relevant yardstick for cost comparison and control than the traditional flexible budget.[1]

EXHIBIT 26-2
Flexible Budget for Evaluation of Overall Performance

ICU, Inc.
Flexible Budget—Watch Division
For the Year Ended December 31

Cost Category	Units Produced* 15,000	17,500	20,000	Variable Cost per Unit†
Direct materials	$306,000	$357,000	$408,000	$20.40
Direct labor	8,850	10,325	11,800	0.59
Variable overhead				
Indirect materials	3,000	3,500	4,000	0.20
Indirect labor	4,500	5,250	6,000	0.30
Utilities	1,500	1,750	2,000	0.10
Other	1,800	2,100	2,400	0.12
Total variable costs	$325,650	$379,925	$434,200	$21.71
Fixed overhead				
Supervisory salaries	$ 4,000	$ 4,000	$ 4,000	
Depreciation	2,000	2,000	2,000	
Utilities	450	450	450	
Other	3,000	3,000	3,000	
Total fixed overhead costs	$ 9,450	$ 9,450	$ 9,450	
Total costs	$335,100	$389,375	$443,650	

Flexible budget formula:

Total Budgeted Costs = (Variable Cost per Unit × Number of Units Produced)
+ Budgeted Fixed Costs
= ($21.71 × Units Produced) + $9,450

*Flexible budgets are commonly used only for overhead costs; when they are, machine hours or direct labor hours are used in place of units produced.
†Computed by dividing the dollar amount in any column by the respective level of output.

by the item's per unit cost. For example, if the Watch Division produces 15,000 units, direct materials will cost $306,000 (15,000 units × $20.40).

Study Note

Flexible budgets allow managers to compare budgeted and actual costs at the same level of output.

An important element in this exhibit is the **flexible budget formula**, an equation that determines the expected, or budgeted, cost for any level of output. Its components include a per unit amount for variable costs and a total amount for fixed costs. (In Exhibit 26-2, the $21.71 variable cost per unit is computed in the far right column, and the $9,450 is found in the section on fixed overhead costs.) Using the flexible budget formula, you can create a budget for the Watch Division for any level of output in the range of levels given.

The performance report in Exhibit 26-3 is based on data from the flexible budget shown in Exhibit 26-2. Variable unit costs have been multiplied by the 19,100 units actually produced to arrive at the total flexible budgeted costs, and fixed overhead information has been carried over from Exhibit 26-2. In this report, actual costs are $29,197 less than the amount budgeted. In other words, when we use a flexible budget at the end of the period, we find that the

EXHIBIT 26-3
Performance Report Using Data from a Flexible Budget

ICU, Inc.
Performance Report—Watch Division
For the Year Ended December 31

Cost Category (Variable Unit Cost)	Budgeted Costs*	Actual Costs	Difference Under (Over) Budget
Direct materials ($20.40)	$389,640	$361,000	$28,640
Direct labor ($0.59)	11,269	11,779	(510)
Variable overhead			
Indirect materials ($0.20)	3,820	3,600	220
Indirect labor ($0.30)	5,730	5,375	355
Utilities ($0.10)	1,910	1,810	100
Other ($0.12)	2,292	2,200	92
Fixed overhead			
Supervisory salaries	4,000	3,500	500
Depreciation	2,000	2,000	—
Utilities	450	450	—
Other	3,000	3,200	(200)
Totals	$424,111	$394,914	$29,197

*Budgeted costs are based on an output of 19,100 units.

performance of the Watch Division in this period actually exceeded budget targets by $29,197.

Using Variance Analysis to Control Costs

As Figure 26-1 shows, using variance analysis to control costs is a four-step process. First, managers compute the amount of the variance. If the amount is insignificant—meaning that actual operating results are close to those anticipated—no corrective action is needed. If the amount is significant, then managers analyze the variance to identify its cause. In identifying the cause, they are usually able to pinpoint the activities that need to be monitored. They then select performance measures that will enable them to track those activities, analyze the results, and determine the action needed to correct the problem. Their final step is to take the appropriate corrective action.

Although computing the amount of a variance is important, it is also important to remember that this computation does nothing to prevent the variance from recurring. To control costs, managers must determine the cause of the variance and select performance measures that will help them track the problem and find the best solution for it.

As we focus on the computation and analysis of cost center variances in the next sections, we follow the steps outlined in Figure 26-1. We limit our analysis to eight variances, two for each of the cost categories of direct materials, direct labor, variable overhead, and fixed overhead. We give examples of operating problems that might cause each of these variances to occur. We also identify some financial and nonfinancial performance measures that can be used to track the cause of a variance and that can be helpful in correcting it.

FIGURE 26-1
Variance Analysis: A Four-Step Approach to Controlling Costs

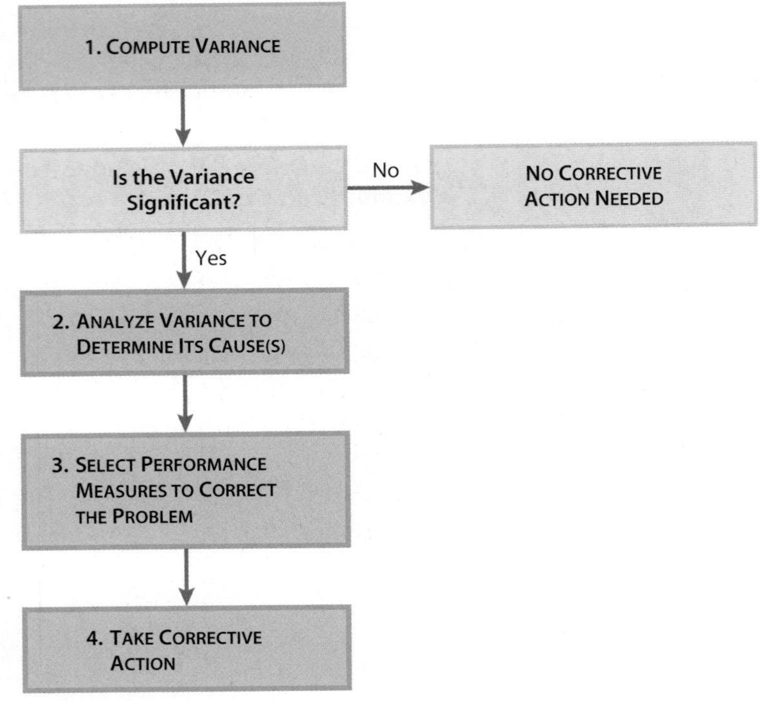

STOP & APPLY >

Keel Company's fixed overhead costs for the year are expected to be as follows: depreciation, $72,000; supervisory salaries, $92,000; property taxes and insurance, $26,000; and other fixed overhead, $14,500. Total fixed overhead is thus expected to be $204,500. Variable costs per unit are expected to be as follows: direct materials, $16.50; direct labor, $8.50; operating supplies, $2.60; indirect labor, $4.10; and other variable overhead costs, $3.20. Prepare a flexible budget for the following levels of production: 18,000 units, 20,000 units, and 22,000 units. What is the flexible budget formula for the year ended December 31?

SOLUTION

Keel Company
Flexible Budget
For the Year Ended December 31

	Units Produced			Variable
Cost Category	**18,000**	**20,000**	**22,000**	**Cost per Unit**
Direct materials	$297,000	$330,000	$363,000	$16.50
Direct labor	153,000	170,000	187,000	8.50
Variable overhead				
Operating supplies	46,800	52,000	57,200	2.60
Indirect labor	73,800	82,000	90,200	4.10
Other	57,600	64,000	70,400	3.20
Total variable costs	$628,200	$698,000	$767,800	$34.90

(continued)

Cost Category	Units Produced 18,000	20,000	22,000	Variable Cost per Unit
Fixed overhead				
Depreciation	$ 72,000	$ 72,000	$ 72,000	
Supervisory salaries	92,000	92,000	92,000	
Property taxes and insurance	26,000	26,000	26,000	
Other	14,500	14,500	14,500	
Total fixed overhead	$204,500	$204,500	$204,500	
Total costs	$832,700	$902,500	$972,300	

Flexible budget formula for the year ended December 31:
Total Budgeted Costs = ($34.90 × Units Produced) + $204,500

Computing and Analyzing Direct Materials Variances

LO3 Compute and analyze direct materials variances.

To control cost center operations, managers compute and analyze variances for whole cost categories, such as total direct materials costs, as well as variances for elements of those categories, such as the price and quantity of each direct material. The more detailed their analysis of direct materials variances is, the more effective they will be in controlling costs.

Computing Direct Materials Variances

The **total direct materials cost variance** is the difference between the standard cost and actual cost of direct materials used to produce the salable units; it is also referred to as the *good units produced*. To illustrate how this variance is computed, let us assume that a manufacturer called Cambria Company makes leather bags to carry the Watch Dog robots. Each bag should use 4 feet of leather (standard quantity), and the standard price of leather is $6.00 per foot. During August, Cambria Company purchased 760 feet of leather costing $5.90 per foot and used the leather to produce 180 bags.

Given these facts, the total direct materials cost variance for Cambria is calculated as follows:

Standard cost

Standard Price × Standard Quantity =
$6.00 per foot × (180 bags × 4 feet per bag) =
$6.00 per foot × 720 feet = $4,320

Less actual cost

Actual Price × Actual Quantity =
$5.90 per foot × 760 feet = 4,484
Total direct materials cost variance = $ 164 (U)

Here, actual cost exceeds standard cost. The situation is unfavorable, as indicated by the U in parentheses after the dollar amount. An F means a favorable situation.

To find the area or people responsible for the variance, the total direct materials cost variance must be broken down into two parts: the direct materials price

Study Note

It is just as important to identify whether a variance is favorable or unfavorable as it is to compute the variance. This information is necessary for analyzing the variance and taking corrective action.

Study Note

The direct materials price variance measures the difference between the standard cost and the actual cost of purchased materials. It is not concerned with the quantity of materials used in the production process.

variance and the direct materials quantity variance. The **direct materials price variance** (also called the *direct material spending* or *rate variance*) is the difference between the standard price and the actual price per unit multiplied by the actual quantity purchased.

For Cambria Company, the direct materials price variance is computed as follows:

Standard price	$6.00
Less actual price	5.90
Difference per foot	$0.10 (F)

Direct Materials Price Variance = (Standard Price − Actual Price) × Actual Quantity
= $0.10 × 760 feet
= $76 (F)

Because the price that the company paid for the direct materials was less than the standard price it expected to pay, the variance is favorable.

The **direct materials quantity variance** (also called the *direct material efficiency* or *usage variance*) is the difference between the standard quantity allowed and the actual quantity used multiplied by the standard price. For Cambria, it is computed as follows:

Standard quantity allowed (180 bags × 4 feet per bag)	720 feet
Less actual quantity	760 feet
Difference	40 feet (U)

Direct Materials Quantity Variance = Standard Price × (Standard Quantity Allowed − Actual Quantity)
= $6 × 40 feet
= $240 (U)

Because more leather than the standard quantity was used in the production process, the direct materials quantity variance is unfavorable.

Summary of Direct Material Variances If the calculations are correct, the net of the direct materials price variance and the direct materials quantity variance should equal the total direct materials cost variance. The following check shows that the variances were computed correctly:

Direct materials price variance	$ 76 (F)
Direct materials quantity variance	240 (U)
Total direct materials cost variance	$164 (U)

Variance analyses are sometimes easier to interpret in diagram form. Figure 26-2 illustrates our analysis of Cambria Company's direct materials variances. Notice that although direct materials are purchased at actual cost, they are entered in the Materials Inventory account at standard price; thus, the direct materials price variance of $76 (F) is obvious when the costs are recorded.

FIGURE 26-2
Diagram of Direct Materials Variance Analysis

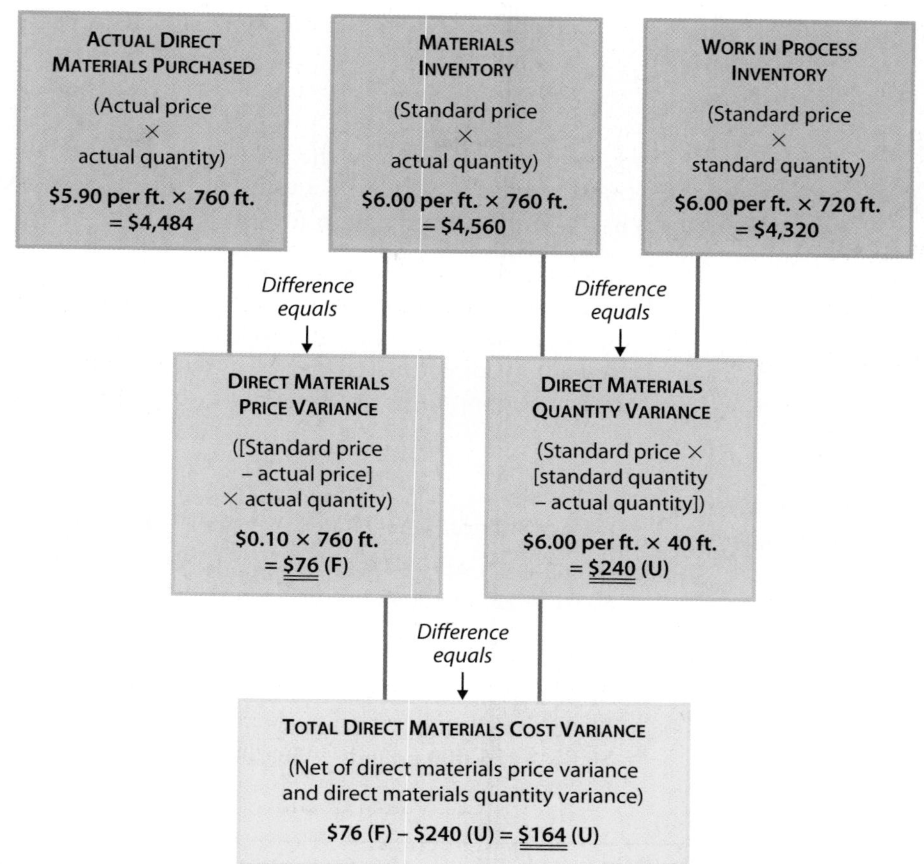

As Figure 26-2 shows, the standard price multiplied by the standard quantity is the amount entered in the Work in Process Inventory account.

Analyzing and Correcting Direct Materials Variances

Cambria Company's managers were concerned because the company had been experiencing direct materials price variances and quantity variances for some time; moreover, as our analysis shows, the price variances were always favorable and the quantity variances were always unfavorable. By tracking the purchasing activity for three months, the managers discovered that the company's purchasing agent, without any authorization, had been purchasing a lower grade of leather at a reduced price. After careful analysis, the engineering manager determined that the substitute leather was not appropriate and that the company should resume purchasing the grade of leather originally specified. In addition, an analysis of scrap and rework revealed that the inferior quality of the substitute leather was causing the unfavorable quantity variance. By tracking the purchasing activity, Cambria's managers were able to solve the problems the company had been having with direct materials variances.

STOP & APPLY >

Using the following information, compare the actual and standard cost and usage data for the production of 5-pound bags of sugar, and compute the direct materials price and direct materials quantity variances using formulas or diagram form:

Direct materials quantity standard	5 pounds per unit
Direct materials price standard	\$0.05 per pound
Direct materials purchased and used	55,100 pounds
Price paid for direct materials	\$0.04 per pound
Number of good units produced	11,000 units

SOLUTION

Direct Materials Price Variance = (Standard Price − Actual Price) × Actual Quantity
= (\$0.05 − \$0.04) × 55,100 pounds
= \$0.01 × 55,100 pounds = \$551 (F)

Direct Materials Quantity Variance = Standard Price × (Standard Quantity − Actual Quantity)
= \$0.05 × [(11,000 × 5 pounds) − 55,100 pounds]
= \$0.05 × (55,000 pounds − 55,100 pounds) = \$5 (U)

Diagram Form:

	Actual Price × Actual Quantity		Standard Price × Actual Quantity		Standard Price × Standard Quantity
Direct Materials	\$2,204[a]	Price Variance	\$2,755[b]	Quantity Variance	\$2.750[c]
		\$551 (F)		\$5 (U)	

[a] \$0.04 × 55,100 = \$2,204
[b] \$0.05 × 55,100 = \$2,755
[c] \$0.05 × (11,000 × 5) = \$2,750

Computing and Analyzing Direct Labor Variances

LO4 Compute and analyze direct labor variances.

The procedure for computing and analyzing direct labor cost variances parallels the procedure for finding direct materials variances. Again, the more detailed the analysis is, the more effective managers will be in controlling costs.

Computing Direct Labor Variances

The **total direct labor cost variance** is the difference between the standard direct labor cost for good units produced and actual direct labor costs. (*Good units* are the total units produced less units that are scrapped or need to be reworked—in other words, the salable units.) At Cambria Company, each leather bag requires 2.4 standard direct labor hours, and the standard direct labor rate is \$8.50 per hour. During August, 450 direct labor hours were used to make 180 bags at an average pay rate of \$9.20 per hour.

Based on these facts, the total direct labor cost variance is computed as follows:

Standard cost

Standard Rate × Standard Hours Allowed =
$8.50 × (180 bags × 2.4 hours per bag) =
$8.50 × 432 hours = $3,672

Less actual cost

Actual Rate × Actual Hours =
$9.20 × 450 hours = 4,140
Total direct labor cost variance = $ 468 (U)

Both the actual direct labor hours per bag and the actual direct labor rate varied from the standard. For effective performance evaluation, management must know how much of the total cost arose from different direct labor rates and how much from different numbers of direct labor hours. This information is found by computing the direct labor rate variance and the direct labor efficiency variance.

The **direct labor rate variance** (also called the *direct labor spending variance*) is the difference between the standard direct labor rate and the actual direct labor rate multiplied by the actual direct labor hours worked. For Cambria, it is computed as follows:

Study Note

The computation of the direct labor rate variance is very similar to the computation of the direct materials price variance. Computations of the direct labor efficiency variance and the direct materials quantity variance are also similar.

Standard rate	$8.50
Less actual rate	9.20
Difference per hour	$0.70 (U)

Direct Labor Rate Variance = (Standard Rate − Actual Rate) × Actual Hours
= $0.70 × 450 hours
= $315 (U)

The **direct labor efficiency variance** (also called the *direct labor quantity* or *usage variance*) is the difference between the standard direct labor hours allowed for good units produced and the actual direct labor hours worked multiplied by the standard direct labor rate. For Cambria, it is computed this way:

Standard hours allowed (180 bags × 2.4 hours per bag)	432 hours
Less actual hours	450 hours
Difference	18 hours (U)

Direct Labor Efficiency Variance = Standard Rate × (Standard Hours Allowed − Actual Hours)
= $8.50 × 18 hours
= $153 (U)

Summary of Direct Labor Variances If the calculations are correct, the net of the direct labor rate variance and the direct labor efficiency variance should equal the total direct labor cost variance. The following check shows that the variances were computed correctly:

Direct labor rate variance	$315 (U)
Direct labor efficiency variance	153 (U)
Total direct labor cost variance	$468 (U)

FIGURE 26-3
Diagram of Direct Labor Variance Analysis

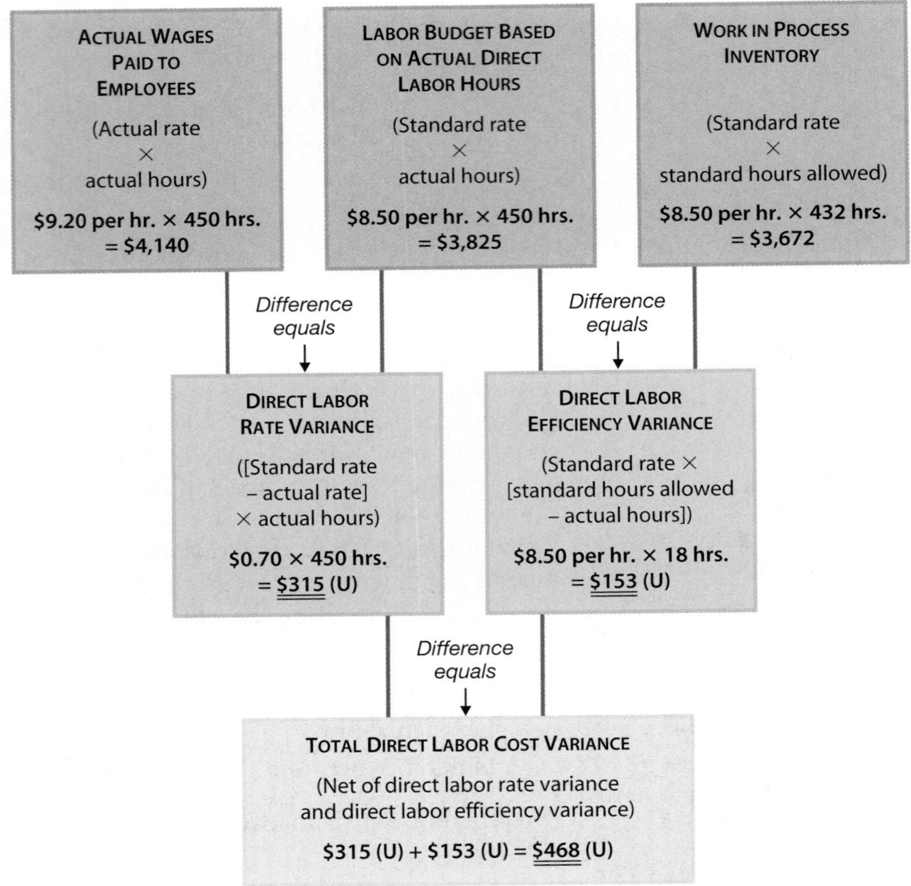

Figure 26-3 summarizes our analysis of Cambria Company's direct labor variances. Unlike direct materials variances, the direct labor rate and efficiency variances are usually computed and recorded at the same time.

Analyzing and Correcting Direct Labor Variances

Because Cambria Company's direct labor rate variance and direct labor efficiency variance were unfavorable, its managers investigated the causes of these variances. An analysis of employee time cards revealed that the Bag Assembly Department had replaced an assembly worker who was ill with a machine operator from another department. The machine operator made $9.20 per hour, whereas the assembly worker earned the standard $8.50 per hour rate. When questioned about the unfavorable efficiency variance, the assembly supervisor identified two causes. First, the machine operator had to learn assembly skills on the job, so his assembly time was longer than the standard time per bag. Second, the materials handling people were partially responsible because they delivered parts late on five different occasions. Because the machine operator was a temporary replacement, Cambria's managers took no corrective action, but they decided to keep a close eye on the materials handling function by tracking delivery times and number of delays for the next three months. Once they have collected and analyzed the new data, they will take whatever action is needed to correct the scheduling problem.

FOCUS ON BUSINESS PRACTICE

What Do You Get When You Cross a Vacuum Cleaner with a Gaming Console?

The transfer of technology ideas used for government purposes to home use is common—for example, the Internet and computers. But, what about transferring technology from home use to the battlefield? **iRobot Corporation** applied the technology it uses in its Roomba vacuum cleaner to create Small Unmanned Ground Vehicles. These robots, such as the PackBot, have cameras that see both during the day and at night, flexible treads that allow it to climb stairs, and radio links that connect it to an operator at a gaming-like console and to the military command center.

Source: IRobot Corporation website: http://www.irobot.com.

& APPLY >

Using the following information, compare the standard cost and usage data for the production of 5-pound bags of sugar, and compute the direct labor rate and direct labor efficiency variances using formulas or diagram form:

Direct labor time standard	0.01 hour per unit
Direct labor rate standard	$10.00 per hour
Direct labor hours used	100 hours
Total cost of direct labor	$1,010
Number of good units produced	11,000 units

SOLUTION

Direct Labor Rate Variance = (Standard Rate − Actual Rate) × Actual Hours
= [$10.00 ÷ ($1,010 ÷ 100 hours)] × 100 hours
= ($10.00 − $10.10) × 100 hours
= $0.10 × 100 hours = $10.00 (U)

Direct Labor Efficiency Variance = Standard Rate × (Standard Hours Allowed − Actual Hours)
= $10.00 × [(11,000 × 0.01 hour) − 100 hours]
= $10.00 × (110 hours − 100 hours)
= $10.00 × 10 hours = $100.00 (F)

Diagram Form:

	Actual Rate × Actual Hours		Standard Rate × Actual Hours		Standard Rate × Standard Hours
Direct Labor	$1,010[a]	Rate Variance	$1,000[b]	Efficiency Variance	$1,100[c]
		$10.00 (U)		$100.00 (F)	

[a] $10.10 × 100 = $1,010
[b] $10.00 × 100 = $1,000
[c] $10.00 × (11,000 × 0.01 hour) = $1,100

Computing and Analyzing Overhead Variances

LO5 Compute and analyze overhead variances.

Many types of variable and fixed overhead costs may contribute to variances from standard costs. Controlling these costs is more difficult than controlling direct materials and direct labor costs because the responsibility for overhead costs is hard to assign. Fixed overhead costs may be unavoidable past costs, such as depreciation and lease expenses; they are therefore not under the control of any department manager. If variable overhead costs can be related to departments or activities, however, some control is possible.

Using a Flexible Budget to Analyze Overhead Variances

Earlier in the chapter, we described the flexible budget that the managers of ICU, Inc., use to evaluate overall performance. That budget, shown in Exhibit 26-2, is based on units of output. Cambria Company's managers also use a flexible budget, but to analyze overhead costs only. As you can see in Exhibit 26-4, Cambria's flexible budget uses direct labor hours as the expression of activity. Thus, variable costs vary with the number of direct labor hours worked. Total fixed overhead costs remain constant. The flexible budget formula in such cases is as follows:

$$\text{Total Budgeted Overhead Costs} = (\text{Variable Costs per Direct Labor Hour} \times \text{Number of Direct Labor Hours}) + \text{Budgeted Fixed Overhead Costs}$$

When applied to Cambria Company's data, the flexible budget formula is as follows:

$$\text{Total Budgeted Overhead Costs} = (\$5.75 \times \text{Number of Direct Labor Hours}) + \$1{,}300$$

Cambria's flexible budget shows monthly overhead costs for 400, 432, and 500 direct labor hours.

To find the total monthly flexible budgeted overhead costs for the 180 bags produced, you simply insert the direct labor hours allowed in the flexible budget formula—for example ($5.75 × 432 direct labor hours) + $1,300 = $3,784.

Computing Overhead Variances

Analyses of overhead variances differ in degree of detail. The basic approach is to compute the **total overhead cost variance,** which is the difference between actual overhead costs and standard overhead costs applied. You may recall from a previous chapter how overhead was applied to production by using a standard overhead rate.

A standard overhead rate has two parts: a variable rate and a fixed rate. For Cambria Company, the standard variable rate is $5.75 per direct labor hour (from the flexible budget). The standard fixed overhead rate is found by dividing total budgeted fixed overhead ($1,300) by normal capacity set by the master budget at the beginning of the period. (Cambria's normal capacity is 400 direct labor hours.) The result is a fixed overhead rate of $3.25 per direct labor hour ($1,300 ÷ 400 hours). So, Cambria's total standard overhead rate is $9.00 per direct labor hour ($5.75 + $3.25).

EXHIBIT 26-4
Flexible Budget for Evaluation of Overhead Costs

Cambria Company
Flexible Budget—Overhead
Bag Assembly Department
For an Average One-Month Period

Cost Category	Direct Labor Hours (DLH) 400	432	500	Variable Cost per DLH
Budgeted variable overhead				
Indirect materials	$ 600	$ 648	$ 750	$1.50
Indirect Labor	800	864	1,000	2.00
Supplies	300	324	375	0.75
Utilities	400	432	500	1.00
Other	200	216	250	0.50
Total budgeted variable overhead costs	$2,300	$2,484	$2,875	$5.75
Budgeted fixed overhead				
Supervisory salaries	$ 600	$ 600	$ 600	
Depreciation	400	400	400	
Other	300	300	300	
Total budgeted fixed overhead costs	$1,300	$1,300	$1,300	
Total budgeted overhead costs	$3,600	$3,784	$4,175	

Flexible budget formula (based on a normal capacity of 400 direct labor hours):
Total Budgeted Overhead Costs = (Variable Costs per Direct Labor Hour × Number of DLH) + Budgeted Fixed Overhead Costs
= ($5.75 × Number of DLH) + $1,300

Cambria Company's total overhead cost variance would be computed as follows:

Standard overhead costs applied to good units produced	
$9.00 per direct labor hour × (180 bags × 2.4 hr. per bag)	$3,888
Less actual overhead costs	4,100
Total overhead cost variance	$ 212 (U)

This amount can be divided into variable overhead variances and fixed overhead variances.

Variable Overhead Variances The **total variable overhead cost variance** is the difference between actual variable overhead costs and the standard variable overhead costs that are applied to good units produced using the standard variable rate. The procedure for finding this variance is similar to the procedure for finding direct materials and labor variances.

Figure 26-4 shows an analysis of Cambria Company's variable overhead variances. At Cambria, each leather bag requires 2.4 standard direct labor hours, and the standard variable overhead rate is $5.75 per direct labor hour. For example, during August, the company incurred $2,500 of variable overhead costs. The total variable overhead cost variance is computed as follows:

Overhead applied to good units produced		
Standard Variable Rate × Standard Labor Hours Allowed	=	
$5.75 per hour × (180 bags × 2.4 hours per bag)	=	
$5.75 × 432 hours	=	$2,484
Less actual cost		2,500
Total variable overhead cost variance	=	$ 16 (U)

Both the actual variable overhead and the direct labor hours per bag may vary from the standard. For effective performance evaluation, managers must know how much of the total cost arose from variable overhead spending deviations and how much from variable overhead application deviations (i.e., applied and actual direct labor hours). This information is found by computing the variable overhead spending variance and the variable overhead efficiency variance.

The **variable overhead spending variance** (also called the *variable overhead rate variance*) is computed by multiplying the actual hours worked by the difference between actual variable overhead costs and the standard variable overhead rate. For Cambria, it is computed as follows:

Variable Overhead, Spending Variance = (Standard Variable Rate × Actual Hours Worked) − Actual Variable Overhead Cost
= ($5.75 × 450 hours) − $2,500.00
= $2,587.50 − $2,500.00
= $87.50 (F)

The **variable overhead efficiency variance** is the difference between the standard direct labor hours allowed for good units produced and the actual hours worked multiplied by the standard variable overhead rate per hour. For Cambria, it is computed as follows:

Standard direct labor hours allowed (180 bags × 2.4 hours per bag)	432 hours
Less actual hours	450 hours
Difference	18 hours (U)

Variable Overhead Efficiency Variance = Standard Variable Rate × (Standard Hours Allowed − Actual Hours)
= $5.75 × 18 hours
= $103.50 (U)

Summary of Variable Overhead Variances If the calculations are correct, the net of the variable overhead spending variance and the variable overhead efficiency variance should equal the total variable overhead variance. The following check shows that these variances have been computed correctly:

Variable overhead spending variance	$ 87.50 (F)
Variable overhead efficiency variance	103.50 (U)
Total variable overhead cost variance	$ 16.00 (U)

FIGURE 26-4
Diagram of Variable Overhead Variance Analysis

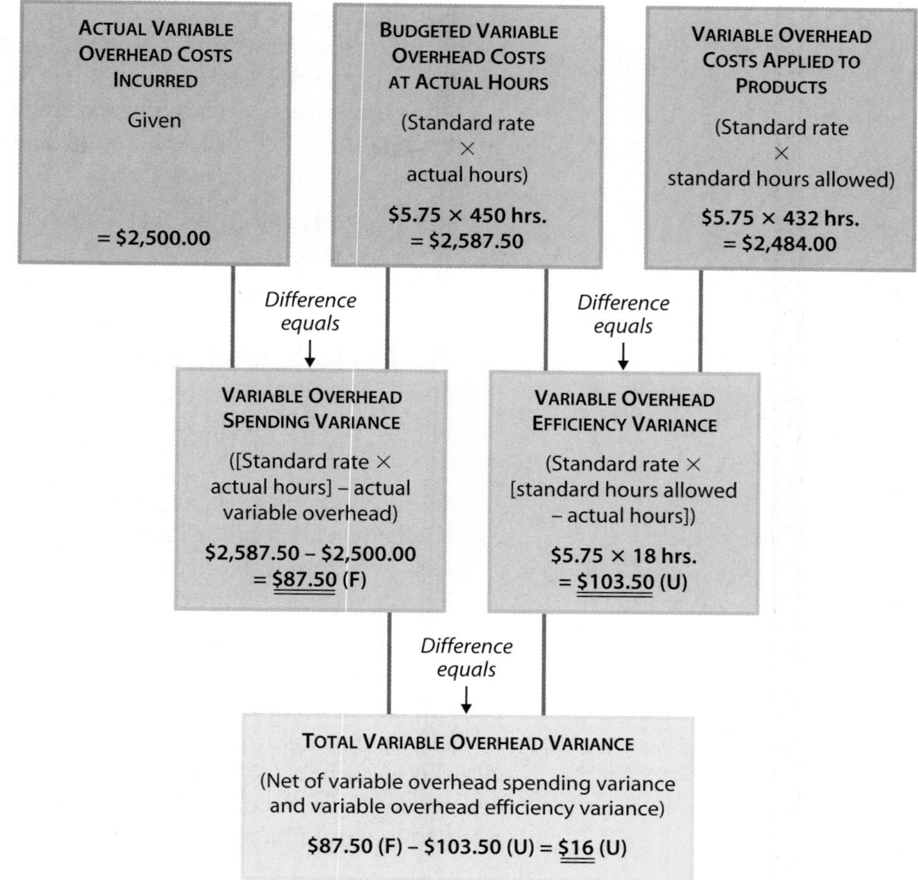

Fixed Overhead Variances The **total fixed overhead cost variance** is the difference between actual fixed overhead costs and the standard fixed overhead costs that are applied to good units produced using the standard fixed overhead rate. The procedure for finding this variance differs from the procedure used for finding direct materials, direct labor, and variable overhead variances.

Figure 26-5 shows an analysis of fixed overhead variances for Cambria Company. At Cambria, each bag requires 2.4 standard direct labor hours, and the standard fixed overhead rate is $3.25 per direct labor hour. As we noted earlier, the standard fixed overhead rate is found by dividing budgeted fixed overhead ($1,300) by normal capacity, which was set by the master budget at the beginning of the period. In this case, because normal capacity is 400 direct labor hours, the fixed overhead rate is $3.25 per direct labor hour ($1,300 ÷ 400 hours). For example, during August, Cambria incurred $1,600 of actual fixed overhead costs. The total fixed overhead variance is computed as follows:

Overhead applied to the good units produced	
Standard fixed rate × Standard direct labor hours allowed=	
$3.25 × (180 bags × 2.4 hours per bag) =	
$3.25 × 432 hours =	$1,404
Less actual cost	1,600
Total fixed overhead cost variance	= $ 196 (U)

For effective performance evaluation, managers break down the total fixed overhead cost variance into two additional variances: the fixed overhead budget variance and the fixed overhead volume variance.

The **fixed overhead budget variance** (also called the *budgeted fixed overhead variance*) is the difference between budgeted and actual fixed overhead costs. For Cambria, it is computed as follows:

Fixed Overhead Budget Variance = Budgeted Fixed Overhead − Actual Fixed Overhead
= $1,300 − $1,600
= $300 (U)

The **fixed overhead volume variance** is the difference between budgeted fixed overhead costs and the overhead costs that are applied to production using the standard fixed overhead rate. For Cambria, the fixed overhead volume variance is computed as follows:

Standard fixed overhead applied to good units produced	
$3.25 per direct labor hour × (180 bags × 2.4 hours per bag)	$1,404
Less total budgeted fixed overhead	1,300
Fixed overhead volume variance	$ 104 (F)

Because the fixed overhead volume variance measures the use of existing facilities and capacity, a volume variance will occur if more or less than normal capacity is used. At Cambria Company, 400 direct labor hours are considered normal use of facilities. Because fixed overhead costs are applied on the basis of standard hours allowed, Cambria Company's overhead was applied on the basis of 432 hours, even though the fixed overhead rate was computed using 400 hours. Thus, more fixed costs would be applied to products than were budgeted.

- When capacity exceeds the expected amount, the result is a favorable overhead volume variance because fixed overhead was overapplied.
- When a company operates at a level below the normal capacity in units, the result is an unfavorable volume variance. Not all of the fixed overhead costs will be applied to units produced. In other words, fixed overhead is underapplied, and the cost of goods produced does not include the full budgeted cost of fixed overhead.

Summary of Variable and Fixed Overhead Variances If our calculations of variable and fixed overhead variances are correct, the net of these variances should equal the total overhead cost variance. Checking the computations, we find that the variable and fixed overhead variances do equal the total overhead cost variance:

Variable overhead spending variance	$ 87.50 (F)
Variable overhead efficiency variance	103.50 (U)
Fixed overhead budget variance	300.00 (U)
Fixed overhead volume variance	104.00 (F)
Total overhead cost variance	$212.00 (U)

Figures 26-4 and 26-5 summarize our analysis of overhead variances. The total overhead cost variance is also the amount of overapplied or underapplied overhead. You may recall from an earlier chapter that actual variable and fixed overhead costs are recorded as they occur, that variable and fixed overhead are applied to products as they are produced, and that the overapplied or underapplied overhead is computed and reconciled at the end of each accounting period. By breaking down the total overhead cost variance into variable and fixed variances, managers can more accurately control costs and reconcile their causes. An analysis of these two overhead variances will help explain why the

FIGURE 26-5
Diagram of Fixed Overhead Variance Analysis

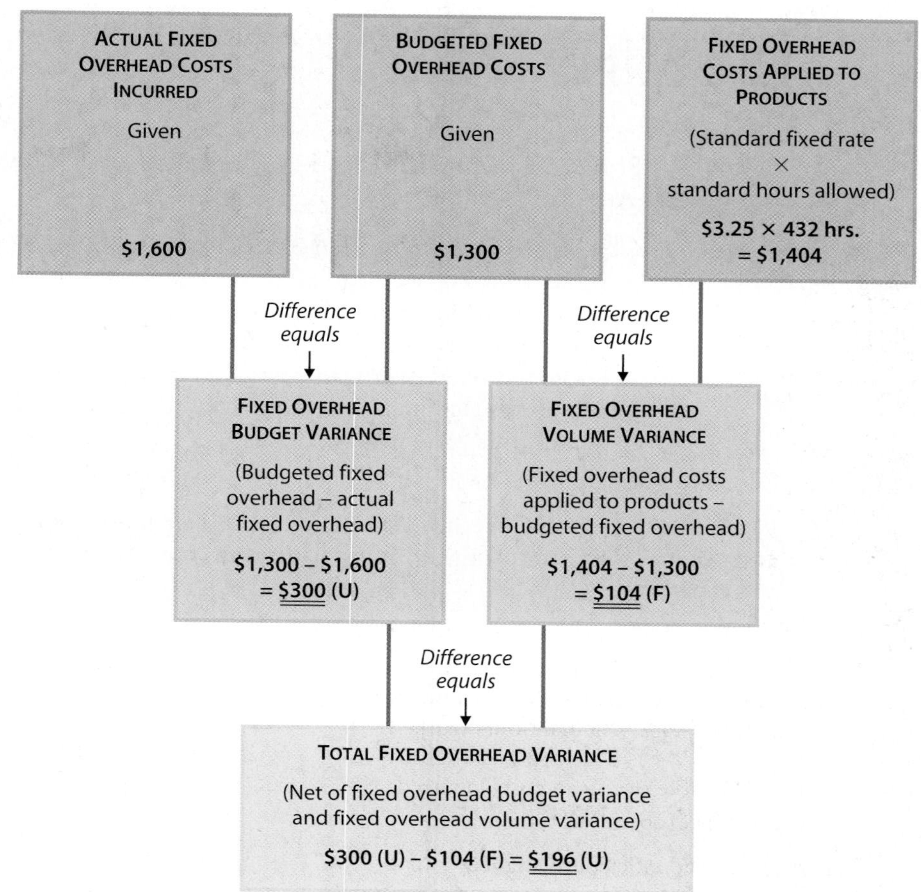

amount of overhead applied to units produced is different from the actual overhead costs incurred.

Analyzing and Correcting Overhead Variances

In analyzing the unfavorable total overhead cost variance of $212, the manager of Cambria Company's Bag Assembly Department found causes for the variances that contributed to it:

- Although the variable overhead spending variance was favorable ($87.50 less than expected because of savings on purchases), the inefficiency of the machine operator who substituted for an assembly worker created unfavorable variances for both direct labor efficiency and variable overhead efficiency. As a result, the manager is going to consider the feasibility of implementing a program for cross-training employees.
- After reviewing the fixed overhead costs, the manager of the Bag Assembly Department concluded that higher-than-anticipated factory insurance premiums were the reason for the unfavorable fixed overhead budget variance and were the result of an increase in the number of insurance claims filed by employees. To obtain more specific information, the manager will study the insurance claims filed over a three-month period.
- Finally, since the 432 standard hours were well above the normal capacity of 400 direct labor hours, fixed overhead was overapplied, and it resulted in a $104(F) volume variance. The overutilization of capacity was traced to high demand that pressed the company to use almost all its capacity. Management decided not to do anything about the fixed overhead volume variance because it fell within an anticipated seasonal range.

Sutherland Products uses standard costing. The following information about overhead was generated during August:

Standard variable overhead rate	\$2 per machine hour
Standard fixed overhead rate	\$3 per machine hour
Actual variable overhead costs	\$443,200
Actual fixed overhead costs	\$698,800
Budgeted fixed overhead costs	\$700,000
Standard machine hours per unit produced	12
Good units produced	18,940
Actual machine hours	228,400

Compute the variable overhead spending and efficiency variances and the fixed overhead budget and volume variances using formulas or diagram form.

SOLUTION

Variable overhead spending variance:	
Budgeted variable overhead for actual hours	
Standard rate × actual hours worked	
(\$2 × 228,400)	\$456,800
Less actual variable overhead costs incurred	443,200
Variable overhead spending variance	\$ 13,600 (F)

Variable overhead efficiency variance:	
Variable overhead applied to good units produced	
Standard rate × standard hours allowed	
[\$2 × (18,940 × 12)]	\$454,560
Less budgeted variable overhead costs for actual hours	
Standard rate × actual hours worked	
(\$2 × 228,400)	456,800
Variable overhead efficiency variance	\$ 2,240 (U)

Diagram Form:

	Actual Variable Overhead Costs		Standard Rate × Actual Hours		Standard Rate × Standard Hours
Variable Overhead	\$443,200	Spending Variance	\$456,800[a]	Efficiency Variance	\$454,560[b]
		\$13,600 (F)		\$2,240 (U)	

[a] \$2 × 228,400 = \$456,800
[b] \$2 × (18,940 × 12) = \$454,560

Fixed overhead budget variance:	
Budgeted fixed overhead	\$700,000
Less actual fixed overhead costs incurred	698,800
Fixed overhead budget variance	\$ 1,200 (F)

Fixed overhead volume variance:	
Fixed overhead applied to good units produced	
Standard rate × standard hours allowed	
[\$3 × (18,940 × 12)]	\$681,840
Less budgeted fixed overhead	700,000
Fixed overhead volume variance	\$ 18,160 (U)

(continued)

Diagram Form:

	Actual Fixed Overhead Costs		Budgeted Fixed Overhead Costs		Standard Rate × Standard Hours
Fixed Overhead	$698,800	Budget Variance	$700,000	Volume Variance	$681,840[a]
		$1,200 (F)		$18,160 (U)	

[a] $3 × (18,940 × 12) = $681,840

Using Cost Variances to Evaluate Managers' Performance

LO6 Explain how variances are used to evaluate managers' performance.

How effectively and fairly a manager's performance is evaluated depends on human factors—the people doing the evaluating—as well as on company policies. The evaluation process becomes more accurate when managerial performance reports include variances from standard costs.

To ensure that the evaluation of a manager's performance is effective and fair, a company's policies should be based on input from managers and employees and should specify the procedures that managers are to use when doing the following:

- Preparing operational plans
- Assigning responsibility for carrying out the operational plans
- Communicating the operational plans to key personnel
- Evaluating performance in each area of responsibility
- Identifying the causes of significant variances from the operational plan
- Taking corrective action to eliminate problems

Because variance analysis provides detailed data about differences between standard and actual costs and thus helps identify the causes of those differences, it is usually more effective at pinpointing efficient and inefficient operating areas than are basic comparisons of budgeted and actual data. A managerial performance report based on standard costs and related variances should identify the causes of each significant variance, the personnel involved, and the corrective actions taken. It should be tailored to the cost center manager's specific areas of responsibility and explain clearly how the manager's department met or did not meet operating expectations. Managers should be held accountable only for the cost areas under their control.

Exhibit 26-5 shows a performance report for the manager of Cambria Company's Bag Assembly Department. The report summarizes all cost data and variances for direct materials, direct labor, and overhead. In addition, it identifies the causes of the variances and the corrective actions taken. Such a report would enable a supervisor to review a cost center manager's actions and evaluate his or her performance.

A point to remember is that the mere occurrence of a variance does not indicate that a manager of a cost center has performed poorly. However, if a variance occurs consistently, and no cause is identified and no corrective action is taken, it may well indicate poor managerial performance.

Exhibit 26-5 shows that the causes of the variances have been identified and corrective actions have been taken, indicating that the manager of the Cambria Company's Bag Assembly Department has the operation under control.

EXHIBIT 26-5 Managerial Performance Report Using Variance Analysis

Cambria Company
Managerial Performance Report
Bag Assembly Department
For the Month Ended August 31

Productivity Summary:

Normal capacity in units	167 bags
Normal capacity in direct labor hours (DLH)	400 DLH*
Good units produced	180 bags
Performance level (standard hours allowed for good units produced)	432 DLH

*Rounded.

Cost and Variance Analysis:

	Standard Costs	Actual Costs	Total Variance	Variance Breakdown: Amount	Variance Breakdown: Type
Direct materials	$ 4,320	$ 4,484	$164 (U)	$ 76.00 (F)	Direct materials price variance
				240.00 (U)	Direct materials quantity variance
Direct labor	3,672	4,140	468 (U)	315.00 (U)	Direct labor rate variance
				153.00 (U)	Direct labor efficiency variance
Variable overhead	2,484	2,500	16 (U)	87.50 (F)	Variable overhead spending variance
				103.50 (U)	Variable overhead efficiency variance
Fixed overhead	1,404	1,600	196 (U)	300.00 (U)	Fixed overhead budget variance
				104.00 (F)	Fixed overhead volume variance
Totals	$11,880	$12,724	$844 (U)	$844.00 (U)	

Causes of Variances	Actions Taken
Direct materials price variance:	
New direct materials purchased at reduced price	New direct materials deemed inappropriate; resumed purchasing materials originally specified
Direct materials quantity variance:	
Poor quality of new direct materials	New direct materials deemed inappropriate; resumed using direct materials originally specified
Direct labor rate variance:	
Machine operator who had to learn assembly skills	Temporary replacement; no action taken on the job
Direct labor efficiency variance:	
Machine operator who had to learn assembly skills	Temporary replacement; no action taken on the job
Late delivery of parts to assembly floor	Material delivery times and number of delays being tracked
Variable overhead spending variance:	
Cost savings on purchases	No action necessary
Variable overhead efficiency variance:	
Machine operator who had to learn assembly skills on the job	A cross-training program for employees now under consideration
Fixed overhead budget variance:	
Large number of factory insurance claims	Study of insurance claims being conducted
Fixed overhead volume variance:	
High number of orders caused by demand	No action necessary

STOP & APPLY >

Jason Ponds, the production manager at WAWA Industries, recently received his performance report from Gina Rolando, the company's controller. The report contained the following information:

	Actual Cost	Standard Cost	Variance
Direct materials	$38,200	$36,600	$1,600 (U)
Direct labor	19,450	19,000	450 (U)
Variable overhead	62,890	60,000	2,890 (U)

Rolando asked Ponds to respond to his performance report. If you were Ponds, how would you respond? What additional information might you need to prepare your response?

SOLUTION

Ponds is responsible only for the direct materials quantity variance, the direct labor efficiency variance, and the variable overhead efficiency variance. Before he answers the controller's query, the total variances given to him need to be broken down into their individual variance amounts. Then, and only then, will Ponds find out how well or poorly he performed.

▸ ICU, INC.: REVIEW PROBLEM

The Decision Point at the beginning of this chapter focused on ICU, Inc., the manufacturer of the home surveillance robot called Watch Dog. It asked these questions:

- How does setting performance standards help managers control costs?
- How do managers use standard costs to evaluate the performance of cost centers?

Managers base standard costs on realistic estimates of operating costs. They use these figures as performance targets and as benchmarks against which they measure actual spending trends. By analyzing variances between standard and actual costs, they gain insight into the causes of those differences. Once they have identified an operating problem that is causing a cost variance, they can devise a solution that results in better control of costs.

When evaluating the performance of cost centers, managers use standard costs to prepare a flexible budget, which will improve the accuracy of their variance analysis. This comparison of actual costs and a budget based on the same amount of output can provide ICU's managers with objective data that they can use to assess the center's performance in terms of its key success factor—cost.

Variance Analysis
LO1 LO3
LO4 LO5

Suppose Cambria Company has discontinued its production of carrier bags for the Watch Dog, and ICU, Inc., has begun producing them itself. ICU's high-quality, heavy-duty bags are made in a single cost center using a standard costing system. The standard variable costs for one bag (a unit) are as follows:

Direct materials (3 sq. meters @ $12.50 per sq. meter)	$37.50
Direct labor (1.2 hours @ $9.00 per hour)	10.80
Variable overhead (1.2 hours @ $5.00 per direct labor hour)	6.00
Standard variable cost per unit	$54.30

The center's master budget was based on its normal capacity of 15,000 direct labor hours. Its budgeted fixed overhead costs for the year were $54,000. During the year, the company produced and sold 12,200 bags, and it purchased and used 37,500 square

meters of direct materials; the purchase cost was $12.40 per square meter. The average labor rate was $9.20 per hour, and 15,250 direct labor hours were worked. The center's actual variable overhead costs for the year were $73,200, and its fixed overhead costs were $55,000.

Required

Using the data given, compute the following using formulas or diagram form:

1. Standard hours allowed for good output
2. Standard fixed overhead rate
3. Direct materials cost variances:
   a. Direct materials price variance
   b. Direct materials quantity variance
   c. Total direct materials cost variance
4. Direct labor cost variances:
   a. Direct labor rate variance
   b. Direct labor efficiency variance
   c. Total direct labor cost variance
5. Variable overhead cost variances:
   a. Variable overhead spending variance
   b. Variable overhead efficiency variance
   c. Total variable overhead cost variance
6. Fixed overhead cost variances:
   a. Fixed overhead budget variance
   b. Fixed overhead volume variance
   c. Total fixed overhead cost variance

Answers to Review Problem

1. Standard Hours Allowed = Good Units Produced × Standard Direct Labor Hours per Unit
   = 12,200 Units × 1.2 Direct Labor Hours per Unit
   = 14,640 Hours

2. Standard Fixed Overhead Rate = $\dfrac{\text{Budgeted Fixed Overhead Cost}}{\text{Normal Capacity}}$
   = $\dfrac{\$54{,}000}{\text{15,000 Direct Labor Hours}}$
   = $3.60 per Direct Labor Hour

3. Direct Materials Cost Variances:
   a. Direct Materials Price Variance:

Price difference:	Standard price	$12.50
	Less actual price	12.40
	Difference	$ 0.10 (F)

   Direct Materials Price Variance = (Standard Price − Actual Price) × Actual Quantity
   = $0.10 × 37,500 Sq. Meters
   = $3,750 (F)

b. Direct Materials Quantity Variance:
Quantity difference: Standard quantity

(12,200 units × 3 sq. meters)	36,600 Sq. Meters
Less actual quantity	37,500 Sq. Meters
Difference	900 Sq. Meters (U)

Direct Materials Quantity Variance = Standard Price × (Standard Quantity − Actual Quantity)
= $12.50 per Sq. Meter × 900 Sq. Meters
= $11,250 (U)

c. Total Direct Materials Cost Variance:
Total Direct Materials Cost Variance = Net of Direct Materials Price Variance and Direct Materials Quantity Variance
= $3,750 (F) − $11,250 (U)
= $7,500 (U)

Diagram Form:

	Actual Price × Actual Quantity		**Standard Price × Actual Quantity**		**Standard Price × Standard Quantity**
Direct Materials	$12.40 × 37,500 = $465,000	**Price Variance**	$12.50 × 37,500 = $468,750	**Quantity Variance**	$12.50 × (12,200 × 3) = $457,500
		$3,750 (F)	**Total Direct Materials Cost Variance**	$11,250 (U)	
			$7,500 (U)		

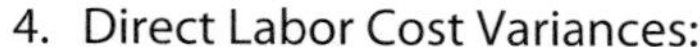

4. Direct Labor Cost Variances:
   a. Direct Labor Rate Variance:
   Rate difference: Standard labor rate

Standard labor rate	$9.00
Less actual labor rate	9.20
Difference	$0.20 (U)

Direct Labor Rate Variance = (Standard Rate − Actual Rate) × Actual Hours
= $0.20 × 15,250 hours
= $3,050 (U)

   b. Direct Labor Efficiency Variance:
   Difference in hours: Standard hours allowed

Standard hours allowed	14,640 hours*
Less actual hours	15,250 hours
Difference	610 hours (U)

Direct Labor Efficiency Variance = Standard Rate × (Standard Hours Allowed − Actual Hours)
= $9.00 per hour × 610 hours (U)
= $5,490 (U)

*12,200 units produced × 1.2 hours per unit = 14,640 hours.

c. Total Direct Labor Cost Variance:

Total Direct Labor Cost Variance = Net of Direct Labor Rate Variance and Direct Labor Efficiency Variance
= $3,050 (U) + $5,490 (U)
= $8,540 (U)

Diagram Form:

	Actual Rate × Actual Hours		Standard Rate × Actual Hours		Standard Rate × Standard Hours
Direct Labor	$9.20 × 15,250 = $140,300	**Rate Variance**	$9.00 × 15,250 = $137,250	**Efficiency Variance**	$9.00 × (12,200 × 1.2) = $131,760
		$3,050 (U)	**Total Direct Labor Cost Variance**	$5,490 (U)	
			$8,540 (U)		

5. Variable Overhead Cost Variances:
   a. Variable Overhead Spending Variance:

Standard variable rate × actual hours worked ($5.00 per hour × 15,250 labor hours)	$76,250
Less actual variable overhead costs incurred	73,200
Variable Overhead Spending Variance	$ 3,050 (F)

   b. Variable Overhead Efficiency Variance:

Variable overhead applied to good units produced (14,640 hours* × $5.00 per hour)	$73,200
Less budgeted variable overhead for actual hours (15,250 hours × $5.00 per hour)	76,250
Variable Overhead Efficiency Variance	$ 3,050 (U)

*12,200 units produced × 1.2 hours per unit = 14,640 hours.

   c. Total Variable Overhead Cost Variance:

Total Variable Overhead Cost Variance = Net of Variable Overhead Spending Variance and Variable Overhead Efficiency Variance
= $3,050 (F) − $3,050 (U)
= $0

Diagram Form:

	Actual Variable Overhead Costs		Standard Rate × Actual Hours		Standard Rate × Standard Hours
Variable Overhead	$73,200	**Spending Variance**	$5.00 × 15,250 = $76,250	**Efficiency Variance**	$5.00 × (12,200 × 1.2) = $73,200
		$3,050 (F)	**Total Variable Overhead Cost Variance**	$3,050 (U)	
			$0		

6. Fixed Overhead Cost Variances:
   a. Fixed Overhead Budget Variance:

Budgeted fixed overhead	\$54,000
Less actual fixed overhead	55,000
Fixed Overhead Budget Variance	\$ 1,000 (U)

   b. Fixed Overhead Volume Variance:

Standard fixed overhead applied (14,640 labor hours × \$3.60* per hour)	\$52,704
Less total budgeted fixed overhead	54,000
Fixed Overhead Volume Variance	\$ 1,296 (U)

   c. Total Fixed Overhead Cost Variance:

      Total Fixed Overhead Cost Variance = Net of Fixed Overhead Budget Variance and Fixed Overhead Volume Variance
      = \$1,000 (U) + \$1,296 (U)
      = \$2,296 (U)

*From answer to requirement **2**.

Diagram Form:

	Actual Fixed Overhead Costs		Budgeted Fixed Overhead Costs		Standard Rate × Standard Hours
Fixed Overhead	\$55,000	**Budget Variance**	\$54,000	**Volume Variance**	\$3.60 × (12,200 × 1.2) = \$52,704
		\$1,000 (U)	**Total Fixed Overhead Cost Variance**	\$1,296 (U)	
			\$2,296 (U)		

LO1 Define *standard costs*, explain how standard costs are developed, and compute a standard unit cost.

Standard costs are realistic estimates of costs based on analyses of both past and projected operating costs and conditions. They provide a standard, or predetermined, performance level for use in standard costing, a method of cost control that also includes a measure of actual performance and a measure of the variance between standard and actual performance.

A standard unit cost has six elements. A total standard unit cost is computed by adding the following costs: direct materials costs (direct materials price standard times direct materials quantity standard), direct labor costs (direct labor rate standard times direct labor time standard), and overhead costs (standard variable and standard fixed overhead rate times standard direct labor hours allowed per unit).

LO2 Prepare a flexible budget, and describe how managers use variance analysis to control costs.

A flexible budget is a summary of anticipated costs for a range of activity levels. It provides forecasted cost data that can be adjusted for changes in level of output. The variable cost per unit and total fixed costs presented in a flexible budget are components of the flexible budget formula, an equation that determines the budgeted cost for any level of output. A flexible budget improves the accuracy of variance analysis, which is a four-step approach to controlling costs. First, managers compute the amount of the variance. If the amount is significant, managers then analyze the variance to identify its cause. They then select performance measures that will enable them to track those activities, analyze the results, and determine the action needed to correct the problem. Their final step is to take the appropriate corrective action.

LO3 Compute and analyze direct materials variances.

The direct materials price variance is computed by finding the difference between the standard price and the actual price per unit and multiplying it by the actual quantity purchased. The direct materials quantity variance is the difference between the standard quantity that should have been used and the actual quantity used, multiplied by the standard price. An analysis of these variances enables managers to identify what is causing them and to formulate plans for correcting related operating problems.

LO4 Compute and analyze direct labor variances.

The direct labor rate variance is computed by determining the difference between the standard direct labor rate and the actual rate and multiplying it by the actual direct labor hours worked. The direct labor efficiency variance is the difference between the standard hours allowed for the number of good units produced and the actual hours worked multiplied by the standard direct labor rate. Managers analyze these variances to find the causes of differences between standard direct labor costs and actual direct labor costs.

LO5 Compute and analyze overhead variances.

The total overhead variance is equal to the amount of under- or overapplied overhead costs for an accounting period. An analysis of the variable and fixed overhead variances will help explain why the amount of overhead applied to units produced differs from the actual overhead costs incurred. The total overhead cost variance can be broken down into a variable overhead spending variance, a variable overhead efficiency variance, a fixed overhead budget variance, and a fixed overhead volume variance.

LO6 Explain how variances are used to evaluate managers' performance.

How effectively and fairly a manager's performance is evaluated depends on human factors—the people doing the evaluating—as well as on company policies. To ensure that performance evaluation is effective and fair, a company's evaluation policies should be based on input from managers and employees and should be specific about the procedures that managers are to follow. The evaluation process becomes more accurate when managerial performance reports for cost centers include variances from standard costs. A managerial performance report based on standard costs and related variances should identify the causes of each significant variance, along with the personnel involved and the corrective actions taken. It should be tailored to the cost center manager's specific areas of responsibility.

REVIEW of Concepts and Terminology

The following concepts and terms were introduced in this chapter:

CHAPTER ASSIGNMENTS

BUILDING Your Basic Knowledge and Skills

Short Exercises

LO1 **Uses of Standard Costs**

SE 1. Lago Corporation is considering adopting the standard costing method. Dan Sarkis, the manager of the Ohio Division, attended a corporate meeting at which Leah Rohr, the controller, discussed the proposal. Sarkis asked, "Leah, how will this new method benefit me? How will I use it?" Prepare Rohr's response to Sarkis.

LO1 **Purposes of Standard Costs**

SE 2. Suppose you are a management consultant and a client asks you why companies include standard costs in their cost accounting systems. Prepare your response, listing several purposes for using standard costs.

LO1 **Computing a Standard Unit Cost**

SE 3. Using the information that follows, compute the standard unit cost of Product MZW:

Direct materials quantity standard	5 pounds per unit
Direct materials price standard	\$10.20 per pound
Direct labor time standard	0.2 hour per unit
Direct labor rate standard	\$10.75 per hour
Variable overhead rate standard	\$7.00 per machine hour
Fixed overhead rate standard	\$11.00 per machine hour
Machine hour standard	3 hours per unit

LO2 **Analyzing Cost Variances**

SE 4. Garden Metal Works produces lawn sculptures. The company analyzes only variances that differ by more than 5 percent from the standard cost. The controller computed the following direct labor efficiency variances for March:

	Direct Labor Efficiency Variance	Standard Direct Labor Cost
Product 4	\$1,240 (U)	\$26,200
Product 6	3,290 (F)	41,700
Product 7	2,030 (U)	34,300
Product 9	1,620 (F)	32,560
Product 12	2,810 (U)	59,740

For each product, determine the variance as a percentage of the standard cost (round to one decimal place). Then identify the products whose variances should be analyzed and suggest possible causes for the variances.

LO2 **Preparing a Flexible Budget**

SE 5. Prepare a flexible budget for 10,000, 12,000, and 14,000 units of output, using the following information:

Variable costs	
Direct materials	\$10.00 per unit
Direct labor	\$3.00 per unit
Variable overhead	\$5.00 per unit
Total budgeted fixed overhead	\$80,800

LO3 Direct Materials Variances

SE 6. Using the standard unit costs that you computed in **SE 3** and the following actual cost and usage data, compute the direct materials price and direct materials quantity variances:

Direct materials purchased and used (pounds)	55,000
Price paid for direct materials	$10.00 per pound
Number of good units produced	11,000 units

LO4 Direct Labor Variances

SE 7. Using the standard unit costs that you computed in **SE 3** and the following actual cost and usage data, compute the direct labor rate and direct labor efficiency variances:

Direct labor hours used	2,250 hours
Total cost of direct labor	$24,750
Number of good units produced	11,000 units

LO5 Overhead Variances

SE 8. Weatherall Products uses standard costing. The following information about overhead was generated during August:

Standard variable overhead rate	$3.00 per machine hour
Standard fixed overhead rate	$3.10 per machine hour
Actual variable overhead costs	$680,100
Actual fixed overhead costs	$698,800
Budgeted fixed overhead costs	$700,000
Standard machine hours per unit produced	12
Good units produced	18,940
Actual machine hours	228,400

Compute the variable overhead spending and efficiency variances and the fixed overhead budget and volume variances.

LO5 Fixed Overhead Rate and Variances

SE 9. To the Point Manufacturing Company uses the standard costing method. The company's main product is a fine-quality fountain pen that normally takes 2.5 hours to produce. Normal annual capacity is 30,000 direct labor hours, and budgeted fixed overhead costs for the year were $15,000. During the year, the company produced and sold 14,000 units. Actual fixed overhead costs were $19,000. Compute the fixed overhead rate per direct labor hour, and determine the fixed overhead budget and volume variances.

LO6 Evaluating Managerial Performance

SE 10. Raul Tempest, the controller at GoTo Products, gave Jim Dodds, the production manager, a report containing the following information:

	Actual Cost	Standard Cost	Variance
Direct materials	$40,200	$38,200	$2,000 (U)
Direct labor	17,550	17,000	550 (U)
Variable overhead	52,860	50,000	2,860 (U)

Tempest asked for a response. If you were Dodds, how would you respond? What additional information might you need to prepare your response?

Exercises

LO1 Uses of Standard Costs

E 1. Summer Diaz has just assumed the duties of controller for Market Research Company. She is concerned that the company's methods of cost planning and control do not accurately track the operations of the business. She plans to suggest to the company's president, Sydney Tyson, that the company start using standard costing for budgeting and cost control. The new method could be incorporated into the existing accounting system. The anticipated cost of adopting it and training managers is around $7,500. Prepare a memo from Summer Diaz to Sydney Tyson that defines standard costing and outlines its uses and benefits.

LO1 Computing Standard Costs

E 2. Normal Corporation uses standard costing and is in the process of updating its direct materials and direct labor standards for Product 20B. The following data have been accumulated:

Direct materials In the previous period, 20,500 units were produced, and 32,800 square yards of direct materials at a cost of $122,344 were used to produce them.

Direct labor During the previous period, 57,400 direct labor hours were worked—34,850 hours on machine H and 22,550 hours on machine K. Machine H operators earned $9.40 per hour, and machine K operators earned $9.20 per hour last period. A new labor union contract calls for a 10 percent increase in labor rates for the coming period.

Using this information as the basis for the new standards, compute the direct materials quantity and price standards and the direct labor time and rate standards for each machine for the coming accounting period.

LO1 Computing a Standard Unit Cost

E 3. Weather Aerodynamics, Inc., makes electronically equipped weather-detecting balloons for university meteorology departments. Because of recent nationwide inflation, the company's management has ordered that standard costs be recomputed. New direct materials price standards are $700 per set for electronic components and $14.00 per square meter for heavy-duty canvas. Direct materials quantity standards include one set of electronic components and 100 square meters of heavy-duty canvas per balloon. Direct labor time standards are 26 hours per balloon for the Electronics Department and 21 hours per balloon for the Assembly Department. Direct labor rate standards are $21 per hour for the Electronics Department and $18 per hour for the Assembly Department. Standard overhead rates are $16 per direct labor hour for the standard variable overhead rate and $12 per direct labor hour for the standard fixed overhead rate. Using these production standards, compute the standard unit cost of one weather balloon.

LO2 Preparing a Flexible Budget

E 4. Keel Company's fixed overhead costs for the year are expected to be as follows: depreciation, $80,000; supervisory salaries, $92,000; property taxes and insurance, $26,000; and other fixed overhead, $14,500. Total fixed overhead is thus expected to be $212,500. Variable costs per unit are expected to be as follows: direct materials, $17.00; direct labor, $9.00; operating supplies, $3.00; indirect labor, $4.00; and other variable overhead costs, $2.50. Prepare a flexible budget for the following levels of production: 15,000 units, 20,000 units, and 25,000 units. What is the flexible budget formula for the year ended December 31?

LO3 **Direct Materials Price and Quantity Variances**

E 5. SITO Elevator Company manufactures small hydroelectric elevators with a maximum capacity of ten passengers. One of the direct materials used is heavy-duty carpeting for the floor of the elevator. The direct materials quantity standard for April was 8 square yards per elevator. During April, the purchasing agent purchased this carpeting at $11 per square yard; the standard price for the period was $12. Ninety elevators were completed and sold during the month; the Production Department used an average of 8.5 square yards of carpet per elevator. Calculate the company's direct materials price and quantity variances for carpeting for April.

LO3 **Direct Materials Variances**

E 6. Diekow Productions manufactured and sold 1,000 products at $11,000 each during the past year. At the beginning of the year, production had been set at 1,200 products; direct materials standards had been set at 100 pounds of direct materials at $2 per pound for each product produced. During the year, the company purchased and used 98,000 pounds of direct materials; the cost was $2.04 per pound. Calculate Diekow Production's direct materials price and quantity variances for the year.

LO4 **Direct Labor Variances**

E 7. At the beginning of last year, Diekow Productions set direct labor standards of 20 hours at $15 per hour for each product produced. During the year, 20,500 direct labor hours were actually worked at an average cost of $16 per hour. Using this information and the applicable information in **E 6**, calculate Diekow Production's direct labor rate and efficiency variances for the year.

LO4 **Direct Labor Rate and Efficiency Variances**

E 8. NEO Foundry, Inc., manufactures castings that other companies use in the production of machinery. For the past two years, NEO's best-selling product has been a casting for an eight-cylinder engine block. Standard direct labor hours per engine block are 1.8 hours. A labor union contract requires that the company pay all direct labor employees $14 per hour. During June, NEO produced 16,500 engine blocks. Actual direct labor hours and costs for the month were 29,900 hours and $433,550, respectively.

1. Compute the direct labor rate variance for eight-cylinder engine blocks during June.
2. Using the same data, compute the direct labor efficiency variance for eight-cylinder engine blocks during June. Check your answer, assuming that the total direct labor cost variance is $17,750 (U).

LO5 **Variable Overhead Variances**

E 9. At the beginning of last year, Diekow Productions set variable overhead standards of 10 machine hours at a rate of $10 per hour for each product produced. During the year, 10,800 machine hours were used at a cost of $10.20 per hour. Using this information and the applicable information in **E 6**, calculate Diekow Production's variable overhead spending and efficiency variances for the year.

LO5 **Fixed Overhead Variances**

E 10. At the beginning of last year, Diekow Productions set budgeted fixed overhead costs at $456,000. During the year, actual fixed overhead costs were $500,000. Using this information and the applicable information in **E 6**, calculate Diekow Production's fixed overhead budget and volume variances for the year. Assume that fixed overhead is applied based on units of product.

LO5 **Variable Overhead Variances for a Service Business**

E 11. Design Architects, LLP, billed clients for 6,000 hours of design work for the month. Actual variable overhead costs for the month were $315,000, and 6,250 hours were worked. At the beginning of the year, a variable overhead standard of $50 per design hour had been developed based on a budget of 5,000 design hours each month. Calculate Design Architects' variable overhead spending and efficiency variances for the month.

LO5 **Fixed Overhead Variances for a Service Business**

E 12. Engineering Associates billed clients for 11,000 hours of engineering work for the month. Actual fixed overhead costs for the month were $435,000, and 11,850 hours were worked. At the beginning of the year, a fixed overhead standard of $40 per engineering hour had been developed based on a budget of 10,000 engineering hours each month. Calculate Engineering Associates' fixed overhead budget and volume variances for the month.

LO5 **Overhead Variances**

E 13. Cedar Key Company produces handmade clamming buckets and sells them to distributors along the Gulf Coast of Florida. The company incurred $9,400 of actual overhead costs ($8,000 variable; $1,400 fixed) in May. Budgeted standard overhead costs for May were $4 of variable overhead costs per direct labor hour and $1,500 of fixed overhead costs. Normal capacity was set at 2,000 direct labor hours per month. In May, the company produced 10,100 clamming buckets by working 1,900 direct labor hours. The time standard is 0.2 direct labor hour per clamming bucket. Compute (1) the variable overhead spending and efficiency variances and (2) the fixed overhead budget and volume variances for May.

LO5 **Overhead Variances**

E 14. Suncoast Industries uses standard costing and a flexible budget for cost planning and control. Its monthly budget for overhead costs is $200,000 of fixed costs plus $5.20 per machine hour. Monthly normal capacity of 100,000 machine hours is used to compute the standard fixed overhead rate. During December, employees worked 105,000 machine hours. Only 98,500 standard machine hours were allowed for good units produced during the month. Actual overhead costs incurred during December totaled $441,000 of variable costs and $204,500 of fixed costs. Compute (1) the under- or overapplied overhead during December and (2) the variable overhead spending and efficiency variances and the fixed overhead budget and volume variances.

LO6 **Evaluating Managerial Performance**

E 15. Ron LaTulip oversees projects for ACE Construction Company. Recently, the company's controller sent him a performance report regarding the construction of the Campus Highlands Apartment Complex, a project that LaTulip supervised. Included in the report was an unfavorable direct labor efficiency variance of $1,900 for roof structures. What types of information does LaTulip need to analyze before he can respond to this report?

Problems

LO1 **Computing and Using Standard Costs**

P 1. Prefabricated houses are the specialty of Affordable Homes, Inc., of Corsicana, Texas. Although Affordable Homes produces many models, the company's best-selling model is the Welcome Home, a three-bedroom, 1,400-square-foot house with an impressive front entrance. Last year, the standard costs for the six basic direct materials used in manufacturing the entrance were as follows: wood framing materials, $2,140; deluxe front door, $480; door hardware, $260; exterior siding, $710; electrical materials, $580; and interior finishing materials, $1,520. Three types of direct labor are used to build the entrance: carpenter, 30 hours at $12 per hour; door specialist, 4 hours at $14 per hour; and electrician, 8 hours at $16 per hour. Last year, the company used an overhead rate of 40 percent of total direct materials cost.

This year, the cost of wood framing materials is expected to increase by 20 percent, and a deluxe front door will cost $496. The cost of the door hardware will increase by 10 percent, and the cost of electrical materials will increase by 20 percent. Exterior siding cost should decrease by $16 per unit. The cost of interior finishing materials is expected to remain the same. The carpenter's wages will increase by $1 per hour, and the door specialist's wages should remain the same. The electrician's wages will increase by $0.50 per hour. Finally, the overhead rate will decrease to 25 percent of total direct materials cost.

Required

1. Compute the total standard cost of direct materials per entrance for last year.
2. Using your answer to item **1**, compute the total standard unit cost per entrance for last year.
3. Compute the total standard unit cost per entrance for this year.

LO2 Preparing a Flexible Budget and Evaluating Performance

P 2. Home Products Company manufactures a complete line of kitchen glassware. The Beverage Division specializes in 12-ounce drinking glasses. Erin Fisher, the superintendent of the Beverage Division, asked the controller to prepare a report of her division's performance in April. The following report was handed to her a few days later:

Cost Category (Variable Unit Cost)	Budgeted Costs*	Actual Costs	Difference Under (Over) Budget
Direct materials ($0.10)	$ 5,000	$ 4,975	$ 25
Direct labor ($0.12)	6,000	5,850	150
Variable overhead			
Indirect labor ($0.03)	1,500	1,290	210
Supplies ($0.02)	1,000	960	40
Heat and power ($0.03)	1,500	1,325	175
Other ($0.05)	2,500	2,340	160
Fixed overhead			
Heat and power	3,500	3,500	—
Depreciation	4,200	4,200	—
Insurance and taxes	1,200	1,200	—
Other	1,600	1,600	—
Totals	$28,000	$27,240	$760

*Based on normal capacity of 50,000 units.

In discussing the report with the controller, Fisher stated, "Profits have been decreasing in recent months, but this report indicates that our production process is operating efficiently."

Required

1. Prepare a flexible budget for the Beverage Division using production levels of 45,000 units, 50,000 units, and 55,000 units.
2. What is the flexible budget formula?
3. Assume that the Beverage Division produced 46,560 units in April and that all fixed costs remained constant. Prepare a revised performance report similar to the one above, using actual production in units as a basis for the budget column.

Manager insight ▶ 4. Which report is more meaningful for performance evaluation, the original one above or the revised one? Why?

LO3 LO4 Direct Materials and Direct Labor Variances

P 3. Winners Trophy Company produces a variety of athletic awards, most of them in the form of trophies. Its deluxe trophy stands 3 feet tall above the base. The company's direct materials standards for the deluxe trophy include 1 pound of metal and 8 ounces of wood for the base. Standard prices for the year were $3.30 per pound of metal and $0.45 per ounce of wood. Direct labor standards for the deluxe trophy specify 0.2 hour of direct labor in the Molding Department and 0.4 hour in the Trimming/Finishing Department. Standard direct labor rates are $10.75 per hour in the Molding Department and $12.00 per hour in the Trimming/Finishing Department.

During January, the company made 16,400 deluxe trophies. Actual production data are as follows:

Direct materials	
Metal	16,640 pounds @ $3.25 per pound
Wood	131,400 ounces @ $0.48 per ounce
Direct labor	
Molding	3,400 hours @ $10.60 per hour
Trimming Finishing	6,540 hours @ $12.10 per hour

Required

1. Compute the direct materials price and quantity variances for metal and wood.
2. Compute the direct labor rate and efficiency variances for the Molding and the Trimming/Finishing Departments.

LO3 LO4 LO5 Direct Materials, Direct Labor, and Overhead Variances

P 4. The Doormat Division of Clean Sweep Company produces all-vinyl mats. Each doormat calls for 0.4 meter of vinyl material; the material should cost $3.10 per meter. Standard direct labor hours and labor cost per doormat are 0.2 hour and $1.84 (0.2 hour × $9.20 per hour), respectively. Currently, the division's standard variable overhead rate is $1.50 per direct labor hour, and its standard fixed overhead rate is $0.80 per direct labor hour.

In August, the division manufactured and sold 60,000 doormats. During the month, it used 25,200 meters of vinyl material; the total cost of the material was $73,080. The total actual overhead costs for August were $28,200, of which $18,200 was variable. The total number of direct labor hours worked was 10,800, and the factory payroll for direct labor for the month was $95,040. Budgeted fixed overhead for August was $9,280. Normal monthly capacity for the year was set at 58,000 doormats.

Required

1. Compute for August the (a) direct materials price variance, (b) direct materials quantity variance, (c) direct labor rate variance, (d) direct labor efficiency

variance, (e) variable overhead spending variance, (f) variable overhead efficiency variance, (g) fixed overhead budget variance, and (h) fixed overhead volume variance.

Manager insight ▶ 2. Prepare a performance report based on your variance analysis, and suggest possible causes for each variance.

LO5 Overhead Variances

P 5. Celine Corporation's accountant left for vacation before completing the monthly cost variance report. George Celine, the corporation's president, has asked you to complete the report. The following data are available to you (capacities are expressed in machine hours):

Actual machine hours	17,100
Standard machine hours allowed	17,500
Actual variable overhead	**a**
Standard variable overhead rate	$2.50
Variable overhead spending variance	$250 (F)
Variable overhead efficiency variance	**b**
Actual fixed overhead	**c**
Budgeted fixed overhead	$153,000
Fixed overhead budget variance	$1,300 (U)
Fixed overhead volume variance	$4,500 (F)
Normal capacity in machine hours	**d**
Standard fixed overhead rate	**e**
Fixed overhead applied	**f**

Required

Analyze the data and fill in the missing amounts. (**Hint:** Use the structure of Figures 26-4 and 26-5 to guide your analysis.)

Alternate Problems

LO1 Computing Standard Costs for Direct Materials

P 6. TickTock, Ltd., assembles clock movements for grandfather clocks. Each movement has four components: the clock facing, the clock hands, the time movement, and the spring assembly. For the current year, the company used the following standard costs: clock facing, $15.90; clock hands, $12.70; time movement, $66.10; and spring assembly, $52.50.

Prices of materials are expected to change next year. TickTock will purchase 60 percent of the facings from Company A at $18.50 each and the other 40 percent from Company B at $18.80 each. The clock hands, which are produced for TickTock by Hardware, Inc., will cost $15.50 per set next year. TickTock will purchase 30 percent of the time movements from Company Q at $68.50 each, 20 percent from Company R at $69.50 each, and 50 percent from Company S at $71.90 each. The manufacturer that supplies TickTock with spring assemblies has announced that it will increase its prices by 20 percent.

Required

1. Determine the total standard direct materials cost per unit for next year.
2. Suppose that because TickTock has guaranteed Hardware, Inc., that it will purchase 2,500 sets of clock hands next year, the cost of a set of clock hands has been reduced by 20 percent. Find the standard direct materials cost per clock.

Manager insight ▶ 3. Suppose that to avoid the increase in the cost of spring assemblies, TickTock purchased substandard ones from a different manufacturer at $50 each; 20 percent of them turned out to be unusable and could not be returned. Assuming that all other data remain the same, compute the standard direct materials unit cost. Spread the cost of the defective materials over the good units produced.

LO2 Flexible Budgets and Performance Evaluation

P 7. Cassen Realtors, Inc., specializes in the sale of residential properties. It earns its revenue by charging a percentage of the sales price. Commissions for sales persons, listing agents, and listing companies are its main costs. Business has improved steadily over the last 10 years. Bonnie Cassen, the managing partner of Cassen Realtors, receives a report summarizing the company's performance each year. The report for the most recent year appears below.

Cassen Realtors, Inc.
Performance Report
For the Year Ended December 31

	Budgeted*	Actual†	Difference Under (Over) Budget
Total selling fees	$2,052,000	$2,242,200	($190,200)
Variable costs			
Sales commissions	$1,102,950	$1,205,183	($102,233)
Automobile	36,000	39,560	(3,560)
Advertising	93,600	103,450	(9,850)
Home repairs	77,400	89,240	(11,840)
General overhead	656,100	716,970	(60,870)
	$1,966,050	$2,154,403	($188,353)
Fixed costs			
General overhead	60,000	62,300	(2,300)
Total costs	$2,026,050	$2,216,703	($190,653)
Operating income	$ 25,950	$ 25,497	$ 453

*Budgeted data are based on 180 units sold.
†Actual data for 200 units sold.

Required

1. Analyze the performance report. What does it say about the company's performance? Is the performance report reliable? Explain your answer.
2. Calculate the budgeted selling fee and budgeted variable costs per home sale.
3. Prepare a performance report using a flexible budget based on the actual number of home sales.

Manager insight ▶ 4. Analyze the report you prepared in requirement **3**. What does it say about the company's performance? Is the report reliable? Explain your answer.

Manager insight ▶ 5. What recommendations would you make to improve the company's performance next year?

LO3 LO4 Direct Materials and Direct Labor Variances

P 8. Fruit Packaging Company makes plastic baskets for food wholesalers. Each basket requires 0.8 gram of liquid plastic and 0.6 gram of an additive that includes color and hardening agents. The standard prices are $0.15 per gram of liquid plastic and $0.09 per gram of additive. Two kinds of direct labor—molding and trimming/packing—are required to make the baskets. The direct labor time and rate standards for a batch of 100 baskets are as follows: molding, 1.0 hour per batch at an hourly rate of $12; and trimming/packing, 1.2 hours per batch at $10 per hour.

During the year, the company produced 48,000 baskets. It used 38,600 grams of liquid plastic at a total cost of $5,404 and 28,950 grams of additive at $2,895. Actual direct labor included 480 hours for molding at a total cost of $5,664 and 560 hours for trimming/packing at $5,656.

Required

1. Compute the direct materials price and quantity variances for both the liquid plastic and the additive.
2. Compute the direct labor rate and efficiency variances for the molding and trimming/packing processes.

LO3 LO4 LO5 LO6

Computing Variances and Evaluating Performance

P 9. Last year, Biomed Laboratories, Inc., researched and perfected a cure for the common cold. Called Cold-Gone, the product sells for $28.00 per package, each of which contains five tablets. Standard unit costs for this product were developed late last year for use this year. Per package, the standard unit costs were as follows: chemical ingredients, 6 ounces at $1.00 per ounce; packaging, $1.20; direct labor, 0.8 hour at $14.00 per hour; standard variable overhead, $4.00 per direct labor hour; and standard fixed overhead, $6.40 per direct labor hour. Normal capacity is 46,875 units per week.

In the first quarter of this year, demand for the new product rose well beyond the expectations of management. During those three months, the peak season for colds, the company produced and sold over 500,000 packages of Cold-Gone. During the first week in April, it produced 50,000 packages but used materials for 50,200 packages costing $60,240. It also used 305,000 ounces of chemical ingredients costing $292,800. The total cost of direct labor for the week was $579,600; direct labor hours totaled 40,250. Total variable overhead was $161,100, and total fixed overhead was $242,000. Budgeted fixed overhead for the week was $240,000.

Required

1. Compute for the first week of April (a) all direct materials price variances, (b) all direct materials quantity variances, (c) the direct labor rate variance, (d) the direct labor efficiency variance, (e) the variable overhead spending variance, (f) the variable overhead efficiency variance, (g) the fixed overhead budget variance, and (h) the fixed overhead volume variance.

Manager insight ▶

2. Prepare a performance report based on your variance analysis, and suggest possible causes for each significant variance.

LO5

Overhead Variances

P 10. Meantime Corporation's accountant left for vacation before completing the monthly cost variance report. Gillian Thornton, the corporation's president, has asked you to complete the report. The following data are available to you (capacities are expressed in machine hours):

Actual machine hours	20,100
Standard machine hours allowed	20,500
Actual variable overhead	a
Standard variable overhead rate	$2.00
Variable overhead spending variance	$200 (F)
Variable overhead efficiency variance	b

Actual fixed overhead	c
Budgeted fixed overhead	$153,000
Fixed overhead budget variance	$500 (U)
Fixed overhead volume variance	$750 (F)
Normal capacity in machine hours	d
Standard fixed overhead rate	e
Fixed overhead applied	f

Required

Analyze the data and fill in the missing amounts. (**Hint:** Use the structure of Figures 26-4 and 26-5 to guide your analysis.)

ENHANCING Your Knowledge, Skills, and Critical Thinking

LO1 An Ethical Question Involving Standard Costs

C 1. Taylor Industries, Inc., develops standard costs for all its direct materials, direct labor, and overhead costs. It uses these costs to price products, cost inventories, and evaluate the performance of purchasing and production managers. It updates the standard costs whenever costs, prices, or rates change by 3 percent or more. It also reviews and updates all standard costs each December; this practice provides current standards that are appropriate for use in valuing year-end inventories on the company's financial statements.

Jody Elgar is in charge of standard costing at Taylor Industries. On November 30, she received a memo from the chief financial officer informing her that Taylor Industries was considering purchasing another company and that she and her staff were to postpone adjusting standard costs until late February; they were instead to concentrate on analyzing the proposed purchase.

In the third week of November, prices on more than 20 of Taylor Industries' direct materials had been reduced by 10 percent or more, and a new labor union contract had reduced several categories of labor rates. A revision of standard costs in December would have resulted in lower valuations of inventories, higher cost of goods sold because of inventory write-downs, and lower net income for the year. Elgar believed that the company was facing an operating loss and that the assignment to evaluate the proposed purchase was designed primarily to keep her staff from revising and lowering standard costs. She questioned the chief financial officer about the assignment and reiterated the need for updating the standard costs, but she was again told to ignore the update and concentrate on the proposed purchase. Elgar and her staff were relieved of the evaluation assignment in early February. The purchase never materialized.

Assess Jody Elgar's actions in this situation. Did she follow all ethical paths to solving the problem? What are the consequences of failing to adjust the standard costs?

LO1 LO2 Standard Costs and Variance Analysis

C 2. Domino's Pizza is a major purveyor of home-delivered pizzas. Although customers can pick up their orders at the shops where Domino's makes its pizzas, employees deliver most orders to customers' homes, and they use their own cars to do it.

Specify what standard costing for a Domino's pizza shop would entail. Where would you obtain the information for determining the cost standards? In what ways would the standards help in managing a pizza shop? If necessary to gain a better understanding of the operation, visit a pizzeria. (It does not have to be a Domino's.)

Your instructor will divide the class into groups to discuss the case. Summarize your group's discussion, and select one person from your group to report the group's findings to the class.

LO2 LO4 LO5 LO6 **Preparing Performance Reports**

C 3. Troy Corrente, the president of Forest Valley Spa, is concerned about the spa's operating performance during March. He budgeted his costs carefully so that he could reduce the annual membership fees. He now needs to evaluate those costs to make sure that the spa's profits are at the level he expected.

He has asked you, the spa's controller, to prepare a performance report on labor and overhead costs for March. He also wants you to analyze the report and suggest possible causes for any problems that you find. He wants to attend to any problems quickly, so he has asked you to submit your report as soon as possible. The following information for the month is available to you:

	Budgeted Costs	Actual Costs
Variable costs		
Operating labor	$10,880	$12,150
Utilities	2,880	3,360
Repairs and maintenance	5,760	7,140
Fixed overhead costs		
Depreciation, equipment	2,600	2,680
Rent	3,280	3,280
Other	1,704	1,860
Totals	$27,104	$30,470

Corrente's budget allows for eight employees to work 160 hours each per month. During March, nine employees worked an average of 150 hours each.

1. Answer the following questions:
   a. Why are you preparing this performance report?
   b. Who will use the report?
   c. What information do you need to develop the report? How will you obtain that information?
   d. When are the performance report and the analysis needed?
2. With the limited information available to you, compute the labor rate variance, the labor efficiency variance, and the variable and fixed overhead variances.
3. Prepare a performance report for the spa for March. Analyze the report, and suggest causes for any problems that you find.

LO2 LO5 **Developing a Flexible Budget and Analyzing Overhead Variances**

C 4. Ezelda Marva is the controller at FH Industries. She has asked you, her new assistant, to analyze the following data related to projected and actual overhead costs for October:

	Standard Variable Costs per Machine Hour (MH)	Actual Variable Costs in October
Indirect materials and supplies	$1.10	$ 2,380
Indirect machine setup labor	2.50	5,090
Materials handling	1.40	3,950
Maintenance and repairs	1.50	2,980
Utilities	0.80	1,490
Miscellaneous	0.10	200
Totals	$7.40	$16,090

(continued)

	Budgeted Fixed Overhead	Actual Fixed Overhead in October
Supervisory salaries	$ 3,630	$ 3,630
Machine depreciation	8,360	8,580
Other	1,210	1,220
Totals	$13,200	$13,430

For October, the number of good units produced was used to compute the 2,100 standard machine hours allowed.

1. Prepare a monthly flexible budget for operating activity at 2,000 machine hours, 2,200 machine hours, and 2,500 machine hours.
2. Develop a flexible budget formula.
3. The company's normal operating capacity is 2,200 machine hours per month. Compute the fixed overhead rate at this level of activity. Then break the rate down into rates for each element of fixed overhead.
4. Prepare a detailed comparative cost analysis for October. Include all variable and fixed overhead costs. Format your analysis by using columns for the following five elements: cost category, cost per machine hour, costs applied, actual costs incurred, and variance.
5. Develop an overhead variance analysis for October that identifies the variable overhead spending and efficiency variances and the fixed overhead budget and volume variances.
6. Prepare an analysis of the variances. Could a manager control some of the fixed costs? Defend your answer.

LO4 LO5 **Standard Costing in a Service Company**

C 5. Annuity Life Insurance Company (ALIC) markets several types of life insurance policies, but P20A—a permanent, 20-year life annuity policy—is its most popular. This policy sells in $10,000 increments and features variable percentages of whole life insurance and single-payment annuities, depending on the policyholder's needs and age. ALIC devotes an entire department to supporting and marketing the P20A policy. Because both the support staff and the sales persons contribute to each P20A policy, ALIC categorizes them as direct labor for purposes of variance analysis, cost control, and performance evaluation. For unit costing, each $10,000 increment is considered one unit; thus, a $90,000 policy is counted as nine units. Standard unit cost information for January is as follows:

Direct labor	
Policy support staff	
3 hours at $12.00 per hour	$ 36.00
Policy sales person	
8.5 hours at $14.20 per hour	120.70
Operating overhead	
Variable operating overhead	
11.5 hours at $26.00 per hour	299.00
Fixed operating overhead	
11.5 hours at $18.00 per hour	207.00
Standard unit cost	$662.70

Actual costs incurred for the 265 units sold during January were as follows:

Direct labor	
Policy support staff	
848 hours at $12.50 per hour	$10,600
Policy sales persons	
2,252.5 hours at $14.00 per hour	31,535
Operating overhead	
Variable operating overhead	78,440
Fixed operating overhead	53,400

Normal monthly capacity is 260 units, and the budgeted fixed operating overhead for January was $53,820.

1. Compute the standard hours allowed in January for policy support staff and policy sales persons.
2. What should the total standard costs for January have been? What were the total actual costs that the company incurred in January? Compute the total cost variance for the month.
3. Compute the direct labor rate and efficiency variances for policy support staff and policy sales persons.
4. Compute the variable and fixed operating overhead variances for January.
5. Identify possible causes for each variance and suggest possible solutions.

LO3 LO4 LO6

Cookie Company (Continuing Case)

C 6. In this segment of our continuing case, assume that you have been using standard costing to plan and control costs at your cookie store. In a meeting with your budget team, which includes managers and employees from the Purchasing, Product Design, and Production departments, you ask all team members to describe any operating problems they encountered in the last quarter. You explain that you will use this information to analyze the causes of significant cost variances that occurred during the quarter.

For each of the following situations, identify the direct materials and/or direct labor variance(s) that could be affected, and indicate whether the variances are favorable or unfavorable:

1. The production department uses highly skilled, highly paid workers.
2. Machines were improperly adjusted.
3. Direct labor personnel worked more carefully than they had in the past to manufacture the product.
4. The Product Design Department replaced a direct material with one that was less expensive and of lower quality.
5. The Purchasing Department bought higher-quality materials at a higher price.
6. A major supplier used a less-expensive mode of transportation to deliver the raw materials.
7. Work was halted for 2 hours because of a power failure.

CHAPTER

27

Short-Run Decision Analysis

The Management Process

PLAN

- ▷ **Discover a problem or a need**
- ▷ **Identify all reasonable courses of action that can solve the problem or meet the need**
- ▷ **Prepare a thorough analysis of each possible solution, identifying its total costs, savings, other financial effects, and any qualitative effects**
- ▷ **Select the best course of action**

PERFORM

- ▷ **Make decisions that affect operations in the current period: outsource or keep in house, special orders, segment profitability, appropriate product mix given a resource constraint, sell a product as is or process further**

EVALUATE

- ▷ **Examine each short-run decision and how it affected the organization**
- ▷ **Identify and prescribe corrective action**

COMMUNICATE

- ▷ **Prepare reports related to short-run decisions throughout the year**

Managers use both financial and nonfinancial quantitative information to analyze the effects of past and potential business actions on their organization's resources and profits. Although many short-term business problems are unique and cannot be solved by following strict rules, managers often take predictable actions when making decisions that will affect their organizations in the short run. In this chapter, we describe those actions. We also explain how managers use incremental analysis in making various types of short-term decisions.

LEARNING OBJECTIVES

DECISION POINT ► A MANAGER'S FOCUS HOME STATE BANK

Home State Bank is a local institution that caters to individuals and small businesses. It has received many awards for its online services and initiatives in preventing online fraud and identity theft. The bank's managers believe the trend to online commerce is good for business, and as customers gain confidence in dealing with their finances online, they plan to offer more online products and services. In looking for safe and innovative ways to meet customers' needs, the managers will make short-run decisions that will affect the bank's profits, resources, and opportunities to increase online banking.

- ► How will managers at Home State Bank decide on new ways to increase business and protect customers' interests?
- ► How can incremental analysis help managers at Home State Bank take advantage of the business opportunities that online banking offers?

Short-Run Decision Analysis and the Management Process

LO1 Describe how managers make short-run decisions using incremental analysis.

Many of the decisions that managers make affect their organization's activities in the short run. Those decisions are the focus of this chapter. In making short-run decisions, managers need historical and estimated quantitative information that is both financial and nonfinancial in nature. Such information should be relevant, timely, and presented in a format that is easy to use in decision making.

Short-run decision analysis is the systematic examination of any decision whose effects will be felt over the course of the next year. The decision analysis must take into account the organization's strategic plan and tactical objectives, the related costs and revenues, as well as any relevant qualitative factors.

Although many business problems are unique and cannot be solved by following strict rules, managers frequently take five predictable actions when making short-run decisions:

1. Discover a problem or need.
2. Identify all reasonable courses of action that can solve the problem or meet the need.
3. Prepare a thorough analysis of each possible solution, identifying its total costs, savings, other financial effects, and any qualitative factors.
4. Select the best course of action.
5. Review each decision to determine whether it produced the forecasted results by examining how each decision was carried out and how it affected the organization. If results fell short, identify and prescribe corrective action. This postdecision audit supplies feedback about the results of the short-run decision. If the solution is not completely satisfactory or if the problem remains, the management process begins again.

In the course of a year, managers may make many short-run decisions, such as whether to make a product or service or buy it from an outside supplier, whether to accept a special order, whether to keep or drop an unprofitable segment, and whether to sell a product as is or process it further. If resources are limited, they may also have to decide on the most appropriate product mix. In making such decisions, managers analyze not only quantitative factors relating to profitability and liquidity; but they also analyze qualitative factors. For example, Home State Bank, the local bank discussed in the Decision Point, would consider these qualitative factors when deciding whether to keep or eliminate a branch location:

- Competition (Do our competitors have a branch office located here?)
- Economic conditions (Is the community growing?)
- Social issues (Will keeping this branch benefit the community we serve?)
- Product or service quality (Can we attract more business because of the quality of service at this branch?)
- Timeliness (Does the branch promote customer service?)

Managers must identify and assess the importance of all such qualitative factors, as well as quantitative factors when they make short-run decisions.

Study Note

Incremental analysis is a technique used not only by businesses but also by individuals to solve daily problems.

Incremental Analysis for Short-Run Decisions

Once managers have determined that a problem or need is worthy of consideration and have identified alternative courses of action, they must evaluate the effect that each alternative will have on their organization. The method of

FOCUS ON BUSINESS PRACTICE

How Much Does It Cost to Process a Check?

Banks today have several options for processing checks. They can outsource the processing of paper checks, use the quasi-paperless system of ATMs, or process transactions over the Internet. Bank managers have found that online banking substantially reduces transaction processing costs. According to a study by an international consulting firm, the cost of processing a transaction is 1 cent if the transaction is completed over the Internet, 27 cents if an ATM is used, or $1.07 if processed by a teller.[1]

comparing alternatives by focusing on the differences in their projected revenues and costs is called **incremental analysis**. If incremental analysis excludes revenues or costs that stay the same or that do not change between the alternatives, it is called *differential analysis.*

> **Study Note**
> Sunk costs cannot be recovered and are irrelevant in short-run decision making.

Irrelevant Costs and Revenues A cost that changes between alternatives is known as a **differential cost** (also called an *incremental cost*). For example, suppose that Home State Bank's managers are deciding which of two ATM machines—C or W—to buy. The ATMs have the same purchase price but different revenue and cost characteristics. The company currently owns ATM B, which it bought three years ago for $15,000 and which has accumulated depreciation of $9,000 and a book value of $6,000. ATM B is now obsolete as a result of advances in technology and cannot be sold or traded in.

A manager has prepared the following comparison of the annual revenue and operating cost estimates for the two new machines:

	ATM C	*ATM W*
Increase in revenue	$16,200	$19,800
Increase in annual operating costs		
Direct materials	4,800	4,800
Direct labor	2,200	4,100
Variable overhead	2,100	3,050
Fixed overhead (depreciation included)	5,000	5,000

Incremental Analysis The first step in the incremental analysis is to eliminate any irrelevant revenues and costs. *Irrelevant revenues* are those that will not differ between the alternatives. *Irrelevant costs* include sunk costs and costs that will not differ between the alternatives. A **sunk cost** is a cost that was incurred because of a previous decision and cannot be recovered through the current decision. An example of a sunk cost is the book value of ATM B. A manager might be tempted to say that the ATM should not be junked because the company still has $6,000 invested in it. However, the manager would be incorrect because the book value of the old ATM represents money that was spent in the past and so does not affect the decision about whether to replace the old ATM with a new one.

The old ATM would be of interest only if it could be sold or traded in, and if the amount received for it would be different, depending on which new ATM was chosen. In that case, the amount of the sale or trade-in value would be relevant to the decision because it would affect the future cash flows of the alternatives. Two examples of an irrelevant cost in the financial data for ATMs C and W are the costs of direct materials and fixed overhead (depreciation included). These costs can also be eliminated from the analysis because they are the same under both alternatives.

Once the irrelevant revenues and costs have been identified, the incremental analysis can be prepared using only the differential revenues and costs that will change between the alternative ATMs, as shown in Exhibit 27-1. The analysis shows that ATM W would produce $750 more in operating income than ATM C. Because the costs of buying the two ATMs are the same, this report would favor the purchase of ATM W.

Opportunity Costs Because incremental analysis focuses on only the quantitative differences among the alternatives, it simplifies management's evaluation of a decision and reduces the time needed to choose the best course of action. However, incremental analysis is only one input to the final decision. Management needs to consider other issues. For instance, the manufacturer of ATM C might have a reputation for better quality or service than the manufacturer of ATM W. **Opportunity costs** are the benefits that are forfeited or lost when one alternative is chosen over another. For example, suppose Home State Bank offers a local plant nursery a high price for the land on which the nursery is located. The interest that could be earned from investing the cash proceeds of the land sale is an opportunity cost for the nursery owner. It is revenue that the nursery owner has chosen to forgo to continue operating the nursery in that location.

Study Note

Opportunity costs arise when the choice of one course of action eliminates the possibility of another course of action.

Opportunity costs often come into play when a company is operating at or near capacity and must choose which products or services to offer. For example, suppose that Home State Bank, which currently services 20,000 debit cards, has the option of offering 15,000 premium debit cards, which is a higher-priced product, but it cannot do both. The amount of income from the 20,000 debit cards is an opportunity cost of the premium debit cards.

EXHIBIT 27-1
Incremental Analysis

Home State Bank
Incremental Analysis

	ATM C	ATM W	Difference in Favor of ATM W
Increase in revenue	$16,200	$19,800	$3,600
Increase in annual operating costs that differ between alternatives			
Direct labor	$ 2,200	$ 4,100	($1,900)
Variable overhead	2,100	3,050	(950)
Total increase in operating costs	$ 4,300	$ 7,150	($2,850)
Resulting change in operating income	$11,900	$12,650	$ 750

STOP & APPLY >

Credit Banc has assembled the following monthly information related to the purchase of a new automated teller machine:

	Machine A	Machine B
Increase in revenue	$4,200	$5,100
Increase in annual operating costs		
Direct materials	1,200	1,200
Direct labor	1,200	1,600
Variable overhead	2,500	2,900
Fixed overhead (including depreciation)	1,400	1,400

Using incremental analysis and only relevant information, compute the difference in favor of the Machine B.

SOLUTION

Credit Banc
Incremental Analysis

	Machine A	Machine B	Difference in Favor of Machine B
Increase in revenue	$4,200	$5,100	$ 900
Increase in operating costs that differ between alternatives			
Direct labor	$1,200	$1,600	($ 400)
Variable overhead	2,500	2,900	(400)
Total increase in operating costs	$3,700	$4,500	($ 800)
Resulting change in operating income	$ 500	$ 600	$ 100

Incremental Analysis for Outsourcing Decisions

LO2 Perform incremental analysis for outsourcing decisions.

Outsourcing is the use of suppliers outside the organization to perform services or produce goods that could be performed or produced internally. **Make-or-buy decisions**, which are decisions about whether to make a part internally or buy it from an external supplier, may lead to outsourcing. However, a company may decide to outsource entire operating activities, such as warehousing or human resources, that have traditionally been performed in-house.

To improve operating income and compete effectively in global markets, many companies are focusing their resources on their core competencies—that is, the activities that they perform best. One way to obtain the financial, physical, human, and technological resources needed to emphasize those competencies is to outsource expensive nonvalue-adding activities. Strong candidates for outsourcing include payroll processing, training, managing fleets of vehicles, sales and marketing, custodial services, and information management. Many such areas involve either relatively low skill levels (such as payroll processing or custodial services) or highly specialized knowledge (such as information management) that could be better acquired from experts outside the company.

Outsourcing production or operating activities can reduce a company's investment in physical assets and human resources, which can improve cash flow. It can also help a company reduce its operating costs and improve operating income. For example, because **Amazon.com** outsources the distribution of most of its products, it has been able to reduce its storage and distribution costs enough to offer product discounts of up to 40 percent off the list price. It is also able to provide additional value-adding services, such as online reviews by customers, personalized recommendations, and discussions and interviews on current products.

Outsourcing Analysis In manufacturing companies, a common decision facing managers is whether to make or to buy some or all of the parts used in product assembly. The goal is to select the more profitable choice by identifying the costs of each alternative and their effects on revenues and existing costs. Managers need the following information for this analysis:

Information About Making	*Information About Buying*
Variable costs of making the item	Purchase price of item
Need for additional machinery	Rent or net cash flow to be generated from vacated space in the factory
Incremental fixed costs	Salvage value of unused machinery

To illustrate a manufacturer's outsourcing decision, let's suppose that for the past five years, Box Company has purchased packing cartons from an outside supplier at a cost of $1.25 per carton.

- The supplier has just informed Box Company that it is raising the price 20 percent, to $1.50 per carton, effective immediately.
- Box Company has idle machinery that could be adjusted to produce the cartons. Annual production and usage would be 20,000 cartons. The company estimates the cost of direct materials at $0.84 per carton. Workers, who will be paid $8.00 per hour, can process 20 cartons per hour ($0.40 per carton). The cost of variable overhead will be $4 per direct labor hour, and 1,000 direct labor hours will be required.
- Fixed overhead includes $4,000 of depreciation per year and $6,000 of other fixed costs.
- The company has space and machinery to produce the cartons; the machines are currently idle and will continue to be idle if the cartons are purchased.

Study Note

When performing an incremental analysis for an outsourcing decision, do not incorporate irrelevant information, such as depreciation and other fixed costs. Include only costs that change between the alternatives.

Should Box Company continue to outsource the cartons?

Exhibit 27-2 presents an incremental analysis of the two alternatives. All relevant costs are listed. Because the machinery has already been purchased and

EXHIBIT 27-2
Incremental Analysis: Outsourcing Decision

Box Company
Outsourcing Decision
Incremental Analysis

	Make	Outsource	Difference in Favor of Make
Direct materials (20,000 × $0.84)	$16,800	—	($16,800)
Direct labor (20,000 × $0.40)	8,000	—	(8,000)
Variable overhead (1,000 hours × $4)	4,000	—	(4,000)
Purchase price (20,000 × $1.50)	—	$30,000	30,000
Totals	$28,800	$30,000	$ 1,200

neither the machinery nor the required factory space has any other use, the depreciation costs and other fixed overhead costs are the same for both alternatives; therefore, they are not relevant to the decision. The cost of making the needed cartons is $28,800. The cost of buying 20,000 cartons at the increased purchase price will be $30,000. Since the company would save $1,200 by making the cartons, management will decide to make the cartons.

& APPLY >

Office Associates, Inc., is currently operating at less than capacity. The company thinks it could cut costs by outsourcing office cleaning to an independent cleaning service for $75 a week. Currently, a general office worker is employed for $10 an hour to do light cleaning and other general office duties. Cleaning the office usually takes one hour a day to perform and consumes $10 of supplies, $2 of variable overhead, and $18 of fixed overhead each week. Should Office Associates, Inc., continue to perform office cleanings, or should it begin to outsource them?

SOLUTION

Costs per Cleaning	Continue to Perform Cleanings	Outsource Cleanings	Difference in Favor of Continuing to Perform Cleanings
Employee labor	$50	—	($50)
Supplies	10	—	(10)
Variable overhead	2	—	(2)
Outside cleaning service	—	$75	75
Totals	$62	$75	$13

Office Associates should continue to perform office cleanings itself.

Incremental Analysis for Special Order Decisions

LO3 Perform incremental analysis for special order decisions.

Managers are often faced with **special order decisions**, which are decisions about whether to accept or reject special orders at prices below the normal market prices. Special orders usually involve large numbers of similar products that are sold in bulk. Before a firm accepts a special product order, it must be sure that excess capacity exists to complete the order and that the order will not reduce unit sales from its full-priced regular product line.

The objective of a special order decision is to determine whether a special order should be accepted. A special order should be accepted only if it maximizes operating income. In many situations, sales commission expenses are excluded from a special order decision analysis because the customer approached the company directly. In addition, the fixed costs of existing facilities usually do not change if a company accepts a special order, and therefore these costs are usually irrelevant to the decision. If additional fixed costs must be incurred to fill the special order, they would be relevant to the decision. Examples of relevant fixed costs are the purchase of additional machinery, an increase in supervisory help, and an increase in insurance premiums required by a specific order.

> **Study Note**
>
> Special order decisions assume that excess capacity exists to accept the order and that the order, if accepted, will not have an impact on regular sales orders.

Special Order Analyses One approach to a special order decision is to compare the price of the special order with the relevant costs of producing, packaging, and shipping the order. The relevant costs include the variable costs, variable selling costs (if any), and other costs directly associated with the special order (e.g., freight, insurance, and packaging and labeling the product). Another approach to this kind of decision is to prepare a special order bid price by calculating a minimum selling price for the special order. The bid price must cover the relevant costs and an estimated profit.

For example, suppose Home State Bank has been approved to provide and service four ATMs at a special event. The event sponsors want the fee reduced to $0.50 per ATM transaction. At past special events, ATM use has averaged 2,000 transactions per machine. Home State Bank has located four idle ATMs and determined the following additional information:

ATM Cost Data for Annual Use of One Machine (400,000 Transactions)

Direct materials	$0.10
Direct labor	0.05
Variable overhead	0.20
Fixed overhead ($100,000 ÷ 400,000)	0.25
Advertising ($60,000 ÷ 400,000)	0.15
Other fixed selling and administrative expenses ($120,000 ÷ 400,000)	0.30
Cost per transaction	$1.05
Regular fee per transaction	$1.50

Should Home State Bank accept the special event offer?

An incremental analysis of the decision in the contribution margin reporting format appears in Exhibit 27-3. The report shows the contribution margin for Home State Bank's operations both with and without the special order. Fixed costs are not included because the only costs affected by the order are direct materials, direct labor, and variable overhead.

- ***Price and relevant cost comparison:*** The net result of accepting the special order is a $1,200 increase in contribution margin (and, correspondingly, in operating income). The analysis reveals that Home State Bank should accept the special order. The $1,200 increase is verified by the following incremental analysis:

EXHIBIT 27-3
Incremental Analysis: Special Order Decision

Home State Bank
Special Order Decision
Incremental Analysis

	Without Order	With Order	Difference in Favor of Accepting Order
Sales	$2,400,000	$2,404,000	$ 4,000
Less variable costs			
Direct materials	$ 160,000	$ 160,800	($ 800)
Direct labor	80,000	80,400	(400)
Variable overhead	320,000	321,600	(1,600)
Total variable costs	$ 560,000	$ 562,800	($ 2,800)
Contribution margin	$1,840,000	$1,841,200	$ 1,200

Special order sales [(2,000 transactions × 4) × $0.50]		$4,000
Less variable costs		
Direct materials (8,000 transactions × $0.10)	$ 800	
Direct labor (8,000 transactions × $0.05)	400	
Variable overhead (8,000 transactions × $0.20)	1,600	
Total variable costs		2,800
Special order contribution margin		$1,200

▶ ***Minimum bid price for special order:*** Now let us assume that the event sponsor asks Home State Bank what its minimum special order price is. If the incremental costs for the special order are $2,800, the relevant cost per transaction is $0.35 ($2,800 ÷ 8,000). The special order price should cover this cost and generate a profit. If Home State Bank would like to earn $800 from the special order, the special order price should be $0.45 [$0.35 cost per transaction plus $0.10 profit per transaction ($800 ÷ 8,000 transactions)].

Of course, the Home State Bank management's decisions must be consistent with the bank's strategic plan and tactical objectives, and it must take into account not only costs and revenues but also relevant qualitative factors. Qualitative factors that might influence the decision are (1) the impact of the special order on regular customers, (2) the potential of the special order to lead into new sales areas, and (3) the customer's ability to maintain an ongoing relationship that includes good ordering and paying practices.

& APPLY >

Sample Company has received an order for Product EZ at a special selling price of $26 per unit (suggested retail price is $30). This order is over and above normal production, and budgeted production and sales targets for the year have already been exceeded. Capacity exists to satisfy the special order. No selling costs will be incurred in connection with this order. Unit costs to manufacture and sell Product EZ are as follows: direct materials, $7.00; direct labor, $10.00; variable overhead, $8.00; fixed manufacturing costs, $5.00; variable selling costs, $3.00; and fixed general and administrative costs, $9.00. Should Sample Company accept the order?

SOLUTION

Variable Costs to Produce Product EZ

Direct materials	$ 7.00
Direct labor	10.00
Variable overhead	8.00
Total variable costs to produce	$25.00

Sample Company should accept the special order because the offered price exceeds the variable manufacturing costs.

Incremental Analysis for Segment Profitability Decisions

LO4 Perform incremental analysis for segment profitability decisions.

Another type of operating decision that management must make is whether to keep or drop unprofitable segments, such as product lines, services, sales territories, divisions, departments, stores, or outlets. Management must select the alternative that maximizes operating income. The objective of the decision analysis is to identify the segments that have a negative segment margin so that managers can drop them or take corrective action.

A **segment margin** is a segment's sales revenue minus its direct costs (direct variable costs and direct fixed costs traceable to the segment). Such costs are assumed to be **avoidable costs**. An avoidable cost could be eliminated if management were to drop the segment.

- If a segment has a positive segment margin—that is, the segment's revenue is greater than its direct costs—it is able to cover its own direct costs and contribute a portion of its revenue to cover common costs and add to operating income. In that case, management should keep the segment.
- If a segment has a negative segment margin—that is, the segment's revenue is less than its direct costs—management should eliminate the segment.

However, certain common costs will be incurred regardless of the decision. Those are unavoidable costs, and the remaining segments must have sufficient contribution margin to cover their own direct costs and the common costs.

Segment Profitability Analysis An analysis of segment profitability includes the preparation of a segmented income statement using variable costing to identify variable and fixed costs. The fixed costs that are traceable to the segments are called *direct fixed costs*. The remaining fixed costs are *common costs* and are not assigned to segments.

Suppose Home State Bank wants to determine if it should eliminate its Safe Deposit Division. Managers prepare a segmented income statement, separating variable and fixed costs to calculate the contribution margin. They separate the total fixed costs of $84,000 further by directly tracing $55,500 to Bank Operations and $16,500 to the Safe Deposit Division; the remaining $12,000 are common fixed costs. The following segmented income statement shows the segment margins for Bank Operations and the Safe Deposit Division and the operating income for the total company:

Home State Bank
Segmented Income Statement
For the Year Ended December 31, 2011

	Bank Operations	Safe Deposit Division	Total Company
Sales	$135,000	$15,000	$150,000
Less variable costs	52,500	7,500	60,000
Contribution margin	$ 82,500	$ 7,500	$ 90,000
Less direct fixed costs	55,500	16,500	72,000
Segment margin	$ 27,000	($ 9,000)	$ 18,000
Less common fixed costs			12,000
Operating income			$ 6,000

EXHIBIT 27-4
Incremental Analysis:
Segment Profitability Decision

Home State Bank
Segment Profitability Decision
Incremental Analysis—Situation 1

	Keep Safe Deposit Division	Drop Safe Deposit Division	Difference in Favor of Dropping Safe Deposit Division
Sales	$150,000	$135,000	($15,000)
Less variable costs	60,000	52,500	7,500
Contribution margin	$ 90,000	$ 82,500	($ 7,500)
Less direct fixed costs	72,000	55,500	16,500
Segment margin	$ 18,000	$ 27,000	$ 9,000
Less common fixed costs	12,000	12,000	0
Operating income	$ 6,000	$ 15,000	$ 9,000

Home State Bank
Segment Profitability Decision
Incremental Analysis—Situation 2

	Keep Safe Deposit Division	Drop Safe Deposit Division	Difference in Opposition to Dropping Safe Deposit Division
Sales	$150,000	$108,000	($42,000)
Less variable costs	60,000	42,000	18,000
Contribution margin	$ 90,000	$ 66,000	($24,000)
Less direct fixed costs	72,000	55,500	16,500
Segment margin	$ 18,000	$ 10,500	($ 7,500)
Less common fixed costs	12,000	12,000	0
Operating income	$ 6,000	($ 1,500)	($ 7,500)

Exhibit 27-4 presents two situations. The first situation demonstrates that dropping the Safe Deposit Division will increase operating income by $9,000. Unless the bank can increase the division's segment margin by increasing sales revenue or by reducing direct costs, management should drop the segment. The incremental approach to analyzing this decision isolates the segment and focuses on its segment margin, as shown in the last column of the exhibit.

The decision to drop a segment also requires a careful review of the other segments to see whether they will be affected.

Situation 2 of Exhibit 27-4 assumes that Bank Operation's sales volume and variable costs will decrease 20 percent if management eliminates the Safe Deposit Division. The reduction in sales volume stems from the loss of customers who purchase products from both divisions. The analysis shows that dropping the division would reduce both the segment margin and the bank's operating income by $7,500. In this situation, Home State Bank would want to keep the Safe Deposit Division.

FOCUS ON BUSINESS PRACTICE

Why Banks Prefer Ebanking

After performing segment analysis of online banking and face-to-face banking, bank managers worldwide are encouraging customers to do their banking over the Internet. Banks have found that linking global Internet access with customer relationship management (CRM), customer-friendly financial software, and online bill payment in a secure banking environment can reduce costs, increase service and product availability, and boost earnings.[2]

STOP & APPLY >

Sample Company is evaluating its two divisions, East Division and West Division. Data for East Division include sales of $500,000, variable costs of $250,000, and fixed costs of $400,000, 50 percent of which are traceable to the division. West Division's data for the same period include sales of $600,000, variable costs of $350,000, and fixed costs of $450,000, 60 percent of which are traceable to the division.

Should either division be considered for elimination?

SOLUTION

	East Division	West Division	Total Company
Sales	$ 500,000	$ 600,000	$1,100,000
Less variable costs	250,000	350,000	600,000
Contribution margin	$ 250,000	$ 250,000	$ 500,000
Less direct fixed costs	200,000	270,000	470,000
Divisional income	$ 50,000	($ 20,000)	$ 30,000
Less common fixed costs			380,000
Operating income (loss)			($ 350,000)

The company should keep East Division because it is profitable. West Division does not seem to be profitable and should be considered for elimination. The home office and its very heavy overhead costs are causing the company's loss.

Incremental Analysis for Sales Mix Decisions

LO5 Perform incremental analysis for sales mix decisions involving constrained resources.

A company may not be able to provide the full variety of products or services that customers demand within a given time. Limits on resources like machine time or available labor may restrict the types or quantities of products or services that are available. Resource constraints can also be associated with other activities, such as inspection and equipment setup. The question is, Which products or services contribute the most to profitability in relation to the amount of capital assets or other constrained resources needed to offer those items? To satisfy customers' demands and maximize operating income, management will choose to offer the most profitable product or service first. To identify such products or services, managers calculate the contribution margin per constrained resource (such as labor hours or machine hours) for each product or service.

Study Note

When resources like direct materials, direct labor, or time are scarce, the goal is to maximize the contribution margin per unit of scarce resource.

Sales Mix Analysis The objective of a **sales mix decision** is to select the alternative that maximizes the contribution margin per constrained resource. The decision analysis, which uses incremental analysis to identify the relevant costs and revenues, consists of two steps:

Step 1. Calculate the contribution margin per unit for each product or service affected by the constrained resource. The contribution margin per unit equals the selling price per unit less the variable costs per unit.

Step 2. Calculate the contribution margin per unit of the constrained resource. The contribution margin per unit of the constrained resource equals the contribution margin per unit divided by the quantity of the constrained resource required per unit.

Suppose Home State Bank offers three types of loans: commercial loans, auto loans, and home loans. The product line data are as follows:

	Commercial Loans	*Auto Loans*	*Home Loans*
Current loan application demand	20,000	30,000	18,000
Processing hours per loan application	2.0	1.0	2.5
Loan origination fee	\$24.00	\$18.00	\$32.00
Variable processing costs	\$12.50	\$10.00	\$18.75
Variable selling costs	\$6.50	\$5.00	\$6.25

The current loan application capacity is 100,000 processing hours.

Question 1. Which loan type should be advertised and promoted first because it is the most profitable for the bank? Which should be second? Which last?

Exhibit 27-5 shows the sales mix analysis. It indicates that the auto loans should be promoted first because they provide the highest contribution margin per processing hour. Home loans should be second, and commercial loans should be last.

Question 2. How many of each type of loan should the bank sell to maximize its contribution margin based on the current loan application capacity of 100,000 processing hours? What is the total contribution margin for that combination?

To begin the analysis, compare the current loan application capacity with the total capacity required to meet the current loan demand. The company needs 115,000 processing hours to meet the current loan demand: 40,000 processing hours for commercial loans (20,000 loans × 2 processing hours per loan), 30,000 processing hours for auto loans (30,000 loans × 1 processing hour per loan), and 45,000 processing hours for home loans (18,000 loans × 2.5 processing hours per loan). Because that amount exceeds the current capacity of 100,000 processing hours, management must determine the sales mix that maximizes the company's contribution margin, which will also maximize its operating income.

EXHIBIT 27-5
Incremental Analysis: Sales Mix Decision Involving Constrained Resources

Home State Bank
Sales Mix Decision: Ranking the Order of Loans
Incremental Analysis

	Commercial Loans	Auto Loans	Home Loans
Loan origination fee per loan	$24.00	$18.00	$32.00
Less variable costs			
Processing	$12.50	$10.00	$18.75
Selling	6.50	5.00	6.25
Total variable costs	$19.00	$15.00	$25.00
Contribution margin per loan (A)	$ 5.00	$ 3.00	$ 7.00
Processing hours per loan (B)	2.0	1.0	2.5
Contribution margin per processing hour (A ÷ B)	$ 2.50	$ 3.00	$ 2.80

Home State Bank
Sales Mix Decision: Number of Units to Make
Incremental Analysis

	Processing Hours
Total processing hours available	100,000
Less processing hours to produce auto loans (30,000 loans × 1 processing hour per loan)	30,000
Balance of processing hours available	70,000
Less processing hours to produce home loans (18,000 loans × 2.5 processing hours per loan)	45,000
Balance of processing hours available	25,000
Less processing hours to produce commercial loans (12,500 loans × 2 processing hours per loan)	25,000
Balance of processing hours available	0

The calculations in the second part of Exhibit 27-5 show that Home State Bank should sell 30,000 auto loans, 18,000 home loans, and 12,500 commercial loans. The total contribution margin is as follows:

Auto loans (30,000 loans × $3.00 per loan)	$ 90,000
Home loans (18,000 loans × $7.00 per loan)	126,000
Commercial loans (12,500 loans × $5.00 per loan)	62,500
Total contribution margin	$278,500

STOP & APPLY >

Surf, Inc., makes three kinds of surfboards, but it has a limited number of machine hours available to make them. Product line data are as follows:

	Fiberglass	Plastic	Graphite
Machine hours per unit	4	1	2
Selling price per unit	$1,500	$800	$1,300
Variable manufacturing cost per unit	500	200	800
Variable selling costs per unit	200	350	200

In what order should the surfboard product lines be produced?

SOLUTION

	Fiberglass	Plastic	Graphite
Selling price per unit	$1,500	$800	$1,300
Less variable costs			
Manufacturing	$ 500	$200	$ 800
Selling	200	350	200
Total unit variable costs	$ 700	$550	$1,000
Contribution margin per unit (A)	$ 800	$250	$ 300
Machine hours per unit (B)	4	1	2
Contribution margin per machine hour (A ÷ B)	$ 200	$250	$ 150

Surf, Inc., should produce plastic first, then fiberglass, and finally graphite surfboards.

Incremental Analysis for Sell or Process-Further Decisions

LO6 Perform incremental analysis for sell or process-further decisions.

Study Note

Products are made by combining materials or by dividing materials, as in oil refining or ore extraction.

Some companies offer products or services that can either be sold in a basic form or be processed further and sold as a more refined product or service to a different market. For example, a meatpacking company processes cattle into meat and meat-related products, such as bones and hides. The company may choose to sell sides of beef and pounds of bones and hides to other companies for further processing. Alternatively, it could choose to cut and package the meat for immediate sale in grocery stores, process bone into fertilizer for gardeners, or tan hides into refined leather for purses.

A **sell or process-further decision** is a decision about whether to sell a joint product at the split-off point or sell it after further processing. **Joint products** are two or more products made from a common material or process that cannot be identified as separate products or services during some or all of the processing. Only at a specific point, called the **split-off point**, do joint products or services become separate and identifiable. At that point, a company may choose to sell the product or service as is or to process it into another form for sale to a different market.

Sell or Process-Further Analysis The objective of a sell or process-further decision is to select the alternative that maximizes operating income. The decision analysis entails calculating the incremental revenue, which is the difference between the total revenue if the product or service is sold at the split-off point and the total revenue if the product or service is sold after further processing. You then compare the incremental revenue with the incremental costs of processing further.

- If the incremental revenue is greater than the incremental costs of processing further, a decision to process the product or service further would be justified.
- If the incremental costs are greater than the incremental revenue, you would probably choose to sell the product or service at the split-off point.

Study Note

The common costs shared by two or more products before they are split off are called *joint costs.* Joint costs are irrelevant in a sell or process-further decision.

Be sure to ignore *joint costs* (or common costs) in your analysis, because they are incurred *before* the split-off point and do not change if further processing occurs. Although accountants assign joint costs to products or services when valuing inventories and calculating cost of goods sold, joint costs are not relevant to a sell or process-further decision and are omitted from the decision analysis.

For example, as part of the company's strategic plan, Home State Bank's management is looking for new markets for banking services, and management is considering whether it would be profitable to bundle banking services. Home State Bank is considering adding two levels of service, Premier Checking and Personal Banker, beyond its current Basic Checking account services. The three levels have the following bundled features:

- Basic Checking: Online checking account, debit card, and online bill payment with a required minimum average balance of $500
- Premier Checking: Paper and online checking, a debit card, a credit card, and a small life insurance policy equal to the maximum credit limit on the credit card for customers who maintain a minimum average balance of $1,000
- Personal Banker: All of the features of Premier Checking plus a safe deposit box, a $5,000 personal line of credit at the prime interest rate, financial investment advice, and a toaster upon opening the account for customers who maintain a minimum average balance of $5,000

Assume that the bank can earn sales revenue of 5 percent on its checking account balances and that the total cost of offering basic checking services is currently $50,000. The bank's accountant provided these data for each level of service:

Product	*Sales Revenue*	*Additional Costs*
Basic Checking	$ 25	$ 0
Premier Checking	50	30
Personal Banker	250	200

The decision analysis in Exhibit 27-6 indicates that the bank should offer Personal Banking services in addition to Basic Checking accounts. Notice that the $50,000 joint costs of Basic Checking were ignored because they are sunk costs that will not influence the decision.

As we noted earlier, the decision analysis must take into account the organization's strategic plan and tactical objectives. In this example, the decision to process services further supports the bank's strategic plan to expand into new markets. In making the final decision, management must also consider other factors, such as the bank's ability to obtain favorable returns on its bank deposit investments.

EXHIBIT 27-6
Incremental Analysis:
Sell or Process-Further Decision

Home State Bank
Sell or Process-Further Decision
Incremental Analysis

	Premier Checking	Personal Banker
Incremental revenue per account if processed further:		
Process further	$50	$250
Split-off—Basic Checking	25	25
Incremental revenue	$25	$225
Less incremental costs	30	200
Operating income (loss) from processing further	($ 5)	$ 25

& APPLY >

In an attempt to provide superb customer service, Home Movie Rentals is considering expanding its product offerings from single movie or game rentals to complete movie or game evenings. Each evening would include a movie or game, candy, popcorn, and drinks. The accountant for Home Movie Rentals has compiled the following relevant information:

Product	Sales Revenue if No Additional Service	Sales Revenue if Processed Further	Additional Processing Costs
Movie	$2	$10	$5
Game	1	6	5

Determine which products Home Movie Rentals should offer.

SOLUTION

Incremental Revenue if Processed Further	Movie Evening	Game Evening
Process further	$10	$6
Split-off	2	1
Incremental revenue	$ 8	$5
Less incremental costs	5	5
Operating income from further processing	$ 3	$0

Home Movie Rentals should promote movie evenings first, then movies, and finally games or game evenings. There is no difference in profitability between the sale of games and the sale of game evenings.

▸ HOME STATE BANK: REVIEW PROBLEM

In this chapter's Decision Point, we commented on Home State Bank's plan to increase its offering of online products and services. We asked the following questions:

- How will managers at Home State Bank decide on new ways to increase business and protect customers' interests?
- How can incremental analysis help managers at Home State Bank take advantage of the business opportunities that online banking offers?

As managers at Home State Bank make short-term decisions about which alternatives to pursue that will increase business and give customers additional protection against fraud and identity theft, they will ask a number of questions—for example: When should bank products and services be outsourced? When should a special order for service be accepted? When is a bank segment profitable? When resource constraints exist, what is the best sales mix? When should bank products be sold as is or processed further into different products?

Segment Profitability
LO4

To answer such questions and determine what could happen under alternative courses of action, the bank's managers need pertinent information that they can use in incremental analysis. On that basis, they can make sound, ethical decisions that will protect the bank's customers and increase both its traditional and online business.

Suppose a loan officer at Home State Bank has been analyzing Home Services, Inc., to determine whether the bank should grant it a loan. Home Services has been in business for ten years, and its services now include tree trimming and auto, boat, and tile floor repair. The following data pertaining to those services were available for analysis:

	A	B	C	D	E	F	G
1				**Home Services, Inc.**			
2				**Segmented Income Statement**			
3				**For the Year Ended December 31, 2011**			
4							
5					**Tile**		
6			**Auto**	**Boat**	**Floor**	**Tree**	**Total**
7			**Repair**	**Repair**	**Repair**	**Trimming**	**Impact**
8	Sales		$297,500	$114,300	$126,400	$ 97,600	$635,800
9	Less variable costs						
10		Direct labor	$119,000	$ 40,005	$ 44,240	$ 34,160	$237,405
11		Operating supplies	14,875	5,715	6,320	4,880	31,790
12		Small tools	11,900	4,572	5,056	7,808	29,336
13		Replacement parts	59,500	22,860	25,280	–	107,640
14		Truck costs	–	11,430	12,640	14,640	38,710
15		Selling costs	44,625	17,145	18,960	9,760	90,490
16		Other variable costs	5,950	2,286	2,528	1,952	12,716
17	Contribution margin		$ 41,650	$ 10,287	$ 11,376	$ 24,400	$ 87,713
18	Less direct fixed costs		35,800	16,300	24,100	5,200	81,400
19	Segment margin		$ 5,850	($ 6,013)	($ 12,724)	$ 19,200	$ 6,313
20	Less common fixed						
21		costs					32,100
22	Operating income						
23		(loss)					($ 25,787)
24							

Home Services' profitability has decreased over the past two years, and to increase the likelihood that the company will qualify for a loan, the loan officer has advised its owner, Dale Bandy, to determine which service lines are not meeting the company's profit targets. Once Bandy has identified the unprofitable service lines, he can either eliminate them or set higher prices. If he sets higher prices, those prices will have to cover all variable and fixed operating, selling, and general administration costs.

Required

1. Analyze the performance of the four service lines. Should Dale Bandy eliminate any of them? Explain your answer.
2. Why might Bandy want to continue providing unprofitable service lines?
3. Identify possible causes of a service's poor performance. What actions do you think Bandy should take to make his company a better loan candidate?

Answers to Review Problem

1. In deciding whether to eliminate any of the four service lines, Dale Bandy should concentrate on those that have a negative segment margin. If the revenues from a service line are less than the sum of its variable and direct fixed costs, then other service lines must cover some of the losing line's costs and carry the burden of the common fixed costs.

   By looking at the segmented income statement, Dale Bandy can see that the company will improve its operating income by $18,737 ($6,013 + $12,724) if he eliminates the boat and tile floor repair services, both of which have a negative segment margin. Bandy's decision can also be supported by the following analysis:

	A	B	C	D	E
1			**Home Services, Inc.**		
2			**Segment Profitability Decision**		
3					
4					**Difference in**
5					**Favor of**
6			**Keep**	**Drop**	**Dropping**
7			**Boat Repair**	**Boat Repair**	**Boat Repair**
8			**and**	**and**	**and**
9			**Tile Floor Repair**	**Tile Floor Repair**	**Tile Floor Repair**
10	Sales		$635,800	$395,100	($240,700)
11	Less variable costs		548,087	329,050	219,037
12	Contribution margin		$ 87,713	$ 66,050	($ 21,663)
13	Less direct fixed costs		81,400	41,000	40,400
14	Segment margin		$ 6,313	$ 25,050	$ 18,737
15	Less common fixed costs		32,100	32,100	—
16	Operating income (loss)		($ 25,787)	($ 7,050)	$ 18,737

2. Bandy may want to continue offering the unprofitable service lines if their elimination would have a negative effect on the sale of the auto repair or tree trimming services.

3. The following are among the possible causes of a service's poor performance:
   a. Service fees set too low
   b. Inadequate advertising
   c. Excessively high direct labor costs
   d. Other variable costs
   e. Poor management of fixed costs
   f. Excessive supervision costs

   To improve profitability and make the company a better candidate for a bank loan, Bandy should eliminate nonvalue-adding costs, increase service fees, or increase the volume of services provided to customers.

LO1 Describe how managers make short-run decisions using incremental analysis.

Both quantitative information and qualitative information are important in short-run decision analysis. Such information should be relevant, timely, and presented in a format that is easy to use in decision making.

Incremental analysis helps managers compare alternative courses of action by focusing on the differences in projected revenues and costs. Any data that relate to future costs, revenues, or uses of resources and that will differ among alternative courses of action are considered relevant decision information. Examples of relevant information are projected sales or estimated costs, such as the costs of direct materials or direct labor, that differ for each alternative. The manager analyzes relevant information to determine which alternative contributes the most to profits or incurs the lowest costs. Only data that differ for each alternative are considered. Differential or incremental costs are costs that vary among alternatives and thus are relevant to the decision. Sunk costs are past costs that cannot be recovered; they are irrelevant to the decision process. Opportunity costs are revenue or income forgone as a result of choosing an alternative.

LO2 Perform incremental analysis for outsourcing decisions.

Outsourcing (including make-or-buy) decision analysis helps managers decide whether to use suppliers from outside the organization to perform services or provide goods that could be performed or produced internally. An incremental analysis of the expected costs and revenues for each alternative is used to identify the best alternative.

LO3 Perform incremental analysis for special order decisions.

A special order decision is a decision about whether to accept or reject a special order at a price below the normal market price. One approach is to compare the special order price with the relevant costs to see if a profit can be generated. Another approach is to prepare a special order bid price by calculating a minimum selling price for the special order. Generally, fixed costs are irrelevant to a special order decision because such costs are covered by regular sales activity and do not differ among alternatives.

LO4 Perform incremental analysis for segment profitability decisions.

Segment profitability decisions involve the review of segments of an organization, such as product lines, services, sales territories, divisions, or departments. Managers often must decide whether to add or drop a segment. A segment with a negative segment margin may be dropped. A segment margin is a segment's sales revenue minus its direct costs, which include variable costs and avoidable fixed costs. Avoidable costs are traceable to a specific segment. If the segment is eliminated, the avoidable costs will also be eliminated.

LO5 Perform incremental analysis for sales mix decisions involving constrained resources.

Sales mix decisions require the selection of the most profitable combination of sales items when a company makes more than one product or service using a common constrained resource. The product or service generating the highest contribution margin per constrained resource is offered and sold first.

LO6 Perform incremental analysis for sell or process-further decisions.

Sell or process-further decisions require managers to choose between selling a joint product at its split-off point or processing it into a more refined product. Managers compare the incremental revenues and costs of the two alternatives. Joint processing costs are irrelevant to the decision because they are identical for both alternatives. A product should be processed further only if the incremental revenues generated exceed the incremental costs incurred.

REVIEW of Concepts and Terminology

The following concepts and terms were introduced in this chapter:

Avoidable costs 1194 (LO4)

Differential cost 1187 (LO1)

Incremental analysis 1187 (LO1)

Joint products 1199 (LO6)

Make-or-buy decisions 1189 (LO2)

Opportunity costs 1188 (LO1)

Outsourcing 1189 (LO2)

Sales mix decision 1197 (LO5)

Segment margin 1194 (LO4)

Sell or process-further decision 1199 (LO6)

Short-run decision analysis 1186 (LO1)

Special order decisions 1191 (LO3)

Split-off point 1199 (LO6)

Sunk cost 1187 (LO1)

CHAPTER ASSIGNMENTS

BUILDING Your Knowledge Foundation

Short Exercises

LO1 Qualitative and Quantitative Information in Short-Run Decision Analysis

SE 1. The owner of Milo's, a Mexican restaurant, is deciding whether to take fish tacos off the menu. State whether each item of decision information that follows is qualitative or quantitative. If the information is quantitative, specify whether it is financial or nonfinancial.

1. The time needed to prepare the fish
2. The daily number of customers who order the tacos
3. Whether competing Mexican restaurants have this entrée on the menu
4. The labor cost of the chef who prepares the fish tacos
5. The fact that the president of a nearby company who brings ten guests with him each week always orders fish tacos

LO1 Using Incremental Analysis

SE 2. Pices Corporation has assembled the following information related to the purchase of a new automated postage machine:

	Posen Machine	Value Machine
Increase in revenue	$44,200	$49,300
Increase in annual operating costs		
Direct materials	12,200	12,200
Direct labor	10,200	10,600
Variable overhead	24,500	26,900
Fixed overhead (including depreciation)	12,400	12,400

Using incremental analysis and only relevant information, compute the difference in favor of the Value machine.

LO2 Outsourcing Decision

SE 3. Marc Company assembles products from a group of interconnecting parts. The company produces some of the parts and buys some from outside vendors. The vendor for Part X has just increased its price by 35 percent, to $10 per unit for the first 5,000 units and $9 per additional unit ordered each year. The company uses 7,500 units of Part X each year. Unit costs if the company makes the part are as follows:

Direct materials	$3.50
Direct labor	2.00
Variable overhead	4.00
Variable selling costs for the assembled product	3.75

Should Marc continue to purchase Part X or begin making it?

LO2 Outsourcing Decision

SE 4. Dental Associates, Inc., is currently operating at less than capacity. The company thinks it could cut costs by outsourcing dental cleaning to an independent dental hygienist for $50 per cleaning. Currently, a dental hygienist is employed for $30 an hour. A dental cleaning usually takes one hour to perform and consumes $10 of dental supplies, $8 of variable overhead, and $16 of fixed overhead. Should Dental Associates, Inc., continue to perform dental cleanings, or should it begin to outsource them?

LO3 Special Order Decision

SE 5. Hadley Company has received a special order for Product R3P at a selling price of $20 per unit. This order is over and above normal production, and budgeted production and sales targets for the year have already been exceeded. Capacity exists to satisfy the special order. No selling costs will be incurred in connection with this order. Unit costs to manufacture and sell Product R3P are as follows: direct materials, $7.60; direct labor, $3.75; variable overhead, $9.25; fixed overhead, $4.85; variable selling costs, $2.75; and fixed general and administrative costs, $6.75. Should Hadley Company accept the order?

LO3 Special Order Decision

SE 6. Smith Accounting Services is considering a special order that it received from one of its corporate clients. The special order calls for Smith to prepare the individual tax returns of the corporation's four-largest shareholders. The company has idle capacity that could be used to complete the special order. The following data have been gathered about the preparation of individual tax returns:

Materials cost per page	$1
Average hourly labor rate	$60
Standard hours per return	4
Standard pages per return	10
Variable overhead cost per page	$0.50
Fixed overhead cost per page	$0.50

Smith Accounting Services would be satisfied with a $40 gross profit per return. Compute the minimum bid price for the entire order.

LO4 Segment Profitability Decision

SE 7. Peruna Company is evaluating its two divisions, North Division and South Division. Data for North Division include sales of $530,000, variable costs of $290,000, and fixed costs of $260,000, 50 percent of which are traceable to the division. South Division's efforts for the same period include sales of $610,000, variable costs of $340,000, and fixed costs of $290,000, 60 percent of which are traceable to the division. Should Peruna Company consider eliminating either division? Is there any other problem that needs attention?

LO5 Sales Mix Decision

SE 8. Snow, Inc., makes three kinds of snowboards, but it has a limited number of machine hours available to make them. Product line data are as follows:

	Wood	Plastic	Graphite
Machine hours per unit	1.25	1.0	1.5
Selling price per unit	$100	$120	$200
Variable manufacturing cost per unit	$45	$50	$100
Variable selling costs per unit	$15	$26	$36

In what order should the snowboard product lines be produced?

LO6 Sell or Process-Further Decision

SE 9. Gomez Industries produces three products from a single operation. Product A sells for $4 per unit, Product B for $6 per unit, and Product C for $10 per unit. When B is processed further, there are additional unit costs of $3, and its new selling price is $10 per unit. Each product is allocated $2 of joint costs from the initial production operation. Should Product B be processed further, or should it be sold at the end of the initial operation?

LO6 Sell or Process-Further Decision

SE 10. In an attempt to provide superb customer service, Richard V. Meats is considering the expansion of its product offerings from whole hams and turkeys to complete ham and turkey dinners. Each dinner would include a carved ham or turkey, two side dishes, and six rolls or cornbread. The accountant for Richard V. Meats has compiled the following relevant information:

Product	Sales Revenue if No Additional Service	Sales Revenue if Processed Further	Additional Processing Costs
Ham	$30	$50	$15
Turkey	20	35	15

A cooked, uncarved ham costs Richard V. Meats $20 to produce. A cooked, uncarved turkey costs $15 to prepare. Use incremental analysis to determine which products Richard V. Meats should offer.

Exercises

LO1 Incremental Analysis

E 1. Max Wayco, the business manager for Essey Industries, must select a new computer system for his assistant. Rental of Model A, which is similar to the model now being used, is $2,200 per year. Model B is a deluxe system that rents for $2,900 per year and will require a new desk for the assistant. The annual desk rental charge is $750. The assistant's salary of $1,200 per month will not change. If Model B is rented, $280 in annual software training costs will be incurred. Model B has greater capacity and is expected to save $1,550 per year in part-time wages. Upkeep and operating costs will not differ between the two models.

1. Identify the relevant data in this problem.
2. Prepare an incremental analysis to aid the business manager in his decision.

LO1 Incremental Analysis

E 2. The managers of Lennox Company must decide which of two mill blade grinders—Y or Z—to buy. The grinders have the same purchase price but different revenue and cost characteristics. The company currently owns Grinder X, which it bought three years ago for $15,000 and which has accumulated depreciation of $9,000 and a book value of $6,000. Grinder X is now obsolete as a result of advances in technology and cannot be sold or traded in.

The accountant has collected the following annual revenue and operating cost estimates for the two new machines:

	Grinder Y	Grinder Z
Increase in revenue	$16,000	$20,000
Increase in annual operating costs		
Direct materials	4,800	4,800
Direct labor	3,000	4,100
Variable overhead	2,100	3,000
Fixed overhead (depreciation included)	5,000	5,000

1. Identify the relevant data in this problem.
2. Prepare an incremental analysis to aid the managers in their decision.
3. Should the company purchase Grinder Y or Grinder Z?

LO2 Outsourcing Decision

E 3. One component of a radio produced by Audio Systems, Inc., is currently being purchased for $225 per 100 parts. Management is studying the possibility of manufacturing that component. Annual production (usage) at Audio is 70,000 units; fixed costs (all of which remain unchanged whether the part is made or purchased) are $38,500; and variable costs are $0.95 per unit for direct materials, $0.55 per unit for direct labor, and $0.60 per unit for variable overhead.

Using incremental analysis, decide whether Audio Systems, Inc., should manufacture the part or continue to purchase it from an outside vendor.

LO2 **Outsourcing Decision**

E 4. Sunny Hazel, the manager of Cyber Web Services, must decide whether to hire a new employee or to outsource some of the web design work to Ky To, a freelance graphic designer. If she hires a new employee, she will pay $32 per design hour for the employee to work 600 hours and incur service overhead costs of $2 per design hour. If she outsources the work to Ky To, she will pay $36 per design hour for 600 hours of work. She can also redirect the use of a computer and server to generate $4,000 in additional revenue from web page maintenance work.

Should Cyber Web Services hire a new designer or outsource the work to Ky To?

LO3 **Special Order Decision**

E 5. Antiquities, Ltd., produces antique-looking books. Management has just received a request for a special order for 2,000 books and must decide whether to accept it. Venus Company, the purchaser, is offering to pay $25.00 per book, which includes $3.00 per book for shipping costs.

The variable production costs per book include $9.20 for direct materials, $4.00 for direct labor, and $3.80 for variable overhead. The current year's production is 22,000 books, and maximum capacity is 25,000 books. Fixed costs, including overhead, advertising, and selling and administrative costs, total $80,000. The usual selling price is $25.00 per book. Shipping costs, which are additional, average $3.00 per book.

Determine whether Antiquities should accept the special order.

LO3 **Special Order Decision**

E 6. Jens Sporting Goods, Inc., manufactures a complete line of sporting equipment. Leiden Enterprises operates a large chain of discount stores. Leiden has approached Jens with a special order for 30,000 deluxe baseballs. Instead of being packaged separately, the balls are to be packed in boxes containing 500 baseballs each. Leiden is willing to pay $2.45 per baseball. Jens knows that annual expected production is 400,000 baseballs. It also knows that the current year's production is 410,000 baseballs and that the maximum production capacity is 450,000 baseballs. The following additional information is available:

Standard unit cost data for 400,000 baseballs	
Direct materials	$ 0.90
Direct labor	0.60
Overhead:	
Variable	0.50
Fixed ($100,000 ÷ 400,000)	0.25
Packaging per unit	0.30
Advertising ($60,000 ÷ 400,000)	0.15
Other fixed selling and administrative expenses ($120,000 ÷ 400,000)	0.30
Product unit cost	$ 3.00
Unit selling price	$ 4.00
Total estimated bulk packaging costs for special order (30,000 baseballs: 500 per box)	$2,500

1. Should Jens Sporting Goods, Inc., accept Leiden's offer?
2. What would be the minimum order price per baseball if Jens would like to earn a profit of $3,000 from the special order?

LO3 **Special Order Decision**

E 7. In September, a nonprofit organization, Toys for Homeless Children (THC), offers Virtually LLC $400 to prepare a custom web page to help the organization attract toy donations. The home page for the THC website will include special animated graphics of toys and stuffed animals. Virtually LLC estimates that it will take 12 design labor hours at $32 per design hour and 2 installation labor hours at $10 per installation hour to complete the job. Fixed costs are already covered by regular business. Should Virtually LLC accept THC's offer?

LO4 **Elimination of Unprofitable Segment Decision**

E 8. Guld's Glass, Inc., has three divisions: Commercial, Nonprofit, and Residential. The segmented income statement for last year revealed the following:

Guld's Glass, Inc.
Divisional Profit Summary and Decision Analysis

	Commercial Division	Nonprofit Division	Residential Division	Total Company
Sales	$290,000	$533,000	$837,000	$1,660,000
Less variable costs	147,000	435,000	472,000	1,054,000
Contribution margin	$143,000	$ 98,000	$365,000	$ 606,000
Less direct fixed costs	124,000	106,000	139,000	369,000
Segment margin	$ 19,000	($ 8,000)	$226,000	$ 237,000
Less common fixed costs				168,000
Operating income				$ 69,000

1. How will Guld's Glass, Inc., be affected if the Nonprofit Division is dropped?
2. Assume the elimination of the Nonprofit Division causes the sales of the Residential Division to decrease by 10 percent. How will Guld's Glass, Inc., be affected if the Nonprofit Division is dropped?

LO4 **Elimination of Unprofitable Segment Decision**

E 9. URL Services has two divisions: Basic Web Pages and Custom Web Pages. Ricky Vega, manager of Custom Web Pages, wants to find out why Custom Web Pages is not profitable. He has prepared the reports that appear on the next page.

1. How will URL Services be affected if the Custom Web Pages Division is eliminated?
2. How will URL Services be affected if the Design segment of Custom Web Pages is eliminated?
3. What should Ricky Vega do? What additional information would be helpful to him in making the decision?

URL Services
Segmented Income Statement
For the Year Ended December 31

	Basic Web Pages (1,000 units)	Custom Web Pages (200 units)	Total Company
Service revenue	$200,000	$150,000	$350,000
Less variable costs			
Direct professional labor: design	$ 32,000	$ 80,000	$112,000
Direct professional labor: install	30,000	4,000	34,000
Direct professional labor: maintain	15,000	36,000	51,000
Total variable costs	$ 77,000	$120,000	$197,000
Contribution margin	$123,000	$ 30,000	$153,000
Less direct fixed costs			
Depreciation on computer equipment	$ 6,000	$ 12,000	$ 18,000
Depreciation on servers	10,000	20,000	30,000
Total direct fixed costs	$ 16,000	$ 32,000	$ 48,000
Segment margin	$107,000	($ 2,000)	$105,000
Less common fixed costs			
Building rent			$ 24,000
Supplies			1,000
Insurance			3,000
Telephone			1,500
Website rental			500
Total common fixed costs			$ 30,000
Operating income			$ 75,000

Custom Web Pages Division
URL Services
Segment Profitability Decision
Incremental Analysis

	Design	Install	Maintain	Total
Service revenue	$60,000	$25,000	$65,000	$150,000
Less variable costs	80,000	4,000	36,000	120,000
Contribution margin	($20,000)	$21,000	$29,000	$ 30,000
Less direct fixed costs	6,000	13,000	13,000	32,000
Segment margin	($26,000)	$ 8,000	$16,000	($ 2,000)

LO5 **Scarce Resource Usage**

E 10. EZ, Inc., manufactures two products that require both machine processing and labor operations. Although there is unlimited demand for both products, EZ could devote all its capacities to a single product. Unit prices, cost data, and processing requirements follow:

	Product E	Product Z
Unit selling price	$70	$230
Unit variable costs	$30	$90
Machine hours per unit	0.4	1.4
Labor hours per unit	2.0	6.0

Next year, the company will be limited to 160,000 machine hours and 120,000 labor hours. Fixed costs for the year are $1,500,000.

1. Compute the most profitable combination of products to be produced next year.
2. Prepare an income statement using the contribution margin format for the product volume computed in **1**.

LO5 **Sales Mix Decision**

E 11. Grady Enterprises manufactures three computer games. They are called Rising Star, Ghost Master, and Road Warrior. The product line data are as follows:

	Rising Star	Ghost Master	Road Warrior
Current unit sales demand	20,000	30,000	18,000
Machine hours per unit	2.0	1.0	2.5
Selling price per unit	$24.00	$18.00	$32.00
Unit variable manufacturing costs	$12.50	$10.00	$18.75
Unit variable selling costs	$6.50	$5.00	$6.25

The current production capacity is 110,000 machine hours.

1. Which computer game should be manufactured first? Which should be manufactured second? Which last?
2. How many of each type of computer game should be manufactured and sold to maximize the company's contribution margin based on the current production activity of 110,000 machine hours? What is the total contribution margin for that combination?

LO5 **Sales Mix Decision**

E 12. Web Services, a small company owned by Simon Orozco, provides web page services to small businesses. His services include the preparation of basic pages and custom pages.

The following summary of information will be used to make several short-run decisions for Web Services:

	Basic Pages	Custom Pages
Service revenue per page	$200	$750
Variable costs per page	77	600
Contribution margin per page	$123	$150

Total annual fixed costs are $78,000.

One of Web Services' two graphic designers, Taylor Campbell, is planning to take maternity leave in July and August. As a result, there will be only one designer available to perform the work, and design labor hours will be a resource constraint. Orozco plans to help the other designer complete the projected 160 orders for basic pages and 30 orders for custom pages for those two months. However, he wants to know which type of page Web Services should advertise and market. Although custom pages have a higher contribution margin per service, each custom page requires 12.5 design hours, whereas basic pages require only 1 design hour per page. On which page type should his company focus? Explain your answer.

LO6 **Sell or Process-Further Decision**

E 13. H & L Beef Products, Inc., processes cattle. It can sell the meat as sides of beef or process it further into final cuts (steaks, roasts, and hamburger). As part of the company's strategic plan, management is looking for new markets for meat or meat by-products. The production process currently separates hides and bones for sale to other manufacturers. However, management is considering whether it would be profitable to process the hides into leather and the bones into fertilizer. The costs of the cattle and of transporting, hanging, storing, and cutting sides of beef are $125,000. The company's accountant provided these data:

Product	Sales Revenue if Sold at Split-Off	Sales Revenue if Sold After Further Processing	Additional Processing Costs
Meat	$100,000	$200,000	$80,000
Bones	20,000	40,000	15,000
Hides	50,000	55,000	10,000

Should the products be processed further? Explain your answer.

LO6 **Sell or Process-Further Decision**

E 14. Six Star Pizza manufactures frozen pizzas and calzones and sells them for $4 each. It is currently considering a proposal to manufacture and sell fully prepared products. The following relevant information has been gathered by management:

Product	Sales Revenue if No Additional Processing	Sales Revenue if Processed Further	Additional Processing Costs
Pizza	$4	$ 8	$5
Calzone	4	10	5

Use incremental analysis to determine which products Six Star should offer.

Problems

LO2 **Outsourcing Decision**

P 1. Stainless Refrigerator Company purchases ice makers and installs them in its products. The ice makers cost $138 per case, and each case contains 12 ice makers. The supplier recently gave advance notice that the price will rise by 50 percent immediately. Stainless Refrigerator Company has idle equipment that with only a few minor changes could be used to produce similar ice makers.

Cost estimates have been prepared under the assumption that the company could make the product itself. Direct materials would cost $100.80 per 12 ice makers. Direct labor required would be 10 minutes per ice maker at a labor rate of $18.00 per hour. Variable overhead would be $4.60 per ice maker. Fixed overhead, which would be incurred under either decision alternative, would be $32,420 a year for depreciation and $234,000 a year for other costs. Production and usage are estimated at 75,000 ice makers a year. (Assume that any idle equipment cannot be used for any other purpose.)

Required

1. Prepare an incremental analysis to determine whether the ice makers should be made within the company or purchased from the outside supplier at the higher price.
2. Compute the variable unit cost to (a) make one ice maker and (b) buy one ice maker.

LO3 Special Order Decision

P 2. On March 26, Sinker Industries received a special order request for 120 ten-foot aluminum fishing boats. Operating on a fiscal year ending May 31, the company already has orders that will allow it to produce at budget levels for the period. However, extra capacity exists to produce the 120 additional boats.

The terms of the special order call for a selling price of $675 per boat, and the customer will pay all shipping costs. No sales personnel were involved in soliciting the order.

The ten-foot fishing boat has the following cost estimates: direct materials, aluminum, two 4′ × 8′ sheets at $155 per sheet; direct labor, 14 hours at $15.00 per hour; variable overhead, $7.25 per direct labor hour; fixed overhead, $4.50 per direct labor hour; variable selling expenses, $46.50 per boat; and variable shipping expenses, $57.50 per boat.

Required

1. Prepare an analysis for the management of Sinker Industries to use in deciding whether to accept or reject the special order. What decision should be made?
2. To make an $8,000 profit on this order, what would be the lowest possible price that Sinker Industries could charge per boat?

LO4 Segment Profitability Decision

P 3. Sports, Inc., is a nationwide distributor of sporting equipment. The corporate president, Wesley Coldwell, is dissatisfied with corporate operating results, particularly those of the Spring Branch, and has asked the controller for more information. The controller prepared the following segmented income statement (in thousands of dollars) for the Spring Branch:

Sports, Inc., Spring Branch
Segmented Income Statement
For the Year Ended December 31
(Amounts in Thousands)

	Football Line	Baseball Line	Basketball Line	Spring Branch
Sales	$3,500	$2,500	$2,059	$8,059
Less variable costs	2,900	2,395	1,800	7,095
Contribution margin	$ 600	$ 105	$ 259	$ 964
Less direct fixed costs	300	150	159	609
Segment margin	$ 300	($ 45)	$ 100	$ 355
Less common fixed costs				450
Operating income (loss)				($ 95)

Coldwell is considering adding a new product line, Kite Surfing. The controller estimates that adding this line to the Spring Branch will increase sales by $300,000, variable costs by $150,000, and direct fixed costs by $20,000. The new product line will have no effect on common fixed costs.

Required

1. How will operating income be affected if the Baseball line is dropped?
2. How will operating income be affected if the Baseball line is kept and a Kite Surfing line is added?

3. If the Baseball line is dropped and the Kite Surfing line is added, sales of the Football line will decrease by 10 percent and sales of the Basketball line will decrease by 5 percent. How will those changes affect operating income?

Manager insight ▶ 4. What decision do you recommend? Explain.

LO5 Sales Mix Decision

P 4. Management at Generic Chemical Company is evaluating its product mix in an attempt to maximize profits. For the past two years, Generic has produced four products, and all have large markets in which to expand market share. Heinz Bexer, Generic's controller, has gathered data from current operations and wants you to analyze them for him. Sales and operating data are as follows:

	Product AZ1	Product BY7	Product CX5	Product DW9
Variable production costs	$71,000	$91,000	$91,920	$97,440
Variable selling costs	$10,200	$5,400	$12,480	$30,160
Fixed production costs	$20,400	$21,600	$29,120	$18,480
Fixed administrative costs	$3,400	$5,400	$6,240	$10,080
Total sales	$122,000	$136,000	$156,400	$161,200
Units produced and sold	85,000	45,000	26,000	14,000
Machine hours used*	17,000	18,000	20,800	16,800

*Generic's scarce resource, machine hours, is being used to full capacity.

Required

1. Compute the machine hours needed to produce one unit of each product.
2. Determine the contribution margin per machine hour for each product.
3. Which product line(s) should be targeted for market share expansion?

LO6 Sell or Process-Further Decision

P 5. Bagels, Inc., produces and sells 20 types of bagels by the dozen. Bagels are priced at $6.00 per dozen (or $0.50 each) and cost $0.20 per unit to produce. The company is considering further processing the bagels into two products: bagels with cream cheese and bagel sandwiches. It would cost an additional $0.50 per unit to produce bagels with cream cheese, and the new selling price would be $2.50 each. It would cost an additional $1.00 per sandwich to produce bagel sandwiches, and the new selling price would be $3.50 each.

Required

1. Identify the relevant per unit costs and revenues for the alternatives. Are there any sunk costs?
2. Based on the information in requirement **1**, should Bagels, Inc., expand its product offerings?
3. Suppose that Bagels, Inc., did expand its product line to include bagels with cream cheese and bagel sandwiches. Based on customer feedback, the company determined that it could further process those two products into bagels with cream cheese and fruit and bagel sandwiches with cheese. The company's accountant compiled the following information:

Product (per unit)	Sales Revenue if Sold with No Further Processing	Sales Revenue if Processed Further	Additional Processing Costs
Bagels with cream cheese	$2.50	$3.50	Fruit: $1.00
Bagel sandwiches	$3.50	$4.50	Cheese: $0.50

Perform an incremental analysis to determine if Bagels, Inc., should process its products further. Explain your findings.

Alternate Problems

LO2 Outsourcing Decision

P 6. Three Brothers Restaurant purchases cheesecakes and offers them as dessert items on its menu. The cheesecakes cost $24 each, and a cake contains 8 pieces. The supplier recently gave advance notice that the price will rise by 20 percent immediately. Three Brothers Restaurant has idle equipment that with only a few minor changes could be used to produce similar cheesecakes.

Cost estimates have been prepared under the assumption that the company could make the product itself. Direct materials would cost $7.00 per cheesecake. Direct labor required would be 0.5 hour per cheesecake at a labor rate of $24.00 per hour. Variable overhead would be $9.00 per cheesecake. Fixed overhead, which would be incurred under either decision alternative, would be $35,200 a year for depreciation and $230,000 a year for other costs. Production and usage are estimated at 3,600 cheesecakes a year. (Assume that any idle equipment cannot be used for any other purpose.)

Required

1. Prepare an incremental analysis to determine whether the cheesecakes should be made within the company or purchased from the outside supplier at the higher price.
2. Compute the variable unit cost to (a) make one cheesecake and (b) buy one cheesecake.

LO3 Special Order Decision

P 7. Keystone Resorts, Ltd., has approached Crystal Printers, Inc., with a special order to produce 300,000 two-page brochures. Most of Crystal's work consists of recurring short-run orders. Keystone Resorts is offering a one-time order, and Crystal has the capacity to handle the order over a two-month period.

The management of Keystone Resorts has stated that the company would be unwilling to pay more than $48 per 1,000 brochures. Crystal Printers' controller assembled the following cost data for this decision analysis: Direct materials (paper) would be $26.80 per 1,000 brochures; direct labor costs would be $6.80 per 1,000 brochures; direct materials (ink) would be $4.40 per 1,000 brochures; variable production overhead would be $6.20 per 1,000 brochures; machine maintenance (fixed cost) is $1.00 per direct labor dollar. Other fixed production overhead amounts to $2.40 per direct labor dollar. Variable packing costs would be $4.30 per 1,000 brochures. Also, the share of general and administrative expenses (fixed costs) to be allocated would be $5.25 per direct labor dollar.

Required

1. Prepare an analysis for Crystal Printers' management to use in deciding whether to accept or reject Keystone Resorts' offer. What decision should be made?
2. What is the lowest possible price Crystal Printers can charge per thousand and still make a $6,000 profit on the order?

LO4 Decision to Eliminate an Unprofitable Product

P 8. Seven months ago, Naib Publishing Company published its first book (Book N). Since then, Naib has added four more books to its product list (Books S, Q, X, and H). Management is considering proposals for three more new books, but editorial capacity limits the company to producing only seven books annually. Before deciding which of the proposed books to publish, management wants you to evaluate the performance of its existing book list. Recent revenue and cost data are as follows:

Naib Publishing Company
Product Profit and Loss Summary
For the Year Ended December 31

	Book N	Book S	Book Q	Book X	Book H	Company Totals
Sales	$813,800	$782,000	$634,200	$944,100	$707,000	$3,881,100
Less variable costs						
Materials and binding	$325,520	$312,800	$190,260	$283,230	$212,100	$1,323,910
Editorial services	71,380	88,200	73,420	57,205	80,700	370,905
Author royalties	130,208	125,120	101,472	151,056	113,120	620,976
Sales commissions	162,760	156,400	95,130	141,615	141,400	697,305
Other selling costs	50,682	44,740	21,708	18,334	60,700	196,164
Total variable costs	$740,550	$727,260	$481,990	$651,440	$608,020	$3,209,260
Contribution margin	$ 73,250	$ 54,740	$152,210	$292,660	$ 98,980	$ 671,840
Less total fixed costs	97,250	81,240	89,610	100,460	82,680	451,240
Operating income loss	($ 24,000)	($ 26,500)	$ 62,600	$192,200	$ 16,300	$ 220,600
Direct fixed costs included in total fixed costs above	$ 51,200	$ 65,100	$ 49,400	$ 69,100	$ 58,800	$ 293,600

Projected data for the three proposed new books are: Book P, sales, $450,000, contribution margin, $45,000; Book T, sales, $725,000, contribution margin, ($25,200); and Book R, sales, $913,200, contribution margin, $115,500. Projected direct fixed costs are: Book P, $5,000; Book T, $6,000; Book R, $40,000.

Required

1. Analyze the performance of the five books that the company is currently publishing.
2. Should Naib Publishing Company eliminate any of its present products? If so, which one(s)?
3. Identify the new books you would use to replace those eliminated. Justify your answer.

LO5 Sales Mix Decision

P 9. Dr. Massy, who specializes in internal medicine, wants to analyze his sales mix to find out how the time of his physician assistant, Consuela Ortiz, can be used to generate the highest operating income.

Ortiz sees patients in Dr. Massy's office, consults with patients over the telephone, and conducts one daily weight-loss support group attended by up to 50 patients. Statistics for the three services are as follows:

	Office Visits	Phone Calls	Weight-Loss Support Group
Maximum number of patient billings per day	20	40	50
Hours per billing	0.25	0.10	1.0
Billing rate	$50	$25	$10
Variable costs	$25	$12	$5

Ortiz works seven hours a day.

Required

1. Determine the best sales mix. Rank the services offered in order of their profitability.
2. Based on the ranking in requirement **1,** how much time should Ortiz spend on each service in a day? (**Hint:** Remember to consider the maximum number of patient billings per day.) What would be the daily total contribution margin generated by Ortiz?
3. Dr. Massy believes the ranking is incorrect. He knows that the daily 60-minute meeting of the weight-loss support group has 50 patients and should continue to be offered. If the new ranking for the services is (1) weight-loss support group, (2) phone calls, and (3) office visits, how much time should Ortiz spend on each service in a day? What would be the total contribution margin generated by Ortiz, assuming the weight-loss support group has the maximum number of patient billings?

Manager insight ▶ 4. Which ranking would you recommend? What additional amount of total contribution margin would be generated if your recommendation were to be accepted?

LO6 **Sell or Process-Further Decision**

P 10. Marketeers, Inc., developed a promotional program for a large shopping center in Sunset Living, Arizona, a few years ago. Having invested $360,000 in developing the original promotion campaign, the firm is ready to present its client with an add-on contract offer that includes the original promotion areas of (1) a TV advertising campaign, (2) a series of brochures for mass mailing, and (3) a special rotating BIG SALE schedule for 10 of the 28 tenants in the shopping center. Presented below are the revenue terms from the original contract with the shopping center and the offer for the add-on contract, which extends the original contract terms.

	Original Contract Terms	Extended Contract Including Add-On Terms
TV advertising campaign	$520,000	$ 580,000
Brochure series	210,000	230,000
Rotating BIG SALE schedule	170,000	190,000
Totals	$900,000	$1,000,000

Marketeers, Inc., estimates that the following additional costs will be incurred by extending the contract:

	TV Campaign	Brochures	BIG SALE Schedule
Direct labor	$30,000	$ 9,000	$7,000
Variable overhead costs	22,000	14,000	6,000
Fixed overhead costs*	12,000	4,000	2,000

*80 percent are direct fixed costs applied to this contract.

Required

1. Compute the costs that will be incurred for each part of the add-on portion of the contract.

Manager insight ▶ 2. Should Marketeers, Inc., offer the add-on contract, or should it ask for a final settlement check based on the original contract only? Defend your answer.

Manager insight ▶ 3. If management of the shopping center indicates that the terms of the add-on contract are negotiable, how should Marketeers, Inc., respond?

ENHANCING Your Knowledge, Skills, and Critical Thinking

LO1 **Management Decision Process**

C 1. Two weeks ago, your cousin Edna moved from New York City to Houston. She needs a car to drive to work and to run errands, but she has no experience in selecting a car and has asked for your help. Using the management process presented in this chapter, write her a letter explaining how she can approach making this decision.

How would your response change if the president of your company asked you to help make a decision about acquiring a fleet of cars for use by the sales personnel?

LO2 **Identification of Sunk Costs and Opportunity Costs**

C 2. Motorola, Inc., originated a $5 billion project, called Iridium, that launched 66 low-earth-orbit satellites for global communication using pagers and mobile phones. After its operations began, the Iridium Project had technical and marketing problems. Instead of the 600,000 subscribers it was expected to have, it had only 55,000. A basic problem with the system was that a subscriber had to buy a mobile phone that cost $3,000 and weighed more than 1 pound. Few potential users wanted to do this. As a result, Iridium had to file for bankruptcy. Motorola, which had an 18 percent ownership of Iridium, had invested $1.6 billion and had to decide if it was willing to invest more in an effort to save the project. Some investors wanted to see Motorola cut its losses and move on. Others were concerned about recouping the enormous expenditure that had already been made.[4]

What are sunk costs, and how do they differ from opportunity costs? How do these concepts apply to the decision by Motorola's management to continue or discontinue support for the Iridium Project?

LO1 **Defining and Identifying Relevant Information**

C 3. Bob's Burgers is in the fast-food restaurant business. One component of its marketing strategy is to increase sales by expanding in foreign markets. It uses both financial and nonfinancial quantitative and qualitative information when deciding whether to open restaurants abroad. Bob's decided to open a restaurant in Prague (Czech Republic) five years ago. The following information helped the managers in making that decision:

Financial Quantitative Information

Operating information

- Estimated food, labor, and other operating costs (e.g., taxes, insurance, utilities, and supplies)
- Estimated selling price for each food item

Capital investment information

- Cost of land, building, equipment, and furniture
- Financing options and amounts

Nonfinancial Quantitative Information

Estimated daily number of customers, hamburgers to be sold, employees to work

High-traffic time periods

Income of people living in the area

Ratio of population to number of restaurants in the market area

Traffic counts in front of similar restaurants in the area

Qualitative Information

Government regulations, taxes, duties, tariffs, political involvement in business operations
Property ownership restrictions
Site visibility
Accessibility of store location
Training process for local managers
Hiring process for employees
Local customs and practices

Bob's Burgers has hired you as a consultant and given you an income statement comparing the operating incomes of its five restaurants in Eastern Europe. You have noticed that the Prague location is operating at a loss (including unallocated fixed costs) and must decide whether to recommend closing that restaurant.

Review the information used in making the decision to open the restaurant. Identify the types of information that would also be relevant in deciding whether to close the restaurant. What period or periods of time should be reviewed in making your decision? What additional information would be relevant in making your decision?

LO1 Identifying Relevant Decision Information

C 4. Select two destinations for a one-week vacation, and gather information about them from brochures, magazines, travel agents, the Internet, and friends. Then list the relevant quantitative and qualitative information in order of its importance to your decision. Analyze the information, and select a destination.

Which factors were most important to your decision? Why? Which were least important? Why? How would the process of identifying relevant information differ if the president of your company asked you to prepare a budget for the next training meeting, to be held at a location of your choice?

Your instructor will divide the class into groups and ask each group to discuss this case. One student from each group will summarize his or her group's findings and debrief the entire class.

LO2 Ethics of a Make-or-Buy Decision

C 5. Tilly Issac is the assistant controller for Tagwell Corporation, a leading producer of home appliances. Her friend Zack Marsh is the supervisor of the firm's Cookware Department. Marsh has the authority to decide whether parts are purchased from outside vendors or manufactured in his department. Issac recently conducted an internal audit of the parts being manufactured in the Cookware Department, including a comparison of the prices currently charged by vendors for similar parts. She found more than a dozen parts that could be purchased for less than they cost the company to produce. When she approached Marsh about the situation, he replied that if those parts were purchased from outside vendors, two automated machines would be idle for several hours a week. Increased machine idle time would have a negative effect on his performance evaluation and could reduce his yearly bonus. He reminded Issac that he was in charge of the decision to make or purchase those parts and asked her not to pursue the matter any further.

What should Issac do in this situation? Discuss her options.

LO3 Special Order Decision

C 6. Metallica Can Opener Company is a subsidiary of Maltz Appliances, Inc. The can opener that Metallica produces is in strong demand. Sales this year are expected to be 1,000,000 units. Full plant capacity is 1,150,000 units, but 1,000,000 units are considered normal capacity for the current year. The following unit price and cost breakdown is applicable:

	Per Unit
Sales price	$22.50
Less manufacturing costs	
Direct materials	$ 6.00
Direct labor	2.50
Overhead, variable	3.50
Overhead, fixed	1.50
Total manufacturing costs	$13.50
Gross margin	$ 9.00
Less selling and administrative expenses	
Selling, variable	$ 1.50
Selling, fixed	1.00
Administrative, fixed	1.25
Packaging, variable*	0.75
Total selling and administrative expenses	$ 4.50
Operating income	$ 4.50

*Three types of packaging are available: deluxe, $0.75 per unit; plain, $0.50 per unit; and bulk pack, $0.25 per unit.

During November, the company received three requests for special orders from large chain-store companies. Those orders are not part of the budgeted 1,000,000 units for this year, but company officials think that sufficient capacity exists for one order to be accepted. Orders received and their terms are as follows: Order 1, 75,000 can openers @ $20.00 per unit, deluxe packaging; Order 2, 90,000 can openers @ $18.00 per unit, plain packaging; Order 3, 125,000 can openers @ $15.75 per unit, bulk packaging.

Because the orders were placed directly with company officials, no variable selling costs will be incurred.

1. Analyze the profitability of each of the three special orders.
2. Which special order should be accepted?

LO4 Decision to Add a New Department

C 7. Management at Transco Company is considering a proposal to install a third production department in its factory building. With the company's existing production setup, direct materials are processed through the Mixing Department to produce Materials A and B in equal proportions. The Shaping Department then processes Material A to yield Product C. Material B is sold as is at $20.25 per pound. Product C has a selling price of $100.00 per pound. There is a proposal to add a Baking Department to process Material B into Product D. It is expected that any quantity of Product D can be sold for $30.00 per pound.

Costs per pound under this proposal appear at the top of the next page.

1. If (a) sales and production levels are expected to remain constant in the foreseeable future and (b) there are no foreseeable alternative uses for the factory space, should Transco Company add a Baking Department and produce Product D, if 100,000 pounds of D can be sold? Show calculations of incremental revenues and costs to support your answer.

	Mixing Department (Materials A and B)	Shaping Department (Product C)	Baking Department (Product D)
Costs from Mixing Department	—	$52.80	$13.20
Direct materials	$20.00	—	—
Direct labor	6.00	9.00	3.50
Variable overhead	4.00	8.00	4.00
Fixed overhead			
Traceable (direct, avoidable)	2.25	2.25	1.80
Allocated (common, unavoidable)	0.75	0.75	0.75
	$33.00	$72.80	$23.25

2. List at least two qualitative reasons why Transco Company may not want to install a Baking Department and produce Product D, even if this decision appears profitable.
3. List at least two qualitative reasons why Transco Company may want to install a Baking Department and produce Product D, even if it appears that this decision is unprofitable. (CMA adapted)

LO3 LO4 LO6 **Cookie Company (Continuing Case)**

C 8. As the CEO of your cookie company, you are interested in how public companies with a segment that includes cookies report their operating results. Because public companies are required to report on their segments, it is possible to evaluate the performance of comparable segments of different companies.

Access the website of **Kraft Foods, Inc.**, which markets Nabisco cookies (www.kraftfoodscompany.com/About), and the website of **Kellogg Company**, which markets Keebler cookies (www2.kelloggs.com). Find information about these companies' major segments. Which segments are comparable, and which are not comparable? Which segments of these companies do you think include their brand of cookies?

CHAPTER 28

Capital Investment Analysis

The Management Process

PLAN

- Carry out capital investment process:
  1. Identify capital investment needs
  2. Prepare formal requests for capital investments
  3. Perform preliminary screening of proposals
  4. Establish the acceptance-rejection standard based on cost of capital
  5. Evaluate proposals
  6. Make decisions based on dollars available for capital investments

PERFORM

- Implement capital investment decisions with proper controls

EVALUATE

- Compare actual results with budget projections
- Conduct postcompletion audit to determine if outcomes were achieved

COMMUNICATE

- Prepare reports related to capital investment process

When deciding when and how much to spend on expensive, long-term projects, such as the construction of a new building or the installation of a new production system, managers apply capital investment analysis to ensure that they use resources wisely and that their choices make the maximum contribution to future profits. This chapter explains the net present value method and other methods of capital investment analysis that managers use when making decisions about long-term capital investments.

LEARNING OBJECTIVES

LO1 **Define *capital investment analysis*, state the purpose of the minimum rate of return, and identify the methods used to arrive at that rate.** (pp. 1226–1231)

LO2 **Identify the types of projected costs and revenues used to evaluate alternatives for capital investment.** (pp. 1231–1234)

LO3 **Apply the concept of the time value of money.** (pp. 1234–1238)

LO4 **Analyze capital investment proposals using the net present value method.** (pp. 1238–1240)

LO5 **Analyze capital investment proposals using the payback period method and the accounting rate-of-return method.** (pp. 1241–1244)

DECISION POINT ► A MANAGER'S FOCUS NEIGHBORHOOD COMMUNICATIONS

Neighborhood Communications provides cell phone service in a small tri-state area. What makes the company competitive is its use of a "lights-out" system—that is, an automated system in which unattended operations are remotely controlled. At Neighborhood Communications, regional operators monitor several cell phone towers from a computer at their homes. If a problem occurs at a tower, the operator can repair it remotely. Only in rare instances does a repair require that an operator visit a tower. The system thus minimizes on-site labor.

Neighborhood Communications is not alone in turning on-site labor's lights off. Using systems that link machines to the Internet so that managers can monitor operations at any time and from anywhere is common in industries that produce identical products in high volume. Automated systems of this kind are expensive, and managers must carefully weigh the risks involved in investing in them.

- ► Why are capital investment decisions critical for a company like Neighborhood Communications?
- ► In evaluating capital investment alternatives, how can managers at Neighborhood Communications ensure a wise allocation of resources and minimize the risks involved in capital investments?

The Capital Investment Process

LO1 Define *capital investment analysis*, state the purpose of the minimum rate of return, and identify the methods used to arrive at that rate.

Among the most significant decisions that management must make are **capital investment decisions**, which are decisions about when and how much to spend on capital facilities and other long-term projects. Capital facilities and projects may include machinery, systems, or processes; new buildings or additions or renovations to existing buildings; entire new divisions or product lines; and distribution and software systems. For example, Neighborhood Communications, the company featured in the Decision Point, will make decisions about installing new equipment, replacing old equipment, expanding service by renovating or adding to existing equipment, buying a building, or acquiring another company.

Capital facilities and projects are expensive. A new production system may cost millions of dollars and require several years to complete. Managers must make capital investment decisions carefully so that they select the alternatives that will contribute the most to future profits.

Capital Investment Analysis

Capital investment analysis, or *capital budgeting*, is the process of making decisions about capital investments. It consists of identifying the need for a capital investment, analyzing courses of action to meet that need, preparing reports for managers, choosing the best alternative, and allocating funds among competing needs. Every part of the organization participates in this process.

> **Study Note**
> Capital investment analysis is a decision process for the purchase of capital facilities, such as buildings and equipment.

- Financial analysts supply a target cost of capital or desired rate of return and an estimate of how much money can be spent annually on capital facilities.
- Marketing specialists predict sales trends and new product demands, which help in determining which operations need expansion or new equipment.
- Managers at all levels help identify facility needs and often prepare preliminary cost estimates for the desired capital investment.
- All then work together to implement the project selected and to keep the results within revenue and cost estimates.

The capital investment process involves the evaluation of alternative proposals for large capital investments, including considerations for financing the projects. Capital investment analyses affect both short-term and long-term planning. Figure 28-1 illustrates the time span of the capital expenditure planning process. Most companies have a long-term plan—that is, a projection of operations for the next five or ten years. Large capital investments should be an integral part of that plan. Anticipated additions or changes to product lines, replacements of equipment, and acquisitions of other companies are examples of items to be included in long-term capital investment plans.

Capital Budgets and Master Budgets One element of budgeting is a capital investment budget. The capital investment budget fits into both the long-term planning process and the capital investment process. Long-term plans are not very specific; they are expressed in broad, goal-oriented terms. Each annual budget must help accomplish the organization's long-term goals. Look again at Figure 28-1. Suppose that in 2015 Neighborhood Communications plans to purchase a large, special-purpose machine.

- When the ten-year capital budget plan was developed, it included only a broad statement about a plan to purchase the machine. Nothing was specified about the cost of the machine or the anticipated operating details and costs.

FIGURE 28-1
Time Span of the Capital Investment Planning Process

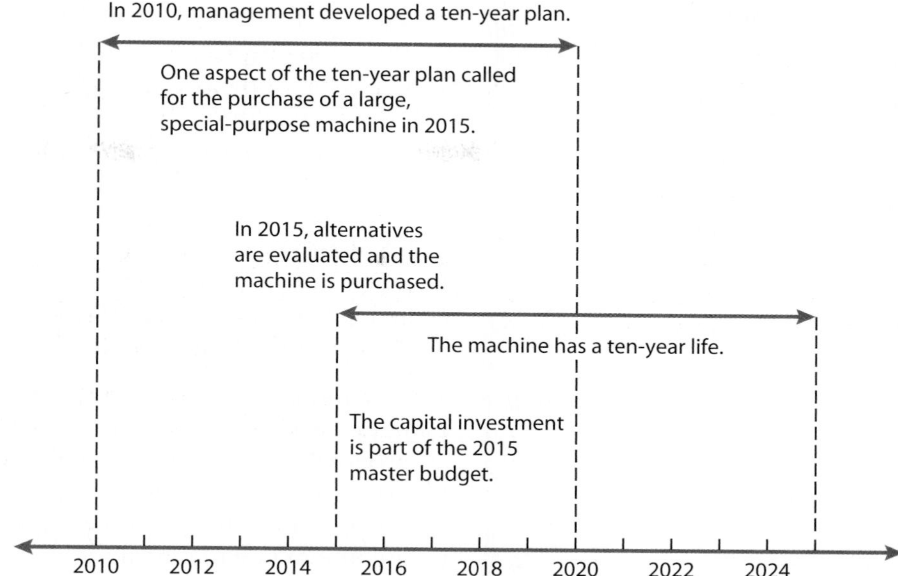

- Those details are contained in the annual master budget for 2015, and it is in 2015 that the capital investment analysis will occur.

So, although capital investment decisions that will affect the company for many years are discussed and estimates of future revenues and expenditures are made when the long-term plan is first developed, the capital investment analysis is performed in the period in which the expenditure will be made. This point is important to the understanding of capital investment analysis.

Capital Investment Analysis in the Management Process

Managers pay close attention to capital investments throughout the management process, as shown at the beginning of the chapter. However, the greatest portion of capital investment analysis takes place when they plan. Each decision made about a capital investment is vitally important because it involves a large amount of money and commits a company to a course of action for years to come. For example, Neighborhood Communications must make capital investment decisions that fit into its strategic plans. A series of poor decisions about capital investments can cause a company to fail.

To ensure high-quality capital investment decisions, managers follow six key steps when they plan.

> **Study Note**
> The six steps of capital investment analysis are performed for both long-term and short-term planning purposes.

Step 1. ***Identification of Capital Investment Needs*** Identifying the need for a new capital investment is the starting point of capital investment analysis. Managers identify capital investment opportunities from past sales experience, changes in sources and quality of materials, employees' suggestions, production bottlenecks caused by obsolete equipment, new production or distribution methods, or customer complaints. In addition, capital investment needs are identified through proposals to:

- Add new products to the product line.
- Expand capacity in existing product lines.

- Reduce production costs of existing products without altering operating levels.
- Automate existing production processes.

Step 2. ***Formal Requests for Capital Investments*** To enhance control over capital investments, managers prepare formal requests for new capital investments. Each request includes a complete description of the investment under review; the reasons a new investment is needed; the alternative means of satisfying the need; the timing, estimated costs, and related cost savings of each alternative; and the investment's engineering specifications, if necessary.

Step 3. ***Preliminary Screening*** Organizations that have several branches and a highly developed system for capital investment analysis require that all proposals go through preliminary screening. The purpose of preliminary screening is to ensure that the only proposals to receive serious review are those that both meet company strategic goals and produce the minimum rate of return set by management.

Step 4. ***Establishment of the Acceptance-Rejection Standard*** To attract and maintain funding for capital investments, an organization establishes an acceptance-rejection standard. Such a standard may be expressed as a minimum rate of return or a minimum cash flow payback period. If the number of acceptable requests for capital investments exceeds the funds available for such investments, the proposals must be ranked according to their rates of return. Acceptance-rejection standards are used to identify projects that are expected to yield inadequate or marginal returns. They also identify proposed projects for which high product demand and high financial returns are expected. Cost of capital information is often used to establish minimum rates of return on investments. The development of such rates is discussed later in this chapter.

Step 5. ***Evaluation of Proposals*** Proposals are evaluated by verifying decision variables and applying established proposal evaluation methods. The key decision variables are (1) expected life, (2) estimated cash flow, and (3) investment cost. Each variable in a proposal should be checked for accuracy. Three commonly used methods of evaluating proposed capital investments are:

- Net present value method
- Payback period method
- Accounting rate-of-return method

Using one or more evaluation methods and the minimum acceptance-rejection standard, management evaluates all proposals. In addition to this quantitative analysis, management will also consider qualitative factors, such as availability and training of employees, competition, anticipated future technological improvements, and the proposal's impact on other company operations.

Step 6. ***Capital Investment Decisions*** The proposals that meet the standards of the evaluation process are given to the appropriate manager for final review. When deciding which requests to implement, the manager must consider the funds available for capital investments. The acceptable proposals are ranked in order of net present value, payback period, or rate of return, and the highest-ranking proposals are funded first. Often there will not be enough money to fund all proposals. The final capital investment budget is then prepared by allocating funds to the selected proposals.

The Minimum Rate of Return on Investment

Most companies set a minimum rate of return, and any capital expenditure proposal that fails to produce that rate of return is automatically refused. The minimum rate of return is often referred to as a *hurdle rate* because it is the rate that must be exceeded, or hurdled. If none of the capital investment requests is expected to meet or exceed the minimum rate of return, or hurdle rate, all requests will be turned down.

Organizations set a minimum rate of return to guard their profitability. If the return from a capital investment falls below the minimum rate of return, the funds can be used more profitably in another part of the organization. Projects that produce poor returns will ultimately have a negative effect on an organization's profitability.

Cost of Capital

> **Study Note**
> Depending on the mixture of sources of capital, a company's cost of capital will vary.

Determining a minimum rate of return is not a simple task. The most widely used measure is the cost of capital. The **cost of capital** is the weighted-average rate of return that a company must pay to its long-term creditors and shareholders for the use of their funds. The components of cost of capital are the cost of debt, the cost of preferred stock, the cost of common stock, and the cost of retained earnings. Sophisticated methods may be used to determine these costs. However, in this discussion, we use a simplified definition of each cost:

- The cost of debt is the after-tax interest on the debt (interest times 1 minus the tax rate). The after-tax amount is used because the interest is tax-deductible.
- The cost of preferred stock is the full dividend rate because dividends are not tax-deductible.
- The cost of equity capital (common stock and retained earnings) is the return required by investors in the company.

Cost of Capital Calculation The cost of capital is computed in four steps:

1. Identify the cost of each source of capital.
2. Compute the proportion (percentage) of the organization's total amount of debt and equity that each source of capital represents.

FOCUS ON BUSINESS PRACTICE

Why Look Beyond the Cost of a Capital Investment?

Cost should not be the only factor when making a capital investment decision. International trade and logistics can also be very important, as **Koss Corporation**, a maker of high-fidelity headphones that is located in Milwaukee, Wisconsin, learned when it moved much of its production to China, where costs were low. However, that caused a problem with making timely deliveries to customers. The just-in-time inventory philosophy was abandoned to avoid customer backorders and dissatisfaction. Now, finished products are stacked in the Milwaukee factory to ensure against dockworker strikes and missed deliveries. Looking beyond the numbers is thus an important consideration in capital investment decisions.[1]

3. Multiply each source's cost by its proportion of the capital.
4. Total the weighted costs computed in Step 3.

For example, suppose Neighborhood Communications' financing structure is as follows:

Cost of Capital	*Source of Capital*	*Amount*	*Proportion of Capital*
6%	Debt financing	$150,000	30%
8%	Preferred stock	50,000	10
12%	Common stock	200,000	40
12%	Retained earnings	100,000	20
	Totals	$500,000	100%

The cost of capital of 9.8 percent would be computed as follows:

Source of Capital	*Cost of Capital*	×	*Proportion of Capital*	=	*Weighted Cost*
Debt financing	0.06		0.30		0.018
Preferred stock	0.08		0.10		0.008
Common stock	0.12		0.40		0.048
Retained earnings	0.12		0.20		0.024
Cost of capital					0.098

Other Measures for Determining Minimum Rate of Return

If cost of capital information is unavailable, management can use one of three less accurate but still useful amounts as the minimum rate of return.

- The first is the average total corporate return on investment. This measure is based on the notion that any capital investment that produces a lower return than the rate that the company has earned historically will negatively affect investors' perception of the firm's future market value.
- A second method is to use the industry's average cost of capital. Most sizable industry associations supply such information.
- As a last resort, a company might use the current bank lending rate. But because most companies are financed by both debt and equity, the bank lending rate seldom reflects an accurate rate of return.

Ranking Capital Investment Proposals

The requests for capital investments that a company receives usually exceed the funds available for capital investments. Even after management evaluates and selects proposals under the minimum acceptance-rejection standard, there are often too many proposals to fund adequately. At that point, managers must rank the proposals according to their rates of return, or profitability, and begin a second selection process.

Suppose that Neighborhood Communications has $4,500,000 to spend this year for capital improvements and that five acceptable proposals are competing for those funds. The company's current minimum rate of return is 18 percent, and it is considering the following proposals:

Project	*Rate of Return*	*Capital Investment*	*Cumulative Investment*
A	32%	$1,460,000	$1,460,000
B	30%	1,890,000	3,350,000
C	28%	460,000	3,810,000
D	24%	840,000	4,650,000
E	22%	580,000	5,230,000
Total		$5,230,000	

The proposals are listed in the order of their rates of return. As you can see, Projects A, B, and C have the highest rates of return and together will cost a total of $3,810,000. That leaves $690,000 in capital funds for other projects. Project D should be examined first to see if it could be implemented for $150,000 less. If not, then Project E should be selected. The selection of Projects A, B, C, and E means that $110,000 in capital funds will be uncommitted for the year.

& APPLY >

Sample Industries is considering investing $20 million in a plant expansion. Management needs to know the average cost of capital to use in evaluating this capital investment decision. The company's capital structure consists of $2,000,000 of debt at 6 percent interest and $3,000,000 of stockholders' equity at 2 percent. What is Sample Industries' average cost of capital?

SOLUTION

The company's average cost of capital is 3.6 percent, which is computed as follows:

Source of Capital	Amount	Proportion of Capital		Cost of Capital		Weighted Cost
Debt	$2,000,000	40%	×	6%	=	0.024
Equity	3,000,000	60	×	2%	=	0.012
Total	$5,000,000	100%				0.036

Measures Used in Capital Investment Analysis

LO2 Identify the types of projected costs and revenues used to evaluate alternatives for capital investment.

When evaluating a proposed capital investment, managers must predict how the new asset will perform and how it will benefit the company. Various measures are used to estimate the benefits to be derived from a capital investment.

Expected Benefits from a Capital Investment

Each capital investment analysis must include a measure of the expected benefit from the investment project. The measure of expected benefit depends on the method of analyzing capital investment alternatives.

Net Income One possible measure is net income, calculated in the usual way. Managers determine increases in net income resulting from the capital investment for each alternative.

Net Cash Flows and Cost Savings A more widely used measure of expected benefit is projected cash flows. **Net cash inflows** are the balance of increases in projected cash receipts over increases in projected cash payments resulting from a capital investment. In some cases, equipment replacement decisions involve situations in which revenues are the same among alternatives. In such cases, **cost savings** measure the benefits, such as reduced costs, from proposed capital investments. Either net cash inflows or cost savings can be used as the basis for an evaluation, but the two measures should not be confused.

- If the analysis involves cash receipts, net cash inflows are used.
- If the analysis involves only cash outlays, cost savings are used.

Managers must measure and evaluate all the investment alternatives consistently.

Equal Versus Unequal Cash Flows

Projected cash flows may be the same for each year of an asset's life, or they may vary from year to year. Unequal annual cash flows are common and must be analyzed for each year of an asset's life. Proposed projects with equal annual cash flows require less detailed analysis. Both a project with equal cash flows and one with unequal cash flows are illustrated and explained later in this chapter.

Carrying Value of Assets

Carrying value is the undepreciated portion of the original cost of a fixed asset—that is, the asset's cost less its accumulated depreciation. Carrying value is also referred to as *book value*. When a decision to replace an asset is being evaluated, the carrying value of the old asset is irrelevant because it is a past, or historical, cost and will not be altered by the decision. Net proceeds from the asset's sale or disposal are relevant, however, because the proceeds affect cash flows and may differ for each alternative.

Depreciation Expense and Income Taxes

The techniques of capital investment analysis discussed in this chapter compare the relative benefits of proposed capital investments by measuring the cash receipts and payments for a facility or project. Income taxes alter the amount and timing of cash flows of projects under consideration by for-profit companies. To assess the benefits of a capital project, a company must include the effects of taxes in its capital investment analyses. Corporate income tax rates vary and can change yearly. Depreciation expense is deductible when determining income taxes. (You may recall that the annual depreciation expense computation using the straight-line method is the asset's cost less its residual value, divided by the asset's useful life.) Thus, depreciation expense strongly influences the amount of income taxes that a company pays and can lead to significant tax savings.

To examine how taxes affect capital investment analysis, assume that Neighborhood Communications has a tax rate of 30 percent on taxable income. It is considering a capital project that will make the following annual contribution to operating income:

Cash revenues	$ 400,000
Cash expenses	(200,000)
Depreciation	(100,000)
Operating income before income taxes	$ 100,000
Income taxes at 30%	(30,000)
Operating income	$ 70,000

The net cash inflows for this project can be determined in either of two ways:

1. Net cash inflows—receipts and disbursements

Revenues (cash inflows)	$ 400,000
Cash expenses (outflows)	(200,000)
Income taxes (outflows)	(30,000)
Net cash inflows	$ 170,000

2. Net cash inflows—income adjustment procedure

Income after income taxes	$ 70,000
Add back noncash expenses (depreciation)	100,000
Less noncash revenues	—
Net cash inflows	$ 170,000

In both computations, the net cash inflows are $170,000, and the total effect of income taxes is to lower the net cash inflows by $30,000.

Disposal or Residual Values

Proceeds from the sale of an old asset are current cash inflows and are relevant to evaluating a proposed capital investment. Projected disposal or residual values of replacement equipment are also relevant because they represent future cash inflows and usually differ among alternatives. Remember that the residual value, sometimes called the *disposal* or *salvage value*, of an asset will be received at the end of the asset's estimated life.

STOP & APPLY >

Sample Company has a tax rate of 25 percent on taxable income. It is considering a capital project that will make the following annual contribution to operating income:

Cash revenues	$ 500,000
Cash expenses	(300,000)
Depreciation	(150,000)
Operating income before income taxes	$ 50,000
Income taxes at 25%	(12,500)
Operating income	$ 37,500

1. Determine the net cash inflows for this project in two different ways. Are net cash flows the same under either approach?
2. What is the impact of income taxes on net cash flows?

(continued)

SOLUTION

1. The net cash inflows for this project can be determined in two ways:

   a. Net cash inflows—receipts and disbursements

Revenues (cash inflows)	$ 500,000
Cash expenses (outflows)	(300,000)
Income taxes (outflows)	(12,500)
Net cash inflows	$ 187,500

   b. Net cash inflows—income adjustment procedure

Income after income taxes	$ 37,500
Add back noncash expenses (depreciation)	150,000
Less noncash revenues	—
Net cash inflows	$ 187,500

   In both computations, the net cash inflows are $187,500.

2. The total effect of income taxes is to lower the net cash inflows by $12,500.

The Time Value of Money

LO3 Apply the concept of the time value of money.

An organization has many options for investing capital besides buying plant assets. Consequently, management expects a plant asset to yield a reasonable return during its useful life. A key question in capital investment analysis is how to measure the return on a plant asset. One way is to look at the cash flows that the asset will generate during its useful life. When an asset has a long useful life, management will usually analyze those cash flows in terms of the time value of money. The **time value of money** is the concept that cash flows of equal dollar amounts separated by an interval of time have different present values because of the effect of compound interest. The notions of interest, present value, future value, and present value of an ordinary annuity are all related to the time value of money.

Interest

Study Note

Interest is a cost associated with the passage of time, whether or not there is a stated interest rate.

Interest is the cost associated with the use of money for a specific period of time. Because interest is a cost associated with time and "time is money," interest is an important consideration in any business decision.

- **Simple interest** is the interest cost for one or more periods when the amount on which the interest is computed stays the same from period to period.
- **Compound interest** is the interest cost for two or more periods when the amount on which interest is computed changes in each period to include all interest paid in previous periods. In other words, compound interest is interest earned on a principal sum that is increased at the end of each period by the interest for that period.

Example: Simple Interest You accept an 8 percent, $30,000 note due in 90 days. How much will you receive in total when the note comes due? The formula for calculating simple interest is as follows:

$$\begin{aligned}\text{Interest Expense} &= \text{Principal} \times \text{Rate} \times \text{Time}\\ &= \$30{,}000 \times 8/100 \times 90/360\\ &= \$600\end{aligned}$$

The total that you will receive is computed as follows:

$$
\begin{aligned}
\text{Total} &= \text{Principal} + \text{Interest} \\
&= \$30{,}000 + \$600 \\
&= \$30{,}600
\end{aligned}
$$

If the interest is paid and the note is renewed for an additional 90 days, the interest calculation will remain the same.

Example: Compound Interest You make a deposit of $5,000 in a savings account that pays 6 percent interest. You expect to leave the principal and accumulated interest in the account for three years. What will be your account total at the end of three years? Assume that the interest is paid at the end of the year, that the interest is added to the principal at that time, and that this total in turn earns interest.

The amount at the end of three years is computed as follows:

(1)	*(2)*	*(3)*	*(4)*
Year	*Principal Amount at Beginning of Year*	*Annual Amount of Interest (col. 2 × 0.06)*	*Accumulated Amount at End of Year (col. 2 + col. 3)*
1	$5,000.00	$300.00	$5,300.00
2	5,300.00	318.00	5,618.00
3	5,618.00	337.08	5,955.08

At the end of three years, you will have $5,955.08 in your savings account. Note that the annual amount of interest increases each year by the interest rate times the interest of the previous year. For example, between year 1 and year 2, the interest increased by $18 ($318 − $300), which exactly equals 6 percent times $300.

Present Value

Suppose that you had the choice of receiving $100 today or one year from today. Intuitively, you would choose to receive the $100 today. Why? You know that if you have the $100 today, you can put it in a savings account to earn interest, so that you will have more than $100 a year from today.

▶ Therefore, we can say that an amount to be received in the future (future value) is not worth as much today as the same amount to be received today (present value) because of the cost associated with the passage of time.

Future value and present value are closely related. **Future value** is the amount that an investment will be worth at a future date if it is invested today at compound interest. **Present value** is the amount that must be invested today at a given rate of compound interest to produce a given future value.

Assume Neighborhood Communications needs $1,000 one year from now. How much should it invest today to achieve that goal if the interest rate is 5 percent? The following equation can be used to answer that question:

$$
\begin{aligned}
\text{Present Value} \times (1.0 + \text{Interest Rate}) &= \text{Future Value} \\
\text{Present Value} \times 1.05 &= \$1{,}000.00 \\
\text{Present Value} &= \$1{,}000.00 \div 1.05 \\
\text{Present Value} &= \$952.38^{*}
\end{aligned}
$$

*Rounded.

Thus, to achieve a future value of $1,000.00, a present value of $952.38 must be invested. Interest of 5 percent on $952.38 for one year equals $47.62, and the two amounts added together equal $1,000.00.

Present Value of a Single Sum Due in the Future

When more than one time period is involved, the calculation of present value is more complicated.

Assume Neighborhood Communications wants to be sure of having $4,000 at the end of three years. How much must the company invest today in a 5 percent savings account to achieve that goal? By adapting the preceding equation, the present value of $4,000 at compound interest of 5 percent for three years in the future may be computed as follows:

Year	*Amount at End of Year*		*Divide by*		*Present Value at Beginning of Year*
3	$4,000.00	÷	1.05	=	$3,809.52
2	3,809.52	÷	1.05	=	3,628.11
1	3,628.11	÷	1.05	=	3,455.34

Neighborhood Communications must invest a present value of $3,455.34 to achieve a future value of $4,000 in three years.

This calculation is made easier by using the appropriate table from the appendix on present value tables. In Table 1, we look down the 5 percent column until we reach period 3. There we find the factor 0.864. Multiplied by $1, this factor gives the present value of $1 to be received three years from now at 5 percent interest. Thus, we solve the previous problem as follows:

$$\text{Future Value} \times \text{Present Value Factor} = \text{Present Value}$$

$$\$4{,}000 \times 0.864 = \$3{,}456$$

Except for a rounding difference of $0.66, this gives the same result as the previous calculation.

Present Value of an Ordinary Annuity

It is often necessary to compute the present value of a series of receipts or payments. When we calculate the present value of equal amounts equally spaced over a period of time, we are computing the present value of an ordinary annuity. An

FOCUS ON BUSINESS PRACTICE

How Would You Decide Whether to Buy Rare Dinosaur Bones?

Not-for-profit organizations can use the techniques of capital investment analysis just as for-profit ones do. For example, the officers of the Field Museum in Chicago applied these techniques when they decided to bid at auction several years ago on the most complete skeleton of a *Tyrannosaurus rex* ever found. The museum bought the bones for $8.2 million and spent another $9 million to restore and install the dinosaur, named Sue. The museum projected that Sue would attract 1 million new visitors, who would produce $5 million in admissions and spend several more million dollars on food, gifts, and the like. After deducting operating costs, museum officials used discounted present values to calculate a return on investment of 10.5 percent. Given that the museum's cost of capital was 8.5 percent, Sue's purchase was considered a financial success. Sue has been extremely popular with the public and more than met the museum's attendance goals in the first year after installation.[2]

Study Note
The first payment of an ordinary annuity is always made at the end of the first year.

ordinary annuity is a series of equal payments or receipts that will begin one time period from the current date.

Suppose that Neighborhood Communications has sold a piece of property and is to receive $15,000 in three equal annual cash payments of $5,000, beginning one year from today. What is the present value of this sale, assuming a current interest rate of 5 percent?

This present value can be determined by calculating a separate present value for each of the three payments (using Table 1 in the appendix on present value tables) and summing the results, as follows:

Future Cash Receipts (Annuity)						
Year 1	*Year 2*	*Year 3*		*Present Value Factor at 5 Percent (from Table 1)*		*Present Value*
$5,000			×	0.952	=	$ 4,760
	$5,000		×	0.907	=	4,535
		$5,000	×	0.864	=	4,320
Total Present Value						$13,615

The present value of this sale is $13,615. Thus, there is an implied interest cost (given the 5 percent rate) of $1,385 associated with the payment plan that allows the purchaser to pay in three installments. We can calculate this present value more easily by using Table 2 in the appendix on present value tables. We look down the 5 percent column until we reach period 3. There we find the factor 2.723. That factor, when multiplied by $1, gives the present value of a series of three $1 payments, spaced one year apart, at compound interest of 5 percent. Thus, we solve the problem as follows:

Periodic Payment	×	Present Value Factor	=	Present Value
$5,000	×	2.723	=	$13,615

This result is the same as the one computed earlier.

To summarize the example, if Neighborhood Communications is willing to accept a 5 percent rate of return, management will be equally satisfied to receive a single cash payment of $13,615 today or three equal annual cash payments of $5,000 spread over the next three years.

STOP & APPLY >

For each of the following situations, identify the correct factor to use from Tables 1 or 2 in the appendix on present value tables. Also, compute the appropriate present value.

1. Annual net cash inflows of $35,000 for five years, discounted at 16 percent
2. An amount of $25,000 to be received at the end of ten years, discounted at 12 percent
3. The amount of $28,000 to be received at the end of two years, and $15,000 to be received at the end of years 4, 5, and 6, discounted at 10 percent

(continued)

SOLUTION

1. From Table 2 in the appendix on present value tables:

$35,000	×	3.274	=	$114,590

2. From Table 1 in the appendix on present value tables:

$25,000	×	0.322	=	$ 8,050

3. From Table 1 in the appendix on present value tables:

$28,000	×	0.826	=	$ 23,128
$15,000	×	0.683	=	10,245
$15,000	×	0.621	=	9,315
$15,000	×	0.564	=	8,460
Total				$ 51,148

The Net Present Value Method

LO4 Analyze capital investment proposals using the net present value method.

The **net present value method** evaluates a capital investment by discounting its future cash flows to their present values and subtracting the amount of the initial investment from their sum. All proposed capital investments are evaluated in the same way, and the projects with the highest net present value—the amount that exceeds the initial investment—are selected for implementation.

Advantages of the Net Present Value Method

Study Note

Because it is based on cash flow, the net present value method is widely used not only in business but also by individuals.

A significant advantage of the net present value method is that it incorporates the time value of money into the analysis of proposed capital investments. Future cash inflows and outflows are discounted by the company's minimum rate of return to determine their present values. The minimum rate of return should at least equal the company's average cost of capital.

When dealing with the time value of money, use discounting to find the present value of an amount to be received in the future. To determine the present values of future amounts of money, use Tables 1 and 2 in the appendix on present value tables. Remember:

- Table 1 deals with a single payment or amount.
- Table 2 is used for a series of equal periodic amounts.

Tables 1 and 2 are used to discount each future cash inflow and cash outflow over the life of the asset to the present. If the net present value is positive (the total of the discounted net cash inflows exceeds the cash investment at the beginning), the rate of return on the investment will exceed the company's minimum rate of return, or hurdle rate, and the project can be accepted. Conversely, if the net present value is negative (the cash investment at the beginning exceeds the discounted net cash inflows), the return on the investment is less than the minimum rate of return and the project should be rejected. If the net present value is zero (if discounted cash inflows equal discounted cash outflows), the project meets the minimum rate of return and can be accepted.

Study Note

If the net present value is zero, the investment will earn the minimum rate of return.

The Net Present Value Method Illustrated

Suppose that Neighborhood Communications is considering the purchase of a new cell phone antenna that will boost the power of cell phone signals in the area.

Study Note

When using the net present value method, remember to consider the present value of the residual or disposal value.

The company's minimum rate of return is 16 percent. Management must decide between two models.

- Model M costs $17,500 and will have an estimated residual value of $2,000 after five years. It is projected to produce cash inflows of $6,000, $5,500, $5,000, $4,500, and $4,000 during its five-year life.
- Model N costs $21,000 and will have an estimated residual value of $2,000. It is projected to produce cash inflows of $6,000 per year for five years.

Because Model M is expected to produce unequal cash inflows, Table 1 in the appendix on present value tables is used to determine the present value of each cash inflow from each year of the machine's life. The net present value of Model M is determined as follows:

Model M

Year	*Net Cash Inflows*	*16% Factor*	*Present Value*
1	$6,000	0.862	$ 5,172.00
2	5,500	0.743	4,086.50
3	5,000	0.641	3,205.00
4	4,500	0.552	2,484.00
5	4,000	0.476	1,904.00
Residual value	2,000	0.476	952.00
Total present value of cash inflows			$17,803.50
Less purchase price of Model M			17,500.00
Net present value			$ 303.50

All the factors for this analysis can be found in the column for 16 percent in Table 1. The factors are used to discount the individual cash flows, including the expected residual value, to the present. The amount of the investment in Model M is deducted from the total present value of the cash inflows to arrive at the net present value of $303.50. Since the entire investment of $17,500 in Model M is a cash outflow at the beginning—that is, at time zero—no discounting of the $17,500 purchase price is necessary.

- Because the net present value is positive, the proposed investment in Model M will achieve at least the minimum rate of return.

Because Model N is expected to produce equal cash receipts in each year of its useful life, Table 2 in the appendix on present value tables is used to determine the combined present value of those future cash inflows. However, Table 1 is used to determine the present value of the machine's residual value because it represents a single payment, not an annuity. The net present value of Model N is calculated as follows:

Model N

Year	*Net Cash Inflows*	*16% Factor*	*Present Value*
1–5	$6,000	3.274	$19,644.00
Residual value	2,000	0.476	952.00
Total present value of cash inflows			$20,596.00
Less purchase price of Model N			21,000.00
Net present value			($ 404.00)

FOCUS ON BUSINESS PRACTICE

What Is Total Cost of Ownership, and Why Is It Important?

The concept of total cost of ownership (TCO) was developed to determine the total lifetime costs of owning an information technology (IT) asset, such as a computer system. TCO includes both the direct and indirect costs associated with the acquisition, deployment, operation, support, and retirement of the asset. Today, TCO is the industry standard for evaluating and comparing the costs associated with long-lived asset acquisitions. For example, if you buy a printer, TCO includes the direct costs of buying the printer, the annual supplies costs of ink and paper, and the indirect costs of maintaining it. Thus, the decision about which printer to buy is not based solely on the cost of the printer, but on all costs related to it over its useful lifetime.

Table 2 is used to determine the factor of 3.274 (found in the column for 16 percent and the row for five periods). Because the residual value is a single inflow in the fifth year, the factor of 0.476 must be taken from Table 1 (the column for 16 percent and the row for five periods). The result is a net present value of ($404).

▶ Because the net present value is negative, the proposed investment in Model N will not achieve the minimum rate of return and should be rejected.

The two analyses show that Model M should be chosen because it has a positive net present value and would exceed the company's minimum rate of return. Model N should be rejected because it does not achieve the minimum rate of return. Model M is the better choice because it is expected to produce cash inflows sooner and will thus produce a proportionately greater present value.

STOP & APPLY >

Sample Communications, Inc., is considering the purchase of a new piece of data transmission equipment. Estimated annual net cash inflows for the new equipment are $575,000. The equipment costs $2 million, has a five-year life, and will have no residual value at the end of the five years. The company's minimum rate of return is 12 percent. Compute the net present value of the equipment. Should the company purchase it?

SOLUTION

Net Present Value = Present Value of Future Net Cash Inflows − Cost of Equipment
= ($575,000 × 3.605*) − $2,000,000
= $2,072,875 − $2,000,000
= $72,875

The solution is positive, so the company should purchase the equipment. A positive answer means that the investment will yield more than the minimum 12 percent return required by the company.

*From Table 1 in the appendix on present value tables.

Other Methods of Capital Investment Analysis

LO5 Analyze capital investment proposals using the payback period method and the accounting rate-of-return method.

The net present value method is the best method for capital investment analysis. However, two other commonly used methods provide rough guides to evaluating capital investment proposals. These methods are the payback period method and the accounting rate-of-return method.

The Payback Period Method

Because cash is an essential measure of a business's health, many managers estimate the cash flow that an investment will generate. Their goal is to determine the minimum time it will take to recover the initial investment. If two investment alternatives are being studied, management should choose the investment that pays back its initial cost in the shorter time. That period of time is known as the payback period, and the method of evaluation is called the **payback period method**. Although the payback period method is simple to use, its use has declined because it does not consider the time value of money.

> **Study Note**
> The payback period method measures the estimated length of time necessary to recover in cash the cost of an investment.

Payback Calculation The payback period is computed as follows:

$$\text{Payback Period} = \frac{\text{Cost of Investment}}{\text{Annual Net Cash Inflows}}$$

To apply the payback period method, suppose that Neighborhood Communications is interested in purchasing a new server that costs $51,000 and has a residual value of $3,000. Assume that estimates for the proposal include revenue increases of $17,900 a year and operating cost increases of $11,696 a year (including depreciation and taxes). To evaluate this proposed capital investment, use the following steps:

Step 1. Determine the cost of the investment. In the example, it is $51,000.

Step 2. Determine the annual net cash inflows, which are the annual cash revenues minus the cash expenses.

- Eliminate the effects of all noncash revenue and expense items included in the analysis of net income to determine cash revenues and cash expenses.
- In this case, the only noncash expense or revenue is machine depreciation. To eliminate it from operating expenses, you must first calculate depreciation expense. To calculate this amount, you must know the asset's life and the depreciation method. Suppose Neighborhood Communications uses the straight-line method of depreciation, and the new server will have a ten-year service life. The annual depreciation is computed using this information and the facts given earlier, as follows:

$$\begin{aligned}\text{Annual Depreciation} &= \frac{\text{Cost} - \text{Residual Value}}{\text{Years}}\\ &= \frac{\$51{,}000 - \$3{,}000}{10\text{ Years}}\\ &= \$4{,}800\text{ per Year}\end{aligned}$$

- Thus, cash expenses are equal to the operating cost of $11,696 reduced by the depreciation expense of $4,800, or $ 6,896.
- The annual net cash inflows are $11,004, or cash revenue increases of $17,900 less cash expenses of $6,896.

Step 3. Compute the payback period.

$$\text{Payback Period} = \frac{\text{Cost of Machine}}{\text{Cash Revenue} - \text{Cash Expenses}}$$

$$= \frac{\$51{,}000}{\$17{,}900 - (\$11{,}696 - \$4{,}800)}$$

$$= \frac{\$51{,}000}{\$11{,}004}$$

$$= 4.6 \text{ Years*}$$

*Rounded.

Study Note

In computing the payback period, depreciation is omitted because it is a noncash expense.

If the company's desired payback period is five years or less, this proposal would be approved.

Unequal Annual Net Cash Inflows If a proposed capital investment has unequal annual net cash inflows, the payback period is determined by subtracting each annual amount (in chronological order) from the cost of the capital facility. When a zero balance is reached, the payback period has been determined. This will often occur in the middle of a year. The portion of the final year is computed by dividing the amount needed to reach zero (the unrecovered portion of the investment) by the entire year's estimated cash inflow. The Review Problem in this chapter illustrates that process.

Advantages and Disadvantages The payback period method is widely used because it is easy to compute and understand. It is especially useful in areas in which technology changes rapidly, such as in Internet companies, and when risk is high, such as when investing in emerging countries. However, the disadvantages of this approach far outweigh its advantages. First, the payback period method does not measure profitability. Second, it ignores differences in the present values of cash flows from different periods; thus, it does not adjust cash flows for the time value of money. Finally, the payback period method emphasizes the time it takes to recover the investment rather than the long-term return on the investment. It ignores all future cash flows after the payback period is reached.

The Accounting Rate-of-Return Method

The **accounting rate-of-return method** is an imprecise but easy way to measure the estimated performance of a capital investment, since it uses financial statement information. This method does not use an investment's cash flows but considers the financial reporting effects of the investment instead. The accounting rate-of-return method measures expected performance using two variables: (1) estimated annual net income from the project and (2) average investment cost.

Accounting Rate-of-Return Calculation The basic equation is as follows:

$$\text{Accounting Rate of Return} = \frac{\text{Average Annual Net Income}}{\text{Average Investment Cost}}$$

Step 1. Compute the average annual net income. Use the cost and revenue data prepared for evaluating the project—that is, revenues minus operating expenses (including depreciation and taxes).

Step 2. Compute the average investment cost in a proposed capital facility as follows:

$$\text{Average Investment Cost} = \left(\frac{\text{Total Investment} - \text{Residual Value}}{2}\right) + \text{Residual Value}$$

Step 3. Compute the accounting rate of return.

To see how the accounting rate-of-return is used in evaluating a proposed capital investment, assume the same facts as before for Neighborhood Communications' interest in purchasing a server. Also assume that the company's management will consider only projects that promise to yield more than a 16 percent return. To determine if the company should invest in the machine, compute the accounting rate of return as follows:

> **Study Note**
> Payback period is expressed in time, net present value is expressed in money, and accounting rate of return is expressed as a percentage.

$$\text{Accounting Rate of Return} = \frac{\$17{,}900 - \$11{,}696}{\left(\frac{\$51{,}000 - \$3{,}000}{2}\right) + \$3{,}000}$$

$$= \frac{\$6{,}204}{\$27{,}000}$$

$$= 23\%^{*}$$

*Rounded.

The projected rate of return is higher than the 16 percent minimum, so management should think seriously about making the investment.

Advantages and Disadvantages The accounting rate-of-return method has been widely used because it is easy to understand and apply, but it does have several disadvantages. First, because net income is averaged over the life of the investment, it is not a reliable figure; actual net income may vary considerably from the estimates. Second, the method is unreliable if estimated annual net incomes differ from year to year. Third, it ignores cash flows. Fourth, it does not consider the time value of money; thus, future and present dollars are treated as equal.

STOP & APPLY >

Sample Communications, Inc., is considering the purchase of new data transmission equipment. Estimated annual net cash inflows from the new equipment are $575,000. The equipment costs $2 million and will have no residual value at the end of its five-year life. Compute the payback period for the equipment. Does this method yield a positive or negative response to the proposal to buy the equipment, assuming that the company has set a maximum payback period of four years?

SOLUTION

$$\text{Payback Period} = \text{Cost of Investment} \div \text{Annual Net Cash Inflows}$$
$$= \$2{,}000{,}000 \div \$575{,}000$$
$$= 3.5 \text{ Years}^{*}$$

*Rounded.

The piece of equipment should be purchased because its payback period is less than the company's maximum payback period of 4 years.

$$\text{Average Investment Cost} = \left(\frac{\text{Total Investment} - \text{Residual Value}}{2}\right) + \text{Residual Value}$$

$$= \left(\frac{\$26{,}000 - \$6{,}000}{2}\right) + \$6{,}000 = \$16{,}000$$

(continued)

Sample Trucking is considering whether to purchase a delivery truck that will cost $26,000, last six years, and have an estimated residual value of $6,000. Average annual net income from the delivery truck is estimated at $4,000. Sample Trucking's owners want to earn an accounting rate of return of 20 percent. Compute the average investment cost and the accounting rate of return. Should the company make the investment?

SOLUTION

$$\text{Accounting Rate-of-Return} = \frac{\text{Average Annual Net Income}}{\text{Average Investment Cost}} = \frac{\$4{,}000}{\$16{,}000} = 25\%$$

The project will exceed the desired return of 20% and should be undertaken.

▶ NEIGHBORHOOD COMMUNICATIONS: REVIEW PROBLEM

In this chapter's Decision Point, we asked the following questions:

- Why are capital investment decisions critical for a company like Neighborhood Communications?
- In evaluating capital investment alternatives, how can managers at Neighborhood Communications ensure a wise allocation of resources and minimize the risks involved in capital investments?

Capital Investment Analysis
LO2 LO3
LO4 LO5

Companies like Neighborhood Communications have many costly equipment needs, and decisions about whether to invest capital to meet those needs can have a positive or negative effect on a company for many years. Capital investment decisions therefore require a systematic approach.

Managers at Neighborhood Communications typically evaluate each proposed investment alternative to determine if it will generate an adequate return for the company before they make far-reaching capital investment decisions. For example, when deciding whether to invest their company's capital in an expensive project like a cell phone tower, they use methods of capital investment analysis, such as the net present value method, the payback period method, or the accounting rate-of-return method. By using these methods, they can ensure a wise allocation of resources and at the same time minimize the risks involved in the investment decision.

Suppose that Neighborhood Communications is considering building a new cell phone tower and has gathered the following information:

Purchase price	$600,000
Residual value	$100,000
Desired payback period	3 years
Minimum rate of return	15%

The cash flow estimates are as follows:

Year	Cash Inflows	Cash Outflows	Net Cash Inflows	Projected Net Income
1	$ 500,000	$260,000	$240,000	$115,000
2	450,000	240,000	210,000	85,000
3	400,000	220,000	180,000	55,000
4	350,000	200,000	150,000	25,000
Totals	$1,700,000	$920,000	$780,000	$280,000

Required

1. Analyze the company's investment in the new tower. In your analysis, use (a) the net present value method, (b) the payback period method, and (c) the accounting rate-of-return method.
2. Summarize your findings from requirement **1**, and recommend a course of action.

Answers to Review Problem

1. a. Net present value method (factors are from Table 1 in the appendix on present value tables):

Year	Net Cash Inflows	Present Value Factor	Present Value
1	$240,000	0.870	$208,800
2	210,000	0.756	158,760
3	180,000	0.658	118,440
4	150,000	0.572	85,800
4	100,000 (residual value)	0.572	57,200
Total present value			$629,000
Less cost of original investment			600,000
Net present value			$ 29,000

b. Payback period method:

Total cash investment		$ 600,000
Less cash flow recovery		
Year 1	$ 240,000	
Year 2	210,000	
Year 3 (5/6 of $180,000)	150,000	(600,000)
Unrecovered investment		$ 0

Payback period: 2.833 (2⅚) Years, or 2 Years, 10 Months.

c. Accounting rate-of-return method:

$$\text{Accounting Rate of Return} = \frac{\text{Average Annual Net Income}}{\text{Average Investment Cost}}$$

$$= \frac{\$280{,}000 \div 4}{\left(\frac{\$600{,}000 - \$100{,}000}{2}\right) + \$100{,}000}$$

$$= \frac{\$70{,}000}{\$350{,}000}$$

$$= 20\%$$

2. Summary of decision analysis:

	Decision Measures	
	Desired	Calculated
Net present value	—	$29,000
Accounting rate of return	15%	20%
Payback period	3 Years	2.833 Years

Based on the calculations in requirement **1,** the company should invest in the tower.

STOP & REVIEW >

LO1 Define *capital investment analysis*, state the purpose of the minimum rate of return, and identify the methods used to arrive at that rate.

Capital investment decisions focus on when and how much to spend on capital facilities and other long-term projects. Capital investment analysis, often referred to as *capital budgeting*, consists of identifying the need for a capital investment, analyzing courses of action to meet that need, preparing reports for management, choosing the best alternative, and dividing funds among competing resource needs.

The minimum rate of return, or hurdle rate, is used as a screening mechanism to eliminate from further consideration capital investment requests with anticipated inadequate returns. It saves executives' time by quickly identifying substandard requests. The most commonly used measure for determining minimum rates of return is cost of capital. Other measures that are used less often are corporate return on investment, industry average return on investment, and bank interest rates.

LO2 Identify the types of projected costs and revenues used to evaluate alternatives for capital investment.

The accounting rate-of-return method requires measures of net income. Other methods of evaluating capital investments evaluate net cash inflows or cost savings. The analysis process must take into consideration whether each period's cash flows will be equal or unequal. Unless the after-income-tax effects on cash flows are being considered, carrying values and depreciation expense of assets awaiting replacement are irrelevant. Net proceeds from the sale of an old asset and estimated residual value of a new facility represent future cash flows and must be part of the estimated benefit of a project. Depreciation expense on replacement equipment is relevant to evaluations based on after-tax cash flows.

LO3 Apply the concept of the time value of money.

Cash flows of equal dollar amounts at different times have different values because of the effect of compound interest. This phenomenon is known as the time value of money. Of the evaluation methods discussed in this chapter, only the net present value method takes into account the time value of money.

LO4 Analyze capital investment proposals using the net present value method.

The net present value method incorporates the time value of money into the analysis of a proposed capital investment. A minimum required rate of return, usually the average cost of capital, is used to discount an investment's expected future cash flows to their present values. The present values are added together, and the amount of the initial investment is subtracted from their total. If the resulting amount, called the net present value, is positive, the rate of return on the investment will exceed the required rate of return, and the investment should be accepted. If the net present value is negative, the return on the investment will be less than the minimum rate of return, and the investment should be rejected.

LO5 Analyze capital investment proposals using the payback period method and the accounting rate-of-return method.

The payback period method of evaluating a capital investment focuses on the minimum length of time needed to get the amount of the initial investment back in cash. With the accounting rate-of-return method, managers evaluate two or more capital investment proposals and then select the alternative that yields the highest ratio of average annual net income to average cost of investment. Both methods are easy to use, but they are very rough measures that do not consider the time value of money. As a result, the net present value method is preferred.

REVIEW of Concepts and Terminology

The following concepts and terms were introduced in this chapter:

Accounting rate-of-return method 1242 (LO5)

Capital investment analysis 1226 (LO1)

Capital investment decisions 1226 (LO1)

Carrying value 1232 (LO2)

Compound interest 1234 (LO3)

Cost of capital 1229 (LO1)

Cost savings 1232 (LO2)

Future value 1235 (LO3)

Interest 1234 (LO3)

Net cash inflows 1232 (LO2)

Net present value method 1238 (LO4)

Ordinary annuity 1237 (LO3)

Payback period method 1241 (LO5)

Present value 1235 (LO3)

Simple interest 1234 (LO3)

Time value of money 1234 (LO3)

CHAPTER ASSIGNMENTS

BUILDING Your Basic Knowledge and Skills

Short Exercises

LO1 Manager's Role in Capital Investment Decisions

SE 1. The supervisor of the Logistics Department has suggested to the plant manager that a new machine costing $285,000 be purchased to improve material handling operations for the plant's newest product line. How should the plant manager proceed with this request?

LO1 Average Cost of Capital

SE 2. Gatwick Industries is considering a $1 million plant expansion. Management needs to know the average cost of capital to use in evaluating this capital investment decision. The company's capital structure consists of $3,000,000 of debt at 4 percent interest and $2,000,000 of stockholders' equity at 6 percent. What is Gatwick Industries' average cost of capital?

LO1 Ranking Capital Investment Proposals

SE 3. Zelolo Corp. has the following capital investment requests pending from its three divisions: Request 1, $60,000, 11 percent projected return; Request 2, $110,000, 14 percent projected return; Request 3, $130,000, 16 percent projected return; Request 4, $160,000, 13 percent projected return; Request 5, $175,000, 12 percent projected return; and Request 6, $230,000, 15 percent projected return. Zelolo's minimum rate of return is 13 percent, and $500,000 is available for capital investment this year. Which requests will be honored, and in what order?

LO2 Capital Investment Analysis and Revenue Measures

SE 4. Daize Corp. is analyzing a proposal to switch its factory over to a lights-out operation similar to the one discussed in this chapter's Decision Point. To do so, it must acquire a fully automated machine. The machine will be able to produce an entire product line in a single operation. Projected annual net cash inflows from the machine are $180,000, and projected net income is $120,000. Why is the projected net income lower than the projected net cash inflows? Identify possible causes for the $60,000 difference.

LO3 Time Value of Money

SE 5. Heidi Layne recently inherited a trust fund from a distant relative. On January 2, the bank managing the trust fund notified Layne that she has the option of receiving a lump-sum check for $200,000 or leaving the money in the trust fund and receiving an annual year-end check for $20,000 for each of the next 20 years. Layne likes to earn at least a 5 percent return on her investments. What should she do?

LO4 Residual Value and Present Value

SE 6. Annelle Coiner is developing a capital investment analysis for her supervisor. The proposed capital investment has an estimated residual value of $5,500 at the end of its five-year life. The company uses an 8 percent minimum rate of return. What is the present value of the residual value? Use Table 1 in the appendix on present value tables.

LO4 **Capital Investment Decision: Net Present Value Method**

SE 7. Noway Jose Communications, Inc., is considering the purchase of a new piece of computerized data transmission equipment. Estimated annual net cash inflows for the new equipment are $590,000. The equipment costs $2 million, it has a five-year life, and it will have no residual value at the end of the five years. The company has a minimum rate of return of 12 percent. Compute the net present value of the piece of equipment. Should the company purchase it? Use Table 2 in the appendix on present value tables.

LO5 **Capital Investment Decision: Payback Period Method**

SE 8. Using the information about Noway Jose Communications, Inc., in **SE 7**, compute the payback period for the piece of equipment. Does this method yield a positive or a negative response to the proposal to buy the equipment, assuming that the company sets a maximum payback period of four years?

LO5 **Capital Investment Decision: Payback Period Method**

SE 9. East-West Cable, Inc., is considering the purchase of new data transmission equipment. Estimated annual cash revenues for the new equipment are $1 million, and operating costs (including depreciation of $400,000) are $825,000. The equipment costs $2 million, it has a five-year life, and it will have no residual value at the end of the five years. Compute the payback period for the piece of equipment. Does this method yield a positive or a negative response to the proposal to buy the equipment if the company has set a maximum payback period of four years?

LO5 **Capital Investment Decision: Accounting Rate-of-Return Method**

SE 10. Best Cleaners is considering whether to purchase a delivery truck that will cost $50,000, last six years, and have an estimated residual value of $5,000. Average annual net income from the delivery service is estimated to be $4,000. Best Cleaners' owners seek to earn an accounting rate of return of 10 percent. Compute the average investment cost and the accounting rate of return. Should the investment be made?

Exercises

LO1 **Capital Investment Analysis**

E 1. Genette Henderson was just promoted to supervisor of building maintenance for the Ford Valley Theater complex. Allpoints Entertainment, Inc., Henderson's employer, uses a company-wide system for evaluating capital investment requests from its 22 supervisors. Henderson has approached you, the corporate controller, for advice on preparing her first proposal. She would also like to become familiar with the entire decision-making process.

1. What advice would you give Henderson before she prepares her first capital investment proposal?
2. Explain the role of capital investment analysis in the management process, including the six key steps taken during planning.

LO1 **Minimum Rate of Return**

E 2. The controller of Olaf Corporation wants to establish a minimum rate of return and would like to use a weighted-average cost of capital. Current data about the corporation's financing structure are as follows: debt financing, 40 percent; preferred stock, 30 percent; common stock, 20 percent; and retained earnings, 10 percent. The cost of debt is 4 percent. The dividend rate on the preferred stock issue is 3 percent. The cost of common stock is 2 percent and the cost of retained earnings is 5 percent.

Compute the weighted-average cost of capital.

LO1 **Ranking Capital Investment Proposals**

E 3. Managers of the Emerald Bay Furniture Company have gathered all of the capital investment proposals for the year, and they are ready to make their final selections. The following proposals and related rate-of-return amounts were received during the period:

Project	Amount of Investment	Rate of Return (Percentage)
AB	$ 450,000	19
CD	500,000	28
EF	654,000	12
GH	800,000	32
IJ	320,000	23
KL	240,000	18
MN	180,000	16
OP	400,000	26
QR	560,000	14
ST	1,200,000	22
UV	1,600,000	20

Assume that the company's minimum rate of return is 15 percent and that $5,000,000 is available for capital investments during the year.

1. List the acceptable capital investment proposals in order of profitability.
2. Which proposals should be selected for this year?

LO2 **Income Taxes and Net Cash Flow**

E 4. Santa Cruz Company has a tax rate of 20 percent on taxable income. It is considering a capital project that will make the following annual contribution to operating income:

Cash revenues	$ 400,000
Cash expenses	(200,000)
Depreciation	(140,000)
Operating income before income taxes	$ 60,000
Income taxes at 20%	(12,000)
Operating income	$ 48,000

1. Determine the net cash inflows for this project in two different ways. Are net cash flows the same under either approach?
2. What is the impact of income taxes on net cash flows?

LO3 **Using the Present Values Tables**

E 5. For each of the following situations, identify the correct factor to use from Tables 1 or 2 in the appendix on present value tables. Also, compute the appropriate present value.

1. Annual net cash inflows of $5,000 for five years, discounted at 6 percent
2. An amount of $25,000 to be received at the end of ten years, discounted at 4 percent
3. The amount of $14,000 to be received at the end of two years, and $8,000 to be received at the end of years 4, 5, and 6, discounted at 10 percent

LO3 **Using the Present Values Tables**

E 6. For each of the following situations, identify the correct factor to use from Tables 1 or 2 in the appendix on present value tables. Also, compute the appropriate present value.

1. Annual net cash inflows of $22,500 for a period of twelve years, discounted at 14 percent
2. The following five years of cash inflows, discounted at 10 percent:

Year 1	$35,000	Year 4	$40,000
Year 2	20,000	Year 5	50,000
Year 3	30,000		

3. The amount of $70,000 to be received at the beginning of year 7, discounted at 14 percent

LO3 **Present Value Computations**

E 7. Two machines—Machine M and Machine P—are being considered in a replacement decision. Both machines have about the same purchase price and an estimated ten-year life. The company uses a 12 percent minimum rate of return as its acceptance-rejection standard. Following are the estimated net cash inflows for each machine.

Year	Machine M	Machine P
1	$12,000	$17,500
2	12,000	17,500
3	14,000	17,500
4	19,000	17,500
5	20,000	17,500
6	22,000	17,500
7	23,000	17,500
8	24,000	17,500
9	25,000	17,500
10	20,000	17,500
Residual value	14,000	12,000

1. Compute the present value of future cash flows for each machine, using Tables 1 and 2 in the appendix on present value tables.
2. Which machine should the company purchase, assuming that both involve the same capital investment?

LO4 **Capital Investment Decision: Net Present Value Method**

E 8. Qen and Associates wants to buy an automated coffee roaster/grinder/brewer. This piece of equipment would have a useful life of six years, would cost $218,500, and would increase annual net cash inflows by $57,000. Assume that there is no residual value at the end of six years. The company's minimum rate of return is 14 percent.

Using the net present value method, prepare an analysis to determine whether the company should purchase the machine. Use Tables 1 and 2 in the appendix on present value tables.

LO4 **Capital Investment Decision: Net Present Value Method**

E 9. H and Y Service Station is planning to invest in automatic car wash equipment valued at $240,000. The owner estimates that the equipment will increase annual net cash inflows by $46,000. The equipment is expected to have a ten-year useful life with an estimated residual value of $50,000. The company requires a 14 percent minimum rate of return.

Using the net present value method, prepare an analysis to determine whether the company should purchase the equipment. How important is the estimate of residual value to this decision? Use Tables 1 and 2 in the appendix on present value tables.

LO4 Capital Investment Decision: Net Present Value Method

E 10. Assume the same facts for H and Y Service Station as in **E 9**, except assume that the company requires a 20 percent minimum rate of return.

Using the net present value method, prepare an analysis to determine whether the company should purchase the equipment. Use Tables 1 and 2 in the appendix on present value tables.

LO5 Capital Investment Decision: Payback Period Method

E 11. Perfection Sound, Inc., a manufacturer of stereo speakers, is thinking about adding a new plastic-injection molding machine. This machine can produce speaker parts that the company now buys from outsiders. The machine has an estimated useful life of 14 years and will cost $425,000. The residual value of the new machine is $42,500. Gross cash revenue from the machine will be about $400,000 per year, and related cash expenses should total $310,050. Depreciation is estimated to be $30,350 annually. The payback period should be five years or less.

Use the payback period method to determine whether the company should invest in the new machine. Show your computations to support your answer.

LO5 Capital Investment Decision: Payback Period Method

E 12. Soaking Wet, Inc., a manufacturer of gears for lawn sprinklers, is thinking about adding a new fully automated machine. This machine can produce gears that the company now produces on its third shift. The machine has an estimated useful life of ten years and will cost $800,000. The residual value of the new machine is $80,000. Gross cash revenue from the machine will be about $520,000 per year, and related operating expenses, including depreciation, should total $500,000. Depreciation is estimated to be $80,000 annually. The payback period should be five years or less.

Use the payback period method to determine whether the company should invest in the new machine. Show your computations to support your answer.

LO5 Capital Investment Decision: Accounting Rate-of-Return Method

E 13. Assume the same facts as in **E 11** for Perfection Sound, Inc. Management has decided that only capital investments that yield at least a 20 percent return will be accepted.

Using the accounting rate-of-return method, decide whether the company should invest in the machine. Show all computations to support your decision.

LO5 Capital Investment Decision: Accounting Rate-of-Return Method

E 14. Assume the same facts as in **E 12** for Soaking Wet, Inc. Management has decided that only capital investments that yield at least a 5 percent return will be accepted.

Using the accounting rate-of-return method, decide whether the company should invest in the machine. Show all computations to support your decision.

LO5 **Capital Investment Decision: Accounting Rate-of-Return Method**

E 15. Boink Corporation manufactures metal hard hats for on-site construction workers. Recently, management has tried to raise productivity to meet the growing demand from the real estate industry. The company is now thinking about buying a new stamping machine. Management has decided that only capital investments that yield at least a 14 percent return will be accepted. The new machine would cost $325,000; revenue would increase by $98,400 per year; the residual value of the new machine would be $32,500; and operating cost increases (including depreciation) would be $75,000.

Using the accounting rate-of-return method, decide whether the company should invest in the machine. Show all computations to support your decision.

Problems

LO1 LO2 **Minimum Rate of Return**

P 1. Capital investment analysis is the main responsibility of Ginny Weiss, the special assistant to the controller of Nazzaro Manufacturing Company. During the previous 12-month period, the company's capital mix and the respective costs were as follows:

	Percentage of Total Financing	Cost of Capital
Debt financing	25%	7
Preferred stock	15%	9
Common stock	50%	12
Retained earnings	10%	12

Plans for the current year call for a 10 percent shift in total financing from common stock financing to debt financing. Also, the cost of debt financing is expected to increase to 8 percent, although the cost of the other types of financing will remain the same.

Weiss has already analyzed several proposed capital investments. Those projects and their projected rates of return are as follows: Project M, 9.5 percent; Equipment Item N, 8.5 percent; Product Line O, 15.0 percent; Project P, 6.9 percent; Product Line Q, 10.5 percent; Equipment Item R, 11.9 percent; and Project S, 11.0 percent.

Required

1. Using the expected adjustments to cost and capital mix, compute the weighted-average cost of capital for the current year.
2. Identify the proposed capital investments that should be implemented based on the cost of capital calculated in requirement **1.**

LO3 LO4 **Net Present Value Method**

P 2. Sonja and Sons, Inc., owns and operates a group of apartment buildings. Management wants to sell one of its older four-family buildings and buy a new building. The old building, which was purchased 25 years ago for $100,000, has a 40-year estimated life. The current market value is $80,000, and if it is sold, the cash inflow will be $67,675. Annual net cash inflows from the old building are expected to average $16,000 for the remainder of its estimated useful life.

The new building will cost $300,000. It has an estimated useful life of 25 years. Net cash inflows are expected to be $50,000 annually.

Assume that (1) all cash flows occur at year end, (2) the company uses straight-line depreciation, (3) the buildings will have a residual value equal to 10 percent of their purchase price, and (4) the minimum rate of return is 14 percent. Use Tables 1 and 2 in the appendix on present value tables.

Required

1. Compute the present value of future cash flows from the old building.
2. What will the net present value of cash flows be if the company purchases the new building?
3. Manager insight ▶ Should the company keep the old building or purchase the new one?

LO3 LO4 **Net Present Value Method**

P 3. The management of Better Plastics has recently been looking at a proposal to purchase a new plastic-injection-style molding machine. With the new machine, the company would not have to buy small plastic parts to use in production. The estimated useful life of the machine is 15 years, and the purchase price, including all setup charges, is $400,000. The residual value is estimated to be $40,000. The net addition to the company's cash inflow as a result of the savings from making the parts is estimated to be $70,000 a year. Better Plastics' management has decided on a minimum rate of return of 14 percent. Use Tables 1 and 2 in the appendix on present value tables.

Required

1. Using the net present value method to evaluate this capital investment, determine whether the company should purchase the machine. Support your answer.
2. Manager insight ▶ If the management of Better Plastics had decided on a minimum rate of return of 16 percent, should the machine be purchased? Show all computations to support your answer.

LO5 **Accounting Rate-of-Return and Payback Period Methods**

P 4. The Raab Company is expanding its production facilities to include a new product line, a sporty automotive tire rim. Tire rims can now be produced with little labor cost using new computerized machinery. The controller has advised management about two such machines. The details about each machine are as follows:

	XJS Machine	HZT Machine
Cost of machine	$500,000	$550,000
Residual value	50,000	55,000
Net income	34,965	40,670
Annual net cash inflows	91,215	90,170

The company's minimum rate of return is 12 percent. The maximum payback period is six years. (Where necessary, round calculations.)

Required

1. For each machine, compute the projected accounting rate of return.
2. Compute the payback period for each machine.
3. Manager insight ▶ Based on the information from requirements **1** and **2**, which machine should be purchased? Why?

LO3 LO4 LO5 **Capital Investment Decision: Comprehensive**

P 5. The Arcadia Manufacturing Company, based in Arcadia, Florida, is one of the fastest-growing companies in its industry. According to Ms. Prinze, the company's production vice president, keeping up-to-date with technological changes is what makes the company successful.

Prinze feels that a machine introduced recently would fill an important need. The machine has an estimated useful life of four years, a purchase price of $250,000, and a residual value of $25,000. The company controller has estimated average annual net income of $11,250 and the following cash flows for the new machine:

	Cash Flow Estimates		
Year	Cash Inflows	Cash Outflows	Net Cash Inflows
1	$325,000	$250,000	$75,000
2	320,000	250,000	70,000
3	315,000	250,000	65,000
4	310,000	250,000	60,000

Prinze uses a 12 percent minimum rate of return and a three-year payback period for capital investment evaluation purposes.

Required

1. Analyze the data about the machine, and decide if the company should purchase it. Use the following evaluation approaches in your analysis: (a) the net present value method, (b) the accounting rate-of-return method, and (c) the payback period method. Use Tables 1 and 2 in the appendix on present value tables.
2. Summarize the information generated in requirement **1**, and make a recommendation to Prinze.

Alternate Problems

LO1 LO2 **Minimum Rate of Return**

P 6. Capital investment analysis is the main responsibility of the controller of Glory Company. During the previous 12-month period, the company's capital mix and the respective costs were as follows:

	Percentage of Total Financing	Cost of Capital
Debt financing	40%	2
Preferred stock	10%	3
Common stock	30%	8
Retained earnings	20%	6

Plans for the current year call for a 10 percent shift in total financing from debt financing to common stock financing. Also, the cost of debt financing is expected to increase to 4 percent, although the cost of the other types of financing will remain the same.

The controller has already analyzed several proposed capital investments. Those projects and their projected rates of return are as follows: Project M, 7.5 percent; Equipment Item N, 6.2 percent; Product Line O, 5.0 percent; Product Line P, 6.9 percent; Product Line Q, 1.5 percent; Equipment Item R, 3.9 percent; and Project S, 6.0 percent.

Required

1. Using the expected adjustments to cost and capital mix, compute the weighted-average cost of capital for the current year.
2. Identify the proposed capital investments that should be implemented based on the cost of capital calculated in requirement **1.**

LO3 LO4 Comparison of Alternatives: Net Present Value Method

P 7. City Sights, Ltd., operates a tour and sightseeing business. Its trademark is the use of trolley buses. Each vehicle has its own identity and is specially made for the company. Gridlock, the oldest bus, was purchased 15 years ago and has 5 years of its estimated useful life remaining. The company paid $25,000 for Gridlock, and the bus could be sold today for $20,000. Gridlock is expected to generate average annual net cash inflows of $24,000 for the remainder of its estimated useful life.

Management wants to replace Gridlock with a modern-looking vehicle called Phantom. Phantom has a purchase price of $140,000 and an estimated useful life of 20 years. Net cash inflows for Phantom are projected to be $40,000 per year.

Assume that (1) all cash flows occur at year end, (2) each vehicle's residual value equals 10 percent of its purchase price, and (3) the minimum rate of return is 10 percent. Use Tables 1 and 2 in the appendix on present value tables.

Required

1. Compute the present value of the future cash flows from Gridlock.
2. Compute the net present value of cash flows if Phantom were purchased.
3. Should City Sights keep Gridlock or purchase Phantom? (Manager insight ▶)

LO3 LO4 Net Present Value Method

P 8. Mansion is a famous restaurant in the French Quarter of New Orleans. Bouillabaisse Sophie is Mansion's house specialty. Management is considering the purchase of a machine that would prepare all the ingredients, mix them automatically, and cook the dish to the restaurant's specifications. The machine will function for an estimated 12 years, and the purchase price, including installation, is $250,000. Estimated residual value is $25,000. This labor-saving device is expected to increase cash flows by an average of $42,000 per year during its estimated useful life. For capital investment decisions, the restaurant uses a 12 percent minimum rate of return. Use Tables 1 and 2 in the appendix on present value tables.

Required

1. Using the net present value method, determine if the company should purchase the machine. Support your answer.
2. If management had decided on a minimum rate of return of 14 percent, should the machine be purchased? Show all computations to support your answer. (Manager insight ▶)

LO5 Accounting Rate-of-Return and Payback Period Methods

P 9. The Cute Car Company is expanding its production facilities to include a new product line, an energy-efficient sporty convertible. The car can be produced with little labor cost using computerized machinery. There are two such machines to choose from. The details about each machine are as follows:

	GoGo Machine	Autom Machine
Cost of machine	$300,000	$325,000
Residual value	30,000	32,500
Net income	25,000	30,000
Annual net cash inflows	60,000	50,000

The company's minimum rate of return is 15 percent. The maximum payback period is six years. (Where necessary, round calculations.)

Required

1. For each machine, compute the projected accounting rate of return.
2. Compute the payback period for each machine.

Manager insight ▶
3. Based on the information from requirements **1** and **2**, which machine should be purchased? Why?

LO3 LO4 LO5 **Capital Investment Decision: Comprehensive**

P 10. Pressed Corporation wants to buy a new stamping machine. The machine will provide the company with a new product line: pressed rubber food trays for kitchens. Two machines are being considered; the data for each machine are as follows:

	ETZ Machine	LKR Machine
Cost of machine	$350,000	$370,000
Net income	$39,204	$48,642
Annual net cash inflows	$64,404	$75,642
Residual value	$28,000	$40,000
Estimated useful life in years	10	10

The company's minimum rate of return is 16 percent, and the maximum allowable payback period is 5.0 years.

Required

1. Compute the net present value for each machine.
2. Compute the accounting rate of return for each machine.
3. Compute the payback period for each machine.

Manager insight ▶
4. From the information generated in requirements **1**, **2**, and **3**, decide which machine should be purchased. Why?

ENHANCING Your Knowledge, Skills, and Critical Thinking

LO1 **Evaluation of Proposed Capital Investments**

C 1. The board of directors of the Tanashi Corporation met to review a number of proposed capital investments that would improve the quality of company products. One production-line manager requested the purchase of new computer-integrated machines to replace the older machines in one of the ten production departments at the Tokyo plant. Although the manager had presented quantitative information to support the purchase of the new machines, the board members asked the following important questions:

1. Why do we want to replace the old machines? Have they deteriorated? Are they obsolete?
2. Will the new machines require less cycle time?
3. Can we reduce inventory levels or save floor space by replacing the old machines?
4. How expensive is the software used with the new machines?

5. Will we be able to find highly skilled employees to maintain the new machines? Or can we find workers who are trainable? What would it cost to train workers? Would the training disrupt the staff by causing relocations?
6. Would the implementation of the machines be delayed because of the time required to recruit and train new workers?
7. How would the new machines affect the other parts of the manufacturing systems? Would the company lose some of the flexibility in its manufacturing systems if it introduced the new machines?

The board members believe that the qualitative information needed to answer their questions could lead to the rejection of the project, even though it would have been accepted based on the quantitative information.

1. Identify the questions that can be answered with quantitative information. Give an example of the quantitative information that could be used.
2. Identify the questions that can be answered with qualitative information. Explain why this information could negatively influence the capital investment decision even though the quantitative information suggests a positive outcome.

LO3 LO4 Using Net Present Value

C 2. The McCall Syndicate owns four resort hotels in Europe. Because the Paris operation (Hotel 1) has been booming over the past five years, management has decided to build an addition to the hotel. This addition will increase the hotel's capacity by 20 percent. A construction company has bid to build the addition at a cost of $30,000,000. The building will have an increased residual value of $3,000,000.

Daj Van Dyke, the controller, has started an analysis of the net present value for the project. She has calculated the annual net cash inflows by subtracting the increase in cash operating expenses from the increase in cash inflows from room rentals. Her partially completed schedule follows:

Year	Net Cash Inflows
1–20 (each year)	$3,900,000

Capital investment projects must generate a 12 percent minimum rate of return to qualify for consideration.

Using net present value analysis, evaluate the proposal and make a recommendation to management. Explain how your recommendation would change if management were willing to accept a 10 percent minimum rate of return. Use Tables 1 and 2 in the appendix on present value tables.

LO4 Capital Investment Analysis

C 3. Automated teller machines (ATMs) have become common in the banking industry. San Angelo Federal Bank is planning to replace some old teller machines and has decided to use the York Machine. Nola Chavez, the controller, has prepared the analysis shown at the top of the opposite page. She has recommended the purchase of the machine based on the positive net present value shown in the analysis.

The York Machine has an estimated useful life of five years and an expected residual value of $35,000. Its purchase price is $385,000. Two existing ATMs, each having a carrying value of $25,000, can be sold to a neighboring bank for a total of $50,000. Annual operating cash inflows are expected to increase in the following manner:

Year 1	$79,900
Year 2	76,600
Year 3	79,900
Year 4	83,200
Year 5	86,500

The San Angelo Federal Bank uses straight-line depreciation. The minimum rate of return is 12 percent.

San Angelo Federal Bank
Capital Investment Analysis
Net Present Value Method

Year	Net Cash Inflows	Present Value Factor	Present Value
1	$ 85,000	0.909	$ 77,265
2	80,000	0.826	66,080
3	85,000	0.751	63,835
4	90,000	0.683	61,470
5	95,000	0.621	58,995
5 (residual value)	35,000	0.621	21,735
Total present value			$ 349,380
Initial investment		$385,000	
Less proceeds from the sale of existing teller machines		50,000	
Net capital investment			(335,000)
Net present value			$ 14,380

1. Analyze Chavez's work. What changes need to be made in her capital investment analysis?
2. What would be your recommendation to bank management about the purchase of the York Machine?

LO4 Net Present Value of Cash Flows

C 4. CPC Corporation is an international plumbing equipment and supply company located in southern California. The manager of the Pipe Division is considering the purchase of a computerized copper pipe machine that costs $120,000.

The machine has a six-year life, and its expected residual value after six years of use will be 10 percent of its original cost. Cash revenue generated by the new machine is projected to be $50,000 in year 1 and will increase by $10,000 each year for the next five years. Variable cash operating costs will be materials and parts, 25 percent of revenue; machine labor, 5 percent of revenue; and overhead, 15 percent of revenue. First-year sales and marketing cash outflows are expected to be $10,500 and will decrease by 10 percent each year over the life of the new machine. Anticipated cash administrative expenses will be $2,500 per year. The company uses a 15 percent minimum rate of return for all capital investment analyses.

1. Prepare an Excel spreadsheet to compute the net present value of the anticipated cash flows for the life of the proposed new machine. Use the following format:

		Projected Cash Outflows							
Future Time Period	Projected Cash Revenue	Materials and Parts	Machine Labor	Overhead	Sales and Marketing	Administrative Expenses	Projected Net Cash Inflows	15% Factor	Present Value

Should the company invest in the new machine?

2. After careful analysis, the controller has determined that the variable rate for materials and parts can be reduced to 22 percent of revenue. Will this reduction in cash outflow change the decision about investing in the new machine? Explain your answer.
3. The marketing manager has determined that the initial estimate of sales and marketing cash expenses was too high and has reduced that estimate by $1,000. The 10 percent annual reductions are still expected to occur. Together with the change in **2**, will this reduction affect the initial investment decision? Explain your answer.

LO4 Ethics, Capital Investment Decisions, and the New Globally Competitive Business Environment

C 5. Marika Jonssen is the controller of Bramer Corporation, a globally competitive producer of standard and custom-designed window units for the housing industry. As part of the corporation's move to become automated, Jonssen was asked to prepare a capital investment analysis for a robot-guided aluminum extruding and stamping machine. This machine would automate the entire window-casing manufacturing line. She has just returned from an international seminar on the subject of qualitative inputs into the capital investment decision process and is eager to incorporate those new ideas into the analysis. In addition to the normal net present value analysis (which produced a significant negative result), Jonssen factored in figures for customer satisfaction, scrap reduction, reduced inventory needs, and reputation for quality. With the additional information included, the analysis produced a positive response to the decision question.

When the chief financial officer finished reviewing Jonssen's work, he threw the papers on the floor and said, "What kind of garbage is this! You know it's impossible to quantify such things as customer satisfaction and reputation for quality. How do you expect me to go to the board of directors and explain your work? I want you to redo the entire analysis and follow only the traditional approach to net present value. Get it back to me in two hours!"

What is Jonssen's dilemma? What ethical courses of action are available to her?

LO2 LO3 LO4 LO5 Cookie Company (Continuing Case)

C 6. Suppose your cookie company is now a corporation that has granted franchises to more than 50 stores. Currently, only 10 of the 50 stores have computerized machines for mixing cookie dough. Because of a tremendous increase in demand for cookie dough, you, as the corporation's president, are considering purchasing 10 more computerized mixing machines by the end of this month. You are writing a memo evaluating this purchase that you will present at the board of directors' meeting next week.

According to your research, the 10 new machines will cost $320,000. They will function for an estimated five years and should have a $32,000 residual value. All of your corporation's capital investments are expected to produce a 20 percent minimum rate of return, and they should be recovered in three years or less. All fixed assets are depreciated using the straight-line method. The forecasted increase in operating results for the aggregate of the 10 new machines is as follows:

	Cash Flow Estimates	
Year	Cash Inflows	Cash Outflows
1	$310,000	$210,000
2	325,000	220,000
3	340,000	230,000
4	300,000	210,000
5	260,000	180,000

1. In preparation for writing your memo, answer the following questions:
   a. What kinds of information do you need to prepare this memo?
   b. Why is the information relevant?
   c. Where would you find the information?
   d. When would you want to obtain the information?
2. Analyze the purchase of the machines, and decide if your corporation should purchase them. Use (a) the net present value method, (b) the accounting rate-of-return method, and (c) the payback period method.

APPENDIX

Accounting for Investments

Many companies invest in the stock or debt securities of other firms. They may do so for several reasons. A company may temporarily have excess funds on which it can earn a return, or investments may be an integral part of its business, as in the case of a bank. A company may also invest in other firms for the purpose of partnering with or controlling them.

Management Issues Related to Investments

The issues of recognition, valuation, classification, and disclosure apply to accounting for investments.

Recognition Recognition of investments as assets follows the general rule for recording transactions that we described earlier in the text. Purchases of investments are recorded on the date on which they are made, and sales of investments are reported on the date of sale. At the time of the transaction, there is either a transfer of funds or a definite obligation to pay. Income from investments is reported as other income on the income statement. Any gains or losses on investments are also reported on the income statement. Gains and losses appear as adjustments in the operating activities section of the statement of cash flows. The cash amounts of purchases and sales of investments appear in the investing activities section of the statement of cash flows.

Valuation Like other purchase transactions, investments are valued according to the *cost principle*—that is, they are valued in terms of their cost at the time they are purchased. The cost, or purchase price, includes any commissions or fees. However, after the purchase, the value of investments on the balance sheet is adjusted to reflect subsequent conditions. These conditions may reflect changes in the market value or fair value of the investments, changes caused by the passage of time (as in amortization), or changes in the operations of the investee companies. Long-term investments must be evaluated annually for any impairment or decline in value that is more than temporary. If such an impairment exists, a loss on the investment must be recorded.

IFRS

Under a new accounting standard, the goal of which is to bring U.S. standards more in line with international financial reporting standards, companies may elect to measure investments at fair value. Recall that *fair value* is defined as the *exchange price* associated with an actual or potential business transaction between market participants. This option applies to all types of investments except in the case of a subsidiary that is consolidated into the statements of the parent company. Generally, companies can elect the investment to which to apply fair value, but having done so, they cannot change the use of fair value in the future. Fair value can be determined when there is a ready market for the security, but determination is more problematic when a ready market does not exist. In the latter case, the fair value must be estimated through a method such as net present value.[1]

Classification Investments in debt and equity securities are classified as either short-term or long-term. *Short-term investments*, also called *marketable securities*, have a maturity of more than 90 days but are intended to be held only until cash is needed for current operations. (As we pointed out in an earlier chapter, investments with a maturity of *less* than 90 days are classified as cash equivalents.) Long-term investments are intended to be held for more than one year. *Long-term investments* are reported in the investments section of the balance sheet, not in the current assets section. Although long-term investments may be just as marketable as short-term assets, management intends to hold them for an indefinite time.

Short-term and long-term investments must be further classified as trading securities, available-for-sale securities, or held-to-maturity securities.[2]

- *Trading securities* are debt or equity securities bought and held principally for the purpose of being sold in the near term.
- *Available-for-sale securities* are debt or equity securities that do not meet the criteria for either trading or held-to-maturity securities. They may be short-term or long-term depending on what management intends to do with them.
- *Held-to-maturity securities* are debt securities that management intends to hold until their maturity date.

Figure 1 illustrates the classification of short-term and long-term investments. Table 1 shows the relationship between the percentage of ownership in a company's stock and the investing company's level of control, as well as the classifications and accounting treatments of these stock investments. These classifications are important because each one requires a different accounting treatment.

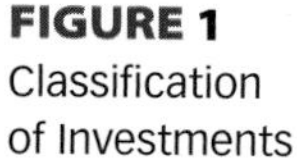
FIGURE 1
Classification of Investments

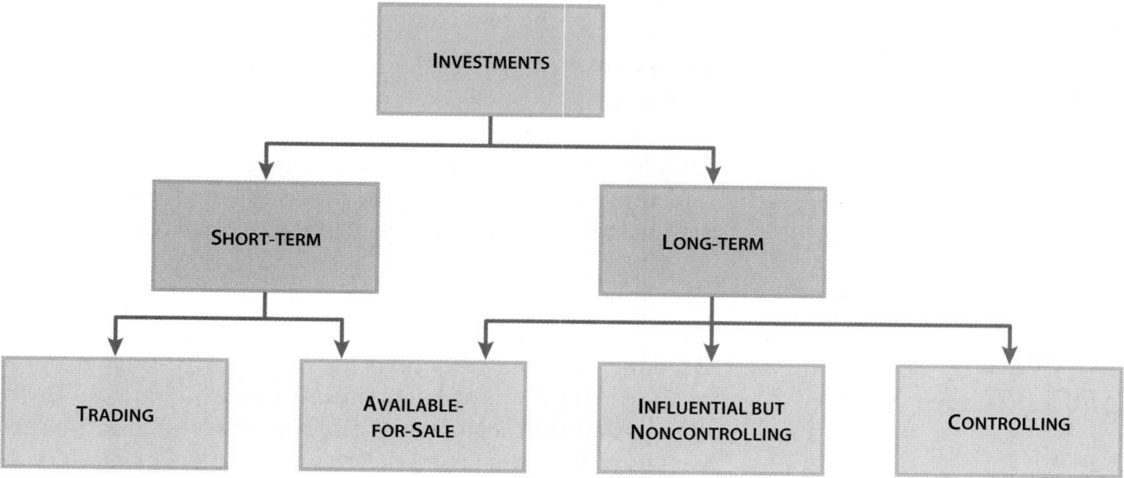

TABLE 1
Accounting for Equity Investments

Level of Control	Percentage of Ownership	Classification	Accounting Treatment
Noninfluential and noncontrolling	Less than 20%	Short-term investments—trading securities	Recorded at cost initially; cost adjusted after purchase for changes in market value; unrealized gains and losses reported on income statement
		Short-term or long-term investments—available-for-sale securities	Recorded at cost initially; cost adjusted for changes in market value with unrealized gains and losses to stockholders' equity
Influential but noncontrolling	Between 20% and 50%	Long-term investments	Equity method: recorded at cost initially; cost subsequently adjusted for investor's share of net income or loss and for dividends received
Controlling	More than 50%	Long-term investments	Financial statements consolidated

In general, the percentage of ownership in another company's stock has the following effects:

- ***Noninfluential and noncontrolling investment:*** A firm that owns less than 20 percent of the stock of another company has no influence on the other company's operations.
- ***Influential but noncontrolling investment:*** A firm that owns between 20 to 50 percent of another company's stock can exercise *significant influence* over that company's operating and financial policies, even though it holds 50 percent or less of the voting stock. Indications of significant influence include representation on the board of directors, participation in policymaking, exchange of managerial personnel, and technological dependency between the two companies.
- ***Controlling investment:*** A firm that owns more than 50 percent of another company's stock.

Disclosure Companies provide detailed information about their investments and the manner in which they account for them in the notes to their financial statements. Such disclosures help users assess the impact of the investments.

Trading Securities

Trading securities are always short-term investments and are frequently bought and sold to generate profits on short-term changes in their prices. They are classified as current assets on the balance sheet and are valued at fair value, which is usually the same as market value. An increase or decrease in the fair value of a company's total trading portfolio (the group of securities it holds for trading purposes) is included in net income in the accounting period in which the increase or decrease occurs.

For example, suppose Jackson Company buys 10,000 shares of **IBM** for $900,000 ($90 per share) and 10,000 shares of **Microsoft** for $300,000 ($30 per share) on October 25, 2010. The purchase is made for trading purposes—that is, Jackson's management intends to realize a gain by holding the shares for only a short period. The entry in journal form to record the investment at cost is as follows:

Purchase

A	=	L	+	OE
+1,200,000				
−1,200,000				

2010			
Oct. 25	Short-Term Investments	1,200,000	
	Cash		1,200,000
	Investment in stocks for trading ($900,000 + $300,000 = $1,200,000)		

Assume that at year end, IBM's stock price has decreased to $80 per share and Microsoft's has risen to $32 per share. The trading portfolio is now valued at $1,120,000:

Security	*Market Value*	*Cost*	*Gain (Loss)*
IBM (10,000 shares)	$ 800,000	$ 900,000	
Microsoft (10,000 shares)	320,000	300,000	
Totals	$1,120,000	$1,200,000	($80,000)

Because the current fair value of the portfolio is $80,000 less than the original cost of $1,200,000, the following adjusting entry is needed:

Year-End Adjustment

A	=	L	+	OE
−80,000				−80,000

2010			
Dec. 31	Unrealized Loss on Investments	80,000	
	Allowance to Adjust Short-Term Investments to Market		80,000
	Recognition of unrealized loss on trading portfolio		

Study Note

The Allowance to Adjust Short-Term Investments to Market account is never changed when securities are sold. It changes only when an adjusting entry is made at year end.

The unrealized loss will appear on the income statement as a reduction in income. The loss is unrealized because the securities have not been sold; if unrealized gains occur, they are treated the same way. The Allowance to Adjust Short-Term Investments to Market account appears on the balance sheet as a contra-asset, as follows:

Short-term investments (at cost)	$1,200,000
Less allowance to adjust short-term investments to market	80,000
Short-term investments (at market)	$1,120,000

or, more simply,

Short-term investments (at market value, cost is $1,200,000)	$1,120,000

If Jackson sells its 10,000 shares of Microsoft for $35 per share on March 2, 2011, a realized gain on trading securities is recorded as follows:

Sale

A	= L +	OE
+350,000		+50,000
−300,000		

2011			
Mar. 2	Cash	350,000	
	Short-Term Investments		300,000
	Realized Gain on Sale of Investments		50,000
	Sale of 10,000 shares of Microsoft for $35 per share; cost was $30 per share		

The realized gain will appear on the income statement. Note that the realized gain is unaffected by the adjustment for the unrealized loss at the end of 2010. The two transactions are treated independently. If the stock had been sold for less than cost, a realized loss on investments would have been recorded. Realized losses also appear on the income statement.

Now let's assume that during 2011, Jackson buys 4,000 shares of **Apple Computer** at $32 per share and has no transactions involving its shares of IBM. Also assume that by December 31, 2011, the price of IBM's stock has risen to $95 per share, or $5 per share more than the original cost, and that Apple's stock price has fallen to $29, or $3 less than the original cost. We can now analyze Jackson's trading portfolio as follows:

Security	*Market Value*	*Cost*	*Gain (Loss)*
IBM (10,000 shares)	$ 950,000	$ 900,000	
Apple (4,000 shares)	116,000	128,000	
Totals	$1,066,000	$1,028,000	$38,000

The market value of Jackson's trading portfolio now exceeds the cost by $38,000 ($1,066,000 − $1,028,000). This amount represents the targeted ending balance for the Allowance to Adjust Short-Term Investments to Market account. Recall that at the end of 2010, that account had a credit balance of $80,000, meaning that the market value of the trading portfolio was less than the cost. Because no entries are made to the account during 2011, it retains its balance until adjusting entries are made at the end of the year. The adjustment for 2011 must be $118,000—enough to result in a debit balance of $38,000 in the allowance account:

Year-End Adjustment

A	= L +	OE
+118,000		+118,000

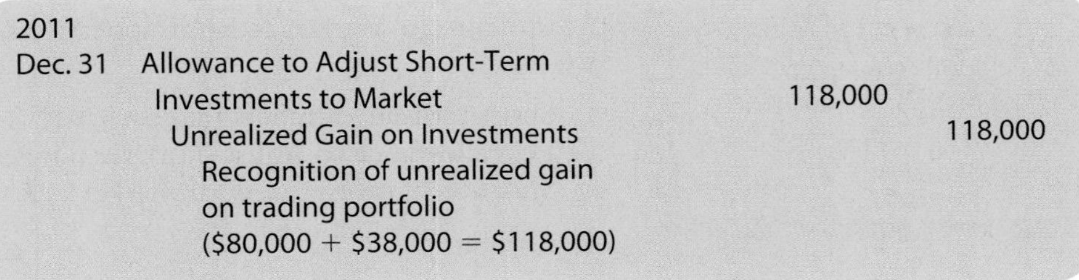

2011			
Dec. 31	Allowance to Adjust Short-Term Investments to Market	118,000	
	Unrealized Gain on Investments		118,000
	Recognition of unrealized gain on trading portfolio ($80,000 + $38,000 = $118,000)		

The 2011 ending balance of Jackson's allowance account can be determined as follows:

ALLOWANCE TO ADJUST SHORT-TERM INVESTMENTS TO MARKET

Dec. 31, 2011 Adj.	118,000	Dec. 31, 2010 Bal.	80,000
Dec. 31, 2011 Bal.	38,000		

The balance sheet presentation of short-term investments is as follows:

Short-term investments (at cost)	$1,028,000
Plus allowance to adjust short-term investments to market	38,000
Short-term investments (at market)	$1,066,000

or, more simply,

Short-term investments (at market value, cost is $1,028,000)	$1,066,000

If the company also has held-to-maturity securities that will mature within one year, they are included in short-term investments at cost adjusted for the effects of interest.

Available-for-Sale Securities

Short-term available-for-sale securities are accounted for in the same way as trading securities with two exceptions: (1) An unrealized gain or loss is reported as a special item in the stockholders' equity section of the balance sheet, not as a gain or loss on the income statement; (2) if a decline in the value of a security is considered permanent, it is charged as a loss on the income statement.

Long-Term Investments in Equity Securities

As indicated in Table 1, the accounting treatment of long-term investments in equity securities, such as common stock, depends on the extent to which the investing company can exercise control over the other company.

Noninfluential and Noncontrolling Investment As noted earlier, available-for-sale securities are debt or equity securities that cannot be classified as trading or held-to-maturity securities. When long-term equity securities are involved, a further criterion for classifying them as available for sale is that they be noninfluential and noncontrolling investments of less than 20 percent of the voting stock. Accounting for long-term available-for-sale securities requires using the *cost-adjusted-to-market method*. With this method, the securities are initially recorded at cost and are thereafter adjusted periodically for changes in market value by using an allowance account.[3]

Available-for-sale securities are classified as long-term if management intends to hold them for more than one year. When accounting for long-term available-for-sale securities, the unrealized gain or loss resulting from the adjustment is not reported on the income statement. Instead, the gain or loss is reported as a special item in the stockholders' equity section of the balance sheet and in the disclosure of comprehensive income.

At the end of each accounting period, the total cost and the total market value of these long-term stock investments must be determined. If the total market value is less than the total cost, the difference must be credited to a contra-asset account called Allowance to Adjust Long-Term Investments to Market. Because of the long-term nature of the investment, the debit part of the entry, which represents a decrease in value below cost, is treated as a temporary decrease and does not appear as a loss on the income statement. It is shown in a contra-stockholders' equity account called Unrealized Loss on Long-Term Investments.* Thus, both of these accounts are balance sheet accounts. If the market value exceeds the cost, the allowance account is added to Long-Term Investments, and the unrealized gain appears as an addition to stockholders' equity.

*If the decrease in market value of a long-term investment is deemed permanent or if the investment is deemed impaired, the decline or impairment is recorded by debiting a loss account on the income statement instead of the Unrealized Loss account.

When a company sells its long-term investments in stock, the difference between the sale price and the cost of the stock is recorded and reported as a realized gain or loss on the income statement. Dividend income from such investments is recorded by a debit to Cash and a credit to Dividend Income. For example, assume the following facts about the long-term stock investments of Nardini Corporation:

June 1, 2010	Paid cash for the following long-term investments: 10,000 shares of Herald Corporation common stock (representing 2 percent of outstanding stock) at $25 per share; 5,000 shares of Taza Corporation common stock (representing 3 percent of outstanding stock) at $15 per share.
Dec. 31, 2010	Quoted market prices at year end: Herald common stock, $21; Taza common stock, $17
Apr. 1, 2011	Change in policy required the sale of 2,000 shares of Herald common stock at $23.
July 1, 2011	Received cash dividend from Taza equal to $0.20 per share.
Dec. 31, 2011	Quoted market prices at year end: Herald common stock, $24; Taza common stock, $13.

Study Note

Nardini's sale of stock on April 1, 2011, was the result of a *change in policy*. This illustrates that intent is often the only difference between long-term investments and short-term investments.

Entries to record these transactions are as follows:

Investment

A	= L +	OE
+325,000		
−325,000		

2010			
June 1	Long-Term Investments	325,000	
	Cash		325,000
	Investments in Herald common stock (10,000 shares × $25 = $250,000) and Taza common stock (5,000 shares × $15 = $75,000)		

Year-End Adjustment

A	= L +	OE
−30,000		−30,000

2010			
Dec. 31	Unrealized Loss on Long-Term Investments	30,000	
	Allowance to Adjust Long-Term Investments to Market		30,000
	To record reduction of long-term investment to market		

This adjustment involves the following computations:

Company	*Shares*	*Market Price*	*Total Market*	*Total Cost*
Herald	10,000	$21	$210,000	$250,000
Taza	5,000	17	85,000	75,000
			$295,000	$325,000

Total Cost − Total Market Value = $325,000 − $295,000 = $30,000

Other entries are as follows:

Sale

A	= L +	OE
+46,000		−4,000
−50,000		

		Debit	Credit
2011			
Apr. 1	Cash	46,000	
	Realized Loss on Sale of Investments	4,000	
	Long-Term Investments		50,000
	Sale of 2,000 shares of Herald common stock 2,000 × $23 = $46,000 2,000 × $25 = 50,000 Loss $ 4,000		

Dividend Received

A	= L +	OE
+1,000		+1,000

		Debit	Credit
2011			
July 1	Cash	1,000	
	Dividend Income		1,000
	Receipt of cash dividend from Taza stock 5,000 × $0.20 = $1,000		

Year-End Adjustment

A	= L +	OE
+12,000		+12,000

		Debit	Credit
2011			
Dec. 31	Allowance to Adjust Long-Term Investment to Market	12,000	
	Unrealized Loss on Long-Term Investments		12,000
	To record the adjustment in long-term investment so it is reported at market		

The adjustment equals the previous balance ($30,000 from the December 31, 2010, entry) minus the new balance ($18,000), or $12,000. The new balance of $18,000 is the difference at the present time between the total market value and the total cost of all investments. It is figured as follows:

Company	*Shares*	*Market Price*	*Total Market*	*Total Cost*
Herald	8,000	$24	$192,000	$200,000
Taza	5,000	13	65,000	75,000
			$257,000	$275,000

Total Cost − Total Market Value = $275,000 − $257,000 = $18,000

The Allowance to Adjust Long-Term Investments to Market and the Unrealized Loss on Long-Term Investments are reciprocal contra accounts, each with the same dollar balance, as shown by the effects of these transactions on the T accounts:

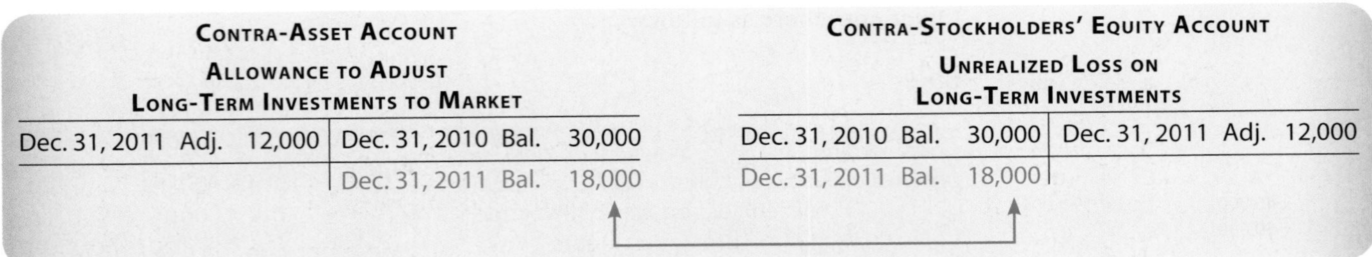

The Allowance account reduces long-term investments by the amount by which the cost of the investments exceeds market; the Unrealized Loss account reduces stockholders' equity by a similar amount. The opposite effects will exist if market value exceeds cost, resulting in an unrealized gain.

Influential but Noncontrolling Investment As we have noted, ownership of 20 percent or more of a company's voting stock is considered sufficient to influence the company's operations. When that is the case, the *equity method* should be used to account for the stock investment. The equity method presumes that an investment of 20 percent or more is not a passive investment and that the investor should therefore share proportionately in the success or failure of the company. The three main features of this method are as follows:

1. The investor records the original purchase of the stock at cost.
2. The investor records its share of the company's periodic net income as an increase in the Investment account, with a corresponding credit to an income account. Similarly, it records its share of a periodic loss as a decrease in the Investment account, with a corresponding debit to a loss account.
3. When the investor receives a cash dividend, the asset account Cash is increased, and the Investment account is decreased.

To illustrate the equity method, suppose that on January 1 of the current year, ITO Corporation acquired 40 percent of Quay Corporation's voting common stock for $180,000. With this share of ownership, ITO can exert significant influence over Quay's operations. During the year, Quay reported net income of $80,000 and paid cash dividends of $20,000. ITO recorded these transactions as follows:

Investment

A	= L	+ OE
+180,000		
−180,000		

Investment in Quay Corporation	180,000	
Cash		180,000
Investments in Quay Corporation common stock		

Recognition of Income

A	= L	+ OE
+32,000		+32,000

Investment in Quay Corporation	32,000	
Income, Quay Corporation Investment		32,000
Recognition of 40% of income reported by Quay Corporation		
40% × $80,000 = $32,000		

Receipt of Cash Dividend

A	= L + OE
+8,000	
−8,000	

Cash	8,000	
Investment in Quay Corporation		8,000
Cash dividend from Quay Corporation 40% × $20,000 = $8,000		

The balance of the Investment in Quay Corporation account after these transactions is $204,000, as shown here:

Investment in Quay Corporation			
Investment	180,000	Dividend Received	8,000
Share of Income	32,000		
Bal.	204,000		

The share of income is reported as a separate line item on the income statement as a part of income from operations. The dividends received affect cash flows from operating activities on the statement of cash flows. The reported income ($32,000) exceeds the cash received by $24,000.

Controlling Investment When a controlling interest exists—usually when one company owns more than 50 percent of the voting stock of another company—consolidated financial statements are required. The investing company is the *parent company*; the other company is a *subsidiary*. Because a parent company and its subsidiaries are separate legal entities, each prepares separate financial statements. However, because of their special relationship, they are viewed for external financial reporting purposes as a single economic entity. For this reason, the FASB requires that they combine their financial statements into a single set of statements called *consolidated financial statements*. The concepts and procedures related to the preparation of consolidated financial statements are the subject of more advanced courses.

Investments in Debt Securities

As noted in previous chapters, debt securities are considered financial instruments because they are claims that will be paid in cash. When a company purchases debt securities, it records them at cost plus any commissions and fees. Like investments in equity securities, short-term investments in debt securities are valued at fair value at the end of the accounting period and are accounted for as trading securities or available-for-sale securities. However, the accounting treatment is different if they qualify as held-to-maturity securities.

Held-to-Maturity Securities As we noted earlier, held-to-maturity securities are debt securities that management intends to hold to their maturity date. Such securities are recorded at cost and are valued on the balance sheet at cost adjusted for the effects of interest. For example, suppose that on December 1, 2010, Webber Company pays $97,000 for U.S. Treasury bills, which are short-term debt of the federal government. The bills will mature in 120 days at $100,000. Webber would make the following entry:

A	= L + OE
+97,000	
−97,000	

2010			
Dec. 1	Short-Term Investments	97,000	
	Cash		97,000
	Purchase of U.S. Treasury bills that mature in 120 days		

At Webber's year end on December 31, the entry to accrue the interest income earned to date would be as follows:

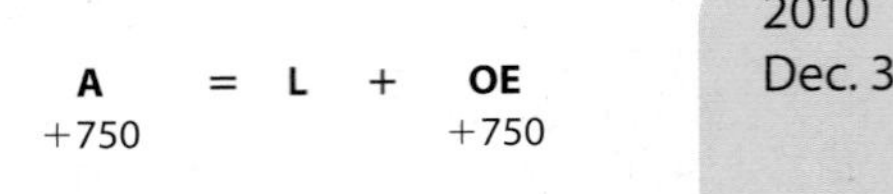

A	=	L	+	OE
+750				+750

2010			
Dec. 31	Short-Term Investments	750	
	Interest Income		750
	Accrual of interest on U.S. Treasury bills $3,000 × 30/120 = $750		

On December 31, the U.S. Treasury bills would be shown on the balance sheet as a short-term investment at their amortized cost of $97,750 ($97,000 + $750). When Webber receives the maturity value on March 31, 2011, the entry is as follows:

A	=	L	+	OE
+100,000 −97,750				+2,250

2011			
Mar. 31	Cash	100,000	
	Short-Term Investments		97,750
	Interest Income		2,250
	Receipt of cash at maturity of U.S. Treasury bills and recognition of related income		

Long-Term Investments in Bonds

Like all investments, investments in bonds are recorded at cost, which, in this case, is the price of the bonds plus the broker's commission. When bonds are purchased between interest payment dates, the purchaser must also pay an amount equal to the interest that has accrued on the bonds since the last interest payment date. Then, on the next interest payment date, the purchaser receives an interest payment for the whole period. The payment for accrued interest should be recorded as a debit to Interest Income, which will be offset by a credit to Interest Income when the semiannual interest is received.

Subsequent accounting for a corporation's long-term bond investments depends on the classification of the bonds. If the company plans to hold the bonds until they are paid off on their maturity date, they are considered held-to-maturity securities. Except in industries like insurance and banking, it is unusual for companies to buy the bonds of other companies with the express purpose of holding them until they mature, which can be in 10 to 30 years. Thus, most long-term bond investments are classified as available-for-sale securities, meaning that the company plans to sell them at some point before their maturity date. Such bonds are accounted for at fair value, much as equity or stock investments are; fair value is usually the market value. When bonds are intended to be held to maturity, they are accounted for not at fair value but at cost, adjusted for the amortization of their discount or premium. The procedure is similar to accounting for long-term bond liabilities, except that separate accounts for discounts and premiums are not used.

- What is the role of fair value in accounting for investments?
- What is the difference between trading securities, available-for-sale securities, and held-to-maturity securities?
- Why are the level and percentage of ownership important in accounting for equity investments?
- How are trading securities valued at the balance sheet date?
- What are unrealized gains and losses on trading securities? On what statement are they reported?
- How does accounting for available-for-sale securities differ from accounting for trading securities?
- At what value are held-to-maturity securities shown on the balance sheet?

Problems

Trading Securities

P 1. Omar Corporation, which has begun investing in trading securities, engaged in the following transactions:

Jan. 6	Purchased 7,000 shares of Quaker Oats stock, $30 per share.
Feb. 15	Purchased 9,000 shares of EG&G, $22 per share.

At year end on June 30, Quaker Oats was trading at $40 per share, and EG&G was trading at $18 per share.

Record the entries in journal form for the purchases. Then record the necessary year-end adjusting entry. (Include a schedule of the trading portfolio cost and market in the explanation.) Also record the entry for the sale of all the EG&G shares on August 20 for $16 per share. Is the last entry affected by the June 30 adjustment?

Methods of Accounting for Long-Term Investments

P 2. Teague Corporation has the following long-term investments:

1. 60 percent of the common stock of Ariel Corporation
2. 13 percent of the common stock of Copper, Inc.
3. 50 percent of the nonvoting preferred stock of Staffordshire Corporation
4. 100 percent of the common stock of its financing subsidiary, EQ, Inc.
5. 35 percent of the common stock of the French company Rue de le Brasseur
6. 70 percent of the common stock of the Canadian company Nova Scotia Cannery

For each of these investments, tell which of the following methods should be used for external financial reporting, and why:

a. Cost-adjusted-to-market method
b. Equity method
c. Consolidation of parent and subsidiary financial statements

Long-Term Investments

P 3. Fulco Corporation has the following portfolio of long-term available-for-sale securities at year end, December 31, 2011:

Company	Percentage of Voting Stock Held	Cost	Year-End Market Value
A Corporation	4	$ 80,000	$ 95,000
B Corporation	12	375,000	275,000
C Corporation	5	30,000	55,000
Total		$485,000	$425,000

Both the Unrealized Loss on Long-Term Investments account and the Allowance to Adjust Long-Term Investments to Market account currently have a balance of $40,000 from the last accounting period. Prepare T accounts with a beginning balance for each of these accounts. Record the effects of the above information on the accounts, and determine the ending balances.

Long-Term Investments: Cost-Adjusted-to-Market and Equity Methods

P 4. On January 1, Rourke Corporation purchased, as long-term investments, 8 percent of the voting stock of Taglia Corporation for $250,000 and 45 percent of the voting stock of Curry Corporation for $2 million. During the year, Taglia Corporation had earnings of $100,000 and paid dividends of $40,000. Curry Corporation had earnings of $300,000 and paid dividends of $200,000. The market value did not change for either investment during the year. Which of these investments should be accounted for using the cost-adjusted-to-market method? Which should be accounted for using the equity method? At what amount should each investment be carried on the balance sheet at year end? Give a reason for each choice.

Held-to-Maturity Securities

P 5. Dale Company experiences heavy sales in the summer and early fall, after which time it has excess cash to invest until the next spring. On November 1, 2011, the company invested $194,000 in U.S. Treasury bills. The bills mature in 180 days at $200,000. Prepare entries in journal form to record the purchase on November 1; the adjustment to accrue interest on December 31, which is the end of the fiscal year; and the receipt of cash at the maturity date of April 30.

Comprehensive Accounting for Investments

P 6. Gulf Coast Corporation is a successful oil and gas exploration business in the southwestern United States. At the beginning of 2011, the company made investments in three companies that perform services in the oil and gas industry. The details of each of these investments follow.

Gulf Coast purchased 100,000 shares of Marsh Service Corporation at a cost of $16 per share. Marsh has 1.5 million shares outstanding and during 2011 paid dividends of $0.80 per share on earnings of $1.60 per share. At the end of the year, Marsh's shares were selling for $24 per share.

Gulf Coast also purchased 2 million shares of Crescent Drilling Company at $8 per share. Crescent has 10 million shares outstanding. In 2011, Crescent paid a dividend of $0.40 per share on earnings of $0.80 per share. During the year, the president of Gulf Coast was appointed to Crescent's board of directors. At the end of the year, Crescent's stock was selling for $12 per share.

In another action, Gulf Coast purchased 1 million shares of Logan Oil Field Supplies Company's 5 million outstanding shares at $12 per share. The president of Gulf Coast sought membership on Logan's board of directors but was rebuffed when a majority of shareholders stated they did not want to be associated with Gulf Coast. Logan paid a dividend of $0.80 per share and reported a net income of only $0.40 per share for the year. By the end of the year, its stock price had dropped to $4 per share.

Required

1. For each investment, make entries in journal form for (a) initial investment, (b) receipt of cash dividend, and (c) recognition of income (if appropriate).
2. What adjusting entry (if any) is required at the end of the year?
3. Assuming that Gulf Coast sells its investment in Logan after the first of the year for $6 per share, what entry would be made?
4. Assuming no other transactions occur and that the market value of Gulf Coast's investment in Marsh exceeds cost by $2,400,000 at the end of the second year, what adjusting entry (if any) would be required?
5. User insight ▶ What principal factors were considered in determining how to account for Gulf Coast's investments? Should they be shown on the balance sheet as short-term or long-term investments? What factors affect this decision?

Long-Term Investments: Equity Method

P 7. Rylander Corporation owns 35 percent of the voting stock of Waters Corporation. The Investment account on Rylander's books as of January 1, 2011, was $720,000. During 2011, Waters reported the following quarterly earnings and dividends:

Quarter	Earnings	Dividends Paid
1	$160,000	$100,000
2	240,000	100,000
3	120,000	100,000
4	(80,000)	100,000
	$440,000	$400,000

Because of the percentage of voting shares Rylander owns, it can exercise significant influence over the operations of Waters Corporation. Therefore, Rylander Corporation must account for the investment using the equity method.

Required

1. Prepare a T account for Rylander Corporation's investment in Waters, and enter the beginning balance, the relevant entries for the year in total, and the ending balance.
2. User insight ▶ What is the effect and placement of the entries in requirement **1** on Rylander Corporation's earnings as reported on the income statement?
3. User insight ▶ What is the effect and placement of the entries in requirement **1** on the statement of cash flows?
4. User insight ▶ How would the effects on the statements differ if Rylander's ownership represented only a 15 percent share of Waters?

APPENDIX

B Present Value Tables

TABLE 1 Present Value of $1 to Be Received at the End of a Given Number of Time Periods

Periods	1%	2%	3%	4%	5%	6%	7%	8%	9%	10%	12%
1	0.990	0.980	0.971	0.962	0.952	0.943	0.935	0.926	0.917	0.909	0.893
2	0.980	0.961	0.943	0.925	0.907	0.890	0.873	0.857	0.842	0.826	0.797
3	0.971	0.942	0.915	0.889	0.864	0.840	0.816	0.794	0.772	0.751	0.712
4	0.961	0.924	0.888	0.855	0.823	0.792	0.763	0.735	0.708	0.683	0.636
5	0.951	0.906	0.883	0.822	0.784	0.747	0.713	0.681	0.650	0.621	0.567
6	0.942	0.888	0.837	0.790	0.746	0.705	0.666	0.630	0.596	0.564	0.507
7	0.933	0.871	0.813	0.760	0.711	0.665	0.623	0.583	0.547	0.513	0.452
8	0.923	0.853	0.789	0.731	0.677	0.627	0.582	0.540	0.502	0.467	0.404
9	0.914	0.837	0.766	0.703	0.645	0.592	0.544	0.500	0.460	0.424	0.361
10	0.905	0.820	0.744	0.676	0.614	0.558	0.508	0.463	0.422	0.386	0.322
11	0.896	0.804	0.722	0.650	0.585	0.527	0.475	0.429	0.388	0.350	0.287
12	0.887	0.788	0.701	0.625	0.557	0.497	0.444	0.397	0.356	0.319	0.257
13	0.879	0.773	0.681	0.601	0.530	0.469	0.415	0.368	0.326	0.290	0.229
14	0.870	0.758	0.661	0.577	0.505	0.442	0.388	0.340	0.299	0.263	0.205
15	0.861	0.743	0.642	0.555	0.481	0.417	0.362	0.315	0.275	0.239	0.183
16	0.853	0.728	0.623	0.534	0.458	0.394	0.339	0.292	0.252	0.218	0.163
17	0.844	0.714	0.605	0.513	0.436	0.371	0.317	0.270	0.231	0.198	0.146
18	0.836	0.700	0.587	0.494	0.416	0.350	0.296	0.250	0.212	0.180	0.130
19	0.828	0.686	0.570	0.475	0.396	0.331	0.277	0.232	0.194	0.164	0.116
20	0.820	0.673	0.554	0.456	0.377	0.312	0.258	0.215	0.178	0.149	0.104
21	0.811	0.660	0.538	0.439	0.359	0.294	0.242	0.199	0.164	0.135	0.093
22	0.803	0.647	0.522	0.422	0.342	0.278	0.226	0.184	0.150	0.123	0.083
23	0.795	0.634	0.507	0.406	0.326	0.262	0.211	0.170	0.138	0.112	0.074
24	0.788	0.622	0.492	0.390	0.310	0.247	0.197	0.158	0.126	0.102	0.066
25	0.780	0.610	0.478	0.375	0.295	0.233	0.184	0.146	0.116	0.092	0.059
26	0.772	0.598	0.464	0.361	0.281	0.220	0.172	0.135	0.106	0.084	0.053
27	0.764	0.586	0.450	0.347	0.268	0.207	0.161	0.125	0.098	0.076	0.047
28	0.757	0.574	0.437	0.333	0.255	0.196	0.150	0.116	0.090	0.069	0.042
29	0.749	0.563	0.424	0.321	0.243	0.185	0.141	0.107	0.082	0.063	0.037
30	0.742	0.552	0.412	0.308	0.231	0.174	0.131	0.099	0.075	0.057	0.033
40	0.672	0.453	0.307	0.208	0.142	0.097	0.067	0.046	0.032	0.022	0.011
50	0.608	0.372	0.228	0.141	0.087	0.054	0.034	0.021	0.013	0.009	0.003

Table 1 is used to compute the value today of a single amount of cash to be received sometime in the future. To use Table 1, you must first know (1) the time period in years until funds will be received, (2) the stated annual rate of interest, and (3) the dollar amount to be received at the end of the time period.

Example—Table 1. What is the present value of \$30,000 to be received 25 years from now, assuming a 14 percent interest rate? From Table 1, the required multiplier is 0.038, and the answer is:

$$\$30,000 \times 0.038 = \$1,140$$

The factor values for Table 1 are:

$$\text{PV Factor} = (1 + r)^{-n}$$

14%	15%	16%	18%	20%	25%	30%	35%	40%	45%	50%	Periods
0.877	0.870	0.862	0.847	0.833	0.800	0.769	0.741	0.714	0.690	0.667	1
0.769	0.756	0.743	0.718	0.694	0.640	0.592	0.549	0.510	0.476	0.444	2
0.675	0.658	0.641	0.609	0.579	0.512	0.455	0.406	0.364	0.328	0.296	3
0.592	0.572	0.552	0.516	0.482	0.410	0.350	0.301	0.260	0.226	0.198	4
0.519	0.497	0.476	0.437	0.402	0.328	0.269	0.223	0.186	0.156	0.132	5
0.456	0.432	0.410	0.370	0.335	0.262	0.207	0.165	0.133	0.108	0.088	6
0.400	0.376	0.354	0.314	0.279	0.210	0.159	0.122	0.095	0.074	0.059	7
0.351	0.327	0.305	0.266	0.233	0.168	0.123	0.091	0.068	0.051	0.039	8
0.308	0.284	0.263	0.225	0.194	0.134	0.094	0.067	0.048	0.035	0.026	9
0.270	0.247	0.227	0.191	0.162	0.107	0.073	0.050	0.035	0.024	0.017	10
0.237	0.215	0.195	0.162	0.135	0.086	0.056	0.037	0.025	0.017	0.012	11
0.208	0.187	0.168	0.137	0.112	0.069	0.043	0.027	0.018	0.012	0.008	12
0.182	0.163	0.145	0.116	0.093	0.055	0.033	0.020	0.013	0.008	0.005	13
0.160	0.141	0.125	0.099	0.078	0.044	0.025	0.015	0.009	0.006	0.003	14
0.140	0.123	0.108	0.084	0.065	0.035	0.020	0.011	0.006	0.004	0.002	15
0.123	0.107	0.093	0.071	0.054	0.028	0.015	0.008	0.005	0.003	0.002	16
0.108	0.093	0.080	0.060	0.045	0.023	0.012	0.006	0.003	0.002	0.001	17
0.095	0.081	0.069	0.051	0.038	0.018	0.009	0.005	0.002	0.001	0.001	18
0.083	0.070	0.060	0.043	0.031	0.014	0.007	0.003	0.002	0.001		19
0.073	0.061	0.051	0.037	0.026	0.012	0.005	0.002	0.001	0.001		20
0.064	0.053	0.044	0.031	0.022	0.009	0.004	0.002	0.001			21
0.056	0.046	0.038	0.026	0.018	0.007	0.003	0.001	0.001			22
0.049	0.040	0.033	0.022	0.015	0.006	0.002	0.001				23
0.043	0.035	0.028	0.019	0.013	0.005	0.002	0.001				24
0.038	0.030	0.024	0.016	0.010	0.004	0.001	0.001				25
0.033	0.026	0.021	0.014	0.009	0.003	0.001					26
0.029	0.023	0.018	0.011	0.007	0.002	0.001					27
0.026	0.020	0.016	0.010	0.006	0.002	0.001					28
0.022	0.017	0.014	0.008	0.005	0.002						29
0.020	0.015	0.012	0.007	0.004	0.001						30
0.005	0.004	0.003	0.001	0.001							40
0.001	0.001	0.001									50

TABLE 2 Present Value of $1 Received Each Period for a Given Number of Time Periods

Periods	1%	2%	3%	4%	5%	6%	7%	8%	9%	10%	12%
1	0.990	0.980	0.971	0.962	0.952	0.943	0.935	0.926	0.917	0.909	0.893
2	1.970	1.942	1.913	1.886	1.859	1.833	1.808	1.783	1.759	1.736	1.690
3	2.941	2.884	2.829	2.775	2.723	2.673	2.624	2.577	2.531	2.487	2.402
4	3.902	3.808	3.717	3.630	3.546	3.465	3.387	3.312	3.240	3.170	3.037
5	4.853	4.713	4.580	4.452	4.329	4.212	4.100	3.993	3.890	3.791	3.605
6	5.795	5.601	5.417	5.242	5.076	4.917	4.767	4.623	4.486	4.355	4.111
7	6.728	6.472	6.230	6.002	5.786	5.582	5.389	5.206	5.033	4.868	4.564
8	7.652	7.325	7.020	6.733	6.463	6.210	5.971	5.747	5.535	5.335	4.968
9	8.566	8.162	7.786	7.435	7.108	6.802	6.515	6.247	5.995	5.759	5.328
10	9.471	8.983	8.530	8.111	7.722	7.360	7.024	6.710	6.418	6.145	5.650
11	10.368	9.787	9.253	8.760	8.306	7.887	7.499	7.139	6.805	6.495	5.938
12	11.255	10.575	9.954	9.385	8.863	8.384	7.943	7.536	7.161	6.814	6.194
13	12.134	11.348	10.635	9.986	9.394	8.853	8.358	7.904	7.487	7.103	6.424
14	13.004	12.106	11.296	10.563	9.899	9.295	8.745	8.244	7.786	7.367	6.628
15	13.865	12.849	11.938	11.118	10.380	9.712	9.108	8.559	8.061	7.606	6.811
16	14.718	13.578	12.561	11.652	10.838	10.106	9.447	8.851	8.313	7.824	6.974
17	15.562	14.292	13.166	12.166	11.274	10.477	9.763	9.122	8.544	8.022	7.120
18	16.398	14.992	13.754	12.659	11.690	10.828	10.059	9.372	8.756	8.201	7.250
19	17.226	15.678	14.324	13.134	12.085	11.158	10.336	9.604	8.950	8.365	7.366
20	18.046	16.351	14.878	13.590	12.462	11.470	10.594	9.818	9.129	8.514	7.469
21	18.857	17.011	15.415	14.029	12.821	11.764	10.836	10.017	9.292	8.649	7.562
22	19.660	17.658	15.937	14.451	13.163	12.042	11.061	10.201	9.442	8.772	7.645
23	20.456	18.292	16.444	14.857	13.489	12.303	11.272	10.371	9.580	8.883	7.718
24	21.243	18.914	16.936	15.247	13.799	12.550	11.469	10.529	9.707	8.985	7.784
25	22.023	19.523	17.413	15.622	14.094	12.783	11.654	10.675	9.823	9.077	7.843
26	22.795	20.121	17.877	15.983	14.375	13.003	11.826	10.810	9.929	9.161	7.896
27	23.560	20.707	18.327	16.330	14.643	13.211	11.987	10.935	10.027	9.237	7.943
28	24.316	21.281	18.764	16.663	14.898	13.406	12.137	11.051	10.116	9.307	7.984
29	25.066	21.844	19.189	16.984	15.141	13.591	12.278	11.158	10.198	9.370	8.022
30	25.808	22.396	19.600	17.292	15.373	13.765	12.409	11.258	10.274	9.427	8.055
40	32.835	27.355	23.115	19.793	17.159	15.046	13.332	11.925	10.757	9.779	8.244
50	39.196	31.424	25.730	21.482	18.256	15.762	13.801	12.234	10.962	9.915	8.305

Table 2 is used to compute the present value of a *series* of *equal* annual cash flows.

Example—Table 2. Arthur Howard won a contest on January 1, 2010, in which the prize was $30,000, payable in 15 annual installments of $2,000 each December 31, beginning in 2010. Assuming a 9 percent interest rate, what is the present value of Howard's prize on January 1, 2010? From Table 2, the required multiplier is 8.061, and the answer is:

$$\$2{,}000 \times 8.061 = \$16{,}122$$

The factor values for Table 2 are:

$$\text{PVa Factor} = \frac{1 - (1 + r)^{-n}}{r}$$

14%	15%	16%	18%	20%	25%	30%	35%	40%	45%	50%	Periods
0.877	0.870	0.862	0.847	0.833	0.800	0.769	0.741	0.714	0.690	0.667	1
1.647	1.626	1.605	1.566	1.528	1.440	1.361	1.289	1.224	1.165	1.111	2
2.322	2.283	2.246	2.174	2.106	1.952	1.816	1.696	1.589	1.493	1.407	3
2.914	2.855	2.798	2.690	2.589	2.362	2.166	1.997	1.849	1.720	1.605	4
3.433	3.352	3.274	3.127	2.991	2.689	2.436	2.220	2.035	1.876	1.737	5
3.889	3.784	3.685	3.498	3.326	2.951	2.643	2.385	2.168	1.983	1.824	6
4.288	4.160	4.039	3.812	3.605	3.161	2.802	2.508	2.263	2.057	1.883	7
4.639	4.487	4.344	4.078	3.837	3.329	2.925	2.598	2.331	2.109	1.922	8
4.946	4.772	4.607	4.303	4.031	3.463	3.019	2.665	2.379	2.144	1.948	9
5.216	5.019	4.833	4.494	4.192	3.571	3.092	2.715	2.414	2.168	1.965	10
5.453	5.234	5.029	4.656	4.327	3.656	3.147	2.752	2.438	2.185	1.977	11
5.660	5.421	5.197	4.793	4.439	3.725	3.190	2.779	2.456	2.197	1.985	12
5.842	5.583	5.342	4.910	4.533	3.780	3.223	2.799	2.469	2.204	1.990	13
6.002	5.724	5.468	5.008	4.611	3.824	3.249	2.814	2.478	2.210	1.993	14
6.142	5.847	5.575	5.092	4.675	3.859	3.268	2.825	2.484	2.214	1.995	15
6.265	5.954	5.669	5.162	4.730	3.887	3.283	2.834	2.489	2.216	1.997	16
6.373	6.047	5.749	5.222	4.775	3.910	3.295	2.840	2.492	2.218	1.998	17
6.467	6.128	5.818	5.273	4.812	3.928	3.304	2.844	2.494	2.219	1.999	18
6.550	6.198	5.877	5.316	4.844	3.942	3.311	2.848	2.496	2.220	1.999	19
6.623	6.259	5.929	5.353	4.870	3.954	3.316	2.850	2.497	2.221	1.999	20
6.687	6.312	5.973	5.384	4.891	3.963	3.320	2.852	2.498	2.221	2.000	21
6.743	6.359	6.011	5.410	4.909	3.970	3.323	2.853	2.498	2.222	2.000	22
6.792	6.399	6.044	5.432	4.925	3.976	3.325	2.854	2.499	2.222	2.000	23
6.835	6.434	6.073	5.451	4.973	3.981	3.327	2.855	2.499	2.222	2.000	24
6.873	6.464	6.097	5.467	4.948	3.985	3.329	2.856	2.499	2.222	2.000	25
6.906	6.491	6.118	5.480	4.956	3.988	3.330	2.856	2.500	2.222	2.000	26
6.935	6.514	6.136	5.492	4.964	3.990	3.331	2.856	2.500	2.222	2.000	27
6.961	6.534	6.152	5.502	4.970	3.992	3.331	2.857	2.500	2.222	2.000	28
6.983	6.551	6.166	5.510	4.975	3.994	3.332	2.857	2.500	2.222	2.000	29
7.003	6.566	6.177	5.517	4.979	3.995	3.332	2.857	2.500	2.222	2.000	30
7.105	6.642	6.234	5.548	4.997	3.999	3.333	2.857	2.500	2.222	2.000	40
7.133	6.661	6.246	5.554	4.999	4.000	3.333	2.857	2.500	2.222	2.000	50

Table 2 is the columnar sum of Table 1. Table 2 applies to *ordinary annuities,* in which the first cash flow occurs one time period beyond the date for which the present value is computed.

An *annuity due* is a series of equal cash flows for N time periods, but the first payment occurs immediately. The present value of the first payment equals the face value of the cash flow; Table 2 then is used to measure the present value of N − 1 remaining cash flows.

Example—Table 2. Determine the present value on January 1, 2010, of 20 lease payments; each payment of $10,000 is due on January 1, beginning in 2010. Assume an interest rate of 8 percent.

Present Value = Immediate Payment + Present Value of 19 Subsequent Payments at 8%

= $10,000 + ($10,000 × 9.604) = $106,040

ENDNOTES

Chapter 1

1. *Statement of Financial Accounting Concepts No. 1,* "Objectives of Financial Reporting by Business Enterprises" (Norwalk, Conn.: Financial Accounting Standards Board, 1978), par. 9.
2. Ibid.
3. CVS Corporation, *Annual Report,* 2008.
4. Ibid.
5. Christopher D. Ittner, David F. Larcker, and Madhav V. Rajan, "The Choice of Performance Measures in Annual Bonus Contracts," *The Accounting Review,* April 1997.
6. National Commission on Fraudulent Financial Reporting, *Report of the National Commission on Fraudulent Financial Reporting* (Washington, D.C.: 1987), p. 2.
7. Target Corporation, Form 10-K, 2008.
8. "Gallup Poll Shows the Public's Opinion of Accounting Profession Is Improving," http://www.picpa.org, August 24, 2005.
9. Robert Johnson, "The New CFO," *Crain's Chicago Business,* July 19, 2004.
10. *Accounting Principles Board Statement No. 4,* "Basic Concepts and Accounting Principles Underlying Financial Statements of Business Enterprises" (New York: AICPA, 1970), par. 138.
11. Securities and Exchange Commission, *Roadmap for the Potential Use of Financial Statements Prepared in Accordance with International Financial Reporting Standards by US Issuers,* August 2008.
12. *Statement Number 1C,* "Standards of Ethical Conduct for Management Accountants" (Montvale, N.J.: Institute of Management Accountants, 1983; revised 1997).
13. Curtis C. Verschoor, "Corporate Performance Is Closely Tied to a Strong Ethical Commitment," *Journal of Business and Society,* Winter 1999; Verschoor, "Does Superior Governance Still Lead to Better Financial Performance?" *Strategic Finance,* October 2004.
14. Costco Wholesale Corporation, *Annual Report,* 2006.
15. Southwest Airlines Co., *Annual Report,* 1996.

Chapter 2

1. The Boeing Company, *Annual Report,* 2008.
2. *Statement of Financial Accounting Standards No. 157,* "Fair Value Measurements" (Norwalk, Conn.: Financial Accounting Standards Board, 2007).
3. Intel Corporation, *Annual Report,* 2008.
4. The Boeing Company, *Annual Report,* 2008.
5. Gary McWilliams, "EDS Accounting Change Cuts Past Earnings by $2.24 Billion," *The Wall Street Journal,* October 28, 2003.
6. Nike, Inc., *Annual Report,* 2008.

Chapter 3

1. Netflix, Inc., *Annual Report,* 2008.
2. "Microsoft Settles with SEC," *CBSNews.com,* June 5, 2002.
3. Christofer Lawson and Don Clark, "Dell to Restate 4 Years of Results," *The Wall Street Journal, August 17, 2007.*
4. Securities and Exchange Commission, *Staff Accounting Bulletin No. 10,* 1999.
5. Ken Brown, "Wall Street Plays Numbers Games with Savings, Despite Reforms," *The Wall Street Journal,* July 22, 2003.
6. Netflix, Inc., *Annual Report,* 2008.
7. Ibid.

Chapter 4

1. Adapted from Robert Half International, Inc., *Annual Report,* 2005.

Chapter 5

1. *Statement of Financial Accounting Concepts No. 1,* "Objectives of Financial Reporting by Business Enterprises" (Norwalk, Conn.: Financial Accounting Standards Board, 1978), pars. 32–54.
2. *Statement of Financial Accounting Concepts No. 2,* "Qualitative Characteristics of Accounting Information" (Norwalk, Conn.: Financial Accounting Standards Board, 1980), par. 20.
3. L. Todd Johnson, "Relevance and Reliability," *The FASB Report,* February 28, 2005.
4. Dell Computer Corporation, Form 10-K for the Fiscal Year Ended February 3, 2006.
5. "Ex-Chief of WorldCom Is Found Guilty in $11 Billion Fraud," *The New York Times,* March 16, 2005.
6. *Accounting Principles Board, Opinion No. 20,* "Accounting Changes" (New York: AICPA, 1971), par. 17.
7. Securities and Exchange Commission, *Staff Accounting Bulletin No. 99,* 1999.
8. http://www.fasb.org, July 12, 2008.
9. Ray J. Groves, "Here's the Annual Report. Got a Few Hours?" *The Wall Street Journal Europe,* August 26–27, 1994.
10. Roger Lowenstein, "Investors Will Fish for Footnotes in Abbreviated' Annual Reports," *The Wall Street Journal,* September 14, 1995.
11. Securities and Exchange Commission, *Staff Accounting Bulletin No. 99,* 1999.
12. Roger Lowenstein, "The 20% Club' Is No Longer Exclusive," *The Wall Street Journal,* May 4, 1995.
13. Albertson's Inc., *Annual Report,* 2008; Great Atlantic & Pacific Tea Company, *Annual Report,* 2008.

Chapter 6

1. Jathon Sapsford, "As Cash Fades, America Becomes a Plastic Nation," *The Wall Street Journal,* July 23, 2004.
2. Helen Leggatt, "Growth Forecast for 2009 On-line Retail Sales," *BizReport,* January 30, 2009.
3. Joel Millman, "Here's What Happens to Many Lovely Gifts After Santa Rides Off," *The Wall Street Journal,* December 26, 2001.
4. Matthew Rose, "Magazine Revenue at Newsstands Falls in Worst Year Ever," *The Wall Street Journal,* May 15, 2001.

Chapter 7

1. Committee of Sponsoring Organizations of the Treadway Commission (COSO), *Internal Control—Integrated Framework, 1985–2005.*
2. Costco Wholesale Corporation, *Annual Report,* 2008.
3. Jonathan Weil, "Accounting Scheme Was Straightforward but Hard to Detect," *The Wall Street Journal,* July 23, 2004.
4. Costco Wholesale Corporation, *Annual Report,* 2008.

5. *Professional Standards,* vol. 1, Sec. AU 325.16.
6. KPMG Peat Marwick, "1998 Fraud Survey," 1998.
7. Elizabeth Woyke, "Attention Shoplifters," *BusinessWeek,* September 11, 2006.
8. Amy Merrick, "Starbucks Accuses Employee, Husband of Embezzling $3.7 Million from Firm," *The Wall Street Journal,* November 20, 2000.

Chapter 8

1. Toyota Motor Corporation, *Annual Report,* 2008.
2. Gary McWilliams, "Whirlwind on the Web," *BusinessWeek,* April 7, 1997.
3. Karen Lundebaard, "Bumpy Ride," *The Wall Street Journal,* May 21, 2001.
4. "Cisco's Numbers Confound Some," *International Herald Tribune,* April 19, 2001.
5. "Kmart Posts $67 Million Loss Due to Markdowns," *The Wall Street Journal,* November 10, 2000.
6. American Institute of Certified Public Accountants, *Accounting Trends & Techniques* (New York: AICPA, 2008).
7. Toyota Motor Corporation., *Annual Report,* 2008.
8. Ernst & Young, *U.S. GAAP vs. IFRS: The Basics,* 2007.
9. American Institute of Certified Public Accountants, *Accounting Trends & Techniques* (New York: AICPA, 2007).
10. American Institute of Certified Public Accountants, *Accounting Trends & Techniques* (New York: AICPA, 2008).

Chapter 9

1. Peter Coy and Michael Arndt, "Up a Creek with Lots of Cash," *BusinessWeek,* November 12, 2001.
2. "So Much for Detroit's Cash Cushion," *BusinessWeek,* November 5, 2001.
3. Jesse Drucker, "Sprint Expects Loss of Subscribers," *The Wall Street Journal,* September 24, 2002.
4. Michael Selz, "Big Customers' Late Bills Choke Small Suppliers," *The Wall Street Journal,* June 22, 1994.
5. Circuit City Stores, Inc., *Annual Report,* 2005.
6. Deborah Solomon and Damian Paletta, "U.S. Drafts Sweeping Plans to Fight Crisis as Turmoil Worsens in Credit Markets," *The Wall Street Journal,* September 19, 2008.
7. Heather Timmons, "Do Household's Numbers Add Up?" *BusinessWeek,* December 10, 2001.
8. Steve Daniels, "Bank One Reserves Feed Earnings," *Crain's Chicago Business,* December 15, 2003.
9. Jonathon Weil, "Accounting Scheme Was Straightforward but Hard to Detect," *The Wall Street Journal,* March 20, 2003.
10. Nike, Inc., *Annual Report,* 2009.
11. Ibid.
12. American Institute of Certified Public Accountants, *Accounting Trends & Techniques* (New York: AICPA, 2007).
13. Tom Lauricella, Shefali Anand, and Valerie Bauerlein, "A $34 Billion Cash Fund to Close Up," *The Wall Street Journal,* December 11, 2007.
14. Jathon Sapsford, "As Cash Fades, America Becomes a Plastic Nation," *The Wall Street Journal,* July 23, 2004.
15. American Institute of Certified Public Accountants, *Accounting Trends & Techniques* (New York: AICPA, 2007).
16. "Bad Loans Rattle Telecom Vendors," *BusinessWeek,* February 19, 2001.
17. Scott Thurm, "Better Debt Bolsters Bottom Lines," *The Wall Street Journal,* August 18, 2003.
18. Information based on promotional brochures of Mitsubishi Corp.
19. Elizabeth McDonald, "Unhatched Chickens," *Forbes,* February 19, 2001.

Chapter 10

1. Pamela L. Moore, "How Xerox Ran Short of Black Ink," *BusinessWeek,* October 30, 2000.
2. Mark Heinzel, Deborah Solomon, and Joann S. Lublin, "Nortel Board Fires CEO and Others," *The Wall Street Journal,* April 29, 2004.
3. Hershey Foods Corporation, *Annual Report,* 2006.
4. Goodyear Tire & Rubber Company, *Annual Report,* 2006.
5. Andersen Enterprise Group, cited in *Crain's Chicago Business,* July 5, 1999.
6. Promomagazine.com, July 6, 2005.
7. Scott McCartney, "Your Free Flight to Mars Is Hobbling the Airline Industry," *The Wall Street Journal,* February 4, 2004.
8. Hershey Foods Corporation, *Annual Report,* 2007.
9. *Statement of Financial Accounting Standards No. 5,* "Accounting for Contingencies" (Norwalk, Conn.: Financial Accounting Standards Board, 1975).
10. American Institute of Certified Public Accountants, *Accounting Trends & Techniques* (New York: AICPA, 2007).
11. Microsoft, *Annual Report,* 2007.
12. American Institute of Certified Public Accountants, *Accounting Trends & Techniques* (New York: AICPA, 2007).
13. *Statement of Financial Accounting Concepts No. 7,* "Using Cash Flow Information and Present Value in Accounting Measurement" (Norwalk, Conn.: Financial Accounting Standards Board, 2000).
14. "Clarifications on Fair-Value Accounting," U.S. Securities and Exchange Commission, *Release 2008-234,* October 1, 2008.
15. Advertisement, *Chicago Tribune,* November 8, 2002.
16. General Motors Corporation, *Annual Report,* 2006.

Chapter 11

1. *Statement of Financial Accounting Standards No. 144,* "Accounting for the Impairment or Disposal of Long-Lived Assets" (Norwalk, Conn.: Financial Accounting Standards Board, 2001).
2. Sharon Young, "Large Telecom Firms, After WorldCom Moves, Consider Writedowns," *The Wall Street Journal,* March 18, 2003.
3. Edward J. Riedl, "An Examination of Long-lived Asset Impairments," *The Accounting Review,* Vol. 79, No. 3, pp. 823–852.
4. *Statement of Financial Accounting Standards No. 34,* "Capitalization of Interest Cost" (Norwalk, Conn.: Financial Accounting Standards Board, 1979), pars. 9–11.
5. American Institute of Certified Public Accountants, *Accounting Trends & Techniques* (New York: AICPA, 2007).
6. Ibid.
7. Jonathan Weil, "Oil Reserves Can Sure Be Slick," *The Wall Street Journal,* March 11, 2004.
8. *Statement of Financial Accounting Standards No. 25,* "Suspension of Certain Accounting Requirements for Oil and Gas Producing Companies" (Norwalk, Conn.: Financial Accounting Standards Board, 1979).
9. "The Top 100 Brands," *BusinessWeek,* August 5, 2002.
10. The New York Times Company, *Annual Report,* 2006.
11. *Statement of Financial Accounting Standards No. 142,* "Goodwill and Other Intangible Assets" (Norwalk, Conn.: Financial Accounting Standards Board, 2001), pars. 11–17.
12. General Motors Corporation, *Annual Report,* 2005.
13. Abbott Laboratories, *Annual Report,* 2005.

14. *Statement of Financial Accounting Standards No. 2,* "Accounting for Research and Development Costs" (Norwalk, Conn.: Financial Accounting Standards Board, 1974), par. 12.
15. *Statement of Financial Accounting Standards No. 86,* "Accounting for the Costs of Computer Software to Be Sold, Leased, or Otherwise Marketed" (Norwalk, Conn.: Financial Accounting Standards Board, 1985).
16. General Mills, Inc., *Annual Report,* 2007; H.J. Heinz Company, *Annual Report,* 2007; Tribune Company, *Annual Report,* 2007.
17. *Statement of Financial Accounting Standards No. 142,* "Goodwill and Other Intangible Assets" (Norwalk, Conn.: Financial Accounting Standards Board, 2001), pars. 11–17.
18. Southwest Airlines Co., *Annual Report,* 2002.
19. Costco Wholesale Corporation, *Annual Report,* 2007.
20. Hilton Hotels Corporation, *Annual Report,* 2006; Marriott International, Inc., *Annual Report,* 2006.

Chapter 12

1. "Stock and Bond Market Shrivels," Wall Street Journal Digital Network, January 2, 2009.
2. Microsoft Corporation, *Annual Report,* 2009.
3. Deborah Solomon, "AT&T Slashes Dividends 83%, Cuts Forecasts," *The Wall Street Journal,* December 21, 2002.
4. Abbott Laboratories, *Annual Report,* 2008.
5. Google, Inc., *Form S-1* (Registration Statement), 2007.
6. Microsoft Corporation, *Annual Report,* 2009.
7. American Institute of Certified Public Accountants, *Accounting Trends & Techniques* (New York: AICPA, 2007).
8. *Statement of Accounting Standards No. 123,* "Stock-Based Payments" (Norwalk, Conn.: Financial Accounting Standards Board, 1995; amended 2004).
9. Google, Inc., *Form S-1* (Registration Statement), 2009.
10. Jonathan Weil, "FASB Unveils Expensing Plan on Option Pay," *The Wall Street Journal,* April 1, 2004.
11. Joseph Weber, "One Share, Many Votes," *BusinessWeek,* March 29, 2004; Google, Inc., *Form S-1* (Registration Statement), 2004.
12. Michael Rapaport and Jonathan Weil, "More Truth-in-Labeling for Accounting Carries Liabilities," *The Wall Street Journal,* August 23, 2003.
13. American Institute of Certified Public Accountants, *Accounting Trends & Techniques* (New York: AICPA, 2007).
14. David Henry, "The Dirty Little Secret about Buybacks," *BusinessWeek,* January 23, 2006; Peter A. McKay and Justin Lahart, "Boom in Buybacks Helps Lift Stocks to Record Heights," *The Wall Street Journal,* July 18, 2007.
15. Mariss Marr, "Dreamworks Shares Rise 38% on First Day," *The Wall Street Journal,* October 10, 2004; *Yahoo Finance,* December 26, 2007.
16. IBM Corporation, *Annual Report,* 2006.
17. Google, Inc., *Form S-1* (Registration Statement), 2004.

Chapter 13

1. *Statement of Financial Accounting Standards No. 13,* "Accounting for Leases" (Norwalk, Conn.: Financial Accounting Standards Board, 1976), par. 10.
2. *Statement of Financial Accounting Standards No. 158,* "Employers' Accounting for Defined Benefit Pension and Other Postretirement Plans" (Norwalk, Conn.: Financial Accounting Standards Board, 2007).
3. General Motors, *Annual Report,* 2007.
4. Deborah Soloman, "After Pension Fund Debacle, San Diego Mired in Probes," *The Wall Street Journal,* October 10, 2005.
5. Mary Williams Walsh, "$53 Billion Shortfall for New Jersey Retiree Care," *The New York Times,* July 25, 2007.
6. *Statement of Financial Accounting Standards No. 106,* "Employers' Accounting for Postretirement Benefits Other than Pensions" (Norwalk, Conn.: Financial Accounting Standards Board, 1990).
7. Southwest Airlines, *Annual Report,* 2008.
8. McDonald's, Inc., *Annual Report,* 2008.
9. Bill Barnhart, "Bond Bellwether," *Chicago Tribune,* December 4, 1996.
10. Accounting Principles Board, *Opinion No. 21,* "Interest on Receivables and Payables" (New York: AICPA, 1971), par. 15.
11. Continental Airlines, *Annual Report,* 2008.
12. Tom Sullivan and Sonia Ryst, "Kodak $1 Billion Issue Draws Crowds," *The Wall Street Journal,* October 8, 2003.
13. Adapted from quotations in *The Wall Street Journal Online,* December 18, 2007.
14. Amazon.com, *Annual Report,* 2007.

Chapter 14

1. Cited in *The Week in Review* (Deloitte Haskins & Sells), February 28, 1985.
2. "Up to the Minute, Down to the Wire," *Twentieth Century Mutual Funds Newsletter,* 1996.
3. "After Charge for Licensing, McDonald's Posts a Record Loss," *The New York Times,* July 25, 2007; Christina Cheddar Berk, "Campbell's Profit Jumps 31 Percent," *The Wall Street Journal,* November 22, 2005.
4. Elizabeth MacDonald, "Pro Forma Puff Jobs," *Forbes,* December 9, 2002.
5. Barbara A. Lougee and Carol A. Marquardt, "Earnings Informativeness and Strategic Disclosure: An Empirical Examination of Pro Forma Earnings," *The Accounting Review,* July 2004.
6. American Institute of Certified Public Accountants, *Accounting Trends & Techniques* (New York: AICPA, 2007).
7. *Statement of Financial Reporting Standards No. 145,* "Rescission and Revision of Various Statements" (Norwalk, Conn.: Financial Accounting Standards Board, 2002).
8. *Statement of Financial Accounting Standards No. 109,* "Accounting for Income Taxes" (Norwalk, Conn.: Financial Accounting Standards Board, 1992).
9. American Institute of Certified Public Accountants, *Accounting Trends & Techniques* (New York: AICPA, 2007).
10. Accounting Principles Board, *Opinion No. 30,* "Reporting the Results of Operations" (New York: AICPA, 1973), par. 20.
11. *Statement of Financial Accounting Standards No. 128,* "Earnings per Share and the Disclosure of Information About Capital Structure" (Norwalk, Conn.: Financial Accounting Standards Board, 1997).
12. *Statement of Financial Accounting Standards No. 130,* "Reporting Comprehensive Income" (Norwalk, Conn.: Financial Accounting Standards Board, 1997).
13. American Institute of Certified Public Accountants, *Accounting Trends & Techniques* (New York: AICPA, 2007).
14. American Institute of Certified Public Accountants, *Accounting Research Bulletin No. 43* (New York: AICPA, 1953), chap. 7, sec. B, par. 10.
15. Ibid., par. 13.
16. Nike, *Annual Report,* 2007.
17. Robert O'Brien, "Tech's Chill Fails to Stem Stock Splits," *The Wall Street Journal,* June 8, 2000.
18. YahooFinance.com, 2007.
19. "Technology Firms Post Strong Earnings but Stock Prices Decline Sharply," *The Wall Street Journal,* January 21,

1988; Donald R. Seace, "Industrials Plunge 57.2 Points—Technology Stocks' Woes Cited," *The Wall Street Journal,* January 21, 1988.

Chapter 15

1. Ian McDonald, "Cash Dilemma: How to Spend It," *The Wall Street Journal,* May 24, 2006; Ian McDonald, "Companies Are Rolling in Cash, Too Bad," *The Wall Street Journal,* August 20, 2006.
2. "Deadweight on the Markets," *BusinessWeek,* February 19, 2001.
3. "Free Cash Flow Standouts," *Upside Newsletter,* October 3, 2001.
4. Amazom.com, *Form 10-K,* 2008.
5. Gary Slutsker, "Look at the Birdie and Say: 'Cash Flow,'" *Forbes,* October 25, 1993.
6. Jonathan Clements, "Yacktman Fund Is Bloodied but Unbowed," *The Wall Street Journal,* November 8, 1993.
7. Jeffery Laderman, "Earnings, Schmearnings—Look at the Cash," *BusinessWeek,* July 24, 1989.
8. Amazom.com, *Form 10-K,* 2008.
9. American Institute of Certified Public Accountants, *Accounting Trends & Techniques* (New York: AICPA, 2006).
10. Martin Peers and Robin Sidel, "WorldCom Causes Analysts to Evaluate EBITDA's Role," *The Wall Street Journal,* July 15, 2002.
11. Richard Passov, "How Much Cash Does Your Company Need?" *Harvard Business Review,* November 2003.
12. "Cash Flow Shortfall in Quarter May Lead to Default on Loan," *The Wall Street Journal,* September 4, 2001.
13. Enron Corporation, *Press Release,* October 16, 2001.
14. Dean Foust, "So Much Cash, So Few Dividends," *BusinessWeek,* January 20, 2003.

Chapter 16

1. David Henry, "The Numbers Game," *BusinessWeek,* May 14, 2001.
2. Jonathan Weil, "Pro Forma in Earnings Reports? . . . As If," *The Wall Street Journal,* April 24, 2003.
3. *Statement of Financial Accounting Standards No. 131,* "Segment Disclosures" (Norwalk, Conn.: Financial Accounting Standards Board, 1997).
4. Starbucks Corporation, *Annual Report,* 2008.
5. Ibid.
6. Ibid.
7. Target Corporation, *Proxy Statement,* May 18, 2005.
8. Starbucks Corporation, *Annual Report,* 2008.
9. Lee Hawkins, Jr., "S&P Cuts Rating on GM and Ford to Junk Status," *The Wall Street Journal,* May 6, 2005.

Chapter 17

1. "Nokia Unveils Plans for Chinese Centre," *Financial Times London,* May 9, 2000.

Chapter 18

1. http://imanet.org/about_ethics_statement.asp.
2. Andrew Ross Sorkin, "Albertsons Nears Deal, Yet Again, to Sell Itself," *The New York Times,* January 23, 2006.
3. Securities and Exchange Commission, "Final Rule: Certification of Disclosure in Companies' Quarterly and Annual Reports," August 28, 2002, http://www.sec.gov/rules/final/33-8124.htm.
4. Andra Gumbus and Susan D. Johnson, "The Balanced Scorecard at Futura Industries," *Strategic Finance,* July 2003.
5. Curtis C. Verschoor, "Economic Crime Results from Unethical Culture," *Strategic Finance,* March 2009.
6. *Statement No. 1A* (New York: Institute of Management Accountants, 1982).

Chapter 20

1. Robert L. Simison, "Toyota Finds Way to Make Custom Car in 5 Days," *The Wall Street Journal,* August 6, 1999.

Chapter 22

1. Lance Thompson, "Examining Methods of VBM," *Strategic Finance,* December 2002.
2. "Just In Time, Toyota Production System & Lean Manufacturing," http://www.strategosinc.com/just_in_time.htm.

Chapter 23

1. http://investor.google.com/conduct.html.

Chapter 24

1. Omar Aguilar, "How Strategic Performance Management Is Helping Companies Create Business Value," *Strategic Finance,* January 2003.
2. Jeremy Hope and Robin Frase, "Who Needs Budgets?" *Harvard Business Review,* February 2003.

Chapter 25

1. Marc J. Epstein and Jean-François Manzoni, "The Balanced Scorecard and Tableau de Bord: Translating Strategy into Action," *Management Accounting,* August 1997.
2. Kerry A. McDonald, "Meyners Does a Reality Check," *Journal of Accountancy,* February 2006.
3. V. G. Narayanan and Ananth Raman, "Aligning Incentives in Supply Chains," *Harvard Business Review,* November 2004.

Chapter 26

1. David E. Keys and Anton Van Der Merwe, "Gaining Effective Organizational Control with RCA," *Strategic Finance,* May 2002.

Chapter 27

1. Stephanie Miles, "What's a Check?" *The Wall Street Journal,* October 21, 2002, p. R5.
2. Alan Fuhrman, "Your e-Banking Future," *Strategic Finance,* April 2002.

Chapter 28

1. Paulette Thomas, "Case Study: Electronics Firm Ends Practice Just in Time," *The Wall Street Journal,* October 29, 2002.
2. From a speech by Jim Croft, vice president of finance and administration of the Field Museum, Chicago, November 14, 2000.

Appendix A

1. *Statement of Financial Accounting Standards No. 157,* "Fair Value Measurements" (Norwalk, Conn.: Financial Accounting Standards Board, 2007). *Statement of Financial Accounting Standards No. 159,* "The Fair Value Option for Financial Assets and Financial Liabilities" (Norwalk, Conn.: Financial Accounting Standards Board, 2007).
2. *Statement of Financial Accounting Standards No. 115,* "Accounting for Certain Investments in Debt and Equity Securities" (Norwalk, Conn.: Financial Accounting Standards Board, 1993).
3. Ibid.

COMPANY NAME INDEX

SUBJECT INDEX

Authors

Randall I. Charles
Professor Emeritus
Department of Mathematics
San Jose State University
San Jose, California

Janet H. Caldwell
Professor of Mathematics
Rowan University
Glassboro, New Jersey

Mary Cavanagh
Mathematics Consultant
San Diego County Office of Education
San Diego, California

Dinah Chancellor
Mathematics Consultant with Carroll ISD
Southlake, Texas
Mathematics Specialist with Venus ISD
Venus, Texas

Juanita V. Copley
Professor
College of Education
University of Houston
Houston, Texas

Warren D. Crown
Associate Dean for Academic Affairs
Graduate School of Education
Rutgers University
New Brunswick, New Jersey

Francis (Skip) Fennell
Professor of Education
McDaniel College
Westminster, Maryland

Alma B. Ramirez
Sr. Research Associate
Math Pathways and Pitfalls WestEd
Oakland, California

Kay B. Sammons
Coordinator of Elementary Mathematics
Howard County Public Schools
Ellicott City, Maryland

Jane F. Schielack
Professor of Mathematics
Associate Dean for Assessment and
Pre K-12 Education, College of Science
Texas A&M University
College Station, Texas

William Tate
Edward Mallinckrodt Distinguished
University Professor in Arts & Sciences
Washington University
St. Louis, Missouri

John A. Van de Walle
Professor Emeritus, Mathematics Education
Virginia Commonwealth University
Richmond, Virginia

Consulting Mathematicians

Edward J. Barbeau
Professor of Mathematics
University of Toronto
Toronto, Canada

Sybilla Beckmann
Professor of Mathematics
Department of Mathematics
University of Georgia
Athens, Georgia

David Bressoud
DeWitt Wallace Professor of Mathematics
Macalester College
Saint Paul, Minnesota

Gary Lippman
Professor of Mathematics and Computer Science
California State University East Bay
Hayward, California

Glenview, Illinois • Boston, Massachusetts • Chandler, Arizona • Upper Saddle River, New Jersey

Consulting Authors

Charles R. Allan
Mathematics Education Consultant
(Retired)
Michigan Department of Education
Lansing, Michigan

Verónica Galván Carlan
Private Consultant Mathematics
Harlingen, Texas

Stuart J. Murphy
Visual Learning Specialist
Boston, Massachusetts

Grant Wiggins
Researcher and Educational Consultant
Hopewell, New Jersey

ELL Consultants/Reviewers

Jim Cummins
Professor
The University of Toronto
Toronto, Canada

Alma B. Ramirez
Sr. Research Associate
Math Pathways and Pitfalls WestEd
Oakland, California

National Math Development Team

Cindy Bumbales
Teacher
Lake in the Hills, IL

Ann Hottovy
Teacher
Hampshire, IL

Deborah Ives
Supervisor of Mathematics
Ridgewood, NJ

Lisa Jasumback
Math Curriculum Supervisor
Farmington, UT

Rebecca Johnson
Teacher
Canonsburg, PA

Jo Lynn Miller
Math Specialist
Salt Lake City, UT

Patricia Morrison
Elementary Mathematics Specialist K-5
Upper Marlboro, MD

Patricia Horrigan Rourke
Mathematics Coordinator
Holliston, MA

Elise Sabaski
Teacher
Gladstone, MO

Math Advisory Board

John F. Campbell
Teacher
Upton, MA

Enrique Franco
Coordinator Elementary Math
Los Angeles, CA

Gladys Garrison
Teacher
Minot AFB, ND

Instructional Resource Teacher
Brookfield, UT

Shari Goodman
Math Specialist
Salt Lake City, UT

Cathy Massett
Math Facilitator
Cobb County SD, GA

Mary Modene
Math Facilitator
Belleville, IL

Kimya Moyo
Math Manager
Cincinnati, OH

Denise Redington
Teacher
Chicago, IL

Arlene Rosowski
Supervisor of Mathematics
Buffalo, NY

Darlene Teague
Director of Core Data
Kansas City, MO

Debbie Thompson
Elementary Math Teaching Specialist
Wichita, KS

Michele Whiston
Supervisor
Curriculum, Instruction, and Assessment
Mobile County, AL

ISBN-13: 978-0-328-48972-5
ISBN-10: 0-328-48972-7

7 8 9 10 11 V082 16 15 14 13 12 11

Topic Titles

Topic 1 Numeration

Topic 2 Adding Whole Numbers

Topic 3 Subtraction Number Sense

Topic 4 Subtracting Whole Numbers to Solve Problems

Topic 5 Multiplication Meanings and Facts

Topic 6 Multiplication Fact Strategies: Use Known Facts

Topic 7 Division Meanings

Topic 8 Division Facts

Topic 9 Patterns and Relationships

Topic 10 Solids and Shapes

Topic 11 Congruence and Symmetry

Topic 12 Understanding Fractions

Topic 13 Decimals and Money

Topic 14 Customary Measurement

Topic 15 Metric Measurement

Topic 16 Perimeter, Area, and Volume

Topic 17 Time and Temperature

Topic 18 Multiplying Greater Numbers

Topic 19 Dividing with 1-Digit Numbers

Topic 20 Data, Graphs, and Probability

Contents

MATH STRAND COLORS

- Number and Operations
- Algebra
- Geometry
- Measurement
- Data Analysis and Probability
- Problem Solving

Mathematical Processes, which include problem solving, reasoning, communication, connections, and representations, are infused throughout all lessons.

Topic 1 Numeration

Topic 2 Adding Whole Numbers

Topic 3 Subtraction Number Sense

Topic 4 Subtracting Whole Numbers to Solve Problems

Topic 5 Multiplication Meanings and Facts

Topic 6 Multiplication Fact Strategies: Use Known Facts

Topic 7 Division Meanings

Topic 8 Division Facts

Topic 9 Patterns and Relationships

Topic 10 Solids and Shapes

Topic 11 Congruence and Symmetry

Topic 12 Understanding Fractions

Topic 13 Decimals and Money

Topic 14 Customary Measurement

Topic 15 Metric Measurement

Topic 16 Perimeter, Area, and Volume

Topic 17 Time and Temperature

Topic 18 Multiplying Greater Numbers

Topic 19 Dividing with 1-Digit Numbers

Topic 20 Data, Graphs, and Probability

enVisionMATH Across the U.S.A.

Problem Solving Using Number and Operations

New Jersey and Outdoor Movies

One of the first drive-in movie theaters opened in 1933. It was in Camden, New Jersey. People could sit in their cars and watch movies. It cost 25¢ to park a car. The first three people in the car paid 25¢ each.

Arizona's Raccoon Relatives

Two animals from the raccoon family live in Arizona. They are the raccoon and the ringtail. The ringtail is Arizona's state mammal. A raccoon can weigh more than 25 pounds. A ringtail weighs about 2 pounds.

ringtail

raccoon

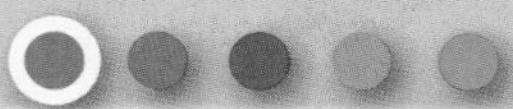

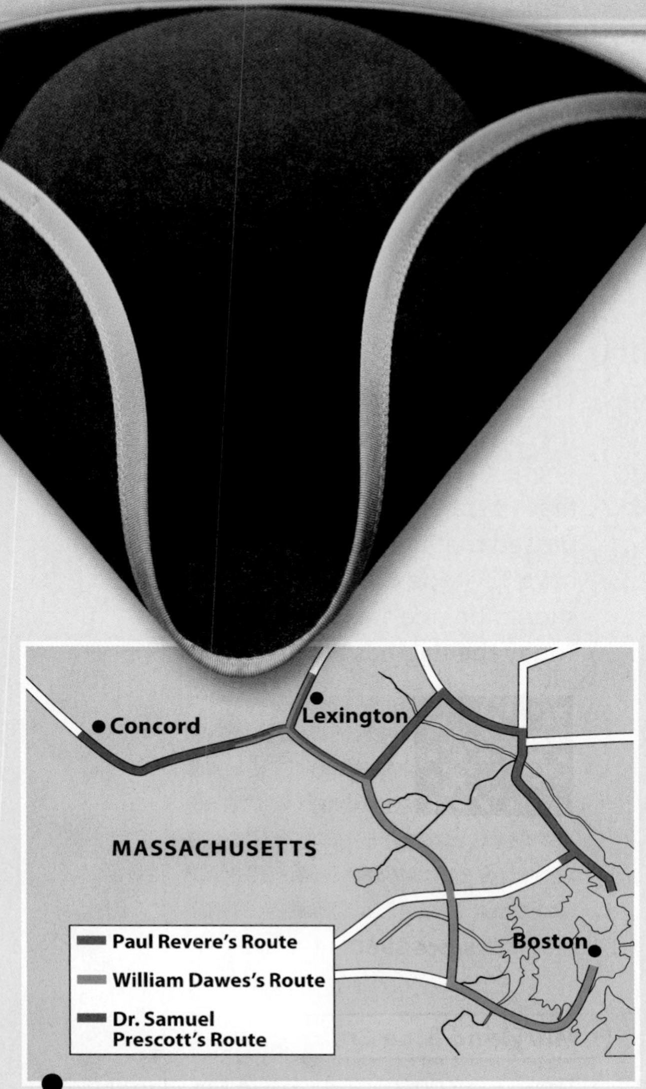

The British Are Coming!

In 1775 two men warned people in Massachusetts that British soldiers were coming. They rode horses from Boston to Lexington. They stopped at houses to give the alarm. Their ride took about two hours. Another man rode from Lexington to warn the town of Concord.

The distance from Boston to Lexington is about 15 miles. Today it would take about 30 minutes to drive a car from Boston to Lexington, a distance of about 15 miles. It would take about 20 minutes to drive about 8 miles from Lexington to Concord.

TEST PREP

Directions: Carefully read questions 1–20. Write your answers on a separate sheet of paper.

1. Rena and Jo paid 80¢ to watch a movie at the Camden drive-in. The two tickets only cost 75¢. How much money should they get back?

A 0¢ **C** 25¢
B 5¢ **D** 50¢

2. Eric drove alone to the Camden drive-in. How much money did he pay to park the car and watch the movie?

A 25¢ **C** 75¢
B 50¢ **D** $1.00

3. Suppose one ringtail weighs 2 pounds. How many pounds would five ringtails weigh all together?

A 3 pounds **C** 7 pounds
B 5 pounds **D** 10 pounds

4. Suppose there is a raccoon that is 42 inches long and a ringtail that is 24 inches long. How much shorter is the ringtail than the raccoon?

A 8 inches **C** 22 inches
B 18 inches **D** 66 inches

5. Pilar drove 15 miles from Boston to Lexington. Then she drove 8 miles to Concord. How many miles was her total trip?

A 7 miles **C** 23 miles
B 15 miles **D** 40 miles

6. Alexi drove for 30 minutes from Boston to Lexington. June drove for 20 minutes from Lexington to Concord. How many more minutes did Alexi drive than June?

A 10 minutes **C** 40 minutes
B 20 minutes **D** 50 minutes

enVisionMATH Across the U.S.A.

Problem Solving Using Geometry

U.S. flag in 1777

The United States Flag

The first official U.S. flag was called the Stars and Stripes. It had 13 stars. There was one star for each of the first 13 states. In 1818 a law was passed that the flag should always have 13 stripes. It also said that there should be one star for each state. Today the flag has 50 stars.

U.S. flag since 1960

Maryland Blue Crab

There is a 400-pound crab in Maryland! The crab is made of many glass pieces. It is at the airport in Baltimore. The glass crab shows travelers one of Maryland's state animals.

7. What is the shape of the U.S. flag?

A Rectangle
B Triangle
C Square
D Circle

8. Name a solid figure that has a side in the shape of the U.S. flag.

A Sphere
B Cone
C Cylinder
D Rectangular prism

9. The shape of the piece of glass shown as part of the crab's claw is a triangle. How many sides and angles does a triangle have?

A 3 sides, 3 angles
B 3 sides, 4 angles
C 3 sides, 5 angles
D 3 sides, 6 angles

Problem Solving Using Measurement

Let Freedom Ring

The Liberty Bell is a symbol of freedom. It has been at the Liberty Bell Center in Philadelphia, Pennsylvania, since 2003. The metal of the bell is 3 inches thick at the bottom. The bell is about 3 feet tall.

Sunlight in Michigan

Lansing, Michigan, can get more than 15 hours of sunlight in summer. In winter, Lansing may only get about 9 hours of sunlight. That's a difference of more than 6 hours!

State Capitol Building in Lansing, Michigan

10. The Liberty Bell is about 3 feet tall. Which object is longer than 3 feet?

A Toothbrush
B Eraser
C Spoon
D Car

11. The metal of the Liberty Bell is about 3 inches thick at the bottom. Which object is about 3 inches long?

A Umbrella
B Bathtub
C Belt
D Crayon

12. Look at the clock. It shows the time the sun set in Lansing, Michigan, on February 19, 2007. What time does the clock show?

A 3:06 P.M.
B 3:30 P.M.
C 6:03 P.M.
D 6:15 P.M.

enVisionMATH Across the U.S.A.

Problem Solving Using Data Analysis and Probability

©1910 USPS

©1962 USPS

©1999 USPS

U.S. Postage

In 1919 it cost 2¢ to mail a letter in the United States. Since then the cost has gone up many times. In May 2007 it cost 41¢ to mail a letter.

13. Ana has five stamps in a box. Four of them are 2¢ stamps. One of them is a 39¢ stamp. What is the likelihood Ana will choose a 39¢ stamp from the box?

A Certain　**C** Unlikely
B Likely　**D** Impossible

14. Ana has ten stamps in a box. All ten stamps are 2¢ stamps. What is the likelihood Ana will choose a 2¢ stamp from the box?

A Certain　**C** Unlikely
B Likely　**D** Impossible

15. Look at the graph of state animals. How many states chose the white-tailed deer?

A 3　**C** 10
B 4　**D** 17

16. Look at the graph of state animals. How many more states chose the white-tailed deer than the black bear?

A 4　**C** 10
B 6　**D** 14

State Symbols

Every state in the United States has state symbols such as state plants, rocks, or animals. Many states have a state animal. Some states picked the same animal. The pictograph shows the three animals that were picked by the most states.

Top Three State Animals

Bison	★ ★ ★
Black Bear	★ ★ ★ ★
White-tailed Deer	★ ★ ★ ★ ★ ★ ★ ★ ★ ★

Each ★ = 1 state.

white-tailed deer

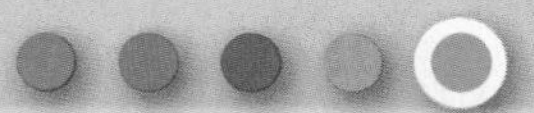

Missouri Caves

There are many caves in Missouri. The longest cave is about 28 miles long. Some animals live in these caves.

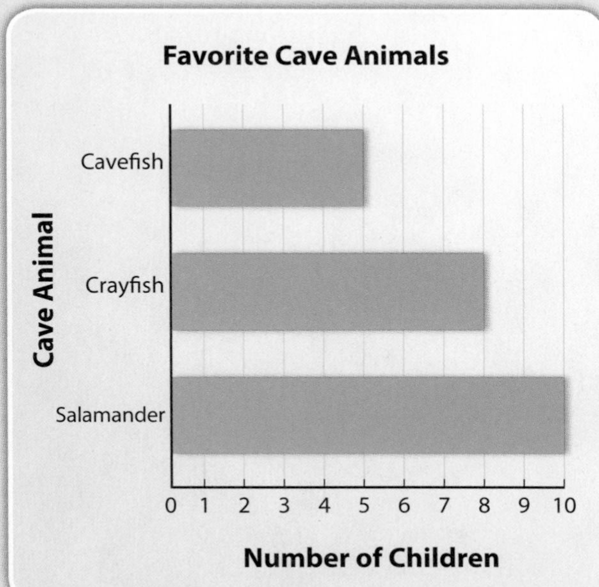

17. Look at the graph of cave animals. How many children chose the cavefish as their favorite cave animal?

A 1
B 3
C 5
D 10

18. Look at the graph of cave animals. How many more children chose the salamander as their favorite cave animal than the crayfish?

A 2
B 8
C 10
D 18

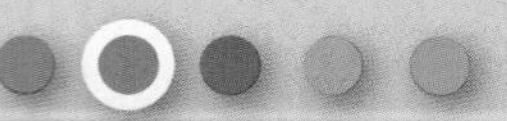

enVisionMATH Across the U.S.A.

Problem Solving Using Algebra

Jim Henson

Jim Henson was born in Mississippi in 1936. His family moved to Maryland when he was in fifth grade. He made the first characters on *Sesame Street®*. One of them was the 98-inch-tall Big Bird®. Jim Henson called these characters "Muppets®." The Muppets® first appeared on *Sesame Street®* in 1969.

19. Big Bird® is 98 inches tall. He stands on a step that is 7 inches above the ground. Which number sentence tells how far the top of Big Bird's® head is above the ground in inches?

A $98 + 7 = \square$
B $98 - 7 = \square$
C $98 \times 7 = \square$
D $98 \div 7 = \square$

20. Big Bird® is about 8 feet tall. Jody is 5 feet tall. Which number sentence tells about how much taller Big Bird® is than Jody?

A $8 + 5 = \square$
B $8 - 5 = \square$
C $8 \times 5 = \square$
D $8 \div 5 = \square$

Problem-Solving Handbook

Scott Foresman · Addison Wesley

enVisionMATH™

Problem-Solving Handbook

Use this Problem-Solving Handbook throughout the year to help you solve problems.

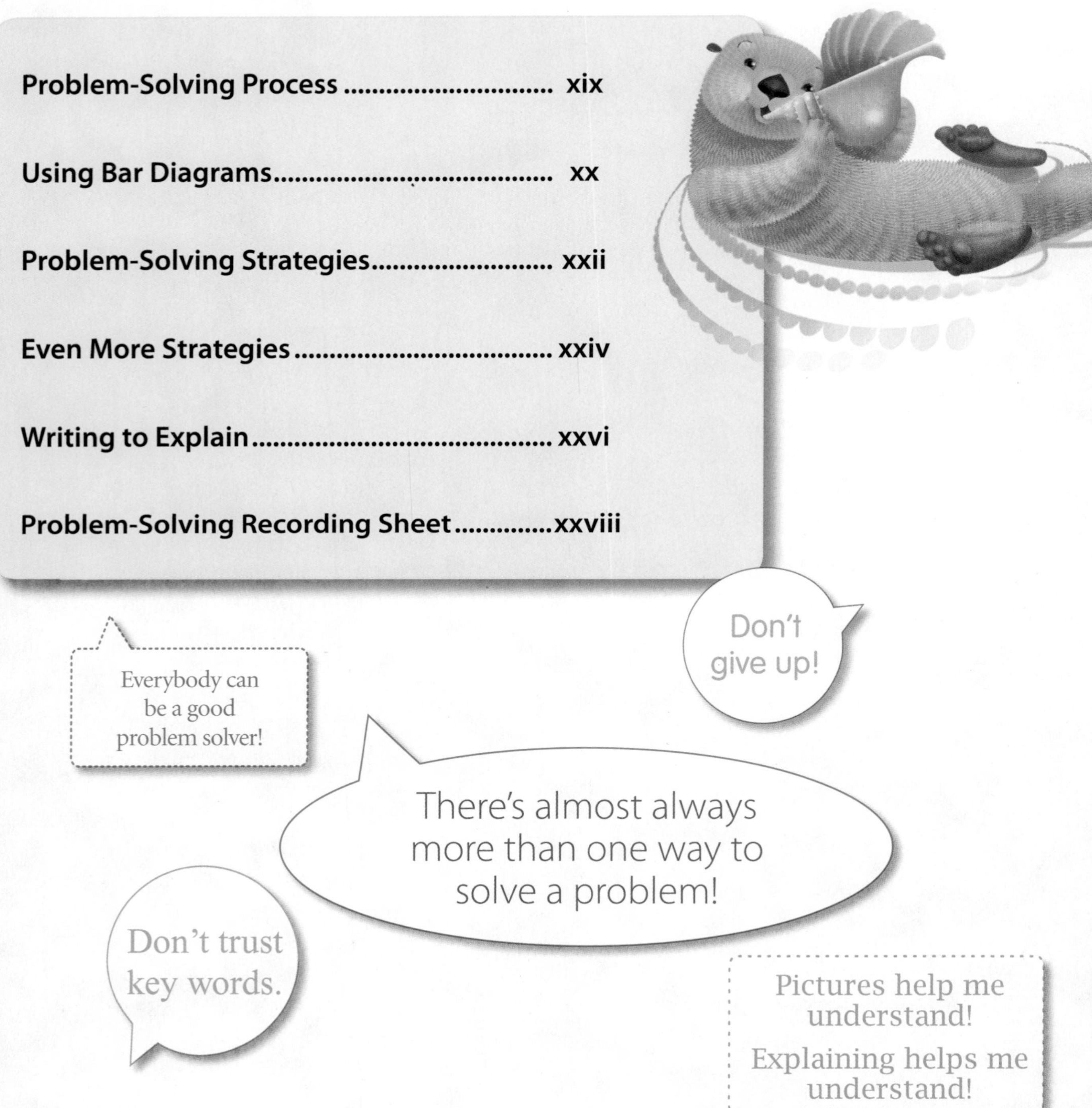

Problem-Solving Process

Read and Understand

What am I trying to find?
- Tell what the question is asking.

What do I know?
- Tell the problem in my own words.
- Identify key facts and details.

Plan and Solve

What strategy or strategies should I try?

Can I show the problem?
- Try drawing a picture.
- Try making a list, table, or graph.
- Try acting it out or using objects.

How will I solve the problem?

What is the answer?
- Tell the answer in a complete sentence.

Strategies
- Show What You Know
  - Draw a Picture
  - Make an Organized List
  - Make a Table
  - Make a Graph
  - Act It Out/ Use Objects
- Look for a Pattern
- Try, Check, Revise
- Write a Number Sentence
- Use Reasoning
- Work Backward
- Solve a Simpler Problem

Look Back and Check

Did I check my work?
- Compare my work to the information in the problem.
- Be sure all calculations are correct.

Is my answer reasonable?
- Estimate to see if my answer makes sense.
- Make sure the question was answered.

Using Bar Diagrams

Use a bar diagram to show how what you know and what you want to find are related. Then choose an operation to solve the problem.

Problem 1

Carrie helps at the family flower store in the summer. She keeps a record of how many hours she works. How many hours did she work on Monday and Wednesday?

Carrie's Work Hours

Data

Days	Hours
Monday	5
Tuesday	3
Wednesday	6
Thursday	5
Friday	5

Bar Diagram

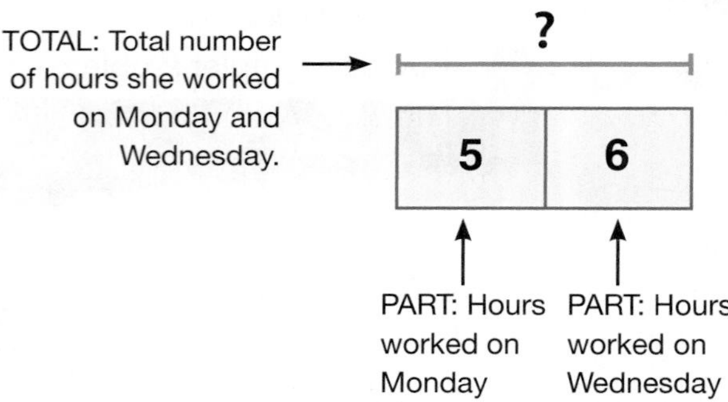

5 + 6 = ☐

I can add to find the total.

Problem 2

Kim is saving to buy a sweatshirt from the college her brother attends. She has $9. How much more money does she need to buy the sweatshirt?

Bar Diagram

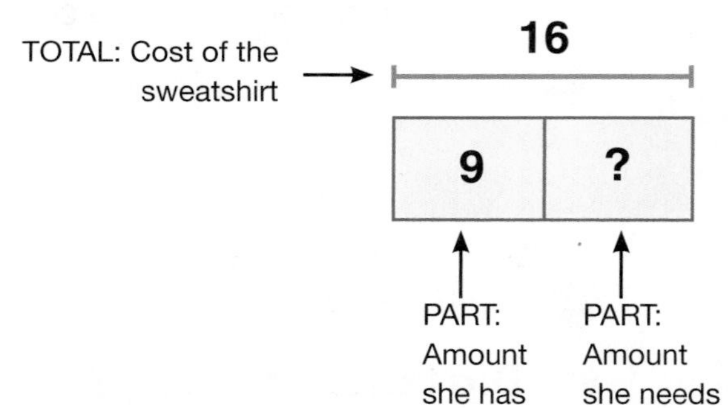

16 − 9 = ☐

I can subtract to find the missing part.

Pictures help me understand!

Don't trust key words!

Problem 3

Tickets to a movie on Saturday cost only $5 each no matter what age you are. What is the cost of tickets for a family of four?

Bar Diagram

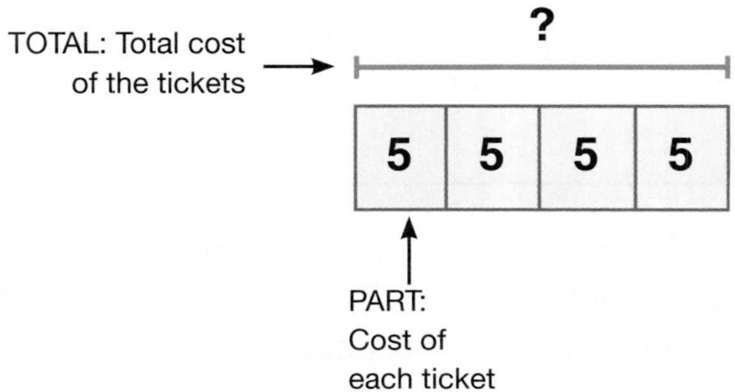

$4 \times 5 = \square$

I can multiply because the parts are equal.

Problem 4

Twelve students traveled in 3 vans to the zoo. The same number of students were in each van. How many students were in each van?

Bar Diagram

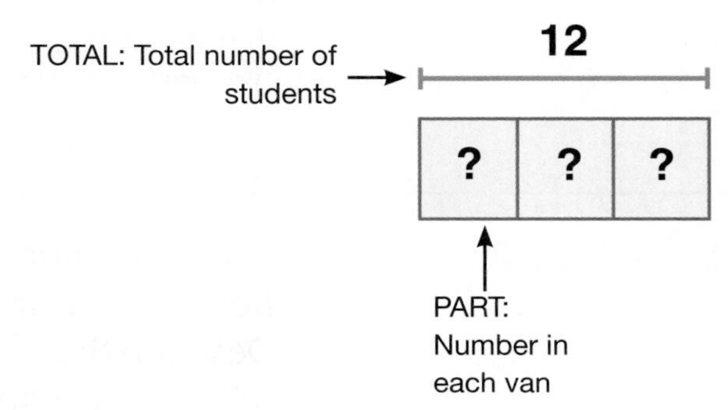

$12 \div 3 = \square$

I can divide to find how many are in each part.

Problem-Solving Strategies

Strategy	Example	When I Use It
Draw a Picture	The race was 5 kilometers. Markers were at the starting line and the finish line. Markers showed each kilometer of the race. Find the number of markers used. Start Line — Finish Line Start Line, 1 km, 2 km, 3 km, 4 km, Finish Line	Try drawing a picture when it helps you visualize the problem or when the relationships such as joining or separating are involved.
Make a Table	Phil and Marcy spent all day Saturday at the fair. Phil rode 3 rides each half hour and Marcy rode 2 rides each half hour. How many rides had Marcy ridden when Phil rode 24 rides?	Try making a table when: • there are 2 or more quantities, • amounts change using a pattern.
Look for a Pattern	The house numbers on Forest Road change in a planned way. Describe the pattern. Tell what the next two house numbers should be. 3, 6, 10, 15, ?, ?	Look for a pattern when something repeats in a predictable way.

Rides for Phil	3	6	9	12	15	18	21	24
Rides for Marcy	2	4	6	8	10	12	14	16

Everybody can be a good problem solver!

Strategy	Example	When I Use It
Make an Organized List	How many ways can you make change for a quarter using dimes and nickels? 1 quarter = 1 dime + 1 dime + 1 nickel 1 dime + 1 nickel + 1 nickel + 1 nickel 1 nickel + 1 nickel + 1 nickel + 1 nickel + 1 nickel	Make an organized list when asked to find combinations of two or more items.
Try, Check, Revise	Suzanne spent \$27, not including tax, on dog supplies. She bought two of one item and one of another item. What did she buy? \$8 + \$8 + \$15 = \$31 \$7 + \$7 + \$12 = \$26 \$6 + \$6 + \$15 = \$27	Use Try, Check, Revise when quantities are being combined to find a total, but you don't know which quantities. **Dog Supplies Sale!** Leash .... \$8 Collar .... \$6 Bowls .... \$7 Medium Beds .... \$15 Toys \$12
Write a Number Sentence	Maria's new CD player can hold 6 discs at a time. If she has 54 CDs, how many times can the player be filled without repeating a CD? Find $54 \div 6 = \blacksquare$.	Write a number sentence when the story describes a situation that uses an operation or operations.

Even More Strategies

Strategy	Example	When I Use It
Act It Out	How many ways can 3 students shake each other's hand?	Think about acting out a problem when the numbers are small and there is action in the problem you can do.
Use Reasoning	Beth collected some shells, rocks, and beach glass. **Beth's Collection** 2 rocks 3 times as many shells as rocks 12 objects in all How many of each object are in the collection?	Use reasoning when you can use known information to reason out unknown information.
Work Backward	Tracy has band practice at 10:15 A.M. It takes her 20 minutes to get from home to practice and 5 minutes to warm up. What time should she leave home to get to practice on time? Time Tracy leaves home ? ← 20 minutes ← Time warm up starts ← 5 minutes ← Time practice starts **10:15**	Try working backward when: • you know the end result of a series of steps, • you want to know what happened at the beginning.

I can think about when to use each strategy.

Strategy	Example	When I Use It
Solve a Simpler Problem 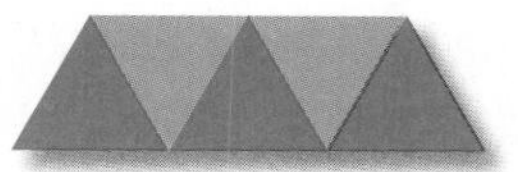	Each side of each triangle in the figure at the left is one centimeter. If there are 12 triangles in a row, what is the perimeter of the figure? I can look at 1 triangle, then 2 triangles, then 3 triangles. 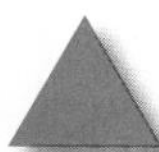 perimeter = 3 cm 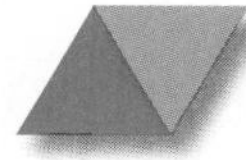 perimeter = 4 cm  perimeter = 5 cm	Try solving a simpler problem when you can create a simpler case that is easier to solve.
Make a Graph	Mary was in a jump rope contest. How did her number of jumps change over the five days of the contest? 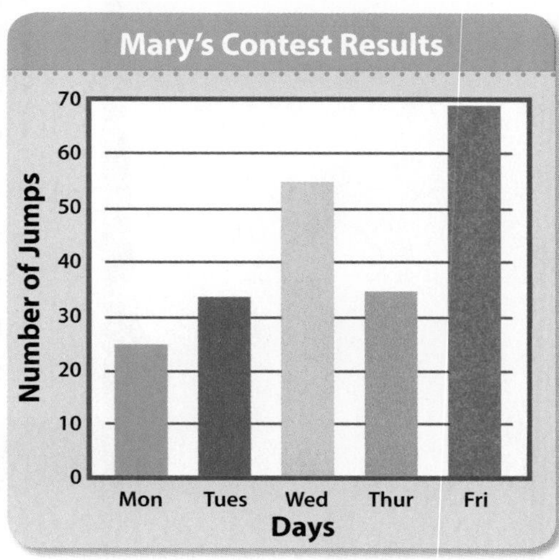	Make a graph when: • data for an event are given, • the question can be answered by reading the graph.

Writing to Explain

Here is a good math explanation.

Writing to Explain What happens to the area of the rectangle if the lengths of its sides are doubled?

▨ = $\frac{1}{4}$ of the whole rectangle

The area of the new rectangle is 4 times the area of the original rectangle.

Tips for Writing Good Math Explanations....

A good explanation should be:

- correct
- simple
- complete
- easy to understand

Math explanations can use:

- words
- pictures
- numbers
- symbols

Explaining helps me understand!

This is another good math explanation.

Writing to Explain Use blocks to show 3 × 24. Draw a picture of what you did with the blocks.

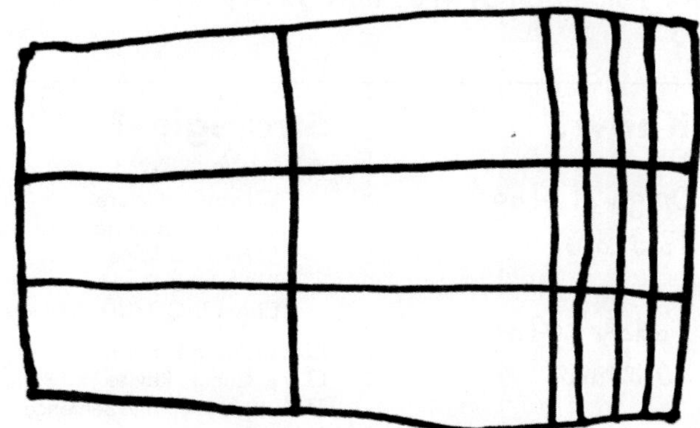

First we made a row of 24 using 2 tens and 4 ones. Then we made 2 more rows. Then we said 3 rows of 2 tens is 3 × 2 tens = 6 tens or 60. Then we said 3 rows of 4 ones is 3 × 4 = 12. Then we added the parts 60 + 12 = 72 So, 3 × 24 = 72.

Problem-Solving Recording Sheet

Name Jane

Teaching Tool 1

Problem-Solving Recording Sheet

Problem:
On June 14, 1777, the Continental Congress approved the design of a national flag. The 1777 flag had 13 stars, one for each colony. Today's flag has 50 stars, one for each state. How many stars were added to the flag since 1777?

Find?
Number of stars added to the flag

Know?
Original flag 13 stars

Today's flag 50 stars

Strategies?
Show the Problem
- ☑ Draw a Picture
- ☐ Make an Organized List
- ☐ Make a Table
- ☐ Make a Graph
- ☐ Act It Out/Use Objects

- ☐ Look for a Pattern
- ☐ Try, Check, Revise
- ☑ Write a Number Sentence
- ☐ Use Reasoning
- ☐ Work Backward
- ☐ Solve a Simpler Problem

Show the Problem?

50	
13	?

Solution?
I am comparing the two quantities.
I could add up from 13 to 50. I can also subtract 13 from 50. I'll subtract.

$$\begin{array}{r} 50 \\ -\ 13 \\ \hline 37 \end{array}$$

Answer?
There were 37 stars added to the flag from 1777 to today.

Check? Reasonable?
37 + 13 = 50 so I subtracted correctly.

50 − 13 is about 50 − 10 = 40
40 is close to 37. 37 is reasonable.

Teaching Tools • 1

Here's a way to organize my problem-solving work.

Name Benton

Problem-Solving Recording Sheet

Problem:

Suppose your teacher told you to open your math book to the facing pages whose page numbers add to 85. To which two pages would you open your book?

Find?

Two facing page numbers

Know?

Two pages.
Facing each other.
Sum is 85.

Strategies?

Show the Problem
- ☑ Draw a Picture
- ☐ Make an Organized List
- ☐ Make a Table
- ☐ Make a Graph
- ☐ Act It Out/Use Objects

- ☐ Look for a Pattern
- ☑ Try, Check, Revise
- ☑ Write a Number Sentence
- ☐ Use Reasoning
- ☐ Work Backward
- ☐ Solve a Simpler Problem

Show the Problem?

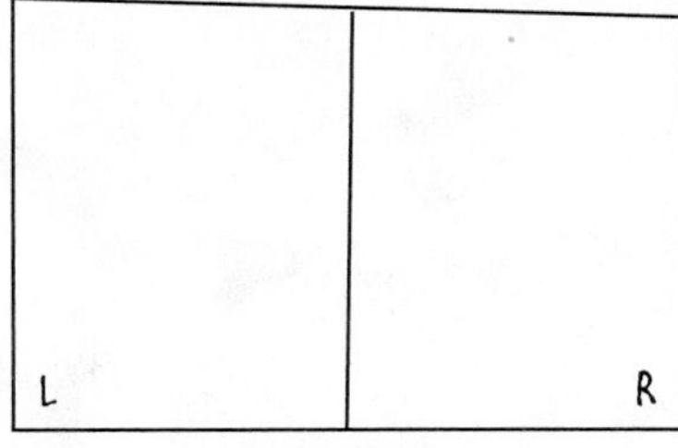

L + R = 85
L is 1 less than R

Solution?

I'll try some numbers in the middle.
40 + 41 = 81, too low
How about 46 and 47?
46 + 47 = 93, too high
Ok, now try 42 and 43.
42 + 43 = 85.

Answer?

The page numbers are 42 and 43.

Check? Reasonable?

I added correctly.
42 + 43 is about 40 + 40 = 80
80 is close to 85.
42 and 43 is reasonable.

Topic 1

Numeration

1 How many dominos were used to set a world record for domino-toppling? You will find out in Lesson 1-3.

2 How much did the world's largest pumpkin weigh? You will find out in Lesson 1-2.

3 How many grooves, or reeds, do some coins have around their edges? You will find out in Lesson 1-6.

4

How tall is the Great Pyramid in Egypt? You will find out in Lesson 1-5.

Review What You Know!

Vocabulary

Choose the best term from the box.

- hundreds
- numbers
- ones
- tens

1. The number 49 has 4 _?_.
2. The number 490 has 4 _?_.
3. The number 54 has 4 _?_.

Place Value

Write each number.

4. 3 tens 5 ones
5. 9 tens
6. forty-six
7. ninety-eight

Money

Write the value of each coin.

8. **9.** **10.** 

Skip count to find the missing amounts.

11. 5¢, 10¢, ▢, ▢, 25¢
12. 10¢, ▢, 30¢, 40¢, ▢

Compare Numbers

13. **Writing to Explain** Which is greater, 95 or 59? How do you know?
14. Write these numbers in order from least to greatest:
 14 54 41

Lesson

1-1 Hundreds

Understand It!
Place value is important when using numbers with more than one digit.

Hands-On
place-value blocks

How can you read and write a number in the hundreds?

All numbers are made from the digits, 0, 1, 2, 3, 4, 5, 6, 7, 8, and 9.

Place value is the value of the place a digit has in a number.

Bicycles with chains have been used for more than 125 years.

Another Example How can you show numbers on a place-value chart?

The place-value chart shows the value of each digit in 850.

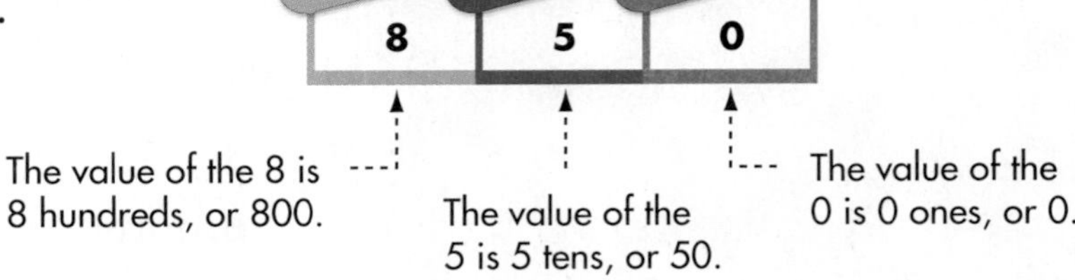

Explain It

1. In expanded form, 850 can be written as 800 + 50. Why are there only 2 addends in this expanded form?

Guided Practice*

Do you know HOW?

For **1–3**, write each number in standard form.

1. 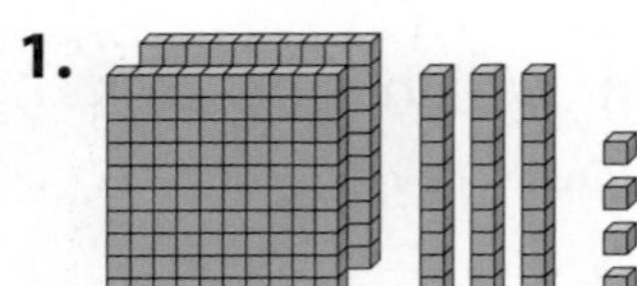

2. 600 + 50 + 3

3. eight hundred seventy-nine

4. Write 156 in expanded form.

Do you UNDERSTAND?

5. How does a place-value chart show the value of a number?

6. The example at the top of the page uses the number 125. What is the value of each digit in 125?

7. How do you know that 37 and 307 do not name the same number?

*For another example, see Set A on page 28.

You can show 125 in different ways.

One way you can show 125 is to use place-value blocks.

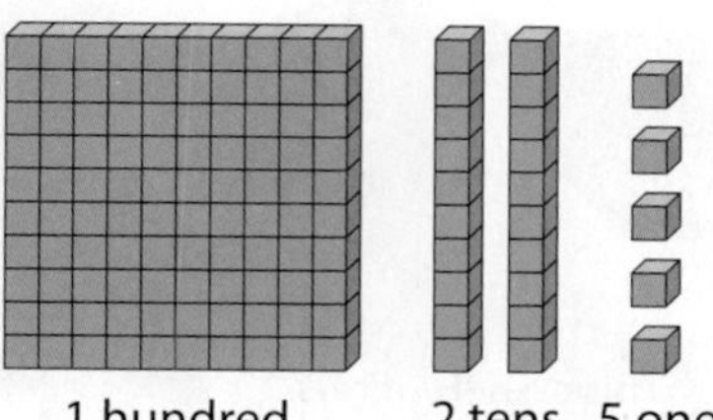

A number written in a way that shows only its digits is in standard form.

125

A number written as the sum of the values of its digits is in expanded form.

100 + 20 + 5

A number written in words is in word form.

one hundred twenty-five

Independent Practice

Write each number in standard form.

8.

9.

10.

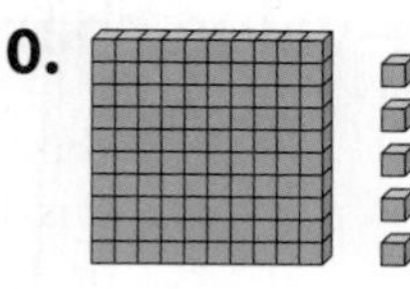

11. 900 + 80 + 5

12. 400 + 70 + 8

13. three hundred four

Write each number in expanded form and word form.

14. 707

15. 683

16. 894

17. 520

18. 251

19. 402

Problem Solving

20. **Reasoning** The sum of the digits in a three-digit number is 4. The ones digit is 3. What is the number?

21. **Algebra** Find the value of the missing number.
389 = ▢ + 80 + 9

22. **Writing to Explain** Which digit has the greatest value in 589? Explain.

23. Which is the standard form of 700 + 50?

A 570 **B** 1,200 **C** 750 **D** 705

24. **Number Sense** What is the greatest three-digit number? the least?

Lesson

1-2

Understand It!
In a four-digit number, each digit tells how many thousands, hundreds, tens, and ones there are.

Thousands

Hands-On
place-value blocks

How can you read and write 4-digit numbers?

Ten hundreds equal one thousand.

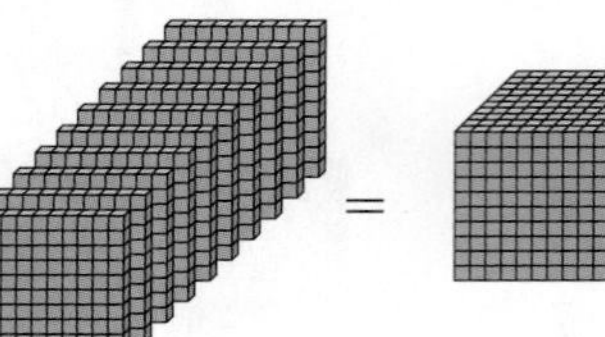
=
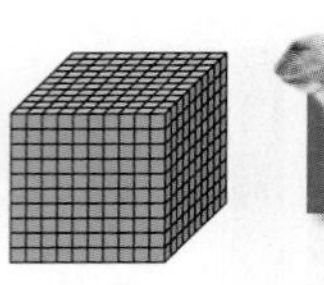

Did you know that a two-humped camel weighs between 1,000 and 1,450 pounds?

This camel weighs 1,350 pounds.

Another Example

How can you show 1,350 on a place-value chart?

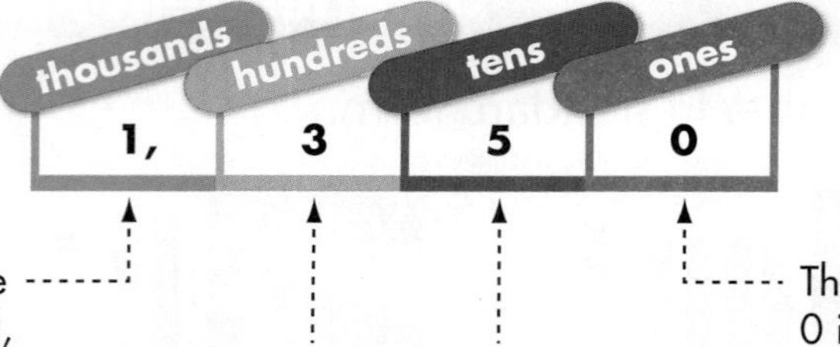

thousands	hundreds	tens	ones
1,	3	5	0

The value of the 1 is 1 thousand, or 1,000.

The value of the 3 is 3 hundreds, or 300.

The value of the 5 is 5 tens, or 50.

The value of the 0 is 0 ones, or 0.

Explain It

1. If you showed 1,305 in a place-value chart, how would it look different from the example above?

Guided Practice*

Do you know HOW?

Write each number in standard form.

1. 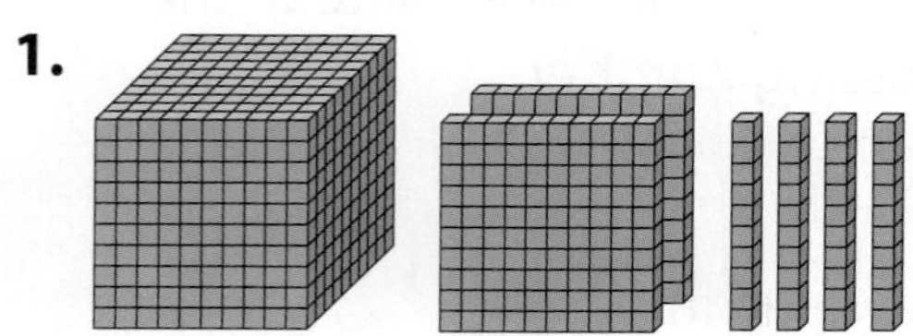

2. 8,000 + 500 + 30 + 9

3. two thousand, four hundred sixty-one

4. four hundred one

Do you UNDERSTAND?

5. Explain the value of each digit in 6,802.

6. Write a 4-digit number that has a tens digit of 5, a hundreds digit of 2, and 6 for each of the other digits.

7. Suppose another animal is three hundred pounds heavier than the camel in the photo. How would you write that weight in expanded form?

*For another example, see Set A on page 28.

You can show 1,350 in different ways.

place-value blocks:

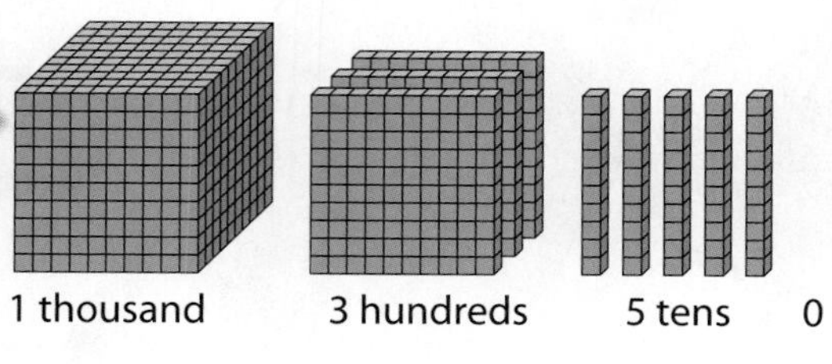

expanded form: 1,000 + 300 + 50

standard form: 1,350

Write a comma between the thousands and the hundreds.

word form: one thousand, three hundred fifty

Write a comma between the thousands and the hundreds.

Independent Practice

For **8–10**, write each number in standard form.

8.

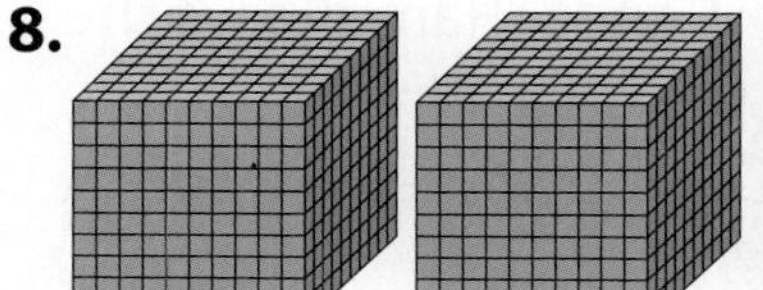

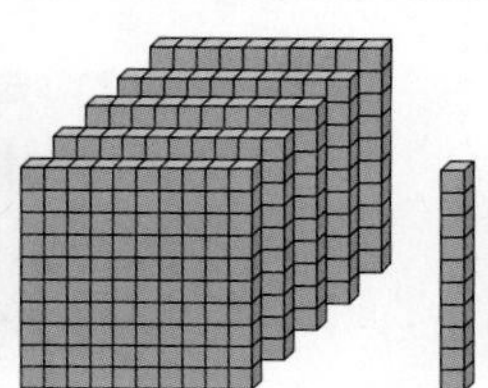

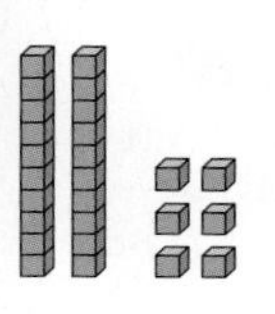

9. 4,000 + 600 + 50 + 8

10. 7,000 + 200 + 1

For **11** and **12**, write each number in expanded form.

11. six thousand, two hundred four

12. 5,033

For **13–17**, write the place of the underlined digit. Then write its value.

13. 4,865 **14.** 3,245 **15.** 9,716 **16.** 5,309 **17.** 7,240

Problem Solving

18. Number Sense Write the greatest possible number and the least possible number using the four digits 5, 2, 8, and 1.

19. In 2005, the world's largest pumpkin weighed 1,469 pounds. Write that number in word form.

20. Which is the word form of 2,406?

A twenty-four thousand, six

B two thousand, four hundred six

C two thousand, forty-six

D two hundred forty-six

21. Writing to Explain Sam used place-value blocks to show the number 3,124. Then he added 2 more thousand cubes. What was the new number? Explain.

Lesson
1-3

Understand It!
Whole numbers greater than 999 have groups of 3 digits separated by commas.

Greater Numbers

How can you read and write greater numbers?

Capitol Reef National Park in Utah covers 241,904 acres of land.

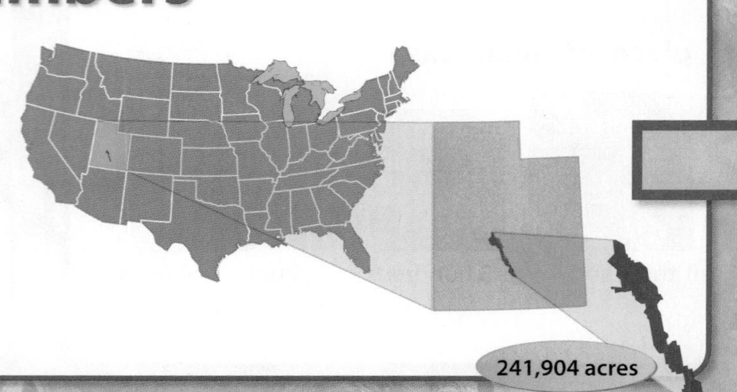

Guided Practice*

Do you know HOW?

For **1–3**, write each number in standard form.

1. three hundred forty-two thousand, six hundred seven

2. ninety-eight thousand, three hundred twenty

3. 500,000 + 40,000 + 600 + 90 + 3

4. What is the value of the 9 in 379,050?

Do you UNDERSTAND?

5. Number Sense Ramos says the value of the digit 7 in 765,450 is 70,000. Do you agree? Why or why not?

6. Writing to Explain Describe how 130,434 and 434,130 are alike and how they are different.

Independent Practice

Write each number in standard form.

7. twenty-seven thousand, five hundred fifty

8. 800,000 + 20,000 + 6,000 + 300 + 50

Write each number in expanded form.

9. 46,354

10. 395,980

Write the place of the underlined digit. Then write its value.

11. 40<u>4</u>,705 **12.** <u>1</u>63,254 **13.** <u>4</u>5,391 **14.** 983,<u>9</u>71 **15.** 6<u>5</u>7,240

*For another example, see Set B on page 28.

How can you show 241,904 in different ways?

place-value chart:

hundred thousands	ten thousands	thousands	hundreds	tens	ones
2	4	1,	9	0	4

thousands period | ones period

A period is a group of 3 digits in a number, starting from the right. Two periods are separated by a comma.

standard form:
241, 904

expanded form:
200,000 + 40,000 + 1,000 + 900 + 4

word form: two hundred forty-one thousand, nine hundred four

Algebra Find each missing number.

16. 26,305 = 20,000 + ■ + 300 + 5

17. 801,960 = 800,000 + 1,000 + ■ + 60

18. 400,000 + ■ + 30 + 2 = 470,032

19. 618,005 = ■ + 10,000 + 8,000 + 5

20. 300,000 + ■ + 600 + 3 = 304,603

21. 200,000 + 4,000 + 60 + 3 = ■

Problem Solving

For **22–24**, use the table.

22. Write the population of each city in the table in expanded form.

23. Write the population of Columbus, OH in word form.

City Populations (Data)

City	Number of People
Austin, TX	681,804
Jacksonville, FL	777,704
Columbus, OH	730,008

24. Which cities listed in the table have more than seven hundred thousand people?

25. A new world record was once set when 303,628 dominos fell. Write 303,628 in expanded form.

26. Which is the word form of the number 805,920?

A eighty-five thousand, ninety-two

B eight hundred five thousand, ninety-two

C eight thousand, five hundred ninety-two

D eight hundred five thousand, nine hundred twenty

Lesson

1-4

Understand It!
There are different uses and different names for numbers.

Ways to Name Numbers

How can you use and name numbers?

In the hobby shop, Jack is looking at a new toy train that has 38 cars. He wants to tell his friend about the train. How can he describe what place the red box car is in? What place is the last car in?

Other Examples

What are different ways to name the number 1,200?

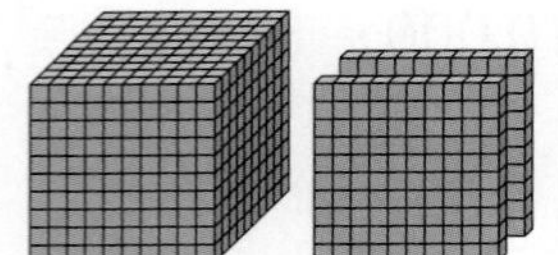

1 thousand = 10 hundreds

one thousand, two hundred

twelve hundred

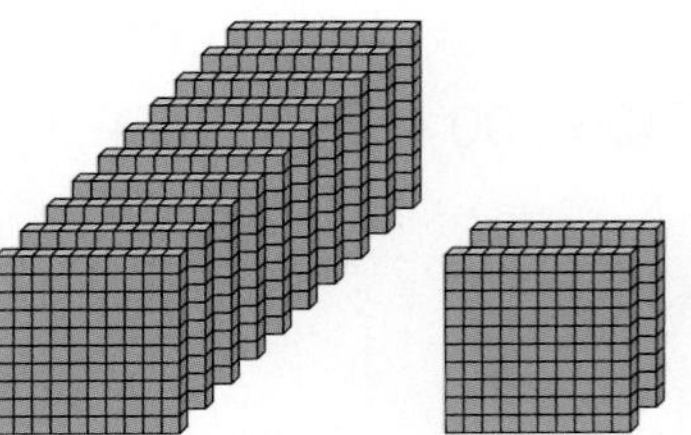

Guided Practice*

Do you know HOW?

Write the ordinal number and ordinal word form of each number.

1. 8
2. 63

Name each number in two ways.

3. 2,400
4. 8,300

Do you UNDERSTAND?

5. Reasoning In the example above, how are the two names for 1,200 the same? different?

6. Lon ran in a race. Sixty people finished the race in front of him. In what place did Lon finish?

Independent Practice

In **7–10**, write the ordinal number and ordinal word form of the number.

7. 18
8. 71
9. 80
10. 93

*For another example, see Set C on page 28.

An ordinal number is used to show the order of people or objects.

1st first | 2nd second | 3rd third | 4th fourth | 5th fifth

Ordinal Number: 4th

Ordinal Word Form: fourth

The red box car is fourth.

There are 38 cars in the train.

Ordinal Number: 38th

Ordinal Word Form: thirty-eighth

The last car is the 38th car in the train.

Here are some other examples of ordinal numbers.

9th ninth | 12th twelfth | 70th seventieth | 91st ninety-first

In **11–14**, name the number in two ways.

11. 5,200 **12.** 6,400 **13.** 9,800 **14.** 4,500

Problem Solving

Use the table at the right for **15** and **16**.

15. Beth wrote down the address she heard—Fifteen thousand, one hundred eight Allen Street. Which place is located at this address?

16. Write two names for the number in the address of Gibson's Market.

Data

Place	Address
Ace Sporting Goods	1518 Allen Street
Central Post Office	15008 Allen Street
Gibson's Market	3900 Allen Street
Tops Bowling Center	15108 Allen Street

17. Ron counted 39 people waiting in line ahead of him. Write the ordinal number and ordinal word form for Ron's place in line.

18. Maris named odd numbers starting with 1. Which is the eighth number in her count?

1, 3, 5, 7, 9, 11, 13, 15, 17, 19, 21

19. **Number Sense** The population of Leon County is 239,452. The population of Dakota County is 355,904. Which county has fewer than three hundred thousand people?

20. Which is another way to write the number 6,200?

A six hundred two

B six hundred two thousand

C sixty-two hundred

D sixty thousand, two hundred

Lesson
1-5

Understand It!
Numbers can be compared using place value or the number line.

Comparing Numbers

How do you compare numbers?

When you compare two numbers you find out which number is greater and which number is less.

Which is taller, the Statue of Liberty or its base?

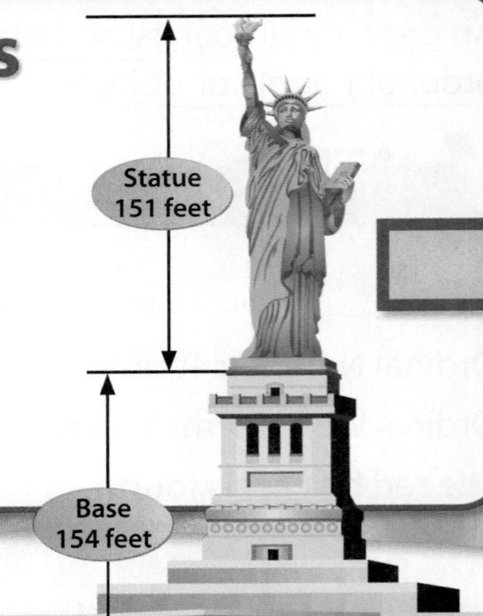

Another Example How can you use place-value charts and number lines to compare numbers?

Compare 3,456 and 3,482 using a place-value chart. Then show these two numbers on a number line.

On a place-value chart, line up the digits by place value. Compare the digits starting from the left.

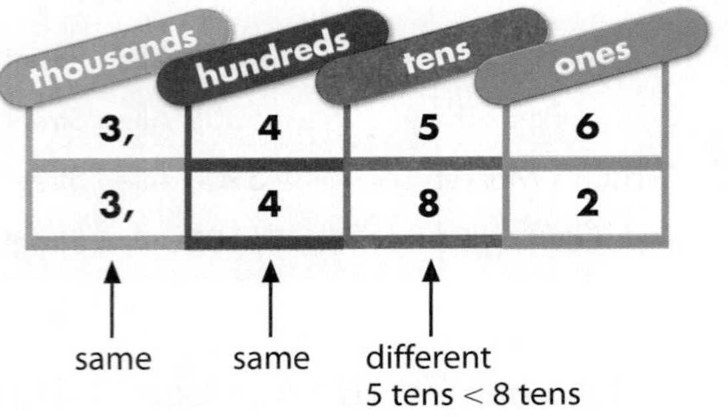

thousands	hundreds	tens	ones
3,	4	5	6
3,	4	8	2
same	same	different 5 tens < 8 tens	

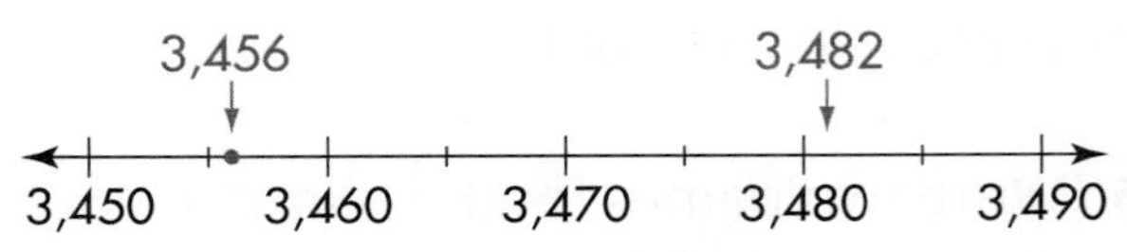

On the number line, 3,456 is to the left of 3,482.

So 3,456 **is less than** 3,482.

3,456 < 3,482

Explain It

1. In this example, why don't you need to compare the digit in the ones place?
2. Why can't you tell which number is greater by just comparing the first digit in each number?

You can use symbols.

Data

Symbol	Meaning
$<$	is less than
$>$	is greater than
$=$	is equal to

You can compare 151 and 154 with place value.

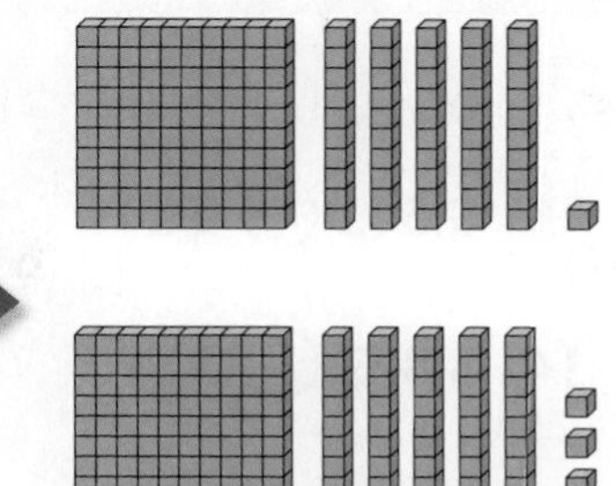

154 is greater than 151.

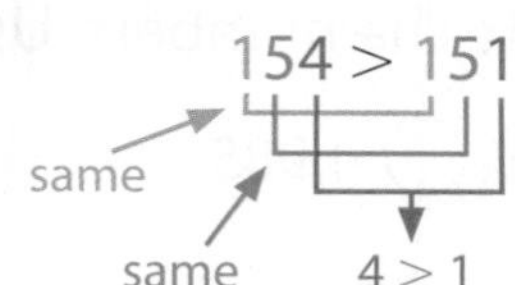

The place-value blocks also show that 151 is less than 154.

$151 < 154$

So, the base is taller than the statue.

Guided Practice*

Do you know HOW?

Compare the numbers. Use $<$, $>$, or $=$.

1. 141 ◯ 64

2. 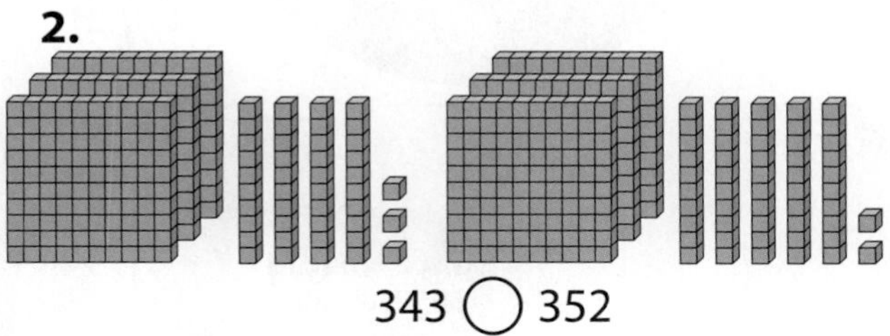

343 ◯ 352

3. 2,561 ◯ 2,261

4. 6,807 ◯ 6,807

Do you UNDERSTAND?

5. **Number Sense** Cara says that since 4 is greater than 1, the number 496 is greater than the number 1,230. Do you agree? Why or why not?

6. **Writing to Explain** The total height of the Statue of Liberty is 305 feet. The Washington Monument is 555 feet tall. Which is taller? Explain how you know.

7. Draw a number line to compare the numbers.

1,462 ◯ 1,521

Independent Practice

Compare the numbers. Use $<$, $>$, or $=$.

8. 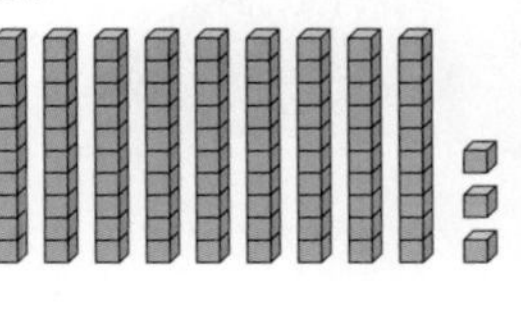

93 ◯ 120

9. 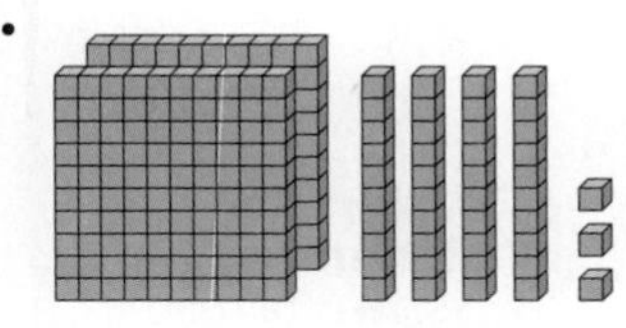 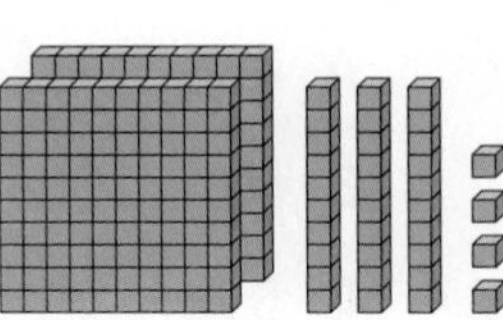

243 ◯ 234

**For another example, see Set D on page 29.*

Independent Practice

Compare the numbers. Use <, >, or =.

10. 679 ○ 4,985 **11.** 9,642 ○ 9,642 **12.** 5,136 ○ 5,163

13. 8,204 ○ 8,402 **14.** 3,823 ○ 3,853 **15.** 2,424 ○ 2,242

Write the missing digits to make each number sentence true.

16. □24 > 896 **17.** 6□7 < 617 **18.** 29□ = 2□0

19. □,000 < 1,542 **20.** 3,□12 > 3,812 **21.** 2,185 > 2,□85

Problem Solving

Use the pictures for **22** and **23**.

22. **Writing to Explain** Which is taller, the Washington Monument or the Great Pyramid in Egypt? How do you know?

23. Which is taller, the Gateway Arch or the Space Needle?

24. **Reasoning** Mark is thinking of a 3-digit number. Rory is thinking of a 4-digit number. Whose number is greater? How do you know?

25. **Number Sense** Suppose you are comparing 1,272 and 1,269. Do you need to compare the ones digits? Which number would be farther to the right on the number line? Explain.

26. Which number sentence is true if the number 537 replaces the box?

A 456 > □

B □ = 256

C 598 < □

D □ > 357

Algebra Connections

Number Patterns

Remember that skip counting can be used to make a number pattern. Skip counting can also be used to find missing numbers in a given pattern.

Copy and complete. Write the number that completes each pattern.

Examples: 2, 4, 6, 8, ▢, 12

Can you skip count by a certain number to get each number in the pattern?

Skip count by 2s for this pattern.

2, 4, 6, 8, 10, 12

1. 3, 6, 9, 12, ▢, 18

2. 14, ▢, 18, 20, 22, 24

3. 20, 30, ▢, 50, 60, 70

4. 25, 50, 75, 100, 125, ▢

5. 3, 8, 13, 18, 23, ▢

6. 9, 19, 29, ▢, 49, 59

7. 7, 9, 11, ▢, 15, 17

8. 12, ▢, 20, 24, 28

9. 90, 80, 70, ▢, 50, 40

10. 22, 20, 18, 16, ▢, 12

11. 86, 81, ▢, 71, 66, 61

12. 150, ▢, 100, 75, 50, 25

For **13** and **14**, copy and complete each pattern. Use the pattern to help solve the problem.

13. Rusty saw that the house numbers on a street were in a pattern. First he saw the number 101. Then he saw the numbers 103, 105, and 107. There was a missing number, and then the number 111. What was the missing number?

101, 103, 105, 107, ▢, 111

14. Alani was skip counting the pasta shapes she made. The numbers she said were 90, 95, 100, 105, 110, 115. She needed to say one more number in the count to finish counting the pasta. How many pasta shapes did Alani make?

90, 95, 100, 105, 110, 115, ▢

15. **Write a Problem** Copy and complete the number pattern below. Write a real-world problem to match the number pattern.

5, 10, 15, 20, 25, 30, ▢

Lesson

1-6

Understand It!
Numbers can be put in order by using place value or the number line.

Ordering Numbers

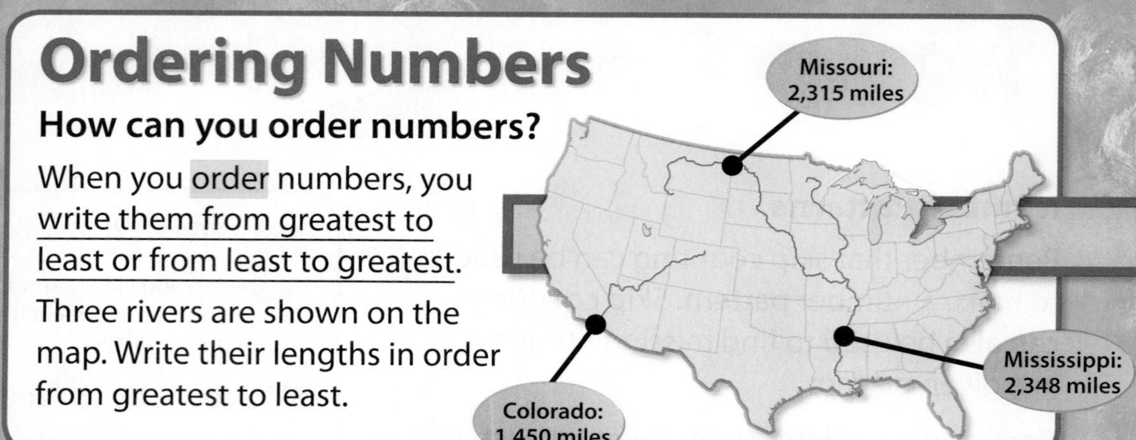

How can you order numbers?

When you order numbers, you write them from greatest to least or from least to greatest.

Three rivers are shown on the map. Write their lengths in order from greatest to least.

Guided Practice*

Do you know HOW?

For **1** and **2**, order the numbers from least to greatest.

1. 769 679 697

2. 359 368 45

For **3** and **4**, order the numbers from greatest to least.

3. 4,334 809 4,350

4. 1,137 1,573 1,457

Do you UNDERSTAND?

5. Writing to Explain The length of another river has a 2 in the hundreds place. Can this river be longer than the Colorado? Why or why not?

6. Copy and complete the number line below to show the numbers 315, 305, and 319 in order.

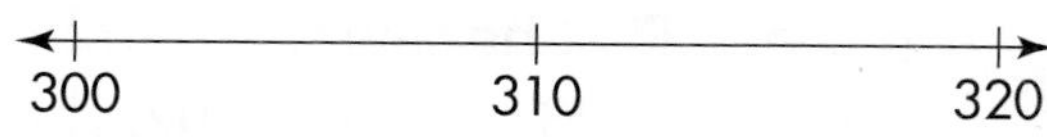

Independent Practice

For **7–9**, order the numbers from least to greatest.

7. 6,743 6,930 6,395 **8.** 995 1,293 1,932 **9.** 8,754 8,700 8,792

For **10–12**, order the numbers from greatest to least.

10. 2,601 967 2,365 **11.** 3,554 3,454 3,459 **12.** 5,304 5,430 5,403

13. Copy and complete the number line below to show 1,020, 965, and 985 in order.

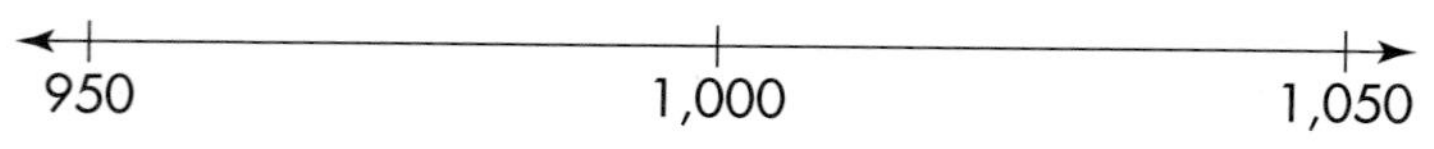

*For another example, see Set D on page 29.

You can use a place-value chart to help you.

thousands	hundreds	tens	ones
1,	4	5	0
2,	3	4	8
2,	3	1	5

1 < 2
So 1,450 is the least number.

3 = 3

4 > 1
So 2,348 is the greatest number.

The lengths of the rivers in order from greatest to least are:

Mississippi: 2,348 miles;
Missouri: 2,315 miles;
Colorado: 1,450 miles.

Problem Solving

Use the pictures for **14–17**.

14. Which animal weighs 100 pounds more than a moose?

Camel weighs 1,521 pounds

Giraffe weighs 4,255 pounds

15. **Number Sense** A ton is equal to 2,000 pounds. Which animals weigh less than 1 ton?

16. Write the names of the animals in the order of their weights from least to greatest.

17. **Reasonableness** Margo says the camel weighs about fifteen hundred pounds. Do you agree or disagree?

18. **Writing to Explain** Describe how you would write the numbers below from least to greatest.

3,456 3,654 2,375

19. Which number is between 5,695 and 6,725?

A 5,659 **B** 6,735 **C** 6,632 **D** 6,728

20. The grooves around the outside of some coins are called reeds. Look at the table at the right. List the coins from the table in order from least to greatest number of reeds.

Data

Coin	Number of Reeds
Susan B. Anthony Dollar	133
Half dollar	150
Quarter	119
Dime	118

Lesson
1-7

Understand It!
The strategy counting on is helpful when finding the total value of a group of coins and bills.

Counting Money

Hands-On
play money

How do you count money?

Here are some familiar bills and coins.

5 dollars
$5 or $5.00

1 dollar
$1 or $1.00

half dollar	**quarter**	**dime**	**nickel**	**penny**
50¢ or $0.50	25¢ or $0.25	10¢ or $0.10	5¢ or $0.05	1¢ or $0.01

Another Example **How can you show the same amount of money in different ways?**

You can show money amounts in more than one way.
Here are two ways to show $2.56.

One Way

$1.00 $2.00 $2.25 $2.50 $2.55 **$2.56**

Another Way

$1.00 $1.50 $2.00 $2.25 $2.35 $2.45 $2.55 **$2.56**

Explain It

1. Could you show $2.56 without using pennies? Explain.
2. How could you show $2.56, using the least number of bills and coins?
3. How do you use skip counting when you count money?

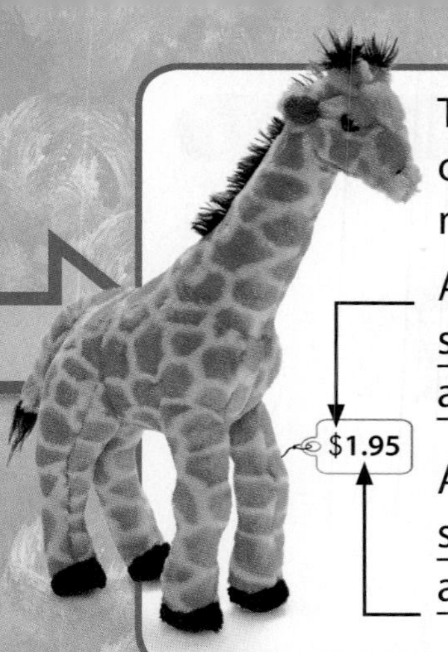

This toy costs one dollar and ninety-five cents.

A dollar sign shows money amounts.

A decimal point separates dollars and cents.

Greg has the money shown below. Does he have enough money to buy the toy giraffe?

To count money, start with the bill or coin of greatest value. Then count on to find the total value.

$1.00 → $1.50 → $1.75 → $1.85 → **$1.90**

Write: $1.90

Say: one dollar and ninety cents

No, Greg does not have enough money.

Guided Practice*

Do you know HOW?

Write the total value in dollars and cents.

1. 

2. 

3. 

Do you UNDERSTAND?

4. How could you show $7.95 using the least number of bills and coins?

5. What coins and bills could you use to show $2.65 two ways?

6. **Number Sense** If you have 195 pennies, do you have enough money to buy the toy giraffe shown above?

Independent Practice

Write the total value in dollars and cents.

7. 

8. 

*For another example, see Set E on page 29.

Independent Practice

Write the total value in dollars and cents.

9.

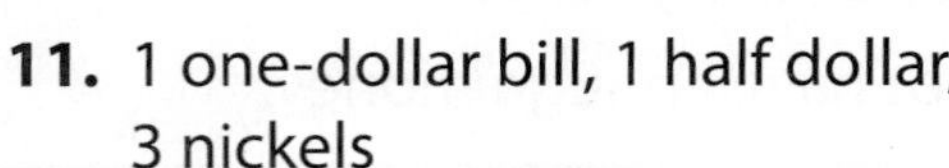

10.

11. 1 one-dollar bill, 1 half dollar, 3 nickels

12. 1 one-dollar bill, 2 half dollars, 1 quarter, 4 dimes, 4 nickels

13. 1 five-dollar bill, 1 one-dollar bill, 2 quarters, 3 dimes, 4 pennies

14. 1 five-dollar bill, 3 quarters, 2 dimes, 2 nickels

Compare the amounts. Write <, >, or =.

15. \$1.01 ○ 1 one-dollar bill

16. \$0.83 ○ 3 quarters, 1 dime

17. 9 dimes, 2 nickels ○ \$0.95

18. \$1.60 ○ 2 half dollars, 3 quarters

19. 10 quarters ○ \$2.50

20. \$3.15 ○ 4 half dollars, 4 quarters

Problem Solving

21. Look at the top of page 19. Keisha says Greg needs 5 more coins to have enough to buy the toy. Reni says he needs only 1 more coin. Explain who is correct.

22. **Reasoning** Bob has 3 quarters, 1 dime, and 1 nickel. What coin does he need to make \$1.00?

23. Show two ways to make \$3.62. Draw rectangles to represent bills. Draw circles with letters to represent coins.

24. Tyler has 5 coins worth \$0.65. All of the coins are either quarters or dimes. How many of each coin does he have?

25. Use the picture at the right. Each minute, the U.S. Treasury Department produces 30,000 coins. Are more coins or bills produced in 1 minute?

Each minute about 24,300 bills are printed.

Use the table for **26–28**.

Data

Ticket Prices for Gateway Arch			
Attraction	**Adults (17 and up)**	**Youth (13–16)**	**Child (3–12)**
Tram Ride	$10.00	$7.00	$3.00
Movie	$7.00	$4.00	$2.50

26. Suppose you had only half dollars and quarters. How many half dollars are needed to buy a child's ticket for the tram ride? How many quarters are needed?

27. If you were using quarters only, how many would you need for a child's movie ticket? If you were using dimes only, how many would you need?

28. Reasoning When the Gateway Arch opened in July 1967, the total cost for 2 adult tram tickets and 1 child's tram ticket was $2.50. What can you buy at the arch for that amount now?

29. What is the total value of the 6 coins below?

A $0.81

B $0.96

C $1.21

D $1.06

30. What is the total value of the 8 coins below?

A $1.02

B $1.20

C $1.07

D $ 0.92

Lesson
1-8

Understand It!
One way to find the amount of change is to count on from the cost to the amount paid.

Making Change

How do you count on to make change?

The Reading Club sold bookmarks at the school book fair. Rodrigo bought one bookmark. He paid with two $1 bills. How much change should he get?

$1.25 for each bookmark

Another Example

Paula bought a notebook for $2.59. She paid with a $5 bill. How much change should she get?

Cost						Amount Paid
$2.59 →	$2.60 →	$2.70 →	$2.75 →	$3.00 →	$4.00 →	**$5.00**

Paula's change should be $2.41.

Guided Practice*

Do you know HOW?

In **1** and **2**, list coins and bills to make the change. Write the amount of the change.

1. Cost: $0.94
Amount paid: $1.00

2. Cost: $2.35
Amount paid: $5.00

Do you UNDERSTAND?

3. **Reasoning** In the notebook example, why does it make sense to start with a penny?

4. Tamara bought some bookmarks for $3.75. She paid with a $5 bill. How much change should she get?

Independent Practice

In **5–7**, list coins and bills to make the change. Write the amount of the change.

5. Cost: $0.79
Amount paid: $1.00

6. Cost: $2.37
Amount paid: $3.00

7. Cost: $3.21
Amount paid: $5.00

*For another example, see Set E on page 29.

Step 1

Start with the cost. Count on from the cost to the amount paid. Use coins that will make skip counting easy.

Cost → Amount Paid

$1.25 → $1.50 → $1.75 → **$2.00**

Step 2

Find the total value of the coins you counted. There were 3 quarters.

3 quarters = $0.75

Rodrigo's change should be $0.75.

Problem Solving

Use the table at the right for **8–10**.

Item	Price
Sharpener	$0.67
Eraser	$1.42
Marker	$1.38
Pencil	$0.56
Sticker	$0.15

8. Writing to Explain Arun paid for a sticker with a $1 bill. The change he received was all nickels. How many nickels did he get? Explain how you found your answer.

9. Mariko bought a marker. She paid with 2 one-dollar bills. List coins and bills that could be her change.

10. Wally paid for an eraser with a $5 bill. List coins and bills that could be his change.

11. Reasonableness Last year, the store sold 1,421 pencils. Walt said that was more than 14 hundred pencils. Is he correct? Explain.

12. A community collected $126,578 to help build a garden. What is the value of the 2 in $126,578?

13. Algebra Keri bought a pen. She paid with a $1 bill. This is the change she got. How much did the pen cost?

14. Rose bought a carton of milk that cost $2.39. She paid with a $5 bill. Which should be her change?

A $7.39 **C** $2.61

B $2.71 **D** $2.41

15. What are two different ways that $3.65 could be given as change?

Lesson
1-9

Understand It!
Making an organized list can help solve some kinds of problems.

Problem Solving

Make an Organized List

Randy is playing a game called *Guess the Number*. What are all the possible numbers that fit the clues shown at the right?

You can make an organized list to find all the possible numbers.

Clues

- It is a 3-digit even number.
- The digit in the hundreds place is greater than 8.
- The digit in the tens place is less than 2.

Guided Practice*

Do you know HOW?

Make an organized list to solve.

1. Rachel has a quarter, a dime, a nickel, and a penny. She told her brother he could take two coins. List all the different pairs of coins her brother can take.

Do you UNDERSTAND?

2. Writing to Explain How did making an organized list help you solve Problem 1?

3. Write a Problem Write and solve a real-world problem by making an organized list.

Independent Practice

For **4** and **5**, make an organized list to solve.

4. List all the 4-digit numbers that fit these clues.

- The thousands digit is less than 2.
- The hundreds digit is greater than 5.
- The tens digit and ones digit both equal $10 - 5$.

5. Jen, Meg, and Emily are standing in line at the movies. How many different ways can they line up? List the ways.

Stuck? Try this....

- What do I know?
- What am I asked to find?
- What diagram can I use to help understand the problem?
- Can I use addition, subtraction, multiplication, or division?
- Is all of my work correct?
- Did I answer the right question?
- Is my answer reasonable?

**For another example, see Set F on page 29.*

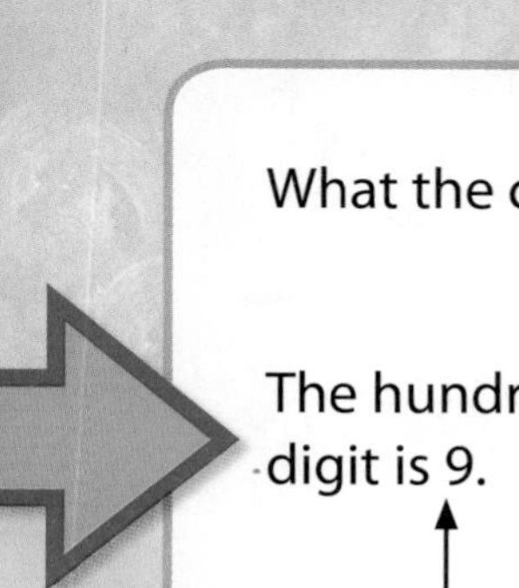

Plan

What the clues tell us:

The hundreds digit is 9.	The tens digit is 0 or 1.	The ones digit is 0, 2, 4, 6, or 8.
↑	↑	↑
greater than 8	less than 2	even number

Solve

Make an organized list to find all the possible numbers.

900	910
902	912
904	914
906	916
908	918

For **6–8**, use the table.

6. How many different kinds of sandwiches can you choose if you want white bread?

7. How many different kinds of sandwiches can you choose if you don't want turkey?

8. Suppose wheat bread was added as a bread choice. How many different kinds of sandwiches could you choose then?

Sandwich Choices

Bread Choices	Filling Choices
White	Ham
Rye	Tuna
	Turkey

9. Jeremy has tan pants and black pants. He also has three shirts: blue, green, and red. List all the different outfits that Jeremy can wear.

10. Dennis bought a 3-pound bag of apples for $3. He also bought some grapes for $4. How much did Dennis spend?

11. How many different ways can you make 15 cents using dimes, nickels, or pennies?

A 15 ways **C** 6 ways

B 9 ways **D** 3 ways

12. Carla bought 4 sheets of poster board. Each sheet cost $2. She paid with a $10 bill. Carla cut each sheet into 2 pieces. How many pieces does Carla have?

There is extra information in the problem.

13. Reasoning What is this 3-digit number?

- The hundreds digit is 3 less than 5.
- The tens digit is greater than 8.
- The ones digit is 1 less than the tens digit.

Test

1. The place-value blocks show the number of students at a school. How many students are there? (1-1)

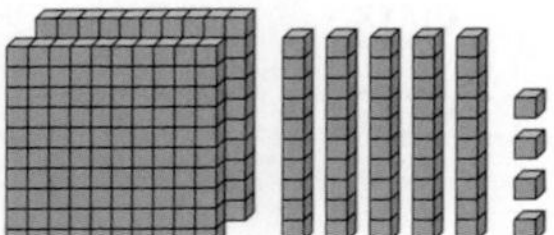

A 2,054

B 254

C 250

D 245

2. On Friday, 1,593 people watched the play *Cinderella*. On Saturday, 1,595 people watched, and on Sunday, 1,586 people watched. Which lists these numbers in order from least to greatest? (1-6)

A 1,586 1,593 1,595

B 1,586 1,595 1,593

C 1,593 1,595 1,586

D 1,595 1,593 1,586

3. The cashier gave Hector the money shown below as change. How much change did he receive? (1-7)

A \$3.82

B \$7.67

C \$7.82

D \$7.87

4. What is the value of the 9 in the number 295,863? (1-3)

A 90

B 9,000

C 90,000

D 900,000

5. The place-value chart shows the depth, in feet, of the deepest lake in the United States, Crater Lake. Which is another way to write this number? (1-2)

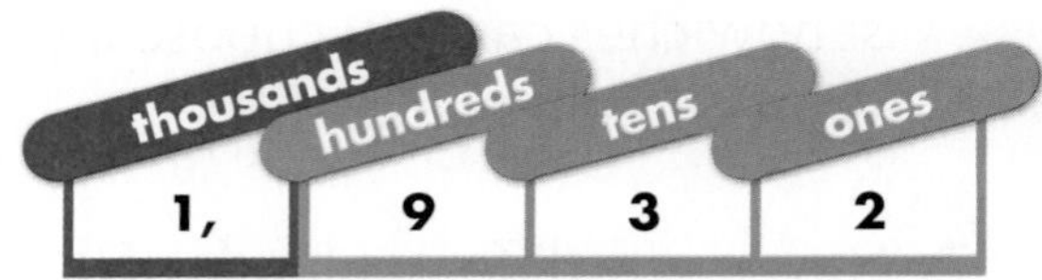

thousands	hundreds	tens	ones
1,	9	3	2

A 100 + 900 + 30 + 2

B 1,000 + 90 + 30 + 2

C 1,000 + 900 + 30

D 1,000 + 900 + 30 + 2

6. Which is the word form of the number 530,450? (1-3)

A Five hundred thirty thousand, forty-five

B Five hundred thirty thousand, four hundred fifty

C Five hundred thirty, four fifty

D Fifty-three thousand, four hundred fifty

7. Which is greater than 4,324? (1-5)

A 4,342

B 4,322

C 4,314

D 3,424

8. Which shows 61 written in ordinal word form? (1-4)

A sixty-first

B sixty-one

C sixteenth

D sixty-oneth

9. Susan is thinking of a number between 3,674 and 5,628. Which of the following could be Susan's number? (1-6)

A 5,629

B 3,673

C 3,629

D 5,575

10. Which is another way to write 3,700? (1-4)

A thirty-seven thousand

B thirty-seven hundred

C three thousand, seven

D three thousand, seventy

11. Which is the standard form of 700 + 8? (1-1)

A 78

B 708

C 780

D 7,008

12. Which group of coins shows 67¢? (1-7)

A

B

C

D

13. Alex, Eric, Josh, and Tony are playing tennis. How many different groups of 2 can they make? (1-9)

A 12

B 8

C 6

D 2

14. The book costs $3.78. Becky gave the cashier $4.00. Which coins are her correct change? (1-8)

A 2 pennies, 2 nickels

B 2 pennies, 2 nickels, 2 dimes

C 2 pennies, 1 nickel, 1 dime

D 2 pennies, 2 dimes

Topic 1

Reteaching

Set A, pages 4–7

Write the number below in standard form, expanded form, and word form.

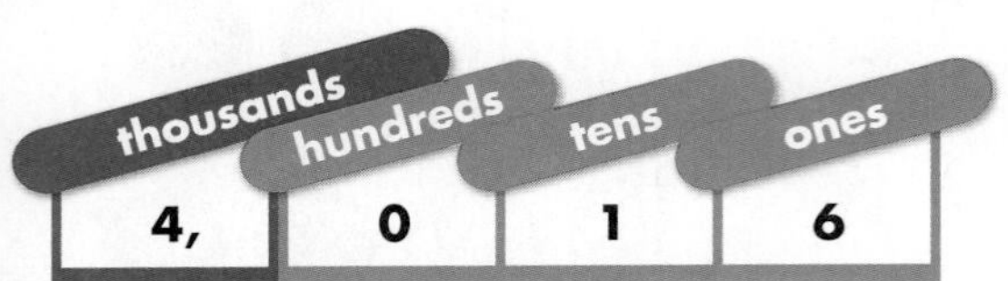

Standard form: 4,016

Expanded form: 4,000 + 10 + 6

Word form: four thousand, sixteen

Remember that the digit 0 is sometimes needed to hold a place in a number.

Write each number in standard form.

1. 1,000 + 5 **2.** 300 + 20 + 7

Write each number in expanded form and word form.

3. 8,214 **4.** 620

Set B, pages 8–9

Find the value of the 4 in 847,193.

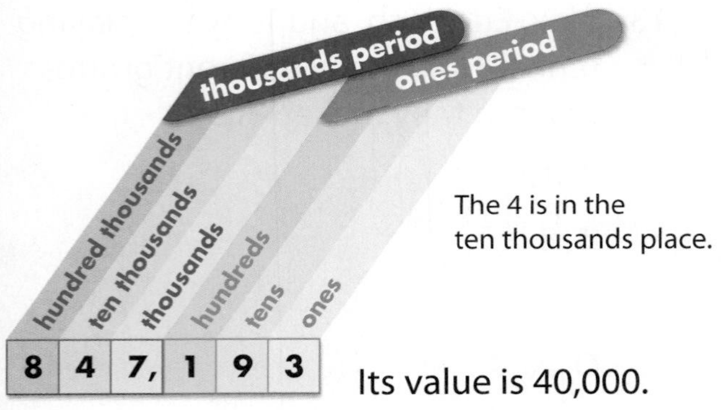

The 4 is in the ten thousands place.

Its value is 40,000.

Remember that 10 thousands equal 1 ten thousand.

Write the place of each underlined digit. Then write its value.

1. $\underline{3}41{,}791$ **2.** $82\underline{9}{,}526$

3. $570{,}\underline{8}90$ **4.** $2\underline{1}5{,}003$

5. $\underline{1}97{,}206$ **6.** $4\underline{7}3{,}069$

7. $628{,}\underline{1}74$ **8.** $78\underline{2}{,}413$

Set C, pages 10–11

The blue car is in the 6th place.

1st

Ordinal Number: 6th **Ordinal Word Form:** sixth

Name 1,300 in two different ways.

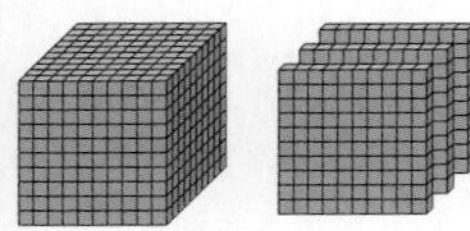

1 thousand + 3 hundreds

one thousand, three hundred

10 hundreds + 3 hundreds

thirteen hundred

Remember that ordinal numbers end with -st, -nd, -rd, or -th.

Write the ordinal number and ordinal word form of each number.

1. 8 **2.** 41

Name each number in two ways.

3. 1,700 **4.** 3,600

Set D, pages 12–14, 16–17

Compare 7,982 and 7,682.
Line up the digits by place value.
Compare the digits starting from the left.

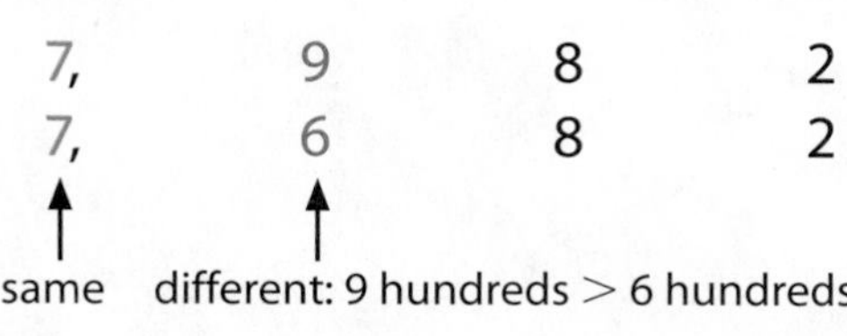

7,982 > 7,682

Remember, when ordering numbers, compare one place at a time.

Compare. Use <, >, or =.

1. 479 ◯ 912 **2.** 1,156 ◯ 156

Write the numbers in order from greatest to least.

3. 393 182 229

4. 1,289 2,983 1,760

Set E, pages 18–23

Write the total value in dollars and cents.

$5.00, $5.25, $5.35, $5.40, $5.45, $5.46

The total is $5.46.

Find the change. Start with the cost. Use coins to count up to the amount paid.

Cost			Amount Paid
$1.60 →	$1.65 →	$1.75 →	**$2.00**

The change is $0.40.

Remember to count on from the bill or coin with the greatest value.

Write the total value in dollars and cents.

1. 

List coins and bills to make the change. Write the amount of the change.

2. Cost: $3.49
Amount paid: $5.00

Set F, pages 24–25

When you make an organized list to solve problems, follow these steps.

Step 1

Carefully read the clues or information from the problem.

Step 2

Choose one clue or piece of information and use it to start your list.

Step 3

Repeat step 2 until you have used all of the clues or information to make an organized list.

Remember that each item on your list must match all of the clues.

1. Pedro has a red marble, a blue marble, a yellow marble, and a green marble. He told Frank to take two marbles. How many different pairs of marbles can Frank take? List the pairs.

Topic 2 Adding Whole Numbers

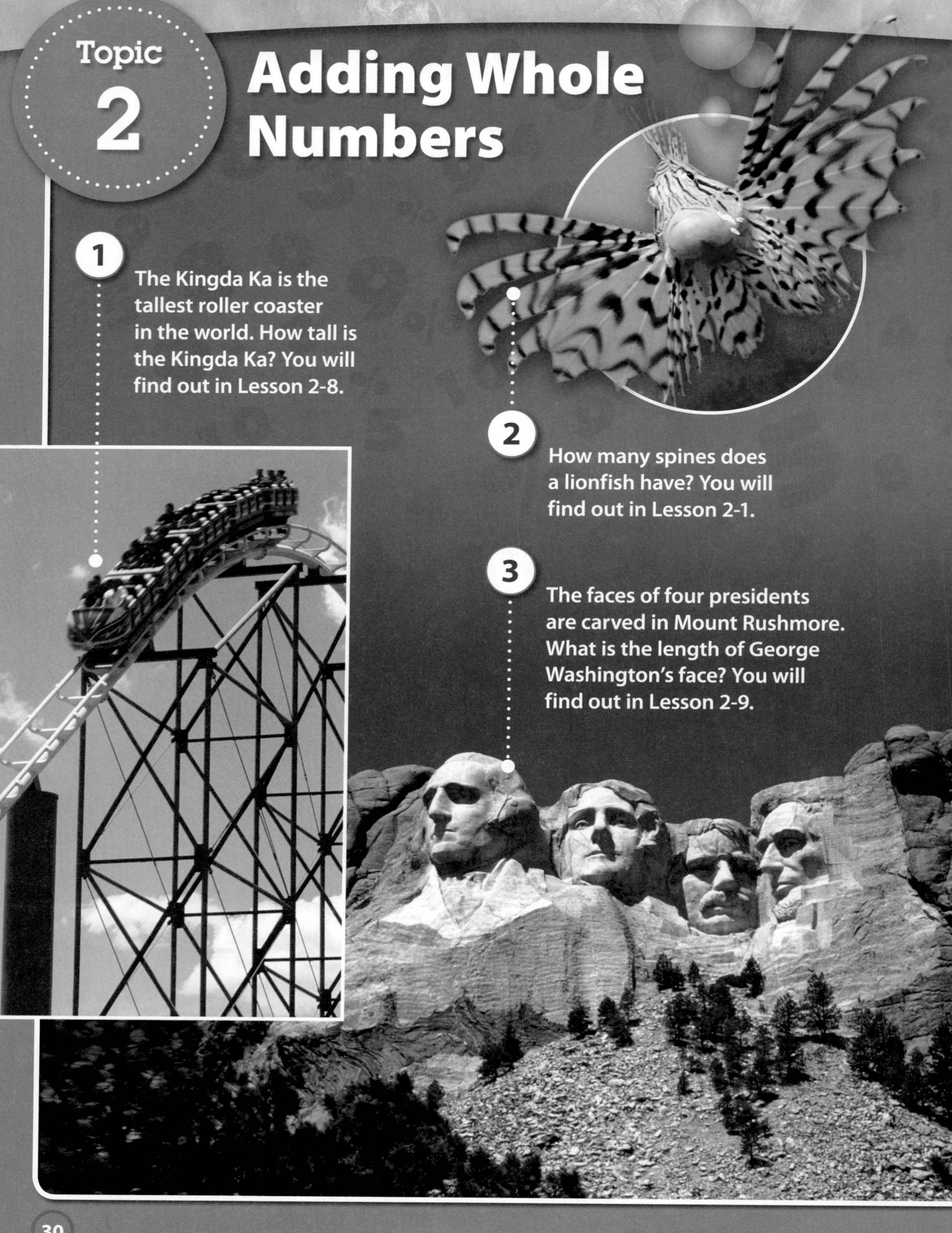

1 The Kingda Ka is the tallest roller coaster in the world. How tall is the Kingda Ka? You will find out in Lesson 2-8.

2 How many spines does a lionfish have? You will find out in Lesson 2-1.

3 The faces of four presidents are carved in Mount Rushmore. What is the length of George Washington's face? You will find out in Lesson 2-9.

4

How many steps lead to the top of the Leaning Tower of Pisa? You will find out in Lesson 2-4.

Review What You Know!

Vocabulary

Choose the best term from the box.

- hundreds
- ones
- sum
- tens

1. In 259, the 2 is in the __?__ place.
2. In 259, the 9 is in the __?__ place.
3. The answer in addition is the __?__.

Place Value

Copy and complete.

4. 35 = ▢ tens ▢ ones
5. 264 = ▢ hundreds ▢ tens ▢ ones
6. 302 = ▢ hundreds ▢ tens ▢ ones

Addition Facts

Write each sum.

7. 3 + 5	8. 1 + 8	9. 6 + 4
10. 4 + 3	11. 8 + 2	12. 6 + 6
13. 7 + 6	14. 8 + 6	15. 9 + 9

16. Janika bought 3 books on Monday and 6 books on Tuesday. How many books did she buy in all?
17. **Writing to Explain** Derrick has 4 red, 2 blue, 2 green, 2 yellow, and 2 orange balloons. Explain how to skip count to find how many balloons he has in all.

Lesson

2-1

Understand It!
Properties are helpful rules that can be used to solve addition problems.

Addition Meaning and Properties

What are some ways to think about addition?

You can use addition to join groups.

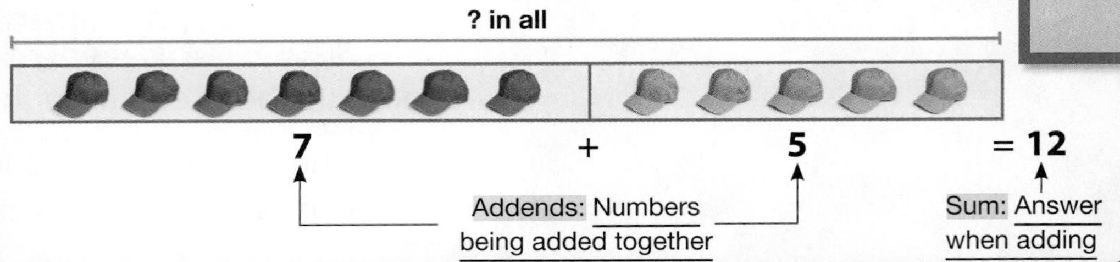

Another Example What is another way to think about addition?

Marda has two pieces of ribbon. One is 4 inches long and the other is 3 inches long. How many inches of ribbon does Marda have all together?

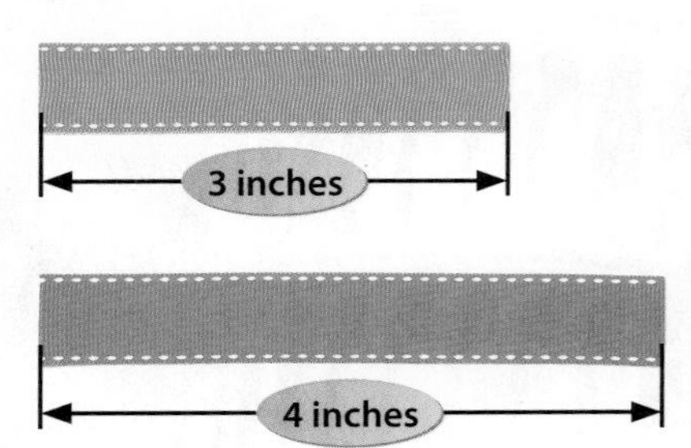

You can use a number line to think about addition.

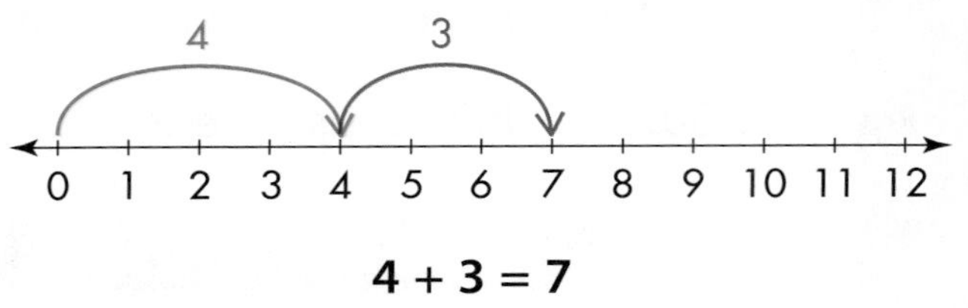

4 + 3 = 7

All together, Marda has 7 inches of ribbon.

Guided Practice*

Do you know HOW?

Write each missing number.

1. ☐ + 9 = 9
2. 4 + 6 = 6 + ☐
3. (2 + ☐) + 6 = 2 + (3 + 6)

Do you UNDERSTAND?

4. Why does it make sense that the Commutative Property is also called the order property?
5. **Writing to Explain** Ralph says you can rewrite (4 + 5) + 2 as 9 + 2. Do you agree? Why or why not?

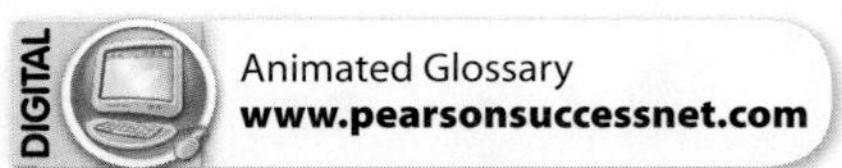

*For another example, see Set A on page 62.

Commutative (Order) Property of Addition: You can add numbers in any order and the sum will be the same.

7 + 5 = 5 + 7

Identity (Zero) Property of Addition: The sum of zero and any number is that same number.

5 + 0 = 5

Associative (Grouping) Property of Addition: You can group addends in any way and the sum will be the same.

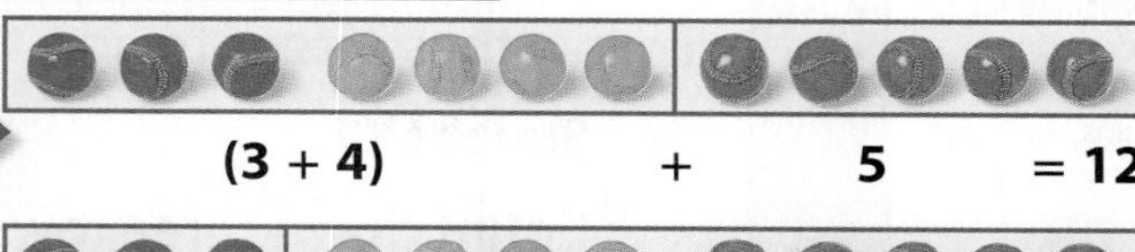

(3 + 4) + 5 = 12

3 + (4 + 5) = 12

(3 + 4) + 5 = 3 + (4 + 5)

Parentheses, (), show what to add first.

Independent Practice

Write each missing number.

6. ☐ + 8 = 8 + 2

7. 19 + ☐ = 19

8. (3 + ☐) + 2 = 2 + 8

9. 4 + (2 + 3) = 4 + ☐

10. 7 + 3 = ☐ + 7

11. ☐ + 25 = 25

12. (3 + ☐) + 6 = 3 + (4 + 6)

13. (6 + 2) + ☐ = 8 + 7

14. (7 + ☐) + 6 = 7 + 6

15. (5 + 6) + 3 = ☐ + (5 + 6)

Problem Solving

16. Reasoning What property of addition is shown in the number sentence 3 + (6 + 5) = (6 + 5) + 3? Explain.

17. Draw objects of 2 different colors to show that 4 + 3 = 3 + 4.

18. A lionfish has 13 spines on its back, 2 near the middle of its underside, and 3 on its underside near its tail. Write two different number sentences to find how many spines a lionfish has in all. What property did you use?

19. Which number sentence matches the picture?

A 3 + 8 = 11

B 11 + 0 = 11

C 11 − 8 = 3

D 11 − 3 = 8

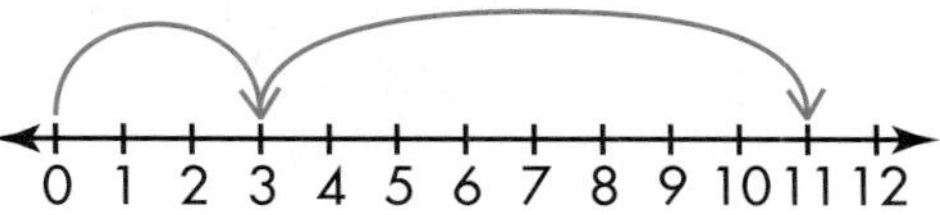

Lesson

2-2

Understand It!
A hundred chart can be used to find sums.

Adding on a Hundred Chart

How can you add on a hundred chart?

Follow these steps to add 17 + 30.

- Start at 17.
- Count down three rows to add 30.
- You end up at 47.

17 + 30 = 47

1	2	3	4	5	6	7	8	9	10
11	12	13	14	15	16	17	18	19	20
21	22	23	24	25	26	27	28	29	30
31	32	33	34	35	36	37	38	39	40
41	42	43	44	45	46	47	48	49	50

Another Example How can you add on a hundred chart by counting backward?

Follow these steps to add 44 + 29:

- Start at 44.
- Move down 3 rows to add 30. You added 30 to 44. But you only needed to add 29, so you need to subtract 1.
- Move left 1 space.
- You end up at 73.

44 + 29 = 73

1	2	3	4	5	6	7	8	9	10
11	12	13	14	15	16	17	18	19	20
21	22	23	24	25	26	27	28	29	30
31	32	33	34	35	36	37	38	39	40
41	42	43	44	45	46	47	48	49	50
51	52	53	54	55	56	57	58	59	60
61	62	63	64	65	66	67	68	69	70
71	72	73	74	75	76	77	78	79	80
81	82	83	84	85	86	87	88	89	90
91	92	93	94	95	96	97	98	99	100

Guided Practice*

Do you know HOW?

Use a hundred chart to add.

1. 34 + 20

2. 78 + 19

3. 53 + 26

4. 68 + 18

5. 37 + 16

6. 44 + 29

7. 26 + 38

8. 57 + 35

Do you UNDERSTAND?

9. **Reasoning** Look at the examples at the top of pages 34 and 35. Compare the steps used to find each sum. How are they the same? How are they different?

10. Allie's mom bought 21 red apples and 18 green apples. How many apples did she buy in all?

*For another example, see Set B on page 62.

Follow these steps to add 56 + 35.

- Start at 56.
- Move down 3 rows to add 30.
- Move right 4 spaces to add 4 more. So far, you have added 34 to 56.
- To add 1 more, go down to the next row and move right 1 space.

51	52	53	54	55	56	57	58	59	60
61	62	63	64	65	66	67	68	69	70
71	72	73	74	75	76	77	78	79	80
81	82	83	84	85	86	87	88	89	90
91	92	93	94	95	96	97	98	99	100

You end up at 91.

56 + 35 = 91

Independent Practice

Use a hundred chart to add.

11. 48 + 50 **12.** 75 + 15 **13.** 73 + 20 **14.** 55 + 34

15. 38 + 15 **16.** 22 + 17 **17.** 68 + 16 **18.** 55 + 29

Number Sense Compare. Use <, >, or =.

19. 23 + 50 ◯ 23 + 65 **20.** 37 + 40 ◯ 47 + 30 **21.** 65 + 34 ◯ 65 + 43

22. 25 + 35 ◯ 35 + 45 **23.** 71 + 20 ◯ 61 + 20 **24.** 82 + 16 ◯ 72 + 26

Problem Solving

25. A horned lizard laid 37 eggs in one place. To the nearest ten, about how many eggs did the lizard lay?

26. **Reasoning** You have learned to add 9 to a number by first adding 10 and then subtracting 1. How could you add 99 to a number using mental math? Try using your method to find 24 + 99.

27. Which number is missing in the pattern below?

0, 50, 100, ▢, 200

A 190 **C** 175

B 180 **D** 150

Lesson

2-3

Understand It!
Addends can be broken apart to find sums using mental math.

Using Mental Math to Add

How can you add with mental math?

Dr. Gomez recorded how many whales, dolphins, and seals she saw. How many whales did she see during the two weeks?

Find 25 + 14.

Data

Marine Animals Seen

Animal	Week 1	Week 2
Whales	25	14
Dolphins	28	17
Seals	34	18

Another Example How can you make tens to add mentally?

How many dolphins did Dr. Gomez see during the two weeks?

You can make a ten to help you find 28 + 17.

- Break apart 17.
  17 = 2 + 15
- Add 2 to 28
  2 + 28 = 30
- Add 15 to 30.
  30 + 15 = 45

? dolphins in all

28	17

28 + 17 = 45

Dr. Gomez saw 45 dolphins.

Explain It

1. How does knowing that 17 = 2 + 15 help you find 28 + 17 mentally?
2. What is another way to make a 10 to add 28 + 17?

One Way

Break apart one of the addends.

- Break apart 14.
  14 = 10 + 4
- Add 10 to 25.
  25 + 10 = 35
- Add 4 to 35.
  35 + 4 = 39

25 + 14 = 39

Dr. Gomez saw 39 whales.

Another Way

Break apart both addends.

- Break apart both addends.
  25 = 20 + 5   14 = 10 + 4
- Add the tens. Add the ones.
  20 + 10 = 30   5 + 4 = 9
- Then add the tens and ones.
  30 + 9 = 39

25 + 14 = 39

Dr. Gomez saw 39 whales.

Guided Practice*

Do you know HOW?

1. Make a ten to add 38 + 26.

38 + 26
26 = 2 + 24
38 + ☐ = 40
40 + ☐ = 64
38 + 26 = ☐

2. Use breaking apart to add 25 + 12.

25 + 12
12 = 10 + 2
25 + 10 = ☐
☐ + 2 = 37
25 + 12 = ☐

Do you UNDERSTAND?

3. **Reasoning** Compare the One Way and Another Way examples above. How are they the same? How are they different?

4. **Number Sense** To find 37 + 28, you could add 37 + 30 = 67. Then what should you do next?

5. Use breaking apart or making tens to find how many seals Dr. Gomez saw during the two weeks. Explain which method you used.

Independent Practice

Leveled Practice Use breaking apart to add mentally.

6. 72 + 18
18 = 10 + ☐
72 + ☐ = 82
82 + ☐ = 90
72 + 18 = ☐

7. 34 + 25
25 = 20 + ☐
34 + ☐ = 54
☐ + 5 = 59
34 + 25 = ☐

8. 53 + 36
36 = ☐ + 6
53 + ☐ = 83
☐ + 6 = 89
53 + 36 = ☐

**For another example, see Set C on page 62.*

Independent Practice

Leveled Practice Make a ten to add mentally.

9. 47 + 9
9 = ▢ + 6
47 + ▢ = 50
▢ + 6 = 56
47 + 9 = ▢

10. 55 + 37
37 = 5 + ▢
▢ + 5 = 60
60 + ▢ = 92
55 + 37 = ▢

11. 49 + 29
29 = ▢ + 28
49 + ▢ = 50
50 + ▢ = 78
49 + 29 = ▢

Find each sum using mental math.

12. 35 + 26 **13.** 50 + 42 **14.** 43 + 4 **15.** 71 + 13

16. 52 + 44 **17.** 7 + 54 **18.** 63 + 12 **19.** 62 + 34

20. 37 + 9 **21.** 5 + 38 **22.** 65 + 15 **23.** 33 + 23

Problem Solving

24. How long can a python be?

25. What is the total length of the iguana?

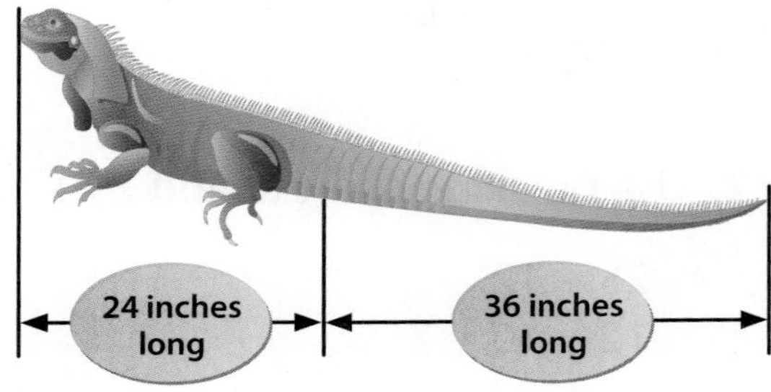

26. **Writing to Explain** Is Bill's work right? If not, tell why and write a correct answer.

Find 38 + 7.
I'll think of 7 as 2 + 5.
38 + 2 = 40
40 + 7 = 47
So, 38 + 7 is 47.

27. How is the number 4,038 written in word form?

A four hundred thirty-eight

B four thousand, three hundred eight

C four thousand, thirty-eight

D forty thousand, thirty-eight

Adding with Mental Math

Use eTools

Place-Value Blocks

Show two ways to make a ten to add 27 + 38.

Step 1 Go to the Place-Value Blocks eTool. Click on the Two-part workspace icon. In the top space, show 27 with place-value blocks. Show 38 in the bottom space.

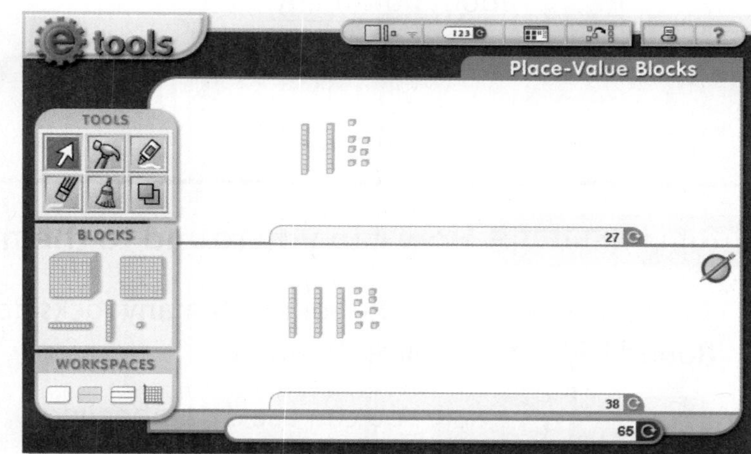

Step 2 Use the arrow tool to select ones from the bottom space and drag them to the top space. Do this until you make a ten on top. The odometers show that you have 30 + 35 = 65. So, 27 + 38 = 65, and 30 + 35 = 65.

Step 3 Use the arrow tool to move the blocks back to show 27 + 38. Then select ones from the top space and drag them to the bottom space until you make a ten on the bottom. The odometers show that you have 25 + 40 = 65. So, 27 + 38 = 65, and 25 + 40 = 65.

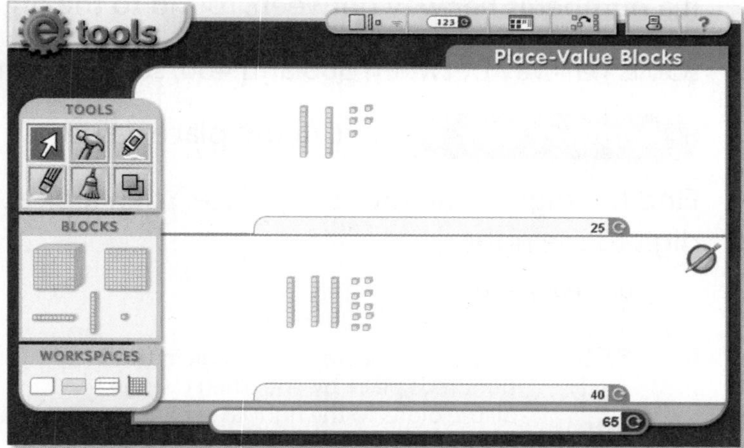

Practice

Use the Place-Value Blocks eTool. Find two ways to make a ten to add.

1. 47 + 29 = ▢ + ▢ = 76
   47 + 29 = ▢ + ▢ = 76

2. 58 + 36 = ▢ + ▢ = 94
   58 + 36 = ▢ + ▢ = 94

Lesson
2-4

Understand It!
Rounded numbers can be used to estimate solutions to problems.

Rounding

How can you round numbers?

To the nearest 10, about how many rocks does Tito have?

Round 394 to the nearest ten. To round, replace a number with a number that tells about how many.

Another Example **How can you round to the nearest hundred?**

To the nearest hundred, about how many rocks does Donna have? Round 350 to the nearest hundred.

One Way You can use a number line.

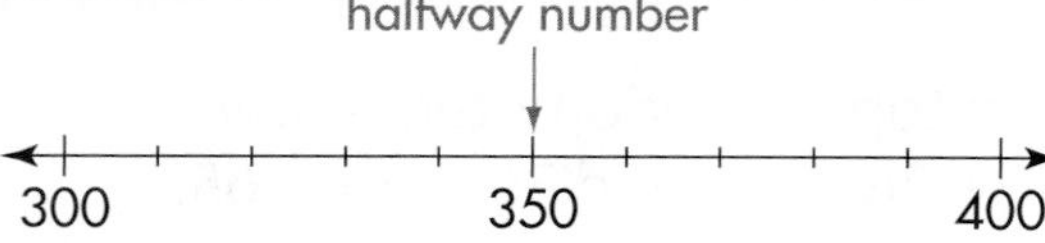

If a number is halfway between, round to the greater number.

350 is halfway between 300 and 400, so 350 rounds to 400.

Another Way You can use place value.

Find the digit in the rounding place. Then look at the next digit to the right.

hundreds place
↓
350
↓↓↓
400

Since $5 = 5$, increase the digit in the hundreds place by one. Then change all the digits to the right to zero.

So, 350 rounds to 400. Donna has about 400 rocks.

Explain It

1. If you round 350 to the nearest ten, would you still say that Donna has about 400 rocks? Why or why not?
2. Explain why 350 is the least number that rounds to 400.

One Way

You can use a number line.

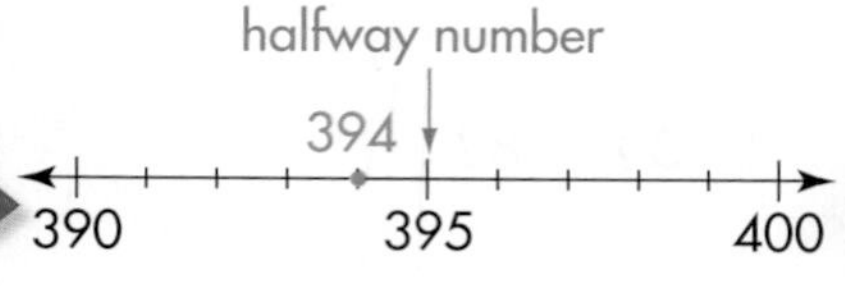

394 is closer to 390 than 400, so 394 rounds to 390.

Tito has about 390 rocks.

Another Way

You can use place value.

- Find the digit in the rounding place.
- Look at the next digit to the right. If it is 5 or greater, add 1 to the rounding digit. If it is less than 5, leave the rounding digit alone.
- Change all digits to the right of the rounding place to 0.

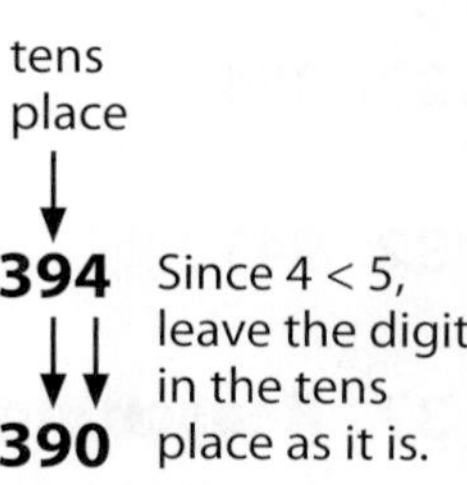

So, 394 rounds to 390.

Tito has about 390 rocks.

Guided Practice*

Do you know HOW?

Round to the nearest ten.

1. 37 **2.** 63 **3.** 85

4. 654 **5.** 305 **6.** 752

Round to the nearest hundred.

7. 557 **8.** 149 **9.** 552

10. 207 **11.** 888 **12.** 835

Do you UNDERSTAND?

13. Number Sense What number is halfway between 250 and 260?

14. Reasoning If Tito adds one more rock to his collection, about how many rocks will he have, rounded to the nearest ten? rounded to the nearest hundred? Explain your answer.

15. Writing to Explain Tell what you would do to round 46 to the nearest ten.

Independent Practice

Round to the nearest ten.

16. 45 **17.** 68 **18.** 98 **19.** 24 **20.** 55

21. 249 **22.** 732 **23.** 235 **24.** 805 **25.** 703

26. Reasoning Round 996 to the nearest ten. Explain your answer.

**For another example, see Set C on page 62.*

Independent Practice

Round to the nearest hundred.

27. 354 **28.** 504 **29.** 470 **30.** 439 **31.** 682

32. 945 **33.** 585 **34.** 850 **35.** 702 **36.** 870

37. Reasoning Round 954 to the nearest hundred. Explain your answer.

Problem Solving

38. Number Sense Write a number that rounds to 200 when it is rounded to the nearest hundred.

39. Writing to Explain Describe the steps you would follow to round 439 to the nearest ten.

40. Number Sense Suppose you are rounding to the nearest hundred. What is the greatest number that rounds to 600? What is the least number that rounds to 600?

41. Number Sense A 3-digit number has the digits 2, 5, and 7. To the nearest hundred, it rounds to 800. What is the number?

42. To the nearest hundred dollars, a computer game costs $100. Which could **NOT** be the actual cost of the game?

A $89 **C** $110

B $91 **D** $150

43. What is the standard form of 700 + 40?

A 740 **C** 470

B 704 **D** 407

44. There are 293 steps to the top of the Leaning Tower of Pisa in Italy. To the nearest hundred, about how many steps are there?

Algebra Connections

Greater, Less, or Equal

Remember that the two sides of a number sentence can be equal or unequal. A symbol $>$, $<$, or $=$ tells how the sides compare. Estimation or reasoning can help you tell if one side is greater.

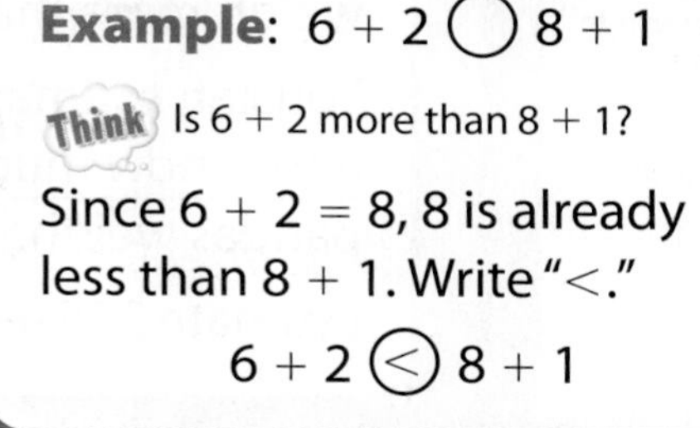

Example: $6 + 2 \bigcirc 8 + 1$

Think: Is $6 + 2$ more than $8 + 1$?

Since $6 + 2 = 8$, 8 is already less than $8 + 1$. Write "$<$."

$6 + 2 < 8 + 1$

$>$	$<$	$=$
is greater than	*is less than*	*is equal to*

Copy and complete. Replace the circle with $<$, $>$, or $=$. Check your answers.

1. $3 + 4 \bigcirc 2 + 7$ **2.** $9 + 1 \bigcirc 5 + 4$ **3.** $5 + 3 \bigcirc 6 + 3$

4. $2 + 9 \bigcirc 1 + 8$ **5.** $4 + 6 \bigcirc 4 + 7$ **6.** $8 + 6 \bigcirc 9 + 5$

7. $18 + 2 \bigcirc 16 + 4$ **8.** $15 + 5 \bigcirc 10 + 8$ **9.** $14 + 4 \bigcirc 12 + 4$

10. $17 + 3 \bigcirc 20 + 1$ **11.** $21 + 2 \bigcirc 19 + 2$ **12.** $27 + 3 \bigcirc 26 + 4$

For **13** and **14**, copy and complete each number sentence. Use it to help solve the problem.

13. Al and Jiro had some toy animals. Al had 8 lizards and 3 frogs. Jiro had 11 lizards and 2 frogs. Who had more toy animals?

14. The number below each block tells how many are in a set. Val used all of the small and large cylinders. Jen used all of the small and large cubes. Who used more blocks?

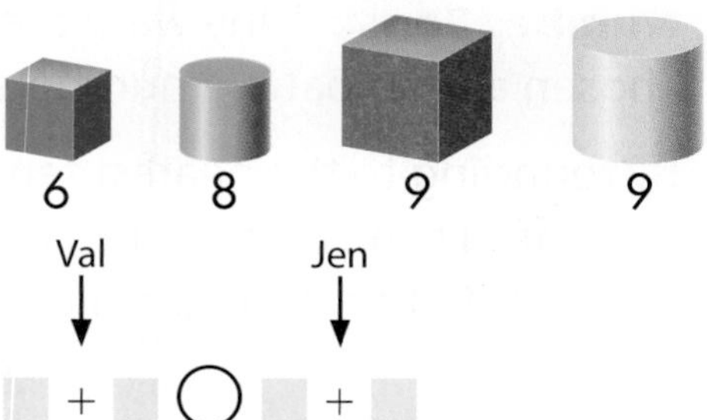

15. **Write a Problem** Write a problem using this number sentence: $9 + 2 > 4 + 5$.

Lesson

2-5

Understand It!
Rounded addends can be used to estimate answers to addition problems.

Estimating Sums

How can you estimate sums?

Do the two pandas together weigh more than 500 pounds?

You can estimate to find out about how much the two pandas weigh.

Estimate 255 + 322.

Another Example **What is another way to estimate sums?**

You can use compatible numbers to estimate.

Compatible numbers are numbers that are close to the addends, but easy to add mentally.

Use compatible numbers to decide if the pandas together weigh more than 500 pounds.

$$\begin{array}{r} 255 \\ +\ 322 \\ \hline \end{array} \longrightarrow \begin{array}{r} 250 \\ +\ 325 \\ \hline 575 \end{array}$$

250 + 325 is about 575.
575 > 500

The pandas together weigh more than 500 pounds.

Explain It

1. **Number Sense** Why were the numbers 250 and 325 chosen as compatible numbers in the example above?
2. By rounding to the nearest ten, everyone gets the same estimated sum. Is this true if compatible numbers are used to estimate the sum? Explain.

One Way

Round to the nearest hundred.

$$\begin{array}{r} 255 \\ +\ 322 \\ \hline \end{array} \longrightarrow \begin{array}{r} 300 \\ +\ 300 \\ \hline 600 \end{array}$$

255 + 322 is about 600.
600 > 500

The pandas together weigh more than 500 pounds.

Another Way

Round to the nearest ten.

$$\begin{array}{r} 255 \\ +\ 322 \\ \hline \end{array} \longrightarrow \begin{array}{r} 260 \\ +\ 320 \\ \hline 580 \end{array}$$

255 + 322 is about 580.
580 > 500

The pandas together weigh more than 500 pounds.

Guided Practice*

Do you know HOW?

Round to the nearest ten to estimate.

1. 28 + 46 **2.** 75 + 17

Round to the nearest hundred to estimate.

3. 114 + 58 **4.** 198 + 426

Use compatible numbers to estimate.

5. 136 + 437 **6.** 654 + 253

Do you UNDERSTAND?

7. Writing to Explain Which estimate in the example above is closer to the actual sum? Explain your thinking.

8. How could you use rounding to estimate 487 + 354?

9. Number Sense If both addends are rounded down, will the estimate be greater or less than the actual sum?

Independent Practice

In **10–13**, round to the nearest ten to estimate.

10. 18 + 43 **11.** 75 + 72 **12.** 39 + 102 **13.** 376 + 295

In **14–17**, round to the nearest hundred to estimate.

14. 403 + 179 **15.** 462 + 251 **16.** 64 + 403 **17.** 539 + 399

In **18–21**, use compatible numbers to estimate.

18. 75 + 26 **19.** 167 + 27 **20.** 108 + 379 **21.** 145 + 394

*For another example, see Set C on page 62.

Independent Practice

Reasonableness Estimate to decide if each answer is reasonable. Write *yes* or *no*. Then explain your thinking.

22. 32 + 58 = 70

23. 83 + 46 = 129

24. 55 + 64 = 99

25. 105 + 23 = 308

26. 713 + 118 = 831

27. 328 + 365 = 693

Problem Solving

In **28–30**, use the table at the right.

Distance from Indianapolis, IN

City	Miles Away
Chicago, IL	187 miles
Cincinnati, OH	112 miles
Columbus, OH	175 miles
Louisville, KY	114 miles

28. Which city is farthest from Indianapolis?

29. Mr. Tyson drove from Indianapolis to Cincinnati and back again. To the nearest ten miles, about how many miles did he drive?

30. Mr. Tyson drove from Chicago to Indianapolis to Louisville. To the nearest 10 miles, about how many miles in all did he drive?

31. Dorinne paid for a pair of socks with a $5 bill. If the socks cost $2.67, what should her change be?

32. **Number Sense** Why might you round to the nearest ten instead of the nearest hundred when you estimate a sum?

33. How could you use rounding to estimate 268 + 354?

34. Write the number 3,500 in word form in two different ways.

35. How could you use compatible numbers to estimate 229 + 672?

36. Think About the Process Jared has 138 marbles. Manny has 132 marbles. Which number sentence is best to estimate how many marbles they have in all?

A 38 + 32 = 70

B 100 + 100 = 200

C 108 + 102 = 210

D 140 + 130 = 270

Mixed Problem Solving

Read the story and then answer the questions.

We Can't Wait!

Jamie and her sisters stared out of the front window of their home. They were talking about all the good stories their grandmother always tells them when she visits. About 10 minutes ago, their dad had called home from the airport. He said that he was exactly 26 blocks away. He needed to make one more stop 12 blocks farther away. Then he would come home.

When Dad finally came around the street corner, the sisters jumped off the sofa and ran to the door. Dad arrived at the door with some grocery bags, a suitcase, and a special visitor. Soon the family would be hearing many good stories.

1. What conclusion can you draw?

2. When the sisters were staring out of the window, their dad had called about 10 minutes ago. Write a number of minutes that rounds to 10 minutes.

3. To the nearest 10 blocks, about how many blocks away from home was Dad when he called home?

4. To the nearest 10 blocks, about how many blocks did Dad travel from his last stop to home?

5. Look at the table below.

Write the distances in order from least to greatest.

Data

Place	Distance from Home
Bakery	38 blocks
Bank	12 blocks
Grocery Store	21 blocks
Toy Store	26 blocks

6. **Strategy Focus** Solve the problem. Use the strategy Make an Organized List.

Jamie earned some money doing chores. She wants to put 70 cents in her bank. What are two different ways she could use coins to make 70 cents?

Lesson

2-6

Understand It!
Place value can be used to regroup when adding 2-digit numbers.

Adding 2-Digit Numbers

Hands-On
place-value blocks

How can you use addition to solve problems?

How many ears of corn are there in all?

- Add to find the total. **58 + 47 =** ☐
- Estimate first. **60 + 50 = 110**
  58 + 47 is about 110.

Guided Practice*

Do you know HOW?

Estimate. Then find each sum. Place-value blocks may help.

1. 42 + 59

2. 64 + 22

3. 93 + 28

4. 57 + 52

5. 47 + 9

6. 84 + 28

Do you UNDERSTAND?

7. Look at the What You Write step in the example above. Why is there a 1 above the 5 in the tens place?

8. Look at the pumpkins above.

a Estimate the total weight of the pumpkins.

b Write and solve a number sentence to find the actual total weight of the pumpkins.

Independent Practice

Estimate. Then find each sum.

9. 77 + 52

10. 19 + 24

11. 57 + 8

12. 72 + 26

13. 75 + 39

14. 33 + 45

15. 88 + 16

16. 24 + 54

17. 17 + 37

18. 59 + 13

19. 83 + 9

20. 71 + 19

21. 45 + 34

DIGITAL eTools www.pearsonsuccessnet.com

*For another example, see Set D on page 63.

What You Think

$58 + 47 = \square$

- Add the ones.
  8 ones + 7 ones = 15 ones
  Regroup.
  15 ones = 1 ten 5 ones
- Add the tens.
  1 ten + 5 tens + 4 tens = 10 tens
  Regroup.
  10 tens = 1 hundred

What You Write

$$\begin{array}{r} \scriptstyle 1 \\ 58 \\ +\ 47 \\ \hline 105 \end{array}$$

105 is close to 110, so 105 is reasonable.

There are 105 ears of corn in all.

Problem Solving

In **22** and **23**, use the table at the right.

22. Follow the steps below to find how many points the Hoop Troop scored all together in Games 1 and 2.

a Write a number sentence to show how to solve the problem.

b Estimate the answer.

c Solve the problem.

d Is your answer reasonable? Explain.

Data

The Hoop Troop

Games	Points Scored
Game 1	66
Game 2	57
Game 3	64

23. List the Hoop Troop's scores in order from the fewest to the most points.

24. Reasonableness Stan added 36 + 29 and got 515. Explain why his answer is not reasonable.

25. Number Sense What is the greatest possible sum of two 2-digit numbers? Explain.

26. Colleen ran 18 miles last week. She ran 26 miles this week. She plans to run 28 miles next week. Which number sentence would find how many miles she has run so far?

A $18 + 28 = \square$ **B** $18 + 26 = \square$ **C** $18 + 26 + 28 = \square$ **D** $28 - 18 = \square$

In **27** and **28**, use the pictures.

27. If the truck is first, which toy is fourth?

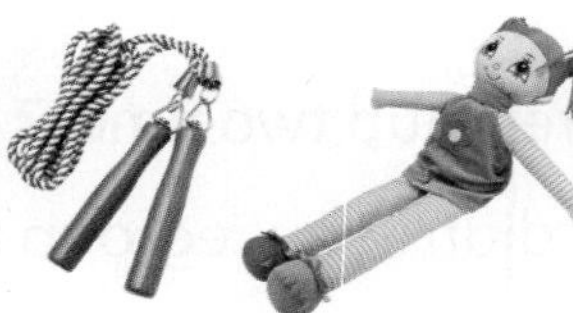

28. The jump rope costs \$3.79. How much change should Susan get if she pays with a \$5 bill?

Lesson
2-7

Understand It!
Place-value blocks can model regroupings in addition problems with greater numbers.

Models for Adding 3-Digit Numbers

Hands-On
place-value blocks

How can you add 3-digit numbers with place-value blocks?

You can add whole numbers by using place value to break them apart.

Find 143 + 285.

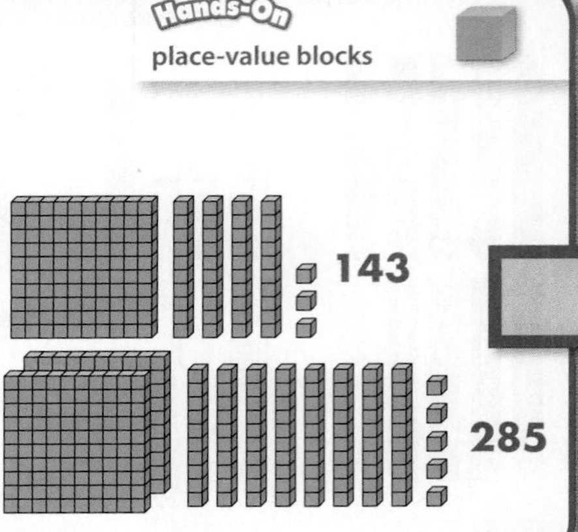

Another Example How do you add with two regroupings?

Find 148 + 276.

Step 1 Add the ones.
8 ones + 6 ones = 14 ones

Regroup.
14 ones = 1 ten 4 ones

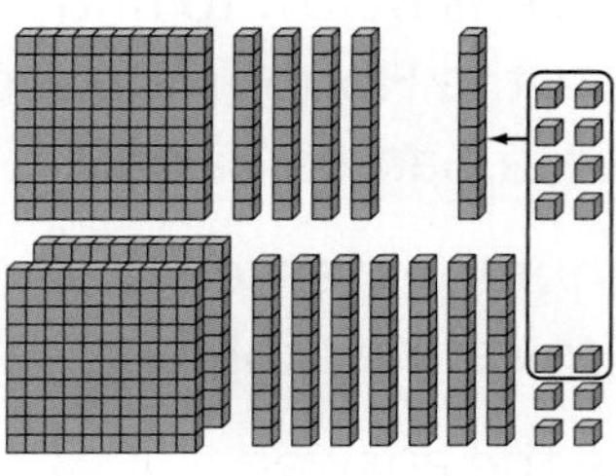

Step 2 Add the tens.
1 ten + 4 tens + 7 tens = 12 tens

Regroup.
12 tens = 1 hundred 2 tens

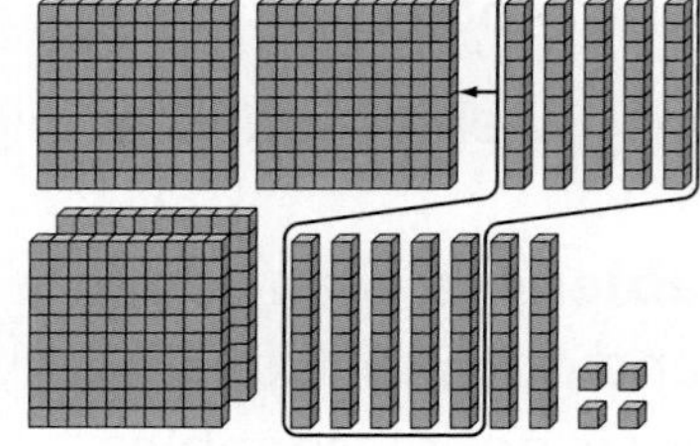

Step 3 Add the hundreds.
1 hundred + 1 hundred +
2 hundreds = 4 hundreds

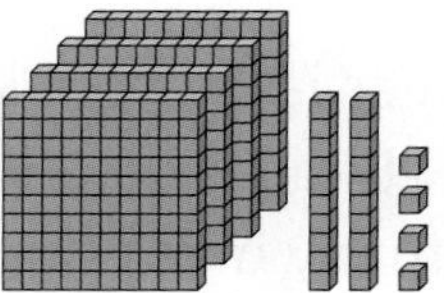

So, 148 + 276 = 424.

Explain It

1. Why did you need to regroup two times?
2. **Number Sense** Why didn't you regroup hundreds?

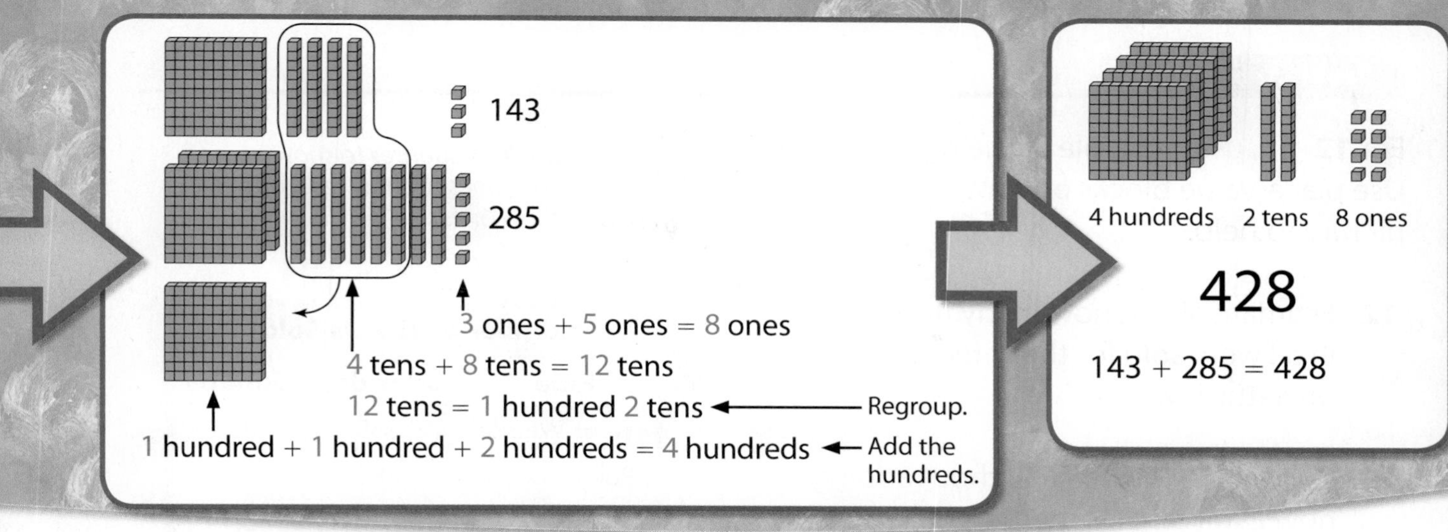

Guided Practice*

Do you know HOW?

1. Write the problem and find the sum.

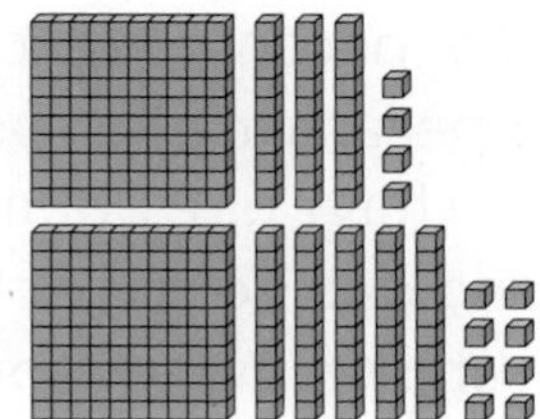

Use place-value blocks or draw pictures to find each sum.

2. 256 + 162

3. 138 + 29

Do you UNDERSTAND?

4. How do you know when you need to regroup?

5. Mr. Wu drove 224 miles yesterday. He drove 175 miles today. Use place-value blocks or draw pictures to find how many miles he drove in all.

Independent Practice

Write each problem and find the sum.

6.

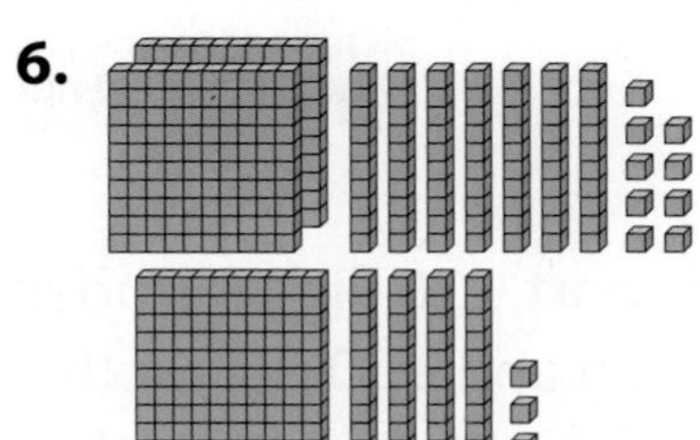

7.

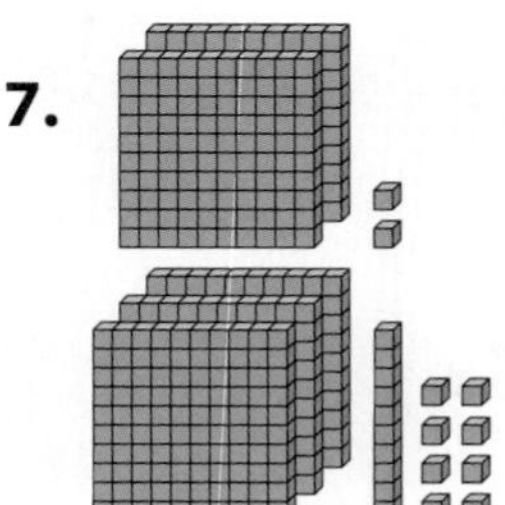

Find each sum. Use place-value blocks or draw pictures to help.

8. 635 + 222

9. 337 + 152

10. 359 + 211

11. 358 + 243

*For another example, see Set E on page 63.

Problem Solving

For **12–15**, use the table at the right. Use place-value blocks or draw a picture to help.

You can draw squares to show hundreds, lines to show tens, and ×s to show ones.

12. Estimate about how many tickets in all were sold for the three rides on Saturday.

13. Writing to Explain Without adding, how can you tell whether more tickets were sold in the two days for the Ferris wheel or the swings?

Number of Tickets Sold

Ride	Saturday	Sunday
Ferris Wheel	368	406
Roller Coaster	486	456
Swings	138	251

14. How many Ferris wheel tickets were sold in the two days?

15. How many roller coaster tickets were sold in the two days?

16. Number Sense Mike wants to use place-value blocks to show 237 + 153. He has 8 tens blocks. Is that enough to show the sum? Explain.

17. One kind of pecan tree produces about 45 pecans in each pound of nuts. If you have one pound of these pecans and one pound of the kind of pecan shown below, how many pecans do you have?

18. Writing to Explain Is the sum of two 3-digit numbers always a 3-digit number? Explain how you know.

19. Which number sentence do these place-value blocks show?

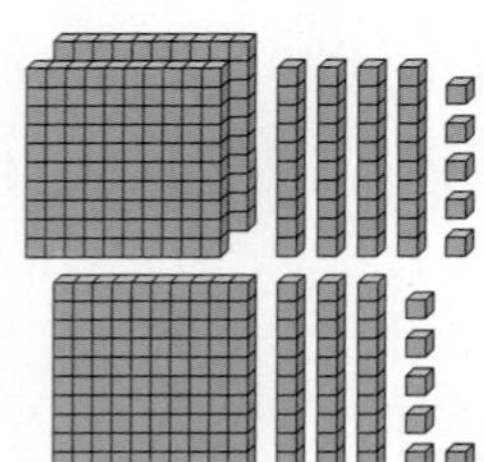

A 254 + 163 = 417

B 245 + 136 = 381

C 245 + 163 = 408

D 254 + 136 = 390

20. At a busy airport, 228 flights landed between noon and 3:00 P.M. On the same day 243 flights landed at that airport between 3 P.M. and 6 P.M. How many flights in all landed between noon and 6 P.M.?

? flights in all

228	243

Adding with Regrouping

Use eTools
Place-Value Blocks

Use the Place-Value Blocks eTool to add 367 + 175 by regrouping.

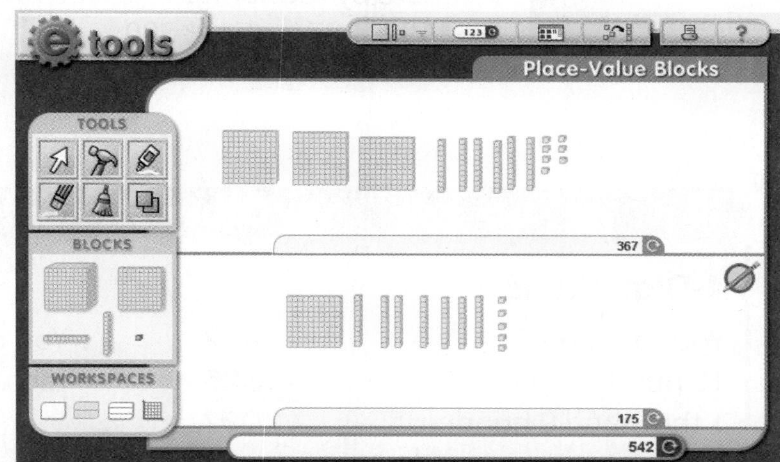

Step 1 Go to the Place-Value Blocks eTool. Click on the Two-part workspace icon. In the top space, show 367 with place-value blocks. Show 175 in the bottom space.

Step 2 Use the arrow tool to move the ones from 175 to the top space. Then use the glue tool to select 10 ones. Click on the group of 10 ones to make one ten.

Step 3 Use the arrow tool to move the tens from 175 to the top space. Use the glue tool to select 10 tens. Click on the group of 10 tens to make one hundred.

Step 4 Use the arrow tool to move the hundred from 175 to the top space. Look at the blocks to find the sum, 367 + 175 = 542.

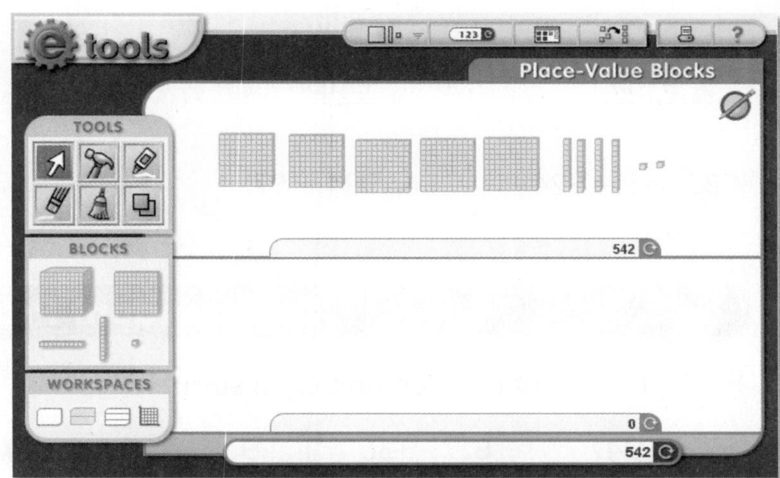

Practice

Use the Place-Value Blocks eTool to find the sums by regrouping.

1. 248 + 374 **2.** 459 + 178 **3.** 566 + 293 **4.** 675 + 189

Lesson
2-8

Understand It!
Place value can be used to regroup when adding greater numbers.

Adding 3-Digit Numbers

How can you use addition to solve problems?

Jason's family drove from Niagara Falls to Albany. How far did they drive in all?

Find 119 + 187.

Estimate by rounding. 100 + 200 = 300
So, 119 + 187 is about 300.

Other Examples

4-Digit Sums

You can regroup 10 hundreds into 1 thousand 0 hundreds.

```
  472
+ 625
1,097
```

You can regroup ones, tens, and hundreds.

```
   1 1
   568
 + 864
 1,432
```

Guided Practice*

Do you know HOW?

Estimate. Then find each sum. Use place-value blocks or drawings to help.

1. 126 + 171

2. 415 + 168

3. 645 + 524

4. 394 + 97

Do you UNDERSTAND?

5. **Reasonableness** In the example about Jason's family, is the answer 306 miles reasonable? Explain.

6. Ms. Lane drove 278 miles on Tuesday and 342 miles on Wednesday. Write and solve a number sentence to find how far she drove in all.

Independent Practice

For **7–15**, estimate. Then find each sum.

7. 347 + 325

8. 136 + 252

9. 564 + 283

10. 731 + 344

11. 324 + 589

12. 324 + 68

13. 709 + 94

14. 496 + 874

15. 526 + 307

*For another example, see Set E on page 63.

Step 1

Add the ones.
9 ones + 7 ones = 16 ones

Regroup.
16 ones = 1 ten 6 ones

```
   1
  119
+ 187
-----
    6
```

Step 2

Add the tens.
1 ten + 1 ten + 8 tens = 10 tens

Regroup.
10 tens = 1 hundred 0 tens

```
  11
  119
+ 187
-----
   06
```

Step 3

Add the hundreds.
1 hundred + 1 hundred + 1 hundred = 3 hundreds

```
  11
  119
+ 187
-----
  306
```

They drove 306 miles in all.

Problem Solving

For **16–19**, use the table at the right.

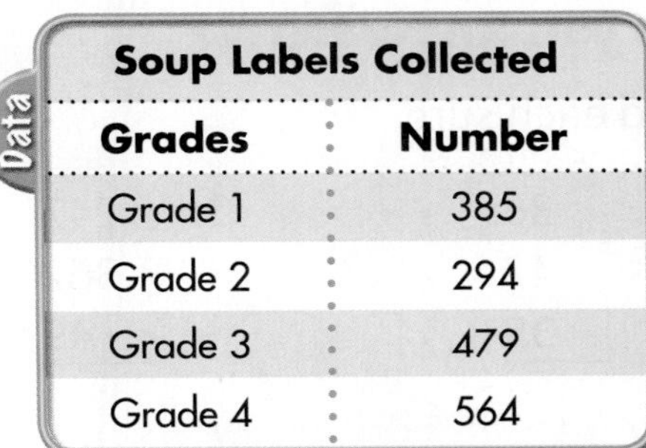

Soup Labels Collected	
Grades	**Number**
Grade 1	385
Grade 2	294
Grade 3	479
Grade 4	564

16. a Write a number sentence to find how many labels the first and second grade collected in all.

b Estimate the answer.

c Solve the problem.

d Is your answer reasonable? Explain.

17. Number Sense Without finding the exact sum, how do you know that Grades 2 and 3 together collected more labels than Grade 4?

18. Write the number of labels collected from least to greatest.

19. Which number sentence shows how many labels Grades 1 and 4 collected in all?

A 385 + 479 = ▭

B 385 + 564 = ▭

C 294 + 479 + 564 = ▭

D 385 + 294 + 479 + 564 = ▭

20. The tallest roller coaster in the world is called Kingda Ka. It is 192 feet higher than the first Ferris wheel. How tall is Kingda Ka?

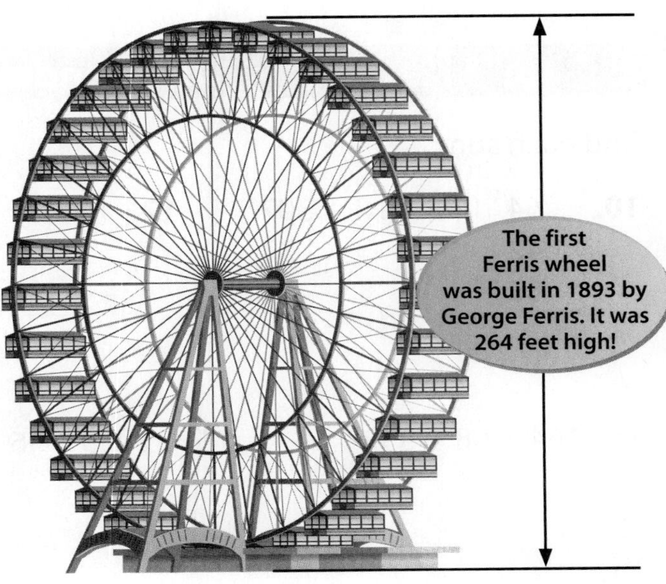

Lesson
2-9

Understand It!
The sum of 3 or more addends can be found using the same rules as for 2 addends.

Adding 3 or More Numbers

How can you use addition to solve problems?

Different kinds of birds are for sale at a pet store. How many birds are for sale in all?

- Find 137 + 155 + 18.
- Estimate: 140 + 160 + 20 = 320

Guided Practice*

Do you know HOW?

Find each sum.

1. 36 + 47 + 35

1.	
	36
	47
	+ 35

2.

	247
	362
	+ 49

3.

	273
	82
	+ 124

4.

	59
	506
	302
	+ 24

5. 9 + 46 + 24

6. 385 + 97 + 34

Do you UNDERSTAND?

For **7–9**, look at the example above.

7. Why is there a 2 above the tens place in Step 2?

8. **Reasonableness** How can you tell that 310 birds is a reasonable answer?

9. Suppose the pet store gets 46 lovebirds to sell. Write and solve a number sentence to show how many birds are for sale now.

Independent Practice

Find each sum.

10. 64, 42, + 88

11. 307, 37, + 234

12. 602, 125, + 231

13. 246, 54, 233, + 205

14. 303, 128, 63, + 149

15. 164 + 68 + 35

16. 32 + 9 + 46 + 8

17. 125 + 36 + 124 + 239

*For another example, see Set E on page 69.

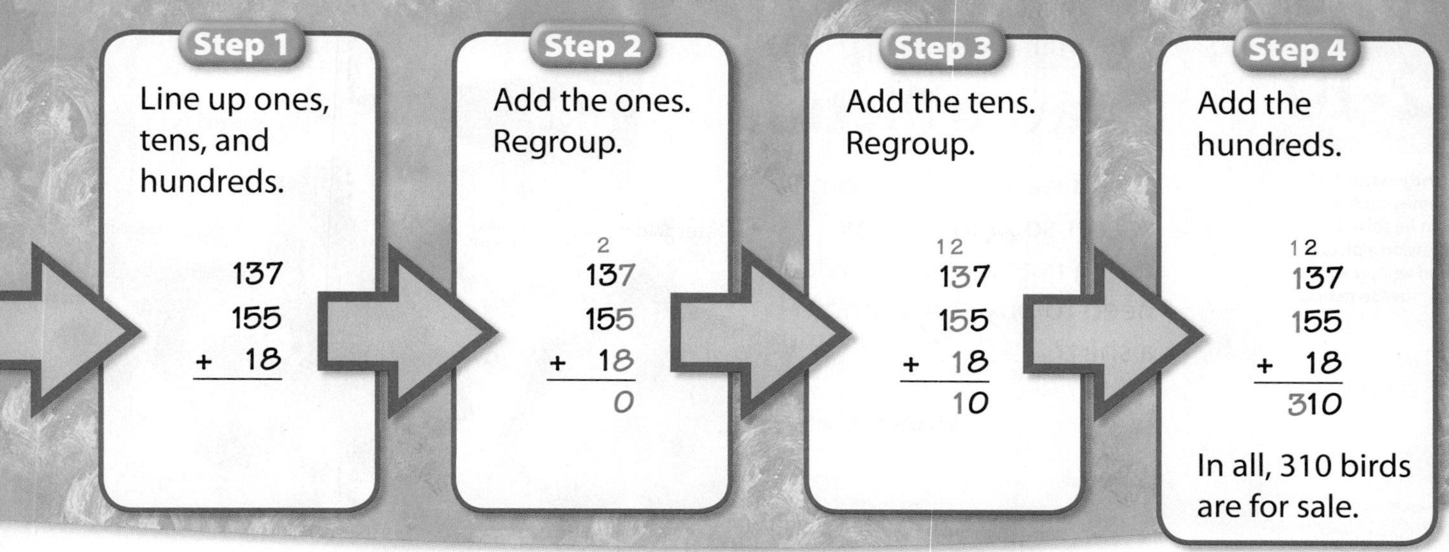

Problem Solving

Calories are used to measure the energy in food. Use the picture for **18** and **19**.

18. Karin had cereal, a glass of milk, and a banana for breakfast. Follow these steps to find how many calories were in the food she ate.

a Write a number sentence to show how to solve the problem.

b Estimate the answer.

c Solve the problem.

d Use the estimate to explain why your answer is reasonable.

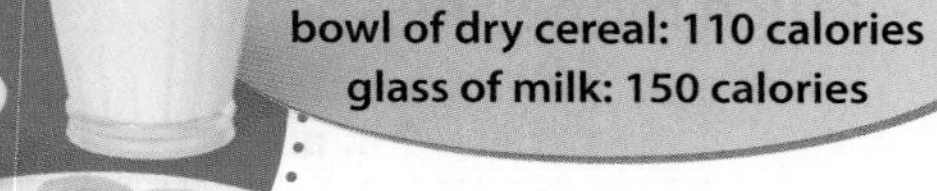

19. Compare the number of calories in a glass of milk with the number of calories in a banana. Use $>$, $<$, or $=$.

20. **Reasonableness** Meg said that $95 + 76 + 86$ is greater than 300. Explain why her answer is not reasonable.

21. Use the picture to find the size of President Washington's head carved in Mt. Rushmore.

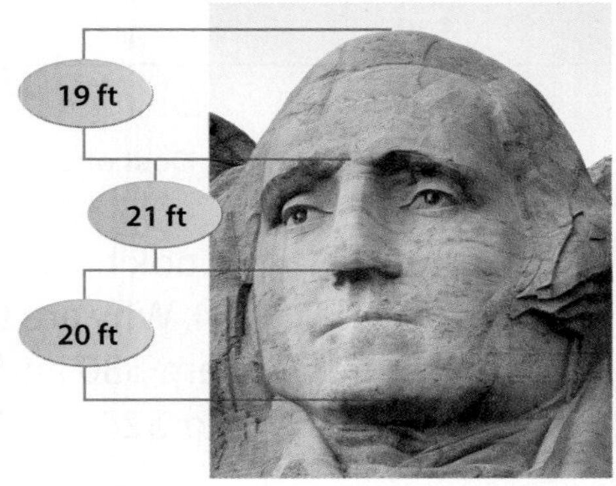

22. Ramos has 225 pennies, 105 nickels, and 65 dimes. How many coins does he have?

A 385 coins

B 395 coins

C 980 coins

D 3,815 coins

Lesson

2-10

Understand It!
Some problems can be solved by drawing a picture and writing a number sentence.

Problem Solving

Draw a Picture

David wants to buy some soccer souvenirs. How much money does David need to buy shorts and a shirt?

Guided Practice*

Do you know HOW?

1. Use the picture above. Cal bought a poster and a pennant. Copy and complete the diagram to find how much money he spent.

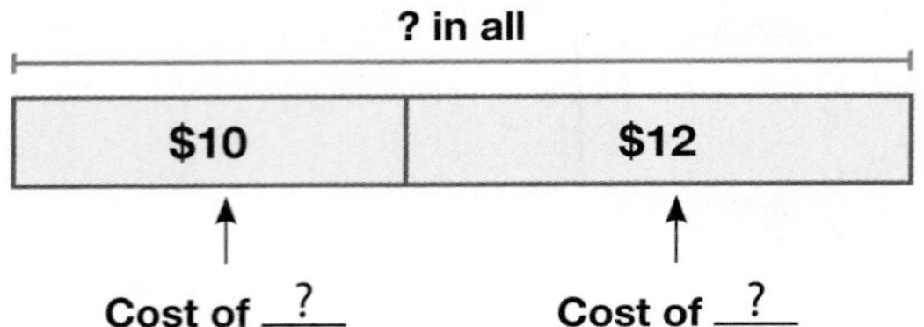

Do you UNDERSTAND?

2. Look at the diagram for Problem 1.
   a What does each box show?
   b What does the line above the whole rectangle show?

3. **Write a Problem** Write and solve a problem that can be solved by drawing a picture.

Independent Practice

4. David's dad spent $27 for tickets to the baseball game. He also spent $24 on food. **About** how much did he spend?

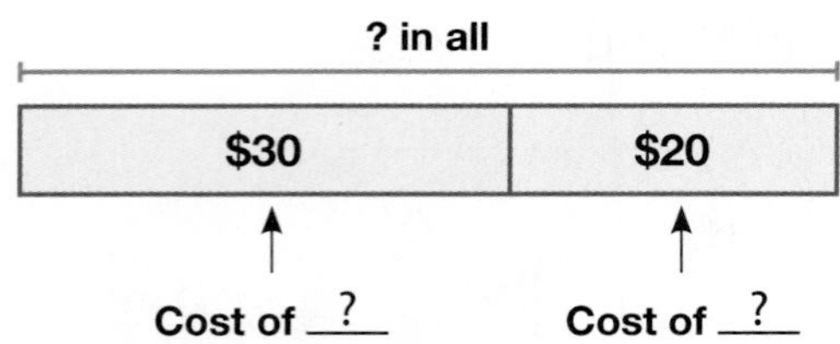

5. **Writing to Explain** Look back at the diagram for Problem 4. Why are the numbers in the diagram $30 and $20 instead of $27 and $24?

Stuck? Try this....

- What do I know?
- What am I asked to find?
- What diagram can I use to help understand the problem?
- Can I use addition, subtraction, multiplication, or division?
- Is all of my work correct?
- Did I answer the right question?
- Is my answer reasonable?

*For another example, see Set F on page 63.

Plan and Solve

Draw a diagram to show what you know.

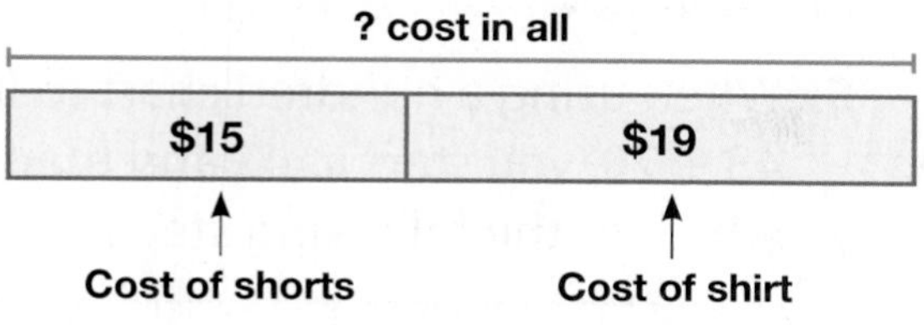

You know the parts. Add to find the total.

$\$15 + \$19 = \square$

$\$15 + \$19 = \$34$

Think $\$15 + \$20 = \$35$
$20 is $1 more than $19.

David needs $34 to buy shorts and a shirt.

Check

Make sure the answer is reasonable.

Estimate.

$\$15 + \$19$ is about $\$20 + \$20$, or $40.

The answer is reasonable because $34 is close to $40.

The table at the right shows the pets owned by third graders at Smith School. Use the table for **6–8**. For **6** and **7**, copy and complete the diagram. Answer the question.

Data

Students' Pets	
Pets	**Number of Students**
Cats	18
Dogs	22
Fish	9
Hamsters	7
Snakes	2

6. How many students have fish or hamsters?

? students in all

?	?

Students with ? Students with ?

7. How many students have cats, dogs, or snakes?

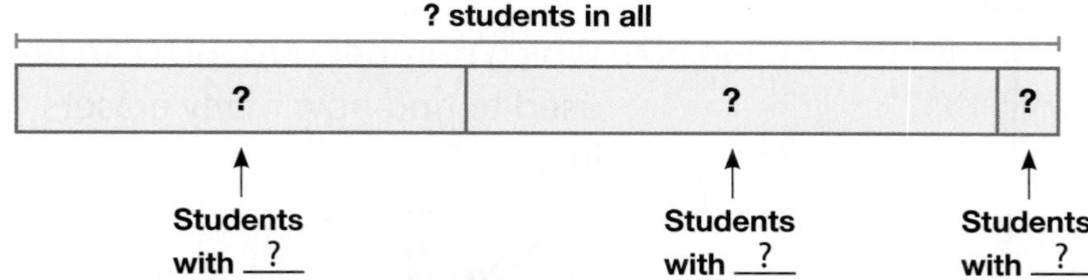

8. Draw a diagram to find about how many students have cats or dogs.

9. Estimation At the aquarium, Janet counted 12 sand sharks, 9 zebra sharks, and 11 nurse sharks. About how many sharks did Janet count?

A 50 sharks **B** 30 sharks **C** 20 sharks **D** 15 sharks

1. To the nearest ten pounds, Riley weighs 90 pounds. Which could be her weight? (2-4)

A 84 pounds

B 86 pounds

C 95 pounds

D 98 pounds

2. Which addition sentence is shown? (2-7)

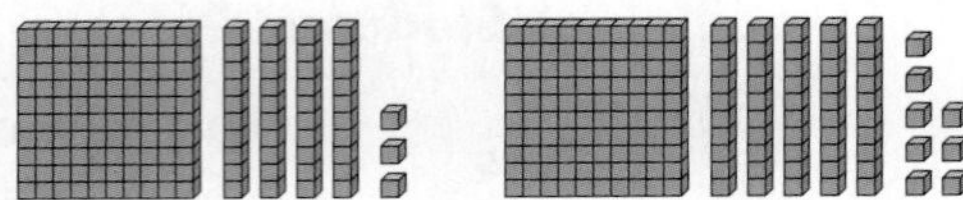

A 143 + 157 = ▢

B 143 + 158 = ▢

C 143 + 147 = ▢

D 8 + 14 = ▢

3. Rex has 252 football cards and 596 baseball cards. Which number sentence shows the best estimate of how many cards Rex has in all, using compatible numbers? (2-5)

A 300 + 550 = 850

B 300 + 500 = 800

C 250 + 550 = 800

D 250 + 600 = 850

4. Between 6 A.M. and 10 A.M., 389 trucks and 599 cars crossed a bridge. How many vehicles is this in all? (2-8)

A 878

B 888

C 978

D 988

5. When using a hundred chart to find 43 + 20, you start at 43 and then do which of the following steps? (2-2)

21	22	23	24	25	26	27	28	29	30
31	32	33	34	35	36	37	38	39	40
41	42	43	44	45	46	47	48	49	50
51	52	53	54	55	56	57	58	59	60
61	62	63	64	65	66	67	68	69	70

A Count down 2 rows.

B Count to the right 2 squares.

C Count to the left 2 squares.

D Count up 2 rows.

6. Tricia spent $35 on a toy bed, $48 on a toy dresser, and $24 on a table. How much did she spend in all? (2-9)

A $107

B $97

C $83

D $72

7. Which number sentence can be used to find how many erasers in all? (2-1)

A 8 + 6 = 14

B 9 + 6 = 15

C 9 + 5 = 14

D 3 + 6 = 9

8. Mr. Kipper's class collected $453 for the local animal shelter. What is $453 rounded to the nearest hundred? (2-4)

A $500

B $460

C $450

D $400

9. Ava swam for 39 minutes on Saturday and 49 minutes on Sunday. To find 39 + 49, Ava made a ten, as shown below. What is the missing number? (2-3)

39 + 49 = 40 + ☐ = 88

A 29

B 30

C 47

D 48

10. Kent has 28 butterflies, 16 beetles, and 12 grasshoppers in his collection. How many butterflies and beetles does he have? (2-6)

A 28

B 40

C 44

D 56

11. The Aztec Ruins monument has about 318 acres. Capulin Volcano has about 793 acres. Which is reasonable for the total size for these two national monuments in New Mexico? (2-8)

A 1,211 acres, because 318 + 793 is about 400 + 800 = 1,200

B 1,111 acres, because 318 + 793 is about 300 + 800 = 1,100

C 1,011 acres, because 318 + 793 is about 300 + 700 = 1,000

D 911 acres, because 318 + 793 is about 300 + 600 = 900

12. Cindy picked 9 roses and then 14 daisies. Which number correctly replaces the question mark in the diagram? (2-10)

? flowers in all

9 roses	14 daisies

A 5

B 23

C 33

D 113

13. Kaitlyn read a 48-page book. Her sister read a 104-page book. Which is the best estimate for the total number of pages the sisters read? (2-5)

A 150

B 140

C 120

D 100

Topic 2

Reteaching

Set A, pages 32–33

Write the missing number.

Use the Associative Property of Addition.

(2 + ☐) + 1 = 2 + (5 + 1)
(2 + 5) + 1 = 2 + (5 + 1)

You can group addends in any way and the sum will be the same.

Use the Commutative Property of Addition.

7 + ☐ = 6 + 7
7 + 6 = 6 + 7

You can add numbers in any order and the sum will be the same.

Remember the Identity Property of Addition: the sum of any number and zero is that same number.

Write each missing number.

1. (2 + 3) + 5 = 2 + (3 + ☐)

2. ☐ + 0 = 6

3. (1 + ☐) + 6 = 1 + (4 + 6)

Set B, pages 34–35

Use a hundred chart to add 14 + 11.

1	2	3	4	5	6	7	8	9	10
11	12	13	14	15	16	17	18	19	20
21	22	23	24	25	26	27	28	29	30
31	32	33	34	35	36	37	38	39	40

Start at 14. Count down 1 row to add 10.
You need to add only 11 so go right 1 space.
14 + 11 = 25

Remember that to add on a hundred chart, first add the tens.

Use a hundred chart to add.

1. 37 + 20 **2.** 52 + 17

3. 18 + 45 **4.** 52 + 30

5. 8 + 29 **6.** 12 + 15

Set C, pages 36–38, 40–42, 44–46

Round 867 to the nearest hundred.

hundreds place

867
900

Since 6 > 5, increase the digit in the hundreds place by one. Then change all the digits to the right to zero.

867 rounds to 900.

Estimate 478 + 134.

Use compatible numbers.

478 ⟶ 470
+ 134 ⟶ + 130
600

Remember that you can break apart addends to use mental math.

Find each sum using mental math.

1. 30 + 56 **2.** 45 + 19

In **3–8**, estimate each sum. Round to the nearest hundred.

3. 367 + 319 **4.** 732 + 110

Round to the nearest ten.

5. 98 + 42 **6.** 459 + 213

Use compatible numbers.

7. 372 + 123 **8.** 211 + 164

Set D, pages 48–49

Find 96 + 68. Estimate: 100 + 70 = 170

Then, add.

$$\begin{array}{r} {}^{1} \\ 96 \\ +\ 68 \\ \hline 164 \end{array}$$

6 + 8 = 14 ones
Regroup into 1 ten 4 ones.
1 ten + 9 tens + 6 tens = 16 tens

164 is close to 170, so 164 is reasonable.

Remember to add ones first. Regroup if necessary. Then add tens.

Estimate. Then find each sum.

1. $\begin{array}{r} 38 \\ +\ 47 \\ \hline \end{array}$

2. $\begin{array}{r} 77 \\ +\ 56 \\ \hline \end{array}$

3. 55 + 89

4. 58 + 33

Set E, pages 50–52, 54–57

Find 125 + 168.

Show 125 and 168 with place-value blocks.

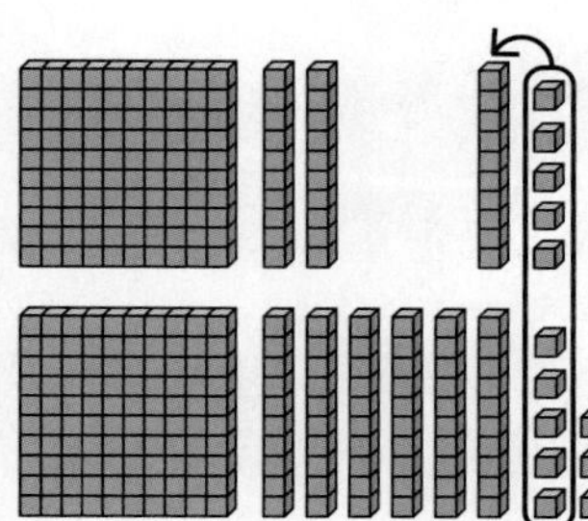

5 ones + 8 ones = 13 ones
Regroup.
13 ones = 1 ten 3 ones

1 ten + 2 tens + 6 tens = 9 tens

1 hundred + 1 hundred = 2 hundreds

So, 125 + 168 = 293.

Find 43 + 187 + 238.
Estimate: 40 + 190 + 240 = 470

$$\begin{array}{r} {}^{1}\ {}^{1} \\ 43 \\ 187 \\ +\ 238 \\ \hline 468 \end{array}$$

Line up ones, tens, and hundreds. Then add each column. Regroup as needed.

The answer 468 is close to 470, so 468 is reasonable.

Remember to add ones, then tens, then hundreds.

Find each sum. Use place-value blocks or draw a picture to help.

1. 265 + 116

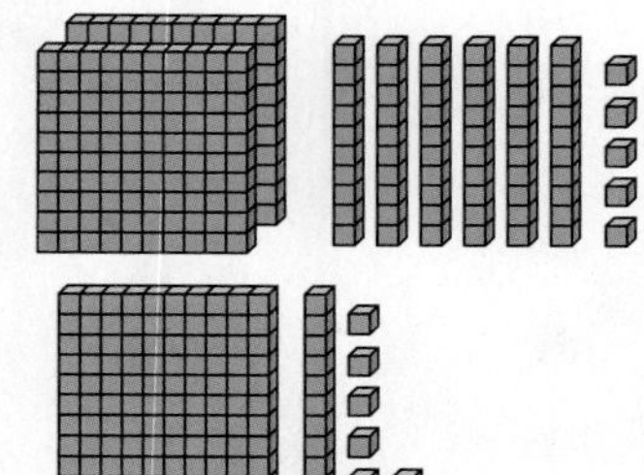

Find each sum.

2. $\begin{array}{r} 718 \\ +\ 156 \\ \hline \end{array}$

3. $\begin{array}{r} 139 \\ 209 \\ +\ 55 \\ \hline \end{array}$

Set F, pages 58–59

Ty's dad spent \$26 for tickets to a game and \$18 for snacks. How much did he spend in all?

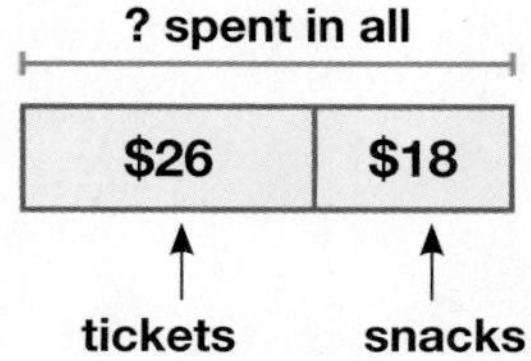

\$26 + \$18 = ▢
\$26 + \$18 = \$44

Remember to draw pictures to show the information you know.

Draw a picture and then solve.

1. Jason had 35 trading cards. Then he bought 27 more. How many does he have in all?

Topic 3 Subtraction Number Sense

1 How much longer was a *Brachiosaurus* than a *Tyrannosaurus rex*? You will find out in Lesson 3-4.

2 In recent years, how many missions from NASA's Jet Propulsion Lab have studied comets? You will find out in Lesson 3-1.

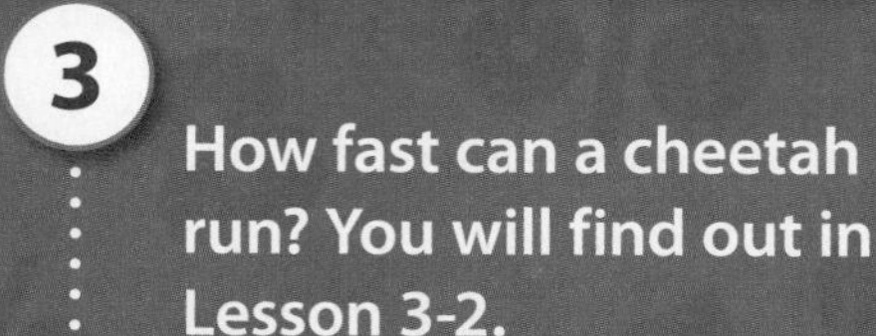

3 How fast can a cheetah run? You will find out in Lesson 3-2.

4 The giant Rafflesia plant has the largest flower in the world. How large is it? You will find out in Lesson 3-3.

Review What You Know!

Vocabulary

Choose the best term from the box.

- add
- round
- skip count
- subtract

1. To take away a part from a whole, you can __?__.

2. You can __?__ to find a number that is close to the actual number.

3. To join parts together, you can __?__.

Subtraction Facts

Find each difference.

4. 9 − 5 **5.** 11 − 3 **6.** 16 − 7

Addition Facts

Find each sum.

7. 4 + 8 **8.** 9 + 8 **9.** 6 + 7

Rounding

Writing to Explain

10. To what two numbers can you round 78? Explain why there is more than one way to round 78.

11. Is the sum of 5 + 8 the same as or different from the sum of 8 + 5? Explain.

Lesson
3-1

Subtraction Meanings

Hands-On
counters

Understand It!
Subtraction can be used to compare amounts or to compare a missing part to the whole.

When do you subtract?

Ms. Aydin's class is making school flags to sell at the school fair.

The table shows how many flags several students have made so far.

Data

Flags for School Fair

Student	Number Made
Brent	12
Devon	9
Keisha	11
Ling	14
Pedro	7
Rick	8

Another Example Subtract to find a missing addend.

Rick plans on making 13 flags. How many more flags does he need?

The parts and the whole show how addition and subtraction are related.

13 flags in all

8	?

$8 + \square = 13$

You can write a fact family when you know the parts and the whole.

A fact family is a group of related facts using the same numbers.

$5 + 8 = 13$ $\quad 13 - 8 = 5$

$8 + 5 = 13$ $\quad 13 - 5 = 8$

The missing part is 5. This means Rick needs to make 5 more flags.

Guided Practice*

Do you know HOW?

Use the table to write and solve a number sentence.

1. How many more flags has Ling made than Devon?

2. How many more flags must Pedro make to have 15 in all? to have the same number as Ling?

Do you UNDERSTAND?

3. Ling sold 8 of the flags she had made. Write a number sentence to find how many flags she has left. Then solve the problem.

4. **Write a Problem** Write and solve a word problem that can be solved by subtracting.

*For another example, see Set A on page 82.

Subtract to take some away and find how many are left.

Brent sold 5 of the flags he made. How many flags did he have left?

12 flags in all	
5	?

$12 - 5 = 7$

Brent had 7 flags left.

Subtract to compare amounts.

How many more flags did Keisha make than Pedro?

Keisha	11	
Pedro	?	7

$11 - 7 = 4$

Keisha made 4 more flags than Pedro.

Independent Practice

Write a number sentence for each situation. Solve.

5. Pat has 15 pins. Chris has 9 pins. How many more pins does Pat have than Chris?

Pat	15	
Chris	9	?

6. How many more orange flags than green flags are there?

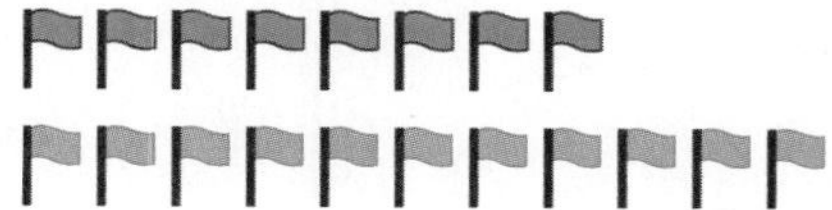

Problem Solving

7. Ching had 12 pies to sell. After she sold some of the pies, she had 4 pies left. How many pies had Ching sold?

8. A pole holding a state flag is 10 feet tall. The height of the flag is 4 feet. How many feet taller is the pole than the flag?

9. The Jet Propulsion Lab had 9 missions between 2003 and 2006. Two of these missions were to study comets. How many of these missions did not study comets?

10. Kevin has 17 spelling words to learn this week. He already knows how to spell 9 of the words. How many words does he still need to learn?

11. Rob had 17 pens. After he gave some of them to his friend, he had 8 pens. Which number sentence shows one way to find how many pens Rob gave to his friend?

A $17 + 8 = \square$ **B** $8 - 1 = \square$ **C** $17 - 1 = \square$ **D** $17 - \square = 8$

Lesson
3-2

Understand It!
A hundred chart can be used to count on or count back to solve a subtraction problem.

Subtracting on a Hundred Chart

How can you subtract on a hundred chart?

Find 38 − 20 on a hundred chart.

Start at 38. To count back 2 tens, move up 2 rows.

38 − 20 = 18

1	2	3	4	5	6	7	8	9	10
11	12	13	14	15	16	17	18	19	20
21	22	23	24	25	26	27	28	29	30
31	32	33	34	35	36	37	38	39	40
41	42	43	44	45	46	47	48	49	50

Another Example **How can you use counting on to find differences?**

The difference is the answer when subtracting two numbers.

Find 43 − 19.

Think 19 + ▢ = 43.

Start at 19.
Move right one square to count on to the next ten.
20

Count on by tens by moving down. Move two rows.
30, 40

Then count on by ones until you reach 43.
41, 42, 43

You counted on: 1 + 20 + 3 = 24.

So, 43 − 19 = 24.

1	2	3	4	5	6	7	8	9	10
11	12	13	14	15	16	17	18	19	20
21	22	23	24	25	26	27	28	29	30
31	32	33	34	35	36	37	38	39	40
41	42	43	44	45	46	47	48	49	50
51	52	53	54	55	56	57	58	59	60
61	62	63	64	65	66	67	68	69	70
71	72	73	74	75	76	77	78	79	80
81	82	83	84	85	86	87	88	89	90
91	92	93	94	95	96	97	98	99	100

Explain It

1. Why do you stop at 20 when you first count on from 19?
2. Why do you add 1 + 20 + 3?

Find 85 − 19.

Think 85 − 20 = ▢

Start at 85 on the hundred chart.

Count back 2 tens to subtract 20. To do this, move up two rows.
75, 65

Since you subtracted 1 more than 19, add 1 by moving to the right one square.
65 + 1 = 66

So, 85 − 19 = 66.

51	52	53	54	55	56	57	58	59	60
61	62	63	64	65 →	(66)	67	68	69	70
71	72	73	74	75 ↑	76	77	78	79	80
81	82	83	84	(85) ↑	86	87	88	89	90
91	92	93	94	95	96	97	98	99	100

Guided Practice*

Do you know HOW?

Use a hundred chart to subtract.

1. 72 − 40

2. 86 − 30

3. 54 − 29

4. 95 − 39

5. 37 − 18

Do you UNDERSTAND?

6. **Writing to Explain** When you move up 2 rows on a hundred chart, how many are you subtracting? Explain.

7. How is subtracting ten on a hundred chart different from adding ten on a hundred chart?

8. Janey has 75 cents. She wants to buy a sticker that costs 39 cents. How much money would she have left? Explain how to use a hundred chart to find the answer.

Independent Practice

Use a hundred chart to subtract.

9. 75 − 30 **10.** 53 − 20 **11.** 68 − 40 **12.** 27 − 10

13. 84 − 50 **14.** 96 − 60 **15.** 47 − 19 **16.** 53 − 28

17. 65 − 39 **18.** 81 − 58 **19.** 76 − 29 **20.** 94 − 38

21. 96 − 17 **22.** 79 − 15 **23.** 81 − 26 **24.** 77 − 48

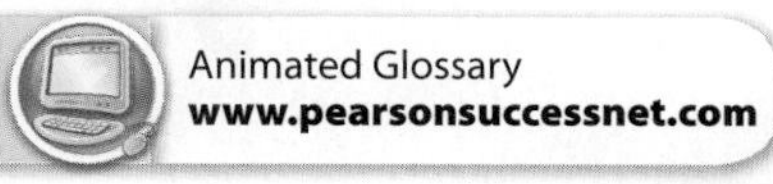

*For another example, see Set B on page 82.

Problem Solving

Use the table for **25–27**.

25. A cottonwood tree in Max's yard is 30 feet shorter than an average cottonwood tree. How tall is the tree in his yard?

26. Write the average heights of the trees from shortest to tallest.

27. A sugar maple tree in the local park is 92 feet tall. How many feet taller is the tree in the park than an average sugar maple tree?

Data

State Trees

State	Kind of Tree	Average Height
Kansas	Cottonwood	75 feet
Michigan	Eastern white pine	70 feet
New York	Sugar maple	80 feet

28. **Writing to Explain** A white pine tree is 52 feet tall. Suppose that during the next 7 years, it grows a total of 10 feet. How tall would it be then? Explain how you found your answer.

29. **Reasonableness** Liam used a hundred chart to find 92 − 62. He said the difference is 40. Is his answer reasonable? Why or why not?

Tip *What addition sentence can help?*

30. The workers in the lunchroom made 234 ham sandwiches and 165 tuna sandwiches. They also made 150 cheese pizzas and 125 veggie pizzas. How many sandwiches did they make in all?

31. For short distances, an elephant can run as fast as 15 miles per hour. How much faster can a cheetah run than an elephant?

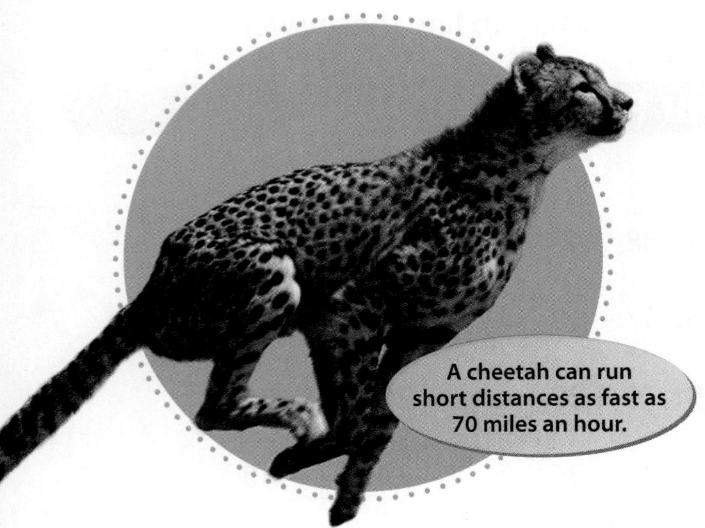

A cheetah can run short distances as fast as 70 miles an hour.

32. John is 56 inches tall. John's father is 72 inches tall. How much taller is John's father than John? Explain how you found your answer.

33. Maya had 15 small rocks. She had 9 large rocks. Which number sentence shows one way to find how many more small rocks than large rocks Maya had?

A 15 − 9 = ▢

B 15 + 6 = ▢

C 15 + 9 = ▢

D 24 − 15 = ▢

Algebra Connections

Addition and Subtraction Number Sentences

The symbol = means "is equal to."
In a number sentence, the symbol = tells you that the value on the left is equal to the value on the right.

Examples: $29 = 20 + 9$

$6 = 11 - 5$

$9 + 4 = 13$

Think The value on the left side of the number sentence is equal to the value on the right side.

Copy and complete. Write the number that makes the number sentence true.

1. $9 + \square = 11$
2. $10 = 3 + \square$
3. $17 - \square = 9$
4. $5 + \square = 13$
5. $8 = 12 - \square$
6. $14 = 5 + \square$
7. $10 = 10 + \square$
8. $6 + \square = 26$
9. $19 + \square = 29$
10. $50 + \square = 60$
11. $30 = 40 - \square$
12. $25 = 5 + \square$
13. $10 + \square = 17$
14. $42 = 45 - \square$
15. $13 - \square = 0$

For **16** and **17**, copy and complete the number sentence below each problem. Use it to solve the problem.

16. Nate had 10 river stones. Chen had 26 river stones. How many more river stones did Chen have than Nate?

$10 + \square = 26$

17. Tania collected 10 more leaves than Gwen. Tania collected 37 leaves. How many leaves did Gwen collect?

$\square + 10 = 37$

18. **Write a Problem** Write and solve a problem to match the number sentence below.

$48 = 20 + \square$

Lesson
3-3

Understand It!
Numbers can be broken apart and combined in different ways to solve subtraction problems using mental math.

Using Mental Math to Subtract

How can you subtract with mental math?

The store is having a sale on jackets. A jacket is on sale for \$17 less than the original price. What is the sale price?

You can use mental math to subtract and solve this problem.

Guided Practice*

Do you know HOW?

In **1–8**, find each difference using mental math.

1. 26 − 18
2. 34 − 19
3. 73 − 16
4. 45 − 27
5. 67 − 28
6. 83 − 39
7. 46 − 18
8. 49 − 19

Do you UNDERSTAND?

9. Writing to Explain In the One Way example above, why do you add 3 to 32 instead of subtract 3 from 32?

10. Suppose a coat has an original price of \$74 and it is on sale for \$18 less than the original price. What is the sale price of the coat? How can you use mental math to solve this problem?

Independent Practice

In **11–30**, find each difference using mental math.

11. 28 − 19
12. 46 − 18
13. 39 − 17
14. 68 − 11
15. 52 − 9
16. 75 − 12
17. 29 − 18
18. 49 − 18
19. 64 − 15
20. 43 − 16
21. 97 − 14
22. 86 − 13
23. 31 − 14
24. 98 − 17
25. 57 − 18
26. 72 − 19
27. 53 − 39
28. 27 − 19
29. 82 − 27
30. 73 − 39

*For another example, see Set C on page 83.

One Way

$52 - 17 = \square$

It's easier to subtract 20.
$52 - 20 = 32$

If you subtract 20, you subtract 3 more than 17. You must add 3 to the answer.

$32 + 3 = 35$

$52 - 17 = 35$

The sale price is $35.

Another Way

$52 - 17 = \square$

Make a simpler problem by changing each number in the same way.

You can change 17 to 20 because it's easy to subtract 20. So, add 3 to both 17 and 52.

$$\begin{array}{ccccc} 52 & - & 17 & = & \square \\ \downarrow +3 & & \downarrow +3 & & \\ 55 & - & 20 & = & 35 \end{array}$$

$52 - 17 = 35$

Problem Solving

31. Number Sense The giant Rafflesia flower can be as wide as shown in the picture. One petal can be 18 inches wide. How can you use mental math to find how much wider the whole flower is than one petal?

36 in.

32. Writing to Explain To subtract 57 − 16, Tom added 4 to each number, while Saul added 3 to each number. Will both methods work to find the correct answer? Explain.

In **33** and **34**, use the photo below.

33. a What is the sale price of the jeans? Describe one way you can use mental math to find the answer.

b Maria bought two pairs of jeans. What was the total sale price of the jeans Maria bought?

34. Which number sentence shows the original price of two pairs of jeans?

A $46 + 46 = \square$

B $46 + 18 = \square$

C $18 + 18 = \square$

D $46 - 18 = \square$

35. Eva saved $38. She bought a book for $17. Which number sentence shows one way to find how much money Eva had left?

A $38 + 17 = \square$

B $38 - 17 = \square$

C $\square - 38 = 17$

D $\square - 17 = 38$

Lesson
3-4

Understand It!
To estimate differences, replace the numbers in the problem with numbers that are close and easy to use with mental math.

Estimating Differences

How can you estimate differences?

All of the tickets for a concert were sold. So far, 126 people have arrived at the concert. About how many people who have tickets have not arrived?

Since you need to find *about* how many, you can estimate.

Estimate 493 − 126 by rounding.

Another Example How can you use compatible numbers to estimate differences?

The Perry family is taking a car trip. The trip is 372 miles long. So far, the family has traveled 149 miles. About how many miles are left to travel?

Use compatible numbers to estimate 372 − 149.

Remember: Compatible numbers are numbers that are close and easy to work with.

$$\begin{array}{r} 372 \\ -\ 149 \\ \hline \end{array} \longrightarrow \begin{array}{r} 375 \\ -\ 150 \\ \hline 225 \end{array}$$

The Perry family still has about 225 miles to travel.

Explain It

1. How are the numbers 375 and 150 easy to work with?
2. Use a different pair of compatible numbers to estimate 372 − 149.
3. Is an estimate enough to solve this problem? Why or why not?

One Way

You can round each number to the nearest hundred.

$$\begin{array}{r} 493 \\ -\ 126 \\ \hline \end{array} \longrightarrow \begin{array}{r} 500 \\ -\ 100 \\ \hline 400 \end{array}$$

About 400 people have not yet arrived.

Another Way

You can round each number to the nearest ten.

$$\begin{array}{r} 493 \\ -\ 126 \\ \hline \end{array} \longrightarrow \begin{array}{r} 490 \\ -\ 130 \\ \hline 360 \end{array}$$

About 360 people have not yet arrived.

Guided Practice*

Do you know HOW?

In **1** and **2**, round to the nearest hundred to estimate each difference.

1. 321 − 112 **2.** 255 − 189

In **3** and **4**, round to the nearest ten to estimate each difference.

3. 579 − 214 **4.** 216 − 97

In **5** and **6**, use compatible numbers to estimate each difference.

5. 328 − 207 **6.** 472 − 148

Do you UNDERSTAND?

7. **Writing to Explain** In the problem above, which way of rounding gives an estimate that is closer to the actual difference? Explain why.

8. The theater sold 415 tickets to the comedy show. So far, 273 people have arrived at the show. About how many more people are expected to arrive? Tell which estimation method you used and how you found your answer.

Independent Practice

In **9–11**, round to the nearest hundred to estimate each difference.

9. 186 − 75 **10.** 704 − 369 **11.** 291 − 93

In **12–17**, round to the nearest ten to estimate each difference.

12. 88 − 32 **13.** 149 − 95 **14.** 361 − 117

15. 75 − 41 **16.** 86 − 38 **17.** 227 − 121

For another example, see Set D on page 83.

Independent Practice

In **18–23**, use compatible numbers to estimate each difference.

18. 77 − 28

19. 202 − 144

20. 611 − 168

21. 512 − 205

22. 342 − 153

23. 904 − 31

Problem Solving

Use the table for **24–27**.

Grand Concert Hall

Day of Concert	Number of Tickets Sold
Wednesday	506
Thursday	323
Friday	251
Saturday	427
Sunday	■

24. The concert hall sold 28 fewer tickets for the Sunday concert than for the Friday concert. About how many tickets were sold for the Sunday concert?

25. About how many tickets in all were sold for Thursday and Friday?

26. **Think About the Process** About how many more tickets were sold for the Wednesday concert than for the Friday concert? Write a number sentence that uses numbers rounded to the nearest ten to estimate how many more. Explain your answer.

27. Which number sentence shows the best way to estimate how many fewer tickets were sold for the Friday concert than the Thursday concert?

A 400 − 200 = 200

B 300 − 300 = 0

C 325 − 200 = 125

D 325 − 250 = 75

28. **Writing to Explain** About how many feet longer was a *Brachiosaurus* than a *T. rex*? Use compatible numbers to estimate. Explain why you chose the numbers you used.

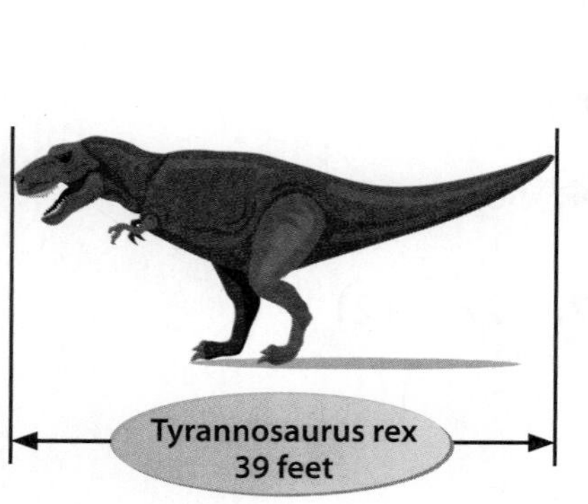

Mixed Problem Solving

The length of one year on a planet is the total time for the planet to make one complete trip around the Sun.

1. About how many fewer Earth days is a year on Mercury than a year on Earth?

2. About how many more Earth days is a year on Mars than a year on Earth?

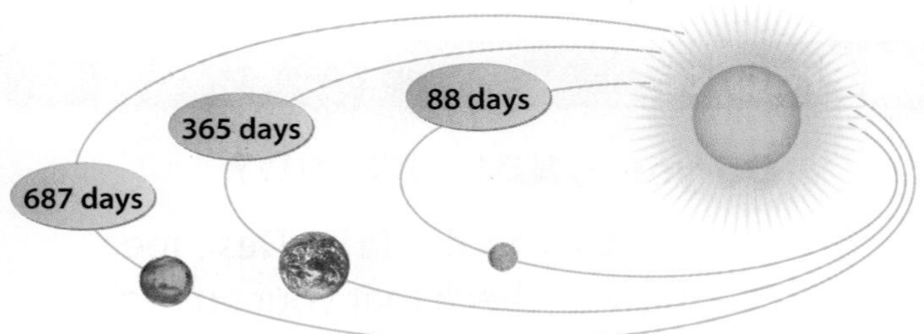

Data

Length of Year

Planet	Length of Year (in Earth Days)
Mercury	88
Venus	225
Earth	365
Mars	687
Jupiter	4,330
Saturn	10,756
Uranus	30,687
Neptune	60,190

3. Which planet has a digit 6 with a value of sixty thousand in the length of its year?

4. Which planet has a year that is about six thousand Earth days more than Jupiter's?

5. Which space object listed in the table at the right has an average surface temperature closest to Mercury's?

6. Write the average surface temperatures in order from least to greatest.

Data

Space Object	Average Surface Temperature
Mercury	332°F
Earth	59°F
The Moon	225°F
Venus	854°F

7. **Strategy Focus** Solve. Use the strategy Make an Organized List.

   Meg's favorite planet has at least 5 letters in its name. The length of its year is less than 10,000 Earth days. List all the planets that fit these clues.

Lesson
3-5

Understand It!
Answers should be checked to see if they make sense.

Problem Solving

Reasonableness

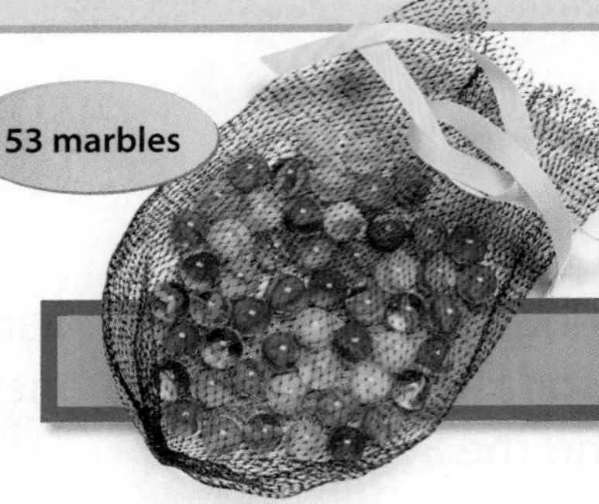

Al had the marbles shown at the right. He gave 18 marbles to his brother. How many marbles does Al have left?

After you solve a problem, ask yourself:

- Is the answer reasonable?
- Did I answer the right question?

53 marbles in all

18 marbles	?

Guided Practice*

Do you know HOW?

1. Rosita is reading a book that is 65 pages long. She has 27 pages left to read. How many pages has she already read?

65 pages in all

?	27

Do you UNDERSTAND?

2. **Writing to Explain** Describe how to check that your answer is reasonable and that you have answered the right question.

3. **Write a Problem** Write and solve a problem. Check that your answer is reasonable.

Independent Practice

Solve. Then check that your answer is reasonable.

4. James is reading a book that is 85 pages long. He read 35 pages yesterday and 24 pages today. How many pages did James read in the two days?

? pages in all

35	24

5. Kyle had 56 model cars. He gave his brother 36 of them. How many model cars does Kyle have now?

- What do I know?
- What am I asked to find?
- What diagram can I use to help understand the problem?
- Can I use addition, subtraction, multiplication, or division?
- Is all of my work correct?
- Did I answer the right question?
- Is my answer reasonable?

*For another example, see Set E on page 83.

Jim's Answer

53 − 18 = 35
Al's brother has 35 marbles.

53 − 18 is about 50 − 20, or 30.

35 is close to 30, so 35 is reasonable.

The number 35 is reasonable, but Jim did not answer the right question.

Sally's Answer

53 − 18 = 45
Al has 45 marbles left.

53 − 18 is about 50 − 20, or 30.

45 is not close to 30, so 45 is not reasonable.

Sally answered the right question, but the number 45 is not reasonable.

Pablo's Answer

53 − 18 = 35
Al has 35 marbles left.

53 − 18 is about 50 − 20, or 30.

35 is close to 30, so 35 is reasonable.

The number 35 is reasonable, and Pablo did answer the right question.

Independent Practice

Use the table to solve **6–8**. Estimate, then check that your answer is reasonable.

Data **Total Points Scored**

Games	Points
Game 1	68
Game 2	74
Game 3	89

6. How many points were scored all together in Games 1 and 2?

? points in all

68	74

7. There were 39 points scored in the first half of Game 1. How many points were scored in the second half?

68 points in all

39	?

8. **Estimation** About how many points were scored all together in the three games?

? points in all

70	70	90

9. Carl practices the piano 45 minutes each day. Today, he practiced 15 minutes after school and 10 minutes before dinner. How much time does he still need to practice?

A 70 minutes
B 60 minutes
C 35 minutes
D 20 minutes

10. Carrie has 15 pennies. Her brother has 10 more pennies than Carrie. How many pennies do they have in all?

A 40 pennies
B 25 pennies
C 10 pennies
D 5 pennies

Test

1. Mario wants to have 15 insects in his collection. He has 8 insects. Which number sentence shows a way to find how many more insects Mario needs to collect? (3-1)

   A 15 − 7 = ▢

   B 15 − ▢ = 7

   C 8 + 15 = ▢

   D 8 + ▢ = 15

2. Tom had $41. He spent $17. Which is the best estimate of how much he had left? (3-4)

   A $60

   B $30

   C $20

   D $10

3. To find 67 − 19 on a hundred chart, Casie started at 67 and then moved up 2 rows. What should she do next? (3-2)

31	32	33	34	35	36	37	38	39	40
41	42	43	44	45	46	47	48	49	50
51	52	53	54	55	56	57	58	59	60
61	62	63	64	65	66	67	68	69	70

   A Move right 1 square.

   B Move left 1 square.

   C Move right 9 squares.

   D Move left 9 squares.

4. Which number sentence is shown? (3-1)

   A 3 + 7 = 10

   B 17 − 7 = 10

   C 7 + 3 = 10

   D 10 − 7 = 3

5. There are 263 children at summer camp. There are 114 boys. Which is the best estimate for the number of girls? (3-4)

   A 250

   B 150

   C 120

   D 100

6. Rosa has 9 pens. Kim has 4 pens. Which number sentence shows how many more pens Rosa has than Kim? (3-1)

   A 9 + 4 = 13

   B 13 − 4 = 9

   C 9 − 5 = 4

   D 9 − 4 = 5

7. Which is the best estimate for 392 − 84? (3-4)

   A 500

   B 400

   C 300

   D 200

8. Tropical Fish Warehouse had 98 goldfish on Monday. By Friday, they had sold 76 of the goldfish. How many goldfish had not been sold? Use mental math to solve. (3-3)

A 22

B 32

C 38

D 174

9. A zoo has 32 kinds of snakes and 22 kinds of lizards. Which number sentence shows the best way to estimate how many more kinds of snakes than lizards are in the zoo? (3-4)

A $30 - 20 = 10$

B $30 + 20 = 50$

C $40 - 20 = 20$

D $40 - 30 = 10$

10. Stacy has 16 spelling words. She already knows how to spell 9 of the words. How many words does she still need to learn how to spell? (3-1)

16 words in all

9	?

A 25

B 9

C 7

D 6

11. Lee drove 348 miles on Monday and 135 miles on Tuesday. Which is the most reasonable answer for how much farther he drove on Monday than on Tuesday? (3-5)

A 113 miles

B 213 miles

C 313 miles

D 483 miles

12. To subtract $62 - 17$ mentally, Talia subtracted $62 - 20 = 42$ first. What should she do next? (3-3)

A Add $42 + 2$.

B Add $42 + 3$.

C Subtract $42 - 2$.

D Subtract $42 - 3$.

13. Mia had $83. She spent $49. To find how much money she has left, Mia used counting on.

$49 + 1 = 50$

$50 + 30 = 80$

$80 + 3 = 83$

How much money does Mia have left? (3-2)

A $49

B $46

C $44

D $34

Set A, pages 66–67

Write a number sentence for the situation. Solve.

Anthony has 10 flags. He gives 7 flags to his friends to wave during a parade on the 4th of July. How many flags does Anthony have left?

10 flags in all

7	?

10 − 7 = 3

Anthony has 3 flags left.

Remember that you can subtract to find how many are left, to compare, or to find a missing addend.

Write a number sentence for each situation. Solve.

1. A band has eight members. Five of the band members sing. How many do not sing?
2. Juanita had 13 flowers. She gave one flower to each of her friends. She had 4 flowers left. How many flowers did Juanita give to her friends?
3. The ceiling in a room is 12 feet high. A ladder is 8 feet tall. How much higher is the ceiling than the top of the ladder?

Set B, pages 68–70

Use a hundred chart to find 76 − 18.

51	52	53	54	55	56	57	58	59	60
61	62	63	64	65	66	67	68	69	70
71	72	73	74	75	76	77	78	79	80
81	82	83	84	85	86	87	88	89	90
91	92	93	94	95	96	97	98	99	100

Start at 76.

Count up 2 rows to subtract 20.

Go right 2 spaces because you only need to subtract 18.

76 − 18 = 58

Remember to first subtract the tens. Then move to the right or left if necessary to adjust the ones.

Use a hundred chart to subtract.

1. 88 − 20
2. 53 − 30
3. 52 − 14
4. 36 − 19
5. 66 − 43
6. 72 − 16

Reteaching

Set C, pages 72–73

Use mental math to find 83 − 16.

Change each number in the same way to make a simpler problem.

20 is easier to subtract than 16.
So, add 4 to each number and then subtract.

83 + 4 = 87 and 16 + 4 = 20

87 − 20 = 67 so 83 − 16 = 67

Remember to change each number in the same way.

Find each difference using mental math.

1. 56 − 14 **2.** 31 − 5

3. 74 − 12 **4.** 97 − 34

Set D, pages 74–76

Estimate 486 − 177.

One Way

$$\begin{array}{r} 486 \\ -\ 177 \\ \hline \end{array} \longrightarrow \begin{array}{r} 500 \\ -\ 200 \\ \hline 300 \end{array}$$

Round each number to the nearest hundred.

Another Way

$$\begin{array}{r} 486 \\ -\ 177 \\ \hline \end{array} \longrightarrow \begin{array}{r} 500 \\ -\ 175 \\ \hline 325 \end{array}$$

Use compatible numbers.

Remember to check place value when rounding.

For **1–6**, estimate each difference.

Round to the nearest hundred.

1. 367 − 319 **2.** 872 − 110

Round to the nearest ten.

3. 78 − 54 **4.** 952 − 227

Use compatible numbers.

5. 472 − 228 **6.** 911 − 347

Set E, pages 78–79

Carla is reading a book that has 87 pages. She has read 49 pages. How many pages does she have left to read?

Estimate: 87 − 49 is about 90 − 50, or 40.
87 − 49 = 38.

Carla has 38 pages left to read. The answer is reasonable because 38 is close to the estimate of 40.

Remember that you can use an estimate to check if your answer is reasonable.

1. Lucy has 45 tulips. There are 27 red tulips. The rest are yellow. How many yellow tulips does Lucy have?

2. Cody had 43 toys. He gave Ty 27 of them. How many toys does Cody have now?

Topic 4

Subtracting Whole Numbers to Solve Problems

1 How much fresh and processed fruit does a person eat in a year? You will find out in Lesson 4-5.

2 The world's largest "basket" is a building in Newark, Ohio. How big is this basket? You will find out in Lesson 4-4.

3 How many days do students in Japan attend school each year? You will find out in Lesson 4-3.

4 How much taller would this statue be if President Lincoln were standing? You will find out in Lesson 4-2.

Review What You Know!

Vocabulary

Choose the best term from the box.

• difference	• order
• estimate	• regroup

1. When you trade 1 ten for 10 ones, you ___?___.
2. The answer in subtraction is the ___?___.
3. When you find an answer that is close to the exact answer, you ___?___.

Estimating Differences

Round to the nearest ten to estimate each difference.

4. 255 − 104 **5.** 97 − 61 **6.** 302 − 38

Round to the nearest hundred to estimate each difference.

7. 673 − 250 **8.** 315 − 96 **9.** 789 − 713

Compatible Numbers

Writing to Explain

10. Use compatible numbers to estimate the difference 478 − 123. Explain why the numbers you chose are compatible.
11. How is rounding to estimate an answer different from using compatible numbers?

Lesson

4-1

Understand It!
Models show how to regroup to subtract.

Models for Subtracting 2-Digit Numbers

Hands-On
place-value blocks

How can you subtract with place-value blocks?

Whole numbers can be subtracted using place value. Subtract the ones first. Then subtract the tens. When needed, a ten can be traded for 10 ones.

Find 43 − 18.

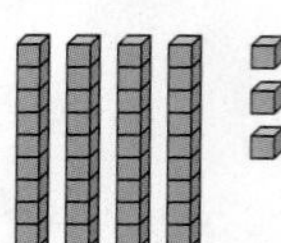

Show 43 with place-value blocks.

Guided Practice*

Do you know HOW?

In **1–6**, use place-value blocks or draw pictures to subtract.

1. 42 − 15

2. 34 − 18

3. 57 − 23

4. 25 − 16

5. 36 − 8

6. 50 − 18

Do you UNDERSTAND?

7. Why is a small 3 written above the 4 in the tens place in the example? Why is a small 13 written above the 3 in the ones place? What do you subtract to get 5 ones in the difference?

8. Nelson had 52 books in his bookcase. He gave away 38 of the books to the community center. How many books did Nelson still have in his bookcase?

Independent Practice

In **9–18**, use place-value blocks or draw pictures to subtract.

You can draw lines to show tens and Xs to show ones. This picture shows 27.

9. 21 − 17

10. 32 − 19

11. 28 − 17

12. 38 − 9

13. 43 − 24

14. 46 − 19

15. 54 − 42

16. 51 − 39

17. 63 − 37

18. 76 − 49

*For another example, see Set A on page 104.

Step 1

Subtract the ones.
3 ones < 8 ones
Regroup 1 ten
into 10 ones.

$$\begin{array}{r} \scriptstyle 3\ 13 \\ \not{4}\ \not{3} \\ -\ 1\ 8 \\ \hline \end{array}$$

1 less ten — 10 more ones

4 tens 3 ones = 3 tens 13 ones

Step 2

Subtract the ones.
13 − 8 = 5 ones

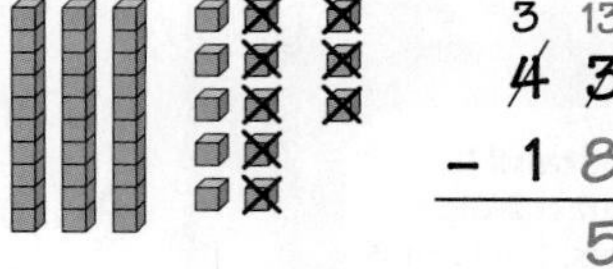

$$\begin{array}{r} \scriptstyle 3\ 13 \\ \not{4}\ \not{3} \\ -\ 1\ 8 \\ \hline 5 \end{array}$$

Subtract the tens.
3 tens − 1 ten = 2 tens

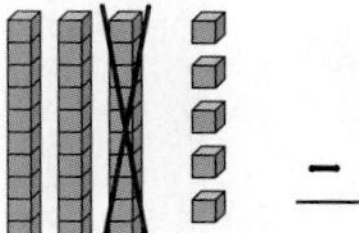

$$\begin{array}{r} \scriptstyle 3\ 13 \\ \not{4}\ \not{3} \\ -\ 1\ 8 \\ \hline 2\ 5 \end{array}$$

43 − 18 = 25

Problem Solving

For **19** and **20**, use the map at the right.

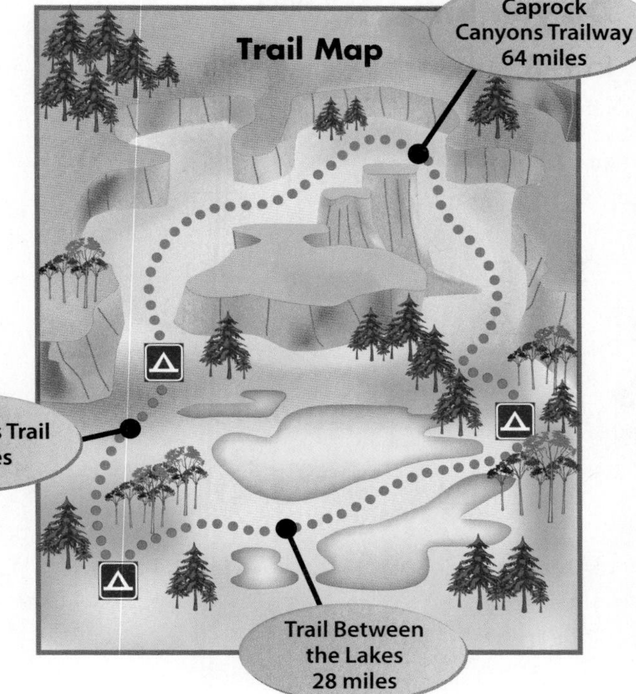

19. Hal wants to hike the Rancherias Trail and the Trail Between the Lakes. So far, he has hiked all of the Rancherias Trail and 19 miles of the Trail Between the Lakes.

a How many miles has Hal hiked so far?

b How many miles does Hal have left?

20. Tamara hiked the Trail Between the Lakes last month. She hiked the Caprock Canyons Trailway this month. How many miles did she hike in all?

21. Writing to Explain To subtract 34 − 18, Max said that 34 is equal to 2 tens and 14 ones. Is he correct? Explain how you know.

22. Ms Jones had 52 colored pencils in a package. She gave 25 of the pencils to her first art class and 18 of the pencils to her second art class. She put the rest of the pencils in a box. How many pencils are in the box?

A 95 **C** 19

B 27 **D** 9

Lesson

4-2 Subtracting 2-Digit Numbers

Understand It!
To subtract 2-digit numbers, 1 ten can be regrouped as 10 ones.

How can you use subtraction?

Animal rescue workers have released 16 of the eagles they have cared for. How many eagles are left?

Find 34 − 16. Use compatible numbers to estimate.

35 − 15 = 20

Guided Practice*

Do you know HOW?

In **1–8**, subtract.

1. 35 − 19

2. 42 − 17

3. 54 − 26

4. 61 − 38

5. 47 − 9

6. 73 − 25

7. 62 − 34

8. 47 − 25

Do you UNDERSTAND?

9. In the example above, why is regrouping needed? What was regrouped?

10. Workers at the park have cared for 52 falcons. If 28 falcons are still at the park, how many of the falcons have left?

a Write a number sentence.

b Estimate the answer.

c Solve the problem.

d Use the estimate to explain why your answer is reasonable.

Independent Practice

In **11–20**, subtract.

11. 26 − 19

12. 45 − 17

13. 37 − 18

14. 56 − 38

15. 83 − 61

16. 75 − 48

17. 22 − 13

18. 31 − 14

19. 53 − 6

20. 48 − 29

*For another example, see Set B on page 104.

Subtract the ones.

6 ones > 4 ones
Regroup 1 ten 4 ones into 14 ones.

14 − 6 = 8 ones

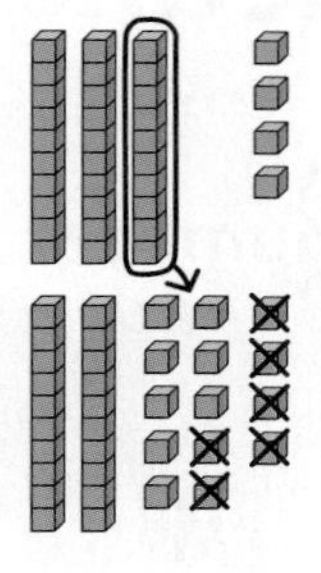

$$\begin{array}{r} \scriptstyle 2\ \ 14 \\ \not{3}\ \not{4} \\ -\ 1\ \ 6 \\ \hline 8 \end{array}$$

Subtract the tens.

2 tens − 1 ten = 1 ten

34 − 16 = 18

$$\begin{array}{r} \scriptstyle 2\ \ 14 \\ \not{3}\ \not{4} \\ -\ 1\ \ 6 \\ \hline 1\ \ 8 \end{array}$$

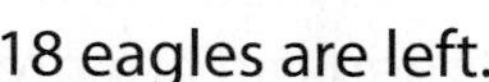

18 eagles are left.

The answer is reasonable because 18 is close to the estimate of 20.

Problem Solving

For **21** and **22**, use the table at the right.

21. Follow the steps below to find how many owls are left at the rescue park.

a Write a number sentence that can be used to solve the problem.

b Estimate the answer.

c Solve the problem.

d Use the estimate to explain why your answer is reasonable.

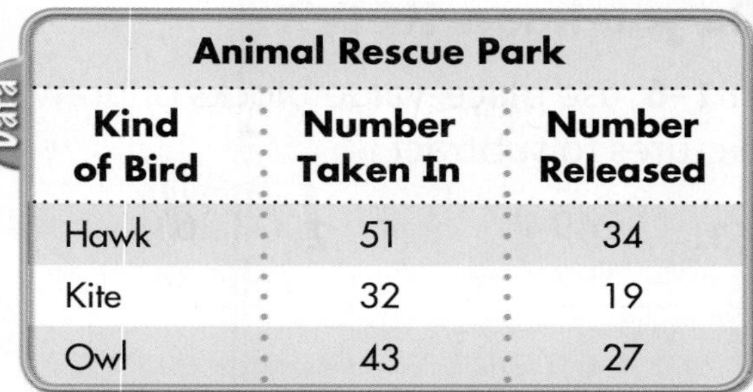

Animal Rescue Park

Kind of Bird	Number Taken In	Number Released
Hawk	51	34
Kite	32	19
Owl	43	27

22. How many fewer kites than hawks have been released from the animal rescue park?

23. Reasonableness Trista subtracted 75 − 48 and got 37. Explain why her answer is not reasonable.

24. This statue would be 25 feet tall if President Lincoln was standing. How much taller is this than the statue in the picture?

25. A sweater costs $29. A shirt costs $18. Meg has $36. Which number sentence can be used to find how much money Meg would have left if she bought the sweater?

A 29 + 36 = ☐ **C** 36 − 29 = ☐

B 29 − 18 = ☐ **D** 36 − 18 = ☐

26. Writing to Explain Do you need to regroup to find 64 − 37? Explain your answer.

Lesson
4-3

Understand It!
Place-value blocks can be used to show regrouping for subtraction.

Models for Subtracting 3-Digit Numbers

Hands-On
place-value blocks

How can you subtract 3-digit numbers with place-value blocks?

Use place value to subtract the ones first, the tens next, and then the hundreds.

Find 237 − 165.

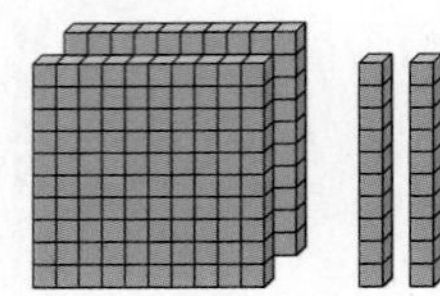

Show 237 with place-value blocks.

Guided Practice*

Do you know HOW?

In **1–6**, use place-value blocks or draw pictures to subtract.

1. 249 − 187

2. 261 − 134

3. 158 − 76

4. 384 − 182

5. 173 − 158

6. 325 − 213

Do you UNDERSTAND?

7. In the example above, why do you need to regroup 1 hundred into 10 tens?

8. Colby saved $256 doing jobs in the neighborhood. He bought a computer printer for $173. How much money did he have left? Draw a picture to help you subtract.

Independent Practice

In **9–18**, use place-value blocks or draw pictures to subtract.

You can draw squares to show hundreds, lines to show tens, and Xs to show ones. This picture shows 127.

9. 347 − 263

10. 196 − 149

11. 218 − 117

12. 251 − 132

13. 423 − 291

14. 123 − 81

15. 265 − 84

16. 539 − 275

17. 376 − 153

18. 417 − 308

DIGITAL
eTools
www.pearsonsuccessnet.com

For another example, see Set C on page 104.

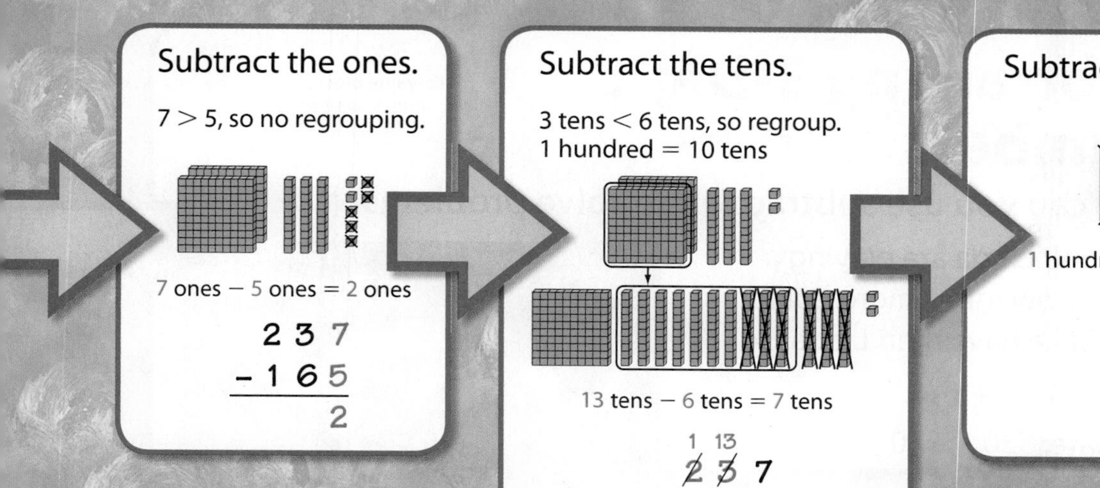

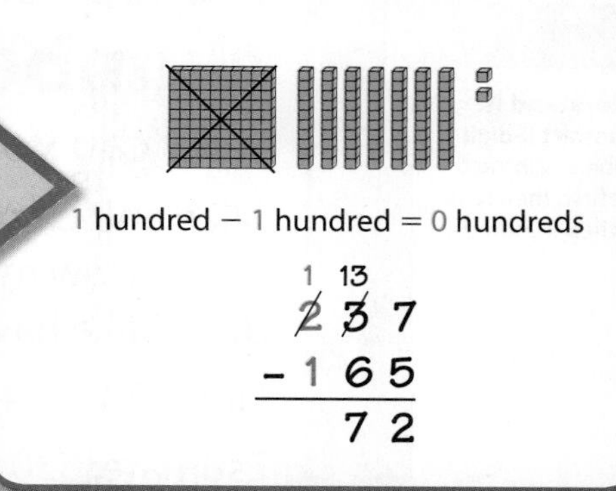

Problem Solving

For **19–21**, use the table at the right.

19. The Wen family drove from Cincinnati to Cleveland. Then the family drove to Chicago. How many miles did the family drive in all?

Trip Distances

Trip	Miles
Cleveland to Chicago	346
Cincinnati to Cleveland	249
Washington, D.C., to Cleveland	372

20. The Miller family is driving from Washington, D.C., to Cleveland and then to Cincinnati. So far the Millers have traveled 127 miles. How many miles are left in their trip?

21. **Writing to Explain** Which city is farther from Cleveland, Chicago or Washington, D.C.? How much farther? Explain your answer.

22. In the United States, students go to school about 180 days per year. Students in Japan go to school about 60 days more per year than students in the United States. About how many days per year do students in Japan attend school?

23. An amusement park ride can hold 120 people. There were 116 people on the ride and 95 people waiting in line. Which number sentence can be used to find how many people in all were on the ride or waiting in line?

A 116 − 95 = ▢

B 120 + 116 + 95 = ▢

C 116 + 95 = ▢

D 120 − 95 = ▢

Lesson
4-4

Understand It!
To subtract 3-digit numbers, subtract ones first, then tens, and then hundreds.

Subtracting 3-Digit Numbers

Hands-On place-value blocks

How can you use subtraction to solve problems?

Mike and Linda are playing a game. How many more points does Mike have than Linda?

Find 528 − 341.

Estimate: 530 − 340 = 190

Another Example How do you subtract with two regroupings?

Find 356 − 189.
Estimate: 400 − 200 = 200

Step 1

Subtract the ones.
Regroup if needed.

6 ones < 9 ones. So, regroup 1 ten into 10 ones.

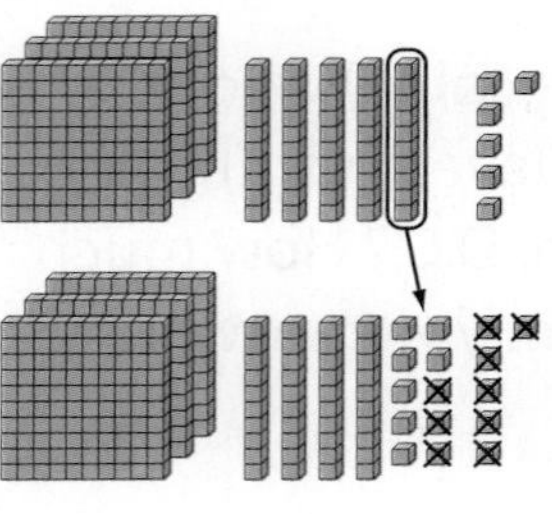

$$\begin{array}{r} \quad {}^{4}\,{}^{16} \\ 3\,\not{5}\,\not{6} \\ -\,1\,8\,9 \\ \hline 7 \end{array}$$

Step 2

Subtract the tens.
Regroup if needed.

4 tens < 8 tens. So, regroup 1 hundred into 10 tens.

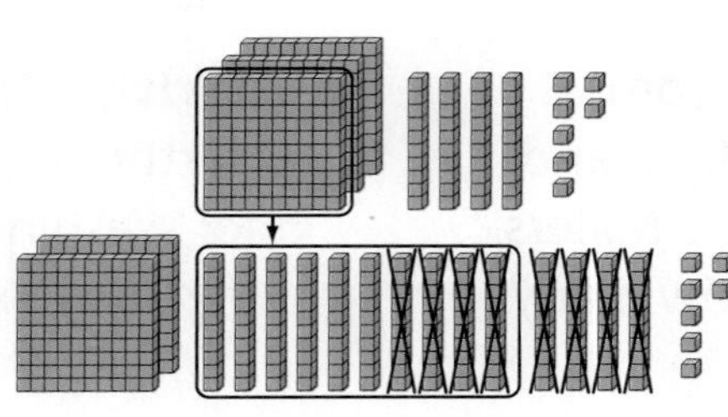

$$\begin{array}{r} {}^{14} \quad \\ {}^{2}\,\not{4}\,{}^{16} \\ \not{3}\,\not{5}\,\not{6} \\ -\,1\,8\,9 \\ \hline 6\,7 \end{array}$$

Step 3

Subtract the hundreds.

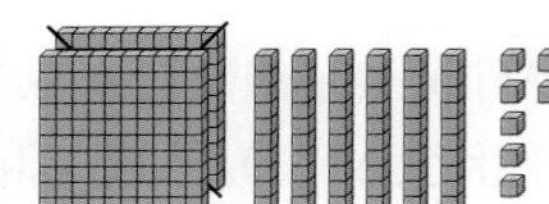

$$\begin{array}{r} {}^{14} \quad \\ {}^{2}\,\not{4}\,{}^{16} \\ \not{3}\,\not{5}\,\not{6} \\ -\,1\,8\,9 \\ \hline 1\,6\,7 \end{array}$$

The answer 167 is reasonable because it is close to the estimate.

Explain It

1. Why do you need to regroup both a ten and a hundred?
2. How is 3 hundreds 5 tens 6 ones the same as 3 hundreds 4 tens 16 ones? How is 3 hundreds 4 tens 16 ones the same as 2 hundreds 14 tens 16 ones?

Subtract the ones.

8 ones > 1 one
You do not regroup.

8 ones − 1 one = 7 ones

$$\begin{array}{r} 528 \\ -\ 341 \\ \hline 7 \end{array}$$

Subtract the tens.

Since 2 tens < 4 tens, regroup 1 hundred into 10 tens.

12 tens − 4 tens = 8 tens

$$\begin{array}{r} \scriptstyle 4\ 12 \\ \not{5}\,\not{2}\,8 \\ -\ 341 \\ \hline 87 \end{array}$$

Subtract the hundreds.

4 hundreds − 3 hundreds = 1 hundred

$$\begin{array}{r} \scriptstyle 4\ 12 \\ \not{5}\,\not{2}\,8 \\ -\ 341 \\ \hline 187 \end{array}$$

Mike has 187 more points.

187 is close to the estimate of 190. The answer is reasonable.

Guided Practice*

Do you know HOW?

In **1–6**, subtract. Use place-value blocks, if you wish.

1. $\begin{array}{r} 374 \\ -\ 176 \\ \hline \end{array}$

2. $\begin{array}{r} 431 \\ -\ 145 \\ \hline \end{array}$

3. $\begin{array}{r} 568 \\ -\ 269 \\ \hline \end{array}$

4. $\begin{array}{r} 327 \\ -\ 238 \\ \hline \end{array}$

5. 574 − 86

6. 410 − 257

Do you UNDERSTAND?

7. In the example above, explain how to decide if regrouping is needed.

8. At the end of their game, Lora had 426 points, and Lou had 158 points. How many more points did Lora have than Lou?

a Write a number sentence.

b Estimate the answer.

c Solve the problem.

d Explain why your answer is reasonable.

Independent Practice

Estimate. Then find each difference. Check answers for reasonableness.

9. $\begin{array}{r} 385 \\ -\ 296 \\ \hline \end{array}$

10. $\begin{array}{r} 276 \\ -\ 97 \\ \hline \end{array}$

11. $\begin{array}{r} 516 \\ -\ 238 \\ \hline \end{array}$

12. $\begin{array}{r} 629 \\ -\ 453 \\ \hline \end{array}$

13. $\begin{array}{r} 948 \\ -\ 569 \\ \hline \end{array}$

DIGITAL eTools www.pearsonsuccessnet.com

For another example, see Set D on page 105.

Independent Practice

Estimate and subtract. Check answers for reasonableness.

14. $392 - 195$ **15.** $754 - 476$ **16.** $819 - 652$ **17.** $123 - 84$ **18.** $435 - 367$

19. 236 − 78 **20.** 568 − 362 **21.** 147 − 58 **22.** 952 − 794

Problem Solving

For **23–25**, use the table at the right.

23. Follow the steps below to find how many more swimmers signed up for the first session at Oak Pool than for the first session at Park Pool.

a Write a number sentence that can be used to solve the problem.

b Estimate the answer.

c Solve the problem.

d Explain why your answer is reasonable.

Data

Swim Class Enrollment

Pool	Number of Swimmers	
	1st session	2nd session
Oak	763	586
Park	314	179
River	256	63

24. At River Pool, late enrollments added 29 swimmers to the second session. The total number of swimmers enrolled in the second session is how many fewer than in the first?

What addition sentence can help?

25. **Write a Problem** Write a problem using the data in the table. Include too much information.

26. The world's largest basket is the building in the photo. It is 186 feet tall from the base to the top of the handles. What is the height of the handles?

27. Ana made 14 hats. After giving some hats to Ty's family and some to Liv's family, she had 3 hats left. If she gave Ty's family 6 hats, which of these shows one way to find how many hats Ana gave to Liv's family?

A $14 + 3 - 6 = \square$

B $14 - 3 - 6 = \square$

C $14 - 3 + 6 = \square$

D $14 + 3 + 6 = \square$

Algebra Connections

Using Properties to Complete Number Sentences

The properties of addition can help you find missing numbers.

Commutative (Order) Property You can add numbers in any order and the sum will be the same. Example: $4 + 3 = 3 + 4$

Identity (Zero) Property The sum of any number and zero is that same number. Example: $9 + 0 = 9$

Associative (Grouping) Property You can group addends in any way and the sum will be the same. Example: $(5 + 2) + 3 = 5 + (2 + 3)$

Example: $26 + \square = 26$

Think: 26 plus what number is equal to 26?

You can use the Identity Property.

$26 + 0 = 26$

Example:

$36 + (14 + 12) = (36 + \square) + 12$

Think: What number makes the two sides equal?

Use the Associative Property.

$36 + (14 + 12) = (36 + 14) + 12$

Copy and complete. Write the missing number.

1. $19 + \square = 19$

2. $15 + 32 = 32 + \square$

3. $28 + (17 + 32) = (28 + \square) + 32$

4. $\square + 27 = 27$

5. $\square + 8 = 8 + 49$

6. $(16 + 14) + \square = 16 + (14 + 53)$

7. $(\square + 9) + 72 = 96 + (9 + 72)$

8. $\square + 473 = 473$

For **9** and **10**, copy and complete the number sentence. Use it to help solve the problem.

9. Vin walked 9 blocks from home to the library. Then he walked 5 blocks farther to the store. Later he walked the same path back to the library. How many more blocks would he need to walk to his home?

$9 + 5 = 5 + \square$

$\square$ blocks

10. Bo scored 7 points in each of two tosses in a game. Then he made one more toss. He had the same total score as Ed. Ed scored 8 points in one toss and 7 points in each of two tosses. How many points did Bo score on his last toss?

$7 + 7 + \square = 8 + 7 + 7$

$\square$ points

Lesson
4-5 Subtracting Across Zero

Understand It!
More than one regrouping may be needed to subtract from a number with a zero.

How do you subtract from a number with one or more zeros?

How much more does the club need?

Find: 305 − 178

305:

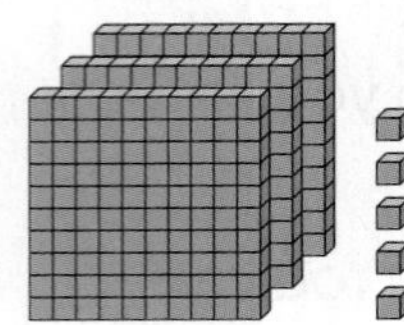

Another Example How do you subtract from a number with two zeros?

Find 600 − 164.

Subtract the ones.
0 ones < 4 ones
So, regroup.

$$\begin{array}{r} \overset{5}{\cancel{6}}\,\overset{10}{\cancel{0}}\,0 \\ -\,1\;6\;4 \\ \hline \end{array}$$

You can't regroup 0 tens.
So, regroup 1 hundred.
6 hundreds 0 tens =
5 hundreds 10 tens

$$\begin{array}{r} \overset{5}{\cancel{6}}\,\overset{10}{\cancel{0}}\,0 \\ -\,1\;6\;4 \\ \hline \end{array}$$

Now regroup tens.
10 tens 0 ones = 9 tens 10 ones
Subtract the ones, the tens, and then the hundreds.

$$\begin{array}{r} \overset{5}{\cancel{6}}\,\overset{\overset{9}{\cancel{10}}}{\cancel{0}}\,\overset{10}{\cancel{0}} \\ -\,1\;6\;4 \\ \hline 4\;3\;6 \end{array}$$

Guided Practice*

Do you know HOW?

In **1–6**, find each difference.

1. 402 − 139

2. 300 − 157

3. 607 − 439

4. 820 − 167

5. 200 − 74

6. 501 − 186

Do you UNDERSTAND?

7. In the examples above, why do you write 10 above the 0 in the tens place?

8. Lia says that she needs to regroup every time she subtracts from a number with a zero. Do you agree? Explain.

*For another example, see Set E on page 105.

Regroup to subtract the ones. There are no tens in 305 to regroup. Regroup 1 hundred.

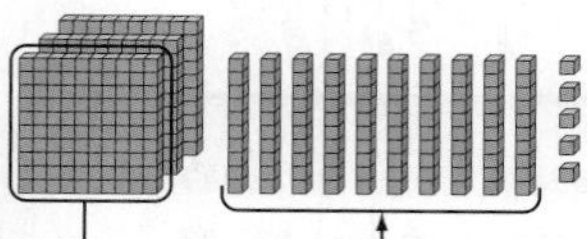

305 is the same as 2 hundreds 10 tens 5 ones.

```
  2 10
  3̸ 0̸ 5
- 1 7 8
```

Regroup the tens.

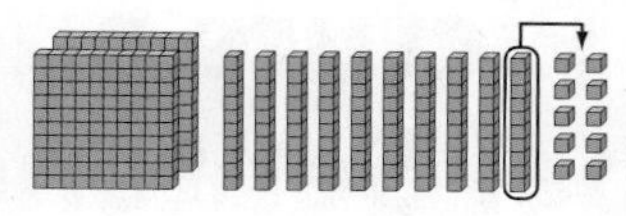

305 is the same as 2 hundreds 9 tens 15 ones.

```
     9
  2 10 15
  3̸ 0̸ 5̸
- 1 7 8
```

Subtract the ones, the tens, and then the hundreds.

```
     9
  2 10 15
  3̸ 0̸ 5̸
- 1 7 8
  1 2 7
```

The Art club needs $127.

Independent Practice

In **9–18**, find each difference.

9. $203 - 157$

10. $400 - 371$

11. $304 - 95$

12. $401 - 282$

13. $500 - 64$

14. $600 - 439$

15. $306 - 248$

16. $705 - 123$

17. $800 - 74$

18. $900 - 506$

Problem Solving

19. The average person eats about 126 pounds of fresh fruit in a year. Write a number sentence to help you find how many pounds of processed fruit you eat. Then solve.

20. Writing to Explain The Art Club needs 605 beads. A large bag of beads has 285 beads. A small bag of beads has 130 beads. Will one large bag and one small bag be enough beads? Explain.

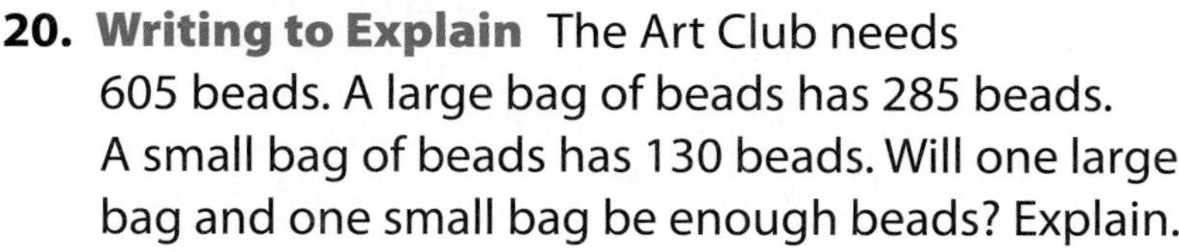

21. Dina counted 204 items on the library cart. There were 91 fiction books, 75 nonfiction books, and some magazines. Which number sentence shows one way to find the number of magazines?

A 204 − 91 − 75 = ▢

B 204 + 91 + 75 = ▢

C 204 − 91 + 75 = ▢

D 204 + 91 − 75 = ▢

Lesson
4-6

Understand It!
Pictures can show how to use information to write a number sentence.

Problem Solving

Draw a Picture and Write a Number Sentence

There are two lunch periods at Central School. If 221 students eat during the first lunch period, how many students eat during the second lunch period?

Central School
Grades K-6
458 Students

Another Example Are there other types of subtraction situations?

There are 85 students in Grade 2. That is 17 more students than in Grade 3. How many students are in Grade 3?

Plan and Solve

Draw a diagram to show what you know.

Gr. 2	85	
Gr. 3	?	17

There are 17 more students in Grade 2 than in Grade 3. Subtract to find the number of students in Grade 3.

Write a number sentence.
$85 - 17 = \square$

Answer

$$\begin{array}{r} \overset{7}{\cancel{8}}\overset{15}{\cancel{5}} \\ -\ 17 \\ \hline 68 \end{array}$$

There are 68 students in Grade 3.

Check

Make sure the answer is reasonable.

$85 - 17$ is about $90 - 20$, or 70.

68 is close to 70, so 68 is reasonable.

The number 68 is reasonable, and the question in the problem was answered.

Explain It

1. Harry wrote $17 + \square = 85$ for the diagram above. Is his number sentence correct? Why or why not?
2. Grade 4 has 72 students. There are 12 more students in Grade 5 than in Grade 4. Would you add or subtract to find the number of students in Grade 5? Write and solve a number sentence.

Plan and Solve

Draw a picture to show what you know.

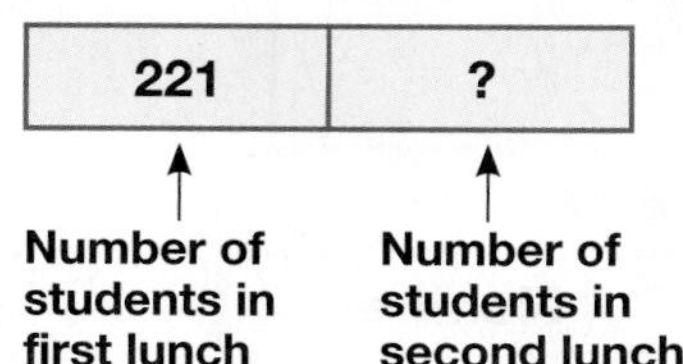

You know the total and one part. Write a subtraction sentence: 458 − 221 = ▢.

Answer

$$\begin{array}{r} 458 \\ -\,221 \\ \hline 237 \end{array}$$

There are 237 students who eat during the second lunch period.

Check

Make sure the answer is reasonable.

458 − 221 is about 460 − 220, or 240.

237 is close to 240, so 237 is reasonable.

The number 237 is reasonable and the right question was answered.

Guided Practice*

Do you know HOW?

1. A total of 254 people entered a bicycle race. So far 135 people have finished the race. How many people are still racing?

254 people in all

135	?

Do you UNDERSTAND?

2. Writing to Explain How do you know what operation to use to solve Problem 1?

3. Write a Problem Write a problem that can be solved by adding or subtracting. Then give your problem to a classmate to solve.

Independent Practice

4. The height of Capote Falls is 175 feet. The height of Madrid Falls is 120 feet. Write and solve a number sentence to find how much taller Capote Falls is than Madrid Falls.

Capote Falls	175	
Madrid Falls	120	?

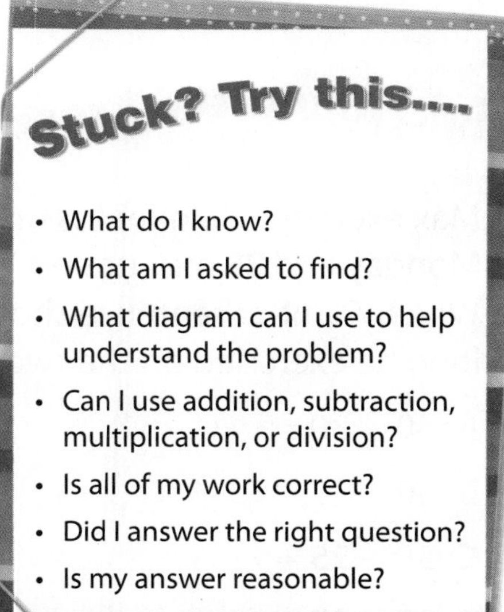

*For another example, see Set F on page 105.

Independent Practice

In the United States House of Representatives, the number of representatives each state has depends upon the number of people who live in the state.

Use the table at the right for **5–7**.

Data

U.S. Representatives	
State	**Number**
California	53
Florida	25
Michigan	15
Texas	32

5. Copy and complete the diagram below. New York has 14 more representatives than Michigan. How many representatives does New York have?

? representatives in New York

15	14

6. Draw a diagram to find how many more representatives Texas has than Florida.

7. How many representatives are there all together from the four states listed in the chart?

8. When the House of Representatives started in 1789, there were 65 members. Now there are 435 members. How many more members are there now?

9. There are 50 states in the United States. Each state has 2 senators. Write and solve a number sentence to find the total number of senators.

Think About the Process

10. Max exercised 38 minutes on Monday and 25 minutes on Tuesday. Which number sentence shows how long he exercised on the two days?

A $40 + 30 = \square$

B $40 - 30 = \square$

C $38 - 25 = \square$

D $38 + 25 = \square$

11. Nancy had $375 in the bank. She took $200 out to buy a scooter that cost $185. Which number sentence shows how much money is left in the bank?

A $\$375 + \$185 = \square$

B $\$375 - \$185 = \square$

C $\$375 - \$200 = \square$

D $\$375 + \$185 + \$200 = \square$

Subtracting with Regrouping

Use eTools

Place-Value Blocks

Use the Place-Value Blocks eTool to subtract 324 − 168.

Step 1 Go to the Place-Value Blocks eTool. Click on the two-part workspace icon. In the top space, show 324 with place-value blocks.

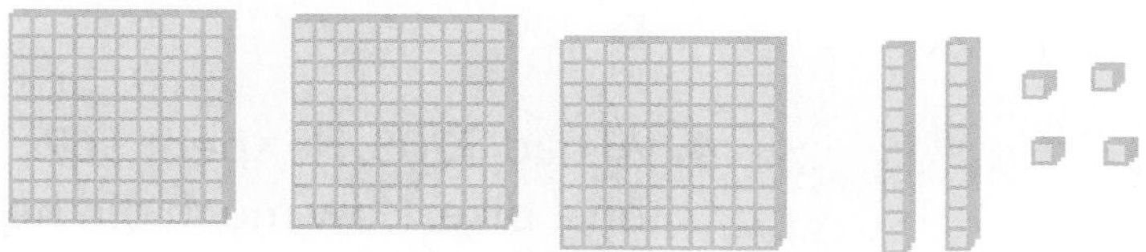

Step 2 Use the hammer tool to break one of the tens blocks into 10 ones. Then use the arrow tool to take away 8 ones and move them to the bottom workspace.

Step 3 Use the hammer tool to break one of the hundreds blocks into 10 tens. Then take away the 6 tens in 168 and move them to the bottom workspace.

Step 4 Use the arrow tool to take away the hundred block in 168. To find the difference, look at all of the blocks that are left.

324 − 168 = 156

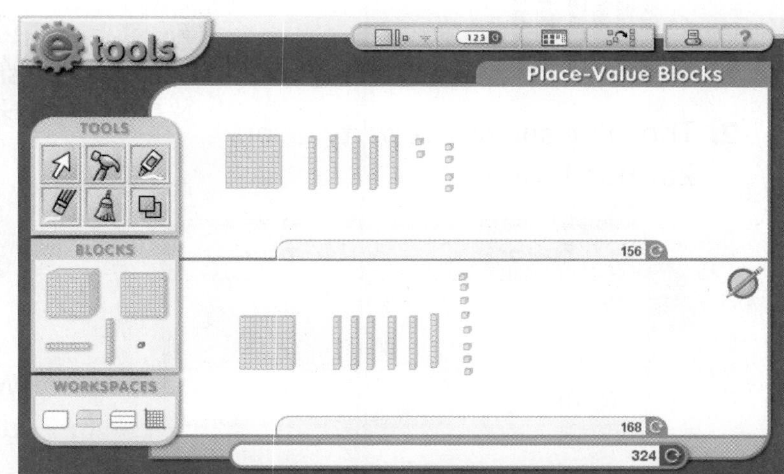

Practice

Use the Place-Value Blocks eTool to subtract.

1. 445 − 176 **2.** 318 − 142 **3.** 546 − 259 **4.** 600 − 473

Test

1. Tracey knows that she will need to regroup to solve 52 − 18. Which picture shows how she should regroup 52? (4-1)

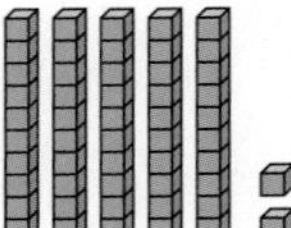

A 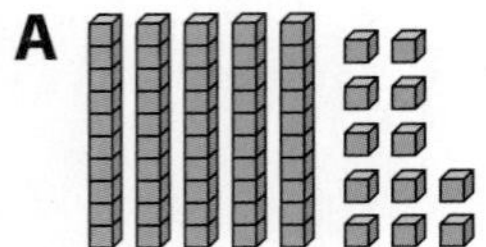

B 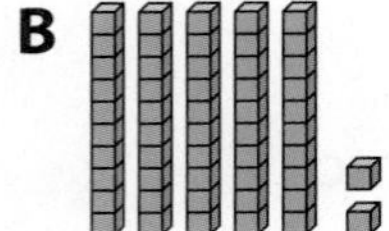

C 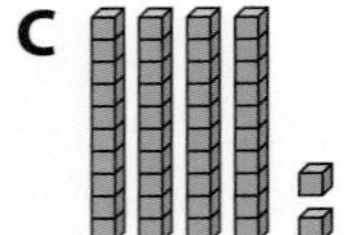

D

2. The table shows the party favors Zac purchased.

Favor	Number
Pencil	36
Kazoo	16
Yo-Yo	8

Which number sentence can be used to find how many more pencils than yo-yos Zac purchased? (4-2)

A 36 − 8 = ☐

B 36 + 8 = ☐

C 36 − 16 = ☐

D 36 + 16 = ☐

3. Cristina scored 485 points on a video game. Olivia scored 196 points. How many more points did Cristina score than Olivia? (4-4)

A 681

B 389

C 299

D 289

4. Al had $205. He spent $67 on a bike. How much did he have left? (4-5)

A $162

B $148

C $138

D $38

5. Mr. Chavez needs to order trophies for the band members. The table shows how many girls and how many boys are in the band.

Band Members	
Boys	32
Girls	28

Which of the following best describes the band members? (4-2)

A There are 4 more boys than girls in the band.

B There are 4 more girls than boys in the band.

C There are 32 more boys than girls in the band.

D There are 28 more girls than boys in the band.

6. Mrs. Wesley bought 325 drinks for a picnic. She bought 135 cartons of milk, 95 bottles of water, and some bottles of juice. Which number sentence shows one way to find how many bottles of juice she bought? (4-4)

A $325 - 135 + 95 = \square$

B $325 - 135 - 95 = \square$

C $325 + 135 - 95 = \square$

D $325 + 135 + 95 = \square$

7. What regrouping is shown? (4-3)

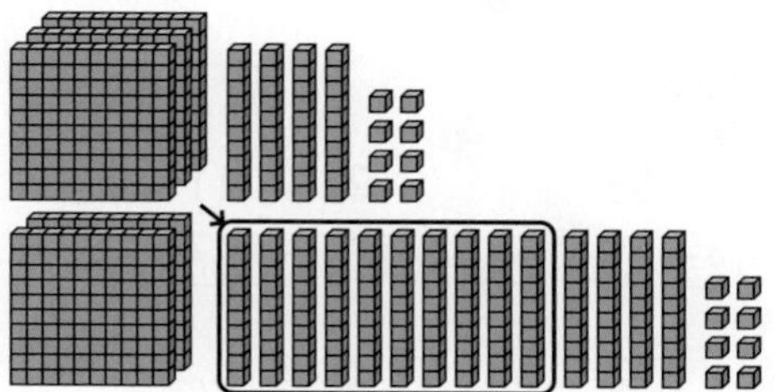

A 3 hundreds 4 tens 8 ones as 2 hundreds 3 tens 18 ones

B 3 hundreds 4 tens 8 ones as 2 hundreds 14 tens 8 ones

C 2 hundreds 4 tens 8 ones as 1 hundreds 14 tens 8 ones

D 2 hundreds 4 tens 8 ones as 2 hundreds 3 tens 18 ones

8. Texas has 254 counties. Georgia has 159 counties. How many more counties does Texas have than Georgia? (4-4)

A 195

B 145

C 105

D 95

9. Which picture shows the problem? Nessie saw 23 deer and 17 squirrels at a national park. How many more deer did she see than squirrels? (4-6)

A

?	
23	17

B

17	
23	?

C

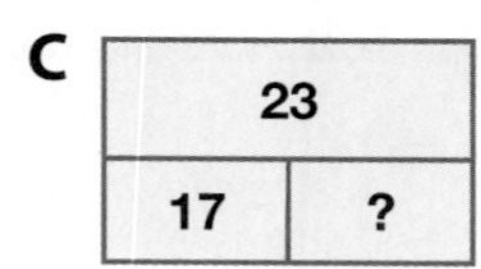

D

23
17

10. Ray had \$41. He spent \$14 for swim goggles and \$19 for admission. How much money did Ray have left? (4-2)

A \$27

B \$12

C \$8

D \$5

11. Trisha had 300 milliliters of water in a beaker. She poured 237 milliliters of the water from the beaker into a test tube. How much water was left in the beaker? (4-5)

A 173 milliliters

B 163 milliliters

C 137 milliliters

D 63 milliliters

Reteaching

Set A, pages 86–87

Find 45 − 18.

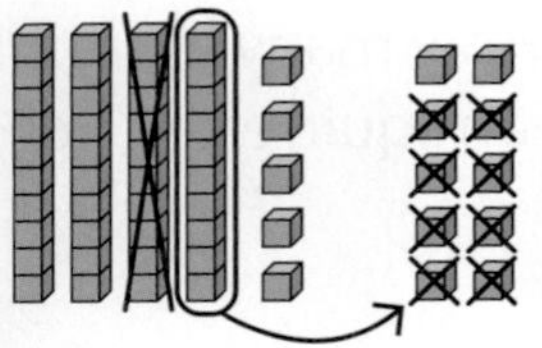

```
  3 15
  4  5
- 1  8
  2  7
```

Remember that you can regroup 1 ten as 10 ones.

Use place-value blocks or draw pictures to subtract.

1. $\begin{array}{r} 52 \\ -\ 17 \\ \hline \end{array}$

2. $\begin{array}{r} 38 \\ -\ 25 \\ \hline \end{array}$

3. 83 − 34

4. 75 − 53

Set B, pages 88–89

Find 31 − 17.

Estimate: 30 − 20 = 10

What You Think

31 = 3 tens 1 one

17 = 1 ten 7 ones

7 ones > 1 one, so regroup.

3 tens 1 one = 2 tens 11 ones

What You Write

```
  2 11
  3  1
- 1  7
  1  4
```

31 − 17 = 14
14 is close to 10, so the answer is reasonable.

Remember to check your answer by comparing it to your estimate.

Subtract.

1. $\begin{array}{r} 53 \\ -\ 29 \\ \hline \end{array}$

2. $\begin{array}{r} 41 \\ -\ 17 \\ \hline \end{array}$

3. $\begin{array}{r} 68 \\ -\ 49 \\ \hline \end{array}$

4. $\begin{array}{r} 34 \\ -\ 28 \\ \hline \end{array}$

5. 92 − 42

6. 70 − 54

Set C, pages 90–91

Find 236 − 127.

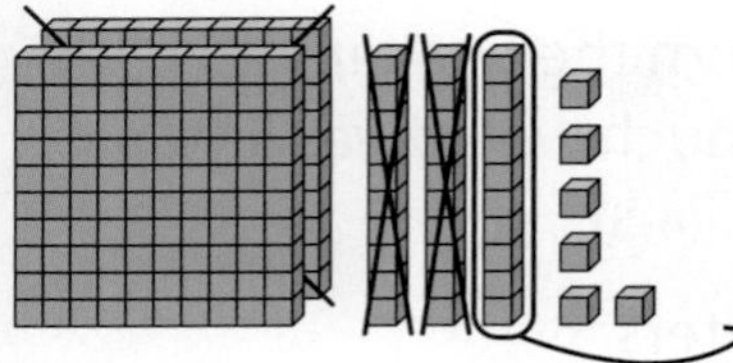

```
    2 16
  2 3  6
- 1 2  7
  1 0  9
```

Remember to subtract ones, then tens, and then hundreds.

Use place-value blocks or draw pictures to subtract.

1. $\begin{array}{r} 435 \\ -\ 217 \\ \hline \end{array}$

2. $\begin{array}{r} 255 \\ -\ 161 \\ \hline \end{array}$

3. 521 − 196

4. 332 − 108

Set D, pages 92–94

Find 312 − 186.

Estimate: 300 − 200 = 100

```
 0 12
3 1 2    Regroup
- 1 8 6  tens.
      6

    10
 2  0 12
3 1 2    Regroup
- 1 8 6  hundreds.
 1 2 6
```

126 is close to 100, so the answer is reasonable.

Remember that sometimes you must regroup twice.

Estimate. Subtract and check answers for reasonableness.

1. 221 − 134
2. 397 − 138
3. 611 − 125
4. 854 − 296

Set E, pages 96–97

Find 306 − 129.

Estimate: 300 − 100 = 200

```
 2 10
3 0 6    There are
- 1 2 9  no tens.
         Regroup
         hundreds.

    9
 2 10 16
3 0 6    Regroup
- 1 2 9  tens.
 1 7 7
```

177 is close to 200, so the answer is reasonable.

Remember that when you need to regroup tens, but have 0 tens, regroup hundreds first.

Find each difference.

1. 308 − 125
2. 105 − 47
3. 200 − 136
4. 602 − 384

Set F, pages 98–100

At the school picnic, 234 students took part in the events. Of those students, 136 students were in the potato sack races. The other students were in the 3-legged races. How many students were in the 3-legged races?

234 students in all

136	?
Number of students in potato sack races	Number of students in 3-legged races

You know the total and one part, so you can subtract to find the other part: 234 − 136 = ▢.

234 − 136 = 98
98 students were in the 3-legged races.

Remember that drawing a picture of the problem can help you write a number sentence.

Draw a picture. Write a number sentence and solve.

1. A total of 293 people entered a running race. So far, 127 people have finished the race. How many people are still racing?

Topic 5 Multiplication Meanings and Facts

1 Monarch butterflies have bright orange wings. How many wings does each monarch butterfly have? You will find out in Lesson 5-4.

2 An armadillo needs more sleep than a horse. How many more hours of sleep does an armadillo need? You will find out in Lesson 5-3.

3 How many hearts does an earthworm have? You will find out in Lesson 5-6.

4 How many wheels are on the bikes of a unicycle relay team? You will find out in Lesson 5-9.

Review What You Know!

Vocabulary

Choose the best term from the box.

- add
- equal groups
- skip count
- subtract

1. If you combine groups to find how many in all, you _?_.

2. _?_ have the same number of items.

3. When you say the numbers 2, 4, 6, 8, you _?_.

Equal Groups

Are the groups equal? Write *yes* or *no*.

4.  

5.  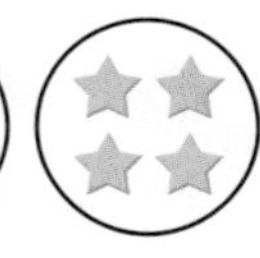

Adding

Find each sum.

6. 5 + 5 + 5
7. 7 + 7
8. 3 + 3 + 3
9. 2 + 2 + 2 + 2
10. 6 + 6 + 6
11. 9 + 9 + 9

Repeated Addition

12. **Writing to Explain** Draw a picture to show how to solve 8 + 8 + 8 = ▢. Then copy and complete the number sentence.

Lesson

5-1

Understand It!
Combining equal groups is one meaning of multiplication.

Multiplication as Repeated Addition

Hands-On
counters

How can you find the total number of objects in equal groups?

Jessie used 3 bags to bring home the goldfish she won at a Fun Fair. She put the same number of goldfish in each bag. How many goldfish did she win?

Guided Practice*

Do you know HOW?

Copy and complete. Use counters.

1. 

2 groups of ▢
4 + 4 = ▢
2 × ▢ = ▢

2. 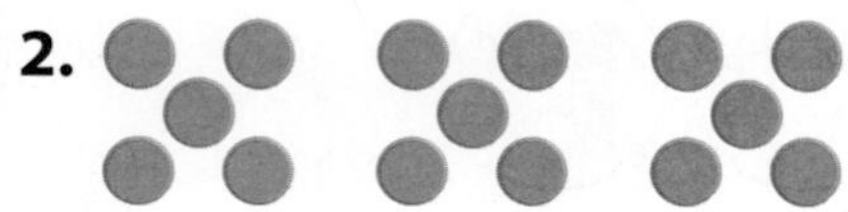

▢ groups of 5
5 + ▢ + ▢ = ▢
3 × ▢ = ▢

Do you UNDERSTAND?

3. Can you write 3 + 3 + 3 + 3 as a multiplication sentence? Explain.

4. Can you write 3 + 5 + 6 = 14 as a multiplication sentence? Explain.

5. Write an addition sentence and a multiplication sentence to solve this problem:

Jessie bought 4 packages of colorful stones to put in the fish bowl. There were 6 stones in each package. How many stones did Jessie buy?

Independent Practice

Copy and complete. Use counters or draw a picture to help.

6. 

2 groups of ▢
6 + ▢ = ▢
2 × ▢ = ▢

7. 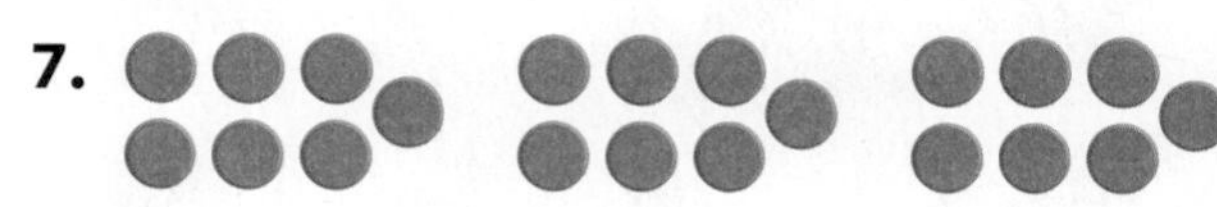

3 groups of ▢
7 + ▢ + ▢ = ▢
3 × ▢ = ▢

*For another example, see Set A on page 136.

The counters show 3 groups of 8 goldfish.

You can use addition to join equal groups.

$8 + 8 + 8 = 24$

Multiplication is an operation that gives the total number when you join equal groups.

What You Say 3 times 8 equals 24

What You Write $3 \times 8 = 24$

factor factor product

Factors are the numbers that are being multiplied. The product is the answer to a multiplication problem.

Addition sentence:
$8 + 8 + 8 = 24$

Multiplication sentence:
$3 \times 8 = 24$

So, $8 + 8 + 8 = 3 \times 8$.

Jessie won 24 goldfish.

Copy and complete each number sentence. Use counters or draw a picture to help.

8. $2 + 2 + 2 + 2 = 4 \times$ ☐

9. ☐ + ☐ + ☐ $= 3 \times 7$

10. 9 + ☐ + ☐ = ☐ $\times 9$

11. $6 + 6 + 6 + 6 + 6 =$ ☐ × ☐

Algebra Write +, −, or × for each ☐.

12. 4 ☐ 3 = 12

13. 3 ☐ 6 = 9

14. 4 ☐ 4 = 0

15. 6 ☐ 4 = 10

16. 5 ☐ 3 = 2

17. 2 ☐ 4 = 8

Problem Solving

18. What number sentence shows how to find the total number of erasers?

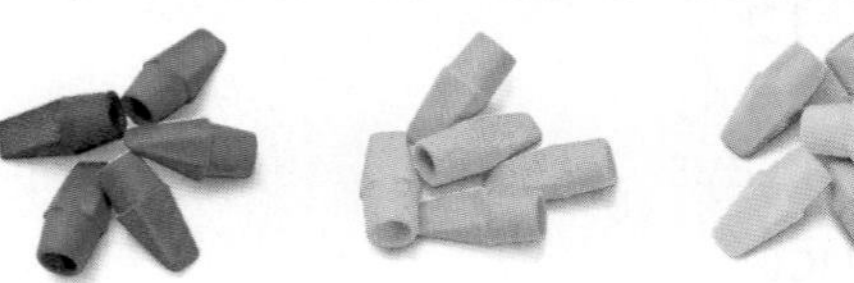

A 5 + 5 = ☐

B 15 − 5 = ☐

C 15 + 5 = ☐

D 3 × 5 = ☐

19. Write an addition sentence and a multiplication sentence to solve the problem below.

Maria has 6 new flashlights. Each flashlight takes 3 batteries. How many batteries will Maria need for the flashlights?

20. **Writing to Explain** Luke says that you can add or multiply to join groups. Is he correct? Explain.

21. Which picture shows 3 groups of 2?

A 

B 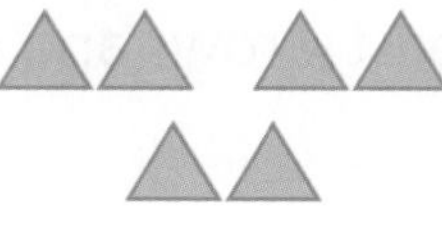

C 

D  

Lesson
5-2

Understand It!
An array is a special kind of arrangement of equal groups. Multiplication can be used to find the total for an array.

Arrays and Multiplication

Hands-On
counters

How does an array show multiplication?

Dana keeps her entire CD collection in a holder on the wall. The holder has 4 rows. Each row holds 5 CDs. How many CDs are in Dana's collection?

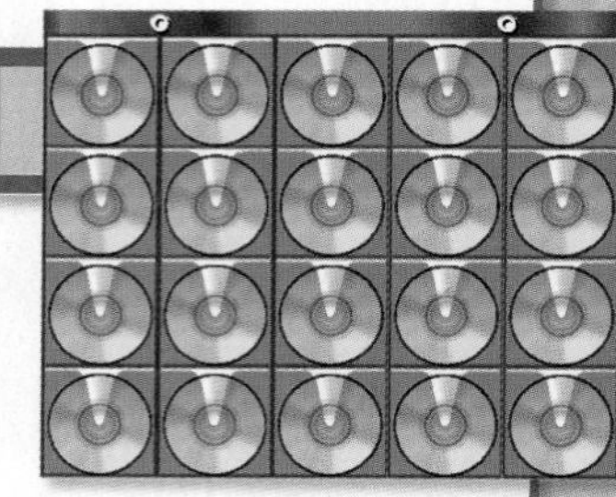

The CDs are in an array. An array shows objects in equal rows.

Another Example **Does order matter when you multiply?**

Libby and Sydney both say their poster has more stickers. Who is correct?

$4 + 4 + 4 = 12$
$3 \times 4 = 12$

Libby's poster has 12 stickers.

$3 + 3 + 3 + 3 = 12$
$4 \times 3 = 12$

Sydney's poster has 12 stickers.

Both poster boards have the same number of stickers.

$$\mathbf{3 \times 4 = 12} \text{ and } \mathbf{4 \times 3 = 12}$$

The Commutative (Order) Property of Multiplication says you can multiply numbers in any order and the product is the same. So, $3 \times 4 = 4 \times 3$.

Explain It

1. Miguel has 5 rows of stickers. There are 3 stickers in each row. Write an addition sentence and a multiplication sentence to show how many stickers he has.
2. Show the Commutative Property of Multiplication by drawing two arrays. Each array should have at least 2 rows and show a product of 6.

The counters show 4 rows of 5 CDs.

Each row is a group. You can use addition to find the total.

$5 + 5 + 5 + 5 = 20$

Multiplication can also be used to find the total in an array.

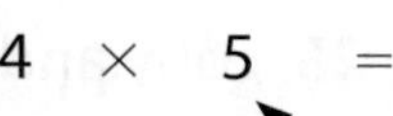

What You Say 4 times 5 equals 20

What You Write $4 \times 5 = 20$

number of rows — number in each row

There are 20 CDs in Dana's collection.

Guided Practice*

Do you know HOW?

In **1** and **2**, write a multiplication sentence for each array.

1. 

2. 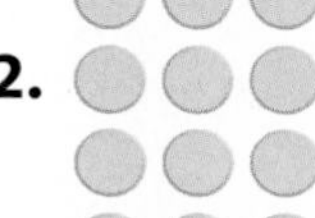

In **3** and **4**, draw an array to show each multiplication fact. Write the product.

3. 3×6

4. 5×4

In **5** and **6**, copy and complete each multiplication sentence. Use counters or draw an array to help.

5. $5 \times \square = 10$
$2 \times \square = 10$

6. $4 \times 3 = \square$
$3 \times \square = 12$

Do you UNDERSTAND?

7. Look at the example above. What does the first factor in the multiplication sentence tell you about the array?

8. Writing to Explain Why is the Commutative Property of Multiplication sometimes called the *order property*?

9. Scott puts some sports stickers in rows. He makes 6 rows with 5 stickers in each row. If he put the same stickers in 5 equal rows, how many would be in each row?

Independent Practice

In **10–12**, write a multiplication sentence for each array.

10. 

11. 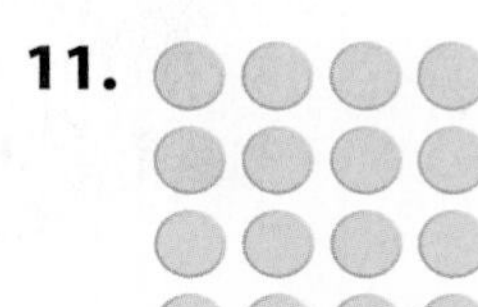

12. 

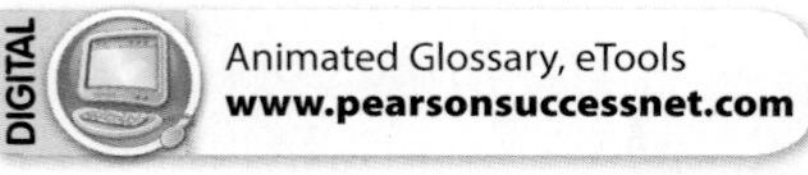

For another example, see Set A on page 136.

Independent Practice

In **13–17**, draw an array to show each multiplication fact. Write the product.

13. 3×3 **14.** 5×6 **15.** 1×8 **16.** 4×3 **17.** 2×9

In **18–23**, copy and complete each multiplication sentence. Use counters or draw an array to help.

18. $4 \times \square = 8$
$2 \times \square = 8$

19. $6 \times 4 = \square$
$4 \times \square = 24$

20. $5 \times \square = 40$
$\square \times 5 = 40$

21. $3 \times 9 = 27$
$9 \times 3 = \square$

22. $7 \times 6 = 42$
$6 \times 7 = \square$

23. $9 \times 8 = 72$
$8 \times 9 = \square$

Problem Solving

24. Writing to Explain How do the arrays at the right show the Commutative Property of Multiplication?

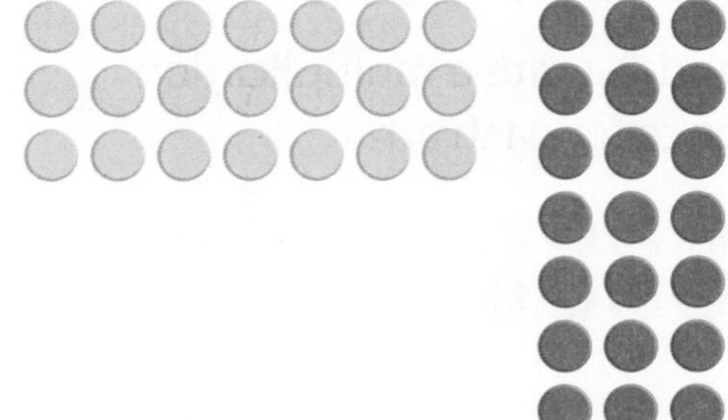

25. Number Sense How does an array show equal groups?

26. Taylor says that the product for 7×2 is the same as the product for 2×7. Is he correct? Explain.

27. Reasoning Margo has 23 pictures. Can she use all of the pictures to make an array with exactly two equal rows? Why or why not?

28. Dan bought the stamps shown at the right. Which number sentence shows one way to find how many stamps Dan bought?

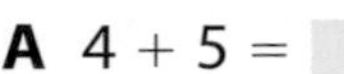

A $4 + 5 = \square$

B $5 \times 4 = \square$

C $5 + 4 = \square$

D $5 - 4 = \square$

Mixed Problem Solving

Josie used stars and circles to make the artwork on the right. Answer the questions about her artwork.

1. Describe the patterns you see in the artwork.

2. How many rows are in each array of stars?

3. Look at one array of circles. How many circles are in each row of the array?

4. Look at one array of stars. Write a number sentence for the array.

5. How many circles did Josie use in her artwork?

6. How many more stars than circles did Josie make?

7. The picture above shows Josie's artwork with 4 rows. Before she started, Josie made a table to plan how many of each shape she would need for different numbers of rows.

Copy and complete Josie's table.

Data

Shapes Needed to Make Artwork

Total Number of Rows	Total Number of Stars	Total Number of Circles
2	42	15
4	84	30
6	126	45
8		

8. If Josie makes her artwork with 10 rows, how many stars will she use in all? how many circles?

9. Mark made 56 stars. He made 18 circles. How many shapes did he make in all?

10. **Strategy Focus** Solve. Use the strategy Write a Number Sentence.

Maggie made a pattern using a total of 92 shapes. Of the 92 shapes Maggie used, 44 were circles and the rest were stars. How many stars did Maggie use?

Lesson

5-3

Understand It!
Multiplication can be used to compare the size of two groups.

Using Multiplication to Compare

Hands-On
counters

How can you use multiplication to compare?

Mike has 5 state quarters. Carl has two times as many, or twice as many as Mike. How many state quarters does Carl have?

Choose an Operation Multiply to find twice as many: $2 \times 5 = \square$

Guided Practice*

Do you know HOW?

Find each amount. You may use drawings or counters to help.

1. 3 times as many as 3
2. 2 times as many as 6
3. Twice as many as 3

Do you UNDERSTAND?

4. **Number Sense** Barry says you can add 5 + 5 to find how many state quarters Carl has. Is he correct? Why or why not?
5. Carl has 4 silver dollars. Mike has twice as many as Carl. How many silver dollars does Mike have?

Independent Practice

In **6–11**, find each amount. You may use drawings or counters to help.

6. 2 times as many as 7
7. 3 times as many as 8
8. Twice as many as 6
9. 4 times as many as 5
10. Twice as many as 9
11. 5 times as many as 4

In **12–15**, which coin or bill matches each value?

12. 2 times as much as 1 nickel
13. 10 times as much as 1 dime
14. 5 times as much as 1 nickel
15. 10 times as much as 1 nickel

dime

quarter

half dollar

one dollar

*For another example, see Set A on page 136.

What You Think

Mike has 5 state quarters.

Carl has 2 times as many.

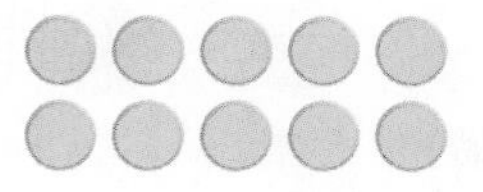

2 times as many is 10.

What You Write

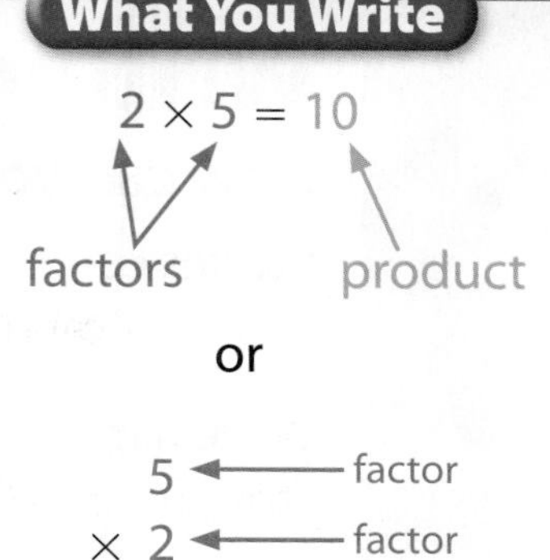

$$\begin{array}{r} 5 \\ \times\ 2 \\ \hline 10 \end{array}$$

10 ← product

Carl has 10 state quarters.

Problem Solving

Number Sense For **16–17**, copy and complete.

16. 6 is twice as many as ▢.

17. 8 is eight times as many as ▢.

18. Reasoning Carol has 4 dolls. Her sister has twice as many. How many dolls do they have in all?

19. Writing to Explain How could this picture help you solve **Exercise 18**?

Carol's sister	**4**	**4**	**twice as many**
Carol	**4**		

20. A horse needs about 3 hours of sleep each day. An armadillo needs 6 times as much sleep as a horse. About how many hours of sleep does an armadillo need each day?

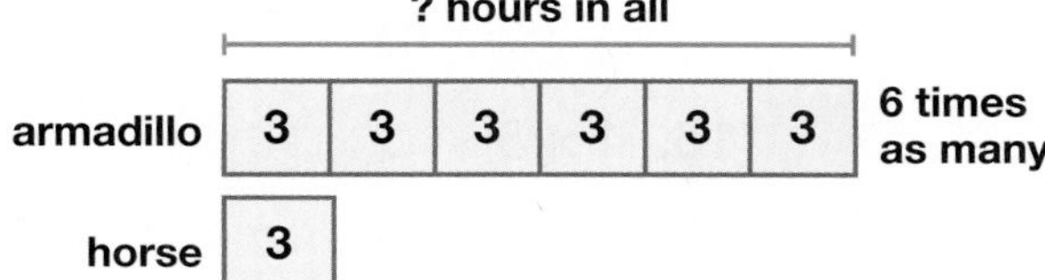

21. Two of the U. S. coins that are worth one dollar are shown below. The Susan B. Anthony coin was first issued in 1979. The Sacagawea coin was issued 21 years later. When was the Sacagawea coin issued?

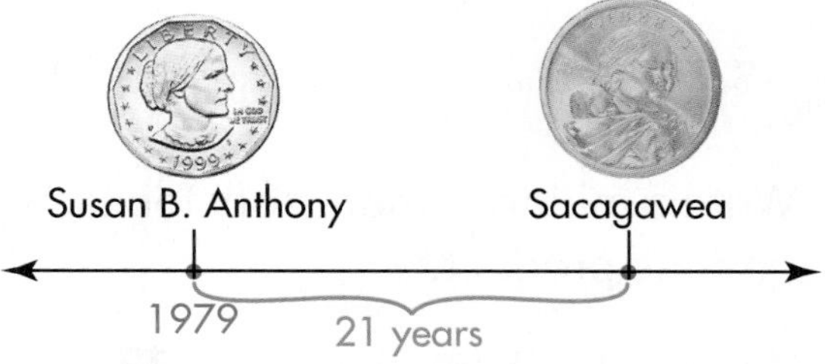

22. What number sentence shows how to find twice as many marbles?

A $8 + 8 + 8 =$ ▢ **B** $1 \times 8 =$ ▢ **C** $2 \times 8 =$ ▢ **D** $3 \times 8 =$ ▢

Lesson

5-4

Understand It!
The different meanings of multiplication can be used to write stories that describe multiplication facts.

Writing Multiplication Stories

How can you describe a multiplication fact?

Stories can be written to describe multiplication facts.

Write a multiplication story for $3 \times 6 = \square$.

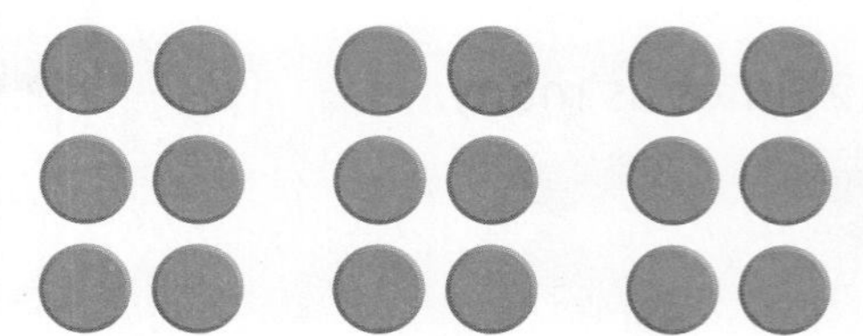

Guided Practice*

Do you know HOW?

In **1–4**, write a multiplication story for each problem. Draw a picture or use objects to find each product.

1. 2×6
2. 3×5
3. 4×2
4. 3×8

Do you UNDERSTAND?

5. How would the story about Randy change if the multiplication sentence $2 \times 6 = \square$ was used?
6. How would the story about Eliza change if the multiplication sentence $3 \times 5 = \square$ was used?
7. **Number Sense** Could the story about carrots also be an addition story? Explain.

Independent Practice

Write a multiplication story for each problem. Draw a picture or use objects to find each product.

8. 7×3
9. 2×9
10. 4×5

Write a multiplication story for each picture. Use the picture to find the product.

11. 

12. 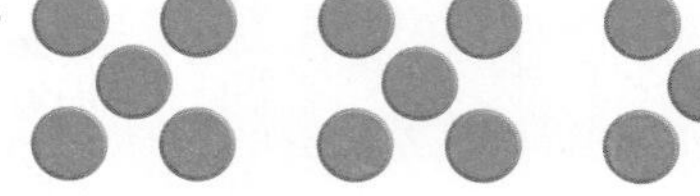

*For another example, see Set B on page 136.

Equal Groups

Randy has 3 packs of 6 buttons. How many buttons does he have?

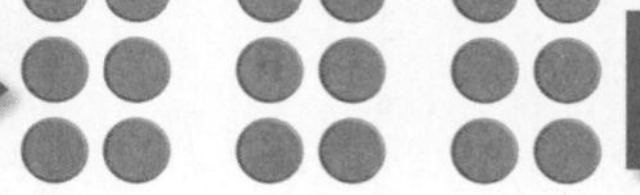

$3 \times 6 = 18$

Randy has 18 buttons.

An Array

Eliza planted 6 lilies in each of 3 rows. How many lilies did she plant?

$3 \times 6 = 18$

Eliza planted 18 lilies.

"Times as Many"

Kanisha has 6 carrots. Jack has 3 times as many. How many carrots does Jack have?

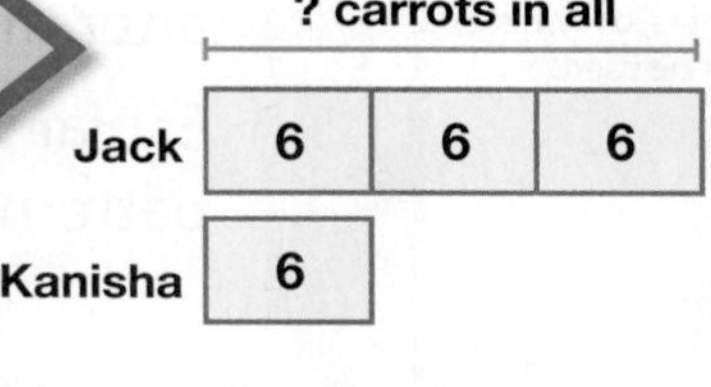

$3 \times 6 = 18$

Jack has 18 carrots.

Problem Solving

Number Sense For **13–15**, describe each story as an addition story, a subtraction story, or a multiplication story.

13. Kay has 6 pencils. She gave 4 of them to her friend. How many pencils does Kay have left?

14. Kay has 6 pencils. She bought 4 more pencils at the school store. How many pencils does Kay have now?

15. Kay has 6 bags of pencils. There are 2 pencils in each bag. How many pencils does Kay have?

16. A soccer team traveled to a soccer game in 4 vans. All four vans were full. Each van held 7 players. How many players went to the game?

A 47 **C** 24

B 28 **D** 11

17. Algebra Steve has some packages of balloons. There are 8 balloons in each package. He has 24 balloons in all. Draw a picture to find how many packages of balloons Steve has.

18. A group of 12 monarch butterflies is getting ready to migrate. How many wings will be moving when the group flies away?

Each monarch butterfly has 4 bright orange wings and 6 legs.

Lesson

5-5

Understand It!
There are different ways to write a good explanation in math. Words, pictures, numbers, or symbols might be used.

Problem Solving

Writing to Explain

Gina's dad gave her 2 pennies on Monday. He promised to double that number of pennies every day after that for one week.

Explain how you can use the pattern to complete the table.

Data

Day	Number of pennies
Monday	2
Tuesday	4
Wednesday	8
Thursday	16
Friday	32
Saturday	
Sunday	

Another Example

Jackie got on an elevator on the first floor. She went up 5 floors. Then she went down 2 floors. Then she went up 4 floors and got off the elevator. What floor is Jackie on?

Use *words, pictures, numbers,* or *symbols* to write a math explanation.

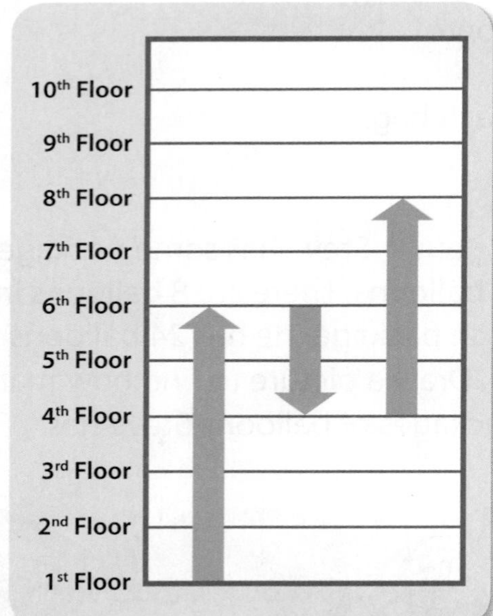

Jackie started on the first floor. Then she went up 5 floors.

$1 + 5 = 6$

Then she went down 2 floors.

$6 - 2 = 4$

Then she went up 4 floors and got off the elevator.

$4 + 4 = 8$

Jackie is on the eighth floor.

Explain It

1. Why is drawing a picture a good way to explain this problem?
2. How do the number sentences explain the problem?

Complete the table. Use *words, pictures, numbers,* or *symbols* to write a math explanation.

The number of pennies doubles each day. That means that Gina will get 2 times as many pennies as she got the day before.

So, I need to double 32.
32 + 32 = 64 pennies
Gina will get 64 pennies on Saturday.

Then, I need to double 64.
64 + 64 = 128 pennies
Gina will get 128 pennies on Sunday.

Data

Day	Number of Pennies
Monday	2
Tuesday	4
Wednesday	8
Thursday	16
Friday	32
Saturday	64
Sunday	128

Guided Practice*

Do you know HOW?

1. Brian bought 3 packs of baseball cards. There are 4 cards in each pack. How many baseball cards did he buy? Explain how you can solve this problem.

Do you UNDERSTAND?

2. If the pattern in the table above continued, how many pennies would Gina get next Monday?

3. **Write a Problem** Write a problem. Explain how to solve it using words, pictures, numbers, or symbols.

Independent Practice

4. Pam is setting up tables and chairs. She puts 4 chairs at each table.

   a Explain how the number of chairs changes as the number of tables changes.

   b Copy and complete the table.

Number of Tables	1	2	3	4	5
Number of Chairs	4	8	12		

5. Aaron cut a log into 5 pieces. How many cuts did he make? Explain how you found the answer.

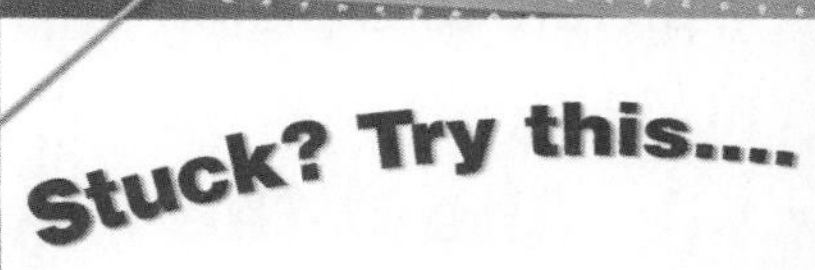

- What do I know?
- What am I asked to find?
- What diagram can I use to help understand the problem?
- Can I use addition, subtraction, multiplication, or division?
- Is all of my work correct?
- Did I answer the right question?
- Is my answer reasonable?

*For another example, see Set B on page 136.

Independent Practice

6. Copy and complete the table below. Then describe how the table helps you explain the pattern.

Cost of School Play Tickets (Data)

Number of Tickets	Cost
1	$5
2	$10
3	$15
4	▢
5	

7. If Margo continues the pattern in the table, what is the first day she will exercise for 1 hour? Explain how you know.

Margo's Exercise Schedule (Data)

Day	Minutes
Monday	20 minutes
Tuesday	30 minutes
Wednesday	40 minutes
Thursday	▢ minutes
Friday	minutes

8. Hank earns $4 for raking lawns and $6 for mowing lawns. How much will Hank earn if he mows and rakes 2 lawns?

9. **a** Describe the pattern below.

   81, 82, 84, 87, 91

   b Write the next two numbers in the pattern and explain how you found them.

10. Jake planted trees in a row that is 20 feet long. He planted a tree at the beginning of the row. Then he planted a tree every 5 feet. How many trees did he plant in this row? Draw a picture to explain.

Think About the Process

11. Alexandra bought 5 bags of oranges. There were 6 oranges in each bag. Then she gave 4 oranges away. Which number sentence shows how many oranges Alexandra bought?

   A $5 + 6 =$ ▢

   B $5 \times 6 =$ ▢

   C $(5 \times 6) - 4 =$ ▢

   D $(5 + 6) - 4 =$ ▢

12. Tara ran 5 miles on Monday and 4 miles on Tuesday. Teresa ran 3 miles on Monday and 6 miles on Tuesday. Which number sentence shows how far Tara ran in all?

   A $3 + 6 =$ ▢

   B $5 + 4 =$ ▢

   C $5 - 4 =$ ▢

   D $5 + 4 + 3 + 6 =$ ▢

Enrichment

Venn Diagrams

In the 1880s, British mathematician John Venn used diagrams with shapes, such as rings or circles, to show how groups of data relate.

Each shape in a **Venn diagram** is named for the group it represents. Shapes overlap, or **intersect,** because some of the data can belong to more than one group.

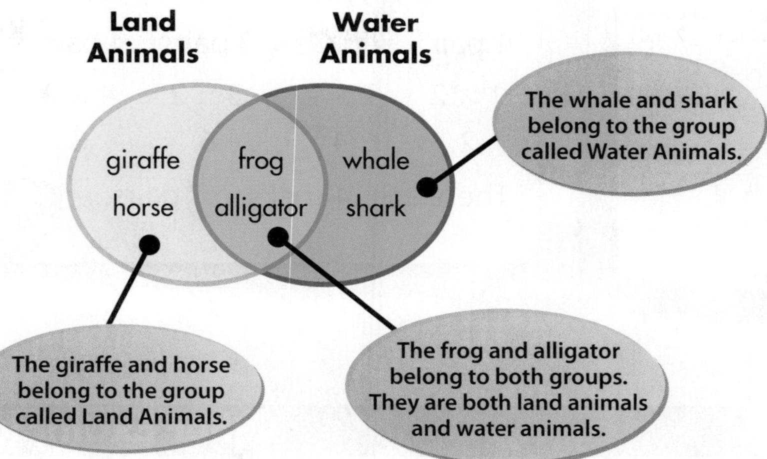

Practice

For **1–4**, use the Venn diagram at the right.

Skip Count by 2s to 12 | **Skip Count by 3s to 12**

Only 2s: 4, 8, 2, 10
Both: 6, 12
Only 3s: 3, 9

1. Which numbers do you name only when you count to 12 by 2s?

2. Which numbers do you name only when you count to 12 by 3s?

3. Which numbers do you name when you count to 12 by both 2s and 3s? How can you tell from the Venn diagram?

4. If you continued counting to 18, where would you place 14? 15? 18?

5. Jamie skip counted by 3s to 36. Oscar skip counted by 4s to 36.

a. Which numbers did Jamie and Oscar both say?

b. Jamie and Oscar used their skip-count numbers to make a Venn diagram. How many numbers did they write in the section where the circles intersect?

6. Use the lists below to make a Venn diagram.

Skip Count to 24

by 4s	by 6s
4	6
8	12
12	18
16	24
20	
24	

Lesson

5-6 2 and 5 as Factors

Understand It!
Skip counting and patterns can be used to multiply by 2 and by 5.

How can you use patterns to multiply by 2 and 5?

How many socks are in 7 pairs of socks? Find 7×2.

1 pair	2 pairs	3 pairs	4 pairs	5 pairs	6 pairs	7 pairs
1×2	2×2	3×2	4×2	5×2	6×2	7×2
2	4	6	8	10	12	14

There are 14 socks in 7 pairs.

Other Examples

What are the patterns in multiples of 2 and 5?

The products for the 2s facts are multiples of 2.
The products for the 5s facts are multiples of 5.
Multiples are the products of a number and other whole numbers.

Data

2s Facts	
$0 \times 2 = 0$	$5 \times 2 = 10$
$1 \times 2 = 2$	$6 \times 2 = 12$
$2 \times 2 = 4$	$7 \times 2 = 14$
$3 \times 2 = 6$	$8 \times 2 = 16$
$4 \times 2 = 8$	$9 \times 2 = 18$

Data

5s Facts	
$0 \times 5 = 0$	$5 \times 5 = 25$
$1 \times 5 = 5$	$6 \times 5 = 30$
$2 \times 5 = 10$	$7 \times 5 = 35$
$3 \times 5 = 15$	$8 \times 5 = 40$
$4 \times 5 = 20$	$9 \times 5 = 45$

Patterns for 2s Facts

- Multiples of 2 are even numbers. Multiples of 2 end in 0, 2, 4, 6, or 8.
- Each multiple of 2 is 2 more than the one before it.

Patterns for 5s Facts

- Each multiple of 5 ends in 0 or 5.
- Each multiple of 5 is 5 more than the one before it.

Explain It

1. Is 83 a multiple of 2? a multiple of 5? How do you know?
2. **Reasoning** How can patterns help you find 10×2?

How many fingers are on 7 gloves?

Choose an Operation Find 7×5.

$1 \times 5 = 5$
$2 \times 5 = 10$
$3 \times 5 = 15$
$4 \times 5 = 20$
$5 \times 5 = 25$
$6 \times 5 = 30$
$7 \times 5 = 35$

There are 35 fingers on 7 gloves.

Guided Practice*

Do you know HOW?

Find each product.

1. 2×6 **2.** 2×3 **3.** 7×2

4. 5×3 **5.** 5×5 **6.** 6×5

7. $\begin{array}{r} 4 \\ \times\ 2 \\ \hline \end{array}$ **8.** $\begin{array}{r} 5 \\ \times\ 2 \\ \hline \end{array}$ **9.** $\begin{array}{r} 8 \\ \times\ 5 \\ \hline \end{array}$

Do you UNDERSTAND?

10. How can you skip count to find the number of socks in 9 pairs? in 10 pairs?

11. How can you skip count to find how many fingers are on 9 gloves? on 10 gloves?

12. **Number Sense** Bert says that 2×8 is 15. How can you use patterns to know that his answer is wrong?

Independent Practice

For **13–22**, find each product.

13. 2×2 **14.** 5×2 **15.** 3×5 **16.** 8×2 **17.** 9×5

18. $\begin{array}{r} 3 \\ \times\ 5 \\ \hline \end{array}$ **19.** $\begin{array}{r} 2 \\ \times\ 4 \\ \hline \end{array}$ **20.** $\begin{array}{r} 4 \\ \times\ 5 \\ \hline \end{array}$ **21.** $\begin{array}{r} 9 \\ \times\ 2 \\ \hline \end{array}$ **22.** $\begin{array}{r} 5 \\ \times\ 7 \\ \hline \end{array}$

23. Find 5 times 6.

24. Multiply 2 by 5.

25. Find the product of 7 and 5.

26. Find 6×2.

DIGITAL Animated Glossary
www.pearsonsuccessnet.com

For another example, see Set C on page 137.

Independent Practice

Algebra Compare. Use $<$, $>$, or $=$.

27. $2 \times 5 \bigcirc 5 \times 2$ **28.** $4 \times 5 \bigcirc 4 \times 6$ **29.** $2 \times 5 \bigcirc 2 \times 4$

30. $6 \times 5 \bigcirc 5 \times 5$ **31.** $9 \times 5 \bigcirc 5 \times 9$ **32.** $7 \times 2 \bigcirc 2 \times 9$

Problem Solving

For **33–35**, use the table at the right.

33. How much does it cost to bowl three games without renting shoes?

34. Maru rented some bowling shoes. She also bowled two games. How much money did she spend?

35. Wendy paid for 2 games with a twenty-dollar bill. How much change did she get back?

Data

Bowling	
Cost per game	\$5
Daily shoe rental	\$2

36. Writing to Explain Eric has some nickels. He says they are worth exactly 34 cents. Can you tell if he is correct or not? Why or why not?

37. April has the coins shown below.

April counted the value of these coins in cents. Which list shows numbers she would have named?

A 5, 10, 16, 20, 25, 26

B 5, 10, 15, 22, 25, 32

C 5, 10, 15, 20, 25, 30

D 10, 15, 22, 25, 30, 35

38. Use the picture below. How many hearts do 3 earthworms have?

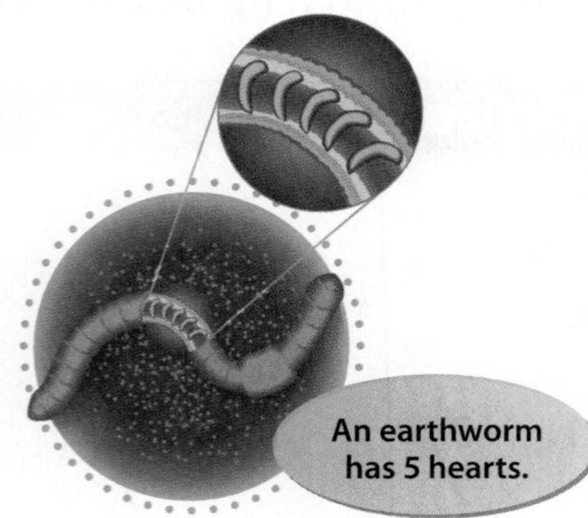

39. Algebra What two 1-digit factors could you multiply to get a product of 30?

40. Jake went bowling. On his first turn, he knocked down 2 pins. On his second turn, he knocked down twice that many. So far, how many pins in all has he knocked down?

Meanings of Multiplication

Use eTools

Counters

Step 1 Go to the Counters eTool. Select a counter shape. Make 4 groups of counters with 3 counters in each group. The odometer tells how many counters in all. Write a number sentence: $4 \times 3 = 12$.

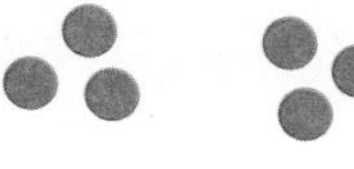

Step 2 Use the broom tool to clear the workspace. Show 3 groups with 8 counters in each and write a number sentence: $3 \times 8 = 24$.

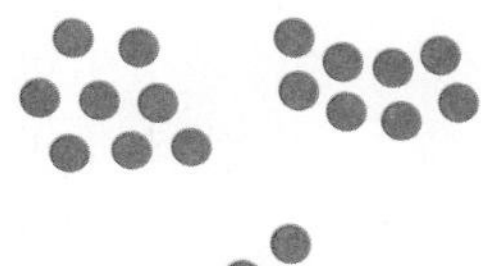

Step 3 Select the array workspace. Drag the button to show 7 rows with 6 counters in each row. Write a number sentence: $7 \times 6 = 42$.

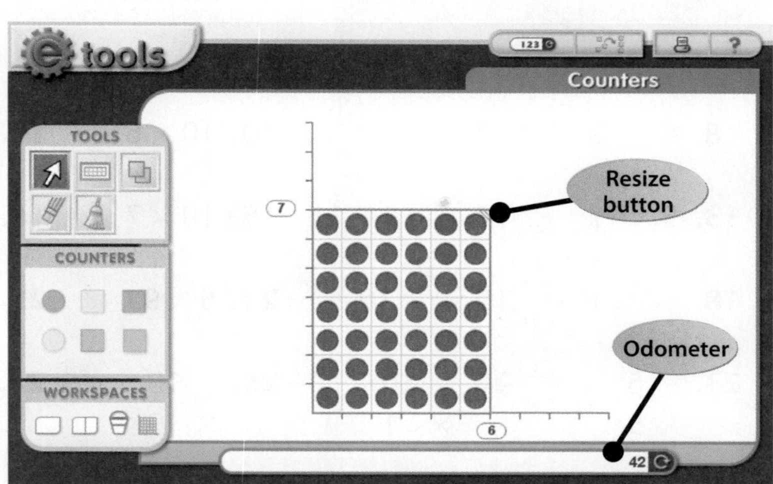

Practice

Use the Counters eTool to draw counters. Write a number sentence.

1. 5 groups with 3 counters in each
2. 7 groups with 4 counters in each
3. 8 rows with 6 counters in each
4. 9 rows with 5 counters in each

Lesson

5-7

Understand It!
Patterns can be used to multiply by 10.

10 as a Factor

What are the patterns in multiples of 10?

Greg wants to train for a race that is 10 weeks away. The chart shows his training schedule. How many miles will Greg run to train for the race?

Data

Weekly Schedule

Activity	Miles
Swimming	4 miles
Running	10 miles
Biking	9 miles

Choose the Operation
Find 10×10.

Guided Practice*

Do you know HOW?

Find each product.

1. 2×10 **2.** 6×10

3. 10×1 **4.** 10×3 **5.** 10×7

Do you UNDERSTAND?

6. Writing to Explain Is 91 a multiple of 10? Explain.

7. How many miles will Greg bike in 10 weeks?

Independent Practice

Find each product.

8. 4×10 **9.** 9×10 **10.** 10×6 **11.** 5×5 **12.** 10×10

13. 5×10 **14.** 8×2 **15.** 10×7 **16.** 2×5 **17.** 6×10

18. 10×10 **19.** 2×10 **20.** 5×9 **21.** 3×10 **22.** 10×8

23. 6×5 **24.** 10×1 **25.** 10×9 **26.** 2×9 **27.** 10×5

28. 10×2 **29.** 7×2 **30.** 10×4 **31.** 10×8 **32.** 0×6

33. 5×8 **34.** 10×0 **35.** 10×3 **36.** 5×7 **37.** 10×7

*For another example, see Set C on page 137.

10s Facts	
$0 \times 10 = 0$	$5 \times 10 = 50$
$1 \times 10 = 10$	$6 \times 10 = 60$
$2 \times 10 = 20$	$7 \times 10 = 70$
$3 \times 10 = 30$	$8 \times 10 = 80$
$4 \times 10 = 40$	$9 \times 10 = 90$
	$10 \times 10 =$

Use patterns to find the product.

- Write the factor you are multiplying by 10.
- Write a zero to the right of that factor. A multiple of 10 will always have a zero in the ones place.

$10 \times 10 = 100$

Greg will run 100 miles.

Problem Solving

Use the table at the right for **38** and **39**. It shows the food that was bought for 70 third graders for a school picnic.

Food Item	Number of Packages	Number in Each Package
Hot dogs	8	10
Rolls	10	9
Juice boxes	7	10

38. Find the total number of each item bought.

a Hot dogs

b Rolls

c Juice boxes

39. How many extra juice boxes were bought?

40. Writing to Explain Look at the table at the top of page 126. Greg multiplied 5×10 to find how many more miles he biked than swam in the 10 weeks. Does that make sense? Why or why not?

41. Strategy Focus Solve. Use the strategy Draw a Picture.

Mai had 3 packs of pens. Each pack had 10 pens. She gave 5 pens to Ervin. How many pens did she have left?

42. Number Sense Raul has only dimes in his pocket. Could he have exactly 45 cents? Explain.

43. Kimmy bought 7 tickets for a concert. Each ticket cost $10. What was the total cost of the tickets Kimmy bought?

? total cost

$10	$10	$10	$10	$10	$10	$10

Cost for each ticket

44. Which sign makes the number sentence true?

8 □ 5 = 40

A +

B −

C ×

D ÷

Lesson
5-8

Understand It!
Use patterns to help you remember multiplication facts for 9.

9 as a Factor

How can patterns be used to find 9s facts?

The owner of a flower shop puts 9 roses in each package. How many roses are in 8 packages?

Use patterns to find 8×9.

Data

9s Facts
$0 \times 9 = 0$
$1 \times 9 = 9$
$2 \times 9 = 18$
$3 \times 9 = 27$
$4 \times 9 = 36$
$5 \times 9 = 45$
$6 \times 9 = 54$
$7 \times 9 = 63$
$8 \times 9 =$ ▢
$9 \times 9 =$

Guided Practice*

Do you know HOW?

Find each product.

1. 9×2 **2.** 5×9 **3.** 7×9

4. 4×9 **5.** 2×8 **6.** 6×9

7. 3×9 **8.** 5×5 **9.** 8×9

Do you UNDERSTAND?

10. Writing to Explain Use the patterns above to find 9×9. Then explain how you found the product.

11. Number Sense Paul thinks that 3×9 is 24. Use a 9s pattern to show that he is wrong.

Independent Practice

Find each product.

12. 9×0 **13.** 5×8 **14.** 9×4 **15.** 8×9

16. 9×9 **17.** 1×9 **18.** 5×9 **19.** 2×9

20. 7×9 **21.** 5×2 **22.** 6×5 **23.** 9×1

24. 6×9 **25.** 9×5 **26.** 9×7 **27.** 9×2

28. 7×9 **29.** 8×2 **30.** 0×9 **31.** 2×3

*For another example, see Set C on page 137.

One Way

Use these patterns. Start with $1 \times 9 = 9$.

The ones digit decreases by 1 each time. So the ones digit in the product after 63 is 2.

The tens digit increases by 1 each time. So the tens digit in the product after 63 is 7.

$8 \times 9 = 72$

There are 72 roses in 8 packages.

Another Way

Use these patterns to find the product.

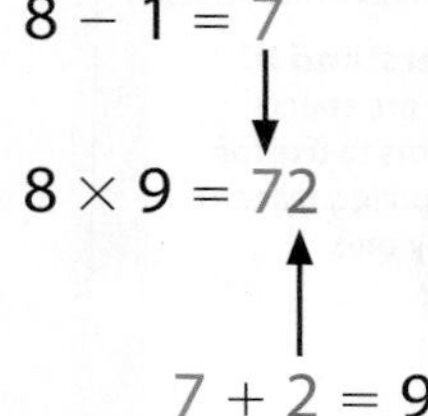

The tens digit is 1 less than the factor being multiplied by 9.

$8 - 1 = 7$

$8 \times 9 = 72$

The digits of the product have a sum of 9.

$7 + 2 = 9$

There are 72 roses in 8 packages.

Algebra Copy and complete. Use +, −, or ×.

32. $2 \times 6 = 10 \square 2$

33. $5 \times 7 = 45 \square 10$

34. $9 \times 9 = 80 \square 1$

35. $20 - 2 = 2 \square 9$

36. $9 \square 3 = 30 - 3$

37. $9 \square 1 = 2 \square 5$

Problem Solving

The library is having a used book sale. For **38–41**, use the table at the right.

38. How much do 4 hardcover books cost?

39. How much more would Chico spend if he bought 3 books on CDs rather than 3 hardcover books?

Data

Library Book Sale	
Paperback Books	$2
Hardcover Books	$5
Books on CDs	$9

40. Maggie bought only paperback books. The clerk told her she owed $15. How does Maggie know that the clerk made a mistake?

41. **Writing to Explain** Mr. Lee bought 2 books on CDs and 9 paperback books. Did he spend more on CDs or on paperback books? Tell how you know.

42. The owner of a flower shop counted the flowers in groups of 9. Which list shows the numbers he named?

A 9, 19, 29, 39, 49, 59

B 6, 12, 18, 24, 36, 42

C 18, 27, 36, 45, 56, 65

D 9, 18, 27, 36, 45, 54

Lesson
5-9

Understand It!
There are special patterns to use for multiplying by zero and by one.

Multiplying with 0 and 1

What are the patterns in multiples of 1 and 0?

Kira has 8 plates with 1 orange on each plate.
How many oranges does Kira have?

Find 8×1.

Guided Practice*

Do you know HOW?

Find each product.

1. 1×7
2. 5×0
3. 5×1
4. 0×0
5. 1×1
6. 8×1
7. 7×0
8. 1×9
9. 0×6

Do you UNDERSTAND?

10. **Writing to Explain** How can you use the properties above to find 375×1 and 0×754?

11. Draw an array to show that $1 \times 8 = 8$.

12. Chad has 6 plates. There is 1 apple and 0 grapes on each plate. How many apples are there? How many grapes are there?

Independent Practice

Find each product.

13. 0×4
14. 1×6
15. 1×3
16. 3×0
17. 4×1
18. 0×9
19. 1×3
20. 1×7
21. 0×7
22. 8×0
23. 8×1
24. 0×2
25. 1×2
26. 9×0
27. 0×1

DIGITAL Animated Glossary **www.pearsonsuccessnet.com**

For another example, see Set E on page 137.

8 groups with 1 in each group equals 8 in all.

$8 \times 1 = 8$

Kira has 8 oranges.

1 plate with 8 oranges also equals 8 oranges.

$1 \times 8 = 8$

The Identity (One) Property of Multiplication: when you multiply a number and 1, the product is that number.

If Kira has 4 plates with 0 oranges on each plate, she has 0 oranges.

$4 \times 0 = 0$

If $4 \times 0 = 0$ then $0 \times 4 = 0$.

The Zero Property of Multiplication: when you multiply a number and 0, the product is 0.

Algebra Copy and complete. Write <, >, or = for each ◯.

28. 1×6 ◯ 8×0 **29.** 8×1 ◯ 1×9 **30.** 1×4 ◯ 4×1

31. 0×654 ◯ 346×0 **32.** 2×9 ◯ 9×1 **33.** 0×754 ◯ 5×1

Algebra Copy and complete. Write ×, +, or − for each □.

34. 4 □ 1 = 4
4 □ 1 = 5
4 □ 1 = 3

35. 4 □ 0 = 4
4 □ 0 = 0

36. 6 □ 1 = 5
6 □ 1 = 6
6 □ 1 = 7

Problem Solving

37. What is the missing factor?
548 × ▢ = 548

A 0 **B** 1 **C** 2 **D** 4

38. Writing to Explain The product of two factors is 0. One of the factors is 0. Can you tell what the other factor is? Explain your answer.

39. A unicycle relay team has 4 riders. Each rider has one unicycle. If each unicycle has 1 wheel, how many wheels does the team have?

40. Reasoning Why do you think the Identity Property of Multiplication is sometimes called the One Property of Multiplication?

41. Tickets for a school concert are free to students. The cost is $1 for each adult. What is the total cost of tickets for 2 adults and 5 students?

A $7 **B** $5 **C** $2 **D** $1

42. The children in the 3rd-grade classes are having a bicycle parade. There are 5 rows of bikes with 8 bikes in each row. How many bikes in all are in the parade?

Lesson
5-10

Understand It!
The answer to one problem might depend on the answer to another problem.

Problem Solving
Two-Question Problems

Sometimes you must use the answer to one problem to solve another problem.

Problem 1: Four girls and five boys went to the movies. How many children went to the movies?

Problem 2: Children's movie tickets cost $5 each. What was the total cost of the tickets for these children?

Movie Plex
Admit One
Child
$5

Guided Practice*

Do you know HOW?

1a. A movie ticket for an adult costs $9. How much do 3 adult tickets cost?

? Total cost

$9	$9	$9

b. Mr. Jones paid for 3 adult tickets with $40. How much change will he get?

$40

$27	?

Do you UNDERSTAND?

2. What operations were used to solve Problems 1a and 1b? Tell why.

3. **Writing to Explain** Why must you solve Problem 1a before solving Problem 1b?

4. **Write a Problem** Write 2 problems that use the answer from the first problem to solve the second one.

Independent Practice

5a. Jared bought a baseball cap for $12 and a T-shirt for $19. How much did the items cost all together?

?

$12	$19

b. Suppose Jared paid with a $50 bill. How much change should he get?

$50

$31	?

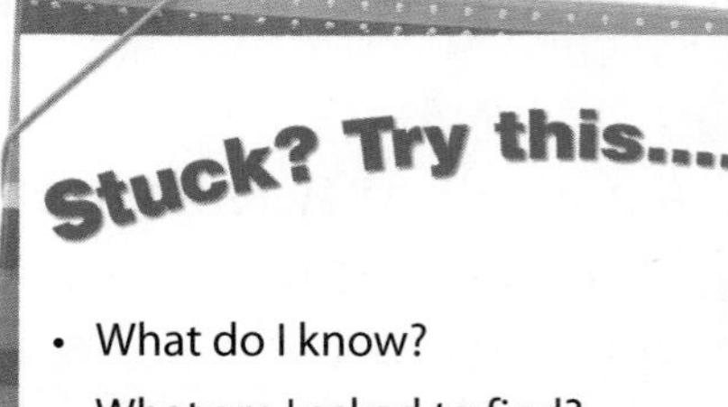

Stuck? Try this....

- What do I know?
- What am I asked to find?
- What diagram can I use to help understand the problem?
- Can I use addition, subtraction, multiplication, or division?
- Is all of my work correct?
- Did I answer the right question?
- Is my answer reasonable?

*For another example, see Set E on page 137.

Solve

Problem 1

Four girls and five boys went to the movies. How many children went to the movies?

? Children in all

4 girls	5 boys

$4 + 5 = 9$

Nine children went to the movies.

Solve

Problem 2

Children's movie tickets cost $5 each. What was the total cost of the tickets for these children?

? Total cost

$5	$5	$5	$5	$5	$5	$5	$5	$5

$9 \times \$5 = \$45$

The total cost of the tickets was $45.

Independent Practice

Cara and some friends bought gifts in a museum shop. The gifts were from Hawaii. In **6**–**8**, use the answer from the first problem to solve the second problem.

6a. Cara bought a poster and a shirt. How much did her gifts cost?

b. Cara gave the clerk $30. How much change should she get?

7a. Dan bought 3 cups. How much did Dan spend on cups?

b. Dan also bought a CD. How much did Dan spend in all?

8a. Teri bought the most expensive and the least expensive gift. How much did she spend?

b. Teri's sister bought a CD. How much did the two girls spend in all?

9. On Monday, Roberta swam 10 laps. On Tuesday, she swam twice as many laps as on Monday. Which pair of number sentences can be used to find:

a how many laps Roberta swam on Tuesday?
b how many laps Roberta swam in all?

A $2 \times 10 = 20$
$20 + 10 = 30$

B $2 \times 10 = 20$
$20 - 10 = 10$

C $10 + 2 = 12$
$12 + 10 = 22$

D $10 + 2 = 12$
$12 - 10 = 2$

Test

1. Which has the same value as 5×2? (5-1)

   A $5 + 2$

   B $2 + 2 + 2 + 2$

   C $2 + 2 + 2 + 5$

   D $2 + 2 + 2 + 2 + 2$

2. Which number sentence shows how to find 4 times as many books as the number of books shown below? (5-3)

   A $4 + 8 = 12$

   B $4 \times 8 = 32$

   C $4 \times 9 = 36$

   D $5 \times 8 = 40$

3. Which story could be solved with 7×8? (5-4)

   A Ben bought 7 bags of apples. Each bag had 8 apples. How many apples did Ben buy?

   B Rob has 7 red fish and 8 orange fish. How many fish does Rob have in all?

   C Tao had 8 math problems to solve. He has solved 7 of them. How many does he have left?

   D Max has 7 pages in his album. He has 8 pictures. How many pictures can he put on each page?

4. Which number makes the second number sentence true? (5-2)

   $9 \times 7 = 63$

   $7 \times \square = 63$

   A 63

   B 56

   C 9

   D 7

5. The 3rd graders at Willow School were put in 9 groups of 10. How many 3rd graders were there? (5-7)

   A 19

   B 90

   C 99

   D 900

6. Alice is buying paper cups for the picnic. Each package has 8 cups. How does the number of cups change as the number of packages increases by 1? (5-5)

Packages	1	2	3	4	5
Cups	8	16	24	32	40

   A There are 40 more cups for each additional package.

   B There are 40 fewer cups for each additional package.

   C There are 8 more cups for each additional package.

   D There are 8 fewer cups for each additional package.

7. Which symbol makes the number sentence true? (5-9)

$5 \times 0 \bigcirc 2 \times 1$

A $>$

B $<$

C $=$

D $\times$

8. For the 4th of July, Ron put flags in his yard as shown below. Which number sentence could be used to find how many flags Ron put in his yard? (5-2)

A $5 + 4 = \square$

B $4 \times 5 = \square$

C $4 + 5 = \square$

D $5 - 4 = \square$

9. Rosa bought all of the ribbon shown below. How many yards of ribbon did she buy? (5-6)

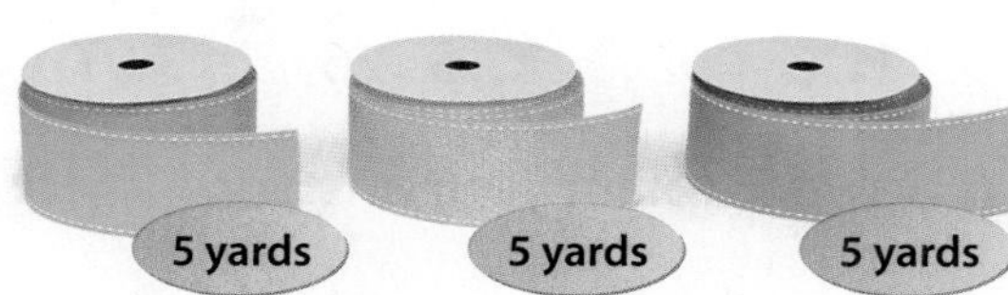

A 8

B 12

C 15

D 18

10. Todd has 7 aquariums. Each aquarium has 9 fish. What is the total number of fish? (5-8)

A 63

B 62

C 27

D 21

11. Len has 3 rolls of quarters. Ryan has 8 rolls. How many more rolls does Ryan have than Len? Each roll has \$10 worth of quarters. In these rolls of quarters, how much more money does Ryan have than Len? (5-10)

A Ryan has 11 more rolls, so he has \$110 more than Len.

B Ryan has 5 more rolls, so he has \$55 more than Len.

C Ryan has 5 more rolls, so he has \$50 more than Len.

D Ryan has 6 more rolls, so he has \$60 more than Len.

12. Which of these best describes all of the snake lengths? (5-6)

Data

Snake	Length in Feet
Black Mamba	14
King Cobra	16
Taipan	10

A They are all greater than 12.

B They are all less than 15.

C They are all multiples of 5.

D They are all multiples of 2.

Topic 5

Reteaching

Set A, pages 108–112, 114–115

Find the total number of squares.

■■ ■■ ■■

There are 3 groups of 2 squares.

Use addition to join groups: $2 + 2 + 2 = 6$

Draw an array to show 3×2.

This array shows 3 rows of 2.

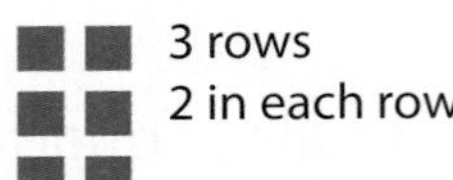

3 rows
2 in each row

$2 + 2 + 2 = 6$ or $3 \times 2 = 6$.

Find twice as many as 6. Multiply by 2 to find *twice as many*.

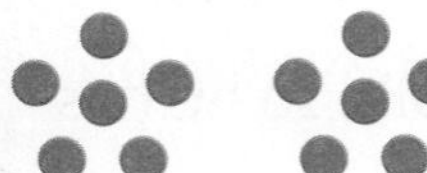

$2 \times 6 = 12$

Remember that multiplication is a quick way of joining equal groups or comparing groups. Use the Commutative (order) Property of Multiplication.

Copy and complete.

1. ●● ●● (2 groups of 5 counters)
   2 groups of ▢
   5 + ▢ = ▢
   2 × ▢ = ▢

Draw an array to show each fact. Write the product.

2. 2×4 **3.** 3×5 **4.** 4×4

Find each amount. You may use drawings or counters to help.

5. 5 times as many as 4
6. Twice as many as 7

Set B, pages 116–120

Write a multiplication story for 3×5. Draw a picture to help find the product.

Jessica is putting pretzels into 3 bags. She will put 5 pretzels in each bag. How many pretzels does Jessica have in all?

 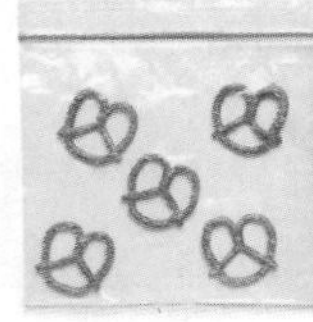 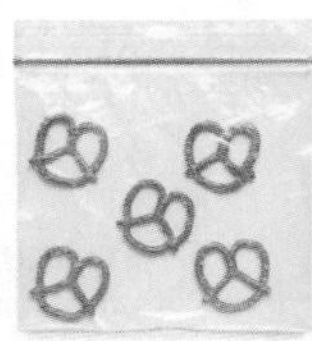

Jessica has 3 bags of pretzels. There are 5 pretzels in each bag.

$5 + 5 + 5 = 15$

Jessica has 15 pretzels.

Remember that another person should be able to follow your explanation.

Write a multiplication story for each problem. Solve. Explain your answer.

1. 3×9 **2.** 5×6 **3.** 7×2

Solve. Explain your answer.

4. Jack is setting up tables for a party. Each table has 6 chairs. How many chairs does he need for 10 tables?

Set C, pages 122–124, 126–129

Find 8×5.

You can use patterns to multiply by 5s.

- You can skip count: 5, 10, 15, 20, and so on.
- Each multiple of 5 ends with a 0 or a 5.
- Each multiple of 5 is 5 more than the one before it.

$8 \times 5 = 40$

Remember that making a table and using a pattern can help you to multiply by 2, 5, 9, or 10.

Find each product.

1. 2×4 **2.** 5×4 **3.** 5×9

4. 10×4 **5.** 9×4 **6.** 9×10

Set D, pages 130–131

Identity Property of Multiplication:
When you multiply a number and 1, the product is that number.

$1 \times 6 = 6$ $12 \times 1 = 12$

Zero Property of Multiplication:
When you multiply a number and 0, the product is 0.

$0 \times 6 = 0$ $12 \times 0 = 0$

Remember that you can think about an array with 1 row when you multiply by 1.

Find each product.

1. 7×0 **2.** 1×10 **3.** 0×9

4. 3×1 **5.** 7×0 **6.** 1×5

Set E, pages 132–133

In two-question problems, you must solve one problem before you can solve the other.

Problem 1: A family of 2 adults and 3 children went to an air show. How many family members went to the air show?
$2 + 3 = 5$

Problem 2: Each pass to the air show cost \$10. How much did the family spend on passes for the air show?
$5 \times \$10 = \$50$

The family spent a total of \$50.

Remember to solve the first problem before you try to solve the second problem.

1. a For lunch, Julia bought a sandwich for \$8 and a glass of juice for \$3. How much did her lunch cost?

b Julia paid with a \$20 bill. How much change will she get?

Topic 6 Multiplication Fact Strategies: Use Known Facts

1 How many feelers do slugs have? You will find out in Lesson 6-2.

2 How many train layouts are at the National Toy Train Museum? You will find out in Lesson 6-3.

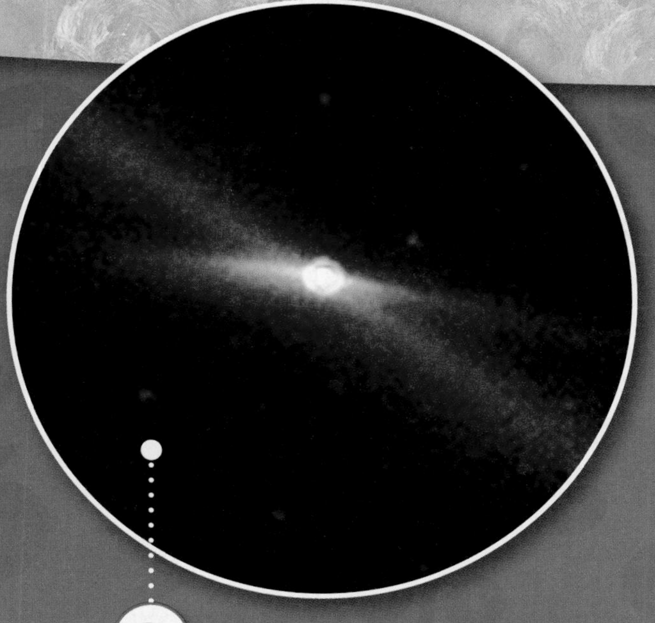

3 How long does Comet Encke take to orbit the Sun? You will find out in Lesson 6-1.

4 How much did miners pay for a glass of water during the California Gold Rush? You will find out in Lesson 6-4.

Review What You Know!

Vocabulary

Choose the best term from the box.

- addend
- array
- factor
- multiply

1. When you put together equal groups to get the total number, you __?__.
2. When numbers are multiplied, each number is called a(n) __?__.
3. When you display objects in rows and columns, you make a(n) __?__.

Multiplication

Find each product.

4. 3×2 **5.** 4×5 **6.** 7×2

7. 6×1 **8.** 8×0 **9.** 5×9

Arrays

Draw an array for each multiplication fact.

10. 6×2 **11.** 4×9

12. Write a multiplication number sentence for the array shown at the right. Explain why you used the numbers you did.

13. **Writing to Explain** Is an array for 2×9 the same as or different from an array for 9×2? Draw a picture and explain your answer.

Lesson

6-1

Understand It!
Facts for 1 and 2 can be used to find facts for 3.

3 as a Factor

Hands-On
counters

How can you break apart arrays to multiply with 3?

The canoes are stored in 3 rows. There are 6 canoes in each row. What is the total number of canoes stored?

Find 3×6.

Choose an Operation Multiply to find the total for an array.

Guided Practice*

Do you know HOW?

In **1–6**, multiply. You may use counters or draw pictures to help.

1. 3×4

2. 3×10

3. 3×5

4. 3×9

5. 12×3

6. 3×6

Do you UNDERSTAND?

7. How can you use $2 \times 8 = 16$ to find 3×8?

8. Selena arranged plants in 3 rows at the community garden. She put 6 plants in each row. How many plants in all did Selena arrange into the rows?

Independent Practice

In **9–28**, find the product. You may draw pictures to help.

9. 3×2 **10.** 4×9 **11.** 10×3 **12.** 2×9 **13.** 1×3

14. 8×3 **15.** 2×7 **16.** 5×3 **17.** 0×3 **18.** 3×8

19. 7×3 **20.** 9×8 **21.** 3×3 **22.** 5×4 **23.** 3×9

24. 1×3 **25.** 6×3 **26.** 9×5 **27.** 3×4 **28.** 3×7

DIGITAL eTools www.pearsonsuccessnet.com

*For another example, see Set A on page 160.

What You Show

Find 3×6.

Use 1s facts and 2s facts to help multiply with 3.

Make an array for each multiplication sentence.

$2 \times 6 = 12$

$1 \times 6 = 6$

$12 + 6 = 18$

What You Think

3×6 is 3 rows of 6. That is 2 sixes plus 1 more six.

2 sixes are 12.
1 six is 6.

$12 + 6 = 18$

$3 \times 6 = 18$

There are 18 canoes in all.

Problem Solving

For **29** and **30**, use the table at the right.

29. What is the total number of stamps in a package of car stamps and a package of outer space stamps?

30. Cara bought 1 package of reptile stamps. What is the total number of reptile stamps she bought? Draw an array.

Data

Number of Stamps in Different Packages

Kind of Stamp	Number of Rows	Number in Each Row
Dinosaurs	3	7
Cars	3	9
Outer Space	3	8
Reptiles	5	6

31. **Number Sense** Suppose you need to find 3×9.

a What two multiplication facts can help you find 3×9?

b How could you use 3×9 to help you find 9×3?

32. It takes about 3 years for Comet Encke to orbit the Sun. About how many years will it take Comet Encke to orbit the Sun 5 times?

A About 5 years

B About 10 years

C About 15 years

D About 20 years

33. Mr. Torres had packages of tomatoes on the counter. Each package had 3 tomatoes in it.

If Mr. Torres counted the tomatoes in groups of 3, which list shows numbers he could have named?

A 6, 12, 16, 19

B 6, 9, 12, 15

C 3, 6, 10, 13

D 3, 7, 11, 15

Lesson
6-2

Understand It!
Facts for 2 can be doubled to find facts for 4.

4 as a Factor

Hands-On
counters

How can you use doubles to multiply with 4?

Anna painted piggy banks to sell at the student art show. She painted a bank on each of the 7 days of the week for 4 weeks. How many piggy banks did she paint in all?

Find 4×7.

Choose an Operation Multiply to find the total for an array.

Guided Practice*

Do you know HOW?

In **1–6**, multiply. You may use counters or draw pictures to help.

1. 4×6

2. 5×4

3. 4×9

4. 1×4

5. 1×4

6. 10×4

Do you UNDERSTAND?

7. Besides the way shown above, what is another way to break apart 4×7 using facts you know?

8. If you know $2 \times 8 = 16$, how can you find 4×8?

9. Nolan made lamps to sell at the school art show. He made 9 lamps each week for 4 weeks. How many lamps did Nolan make in all?

Independent Practice

In **10–29**, find the product. You may draw pictures to help.

10. 4×8 **11.** 3×8 **12.** 4×3 **13.** 6×4 **14.** 9×6

15. 4×4 **16.** 5×9 **17.** 1×4 **18.** 0×4 **19.** 2×10

20. 3×4 **21.** 2×8 **22.** 4×5 **23.** 7×4 **24.** 4×1

25. 2×4 **26.** 7×4 **27.** 9×4 **28.** 10×7 **29.** 4×8

*For another example, see Set B on page 160.

What You Show

Find 4×7.

To multiply by 4, you can think of a 2s fact, then double it.

You can make arrays.

$2 \times 7 = 14$

$2 \times 7 = 14$

$14 + 14 = 28$

What You Think

4×7 is 4 rows of 7. That is 2 sevens plus 2 sevens.

2 sevens are 14.

$14 + 14 = 28$

So, $4 \times 7 = 28$.

Anna painted 28 piggy banks in all.

Problem Solving

For **30** and **31**, use the table at the right for the supplies James needs to buy for the Trail Walk trip.

30. What is the total number of cereal bars he needs to buy?

31. How many more apples than juice drinks does James need?

Data

Trail Walk Trip Supplies

Item	Number of Packages Needed	Number of Items in Each Package
Apples	2	8
Cereal Bars	4	6
Juice Drinks	4	3

32. Martin studied slugs in science class. He learned that each slug has 4 feelers. That evening, he saw 8 slugs. How many feelers did the slugs have in all?

33. **Writing to Explain** Lila had 9 weeks of rock climbing lessons. She had 4 lessons each week. Explain why Lila can use 4×9 to find the product of 9×4.

34. Which of these best describes all the numbers on the shirts?

A They are all even numbers.

B They are all multiples of 3.

C They are all greater than 10.

D They are all 2-digit numbers.

35. Bess had boxes of candles on the table. Each box had 4 candles in it.

If Bess counted the candles in groups of 4, which list shows numbers she could have named?

A 8, 12, 16, 20

B 8, 12, 14, 18

C 4, 6, 12, 14

D 4, 8, 10, 14

Lesson
6-3

Understand It!
Facts for 5 can be used to help find facts for 6 and 7.

6 and 7 as Factors

Hands-On
counters

How can you break apart arrays to multiply?

The members of the band march in 6 equal rows. There are 8 band members in each row. How many are in the band?

Find 6×8.

Choose an Operation Multiply to find the total for an array.

Another Example **How can you break apart arrays to multiply by 7?**

The singers in the chorus are standing in equal rows.
There are 8 singers in each row. There are 7 rows.
How many singers are in the chorus?

What You Show

Find 7×8.

Use 5s facts and 2s facts to help multiply with 7.
Make an array for each multiplication sentence.

$5 \times 8 = 40$

$2 \times 8 = 16$

What You Think

7×8 is 7 rows of 8.

That is 5 eights plus 2 eights.

5 eights are 40.
2 eights are 16.

$40 + 16 = 56$

So, $7 \times 8 = 56$.

The chorus has 56 singers.

Explain It

1. What other multiplication facts might help to find 7×8?
2. How could you use 5×7 and 2×7 to find 7×7?

What You Show

Find 6×8.

Use 5s facts and 1s facts.

Make an array for each multiplication sentence.

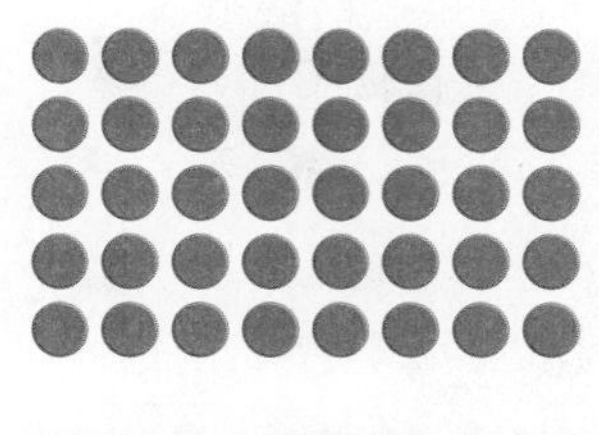

$5 \times 8 = 40$

$1 \times 8 = 8$

What You Think

6×8 is 6 rows of 8. That is 5 eights plus 1 more eight.

5 eights are 40.
8 more is 48.
$40 + 8 = 48$

So, $6 \times 8 = 48$.

The band has 48 members.

Guided Practice*

Do you know HOW?

In **1–6**, multiply. You may draw pictures or use counters to help.

1. 6×10

2. 7×6

3. 7×6

4. 9×7

5. Find 4 times 7.

6. Multiply 6 and 5.

Do you UNDERSTAND?

7. Writing to Explain Draw a picture of two arrays that show that 6×9 is equal to 5×9 plus 1×9. Explain your drawing.

8. The students who are graduating are standing in 7 equal rows. There are 9 students in each row. How many students are graduating?

Independent Practice

In **9–23**, find the product. You may draw pictures to help.

9. 6×7 **10.** 7×9 **11.** 9×6 **12.** 8×7 **13.** 6×4

14. 6×6 **15.** 10×7 **16.** 8×6 **17.** 7×7 **18.** 7×3

19. 5×7 **20.** 3×6 **21.** 4×7 **22.** 7×8 **23.** 10×6

DIGITAL eTools **www.pearsonsuccessnet.com**

*For another example, see Set C on page 160.

Problem Solving

24. The National Toy Train Museum has 5 large layouts for trains. One day, each layout had the same number of trains. Use the picture on the right to find how many trains were on display at the museum that day.

6 trains in each layout

25. **Number Sense** Marge says that 1×0 is equal to $1 + 0$. Is she correct? Why or why not?

26. Miguel had baskets of oranges. Each held 6 oranges.

If Miguel counted the oranges in groups of 6, which list shows the numbers he would have named?

A 6, 12, 21, 26, 32

B 6, 11, 16, 21, 26

C 12, 16, 20, 24, 28

D 6, 12, 18, 24, 30

27. **Writing to Explain** Nan made the arrays shown to find 6×3. Explain how to change the arrays to find 7×3. Use objects and draw a picture.

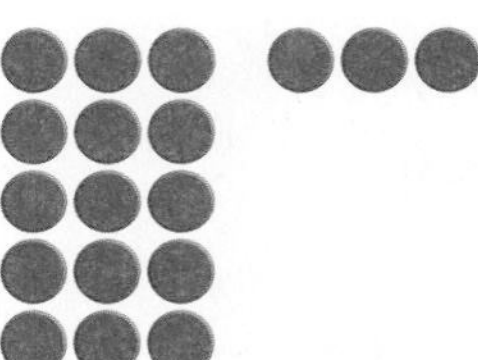

For **28** and **29**, use the drawings of the trains below.

28. A group of tourists needs 7 rows of seats in Car 5 of the Réseau train.

a How many seats will this group need?

b How many seats are left on this train for other passengers?

29. **Estimation** Use rounding to the nearest ten to find about how many seats in all are on the Réseau and the Sud-Est trains.

Réseau
377 total seats

3 seats each row | 3 seats each row | 3 seats each row | 4 seats each row | 4 seats each row

Sud-Est
345 total seats

3 seats each row | 3 seats each row | 3 seats each row | 4 seats each row | 4 seats each row

Algebra Connections

Missing Operations

In a number sentence with the = symbol, both sides of the number sentence must have the same value. An operation symbol such as +, −, or × tells how to find that value. Reasoning can help you decide which operation symbol is missing.

Example: 72 = 8 ☐ 9

Think: 72 is equal to 8 (plus or minus or multiplied by) 9?

Since 8 × 9 = 72, write "×."

72 = 8 ☒ 9

Copy and complete. Replace the square with +, −, or ×. Check your answers.

1. 9 ☐ 36 = 45

2. 24 ☐ 17 = 7

3. 16 = 2 ☐ 8

4. 8 = 32 ☐ 24

5. 7 ☐ 5 = 35

6. 50 = 12 ☐ 38

7. 18 = 9 ☐ 2

8. 64 ☐ 36 = 28

9. 30 = 6 ☐ 5

10. 47 ☐ 37 = 84

11. 63 = 9 ☐ 7

12. 12 ☐ 1 = 12

For **13** and **14**, copy and complete the number sentence below each problem. Use it to help find your answer.

13. Lisa had some pens left after she gave 27 pens to her friends. She started with a package of 36 pens. What operation can you use to find the number of pens Lisa had left?

9 = 36 ☐ 27

14. The picture below shows the number of each kind of button in a package. What operation can you use to find the total number of buttons in one package?

45 = 5 ☐ 9

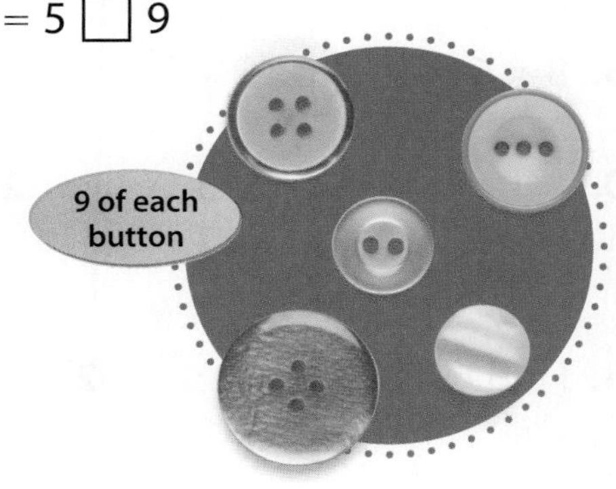

15. Write a Problem Write a problem using the number sentence below.

48 = 26 + 22

Lesson

6-4

Understand It!
Facts for 2 or 4 can be used to find facts for 8.

8 as a Factor

How can you use doubles to multiply with 8?

At the school fun fair, students try to toss a table tennis ball into a bowl. There are 8 rows of bowls. There are 8 bowls in each row. How many bowls are there in all?

Choose an Operation Multiply to find the total for an array. Find 8×8.

Guided Practice*

Do you know HOW?

In **1–6**, multiply.

1. 8×7

2. 8×4

3. 6×8

4. 10×8

5. $\begin{array}{r} 9 \\ \times 8 \\ \hline \end{array}$

6. $\begin{array}{r} 8 \\ \times 3 \\ \hline \end{array}$

Do you UNDERSTAND?

7. How could the fact that $5 \times 8 = 40$ help you find 8×8?

8. How can you use 4×7 to find 8×7?

9. Mrs. Reyes needs to order bricks for her garden. She needs 8 rows of bricks. Each row will have 7 bricks. How many bricks in all should Mrs. Reyes order?

Independent Practice

In **10–27**, find the product.

10. 8×4 **11.** 1×8 **12.** 2×9 **13.** 5×7 **14.** 8×2

15. 8×6 **16.** 5×9 **17.** 8×5 **18.** 0×8 **19.** 4×9

20. $\begin{array}{r} 10 \\ \times\ 8 \\ \hline \end{array}$ **21.** $\begin{array}{r} 3 \\ \times 7 \\ \hline \end{array}$ **22.** $\begin{array}{r} 8 \\ \times 8 \\ \hline \end{array}$ **23.** $\begin{array}{r} 2 \\ \times 4 \\ \hline \end{array}$ **24.** $\begin{array}{r} 9 \\ \times 8 \\ \hline \end{array}$

25. Find 6 times 9. **26.** Multiply 8 and 1. **27.** Find 9 times 8.

For another example, see Set C on page 160.

One Way

Use 2s facts to find 8×8.

8×8 is 4 groups of 2 eights.

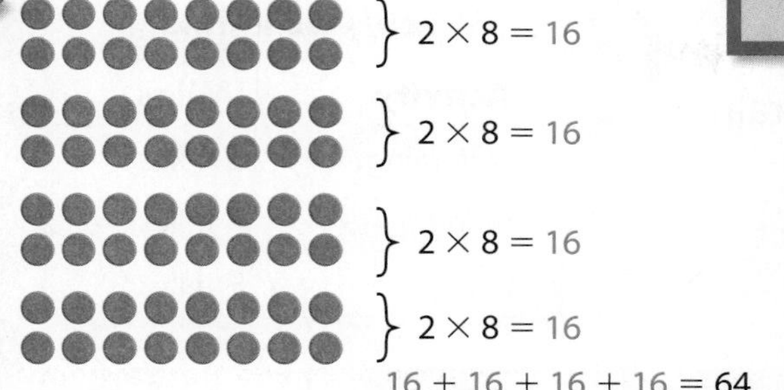

$16 + 16 + 16 + 16 = 64$

Another Way

Double a 4s fact to find 8×8.

8×8 is 4 eights plus 4 eights.

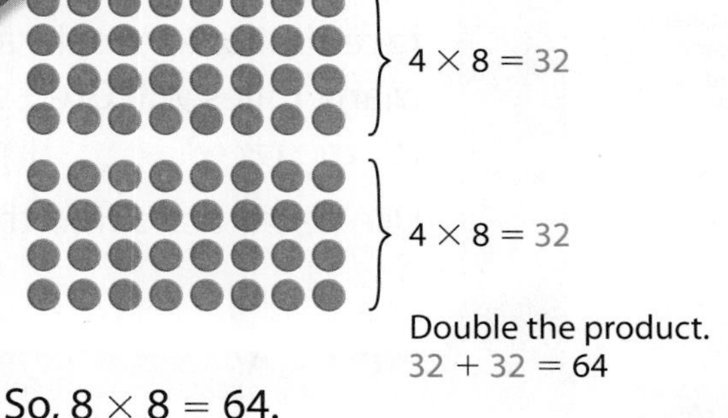

Double the product.
$32 + 32 = 64$

So, $8 \times 8 = 64$.
There are 64 bowls in all.

Problem Solving

For **28–30**, find the total number of tiles.

28. Mischa bought 8 boxes of orange tiles.

29. Aaron bought 6 boxes of yellow tiles.

30. Liz bought 7 boxes of green tiles.

8 tiles in each box

9 tiles in each box

7 tiles in each box

31. Writing to Explain Sophi says, "To find 8×8, I can find 2×8 and double it." Do you agree? Explain.

For **32** and **33**, use the table at the right.

32. Algebra The total amount of money Nate spent at the clothing sale is $(2 \times \$9) + \$42$. What did he buy?

Data

Clothing Sale	
Shirt	$23
Belt	$9
Sweater	$38
Pair of jeans	$42

33. Willa bought a shirt and a sweater. She had $14 left. How much money did she start with?

34. Ms. Vero had boxes of crayons in a closet. Each box had 8 crayons in it. If Ms. Vero counted the crayons in groups of 8, which list shows the numbers she would have named?

A 8, 16, 28, 32, 40, 48

B 8, 14, 18, 24, 32, 40

C 16, 20, 24, 28, 32, 36

D 8, 16, 24, 32, 40, 48

35. During the California Gold Rush, miners sometimes paid $10 for a glass of water. What was the total cost if 8 miners each bought one glass of water?

Lesson
6-5

Understand It!
Patterns can be used to remember multiplication facts for 11 and 12.

11 and 12 as Factors

What are the patterns in multiples of 11 and 12?

Greg's training schedule is for a race that is 11 weeks away. How many miles will Greg swim to train for the race?

Use patterns to find the product 8×11.

Data

Weekly Schedule

Activity	Miles
Swimming	8 miles
Running	7 miles
Biking	9 miles

Another Example What are the patterns in multiples of 12?

Data

$0 \times 12 = 0$	$7 \times 12 =$
$1 \times 12 = 12$	$8 \times 12 =$
$2 \times 12 = 24$	$9 \times 12 =$
$3 \times 12 = 36$	$10 \times 12 =$
$4 \times 12 = 48$	$11 \times 12 =$
$5 \times 12 = 60$	$12 \times 12 =$
$6 \times 12 = 72$	

To multiply any factor by 12, first multiply that factor by 10. Then multiply that factor by 2 and add the two products.

Example: $3 \times 12 = (3 \times 10) + (3 \times 2)$

Find: 7×12.

$7 \times 10 = 70$ and $7 \times 2 = 14$

$70 + 14 = 84$

So, $7 \times 12 = 84$.

Guided Practice*

Do you know HOW?

Use patterns to find each product.

1. 8×12 **2.** 9×12

3. 9×11 **4.** 11×11

Do you UNDERSTAND?

5. **Writing to Explain** How can you use a pattern to find 12×11?

6. How many miles will Greg bike in 12 weeks?

Independent Practice

Use patterns to find each product.

7. 7×11 **8.** 11×9 **9.** 6×11 **10.** 12×11 **11.** 8×11

12. 11×12 **13.** 10×12 **14.** 11×5 **15.** 10×11 **16.** 12×12

*For another example, see Set D on page 161.

0 × 11 = 0	6 × 11 = 66
1 × 11 = 11	7 × 11 = 77
2 × 11 = 22	8 × 11 =
3 × 11 = 33	9 × 11 =
4 × 11 = 44	10 × 11 =
5 × 11 = 55	11 × 11 =

Look at the patterns in the table.

$2 \times 11 = 20 + 2$ (20 = 2×10)

$3 \times 11 = 30 + 3$ (30 = 3×10)

To multiply any factor by 11, first multiply that factor by 10. Then add that factor to the product.

$8 \times 10 = 80 \rightarrow 80 + 8 = 88 \rightarrow 8 \times 11 = 88$

Greg will swim 88 miles.

Problem Solving

Use the table at the right for **17** and **18**. It shows the food that was bought for 96 third graders for a school picnic.

Food Item	Number of Packages	Number in Each Package
Hot Dogs	8	12
Rolls	12	9
Juice Boxes	12	11

17. Find the total number of each item bought.

a Hot dogs

b Rolls

c Juice boxes

18. How many extra juice boxes were bought?

19. Writing to Explain Look at the table at the top of page 150. Greg multiplied 2 × 11 to find how many more miles he biked than he ran in 11 weeks. Does that make sense? Why or why not?

20. Strategy Focus Solve. Use the strategy Draw a Picture.

Mai had 3 packs of pens. Each pack had 11 pens. She gave 5 pens to Ervin. How many pens did she have left?

21. Number Sense Raul has only dimes in his pocket. Could he have exactly 45 cents? Explain.

22. Algebra Which symbol makes the number sentence true?

8 ☐ 5 = 40

A + **B** − **C** × **D** ÷

23. Suppose a worker building one of the first railroads hammered 10 spikes into each railroad tie. How many spikes did he need for 7 ties?

Lesson

6-6

Understand It!
To multiply 3 numbers, start with any 2 factors.

Multiplying with 3 Factors

How can you multiply 3 numbers?

Drew is joining 3 sections of a quilt. Each section has 2 rows with 4 squares in each row. How many squares in all are in these 3 sections?

Find $3 \times 2 \times 4$.

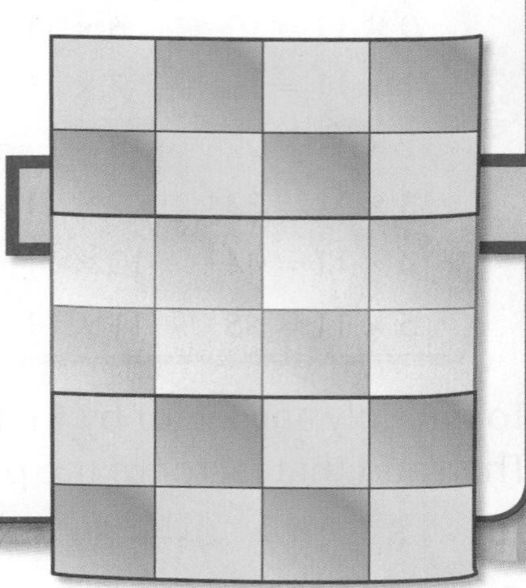

Guided Practice*

Do you know HOW?

In **1–6**, multiply. You may use objects or draw a picture to help.

1. $2 \times 4 \times 2$

2. $3 \times 4 \times 3$

3. $2 \times 2 \times 3$

4. $2 \times 5 \times 2$

5. $3 \times 2 \times 4$

6. $2 \times 6 \times 2$

Do you UNDERSTAND?

7. In the example above, if you find 3×4 first, do you get the same product? Explain.

8. Sara has 4 quilt pieces. Each piece has 3 rows with 3 squares in each row. How many squares are in Sara's quilt pieces?

Independent Practice

In **9–16**, find the product. You may draw a picture to help.

9. $2 \times 3 \times 2$

10. $5 \times 2 \times 2$

11. $3 \times 6 \times 1$

12. $3 \times 3 \times 2$

13. $2 \times 2 \times 2$

14. $2 \times 3 \times 4$

15. $3 \times 3 \times 3$

16. $6 \times 2 \times 2$

In **17–22**, write the missing number.

17. $3 \times (2 \times 5) = 30$, so $(3 \times 2) \times 5 = \square$

18. $5 \times (7 \times 2) = (7 \times 2) \times \square$

19. $4 \times (2 \times 2) = 16$, so $(4 \times 2) \times 2 = \square$

20. $8 \times (3 \times 6) = (8 \times 3) \times \square$

21. $(7 \times 3) \times 4 = \square \times (3 \times 4)$

22. $5 \times (2 \times 9) = (5 \times \square) \times 9$

DIGITAL Animated Glossary **www.pearsonsuccessnet.com**

**For another example, see Set E on page 161.*

One Way

Find 3×2 first.

$(3 \times 2) \times 4$

$6 \quad \times 4 = 24$

6 rows, 4 squares in each row

There are 24 squares in all.

Another Way

Find 2×4 first.

$3 \times (2 \times 4)$

$3 \times \quad 8 = 24$ 3 sections, 8 squares in each section

There are 24 squares in Drew's quilt.

The Associative (Grouping) Property of Multiplication says that you can change the grouping of the factors and the product will be the same.

Problem Solving

For **23–25**, find the total number of eggs.

23. There are 8 mockingbird nests at a park. Each nest has 5 eggs.

24. At another park, there are 3 mockingbird nests with 4 eggs in each nest, and 2 more nests with 3 eggs in each.

25. **Estimation** About how many eggs would you find in 10 nests?

26. **Reasonableness** Anita says the product of $5 \times 2 \times 3$ is less than 20. Do you agree? Explain.

For **27** and **28**, use the table at the right.

27. Ellis bought 3 packs of baseball cards and 2 packs of basketball cards. How many cards did he buy in all?

28. Mandy bought 1 pack of each of the four kinds of cards. What is the total number of cards she bought?

Sports Card Sale (Data)

Kind of Cards	Number of Cards in Each Pack
Baseball	8
Basketball	5
Football	7
Hockey	6

29. Which number makes this number sentence true?

$4 \times (3 \times 2) = (4 \times \square) \times 2$

A 12 **B** 7 **C** 3 **D** 2

Lesson
6-7

Understand It!
Word problems tell what is known and what needs to be figured out.

Problem Solving

Multiple-Step Problems

Some word problems have hidden questions that need to be answered before you can solve the problem.

Keisha bought 2 yards of felt to make some puppets. Tanya bought 6 yards of felt. The felt cost \$3 a yard. How much did the two girls spend on felt?

Another Example

Keisha plans to make 3 puppets. Tanya will make 3 times as many puppets as Keisha. Each puppet needs 2 buttons for its eyes. How many buttons will Tanya need?

Find and solve the hidden question.

How many puppets will Tanya make?

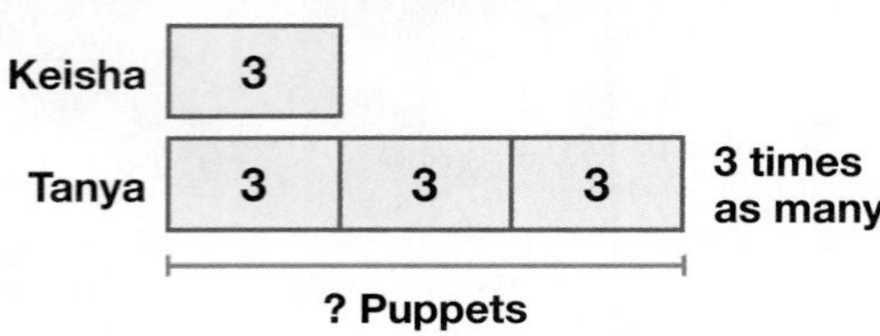

3×3 puppets $= 9$ puppets

Tanya will make 9 puppets.

Use the answer to the hidden question to solve the problem.

How many buttons will Tanya need?

? Buttons in all

2	2	2	2	2	2	2	2	2

Buttons for each puppet

9×2 buttons $= 18$ buttons

Tanya will need 18 buttons.

Explain It

1. Philip wrote $3 + 3 + 3 = \square$ instead of $3 \times 3 = \square$ for the diagram for the hidden question. Is his number sentence correct? Why or why not?

2. **Number Sense** What number sentences could you write to find how many buttons both girls need? Explain your thinking.

Find and solve the hidden question.

How much felt did the girls buy in all?

? Yards in all	
2 yards	6 yards

2 yards + 6 yards = 8 yards

The girls bought 8 yards of felt.

Use the answer to the hidden question to solve the problem.

How much did the girls spend in all?

? Total cost							
$3	$3	$3	$3	$3	$3	$3	$3

$8 \times \$3 = \$24$

The two girls spent $24 on felt.

Guided Practice*

Do you know HOW?

1. Keisha bought glue for $3, sequins for $6, and lace for $4 to decorate her puppets. She paid for these items with a $20 bill. How much change should she get?

The hidden question is "What is the total cost of the three items?"

Do you UNDERSTAND?

2. Describe another way to solve the problem above about buying felt.

3. **Write a Problem** Write a problem that has a hidden question. Then solve your problem.

Independent Practice

4. The library has 4 videos and some books about dinosaurs. There are 5 times as many books as videos. After 3 of the books were checked out, how many were left? The diagram below helps you answer the hidden question. Draw a diagram and solve the problem.

Videos	4					
Books	4	4	4	4	4	5 times as many
	? Books					

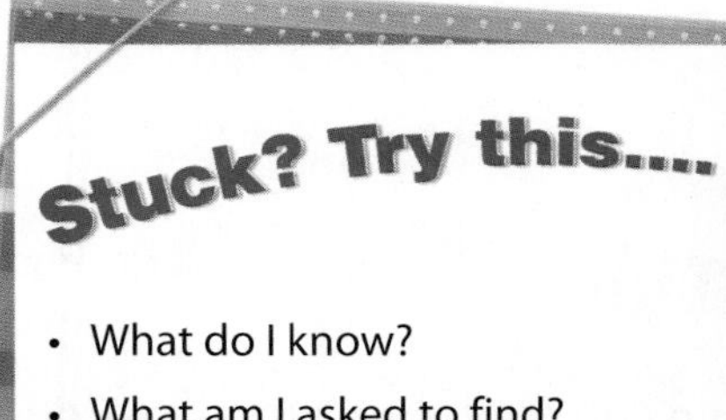

- What do I know?
- What am I asked to find?
- What diagram can I use to help understand the problem?
- Can I use addition, subtraction, multiplication, or division?
- Is all of my work correct?
- Did I answer the right question?
- Is my answer reasonable?

For another example, see Set F on page 161.

Independent Practice

Use the pictures for **5–8**.

5. Craig bought 2 bags of oranges. After he ate 3 of the oranges, how many oranges were left?

First find how many oranges Craig bought.

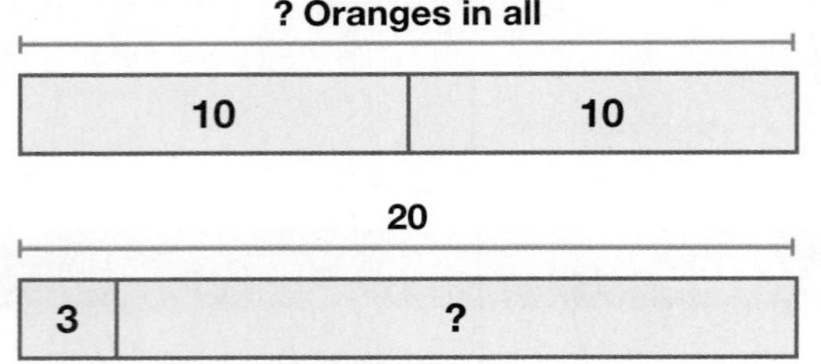

6. Delia bought 2 bags of lemons and 3 bags of apples. How much did she spend on fruit?

7. Mrs. Evans bought 2 bags of oranges and 2 bags of lemons. How many pieces of fruit did she buy?

8. Mr. Day bought a bag each of apples, oranges, and lemons. He paid with a $20 bill. What change should he get?

9. **Writing to Explain** Which costs more, 30 oranges or 30 lemons? How much more? Explain how you found your answer.

Think About the Process

10. Al had $38. He spent $4 on an action figure and $10 on a board game. Which number sentence shows how much money Al has left?

A $38 + $4 + $10 = ▢

B $38 − ($4 + $10) = ▢

C $38 − $4 = ▢

D 38 + $10 = ▢

11. Jose has 4 action figures. His brother has 3 times as many action figures. Which number sentence shows how many figures the boys have in all?

A $4 + 3 =$ ▢

B $4 \times 3 =$ ▢

C $4 - 3 =$ ▢

D $4 + (3 \times 4) =$ ▢

Using Known Facts

Use eTools

Counters

Use known facts to find 4×6 and 6×7.

Step 1 Go to the Counters eTool. Select the two-part workspace. Use 2×6 to find 4×6. Select a counter. Show two rows of 6 counters in the left side. Look at the odometer. You see that $2 \times 6 = 12$. Show the same rows on the right side. There are 4 rows of 6 counters in all. $4 \times 6 = 24$, and $12 + 12 = 24$.

Step 2 Use the broom tool to clear one side of the workspace. Select the other side and use the broom tool again, to clear it. Use 5×7 and 1×7 to find 6×7. Show 5 rows of 7 counters on one side of the workspace. Look at the odometer to find that $5 \times 7 = 35$. Show 1 row of 7 counters on the other side. There are 6 rows of 7 counters in all. $6 \times 7 = 42$, and $35 + 7 = 42$.

Practice

Use the Counters eTool and known facts to find each product. Explain how you found the product.

1. 4×9

2. 8×8

3. 6×8

4. 7×7

Test

1. Last summer, Martin walked the 8-mile Wolf Mountain Trail 7 times. How many total miles did he walk on the trail? (6-3)

A 15

B 54

C 56

D 78

2. There are 3 periods in a hockey game. How many periods are there in 5 hockey games? (6-1)

A 8

B 12

C 15

D 18

3. Which shows a way to find 4×6? (6-2)

A $4 + 6$

B $12 + 12$

C $6 + 6 + 6$

D $12 + 2$

4. Jon bought 3 packages of invitations. Each package had 8 invitations. He sent out 20 invitations. Which shows one way to find how many are left? (6-7)

A Multiply 3 by 8 and then subtract 20.

B Multiply 3 by 20 and then subtract 8.

C Multiply 5 by 8 and then add 20.

D Multiply 3 by 8 and then add 20.

5. If you count the muffins below in groups of 6, which list shows numbers you would name? (6-3)

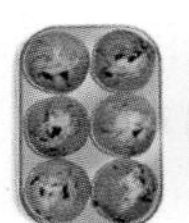   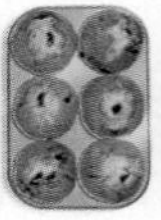 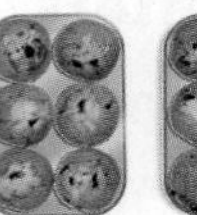 

A 6, 12, 16, 24

B 6, 12, 16, 22

C 12, 18, 24, 32

D 12, 18, 24, 30

6. Sven feeds his fish 2 food pellets 3 times a day. How many pellets does he feed them in 7 days? (6-6)

A 13

B 14

C 21

D 42

$2 \times 3 = 6$
$6 \times 7 = 42$

7. What number makes the number sentence true? (6-6)

$6 \times (9 \times 2) = (6 \times 9) \times \square$

A 2

B 6

C 9

D 54

8. The 3rd graders formed 11 groups with 10 in each group. How many 3rd graders were there in all? (6-5)

A 111

B 110

C 101

D 100

9. Mr. Hernandez bought 8 bags of limes. Each bag had 4 limes. How many limes did he buy? (6-2)

A 32

B 28

C 24

D 12

10. Mrs. Chavez put new light switch covers in her house. She put in 8 plastic covers and 7 wooden covers. Each cover uses 2 screws. How many screws did she use? (6-7)

A 14

B 15

C 16

D 30

8 + 7 = 15
15 × 2 = 30

11. A marching band was in a parade. The band members marched in 8 rows. There were 6 band members in each row. Which shows a way to find 8×6? (6-4)

A $8 + 6$

B $24 + 24 + 24$

C $12 + 12 + 12 + 12$

D $16 + 16 + 16 + 16$

12. The Cougars basketball team has 8 players. The coach ordered 3 pairs of socks for each player. How many pairs did he order? (6-4)

A 16

B 24

C 32

D 48

13. Which of these best describes all the numbers on the mileage sign? (6-1)

Center City	9 mi
Springfield	15 mi
Lakewood	30 mi
Newton	33 mi

A They are all greater than 18.

B They are all multiples of 5.

C They are all multiples of 3.

D They are all less than 30.

14. Which is a way to find 7×6? (6-3)

A $35 + 14$

B $30 + 12$

C $35 + 6$

D $30 + 14$

15. Mrs. Kent drives 12 miles 6 times a week for her part-time job. How many miles is this in all? (6-5)

A 18 miles

B 36 miles

C 48 miles

D 72 miles

Reteaching

Set A, pages 140–141

Find 3×7.

You can break an array into facts you know.

$3 \times 7 = 3$ groups of 7
That is 2 sevens plus 1 more seven.

$2 \times 7 = 14$
$1 \times 7 = 7$
$14 + 7 = 21$

So, $3 \times 7 = 21$.

Remember that you can use facts you already know to help you multiply.

Find the product.

1. 3×8
2. 6×3
3. 4×3
4. 3×3
5. 3×5
6. 10×3

Set B, pages 142–143

Find 4×7.

Think of a 2s fact, then double the product.

$4 \times 7 = 4$ groups of 7.

$2 \times 7 = 14$
$2 \times 7 = 14$
$14 + 14 = 28$

So, $4 \times 7 = 28$.

Remember that you can draw arrays to solve multiplication facts.

Find the product.

1. 4×10
2. 3×4
3. 6×4
4. 8×4
5. 4×2
6. 9×4

Set C, pages 144–146, 148–149

Find 7×6.

$5 + 2 = 7$, so use 5s facts and 2s facts to multiply with 7.

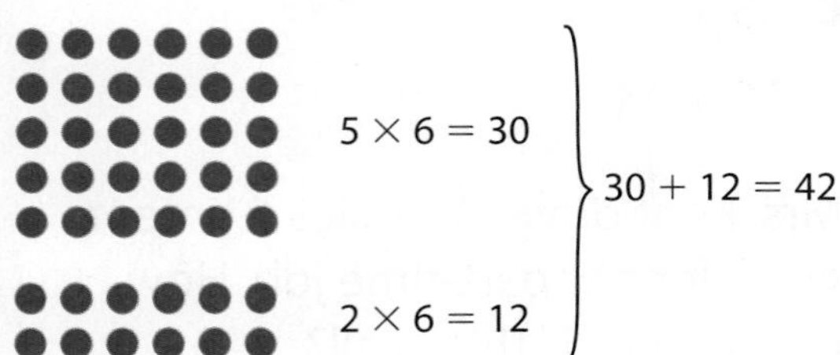

So, $7 \times 6 = 42$.

To find 8×6, you can double a 4s fact.
Find 4×6. Then double the product.
$4 \times 6 = 24$, and $24 + 24 = 48$.
So, $8 \times 6 = 48$.

Remember that you can use known facts to multiply with 6, 7 and 8.

Find the product.

1. 7×9
2. 8×7
3. 6×9
4. 3×6
5. 7×4
6. 8×6
7. 8×7
8. 6×2
9. 3×8

Set D, pages 150–151

Find 5×12. Use a pattern.

Multiply the factor that is not 12 by 10.
$5 \times 10 = 50$

Then multiply the same factor by 2.
$5 \times 2 = 10$

Then add the two products.
$50 + 10 = 60$

$5 \times 12 = 60$

Remember that you can use a 10s fact plus another fact to help.

Use patterns to find each product.

1. 11×4
12×4

2. 11×7
12×7

3. 6×12

4. 11×12

Set E, pages 152–153

Find $4 \times 5 \times 2$.

The Associative Property of Multiplication says that you can change the grouping of the factors, and the product will be the same.

One Way

$(4 \times 5) \times 2$
↓
$20 \quad \times 2 = 40$

Another Way

$4 \times (5 \times 2)$
↓
$4 \times \quad 10 = 40$

So, $4 \times 5 \times 2 = 40$.

Remember you may draw a picture to help you multiply 3 factors.

Find the product.

1. $3 \times 2 \times 5$

2. $5 \times 3 \times 4$

3. $1 \times 9 \times 8$

4. $7 \times 2 \times 5$

5. $6 \times 3 \times 4$

6. $4 \times 3 \times 2$

Set F, pages 154–156

Some problems have hidden questions.

Jeff charged \$10 to wash a car and \$7 to walk a dog. How much money did Jeff earn for washing 6 cars and walking 1 dog?

Find and solve the hidden question.
How much money did Jeff earn washing 6 cars?
$6 \times \$10 = \$60$
Then solve the problem.
How much money did Jeff earn in all?
$\$60 + \$7 = \$67$
Jeff earned \$67.

Remember to carefully read the order in which things happen.

1. At the fair, Bonnie wants to get 2 rings and 1 pen. Each ring costs 8 tickets, and each pen costs 6 tickets. How many tickets does she need in all?

2. Mrs. Green bought 2 bags of apples. Each bag had 10 apples. She used 4 apples. How many apples did she have left?

Topic 7

Division Meanings

1 How many strings are on the guitars used by Tejano musicians? You will find out in Lesson 7-2.

2 These three astronauts orbited the Moon on Apollo 11. How many astronauts in all orbited the Moon on Apollo space missions? You will find out in Lesson 7-1.

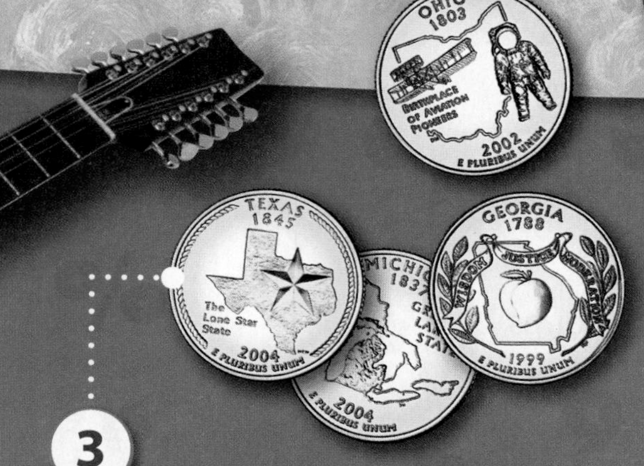

3 In 1999, the United States Mint began circulating new state quarters. How many states have new quarters every year? You will find out in Lesson 7-3.

4 About how many baseballs are used during one inning of a major league game? You will find out in Lesson 7-4.

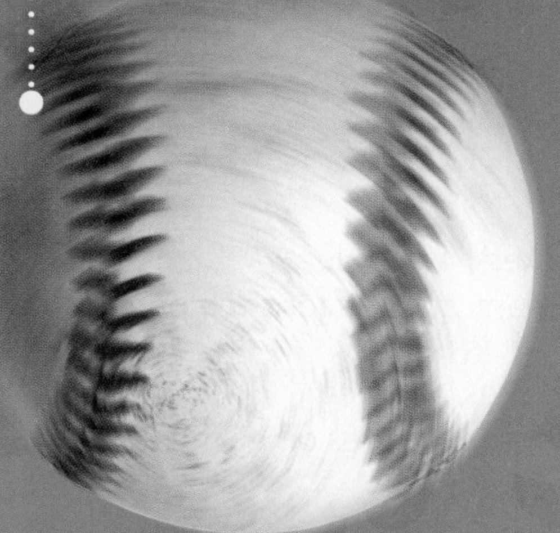

Review What You Know!

Vocabulary

Choose the best term from the box.

- array
- difference
- factor
- product

1. The answer in multiplication is the _?_.

2. In $3 \times 5 = 15$, 5 is a(n) _?_.

3. When objects are placed in equal rows they form a(n) _?_.

Subtraction

Subtract.

4. $21 - 7$
$14 - 7$
$7 - 7$

5. $15 - 5$
$10 - 5$
$5 - 5$

6. $27 - 9$
$18 - 9$
$9 - 9$

Multiplication Facts

7. 5×4 **8.** 7×3 **9.** 3×8

10. 9×2 **11.** 6×5 **12.** 4×7

13. 6×7 **14.** 8×4 **15.** 5×9

Equal Groups

16. Writing to Explain The picture has 9 counters. Describe why this picture doesn't show equal groups. Then show how to change the drawing so it does show equal groups.

Lesson
7-1

Division as Sharing

Hands-On
counters

Understand It!
One way to think of division is as sharing equally.

How many are in each group?

Three friends have 12 toys to share equally. How many toys will each person get?

Think of putting 12 toys into 3 equal groups.

Division is an operation that is used to find how many equal groups or how many are in each group.

Guided Practice*

Do you know HOW?

Use counters or draw a picture to solve.

1. 15 bananas, 3 boxes
   How many bananas in each box?

2. 16 plants, 4 pots
   How many plants in each pot?

Do you UNDERSTAND?

3. Copy and complete the division sentence. Use the picture to help.

   18
?	?	?

   $18 \div 3 = \square$

4. Can 12 grapes be shared equally among 5 children? Explain.

Independent Practice

Use counters or draw a picture to solve.

5. 18 marbles, 6 sacks
   How many marbles in each sack?

6. 36 stickers, 4 people
   How many stickers for each person?

7. 16 crayons, 2 people
   How many crayons for each person?

8. 12 pictures, 4 pages
   How many pictures on each page?

9. 24 bottles, 4 cases
   How many bottles in each case?

10. 27 CDs, 9 packages
    How many CDs in each package?

Complete each division sentence.

11. 12
?	?

    $12 \div 2 = \square$

12. 16
?	?	?	?	?	?	?	?

    $16 \div 8 = \square$

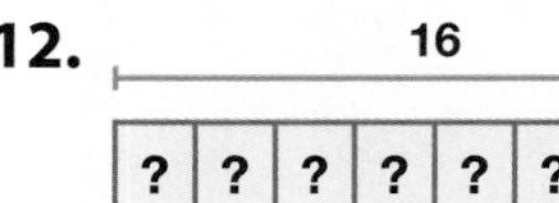
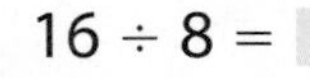
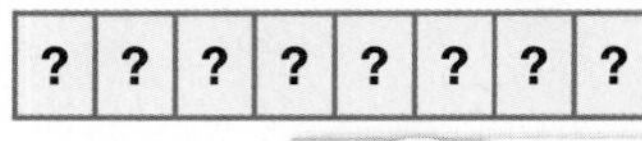
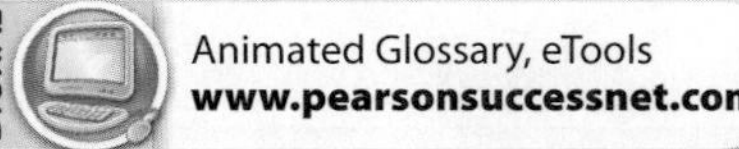

*For another example, see Set A on page 180.

What You Think

Put one at a time in each group.

When all the toys are grouped, there will be 4 in each group.

What You Write

You can write a division sentence to find the number in each group.

12	÷	3	=	4
↑		↑		↑
Total		Number of equal groups		Number in each group

Each person will get 4 toys.

Problem Solving

13. **Writing to Explain** Jim is putting 18 pens into equal groups. He says that there will be more pens in each of 2 equal groups than in each of 3 equal groups. Is he correct? Explain.

14. Joy has 12 shells. She gives 2 to her mom. Then she and her sister share the rest equally. How many shells does Joy get? How many shells does her sister get?

15. Three astronauts were on each *Apollo* spacecraft. How many astronauts in all were on the nine *Apollo* spacecraft that orbited the Moon?

16. Max has the stickers shown. He wants to put an equal number of stickers on each of 2 posters. Which number sentence shows how to find the number of stickers Max should put on each poster?

A $14 + 2 = \square$

B $14 \times 2 = \square$

C $14 - 2 = \square$

D $14 \div 2 = \square$

17. The flag bearers march in 9 rows with 5 people in each row. Each person is carrying one flag. Write a number sentence to show how many flags there are.

Lesson
7-2

Understand It!
Some division problems show equal groups with some left over.

Understanding Remainders

counters

How many are left over?

Luisa is packing soccer balls into crates. Each crate will hold 5 soccer balls. How many crates will she fill? Are any soccer balls left?

Choose an Operation You want to separate 23 into equal groups of 5, so you can divide.

Another Example What do you do with the remainder?

Sometimes a problem asks for the amount in the remainder. Sometimes a problem asks about the number of groups.

Ned has 27 soccer cards to put in an album. He can put 6 cards on each page.

Example A

How many pages can Ned fill?

Find how many groups of 6 there will be.

Ned can fill 4 pages.

Example B

How many pages will Ned work on?

Find how many groups are filled or started.

Ned will work on 5 pages.

Example C

How many cards will Ned put on the 5th page?

Find how many are left after 4 pages are filled.

Ned will put 3 cards on the 5th page.

Explain It

1. Why are the answers to the examples different?
2. Janie has 34 photos to put in an album. She can put 4 photos on each page. How many photos will be on the 9th page?

Animated Glossary, eTools
www.pearsonsuccessnet.com

Step 1

Show the total number of items.

Use counters to show 23.

Step 2

Divide them into equal groups.

Make equal groups with 5 counters in each group.

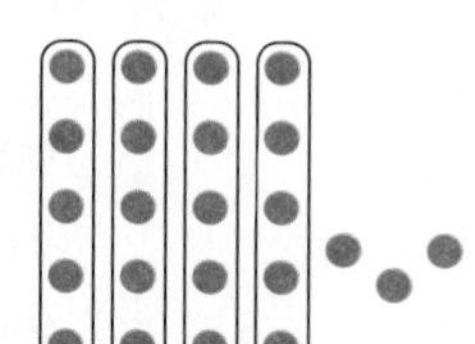

Step 3

Write the number of equal groups and the number left over.

23 ÷ 5 = 4 with 3 left over

Luisa will fill 4 crates. There will be 3 soccer balls left over.

The part that is left over when we divide is called the remainder.

Guided Practice*

Do you know HOW?

Use counters or draw a picture to find the number of groups and the number left over.

1. 17 oranges, 3 oranges in each box

17 ÷ 3 = ▢ with ▢ left over

2. 9 ÷ 2 = ▢ with ▢ left over

Do you UNDERSTAND?

3. In the example above, how do you find the remainder?

4. Dave is packing 23 sweaters into boxes. Each box will hold 3 sweaters. How many boxes will he fill? How many sweaters will be left over?

Independent Practice

For **5–10**, find the number of groups and the number left over. Use counters or draw a picture to help.

5. 18 jars, 4 jars in each box
18 ÷ 4 = ▢ with ▢ left over

6. 22 shirts, 6 shirts in each box
22 ÷ 6 = ▢ with ▢ left over

7. 27 books, 7 books in each box
27 ÷ 7 = ▢ with ▢ left over

8. 13 ÷ 2 = ▢ with ▢ left

9. 31 ÷ 8 = ▢ with ▢ left

10. 32 ÷ 9 = ▢ with ▢ left

11. 7 football cards, 3 cards on each page
How many pages can Alex complete?

12. 11 baseball cards, 4 cards on each page
How many cards are on the 3rd page?

13. 34 stickers, 5 stickers on each page
How many pages will have some stickers?

For another example, see Set B on page 180.

Problem Solving

Use the table for **14–16**.

14. Samuel has 45 prize tickets. How many marbles can he get?

15. Inez got 3 rings and 2 stickers. How many tickets did she use?

16. Milt had 28 prize tickets. He traded tickets for 3 yo-yos. How many prize tickets does he have left?

Data

Trade Tickets for Prizes!

Prize	Number of Tickets
Yo-yo	8 tickets
Ring	9 tickets
Marble	7 tickets
Sticker	4 tickets

17. **Strategy Focus** Solve. Use the Draw a Picture strategy.

Keiko makes necklaces like the one in the picture on the right. She has 19 blue beads and 13 red beads.

a How many more blue beads than red beads does Keiko have?

b How many necklaces can she make?

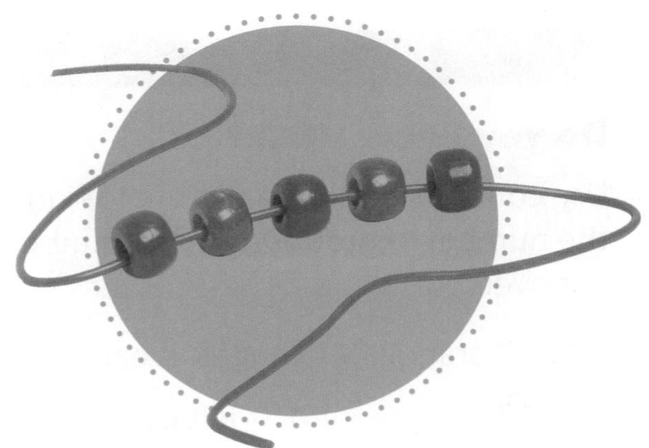

18. There are 38 students going to a museum. Each van can hold 8 students. How many vans will be needed?

19. Jack is making muffins. He will use 5 raisins to decorate each muffin. If he has 21 raisins, how many muffins can he decorate?

20. Jada bought a bag of 8 apples. She and her 3 sisters will share the apples equally. How many apples will each person get? Will there be any apples left over? If so, how many?

21. How many strings in all are used to make 4 guitars like the ones in the picture below?

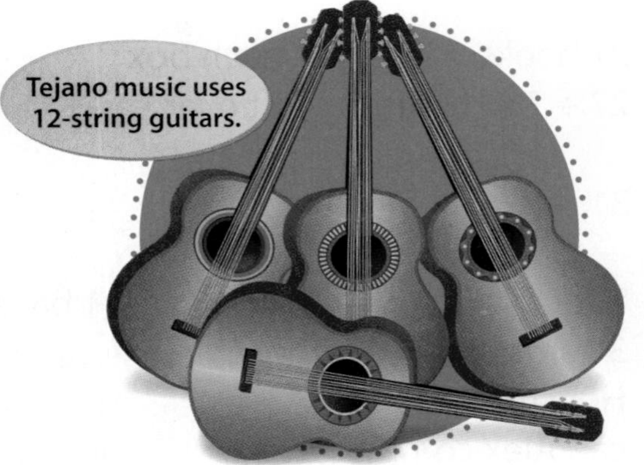

22. There are 39 children at a park. They want to make teams with 9 children on each team. How many teams can they make?

A 4 **C** 9

B 5 **D** 28

Mixed Problem Solving

Animals get special features, called inherited traits, from their parents. Use the table on the right to answer the questions.

Data

Some Traits of Animals

Kind of Animal	Inherited Trait
Birds	2 eyes, 2 legs, 2 wings
Fish	2 eyes
Insects	2 antennas, 6 legs, 3 body parts
Apes	2 hands, 5 fingers on each hand, 2 legs, 5 toes on each foot, 2 eyes

1. A mother and her two babies are on a tree branch. They have six wings in all. Which kind of animal listed in the table could they be?

2. Two adult apes and two baby apes are near the water. How many fingers do the apes have in all?

3. One of these animals is on a tree branch. It has six legs in all. Which kind of animal listed in the table could it be?

4. Which has more legs—two birds or one insect? How many more?

5. Look at the table below.

Data

Kind of Animal	Number of Body Parts	Number of Legs
Insect	3	6
Spider	2	8

Danny saw three of the same kind of animal on the sidewalk. He counted six body parts in all. Did Danny see 3 spiders or 3 insects?

6. **Strategy Focus** Solve. Use the strategy Draw a Picture.

Trini had 31 baby fish and 5 adult fish in a fish tank. She put 18 of the baby fish in another tank, and all of the adult fish in a third tank. How many baby fish are left in the first tank? Check if your answer is reasonable.

Lesson
7-3

Understand It!
One way to think of division is as repeated subtraction.

Division as Repeated Subtraction

Hands-On
counters

How many equal groups?

June has 10 strawberries to serve to her guests. If each guest eats 2 strawberries, how many guests can June serve?

Guided Practice*

Do you know HOW?

Use counters or draw a picture to solve.

1. 16 gloves
2 gloves in each pair
How many pairs?

2. 15 tennis balls
3 balls in each can
How many cans?

Do you UNDERSTAND?

3. Suppose June had 12 strawberries and each guest ate 2 strawberries. How many guests could she serve? Use counters or draw a picture to solve.

4. **Number Sense** Show how you can use repeated subtraction to find how many groups of 4 there are in 20. Then write the division sentence for the problem.

Independent Practice

Use counters or draw a picture to solve.

5. 12 wheels
4 wheels on each wagon
How many wagons?

6. 30 markers
5 markers in each package
How many packages?

7. 8 apples
4 apples in each bag
How many bags?

8. 18 pencils
2 pencils on each desk
How many desks?

*For another example, see Set A on page 180.

One Way

You can use repeated subtraction to find how many groups of 2 are in 10.

$10 - 2 = 8$
$8 - 2 = 6$
$6 - 2 = 4$
$4 - 2 = 2$
$2 - 2 = 0$

You can subtract 2, five times. There are five groups of 2 in 10.

There are no strawberries left.

June can serve 5 guests.

Another Way

You can write a division sentence to find the number of groups.

Write: $10 \div 2 = 5$

Read: Ten divided by 2 equals 5.

June can serve 5 guests.

Problem Solving

9. **Number Sense** Raymond has 16 model planes that he wants to display. Will he need more shelves if he puts 8 on a shelf or 4 on a shelf? Explain.

For **10–12**, match each problem to a picture or a repeated subtraction. Then write the division sentence to solve.

10. 24 books
6 in a box
How many boxes?

11. 24 books
3 in a box
How many boxes?

12. 24 books
8 in a box
How many boxes?

a

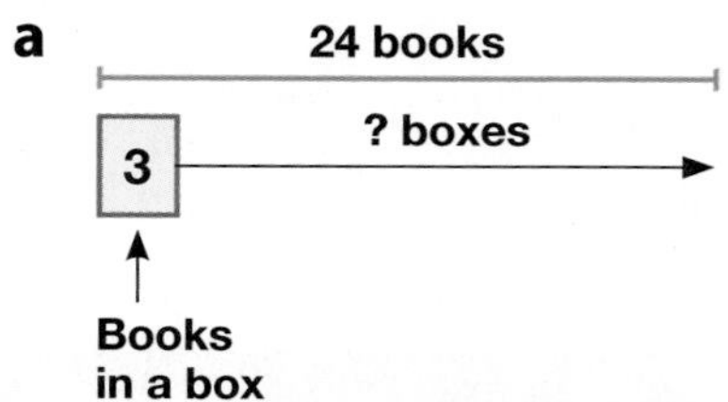

b

$24 - 8 = 16$
$16 - 8 = 8$
$8 - 8 = 0$

c

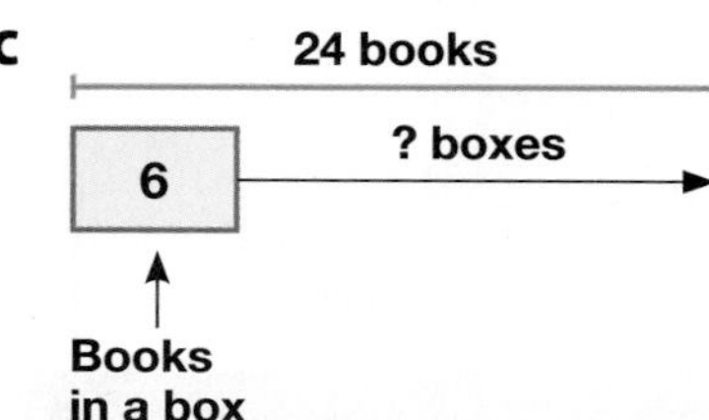

13. In 1999, the United States Mint began circulating state quarters. New quarters for 5 states are released each year. How many years will it take for quarters to be released for all 50 states? Write a number sentence to solve.

14. Toni has 6 tulips and 6 daisies. She wants to put 4 flowers in each vase. Which number sentence shows how many vases she needs?

A $12 + 4 = 16$ **B** $12 - 4 = 8$ **C** $6 \times 4 = 24$ **D** $12 \div 4 = 3$

Lesson

7-4

Understand It!
Division can be used to find the number in each group or the number of equal groups.

Writing Division Stories

Hands-On
counters

What is the main idea of a division story?

Mrs. White asked her students to write a division story for $15 \div 3 = \square$.

Mike and Kia decided to write stories about putting roses in vases.

Guided Practice*

Do you know HOW?

Write a division story for each number sentence. Then use counters or draw a picture to solve.

1. $8 \div 4 = \square$

2. $10 \div 2 = \square$

3. $20 \div 5 = \square$

4. $14 \div 7 = \square$

Do you UNDERSTAND?

5. How are Mike's and Kia's stories alike? How are the two stories different?

6. **Writing to Explain** When you write a division story, what two pieces of information do you need to include? What kind of information do you ask for?

Independent Practice

Write a division story for each number sentence. Then use counters or draw a picture to solve.

7. $18 \div 3 = \square$ **8.** $25 \div 5 = \square$ **9.** $16 \div 4 = \square$ **10.** $30 \div 6 = \square$

11. **Number Sense** Choose two of the stories you wrote for the exercises above. For each, tell whether you found the number in each group or the number of equal groups.

*For another example, see Set C on page 181.

Mike's Story

I have 15 roses. I want an equal number of roses in each of 3 vases. How many roses should I put in each vase?

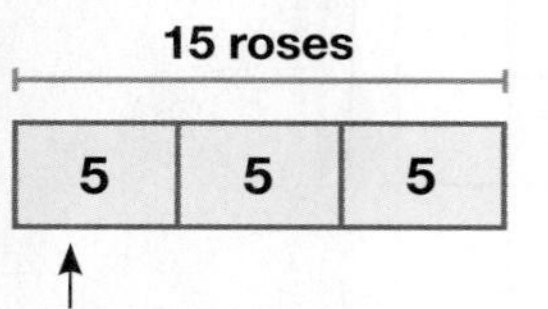

Main idea: How many are in each group?

$15 \div 3 = 5$

I should put 5 roses in each vase.

Kia's Story

I have 15 roses to put into vases. I want to put 3 roses into each vase. How many vases will I need?

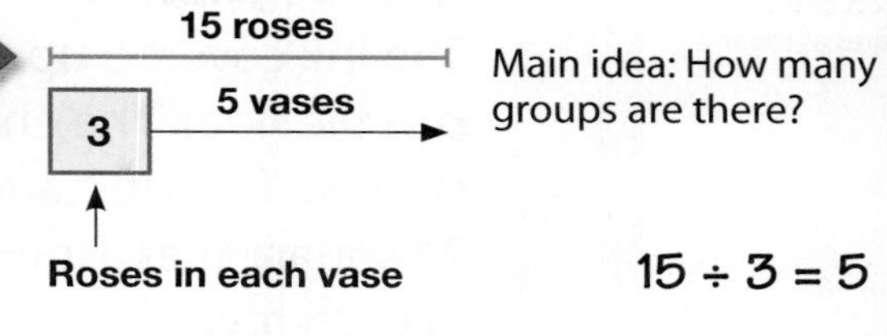

$15 \div 3 = 5$

I will need 5 vases.

Problem Solving

The table shows the number of players needed for each kind of sports team. Use the table for **12–15**.

There are 36 third graders at sports camp who want to play on different teams.

Data

Sports Team	Number
Baseball	9 players
Basketball	5 players
Doubles Tennis	2 players

12. If everyone wants to play baseball, how many teams will there be?

13. **Writing to Explain** Could everyone play basketball at the same time? Why or why not?

14. Twenty of the third graders went swimming. The rest of them played doubles tennis. How many doubles tennis teams were there?

15. Two baseball teams are playing a game. At the same time, two basketball teams are playing a game. The rest of the campers are playing tennis. How many campers are playing tennis?

16. Carmen rides her bike to school from 3 to 5 times a week. Which is a reasonable number of times Carmen will ride her bike in 4 weeks?

A More than 28

B From 12 to 20

C From 14 to 28

D Fewer than 12

17. In one inning, each baseball was used for 7 pitches. Write a number sentence that shows the total number of pitches thrown that inning.

4 baseballs are used each inning.

Lesson

7-5

Understand It!
Some problems can be solved by using objects or drawing pictures as models.

Problem Solving

Use Objects and Draw a Picture

Hands-On
square tiles
grid paper

Naomi spilled some ink on her paper. The ink covered up part of her picture of a tile floor. The entire floor was shaped like a rectangle covered by 24 square tiles. How many tiles were in each row?

Another Example How can drawing a picture help you solve a problem?

Some ink spilled and covered up part of a picture of a tile floor. The tile floor was shaped like a rectangle. There were 21 square tiles in the whole floor. How many tiles were in each row?

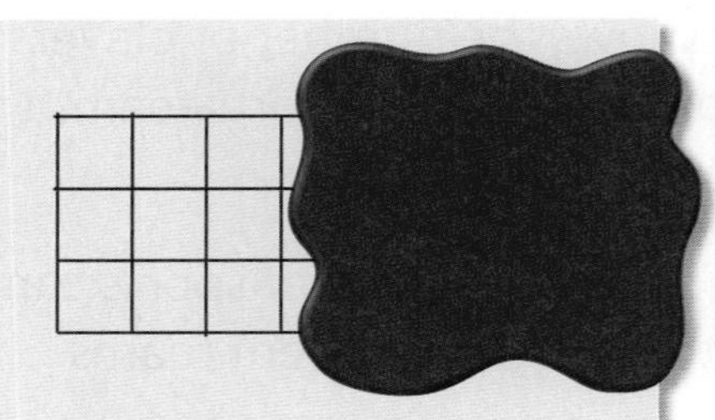

Plan

What strategy can I use?

I can draw a picture to show what I know.

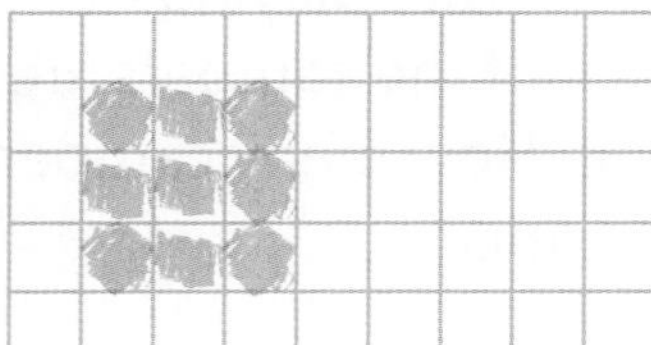

Solve

I can finish the picture to solve the problem.

There should be 21 squares in all.

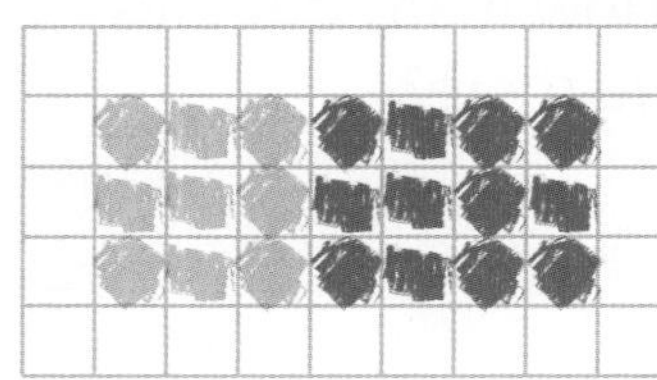

$7 + 7 + 7 = 21$
There were 7 tiles in each row.

Explain It

1. How do you know how many tiles to draw to finish the picture in the problem above?
2. Explain how to check the solution to this problem.

eTools
www.pearsonsuccessnet.com

Understand and Plan

What strategy can I use?

I can act it out by using objects to show what I know.

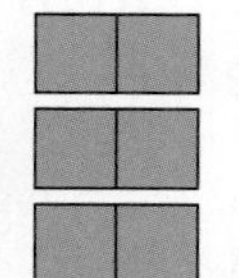

These tiles were not covered.

Solve

Now I will add tiles to each row to solve the problem. I'll add the same number of tiles to each row until there are 24 tiles in all.

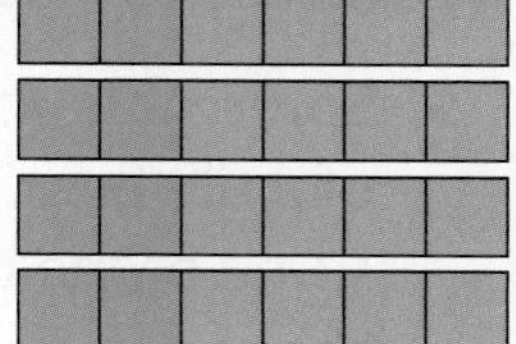

$6 + 6 + 6 + 6 = 24$

There were 6 tiles in each row.

Guided Practice*

Do you know HOW?

Solve. Use objects or draw a picture.

1. Paint covered part of a tile floor. The square floor had 16 tiles. How many tiles had paint on them?

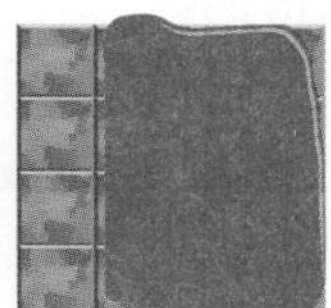

Do you UNDERSTAND?

2. What strategy did you use to find the number of tiles covered by paint in Exercise 1?

3. **Write a Problem** Write and solve a problem that you can solve by using objects or drawing a picture.

Independent Practice

Solve. Use objects or draw a picture.

4. Kim painted part of a tiled section of a wall. The whole section of tiles was shaped like a rectangle. There were 27 square tiles. How many tiles were in each row?

Stuck? Try this....

- What do I know?
- What am I asked to find?
- What diagram can I use to help understand the problem?
- Can I use addition, subtraction, multiplication, or division?
- Is all of my work correct?
- Did I answer the right question?
- Is my answer reasonable?

For another example, see Set D on page 181.

Independent Practice

5. Some glue spilled on Ana's drawing of a tile floor. The glue covered up some of the tiles. The tile floor was shaped like a rectangle. There were 20 square tiles in the whole floor. How many of the tiles had glue on them?

6. Joyce wants to make a design using the pattern of square tiles shown below. She wants to use this pattern four times. How many white tiles does she need?

7. Jeff's family took a car trip for a summer vacation. The family drove 362 miles to a national park. Then the family drove 174 miles to hike in the mountains. How many miles did the family drive all together?

? miles in all

362 miles	174 miles

8. Mari needs to make 215 programs in all for the class play. So far, she has made 89 programs. How many more programs does she still need to make?

215 programs in all

89 made	?

Think About the Process

9. Which of the following can be used to find how many days there are in 8 weeks?

A 8×7

B $8 \div 2$

C $8 + 7$

D $8 - 2$

10. Mrs. Clay bought 28 picture frames packed equally into 4 boxes. Which number sentence shows how to find the number of frames in each box?

A $28 - 4 = \square$

B $28 + 4 = \square$

C $28 \times 4 = \square$

D $28 \div 4 = \square$

Stop and Practice

Write each number in expanded form.

1. 7,409 **2.** 38,617 **3.** 926,054

Order the numbers from least to greatest.

4. 918 909 1,062 **5.** 934 1,121 1,119

6. 5,609 5,600 5,610 **7.** 8,736 8,832 8,734

Estimate and then find each sum. Check that your answer is reasonable.

8. $73 + 59$ **9.** $386 + 94$ **10.** $869 + 253$ **11.** $925 + 678$ **12.** $215 + 499$

Estimate and then find each difference. Check that your answer is reasonable.

13. $64 - 39$ **14.** $213 - 95$ **15.** $502 - 317$ **16.** $756 - 359$ **17.** $308 - 179$

Find each product.

18. 6×8 **19.** 10×1 **20.** $2 \times 2 \times 2$ **21.** 4×7 **22.** 9×0

Error Search Find each sum or difference that is not correct. Write it correctly and explain the error.

23. $95 + 18 = 103$ **24.** $207 + 536 = 743$ **25.** $630 - 472 = 228$ **26.** $849 + 205 = 1{,}044$ **27.** $534 - 427 = 107$

Number Sense

Estimating and Reasoning Write true or false for each statement. If it is false, explain why.

28. $67 + 45 < 100$ **29.** $8 \times 10 > 18$

30. $218 - 53 < 100$ **31.** $969 - 837 > 100$

32. $342 + 519 < 1{,}000$ **33.** $0 \times 9 > 1 \times 9$

Topic 7

Test

1. Martin has 12 pinecones. His birdfeeder design uses 3 pinecones. Which number sentence shows how many birdfeeders he can make? (7-3)

A $12 + 3 = 15$

B $12 \div 3 = 4$

C $12 - 3 = 9$

D $12 \times 3 = 36$

2. Which story could be solved with $20 \div 4$? (7-4)

A Harold caught 20 fish. All but 4 of them were catfish. How many of the fish were something other than catfish?

B Becky bought 20 bags of crystal beads. Each bag had 4 crystal beads. How many crystal beads did she buy?

C Batina has made 20 doll dresses. If she makes 4 more, how many doll dresses will she have made?

D Coach Sid has 20 baseballs. Each group needs 4 balls for the practice drill. How many groups can he form?

3. Five friends have 15 pencils to share equally. Which number sentence shows how many pencils each friend will get? (7-1)

A $15 \div 5 = 3$

B $15 + 5 = 20$

C $15 \times 5 = 75$

D $15 - 5 = 10$

4. Mrs. Vincent bought 16 kiwis for her 4 children to share equally. How many kiwis will each child get? (7-1)

A 3

B 4

C 5

D 12

5. Each fence board requires 4 nails. How many boards can Mason put up with one package of 30 nails? (7-2)

A 2

B 6

C 7

D 8

Topic 7

Test

6. Which division sentence is shown by the repeated subtraction? (7-3)

$$15 - 3 = 12$$
$$12 - 3 = 9$$
$$9 - 3 = 6$$
$$6 - 3 = 3$$
$$3 - 3 = 0$$

A $15 \div 3 = 5$

B $15 \div 3 = 0$

C $18 \div 3 = 6$

D $18 \div 6 = 3$

7. The pet store had 24 parakeets to put equally in 8 cages. How many birds should be put in each cage? (7-1)

24 parakeets

?	?	?	?	?	?	?	?

Birds in each cage

A 6

B 4

C 3

D 2

8. While on vacation, Ginny bought 22 postcards. She can put 4 postcards on each page in her memory book. How many postcards will Ginny put on the 6th page? (7-2)

A 6

B 5

C 4

D 2

9. Which story could be solved with $36 \div 6$? (7-4)

A Carla used 36 seashells to make 6 necklaces. Each necklace had the same number of shells. How many shells were on each necklace?

B Patrick planted 36 trees on Arbor Day. If he plants 6 more, how many trees will he have planted?

C The zoo's gift shop ordered 36 bags with 6 plastic animals in each. How many plastic animals did the gift shop order?

D Ray counted 36 coins in his bank. All but 6 of them were quarters. How many of the coins were something other than quarters?

10. The pictures below are examples of a triangle in several different positions.

Which of the following shapes can **NOT** be made by joining two of the triangles? (7-5)

A A rectangle

B A parallelogram

C A triangle

D A square

Reteaching

Set A, pages 164–165, 170–171

There are 12 toys. If 4 toys are put in each box, how many boxes are needed?

$12 - 4 = 8$
$8 - 4 = 4$
$4 - 4 = 0$

Use repeated subtraction to find how many groups.

You can subtract 4 three times.

$12 \div 4 = 3$ You can also divide to find the number of groups.

Three boxes are needed.

Remember that you can also think of division as sharing equally.

Use counters or draw a picture to solve each problem.

1. 6 books
3 shelves
How many books are on each shelf?

2. 18 students
2 students in each group
How many groups are there?

Set B, pages 166–168

Tom has 14 apples to put into bags. Each bag holds 4 apples. How many bags can Tom fill? Are any apples left?

- Show the total number of items.
- Divide them into equal groups.
- Write the number of equal groups and the number left over.

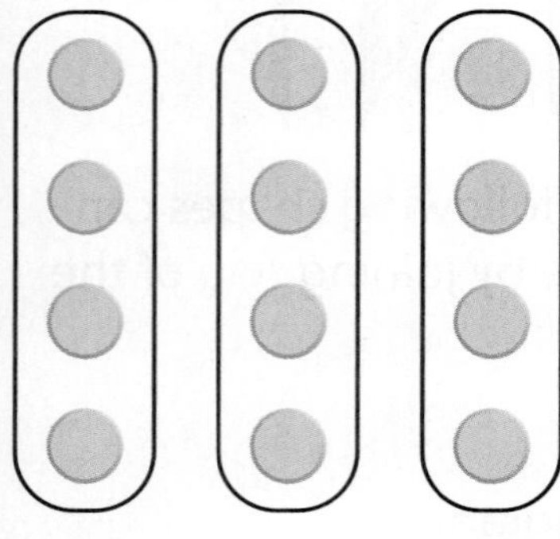

$14 \div 4 = 3$ with 2 left over

Tom can fill 3 bags. There will be 2 apples left over.

Remember to make sure you put the correct number of items in each group.

Find each number of equal groups and the number left over.

1. 21 books,
5 books in each box

$21 \div 5 =$ ☐ with ☐ left over

2. 20 muffins,
3 muffins in each box

$20 \div 3 =$ ☐ with ☐ left over

3. 40 stickers
6 stickers on each page

$40 \div 6 =$ ☐ with ☐ left over

4. 23 days
7 days in each week

$23 \div 7 =$ ☐ with ☐ left over

Set C, pages 172–173

Write a division story for 20 ÷ 5.

If 20 children form 5 equal teams, how many children are on each team?

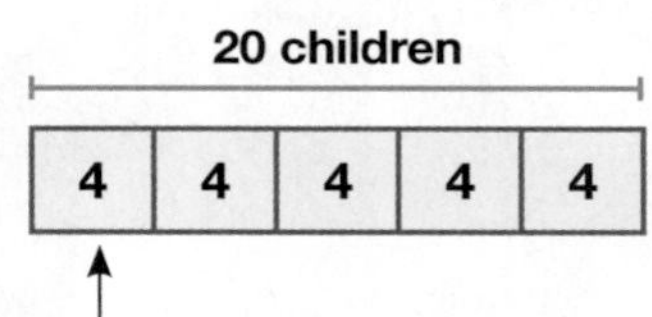

20 ÷ 5 = 4

There are 4 children on each team.

Remember that division stories can ask for the number in each group or the number of equal groups.

Write a division story for each number sentence. Draw a picture to help.

1. 15 ÷ 3 = ▢
2. 21 ÷ 7 = ▢
3. 24 ÷ 6 = ▢
4. 30 ÷ 5 = ▢

Set D, pages 174–176

Some blue paint spilled on a tile floor. The tile floor was in the shape of a square. There were 9 tiles in the whole floor. How many of the tiles had blue paint on them?

Draw a picture to show what you know.

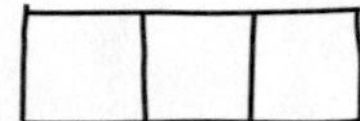

Finish the picture to solve. Show 9 tiles in all.

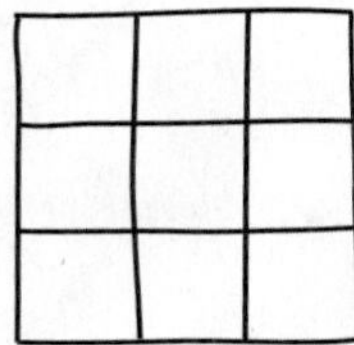

Six tiles had blue paint on them.

Remember to check that your picture matches the information in the problem.

1. Carmela painted over a part of some tiles. The whole group of tiles was in the shape of a rectangle. There were 28 tiles in the whole group. How many tiles did Carmela paint over?

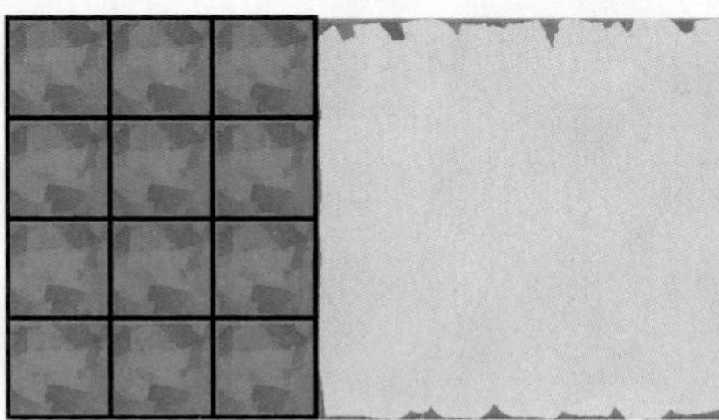

Topic 8

Division Facts

1

A dollhouse was made for Queen Mary of England. How do the objects in the dollhouse compare in size to the objects in her real-life castle? You will find out in Lesson 8-5.

2

The public subway in London is called the Underground, or the Tube. How long is the East London tube line? You will find out in Lesson 8-4.

3 How much water might you use when you brush your teeth? You will find out in Lesson 8-2.

4 A mosaic is a type of art made with tiles. How does this mosaic show multiplication and division? You will find out in Lesson 8-1.

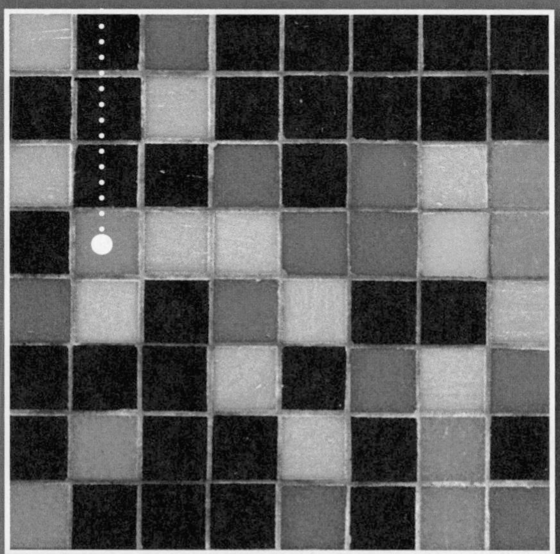

Review What You Know!

Vocabulary

Choose the best term from the box.

- addends
- factors
- difference
- product

1. The numbers you multiply are __?__.
2. The answer in a subtraction problem is the __?__.
3. The answer in a multiplication problem is the __?__.

Fact Families

Copy and complete each fact family.

4. 7 + 6 = ▢   13 − 6 = ▢
   6 + 7 = ▢   ▢ − 7 = 6
5. 8 + ▢ = 17   17 − 8 = ▢
   9 + 8 = ▢   ▢ − 9 = 8
6. Write the fact family for 2, 6, and 8.

Multiplication

Copy and complete.

7. 6 × 8 = ▢ × 6
8. 10 × ▢ = 0
9. ▢ × 1 = 7
10. **Writing to Explain** Explain how to find how many items are in 3 groups if there are 4 items in each group. Draw a picture to help.

Lesson
8-1

Understand It!
Fact families show how multiplication and division are related.

Relating Multiplication and Division

Hands-On
counters

How can multiplication facts help you divide?

This array can show multiplication and division.

Multiplication	Division
5 rows of 6 drums	30 drums in 5 equal rows
$5 \times 6 = 30$	$30 \div 5 = 6$
30 drums	6 drums in each row

Guided Practice*

Do you know HOW?

Copy and complete. Use counters or draw a picture to help.

1. $4 \times \square = 28$
$28 \div 4 = \square$

2. $6 \times \square = 36$
$36 \div 6 = \square$

3. $2 \times \square = 18$
$18 \div 2 = \square$

4. $8 \times \square = 32$
$32 \div 8 = \square$

Do you UNDERSTAND?

5. Number Sense What multiplication fact can help you find $54 \div 6$?

6. Look at the fact family for 5, 6, and 30. What do you notice about the products and the dividends?

7. Writing to Explain Is $4 \times 6 = 24$ part of the fact family for 3, 8, and 24? Explain.

Independent Practice

Copy and complete. Use counters or draw a picture to help.

8. $8 \times \square = 16$
$16 \div 8 = \square$

9. $5 \times \square = 35$
$35 \div 5 = \square$

10. $6 \times \square = 48$
$48 \div 6 = \square$

11. $9 \times \square = 36$
$36 \div 9 = \square$

12. $3 \times \square = 27$
$27 \div 3 = \square$

13. $8 \times \square = 56$
$56 \div 8 = \square$

14. $\square \times 7 = 42$
$42 \div 7 = \square$

15. $\square \times 8 = 72$
$72 \div 8 = \square$

16. $\square \times 9 = 45$
$45 \div 9 = \square$

17. Write the fact family for 5, 8, and 40.

*For another example, see Set A on page 202.

A fact family shows how multiplication and division are related.

Fact family for 5, 6, and 30:

$5 \times 6 = 30$		$30 \div 5 = 6$
$6 \times 5 = 30$		$30 \div 6 = 5$

dividend → 30, divisor → 6, quotient → 5

The dividend is the number of objects to be divided.

The divisor is the number by which another number is divided.

The quotient is the answer to a division problem.

Problem Solving

18. **Writing to Explain** Why does the fact family for $2 \times 2 = 4$ have only two facts?

For **19** and **20**, write the rest of the fact family for each array.

19.

$3 \times 4 = 12$ $\quad$ $12 \div 3 = 4$

20.

$4 \times 5 = 20$ $\quad$ $20 \div 4 = 5$

21. There were 3 lines of clowns in a parade. Each line had 8 clowns in it. Near the end of the parade, 3 of the clowns had to leave. How many clowns were still in the parade?

22. Write a fact family to describe the array of tiles in the mosaic shown at the right.

23. What number makes this number sentence true?

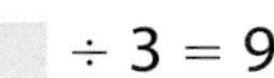 $\div 3 = 9$

A 3 $\quad$ **B** 12 $\quad$ **C** 18 $\quad$ **D** 27

Lesson

8-2

Understand It!
Multiplication facts can be helpful in solving division problems.

Fact Families with 2, 3, 4, and 5

What multiplication fact can you use?

Dee has 14 noisemakers. She puts the same number on each of 2 tables. How many will be on each table?

What You Think	What You Write
2 times what number is 14? $2 \times 7 = 14$	$14 \div 2 = 7$ There will be 7 noisemakers on each table.

Another Example **What is another way to write a division problem?**

Dee is making balloon animals for her party. She has 24 balloons. It takes 4 balloons to make each animal. How many balloon animals can she make?

4 times what number is 24?
$4 \times 6 = 24$

There are two ways to write a division problem.

$24 \div 4 = 6$

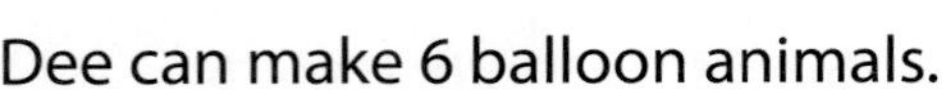

dividend   divisor   quotient

6 ← quotient
divisor → $4\overline{)24}$ ← dividend

Dee can make 6 balloon animals.

Explain It

1. Copy and complete the fact family:

   $4 \times 6 = 24$
   $24 \div 4 = 6$

2. How do you know what multiplication fact to use to find $24 \div 4$?

3. **Number Sense** Dee says she could make more than 10 balloon animals if she was able to make an animal using only 3 balloons. Do you agree? Why or why not?

Dee has 40 stickers. She puts 5 stickers on each bag. How many bags can she decorate?

What You Think	What You Write
5 times what number is 40? $5 \times 8 = 40$	$40 \div 5 = 8$ Dee can decorate 8 bags.

Dee wants to put 15 cups in 3 rows on the table. How many cups will she put in each row?

What You Think	What You Write
3 times what number is 15? $3 \times 5 = 15$	$15 \div 3 = 5$ Dee will put 5 cups in each row.

Guided Practice*

Do you know HOW?

In **1–2**, copy and complete each fact family.

1. $2 \times 7 = 14$
$14 \div 2 = 7$

2. $5 \times 8 = 40$
$40 \div 5 = 8$

In **3–8**, find each quotient.

3. $27 \div 3$ **4.** $16 \div 4$ **5.** $40 \div 4$

6. $2\overline{)18}$ **7.** $4\overline{)28}$ **8.** $5\overline{)30}$

Do you UNDERSTAND?

9. Identify the dividend, divisor and quotient in Exercise 8.

10. **Number Sense** How can you tell without dividing that $15 \div 3$ will be greater than $15 \div 5$?

11. How can you use multiplication to help you find 36 divided by 4?

12. Dee has planned 4 games for her party. If she has 12 prizes, how many prizes can she give for each game?

Independent Practice

Find each quotient.

13. $10 \div 2$ **14.** $25 \div 5$ **15.** $21 \div 3$ **16.** $18 \div 3$

17. $2\overline{)16}$ **18.** $5\overline{)50}$ **19.** $3\overline{)24}$ **20.** $4\overline{)36}$

21. $12 \div 4$ **22.** $45 \div 5$ **23.** $4\overline{)16}$ **24.** $5\overline{)40}$

25. Find 12 divided by 2. **26.** Divide 20 by 5. **27.** Find 32 divided by 4.

For another example, see Set B on page 202.

Independent Practice

Algebra Find each missing number.

28. $2 \times \square = 8$

29. $15 \div 3 = \square$

30. $\square \div 3 = 2$

31. $7 \times 4 = \square$

32. $\square \times 5 = 40$

33. $32 \div \square = 8$

Number Sense Write < or > to compare.

34. $4 \times 2 \bigcirc 4 \div 2$

35. $2 \times 3 \bigcirc 6 \div 2$

36. $5 + 8 \bigcirc 5 \times 8$

Problem Solving

37. Writing to Explain Joey says, "I can't solve $8 \div 2$ by using the fact $2 \times 8 = 16$." Do you agree or disagree? Explain.

38. Anna wants to make one array with 2 rows of 8 tiles and another array with 3 rows of 5 tiles. How many tiles does she need all together?

39. You might use 2 gallons of water when you brush your teeth. There are 16 cups in 1 gallon. About how many cups of water might you use when brushing your teeth?

40. Bob has 15 pennies and 3 dimes. Miko has the same amount of money, but she has only nickels. How many nickels does Miko have?

41. Which number sentence is in the same fact family as $3 \times 6 = 18$?

A $3 \times 3 = 9$

B $2 \times 9 = 18$

C $6 \div 3 = 2$

D $18 \div 6 = 3$

42. Mike bought 3 bags of marbles with 5 marbles in each bag. He gave 4 marbles to Marsha. How many marbles did Mike have left?

A 11

B 15

C 19

D 21

43. Sammy wants to buy one remote control car for $49 and three small cars for $5 each. What is the total amount he will spend?

44. Annie helped her friend set up 40 chairs for a meeting. They set up the chairs in 5 equal rows. Write a division sentence to show the number of chairs in each row. What multiplication fact could you use to help you divide?

Algebra Connections

Division and Number Sentences

Remember that the two sides of a number sentence can be equal or unequal. A symbol $>$, $<$, or $=$ tells how the sides compare. Estimation or reasoning can help you tell if one side is greater without doing any computations.

$>$ means *is greater than*
$<$ means *is less than*
$=$ means *is equal to*

Example: $10 \div 2 \bigcirc 8 \div 2$

Each whole is being divided into 2 equal groups. The greater whole will have a greater number of items in each group.

Since 10 is greater than 8, the quotient on the left side is greater. Write the symbol $>$.

$10 \div 2 \ (>) \ 8 \div 2$

Copy and complete by writing $>$, $<$, or $=$.

1. $20 \div 5 \bigcirc 25 \div 5$ **2.** $12 \div 3 \bigcirc 12 \div 4$ **3.** $3 \times 18 \bigcirc 3 \times 21$

4. $24 \div 2 \bigcirc 8$ **5.** $19 + 19 \bigcirc 2 \times 19$ **6.** $100 \bigcirc 5 \times 30$

7. $1 \times 53 \bigcirc 1 \times 43$ **8.** $9 \bigcirc 36 \div 4$ **9.** $9 \div 3 \bigcirc 18 \div 3$

10. $16 \div 2 \bigcirc 1 + 9$ **11.** $35 \div 5 \bigcirc 2 + 3$ **12.** $24 \div 4 \bigcirc 24 \div 2$

In **13** and **14**, copy and complete the number sentence below each problem. Use it to help explain your answer.

13. Mara and Bobby each have 40 pages to read. Mara will read 4 pages each day. Bobby will read 5 pages each day. Who needs more days to read 40 pages?

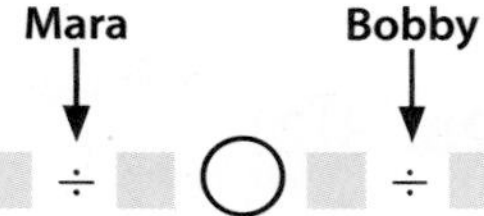

14. Tim had a board that was 12 feet long. He cut the board into 3 equal pieces. Ellen had a board that was 18 feet long. She cut the board into 3 equal pieces. Who had the longer pieces?

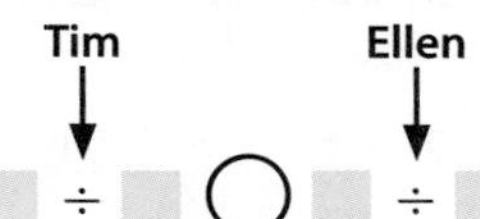

15. Write a Problem Write a problem described by $16 \div 2 > 14 \div 2$.

Lesson

8-3

Understand It!
Multiplication facts for 6 and 7 can be used to divide with 6 and 7.

Fact Families with 6 and 7

How do you divide with 6 and 7?

There are 48 dogs entered in a dog show. The judge wants 6 dogs in each group. How many groups will there be?

Choose an Operation Divide to find how many groups.

Guided Practice*

Do you know HOW?

1. Copy and complete the fact family.

$8 \times 6 = 48$
$48 \div 6 = 8$

In **2–10**, find each quotient.

2. $12 \div 6$ **3.** $30 \div 6$ **4.** $42 \div 6$

5. $14 \div 7$ **6.** $77 \div 7$ **7.** $63 \div 7$

8. $6\overline{)24}$ **9.** $6\overline{)54}$ **10.** $7\overline{)49}$

Do you UNDERSTAND?

11. **Number Sense** How can you tell without dividing that $42 \div 6$ will be greater than $42 \div 7$?

12. Write the fact family for 7, 8, and 56.

13. There are 54 children in 6 ballet classes. Each class is the same size. How many children are in each class?

Independent Practice

Find each quotient.

14. $18 \div 6$ **15.** $6 \div 6$ **16.** $21 \div 7$ **17.** $36 \div 6$ **18.** $84 \div 7$

19. $6\overline{)48}$ **20.** $5\overline{)30}$ **21.** $7\overline{)56}$ **22.** $7\overline{)35}$ **23.** $6\overline{)36}$

24. $6\overline{)42}$ **25.** $7\overline{)63}$ **26.** $6\overline{)18}$ **27.** $7\overline{)42}$ **28.** $3\overline{)21}$

29. Find 49 divided by 7. **30.** Divide 72 by 6. **31.** Find 56 divided by 7.

32. Find 60 divided by 6. **33.** Divide 28 by 7. **34.** Find 48 divided by 6.

*For another example, see Set C on page 202.

Find 48 ÷ 6.

What You Think	What You Write
What number times 6 is 48? $8 \times 6 = 48$	$48 \div 6 = 8$ There will be 8 groups.

Another dog was entered. There will now be 7 dogs in each group. How many groups will there be now?

Find 49 ÷ 7.

What You Think	What You Write
What number times 7 is 49? $7 \times 7 = 49$	$49 \div 7 = 7$ There will be 7 groups.

Problem Solving

Use the pictures below for **35–38**.

35. Rita needs 15 gold beads for an art project.

a How many packages of beads does she need?

b How much do the beads cost?

36. Eve bought 2 packages of red beads and 2 packages of blue beads.

a How many beads did she buy?

b How much did she spend?

37. **Writing to Explain** Guy bought 28 red beads and 18 blue beads. How many packages did he buy? Explain how you solved the problem.

38. **Number Sense** Andy bought exactly 35 beads, all the same color. Which color beads could he have bought? Explain your thinking.

39. There are 6 rafts on the river. Each raft holds 8 people. Which number sentence is in the fact family for these numbers?

A $48 - 6 = 42$ **C** $48 + 6 = 54$

B $48 \div 6 = 8$ **D** $48 - 8 = 40$

40. The school auditorium has 182 seats. People are sitting in 56 of the seats. Which is the best estimate of the number of seats that do **NOT** have people sitting in them?

A 20 **B** 120 **C** 240 **D** 250

Lesson
8-4

Understand It!
Multiplication facts for 8 and 9 can be used to divide with 8 and 9.

Fact Families with 8 and 9

What multiplication fact can you use?

John has 56 straws. How many spiders can he make?

Find 56 ÷ 8.

What number times 8 is 56?

$7 \times 8 = 56$

John can make 7 spiders.

Guided Practice*

Do you know HOW?

Find each quotient.

1. 16 ÷ 8 **2.** 64 ÷ 8 **3.** 36 ÷ 9

4. 27 ÷ 9 **5.** 45 ÷ 9 **6.** 63 ÷ 9

7. $8\overline{)24}$ **8.** $8\overline{)72}$ **9.** $8\overline{)8}$

Do you UNDERSTAND?

10. What multiplication fact could you use to find 18 ÷ 9?

11. **Number Sense** Carla and Jeff each use 72 straws. Carla makes animals with 9 legs. Jeff makes animals with 8 legs. Who makes more animals? Explain.

Independent Practice

Find each quotient.

12. 32 ÷ 8 **13.** 28 ÷ 7 **14.** 18 ÷ 9 **15.** 48 ÷ 8 **16.** 81 ÷ 9

17. $5\overline{)45}$ **18.** $9\overline{)54}$ **19.** $7\overline{)56}$ **20.** $4\overline{)28}$ **21.** $8\overline{)56}$

22. $9\overline{)27}$ **23.** $9\overline{)72}$ **24.** $8\overline{)16}$ **25.** $8\overline{)64}$ **26.** $8\overline{)48}$

27. Find 90 divided by 9. **28.** Divide 40 by 8. **29.** Find 56 divided by 8.

30. Find 81 divided by 9. **31.** Divide 45 by 9. **32.** Find 88 divided by 8.

33. Write fact families for the numbers in **30** and **31**. How are the fact families different?

*For another example, see Set D on page 203.

Luz made 9 animals. She used 54 straws. She used the same number of straws for each animal. How many straws did Luz use for each animal?

Find $54 \div 9$.

54 straws

?	?	?	?	?	?	?	?	?

Number of straws for one animal

What You Think	What You Write
9 times what number is 54?	$54 \div 9 = 6$
$9 \times 6 = 54$	Luz used 6 straws for each animal.

Problem Solving

Algebra Write < or > to compare.

34. $36 \div 9$ ◯ 9

35. 65 ◯ 8×8

36. $63 \div 9$ ◯ 8

Use the ticket prices at the right for **37–39**.

37. Writing to Explain Mr. Stern bought 4 children's tickets and 2 adult tickets. How much more did he spend for the adult tickets than the children's tickets? Explain.

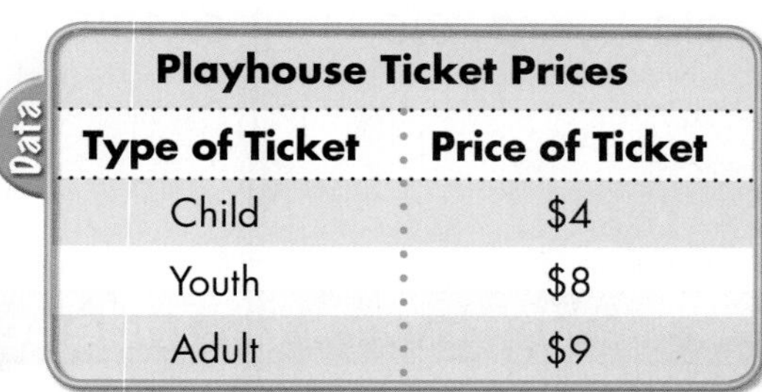

Playhouse Ticket Prices

Type of Ticket	Price of Ticket
Child	$4
Youth	$8
Adult	$9

38. What is the total cost of 2 children's tickets and 2 adult tickets?

39. Reasoning The clerk at the playhouse sold $72 worth of adult tickets. Ten people bought adult tickets online. Did more people buy tickets at the playhouse or online? Tell how you know.

40. Which number sentence is **NOT** in the same fact family as the others?

A $8 \times 4 = 32$

B $32 \div 8 = 4$

C $2 \times 4 = 8$

D $4 \times 8 = 32$

41. The London Underground has 12 lines. The District line is 8 times as long as the East London line. Use the diagram to write a number sentence to find the length of the East London line.

64 km

?	?	?	?	?	?	?	?

8 times as long

?

length of East London line

Lesson

8-5

Understand It!
Multiplication facts can help explain the division rules for 0 and 1.

Dividing with 0 and 1

How do you divide with 1 or 0?

Dividing by 1

Find $3 \div 1$

What number times 1 is 3?

$3 \times 1 = 3$

So, $3 \div 1 = 3$.

Rule: Any number divided by 1 is itself.

Guided Practice*

Do you know HOW?

Find each quotient.

1. $8 \div 8$ **2.** $2 \div 1$ **3.** $0 \div 5$

4. $1\overline{)8}$ **5.** $6\overline{)6}$ **6.** $10\overline{)0}$

Do you UNDERSTAND?

7. How can you tell without dividing that $375 \div 375 = 1$?

8. **Writing to Explain** Describe how you can find $0 \div 267$, without dividing.

Independent Practice

Find each quotient.

9. $7 \div 7$ **10.** $0 \div 4$ **11.** $10 \div 1$ **12.** $0 \div 6$ **13.** $10 \div 10$

14. $4 \div 1$ **15.** $7 \div 1$ **16.** $0 \div 8$ **17.** $5 \div 5$ **18.** $5 \div 1$

19. $14 \div 2$ **20.** $70 \div 7$ **21.** $56 \div 7$ **22.** $24 \div 4$ **23.** $90 \div 9$

24. $6\overline{)36}$ **25.** $7\overline{)49}$ **26.** $8\overline{)64}$ **27.** $9\overline{)81}$ **28.** $5\overline{)20}$

29. $7\overline{)56}$ **30.** $8\overline{)48}$ **31.** $7\overline{)42}$ **32.** $5\overline{)25}$ **33.** $4\overline{)32}$

34. Divide 0 by 9. **35.** Find 9 divided by 9. **36.** Find 6 divided by 1.

37. Divide 3 by 3. **38.** Find 0 divided by 8. **39.** Find 7 divided by 1.

*For another example, see Set E on page 203.

1 as a Quotient

Find $3 \div 3$.

Think 3 times what number equals 3?

$3 \times 1 = 3$

So, $3 \div 3 = 1$.

Rule: Any number (except 0) divided by itself is 1.

Dividing 0 by a Number

Find $0 \div 3$.

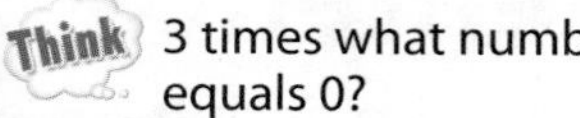

3 times what number equals 0?

$3 \times 0 = 0$

So, $0 \div 3 = 0$.

Rule: 0 divided by any number (except 0) is 0.

Dividing by 0

Find $3 \div 0$.

0 times what number equals 3?

There is no such number.

So, $3 \div 0$ can't be done.

Rule: You cannot divide any number by 0.

Problem Solving

Algebra In **40–43**, copy and complete. Use $<$, $>$, or $=$.

40. $3 \div 3 \bigcirc 3 \times 0$

41. $17 \div 17 \bigcirc 1 \div 1$

42. $0 \div 6 \bigcirc 0 \div 1$

43. $6 \times 1 \bigcirc 6 \div 1$

Use the sign at the right for **44–47**.

44. Paul hiked one trail 3 times for a total distance of 12 miles. Which trail did he hike?

45. Reasoning Addie hiked 3 different trails for a total distance of 11 miles. Which trails did she hike?

46. Yoko hiked the blue trail once and the green trail twice. How many miles did she hike on the green trail?

47. Writing to Explain Marty hiked one trail 4 times. He hiked more than 10 miles but less than 16 miles. Which trail did he hike? Explain.

48. Objects in Windsor Castle are 12 times the size of the miniature versions in Queen Mary's dollhouse. How tall is a real-life painting if it is 1 inch tall in the dollhouse?

49. Which number will make the number sentence below true?

$54 \div \square = 9$

A 5 **B** 6 **C** 7 **D** 8

Lesson

8-6

Understand It!
A picture can show information that is used to write a number sentence.

Problem Solving

Draw a Picture and Write a Number Sentence

Jeff is setting up the sand-painting booth at the school carnival. He put the sand from one bag of sand into 5 buckets. If each bucket has the same amount of sand, how much sand is in each bucket?

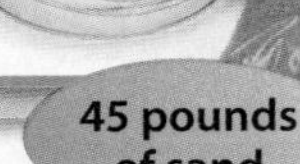

Another Example Are there other types of division situations?

Alison is setting up the prize booth. She has 48 prizes. She will put 8 prizes in each row. How many rows can she make?

Plan and Solve

Use a diagram to show what you know.

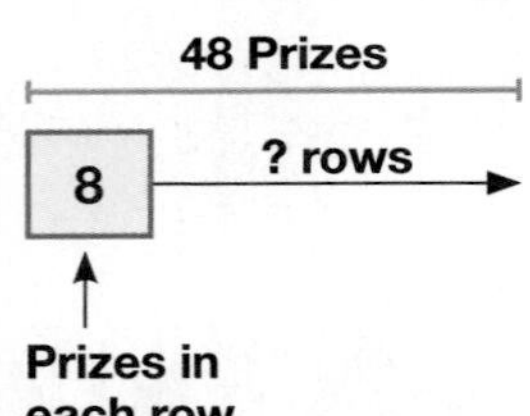

Answer

Write a number sentence

$48 \div 8 = 6$

Alison can make 6 rows.

Check

Make sure the answer is reasonable.

Use multiplication or repeated addition to check.

$6 \times 8 = 48$

or

$8 + 8 + 8 + 8 + 8 + 8 = 48$

Explain It

1. Explain how you can check the quotient in division by using either multiplication or addition. **See margin.**
2. **Number Sense** If Alison wants fewer than 6 rows of prizes, should she put more or fewer prizes in each row? Explain your thinking. **See margin.**

Plan and Solve

Use a diagram to show what you know.

45 pounds

Amount of sand in each bucket

You know the total amount of sand and that there are 5 buckets. Divide to find how much sand is in each bucket.

Answer

Write a number sentence.

$45 \div 5 = 9$

There are 9 pounds of sand in each bucket.

Check

Make sure the answer is reasonable.

Use multiplication or repeated addition to check.

$5 \times 9 = 45$

or

$9 + 9 + 9 + 9 + 9 = 45$

Guided Practice*

Do you know HOW?

1. Larry and Pat made 18 posters. Each made the same number. How many did each make? Write a number sentence and solve.

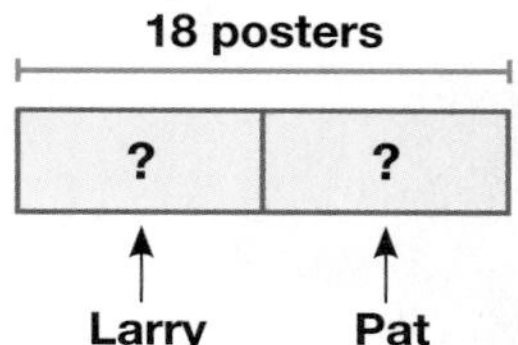

Do you UNDERSTAND?

2. What operation did you use for Problem 1? Tell why.

3. **Write a Problem** Write a real-world problem that you can solve by subtracting. Draw a diagram. Write a number sentence and solve.

Independent Practice

For **4** and **5**, draw a diagram to show what you know. Then write a number sentence and solve.

4. There are 8 cars on a Ferris wheel. Each car holds 3 people. How many people can ride the Ferris wheel at the same time?

5. There were 24 children in a relay race. There were 6 teams in all. How many children were on each team?

6. Austin is 8 years old. Grace is twice as old as Austin. How old is Grace?

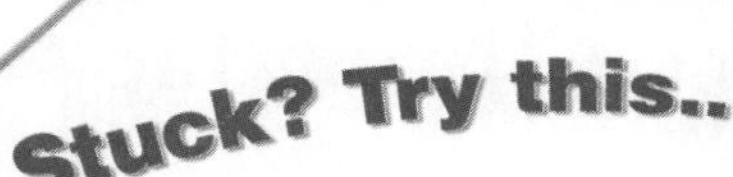

- What do I know?
- What am I asked to find?
- What diagram can I use to help understand the problem?
- Can I use addition, subtraction, multiplication, or division?
- Is all of my work correct?
- Did I answer the right question?
- Is my answer reasonable?

For another example, see Set F on page 203.

Independent Practice

Use the table at the right for **7** and **8**. Solve each problem.

Cost of Tickets	
Adult	$10
Youth	$5
Child	$3

7. Mr. Niglio bought 2 youth tickets and 2 adult tickets. He gave the clerk a $50 bill. How much change did he get back?

8. **Number Sense** Dan, Sue, and Joe each bought a different kind of ticket. Dan spent the least. Sue spent twice as much as Joe. How much did Joe spend?

For **9** and **10**, use the animal pictures at the right. Write a number sentence and solve.

9. About how many hours is a sloth awake each day?

Tip *There are 24 hours in a day.*

10. About how many hours is a koala bear awake each day?

Tip *There are 7 days in a week.*

Think About the Process

11. Alma bought 2 bracelets for $6 at the craft fair. Each bracelet cost the same amount. Which number sentence shows how to find the cost of each bracelet?

A $2 \times \$6 = \square$

B $2 + \$6 = \square$

C $\$6 - 2 = \square$

D $\$6 \div 2 = \square$

12. Tomas bought a book for $4, crayons for $2, and a pen for $1. He gave the clerk $10. Which number sentence shows how to find his change?

A $\$4 + \$2 + \$1 = \square$

B $\$4 \times \$2 \times \$1 = \square$

C $\$10 - \$6 = \square$

D $\$10 - (\$4 + \$2 + \$1) = \square$

Choosing an Operation and a Computation Method

The tallest building in a city is on Central Avenue. It is 921 feet tall. The second tallest building is on Main Street. It is 886 feet tall. How much taller is the building on Central Avenue than the building on Main Street?

Step 1 Choose an operation.

You are comparing the heights, so subtract. Find 921 − 886.

Step 2 Choose the best computation method. Decide whether to use mental math, paper and pencil, or a calculator.

Since there is more than 1 regrouping, use a calculator.

Step 3 Solve.

Press: 921 [−] 886 [ENTER =]

Display: 35

The building on Central Avenue is 35 feet taller than the building on Main Street.

Practice

For each problem, choose an operation. Then use the best computation method to solve.

1. The building on Central Avenue has 72 floors. An elevator stopped at every 9th floor as it came down from the top floor to the bottom. How many times did it stop?

2. An office building on Elm Street could be divided into 3 sections with 25 floors in each section. How many floors does the office building have?

3. The Plaza skyscraper is 579 feet tall. The Fountain skyscraper is 142 feet taller. How tall is the Fountain skyscraper?

4. The Morgan building is 1,002 feet tall. The Plaza Tower is 972 feet tall. How much taller is the Morgan building than the Plaza Tower?

Test

1. Which number makes both number sentences true? (8-1)

$9 \times \square = 54$
$54 \div 9 = \square$

A 8

B 7

C 6

D 5

2. Which number sentence is true? (8-5)

A $6 \div 6 = 0$

B $5 \div 1 = 1$

C $0 \div 4 = 4$

D $7 \div 1 = 7$

3. Nancy has 4 CDs. Each CD has 8 songs. Which number sentence is in the same fact family as $4 \times 8 = 32$? (8-2)

A $32 \div 4 = 8$

B $32 - 8 = 24$

C $8 - 4 = 4$

D $2 \times 4 = 8$

4. Gavin has 7 pages of his picture album filled. Each page has 6 pictures, for a total of 42 pictures. Which number sentence is **NOT** in the same fact family as the others? (8-3)

A $7 \times 6 = 42$

B $6 \times 7 = 42$

C $42 \div 7 = 6$

D $5 \times 7 = 35$

5. Mrs. Hendrix bought 45 pounds of modeling clay. She wants to divide it evenly among her 5 art classes. How many pounds of modeling clay will each class get? (8-2)

A 40

B 9

C 8

D 7

6. Beth bought a box of dog treats. The box had 48 treats. If Beth gives her dog 6 treats a day, how many days will the box of treats last? (8-3)

A 6

B 7

C 8

D 9

7. What number makes this number sentence true? (8-4)

$\square \div 9 = 8$

A 81

B 72

C 17

D 8

8. Peg put 18 rocks into 2 equal piles. How many rocks were in each pile? (8-2)

A 6

B 8

C 9

D 36

9. Neil has 30 nails and 6 boards. Which number sentence shows how many nails he can put in each board if he puts the same number in each? (8-6)

30 nails

?	?	?	?	?	?

Nails in each board

A $30 + 6 = 36$

B $30 - 6 = 24$

C $30 \div 6 = 5$

D $6 \times 30 = 180$

10. The drawing below shows how Janet planted 18 daisies in her flowerbed.

$6 \times 3 = 18$

Which division sentence can be written using the drawing of Janet's daisies? (8-1)

A $6 \div 3 = 2$

B $18 \div 9 = 2$

C $24 \div 3 = 8$

D $18 \div 6 = 3$

11. Mrs. Manchez bought 3 boxes of tissue. How many rooms will get a box of tissue if she puts 1 box in each room? (8-5)

A 9

B 3

C 1

D 0

12. A league has 7 basketball teams. Each team has 8 players, for a total of 56 players. Which number sentence is **NOT** in the same fact family as the others? (8-4)

A $9 \times 7 = 63$

B $8 \times 7 = 56$

C $56 \div 8 = 7$

D $7 \times 8 = 56$

13. Mr. Yarbrough bought 20 pounds of sand. Each bag contained 5 pounds of sand. Which number sentence shows how to find the number of bags of sand Mr. Yarbrough bought? (8-6)

A $20 \div 5 = 4$

B $5 \times 20 = 100$

C $20 - 5 = 15$

D $20 + 5 = 25$

14. What is $24 \div 8$? (8-4)

A 16

B 6

C 4

D 3

Reteaching

Set A, pages 184–185

Use the array to help you find the fact family for 4, 7, and 28.

Multiplication

$4 \times 7 = 28$
$7 \times 4 = 28$

Division

$28 \div 4 = 7$
$28 \div 7 = 4$

Remember that a fact family shows how multiplication and division are related.

Copy and complete.

1. $3 \times \square = 27$
$27 \div 3 = \square$

2. $\square \times 7 = 49$
$49 \div 7 = \square$

3. $7 \times \square = 56$
$56 \div 7 = \square$

4. $5 \times \square = 25$
$25 \div 5 = \square$

Set B, pages 186–188

Hanna read 21 pages of a book in 3 days. If Hanna read the same number of pages each day, how many pages did she read each day?

Find $21 \div 3$.

What number times 3 equals 21?

$7 \times 3 = 21$

Write: $21 \div 3 = 7$

Hanna read 7 pages each day.

Remember to think of a related multiplication fact to solve a division problem.

Find each quotient.

1. $27 \div 3$ **2.** $12 \div 2$

3. $32 \div 4$ **4.** $35 \div 5$

5. $50 \div 5$ **6.** $8 \div 2$

7. $20 \div 4$ **8.** $18 \div 3$

Set C, pages 190–191

Joseph has 24 spelling words to practice in the next 6 days. How many words does he need to practice each day?

Find $24 \div 6$.

What number times 6 equals 24?

$4 \times 6 = 24$

Write: $24 \div 6 = 4$

Joseph has 4 words to practice each day.

Remember that division problems can be written in two ways.

Find the quotient.

1. $63 \div 7$ **2.** $36 \div 6$

3. $42 \div 6$ **4.** $60 \div 6$

5. $7\overline{)14}$ **6.** $6\overline{)30}$

7. $6\overline{)48}$ **8.** $7\overline{)42}$

Set D, pages 192–193

There are 36 students who want to play baseball. Each team needs 9 players. How many teams will there be?

Find 36 ÷ 9.

 What number times 9 equals 36?

4 × 9 = 36

Write: 36 ÷ 9 = 4

There will be 4 teams.

Remember that you can divide to find how many equal groups.

Find the quotient.

1. 64 ÷ 8
2. 18 ÷ 9
3. $9\overline{)54}$
4. $8\overline{)32}$
5. Divide 24 by 8.
6. Find 45 divided by 9.

Set E, pages 194–195

Find 8 ÷ 1, 8 ÷ 8, and 0 ÷ 8.

When any number is divided by 1, the quotient is that number. **8 ÷ 1 = 8**

When any number (except 0) is divided by itself, the quotient is 1. **8 ÷ 8 = 1**

When zero is divided by any number (except 0), the quotient is 0. **0 ÷ 8 = 0**

Remember that you cannot divide any number by 0.

Find each quotient.

1. 4 ÷ 1
2. 7 ÷ 7
3. 0 ÷ 5
4. $1\overline{)5}$
5. $3\overline{)0}$
6. $9\overline{)9}$
7. $6\overline{)6}$
8. $1\overline{)7}$
9. $4\overline{)0}$

Set F, pages 196–198

Carl has 48 balloons to tie in 6 equal groups. How many balloons will be in each group?

48 balloons					
?	?	?	?	?	?

↑ Balloons in each group

Draw a diagram to show what you know.

Write a number sentence.
48 ÷ 6 = 8
There will be 8 balloons in each group.

Remember to read carefully.

Draw a diagram and write a number sentence to solve.

1. A roller coaster has 10 cars that each hold 6 people. How many people can ride the roller coaster at one time?
2. There were 36 children on a field trip. The children formed 6 equal groups. How many children were in each group?

Topic 9

Patterns and Relationships

1 How many years will it take an animal symbol to repeat in the Chinese calendar? You will find out in Lesson 9-2.

2 How fast can a penguin swim? You will find out in Lesson 9-3.

3 Are the rocks of Stonehenge arranged in a pattern? You will find out in Lesson 9-6.

4

How many eggs can an ostrich hen lay in a year? You will find out in Lesson 9-4.

Review What You Know!

Vocabulary

Choose the best term from the box.

- compare
- divide
- multiply
- regroup

1. To put together equal groups to find the total number, you __?__.

2. To decide if 4 has more ones or fewer ones than 8, __?__ the numbers.

3. To separate into equal groups, you __?__.

Number Patterns

Write the missing number in each pattern.

4. 3, 6, 9, 12, ▒, 18

5. 4, 8, 12, ▒, 20, 24

6. 8, 7, 6, ▒, 4, 3

7. 30, 25, 20, 15, ▒, 5

Multiplication Facts

Find each product.

8. 4×3 **9.** 3×5 **10.** 7×2

11. 5×6 **12.** 2×4 **13.** 3×7

Division Facts

Find each quotient.

14. $20 \div 4$ **15.** $10 \div 5$ **16.** $18 \div 6$

17. $28 \div 4$ **18.** $24 \div 6$ **19.** $56 \div 8$

20. Writing to Explain Janelle bought 4 cans of tennis balls. There are 3 balls in each can. How many tennis balls did she buy? Explain how you solved the problem.

Lesson

9-1

Understand It!
Some problems can be solved by finding patterns.

Repeating Patterns

How can you continue a repeating pattern?

Rashad is making patterns with shapes. What three shapes should come next in this pattern?

A repeating pattern is made up of shapes or numbers that form a part that repeats.

Guided Practice*

Do you know HOW?

1. Draw the next three shapes to continue the pattern.

2. Write the next three numbers to continue the pattern.
9, 2, 7, 6, 9, 2, 7, 6, 9

Do you UNDERSTAND?

3. In the example above, describe the pattern using words.

4. What is the 10th shape in the pattern below? How do you know?

Independent Practice

In **5–8**, draw the next three shapes to continue the pattern.

5.

6.

7.

8.

In **9–12**, write the next three numbers to continue the pattern.

9. 1, 1, 2, 1, 1, 2, 1, 1, 2

10. 5, 7, 4, 8, 5, 7, 4, 8, 5, 7, 4

11. 2, 8, 2, 9, 2, 8, 2, 9, 2, 8, 2, 9

12. 4, 0, 3, 3, 4, 0, 3, 3, 4, 0, 3

DIGITAL Animated Glossary
www.pearsonsuccessnet.com

For another example, see Set A on page 230.

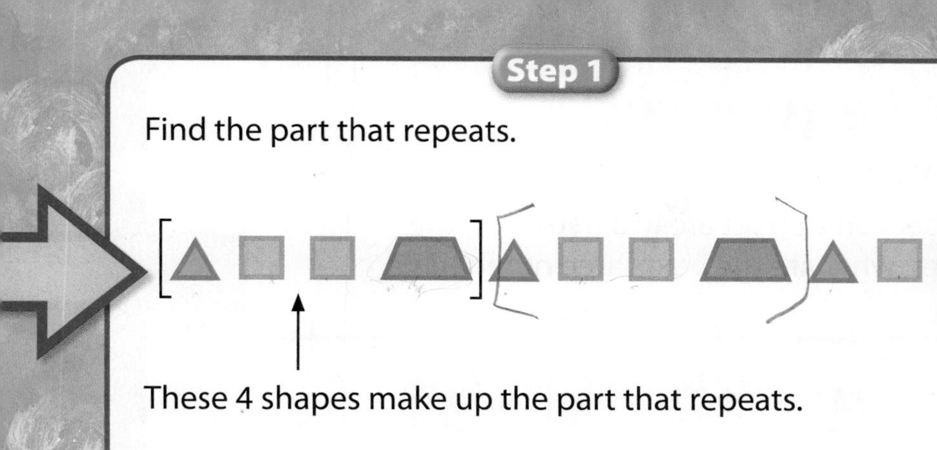

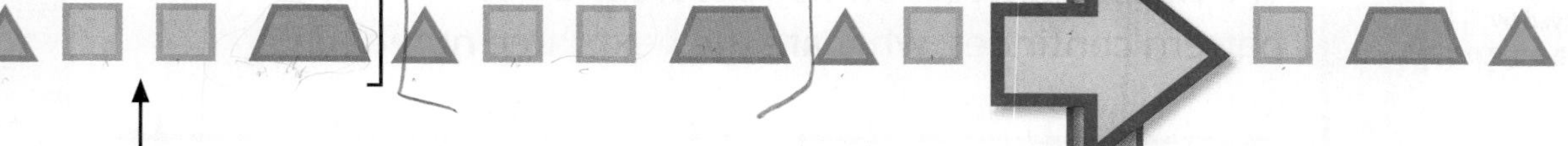

Step 2

Continue the pattern.

Problem Solving

13. Hilda is making a pattern with the shapes below. If she continues the pattern, what will the 11th shape in the pattern be? Draw a picture to show the shape.

14. Marcus is using shapes to make the pattern below. He wants the completed pattern to show the part that repeats 5 times. How many circles will be in Marcus' finished pattern?

15. Louisa put beads on a string to make a bracelet. She used a blue bead, then three green beads, then a blue bead, then three green beads, and so on, until she used 18 green beads. How many beads did she use in all?

16. **Estimation** A box of toy blocks has 108 blocks. Jiang used 72 of the blocks to make a building. About how many blocks are left in the box? Explain how you estimated.

17. The table shows the number of students in each grade at a school.

Which grade has more than 145 but fewer than 149 students?

A First **C** Second

B Third **D** Fourth

Data

Grade	Number of Students
First	142
Second	158
Third	146
Fourth	139

18. **Writing to Explain** Balloons are sold in bags of 30. There are 5 giant balloons in each bag. How many giant balloons will you get if you buy 120 balloons? Explain.

Lesson

9-2

Understand It!
Some problems can be solved by continuing patterns.

Number Sequences

What is the pattern?

The house numbers on a street are in a pattern. If the pattern continues, what are the next three numbers?

Guided Practice*

Do you know HOW?

In **1** and **2**, find a rule for the pattern. Use your rule to continue each pattern.

1. 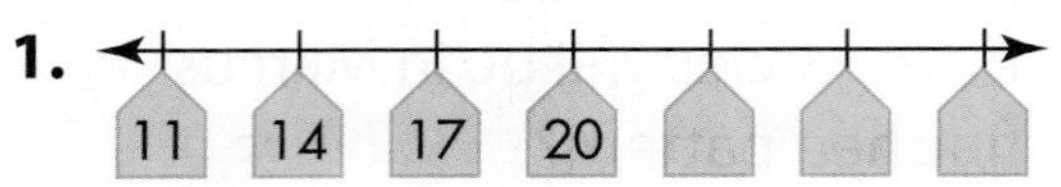

2. 48, 42, 36, 30, 24, ▢, ▢, ▢

Do you UNDERSTAND?

3. In the example above, suppose 16 is the 1st number in the pattern. What is the 10th number?

4. Rudy is using "add 2" as his rule to make a pattern. He started with 4 and wrote the numbers below for his pattern. Which number does not belong in this pattern? Explain.

4, 6, 8, 9, 10, 12

Independent Practice

In **5–16**, find a rule for the pattern. Use your rule to continue each pattern.

5. 21, 18, 15, ▢, ▢

6. 4, 11, 18, ▢, ▢

7. 5, 10, 15, ▢, ▢

8. 5, 7, 9, ▢, ▢, 15

9. 250, 300, 350, ▢, ▢

10. 92, 80, 68, ▢, ▢

11. 790, 780, 770, ▢, ▢

12. 16, 27, 38, ▢, ▢

13. 96, 101, 106, ▢, 116, ▢

14. 43, 47, 51, ▢, ▢, 63

15. 120, 105, 90, ▢, ▢, 45

16. 99, 90, 81, 72, ▢, ▢

**For another example, see Set B on page 230.*

Step 1

Find a rule for the pattern.

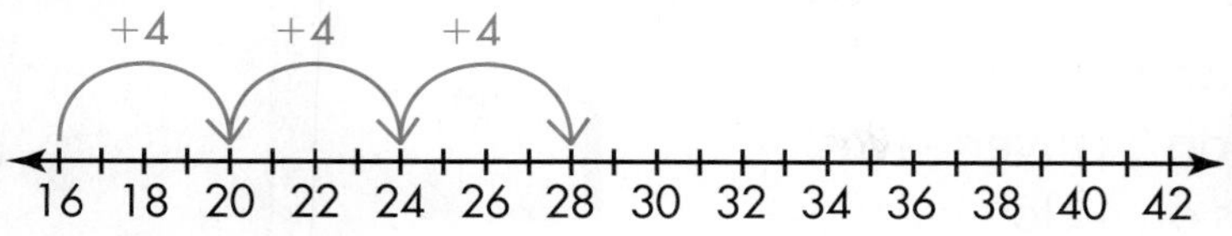

Each number is 4 more than the number before it.

Step 2

Use your rule to continue the pattern.

Rule: Add 4.

$28 + 4 = 32$
$32 + 4 = 36$
$36 + 4 = 40$

The next numbers in the pattern are 32, 36, and 40.

Problem Solving

17. Orlando delivers mail. He sees that one mailbox does not have a number. If the numbers are in a pattern, what is the missing number?

18. In the Chinese calendar, each year has an animal as a symbol. There are 12 animals. It was the year of the snake in 2001 and will be again in 2013. The year 2005 was the year of the rooster. When is the next year of the rooster?

19. Suppose you were born in the year of the snake. How old will you be the next time the year of the snake is celebrated?

The pattern of animals repeats every 12 years.

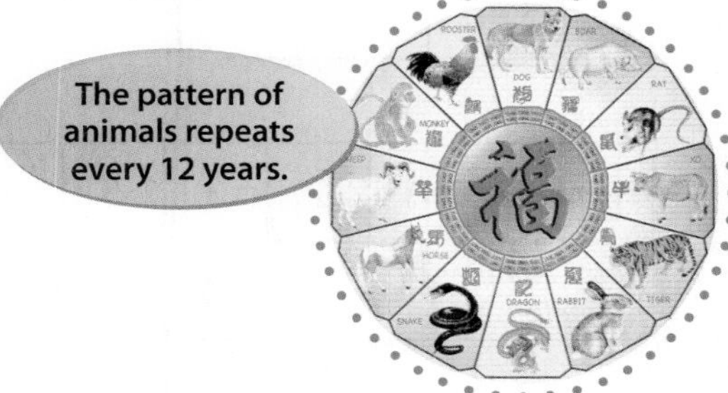

20. **Reasoning** The numbers below are in a pattern.

24, 27, 30, 33

Which number would be part of the pattern?

A 34 **C** 39

B 38 **D** 44

21. Mia counted the pencils in groups of 6.

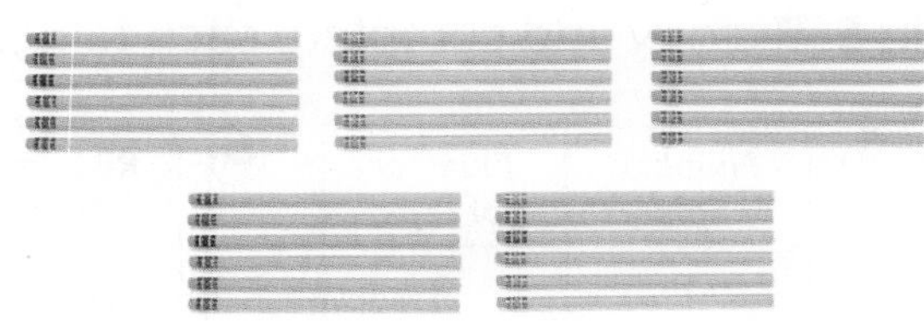

Which list shows numbers Mia named?

A 24, 36, 48, 52 **C** 6, 12, 24, 32

B 6, 24, 48, 56 **D** 12, 18, 24, 30

Lesson

9-3

Understand It!
Number pairs that fit a pattern can be organized in a table.

Extending Tables

What pairs of numbers fit a pattern?

There are 3 leaflets on 1 cloverleaf.
There are 9 leaflets on 3 cloverleaves.
There are 12 leaflets on 4 cloverleaves.
How many leaflets are there on 2 cloverleaves? on 5 cloverleaves?

A cloverleaf has 3 leaflets.

Guided Practice*

Do you know HOW?

In **1** and **2**, copy and complete each table.

1.

Number of Boxes	*Total Number of Hats*
2	6
5	15
7	21
▢	27

2.

Number of Cars	2	3	5	9
Total Number of Wheels	8	12	20	▢

Do you UNDERSTAND?

3. In the example above, 4 and 12 are a pair of numbers that fit the pattern. Does the pair 6 and 16 fit the pattern? Explain.

4. **Reasonableness** A rule for this table is "add 5 to my age."

My Age	*Joe's Age*
5	10
8	13
9	15

Which number does not belong?

Independent Practice

In **5–7**, copy and complete each table.

5.

Number of Spiders	*Number of Legs*
1	8
2	▢
3	24
4	32
▢	56

6.

Regular Price	*Sale Price*
$29	$22
$25	$18
▢	$16
$22	▢
$19	$12

7.

Weight of Book in Ounces	9	11	12	16
Total Weight of Carton in Ounces	18	20	21	▢

8. For each table in 5–7, write another pair of numbers that could be in the table.

*For another example, see Set C on page 230.

Draw pictures to show what you know.

3 leaflets 9 leaflets

12 leaflets

Fill in a table by using a rule.

Rule: Multiply by 3

Number of Cloverleaves	*Number of Leaflets*
1	3
2	6
3	9
4	12
5	15

Problem Solving

For **9** and **10**, the table at the right shows the number of batteries needed for different numbers of one kind of flashlight.

Batteries for Flashlights

Number of Flashlights	Number of Batteries
1	3
4	12
7	21

9. How many batteries do 8 flashlights need? 10 flashlights?

10. Writing to Explain How many more batteries do 6 flashlights need than 4 flashlights? Explain how you found your answer.

11. Number Sense What is the greatest number you can make using each of the digits 1, 7, 0, and 6 once?

12. A penguin can swim 11 miles per hour. At this speed, how far can it swim in 3 hours? Use a table to help.

13. Alan has 35 fewer coins than Suzy has. Which of these shows the number of coins that Alan and Suzy could have?

A Alan 65, Suzy 105 **C** Alan 105, Suzy 65

B Alan 105, Suzy 70 **D** Alan 70, Suzy 105

14. If the pattern at the right continues, how long will each side of the next square be?

A 8 feet **C** 10 feet

B 9 feet **D** 11 feet

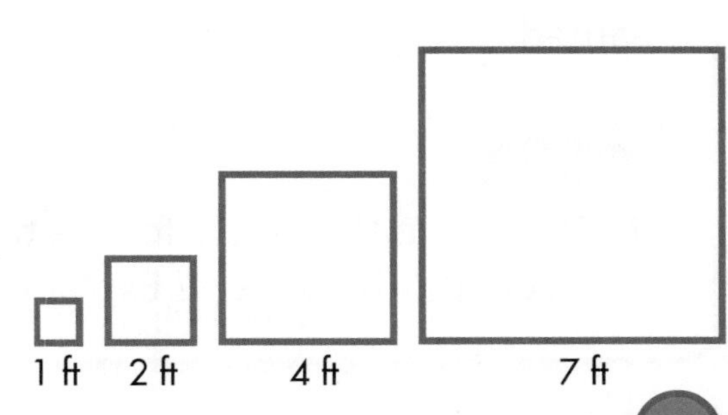

Lesson
9-4

Understand It!
A rule can be used to describe patterns in a table.

Writing Rules for Situations

What is a math rule for the situation?

Alex and his older brother Andy have the same birthday. If you know Alex's age, how can you find Andy's age? Look for a pattern in the table and find a rule.

Alex's age	2	4	6	7	9
Andy's age	8	10	12	13	15

Another Example **What other rules are there for pairs of numbers?**

Nell saves some of the money she earns. The table shows how much she earned and how much she saved for five days. What is a rule for the table? What are the missing numbers?

Earned	65¢	45¢	50¢	30¢	
Saved	50¢	30¢		15¢	25¢

Step 1

Find a rule for the table.

Look for a pattern.

Earned	65¢	45¢	50¢	30¢	
Saved	50¢	30¢		15¢	25¢

Each time, the amount saved is 15¢ less than the amount earned.

Rule: Subtract 15¢ from the amount earned.

Step 2

Check that your rule works for all pairs.

65¢ − 15¢ = 50¢
45¢ − 15¢ = 30¢
30¢ − 15¢ = 15¢

Your rule works for each pair.

What amount is 15¢ less than 50¢?
50¢ − 15¢ = 35¢

25¢ is 15¢ less than what amount?
25¢ = ▢ − 15¢   15¢ + 25¢ = 40¢

The missing amounts are 35¢ saved and 40¢ earned.

Explain It

1. David said that a rule for the table above is "Add 15¢." Could this be correct? Explain.

Step 1

Find a rule for the table.

Compare each pair of numbers. Look for a pattern.

Alex's age	2	4	6	7	9
Andy's age	8	10	12	13	15

In each pair, Andy's age is 6 more than Alex's age. You say a rule for the table is "add 6."

Step 2

Check that your rule works for all pairs.

Rule: Add 6.

$2 + 6 = 8$
$4 + 6 = 10$
$6 + 6 = 12$
$7 + 6 = 13$
$9 + 6 = 15$

Your rule works for each pair.

Guided Practice*

Do you know HOW?

In **1** and **2**, use the table below.

Hours Worked	4	8	7	2	6
Amount Earned	$24	$48		$12	

1. Write a rule for the table.

2. What are the missing numbers?

Do you UNDERSTAND?

3. In the example above, what does the rule "add 6" mean in the problem?

4. Marty uses the rule "subtract 9" for his table. If the first number in Marty's table is 11, what is the second number in that pair?

Independent Practice

In **5–9**, find a rule for the table. Use your rule to complete the table.

5.

Earned	$15	$12	$17	$9	$11
Spent	$7		$9		$3

6.

Earned	$14	$18	$12	$16	$8
Saved	$7	$9			$4

7.

Price	$36	$28	$33	$40	$25
Discount	$24	$16		$28	

8.

Number of Chairs	*Number of Legs*
3	12
2	8
5	20
7	
	36

9.

Number of Teams	*Number of Players*
4	20
3	15
5	
6	30
8	

**For another example, see Set C on page 230.*

Problem Solving

For **10** and **11**, use the table at the right.

10. The table shows the ages of a velvet mesquite tree and a saguaro cactus plant at a garden. When the velvet mesquite tree was 48 years old, how old was the saguaro cactus?

Plant's Age in Years

Velvet Mesquite Tree	Saguaro Cactus
1 year	36
15	50
67	102
48	

11. **Reasonableness** Phil says the saguaro cactus is about 100 years older than the velvet mesquite tree. Is his estimate reasonable? Explain.

12. Use the table below. How many eggs can 4 ostrich hens lay in one year? 5 ostrich hens?

Number of Ostrich Hens	1	2	3	4	5
Number of Eggs	50	100	150		

An ostrich hen can lay 50 eggs in a year. A male ostrich helps care for the eggs.

For **13** and **14**, the table shows the number of baskets that Betty needs for different numbers of apples. She needs to put an equal number of apples into each basket.

Betty's Apple Baskets

Number of Apples	28	56	7	21	14
Number of Baskets	4		1	3	2

13. How many baskets does Betty need for 56 apples?

A 8 **B** 7 **C** 6 **D** 5

14. What is a rule for the table?

A Subtract 24. **C** Divide by 7.

B Subtract 6. **D** Add 12.

15. An art museum has 47 paintings in one room and 24 paintings in another room. Which is the best estimate of the total number of paintings in these two rooms?

A 50 **C** 80

B 70 **D** 100

16. Esther is 8 years older than Manuel. Which of these shows the ages that Esther and Manuel could be?

A Esther 15, Manuel 23

B Esther 16, Manuel 15

C Esther 15, Manuel 7

D Esther 7, Manuel 15

Mixed Problem Solving

In the 1800s and 1900s, several inventions helped to change life around the world. The time line shows the dates of some of these inventions and discoveries.

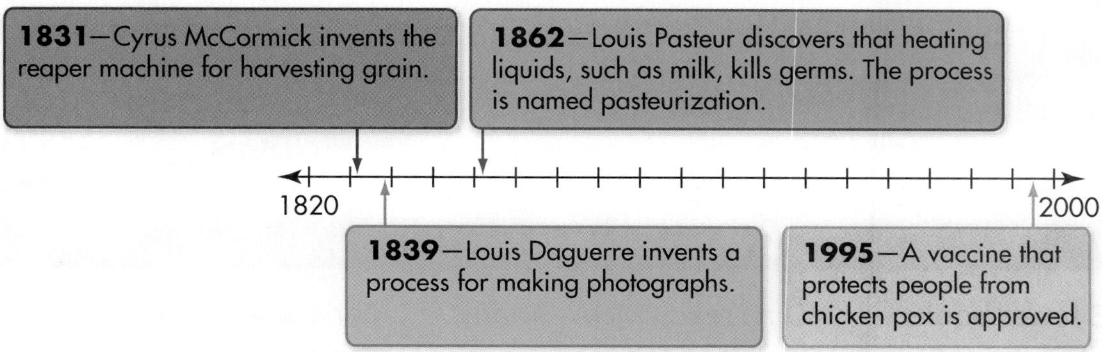

1. Which invention was made about 10 years before a process for making photographs was invented?

2. How many years after the discovery of pasteurization was the chicken pox vaccine approved?

3. Which invention or discovery was made before 1900 but after 1850?

4. How many years have passed since the year that a chicken pox vaccine was approved?

For **5** and **6**, use the table below.

Data

Year	Invention
1804	Steam Locomotive
1885	Gasoline-powered Automobile
1934	Diesel Train in U.S.

5. How many years passed between the first steam locomotive and U.S. diesel train?

6. How many years ago was the gasoline-powered automobile invented?

7. **Strategy Focus** Solve the problem. Use the strategy Make a Table.

   The reaper machine could cut wheat and move it to the side for harvesting. One reaper machine could do the work of 5 people. How many reapers could do the work of 20 people?

Lesson
9-5

Understand It!
A relationship can be described using words or symbols.

Translating Words to Expressions

How can you translate words to numerical expressions?

Jon read 8 books.

In a reading contest, Kara read 5 more books than Jon. What numerical expression shows how many books Kara read?

A numerical expression is made up of numbers and at least one operation symbol.

Other Examples

Teri read 3 fewer books than Jon read.

Word phrase
"3 fewer books than the 8 books Jon read"

Numerical expression
$8 - 3$

Dina read twice as many books as Jon read.

Word phrase
"twice as many as the 8 books Jon read"

Numerical expression
2×8

For 4 weeks, Jon read the same number of books each week.

Word phrase
"the 8 books Jon read, put into 4 equal groups"

Numerical expression
$8 \div 4$

Guided Practice*

Do you know HOW?

Write a numerical expression for each.

1. 18 less than 25

2. half of 14

"Half" means 2 equal groups.

3. the total of 24, 16, and 32

Do you UNDERSTAND?

4. Jon read 7 fewer books than Jamal. Use the examples above to write a numerical expression to show how many books Jamal read.

5. **Reasoning** Does the word "fewer" always tell you to subtract? Explain.

Independent Practice

In **6–9**, write a numerical expression for each word phrase.

6. 7 times as many as 8

7. the product of 9 and 8

8. the difference of 56 and 48

9. the sum of 15, 24, and 18

*For another example, see Set D on page 231.

What You Think

Word phrase:
"5 more books than the 8 books Jon read"
To find 5 more than a number, use addition.

What You Write

To show the number of books Kara read, write "the sum of 8 and 5" as a numerical expression.

Numerical expression:
$8 + 5$

Problem Solving

In **10–17,** write a numerical expression for each word phrase.

10. 8 points taken away from 16 points

11. 28 players separated into 4 equal teams

12. \$15 less than \$35

13. 4 times as long as 9 inches

14. twice as old as 7 years old

15. 24 grapes shared equally by 4 people

16. the total of 18 children and 13 adults

17. 45 yards shorter than 120 yards

There are 10 cars in a parking lot. For **18–21,** write a numerical expression for the number of cars described in each word phrase.

18. 7 fewer cars

19. half the number of cars

20. 5 times as many cars

21. 12 more cars

22. **Geometry** Juana has a wooden block that is 12 inches long. Juana cut the block into 6 pieces that are all the same length. How long is each piece?

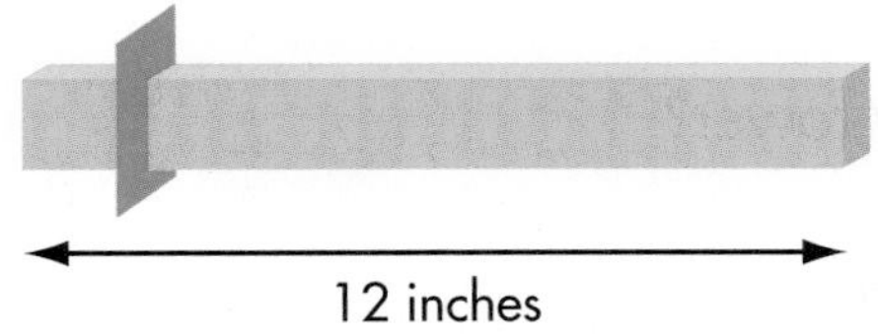

23. Walt bought 16 muffins packed equally into 4 boxes. Which numerical expression shows how to find the number of muffins in each box?

A $16 \div 4$ **C** $16 - 4$

B 16×4 **D** $16 + 4$

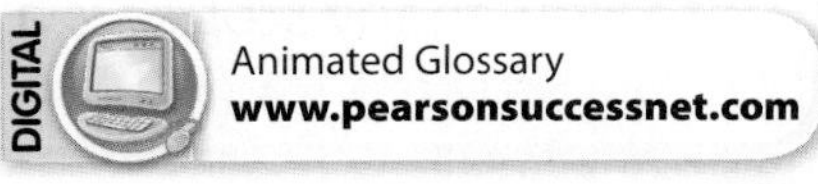

Lesson
9-6

Understand It!
Patterns can be used to make predictions.

Geometric Patterns

Hands-On
grid paper
cubes

How can you describe block towers?

Talisa made three block towers. She recorded her pattern. If she continued the pattern, how many blocks would be in a 10-story tower? a 100-story tower?

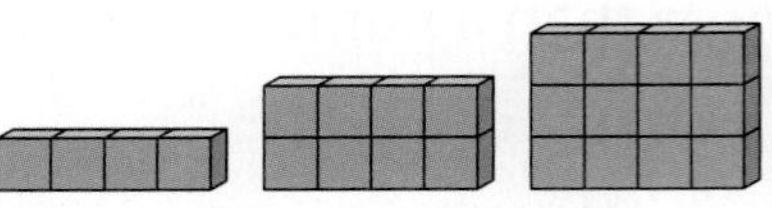

Stories:	1	2	3
Blocks:	4	8	12

Another Example Making Another Block Tower

Luis made three more block towers. He recorded his pattern. If he continued the pattern, how many blocks would a 5-story tower have?

Number of Stories	1	2	3
Number of Blocks	1	3	6

Build the next two towers.

Number of Stories	1	2	3	4	5
Number of Blocks	1	3	6		

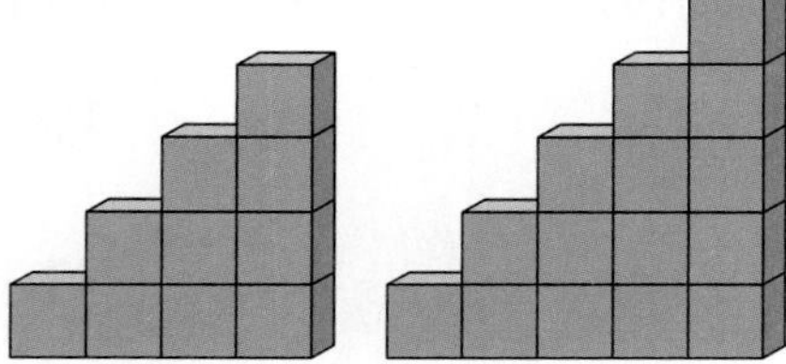

A 4-story tower has 10 blocks, and a 5-story tower has 15 blocks.

Explain It

1. How many blocks would Luis need for a 6-story tower? Explain.
2. How many stories is a tower made of 36 blocks?

Build the next two towers.

Number of Stories	1	2	3	4	5
Number of Blocks	4	8	12		

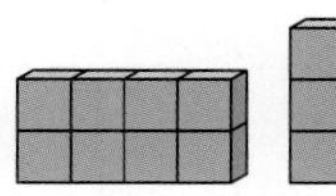
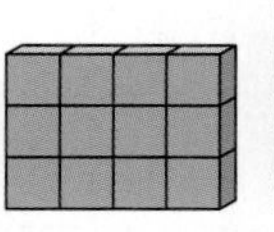
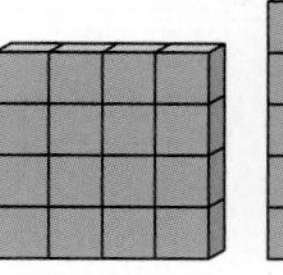
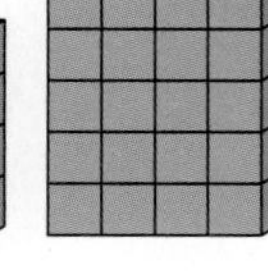

1 story 4 blocks | 2 stories 8 blocks | 3 stories 12 blocks | 4 stories 16 blocks | 5 stories 20 blocks

A rule for the pattern in the table is "multiply by 4."

$$5 \times 4 = 20$$
$$10 \times 4 = 40$$
$$100 \times 4 = 400$$

A 10-story tower would have 40 blocks.

A 100-story tower would have 400 blocks.

Guided Practice*

Do you know HOW?

In **1** and **2**, draw the next two towers in the pattern. Use grid paper. Find the missing numbers in each table.

1.

Number of Stories	1	2	3	4	5
Number of Blocks	2	4	6		

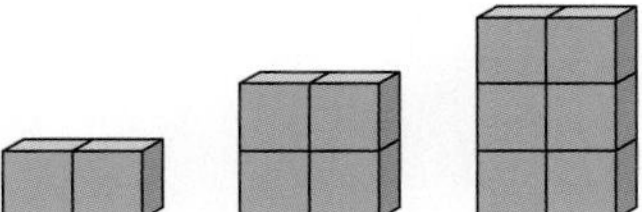

2.

Number of Stories	1	2	3	4	5	
Number of Blocks	2	3	4	5		7

Do you UNDERSTAND?

3. In the example above, why does multiplication work to get from the first number to the second number in a number pair?

4. In Exercise 1, how many blocks would a 10-story tower have?

5. Lionel made the three block towers below. If he continued the pattern, how many blocks would a 100-story tower have?

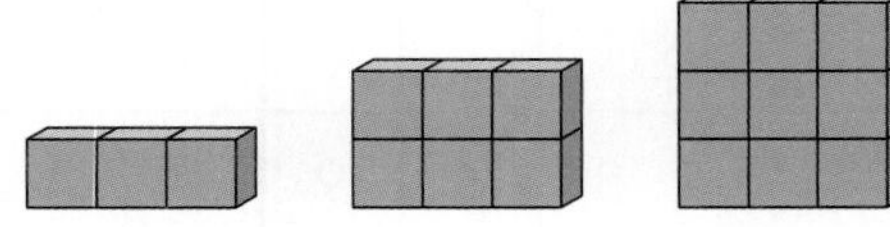

6. Writing to Explain How many blocks would you need to make a 15-story tower in Exercise 2? Explain how you know.

DIGITAL eTools **www.pearsonsuccessnet.com**

For another example, see Set C on page 230.

Independent Practice

In **7–10**, use patterns to find the missing numbers in each table. You may draw the next two figures on grid paper to help.

7.

Number of Stories	7	6	5	4	3
Number of Blocks	21	18	15		

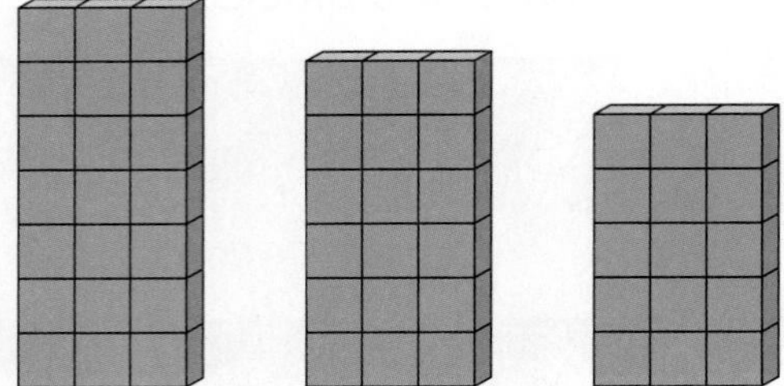

8.

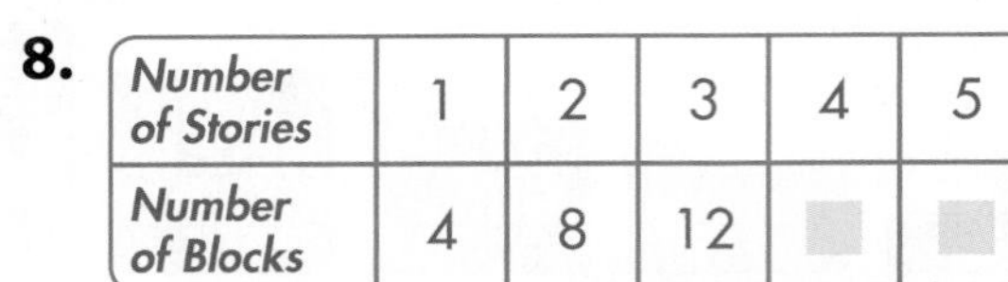

Number of Stories	1	2	3	4	5
Number of Blocks	4	8	12		

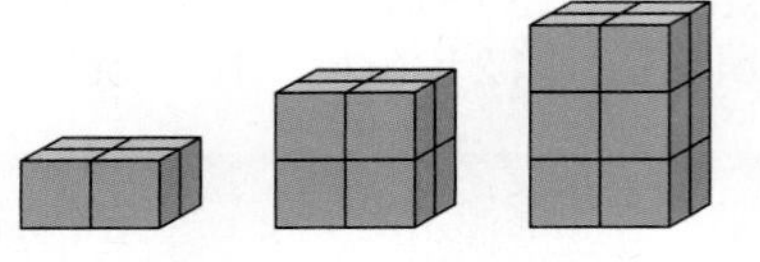

9.

Number of Rows	2	3	4	5	6
Number of Squares	3	5	7		

10.

Number of Rows	1	2	3	4	5
Number of Small Triangles	1	4	9		

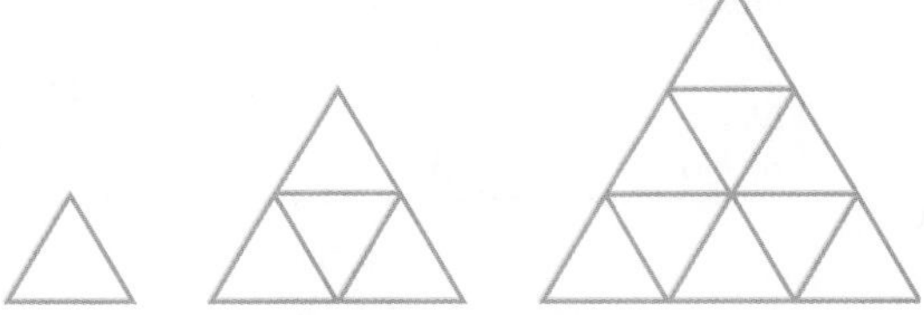

In **11–13**, use the patterns in the block towers or squares to copy and complete each table.

11.

Number of Stories	1	2	3	4	5	
Number of Blocks	3	6	9			30

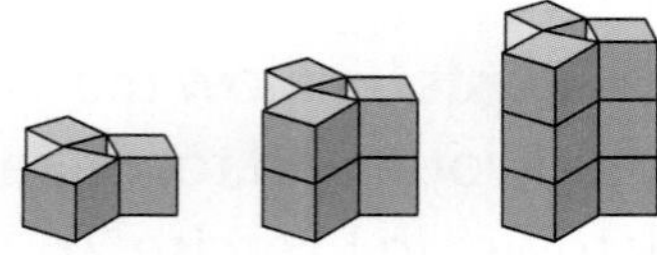

12.

Length of Each Side	1	2	4	6	9
Sum of All Sides	4	8	16		

13.

Number of Stories	1	2	3	4	5
Number of Blocks	2	6	12		

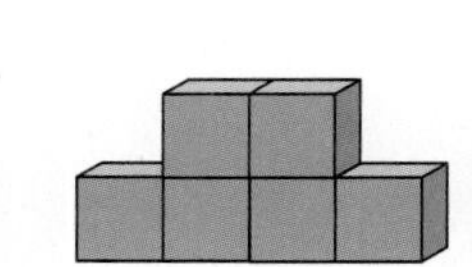

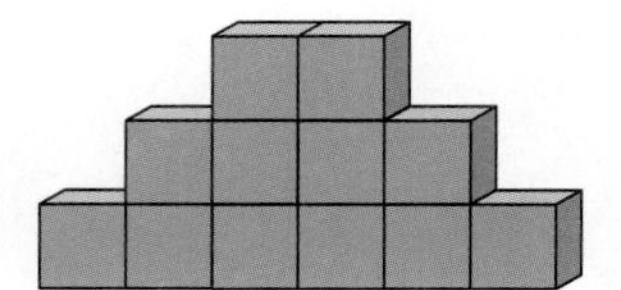

Problem Solving

14. Jon used 15 blocks to make a tower. Next he used 12 blocks to make a tower, and then 9 blocks to make a tower. If he continued the pattern, what rule could he use for this table?

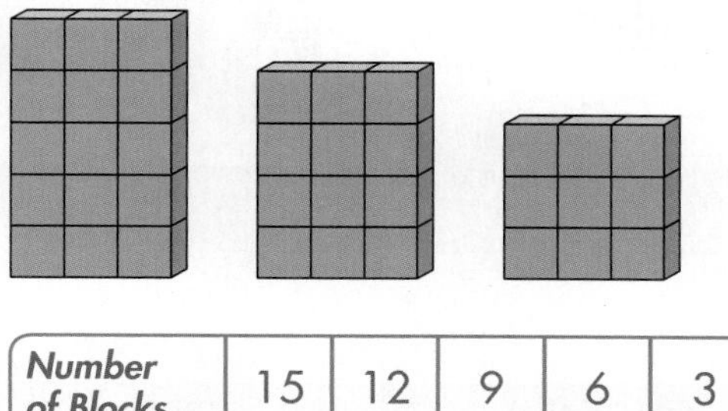

Number of Blocks	15	12	9	6	3
Number of Stories	5	4	3	2	1

15. Dean is making picture frames. He uses the same number of wood pieces in each frame. The table shows the number of wood pieces that he needs for different numbers of frames.

Number of Frames	6	7	8	9	10
Number of Wood Pieces	24	28	■	36	40

How many wood pieces does Dean need for 8 picture frames?

A 30 **C** 34

B 32 **D** 36

16. Stonehenge is an ancient monument in England made up of a pattern of rocks that looks like this:

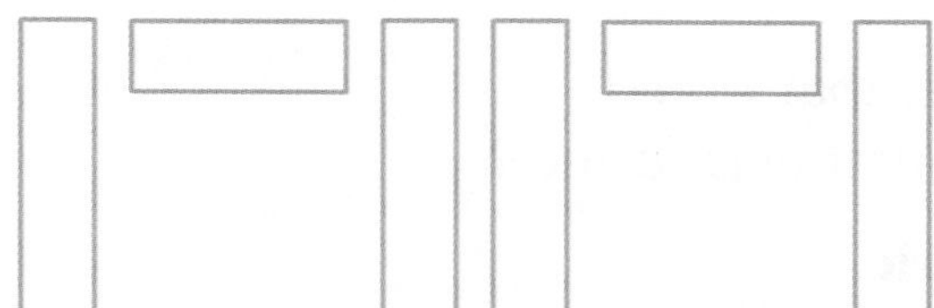

Draw the shape that comes next.

17. Maura made these three block towers. If she continued the pattern, how many blocks would a 10-story tower have? How many blocks would a 100-story tower have?

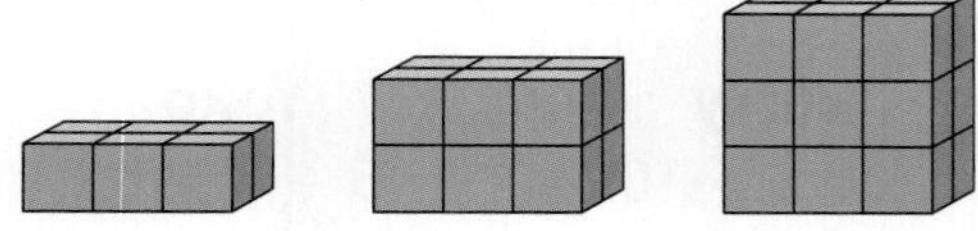

18. **Algebra** What two 1-digit factors could you multiply to get a product of 48?

19. **Number Sense** Which product is greater, 9×15 or 9×17? Explain how you can tell without finding the products.

20. **Estimation** Lily has 75¢. A stamp costs 39¢. Does she have enough money to buy 2 stamps? Explain.

21. Leon ran twice as many laps around the track as Sam. Sam ran 6 laps. How many laps did they run in all?

22. **Writing to Explain** Eduardo spent \$3.78 on groceries. He paid with a \$5 bill. How do you know that his change included at least two pennies?

Lesson

9-7

Understand It!
Expressions can be compared using =, >, and <.

Equal or Unequal

How can you compare two expressions?

Max and Julie each have the books shown in the bookcase. If Max gets 2 more books and Julie gives away 3 of her books, how can you compare the numbers of books they will have?

A numerical expression contains numbers and at least one operation.

Other Examples

An equation is a number sentence that says two expressions are equal.

$$5 + 3 = 10 - 2$$
$$8 = 8$$

An inequality is a number sentence that uses < or >. An inequality shows that two expressions are not equal.

$$5 + 1 < 10 - 1$$
$$6 < 9$$

$$3 + 4 + 1 > 12 - 6$$
$$8 > 6$$

Jerry, Yoko, and Eric each tried to find a number that would make the inequality 5 + ▭ > 10 true. Whose number is correct?

Jerry	Yoko	Eric
$5 + 6 > 10$	$5 + 8 > 10$	$5 + 3 > 10$
$11 > 10$	$13 > 10$	$8 > 10$
True	True	False

Jerry's and Yoko's numbers are correct.

Guided Practice*

Do you know HOW?

Compare. Write <, >, or = for each ◯.

1. 12 + 5 ◯ 20 − 2

2. 46 + 10 ◯ 50

3. 27 + 8 ◯ 6 + 29

Do you UNDERSTAND?

4. **Reasoning** Find a third number that makes 5 + ▭ > 10 true.

5. Tom had 9 rocks and then got 3 more. Ira had 11 rocks but lost 2 of them. Write a number sentence to compare their numbers of rocks.

*For another example, see Set E on page 231.

Step 1

Write an expression for each person's number of books.

Max	Julie
6 + 2	12 − 3

Step 2

Do the operation for each expression to find how the expressions compare.

Max	Julie
6 + 2 → 8	12 − 3 → 9

Step 3

Use <, >, or = to compare the expressions.

$8 < 9$ so

$6 + 2 < 12 - 3$

Independent Practice

In **6–8**, compare. Write <, >, or = for each ◯.

6. 34 + 17 ◯ 45 **7.** 18 + 9 ◯ 6 + 21 **8.** 41 + 7 ◯ 53 − 4

In **9–11**, write a number that makes each number sentence true.

9. 4 + ▢ = 12 **10.** 16 − ▢ > 10 **11.** 5 + ▢ < 18

Problem Solving

For **12–14**, the table at the right shows the number of rocks in each friend's collection last month.

Rock Collections (Data)

Name	Number of Rocks
Ana	29
Julio	32
Rashad	27
Sally	45

12. How many more rocks did Sally have than Ana?

13. This month, Rashad collected 7 more rocks and Ana gave away 3 rocks. Write a number sentence to compare their numbers of rocks.

14. This month, Sally gave away 6 rocks and Julio got 8 more rocks. Write a number sentence to compare their numbers of rocks.

15. Estimation Boris put 18 lemons on one shelf. He put 34 lemons on another shelf. About how many lemons in all did he put on the shelves?

16. Which symbol makes the number sentence true?

34 − 17 ◯ 5 + 11

A + **B** = **C** < **D** >

Lesson
9-8

Understand It!
Sometimes you can use objects to act out a problem and then use reasoning to find the answer.

Problem Solving

Act It Out and Use Reasoning

Hands-On
counters

Juana collected old pennies, nickels, and dimes. Her collection has at least one of each kind of coin.

How many of each kind of coin does Juana have?

nickel penny dime

Juana's Collection
2 pennies
2 fewer nickels than dimes
10 coins in all

Another Example What are other kinds of relationships?

Ken's Collection of Dimes, Nickels, and Pennies
3 nickels
4 more dimes than nickels
15 coins in all

How many of each coin are in his collection?

Read and Understand

What do I know? There are 15 coins in all, and 3 of the coins are nickels.

There are 4 more dimes than nickels.

Use objects to show what you know.

Plan and Solve

Use reasoning to make conclusions.

Since there are 3 nickels, there are 12 pennies and dimes together.

Try 3 nickels, 7 dimes, and 5 pennies. Since $3 + 7 + 5 = 15$, this is correct.

There are 5 pennies, 3 nickels, and 7 dimes in the collection.

Explain It

1. Which number of coins in Ken's collection is given to you? Which information do you need to find?
2. Explain how you know 7 is the number of dimes in the solution above.

Read and Understand

What do I know? Juana has 10 coins in all, and 2 of the coins are pennies.

There are 2 fewer nickels than dimes.

Use objects to show what you know.

Plan and Solve

Use reasoning to make conclusions.

She has 2 pennies, so there are 8 nickels and dimes together.

Try 1 nickel and 7 dimes.
$2 + 1 + 7 = 10$, but 1 nickel is not 2 fewer than 7.

Try 3 nickels and 5 dimes.
Since $2 + 3 + 5 = 10$, this is correct.

There are 2 pennies, 3 nickels, and 5 dimes in Juana's collection.

Guided Practice*

Do you know HOW?

Find the number of each kind of stamp in the collection. Use counters.

1. Ricardo has 9 stamps in all. He has 2 nation stamps and 3 more inventor stamps than flower stamps.

   Nation Stamps = ▢
   Inventor Stamps = ▢
   Flower Stamps = ▢

Do you UNDERSTAND?

2. What did you do to find the number of inventor stamps in Ricardo's collection?

3. **Write a Problem** Write a problem about coin collections that you can solve by using reasoning.

Independent Practice

Find the number of each kind of object in Anya's collection. Use counters or draw pictures to help.

4. **Anya's Collection of Minerals, Gemstones and Rocks**
   6 minerals
   3 fewer gemstones than rocks.
   15 objects in all.

   Minerals = ▢
   Gemstones = ▢
   Rocks = ▢

Stuck? Try this....

- What do I know?
- What am I asked to find?
- What diagram can I use to help understand the problem?
- Can I use addition, subtraction, multiplication, or division?
- Is all of my work correct?
- Did I answer the right question?
- Is my answer reasonable?

**For another example, see Set F on page 231.*

Independent Practice

5. There are 10 fish in all in Percy's fish tank. Four of the fish are angel fish. There are 4 more mollie fish than tetra fish. How many of each kind of fish are in the tank?

6. Norah's dog weighs 9 pounds more than her cat. Her dog weighs 6 pounds less than Jeff's dog. Norah's cat weighs 7 pounds. How much does Jeff's dog weigh?

The students in Mr. Cole's class voted on which kind of collection their class should start. The graph shows the results. Use the graph for **7–9**.

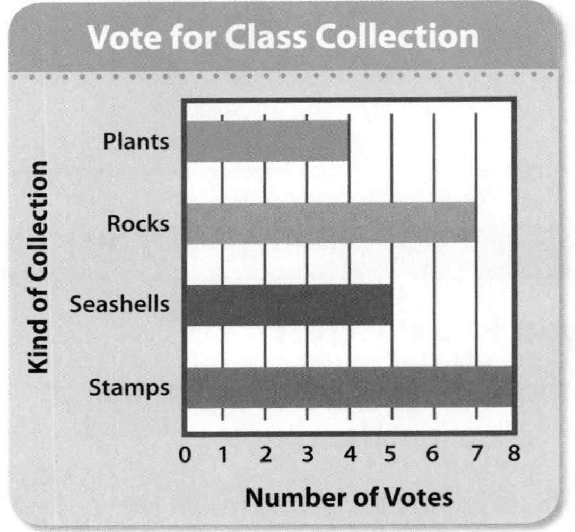

7. Which collection got five votes?

8. Which collection got the greatest number of votes?

9. How many more votes did the collection with the most of votes get than the collection with the fewest votes?

10. Isadora has 15 seashells in her collection. She has some oyster shells, some conch shells, and 6 clam shells. She has 2 fewer clam shells than oyster shells. How many conch shells does she have?

11. Lyn, Kurt, and Steve wrote a riddle about their ages. Lyn is 7 years older than Steve. Steve is 5 years old. The sum of their ages is 25 years. How old is Kurt?

12. Sondra wants to buy 2 plates and 3 towels. What is the total cost of her items?

Data

Item	Price
Flashlight	$9
Plate	$7
Towel	$4
Fishing net	$8
Umbrella	$3

13. **Think About the Process** At the town pet show, Dina saw 48 pets. There were 6 birds and 7 cats. The remaining pets were dogs. Which number sentence shows one way to find the number of pets that were dogs?

A $48 - 6 - 7 = \square$

B $48 + 6 \div 7 = \square$

C $48 - 6 \times 7 = \square$

D $6 \times 7 \times 48 = \square$

Extending Tables

Use eTools

Spreadsheet/Data/Grapher eTool

Use a rule to complete the table.

Number of Lions	1	2	3	4	5
Number of Legs	4	8		16	20

Step 1 Go to the Spreadsheet/Data/Grapher eTool. Use the arrow tool to select at least 2 rows and 6 columns. Set the number of decimal places at zero using the .00 pull-down menu. Enter *Lions*, *1*, *2*, *3*, *4*, *5* in row A. Enter *Legs* in the first column of row B.

Step 2 Try the rule "multiply by 4." Cell B2 is in column B, row 2. In cell B2, type = *4*B1*. This means "multiply 4 by the value in cell B1." The product will be shown in cell B2. In cell C2, type = *4*C1*. In cell D2, type = *4*D1* and so on for cells E2 and F2.

Step 3 Check that the numbers match those in the table above. This means the rule "multiply by 4" is correct. The missing number is 12.

F2 20

	A	B	C	D	E	F
1	Lions	1.00	2.00	3.00	4.00	5.00
2	Legs	4.00	8.00	12.00	16.00	20.00

Practice

Copy each table, find a rule, and fill in the missing cell.

1.

Bud's Age	2	4	6	9
Spot's Age	7	9		14

2.

Days	1	2	3	4
Toys Made	7		21	28

Topic 9

Test

1. Football players came out of the tunnel in the pattern shown below.

What number belongs on the blank jersey? (9-2)

A 26

B 25

C 24

D 22

2. What are the next three numbers in this pattern? (9-1)

6, 5, 3, 1, 6, 5, 3, 1, 6, 5, 3

A 6, 3, 1

B 6, 5, 3

C 1, 5, 3

D 1, 6, 5

3. What rule can be used to find the number of legs on 7 grasshoppers? (9-4)

Number of Grasshoppers	3	5	7	9
Number of Legs	18	30		54

A Add 15.

B Divide by 5.

C Multiply by 5.

D Multiply by 6.

4. Kayla is cutting ribbon to go around cards. Each card is shaped like a triangle with all sides the same length. How many inches of ribbon does she need for a card with each side 7 inches long? (9-6)

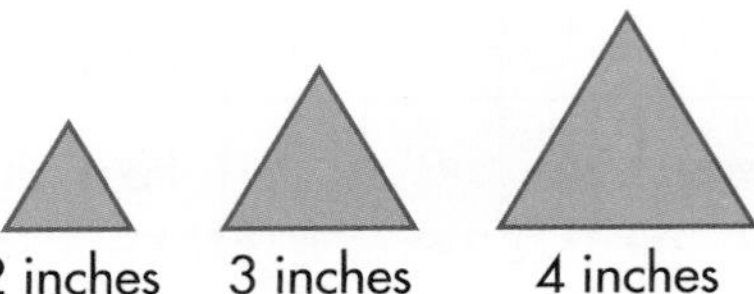

Side Length in Inches	2	3	4	7
Inches of Ribbon	6	9	12	

A 15

B 18

C 21

D 24

5. Coach Kim needs to form teams that all have the same number of players. The table shows the number of teams formed for different numbers of players.

Number of Players	24	32	40	72
Number of Teams	3	4		9

What rule can be used to find how many teams are formed if there are 40 players? (9-4)

A Divide by 8.

B Divide by 6.

C Subtract 21.

D Multiply by 6.

6. Hank had a party at the zoo. He used the table below to find the total price of admission for groups of different sizes.

Total Number of Children	*Total Admission Price*
3	$21
5	$35
7	▢
9	$63

What is the total cost of admission for 7 children? (9-3)

A $37

B $48

C $49

D $56

7. Joe has 18 pets. His pets are birds, hamsters, and 10 fish. He has 2 fewer birds than hamsters. How many birds does he have? (9-8)

A 2

B 3

C 4

D 5

8. Which is a rule for the pattern? (9-2)

29, 24, 19, 14, 9

A Subtract 4.

B Subtract 5.

C Add 4.

D Subtract 10.

9. Fran has 3 grapes. Ivan has 6 times as many grapes as Fran. Which numerical expression shows how to find the number of grapes Ivan has? (9-5)

A $6 + 3$

B $6 - 3$

C 6×3

D $6 \div 3$

10. Which symbol makes the number sentence true? (9-7)

$24 + 9 \bigcirc 36 - 4$

A $>$

B $<$

C $=$

D $\times$

11. Which numerical expression shows 2 feet shorter than 18 feet? (9-5)

A $2 - 18$

B $18 \div 2$

C $18 + 2$

D $18 - 2$

12. Which number makes the number sentence true? (9-7)

$9 + \square = 16$

A 25

B 7

C 6

D 5

Reteaching

Set A, pages 206–207

Draw the next three shapes to continue the pattern.

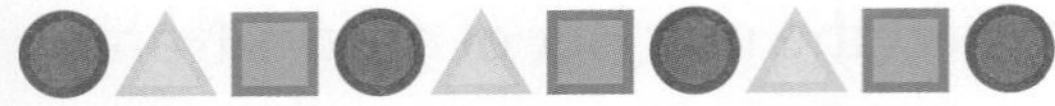

Find the part that repeats.

Then continue the pattern.

Remember to first find the part of the pattern that repeats.

Draw the next three shapes or numbers to continue the pattern.

1. ➡⬆⬆➡⬆⬆➡⬆⬆➡
2. 3, 5, 7, 9, 3, 5, 7, 9, 3, 5, 7

Set B, pages 208–209

Find a rule to use to continue the pattern.

24, 21, 18, 15, 12, ▢, ▢, ▢,

−3 −3 −3 −3 −3 −3 −3

Rule: Subtract 3
The next numbers in the pattern are 9, 6, and 3.

Remember to check that your rule works with all of the given numbers.

Write a rule and continue the pattern.

1. 5, 7, 9, ▢, ▢, ▢
2. 22, 18, 14, ▢, ▢, ▢

Set C, pages 210–214, 218–221

If Sam continues the pattern, how many blocks would a 5-story tower have? a 10-story tower?

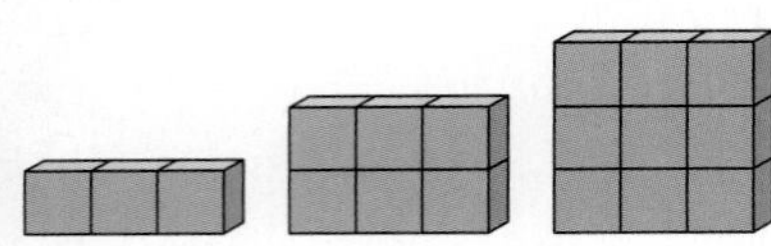

Stories	1	2	3
Blocks	3	6	9

A pattern in the table is multiply by 3. So, use 5×3 to find the number of blocks in a 5-story tower.
$5 \times 3 = 15$
There are 15 blocks in a 5-story tower.

A 10-story tower would have 10×3 or 30 blocks.

Remember to use the number pairs in a table to find a rule or make predictions.

In 1 and 2, write the missing numbers and a rule.

1.

Cars	1	2	3	4
Wheels	4	8	▢	▢

2. Draw the next two figures in the pattern. Use grid paper.

Stories	1	2	3	4	5
Blocks	6	12	18	▢	▢

Set D, pages 216–217

Some friends made posters for a music night. Kelli made 3 times as many posters as Rob. Suppose ▢ stands for the number of posters Rob made. Write a numerical expression to show how many posters Kelli made.

Think *Word phrase*
"3 times as many posters as Rob made"

Numerical expression: 3 × ▢

Remember that ▢ stands for a value in the problem.

1. Suppose ▢ stands for the number of friends who will share 16 peaches equally. Write a numerical expression to show how many peaches each friend will get.

Set E, pages 222–223

Compare the expressions.

3 + 4 ◯ 8 − 2

Do the operation for each expression,
3 + 4 = 7   8 − 2 = 6

Compare. 7 > 6

3 + 4 > 8 − 2

Remember to do each operation.

Copy and complete. Use >, <, or = to compare.

1. 18 − 11 ◯ 7 + 1
2. 25 + 9 ◯ 46 − 12

Write a number that makes the number sentence true.

3. 13 − ▢ > 9

Set F, pages 224–226

When you solve a problem by acting it out, follow these steps.

Step 1

Choose objects to act out the problem.

Step 2

Show what you know using the objects.

Step 3

Act out the problem.

Step 4

Find the answer.

Remember to decide what the objects represent before you begin.

Solve. Find the number of each kind of sticker in Ben's collection.

1. **Ben's Sticker Collection**
   - 3 kinds of stickers with 17 stickers in all
   - 6 star stickers
   - 3 fewer smiley face stickers than planet stickers

Topic 10

Solids and Shapes

1 A sculpture in Madrid, Spain, is made from 6 tons of bananas! Which solid figure best describes the shape of this sculpture? You will find out in Lesson 10-1.

2 Which geometric term describes the wings of a biplane? You will find out in Lesson 10-3.

3

Which polygons did famous architect Frank Lloyd Wright use in designing this building ? You will find out in Lesson 10-5.

4

When was this unusual bicycle designed? You will find out in Lesson 10-7.

Review What You Know!

Vocabulary

Choose the best term from the box.

- circle
- cube
- square
- triangle

1. A shape that has 4 sides all the same length is called a ___?___.
2. A solid that has six square faces is called a ___?___.
3. A shape with 3 sides is called a ___?___.

Name Solids and Shapes

Write the name of each figure.

4. 

5. 

6. 

7. 

Shapes

Write the number of sides each figure has.

8. 

9. 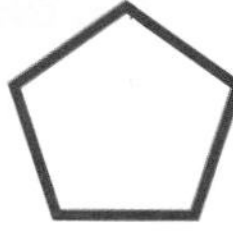

10. 

11. 

12. **Writing to Explain** Which solid rolls, a cone or a cube? Explain why it rolls.

Lesson

10-1

Understand It!
Solid figures in the world around us come in many shapes and sizes.

Solid Figures

What is a solid figure?

A solid figure is a geometric figure that has length, width, and height.

Some common solid figures and their names are shown at the right.

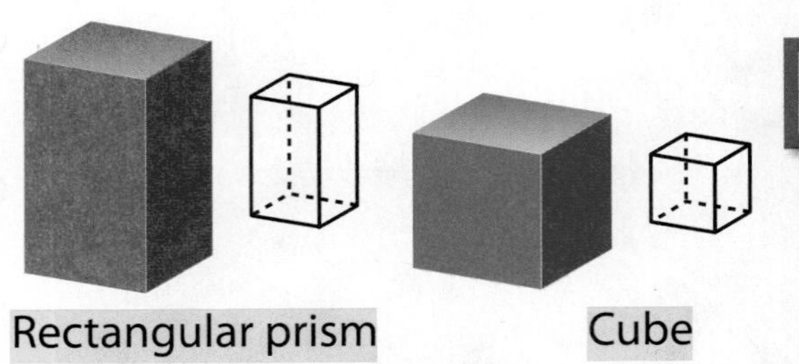

Rectangular prism

Cube

Another Example **How do solid figures help you describe objects in the world around you?**

Many things in the real world are shaped like the solid figures shown above. Name the solid figure each object looks like.

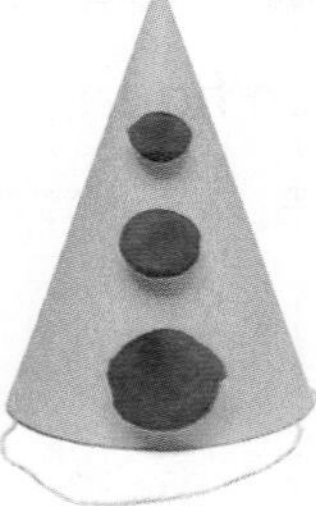

The clown's hat looks like a cone.

The cereal box looks like a rectangular prism.

The tennis ball looks like a sphere.

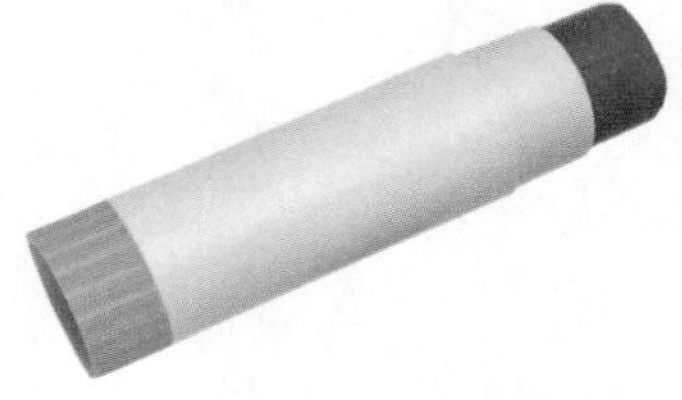

The glue stick looks like a cylinder.

Explain It

1. Explain why the clown's hat looks like a cone.
2. Why is it wrong to say that the cereal box looks like a cube?
3. Which of the 4 objects pictured can roll? Explain.

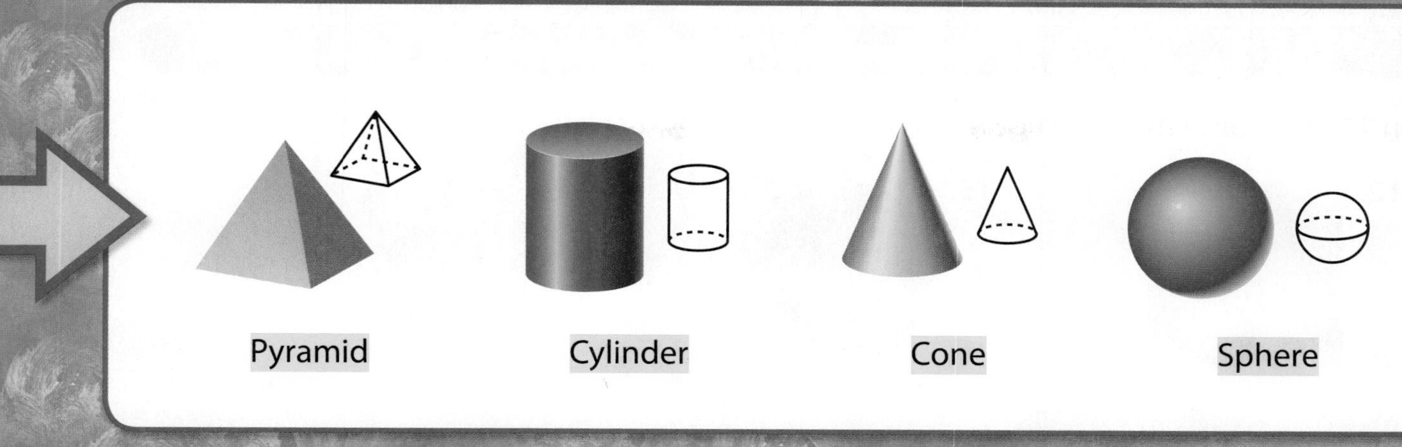

Guided Practice*

Do you know HOW?

Name the solid figure.

1. 

2. 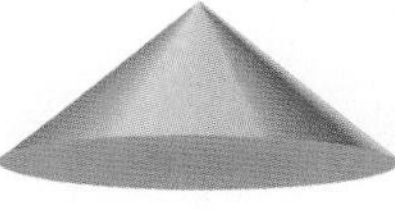

Name the solid figure that each object looks like.

3. 

4. 

5. 

6. 

Do you UNDERSTAND?

For **7–10**, look at the solid figures above.

7. Which solid figure has no flat surfaces?

8. Which solid figures can roll? Which cannot roll?

9. How are the cone and the cylinder alike? How are they different?

10. How are the cone and the pyramid alike? How are they different?

11. **Writing to Explain** Look at the pictures below. Does the name of a solid figure change if the figure is turned on its side? Explain.

DIGITAL Animated Glossary **www.pearsonsuccessnet.com**

For another example, see Set A on page 256.

Independent Practice

In **12–17**, name the solid figure.

12. 

13. 

14. 

15. 

16. 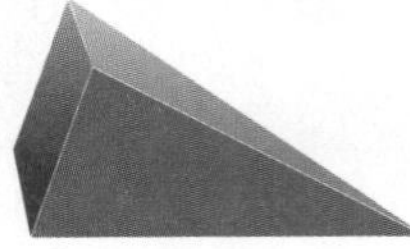

17. 

In **18–26**, name the solid figure that each object looks like.

18. 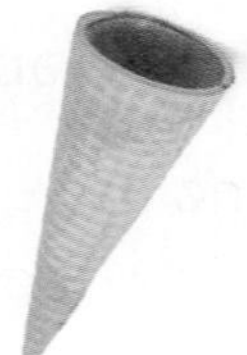

19. 

20. 

21. 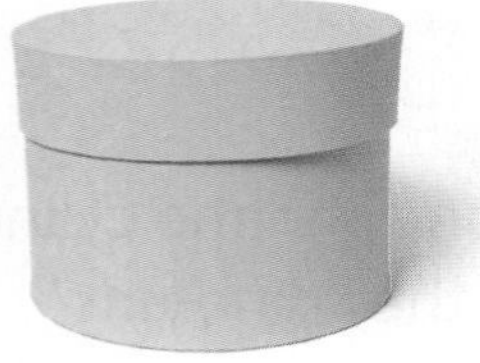

22. 

23. 

24. 

25. 

26. 

In **27–32**, name an object in your classroom or at home that is shaped like each solid figure.

27. Sphere

28. Cube

29. Cylinder

30. Rectangular prism

31. Pyramid

32. Cone

Problem Solving

33. Kayla used blocks to make this train. Give the solid figure name for each type of block. Tell how many blocks of each type Kayla used.

34. What solid figures do you get if you cut a cube as shown?

35. Three pizzas were cut into 8 slices each. Six friends ate all of the pizza, and each person ate the same number of slices. How many slices did each person eat?

36. **Writing to Explain** Spheres and cylinders are both solid figures that can roll. Why are so many sports played with objects shaped like spheres rather than objects shaped like cylinders?

37. What solid figure would you make if you stacked two rectangular prisms of the same size?

38. What solid figures can be stacked to make a round tower with a flat top?

39. Which solid figure name best describes the shape of the banana sculpture shown at the right?

A Cylinder

B Pyramid

C Rectangular prism

D Sphere

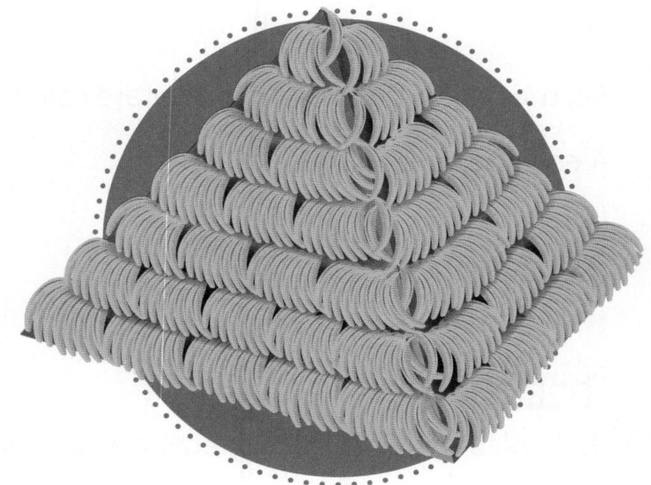

40. **Number Sense** There are 10 girls and 9 boys in Catherine's class. Which number sentence can be used to find how many children are in the class?

A $10 \times 9 = \square$ **C** $10 - 9 = \square$

B $10 \div 9 = \square$ **D** $10 + 9 = \square$

Lesson
10-2

Understand It!
A solid figure can be described by telling about its parts.

Relating Solids and Shapes

How can you describe parts of solid figures?

Some solid figures have faces, vertices, and edges.

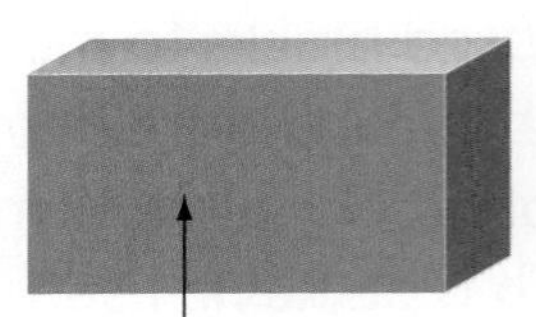

Each flat surface is a face.

A rectangular prism has 6 faces. The shape of each face is a rectangle.

Another Example **How can you describe parts of solid figures that roll?**

Flat surfaces of solid figures that can roll are called bases.

A cylinder has two flat surfaces.

A cylinder can roll.

So, the flat surfaces of a cylinder are called bases.

A cone has one vertex.

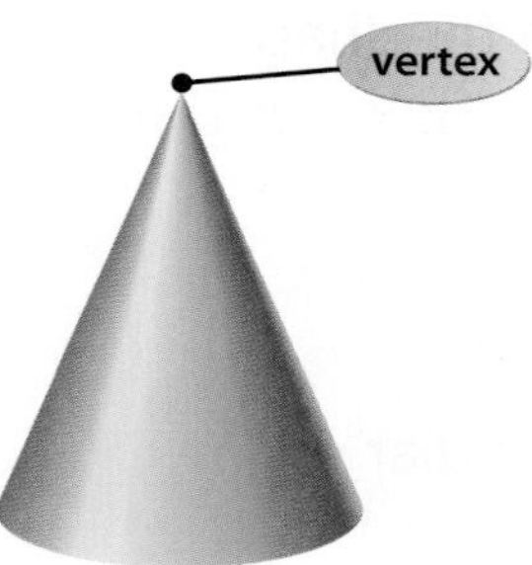

Explain It

1. Explain why the flat surface of a cone is called a base.
2. Do you think that the flat surfaces of a pyramid are called faces? Explain.

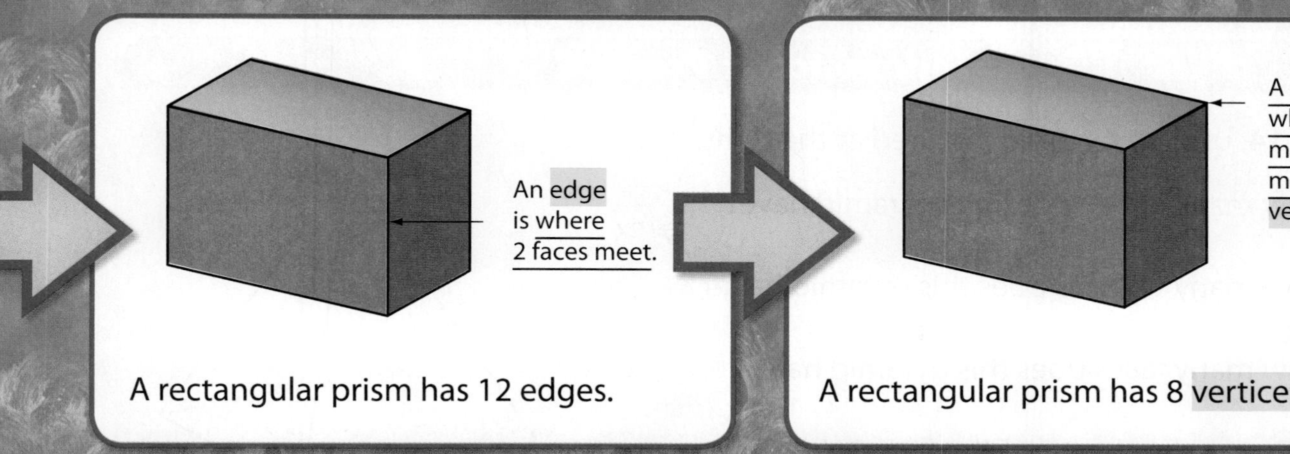

Guided Practice*

Do you know HOW?

For **1–6**, use the cube and cone pictured below.

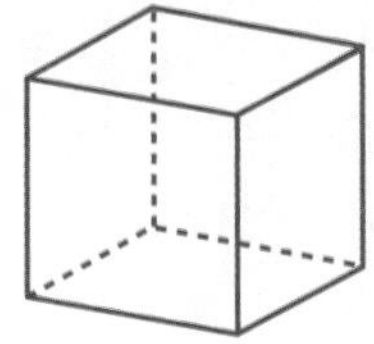
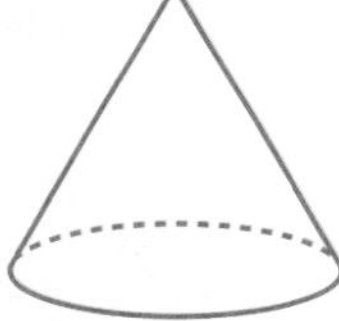

1. How many faces does the cube have in all?
2. What is the shape of each face of the cube?
3. How many edges does the cube have?
4. How many vertices does the cube have?
5. How many bases does the cone have?
6. How many vertices does the cone have?

Do you UNDERSTAND?

For **7–10**, use the solids pictured below.

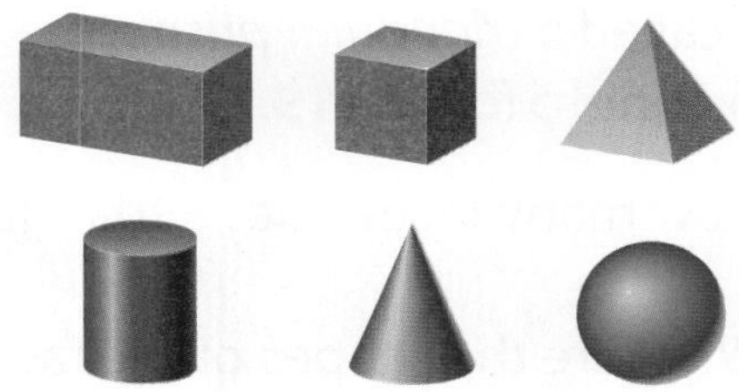

7. Which solid has faces that are all the same size and shape? What is the shape of the faces?
8. Which two solids have the same number of edges?
9. Which of these solid figures roll?
10. Besides the rectangular prism, which solid has 6 faces, 12 edges, and 8 vertices?

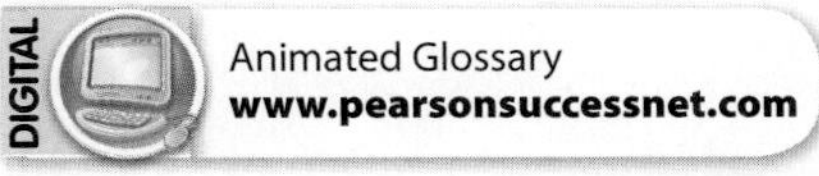

**For another example, see Set B on page 256.*

Independent Practice

For **11–14**, use the pyramid pictured at the right.

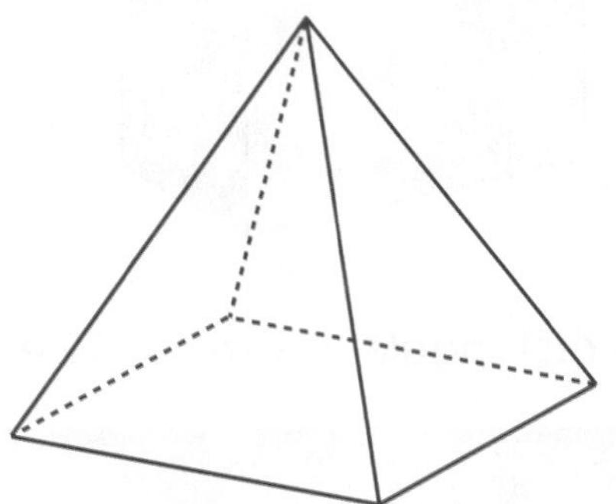

11. How many edges does this pyramid have?

12. How many vertices does this pyramid have?

13. How many faces does this pyramid have?

14. What are the shapes of the faces? How many faces of each shape are there?

Problem Solving

15. Writing to Explain Why does a cube have the same number of faces, edges, and vertices as a rectangular prism?

This wedge of cheese looks like a solid figure called a *triangular prism.* Use the photo for **16–19**.

16. How many faces does a triangular prism have?

17. What are the shapes of the faces?

18. How many vertices does a triangular prism have?

19. How many edges does a triangular prism have?

20. Tran bought a bag of 24 stickers. He plans to put one sticker on each face of this cube. How many stickers will be left over?

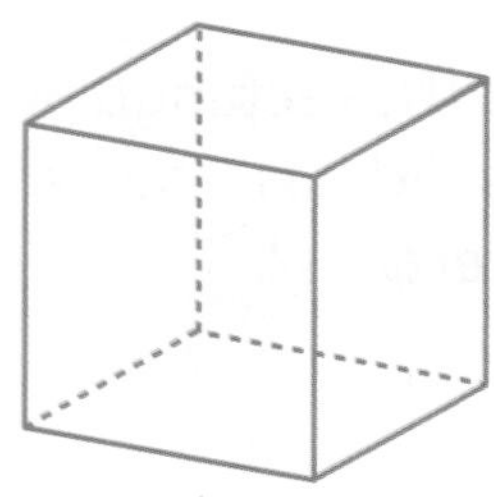

A 12 **C** 18

B 16 **D** 21

21. What is the total value of the 8 coins shown below?

A 36¢ **C** 56¢

B 46¢ **D** 71¢

Enrichment

Nets

A **net** is a flat pattern that can be folded to make a solid figure.

The pictures below show how to fold the net at the right into a rectangular prism.

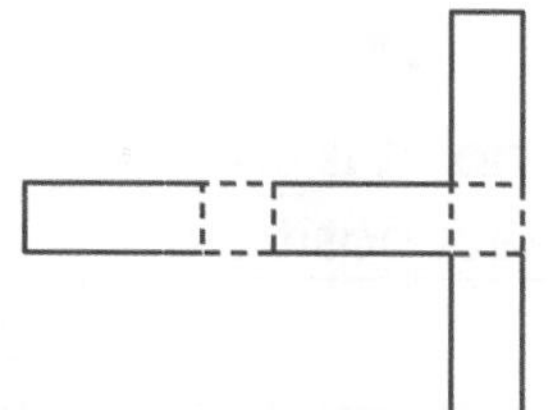

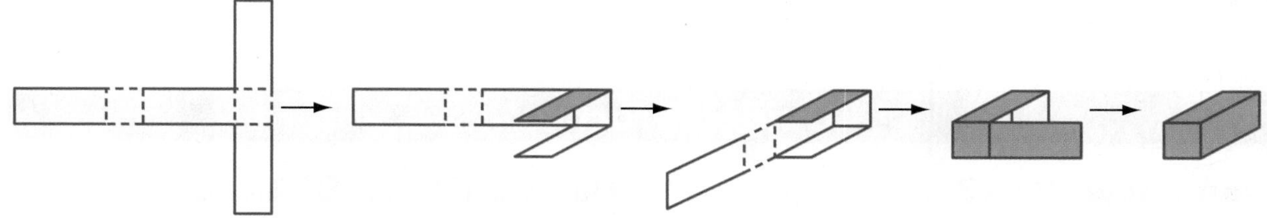

Practice

Match each net to the solid figure it makes below.

1. 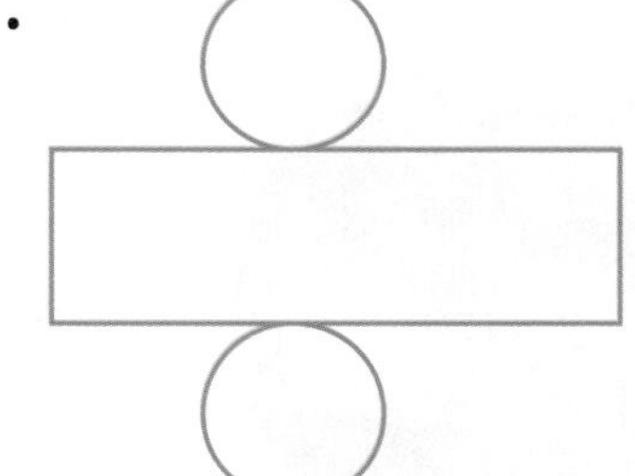

2. 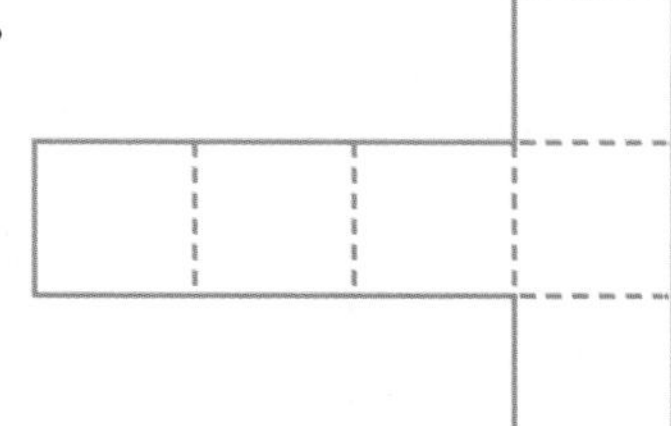

3. 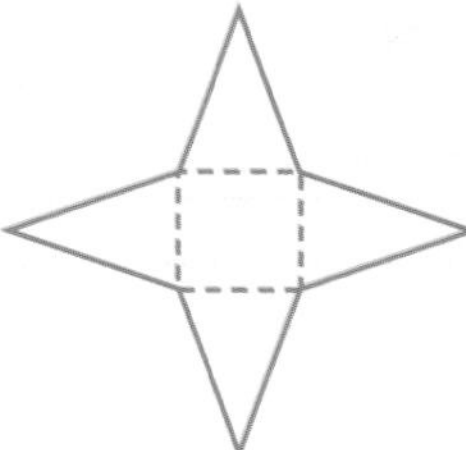

a. 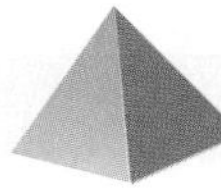

b. 

c. 

4. Draw a net for a cube. Use a design that is different from the net that matched Picture **c**. How many faces does a cube have? What is the shape of each face?

5. Bruce made the net below by tracing around each face of a solid figure. What solid figure did he use?

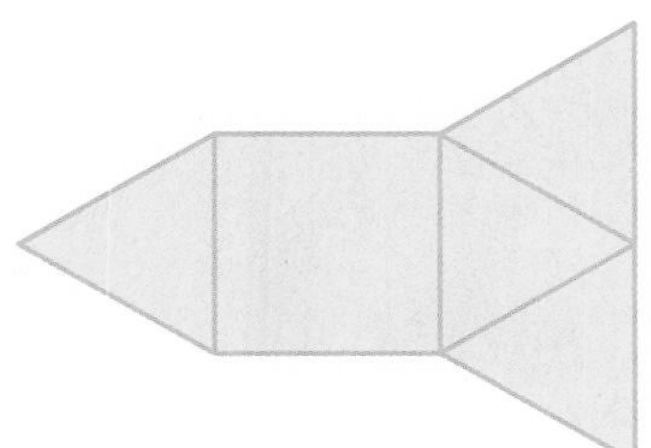

Lesson
10-3

Understand It!
Lines and line segments are made up of points.

Lines and Line Segments

What is important to know about lines?

Lines and parts of lines are used to describe shapes and solid figures.

A point is an exact position.

A line is a set of points that is endless in two directions.

A line segment is a part of a line with two endpoints.

Guided Practice*

Do you know HOW?

Write the name for each.

1.

2.

3.

Do you UNDERSTAND?

4. What do the arrows in the drawing of a line tell you?

5. What type of lines do the railroad tracks look like?

Independent Practice

Write the name for each.

6.

7.

8.

9.

10.

11.

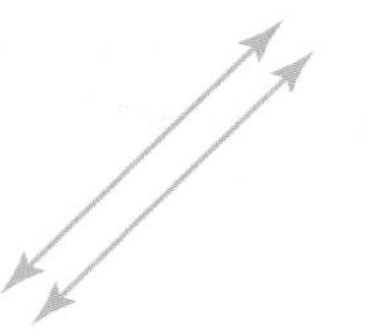

*For another example, see Set C on page 256.

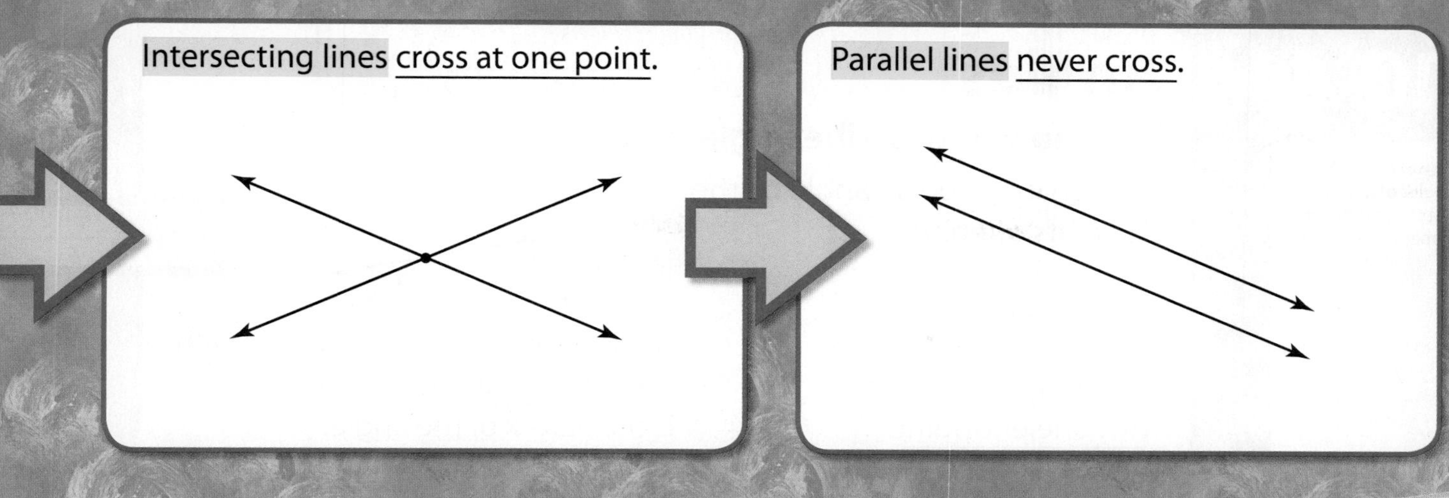

Draw and label a picture of each.

12. Line segment **13.** Line **14.** Parallel lines **15.** Intersecting lines

Problem Solving

For **16** and **17**, use the map at the right. Tell if the two streets named look like intersecting lines or parallel lines.

Park
Elm Street
Birch Street
Oak Street
School

16. Oak Street and Birch Street

17. Birch Street and Elm Street

18. **Writing to Explain** Rosa bought 3 packs of 6 baseball cards. Luis bought 4 packs of 3 baseball cards. Who bought more baseball cards? Explain.

19. Look at the wings on the plane. What geometric term can you use to describe them?

20. Which best describes the place where these two lines intersect?

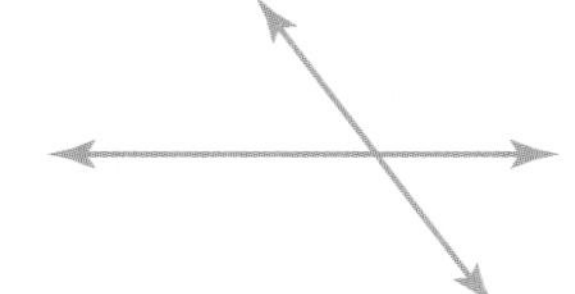

A Line

B Point

C Line segment

D Parallel line

Lesson

10-4

Understand It!
Angles of different sizes have different names.

Angles

How do you describe angles?

You can describe an angle by the size of its opening.

A ray is a part of a line with one endpoint.

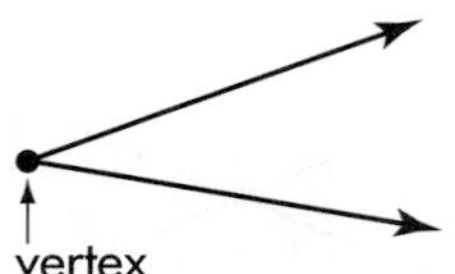

An angle is formed by two rays with the same endpoint. That endpoint is the vertex of the angle.

Guided Practice*

Do you know HOW?

Write the name for each.

1. 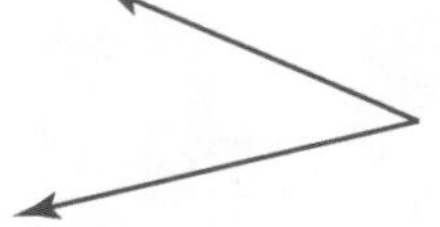

2. 

Tell if each angle is right, acute, or obtuse.

3. 

4. 

Do you UNDERSTAND?

5. How can you use the corner of a note card to decide if an angle is acute, right, or obtuse?

6. Explain why these two rays do not form an angle.

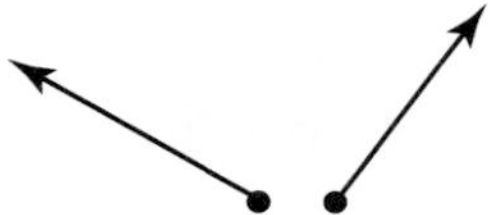

7. Describe something in your classroom that reminds you of perpendicular line segments.

Independent Practice

Tell if each angle is right, acute, or obtuse.

8. 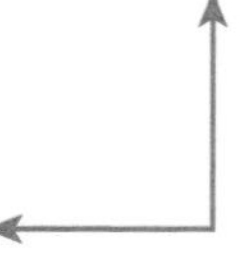

9. 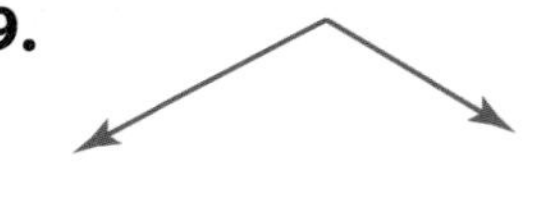

10. 

11. 

In **12–15**, draw a picture of each.

12. Obtuse angle **13.** Right angle **14.** Ray **15.** Acute angle

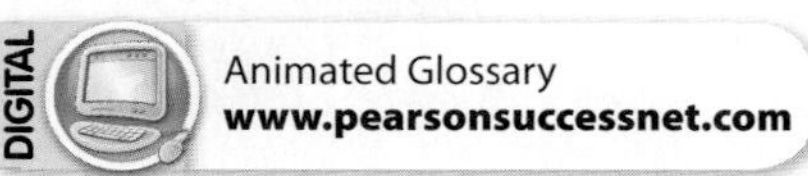

*For another example, see Set D on page 256.

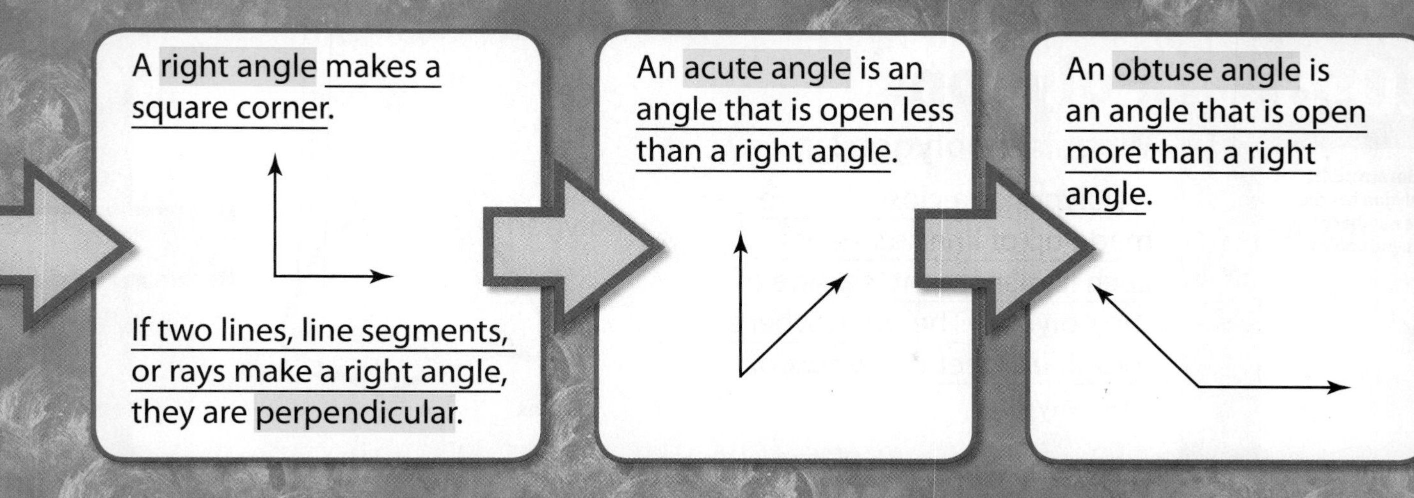

Problem Solving

In **16–18**, tell the time on each clock. Then tell what type of angle is formed by the hands of the clock.

16. 

17. 

18. 

19. Writing to Explain Are all obtuse angles the same size? Draw a picture to explain your answer.

20. Which picture shows a pair of perpendicular line segments?

A 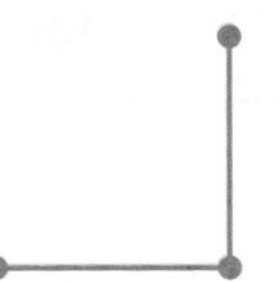

B 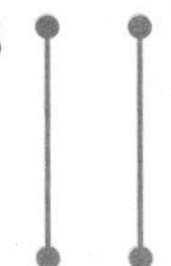

C 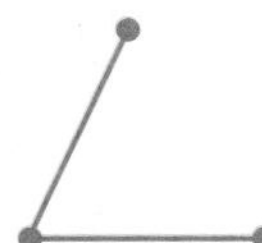

D 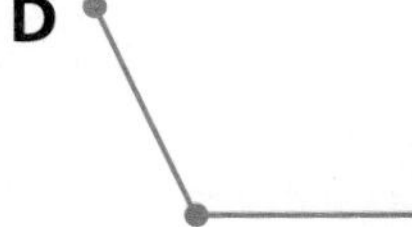

21. Reasoning Are these lines parallel or intersecting? Explain.

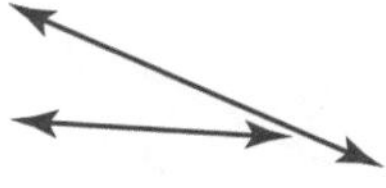

Tip *Remember that a line does not end.*

22. Which number is greater than 1,051?

A 1,005 **C** 947

B 1,073 **D** 1,021

23. Dori counted 8 children waiting in line ahead of her at the drinking fountain. Write the ordinal number and the ordinal word form for Dori's place in line.

Lesson
10-5

Understand It!
A polygon has the same number of sides and angles.

Polygons

What is a polygon?

A polygon is a closed figure made up of line segments. Each line segment is a side of the polygon. The point where two sides meet is a vertex of the polygon.

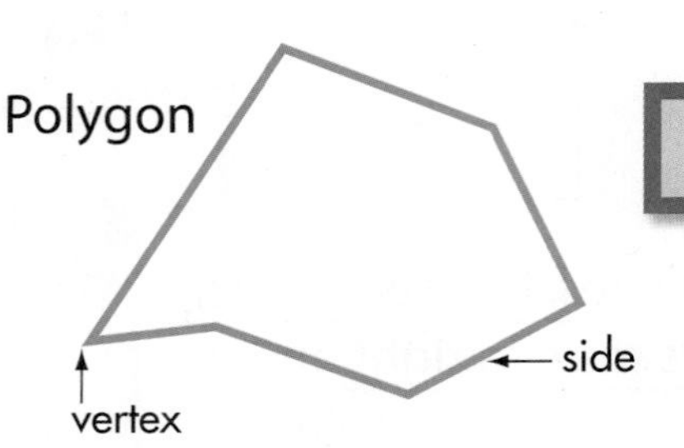

Guided Practice*

Do you know HOW?

Name the polygon.

1. 

2. 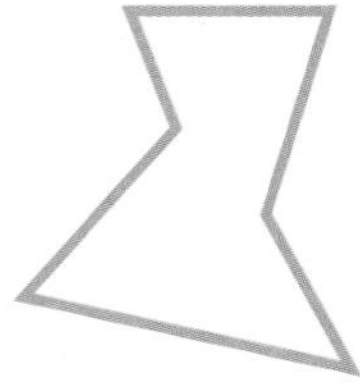

Is each figure a polygon? If it is not, explain why.

3. 

4. 

Do you UNDERSTAND?

Draw a polygon with 3 sides. Use the polygon for Exercises **5–7**.

5. How many vertices are there?
6. How many angles are there?
7. What is the name of the polygon?
8. Suppose that a polygon has 10 sides. How many angles does it have?
9. Describe an everyday object that is a model of a polygon. What is the name of the polygon?

Independent Practice

Name the polygon.

10. 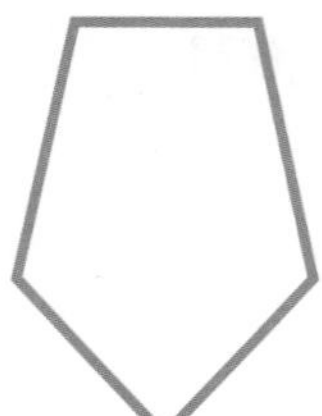

11. 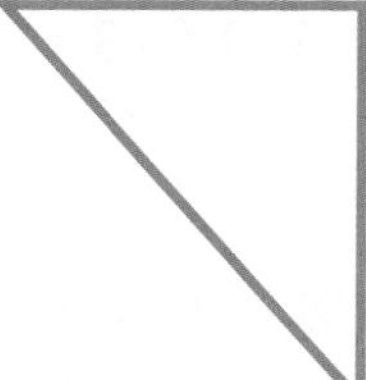

12. 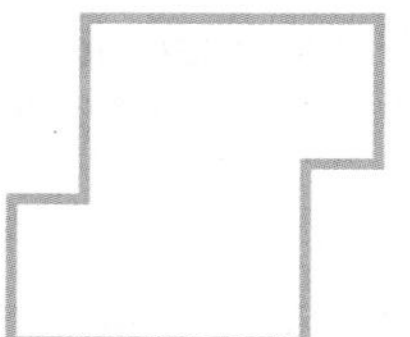

13. 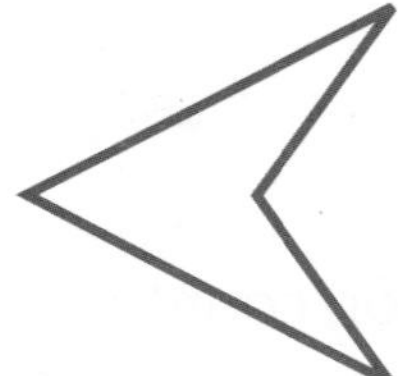

*For another example, see Set E on page 257.

Polygons are named for the number of sides they have. Two sides meet to form an angle at each vertex.

Some commonly used polygons are named and described in the table.

Data

Polygon	Number of Sides	Number of Vertices
Triangle	3	3
Quadrilateral	4	4
Pentagon	5	5
Hexagon	6	6
Octagon	8	8

Is each figure a polygon? If not, explain why.

14. 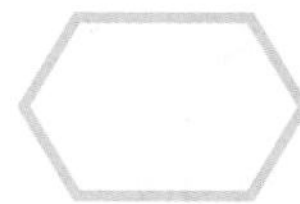

15. 

16. 

17. 

Problem Solving

In **18–21**, name the polygon that each traffic sign looks most like.

18. 

19. 

20. 

21. 

22. Reasoning Which polygon comes next in the pattern? Explain your answer.

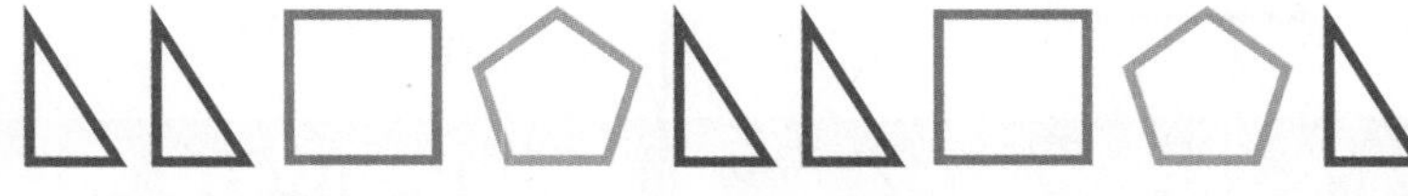

23. What polygons were used to design this house?

24. Which polygon best represents the top of the box?

A Quadrilateral **C** Pentagon

B Octagon **D** Hexagon

Lesson
10-6

Understand It!
There are two different ways to describe triangles.

Triangles

How can you describe triangles?

Triangles can be described by their sides.

Equilateral triangle

All three sides are the same length.

Isosceles triangle

At least two sides are the same length.

Scalene triangle

No sides are the same length.

Guided Practice*

Do you know HOW?

Tell if each triangle is equilateral, isosceles, or scalene.

1. 

2. 

Tell if each triangle is right, acute, or obtuse.

3. 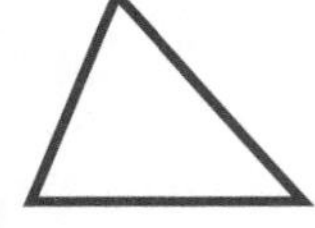

4. 

Do you UNDERSTAND?

5. How many acute angles are in an acute triangle?

6. How many obtuse angles are in an obtuse triangle?

7. Can a right triangle also be

a an isosceles triangle? Explain.

b an equilateral triangle? Explain.

8. Can an isosceles triangle also be equilateral? Explain.

Independent Practice

In **9–12**, tell if each triangle is equilateral, isosceles, or scalene. If a triangle has two names, give the name that best describes it.

9. 

10. 

11. 

12. 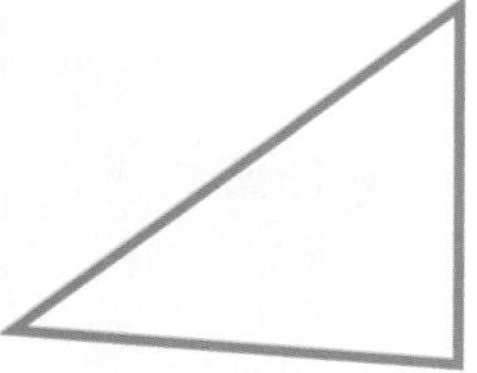

*For another example, see Set F on page 257.

Triangles can be described by their angles.

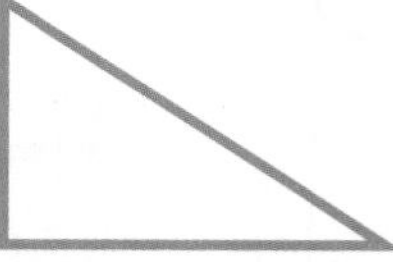

Right triangle

One angle is a right angle.

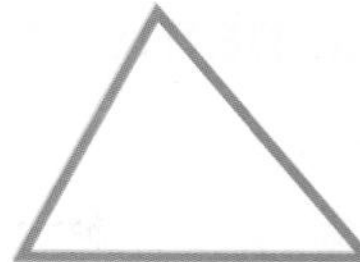

Acute triangle

All three angles are acute angles.

Obtuse triangle

One angle is an obtuse angle.

In **13–16**, tell if each triangle is right, acute, or obtuse.

13. 

14. 

15. 

16. 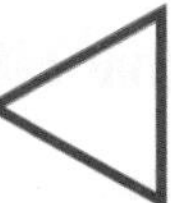

Problem Solving

For **17** and **18**, use the picture of the musical triangle.

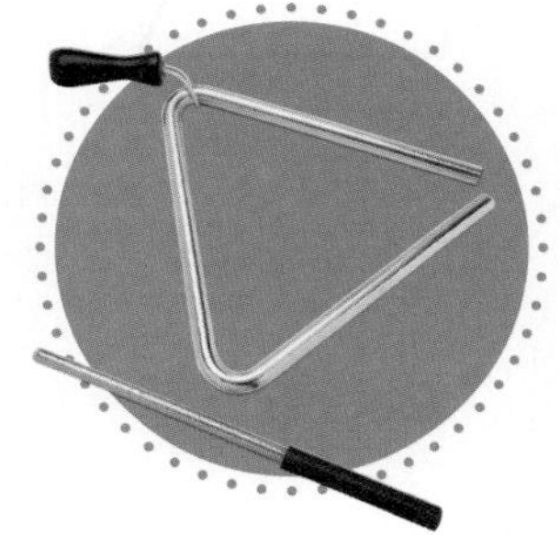

17. Does the musical triangle look most like an equilateral triangle, an isosceles triangle, or a scalene triangle?

18. **Reasoning** The shape of the musical triangle is not a geometric triangle. Explain why not.

19. Look at the sentence below. Write the word that will make it true.

An obtuse triangle has one obtuse angle and two __?__ angles.

20. Draw a picture to show how you could make one straight cut in a rectangle to form two right triangles.

21. Which pair of triangle names best describes this pennant?

A Equilateral triangle, acute triangle

B Equilateral triangle, right triangle

C Isosceles triangle, acute triangle

D Isosceles triangle, obtuse triangle

22. **Writing to Explain** Why is it impossible for a triangle to have two right angles?

Lesson

10-7

Understand It!
There are many different kinds of quadrilaterals. Some have special names.

Quadrilaterals

What are some special names for quadrilaterals?

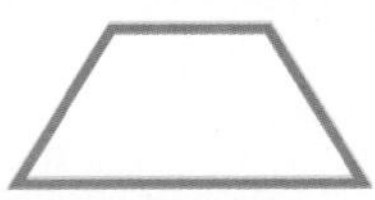

Trapezoid

Exactly one pair of parallel sides

Parallelogram

Two pairs of parallel sides

Opposite sides are the same length.
Opposite angles are the same size.

Guided Practice*

Do you know HOW?

In **1–4**, write as many special names as possible for each quadrilateral.

1.

2.

3.

4.

Do you UNDERSTAND?

5. This figure is a rectangle, but it is not a square. Why?

6. Draw a parallelogram with all four sides the same length. What is its special name?

7. Why is a square a parallelogram?

Independent Practice

In **8–13**, write as many special names as possible for each quadrilateral.

8.

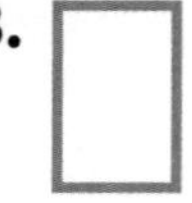

9.

10.

11.

12.

13.

DIGITAL Animated Glossary **www.pearsonsuccessnet.com**

For another example, see Set G on page 257.

Some quadrilaterals have more than one special name.

Rectangle

Four right angles

A *rectangle* is a special *parallelogram*.

Rhombus

All sides the same length

A *rhombus* is a special *parallelogram*.

Square

Four right angles and all sides the same length

A *square* is a special *parallelogram*. It is a combination of a *rectangle* and a *rhombus*.

In **14–17**, write the name that best describes the quadrilateral. Draw a picture to help.

14. A rectangle with all sides the same length

15. A quadrilateral with only one pair of parallel sides

16. A parallelogram with four right angles

17. A rhombus with four right angles

Problem Solving

18. The bike in the photo was designed in 1997. What is the shape of the wheels? How is the shape different from the wheels on most bikes? How is a square different from a circle?

19. Reasoning I am a special quadrilateral with opposite sides the same length. What special quadrilateral could I be? (*Hint:* There is more than one correct answer.)

20. Writing to Explain How are a rectangle and a rhombus alike? How are they different?

21. Which picture shows more than $\frac{5}{8}$ of the square shaded?

A 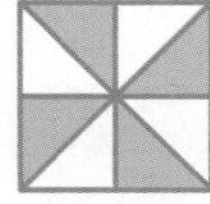

B 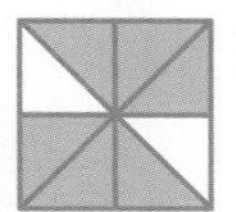

C 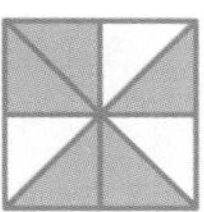

D 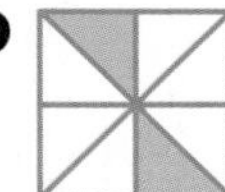

Lesson
10-8

Understand It!
In math, a generalization must be tested to show that it is correct.

Problem Solving

Make and Test Generalizations

What is the same in these three polygons?

Guided Practice*

Do you know HOW?

Make and test a generalization for each set of polygons.

1.

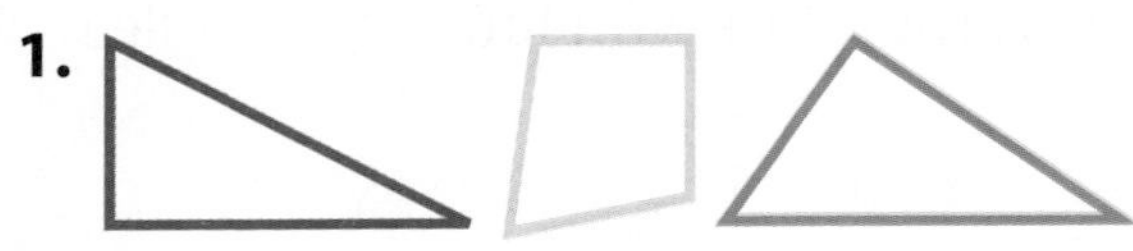

2.

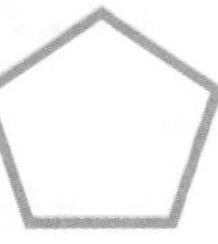

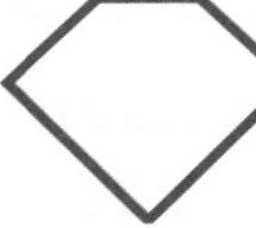

Do you UNDERSTAND?

3. Look at the polygons above. All sides of the second and third polygons **are** the same length. So why is the friend's generalization incorrect?

4. Draw a set of polygons that you can make a generalization about. Include a picture.

Independent Practice

In **5–7**, make a generalization for each set of polygons.

5.

6.

7.

Stuck? Try this....

- What do I know?
- What am I asked to find?
- What diagram can I use to help understand the problem?
- Can I use addition, subtraction, multiplication, or division?
- Is all of my work correct?
- Did I answer the right question?
- Is my answer reasonable?

*For another example, see Set H on page 257.

Make a Generalization

Your friend says that the sides are all the same length.

You say that they all have 4 sides.

Test the Generalization

Notice that the top and bottom of this polygon are not the same length. Your friend's generalization is not correct!

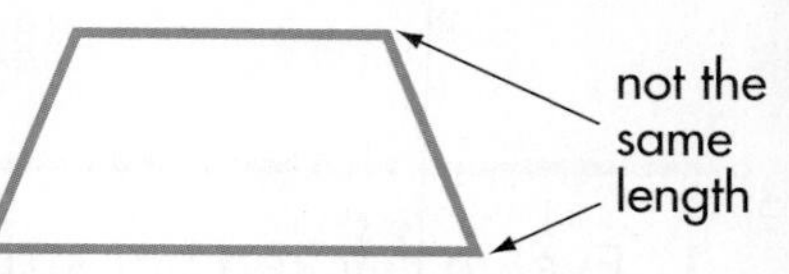

You see that the first polygon has 4 sides. The second has 4 sides. So does the third. Your generalization is correct!

8. Mr. Redbird makes tables that have 3 legs and tables that have 4 legs. The tables that he made this month have 18 legs in all. How many tables of each kind did he make?

9. Anna earns $4 for each hour that she babysits. She babysat for 2 hours last week and 5 hours this week. How much did she earn in all?

10. How are the four numbers 18, 24, 16, and 40 alike?

11. Compare each sum to its addends in these number sentences:

$34 + 65 = 99$ $8 + 87 = 95$ $435 + 0 = 435$

Make a generalization about addends and sums for whole numbers.

12. **Writing to Explain** Is this generalization true? If not, draw a picture to show why not.

If a shape is made up of line segments, then it is a polygon.

13. Ari gave his friends these clues about a secret number.

- The number has three digits.
- The hundreds digit is less than 3.
- The tens digit is twice the ones digit.
- The number is odd.

What are all the possible secret numbers?

14. What is the same in all these polygons?

A All have a pair of parallel sides.

B All have two right angles.

C All have one acute angle.

D All have four sides.

Topic 10 Test

1. Evelyn packed her stuffed animals in the box shown below. Which solid best describes the box? (10-1)

A Cylinder

B Cube

C Pyramid

D Cone

2. The angles below are examples of acute angles. (10-4)

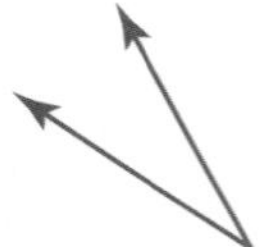  

Which clock face below shows the hands in an acute angle?

A

B

C

D

3. Keenan bought a yo-yo in an unusually shaped box. Which best describes the shape of the top of the box? (10-5)

A Hexagon

B Pentagon

C Octagon

D Quadrilateral

4. Which best describes the triangles? (10-8)

A They are all acute triangles.

B They are all isosceles triangles.

C They are all obtuse triangles.

D They are all scalene triangles.

5. Which figure is a polygon? (10-5)

A

B

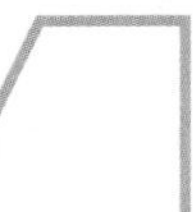

C

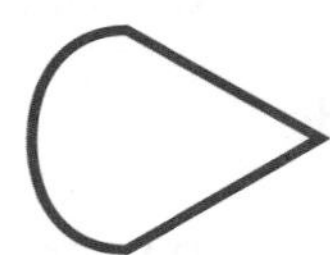

D

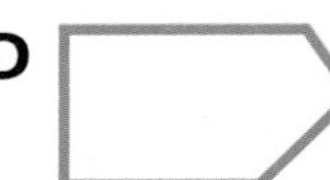

6. Four friends made quadrilateral shapes out of colored paper. Whose shape has only one set of parallel sides? (10-7)

A Melissa's

B Nigel's

C Pat's

D Rahmi's

7. Below is part of a nature trail map. Which two trails represent parallel lines? (10-3)

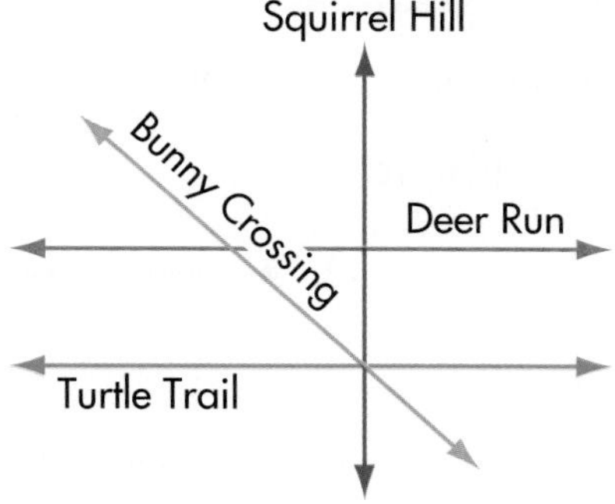

A Deer Run and Turtle Trail

B Deer Run and Squirrel Hill

C Bunny Crossing and Squirrel Hill

D Bunny Crossing and Deer Run

8. The students ran a course from the flag to the tree, to the trash can, and then back to the flag. What type of triangle did the course form? (10-6)

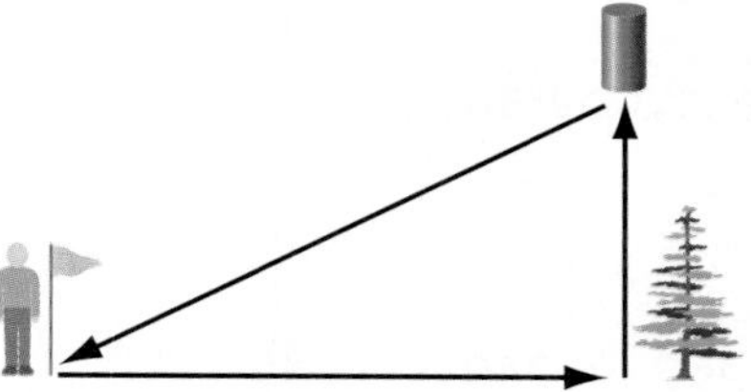

A Scalene

B Isosceles

C Equilateral

D Acute

9. What two quadrilaterals did Kim use to make up the rug design? (10-7)

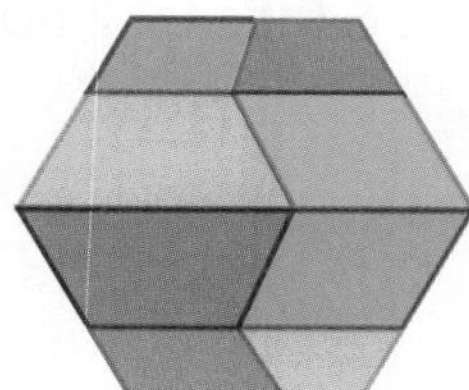

A Rhombus and parallelogram

B Rhombus and trapezoid

C Parallelogram and trapezoid

D Parallelogram and hexagon

10. A decorative pillow is shaped like a rectangular prism with a tassel at each vertex. How many tassels are there? (10-2)

A 4

B 6

C 7

D 8

Reteaching

Set A, pages 234–236

Name this solid figure.

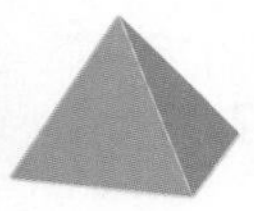
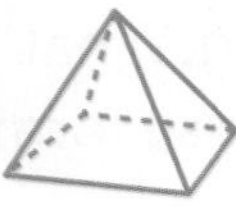

The figure has flat surfaces and a point at the top.

The figure is a pyramid.

Remember that some solid figures roll and some do not.

Name the solid figure.

1. 

2. 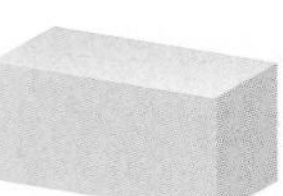

Set B, pages 238–240

How many faces, edges, and vertices does the following solid figure have?

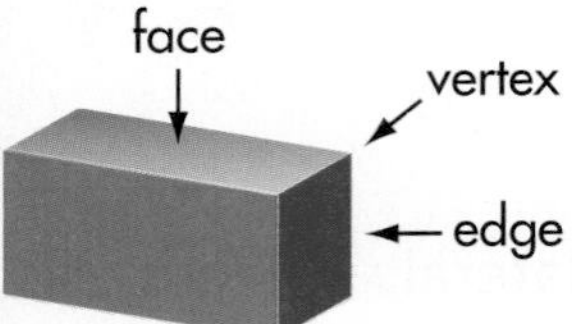

A rectangular prism has 6 faces, 12 edges, and 8 vertices.

Remember that a vertex is where three or more edges meet.

For **1** and **2**, use the cube below.

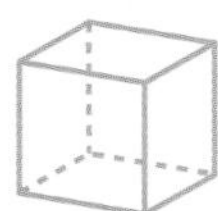

1. How many faces, edges, and vertices does this cube have?
2. Describe the shape of each face.

Set C, pages 242–243

Write the name for the following.

The lines cross at one point. They are intersecting lines.

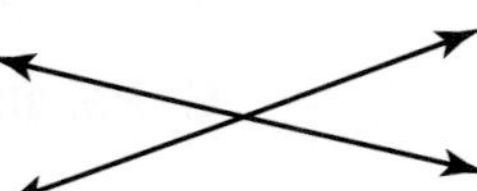

Remember that a line never ends.

Write the name for each.

1. •

2. •———•

Set D, pages 244–245

Describe the angle as right, acute, or obtuse.

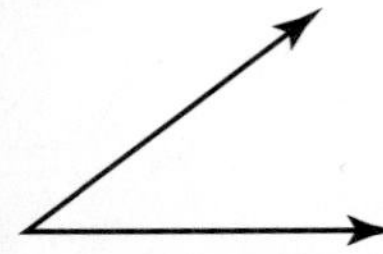

The angle is open less than a right angle.

It is an acute angle.

Remember that the opening of a right angle makes a square corner.

Describe each angle.

1. 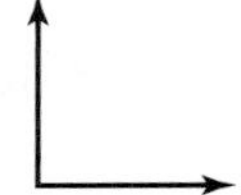

2. 

Set E, pages 246–247

Is the figure a polygon? If it is a polygon, give its name. If not, explain why.

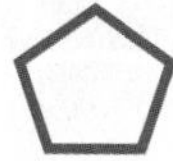

The figure is closed and is made up of line segments. It is a polygon.

The figure has 5 sides. It is a pentagon.

Remember that a polygon is made up of line segments.

Is each figure a polygon? If so, give its name. If not, explain why.

1. 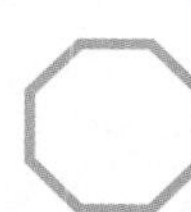

2. 

Set F, pages 248–249

Tell if the triangle below is equilateral, isosceles, or scalene. Then tell if the triangle is right, acute, or obtuse.

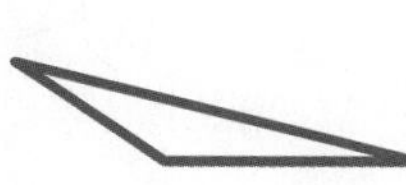

None of the sides are the same length. The triangle is a scalene triangle. One angle is an obtuse angle.

The triangle is an obtuse triangle.

Remember that no sides of a scalene triangle are congruent.

Describe each triangle by its sides and by its angles.

1. 

2. 

Set G, pages 250–251

Name the following quadrilateral.

Opposite sides are parallel and opposite sides have the same length.

The figure is a parallelogram.

Remember that all quadrilaterals have four sides.

Write as many special names as possible for each quadrilateral.

1.

2. 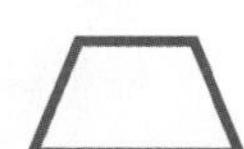

Set H, pages 252–253

Make and test a generalization for the set of polygons.

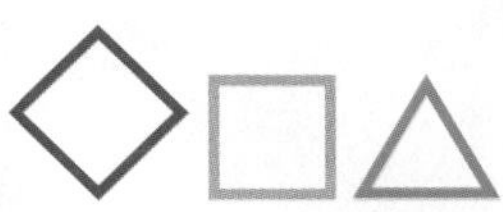

Make a generalization. *Each polygon has sides that are the same length.*

Test the generalization. *All of the polygons have sides that are the same length.*

Remember that a generalization must apply to the entire set.

Make and test a generalization for this set of polygons.

1. 

Topic 11

Congruence and Symmetry

1 Are snowflakes symmetric? You will find out in Lesson 11-3.

2 Are the windows of the Taj Mahal congruent? You will find out in Lesson 11-1.

3

Where is the line of symmetry in the picture of a mountain and its reflection? You will find out in Lesson 11-2.

4

Does fruit such as an orange, a grapefruit, or a starfruit have lines of symmetry? You will find out in Lesson 11-3.

Review What You Know!

Vocabulary

Choose the best term from the box.

- difference
- estimate
- line
- rounding

1. When you subtract two numbers, the answer is called the _?_.
2. When you replace a number with a number that tells about how many to the nearest ten, you are _?_ the number.
3. A _?_ is a straight path of points that is endless in both directions.

Repeating Patterns

Draw the next three shapes to continue each pattern.

4. ○ ◯ △ △ ○ ◯ △

5. □ ▯ □ ○ □ ▯ □

Division Facts

Find each quotient.

6. 24 ÷ 3 7. 36 ÷ 9 8. 16 ÷ 4

9. 54 ÷ 6 10. 81 ÷ 9 11. 48 ÷ 8

12. **Writing to Explain** Is the figure below a polygon? Explain how you can draw the figure to make it a polygon.

Lesson
11-1

Congruent Figures and Motion

Understand It!
Sliding, flipping, or turning a figure forms a figure that is the same size and shape as the original figure.

What are congruent figures?

Figures that have the same size and shape are congruent figures. You can move a figure to make a new figure that is congruent to it.
A slide or translation moves a figure up, down, left, or right.

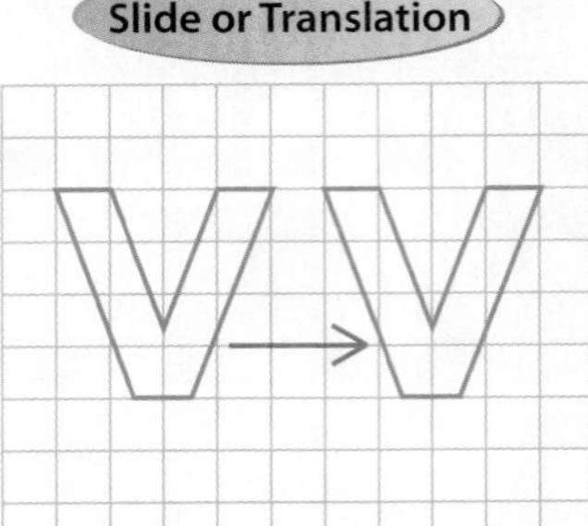

Another Example How can you decide if two figures are congruent?

To decide if two figures are congruent, trace one of the figures and place the tracing on top of the other figure.

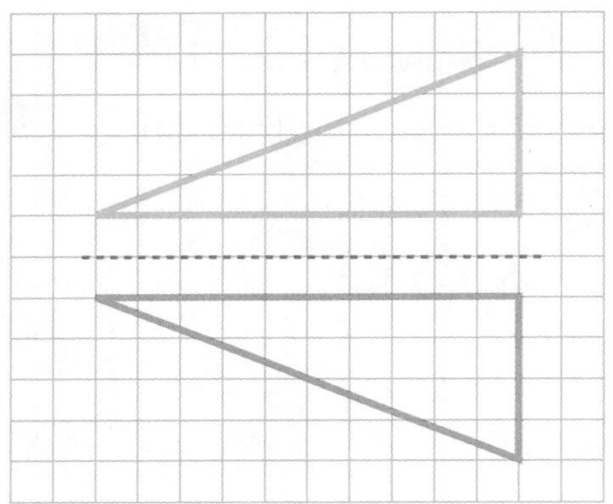

Yes, the figures are congruent.

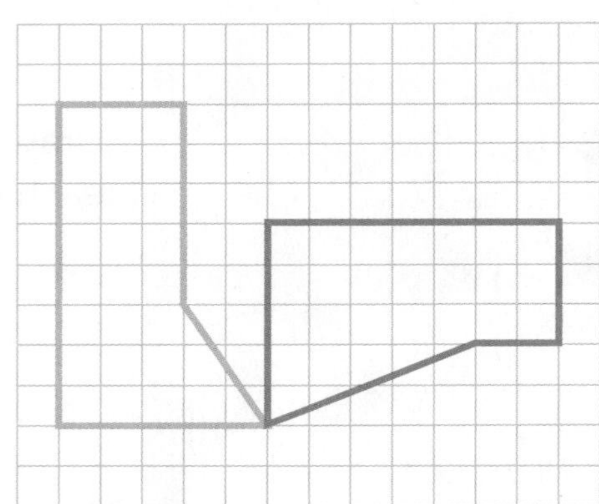

No, the figures are not congruent.

Explain It

1. Look at the two triangles. How could you move one triangle to match it to the other?
2. Look at the two pentagons. How could you move one to show that it does not match the other?

A flip or reflection picks up and moves a figure to give a mirror image.

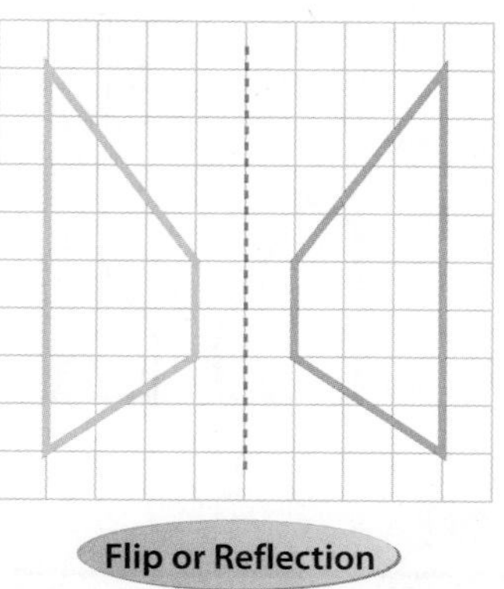

Flip or Reflection

A turn or rotation moves a figure around a point.

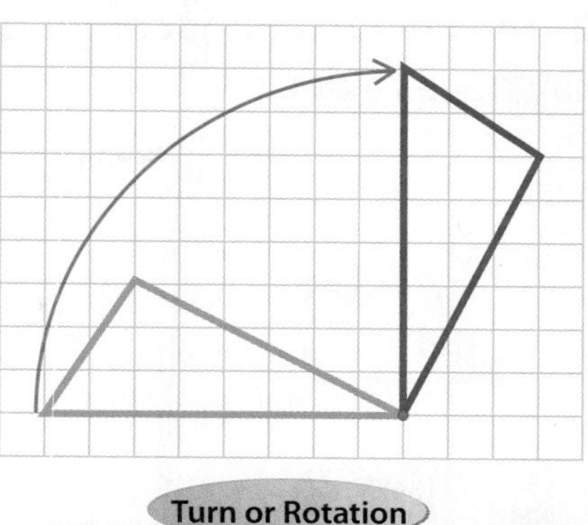

Turn or Rotation

Guided Practice*

Do you know HOW?

Write *slide, flip,* or *turn* for each.

1. **2.**

Are the figures congruent? Write *yes* or *no*. You may trace to decide.

3.

4.

Do you UNDERSTAND?

5. Could a triangle and a square be congruent? Explain your answer.

6. Are all triangles congruent? Explain your answer.

7. Are all squares congruent? Explain your answer.

8. Trace this pentagon. Then show what it would look like after reflecting it to the right.

Independent Practice

For **9–11**, write *slide, flip,* or *turn* for each pair of congruent figures.

9.

10.

11.

DIGITAL Animated Glossary **www.pearsonsuccessnet.com**

**For another example, see Set A on page 272.*

Independent Practice

For **12–14**, are the figures congruent? Write *yes* or *no*. You may trace to decide.

12.

13.

14.

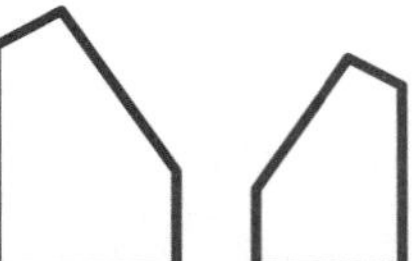

Problem Solving

15. Manny says the windows of the Taj Mahal are congruent because they are all shaped like the window in the picture below. Do you agree? Why or why not?

16. Think About the Process Samantha arranged some pennies in the pattern shown below. Which numerical expression best shows how she arranged them?

A $3 + 6$

B $3 + 9$

C 3×6

D 3×9

17. Draw a rectangle. Then draw a line segment that divides the rectangle into two congruent figures. Describe the two figures.

18. **Writing to Explain** Are all rectangles congruent? Explain your answer.

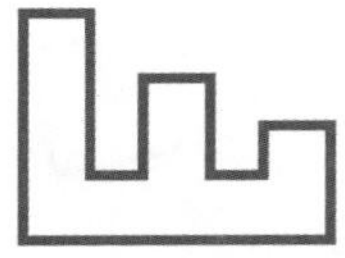

19. Which figure below is congruent to the figure at the right?

A

B

C

D

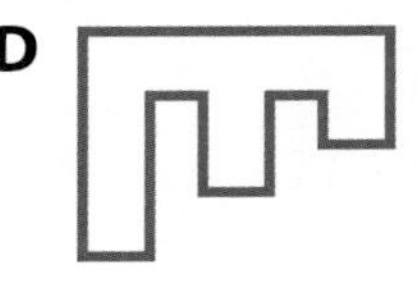

Motions

Use e tools

Geometry Shapes

Write *translation*, *reflection*, or *rotation* for each pair of figures.

Step 1 Go to the Geometry Shapes eTool. Click on the pentagon, and then click in the workspace twice to create two pentagons side-by-side.

Step 2 Click on the rotate tool and then click on the second pentagon until it looks like the second pentagon pictured above. This shows that the second pentagon is the result of rotating the first. Write *rotation*.

Step 3 Make two copies of the right triangle in the workspace. Click on the reflection (flip vertical) tool and then on the second triangle. This shows that the second triangle is a reflection of the first. Write *reflection*.

Step 4 Make two copies of the trapezoid in the workspace. Use the arrow tool to move the second trapezoid like the one pictured above. This shows that the second trapezoid is a translation of the first. Write *translation*. Use the broom tool to clear the workspace.

Practice

Write *translation, reflection,* or *rotation* for each pair of figures.

1. 

2. 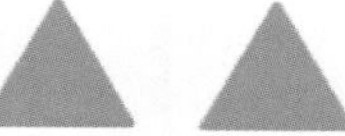

3. 

Lesson

11-2

Understand It!
A figure is symmetric when two halves of the figure match. The line of symmetry divides the two halves.

Line Symmetry

What are symmetric figures?

A line of symmetry is a line on which a figure can be folded so the two parts match exactly. A symmetric figure has at least one line of symmetry.

A figure can have just one line of symmetry.

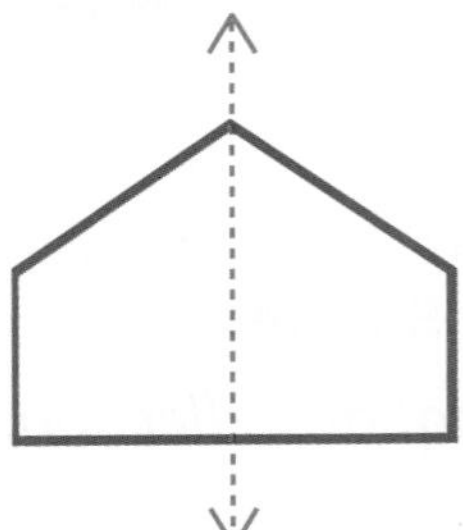

Guided Practice*

Do you know HOW?

Is the figure symmetric? Write *yes* or *no*. You may trace to decide.

1. 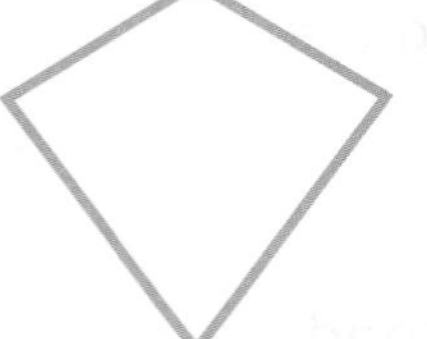

2. 

3. 

4. 

Do you UNDERSTAND?

5. Explain how you can test a figure to decide if it has a line of symmetry.

6. Is the dashed line a line of symmetry for the rectangle? Explain.

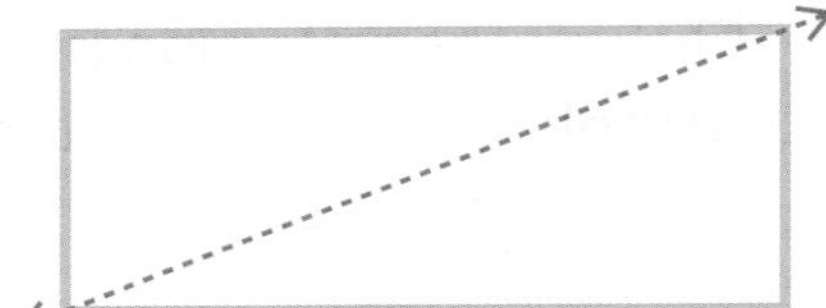

Independent Practice

Is the figure symmetric? Write *yes* or *no*. You may trace to decide.

7. 

8. 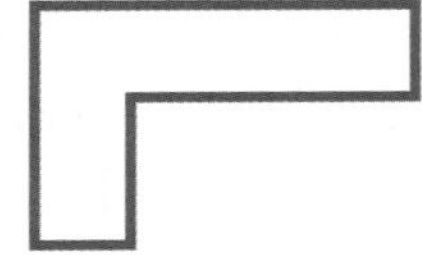

9. 

10. 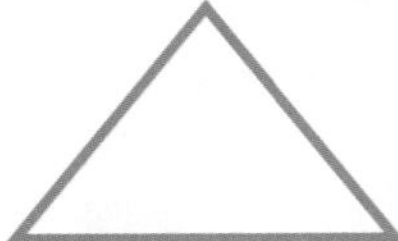

*For another example, see Set B on page 272.

A figure can have no lines of symmetry.

A figure can have more than one line of symmetry.

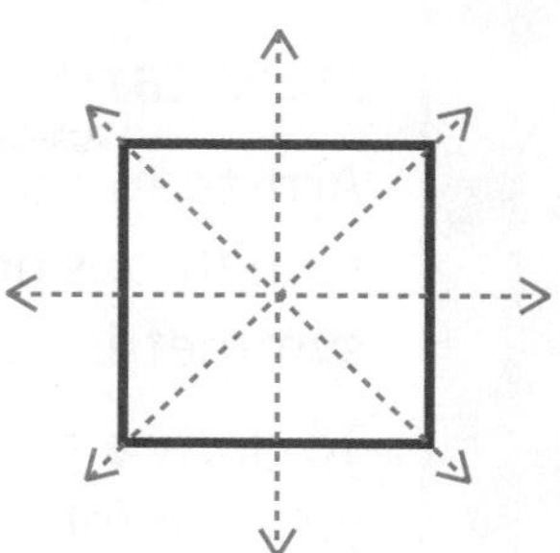

Tell whether each object is symmetric. Write *yes* or *no*.

11. 

12. 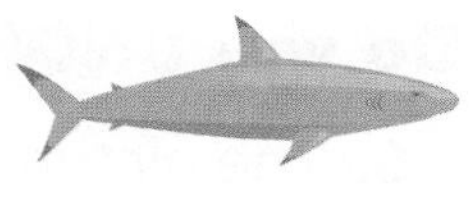

13. 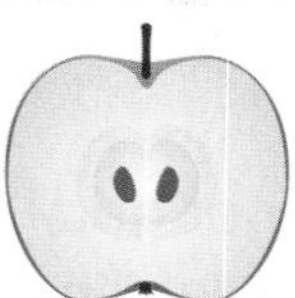

14. 

Problem Solving

15. Trace this picture of a mountain and its reflection. Then fold your tracing and draw the line of symmetry.

16. Which figure below does **NOT** have at least one line of symmetry?

A 

C 

B 

D 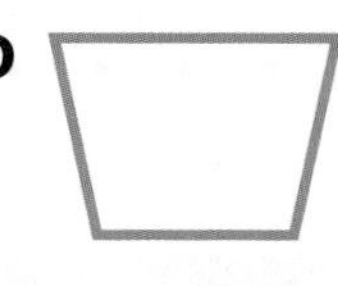

17. **Writing to Explain** You have learned that a square is a type of rectangle. Do all rectangles have the same number of lines of symmetry as all squares? Explain your answer.

18. Sue has some nickels, dimes, and quarters in her pocket.

- There are 3 quarters.
- There are 2 more dimes than nickels.
- There are 15 coins in all.

What is the total value of the coins?

Lesson

11-3

Understand It!
The two parts of a symmetric figure match exactly when the figure is folded along a line of symmetry.

Drawing Shapes with Lines of Symmetry

Hands-On
grid paper

How can you draw a figure with a line of symmetry?

Artists and other workers sometimes need to draw symmetric figures.

To draw a symmetric figure, you can follow these steps.

Step 1

Draw a line segment as part of the line of symmetry.

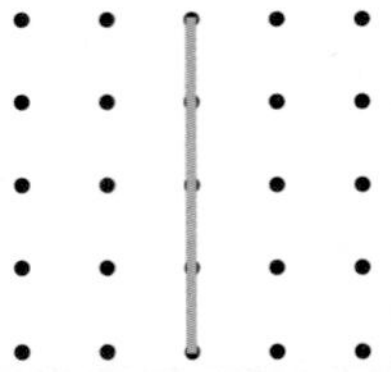

Guided Practice*

Do you know HOW?

Trace the figure onto dot paper or grid paper. Then complete it so the blue line segment is part of a line of symmetry.

1.

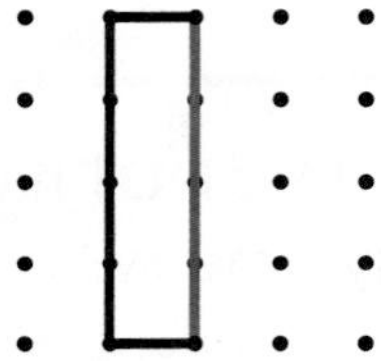

2.

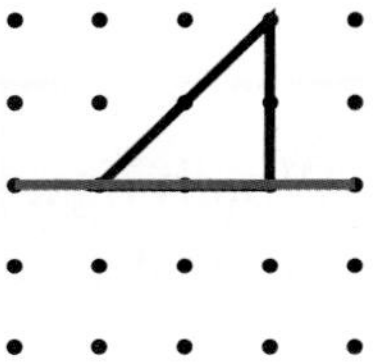

3.

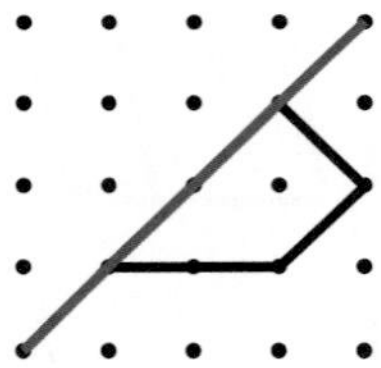

4.

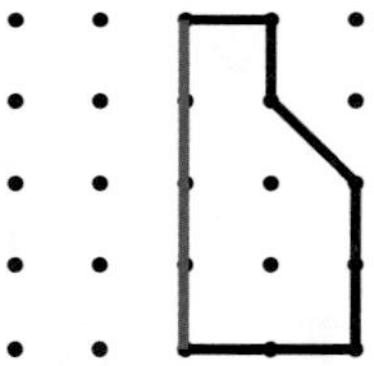

Do you UNDERSTAND?

5. The picture below shows two parts of a figure on dot paper.

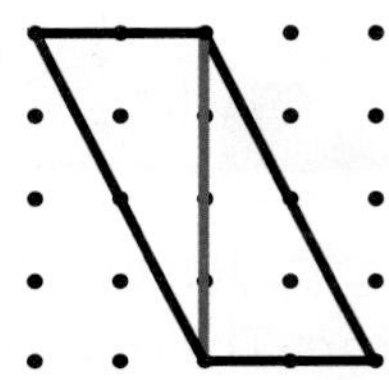

Explain why the blue line segment is not part of a line of symmetry.

6. How would you draw a figure that has two lines of symmetry?

Independent Practice

Trace the figure. Then complete it so the blue line segment is part of a line of symmetry. You may use dot paper or fold and trace.

7.

8.

9.

10.

DIGITAL eTools **www.pearsonsuccessnet.com**

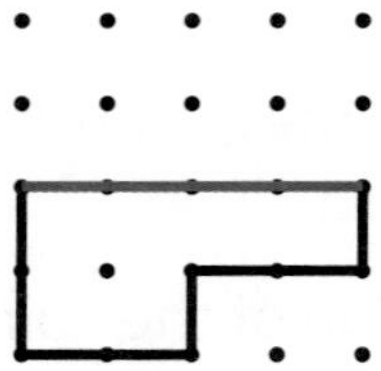

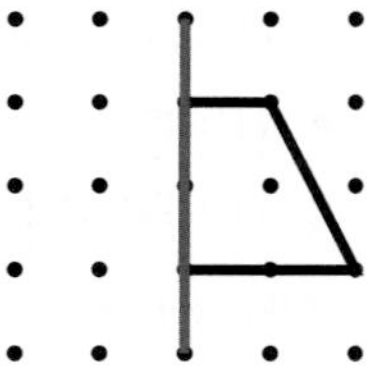

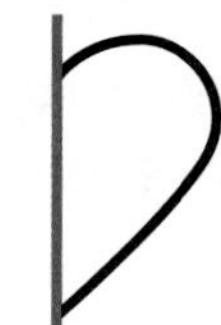

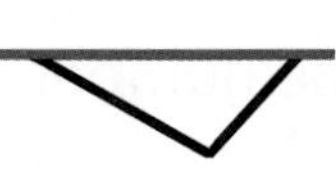

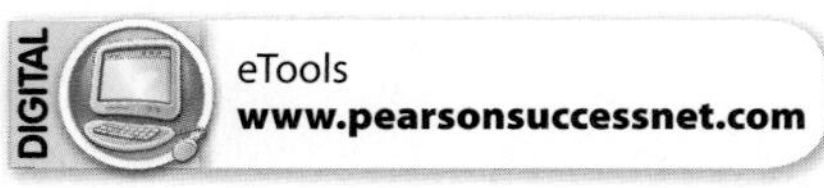

*For another example, see Set C on page 273.

Step 2

Draw the first part of the figure on one side of the line segment.

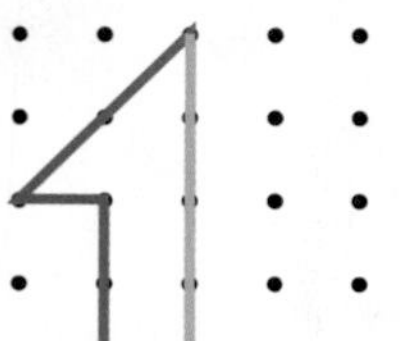

Step 3

Copy the first part exactly on the other side of the line segment.

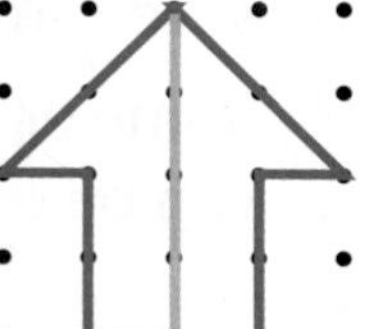

Problem Solving

11. **Estimation** Jeremy is reading a book that has 121 pages. He read 19 pages yesterday and 33 pages today. About how many more pages are left to read?

12. A perfectly formed snowflake has 6 sides and is symmetric.

Draw your own snowflake. Color the lines of symmetry on your drawing. How many lines of symmetry does it have?

13. **Writing to Explain** Explain how you can use this shape to make a symmetric quadrilateral. What type of quadrilateral will it be?

14. The picture shows a sliced ruby red grapefruit and an outline of part of the grapefruit sections.

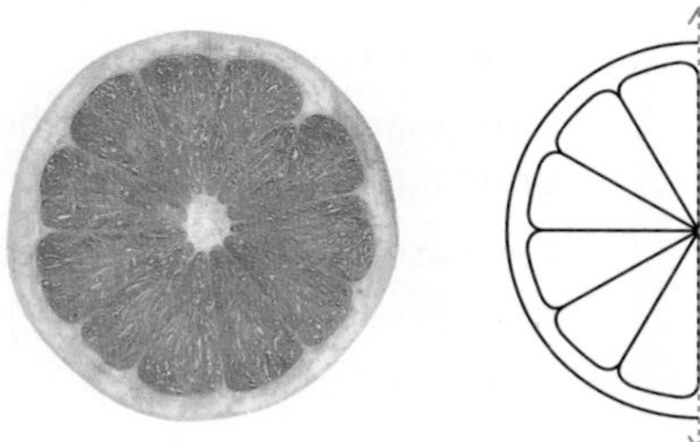

Trace the outline onto a sheet of paper. Complete the outline so the dashed line is a line of symmetry.

15. The green line segment is part of a line of symmetry. Which picture below shows the complete figure?

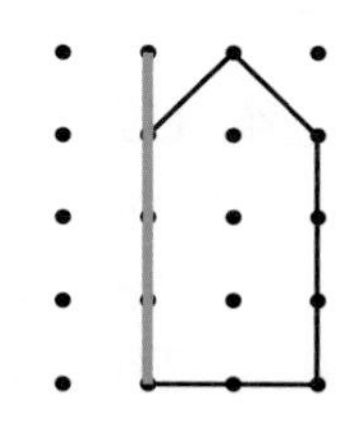

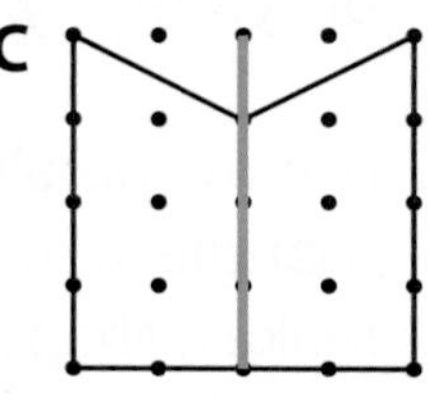

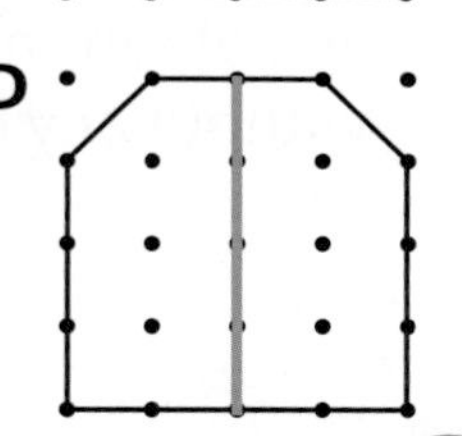

Lesson
11-4

Understand It!
Shapes can be broken apart and put together in different ways.

Problem Solving

Use Objects

A tangram is a square made up of seven smaller shapes.

Some or all of the smaller shapes can be used to make other shapes.

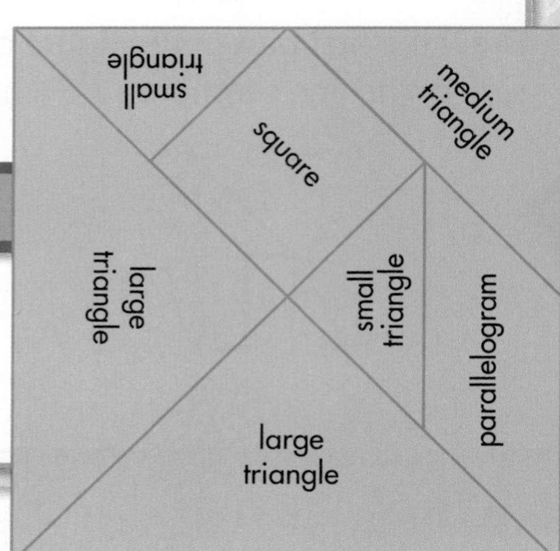

Guided Practice*

Do you know HOW?

Use tangram pieces to make the shapes described. Draw what you made.

1. Use the parallelogram and one small triangle. Make a shape that has at least one line of symmetry. Then make a shape without any lines of symmetry.

Do you UNDERSTAND?

For **2** and **3**, look at the problem above.

2. Where are the two lines of symmetry in the rectangle?

3. **Write a Problem** Write a problem that you can solve by making a shape from tangram pieces.

Independent Practice

For **4** and **5**, use tangram pieces to make the shapes described. Draw what you made.

4. Use the parallelogram and the medium triangle. Make a shape that has at least one line of symmetry. Then make a shape without any lines of symmetry.

5. Use the parallelogram, one small triangle, and the medium triangle. Make a shape that has at least one line of symmetry. Then make a shape without any lines of symmetry.

Stuck? Try this....

- What do I know?
- What am I asked to find?
- What diagram can I use to help understand the problem?
- Can I use addition, subtraction, multiplication, or division?
- Is all of my work correct?
- Did I answer the right question?
- Is my answer reasonable?

*For another example, see Set D on page 273.

Read and Understand

Make two different shapes using the two small triangles and the medium triangle.

- Make one shape that has at least one line of symmetry.
- Make the other shape without any lines of symmetry.

Plan and Solve

This shape is a rectangle. It has two lines of symmetry.

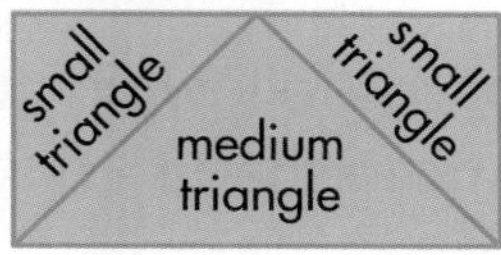

This shape is a parallelogram. It does not have a line of symmetry.

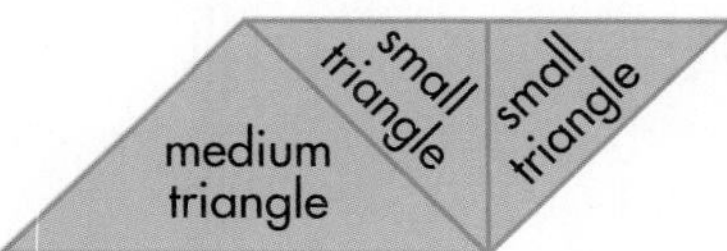

For **6–8**, use the two small triangles and the parallelogram to make each shape. For each shape, use all three pieces. Then draw what you made.

6. A rectangle **7.** A triangle **8.** A parallelogram

For **9–11**, use the two small triangles, the parallelogram, and the square. Make each shape using all four pieces. Then draw what you made.

9. A rectangle **10.** A parallelogram **11.** A hexagon

12. Writing to Explain Show and explain how you can make a triangle and two types of quadrilaterals using just the two small triangles.

13. Use all five triangles from a set of tangram shapes. Make at least three different shapes. Draw what you made.

14. Timothy sold some tickets to the school play. The tickets were numbered in order. The numbers started at 16 and ended at 45. How many tickets did Timothy sell?

15. Jessica is standing in a line of 10 people. There are twice as many people ahead of her as there are behind her. How many people are ahead of Jessica in the line?

16. David's mother brought 24 cartons of orange and grape juice to the class picnic. There were twice as many cartons of orange juice as cartons of grape juice. How many of each kind were there?

A 12 orange, 6 grape
B 12 grape, 6 orange
C 16 orange, 8 grape
D 16 grape, 8 orange

Test

1. Which of the following numbers is symmetric in shape? (11-2)

   A 2

   B 5

   C 0

   D 7

2. Which moves one arrow to match the other one? (11-1)

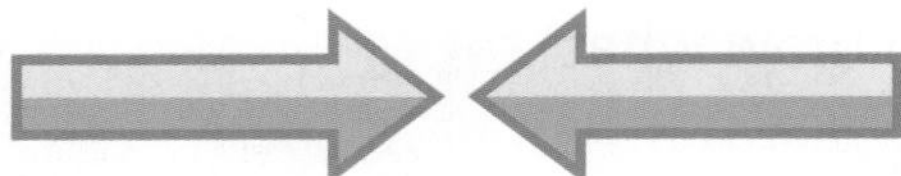

   A Flip

   B Symmetry

   C Slide

   D Turn

3. Below are examples of the small triangle tangram shape turned to several different positions.

   Which of the following shapes can **NOT** be made by joining two of the triangles? (11-4)

   A A square

   B A parallelogram

   C A triangle

   D A trapezoid

4. Katherine designed the body of a kite.

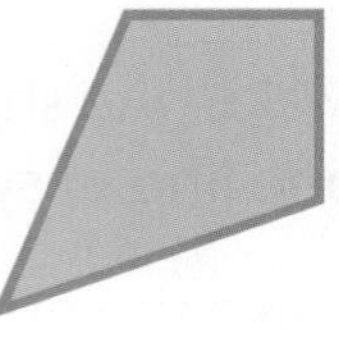

   Which shape is congruent to her kite design? (11-1)

   A

   B

   C

   D

5. Which of the following shows a rotation (turn)? (11-1)

   A

   B

   C

   D

6. While on a nature hike, Nolan saw the items below. Which item does **NOT** show a line of symmetry? (11-2)

A

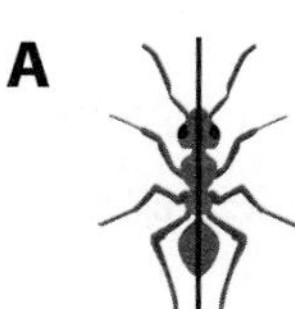

B

C

D

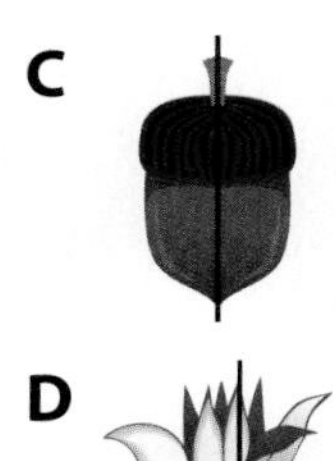

7. Which moves one flag to match the other one? (11-1)

A Slide

B Turn

C Congruent

D Flip

8. Danny drew the left half of his playground design on dot paper.

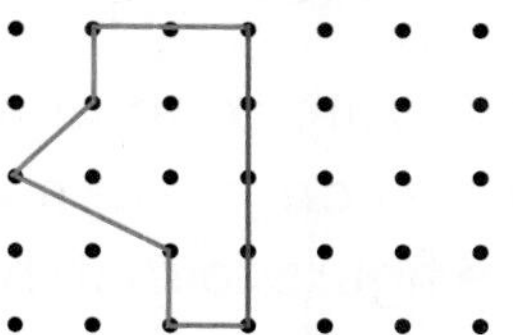

Which shows the right half of his design if the blue segment is part of a line of symmetry? (11-3)

A

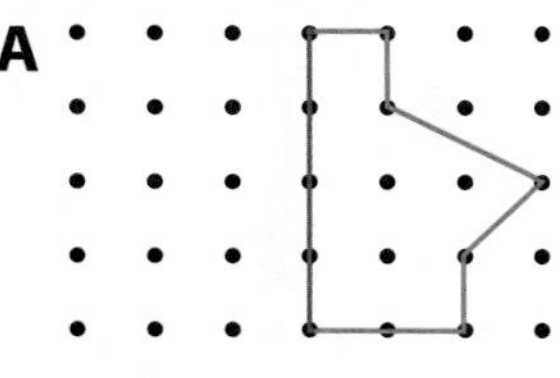

B

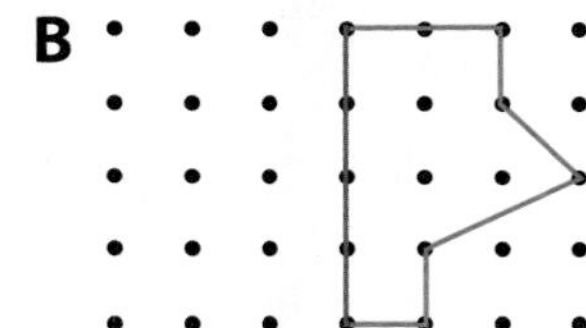

C

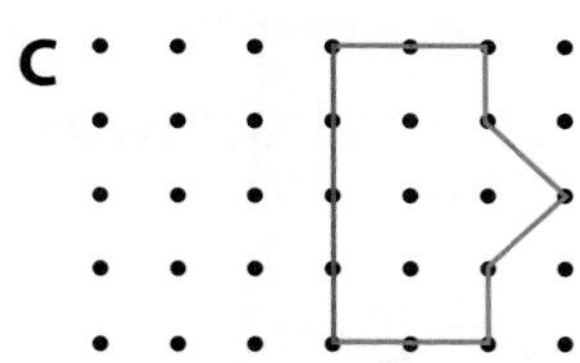

D

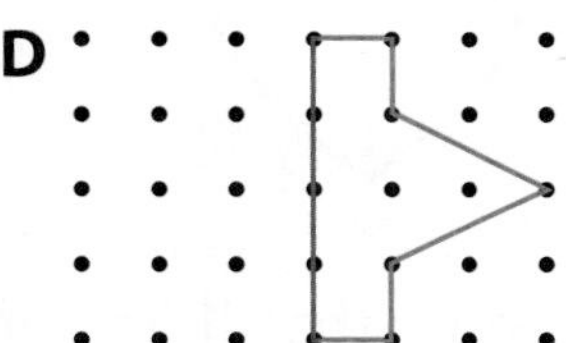

9. How many letters in the word below have at least one line of symmetry? (11-2)

TAXES

A 0

B 2

C 4

D 5

Reteaching

Set A, pages 260–262

Figures that have the same size and same shape are congruent figures.

You can check if figures are congruent by moving them. They are congruent if you can slide, flip, or turn one figure to match the other.

This reflection shows that these two figures are congruent.

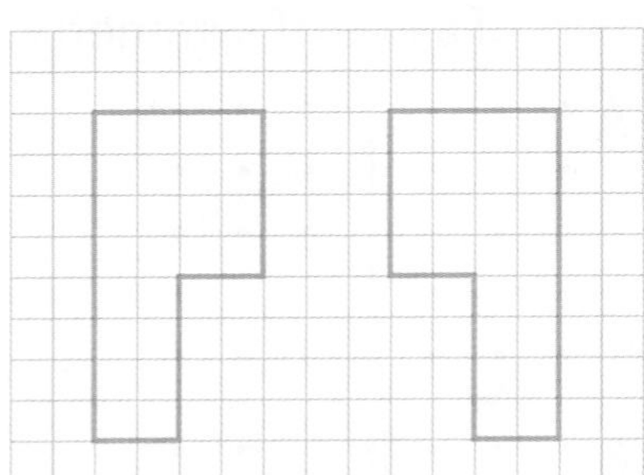

Flip

Remember that figures need to be the same shape and same size to be congruent.

Are the figures congruent? Write *yes* or *no*. If yes, write *slide*, *turn*, or *flip* for each.

1. 

2. 

Set B, pages 264–265

A symmetric figure has at least two parts that match exactly.

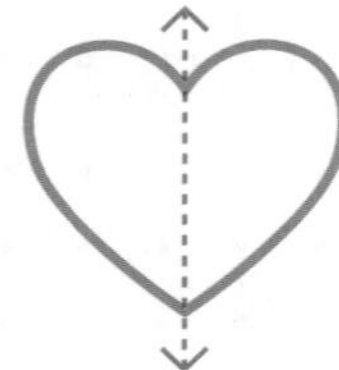

A figure can have more than 1 line of symmetry.

This figure has 5 lines of symmetry.

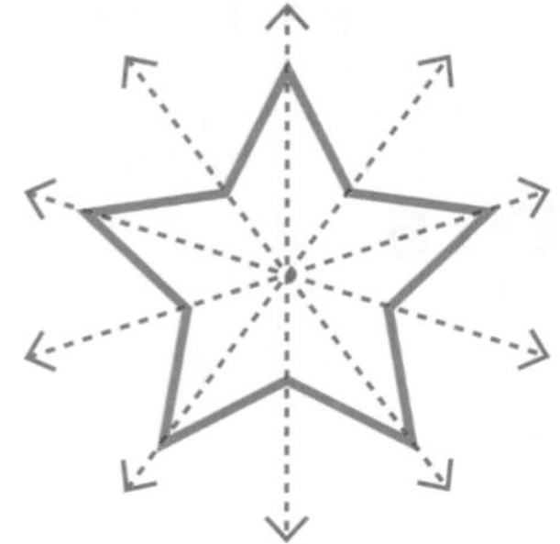

Remember that a symmetric figure has at least 1 line of symmetry, showing two parts that match exactly.

Tell whether each figure is symmetric. Write *yes* or *no*.

1. 

2. 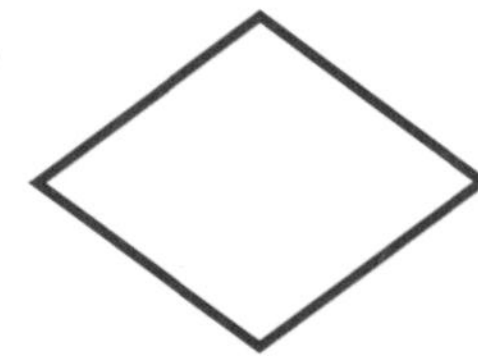

Set C, pages 266–267

To draw a symmetric figure, draw the first part of the figure on one side of a line segment.

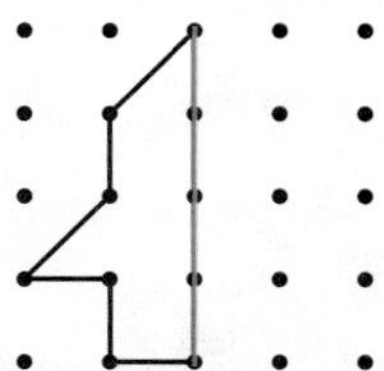

Copy the first part exactly on the other side of the line segment.

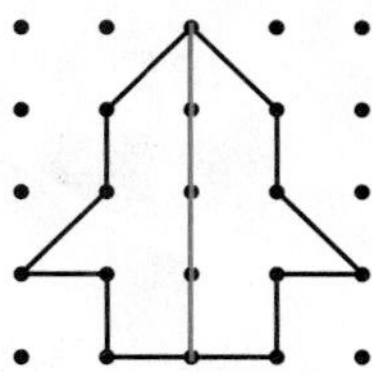

Remember to match each part of the figure exactly.

Copy the figure onto dot paper. Then complete it so the red line segment is part of a line of symmetry.

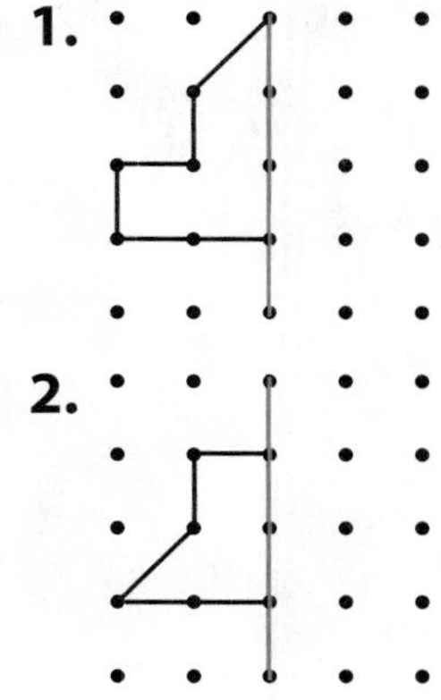

Set D, pages 268–269

Use the two large triangle tangram shapes. Make one shape that has at least one line of symmetry. Make another shape that does not have a line of symmetry.

This shape is a triangle. It has one line of symmetry.

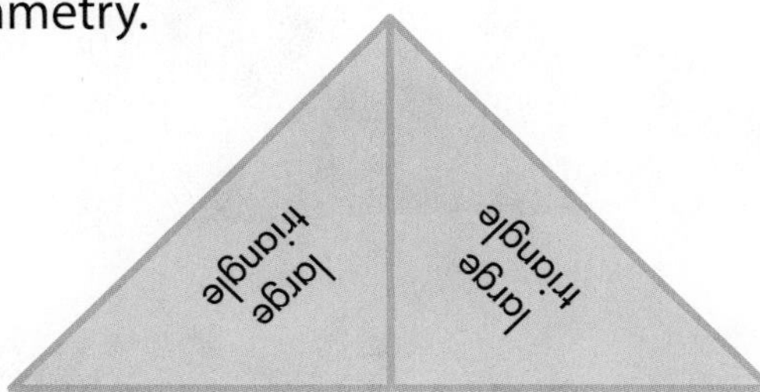

This shape is a polygon. It does not have a line of symmetry.

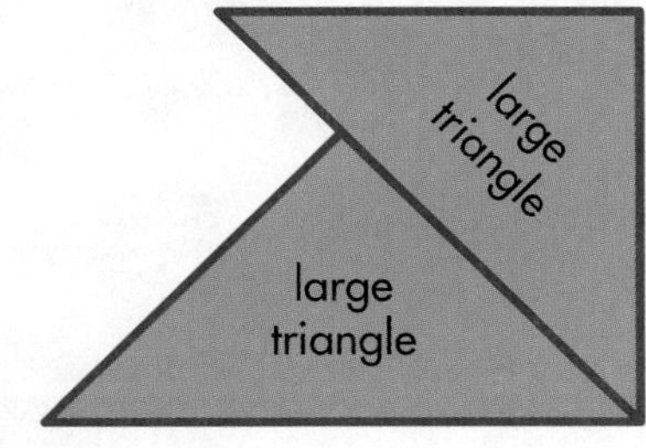

Remember to check that your new shape matches the directions given.

From a tangram, use the two small triangles and the square. Make the shape described. Draw what you made.

1. A shape with a line of symmetry
2. A parallelogram
3. A trapezoid

Topic 12

Understanding Fractions

1 The tiger beetle and the caterpillar hunter beetle are helpful insects. Which type of beetle is longer? You will find out in Lesson 12-9.

2 What fraction of Earth's land surface is desert? You will find out in Lesson 12-5.

3

What fraction of the bones in your body are in your feet? You will find out in Lesson 12-4.

4

Is the flag of Nigeria made up of equal parts? You will find out in Lesson 12-1.

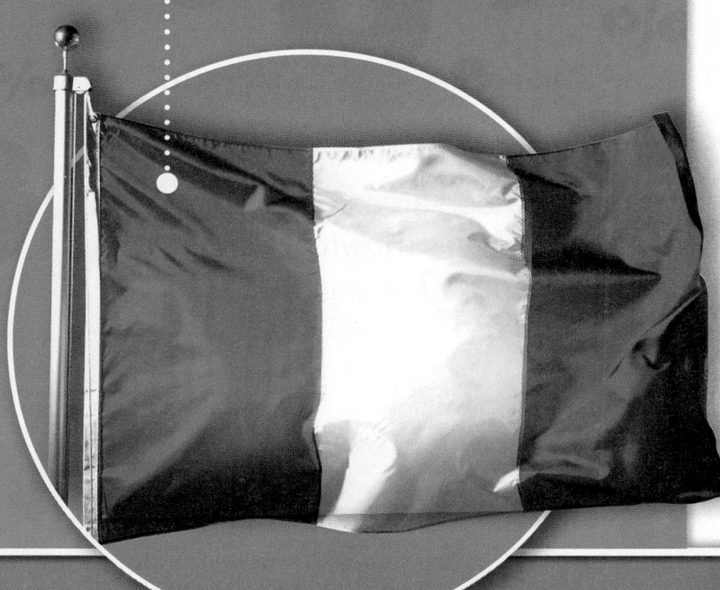

Review What You Know!

Vocabulary

Choose the best term from the box.

- compare
- greater
- less
- multiply

1. The number 219 is _?_ than the number 392.
2. The number 38 is _?_ than the number 19.
3. When you decide if 15 has more tens or fewer tens than 24, you _?_ the numbers.

Arrays

Find the product for each array.

4. ● ● ●
   ● ● ●

5. ● ● ● ●
   ● ● ● ●
   ● ● ● ●

Compare Numbers

Compare. Write >, <, or =.

6. 427 ◯ 583
7. 910 ◯ 906
8. 139 ◯ 136
9. 4,500 ◯ 4,500
10. 693 ◯ 734
11. 1,050 ◯ 1,005
12. **Writing to Explain** Which number is greater, 595 or 565? Explain which digits you used to decide.

Lesson

12-1

Understand It!
A whole can be divided into equal parts in different ways.

Dividing Regions into Equal Parts

Hands-On
grid paper

How can you divide a whole into equal parts?

Show two ways to divide the grid paper into equal parts.

When a region is divided into two equal parts, the parts are called halves.

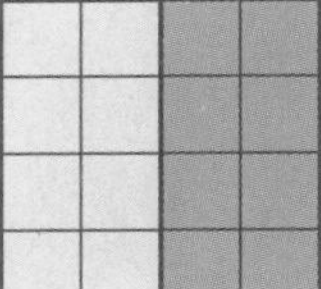

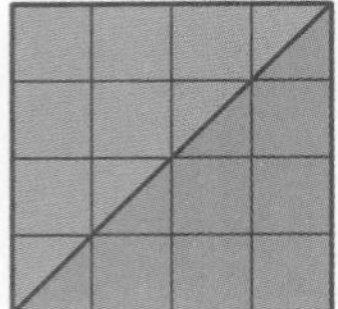

Other Examples

The parts do not need to be the same shape, but they must be equal in area.

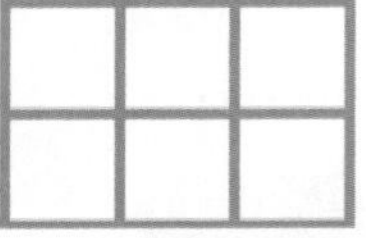

6 equal parts
sixths

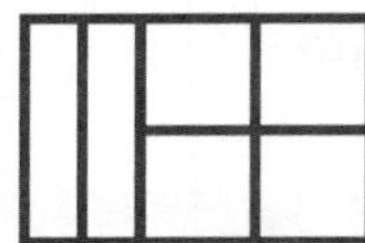

6 equal parts
sixths

10 equal parts
tenths

10 equal parts
tenths

Guided Practice*

Do you know HOW?

In **1–4**, tell if each shows equal or unequal parts. If the parts are equal, name them.

1. 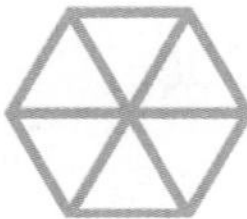

2. 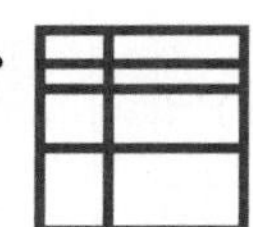

3. 

4. 

Do you UNDERSTAND?

5. In the examples on grid paper above, explain how you know the two parts are equal.

6. Use grid paper. Draw a picture to show sixths.

7. Amar divided his garden into equal areas, as shown below. What is the name of the equal parts of the whole?

*For another example, see Set A on page 302.

Here are some names of equal parts of a whole.

2 equal parts halves	3 equal parts thirds	4 equal parts fourths	5 equal parts fifths
6 equal parts sixths	8 equal parts eighths	10 equal parts tenths	12 equal parts twelfths

Independent Practice

In **8–11**, tell if each shows equal or unequal parts. If the parts are equal, name them.

8. **9.** **10.** **11.**

In **12–15**, use grid paper. Draw a region showing the equal parts named.

12. fourths **13.** halves **14.** tenths **15.** eighths

Problem Solving

In **16–18**, use the table of flags.

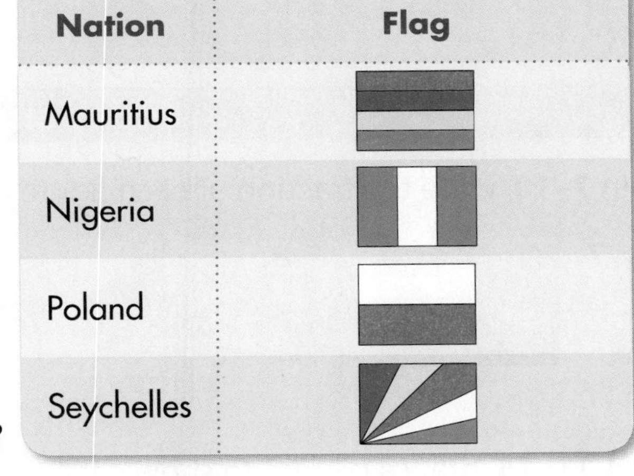

16. **Reasoning** The flag of this nation has more than three parts. The parts are equal. Which nation is this?

17. The flag of Nigeria is made up of equal parts. What is the name of the parts of this flag?

18. Which flag does **NOT** have equal parts?

19. Which shape does **NOT** show equal parts?

A
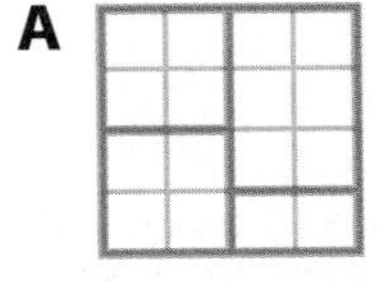

B
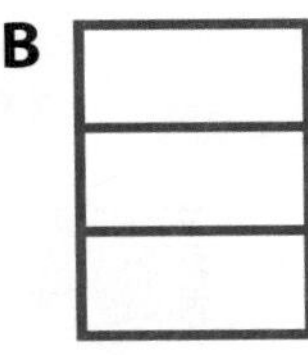

C
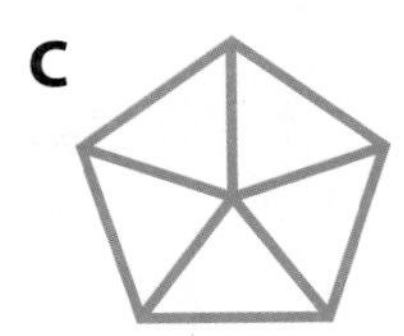

D

Lesson

12-2 Fractions and Regions

Understand It!
A fraction can be used to describe equal parts of a whole.

How can you show and name part of a region?

Mr. Kim made a pan of fruit bars. He served part of the pan of bars to friends. What part of the whole pan was served? What part was left?

A fraction is a symbol, such as $\frac{1}{2}$ or $\frac{2}{3}$, that names equal parts of a whole.

Guided Practice*

Do you know HOW?

In **1** and **2**, write the fraction of each figure that is orange.

1. 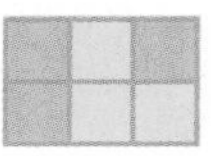

2. 

In **3** and **4**, draw a picture to show each fraction.

3. $\frac{3}{4}$

4. $\frac{4}{7}$

Do you UNDERSTAND?

5. In the example above, what fraction names all of the parts in the pan of bars?

6. Mrs. Gupta bought a pizza. The picture shows what part of it she ate. What fraction of the pizza did she eat? What fraction of the pizza was left?

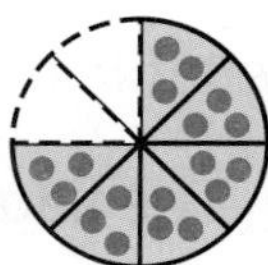

Independent Practice

In **7–10**, write the fraction of each figure that is green.

7. 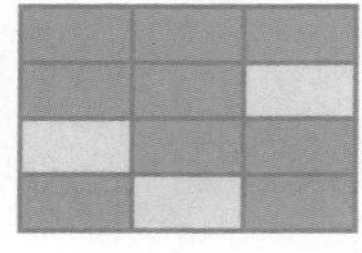

8. 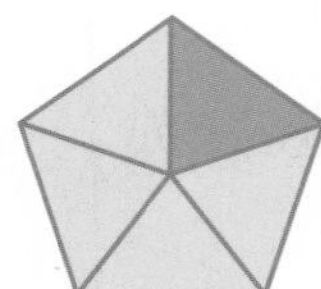

9. 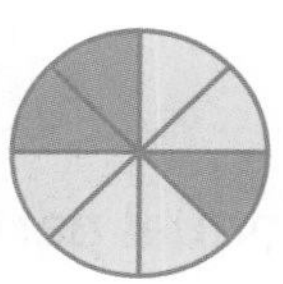

10. 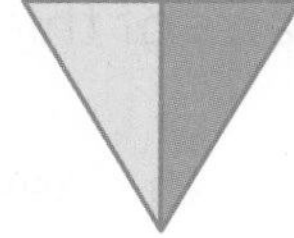

In **11–15**, draw a picture to show each fraction.

11. $\frac{1}{3}$ **12.** $\frac{2}{4}$ **13.** $\frac{1}{6}$ **14.** $\frac{7}{10}$ **15.** $\frac{2}{2}$

*For another example, see Set A on page 302.

What You Write

Numerator → $\frac{4}{9}$ ← 4 equal parts served
Denominator → ← 9 equal parts **in all**

Numerator → $\frac{5}{9}$ ← 5 equal parts left
Denominator → ← 9 equal parts **in all**

The numerator tells how many equal parts are described. It is the number above the fraction bar.

The denominator tells the total number of equal parts. It is the number below the bar.

What You Say

Four ninths of the pan of fruit bars was served.

Five ninths of the pan of fruit bars was left.

Problem Solving

For **16–19**, use the sign at the right.

Size of Pizza	Price
Small	$7
Medium	$9
Large	$11

16. Ben and his friends ordered a medium pizza. Ben ate 1 slice of the pizza. What fraction of the pizza did Ben eat?

17. Aida's family bought a large pizza. The family ate 4 slices of the pizza. What fraction of the pizza was left?

18. Tami's family bought 3 small pizzas. Leo's family bought 2 medium pizzas. How much more did Tami's family spend than Leo's family?

19. Which costs more, 6 small pizzas or 4 large pizzas? How much more?

20. **Writing to Explain** A pan of cornbread is divided into 12 unequal parts. Alana serves 3 of the parts. Is it reasonable to say she has served $\frac{3}{12}$ of the cornbread? Explain.

21. Look at the grid at the right. What fraction of the grid is white?

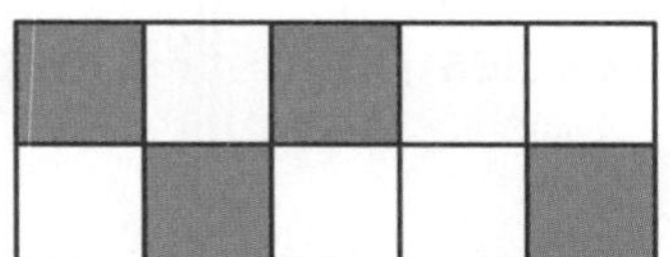

A 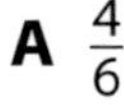 $\frac{4}{6}$ **C** $\frac{6}{10}$

B $\frac{6}{6}$ **D** $\frac{2}{5}$

Lesson
12-3

Understand It!
A fraction can be used to describe parts of a group.

Fractions and Sets

Hands-On
counters

How can a fraction name part of a group?

A group of 12 people is in line for movie tickets. What fraction of the group of people are wearing red? What fraction of the people are not wearing red?

A fraction can name parts of a set, or group, of objects or people.

8 of the people are wearing red.

Guided Practice*

Do you know HOW?

In **1** and **2**, write the fraction of the counters that are red.

1.

2.

In **3** and **4**, draw counters to show the fraction given.

3. $\frac{4}{5}$

4. $\frac{3}{8}$

Do you UNDERSTAND?

5. In the example above, why is the denominator the same for the part of the group wearing red and for the part of the group not wearing red?

6. A group of 9 students is waiting for a bus. Six of them are wearing jackets. What fraction of the students in the group are wearing jackets? What fraction of the students are not wearing jackets?

Independent Practice

In **7–9**, write the fraction of the counters that are yellow.

7.

8. 

9. 

In **10–12**, draw a picture of the set described.

10. 5 shapes, $\frac{3}{5}$ of the shapes are circles

11. 8 shapes, $\frac{5}{8}$ of the shapes are triangles

12. 2 shapes, $\frac{1}{2}$ of the shapes are squares

DIGITAL
eTools
www.pearsonsuccessnet.com

For another example, see Set A on page 302.

What You Write	What You Say
$\frac{8}{12}$ ← Number of people wearing red ← Total number of people	*Eight twelfths* of the people are wearing red.
$\frac{4}{12}$ ← Number of people **not** wearing red ← Total number of people	*Four twelfths* of the people are not wearing red.

Problem Solving

For **13–15**, write the fraction of the group of buttons described.

13. Pink buttons

14. Blue buttons

15. Buttons with only two holes

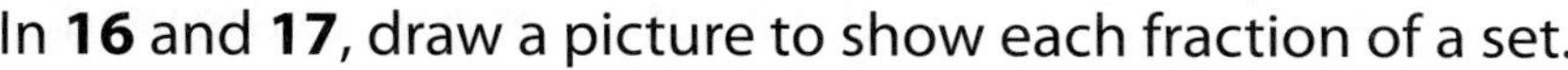

In **16** and **17**, draw a picture to show each fraction of a set.

16. Flowers: $\frac{3}{4}$ are yellow

17. Apples: $\frac{1}{2}$ are green

18. The picture below shows six statues of children. How many are statues of girls?

19. **Number Sense** A family of 5 is buying concert tickets. If $\frac{2}{5}$ of the tickets they buy are for adults, how many adult tickets does the family need?

20. What fraction of the flower petals have fallen off the flower?

A $\frac{3}{5}$

B $\frac{2}{8}$

C $\frac{8}{10}$

D $\frac{2}{10}$

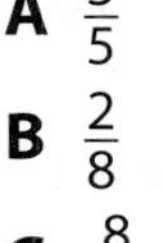

Lesson
12-4

Understand It!
Benchmark fractions are helpful in estimating fractional amounts.

Benchmark Fractions

How do you estimate parts?

Mr. Anderson is harvesting wheat on his farm. About what part of the wheat field does he still need to harvest?

Guided Practice*

Do you know HOW?

1. Estimate the fractional part that is yellow. Use a benchmark fraction.

2. What benchmark fraction should be written at point *P*?

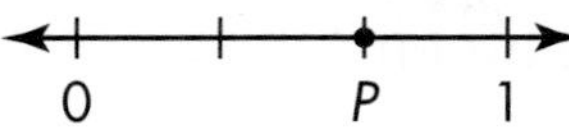

Do you UNDERSTAND?

3. In the example above, what benchmark fraction can you use for the part of the wheat field that Mr. Anderson has harvested?

4. Geena is raking the leaves in her yard. About what part of the yard still needs to be raked?

Independent Practice

In **5–7**, estimate the fractional part that is green. Use a benchmark fraction.

5.   **6.**   **7.**

In **8–10**, what benchmark fraction is closest to each point? Choose from the benchmark fractions $\frac{1}{2}$, $\frac{1}{3}$, $\frac{2}{3}$, $\frac{1}{4}$, and $\frac{3}{4}$.

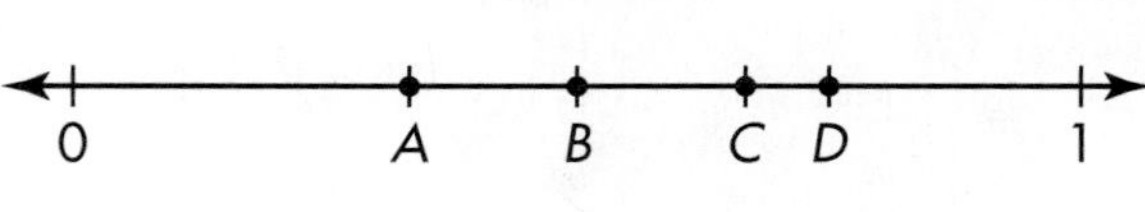

8. *A*   **9.** *B*   **10.** *C*   **11.** *D*

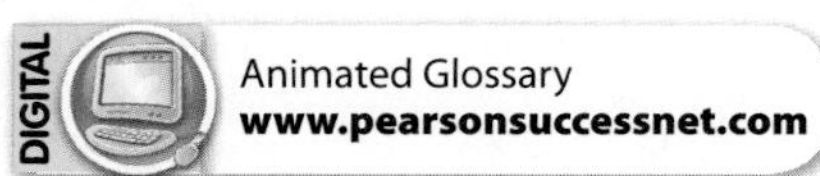

Animated Glossary
www.pearsonsuccessnet.com

**For another example, see Set B on page 302.*

Step 1

You can use benchmark fractions to estimate fractional parts.

Benchmark fractions are commonly used fractions. Some benchmark fractions are $\frac{1}{4}$, $\frac{1}{3}$, $\frac{1}{2}$, $\frac{2}{3}$, and $\frac{3}{4}$.

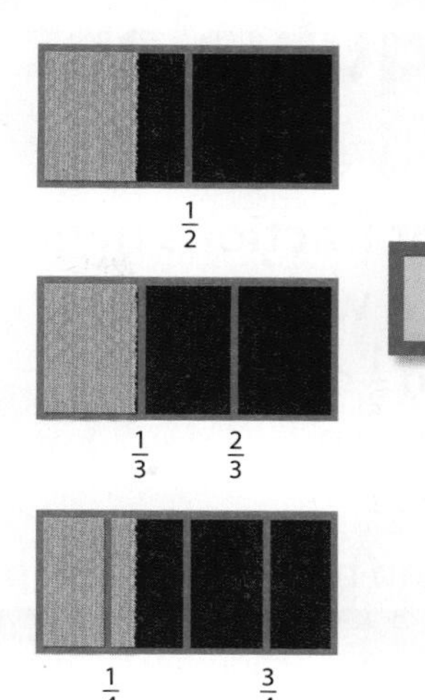

Step 2

Find the benchmark fraction that is closest to the fraction in the problem.

The part of the field that still has wheat is closest to $\frac{1}{3}$.

Mr. Anderson still needs to harvest about $\frac{1}{3}$ of the wheat field.

Problem Solving

In **12–14**, estimate the part of each garden that has flowers.

12. Garden A

13. Garden B

14. Garden C

Use the table at the right for **15–17**.

15. In which months did the garden sell more tickets—May and June combined or July and August combined?

16. Estimation About how many tickets in all were sold in the four months? Explain how you estimated.

17. Which shows the numbers in the table from least to greatest?

A 583, 947, 815, 726

B 947, 815, 726, 583

C 947, 726, 815, 583

D 583, 726, 815, 947

Data

Children's Garden Tickets Sold	
May	583
June	947
July	815
August	726

18. What fraction of your body's bones are **NOT** in your feet? Use the picture at the right.

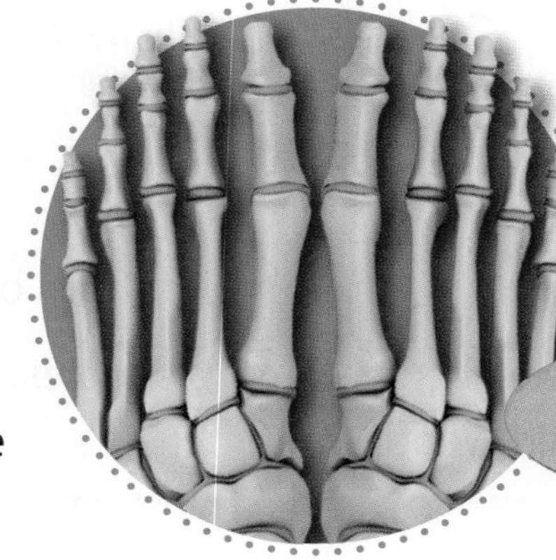

One fourth of your body's bones are in your feet.

Lesson

12-5

Understand It!
The same fractional amount can be named in different ways.

Finding Equivalent Fractions

Hands-On
fraction strips

How can different fractions name the same part of a whole?

Sonya has decorated $\frac{1}{2}$ of the border. What are two other ways to name $\frac{1}{2}$?

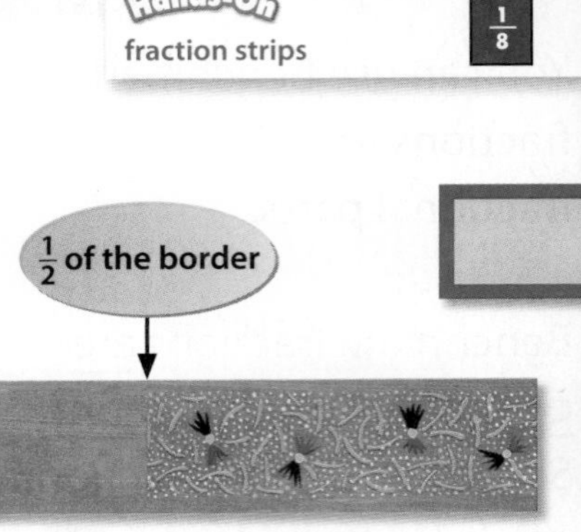

Different fractions can name the same part of a whole.

Another Example How can you write a fraction in simplest form?

Division facts that you know will help you find equivalent fractions.

Mario has colored $\frac{4}{6}$ of a border. What is the simplest form of $\frac{4}{6}$?

The simplest form of a fraction is a fraction with a numerator and denominator that cannot be divided by the same divisor, except 1.

$\frac{4}{6}$ of the length of the border

One Way

Use models.

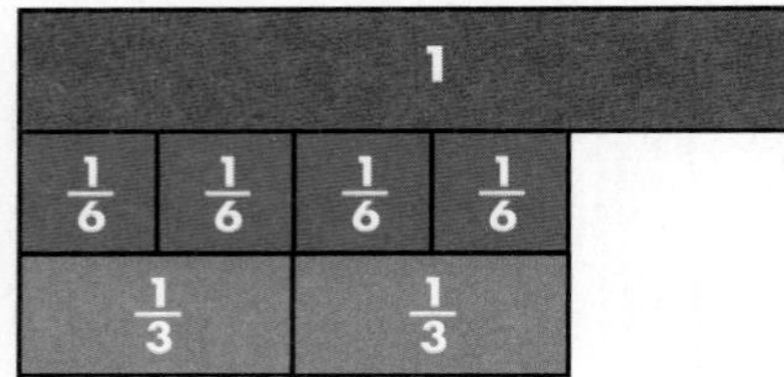

$\frac{4}{6} = \frac{2}{3}$

The simplest form of $\frac{4}{6}$ is $\frac{2}{3}$.

Another Way

Divide the numerator and denominator by the same number.

Find a divisor that both the numerator and denominator can be divided by evenly.

Both 4 and 6 can be evenly divided by 2.

$$\frac{4 \div 2}{6 \div 2} = \frac{2}{3}$$

The numerator and denominator of $\frac{2}{3}$ cannot be divided evenly by the same divisor except 1. The simplest form of $\frac{4}{6}$ is $\frac{2}{3}$.

Explain It

1. **Number Sense** Is $\frac{1}{3}$ the simplest form of $\frac{2}{6}$? Why or why not?
2. Wendi colored $\frac{2}{4}$ of a banner. In simplest form, what fraction of the banner did Wendi color?

$\frac{1}{2} = \frac{\square}{8}$

You can use fraction strips. The denominators of the fractions tell which fraction strips to use.

Find how many $\frac{1}{8}$s are equal to $\frac{1}{2}$.

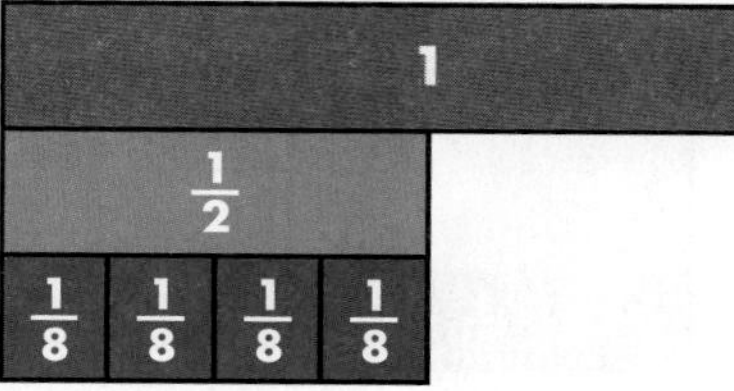

Four $\frac{1}{8}$ strips are equal to $\frac{1}{2}$, so $\frac{1}{2} = \frac{4}{8}$.

Another name for $\frac{1}{2}$ is $\frac{4}{8}$.

$\frac{1}{2} = \frac{\square}{6}$

You can use fraction strips. The denominator is 6 so use $\frac{1}{6}$ strips.

Find how many $\frac{1}{6}$s are equal to $\frac{1}{2}$.

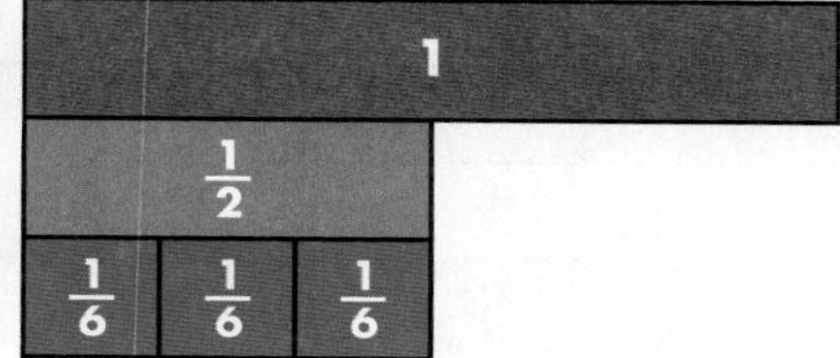

Three $\frac{1}{6}$ strips are equal to $\frac{1}{2}$, so $\frac{1}{2} = \frac{3}{6}$.

Another name for $\frac{1}{2}$ is $\frac{3}{6}$.

Guided Practice*

Do you know HOW?

1. Copy and complete the number sentence. Use fraction strips or make drawings on grid paper.

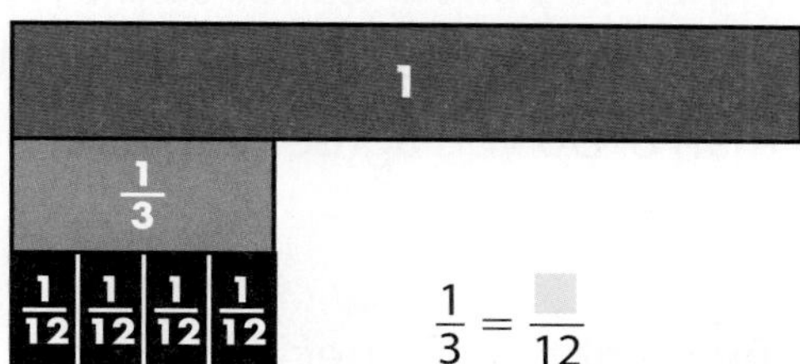

$\frac{1}{3} = \frac{\square}{12}$

Find the simplest form of each fraction.

2. $\frac{5}{10}$ 3. $\frac{6}{9}$ 4. $\frac{2}{4}$

Do you UNDERSTAND?

5. In the example above, what pattern do you see in the numerator and denominator of fractions that name $\frac{1}{2}$?

6. Vijay folded a rope into fourths. Then he showed $\frac{1}{4}$ of the length. Write $\frac{1}{4}$ one other way.

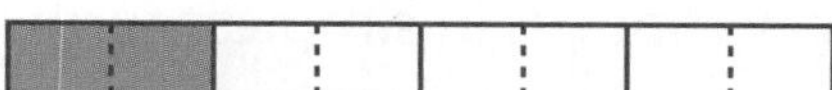

Independent Practice

In **7–9**, copy and complete each number sentence. Use fraction strips or make drawings on grid paper to help.

7.

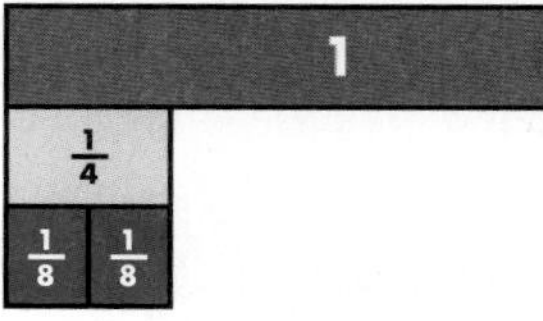

$\frac{1}{4} = \frac{\square}{8}$

8.

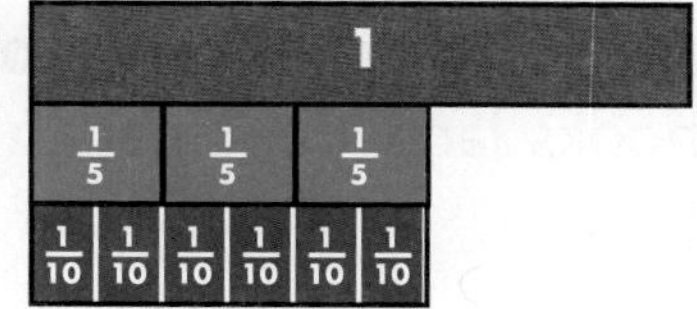

$\frac{3}{5} = \frac{\square}{10}$

9.

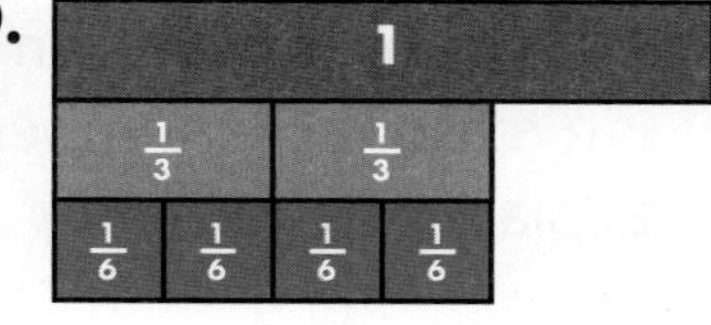

$\frac{2}{3} = \frac{\square}{6}$

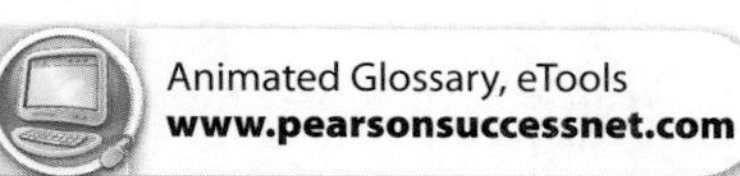

For another example, see Set A on page 302.

Independent Practice

For **10–12**, copy and complete each number sentence. Use fraction strips or make drawings on grid paper to help.

10.

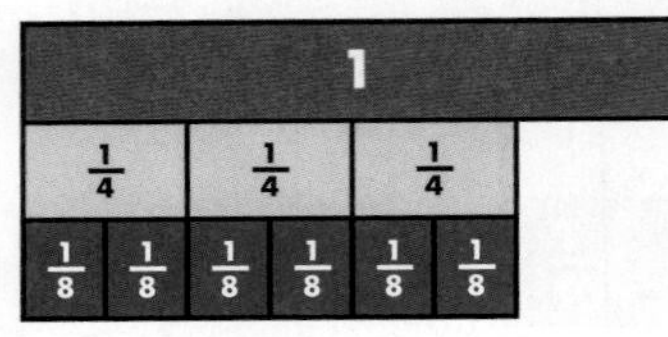

$\frac{6}{8} = \frac{\square}{4}$

11.

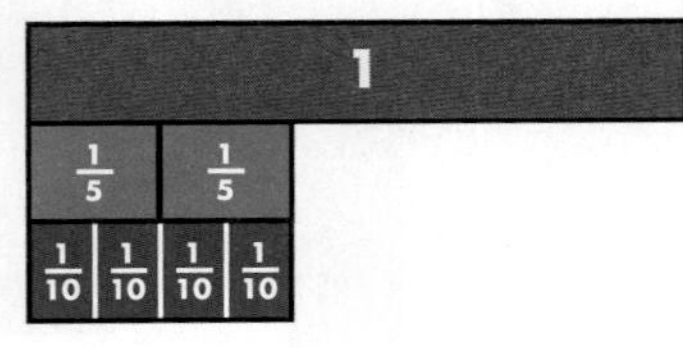

$\frac{2}{5} = \frac{\square}{10}$

12.

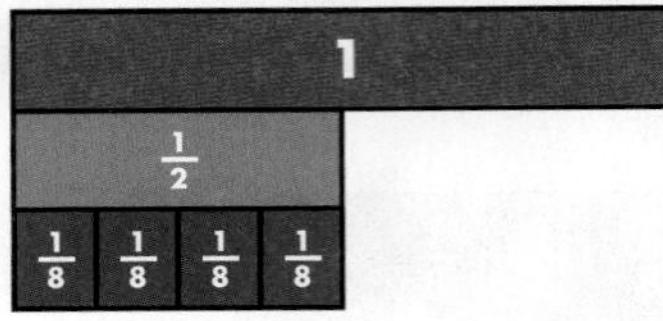

$\frac{1}{2} = \frac{\square}{8}$

For **13–20**, write each fraction in simplest form.

13. $\frac{3}{6}$ **14.** $\frac{9}{12}$ **15.** $\frac{8}{12}$ **16.** $\frac{5}{15}$

17. $\frac{2}{10}$ **18.** $\frac{7}{8}$ **19.** $\frac{8}{10}$ **20.** $\frac{6}{12}$

Problem Solving

21. Evie painted $\frac{1}{6}$ of a board. What is one other way to name $\frac{1}{6}$?

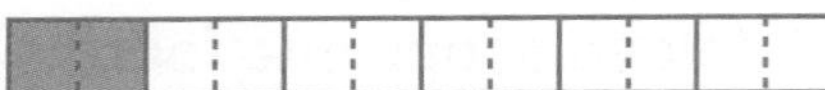

22. **Number Sense** Carlos said that $\frac{3}{4}$ must be less than $\frac{3}{8}$ because 4 is less than 8. Do you agree? Explain.

23. **Writing to Explain** How do you know that $\frac{2}{3}$ is in simplest form?

24. Two eighths of a necklace is red. What part of the necklace is not red?

25. The shaded part of which rectangle is a fraction equal to $\frac{1}{4}$?

A

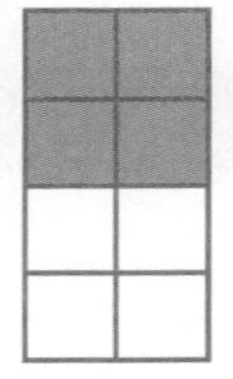

B

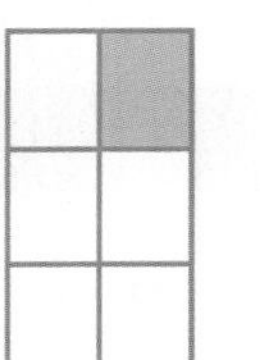

C

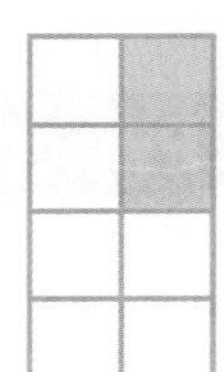

D

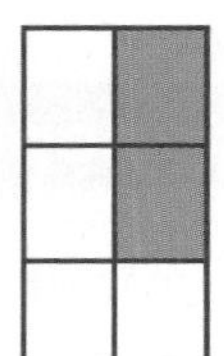

26. **Reasonableness** Jan reads 4 to 6 books every month. What is a reasonable number of books Jan would read in 7 months? Explain your answer.

27. In simplest form, what fraction of the Earth's land surface is desert? Use the picture.

A $\frac{1}{2}$ **B** $\frac{1}{3}$ **C** $\frac{1}{5}$ **D** $\frac{4}{6}$

About $\frac{2}{6}$ of Earth's land surface is desert.

Circle Graphs

Kara earned \$20 last week. The circle graph shows how she earned money and what part of the total was earned for each kind of job.

Kara's Earnings

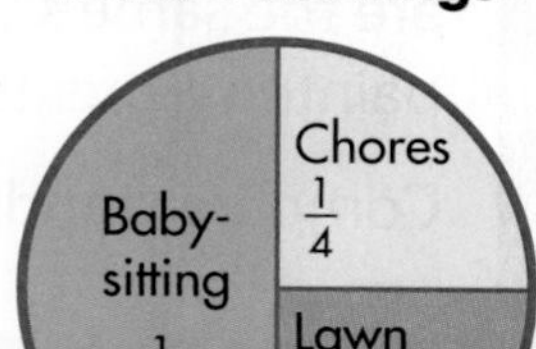

The part for babysitting is half of the circle. Kara earned more by babysitting than by doing chores or lawn work.

One half of the \$20 Kara earned was from babysitting.

$\frac{1}{2} = \frac{10}{20}$ So, Kara earned \$10 by babysitting.

One fourth of the amount Kara earned was from doing chores, and one fourth was from doing lawn work.

$\frac{1}{4} = \frac{5}{20}$ Kara earned \$5 doing chores and \$5 doing lawn work.

Practice

Tom spent a total of \$12 on supplies for Hammy, his pet hamster. For **1–5**, use the circle graph that Tom made.

Supplies for Hammy

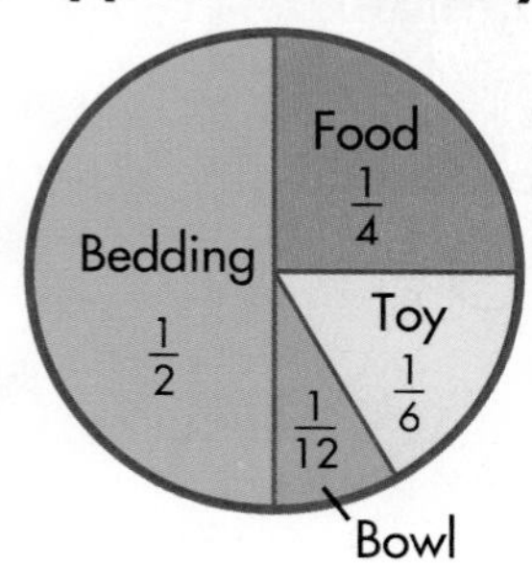

1. Which item cost one fourth of the total? How much money is that?

2. How much did Tom spend on bedding?

3. Which item cost one sixth of the total? How much money is that?

4. List the items Tom bought from least to greatest cost.

5. How could thinking about a clock help Tom make the circle graph for Hammy's supplies?

For **6** and **7**, use the table at the right that shows the voting results for class color.

Class Color (Data)

Color	Votes
Blue	9
Green	3
Silver	6

6. a. What is the total number of votes?

b. Write a fraction that describes the votes for each color.

7. Make a circle graph showing the votes.

Lesson
12-6

Understand It!
There are different ways to compare fractions.

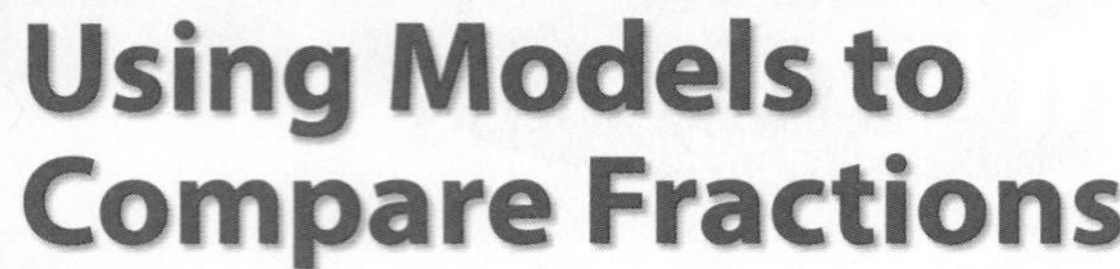

Using Models to Compare Fractions

Hands-On
fraction strips

How can you compare fractions?

Nola and Edwin are painting two boards that are the same size and the same shape. Who painted a greater amount—Nola or Edwin?

Compare $\frac{1}{2}$ and $\frac{2}{5}$.

Nola painted $\frac{1}{2}$ of one board.

Edwin painted $\frac{2}{5}$ of the other board.

Guided Practice*

Do you know HOW?

In **1** and **2**, compare. Write >, <, or =. Use fraction strips to help.

1. 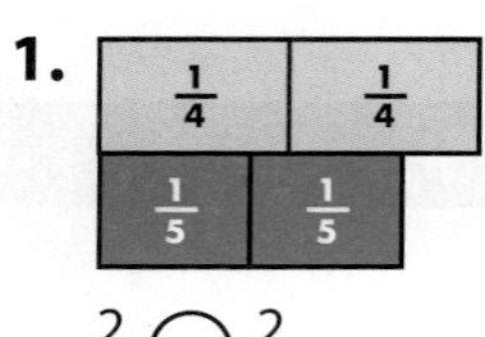

$\frac{2}{4} \bigcirc \frac{2}{5}$

2. 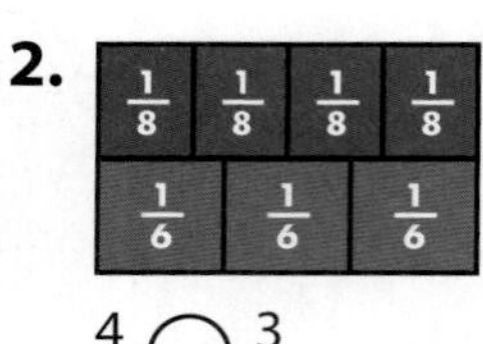

$\frac{4}{8} \bigcirc \frac{3}{6}$

Do you UNDERSTAND?

3. In the problem above about Zoe and Nat, can you tell who painted a greater area of board? Explain.

4. Bob and Irene are painting two walls that are the same size and shape. Irene painted $\frac{2}{3}$ of one wall. Bob painted $\frac{3}{4}$ of the other wall. Who painted a greater amount?

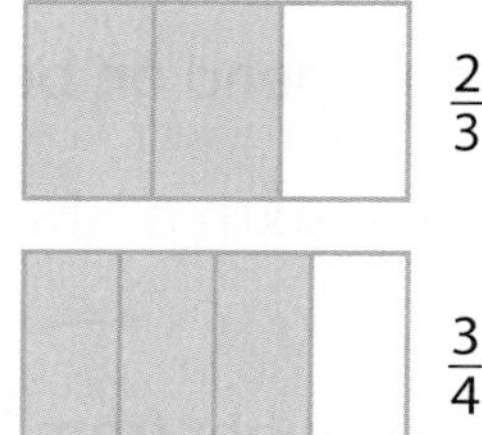

$\frac{2}{3}$

$\frac{3}{4}$

Independent Practice

In **5–7**, compare. Write >, <, or =. Use fraction strips to help.

5. 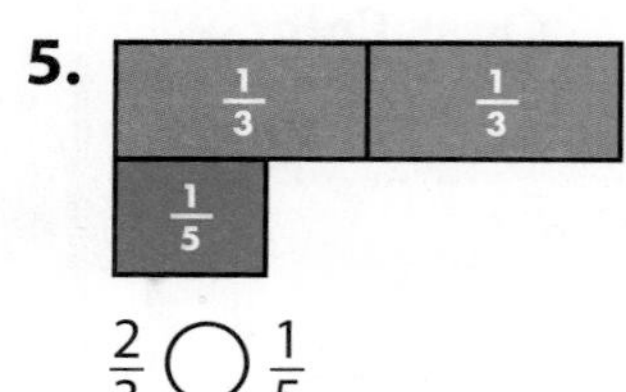

$\frac{2}{3} \bigcirc \frac{1}{5}$

6. $\frac{1}{12}$ $\frac{1}{12}$ $\frac{1}{12}$ / $\frac{1}{4}$

$\frac{3}{12} \bigcirc \frac{1}{4}$

7. $\frac{1}{6}$ $\frac{1}{6}$ / $\frac{1}{2}$

$\frac{2}{6} \bigcirc \frac{1}{2}$

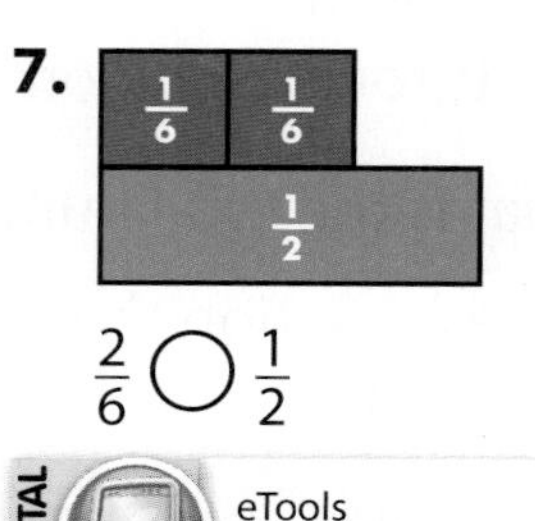

DIGITAL eTools **www.pearsonsuccessnet.com**

*For another example, see Set C on page 302.

You can use fraction strips.

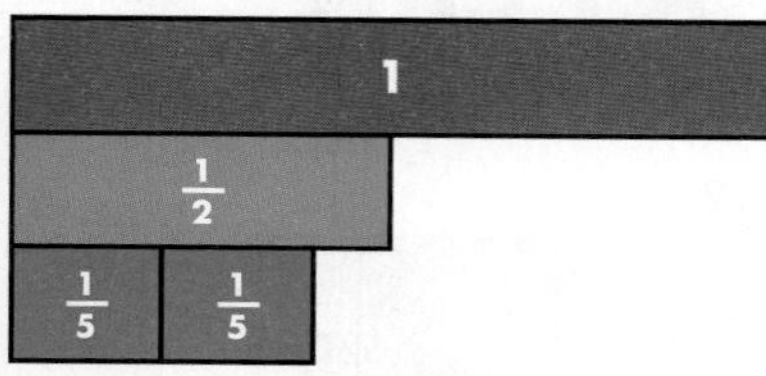

Compare the fraction strips.

$\frac{1}{2}$ is greater than $\frac{2}{5}$.

$\frac{1}{2} > \frac{2}{5}$

Nola painted a greater amount.

Zoe painted $\frac{1}{2}$ of one board. Nat painted $\frac{1}{2}$ of a board with a different area. Is the half Zoe painted equal to the half Nat painted?

Draw a picture.

$\frac{1}{2}$ of each board is painted

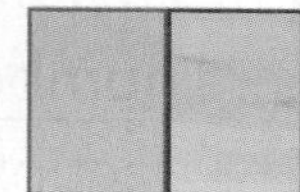

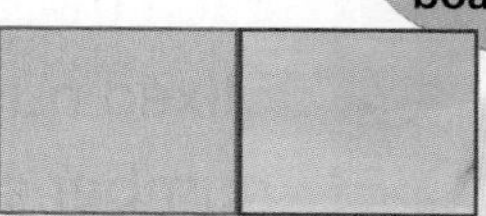

The boards have different areas. Zoe's half is not equal to Nat's half.

Problem Solving

The fraction strips at the right represent three loaves of bread that Mrs. Rai sliced for a meal. The 1 strip represents a whole loaf. The other strips show how much of each loaf was left after the meal.

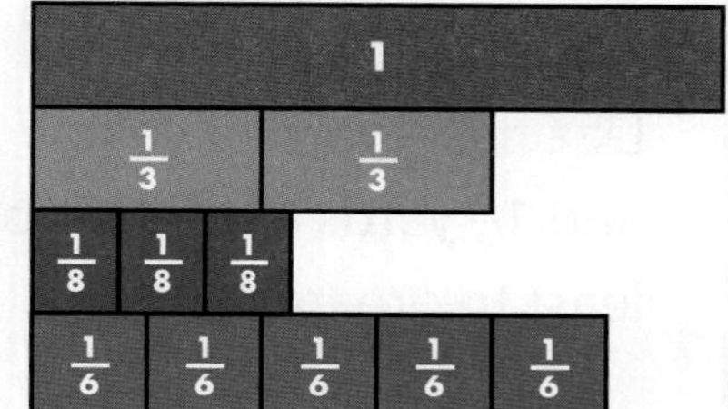

For **8** and **9**, copy and complete each number sentence to find the loaf with the greater amount left.

8. The loaf cut in sixths or the loaf cut in thirds

$\frac{5}{6} \bigcirc \frac{2}{3}$

9. The loaf cut in eighths or the loaf cut in thirds

$\frac{3}{8} \bigcirc \frac{2}{3}$

10. **Writing to Explain** Lupe ate $\frac{1}{3}$ of a sandwich. Jed ate $\frac{1}{3}$ of a different sandwich. Jed ate more than Lupe. How is that possible?

11. Kobe fed his hamster and his rabbit. He gave the rabbit 3 carrot pieces for each 2 carrot pieces he gave the hamster. If the hamster got 8 carrot pieces, how many carrot pieces did the rabbit get?

12. Which group shows more than $\frac{5}{7}$ of the shapes shaded?

A 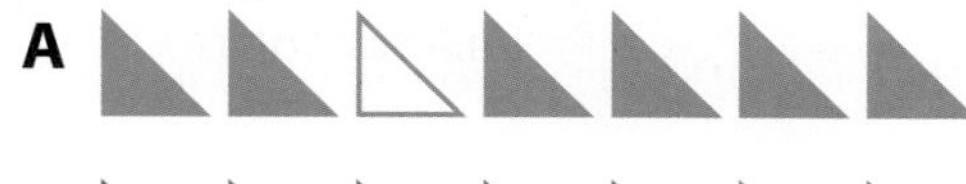

C 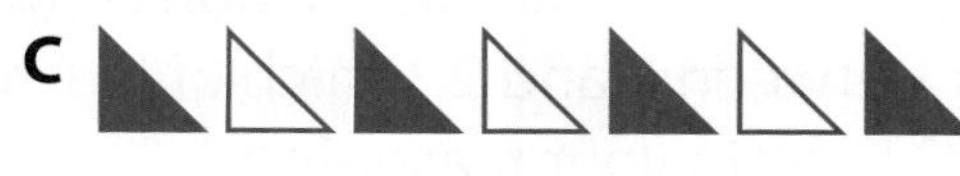

B 

D 

Lesson

12-7

Understand It!
Number lines can be used to compare and to order fractions and mixed numbers.

Fractions on the Number Line

How can you locate and compare fractions and mixed numbers on a number line?

Each fraction names a point on a number line. Mixed numbers are numbers that have a whole number part and a fraction part. For example, $1\frac{3}{4}$ and $1\frac{1}{2}$ are mixed numbers.

Is there more red ribbon or more blue ribbon?

Another Example **How can you order fractions and mixed numbers?**

Liza has $\frac{3}{4}$ yard of yellow ribbon, $\frac{1}{2}$ yard of green ribbon, and $1\frac{3}{4}$ yards of pink ribbon. Write the lengths in order from least to greatest.

You can use a number line to order fractions and mixed numbers.

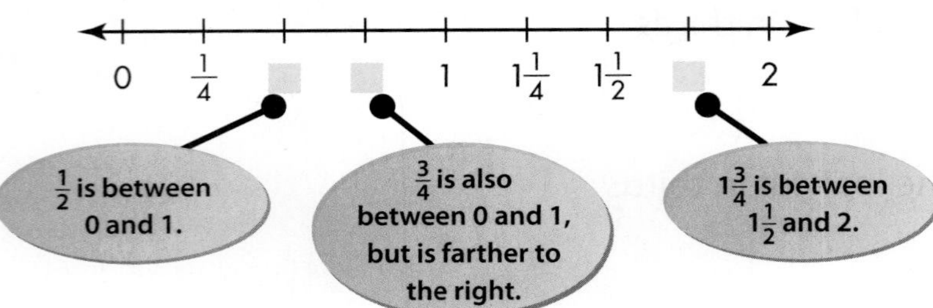

The order of the lengths of ribbon from least to greatest is $\frac{1}{2}$ yard, $\frac{3}{4}$ yard, $1\frac{3}{4}$ yards.

Explain It

1. Describe how you would order $\frac{3}{4}$, $2\frac{3}{4}$, and $2\frac{2}{4}$ from greatest to least.
2. Suppose there are two unit fractions and one mixed number between 1 and 2. Which of them is the greatest? Explain your reasoning.

The numerator of every unit fraction is 1.

Use a number line to compare $1\frac{1}{2}$ and $1\frac{3}{4}$.

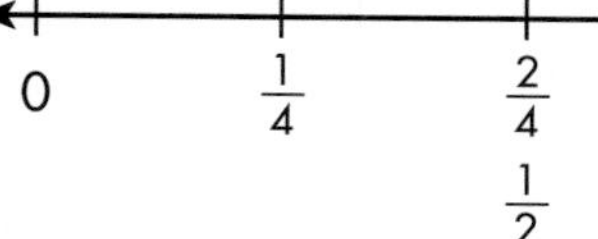

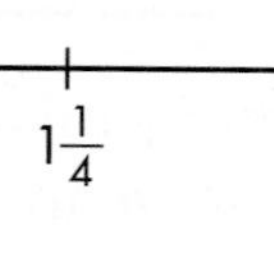

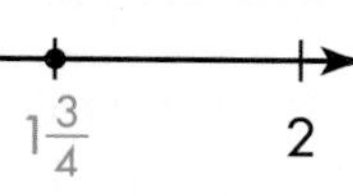

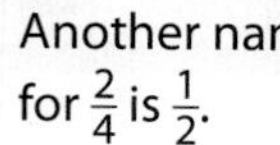

0, $\frac{1}{4}$, $\frac{2}{4}$ ($\frac{1}{2}$), $\frac{3}{4}$, 1, $1\frac{1}{4}$, $1\frac{2}{4}$ ($1\frac{1}{2}$), $1\frac{3}{4}$, 2

Another name for $\frac{2}{4}$ is $\frac{1}{2}$.

Another name for $1\frac{2}{4}$ is $1\frac{1}{2}$.

On the number line, $1\frac{3}{4}$ is farther to the right than $1\frac{1}{2}$.

$1\frac{3}{4} > 1\frac{1}{2}$

There is more blue ribbon than red ribbon.

Guided Practice*

Do you know HOW?

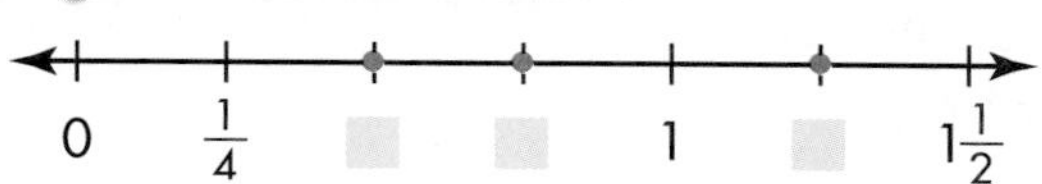

1. Write the missing fractions or mixed numbers for the number line above.

2. Write the answers for Exercise 1 in order from greatest to least.

Compare. Write <, >, or =. Use a number line to help.

3. $\frac{1}{2} \bigcirc \frac{3}{4}$ **4.** $4\frac{1}{2} \bigcirc 4\frac{2}{4}$

Do you UNDERSTAND?

5. In the example above, could you compare $1\frac{3}{4}$ and $1\frac{1}{2}$ by just comparing $\frac{3}{4}$ and $\frac{1}{2}$? Explain.

6. A number line is divided into fourths. What is the next mixed number to the right of $2\frac{2}{4}$?

7. **Number Sense** In Exercise 2, how do you know which fraction or mixed number is greatest?

Independent Practice

8. Copy and complete the number line by writing the missing fractions and mixed numbers.

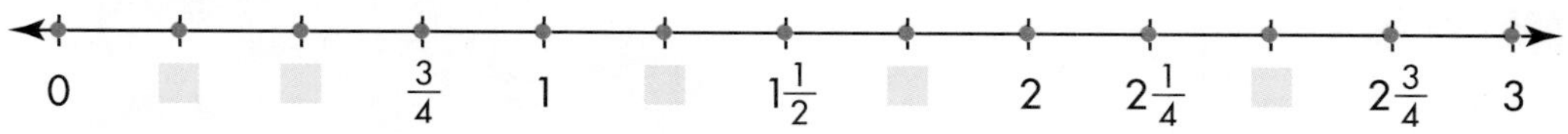

Compare. Write <, >, or =. Use a number line to help.

9. $\frac{2}{4} \bigcirc 1$ **10.** $\frac{2}{4} \bigcirc \frac{1}{2}$ **11.** $2\frac{3}{4} \bigcirc 2\frac{1}{4}$ **12.** $1\frac{3}{4} \bigcirc 2\frac{1}{3}$

13. Write $2\frac{1}{2}$, $\frac{1}{4}$, and $1\frac{3}{4}$ in order from least to greatest.

*For another example, see Set D on page 303.

Problem Solving

The number line below shows how many miles different places are from Oliver's house. Use the number line for **14** and **15**.

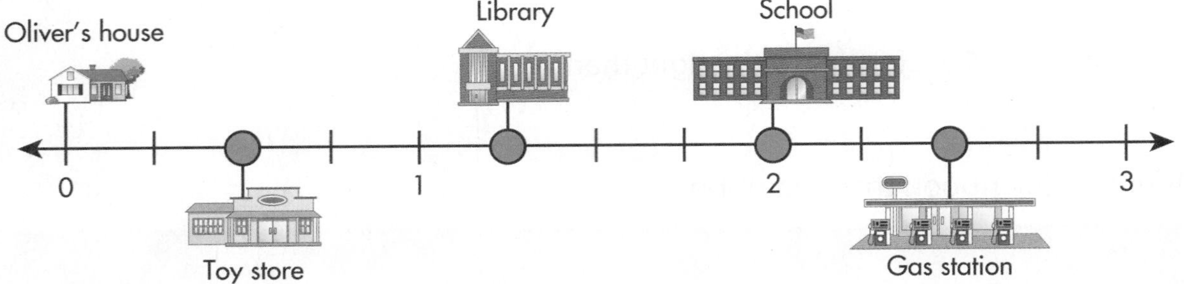

14. The school is 2 miles from Oliver's house. How many miles from Oliver's house are these places?

a library **b** toy store **c** gas station

15. A bank is twice as far from Oliver's house as the toy store. How many miles from Oliver's house is the bank?

16. Geometry Teresa drew this shape.

a How many acute angles does the shape have?

b What is the best name for this shape?

17. Reasonableness Mr. Smith has 38 sheets of drawing paper. Does he have enough paper to give 4 sheets to each of 9 students? Explain.

18. Which lettered point on the ruler below could represent the number of centimeters that the shore of Iceland grows in a year?

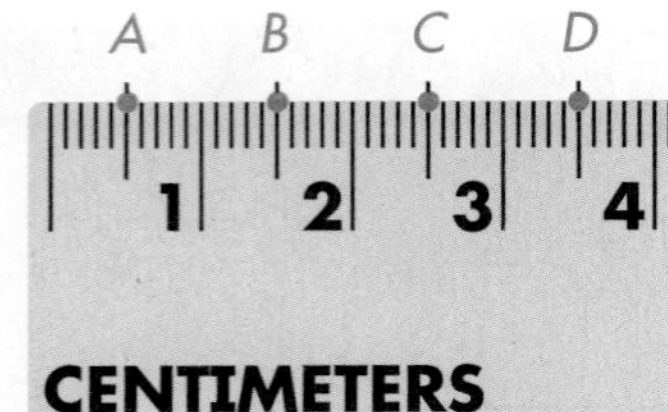
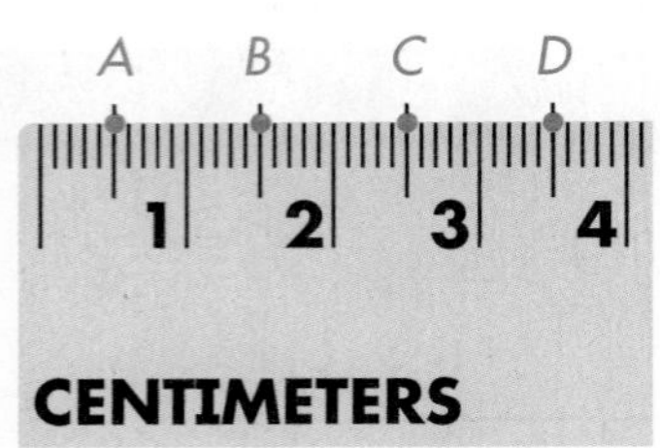

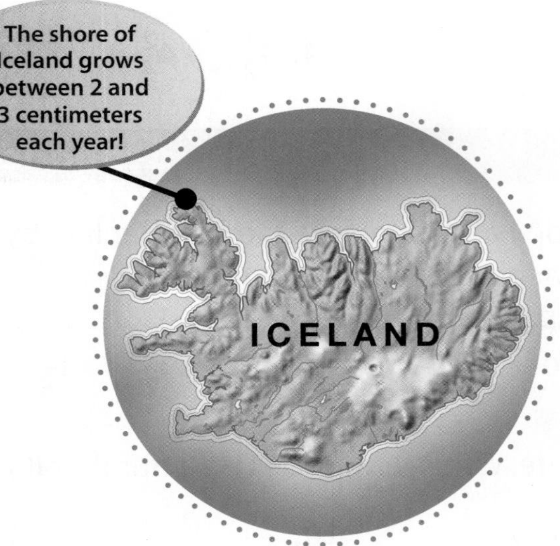

19. Which number makes this number sentence true?

$\square \div 9 = 6$

A 18 **B** 28 **C** 36 **D** 54

Use the pictures and number line below for **20** through **23**.

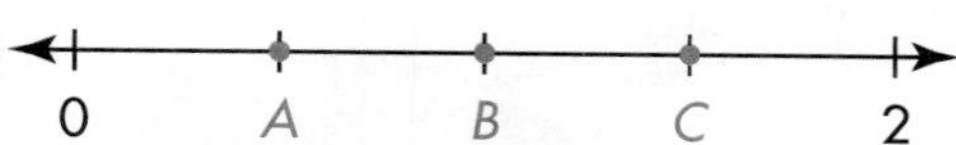

Bumblebee: 1 inch long

Firefly: $\frac{1}{2}$ inch long

Eyed Click Beetle: $1\frac{1}{2}$ inches long

20. Write the name of the insect whose length in inches matches each lettered point on the number line.

a Point *A*

b Point *B*

c Point *C*

21. Writing to Explain How does the number line show which insect is the longest?

22. Which is longer—the firefly or the bumblebee?

23. Which insect is the shortest?

24. Show 3 different ways to divide a square into fourths.

25. What fraction of the letters in the word *TENNESSEE* are *E*s?

26. What kind of angle do the clock hands form at 4:00?

A acute **C** square

B obtuse **D** right

27. What number is missing from the pattern below?

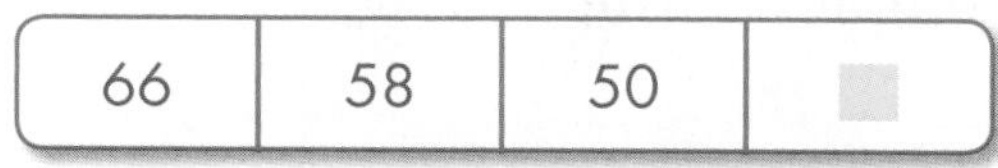

A 48 **B** 46 **C** 44 **D** 42

28. Janet had the coins and bills shown at the right. How much money did she have in all?

Lesson
12-8

Understand It!
To find the sum of fractions with the same denominator, add the numerators and keep the same denominator. Then write the answer in simplest form.

Using Models to Add Fractions

Hands-On
fraction strips

How can you add fractions?

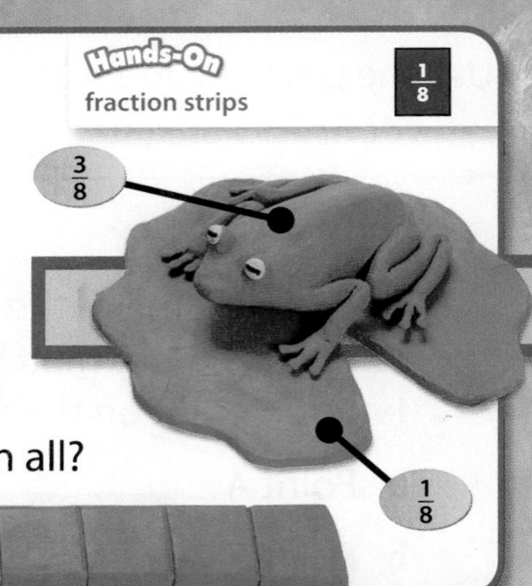

Mia used $\frac{3}{8}$ of the block of clay to make the frog. She used $\frac{1}{8}$ of the block to make the lily pad. What fraction of the block did she use in all?

Find $\frac{3}{8} + \frac{1}{8}$.

Guided Practice*

Do you know HOW?

In **1** and **2**, add. Write the sum in simplest form. You may use fraction strips or draw a picture to help.

1. $\frac{2}{5} + \frac{1}{5}$ $\frac{1}{5}$ $\frac{1}{5}$ $\frac{1}{5}$

2. $\frac{2}{12} + \frac{4}{12}$

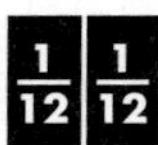

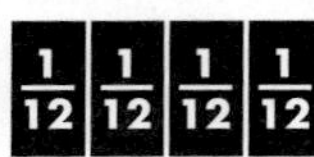

Do you UNDERSTAND?

3. Suppose you add two fractions with the same denominator. What can you say about the sum before you write it in simplest form?

4. Alonso used $\frac{2}{6}$ of a loaf of bread to make peanut butter sandwiches. He used $\frac{2}{6}$ of the loaf to make tuna sandwiches. What fraction of the bread loaf did he use in all?

Independent Practice

Leveled Practice In **5–14**, add. Write the sum in simplest form. You may draw a picture to help.

5. $\frac{3}{6} + \frac{2}{6}$ $\frac{1}{6}$ $\frac{1}{6}$ $\frac{1}{6}$

6. $\frac{2}{8} + \frac{4}{8}$

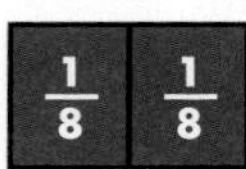

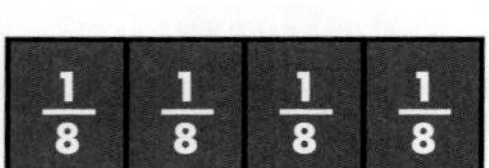

7. $\frac{1}{4} + \frac{2}{4}$

8. $\frac{1}{3} + \frac{1}{3}$

9. $\frac{3}{10} + \frac{5}{10}$

10. $\frac{2}{5} + \frac{1}{5}$

11. $\frac{3}{12} + \frac{5}{12}$

12. $\frac{1}{6} + \frac{2}{6}$

13. $\frac{5}{8} + \frac{2}{8}$

14. $\frac{4}{10} + \frac{3}{10}$

DIGITAL eTools **www.pearsonsuccessnet.com**

*For another example, see Set E on page 303.

Step 1

Add.

1

$\frac{1}{8}$ $\frac{1}{8}$ $\frac{1}{8}$ $\frac{1}{8}$

$\frac{3}{8} + \frac{1}{8} = \frac{4}{8}$

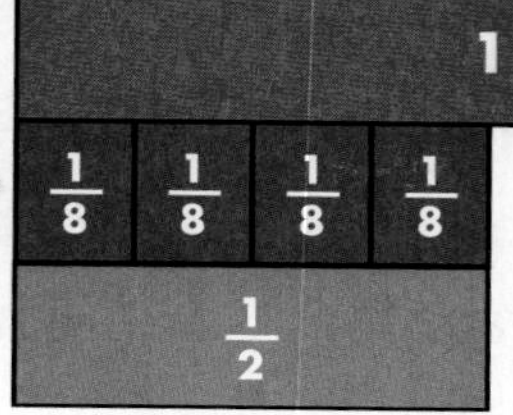

Step 2

Write the sum in simplest form.

1

$\frac{1}{8}$ $\frac{1}{8}$ $\frac{1}{8}$ $\frac{1}{8}$

$\frac{1}{2}$

$\frac{4}{8} = \frac{1}{2}$

So, in simplest form, $\frac{3}{8} + \frac{1}{8} = \frac{4}{8}$, or $\frac{1}{2}$.

All together, Mia used $\frac{1}{2}$ of the block of clay.

Problem Solving

15. Ken ate $\frac{2}{4}$ of a large sandwich and Janet ate $\frac{1}{4}$ of it. Write an addition sentence that shows the fraction of the sandwich they ate all together.

16. Chad found 12 seashells. Four of them were bubble shells. The rest were jingle shells. In simplest form, what fraction of the shells were jingle shells?

17. Rashad colored $\frac{3}{5}$ of a flag red and $\frac{1}{5}$ of the same flag green. What fraction of the flag did he color in all?

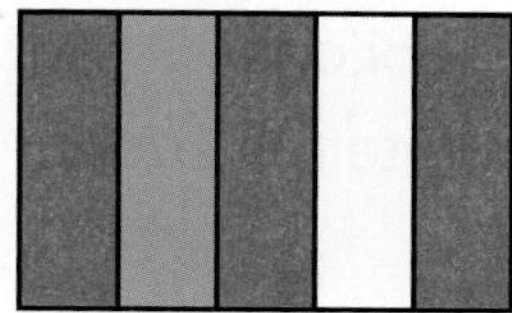

18. Nia painted $\frac{4}{8}$ of a fence rail and Tracy painted $\frac{2}{8}$ of it. What simplest form fraction names the part of the rail they painted in all?

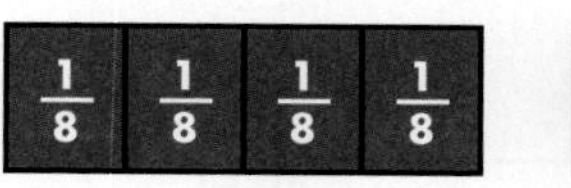

A $\frac{6}{4}$ **B** $\frac{3}{4}$ **C** $\frac{1}{2}$ **D** $\frac{2}{8}$

19. Diane's hair grew $\frac{2}{5}$ inch in one month and $\frac{3}{5}$ inch the next month. How much did it grow in the two months?

20. **Writing to Explain** Cassie drank $\frac{5}{8}$ of a glass of juice. Julie drank $\frac{3}{4}$ of the same size glass of juice. Who drank more juice? Explain.

21. Which fraction comes next in the pattern?

$\frac{1}{2}, \frac{2}{4}, \frac{3}{6}, \frac{4}{8},$ ▢

A $\frac{5}{15}$ **B** $\frac{3}{7}$ **C** $\frac{5}{10}$ **D** $\frac{5}{9}$

22. Estela cut a rectangle into sixths. Draw a picture of a rectangle divided into sixths. Use grid paper to help.

Lesson

12-9

Understand It!
To find the difference of two fractions with the same denominator, subtract the numerators and keep the same denominator. Then write the answer in simplest form.

Using Models to Subtract Fractions

Hands-On
fraction strips

How can you subtract fractions?

Helen had $\frac{5}{8}$ of a yard of cloth. She cut $\frac{1}{8}$ of a yard for a scarf. What fraction of a yard of cloth was left?

Choose an Operation $\frac{5}{8} - \frac{1}{8} = \square$

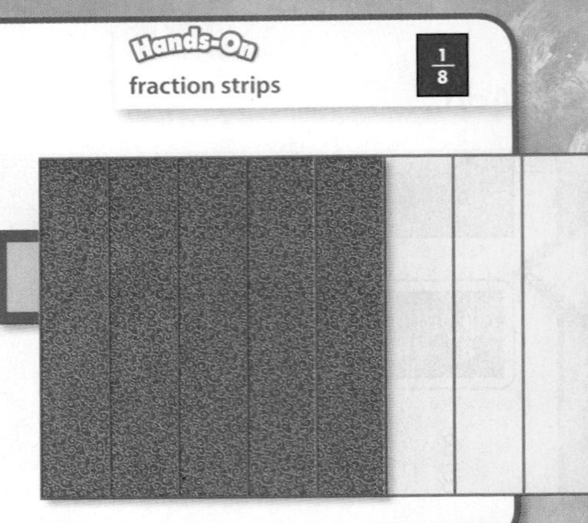

Guided Practice*

Do you know HOW?

In **1** and **2**, subtract. Write the difference in simplest form. You may use fraction strips or draw a picture to help.

1. $\frac{6}{8} - \frac{4}{8}$

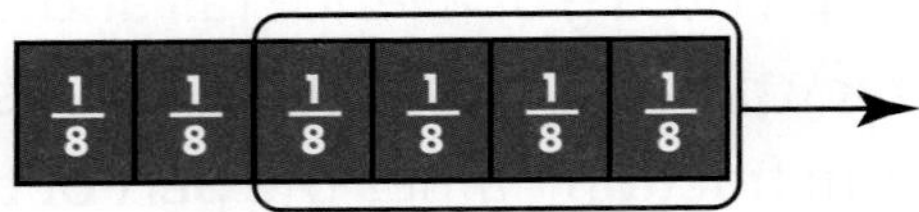

2. $\frac{3}{4} - \frac{1}{4}$

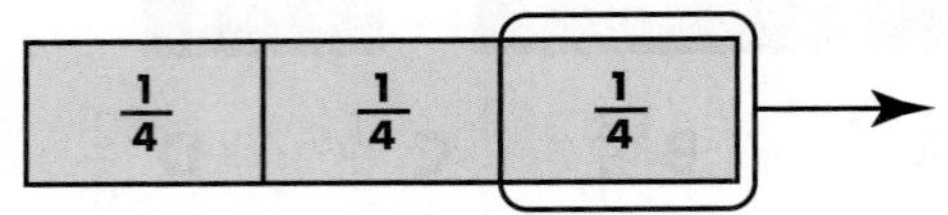

Do you UNDERSTAND?

3. Suppose you subtract two fractions with the same denominator. What can you say about the difference before you write it in simplest form?

4. Ethan lives $\frac{9}{10}$ of a mile from school. His friend Luis lives $\frac{3}{10}$ of a mile from school. How much farther from school does Ethan live than Luis? Write the answer in simplest form.

Independent Practice

Leveled Practice In **5–10**, subtract. Write the difference in simplest form. You may draw a picture to help.

5. $\frac{2}{3} - \frac{1}{3}$ [strip: $\frac{1}{3}$ $\frac{1}{3}$]

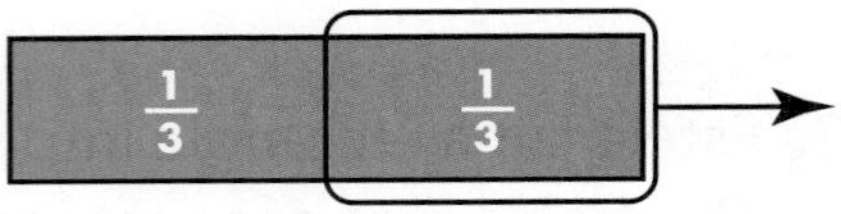

6. $\frac{4}{6} - \frac{2}{6}$ [strip: $\frac{1}{6}$ $\frac{1}{6}$ $\frac{1}{6}$ $\frac{1}{6}$]

7. $\frac{4}{5} - \frac{2}{5}$

8. $\frac{7}{9} - \frac{4}{9}$

9. $\frac{10}{12} - \frac{4}{12}$

10. $\frac{3}{4} - \frac{2}{4}$

*For another example, see Set E on page 303.

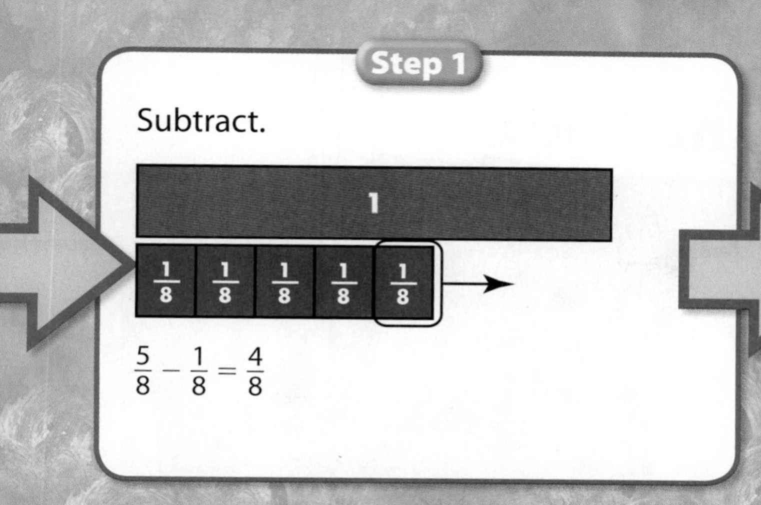

Write the difference in simplest form.

$\frac{4}{8} = \frac{1}{2}$

$\frac{5}{8} - \frac{1}{8} = \frac{4}{8}$, or $\frac{1}{2}$

One half yard of cloth was left.

Problem Solving

11. Selena had $\frac{3}{4}$ of a whole sheet of grid paper. She cut off $\frac{2}{4}$ of the whole sheet. Write a subtraction sentence that shows the fraction of the whole sheet that was left.

12. **Number Sense** There are 56 crayons. The crayons are placed onto 8 tables so that the same number of crayons is on each table. How many crayons in all would be on 3 tables?

13. Ted saw that there was $\frac{5}{8}$ of a pizza in the refrigerator. He ate $\frac{1}{8}$ of the pizza. What fraction of the original pizza was left? Write the fraction in simplest form.

14. A diner had $\frac{8}{12}$ of a supreme pizza on the warming shelf. Then Marion served $\frac{4}{12}$ of the pizza to customers. In simplest form, what fraction of the pizza was left?

A $\frac{4}{4}$ **C** $\frac{1}{4}$

B $\frac{1}{3}$ **D** $\frac{2}{12}$

15. Use the pictures of beetles at the right. How much longer is the caterpillar hunter beetle than the tiger beetle?

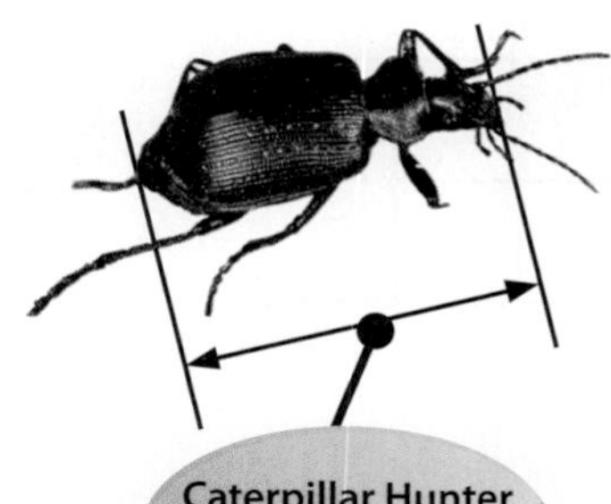

Lesson
12-10

Understand It!
A table can help organize information and make it easier to find patterns to solve problems.

Problem Solving

Make a Table and Look for a Pattern

A video game company tested 20 games. Three of the games did not work. If 120 games are tested, how many of them might not work?

Guided Practice*

Do you know HOW?

Copy and complete the table to solve.

1. Ms Simms is buying bags of blocks. Out of the 50 blocks in each bag, 3 are cubes. If she buys 250 blocks, how many cubes will she get?

Cubes	3	■	■	■	■
Total Blocks	50	■	■	■	■

Do you UNDERSTAND?

2. Look at the example above. If the video game store bought 50 games, about how many games might not work? Explain.

3. **Write a Problem** Write a problem that can be solved by making a table and using a pattern. Then solve the problem.

Independent Practice

Copy and complete the table to solve.

4. Erasers are sold in packages of 6. In each package, 2 of the erasers are pink. How many pink erasers will Andrea get if she buys 30 erasers?

Pink Erasers	2	■	■	■	■
Total Erasers	6	■	■	■	■

Stuck? Try this....

- What do I know?
- What am I asked to find?
- What diagram can I use to help understand the problem?
- Can I use addition, subtraction, multiplication, or division?
- Is all of my work correct?
- Did I answer the right question?
- Is my answer reasonable?

*For another example, see Set F on page 303

Plan

Make a table.

Then, write in the information you know.

Might Not Work	3					
Total Games	20					

Solve

Extend the table. Look for a pattern to help. Then find the answer in the table.

Might Not Work	3	6	9	12	15	18
Total Games	20	40	60	80	100	120

If 120 games are tested, 18 might not work.

Copy and complete the tables in **5** and **7**. Use the tables to help solve.

5. Sue planted 8 daffodil bulbs. Two of the bulbs didn't grow. Suppose that pattern continues and Sue plants 32 bulbs. How many bulbs most likely won't grow?

Didn't Grow	2	■	■	■
Total Bulbs	8	■	■	■

6. **Reasoning** Look back at Problem 5. Suppose Sue decided to plant 20 daffodil bulbs.

a How many bulbs would most likely not grow?

b How many bulbs would most likely grow?

7. Sue planted 12 tulip bulbs of mixed colors. When the bulbs grew, there were 4 red tulips. Suppose that pattern continues and Sue plants 48 bulbs. How many of the tulips will likely be red? How many will NOT be red?

Red Tulips	4	■	■	■
Total Tulips	12	■	■	■

8. **Reasoning** Tad planted 15 tulips in a row. He followed the pattern shown below. What is the color of the last tulip in the row?

9. **Number Sense** See Problem 8. Suppose Tad planted 30 tulips in this pattern. How many would be red?

10. Which equivalent fraction completes the pattern below?

$\frac{1}{4}$ $\frac{2}{8}$ $\frac{3}{12}$ $\frac{■}{■}$

A $\frac{3}{14}$ **B** $\frac{4}{14}$ **C** $\frac{3}{16}$ **D** $\frac{4}{16}$

Topic 12

Test

1. What is the name of the equal parts of the whole pizza? (12-1)

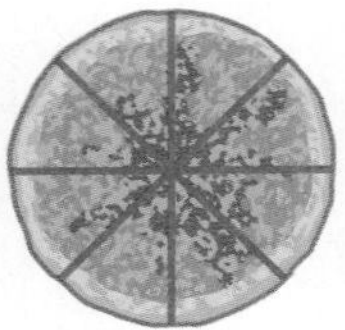

A Sixths

B Sevenths

C Eighths

D Ninths

2. The stage was divided into equal parts. What fraction names the part of the stage used for flute players? (12-2)

Trombones	Drums	Trombones
Clarinets	Trombones	Clarinets
Flutes	Triangles	Flutes

A $\frac{1}{9}$

B $\frac{2}{9}$

C $\frac{2}{7}$

D $\frac{3}{9}$

3. Blair bought the fruit shown below. What fraction of the pieces of fruit are oranges? (12-3)

A $\frac{5}{7}$

B $\frac{6}{12}$

C $\frac{5}{12}$

D $\frac{1}{5}$

4. Stacy rode her bike $\frac{1}{5}$ mile to her grandmother's house. Then she rode $\frac{3}{5}$ mile to her aunt's house. How far did Stacy ride? (12-8)

$\frac{1}{5}$	$\frac{1}{5}$	$\frac{1}{5}$	$\frac{1}{5}$

A $\frac{5}{4}$ miles

B $\frac{4}{5}$ mile

C $\frac{2}{5}$ mile

D $\frac{4}{10}$ mile

5. Which fraction is in simplest form? (12-5)

A $\frac{2}{3}$

B $\frac{6}{8}$

C $\frac{2}{4}$

D $\frac{9}{12}$

6. The number line shows four friends' guesses for the average length, in inches, of the striped bark scorpion. Ty's guess was correct. Which number did Ty guess? (12-7)

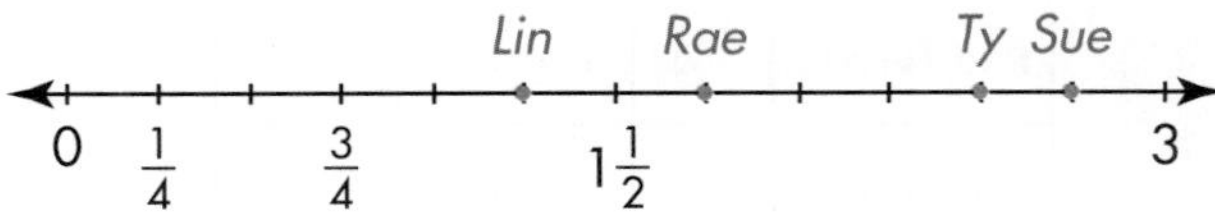

A $1\frac{1}{4}$

B $1\frac{3}{4}$

C $2\frac{1}{2}$

D $2\frac{3}{4}$

7. During the time allowed, Delia swam $\frac{3}{4}$ of the length of the pool. Loren swam $\frac{4}{5}$ of it. Use the models to find which is the correct symbol to compare the fractions. (12-6)

$\frac{3}{4} \bigcirc \frac{4}{5}$

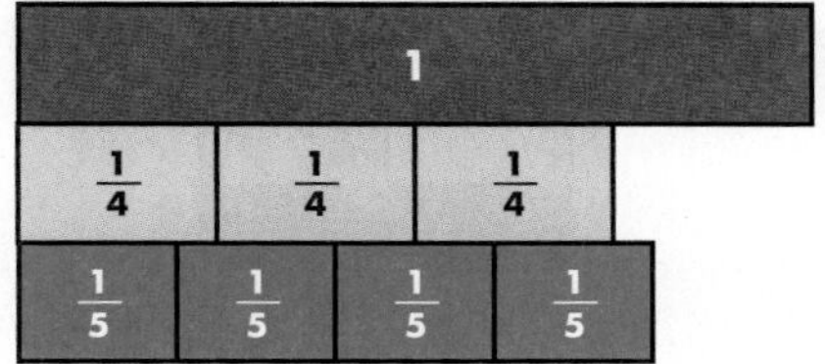

A $=$

B $\times$

C $>$

D $<$

8. Allison is buying packages of sliced meat for the picnic. Each package has 20 slices of meat. Out of the 20 slices, 5 are turkey. If Allison buys 80 slices, how many are turkey? (12-10)

Turkey Slices	5	10		
Total Slices	20	40	60	80

A 11

B 15

C 16

D 20

9. About how much of Trenton's garden is corn? (12-4)

A About $\frac{1}{2}$

B About $\frac{1}{3}$

C About $\frac{1}{4}$

D About $\frac{3}{4}$

10. Bethany bought $\frac{7}{8}$ yard of ribbon. She used $\frac{5}{8}$ yard to decorate a costume. In simplest form, how much ribbon does she have left? (12-9)

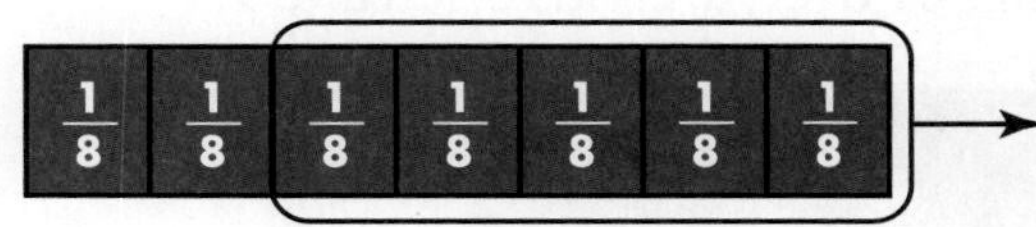

A $\frac{1}{4}$ yard

B $\frac{1}{3}$ yard

C $\frac{3}{4}$ yard

D $\frac{4}{3}$ yards

11. Rachel's scarf is $2\frac{1}{2}$ feet long. Elle's scarf is longer. Which could be the length of Elle's scarf? (12-7)

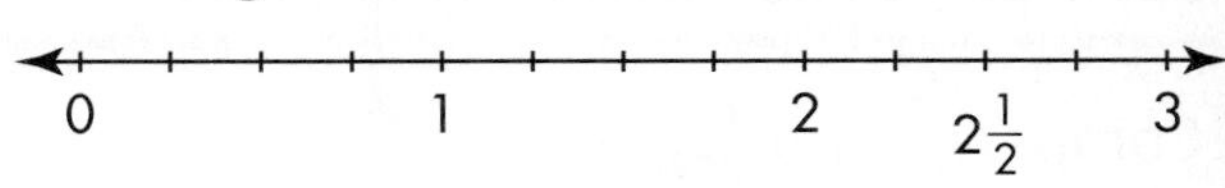

A $2\frac{3}{4}$ feet

B $1\frac{3}{4}$ feet

C 2 feet

D $2\frac{1}{4}$ feet

Reteaching

Set A, pages 276–281, 284–286

What fraction of the triangles are pink?

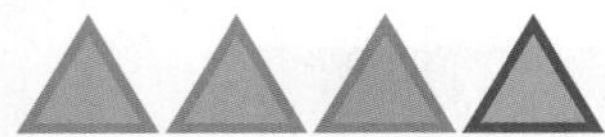

$\frac{\text{numerator}}{\text{denominator}} = \frac{\text{number of pink triangles}}{\text{total number of triangles}} = \frac{3}{4}$

$\frac{3}{4}$ of the triangles are pink.

What is another name for $\frac{3}{4}$?

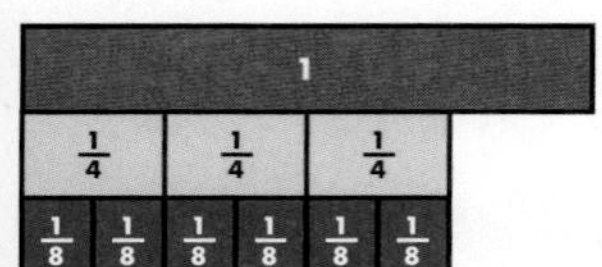

$\frac{3}{4} = \frac{\square}{8}$

$\frac{3}{4} = \frac{6}{8}$

Remember that fractions can name parts of a whole or a set.

Write the fraction that is red.

1. 

2.  

Copy and complete.

3. $\frac{2}{3} = \frac{\square}{6}$

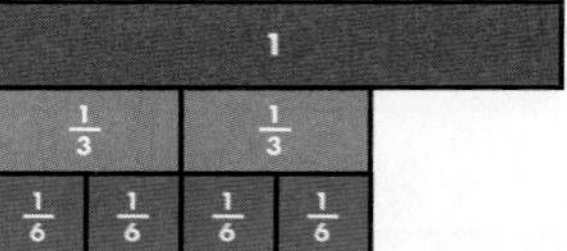

Set B, pages 282–283

Lisa is raking the leaves in her yard. About what part of the yard has she raked?

Find the benchmark fraction that is closest to the fraction in the problem.

Try $\frac{1}{2}, \frac{1}{3}, \frac{2}{3}, \frac{1}{4}$, or $\frac{3}{4}$.

Lisa has raked about $\frac{1}{4}$ of the yard.

Remember that benchmark fractions are commonly used fractions such as $\frac{1}{4}, \frac{1}{3}, \frac{1}{2}, \frac{2}{3}$, and $\frac{3}{4}$.

Estimate the fractional part that is yellow. Use a benchmark fraction.

1. 

2.

Set C, pages 288–289

Compare $\frac{3}{8}$ and $\frac{1}{2}$.

$\frac{3}{8} \bigcirc \frac{1}{2}$

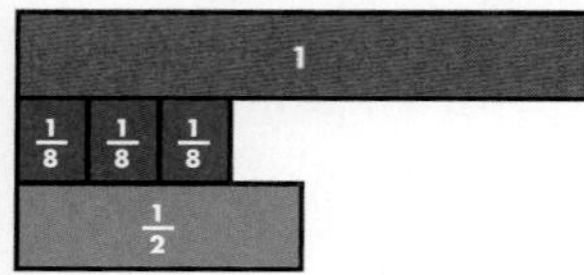

$\frac{3}{8} < \frac{1}{2}$

Remember that if two fractions have the same denominator, the fraction with the greater numerator is the greater fraction.

1. Compare. Write <, >, or =.

$\frac{7}{8} \bigcirc \frac{2}{5}$

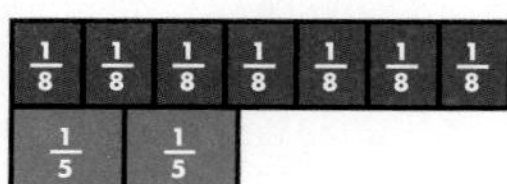

Topic 12

Reteaching

Set D, pages 290–293

What fraction and what mixed number are missing on the number line?

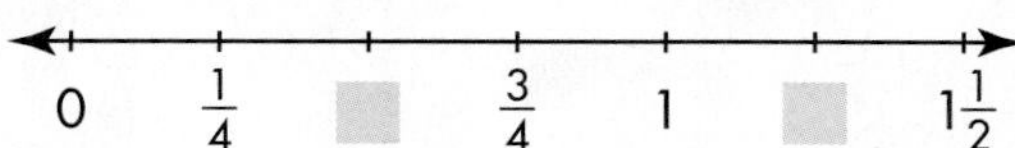

Each section of the number line is $\frac{1}{4}$.

So $\frac{2}{4}$, or $\frac{1}{2}$, and $1\frac{1}{4}$ are missing.

Which is greater, $1\frac{1}{4}$ or $\frac{3}{4}$?

Since $1\frac{1}{4}$ is farther to the right, $1\frac{1}{4} > \frac{3}{4}$.

Remember to look for a pattern in the fractions on your number line.

Write the missing fraction or mixed number for the number line.

1. 0 $\quad \frac{1}{4} \quad \frac{2}{4} \quad$ ▢ $\quad 1 \quad 1\frac{1}{4} \quad$ ▢ ▢

Compare. Write <, >, or =.

2. $\frac{1}{4}$ ◯ $\frac{1}{2}$ **3.** $5\frac{2}{4}$ ◯ $5\frac{1}{4}$

Set E, pages 294–297

Find the sum $\frac{1}{6} + \frac{3}{6}$ in simplest form.

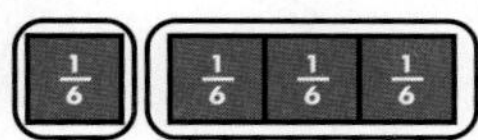

$\frac{1}{6} + \frac{3}{6} = \frac{4}{6}$ and $\frac{4}{6} = \frac{2}{3}$, so $\frac{1}{6} + \frac{3}{6} = \frac{2}{3}$

Find $\frac{6}{8} - \frac{2}{8}$ in simplest form.

$\frac{6}{8} - \frac{2}{8} = \frac{4}{8}$ and $\frac{4}{8} = \frac{1}{2}$, so $\frac{6}{8} - \frac{2}{8} = \frac{1}{2}$.

Remember to check your work.

Find each answer in simplest form.

1. $\frac{3}{10} + \frac{2}{10}$

2. $\frac{5}{6} - \frac{3}{6}$

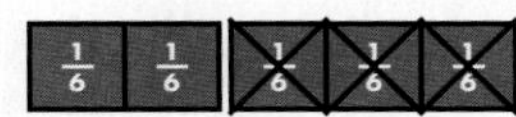

Set F, pages 298–299

Make a table and find a pattern to solve.

Each bag of 20 marbles has 4 green marbles. If Ed buys 80 marbles, how many are green?

Make a table. Look for a pattern.

Green	4	8	12	16
Total	20	40	60	80

16 marbles are green.

Remember that making a table can help you find a pattern.

1. Each box of pens has 2 red pens. How many red pens will you get if you buy 40 pens?

Red	2				
Total	8				

Topic 13

Decimals and Money

1

On March 1, 2002, the euro became the official money in several countries in Europe. What was the value of 1 U.S. dollar in euros? You will find out in Lesson 13-3.

2 In one minute, does the United States Treasury Department produce more coins or more bills? You will find out in Lesson 13-5.

3 How much does it cost the United States Mint to make a quarter? You will find out in Lesson 13-2.

Review What You Know!

Vocabulary

Choose the best term from the box.

- digits
- place
- one thousand
- tens

1. All of the numbers are made from __?__.
2. The number 328 has a 3 in the hundreds __?__.
3. Ten hundreds equal __?__.

Fractions

Name the equal parts of the whole.

4. 
5. 

Fractions and Regions

Write the fraction that is blue.

6. 
7. 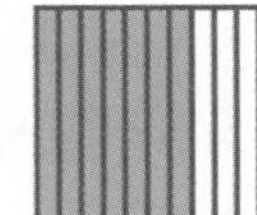

Place Value

Write each number in standard form.

8. 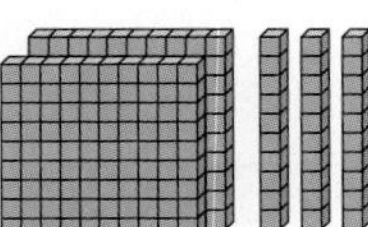
9. 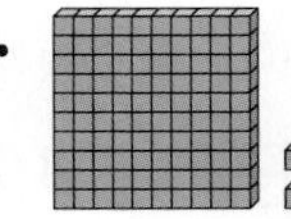

10. **Writing to Explain** Show the number 180 in a place-value chart. Explain how the chart helps show the value of a number.

Lesson

13-1

Understand It!
Decimals show fractional parts of a whole.

Fractions and Decimals

How can you write a decimal and a fraction for the same part of a whole?

Amy has a set of ten markers. Three of the markers are green. What part of the set of markers is green?

Guided Practice*

Do you know HOW?

In **1** and **2**, write a fraction and a decimal for each shaded part.

1. 

2. 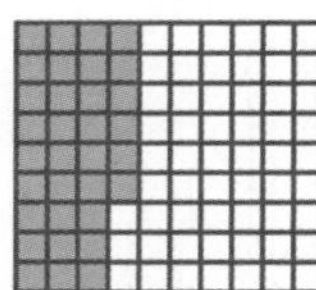

Do you UNDERSTAND?

In **3** and **4**, use the example above.

3. What part of the set is NOT green? Write your answer in three ways.

4. What part of the set is blue? Write your answer in three ways.

Independent Practice

In **5–12**, write a fraction and a decimal for each shaded part.

5. 

6. 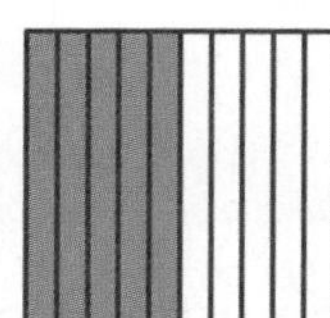

7. 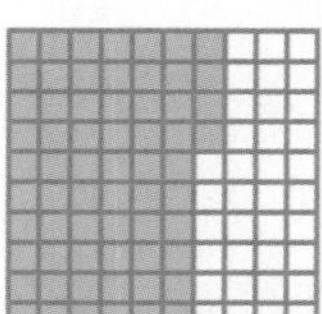

8. 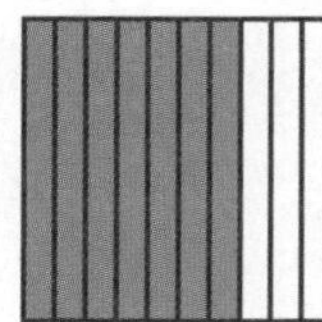

9. 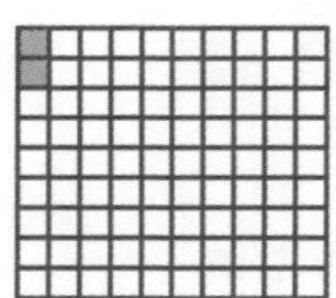

10. 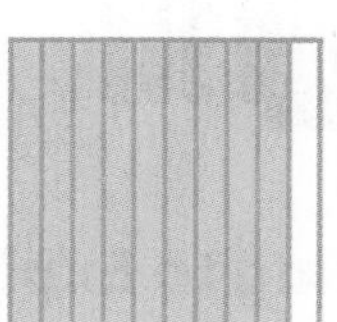

11. 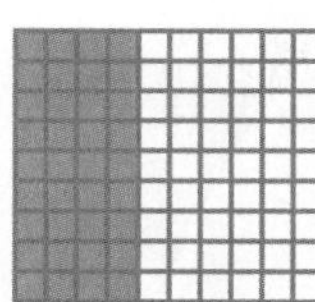

12. 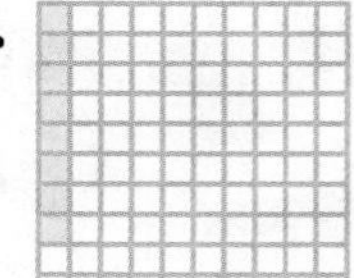

DIGITAL Animated Glossary
www.pearsonsuccessnet.com

*For another example, see Set A on page 324.

Tenths are ten equal parts of a whole or a set.

A decimal point is a dot used to separate ones from tenths in a number.

A decimal is a number with one or more digits to the right of the decimal point. Tenths can be written as a fraction or a decimal.

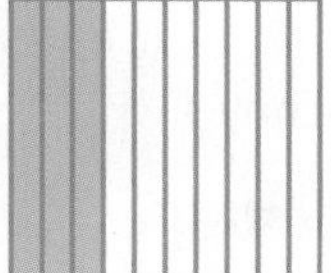

Three tenths of the set of markers is green. Three tenths can be written as $\frac{3}{10}$ or 0.3.

A tiled wall is made up of 100 tiles that are the same size and shape. Joel painted 27 of the tiles orange. What part of the whole wall did he paint orange?

Hundredths are one hundred equal parts of a whole or a set.

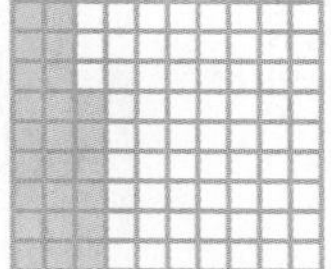

Joel painted $\frac{27}{100}$ or 0.27 of the wall.

In **13–15**, use the pictures below. Mike cut each kind of food he served at a party into tenths. For each kind of food, write a fraction and a decimal for the part that is left.

13. Rice

14. Pasta

15. Potatoes

Rice

Pasta

Potatoes

For **16** and **17**, use the sign at the right.

16. **Estimation** Which costs more, boots and one jacket or one winter coat? Use estimation to decide. Explain how you got your answer.

17. Mr. Murti wants to buy a winter coat for himself and one for his son. What is the total cost of the coats?

Data

Ace Clothing Shop Sale

Item	Cost
Boots	$129
Jacket	$87
Pants	$64
Winter Coat	$238

18. A fairy fly is the world's smallest insect. It is $\frac{1}{100}$ inch long. Write the length of a fairy fly as a decimal.

19. Jeremy shaded $\frac{4}{10}$ of the figure at the right. Which decimal equals $\frac{4}{10}$?

A 4.0 **B** 0.440 **C** 0.4 **D** 0.04

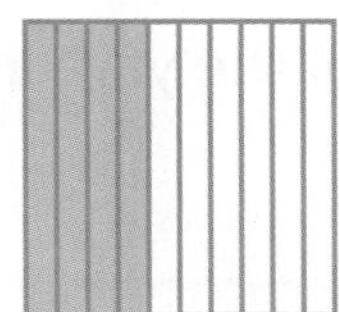

Lesson

13-2

Understand It!
A dime is one tenth of a dollar, and a penny is one hundredth of a dollar.

Using Money to Understand Decimals

Hands-On
money

How are decimals and fractions related to money?

How could Ben pay for the popcorn with only dollars, dimes, and pennies?

$1.24

dollar bill
1 dollar
$1 or $1.00

quarter
25 cents
25¢ or $0.25

dime
10 cents
10¢ or $0.10

nickel
5 cents
5¢ or $0.05

penny
1 cent
1¢ or $0.01

Another Example **What are other ways to write money amounts?**

You can use what you have learned about place value for whole numbers to help you understand place value for money amounts.

Ten dimes are equal to one dollar.
A dime is one tenth of a dollar.
Each dime has a value of $0.10 or 10¢.

One hundred pennies are equal to one dollar.
A penny is one hundredth of a dollar.
Each penny has a value of $0.01 or 1¢.

The amount $4.95 can be made in different ways.

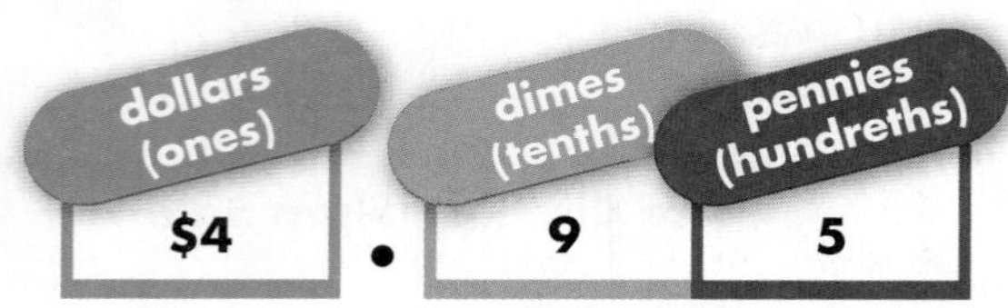

The decimal point is read by saying *and*.
So $4.95 is read as *4 dollars and 95 cents*.

$4.95 = 4 dollars + 9 dimes + 5 pennies ← **Expanded Form**
4.95 = 4 ones + 9 tenths + 5 hundredths

$4.95 = 4 dollars + 95 pennies
4.95 = 4 ones + 95 hundredths

Explain It

1. How is a dime one tenth of a dollar?
2. How is a penny one hundredth of a dollar?
3. Write the cost of the yarn in expanded form.

One Way

Ben can use 1 dollar, 2 dimes, and 4 pennies.

$1.24

Another Way

Ben can use 1 dollar and 24 pennies.

$1.24

Other Examples

Four quarters make a dollar. So each quarter is $\frac{1}{4}$ of a dollar.

Write $\frac{1}{4}$ of a dollar using a decimal point.

One quarter is $\frac{1}{4}$ of a dollar.

$\frac{1}{4} = \frac{25}{100}$

$\frac{1}{4}$ of a dollar = $0.25

Write $\frac{1}{2}$ of a dollar using a decimal point.

Two quarters are $\frac{1}{2}$ of a dollar.

$\frac{1}{2} = \frac{50}{100}$

$\frac{1}{2}$ of a dollar = $0.50

Write $\frac{3}{4}$ of a dollar using a decimal point.

Three quarters are $\frac{3}{4}$ of a dollar.

$\frac{3}{4} = \frac{75}{100}$

$\frac{3}{4}$ of a dollar = $0.75

Guided Practice*

Do you know HOW?

1. Copy and complete. $3.62 = ▒ dollars + ▒ dimes + ▒ pennies

   3.62 = ▒ ones + ▒ tenths + ▒ hundredths

   3.62 = ▒ ones + ▒ hundredths

2. Write one and four hundredths as a decimal.

Do you UNDERSTAND?

3. In the example above, what is another way to show $1.24?

4. How could you show $4.17 with only dollars, dimes, and pennies?

*For another example, see Set A on page 324.

Independent Practice

Leveled Practice In **5–10**, copy and complete.

5. \$6.45 = dollars + 4 dimes + 5 pennies or 6 dollars + 45 pennies
6.45 = 6 ones + tenths + hundredths or ones + hundredths

6. \$8.09 = dollars + dimes + pennies or dollars + 9 pennies
8.09 = ones + tenths + hundredths or ones + hundredths

7. \$2.39 = dollars + dimes + pennies or dollars + pennies
2.39 = ones + tenths + hundredths or ones + hundredths

8. \$5.07 = dollars + dimes + pennies or dollars + pennies
5.07 = ones + tenths + hundredths or ones + hundredths

9. \$4.80 = dollars + dimes + pennies or dollars + pennies
4.80 = ones + tenths + hundredths or ones + hundredths

10. \$9.65 = dollars + dimes + pennies or dollars + pennies
9.65 = ones + tenths + hundredths or ones + hundredths

In **11–14**, write each number with a decimal point.

11. seven and fifty-two hundredths

12. eight and twelve hundredths

13. one and ninety-six hundredths

14. three and six hundredths

Problem Solving

In **15** and **16**, draw a picture of bills and coins that equal the amount of each price.

Draw rectangles for dollars and circles with letters for coins.

15.

16.

17. **Writing to Explain** Marnie has two dollars and fifteen pennies. Alfred has two dollars, one dime, and eight pennies. Who has a greater amount of money? Explain how you decided.

18. **Reasoning** Carl has two dollar bills, nine dimes, and 6 pennies. What coins does he need to make $3.00?

19. Tamiya has 23 pennies. How many hundredths of a dollar does she have?

20. Lars and Evelyn each have $1.38 in bills and coins. They have different coins. Show two ways to make $1.38. Draw a picture of each set of bills and coins.

21. Use a piece of grid paper. Draw a shape with one line of symmetry.

Use the table at the right for **22** and **23**.

22. Ms. Evans bought one quart of paint. She paid the exact price with six dollar bills and fourteen pennies. From which store did she buy the paint?

23. Mr. Park bought one quart of paint. He paid the exact price with dollars and coins. He used only one penny. From which store did he buy the paint?

1 Quart of Paint

Store	Price
A-1 Supplies	$6.48
Crafts and More	$6.14
Paint Station	$6.04
Wagner's	$6.41

24. Draw another set of bills and coins to make the same amount as shown.

25. It costs the United States Mint about 4 hundredths of a dollar to make a quarter. Write 4 hundredths using a decimal point.

26. Which money amount represents $\frac{1}{4}$ of a dollar?

   A $1.40 **C** $0.25

   B $0.40 **D** $0.14

27. Which money amount represents 4 dollars, 7 dimes, and 3 pennies?

   A $4.38 **C** $40.73

   B $4.73 **D** $47.03

Lesson
13-3

Understand It!
You can use the same rules for adding and subtracting whole numbers to add and subtract money.

Adding and Subtracting Money

How can you add and subtract money?

Neta wants to buy a flower pot and a picture frame. What is the total cost of the two items?

? cost in all	
$5.47	$6.89

Choose an Operation
$5.47 + $6.89 = ▢

Another Example How can you subtract money?

The items Nancy bought cost a total of $12.36. She pays with $20. How much change should she get?

You can use what you have learned about subtracting across zero in Lesson 4-5 to help you understand subtracting money amounts.

$20	
$12.36	?

Step 1

Line up the decimal points. Write $20 as $20.00. Subtract as you would with whole numbers.

```
     9  9
  1 10 10 10
 $2̸ 0̸. 0̸ 0̸
-  1 2. 3 6
 ----------
     7  6 4
```

Step 2

Write the answer in dollars and cents.

```
     9  9
  1 10 10 10
 $2̸ 0̸. 0̸ 0̸
-  1 2. 3 6
 ----------
    $7. 6 4
```

Write the dollar sign and the decimal point.

Nancy should get $7.64 in change.

Explain It

1. Suppose the total cost of the items Nancy bought was $19.36. Write the change she should get from $20 in two ways.

2. Use the prices at the top of the page. Maurice wants to buy a radio and a calculator. How much change should he get from $50?

Step 1

Line up the decimal points in the addends. Add as you would with whole numbers.

$$\begin{array}{r} \scriptstyle 1\ 1\ \ \\ \$5.47 \\ +\ \ 6.89 \\ \hline 12\ 36 \end{array}$$

Remember to regroup if needed.

Step 2

Write the answer in dollars and cents.

$$\begin{array}{r} \scriptstyle 1\ 1\ \ \\ \$5.47 \\ +\ \ 6.89 \\ \hline \$12.36 \end{array}$$

Write the dollar sign and the decimal point.

The total cost of the flower pot and the picture frame is $12.36.

Guided Practice*

Do you know HOW?

In **1–4**, find the sum or difference.

1. $\begin{array}{r} \$3.85 \\ +\ \ 9.76 \\ \hline \end{array}$

2. $\begin{array}{r} \$10.07 \\ -\ \ 1.68 \\ \hline \end{array}$

3. $17.62 + $4.93

4. $20.00 − $3.64

Do you UNDERSTAND?

5. In the example above, Neta estimated that $13.00 would be enough to pay for the total cost of her items. Would $13.00 be enough? Explain.

6. Use the prices on page 312. Bo wants to buy a clock and a radio. What is the total cost of these items?

Independent Practice

In **7–20**, find each sum or difference.

7. $\begin{array}{r} \$2.87 \\ +\ \ 5.46 \\ \hline \end{array}$

8. $\begin{array}{r} \$6.24 \\ +\ \ 9.97 \\ \hline \end{array}$

9. $\begin{array}{r} \$10.00 \\ -\ \ 7.23 \\ \hline \end{array}$

10. $\begin{array}{r} \$25.00 \\ -\ 14.39 \\ \hline \end{array}$

11. $\begin{array}{r} \$30.00 \\ -\ 27.14 \\ \hline \end{array}$

12. $\begin{array}{r} \$13.06 \\ +\ \ 9.56 \\ \hline \end{array}$

13. $\begin{array}{r} \$0.75 \\ +\ \ 8.49 \\ \hline \end{array}$

14. $\begin{array}{r} \$10.50 \\ -\ \ 3.62 \\ \hline \end{array}$

15. $4.00 − $2.64

16. $20.00 − $6.81

17. $3.75 + $9.82

18. $1.00 − $0.36

19. $40.00 − $28.15

20. $9.09 + $2.83

For another example, see Set B on page 324.

Independent Practice

In **21–27**, find each sum or difference.

21. $20.00 − 15.37

22. $14.69 + 8.72

23. $0.58 + 6.73

24. $10.00 − 4.91

25. $5.00 − $3.74

26. $15.74 + $7.26

27. $40.20 − $23.10

Problem Solving

Norma and Devon compared the prices of four backpacks. The table at the right shows the prices. Use the table for **28–31**.

Cost of Backpacks

Brand	Cost
A	$24.19
B	$26.09
C	$22.99
D	$20.39

28. Which brand costs more, Brand A or Brand B? Find how much more.

29. Norma will buy Brand B and Brand D. She will pay with $50. How much change should she get?

30. Devon decided to buy Brand A. He paid with $40. How much change should he get?

31. What is the total cost of Brand C and Brand D?

? cost in all

$22.99	$20.39

32. **Algebra** Copy and complete by writing the missing number in each pattern.

25, 50, 75, 100, ▭, 150
75, 70, 65, 60, ▭, 50

33. When the euro became the official money of Europe, $1 U.S. was equal to 0.87 euro. How many euros would you receive for $2 U.S.?

34. Lou used a $5 bill to buy a box of cereal that cost $4.62. How much change did he get?

A $9.62 **B** $1.38 **C** 62¢ **D** 38¢

35. **Think About the Process** Deena bought a pair of socks that cost $3.72. She paid with $10.00. Which number sentence shows how to find how much change she should get back?

A $10.00 − $3.72 = ▭

B $10.00 + $3.72 = ▭

C $10.00 ÷ $3.72 = ▭

D $10.00 × $3.72 = ▭

Enrichment

At Most and At Least

The symbol $\leq$ is read "is less than or equal to."

What whole numbers make this number sentence true?

$$\square \leq 6$$

The whole numbers 0, 1, 2, 3, 4, 5, and **6** make this number sentence true. The greatest whole number that makes this number sentence true is 6.

The value of $\square$ is ***at most*** 6.

The symbol $\geq$ is read "is greater than or equal to."

What whole numbers make this number sentence true?

$$\square \geq 4$$

The whole numbers **4**, 5, 6, 7, 8, and so on, make this number sentence true. The least whole number that makes this number sentence true is 4.

The value of $\square$ is ***at least*** 4.

Practice

List the whole numbers that make each number sentence true.

1. $\square \leq 2$ **2.** $\square \geq 5$ **3.** $\square \leq 7$

4. $\square \geq 8$ **5.** $\square \geq 13$ **6.** $\square \leq 1$

7. $\square \leq 6$ **8.** $\square \leq 10$ **9.** $\square \geq 15$

Describe each list of numbers using ***at most*** or ***at least***. Then use $\geq$ or $\leq$ to write a number sentence for each list.

10. 0, 1, 2, 3, 4 **11.** 9, 10, 11, 12, and so on **12.** 0, 1, 2, 3, 4, 5, 6, 7, 8, 9

13. 3, 4, 5, 6, 7, and so on **14.** 20, 21, 22, 23, and so on **15.** 0, 1, 2, 3, 4, 5, 6

16. Sara started with a package of 12 pens. She gave at least 2 of the pens to friends. How many pens might Sara have left? List all the possible answers. Describe your list using ***at most*** or ***at least***.

17. Miguel is in at least 3 scenes in the school play. The play has 6 scenes in all. Is Miguel in at least half of the scenes? Explain.

Lesson

13-4

Understand It!
Drawing a picture helps when choosing which operation to use for solving a problem.

Problem Solving

Draw a Picture and Write a Number Sentence

Alex earns money by walking dogs. The table shows how much he earned and how much he spent for each of three months. What were Alex's total earnings for May and June?

Data

Month	Earned	Spent
May	\$11.25	\$4.35
June	\$20.25	\$7.80
July	\$13.50	\$5.95

Another Example **In what other kinds of situations can you draw pictures to help choose an operation?**

Use Alex's table at the top of the page. In May, how much more was the amount Alex earned than the amount he spent?

Read and Understand

Use a diagram to show what you know.

\$11.25		← Earned
?	\$4.35	← Spent

Since you are comparing amounts, you can subtract.

$\$11.25 - \$4.35 = \square$

Plan and Solve

Subtract to solve the problem.

$$\begin{array}{r} \overset{0}{\cancel{1}}\overset{10}{\cancel{1}}.\overset{12}{\cancel{2}}5 \\ -\ \ 4.35 \\ \hline \$6.90 \end{array}$$

Alex earned \$6.90 more than he spent.

Explain It

1. Suppose Tammy wrote \$4.35 + ? = \$11.25 for the diagram above. Is this number sentence correct? Explain.

2. Once a month Alex puts \$5 into a savings account. How much does he put into the account in 1 year? Draw a picture and write a number sentence to solve.

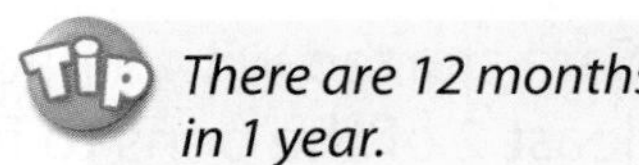

Plan and Solve

Use a diagram to show what you know. Then write a number sentence.

Total Earnings

$11.25	$20.25

You know the two parts. Add to find the total.

$11.25 + $20.25 = ▢

Solve and Answer

Add to solve the problem.

$$\begin{array}{r} \scriptstyle 1 \\ \$11.25 \\ +\ 20.25 \\ \hline \$31.50 \end{array}$$

In May and June, Alex earned a total of $31.50.

Guided Practice*

Do you know HOW?

Draw a picture and write a number sentence to solve.

1. Miyoko had a piece of ribbon that was $\frac{7}{8}$ yard long. She cut off $\frac{2}{8}$ yard to make a bow. She used the rest of the ribbon to make a tail for her kite. How much ribbon did she use for the kite?

Do you UNDERSTAND?

2. Anna needs $\frac{3}{8}$ yard of yarn for each bracelet she makes. Explain how to find how much yarn she needs for 2 bracelets.

3. **Write a Problem** Write a problem with fractions that you can solve by drawing a picture and writing a number sentence.

Independent Practice

For **4–5**, draw a picture and write a number sentence to solve.

4. Gus had $10. He spent $3.87 at the hobby shop. How much money does Gus have left?

5. Last week Bev earned $5.75. This week she earned $6.50. How much did she earn in the 2 weeks?

Stuck? Try this....

- What do I know?
- What am I asked to find?
- What diagram can I use to help understand the problem?
- Can I use addition, subtraction, multiplication, or division?
- Is all of my work correct?
- Did I answer the right question?
- Is my answer reasonable?

For another example, see Set C on page 325.

Independent Practice

6. Josh wants to buy some art supplies. How much money does Josh need to buy a paint brush and 4 jars of paint?

Tip *First find the cost of 4 jars of paint.*

Art Supplies	
Jar of paint	\$4
Marker	\$3
Paint brush	\$6

7. Gloria and Louisa both walk to school. Gloria lives 9 blocks from school. Louisa lives 6 blocks from school. How much farther does Gloria have to walk than Louisa?

For **8** and **9**, use the pictograph.

8. Mrs. Riley's class voted on which kind of activity they should do during gym time. The pictograph shows the results. Which activity received the most votes?

9. Writing to Explain How do you know that two activities did not receive the same number of votes?

Votes for Gym Time Activity	
Basketball	☺☺☺☺☺☺☺
Races	☺☺☺☺☺☺
Skip Rope	☺☺☺☺☺
Volleyball	☺☺☺☺☺☺☺☺

Each ☺ = 1 vote.

10. Leo colored $\frac{3}{5}$ of a flag blue. Then he colored another $\frac{1}{5}$ of the same flag yellow. What fraction of the flag did he color in all?

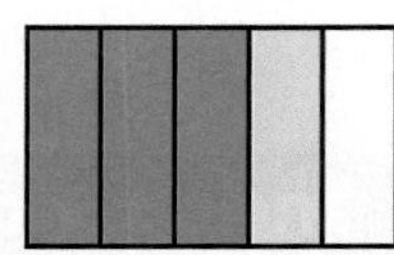

Think About the Process

11. Each week has 7 days. Which of the following is used to find out how many days are in 2 weeks?

A $7 - 2$

B $2 + 7$

C $7 \div 2$

D 2×7

12. Mr. Wilson's class has 27 students. Mrs. Pak's class has 32 students. Which number sentence shows how many more students are in Mrs. Pak's class than are in Mr. Wilson's class?

A $32 - 27 = \square$

B $32 + 27 = \square$

C $32 \div 27 = \square$

D $32 \times 27 = \square$

Estimate and then find each sum. Check that your answer is reasonable.

1. $\begin{array}{r} 24 \\ +\ 65 \\ \hline \end{array}$ 2. $\begin{array}{r} 39 \\ +\ 76 \\ \hline \end{array}$ 3. $\begin{array}{r} 638 \\ +\ 823 \\ \hline \end{array}$ 4. $\begin{array}{r} 4{,}207 \\ +\ 1{,}985 \\ \hline \end{array}$

Estimate. Then find each difference. Check that your answer is reasonable.

5. $\begin{array}{r} 83 \\ -\ 27 \\ \hline \end{array}$ 6. $\begin{array}{r} 285 \\ -\ 89 \\ \hline \end{array}$ 7. $\begin{array}{r} 602 \\ -\ 234 \\ \hline \end{array}$ 8. $\begin{array}{r} 5{,}413 \\ -\ 2{,}278 \\ \hline \end{array}$

Find each product.

9. 4×7 **10.** 7×9 **11.** 0×8 **12.** 10×6 **13.** 8×5

14. 7×8 **15.** 5×9 **16.** 4×3 **17.** 3×9 **18.** 2×10

Find each quotient.

19. $54 \div 6$ **20.** $40 \div 8$ **21.** $18 \div 3$ **22.** $45 \div 5$ **23.** $72 \div 9$

24. $36 \div 9$ **25.** $63 \div 7$ **26.** $42 \div 6$ **27.** $21 \div 7$ **28.** $18 \div 9$

Error Search Find each sum or difference that is not correct. Write it correctly and explain the error. For **31** and **32**, you may use fraction strips or draw a picture to help.

29. $\begin{array}{r} 183 \\ +\ 127 \\ \hline 310 \end{array}$ **30.** $\begin{array}{r} 685 \\ -\ 289 \\ \hline 404 \end{array}$ **31.** $\frac{2}{5} + \frac{1}{5} = \frac{1}{5}$ **32.** $\frac{7}{8} - \frac{3}{8} = \frac{1}{4}$

Number Sense

Estimating and Reasoning Write true or false for each statement. If it is false, explain why.

33. $3 \times 10 > 300$ **34.** $27 \div 3 > 10$

35. $90 + 8 < 100$ **36.** $\frac{1}{4} + \frac{2}{4} > 1$

37. $\$3.65 + 2.95 > \$5.00$ **38.** $\$6.84 - \$5.00 > \$1.00$

Lesson
13-5

Understand It!
Some problems do not have all of the information needed to solve them. Some problems have extra information that is not used.

Problem Solving

Missing or Extra Information

Ruth bought one CD, one DVD, and one package of blank tapes. She spent a total of $25 on the CD and DVD. If Ruth started with $45, how much money did she have left?

Guided Practice*

Do you know HOW?

Tell what information is missing.

1. Brad bought 3 tapes for a total of $9. He also bought some CDs that cost $10 each. How much did Brad spend in all?

Do you UNDERSTAND?

2. For Problem 1, make up the missing information and solve.

3. **Write a Problem** Write a problem that has extra information about the cost of school supplies.

Independent Practice

Decide if the problem has extra or missing information. Solve if you have enough information.

4. Pablo collects coins. He has 24 coins from Mexico, 14 coins from Canada, and 6 coins from Italy. How many more coins does he have from Mexico than from Canada?

5. Each minute, the U.S. Treasury Department makes about 30,000 coins and prints about 24,300 bills. What is the total value of the money produced each minute?

Stuck? Try this....

- What do I know?
- What am I asked to find?
- What diagram can I use to help understand the problem?
- Can I use addition, subtraction, multiplication, or division?
- Is all of my work correct?
- Did I answer the right question?
- Is my answer reasonable?

*For another example, see Set D on page 325.

Plan and Solve

Draw a diagram to show what you know and what you want to find.

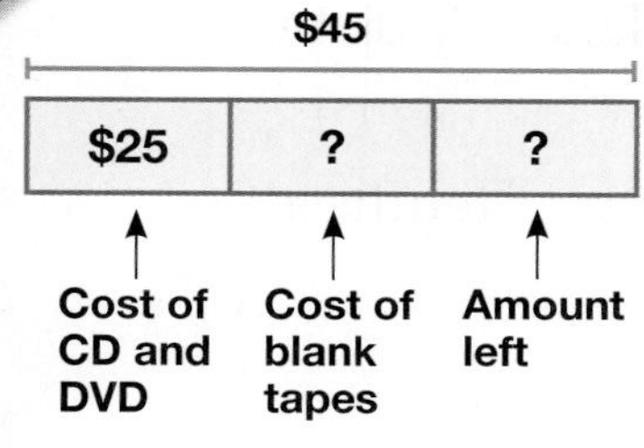

Is any information missing that you need before you can solve the problem?

Yes, I need to know the cost of the blank tapes so I can find the total Ruth spent. Then I can find how much she had left.

Is there extra information not needed to solve the problem?

No, there is no extra information.

For **6–9**, decide if each problem has extra or missing information. If information is missing, make up the information. Then solve.

Use the pictograph for **6** and **7**.

Trees Planted by Scouts

Oak	🌳 🌳
Maple	🌳 🌳 🌳
Walnut	🌳 🌳 🌳 🌳 🌳

🌳 stands for 3 trees

6. The scouts spent 2 hours planting oak trees and 4 hours planting maple trees. How many oak and maple trees did they plant?

7. The scouts also planted twice as many pine trees as walnut trees. How many pine trees did they plant?

8. Stacy spent $24 on 20 yards of material to make curtains. She used all of the material to make 4 curtains, all the same size. How much material did she use for each curtain?

9. Nick is planting 36 flowers in rows in his garden. His garden is 10 feet long and 2 feet wide. How many rows of flowers can Nick plant?

10. Frances has 24 colored pencils and 14 markers. What information is needed to find the number of her pencils that are **NOT** red?

A The total number of pencils and markers

B The number of pencils that are red

C The number of markers that are blue

D The number of markers that are red

Test

1. In the talent show, 6 out of the 10 acts were singing. Larry shaded $\frac{6}{10}$ in the figure. (13-1)

Which decimal equals $\frac{6}{10}$?

A 0.006

B 0.06

C 0.6

D 6.6

2. Jamison found 4 dimes under his bed. How do you write the value of 4 dimes? (13-2)

A 0.4

B 0.04

C $0.40

D $0.04

3. Elena has 6 tennis balls, 12 golf balls, 2 basketballs, and some softballs in the gym closet. What other information is needed to find how many softballs Elena has? (13-5)

A How many balls she has in all

B How many soccer balls she has

C How big the gym closet is

D How often she plays softball

4. What is the missing number? (13-2)

$3.49 = 3 dollars + ▢ dimes + 9 pennies

3.49 = 3 ones + ▢ tenths + 9 hundredths

A 3

B 4

C 6

D 9

5. Celia spent $24.36 on one pair of jeans and $28.65 on a second pair. How much more did the second pair cost than the first? (13-3)

A $53.01

B $5.29

C $4.79

D $4.29

6. How much is $\frac{1}{4}$ of a dollar? (13-2)

A $0.25

B $0.40

C $0.50

D $0.75

7. How much change should Lucia get back from $20 if she spent $9.48? (13-3)

A $9.52

B $10.52

C $11.42

D $11.52

8. Maria spent $11 on a shirt, $25 on pants, $12 on a CD, and $19 on sandals. How much did Maria spend in all on things to wear? (13-5)

A $48

B $55

C $56

D $67

9. Jason wants a shirt that costs $13.89 and a CD that costs $9.95. How much is his total before tax? (13-3)

A $24.84

B $23.85

C $23.84

D $23.74

10. What fraction and decimal represent the part that is blue? (13-1)

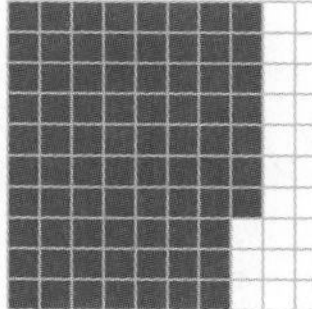

A $\frac{77}{10}$ and 0.77

B $\frac{77}{100}$ and 0.077

C $\frac{77}{100}$ and 7.7

D $\frac{77}{100}$ and 0.77

11. Each day the Video Shop has early morning special prices. From 8:00 A.M. to 10:00 A.M., a CD costs $12.75 and a DVD costs $16.35. At 9:00 A.M., Tia buys a DVD and gives the clerk a $20 bill. What information is not needed to find how much change Tia gets? (13-5)

A The cost of a CD

B The cost of a DVD

C How much Tia gave the clerk

D The time of day

12. Chelle used ham or turkey to make sandwiches. She spent $9.75 on turkey and $3.25 on ham. Which picture models how much Chelle spent on meat for sandwiches? (13-4)

A

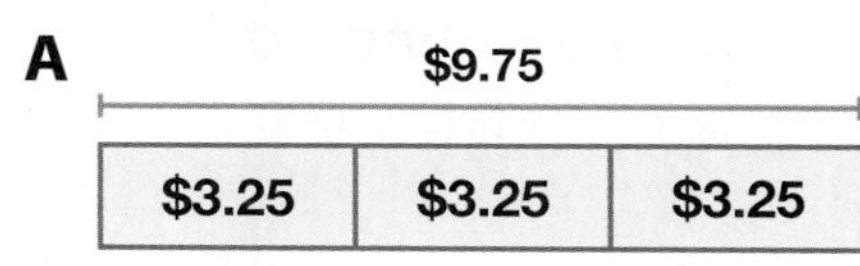

B

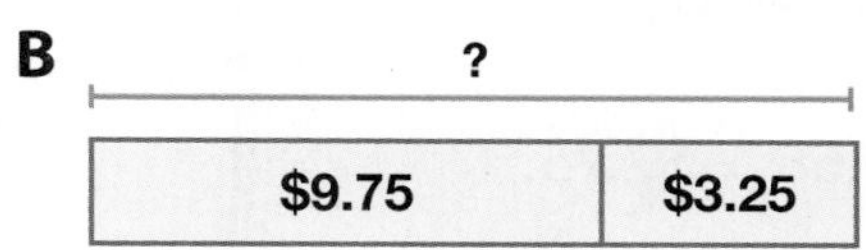

C

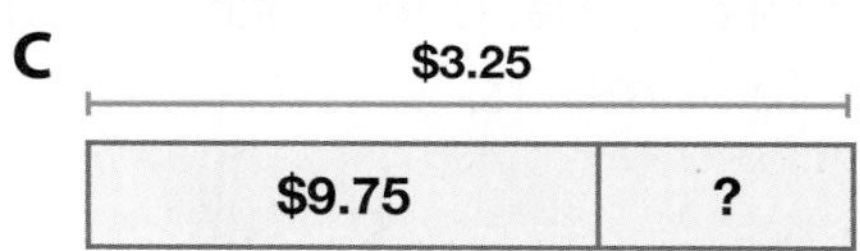

D

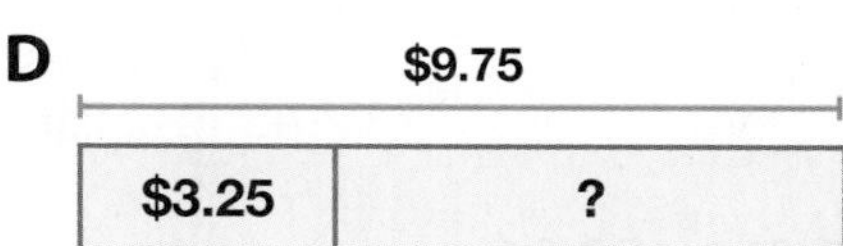

Reteaching

Set A, pages 306–311

Tenths can be written as fractions or as decimals.

$\frac{4}{10}$ or 0.4

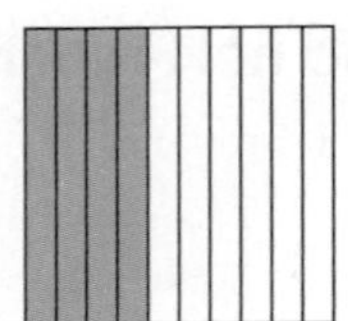

Hundredths can be written as fractions or as decimals.

$\frac{23}{100}$ or 0.23

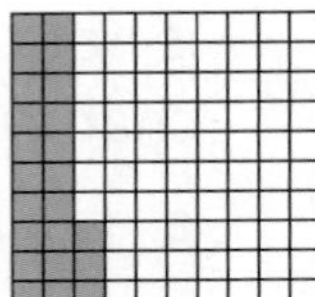

Money amounts are written as decimals.

$3.79 = 3 dollars + 7 dimes + 9 pennies or
3 ones + 79 pennies

3.79 = 3 ones + 7 tenths + 9 hundredths or
3 ones + 79 hundredths

Remember that tenths are 10 equal parts of a whole. Hundredths are 100 equal parts of a whole.

In **1** and **2**, write a fraction and a decimal for each shaded part.

1. 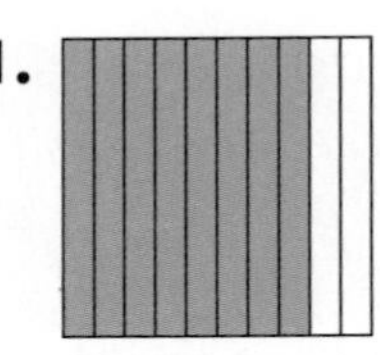

2.

In **3** and **4**, copy and complete.

3. $5.36 = ▢ dollars + ▢ dimes + ▢ pennies
5.36 = ▢ ones + ▢ tenths + ▢ hundredths

4. $7.04 = ▢ dollars + ▢ dimes + ▢ pennies
7.04 = ▢ ones + ▢ tenths + ▢ hundredths

Set B, pages 312–314

Find $9.68 + $2.75.

Line up the decimal points. Add as you would with whole numbers.

```
   1 1
  $9.68
+  2.75
 $12.43
```

Write the answer in dollars and cents.

Find $10.00 − $3.26.

Line up the decimal points. Subtract as you would with whole numbers.

```
    9  9
 0 10 10 10
$1  0. 0  0
 −  3. 2  6
   $6. 7  4
```

Write the answer in dollars and cents.

Remember to regroup as needed.

Find the sum or difference.

1. $4.97 + 5.36

2. $20.00 + 9.28

3. $18.54 + 4.76

4. $30.00 − 7.19

5. $25.00 − 14.38

6. $12.00 − 9.82

Set C, pages 316–318

Ed has $6.95. Al has $8.89. How much more does Al have than Ed?

Use a diagram to show what you know. You are comparing amounts, so subtract.

Al	$8.89	
Ed	$6.95	?

```
  7 18
 $8. 8 9
-  6. 9 5
 --------
 $1. 9 4
```

Al has $1.94 more than Ed.

Remember to draw a picture.

Solve. Draw a picture and write a number sentence.

1. Ira had $20. He gave $7.50 to Tom. How much did Ira have left?
2. Kate babysat 3 times last month. She earned $9.50, $16.75, and $12. How much did she earn in all?

Set D, pages 320–321

To solve a problem with a lot of information, follow these steps.

Step 1 Find the main idea and the key facts and details in the problem.

Step 2 Cross out any extra information.

Step 3 Solve the problem if you have enough information.

Does this problem have extra information? Is there missing information that is needed?

Meg collects stamps. She has 36 flower stamps, 24 bird stamps, and more than 20 fish stamps. How many bird and fish stamps does she have?

The number of flower stamps is extra information. The exact number of fish stamps is missing information that is needed to solve the problem.

Remember to make sure you understand what information is needed to solve the problem.

Decide if each problem has extra information or missing information. If there is enough information, solve the problem. If not, tell what is missing.

1. Three friends spent $24 to buy lunch. They also bought a magazine for $4. They shared the cost of buying lunch equally. How much did each person spend on lunch?
2. Anna bought 4 yards of cloth to make pillows. She paid $4 per yard for the cloth. How many pillows can Anna make?

Topic 14

Customary Measurement

1 What is the record length of the "World's Longest Apple Peel?" You will find out in Lesson 14-3.

2 This kind of hat is sometimes called a 10-gallon hat. Does it really hold ten gallons? You will find out in Lesson 14-4.

3

Mark Twain is a famous author. What does his name have to do with a unit of measure? You will find out in Lesson 14-1.

4

Owen, a baby hippo, and Mzee, a giant tortoise, met after a tsunami. When they first met, how much more did Mzee weigh than Owen? You will find out in Lesson 14-5.

Review What You Know!

Vocabulary

Choose the best term from the box.

- estimate
- fraction
- factor
- multiply

1. When you find 3×4, you _?_.
2. When you find a number that is about how many, you _?_.
3. If a whole is divided into equal parts, each part is a _?_ of the whole.

Fractions and Length

Find what part of the length of the 1 strip the other strips show. Write the fraction.

4. 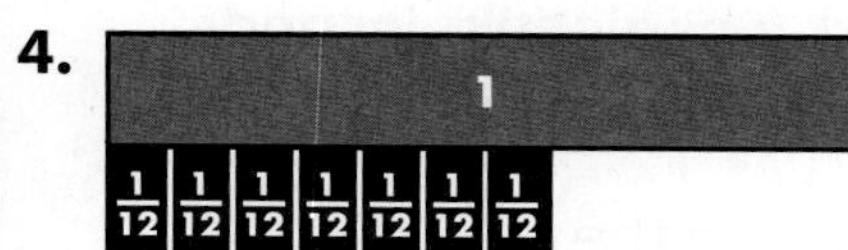

5. 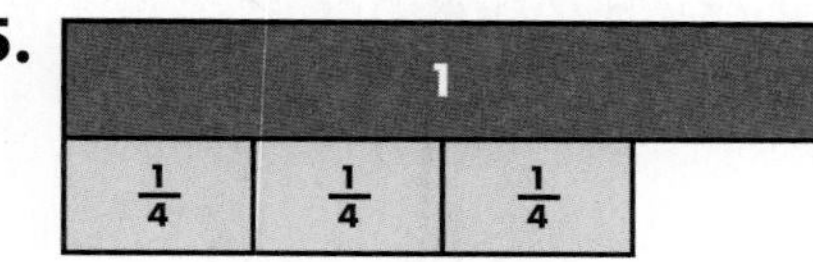

Multiplication

Find each product.

6. 3×12 7. 6×10 8. 5×3

9. 2×11 10. 4×6 11. 6×12

12. **Writing to Explain** Kim has had 3 skating lessons each month for 12 months. How many lessons has she had? Explain how an array could help you solve this problem. Then solve the problem.

Lesson
14-1

Understand It!
Objects can be used as units of measurement, but a standard unit, such as the inch, is always the same length.

Understanding Measurement

Hands-On
inch ruler

How can you describe the length of an object in different ways?

Measure the length of your desktop in pencil-lengths and in crayon-lengths.

Another Example How can you use inches to measure?

Find the length of the desktop in inches.

To use a ruler, line up the object with the 0 mark.

You may need to move the ruler to continue measuring. If so, make sure that you mark where the ruler ends before you move it.

When the ruler on the desk is moved, it will show about 6 more inches.

12 + 6 = 18

To the nearest inch, this desktop is 18 inches long.

Explain It

1. Estimate the length of your shoe in inches. Explain how you got your estimate.
2. Find the length of a pen to the nearest inch.
3. Explain why using a ruler is a better way to measure length than using a crayon.

Find the length.

More crayon-lengths than pencil-lengths equal the length of the desktop.

The desktop is 3 pencil-lengths or 6 crayon-lengths long.

Compare the units.

The crayon-length is a smaller unit than the pencil-length.

The smaller the unit used, the more units are needed to equal a given length.

Use a standard unit.

People use standard units to describe measurements.

A standard unit for measuring length is the inch (in.).

1 inch

Guided Practice*

Do you know HOW?

Estimate each length. Then measure to the nearest inch.

1. 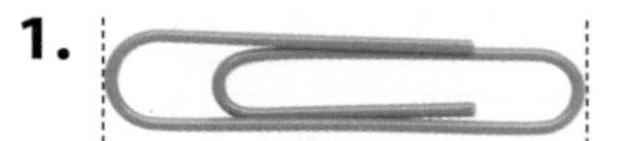

2. 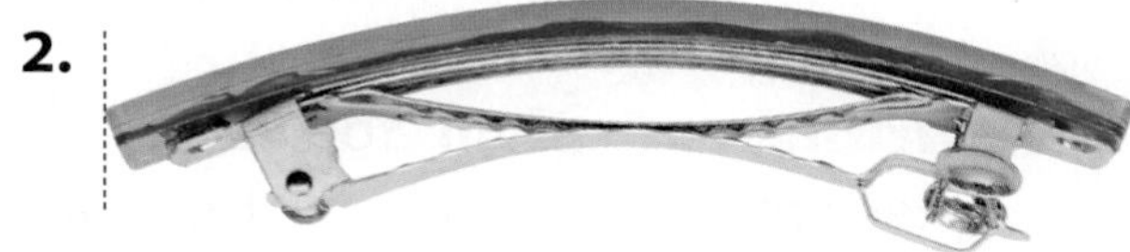

3. 

Do you UNDERSTAND?

4. In the example above, are more pencil-lengths or crayon-lengths equal to the length of the desktop?

5. Find the length of your desktop in paper clip-lengths. First estimate the length in paper clips.

6. What is the length of the candle to the nearest inch?

Independent Practice

In **7–10**, estimate each length. Then measure to the nearest inch.

7. 

8. 

9.

10. 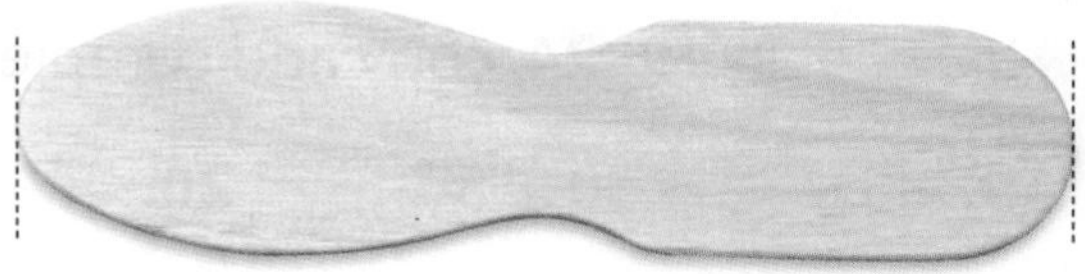

*For another example, see Set A on page 346.

Independent Practice

In **11–13**, estimate each length. Then measure to the nearest inch.

11.

12.

13.

Problem Solving

14. A marker is 4 times as long as a piece of chalk. The piece of chalk is 2 inches long. How long is the marker?

marker |—|—|—|—|
chalk |—|

15. Kevin's father is 72 inches tall. He is 26 inches taller than Kevin. How tall is Kevin?

Kevin's father	72	
Kevin	?	26

16. **Number Sense** Jeff's hand is 3 large paper clips long. Alan's hand is 8 small paper clips long. Could their hands be the same size? Explain. How would standard units help?

17. **Writing to Explain** You have a piece of string and a ruler. How can you decide how long this curve is?

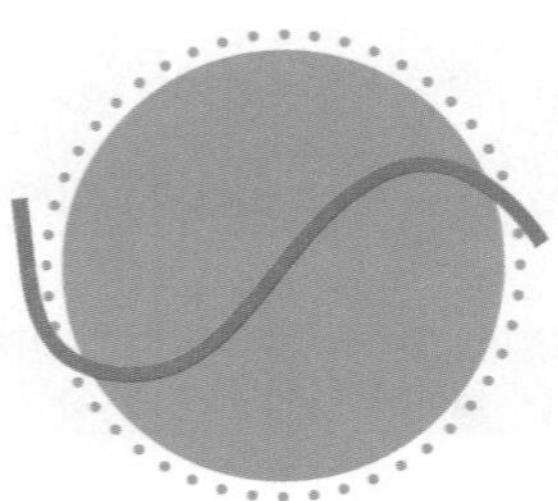

18. **Reasoning** The author Mark Twain's name is taken from riverboat slang. "Mark twain" meant "Mark two" for 2 fathoms. Two fathoms are equal to 12 feet. Which measurement unit is longer, a fathom or a foot?

Algebra In **19–24**, copy and complete each number sentence.

19. 35 + ▢ = 50 + 5

20. ▢ − 10 = 38 + 1

21. 40 − ▢ = 30 + 1

22. ▢ + 22 = 30 − 2

23. 50 − ▢ = 46 + 3

24. 32 − ▢ = 20 + 4

25. Without using a ruler, draw a line segment about 4 inches long. Then measure it to the nearest inch.

26. Al fed his friend's dog for 4 days. He used 2 cups of food 2 times each day. How many cups of food did he use?

27. Juan has 15 pennies and 3 dimes. Olivia has the same amount of money, but she has only nickels. How many nickels does Olivia have?

28. Alberto had 104 peacock stickers. He put 68 of them in his old sticker book and gave 18 away. How many peacock stickers does Alberto have left to put in his new sticker book?

29. **Number Sense** Suppose two pizzas are the same size. One pizza is cut into eighths and the other pizza is cut into tenths. Which pizza has larger pieces?

30. **Reasoning** Ken has 8 quarters, 5 dimes, 5 nickels, and 5 pennies. This is all the money he has. Explain why the total value of all of Ken's coins could not be $2.81. Then find the correct amount he had.

31. Which of the pencil stickers below is 2 inches high? Use a ruler to measure.

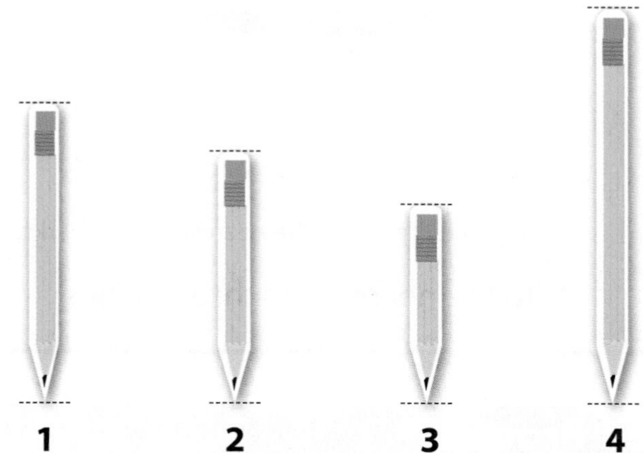

A Sticker 1
B Sticker 2
C Sticker 3
D Sticker 4

32. Ruth did 63 extra math problems in 7 days. She did the same number of problems each day. Which number sentence would you use to find the number of problems she did each day?

A $63 + 7 = \square$
B $63 - 7 = \square$
C $63 \times 7 = \square$
D $63 \div 7 = \square$

Lesson
14-2

Understand It! Using fractions of an inch gives measurements that are closer to the actual length than using inches.

Fractions of an Inch

Hands-On
inch ruler

How do you measure to a fraction of an inch?

In the picture, what is the length of the red pepper to the nearest $\frac{1}{2}$ inch and to the nearest $\frac{1}{4}$ inch?

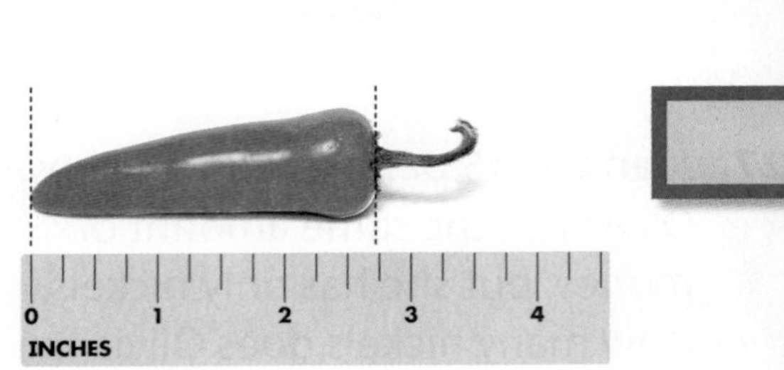

Other Examples

The nearest $\frac{1}{2}$ inch and $\frac{1}{4}$ inch can be the same.

In the picture, the length of the green bean is measured to the nearest $\frac{1}{2}$ inch and to the nearest $\frac{1}{4}$ inch.

To the nearest $\frac{1}{2}$ inch:

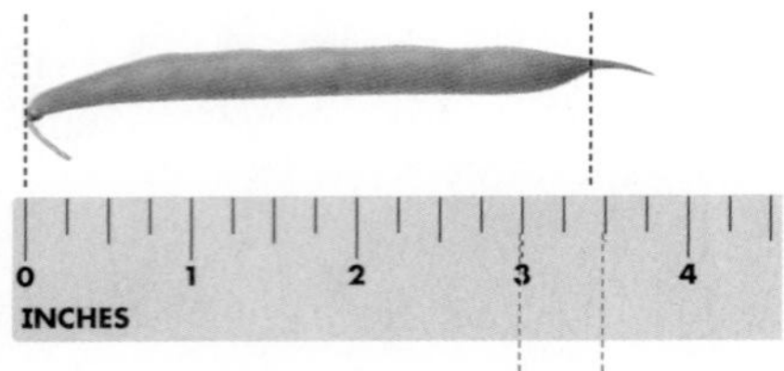

The red marks are the nearest $\frac{1}{2}$-inch marks.

To the nearest $\frac{1}{2}$ inch: $3\frac{1}{2}$ inches

To the nearest $\frac{1}{4}$ inch:

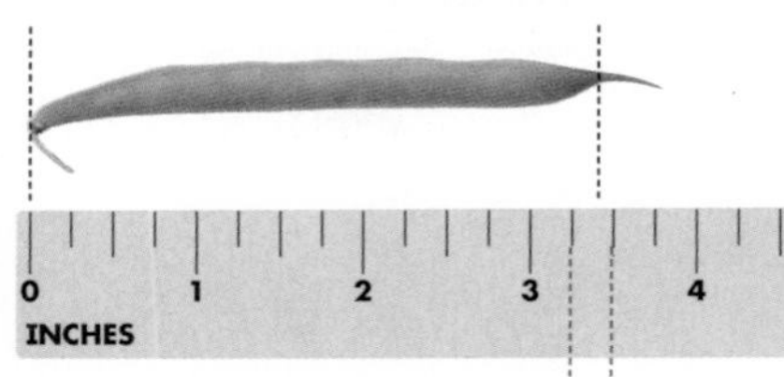

The blue marks are the nearest $\frac{1}{4}$-inch marks.

To the nearest $\frac{1}{4}$ inch: $3\frac{1}{2}$ inches

Guided Practice*

Do you know HOW?

Measure each length to the nearest $\frac{1}{2}$ inch and to the nearest $\frac{1}{4}$ inch.

1. 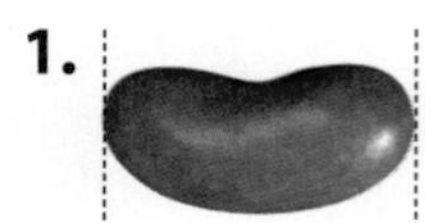

2. 

Do you UNDERSTAND?

3. In measuring the red pepper above, between which two $\frac{1}{2}$-inch marks does the pepper end?

4. Is $2\frac{1}{2}$ inches or $2\frac{3}{4}$ inches nearer to the actual length of the pepper? Explain.

*For another example, see Set B on page 346.

Measure to the nearest $\frac{1}{2}$ inch.

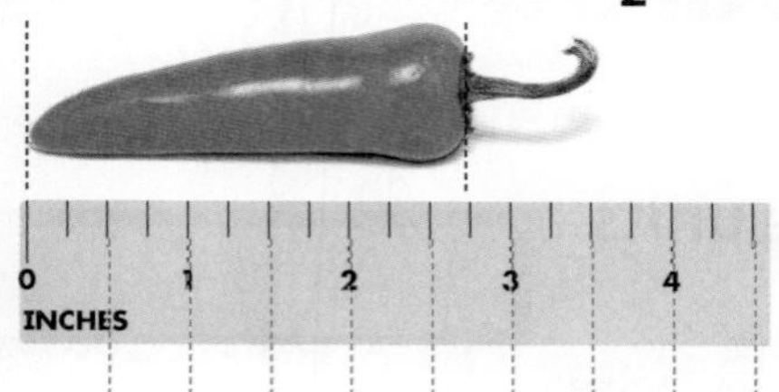

The red marks are all $\frac{1}{2}$-inch marks. The nearest $\frac{1}{2}$-inch marks are $2\frac{1}{2}$ inches and 3 inches.

To the nearest $\frac{1}{2}$ inch: $2\frac{1}{2}$ inches

Measure to the nearest $\frac{1}{4}$ inch.

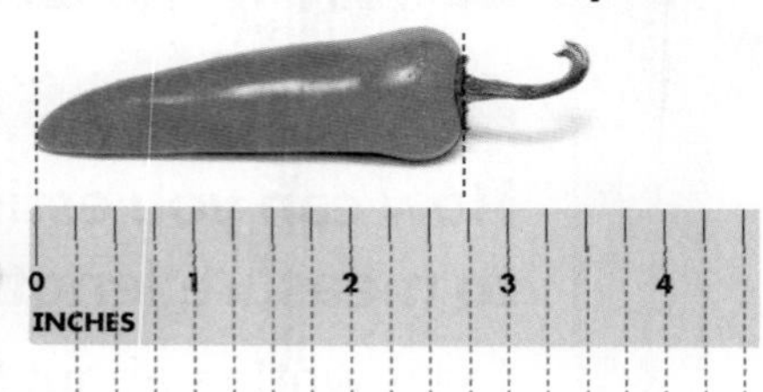

The blue marks are all $\frac{1}{4}$-inch marks. The nearest $\frac{1}{4}$-inch marks are $2\frac{1}{2}$ inches and $2\frac{3}{4}$ inches.

To the nearest $\frac{1}{4}$ inch: $2\frac{3}{4}$ inches

Independent Practice

Measure the length of each object to the nearest $\frac{1}{2}$ inch and to the nearest $\frac{1}{4}$ inch.

5. 

6. 

7. 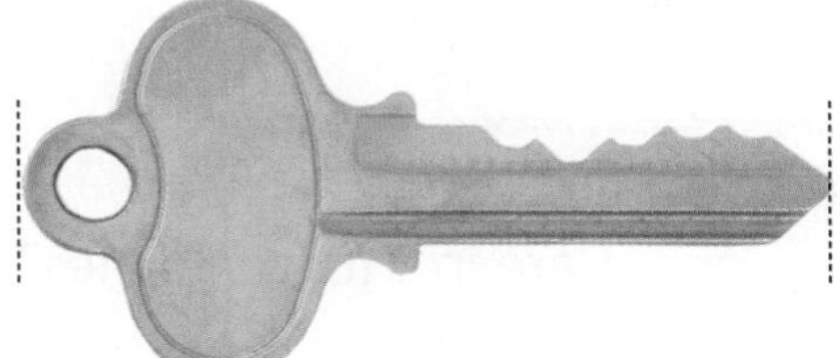

8. 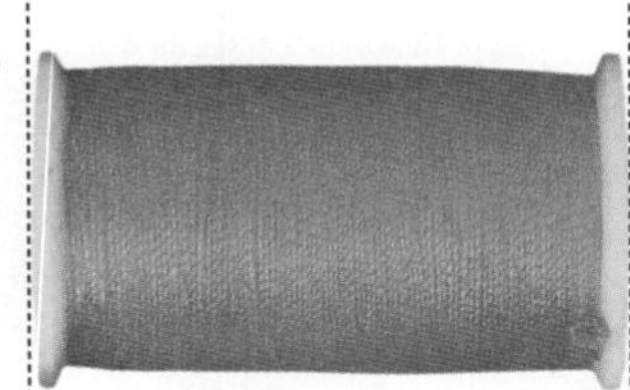

Problem Solving

9. Reasoning Can a piece of carrot be 3 inches long to the nearest inch, nearest $\frac{1}{2}$ inch, and nearest $\frac{1}{4}$ inch? Explain.

10. Karina has 3 rows of tomato plants in her garden. There are 9 plants in each row. How many tomato plants are in her garden?

11. What is the length of the asparagus to the nearest $\frac{1}{2}$ inch? Use a ruler to measure.

A 5 inches **B** $5\frac{1}{2}$ inches **C** 6 inches **D** $6\frac{1}{2}$ inches

Lesson

14-3 Using Inches, Feet, Yards, and Miles

Understand It!
Inches, feet, yards, and miles are all units of length. Using a table of equal measures can help you change units.

How can you estimate and choose units to measure length?

Joe is writing about fire trucks. What units of length or distance might he use?

Another Example How can you change from one unit of length to a different unit of length?

The table at the right shows how some units of length are related.

Customary Units of Length
12 inches = 1 foot (ft)
3 feet = 1 yard (yd)
36 inches = 1 yard
5,280 feet = 1 mile (mi)
1,760 yards = 1 mile

How many feet are in 4 yards?

1 yard = 3 feet

Multiply:
4 × 3 feet = 12 feet

There are 12 feet in 4 yards.

How many inches are in 3 feet, 2 inches?

1 foot = 12 inches

Multiply, then add:
3 × 12 inches = 36 inches
36 inches + 2 inches = 38 inches

3 feet, 2 inches = 38 inches

Explain It

1. How could you make a table to help find the number of inches in 3 feet, 2 inches?
2. How many inches are in 2 feet, 7 inches?

Besides the inch, some customary units of length are the foot (ft), yard (yd), and mile (mi).

A loaf of bread is about a foot long.

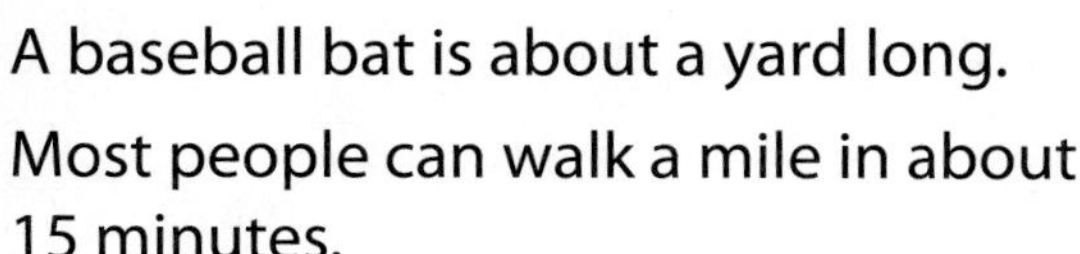

A baseball bat is about a yard long.

Most people can walk a mile in about 15 minutes.

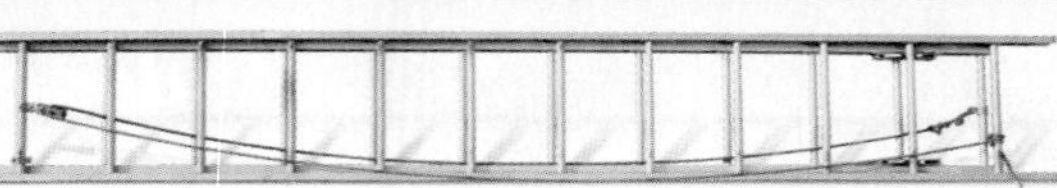

The length of the ladder on the fire truck is best measured in feet.

The length of the fire hose is best measured in yards. The width of the fire hose is best measured in inches.

The distance a fire truck travels is best measured in miles.

Guided Practice*

Do you know HOW?

Which is the best unit to use? Choose inches, feet, yards, or miles.

1. The distance between two cities
2. The length of your classroom

Do you UNDERSTAND?

3. In the example above, why would the width of the hose be measured in inches instead of feet?
4. What unit is best used for the height of a bookcase? Why?

Independent Practice

In **5–7**, tell which is the best unit to use. Choose inches, feet, yards, or miles.

5. The length of a toothbrush
6. The distance driven on a road trip
7. The length of a playground

Leveled Practice In **8–11**, change the units.

8. Change 2 feet, 9 inches to inches.
   1 foot = 12 inches
   2×12 inches = 24 inches
   24 inches + ☐ inches = ☐ inches

9. Change 2 yards, 2 feet to feet.
   1 yard = 3 feet
   2×3 feet = ☐ feet
   ☐ feet + 2 feet = ☐ feet

10. How many feet are in 6 yards?

11. 4 feet, 5 inches = ☐ inches

DIGITAL Animated Glossary
www.pearsonsuccessnet.com

*For another example, see Set C on page 346.

Independent Practice

In **12–15**, choose the better estimate.

12. A child's height
4 feet or 9 feet

13. The distance you travel on a train
70 yards or 70 miles

14. The length of a car's license plate
9 inches or 9 yards

15. The distance across your hand
3 inches or 8 inches

Problem Solving

16. Mr. Berry put up the fence shown below. How many inches long is the fence?

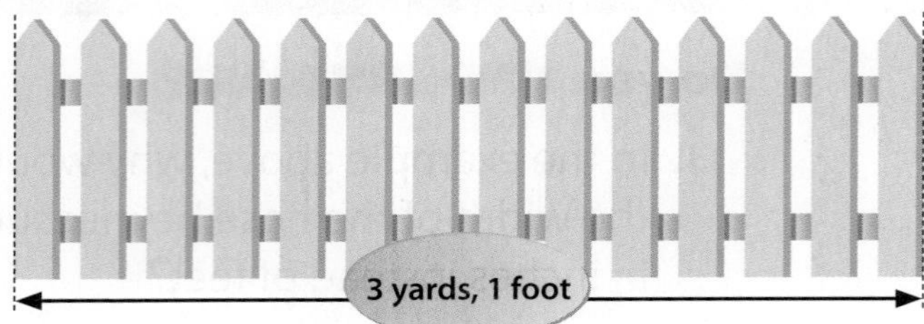

17. Angie needs 8 inches of ribbon for each of the 9 bows she is making. The ribbon is sold by the yard. How many yards of ribbon should Angie buy?

18. **Writing to Explain** West Side Park is 2,000 feet long. East Side Park is 1 mile long. Which park is longer? Explain your answer.

19. Look at the poster below. What fraction of the squares on this poster show food?

A $\frac{1}{15}$

B $\frac{7}{15}$

C $\frac{8}{15}$

D $\frac{3}{5}$

20. Writing to Explain Judy broke one of her shoelaces. She measured the unbroken lace and found it was 2 feet long. She bought a pair of 27-inch shoelaces. How does the length of her new laces compare to the length of her old laces? Explain.

21. Number Sense Would you measure the length of a soccer field in yards or inches? Explain.

22. Geometry Which shape is a scalene triangle?

A  **B** **C** **D**

23. In 1976, the world record was set for the "World's Longest Apple Peel," measuring at about 170 feet. Which lettered point best represents the length of the "World's Longest Apple Peel"?

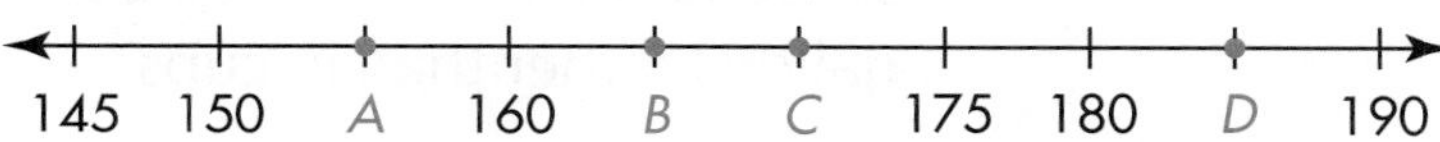

24. The table at the right shows the long-jump distances for Juanita, Tom, and Margo. Write these distances in order from shortest to longest.

Data

Long Jump

Student	Distance
Juanita	2 ft, 4 in.
Tom	23 in.
Margo	2 ft

25. Which measurement best describes the length of a couch?

A 6 miles

B 6 yards

C 6 feet

D 6 inches

26. Which measurement best describes the height of a kitchen table?

A 1 foot

B 3 feet

C 6 feet

D 12 feet

Algebra In **27–29**, use >, <, or = to compare.

27. 2 yd ◯ 5 ft

28. 3 ft ◯ 36 in.

29. 1 mi ◯ 1,000 in.

Lesson

14-4

Understand It!
The cup, pint, quart and gallon are customary units of capacity that are related by multiples of 2.

Customary Units of Capacity

What customary units describe how much a container holds?

The capacity of a container is the volume of a container measured in liquid units. What is the capacity of this pail?

Guided Practice*

Do you know HOW?

For **1** and **2**, choose the better estimate for each.

1.

1 c or 1 qt

2.

3 pt or 3 gal

Do you UNDERSTAND?

3. Number Sense Why does it make sense to measure the pail above in gallons rather than in cups?

4. Find a container that you think holds about 1 gallon and another that holds about 1 cup. Then use measuring containers to see how well you estimated each capacity.

Independent Practice

For **5–12**, choose the better estimate for each.

5.

1 pt or 1 gal

6.

1 c or 1 pt

7.

1 c or 1 pt

8.

1 c or 1 qt

9. kitchen sink
22 c or 22 qt

10. water glass
1 c or 1 qt

11. baby bottle
1 qt or 1 c

12. tea kettle
3 qt or 3 c

*For another example, see Set D on page 347.

Step 1

Cups, pints, quarts, and gallons are customary units of capacity.

Choose an appropriate unit and estimate.

The cup, pint, and quart are too small. Use gallons.

The pail looks like it will hold more than 1 gallon.

Data

Units of Capacity
1 pint = 2 cups
1 quart = 2 pints
1 gallon = 4 quarts

Step 2

Measure the capacity of the pail.

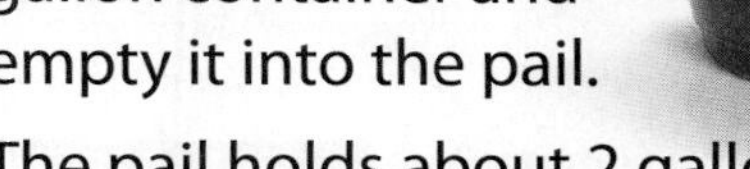

Count how many times you can fill a gallon container and empty it into the pail.

The pail holds about 2 gallons.

Choose the better unit to measure the capacity of each.

13. teacup
pt or c

14. swimming pool
pt or gal

15. water bottle
pt or gal

16. pitcher of juice
c or qt

Problem Solving

17. **Writing to Explain** Can containers with different shapes have the same capacity? Why or why not?

18. Look at the hat at the right. It is sometimes called a ten-gallon hat!

a Can this hat really hold 10 gallons? How do you know?

b Can this hat hold 1 gallon? How do you know?

This ten-gallon hat has a capacity of about 3 quarts!

19. Which measurement best describes the capacity of a bathtub?

A 50 cups

B 50 quarts

C 50 gallons

D 50 pints

20. Which of the objects below holds about 1 pint?

A bowl of soup

B punch bowl

C gas tank

D pool

21. Jeanne made 5 pitchers of lemonade. Each pitcher served 9 customers at her lemonade stand. If Jeanne had 1 pitcher of lemonade left, how many customers did Jeanne serve?

Lesson
14-5

Understand It!
The ounce, pound, and ton are customary units of weight that are used to measure all kinds of objects.

Units of Weight

What customary units describe how heavy something is?

The weight of an object is a measure of how heavy the object is. What is the weight of this apple?

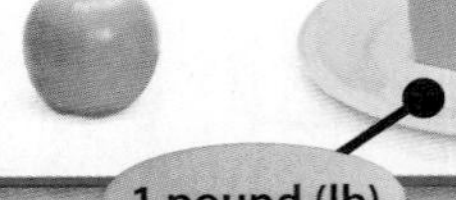

1 ounce (oz)

1 pound (lb)

about 1 ton (T)

Guided Practice*

Do you know HOW?

For **1** and **2**, choose the better estimate for each.

1. 

1 oz or 1 lb

2. 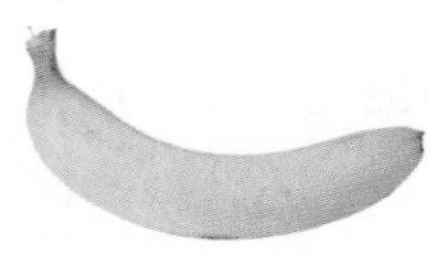

6 oz or 6 lb

Do you UNDERSTAND?

3. Number Sense If you buy a bag of 6 apples, what unit would you use for its weight? Explain.

4. Find an object that you think weighs about 1 pound and another that weighs about 1 ounce. Then weigh the objects to see how well you estimated.

Independent Practice

For **5–12**, choose the better estimate for each.

5. 

10 oz or 10 lb

6. 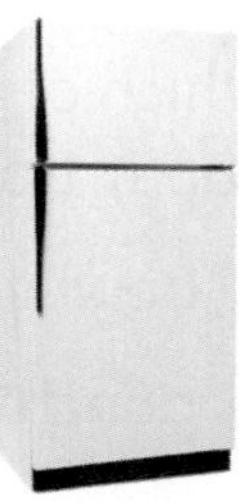

300 lb or 300 T

7. 

200 lb or 2 T

8. 

2 oz or 2 lb

9. cracker
1 oz or 1 lb

10. television set
30 oz or 30 lb

11. baseball hat
5 oz or 5 lb

12. elephant
30 lb or 3 T

*For another example, see Set E on page 347.

Step 1

Ounces, pounds, and tons are units of weight.

Choose a unit and estimate.

The units pound and ton are too big. Use ounces.

The apple weighs less than 1 pound but more than 1 ounce.

Units of Weight
16 ounces = 1 pound
2,000 pounds = 1 ton

Step 2

Weigh the apple.

Three stacks of three 1-ounce weights balance with the apple.

The apple weighs about 9 ounces.

For **13–16**, choose the better unit to measure the weight of each.

13. student desk
lb or T

14. lemon
oz or lb

15. bicycle
oz or lb

16. truck
oz or T

Problem Solving

17. How much does the orange weigh?

18. When would you use this scale instead of a pan balance?

19. **Number Sense** Which weighs more—a pound of rocks or a pound of feathers? Explain your thinking.

20. **Writing to Explain** Do small objects always weigh less than large objects? Use examples to explain your thinking.

21. When Owen and Mzee first met, Owen weighed 600 pounds. Mzee weighed 661 pounds. How much more did Mzee weigh than Owen when they first met?

22. Which animal weighs about 1 ton?

A squirrel
B giraffe
C wolf
D monkey

Lesson
14-6

Understand It!
Acting out a problem can be helpful when using reasoning to find the answer.

Problem Solving

Act It Out and Use Reasoning

Hands-On
cubes

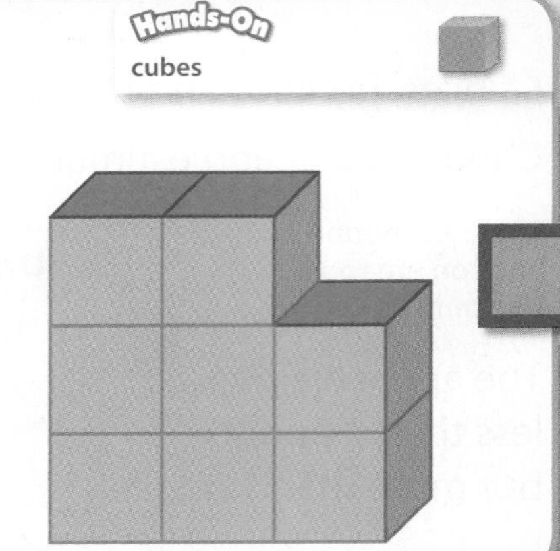

You can use different views of a figure to tell what the figure looks like.

Janet built this figure out of cubes. Then she colored the faces she could see.

Guided Practice*

Do you know HOW?

1. Use cubes to build the figure shown in these pictures.

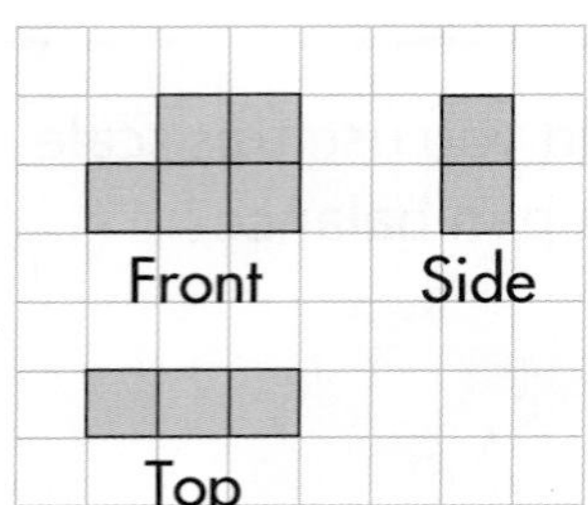

Do you UNDERSTAND?

2. **Writing to Explain** Would a drawing showing the right side of Janet's figure be the same as the drawing showing the left side?

3. Add one more block any place you wish to Janet's figure. Then make drawings to show how each view would change.

Independent Practice

Use grid paper. Draw the front, side, and top views of the figures shown below.

4.

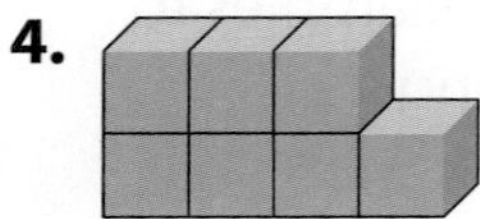

5.

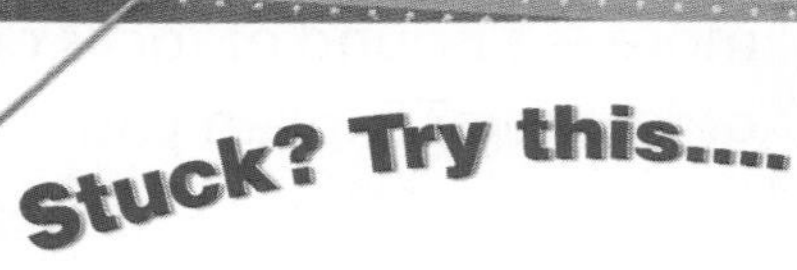

Stuck? Try this....

- What do I know?
- What am I asked to find?
- What diagram can I use to help understand the problem?
- Can I use addition, subtraction, multiplication, or division?
- Is all of my work correct?
- Did I answer the right question?
- Is my answer reasonable?

*For another example, see Set F on page 347.

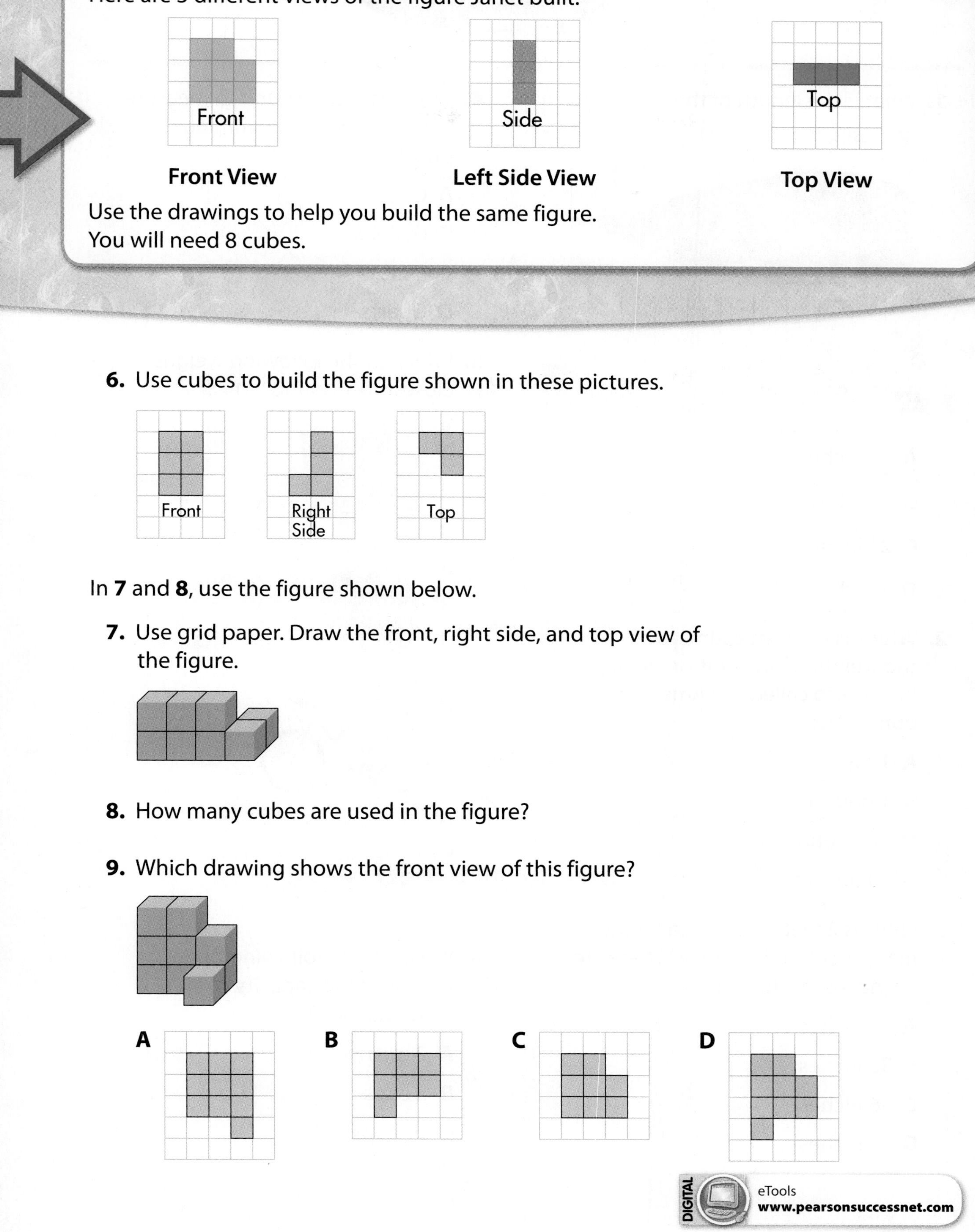

Here are 3 different views of the figure Janet built.

Front View **Left Side View** **Top View**

Use the drawings to help you build the same figure. You will need 8 cubes.

6. Use cubes to build the figure shown in these pictures.

In **7** and **8**, use the figure shown below.

7. Use grid paper. Draw the front, right side, and top view of the figure.

8. How many cubes are used in the figure?

9. Which drawing shows the front view of this figure?

DIGITAL eTools **www.pearsonsuccessnet.com**

Topic 14

Test

1. What is the length of the leaf to the nearest $\frac{1}{2}$ inch? (14-2)

A $1\frac{1}{2}$ inches

B 2 inches

C $2\frac{1}{2}$ inches

D 3 inches

2. Which is the best estimate of the weight of an adult American bison, also called the American buffalo? (14-5)

A 1 ton

B 1 pound

C 10 pounds

D 10 ounces

3. Emily is 2 feet, 8 inches tall. How many inches tall is Emily? There are 12 inches in a foot. (14-3)

A 28 inches

B 32 inches

C 36 inches

D 98 inches

4. Which is the best unit to measure the capacity of a swimming pool? (14-4)

A Cups

B Gallons

C Pints

D Quarts

5. Which of the following weighs closest to 1 pound? (14-5)

A

B

C

D

6. Which of the following best describes the capacity of a water balloon? (14-4)

A 2 quarts

B 2 cups

C 20 cups

D 20 pints

7. Which is the best unit to measure the length of the Mississippi River? (14-3)

A Miles **C** Feet

B Yards **D** Inches

8. Juana's goldfish is 2 inches long. Which could be Juana's goldfish? (14-1)

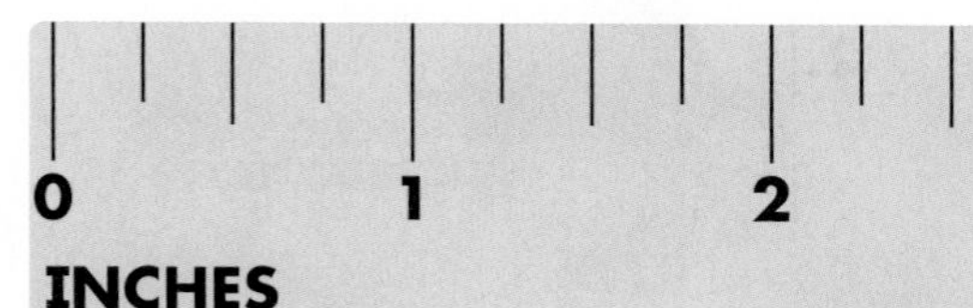

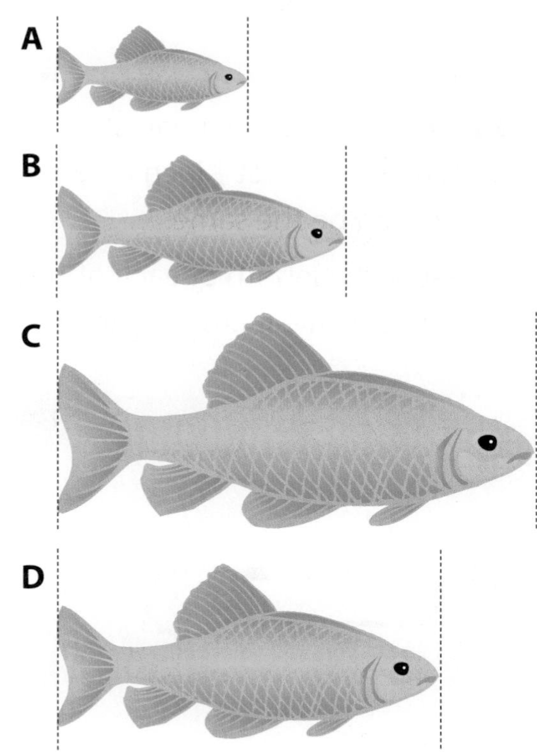

9. Which best describes the length of a large school bus? (14-3)

A 12 inches

B 12 feet

C 12 yards

D 12 miles

10. What is the length of the screwdriver to the nearest $\frac{1}{2}$ inch? (14-2)

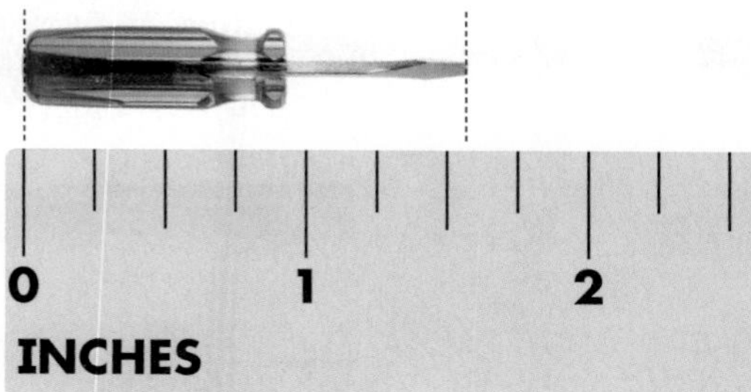

A $1\frac{1}{4}$ inches **C** $1\frac{3}{4}$ inches

B $1\frac{1}{2}$ inches **D** 2 inches

11. Which drawing shows the front view of this figure? (14-6)

A

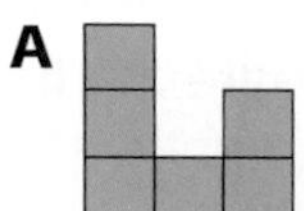

B

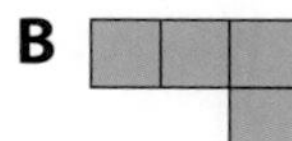

C

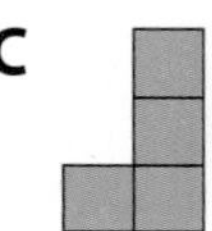

D

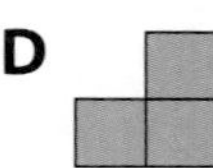

12. Which is the best estimate of the length of the almond? (14-1)

A 4 inches

B 3 inches

C 2 inches

D 1 inch

Reteaching

Set A, pages 328–331

You can use different units to measure length.

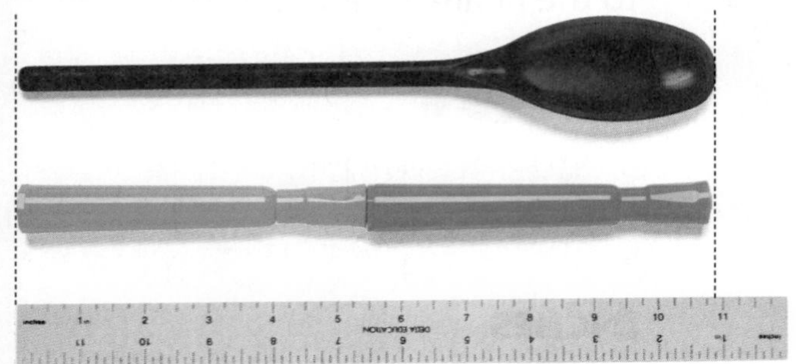

The spoon is about 2 marker-lengths long. To the nearest inch, it is about 11 inches long.

Remember to line up the object with the 0 mark on the ruler.

Use an inch ruler to measure each length to the nearest inch.

1. 

2. 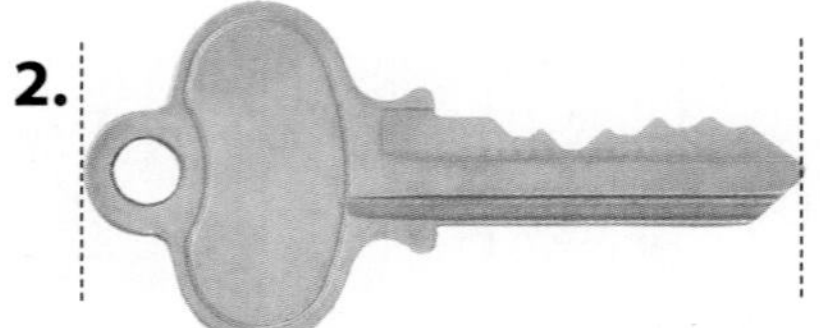

Set B, pages 332–333

Use the picture to measure the ribbon to the nearest $\frac{1}{2}$ inch and to the nearest $\frac{1}{4}$ inch.

Look for the two nearest $\frac{1}{2}$ inch marks.

To the nearest $\frac{1}{2}$ inch: $3\frac{1}{2}$ inches

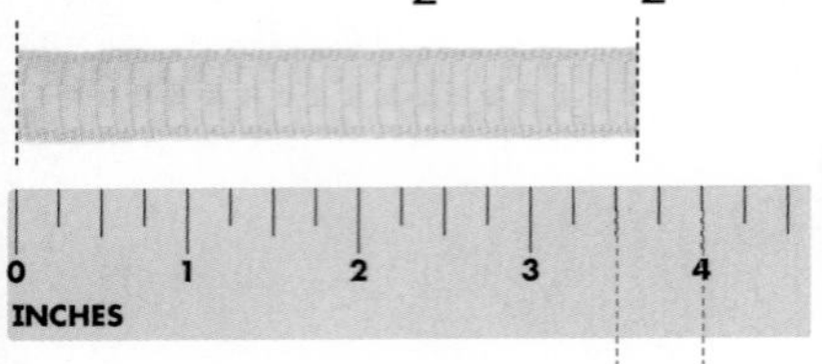

Look for the two nearest $\frac{1}{4}$ inch marks.

To the nearest $\frac{1}{4}$ inch: $3\frac{3}{4}$ inches

Remember that the nearest $\frac{1}{2}$ inch and nearest $\frac{1}{4}$ inch for an object can be the same.

Measure the length of each object to the nearest $\frac{1}{2}$ inch and $\frac{1}{4}$ inch.

1. 

2. 

Set C, pages 334–337

Change the units.

2 feet, 6 inches = ☐ inches  *1 foot = 12 inches*

Multiply: 2 × 12 inches = 24 inches
Then add: 24 inches + 6 inches = 30 inches

2 feet, 6 inches = 30 inches

Remember that 1 yard equals 3 feet.

Change the units.

1. 4 feet, 3 inches = ☐ inches
2. 6 feet, 4 inches = ☐ inches
3. 5 yards, 2 feet = ☐ feet

Set D, pages 338–339

What is the capacity of this teapot?

Choose an appropriate unit and estimate.

Gallon and quart are too big. The teapot holds more than 1 pint but fewer than 2 pints.

If you estimate using cups, the teapot looks like it holds about 3 cups.

Remember to use the examples of a cup, pint, quart, and gallon to help you estimate.

1. 

1 c or 1 qt

2. 

30 pt or 30 gal

Set E, pages 340–341

What is the weight of a tennis ball?

Choose a unit and estimate.

A tennis ball does not weigh as much as a ton or even a pound, so estimate using ounces.

The tennis ball weighs about as much as 4 small cubes of cheese, or about 4 ounces.

Remember to use the examples of an ounce, pound, and ton to help you estimate.

Choose the better estimate.

1. 8 oz or 8 lb

2. 20 lb or 20 T

Set F, pages 342–343

Les built this figure with cubes. How can you draw the front, side, and top view of the figure?

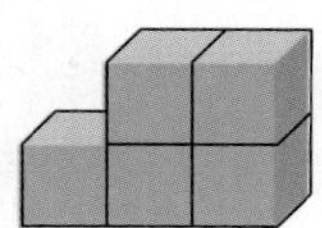

Turn the front of the figure to face you.

Front View

Then turn the figure to the side.

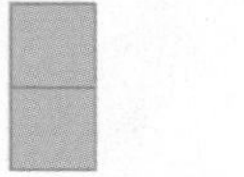

Side View

Then look at the figure from above.

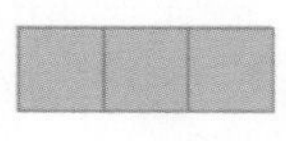

Top View

Remember to check your solution.

Use grid paper. Draw the front, side, and top view of each figure.

1. 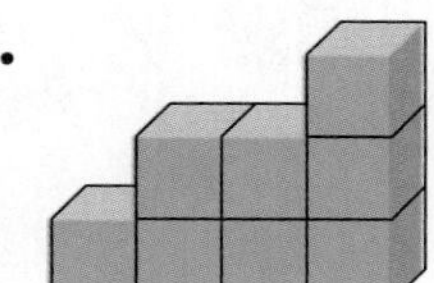

2. 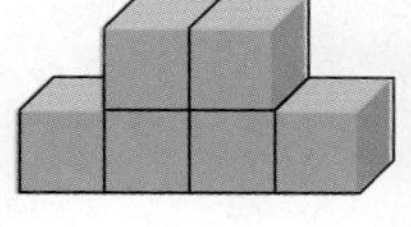

Topic 15

Metric Measurement

1 The sandgrouse soaks up water in its fluffy feathers and carries it many kilometers to its chicks. About how much water can a sandgrouse carry in its feathers? You will find out in Lesson 15-3.

2 What is the length in meters and centimeters of the footbridge on Tower Bridge in London, England? You will find out in Lesson 15-2.

3 Do you know how many grains of sand equal 1 gram? You will find out in Lesson 15-4.

4 What is the length of the world's smallest seahorse? You will find out in Lesson 15-1.

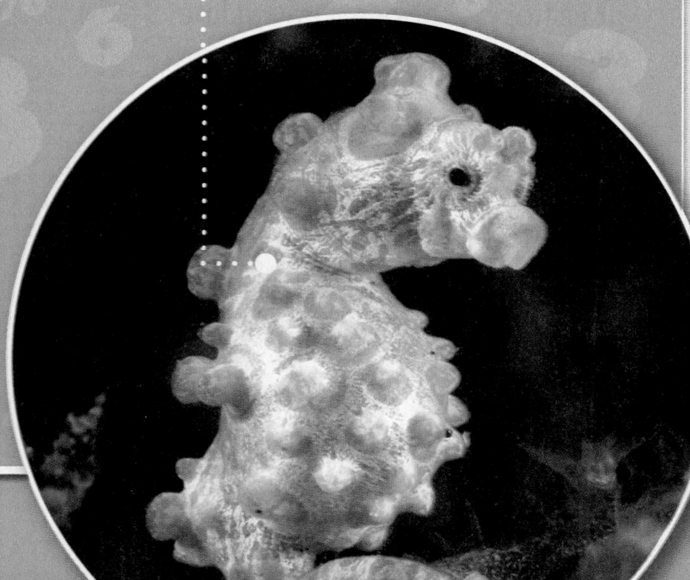

Review What You Know!

Vocabulary

Choose the best term from the box.

- cubes
- feet
- pounds
- quarts

1. You can measure weight in __?__.
2. You can measure a liquid in __?__.
3. You can measure length in __?__.

Compare Measurements

Choose the greater amount.

4. 3 inches or 3 feet
5. 20 quarts or 2 quarts
6. 6 pounds or 60 pounds

Add

Find each sum.

7. 400 + 57
8. 100 + 100 + 36
9. 10 + 10 + 5
10. 1,000 + 1,000 + 1,000

Arrays

Writing to Explain Use the array for **11** and **12**. Write an answer for each question.

11. How can you find the number of dots in the array?

12. Suppose there were 6 dots in each row. How could you find the number of dots in the array?

Lesson

15-1

Understand It!
Centimeters and decimeters are metric units that are used to describe small objects and short distances.

Using Centimeters and Decimeters

Hands-On
metric ruler

How can you estimate and measure in metric units?

What is the length of the grasshopper, to the nearest centimeter?

Other Examples

Some other metric units of length are the decimeter (dm) and the millimeter (mm).

10 centimeters = 1 decimeter
10 cm = 1 dm

This wrench is 1 dm long.

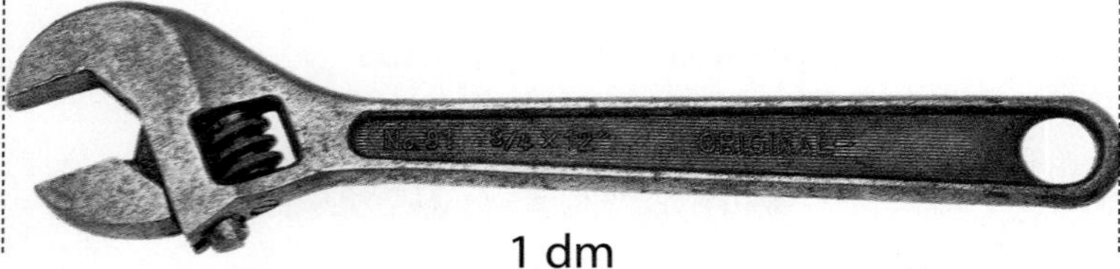

1 dm

10 millimeters = 1 centimeter
10 mm = 1 cm

A dime is about 1 mm thick.

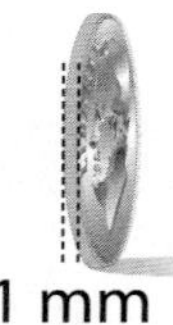

1 mm

Guided Practice*

Do you know HOW?

In **1** and **2**, estimate each length. Then measure to the nearest centimeter.

1. 

2. 

Do you UNDERSTAND?

3. A cricket is 1 cm shorter than the grasshopper above. Draw a line segment that is the same length as the cricket.

4. What is the length of the clamshell to the nearest centimeter?

*For another example, see Set A on page 364.

A metric unit for measuring length is the centimeter (cm).

Your finger is about 1 cm wide. Use your finger width to help estimate lengths.

1 cm

Use the centimeter ruler to measure.

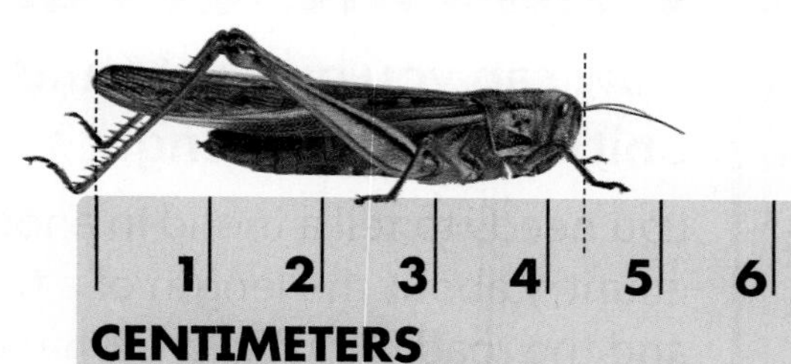

The grasshopper is 4 cm long, to the nearest centimeter.

Independent Practice

In **5–7**, estimate each length. Then measure to the nearest centimeter.

5. 

6. 

7. 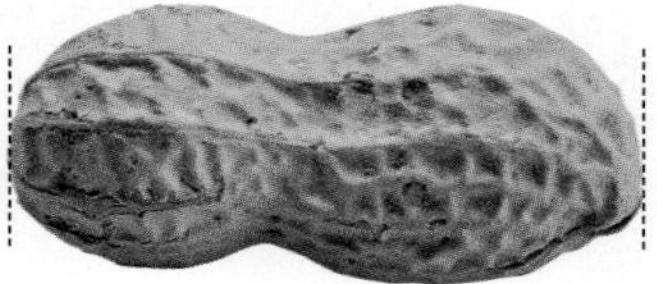

Problem Solving

8. What is the length of the flower to the nearest centimeter?

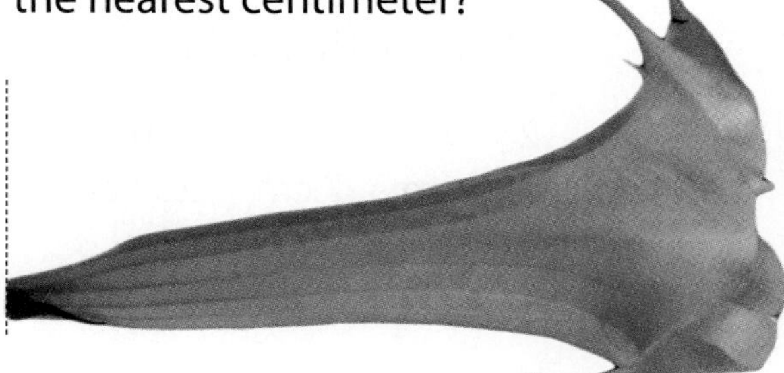

9. What is the length of the world's smallest seahorse to the nearest centimeter?

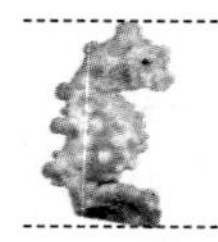

Algebra In **10–12**, copy and complete each number sentence.

10. 36 = 9 × ▢

11. 7 × ▢ = 56

12. 60 = ▢ × 10

13. Which is the length of the crayon below? Use a centimeter ruler to measure.

A 1 cm **B** 4 cm **C** 8 cm **D** 1 dm

Lesson

15-2 Using Meters and Kilometers

Understand It!
Meters and kilometers are metric units of length. A table of equal measures can help you change units.

How can you estimate and choose units to measure length?

Lou needs to tell a friend in another country about the length of a truck and the road it travels on. What units can Lou use?

Another Example How can you change units?

Metric Units of Length (Data)

Metric Units of Length
1 meter (m) = 100 centimeters (cm)
1 kilometer (km) = 1,000 meters (m)

2 meters, 7 centimeters = ▢ centimeters

One Way

Make a table that relates meters and centimeters.

Meters	1	2	3	4
Centimeters	100	200	300	400

2 meters, 7 centimeters = 207 centimeters

Another Way

Multiply. Then add.

2×100 cm = 200 cm
200 cm + 7 cm = 207 cm

Explain It

1. How could you make a table to help find the number of centimeters in 6 meters, 5 centimeters?
2. How many centimeters are 4 meters, 17 centimeters?

Metric units used for measuring longer lengths are the meter (m) and the kilometer (km).

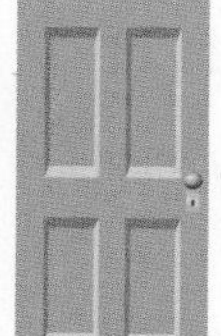

A doorknob is about 1 meter above the floor.

Most people can walk a kilometer in about 10 minutes.

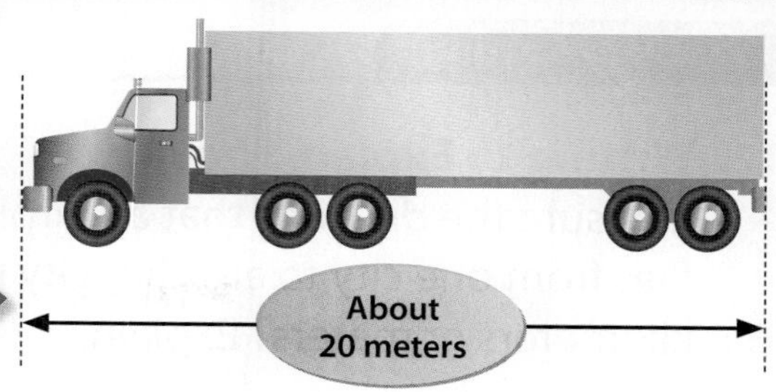

About 20 meters

The length of a truck is best measured in meters.

The distance a truck travels on a road is best measured in kilometers.

Guided Practice*

Do you know HOW?

Which is the best unit to use? Choose meter or kilometer.

1. The length of a classroom

2. The length of a table in the lunchroom

3. The distance across your state

Do you UNDERSTAND?

4. In the example above, why is a kilometer the better unit to use to measure the length of the road?

5. **Writing to Explain** Which distance is greater, 850 meters or 1 kilometer? How do you know?

Independent Practice

In **6** and **7** tell if meter or kilometer is the better unit to use.

6. The height of a flagpole

7. The length of a bike trail

In **8** and **9**, change the units. Copy and complete.

8. How many centimeters are in 3 meters, 8 centimeters?

9. 4 meters = ▢ centimeters

In **10** and **11**, choose the better estimate.

10. The height of an adult
2 kilometers or 2 meters

11. The length of your foot
20 centimeters or 20 meters

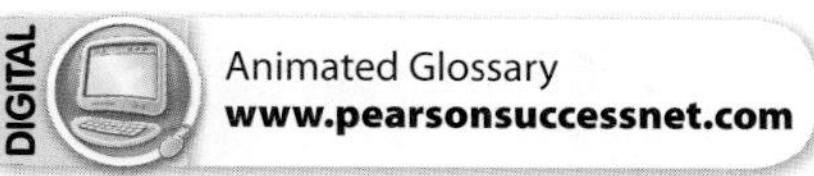

**For another example, see Set A on page 364.*

Problem Solving

12. **Writing to Explain** Would you measure the distance that an airplane flies from one city to another city in kilometers or meters? Explain.

13. **Number Sense** A tree is 4 meters, 10 centimeters tall. Is this more than or less than 500 centimeters? Explain.

14. Change the units. Copy and complete the table to help.

Meters	1	2	3	4
Centimeters	100	200		

a 3 meters, 15 centimeters = ▢ centimeters

b 4 meters, 63 centimeters = ▢ centimeters

In **15** and **16**, use the table at the right.

15. **Estimation** About how much would it cost to buy two 1-meter railings and two 2-meter railings?

16. How much more is the price of one 150-centimeter railing than the price of one 1-meter railing?

Data

Sale on Railings

Length	Price
1 meter	$8
2 meters	$19
150 centimeters	$11

17. Which measurement best describes the length of a car?

A 5 centimeters **C** 5 meters

B 5 kilometers **D** 5 millimeters

Use the photo at the right for **18** and **19**.

18. The footbridge on Tower Bridge was built so workers could cross the River Thames in London, even when the main part of the bridge was open to let a boat pass. How many centimeters long is the footbridge?

19. Which measurement is a reasonable estimate of the height of each tower?

A 65 m **C** 65 dm

B 65 km **D** 65 cm

Changing Metric Units

How many centimeters are in 2 meters, 45 centimeters?

There are 100 centimeters in a meter. To find how many centimeters are in 2 meters, 45 centimeters, multiply 2 × 100 and then add 45.

Press: 2 [×] 100 [+] 45 [ENTER =]

Display: 245

2 meters, 45 centimeters = 245 centimeters

Changing Customary Units

How many inches are in 4 feet, 8 inches?

There are 12 inches in a foot. To find how many inches are in 4 feet, 8 inches, multiply 4 × 12 and then add 8.

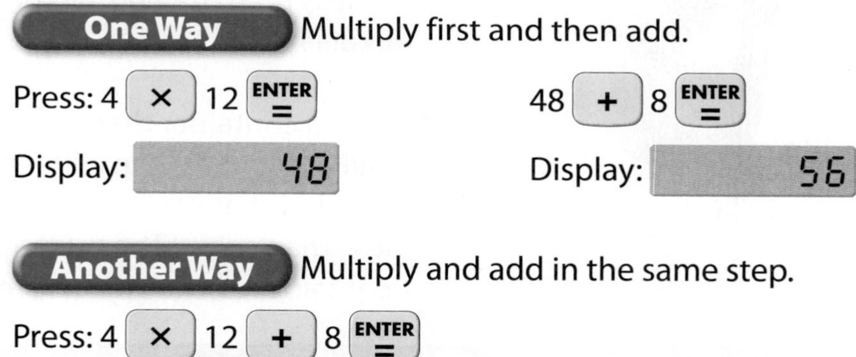

One Way Multiply first and then add.

Press: 4 [×] 12 [ENTER =]

Display: 48

48 [+] 8 [ENTER =]

Display: 56

Another Way Multiply and add in the same step.

Press: 4 [×] 12 [+] 8 [ENTER =]

Display: 56

4 feet, 8 inches = 56 inches

Practice

1. How many inches are in 3 feet, 9 inches?
2. How many centimeters are in 2 meters, 74 centimeters?
3. How many inches are in 7 yards, 16 inches?
4. How many feet are in 4 yards, 2 feet?
5. How many meters are in 5 kilometers, 25 meters?

Lesson

15-3

Understand It!
A liter and a milliliter are metric units that measure capacity.

Metric Units of Capacity

What metric units describe how much a container holds?

Two metric units of capacity are milliliters and liters. What is the capacity of this pail?

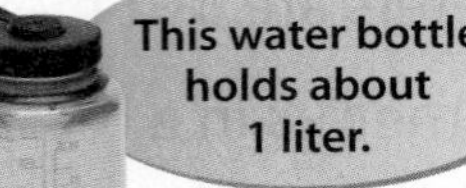

A milliliter is about 20 drops from this eyedropper.

Milliliter (mL)

This water bottle holds about 1 liter.

Liter (L)

Guided Practice*

Do you know HOW?

Choose the better estimate for each.

1.

250 mL or 2 L

2.

5 mL or 1 L

Do you UNDERSTAND?

3. Writing to Explain Suppose the capacity of the pail above is given in milliliters. Is this number greater or less than the number of liters? Explain.

4. Find a container that you predict will hold more than a liter and another that you predict will hold less than a liter. Then use a liter container to check your predictions.

Independent Practice

In **5–12**, choose the better estimate for each.

5.

40 mL or 40 L

6.

15 mL or 1 L

7.

14 mL or 14 L

8.

250 mL or 250 L

9. teacup

15 L or 150 mL

10. bathtub

115 mL or 115 L

11. bottle cap

3 mL or 3 L

12. teapot

1 L or 10 L

Animated Glossary
www.pearsonsuccessnet.com

*For another example, see Set B on page 364.

Step 1

Choose an appropriate unit and estimate.

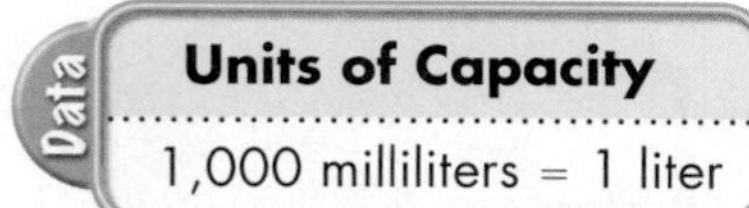

A milliliter is too small. So use liters.

The pail will hold several liters.

Step 2

Measure the capacity.

Count how many times you can fill a liter container and empty it into the pail.

The pail holds about 8 liters.

In **13–16**, choose the unit you would use to measure the capacity of each.

13. soup can
mL or L

14. water pitcher
mL or L

15. swimming pool
mL or L

16. baby bottle
mL or L

Problem Solving

Estimation For **17–20**, is the capacity of each container more than a liter or less than a liter?

17. large pot

18. glass of juice

19. washing machine

20. mug

21. Reasoning Which cooler has a greater capacity? Explain your thinking.

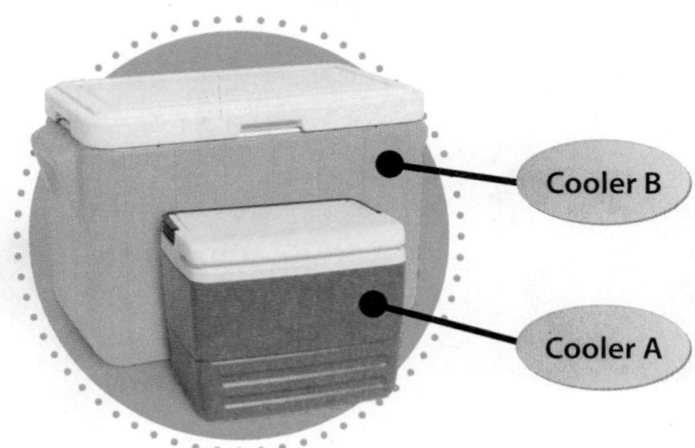

22. Which measurement best describes the capacity of a can of paint?

A 4 mL

B 4 L

C 40 L

D 40 mL

23. Number Sense A sandgrouse can soak up water in its fluffy feathers. It can carry the water many kilometers to its chicks. Does a sandgrouse carry 20 milliliters of water or 2 liters of water?

Lesson
15-4 Units of Mass

Understand It!
The gram and the kilogram are metric units of mass. They are used to describe how heavy an object seems.

What metric units describe mass?

Mass is a measure of the amount of matter in an object. Grams and kilograms are two metric units of mass. What is the mass of this apple?

Guided Practice*

Do you know HOW?

Choose the better estimate for each.

1.

5 g or 5 kg

2.

40 g or 4 kg

Do you UNDERSTAND?

3. Writing to Explain There are 10 weights on the pan balance above. Why isn't the mass of the apple 10 grams?

4. Find an object that you think has a mass more than a kilogram and another that has a mass less than a kilogram. Then use a pan balance to see if you are correct.

Independent Practice

For **5–12**, choose the better estimate for each.

5.

100 g or 10 kg

6.

15 g or 15 kg

7.

4 g or 400 g

8.

400 g or 4 kg

9. bicycle
2 kg or 12 kg

10. feather
1 g or 1 kg

11. horse
5 kg or 550 kg

12. penny
3 g or 300 g

*For another example, see Set C on page 365.

Step 1

Choose a unit and estimate.

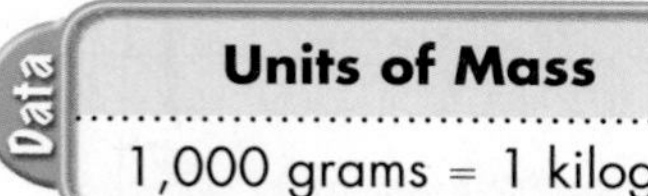
Units of Mass

1,000 grams = 1 kilogram

The unit kilogram is too big. Use grams.

The mass of the apple is less than 1 kilogram but more than 1 gram.

Step 2

Measure the mass of the apple.

Two 100-gram weights, six 10-gram weights, and two 1-gram weights balance with the apple.

The apple has a mass of 262 grams.

Problem Solving

For **13–17**, choose the best tool to measure each.

13. the capacity of a glass

14. the temperature of water

15. the length of a box

16. the weight of a pear

17. the length of time you sleep

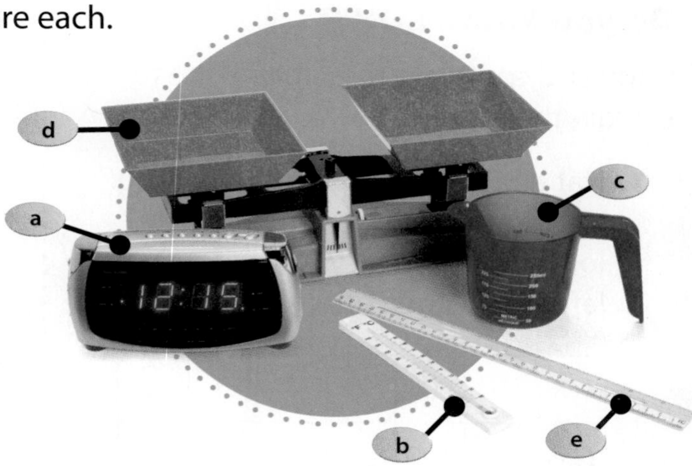

18. What is the mass of the orange?

19. Correct the mistakes in the shopping list below.

Shopping List
2 L of apples
3 kg of milk
5 cm of flour

20. A bag holds 500 grams of sand. About how many grains of sand are in the bag?

There are about 1,000 grains of sand in 1 gram.

21. Which measurement best describes the mass of a rabbit?

A 2 grams

B 2 kilograms

C 2 liters

D 2 meters

Lesson

15-5

Understand It!
One way to organize information is to make a table. The table can be used to find patterns that can help solve problems.

Problem Solving

Make a Table and Look for a Pattern

Livia is training for a 25 km walk. She recorded how far she walked each day. If she continues the pattern, how far will Livia walk on Day 4? How far will she walk on Day 5?

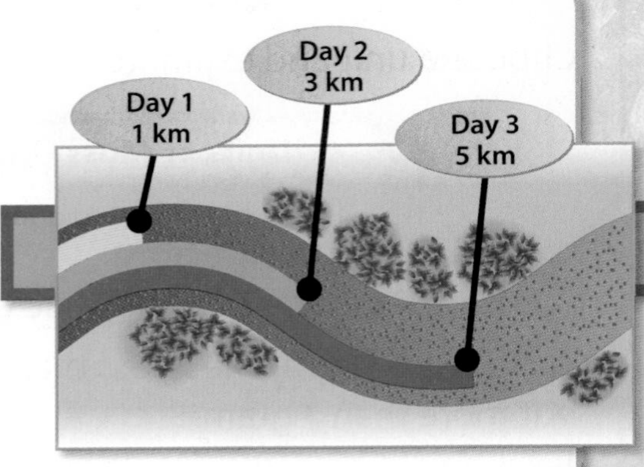

Guided Practice*

Do you know HOW?

Copy and complete the table. Write to explain the pattern. Solve.

1. Nat has a pole that is 1 meter long. He is cutting it into 20-centimeter long pieces. What length of pole is left after 3 cuts? after 4 cuts?

Cuts	0	1	2	3	4
Length (cm)	100	80	60		

Do you UNDERSTAND?

2. In the example above, how did the table help you to explain the pattern?

3. Write a Problem Write a problem that you can solve by writing an explanation of a pattern.

Independent Practice

In **4–7**, Copy and complete the table. Write to explain the pattern. Solve.

4. Nola is putting tiles in a row. Each tile is a square and the length of its side is 4 centimeters. What is the length of 4 tiles together? 5 tiles?

Number of Tiles	1	2	3	4	5
Total Length (cm)	4	8	12		

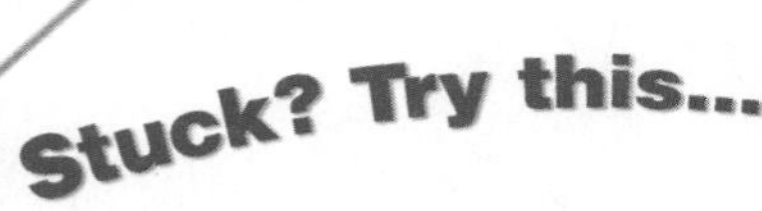

- What do I know?
- What am I asked to find?
- What diagram can I use to help understand the problem?
- Can I use addition, subtraction, multiplication, or division?
- Is all of my work correct?
- Did I answer the right question?
- Is my answer reasonable?

**For another example, see Set D on page 365.*

Plan

You can make a table to show what you know. Then look for a pattern.

Day	1	2	3	4	5
Distance walked (km)	1	3	5		

Explain the pattern you see.

Each day Livia increased the distance she walked by 2 km.

Solve

Use your pattern to complete the table and solve the problem.

Day 3: 5 km
Day 4: 5 km + 2 km = 7 km
Day 5: 7 km + 2 km = 9 km

Day	1	2	3	4	5
Distance walked (km)	1	3	5	7	9

Livia will walk 7 km on Day 4 and 9 km on Day 5.

5. Talia is cutting up a sheet of paper that is 24 centimeters long. She is cutting the sheet into pieces that are each 3 centimeters long. What is the length of the sheet that is left after Talia has made 3 cuts? 4 cuts?

Number of Cuts	0	1	2	3	4
Length Left (cm)	24	21	18		

6. Mr. Lum is putting fence rails together in a row. Each rail is 2 meters long. What is the length of 5 rails together? 6 rails?

Number of Rails	1	2	3	4	5	6
Total Length (m)	2	4	6	8		

7. Evan makes picture frames using wood. For each frame, he needs 60 cm of wood. What is the total length of wood he needs to make 4 frames? 5 frames?

Number of Frames	1	2	3	4	5
Total Length (cm)	60	120	180		

8. Nick earns money doing chores. How much would he earn if he washes windows, washes dishes, and does laundry?

Data

Item	Price
Clean yard	\$8
Do laundry	\$5
Vacuum floors	\$3
Wash dishes	\$2
Wash windows	\$7

9. In the morning, Ray painted 12 windows. By the end of the day he had painted all 26 windows in the house. Which expression shows one way to find how many windows he painted in the afternoon?

A $26 + 12$ **B** $26 - 12$ **C** 26×12 **D** $26 \div 12$

Test

1. Which unit would be best to measure the mass of a mouse? (15-4)

A Gram

B Kilogram

C Liter

D Milliliter

2. Pat bought a sub sandwich that was 36 centimeters long. She cut 4-centimeter slices. What was the length of the sandwich left after Pat cut off 5 slices? (15-5)

Slices Cut Off	0	1	2	3	4	5
Centimeters Left	36	32	28	24		

A 20 centimeters

B 18 centimeters

C 16 centimeters

D 12 centimeters

3. Which animal could be about a decimeter long? (15-1)

A a turtle

B a whale

C an ant

D a ladybug

4. Which of the following best describes the mass of an orange? (15-4)

A 20 kilograms

B 200 kilograms

C 20 grams

D 200 grams

5. Which of the following is about 2 meters? (15-2)

A The length of a bumblebee

B The distance from your home to your school

C The height of a one-story house

D The height of a classroom door

6. What is the length of the apple core to the nearest centimeter? (15-1)

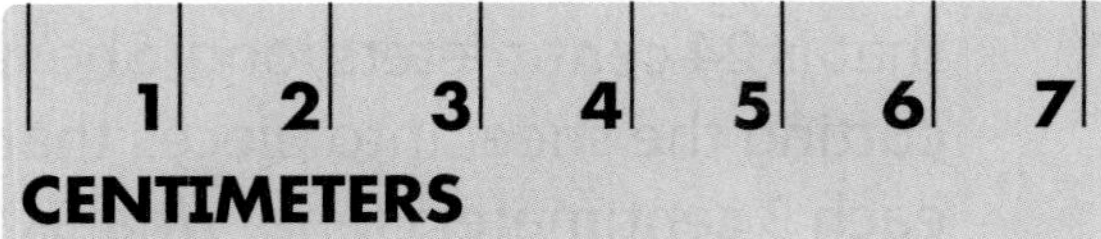

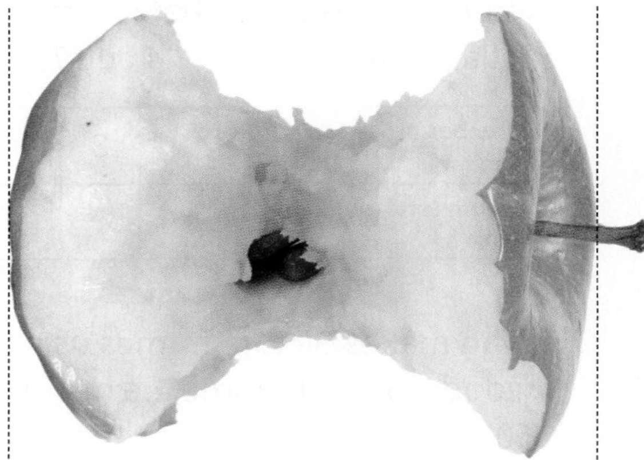

A 3 centimeters

B 6 centimeters

C 7 centimeters

D 8 centimeters

7. Which is the best estimate of the capacity of a bottle of syrup? (15-3)

A 709 pints

B 709 liters

C 709 cups

D 709 milliliters

8. Which best describes the length of a crayon? (15-2)

A 7 centimeters

B 7 decimeters

C 7 meters

D 7 kilometers

9. Which of the following would you measure in milliliters? (15-3)

A Capacity of an aquarium

B Capacity of an eyedropper

C Capacity of a coffee pot

D Capacity of a bathtub

10. Which insect could be about 5 centimeters long? (15-1)

A Ladybug

B Flea

C Ant

D Dragonfly

11. Which would be the best to measure in meters? (15-2)

A the distance from California to Hawaii

B the length of a toothbrush

C the length of a soccer field

D the distance a snail can crawl in one minute

12. Trey is practicing for a swim meet. If he continues the pattern, how many laps will he swim on the 6th day? (15-5)

Day	1	2	3	4	5	6
Laps Swam	25	29	33	37		

A 46 laps

B 45 laps

C 44 laps

D 39 laps

13. Which of the following can hold only about 2 liters of water? (15-3)

A Bathtub

B Swimming pool

C Coffeepot

D Medicine dropper

14. Which unit would be best to use for the distance from New York to Chicago? (15-2)

A centimeter

B kilometer

C meter

D millimeter

15. Which is the best estimate of the mass of a golf ball? (15-4)

A 450 kilograms

B 450 grams

C 45 kilograms

D 45 grams

Reteaching

Set A, pages 350–354

Estimate the length of the bead in centimeters. Then measure to the nearest centimeter.

You can use your finger width as 1 centimeter to help estimate.

Estimate: about 3 centimeters long

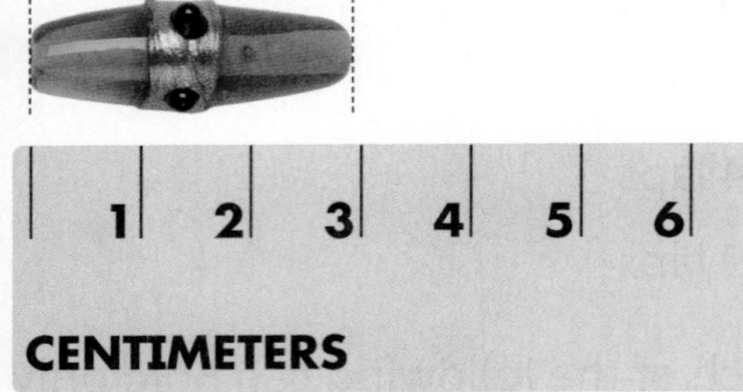

The bead is 3 centimeters long, to the nearest centimeter.

Remember to line up the object with the 0 mark on the ruler.

Estimate the length. Then measure to the nearest centimeter.

1. 

Choose the better estimate.

2. The length of a truck
10 meters or 10 kilometers

3. The height of a house
4 centimeters or 4 meters

Change the units.

4. 5 meters = ▢ centimeters

5. How many centimeters are in 4 meters, 3 centimeters?

Set B, pages 356–357

What is the capacity of this pitcher?

Choose an appropriate unit and estimate.

A milliliter is too small, so estimate using liters.

The pitcher looks like it will hold about 2 liters.

Remember that more than one unit can be used to measure the capacity of a container.

Choose the better estimate.

1. 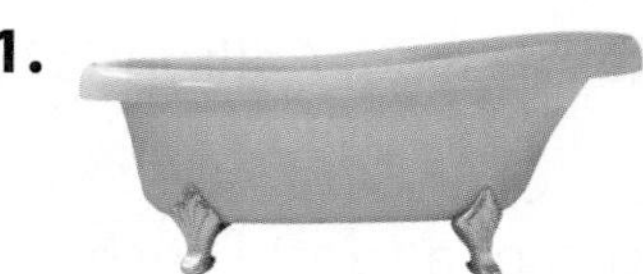

150 mL or 150 L

2. 

5 mL or 5 L

Set C, pages 358–359

What is the mass of this bar of soap?

Choose a unit and estimate.

A kilogram is too much, so estimate using grams.

The bar of soap has about the same mass as 100 grapes, or about 100 grams.

Remember to use the examples of a gram and kilogram to help you estimate.

Choose the better estimate.

1. 

15 g or 15 kg

2. 

2 g or 2 kg

Set D, pages 360–361

Vita makes bows using ribbon. She needs 30 cm of ribbon for each bow. What is the total length of ribbon she needs to make 4 bows? 5 bows?

Make a table and look for a pattern.

Explain the pattern you see.
Solve the problem.

Number of Bows	1	2	3	4	5
Total Length of Ribbon	30 cm	60 cm	90 cm	120 cm	150 cm

Vita needs 30 cm of ribbon for each bow she makes. For 2 bows, she needs 30 cm + 30 cm of ribbon. I continued the pattern to find how much ribbon Vita needs for 4 bows and for 5 bows.

Vita needs 120 cm for 4 bows and 150 cm for 5 bows.

Remember to check your answers. Make sure all of your numbers fit the pattern.

Copy and complete the table.
Write to explain the pattern.
Solve the problem.

Ned is training for a 40 km bike race. If he continues his pattern, how far will he ride on Day 4? On Day 5?

Day	1	2	3	4	5
Distance Ned Rode	1 km	4 km	7 km		

Topic 16

Perimeter, Area, and Volume

1 How far would you need to walk to go around the outside of this maze in Williamsburg, Virginia? You will find out in Lesson 16-1.

2 How many different kinds of alligators and crocodiles are there? You will find out in Lesson 16-4.

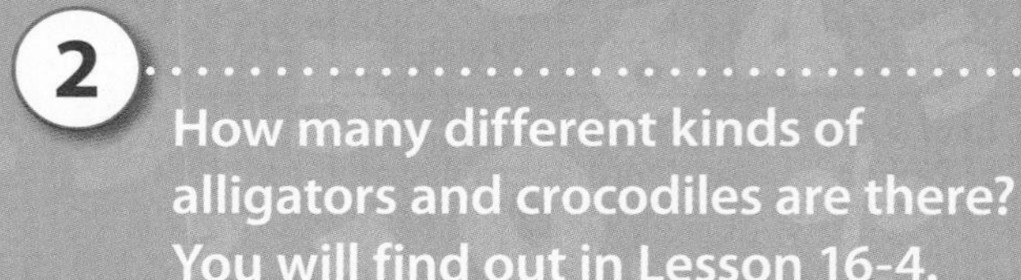

3 How long is one side of this small chessboard? You will find out in Lesson 16-6.

Review What You Know!

Vocabulary

Choose the best term from the box.

- equilateral
- quadrilateral
- pentagon
- trapezoid

1. A __?__ has 5 sides.

2. A triangle with all three sides the same length is called a(n) __?__ triangle.

3. A rectangle is a special __?__ with 4 right angles.

Multiplication Facts

Find each product.

4. 3×8	**5.** 6×4	**6.** 5×7
7. 2×9	**8.** 7×3	**9.** 4×8
10. 7×5	**11.** 4×4	**12.** 9×8

Geometry

Write the name that best describes each figure.

13. A quadrilateral with only one pair of parallel sides

14. A quadrilateral with four right angles and all sides the same length

15. A triangle with no sides the same length

Arrays

16. **Writing to Explain** Explain how to draw an array to show 3×6. Draw the array.

Lesson
16-1 Understanding Perimeter

Understand It!
The perimeter of a figure is the sum of the lengths of its sides.

Hands-On
grid paper

How do you find perimeter?

Gus wants to make a playpen for his dog and put a fence around it. He made drawings of two different playpens. What is the perimeter of the playpen in each drawing?

The distance around a figure is its perimeter.

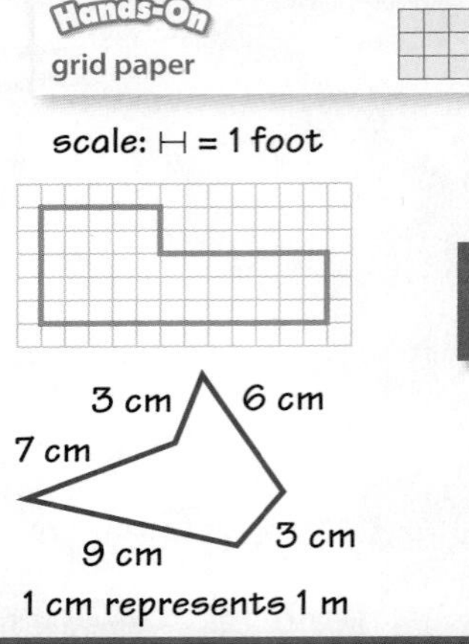

Guided Practice*

Do you know HOW?

In **1** and **2**, find the perimeter.

1.

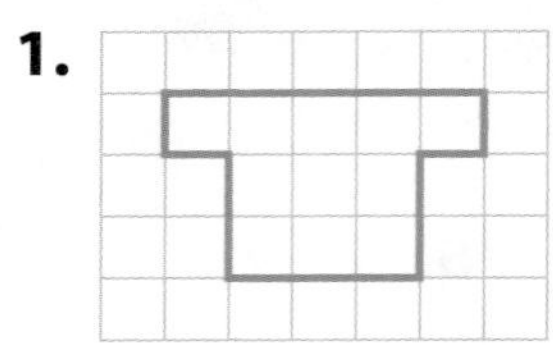

2.

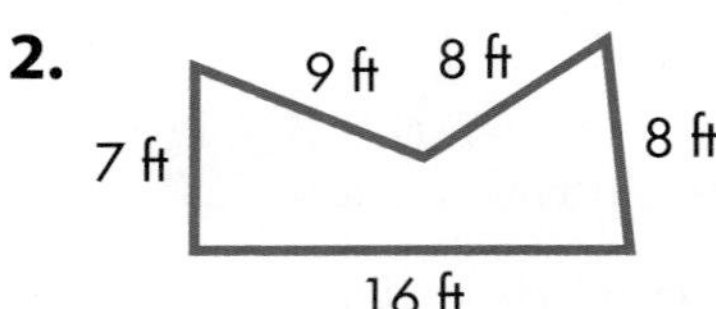

Do you UNDERSTAND?

3. In the example above, how do you know what unit Gus used for the first playpen?

4. What is the perimeter of the garden shown in the diagram below?

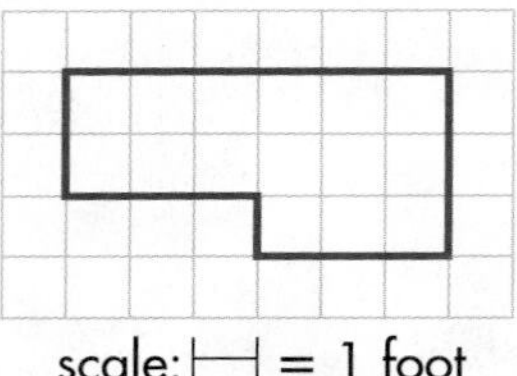

Independent Practice

In **5–7**, find the perimeter of each polygon.

5.

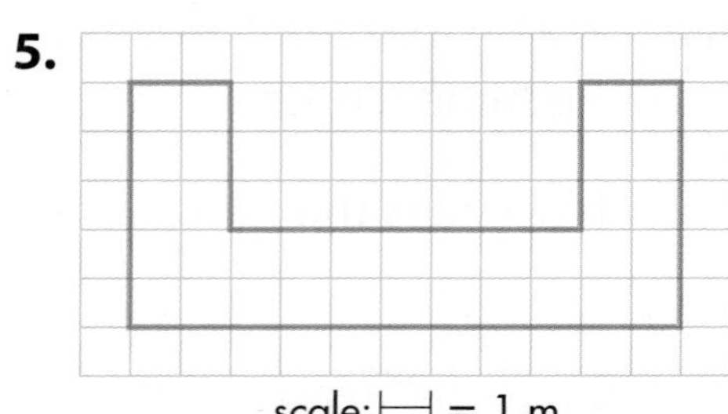

6.

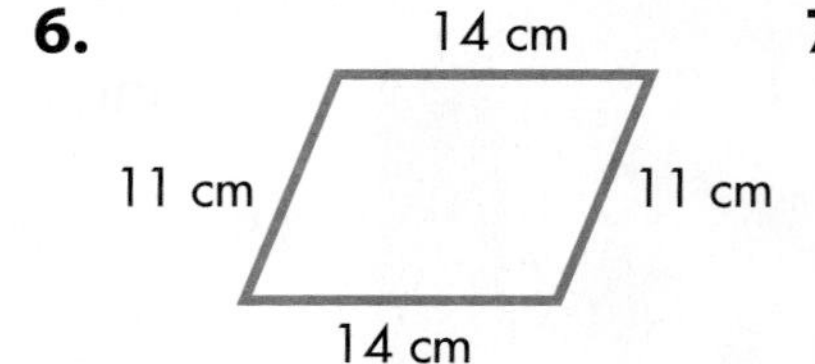

7.

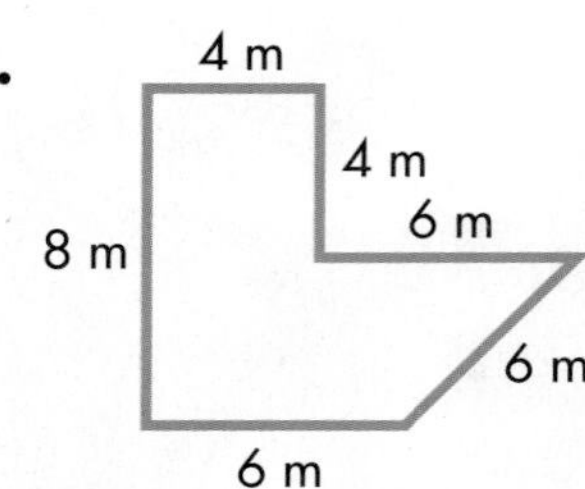

In **8–10**, draw a figure with the given perimeter. Use grid paper.

8. 14 units **9.** 8 units **10.** 20 units

*For another example, see Set A on page 388.

One Way

You can find the perimeter by counting unit segments.

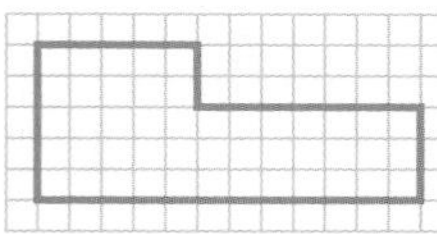

scale: ├┤ = 1 foot

The perimeter of this playpen is 34 feet.

Another Way

Add the lengths of the sides to find the perimeter.

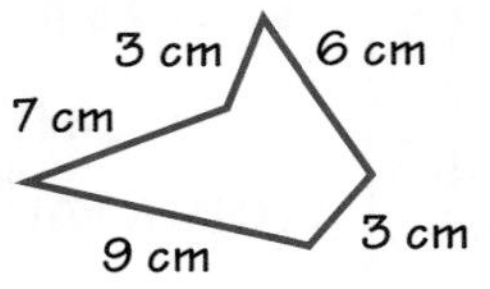

$3 + 9 + 7 + 3 + 6 = 28$

The perimeter of the drawing is 28 cm.
The perimeter of this playpen is 28 meters.

Problem Solving

11. Mr. Karas needs to find the perimeter of the playground to build a fence around it. What is the perimeter of the playground?

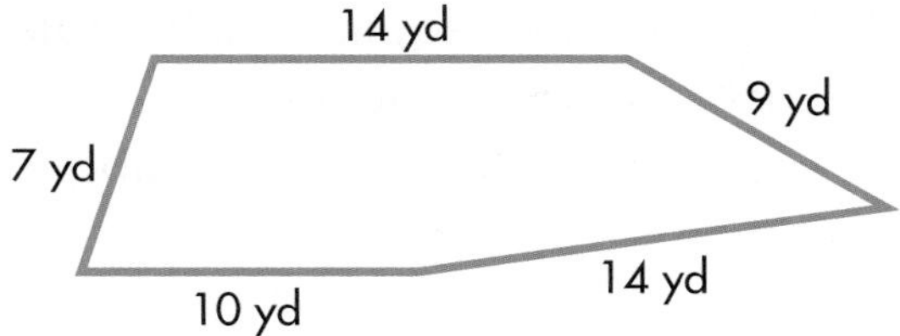

12. Mike needs to find the perimeter of the pool so he knows how many tiles to put around the edge. What is the perimeter of the pool?

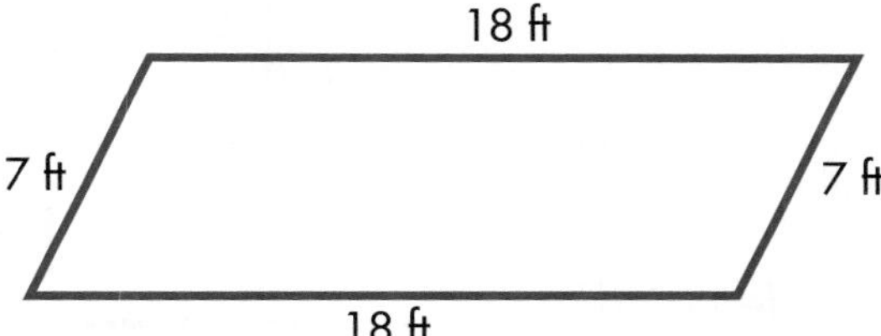

13. The distance around the outside of this maze in Williamsburg, Virginia, is the same as the perimeter of a rectangle. The picture shows the lengths of the sides of the rectangle. What is the perimeter of the maze?

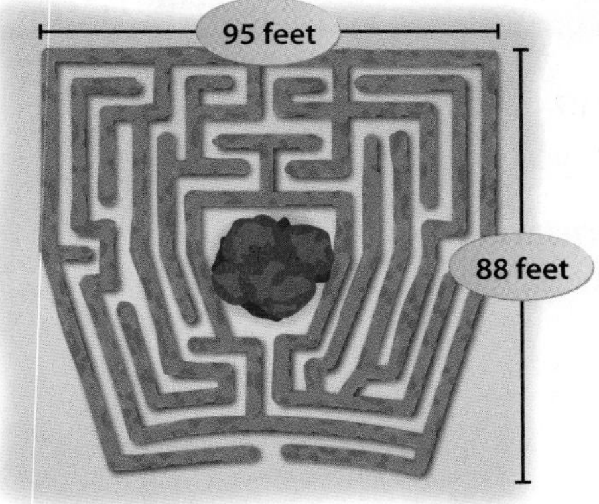

14. Jani has the magnet shown below.

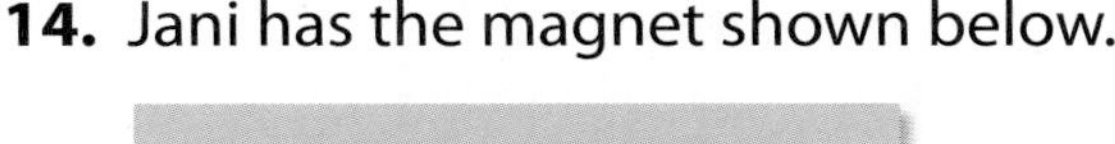

What is the perimeter of Jani's magnet to the nearest inch? Use a ruler to measure.

A 2 in. **B** 4 in. **C** 5 in. **D** 6 in.

15. Writing to Explain Roberto has a magnet that is twice as long and twice as wide as Jani's magnet in Problem 14. Find the perimeter of Roberto's magnet. Explain your work.

Lesson
16-2

Understand It!
For some polygons, knowing the length of just one or two sides is enough to find the perimeter.

Perimeter of Common Shapes

How can you find the perimeter of common shapes?

Mr. Coe needs to find the perimeter of two swimming pool designs. One pool shape is a rectangle. The other pool shape is a square. What is the perimeter of each pool?

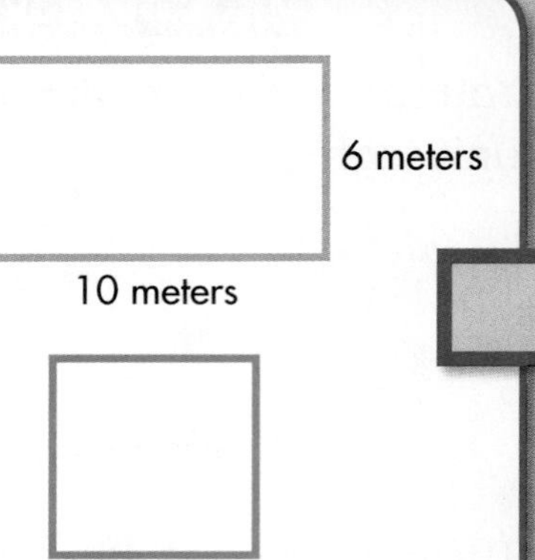

Guided Practice*

Do you know HOW?

For **1** and **2**, find the perimeter.

1. Rectangle

8 feet

4 feet

2. Square

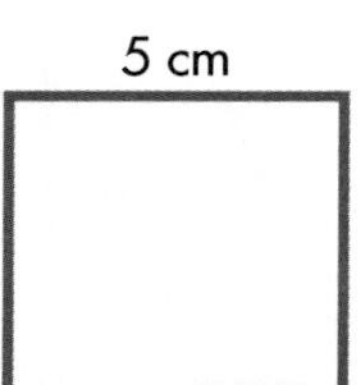

Do you UNDERSTAND?

3. In the examples above, explain how to find the missing lengths.

4. Darla drew an equilateral triangle. Each side was 9 inches long. What was the perimeter of the triangle?

Independent Practice

In **5** and **6**, use an inch ruler to measure the length of the sides of the polygon. Find the perimeter.

5. Square

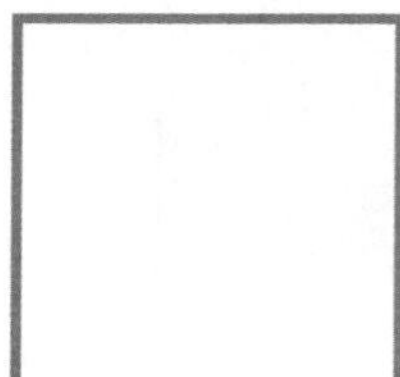

6. Rectangle

In **7** and **8**, find the perimeter of each polygon.

7. Rectangle

15 m

3 m

8. Equilateral triangle

4 yd

*For another example, see Set A on page 388.

Find the perimeter of the pool that has a rectangle shape.

Remember: Opposite sides of a rectangle are the same length.

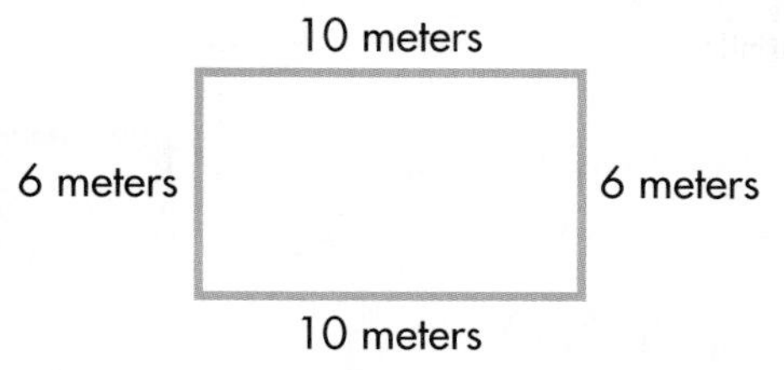

$10 + 6 + 10 + 6 = 32$

The perimeter of this pool is 32 meters.

Find the perimeter of the pool that has a square shape.

Remember: All four sides of a square are the same length.

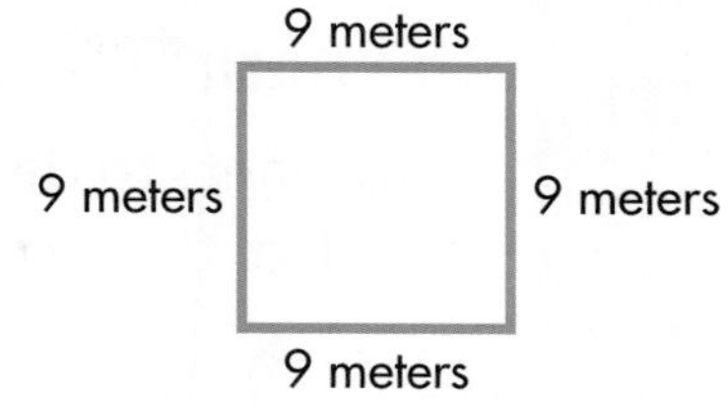

$9 + 9 + 9 + 9 = 36$ or $4 \times 9 = 36$

The perimeter of this pool is 36 meters.

Problem Solving

9. Writing to Explain Cora uses ribbons to make three different sizes of bows. How much more ribbon does it take to make 2 large bows than 2 small bows? Explain how you found your answer.

Data

Size of Bow	Length of Ribbon
Small	27 in.
Medium	36 in.
Large	49 in.

10. The base of Philip Johnson's glass house in New Canaan, Connecticut, is a rectangle. What is the perimeter of the base of the glass house?

11. What is the perimeter of the cloth patch outlined below?

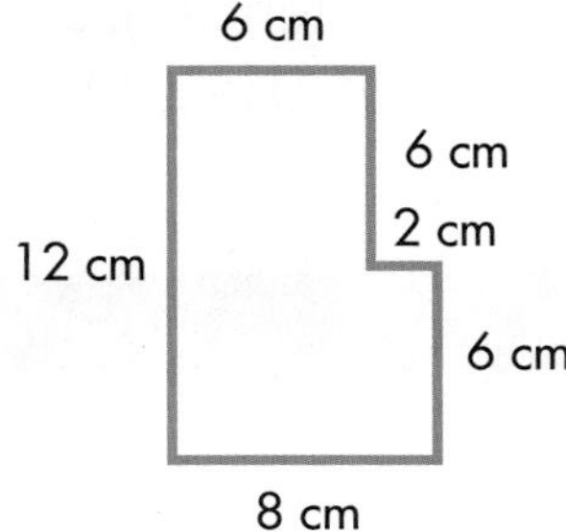

A 96 cm **C** 38 cm

B 40 cm **D** 32 cm

12. Ami's room is in the shape of a square. What is the perimeter of the room?

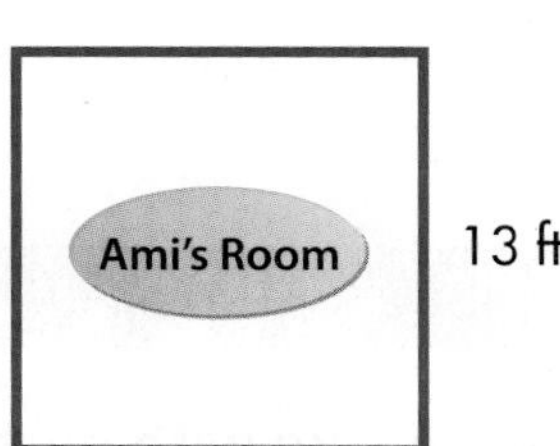

Lesson

16-3

Understand It!
Different kinds of polygons can have the same perimeter.

Different Shapes with the Same Perimeter

Hands-On
grid paper

What shapes can you make when you know the perimeter?

Kara wants to design a shape for her garden. She will use all of the fencing shown. What shape can she make?

Other Examples

Each of these shapes also has a perimeter of 14 yards.

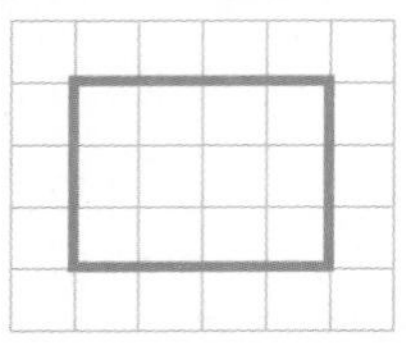

scale: ⊢⊣ = 1 yard

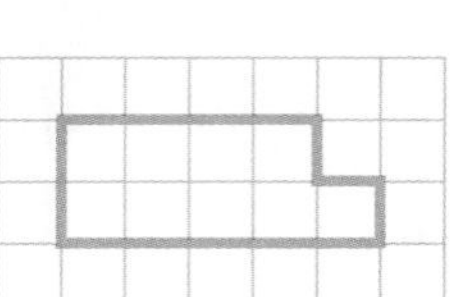

scale: ⊢⊣ = 1 yard

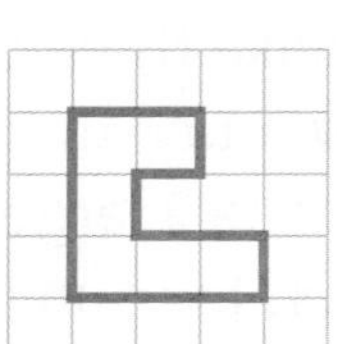

scale: ⊢⊣ = 1 yard

Guided Practice*

Do you know HOW?

Copy and complete each figure to show the given perimeter. Use grid paper.

1. A square
Perimeter = 16 ft

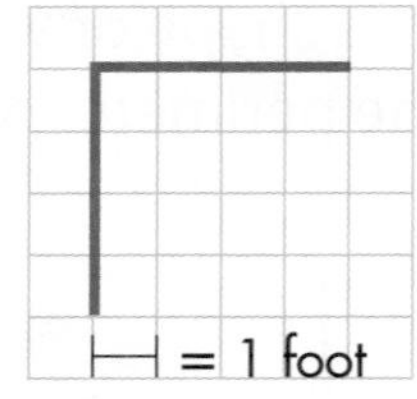

2. A 6-sided figure
Perimeter = 10 m

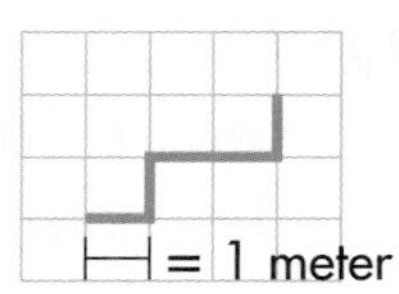

Do you UNDERSTAND?

3. Look at the examples above. Describe the lengths of the sides of a third rectangle that has a perimeter of 14 yards.

4. Mike wants to design a shape for his garden. He wants to use exactly 18 meters of fencing. Draw a shape he can make. Use grid paper.

Independent Practice

In **5–7**, draw a figure with each perimeter. Use grid paper.

5. 12 units **6.** 4 units **7.** 22 units

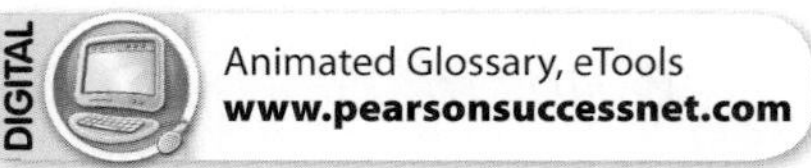

*For another example, see Set A on page 388.

Step 1

Draw a picture or use straws to act out the problem.

Each straw is 1 unit. Use 14 straws to make a shape. The perimeter of the shape is 14 units.

Then describe the shape and the length of each side.

The figure is a rectangle. Two sides are each 6 units long, and two sides are each 1 unit long.

Step 2

Check that the shape has the correct perimeter.

Add the side lengths.
6 + 1 + 6 + 1 = 14 units

Kara needs exactly 14 yards of fencing to make a rectangle with sides that are 6 yards and 1 yard.

Problem Solving

8. Darius wants to design a birthday card. He has exactly 18 inches of yarn that he wants to glue around the edge of the card. Draw a card design he can make. Use grid paper.

9. Draw 2 different shapes that have a perimeter of 24 units. Use grid paper to help.

Use the pictures at the right for **10** and **11**.

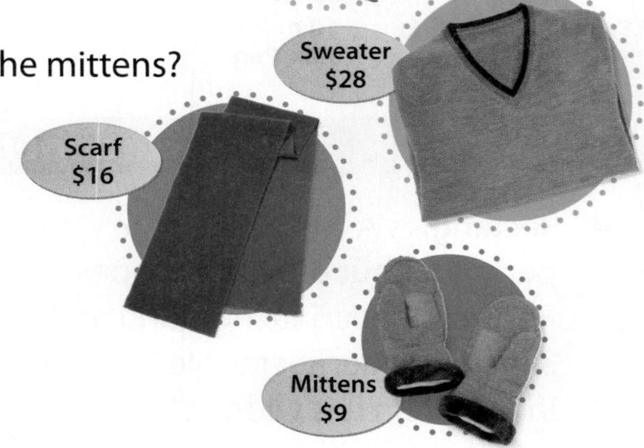

10. Aleesa bought one scarf and three hats. What was the total cost of these items?

11. How much more does a sweater cost than the mittens?

12. **Algebra** Look for a pattern in the table. Copy and complete.

Number of Tables	1	2	3	4	5	6
Number of Chairs	8	16	■	32	■	48

13. Which pair of shapes have the same perimeter?

A
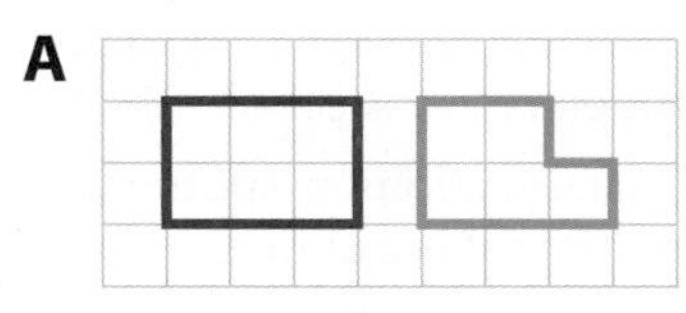

C
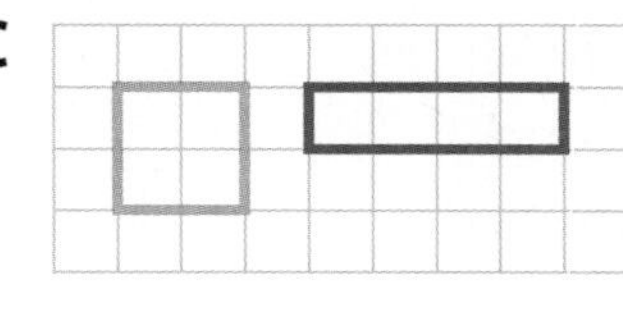

B
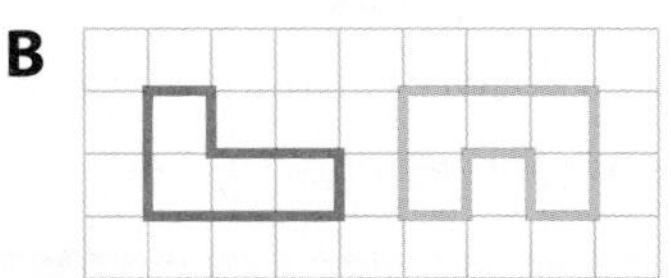

D
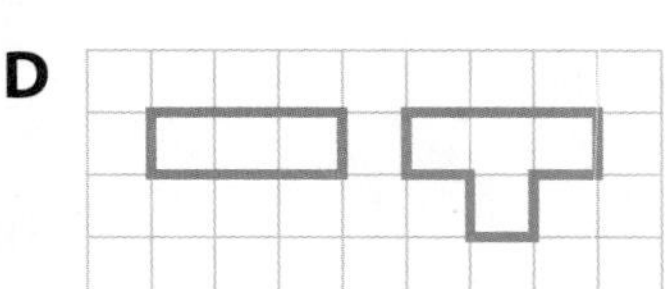

Lesson
16-4

Understand It!
The strategy Try, Check, and Revise can help you solve problems.

Problem Solving

Try, Check, and Revise

Tad, Holly, and Shana made 36 posters all together. Shana made 3 more posters than Holly.

Tad and Holly made the same number of posters. How many posters did Shana make?

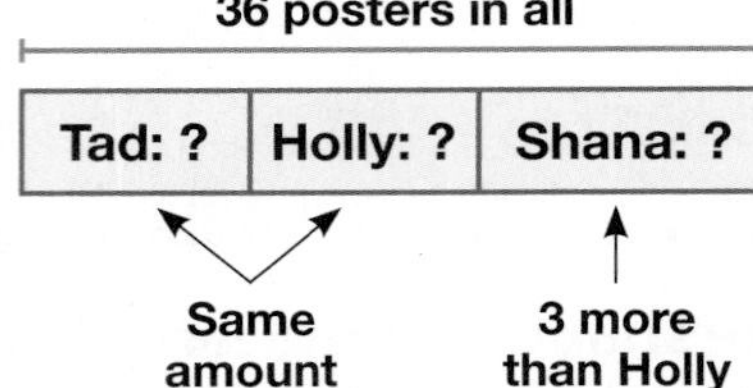

Guided Practice*

Do you know HOW?

1. Peg and Pat are sharing 64 crayons. Pat has 10 more crayons than Peg. How many crayons does each girl have?

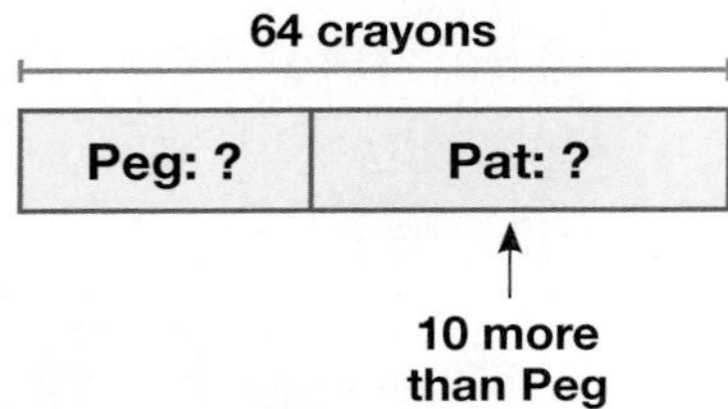

Do you UNDERSTAND?

2. Look at the diagram for Problem 1. Why aren't the two parts of the rectangle the same size?

3. **Write a Problem** Write a problem that can be solved by using reasoning to make good tries.

Independent Practice

4. Rectangles A and B have the same perimeter but different shapes. Rectangle A is 5 inches long and 3 inches wide. Rectangle B is 6 inches longer than it is wide. What are the length and width of Rectangle B?

5. Hanna has 6 coins worth 50¢ in all. Some of the coins are nickels and some are dimes. What coins does Hanna have?

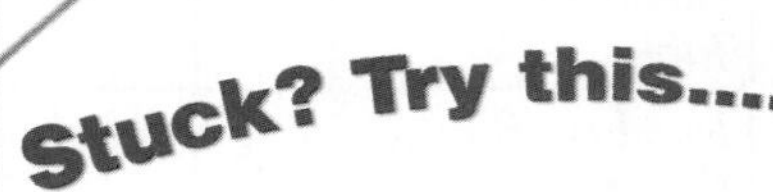

- What do I know?
- What am I asked to find?
- What diagram can I use to help understand the problem?
- Can I use addition, subtraction, multiplication, or division?
- Is all of my work correct?
- Did I answer the right question?
- Is my answer reasonable?

*For another example, see Set B on page 388.

Plan

Use reasoning to make good tries.
Then check.

Try: $10 + 10 + 13 = 33$

Check: $33 < 36$
Too low, I need 3 more.

Try: $12 + 12 + 15 = 39$

Check: $39 > 36$
Too high, I need 3 less.

Solve

Revise, using what you know.

Try: $11 + 11 + 14 = 36$

Check: $36 = 36$
This is correct.

Shana made 14 posters.

Use the pictures at the right for **6** and **7**.

6. The clerk at the flower store puts all the roses into two vases. One vase has 2 more roses than the other vase. How many roses are in each vase?

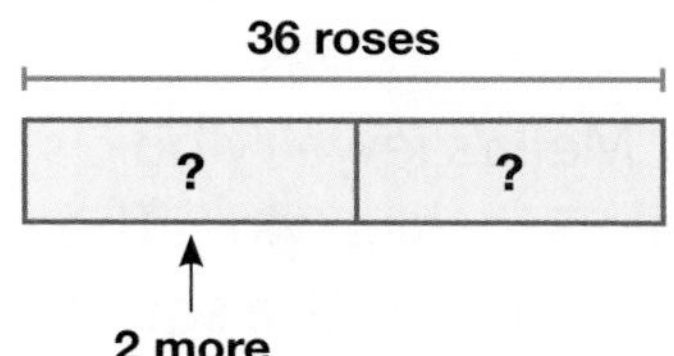

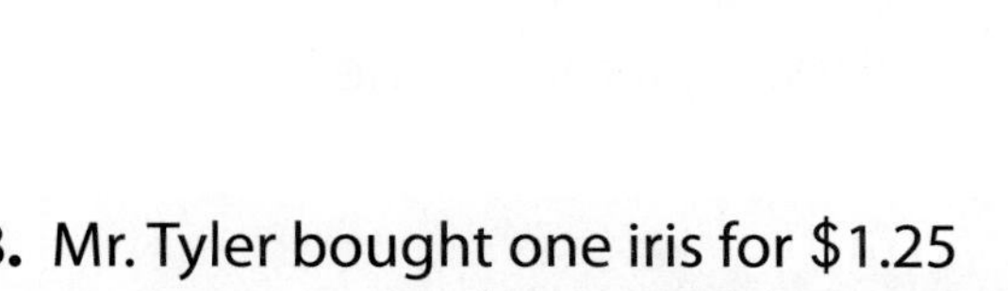

7. Edna, Jay, and Bob bought all of the carnations in the flower store. Edna bought 2 more than Jay. Bob and Jay bought the same number. How many carnations did Edna buy?

8. Mr. Tyler bought one iris for $1.25 and 3 roses for $3 each. How much did Mr. Tyler spend for the roses?

9. Cam bought an iris for $1.25. He paid with 6 coins. What coins did he use?

10. A rectangle has a perimeter of 48 inches. Which of the following pairs of numbers could be the length and width of the rectangle?

A 12 inches and 10 inches

B 8 inches and 6 inches

C 20 inches and 4 inches

D 15 inches and 5 inches

11. Kevin read that there are 22 types of crocodiles and alligators in all. There are 6 more types of crocodiles than alligators. How many types of crocodiles are there? How many types of alligators are there?

Lesson

16-5

Understand It!
Area is measured in square units.

Understanding Area

Hands-On: square tiles

How do you find area?

Raj needs to know how many tiles to buy to cover a floor. What is the area of the floor?

Area is the number of square units needed to cover the region inside a figure. A square unit is a square with sides that are each 1 unit long.

☐ = 1 square unit

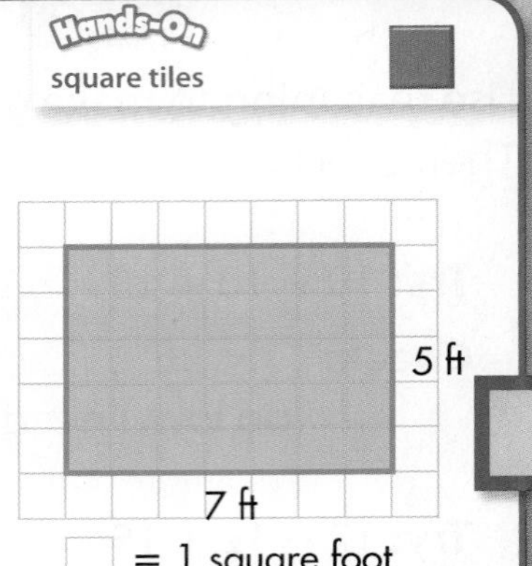

Guided Practice*

Do you know HOW?

In **1** and **2**, find the area of each figure. Use square tiles or grid paper to help.

1.

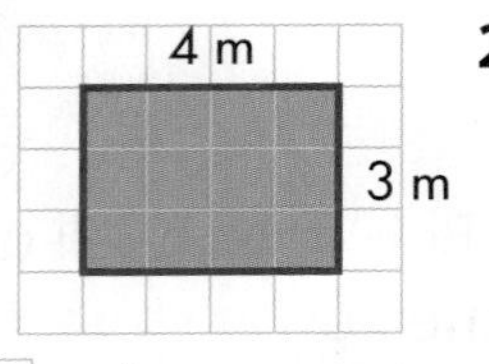

2.

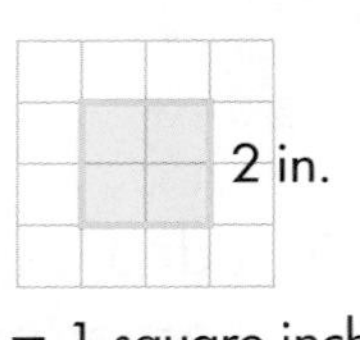

Do you UNDERSTAND?

3. Use the example above. Explain how finding the area of a figure is different from finding the perimeter.

4. The lid of Mella's jewelry box is a rectangle 3 inches wide. The area is 15 square inches. Use square tiles to make a model or grid paper to draw a picture of the lid.

Independent Practice

In **5–10**, find the area of each figure.

5.

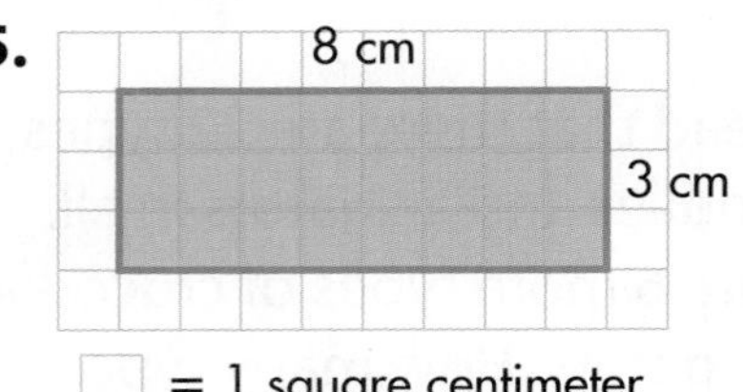

6.

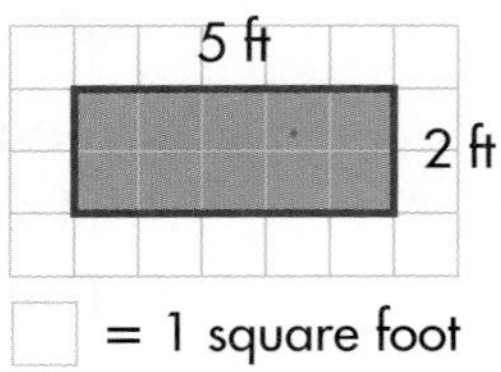

7.

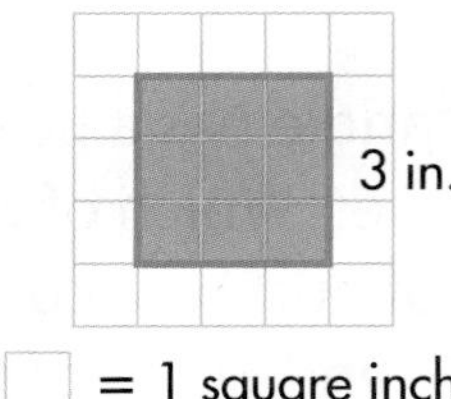

8.

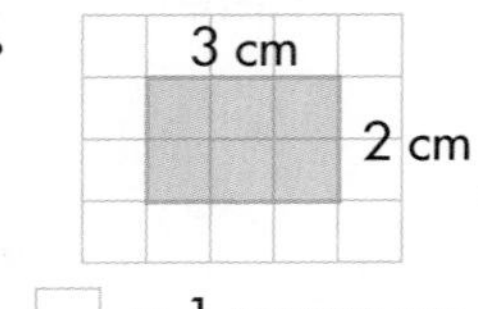

9.

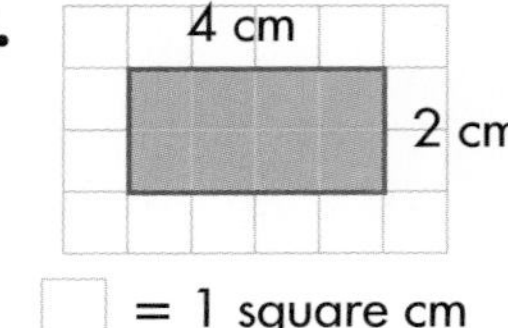

10.

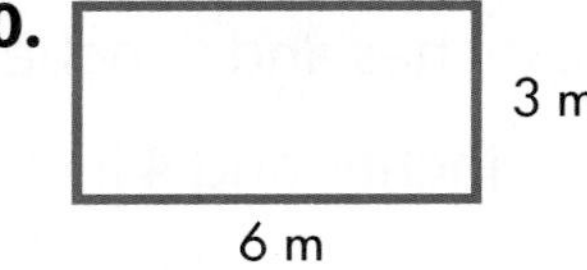

*For another example, see Set C on page 389.

One Way

Count the square units.

There are 35 square units inside the figure.

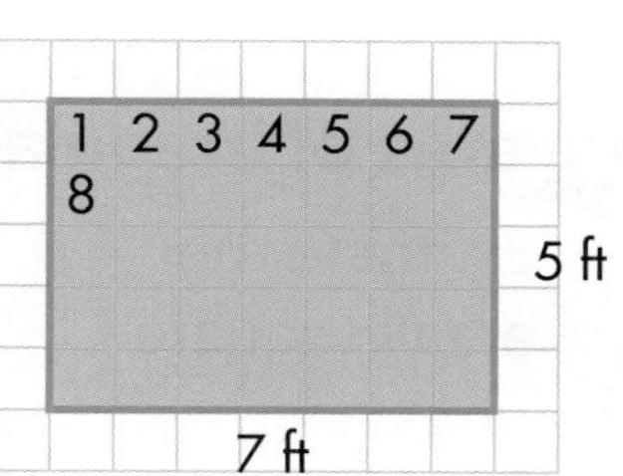

The lengths are given in feet. The area of the floor is 35 square feet.

Another Way

When you find the area of a rectangle or square, you can think of the grid squares as an array.

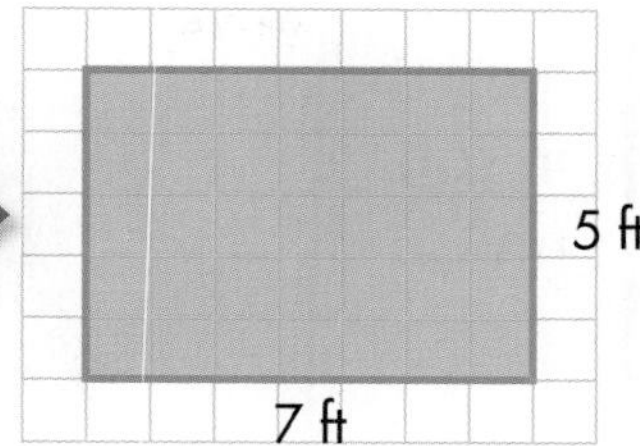

There are 5 rows with 7 squares in each row.

$5 \times 7 = 35$

The area of the floor is 35 square feet.

Problem Solving

A gallery is planning a display of animal photographs. Use the picture at the right for **11–13**.

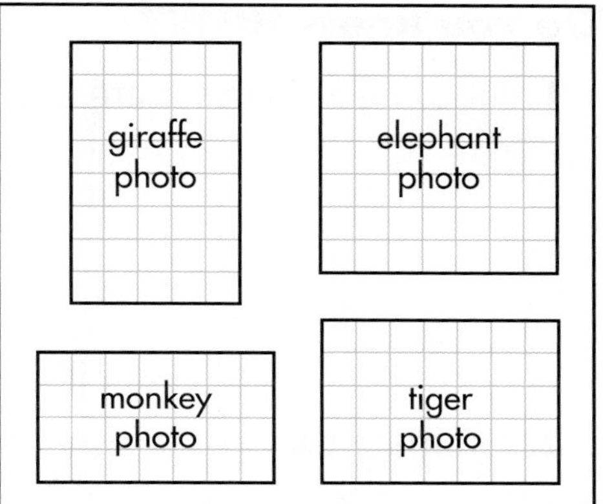

11. Find the area of each photo in square units.

12. Use grid paper. Draw a rectangle that has a smaller area than the giraffe photo and a greater area than the monkey photo.

13. Which has the greater perimeter, the photo of the giraffe or the photo of the tiger? How many units greater is it?

14. Use grid paper. Draw two different figures, each with an area of 24 square units. Find the perimeter of each figure.

15. **Writing to Explain** Tamiya cut a 12-inch piece of string into 3 equal parts. She also cut a 24-inch piece of ribbon into 8 equal parts. Which was longer, a piece of the string or a piece of the ribbon? Explain how you decided.

16. What is the area of the picture Abe made with square tiles?

A 20 square inches

B 21 square inches

C 24 square inches

D 30 square inches

□ = 1 square inch

Lesson

16-6

Understand It!
To find area, count squares. If there are partial squares, combine them to estimate area.

Estimating and Measuring Area

Hands-On
grid paper

How do you find and estimate area of irregular shapes?

Find the area in square units.

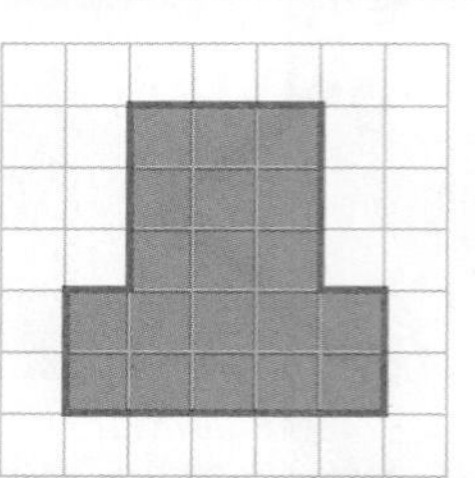

Estimate the area in square units.

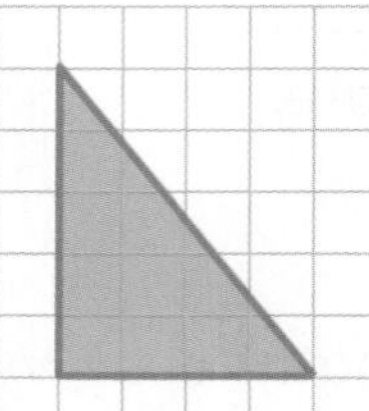

Guided Practice*

Do you know HOW?

1. Find the area in square units.

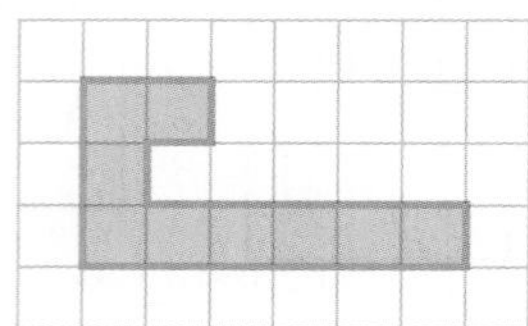

2. Estimate the area in square units.

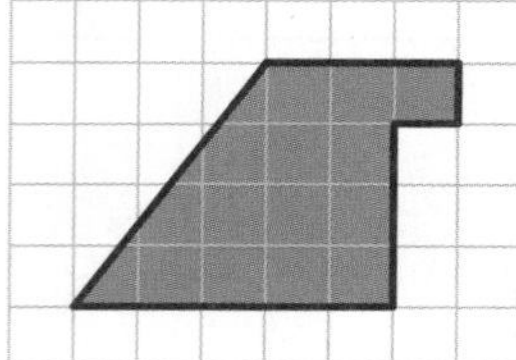

Do you UNDERSTAND?

3. Will partial squares always combine to form whole squares? Why or why not?

4. Kev needs to find the area of the floor so that he knows the number of tiles to buy to cover it. What is the area of the floor?

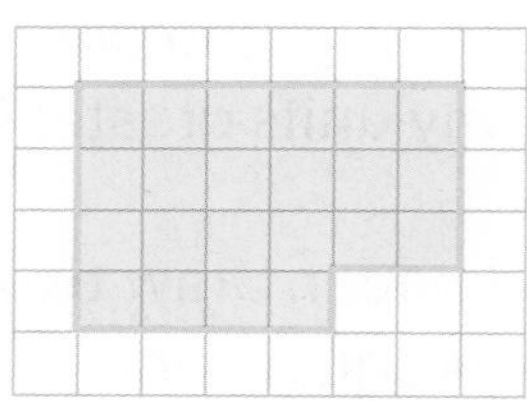

Independent Practice

In **5–7**, find each area in square units.

5.

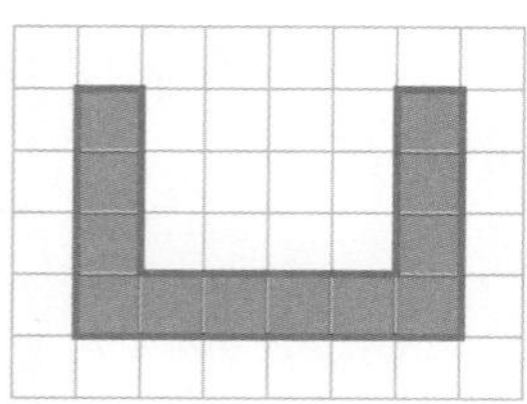

6.

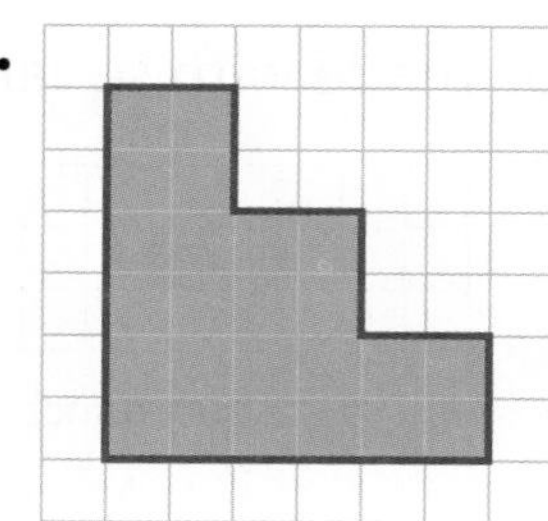

7.

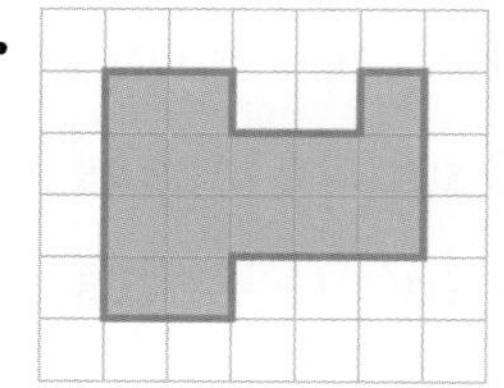

*For another example, see Set C on page 389.

To find the area, count the squares.

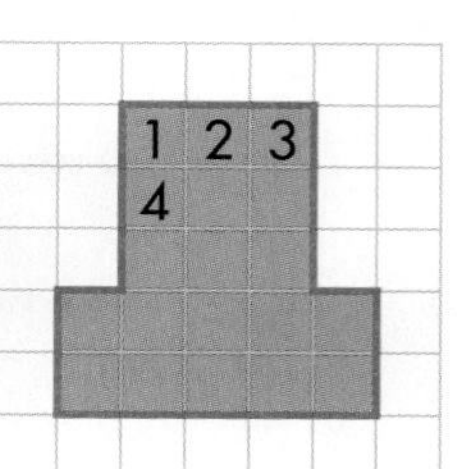

There are 19 square units.

The area is 19 square units.

To estimate the area, count whole squares first.

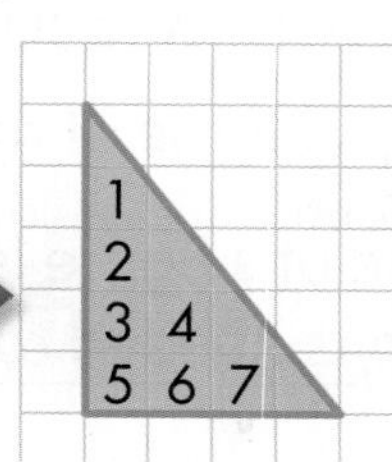

There are 7 whole squares.

Combine partial squares to make whole squares.

The partial squares make up about 3 whole squares.

$7 + 3 = 10$

The area is about 10 square units.

In **8–10**, estimate each area in square units.

8.

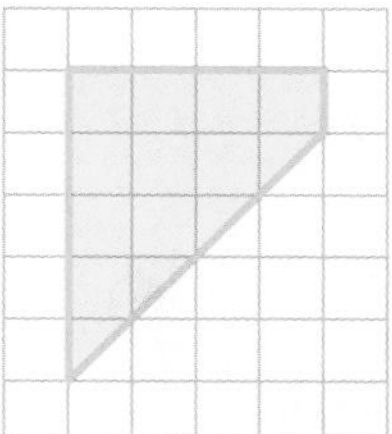

9.

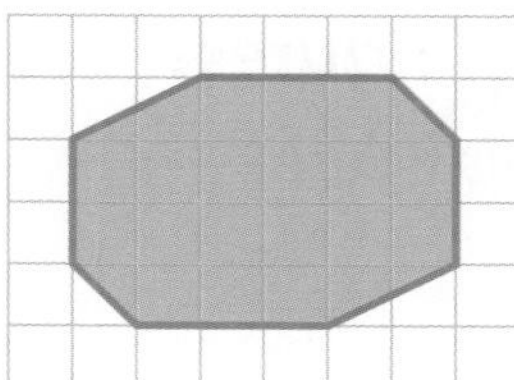

10.

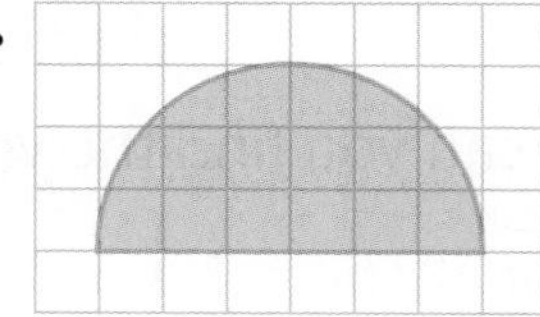

Problem Solving

11. Chen will use tiles to make a picture. He needs to estimate the area of the picture so that he buys enough tiles. Estimate the area of Chen's picture.

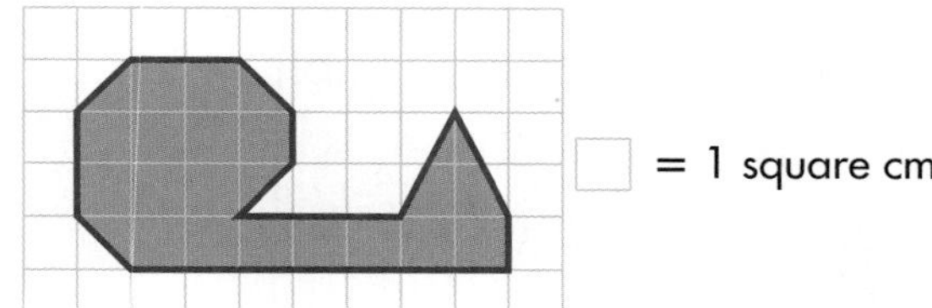

12. Suni put blue tiles on a wall. What is the area of the part of the wall with blue tiles?

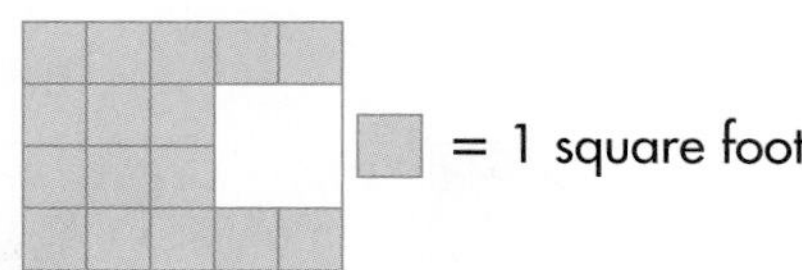

A 4 square feet

B 12 square feet

C 16 square feet

D 20 square feet

13. **Writing to Explain** Joe says the area of this chessboard is between 1 and 2 square inches. Do you agree? Explain.

Each side of this chessboard is $1\frac{1}{4}$ inches long.

scale: ☐ = 1 sq. in.

14. **Reasonableness** Bobby estimated that the sum of $138 and $241 is about $480. Is his estimate reasonable? Explain.

Lesson
16-7

Understand It!
Volume is measured in cubic units.

Volume

Hands-On
unit cubes

How can you measure the space inside a solid figure?

What is the volume of the box?

The volume of a figure is the number of cubic units needed to fill it.

A cubic unit is a cube with edges that are 1 unit long.

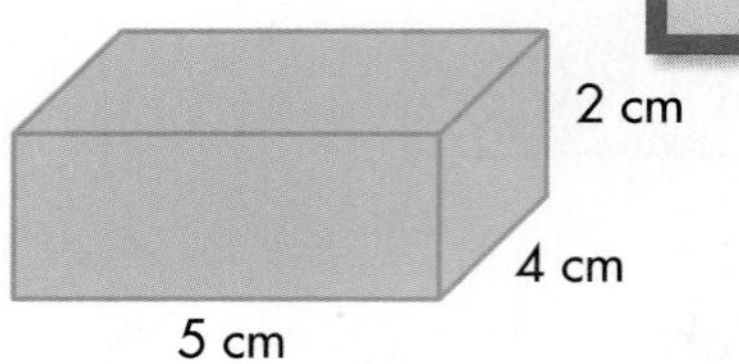

Another Example How can you measure the volume of other kinds of figures?

How can you find the volume of this figure?

Count all the cubes.

The figure has 2 rows of cubes.
There are 8 cubes in the back row.
There are 2 more cubes in the front row.
8 cubes + 2 cubes = 10 cubes

So the volume is 10 cubic units.

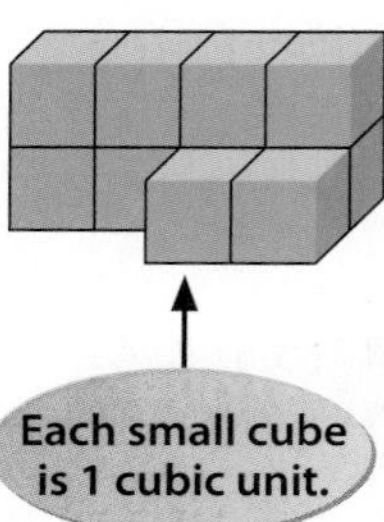

Each small cube is 1 cubic unit.

Explain It

1. Describe how to find the volume of the figure below.

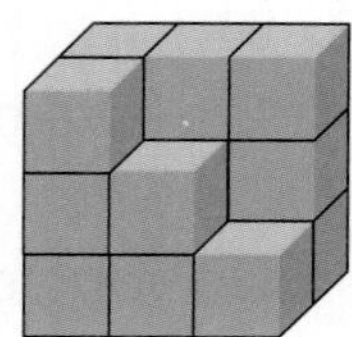

For **2** and **3**, use the figures at the right.

2. How are these two figures the same? How are they different?
3. Find the volume of each of the two figures.

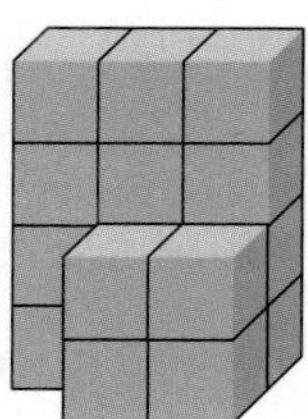

Step 1

Make a model of the box using cubes.

The box is measured in centimeters.

The volume will be in cubic centimeters.

Step 2

Count all the cubes in 1 layer.

There are 20 cubes in each layer.
There are 2 layers.
20 cubes + 20 cubes = 40 cubes

Since there are 40 cubes, the volume is 40 cubic centimeters.

Guided Practice*

Do you know HOW?

Find the volume of each figure in cubic units. You may use unit cubes to help.

1. 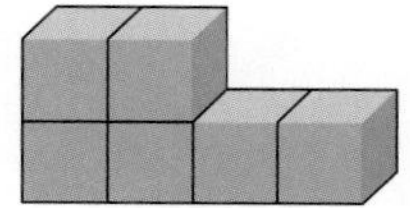

2. 

3. 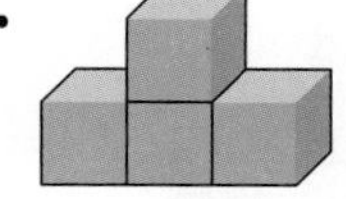

4. 

Do you UNDERSTAND?

5. How do you know the volume of the box above is 40 cubic centimeters and not 40 cubic meters?

6. Pedro has a box that is 4 inches long, 4 inches wide, and 2 inches tall. A model of the box is shown below. What is the volume of the box?

Each cube is one cubic inch.

Independent Practice

For **7–9**, find the volume of each figure in cubic units.

7. 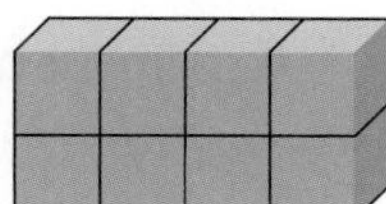

8. 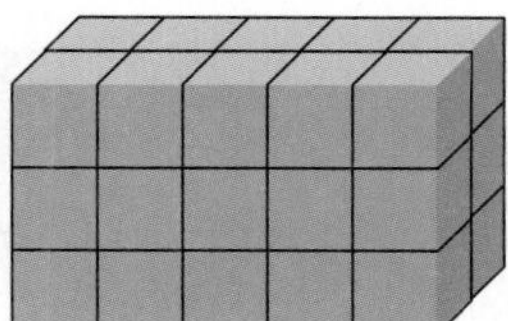

9. 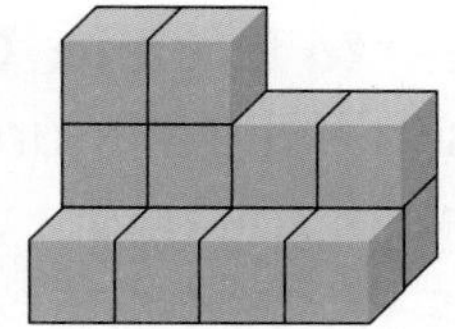

Animated Glossary, eTools
www.pearsonsuccessnet.com

*For another example, see Set D on page 389.

Independent Practice

For **10–12**, find the volume of each figure in cubic units.

10. 

11. 

12. 

Problem Solving

13. Estimation Use the cubes shown at the right to estimate the volume of the rectangular prism.

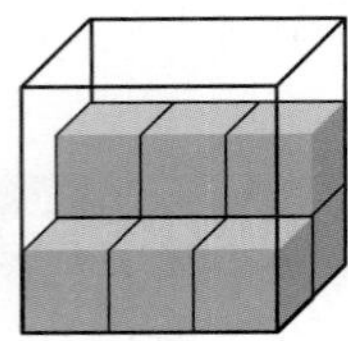

14. Derek made a rectangular prism with 4 layers of cubes. He put 5 cubes in each layer. What is the volume of the rectangular prism?

15. Draw or describe two different solid figures, each with a volume of 16 cubic units.

16. Reasoning One rectangular prism has 3 cubes in each of 7 layers. Another rectangular prism has 7 cubes in each of 3 layers. Which prism has the greater volume?

17. Dana has a jewelry box that looks like the model at the right. What is the volume of the jewelry box?

Each [cube] = 1 cubic inch.

A 25 cubic inches

B 34 cubic inches

C 39 cubic inches

D 45 cubic inches

18. Writing to Explain Carmen used cubes to build a figure. She said the volume of the figure was 15 square inches. Was she correct? Explain why or why not.

19. Tessa drinks 9 cups of water each day. In one week, how many cups of water does Tessa drink?

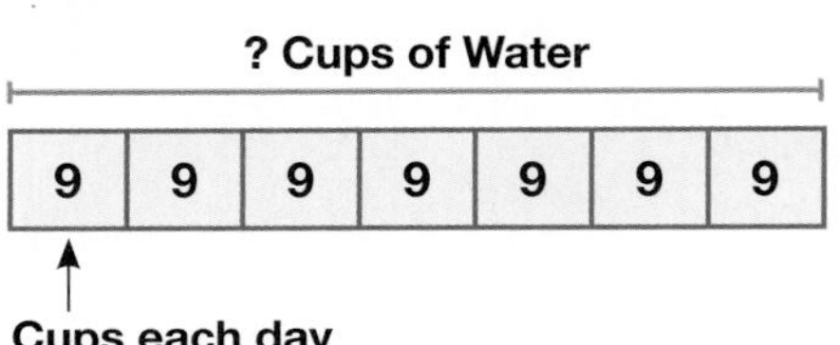

Perimeter and Area

Use e tools

Geometry Drawing

Draw a polygon with an area of 8 square units. Find the perimeter.

Step 1 Go to the Geometry Drawing eTool. Select the Geoboard workspace. Then click on the polygon drawing tool. Click on one point in the workspace. Drag the mouse to a second point 4 units down and click again. Drag the mouse to a point 2 units to the right and click. Drag the mouse 4 units up and click. Finally, drag the mouse 2 units left and click on point A.

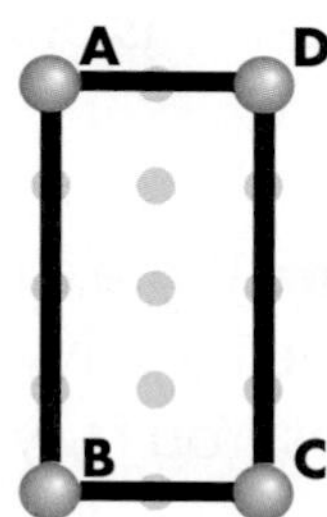

Step 2 Click on the area measurement tool icon and then on the rectangle you just drew. In the lower right corner, under Measurements, the area will appear. Make sure it is 8.00 square units. The area is 8 square units.

Step 3 Click on the perimeter measurement tool icon and then on the rectangle you just drew. In the lower right corner, under Measurements, the perimeter will appear. Make sure it is 12.00 units. The perimeter is 12 units.

Practice

1. Draw two other polygons with an area of 8 square units each. Find the perimeter of each.

2. Use the broom icon to clear the workspace. Draw two polygons with an area of 9 square units each. Find the perimeter of each.

Lesson
16-8

Understand It!
Some problems can be solved by solving a simpler problem first.

Problem Solving

Solve a Simpler Problem

Janet wants to paint the door to her room. The shaded part of the figure shows the part of the door that needs paint.

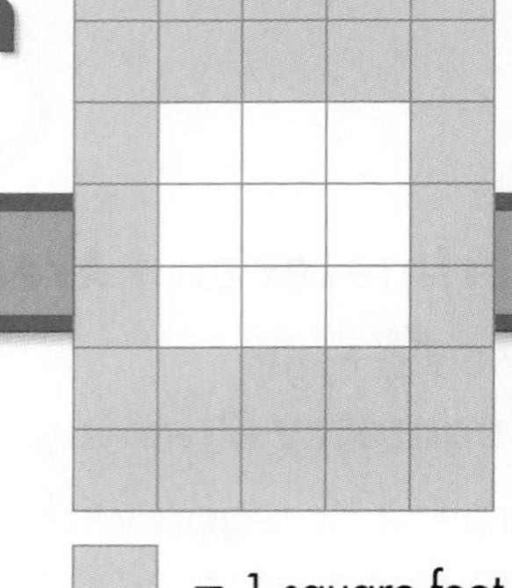

What is the area of the part of the door that needs paint?

Guided Practice*

Do you know HOW?

Solve. Use simpler problems.

1. Lil glued square beads on the shaded part of the frame. What is the area of the part she decorated?

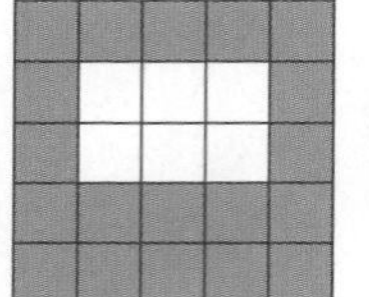

Do you UNDERSTAND?

2. What simpler problems did you use to solve Exercise 1?

3. **Write a Problem** Write a problem that you can solve by solving simpler problems. You may draw a picture to help.

Independent Practice

For **4–8**, solve. Use simpler problems.

4. Reg wants to put tiles on a wall. The shaded part of the figure shows the part that needs tiles. What is the area of the shaded part?

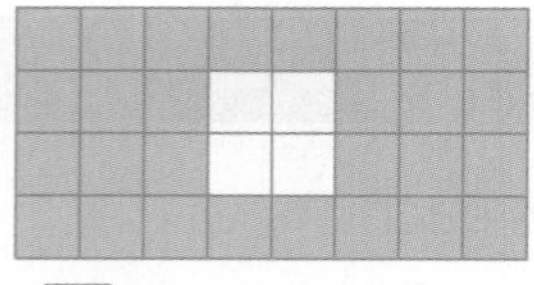

Stuck? Try this....

- What do I know?
- What am I asked to find?
- What diagram can I use to help understand the problem?
- Can I use addition, subtraction, multiplication, or division?
- Is all of my work correct?
- Did I answer the right question?
- Is my answer reasonable?

*For another example, see Set E on page 389.

Plan

I can solve simpler problems.

I can find the area of the whole rectangle and then the area of the square.

Then I can subtract to find the area of the shaded part.

Solve

Area of the whole rectangle
7 rows with 5 squares in each row
$7 \times 5 = 35$

Area of the square
3 rows with 3 squares in each row
$3 \times 3 = 9$

Subtract
$35 - 9 = 26$

The area of the part of the door that needs paint is 26 square feet.

5. Jim wants to tile the floor. The shaded part of the figure shows the part of the floor that needs tiles. What is the area of the shaded part?

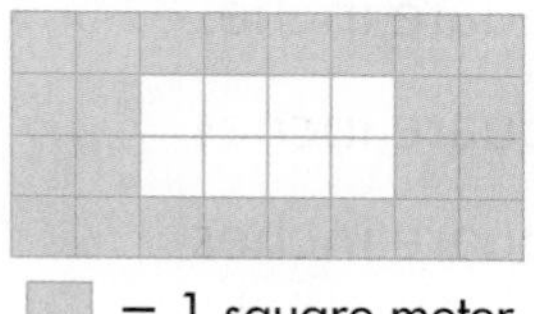

= 1 square meter

6. Dan wants to paint the bottom of a pool. The shaded part of the figure shows the part that needs paint. What is the area of the shaded part?

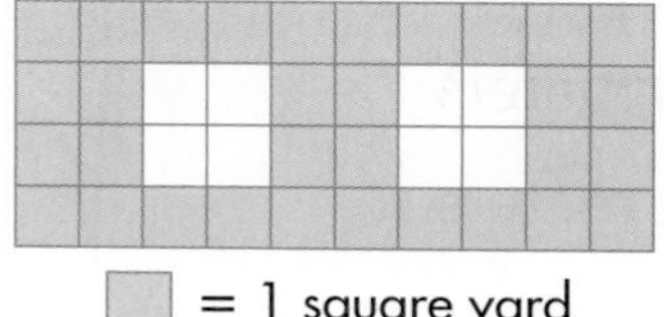

= 1 square yard

7. Macy drew two designs. How much greater is the area of the yellow figure than the area of the green figure?

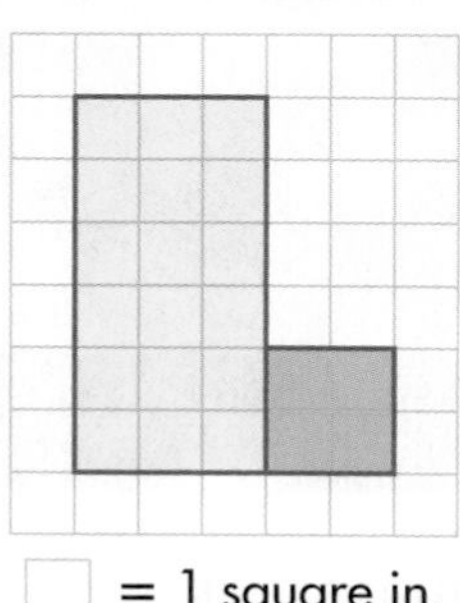

= 1 square in.

8. Mr. Eli grows vegetables in different fields on his farm. What is the total area of the corn and bean fields?

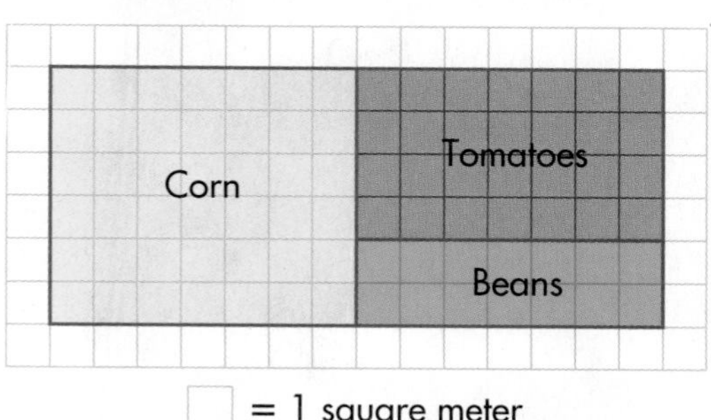

= 1 square meter

9. Neva built these figures using toothpicks. If she continues the pattern, how many toothpicks in all will she use for the 4th figure? the 5th figure?

1st figure

2nd figure

3rd figure

Test

1. A drawing of the rose garden in the park is shown. What is the perimeter of the rose garden? (16-1)

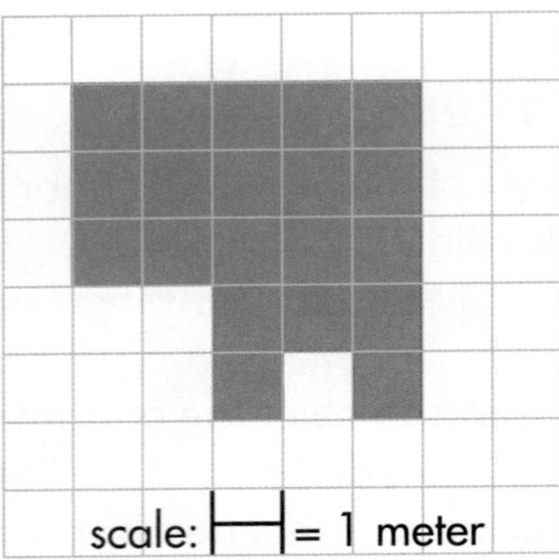

A 26 meters

B 24 meters

C 22 meters

D 20 meters

2. The patio in Marta's backyard is in the shape of a square. What is the perimeter of the patio? (16-2)

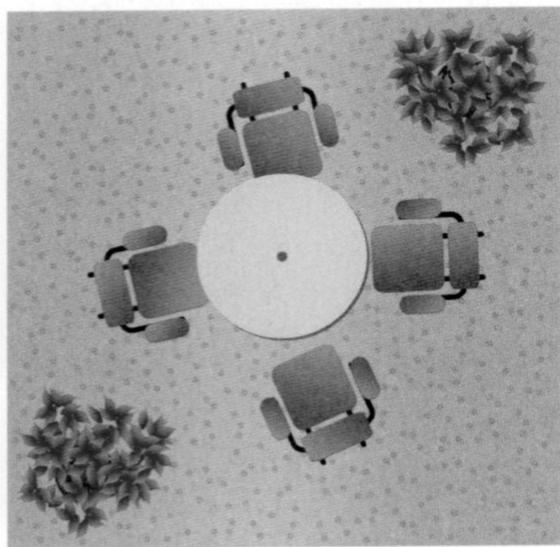

A 144 feet

B 48 feet

C 36 feet

D 24 feet

3. Mrs. Gomez made a quilt for her daughter's doll. What is the area of the doll's quilt? (16-5)

= 1 square inch

A 50 square inches

B 45 square inches

C 40 square inches

D 30 square inches

4. A swimming pool is drawn below. How many square feet of green tile are around the pool? (16-8)

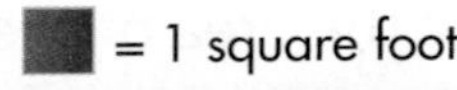

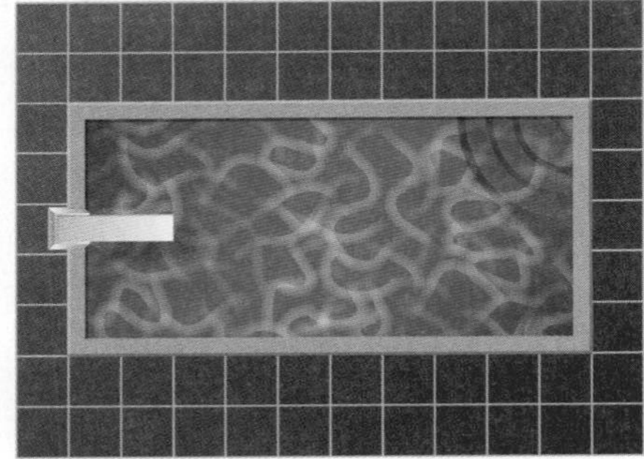

A 108 square feet

B 63 square feet

C 58 square feet

D 50 square feet

5. A model of the box that a toy came in is shown below. What is the volume of the box? (16-7)

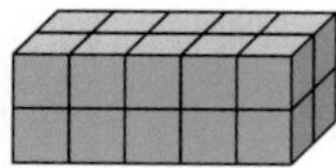

A 15 cubic units

B 16 cubic units

C 20 cubic units

D 24 cubic units

6. Which is the best estimate of the area of the shape shown below? (16-6)

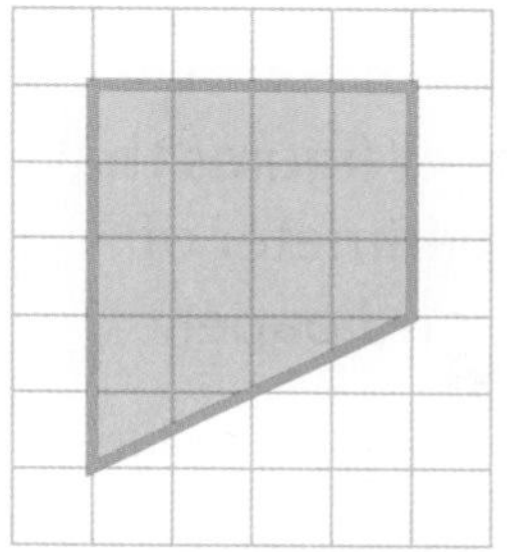

A 23 square inches

B 20 square inches

C 18 square inches

D 16 square inches

7. What is the volume of this figure? (16-7)

A 24 cubic units

B 18 cubic units

C 14 cubic units

D 8 cubic units

8. Each of the 26 students in Carrie's class chose either drums or horns to play during music class. If 4 more students chose drums than horns, how many chose each? (16-4)

A 16 chose drums, 10 chose horns

B 15 chose drums, 11 chose horns

C 14 chose drums, 12 chose horns

D 14 chose drums, 10 chose horns

9. Eugene's garden design is shown below.

Which other design has the same perimeter as Eugene's garden design? (16-3)

A

B

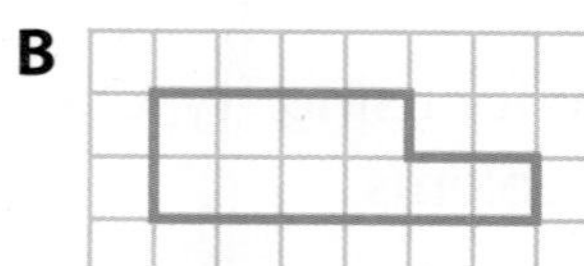

C

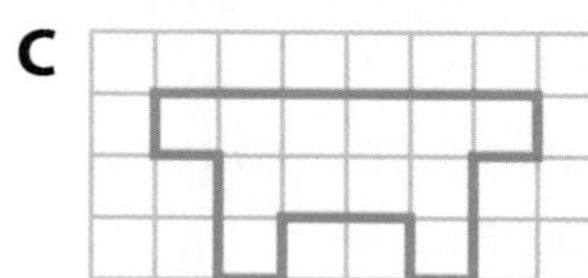

D

Reteaching

Set A, pages 368–373

What is the perimeter of each figure?

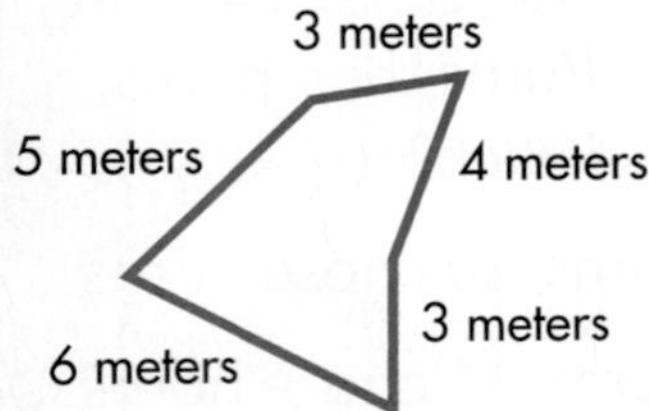

Add the lengths of the sides.

3 + 4 + 3 + 6 + 5 = 21 meters

The perimeter is 21 meters.

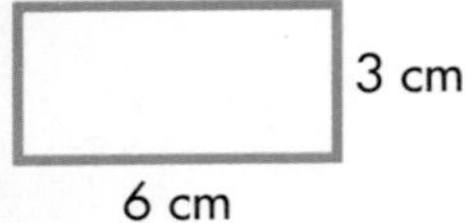

Opposite sides of a rectangle are the same length.

6 + 3 + 6 + 3 = 18

The perimeter is 18 centimeters.

Remember that different shapes can have the same perimeter.

Find the perimeter.

1.

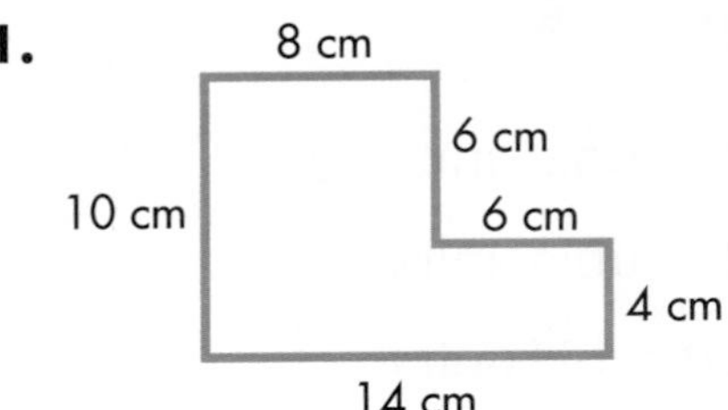

2.

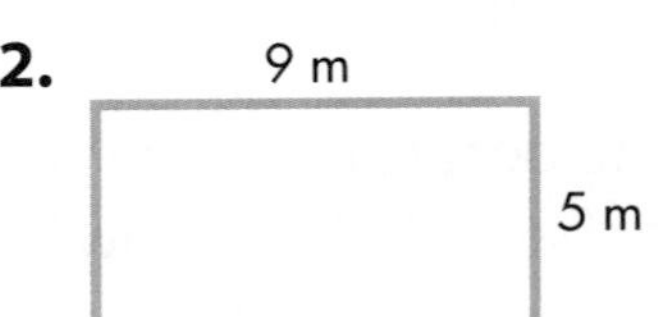

3. Draw 2 different figures that each have a perimeter of 16 units. Use grid paper.

Set B, pages 374–375

Follow these steps for using Try, Check, and Revise to solve problems.

Step 1 Think to make a reasonable first try.

Step 2 Check, using information from the problem.

Step 3 Revise. Use your first try to make a reasonable second try. Check.

Step 4 Continue trying and checking until you find the correct answer.

Remember to check each try.

Use Try, Check, and Revise to solve.

1. Ray and Tony have 32 markers. Ray has 2 more markers than Tony. How many markers does each boy have?

2. The soccer club has 28 members. There are 4 more girls than boys. How many boys are in the soccer club?

Set C, pages 376–379

What is the area of the rectangle?

For a rectangle or square, think of an array.
To estimate area, you can count whole squares and combine partial squares to make whole squares.

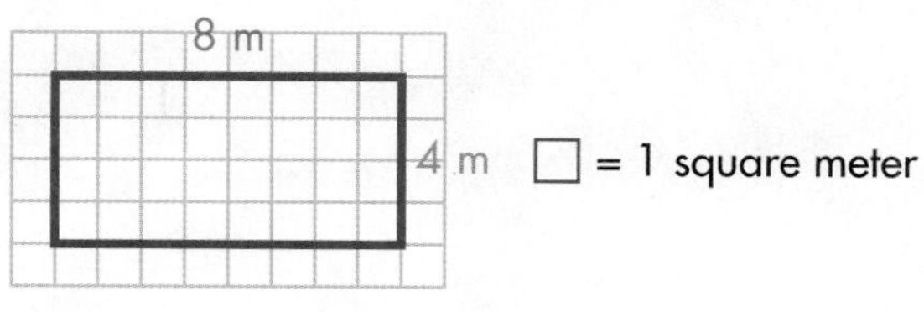

$4 \times 8 = 32$

The area of the rectangle is 32 square meters.

Remember to give area measurements in square units.

1. Find the area of this figure.

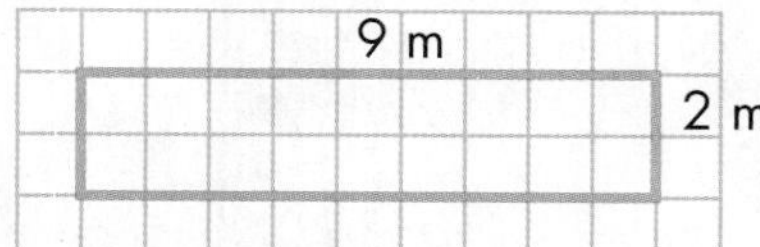

2. Estimate the area of this figure in square units.

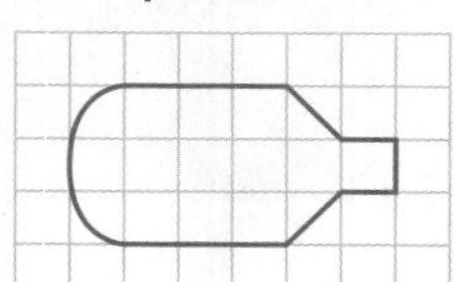

Set D, pages 380–382

What is the volume of the figure in cubic units?

Count the cubes in each floor. Then add.

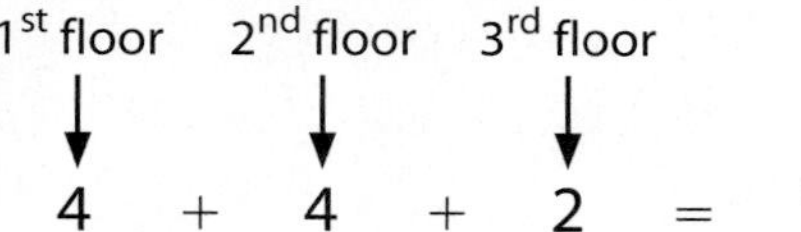

The volume is 10 cubic units.

Remember to count all the cubes, even the ones you can't see.

Find the volume of each figure. Write your answers in cubic units.

1. 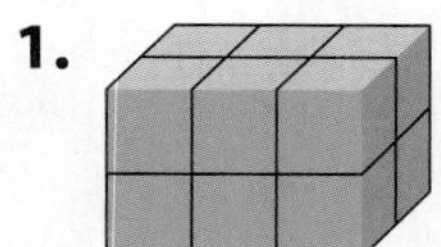

2. 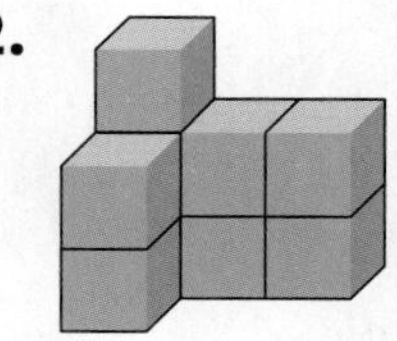

Set E, pages 384–385

Use simpler problems to find the area of the shaded part of the rectangle.

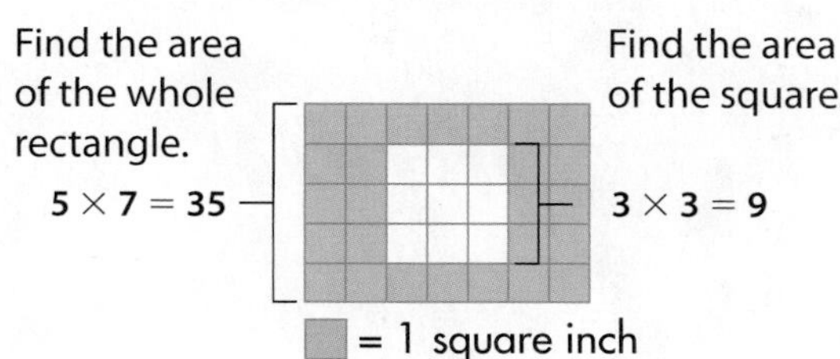

Subtract: $35 - 9 = 26$

The area of the shaded part of the rectangle is 26 square inches.

Remember to use the answers to the simpler problems.

1. Solve. Use simpler problems.

   Walt wants to paint a wall. The shaded part of the wall is the part that needs blue paint. What is the area of the shaded part?

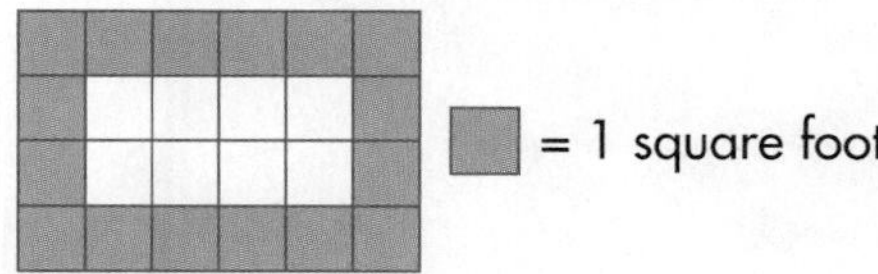

Topic 17

Time and Temperature

1 The sailfish is the fastest swimmer of all fish. How fast can a sailfish swim? You will find out in Lesson 17-3.

2 How quickly does a Venus flytrap close after catching its next meal? You will find out in Lesson 17-6.

3

How long does the Hubble Telescope take to orbit Earth? You will find out in Lesson 17-2.

4

What is the year-round temperature in Carlsbad Caverns? You will find out in Lesson 17-5.

Review What You Know!

Vocabulary

Choose the best term from the box.

- hour
- o'clock
- minute
- thermometer

1. Luz read the time. She saw that the time was nine ___?___.
2. It takes about one ___?___ for Anita to tie her shoelaces.
3. Corey will read the ___?___ to tell his friend in another state how warm it is.

Time

Write each time.

4. 

5. 

Temperature

Write whether each temperature is hot or cold.

6. 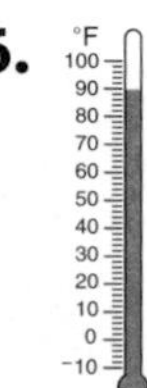

7. 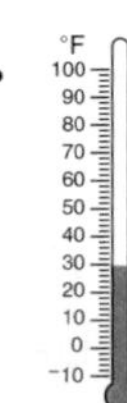

8. **Writing to Explain** Draw a clock face. Draw the hour hand on the 8 and the minute hand on the 12. Write the time. Explain how to read the time on a clock.

Lesson

17-1

Understand It!
Time can be measured in half hours and in quarter hours.

Time to the Half Hour and Quarter Hour

How do you tell time to the nearest half hour or quarter hour?

The clocks show the time that the bus arrives at school and the time it leaves.

Data

Units of Time		
1 day	=	24 hours
1 hour	=	60 minutes
1 half hour	=	30 minutes
1 quarter hour	=	15 minutes
1 minute	=	60 seconds

Bus Arrives

8:30

Bus Leaves

2:45

Another Example **How do you decide whether the time is A.M. or P.M.?**

The hours of the day between midnight and noon are A.M. hours.
The hours between noon and midnight are P.M. hours.

Would the time the bus arrives at school more likely be 8:30 A.M. or 8:30 P.M.?

8:30 P.M. is in the evening. The bus probably would not arrive at school in the evening. 8:30 A.M. is in the morning.

The bus would more likely arrive at school at 8:30 A.M.

Would the time the bus leaves school more likely be 2:45 A.M. or 2:45 P.M.?

2:45 A.M. is in the middle of the night. The bus probably would not be leaving school at that time. 2:45 P.M. is in the afternoon.

The bus would more likely leave school at 2:45 P.M.

Explain It

1. Why might it be important to use A.M. or P.M. when you give a time?
2. Would you be more likely to leave your home to go to school at 8:15 A.M. or 8:15 P.M.?
3. Would you be more likely to eat lunch at 12:30 A.M. or 12:30 P.M.?

Tell the time the bus arrives.

Write 8:30 in three other ways.

When the minute hand is on the 6, you can say the time is "half past" the hour.

The bus arrives at *eight thirty*, or *half past eight*, or *30 minutes past eight*.

Tell the time the bus leaves.

Write 2:45 in three other ways.

When the minute hand is on the 9, you can say the time is "15 minutes to" or "quarter to" the hour.

The bus leaves at *two forty-five*, or *15 minutes to three*, or *quarter to three*.

Guided Practice*

Do you know HOW?

In **1** and **2**, write the time shown on each clock in two ways.

1. 

2. 

Do you UNDERSTAND?

3. In the example above, why do you think the fraction word "quarter" is used for the time when the minute hand is on the 9?

4. The clock shows the time that Etta's skating lesson starts. What time does it start? Give the time in 3 ways.

Independent Practice

In **5–7**, write the time shown on each clock in two ways.

5. 

6. 

7. 

DIGITAL Animated Glossary **www.pearsonsuccessnet.com**

**For another example, see Set A on page 408.*

Independent Practice

In **8–10**, write the time shown on each clock in two ways.

8. 

9. 

10. 

Problem Solving

11. The clocks below show the time that the Flying Horse Carousel in Rhode Island opens and closes. What time does the carousel open? What time does it close?

Opens 

Closes 

12. Writing to Explain Mr. Boyd gave his students a math test at 10:45. Explain why this time is most likely an A.M. time.

For **13–16**, use the table at the right.

13. Estimation Whose bowling score was about 20 points less than Beth's?

14. Whose bowling score was 15 points more than Cal's?

15. What is the order of the friends' names from greatest to least score?

Data

Bowling Scores

Name	Score
Cal	63
Beth	78
Rusty	59
Pang	82

16. Algebra Write a number sentence that compares the total of Cal's and Beth's scores with the total of Rusty's and Pang's scores.

17. Ronaldo delivers a newspaper to the Hong family between 7:00 A.M. and 8:00 A.M. each day. Which clock shows a time between 7:00 A.M. and 8:00 A.M.?

A 

B 

C 

D 

Enrichment

Roman Numerals

The symbols for numbers, or numerals, used by the ancient Romans are still seen today on some clock faces and buildings. They are used as page numbers at the front of many books, including this one.

Roman numeral	I	V	X	L	C	D	M
Decimal value	1	5	10	50	100	500	1,000

Our number system is called the decimal system. It is based on place value. Roman numerals are based on addition and subtraction.

How to read Roman numerals:

VI = 5 + 1 = 6 When the symbol for the smaller number is written to the right of the greater number, add. No more than three symbols for smaller numbers are used this way.

IV = 5 − 1 = 4 When the symbol for a smaller number is to the left of the greater number, subtract. No more than one symbol for a smaller number is used this way.

Practice

Write each as a decimal number.

1. VII **2.** XX **3.** CV **4.** XIV **5.** LI

6. XXI **7.** XIX **8.** DC **9.** CM **10.** MC

Write each as a Roman numeral.

11. 15 **12.** 30 **13.** 9 **14.** 52 **15.** 60

16. 6 **17.** 110 **18.** 400 **19.** 550 **20.** 40

21. In Roman numerals, the year 1990 is written as MCMXC, and 2007 is written as MMVII. Write the current year using Roman numerals.

22. One movie was made in the year MMIV. Another movie was made in the year MCML. How many years passed between these years?

Lesson
17-2

Understand It!
Time can be measured to the minute and read on a clock by skip counting by 5s and counting on by 1s.

Time to the Minute

How do you tell time to the nearest minute?

The clock shows the time a train is scheduled to arrive at Pinewood Station. What time is the train scheduled to arrive? Give the time in digital form and in two other ways.

Guided Practice*

Do you know HOW?

In **1** and **2**, write the time shown on each clock in two ways.

1.

2.

Do you UNDERSTAND?

3. **Reasoning** In the example above, why is 42 minutes past 12 the same as 18 minutes to 1? Explain.

4. The clock below shows the time that an airplane landed. Write the time in two ways.

Independent Practice

In **5–7**, write the time shown on each clock in two ways.

5.

6.

7.

*For another example, see Set A on page 408.

Step 1

The hour hand is between 12 and 1. The time is after 12:00 and before 1:00.

Step 2

In 5 minutes, the minute hand moves from one number to the next.

Count by 5s from the 12 to the 8: 40 minutes

Step 3

In 1 minute, the minute hand moves from one mark to the next. After counting by 5s, count two minutes more.

The digital time is 12:42. It is 42 minutes past 12 or 18 minutes to 1.

Problem Solving

8. Toya's family went to see a movie. The clock shows the time that the movie ended. Write the digital time.

9. The Hubble Space Telescope has been moving in its orbit for 1 hour. In 37 more minutes it will complete an orbit. How many minutes does it take the Hubble Space Telescope to complete 1 orbit?

10. **Geometry** Enzo used grid paper to draw a model of a triangle he will paint on a wall. His drawing is shown at the right. Estimate the area of the figure.

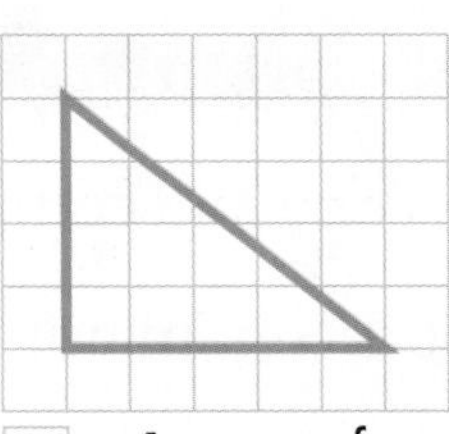

11. **Writing to Explain** Which figure has a greater area, a square with a side length of 4 feet or the triangle Enzo drew? Explain how you found your answer.

12. Ross walks his dog between 3:15 P.M. and 4:00 P.M. Which clock shows a time between 3:15 P.M. and 4:00 P.M.?

A

B

C

D

Lesson
17-3

Understand It!
There are relationships that make it possible to change between any two units of time.

Units of Time

How can you change units of time?

The class is growing a plant from a seed. The project will last for 5 weeks. How many days are in 5 weeks? The picture shows how long the seed has been growing. How many hours is this?

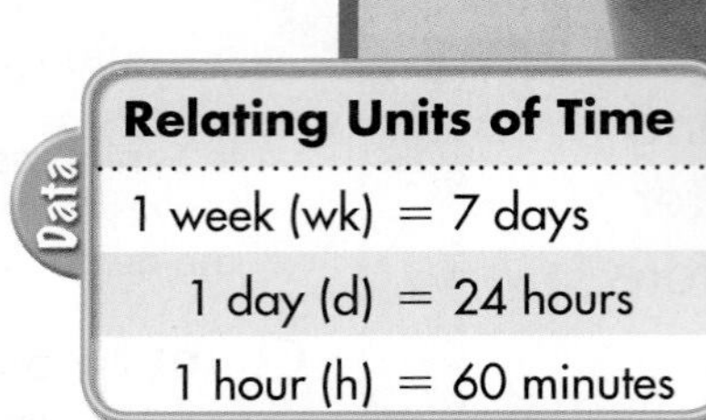

Data

Relating Units of Time
1 week (wk) = 7 days
1 day (d) = 24 hours
1 hour (h) = 60 minutes

Guided Practice*

Do you know HOW?

For **1–3**, copy and complete to change the units.

1. 8 weeks = ☐ days

2. 2 days = ☐ hours

3. How many days are in 2 weeks, 4 days?

Do you UNDERSTAND?

4. In the example above, why do you multiply the number of weeks by 7?

5. At the end of the first week, the class had worked on the science experiment for 6 hours. How many minutes did the class work on the experiment?

Independent Practice

For **6–15**, copy and complete to change the units.

6. 3 hours = ☐ minutes

7. 5 days = ☐ hours

8. 4 hours = ☐ minutes

9. 7 weeks = ☐ days

10. 3 weeks = ☐ days

11. 7 days = ☐ hours

12. How many hours are in 3 days, 5 hours?

13. How many minutes are in 5 hours, 10 minutes?

14. How many days are in 10 weeks?

15. How many hours are in 9 days?

**For another example, see Set B on page 408.*

Since there are 7 days in 1 week, the number of days in 5 weeks is 5×7.

5×7 days = ☐ days

$$\begin{array}{r} 7 \\ \times\ 5 \\ \hline 35 \end{array}$$

5 weeks = 35 days

Make a table to find the number of hours in 8 days.

Number of Days	1	2	3	4	5	6	7	8
Number of Hours	24	48	72	96	120	144	168	192

There are 192 hours in 8 days.

Problem Solving

16. In 30 more minutes, the International Space Station will complete an orbit. It has been in this orbit for 1 hour. How many minutes does it take the International Space Station to complete 1 orbit?

17. A group of high school students helped to prepare samples of materials to send to the International Space Station in 2001. The samples were returned to Earth from space after 4 years. In what year were the samples returned?

For **18** and **19**, use the table at the right.

18. Astronauts at the International Space Station took a spacewalk to do tasks outside the station. They finished their tasks in less time than was planned. How many minutes of actual time did the astronauts need?

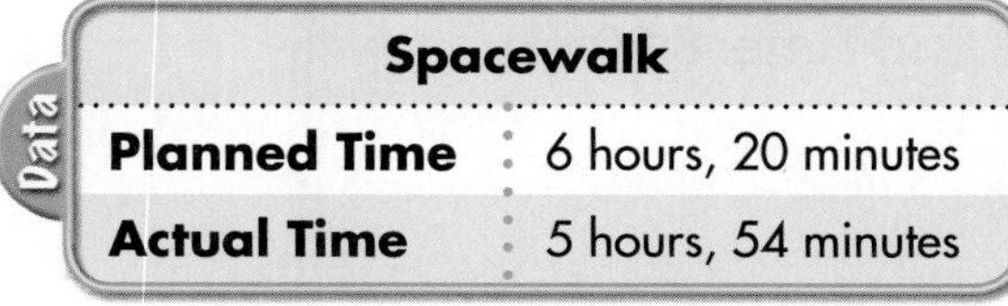

Spacewalk	
Planned Time	6 hours, 20 minutes
Actual Time	5 hours, 54 minutes

19. Writing to Explain How many fewer minutes than planned did the astronauts need? Explain how you found your answer.

20. Number Sense A sailfish can swim as fast as 68 miles per hour. In 1 minute can a sailfish swim as far as 1 mile? Explain your answer.

21. What fraction of an hour is 20 minutes? Write your answer in simplest form.

22. How many days are in 6 weeks?

A 42 **B** 36 **C** 13 **D** 7

Lesson
17-4

Understand It!
Elapsed time tells how long something takes.

Elapsed Time

How can you find elapsed time?

Janey took part in a charity walk. The walk started at 7:00 A.M. It ended at 11:20 A.M. How long did the walk last?

Elapsed time is the total amount of time that passes from the starting time to the ending time.

Guided Practice*

Do you know HOW?

For **1–3**, find the elapsed time.

1. Start Time: 11:00 A.M.
End Time: 5:00 P.M.

2. Start Time: 1:00 P.M.
End Time: 4:45 P.M.

3. Start Time: 7:10 A.M.
End Time: 8:00 A.M.

Do you UNDERSTAND?

4. In the example above, why do you count the minutes by 5s as the minute hand moves to each number on the clock?

5. During the charity walk, lunch was served from 12:00 P.M. until 2:10 P.M. How long was lunch served?

6. A movie started at 2:30 P.M. and ran for 1 hour, 45 minutes. What time did the movie end?

Independent Practice

For **7–15**, find the elapsed time.

7. Start Time: 6:30 P.M.
End Time: 9:50 P.M.

8. Start Time: 11:00 A.M.
End Time: 3:55 P.M.

9. Start Time: 5:40 P.M.
End Time: 6:00 P.M.

10. Start Time: 8:10 A.M.
End Time: 10:45 A.M.

11. Start Time: 9:15 A.M.
End Time: 10:45 A.M.

12. Start Time: 10:00 A.M.
End Time: 3:00 P.M.

13. Start Time: 3:20 P.M.
End Time: 6:00 P.M.

14. Start Time: 7:30 A.M.
End Time: 9:45 A.M.

15. Start Time: 12:45 P.M.
End Time: 2:20 P.M.

*For another example, see Set C on page 409.

Problem Solving

16. The picnic started at 12:10 P.M. and ended at 5:00 P.M. How long did the picnic last?

17. The baseball game started at 1:15 P.M. It lasted 2 hours, 45 minutes. What time did the game end?

18. The picnic started at 12:10 P.M. Kevin's family had arrived at the picnic 30 minutes earlier. What time did Kevin's family arrive at the picnic?

19. Mr. Parker had $\frac{5}{6}$ of a sandwich. He gave $\frac{2}{6}$ of the sandwich to Mikey. He gave the rest of the sandwich to Ben. What fraction of the sandwich did he give to Ben? Draw a picture.

Mrs. Flores keeps a list of the amount of time it takes for different items to bake. Use the table at the right for **20** and **21**.

20. Which items take less than $\frac{1}{2}$ hour to bake?

21. **Estimation** About how many more minutes does it take to bake the pasta dish than to bake the granola bars?

Item	Baking Time in Minutes
Bread	26
Granola Bars	21
Pasta Dish	48
Vegetables	24

22. The train leaves Carlton at 9:25 A.M. and arrives at Longview at 10:55 A.M. How long is the train ride?

A 1 hour, 20 minutes

B 1 hour, 25 minutes

C 1 hour, 30 minutes

D 1 hour, 35 minutes

Lesson

17-5

Understand It!
Temperatures can be read in degrees Fahrenheit or in degrees Celsius.

Temperature

How are temperatures measured?

A thermometer is a tool that measures temperature on the Fahrenheit or Celsius scale. Degrees Fahrenheit (°F) and degrees Celsius (°C) are units that are used to measure temperature.

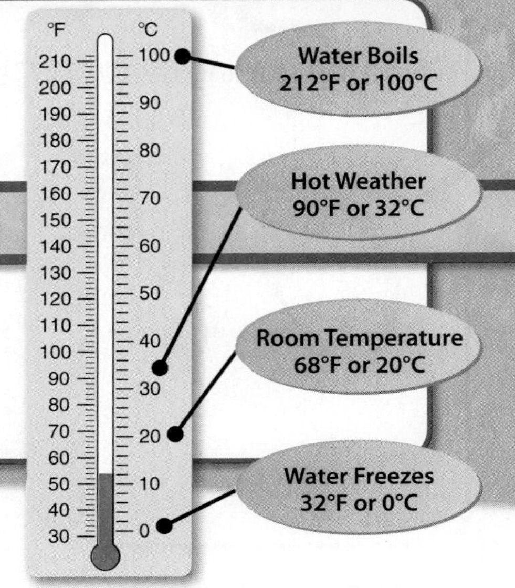

Guided Practice*

Do you know HOW?

In **1** and **2**, write each temperature in °F and in °C.

1.

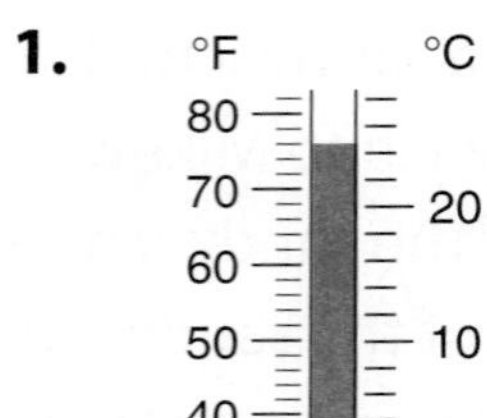

2.

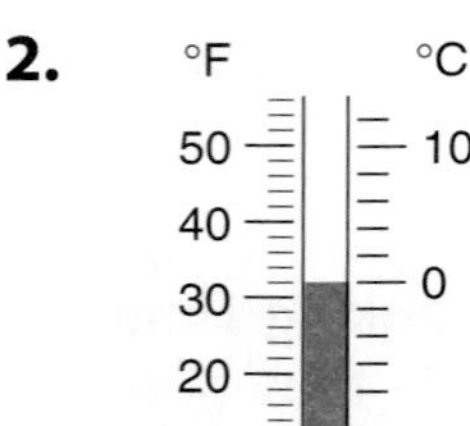

Do you UNDERSTAND?

3. Look at the thermometer above. Would you swim outside if the temperature was 28°C? Explain.

4. **Writing to Explain** Which is the better temperature for bicycling outside, 15°F or 50°F? Explain.

5. Mateo needs to wear a coat to go outside today. The thermometer shows the temperature. What is the temperature in degrees Fahrenheit?

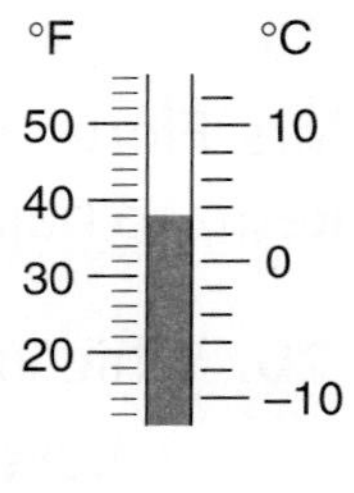

Independent Practice

In **6–8**, write each temperature in °F and °C.

6.

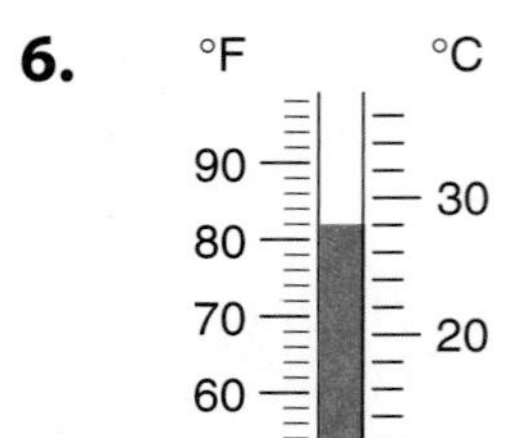

7.

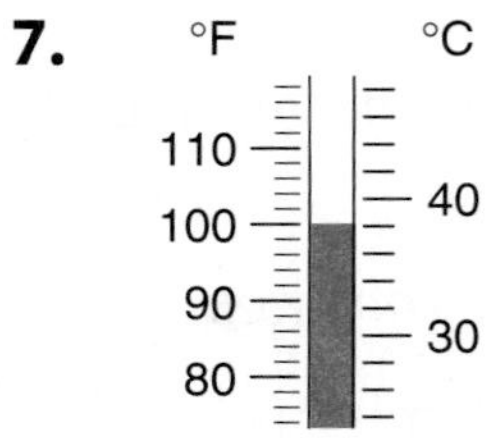

8.

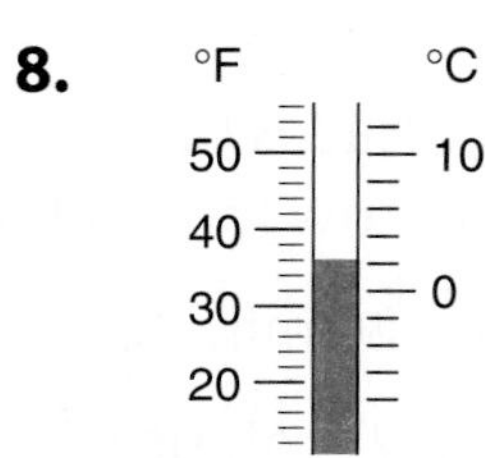

*For another example, see Set D on page 409.

Rita will wear a jacket outside today. What is the temperature outside, shown on the thermometer?

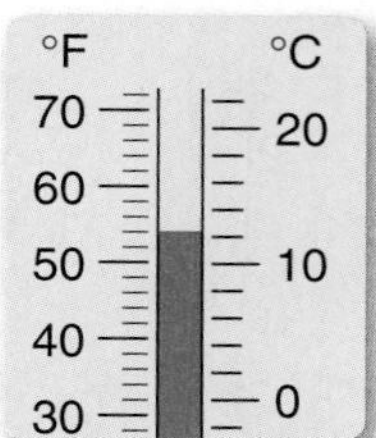

Each line on the scale is 2 degrees. The top of the red column is at 54 on the Fahrenheit scale and at 12 on the Celsius scale.

The temperature is 54°F or 12°C.

Dave will wear a T-shirt outside today. What is the temperature outside, shown on the thermometer?

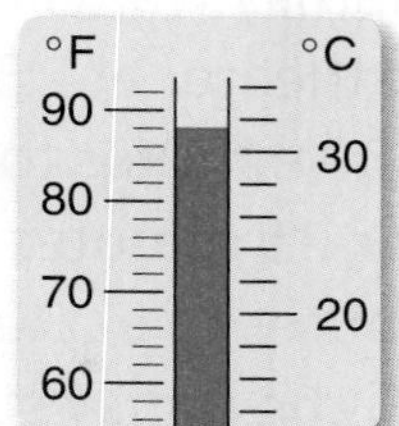

The top of the red column is at 88 on the Fahrenheit scale and at 31 on the Celsius scale.

The temperature is 88°F or 31°C.

Problem Solving

9. The year-round temperature in Mammoth Cave is shown on the thermometer below. What is that temperature in degrees Fahrenheit?

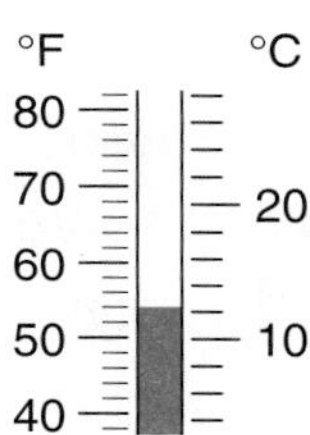

10. Algebra The year-round temperature in Carlsbad Caverns in New Mexico is 56°F. Copy and complete the number sentence to compare the temperature in Carlsbad Caverns with the temperature in Mammoth Cave.

56 ◯ ▢

For **11** and **12**, use the sign at the right.

11. Reasonableness Roy says that a scarf and a hat together cost about the same as 2 blankets. Is his estimate reasonable? Explain.

12. Algebra What did Jorge buy at the sale if $(3 \times \$19) + \$23$ stands for the total cost?

13. The temperature in Sonora Caverns is always about 70°F. Which thermometer shows this temperature?

A

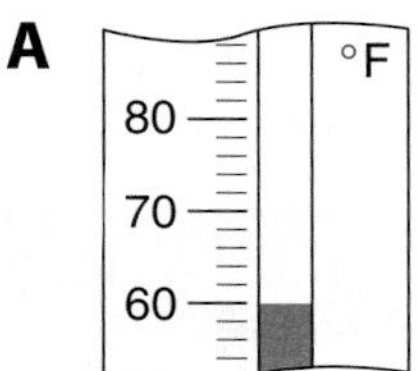

B

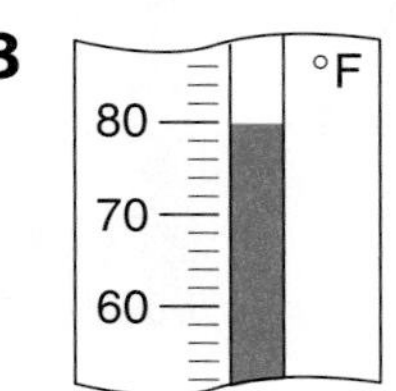

C

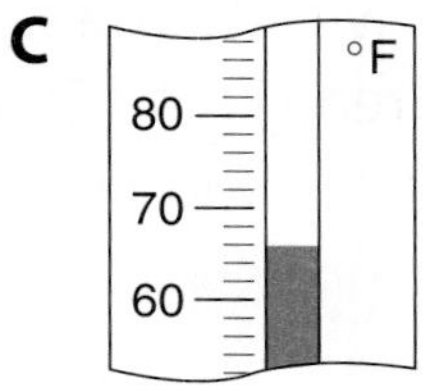

D

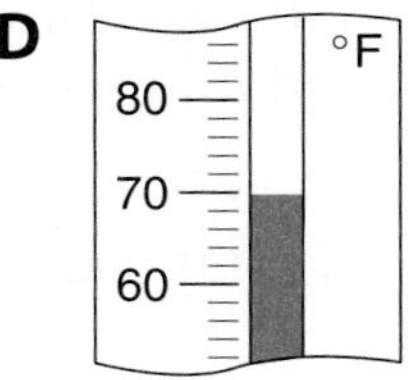

Lesson

17-6

Understand It!
Some problems can be solved by starting with the end result and working backward step-by-step to the beginning.

Problem Solving

Work Backward

Eric's family wants to arrive at the movie theater at 2:30 P.M. It takes them 30 minutes to travel to the theater, 15 minutes to get ready, and 30 minutes to eat lunch. What time should the family start eating lunch?

Arrive at Theater

Guided Practice*

Do you know HOW?

Solve the problem by drawing a picture and working backward.

1. The swim meet starts at 10:15 A.M. It takes Abby 15 minutes to walk to the pool. On her way, she needs 15 minutes to shop. It takes her 30 minutes to get ready. What time should Abby start getting ready?

Do you UNDERSTAND?

2. In the example above, why do the arrows in the Solve step move to the left?

3. **Write a Problem** Write a problem that you can solve by working backward.

Independent Practice

In **4** and **5**, solve the problem by drawing a picture and working backward.

4. Emilio read the thermometer one evening. The temperature was 56°F. This temperature was 9°F less than the temperature that afternoon. The afternoon temperature was 7°F greater than the temperature in the morning. What was the temperature in the morning?

5. Jana's dentist appointment is at 4:30 P.M. It takes Jana 20 minutes to walk to the dentist's office, 20 minutes to get ready, and 30 minutes to clean her room. What time should she start cleaning her room?

- What do I know?
- What am I asked to find?
- What diagram can I use to help understand the problem?
- Can I use addition, subtraction, multiplication, or division?
- Is all of my work correct?
- Did I answer the right question?
- Is my answer reasonable?

*For another example, see Set E on page 409.

Read and Understand

What do I know? Arrive 2:30 P.M., 30 minutes to travel, 15 minutes to get ready, 30 minutes to eat lunch

What am I being asked to find? The time the family should start eating lunch

Plan and Solve

Draw a picture to show each change.

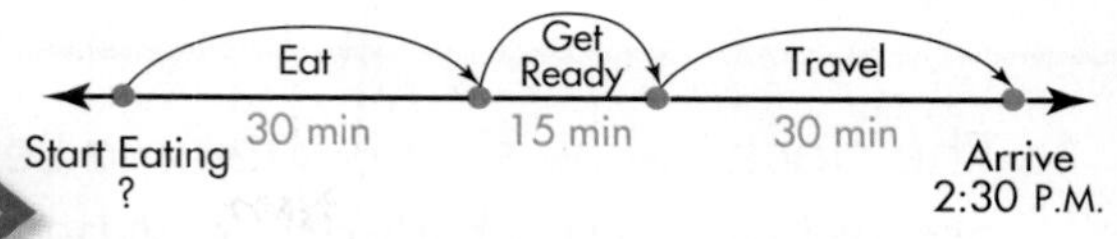

Work backward from the end.

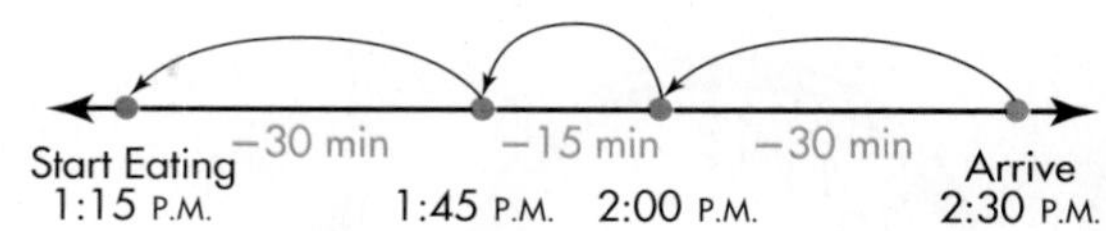

Eric's family should start eating lunch at 1:15 P.M.

6. Kent read the thermometer this evening. The temperature was 65°F. This temperature was 15°F less than the temperature in the afternoon. The afternoon temperature was 14°F greater than the temperature in the morning. What was the temperature in the morning?

7. Corinna read the thermometer at 7:00 P.M. The temperature was 16°C. This temperature was 9°C less than the temperature at 2:00 P.M. The temperature at 2:00 P.M. was 10°C higher than the temperature at 8:00 A.M. What was the temperature at 8:00 A.M.?

8. Wan-li drew these polygons. What is the same in all three polygons?

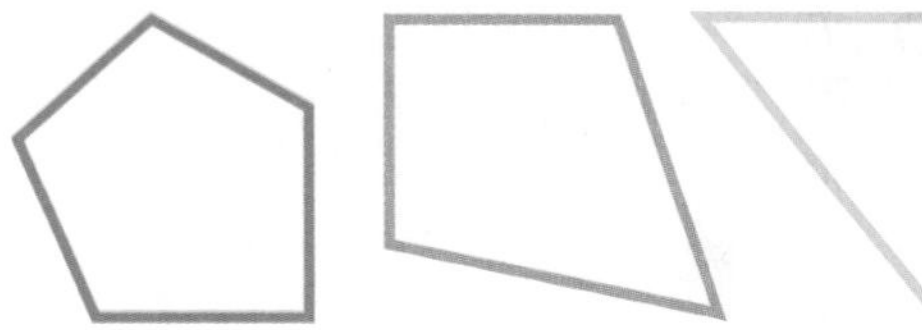

9. School starts at 8:15 A.M. It takes Shane 15 minutes to walk to school, 20 minutes to eat, 15 minutes to walk his dog, and 15 minutes to get ready. What time should he get up?

10. A scientist recorded the data shown in the table. About how long does it take a Venus flytrap to close after an insect or spider lands on it?

A Less than 1 second

B More than 1 second

C More than 1 minute

D More than 2 minutes

Data

Time Prey Landed	Time Flytrap Closed
2:07	$\frac{1}{2}$ second after 2:07
2:49	$\frac{3}{4}$ second after 2:49
2:53	$\frac{1}{2}$ second after 2:53

Test

1. The clock below shows the time Levi arrived at the doctor's office. What time did he arrive? (17-2)

A 3:42

B 3:37

C 3:35

D 2:37

2. What is one way to write the time shown on the clock? (17-1)

A Quarter to 1

B 15 past 1

C Quarter past 2

D Quarter to 2

3. Anita got to school at 8:05 A.M. She was on the bus 15 minutes, stood at the bus stop for 10 minutes, and took 40 minutes to get ready after she got up. What time did Anita get up? (17-6)

A 9:10 A.M.

B 7:05 A.M.

C 7:00 A.M.

D 6:55 A.M.

4. The temperature outside on Mikal's birthday was 54°F. Which thermometer shows this temperature? (17-5)

A
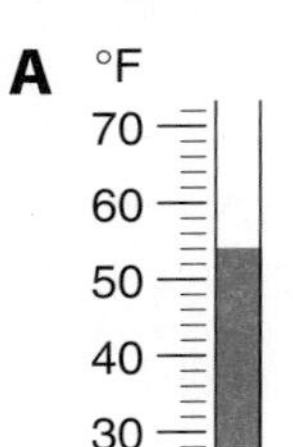

B
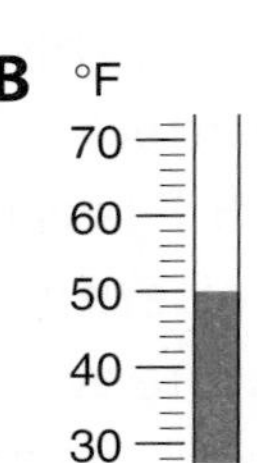

C
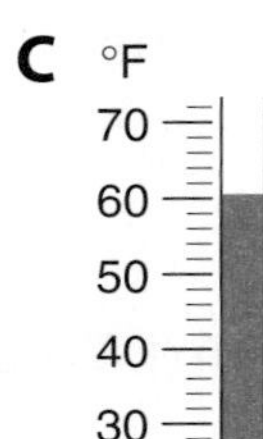

D
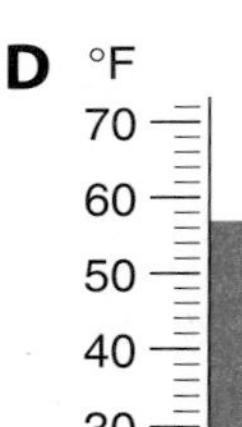

5. Which of the following is a time that Jose would be asleep during the night? (17-1)

A 3:15 P.M.

B 11:45 P.M.

C 10:45 A.M.

D 12:30 P.M.

6. What temperature in °F is shown? (17-5)

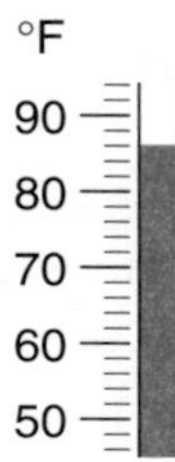

A 88°F

B 86°F

C 84°F

D 83°F

7. Jon arrived home from school at the time shown on the clock.

What time did Jon arrive? (17-2)

A 12:03

B 2:02

C 6:35

D 3:24

8. Olivia left her house at 6:30 to go to the movies. Which is another way to write 6:30? (17-1)

A quarter to 6

B quarter past 6

C half past 6

D quarter to 7

9. The concert in the park started at 11:15 A.M. and ended at 1:50 P.M. How long did the concert last? (17-4)

A 1 hour, 35 minutes

B 2 hours, 25 minutes

C 2 hours, 30 minutes

D 2 hours, 35 minutes

10. How many hours are in 4 days? (17-3)

A 52

B 84

C 96

D 100

11. The 3:00 P.M. temperature was 93°F. This was 8° warmer than the temperature at noon. The noon temperature was 13° warmer than the 9:00 A.M. temperature. What was the 9:00 A.M. temperature in °F? (17-6)

A 72°F

B 73°F

C 88°F

D 114°F

12. Jen was playing in a soccer game. The game started at 11:10 A.M. and ended at 12:40 P.M. How long did the game last? (17-4)

A 30 minutes

B 1 hour, 10 minutes

C 1 hour, 30 minutes

D 2 hours, 30 minutes

Reteaching

Set A, pages 392–394, 396–397

To tell the time, find where the hour hand points and where the minute hand points. When the minute hand is on the 9, you can say "15 minutes to" the hour. You can also say "quarter to" the hour.

What is the time to the nearest minute?

The hour hand is between 10 and 11. The time is after 10:00.

Count by 5s from the 12 to the 5.
5, 10, 15, 20, 25 minutes.

After counting by 5s, count the marks by 1.
5, 10, 15, 20, 25, 26, 27 minutes.

The digital time is 10:27.
It is 27 minutes past 10 or 33 minutes to 11.

Remember that the hours between midnight and noon are A.M. hours. The hours between noon and midnight are P.M. hours.

Write the time shown on each clock in two ways.

1. 

2. 

3. 

4. 

5. Lucy saw the sun rise at 6:10. Was this an A.M. time or a P.M. time?
6. At which time is it more likely to be dark outside, 11:00 A.M. or 11:00 P.M.?

Set B, pages 398–399

Change 9 weeks to days.

9 weeks = ▭ days
Change to days.

You know that 1 week equals 7 days.

Multiply: 9 × 7 days = 63 days

9 weeks = 63 days

Remember to use the correct factors for the units you are changing.

1. 6 hours = ▭ minutes
2. 2 weeks = ▭ days
3. 3 days = ▭ hours
4. 1 hour, 41 minutes = ▭ minutes
5. 2 days, 3 hours = ▭ hours
6. 3 hours, 15 minutes = ▭ minutes

Set C, pages 400–401

How long does the hockey game last?
Start Time: 11:00 a.m
End Time: 2:35 pm

- Find the starting time: **11:00 a.m**
- Count the hours: **12, 1, 2.**
- Count the minutes: **5, 10, 15, 20, 25, 30, 35.**

The game lasted 3 hours, 35 minutes.

Remember to count hours and then minutes.

Find the elapsed time.

1. Start Time: 9:00 A.M.
   End Time: 12:15 P.M.
2. Start Time: 5:00 P.M.
   End Time: 9:50 P.M.

Set D, pages 402–403

The thermometer shows the temperature outside. What is the temperature?

Each line on the scale is 2 degrees.

Count by 2s from the 70 mark up to where the red column ends.
70, 72, 74, 76, 78
Then count on by 1.
79

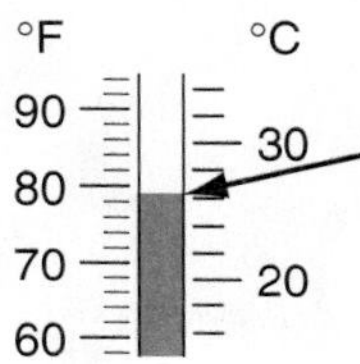

On the Celsius scale, count by 2s from 20.
20, 22, 24, 26

The temperature is 79°F or 26°C.

Remember that each line on the scale on these thermometers is 2 degrees.

Write each temperature in °F and °C.

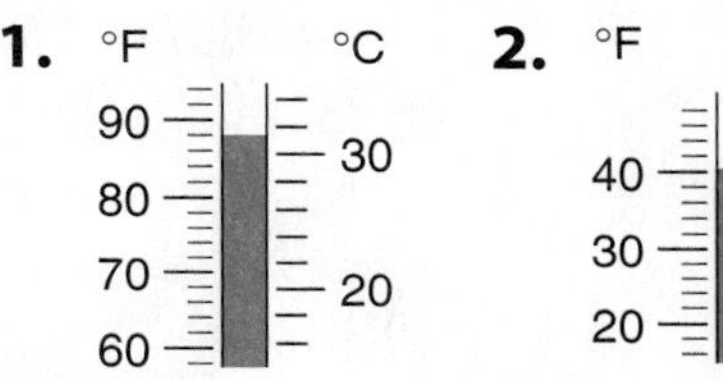

Set E, pages 404–405

Jay's soccer practice begins at 10:00 a.m He takes 30 minutes to walk to the field. He takes 10 minutes to walk his dog and 10 minutes to get ready. When should Jay start getting ready?

Work backward from the end using the opposite of each change.

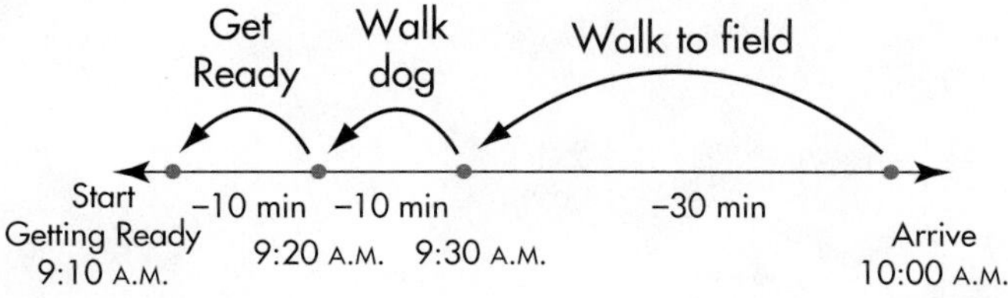

Jay should start getting ready at 9:10 a.m

Remember to check your solution by working forward.

Solve each problem by drawing a picture and working backward.

1. Hal needs to meet Lou at 1:00 P.M. It takes him 10 minutes to walk to Lou's house, 10 minutes to get ready, and 20 minutes to eat lunch. What time should Hal start eating lunch?

Topic 18

Multiplying Greater Numbers

1 Solar cells on a Solar Array Wing are used to produce electricity for the International Space Station. How many solar cells are there? You will find out in Lesson 18-3.

2 About how much does a manatee weigh compared to a golden eagle? You will find out in Lesson 18-1.

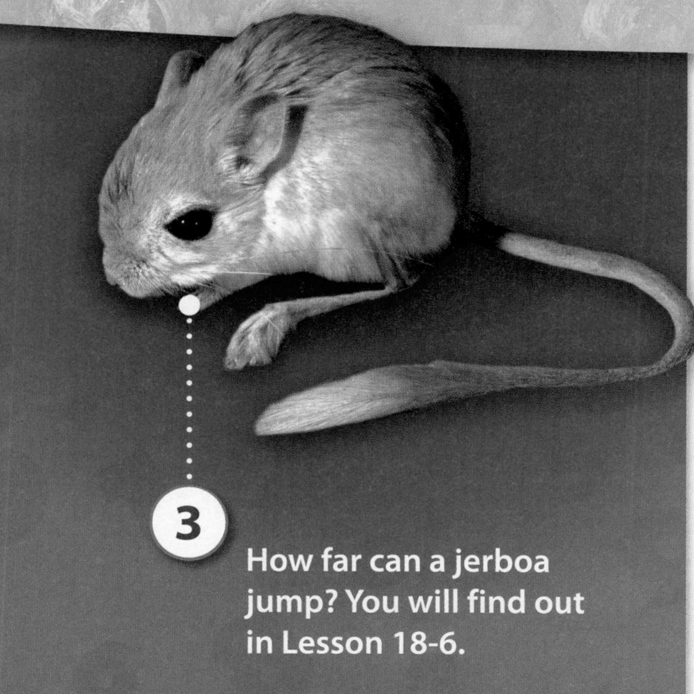

3 How far can a jerboa jump? You will find out in Lesson 18-6.

4 Which has more members, the world's largest accordion band or the world's largest trombone band? You will find out in Lesson 18-5.

Review What You Know!

Vocabulary

Choose the best term from the box.

- addends
- factors
- product
- sum

1. When you add to combine numbers, another name for the total is the ___?___.

2. The Commutative Property of Multiplication says that the ___?___ can be multiplied in any order and the answer will be the same.

3. In the number sentence $9 \times 6 = 54$, the number 54 is called the ___?___.

Multiplication

Multiply.

4. 3×9	**5.** 8×7	**6.** 6×6
7. 4×8	**8.** 7×5	**9.** 4×2
10. 7×6	**11.** 8×9	**12.** 6×8

Arrays

Draw an array of dots for each multiplication.

13. 3×9 **14.** 4×8

15. Write a Problem Write a problem for the number sentence $7 \times 6 = \square$.

Lesson

18-1

Understand It!
Place value, multiplication facts, and patterns can help multiply numbers using mental math.

Using Mental Math to Multiply

Hands-On
place-value blocks

How can you multiply by multiples of 10, 100, and 1,000?

You already know how to multiply by 10, as in 5 × 10 = 50.

5 × 100 is 5 groups of 1 hundred or 500.

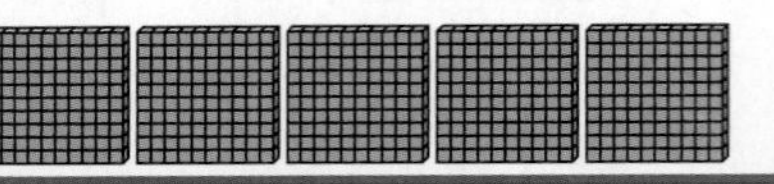

5 × 1,000 is 5 groups of 1 thousand or 5,000.

Guided Practice*

Do you know HOW?

In **1–8**, use place-value blocks or patterns to find each product.

1. 8 × 100

2. 7 × 1,000

3. 6 × 1,000

4. 9 × 100

5. 6 × 40

6. 3 × 700

7. 9 × 50

8. 5 × 3,000

Do you UNDERSTAND?

9. In the examples above, what pattern do you see when you multiply a number by 10? by 100? by 1,000?

10. The memory card for Jay's digital camera holds 70 pictures. How many pictures can 4 memory cards hold?

11. Your friend says, "The product 6 × 5 is 30, so 6 × 500 is 300." Is he correct? Explain.

Independent Practice

In **12–27,** use mental math to find the product.

12. 4 × 10

13. 9 × 100

14. 2 × 1,000

15. 3 × 60

16. 8 × 80

17. 6 × 50

18. 40 × 7

19. 900 × 4

20. 500 × 9

21. 70 × 5

22. 100 × 8

23. 2 × 6,000

24. 200 × 8

25. 300 × 6

26. 4 × 500

27. 3 × 400

DIGITAL eTools
www.pearsonsuccessnet.com

For another example, see Set A on page 432.

Find 3×70.

Use place-value blocks. Remember, $70 = 7$ tens.

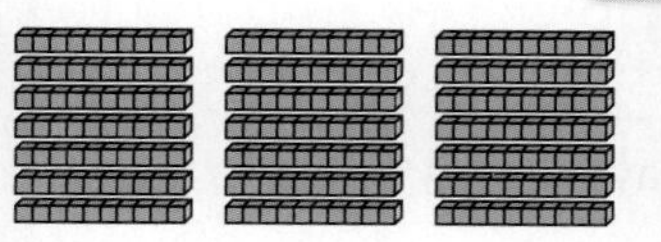

3 groups of 7 tens = 21 tens

$3 \times 70 = 210$

Find 4×300.

Use place-value blocks. Remember, $300 = 3$ hundreds.

4 groups of 3 hundreds = 12 hundreds

$4 \times 300 = 1{,}200$

Find $2 \times 4{,}000$.

Use a pattern.

$2 \times 4 = 8$

$2 \times 40 = 80$

$2 \times 400 = 800$

$2 \times 4{,}000 = 8{,}000$

Notice the pattern of zeros.

Problem Solving

For **28** and **29**, use the table at the right.

28. If you used a washing machine for 3 loads, how many gallons of water would you use? Draw pictures of place-value blocks to show the problem.

29. **Writing to Explain** How much water would you save if you took a 10-minute shower instead of a bath each day for 5 days? Explain how you solved the problem.

Data

Use of Water

Use	Estimated Number of Gallons
Bath	50
Dishwasher (1 load)	10
Shower (10 minutes)	20
Toilet (1 flush)	5
Washing Machine (1 load)	50

30. Each person in the United States uses about 200 gallons of water each day. About 125 gallons are used in the bathroom. How many gallons of water are used in other ways?

31. A golden eagle weighs about 11 pounds. A manatee can weigh 100 times as much as a golden eagle. How much can a manatee weigh?

32. An African elephant drinks about 50 gallons of water each day. How many gallons of water does the elephant drink in 7 days?

33. There are 6 floors in a building. Each floor has 20 windows. Some windows have 2 curtains. How many windows in all does the building have?

A 240 **C** 120

B 122 **D** 28

Lesson

18-2

Understand It!
One way to estimate a product is to round the greater factor and multiply.

Estimating Products

How can you estimate products?

Bamboo is one of the fastest growing plants on Earth. It can grow about 36 inches a day. Can it grow more than 200 inches in a week?

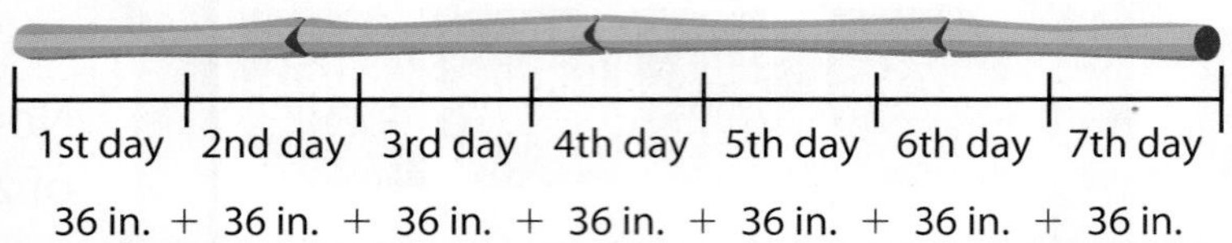

36 in. + 36 in. + 36 in. + 36 in. + 36 in. + 36 in. + 36 in.

Guided Practice*

Do you know HOW?

In **1–6**, estimate each product.

1. 6×18

2. 3×52

3. 5×79

4. 4×65

5. 7×23

6. 9×37

Do you UNDERSTAND?

7. In the example above, is the exact answer more than or less than the estimate of 280? How do you know?

8. The kudzu plant is a vine that can grow about 12 inches each day. Can it grow more than 100 inches in a week? Explain how to round to estimate.

Independent Practice

In **9–28**, estimate each product.

9. 2×46

10. 8×31

11. 5×84

12. 7×26

13. 4×58

14. 6×19

15. 3×67

16. 9×23

17. 8×44

18. 5×32

19. 9×47

20. 2×64

21. 71×4

22. 98×7

23. 85×6

24. 31×4

25. 56×2

26. 73×5

27. 29×3

28. 47×6

*For another example, see Set B on page 432.

Step 1

An estimate is enough to find out if the plant can grow more than 200 inches in a week.

Estimate 7×36.

Round 36 to the nearest ten.

7×36

↓ 36 rounds to 40.

$7 \times 40 = 280$

7×36 is about 280.

Step 2

Compare the estimate to 200 inches.

$280 > 200$

So, a bamboo plant can grow more than 200 inches in a week.

Problem Solving

For **29–31**, use the graph at the right.

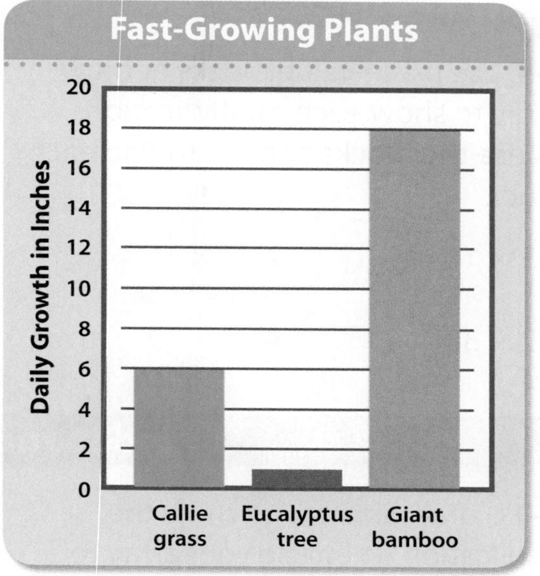

29. Writing to Explain Does a giant bamboo plant grow more than 100 inches in 6 days? Explain how to round to estimate the answer.

30. Reasonableness Jim says a eucalyptus tree grows more in 8 days than Callie grass grows in 2 days. Is his statement reasonable? Explain.

31. How much more does giant bamboo grow in one day than Callie grass?

32. Algebra Look for patterns in the table. Copy and complete.

2	3	4	5	7	9
40	60	■	100	■	■

33. There are 22 rows of seats on an airplane. Each has 6 seats. Which is the best estimate of the number of seats on the plane?

A 20 **B** 60 **C** 120 **D** 200

34. Think About the Process Jamal is buying 5 books. Each book costs \$19. Which number sentence shows the best estimate of the total cost of the books?

A $5 \times \$10 = \$50$

B $\$5 + \$20 = \$25$

C $5 \times \$20 = \$100$

D $\$10 + \$20 = \$30$

Lesson
18-3

Understand It!
An array or a picture can model multiplication with greater numbers.

Multiplication and Arrays

Hands-On
place-value blocks

How can you use arrays to show how to multiply with greater numbers?

Lava lamps in a store are arranged in 4 equal rows. What is the total number of lava lamps?

Choose an Operation Multiply to find the total for an array.

4 rows

13 lamps in each row

Guided Practice*

Do you know HOW?

In **1–4**, use place-value blocks or draw an array to show each multiplication. Then use the blocks or array to find each product.

1. 5×14 **2.** 3×21

3. 2×38 **4.** 4×29

Do you UNDERSTAND?

5. In the example above, what multiplication fact could you use to find the total number of ones?

6. Light bulbs are arranged in 3 equal rows on a shelf in the store. There are 17 bulbs in each row. What is the total number of bulbs on the shelf?

Independent Practice

In **7–11**, draw an array to show the multiplication. Then use your array to find the product.

Tip *You can draw lines to show tens, and Xs to show ones. This picture shows 23.*

——— ——— × ×

7. 3×26 **8.** 5×15 **9.** 2×18 **10.** 4×16 **11.** 7×21

In **12–21**, find each product. You may use place-value blocks or draw a picture to help.

12. 2×47 **13.** 6×28 **14.** 5×31 **15.** 3×45 **16.** 4×32

17. 8×15 **18.** 3×29 **19.** 5×22 **20.** 2×38 **21.** 4×19

DIGITAL eTools www.pearsonsuccessnet.com

*For another example, see Set C on page 432.

Step 1

Use an array to show 4×13.

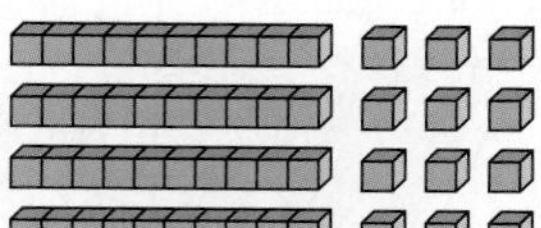

4 rows with 1 ten and 3 ones in each row.

Step 2

Find how many in all.

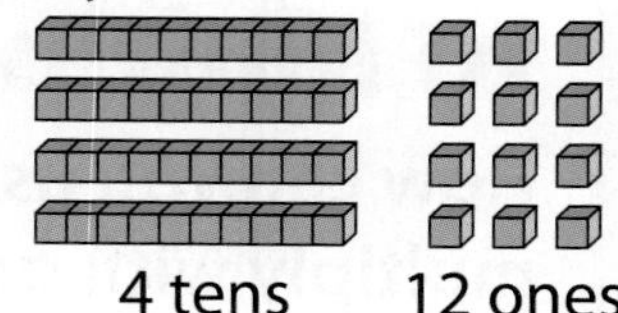

Count by tens and then count on with the ones to find the total.

10, 20, 30, 40

41, 42, 43, 44, 45, 46, 47, 48, 49, 50, 51, 52

There are 52 lava lamps.

Problem Solving

For **22** and **23**, use the table and the tip at the right.

22. Jake walked for 1 minute. How many times did Jake's heart beat?

23. **Strategy Focus** Solve. Use the strategy Try, Check, and Revise.

While doing one of the activities, Jake counted his heartbeats. He found that his heart rate in one minute was greater than 120, but less than 130. Which activity was he doing? Explain how you know.

Data

Jake's Heart Rate

Activity	**Number of Heartbeats in 10 Seconds**
Bicycling	21
Resting	13
Running	22
Walking	18

The number of heartbeats in 1 minute is 6 times as many as in 10 seconds.

24. The soup cans in a store display were arranged in 3 rows. There were 27 cans in each row. Which number sentence describes the array of soup cans?

A $3 \times 27 = 81$ **B** $6 \times 21 = 126$ **C** $6 + 21 = 27$ **D** $2 \times 27 = 54$

25. A solar array wing on the International Space Station has 3,280 rows of solar cells. There are 10 solar cells in each row. Write an expression that describes how many solar cells are in the array.

26. What multiplication sentence could you write for the array shown at the right?

Lesson

18-4

Understand It!
For multiplication, greater numbers can be broken apart using place value.

Breaking Apart to Multiply

Hands-On
place-value blocks

How can you use place value to multiply with greater numbers?

A parking lot has the same number of spaces in each row. How many spaces are in the lot?

Choose an Operation Multiply to find the total for an array.

Another Example

The Distributive Property says you can break a factor apart to find partial products. The sum of the partial products is the product of the two factors.

Find 3 × 16.

$3 \times 16 = 3 \times (10 + 6)$	Break 16 into tens and ones.
$= (3 \times 10) + (3 \times 6)$	Use the Distributive Property.
$= 30 + 18$	Find the partial products.
$= 48$	Add the partial products.

Guided Practice*

Do you know HOW?

In **1** and **2**, copy and complete. You may use place-value blocks or drawings to help.

1. 4 × 36
4 × 3 tens = ☐ tens or 120
4 × 6 ones = 24 ones or ☐
☐ + ☐ = ☐

2. 5 × 27
5 × (20 + 7) = (5 × 20) + (5 × 7)
☐ + ☐ = ☐

Do you UNDERSTAND?

3. In the parking lot example, what two groups are in the array?

4. The buses at a bus garage are parked in 4 equal rows. There are 29 buses in each row. How many buses are parked at the garage?

5. Writing to Explain Why can you break apart numbers to multiply without changing the product?

*For another example, see Set D on page 433.

Step 1

Use an array to show 4×24.

Break 24 into tens and ones.
24 = 2 tens 4 ones

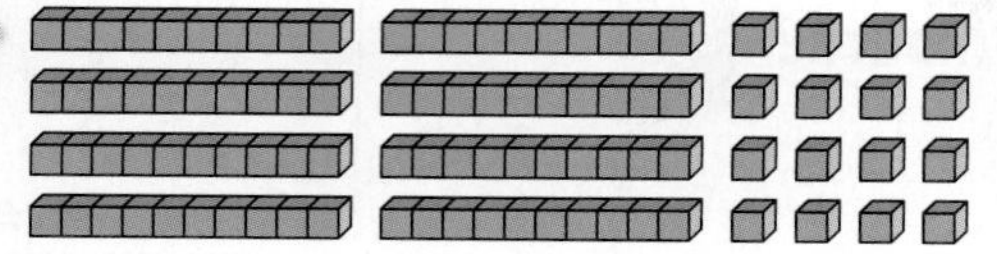

4 × 2 tens — 4 × 4 ones

$4 \times 20 = 80$ — $4 \times 4 = 16$

Step 2

Add each part to get the product.

$4 \times 20 = 80$ — $4 \times 4 = 16$

$80 + 16 = 96$

80 and 16 are called partial products because they are parts of the product.

$4 \times 24 = 96$

There are 96 spaces in the parking lot.

Independent Practice

In **6–15**, find each product. You may use place-value blocks or drawings to help.

6. 3×19 **7.** 4×31 **8.** 6×23 **9.** 5×25 **10.** 2×54

11. 3×49 **12.** 6×27 **13.** 5×43 **14.** 7×35 **15.** 4×62

Problem Solving

For **16–18**, find the total number of miles walked in the number of weeks given.

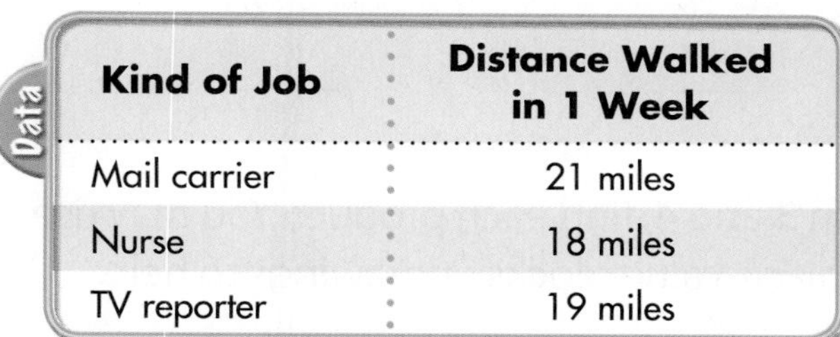

Data

Kind of Job	Distance Walked in 1 Week
Mail carrier	21 miles
Nurse	18 miles
TV reporter	19 miles

16. Nurse: 6 weeks

17. Mail carrier: 7 weeks

18. TV reporter: 2 weeks

Use the picture at the right for **19** and **20**.

19. Estimation Is $80 enough money to buy a chair and a desk? Explain how to round to estimate.

20. Nilda bought a bookcase, a lamp, and a desk. What was the total cost?

A $77 **C** $109

B $104 **D** $123

Lesson

18-5

Understand It! Partial products can be recorded and added using place value.

Using an Expanded Algorithm

How do you record partial products when you multiply greater numbers?

How many calories are in 3 peaches?

Find 3 × 46.

Estimate: 3 × 50 = 150

Data

Calories	
Fruit	Number of calories in 1 piece
Peach	46
Orange	35
Pear	40

Guided Practice*

Do you know HOW?

In **1** and **2**, copy and complete. Use place-value blocks or draw pictures to help.

1. $\begin{array}{r} 16 \\ \times\ 3 \\ \hline 18 \\ \square\square \\ \hline \square\square \end{array}$

2. $\begin{array}{r} 34 \\ \times\ \ 5 \\ \hline 20 \\ \square\square\square \\ \hline \square\square\square \end{array}$

In **3** and **4**, find each product. You may use place-value blocks or drawings to help.

3. $\begin{array}{r} 67 \\ \times\ 2 \\ \hline \end{array}$

4. $\begin{array}{r} 54 \\ \times\ 7 \\ \hline \end{array}$

Do you UNDERSTAND?

For **5–7**, use the example above.

5. What factors give the partial product 18? What factors give the partial product 120?

6. What is the next step after you write the partial products?

7. How many calories are in 2 oranges?

Independent Practice

Leveled Practice In **8** and **9**, copy and complete. In **10–12**, find each product. You may use place-value blocks or drawings to help.

You can draw lines to show tens, and Xs to show ones. This picture shows 27.

—— —— ×××××××

8. $\begin{array}{r} 36 \\ \times\ \ 2 \\ \hline 12 \\ \square\square \\ \hline \square\square \end{array}$

9. $\begin{array}{r} 53 \\ \times\ \ \ 4 \\ \hline 12 \\ \square\square\square \\ \hline \square\square\square \end{array}$

10. $\begin{array}{r} 18 \\ \times\ 7 \\ \hline \end{array}$

11. $\begin{array}{r} 42 \\ \times\ 6 \\ \hline \end{array}$

12. $\begin{array}{r} 65 \\ \times\ 3 \\ \hline \end{array}$

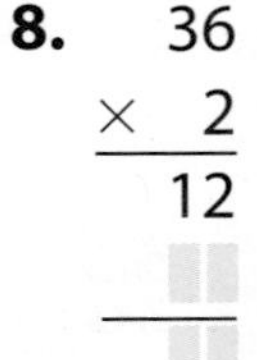

*For another example, see Set E on page 433.

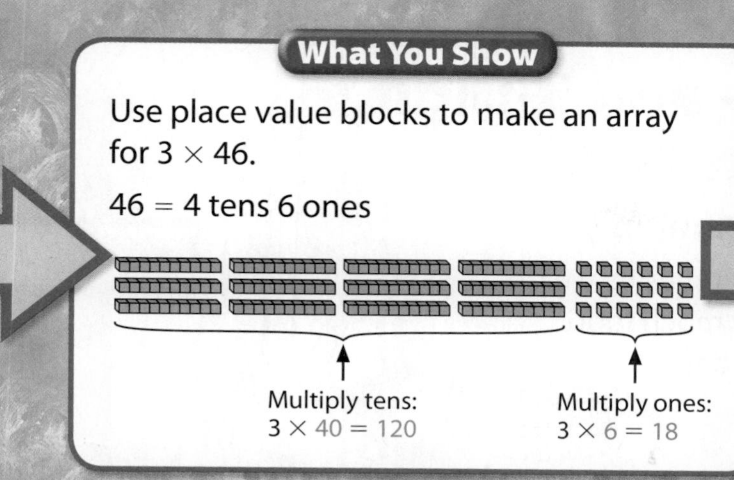

What You Write

$$\begin{array}{r} 46 \\ \times \quad 3 \\ \hline 18 \\ +\ 120 \\ \hline 138 \end{array}$$

Write the partial products. Line up the ones, tens, and hundreds. Add.

There are 138 calories in 3 peaches.

The answer is reasonable because 138 is close to the estimate of 150.

Problem Solving

13. Sam's family is planning a vacation. The table shows the cost of each one-way plane ticket from his town to three different cities.

a How much more is a one-way ticket to Atlanta than a one-way ticket to Chicago?

b How much would Sam's family spend for 3 round-trip tickets to Kansas City?

Tip *A round-trip ticket costs twice as much as a one-way ticket.*

Data

Airfare	
City	Cost of One-Way Ticket
Atlanta	$87
Chicago	$59
Kansas City	$49

14. Reasoning How can knowing that $5 \times 14 = 70$ help you find 5×16? Explain your strategy.

15. Algebra The product of this whole number and 25 is greater than 50 but less than 100. What's the number?

16. Estimation Round to the nearest hundred to estimate how many more musicians are in the world's largest accordion band than in the world's largest trombone band.

Data

World's Largest Bands	
Trombone	284 musicians
Accordion	625 musicians

17. Writing to Explain To find 24×7, Joel adds the partial products 28 and 14. Is he correct? Explain.

18. Mr. Cruz weighed 8 cartons. Each carton weighed 17 pounds. How many pounds was this in all?

A 25 pounds
B 136 pounds
C 856 pounds
D 8,056 pounds

Lesson

18-6

Understand It!
You can regroup ones, tens, and hundreds when you multiply 2- and 3-digit numbers by 1-digit numbers.

Multiplying 2- and 3-Digit by 1-Digit Numbers

How do you regroup to multiply?

The grass carp fish can eat 3 times its weight in plant food each day. How much food can this grass carp eat each day?

This grass carp weighs 26 pounds.

Find 3×26.

Estimate: $3 \times 30 = 90$

Another Example How do you multiply 3-digit numbers?

An aquarium in a large city has about 605 visitors each hour. How many visitors is that in an 8-hour day?

Find 8×605.

Use what you know about multiplying 2-digit numbers for 3-digit numbers.

Step 1

Multiply the ones.
8 × 5 ones = 40 ones
Regroup.

$$\begin{array}{r} {\scriptstyle 4} \\ 605 \\ \times \quad 8 \\ \hline 0 \end{array}$$

Step 2

Multiply the tens.
8 × 0 tens = 0 tens
Add the regrouped tens.

$$\begin{array}{r} {\scriptstyle 4} \\ 605 \\ \times \quad 8 \\ \hline 40 \end{array}$$

Step 3

Multiply the hundreds.
8 × 6 hundreds = 48 hundreds

$$\begin{array}{r} {\scriptstyle 4} \\ 605 \\ \times \quad 8 \\ \hline 4,840 \end{array}$$

There are 4,840 visitors in an 8-hour day.

If aquarium tickets cost $4.75 each, how much would 5 tickets cost?

Find 5 × $4.75.

$$\begin{array}{r} {\scriptstyle 3\ 2} \\ \$4.75 \\ \times \quad 5 \\ \hline \$23.75 \end{array}$$

Multiply as with whole numbers.
Find 5 × 475.
Write the answer in dollars and cents.

$? in all

$4.75	$4.75	$4.75	$4.75	$4.75

Explain It

1. How is multiplying money the same as multiplying whole numbers? How is it different?

Step 1

Multiply the ones. Regroup, if needed.

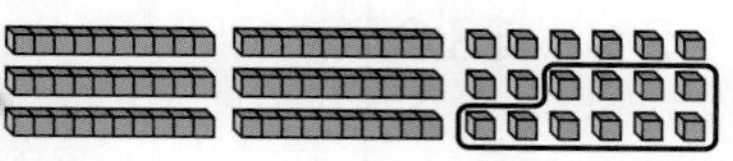

$$\begin{array}{r} \scriptstyle 1 \\ 26 \\ \times \ \ 3 \\ \hline 8 \end{array}$$

$3 \times 6 = 18$ ones

Regroup 18 ones as 1 ten 8 ones.

Step 2

Multiply the tens. Add regrouped tens.

3×2 tens $= 6$ tens

6 tens $+ 1$ ten $= 7$ tens

$$\begin{array}{r} \scriptstyle 1 \\ 26 \\ \times \ \ 3 \\ \hline 78 \end{array}$$

The fish would eat 78 pounds of food.

Guided Practice*

Do you know HOW?

In **1** and **2**, copy and complete. You may use drawings to help.

1. $\begin{array}{r} \square \\ 13 \\ \times \ \ 6 \\ \hline \end{array}$

2. $\begin{array}{r} \square\square \\ 124 \\ \times \ \ 7 \\ \hline \end{array}$

In **3–6**, find each product.

3. $\begin{array}{r} 78 \\ \times \ \ 4 \\ \hline \end{array}$

4. $\begin{array}{r} \$2.35 \\ \times \ \ 8 \\ \hline \end{array}$

5. $6 \times \$1.49$

6. 3×209

Do you UNDERSTAND?

For **7** and **8**, use the example above.

7. Why is the estimate greater than the exact answer?

8. How much food could this grass carp eat in 4 days?

9. A blue shark can swim 36 feet in 1 second. At this speed, how far would it swim in 3 seconds?

10. Find the total cost of 7 tickets that cost $2.95 each.

Independent Practice

In **11–20**, estimate and then find each product. You may use drawings to help.

11. $\begin{array}{r} 49 \\ \times\ 2 \\ \hline \end{array}$

12. $\begin{array}{r} 37 \\ \times\ 3 \\ \hline \end{array}$

13. $\begin{array}{r} 64 \\ \times\ 5 \\ \hline \end{array}$

14. $\begin{array}{r} 52 \\ \times\ 9 \\ \hline \end{array}$

15. $\begin{array}{r} 46 \\ \times\ 7 \\ \hline \end{array}$

16. 6×53

17. 7×38

18. 4×44

19. 5×42

20. 2×48

For another example, see Set E on page 433.

Independent Practice

In **21–28**, find each product.

21. $\begin{array}{r} 423 \\ \times \quad 9 \\ \hline \end{array}$

22. $\begin{array}{r} 185 \\ \times \quad 4 \\ \hline \end{array}$

23. $\begin{array}{r} \$5.19 \\ \times \quad 6 \\ \hline \end{array}$

24. $\begin{array}{r} \$8.95 \\ \times \quad 2 \\ \hline \end{array}$

25. 291×3

26. 145×5

27. $8 \times \$0.65$

28. $2 \times \$6.85$

Problem Solving

29. The ostrich is the fastest bird on land. An ostrich can run 66 feet in 1 second. The cheetah is the fastest mammal on land. A cheetah can run 94 feet in 1 second. How many fewer feet can an ostrich run in 1 second than a cheetah?

30. The length of the body of this jerboa is shown in the picture. How far can this jerboa jump?

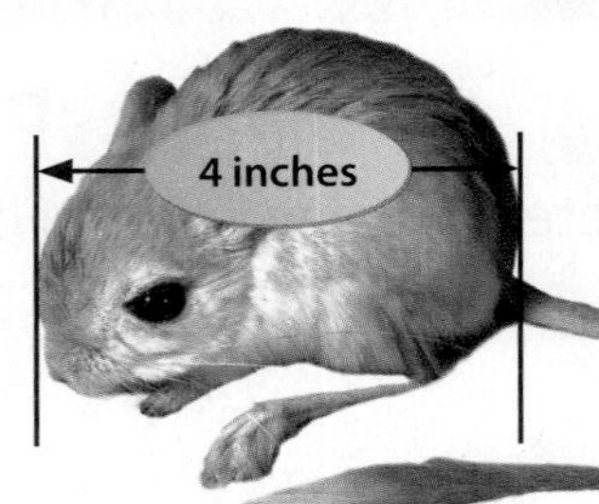

A jerboa can jump 25 times its body length.

31. **Estimation** Dionne used rounding to estimate the product of 198 and another number. Her estimate of the product was 800. Which number is the best choice for the other factor?

A 3 **B** 4 **C** 8 **D** 10

Algebra For **32–34**, copy and complete. Use <, >, or =.

32. 53×6 ◯ 308 **33.** 19×5 ◯ 145 **34.** 24×4 ◯ 12×8

35. Wanda bought 3 concert tickets that cost $9.75 each. How much did she spend on tickets?

36. Use your answer to Exercise 35. Find how much change Wanda got if she paid with a $20 bill and a $10 bill.

37. At a museum, the visitors formed 8 tour groups to go on tours. Each group had 32 visitors. How many visitors were going on tours?

A 40 **C** 246

B 256 **D** 2,416

38. The Great Pyramid of Khufu is square at the bottom. Each side of the square is 751 feet long. What is the perimeter of the pyramid at the bottom?

Algebra Connections

Using Multiplication Properties

Remember to use the properties of multiplication to help you complete number sentences.

Commutative (Order) Property You can multiply factors in any order and the product is the same. $5 \times 9 = 9 \times 5$

Identity (One) Property When you multiply a number and 1, the product is that number. $1 \times 8 = 8$

Zero Property When you multiply a number and 0, the product is 0. $0 \times 7 = 0$

Associative (Grouping) Property You can change the grouping of the factors, and the product is the same. $(3 \times 2) \times 4 = 3 \times (2 \times 4)$

Example: $\square \times 8 = 0$

Think: What number multiplied by 8 is equal to 0?

You can use the Zero Property.

$\underline{0} \times 8 = 0$

Example:

$6 \times (9 \times 7) = (6 \times \square) \times 7$

Think: What number makes the two sides equal?

Use the Associative Property.

Copy and complete with the number that makes the two sides equal.

1. $10 \times \square = 10$

2. $12 \times 8 = 8 \times \square$

3. $6 \times (2 \times 5) = (6 \times \square) \times 5$

4. $\square \times 8 = 0$

5. $\square \times 7 = 7 \times 11$

6. $(4 \times 3) \times \square = 4 \times (3 \times 8)$

7. $6 \times \square = 9 \times 6$

8. $\square \times 9 = 9$

9. $(\square \times 7) \times 2 = 5 \times (7 \times 2)$

In **10** and **11**, copy and complete the number sentence. Solve the problem.

10. Gemma made 8 rows of stickers on a sheet with 19 stickers in each row. How could she use the Distributive Property to find the total number of stickers?

$8 \times 19 = 8 \times (10 + 9)$
$= (8 \times \square) + (8 \times \square)$

How many stickers did she have in all?

11. Hal and Den each have copies of the same photos. Hal arranges 5 photos on each of 6 pages in 2 albums. Den needs 5 pages in 2 albums for the same photos. How many photos are on each page in Den's albums?

$(6 \times 5) \times 2 = (5 \times \square) \times 2$

How many photos does each boy have?

12. Write a Problem Write a real-world problem to match the number sentence on the right.

$\square \times 12 = 12 \times 3$

Lesson
18-7

Understand It!
Draw a picture to decide what number sentence can be used to solve a problem.

Problem Solving

Draw a Picture and Write a Number Sentence

Oscar bought 5 cases of bottled water. How many bottles of water did Oscar buy?

Another Example

Melody wants to buy a case of juice boxes. There are 3 times as many boxes in a jumbo case as in a regular case. How many juice boxes are in a jumbo case?

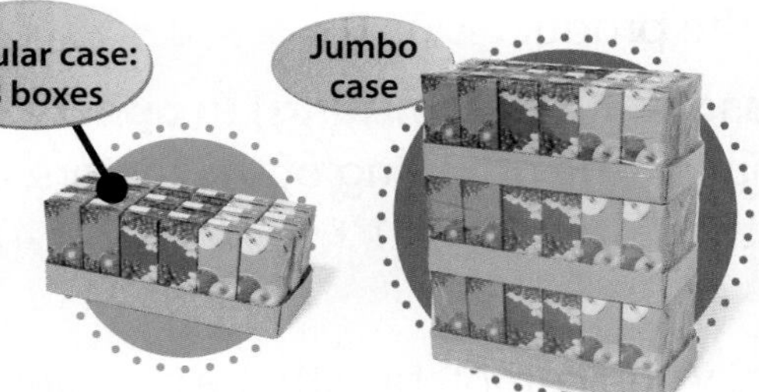

Plan

Use a picture or a diagram to show what you know.

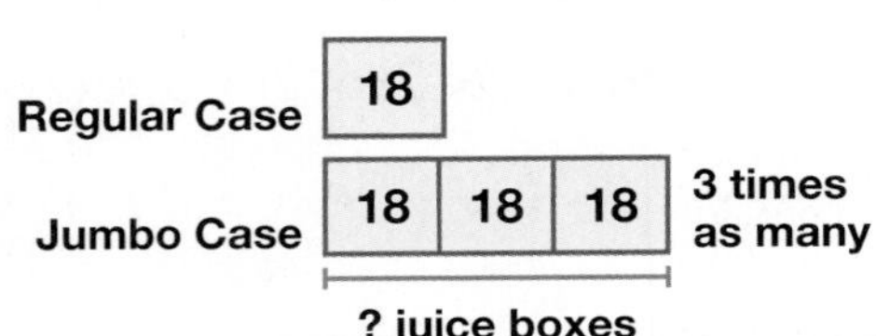

Write a number sentence to find the number that is 3 times as many as 18.

$3 \times 18 = \square$

Solve

Find 3×18.

$$\begin{array}{r} \overset{2}{1}8 \\ \times \;\; 3 \\ \hline 54 \end{array}$$

A jumbo case has 54 juice boxes.

Check

Make sure the answer is reasonable.

Estimate to check.

Round 18 to 20.

$3 \times 20 = 60$

The answer is reasonable because 54 is close to the estimate of 60.

Explain It

1. **Number Sense** Why can't you use the same type of diagram for this problem as you used for the problem at the top of the page?
2. Describe another way that you could check that the answer to the problem above is correct.

Plan

Use a picture or a diagram to show what you know.

The groups are equal, so multiply to find the total. Write a number sentence.

$5 \times 24 = \square$

Solve

Find 5×24.

$$\begin{array}{r} \scriptsize{2} \\ 24 \\ \times \ \ 5 \\ \hline 120 \end{array}$$

Oscar bought 120 bottles of water.

Check

Make sure the answer is reasonable.

Estimate to check.

Round 24 to 20.

$5 \times 20 = 100$

The answer 120 is reasonable because it is close to the estimate.

Guided Practice*

Do you know HOW?

1. A doll collection is displayed in 8 rows with 16 dolls in each row. How many dolls are in the collection?

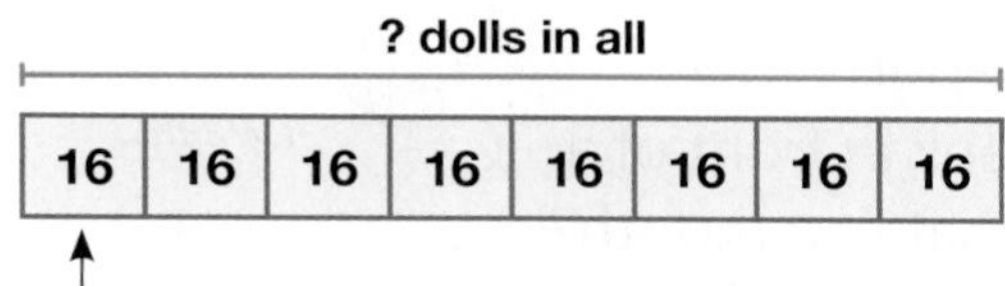

Do you UNDERSTAND?

2. **Writing to Explain** Why do you multiply to solve Problem 1?

3. **Write a Problem** Write a problem that can be solved by drawing a picture. Draw the picture. Solve.

Independent Practice

4. Eduardo has 36 football cards. He has 3 times as many baseball cards. How many baseball cards does he have?

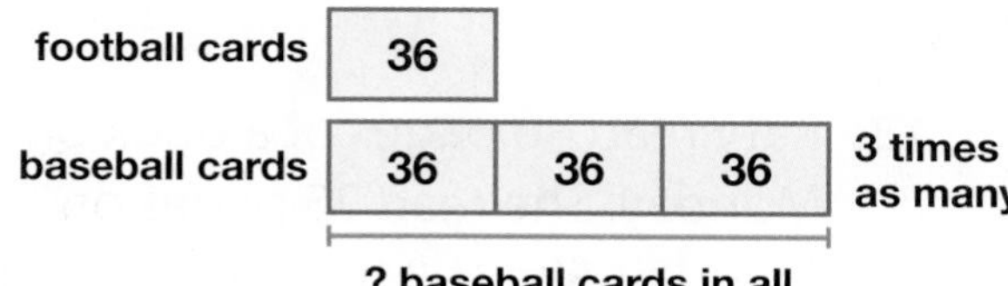

5. **Writing to Explain** Noah has 95 books to put on 4 shelves. If he puts 24 books on each shelf, will all the books fit on the shelves?

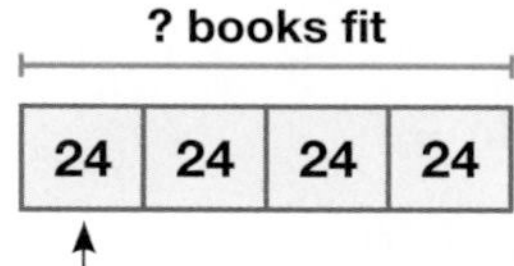

Stuck? Try this....

- What do I know?
- What am I asked to find?
- What diagram can I use to help understand the problem?
- Can I use addition, subtraction, multiplication, or division?
- Is all of my work correct?
- Did I answer the right question?
- Is my answer reasonable?

For another example, see Set F on page 433.

Independent Practice

The table shows about how many calories a 150-pound adult uses doing different activities. Use the table for **6–8**.

6. Martha's mother went jogging for 15 minutes. How many calories did she use?

? calories in all

8	8	8	8	8	8	8	8	8	8	8	8	8	8	8

Number of calories used each minute

Data

Calories Used in 1 Minute	
Activity	**Number of Calories**
Swimming	10
Jogging	8
Rollerblading	4
Running	9

7. Mr. Lee ran for 25 minutes. Then he swam for 20 minutes. How many calories did he use in all?

8. Miss Nunez plans to swim for 15 minutes every day. How many calories will she use in a week?

9. Frank rode his bike for an hour. Then he went rollerblading for 25 minutes. How many more minutes did he spend riding his bike than rollerblading?

10. **Estimation** The U.S. Department of Health reports that many children spend about 32 hours each week in front of a computer screen. About how many hours is that in a month?

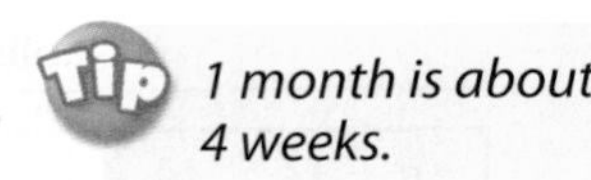

1 month is about 4 weeks.

11. Stacy has 3 bags of red beads. Cynthia has 2 more bags than Stacy. There are 24 beads in each bag.

a How many beads does each girl have?

b How many beads do the girls have all together?

Think About the Process

12. Mike earns \$4 an hour doing yard work. He worked 12 hours last week and 23 hours this week. Which number sentence shows how much he earned this week?

A $\$23 + \$12 = \square$

B $12 \times \$4 = \square$

C $23 \times \$4 = \square$

D $(23 \times \$4) \times 7 = \square$

13. Katy read 46 pages of a book on Monday. She read 25 pages on Tuesday. She still has 34 pages to read. Which number sentence shows how many pages are in the book?

A $46 + 25 = \square$

B $46 - 34 = \square$

C $(46 + 25) - 34 = \square$

D $46 + 25 + 34 = \square$

Arrays and Partial Products

Use eTools

Place-Value Blocks

Find 4×37. Use an array to tell the partial products.

Step 1 Go to the Place-Value Blocks eTool. Select a horizontal tens block. Click in the workspace 3 times to show the 3 tens in 37. Select a ones block. Click in the workspace 7 times to show the 7 ones in 37. Put all these blocks in one row.

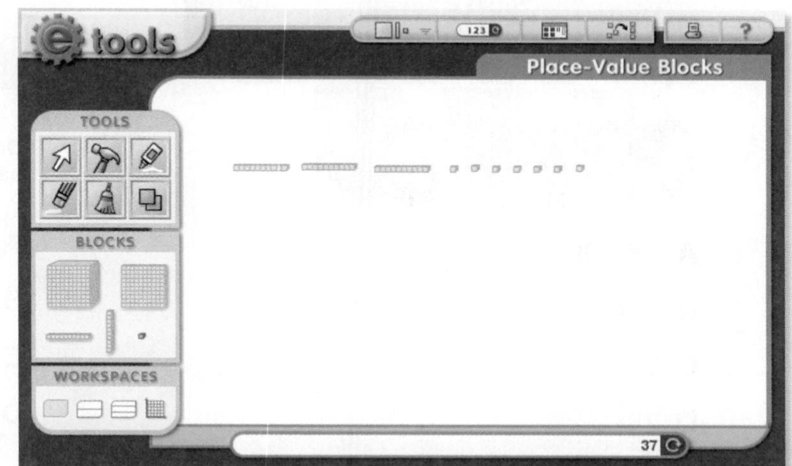

Step 2 Make 3 more rows with 37 in each, so you have 4 rows in all. Click on the odometer style button until you see the partial products 120 + 28 in the odometer. Click on the odometer style button again until the product is shown. The odometer should show 148. Now write a number sentence that shows the partial products and the product.
$4 \times 37 = 120 + 28 = 148$

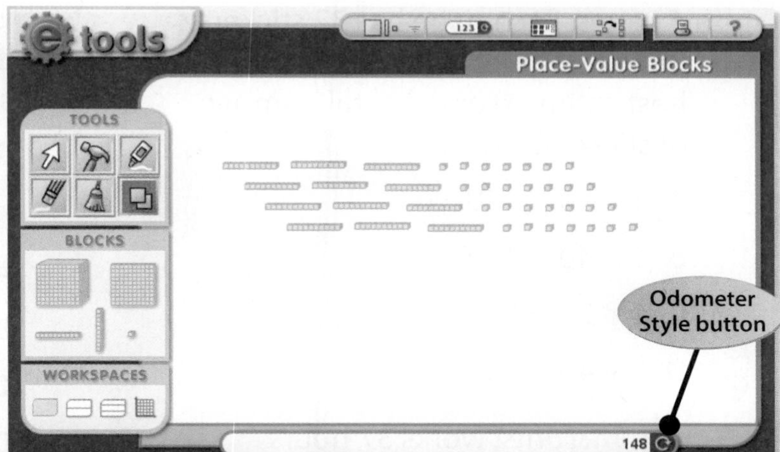

Practice

Use the Place-Value Blocks eTool to find the partial products and the product for each.

1. 3×56 **2.** 3×29 **3.** 2×68

4. 2×87 **5.** 3×98 **6.** 5×17

Topic 18
Test

1. Jillian bought 7 packages of paper. Each package had 400 sheets. How many sheets of paper did Jillian buy? (18-1)

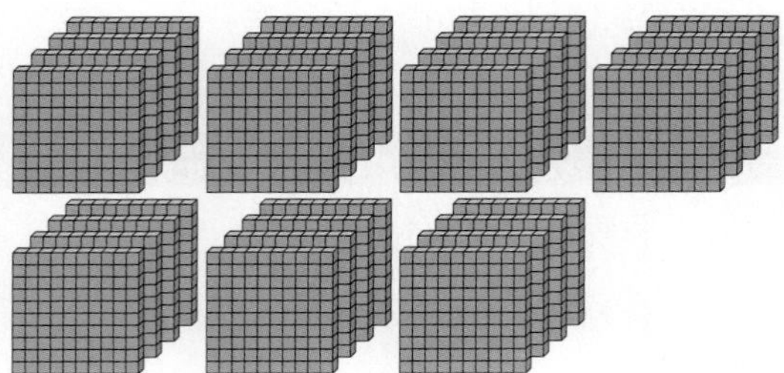

A 28,000

B 2,800

C 128

D 28

2. A package of stickers contains 4 pages. Each page has 32 stickers. Which number sentence shows the best estimate of the total number of stickers? (18-2)

A $4 \times 30 = 120$

B $4 \times 40 = 160$

C $4 + 30 = 34$

D $4 + 40 = 44$

3. Mrs. Martinez works 37 hours each week. How many hours does she work in 6 weeks? Find the product. (18-5)

$$\begin{array}{r} 37 \\ \times \ 6 \\ \hline \end{array}$$

A 60

B 122

C 192

D 222

4. Vella's bookcase has 6 shelves. Each shelf displays 3 dolls. Which number sentence shows how many dolls are displayed in the bookcase? (18-7)

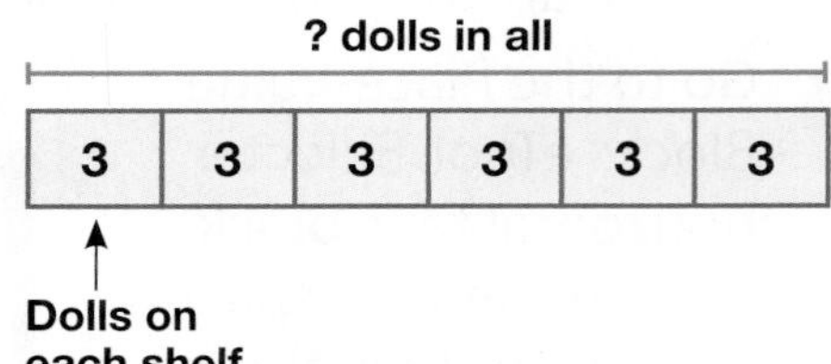

A $6 + 3 = 9$

B $6 - 3 = 3$

C $6 \times 3 = 18$

D $6 \div 3 = 2$

5. Henry bought 3 bags of oranges. Each bag had 16 oranges. How many oranges did he buy? Use the array to solve. (18-3)

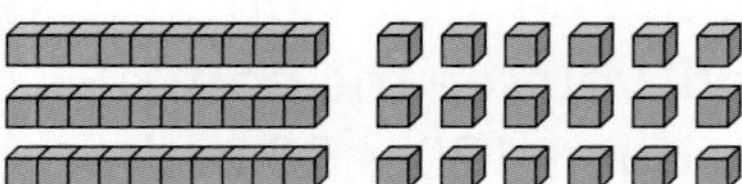

A 19

B 38

C 48

D 54

6. Mr. Gomez bought 26 packages of juice boxes for the school picnic. Each package had 8 juice boxes. How many juice boxes did he buy? (18-6)

A 214

B 208

C 202

D 168

7. Which addition sentence shows how to use partial products to find 5×17? (18-4)

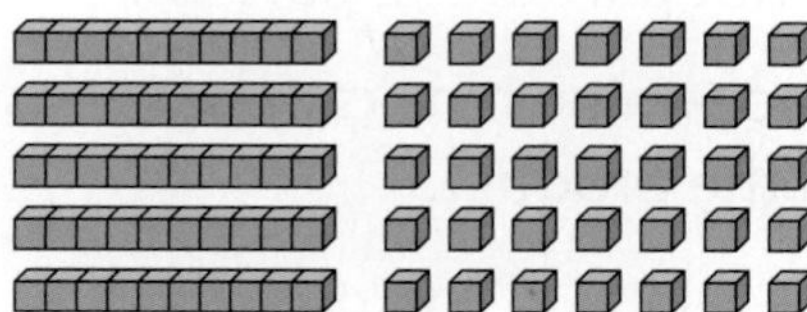

A $50 + 35 = 85$

B $5 + 35 = 38$

C $50 + 45 = 95$

D $50 + 5 = 55$

8. There are 46 students in Grade 3. Each student brought 6 balloons to use on the Grade 3 float in the parade. Which is the best estimate of the number of balloons that will be used on the float? (18-2)

A 50

B 100

C 150

D 300

9. One kind of hippopotamus can eat 130 pounds of food a day. How many pounds of food can this hippopotamus eat in 7 days? (18-6)

A 28

B 91

C 910

D 9,100

10. Which number sentence comes next in the pattern? (18-1)

$8 \times 6 = 48$
$8 \times 60 = 480$
$8 \times 600 = 4{,}800$

A $8 \times 600 = 48{,}000$

B $8 \times 6{,}000 = 48{,}000$

C $80 \times 60 = 4{,}800$

D $80 \times 600 = 48{,}000$

11. Jo drinks 2 to 3 glasses of milk a day. Which is a reasonable number of glasses of milk Jo will drink in 7 days? (18-2)

A Fewer than 14

B Between 14 and 21

C Between 22 and 35

D More than 35

12. Ann needs 20 ceramic tiles to decorate one stepping stone. If she wants to decorate 4 stepping stones for her garden, how many ceramic tiles does she need? (18-1)

A 80

B 24

C 16

D 5

Reteaching

Set A, pages 412–413

Find $7 \times 5{,}000$.

Use basic facts and patterns.

$7 \times 5 = 35$ ← basic fact
$7 \times 50 = 350$
$7 \times 500 = 3{,}500$
$7 \times 5{,}000 = 35{,}000$
} Pattern of zeros

Remember that when the product of a basic fact contains a zero, that zero is not part of the pattern.

Use place-value blocks or patterns to find the product.

1. 7×300 **2.** $9 \times 6{,}000$

3. $4 \times 5{,}000$ **4.** 5×200

5. 8×900 **6.** $3 \times 3{,}000$

Set B, pages 414–415

Estimate 6×57.

Round 57 to the nearest ten.
Then multiply.

6×57
↓ 57 rounds to 60.
$6 \times 60 = 360$

6×57 is about 360.

Remember that you round to the greater ten if the digit in the ones place is 5 or greater. Round to the lesser ten if the ones digit is 4 or less.

Estimate each product.

1. 5×39 **2.** 8×67

3. 7×42 **4.** 2×76

5. 4×83 **6.** 9×25

Set C, pages 416–417

Draw an array to find 3×24.

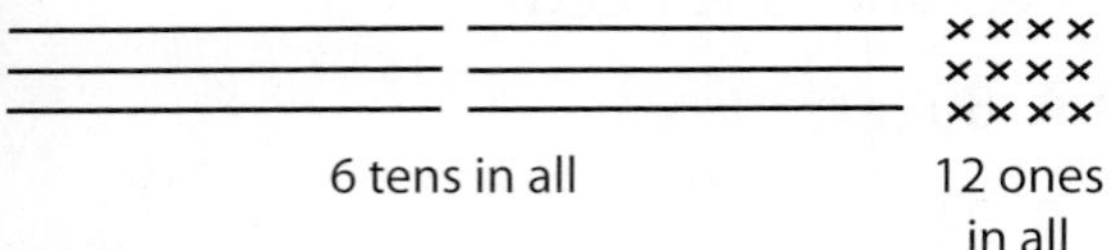

Count by tens.
10, 20, 30, 40, 50, 60

Then count by ones to find the total.
61, 62, 63, 64, 65, 66, 67, 68, 69, 70, 71, 72

So, $3 \times 24 = 72$.

Remember to keep your drawings simple.

Find each product. Use place-value blocks or draw a picture to help.

1. 3×27 **2.** 4×18

3. 5×14 **4.** 3×32

5. 7×31 **6.** 4×42

7. 8×22 **8.** 5×62

Set D, pages 418–419

Find 2×17 by breaking 17 into tens and ones.

×××××××
×××××××

Two rows of 1 ten = 2 tens or 20
Two rows of 7 ones = 14 ones or 14

20 and 14 are partial products.

$20 + 14 = 34$ Add the partial products.

So, $2 \times 17 = 34$.

Remember to include a zero when you record the value of the tens.

Find each product. You may draw a picture to help.

1. 4×73 **2.** 2×59

3. 6×35 **4.** 3×81

5. 7×25 **6.** 5×34

Set E, pages 420–424

Find 27×6.

One Way

$$\begin{array}{r} 27 \\ \times \quad 6 \\ \hline 42 \\ +\ 120 \\ \hline 162 \end{array}$$

42 and 120: partial products

Another Way

$$\begin{array}{r} {}^{4} \\ 27 \\ \times \quad 6 \\ \hline 162 \end{array}$$

Multiply ones.
Regroup.
Multiply tens.

So, $27 \times 6 = 162$.

Remember you can estimate to check that your answer is reasonable.

Find each product.

1. 29×6 **2.** 42×5 **3.** 79×4

4. 9×163 **5.** 8×240

6. $3 \times \$9.67$ **7.** $2 \times \$1.98$

Set F, pages 426–428

Beth has 24 planet stickers. She has 4 times as many flower stickers as planet stickers. How many flower stickers does Beth have?

The groups are equal, so multiply.

$4 \times 24 = 96$
Beth has 96 flower stickers.

Remember that drawing a picture can help you write a number sentence.

Draw a picture to show what you know. Write a number sentence and solve the problem.

1. Ty has his model car collection on shelves in his room. There are 9 shelves with 18 model cars on each shelf. How many model cars are on the shelves?

Topic 19

Dividing with 1-Digit Numbers

1. When Little League began in 1939, there were 30 players. How many teams did they form? You will find out out in Lesson 19-4.

2. The world's largest American flag is 505 feet long. Each star is 17 feet high. About how wide is the flag? You will find out in Lesson 19-6.

3 Skateboarding began in the 1950s. How many skateboards can be made from 38 wheels? You will find out in Lesson 19-5.

4 How much air does a person breathe each day? You will find out in Lesson 19-2.

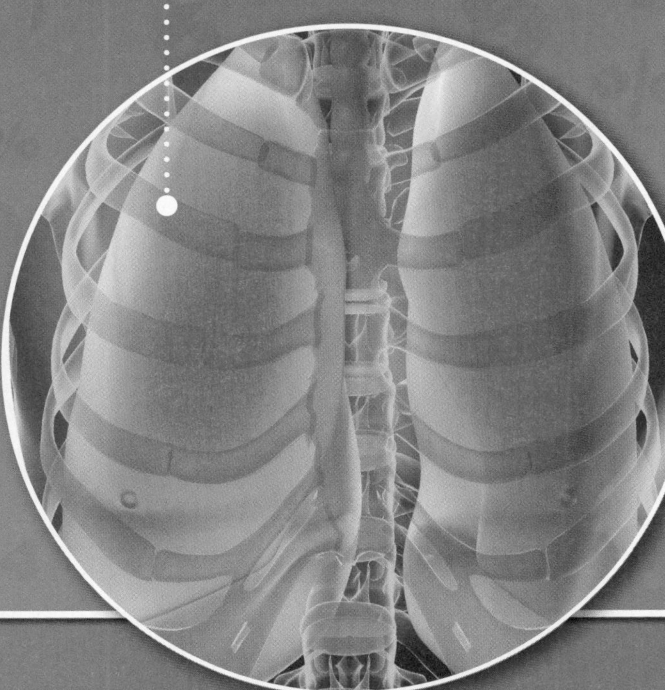

Review What You Know!

Vocabulary

Choose the best term from the box.

- division
- fact
- quotient
- regroup

1. The answer in division is called the __?__.
2. A __?__ family shows how multiplication and division are related.
3. When there are not enough ones to subtract, you can __?__ tens for ones.

Division Facts

Divide.

4. 12 ÷ 3 **5.** 18 ÷ 2 **6.** 30 ÷ 6

7. 54 ÷ 9 **8.** 64 ÷ 8 **9.** 63 ÷ 7

Multiplication

Multiply.

10. 4 × 19 **11.** 7 × 14 **12.** 4 × 23

Subtraction

Subtract.

13. 72 − 60 **14.** 346 − 200

15. 1,308 − 1,200 **16.** 4,275 − 3,000

17. **Writing to Explain** Lea poured 40 ounces of paint into 5 jars. Each jar had the same amount of paint. How much paint was in each jar? Draw a picture and solve. Explain why your drawing helps.

Lesson

19-1

Understand It!
Basic facts and place-value patterns can be used to find some quotients.

Mental Math

How can you divide multiples of 10, 100, and 1,000 using patterns?

You know that 12 ÷ 3 = 4.

120 ÷ 3 = 40

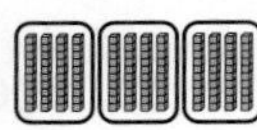

1,200 ÷ 3 = 400

12,000 ÷ 3 = 4,000

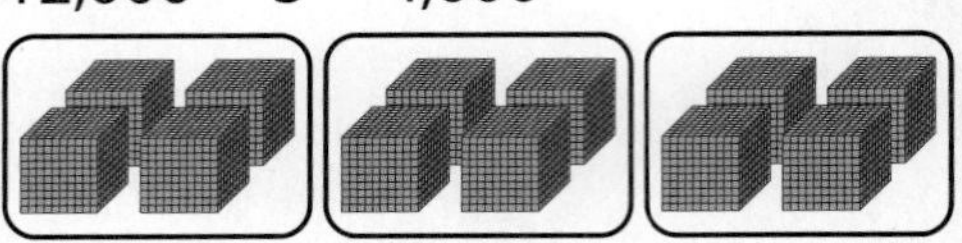

Guided Practice*

Do you know HOW?

In **1–4**, use patterns and mental math to find each quotient.

1. 36 ÷ 4
360 ÷ 4
3,600 ÷ 4

2. 40 ÷ 8
400 ÷ 8
4,000 ÷ 8

3. 180 ÷ 6

4. 1,400 ÷ 2

Do you UNDERSTAND?

5. Look at Another Way above. Why are 2 zeros written to the right of 4?

6. What basic fact can you use to find the quotient of 1,800 ÷ 3?

7. Jay says, "28 ÷ 4 is 7, so 2,800 ÷ 4 is 700." Do you agree? Explain.

Independent Practice

In **8–15**, use patterns to find each quotient.

8. 15 ÷ 3
150 ÷ 3
1,500 ÷ 3

9. 54 ÷ 9
540 ÷ 9
5,400 ÷ 9

10. 32 ÷ 4
320 ÷ 4
3,200 ÷ 4

11. 72 ÷ 8
720 ÷ 8
7,200 ÷ 8

12. 21 ÷ 7
210 ÷ 7
2,100 ÷ 7

13. 12 ÷ 6
120 ÷ 6
1,200 ÷ 6

14. 20 ÷ 5
200 ÷ 5
2,000 ÷ 5

15. 63 ÷ 9
630 ÷ 9
6,300 ÷ 9

In **16–25**, use mental math to find each quotient.

16. 160 ÷ 2 **17.** 4,900 ÷ 7 **18.** 60 ÷ 3 **19.** 350 ÷ 5 **20.** 5,600 ÷ 8

21. 3,200 ÷ 8 **22.** 120 ÷ 6 **23.** 80 ÷ 4 **24.** 360 ÷ 6 **25.** 8,100 ÷ 9

*For another example, see Set A on page 454.

One Way

Find 2,400 ÷ 6.

Use place value.

2,400 is the same as 24 × 100 or 24 hundreds.

24 ÷ 6 = 4
So, 24 hundreds ÷ 6 = 4 hundreds.

2,400 ÷ 6 = 400

Another Way

Find 2,400 ÷ 6.

Use a rule.

24 ÷ 6 = 4

2,400 ÷ 6 is 4 followed by 2 zeros.

2,400 ÷ 6 = 400

Problem Solving

For **26–30**, use the table at the right.

Animal Heart Rates

Animal	Number of Heartbeats in 5 Minutes
Bat	3,500
Chicken	1,500
Frog	150
Horse	200
Mouse	3,100

26. How many times does a horse's heart beat in one minute?

27. How many times does a chicken's heart beat in one minute?

28. In 5 minutes, how many more times does a bat's heart beat than a chicken's heart?

29. In 5 minutes, which animal has 10 times as many heartbeats as a frog?

30. Write the animals' names in order from fewest to most heartbeats in 5 minutes.

31. Kara leads tours in a museum. During 2 tours she climbed a total of 800 stairs. If the tours were exactly the same, how many stairs did she climb during each tour?

32. The 1,400 people who attended a music concert were equally divided into 7 seating areas. How many people were in each seating area?

A 140 **B** 200 **C** 1,393 **D** 1,407

33. **Number Sense** How many $5 bills make $30? How many make $300?

Lesson
19-2

Understand It!
Basic division facts can be helpful in estimating quotients.

Estimating Quotients

How do you estimate with division?

The Mills family is planning a car trip that will be 1,764 miles long. The family wants to drive an equal number of miles on each of 6 days. About how many miles should the family drive each day?

1,764 miles

Estimate You need to know *about* how many miles, so an estimate is enough.

Guided Practice*

Do you know HOW?

In **1–8**, estimate each quotient.

1. 83 ÷ 4

2. 248 ÷ 5

3. 572 ÷ 7

4. 4,138 ÷ 6

5. 91 ÷ 9

6. 306 ÷ 5

7. 2,293 ÷ 8

8. 2,710 ÷ 4

Do you UNDERSTAND?

9. In the example above, why is 1,800 ÷ 6 equal to 300 and not 30?

10. What division could you use to estimate 317 ÷ 4?

11. Timmy wants to put 346 toy cars into 5 equal groups. About how many cars should he put in each group?

Independent Practice

In **12–35**, estimate each quotient.

12. 73 ÷ 7

13. 164 ÷ 2

14. 479 ÷ 8

15. 172 ÷ 3

16. 416 ÷ 5

17. 1,983 ÷ 4

18. 361 ÷ 9

19. 505 ÷ 7

20. 7,168 ÷ 9

21. 1,329 ÷ 6

22. 324 ÷ 8

23. 546 ÷ 9

24. 729 ÷ 8

25. 2,036 ÷ 5

26. 697 ÷ 7

27. 812 ÷ 9

28. 364 ÷ 4

29. 206 ÷ 4

30. 427 ÷ 7

31. 489 ÷ 6

32. 278 ÷ 7

33. 8,097 ÷ 9

34. 2,536 ÷ 5

35. 4,917 ÷ 7

For another example, see Set A on page 454.

Use a division fact.

The family will drive for 6 days. What numbers can be divided evenly by 6?

6, 12, 18, and so on.

1,764 miles is about 1,800 miles.

For division, 1,800 and 6 are numbers that are easy to work with.

Then use mental math.

Find 1,800 ÷ 6.

18 ÷ 6 = 3

1,800 ÷ 6 = 300

The family should drive about 300 miles each day.

Problem Solving

For **36–38**, use the table at the right.

Data

Ramos Family Vacation Ideas Car Trip Distances

Trip	Number of Miles
Blue Mountain	1,135
Camp Carlson	1,589
Forest Park	473
River Land	766
Sands Point Beach	2,740

36. The Ramos family wants to take 4 days to drive to River Land. The family wants to drive an equal number of miles each day. About how many miles should the family drive each day?

37. About how many more miles is the trip to Camp Carlson than to Forest Park?

38. **Reasonableness** The Ramos family wants to take 4 days to drive to Blue Mountain. They plan to drive about 300 miles each day. Is this reasonable? Explain.

39. Ashley has 87 insects in her nature collection. She has three times as many leaves as insects in her collection. How many leaves does Ashley have in her collection?

40. Mr. Lowell bought 8 baseball caps. All of the caps were the same price. The total cost was $72. What is the cost of each baseball cap?

A $576 **B** $80 **C** $64 **D** $9

41. **Algebra** What number makes the number sentence true?

179 × ▢ = 179

42. In 3 days, a person breathes about 9,100 gallons of air. About how many gallons of air does a person breathe in 1 day?

Lesson
19-3

Understand It!
Place-value blocks can be used to model division with 2-digit numbers.

Connecting Models and Symbols

Hands-On
place-value blocks

How can you model division with greater numbers?

The third graders made 56 sandwiches for a picnic. They put an equal number of sandwiches on each of 4 plates. How many sandwiches are on each plate?

56 sandwiches

Another Example How can place value help you divide?

Helen has 54 baseball cards. She wants to put an equal number of cards in each of 3 albums. How many cards will go in each album?

Choose an Operation Division is used to find the size of equal groups. Helen needs to find $54 \div 3$.

You have used place value to help subtract. Now you will use place value to help divide.

Estimate Use numbers that are easy to divide: 60 is close to 54 and $60 \div 3 = 20$. There should be about 20 cards in each album.

Draw place-value blocks to show 54.

$3\overline{)54}$

Divide the tens into 3 equal groups.

$$\begin{array}{r} 1 \\ 3\overline{)54} \\ -3 \\ \hline \end{array}$$

1 ten in each group

3 tens used

Regroup the extra tens as ones.

$$\begin{array}{r} 1 \\ 3\overline{)54} \\ -3 \\ \hline 2 \end{array}$$

2 tens are left

Divide the ones into 3 equal groups.

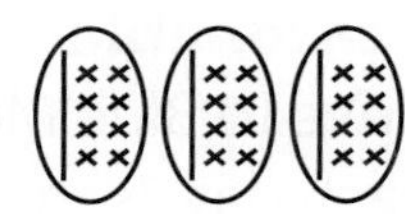

$$\begin{array}{r} 18 \\ 3\overline{)54} \\ -3\downarrow \\ \hline 24 \\ -24 \\ \hline 0 \end{array}$$

8 ones in each group

24 ones used

No ones left

There will be 18 cards in each album.

Explain It

1. Why do you trade the tens for ones?

Step 1

Model the problem.

Use place-value blocks.

56: 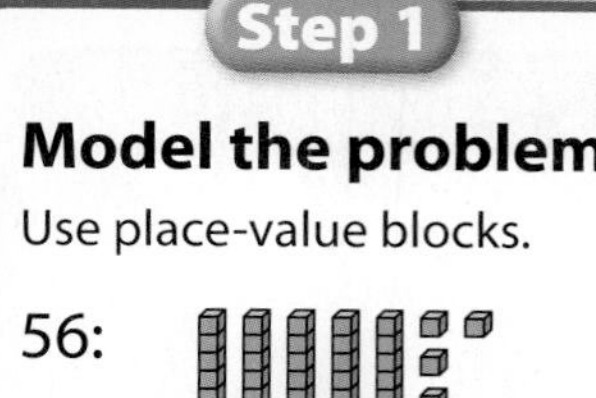

Draw rings to show how many equal groups you need.

Step 2

Divide the tens.

Put an equal number of tens in each ring. 1 ten and 6 ones are left.

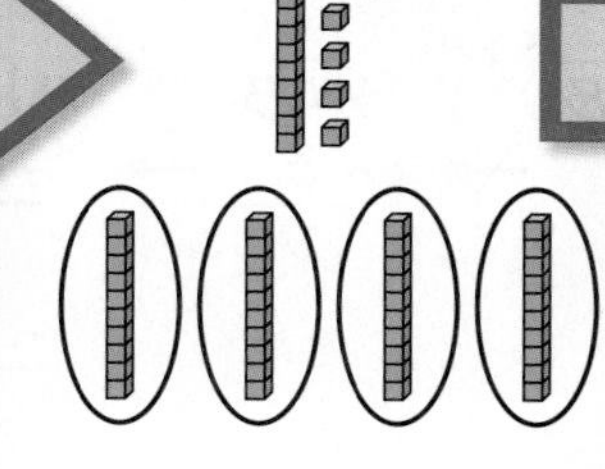

Step 3

Regroup the leftover tens as ones and divide the ones.

1 ten regrouped as 10 ones plus the 6 ones is 16 ones.

Place an equal number of ones in each ring.

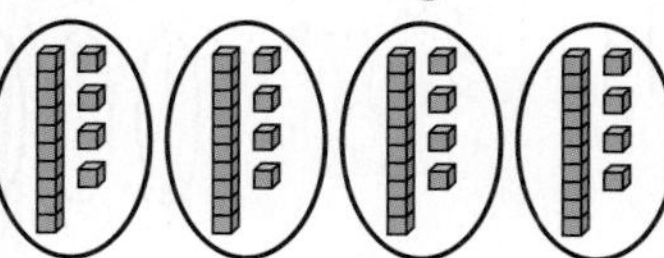

Each plate has 14 sandwiches.

Guided Practice*

Do you know HOW?

Use place-value blocks or the pictures. Copy and complete to find the quotient.

1. $32 \div 2$

a Draw place-value blocks to show 32.

$2\overline{)32}$

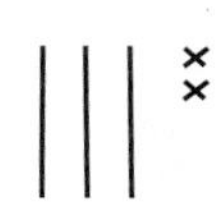

b Divide the tens into 2 equal groups.

c Regroup the extra ten as ones.

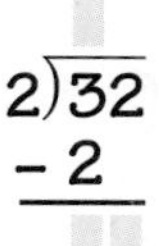

d Divide the ones.

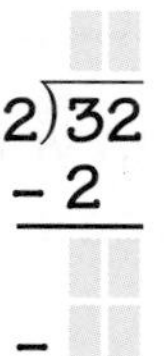

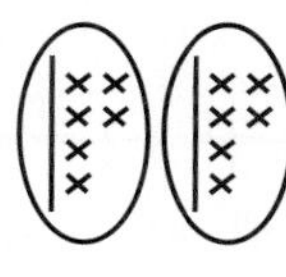

Do you UNDERSTAND?

2. In Exercise 1, how do the pictures help you divide?

3. **Writing to Explain** In the example above, why do you draw four rings?

In **4** and **5**, solve. Use place-value blocks or draw pictures to help.

4. In the example above, suppose the 3rd graders made 68 sandwiches for the picnic. How many would they need to put on each plate?

5. The third graders have 42 straws for a picnic. They want to put an equal number of straws in each of three cups. How many straws should they put in each cup?

*For another example, see Set B on page 454.

Independent Practice

Leveled Practice In **6–9**, use place-value blocks or the pictures to help you find each quotient.

6. 48 ÷ 3

3)48 → 3)48 − 3 → 3)48 − 3, −, 0

7. 34 ÷ 2

2)34 → 2)34 − 2 → 2)34 − 2, −, 0

8. 51 ÷ 3

3)51 → 3)51 − 3 → 3)51 − 3, −, 0

9. 72 ÷ 4

4)72 → 4)72 − 4 → 4)72 − 4, −, 0

In **10–19**, draw pictures to help find each quotient.

10. 36 ÷ 2 **11.** 68 ÷ 4 **12.** 90 ÷ 9 **13.** 65 ÷ 5 **14.** 84 ÷ 6

15. 42 ÷ 3 **16.** 80 ÷ 5 **17.** 76 ÷ 4 **18.** 42 ÷ 2 **19.** 91 ÷ 7

Problem Solving

20. There are 64 children playing games. They want to make 4 equal teams. How many children should be on each team?

21. **Number Sense** How can you tell if the quotient 46 ÷ 2 is greater than 20 without dividing?

22. Mr. Wen has $42. He wants to give an equal amount to each of his three children. What amount should he give to each child?

23. Indira painted $\frac{1}{4}$ of the length of a board. What is one other way to name $\frac{1}{4}$?

$\frac{1}{4}$ painted

Use the table for **24–26**.

Number of Items in Package

Item	Small	Medium	Large
Paper Plates	36	52	90
Paper Cups	24	48	96

24. Marisol has a medium package of paper plates. She wants to put an equal number of plates on each of four tables. How many plates should she put on each table?

25. Marisol has a large package of paper cups. She wants to put an equal number of cups on each of six tables. How many cups should she put on each table?

26. Suppose Bruce buys a small package and a medium package of paper plates. How many fewer paper plates would he have than if he bought a large package of paper plates?

27. Leslie estimates that it will take 150 hours to paint her house. If Leslie paints for 8 hours each day, about how many days will it take her to paint the house?

A 10 **C** 40

B 20 **D** 60

28. Malik is displaying baseball cards in an album. He can fit 4 cards on a page. How many pages does he need to display 96 baseball cards?

A 20 **C** 24

B 22 **D** 25

29. For a cooking contest, 85 chefs were equally divided into 5 different teams. How many chefs were on each team?

A 17 **C** 80

B 18 **D** 90

30. Mr. Mason bought 3 folding chairs. All of the chairs were the same price. The total cost was $57. How much money did each chair cost?

A $60 **C** $19

B $54 **D** $18

Lesson

19-4

Understand It!
Numbers can be broken apart into tens and ones to divide.

Dividing 2-Digit Numbers

How do you divide with paper and pencil?

Dara and Toby are dividing each kind of fruit equally into four boxes. How many apples should they put in each box?

Kind of Fruit	Number
Apples	76
Pears	56
Oranges	92

Choose an Operation Division is used to find the size of equal groups. Find 76 ÷ 4.

Estimate There are about 80 apples, and 80 ÷ 4 = 20. They should put about 20 apples in each box.

Guided Practice*

Do you know HOW?

In **1–4**, copy and complete. Find each quotient. Check your answers.

1.
```
   1□
 3)48
 - 3
   1□
 - □□
```

2.
```
   1□
 6)84
 - 6
   2□
 - □□
```

3.
```
   1□
 2)38
 - 2
   □□
 - □□
```

4.
```
   1□
 5)85
 - 5
   □□
 - □□
```

Do you UNDERSTAND?

5. In the example above, why is a 1 written above the 7?

6. **Number Sense** Charles says that 68 ÷ 4 = 18. Multiply to find out if he is correct.

7. Use the table above. Dara and Toby are dividing the pears and the oranges equally into four boxes.

a How many pears should they put in each box?

b How many oranges?

Independent Practice

In **8–12**, copy and complete to find each quotient. Check your answers.

8.
```
   3□
 2)76
 - 6
   □6
 - □□
```

9.
```
   □□
 6)78
 - □
   □8
 - □□
```

10.
```
   2□
 3)81
 - 6
   □1
 - □□
```

11.
```
   □□
 4)92
 - □
   □2
 - □□
```

12.
```
   1□
 5)95
 - 5
   □5
 - □□
```


*For another example, see Set B on page 454.

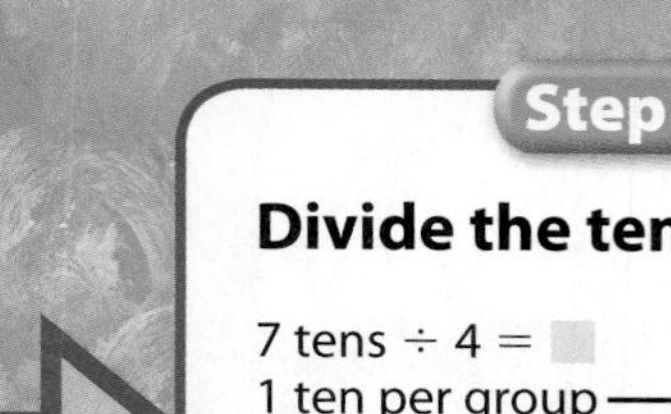

Step 1

Divide the tens.

7 tens ÷ 4 = ▢

1 ten per group → 1

4)76

4 tens used → − 4

3 tens left → 3

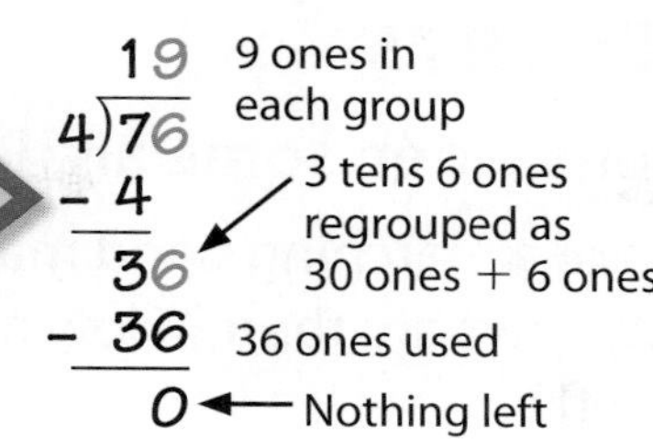

Step 2

Divide the ones.

19 — 9 ones in each group

4)76

− 4

36 — 3 tens 6 ones regrouped as 30 ones + 6 ones

− 36 — 36 ones used

0 ← Nothing left

$76 \div 4 = 19$

They should put 19 apples in each box.

Step 3

Check by multiplying.

$$\begin{array}{r} \scriptstyle 3 \\ 19 \\ \times\ 4 \\ \hline 76 \end{array}$$

Also, the answer 19 is close to the estimate of 20.

Problem Solving

For **13–15**, use the table at the right.

Fruits Picked (Data)

Kind of Fruit	Number
Lemons	84
Peaches	96
Pears	72
Oranges	79

13. Carla picked the peaches. She put an equal number of peaches into each of eight crates. How many peaches did Carla put in each crate?

14. Justine picked the lemons and put an equal number of lemons into each of three crates. How many lemons did she put in each crate?

15. **Estimation** About how many pears and oranges were picked in all?

16. For the concert, the 64 band members were divided equally into 4 different groups. How many band members were in each group?

17. Little League baseball began in 1939 in Pennsylvania. There were 30 players equally divided among 3 teams. How many players were on each team?

18. **Algebra** Which of the following numbers makes this number sentence true?

$8 \times 9 > 4 \times$ ▢

A 17

B 18

C 19

D 21

19. Mrs. Adams bought 5 blankets. All of the blankets were the same price. The total cost was $95. How much did each blanket cost?

A $475

B $90

C $19

D $18

Lesson

19-5

Understand It!
Division problems can have something left over.

Dividing with Remainders

Hands-On
counters

What happens when some are left?

If 23 members of a marching band march in rows of 4, how many rows are there? How many band members are left?

Division is used to find how many groups. The number left over after dividing is the remainder.

Guided Practice*

Do you know HOW?

In **1–6**, use counters or draw a picture to find each quotient and remainder.

1. 17 ÷ 3 **2.** 22 ÷ 6

3. 25 ÷ 4 **4.** 18 ÷ 5

5. 15 ÷ 2 **6.** 19 ÷ 7

Do you UNDERSTAND?

7. In the example above, what does the quotient 5 R3 mean?

8. There are 20 members in the marching band. Suppose they march in rows of 3. How many full rows of band members would there be? How many band members would be left?

Independent Practice

Leveled Practice In **9–12**, copy and complete. Check your answers.

9. ▢ R▢ $3\overline{)14}$ − ▢▢

10. ▢ R▢ $2\overline{)17}$ − ▢▢

11. ▢ R▢ $7\overline{)27}$ − ▢▢

12. ▢ R▢ $8\overline{)55}$ − ▢▢

In **13–22**, find each quotient and remainder. Check your answers.

13. $4\overline{)21}$ **14.** $6\overline{)46}$ **15.** $5\overline{)48}$ **16.** $9\overline{)41}$ **17.** $9\overline{)64}$

18. $5\overline{)52}$ **19.** $8\overline{)58}$ **20.** $4\overline{)35}$ **21.** $6\overline{)39}$ **22.** $7\overline{)70}$

DIGITAL Animated Glossary, eTools
www.pearsonsuccessnet.com

*For another example, see Set C on page 455.

What You Show

What You Think

If I put 23 counters in rows of 4, I get 5 full rows.

I used 5 × 4, or 20 counters. The 3 counters I have left are not enough for another group of 4, so the remainder is 3.

I can check by multiplying 5 × 4 and then adding 3.

What You Write

$$\begin{array}{r} 5 \text{ R}3 \\ 4\overline{)23} \\ -\ 20 \\ \hline 3 \end{array}$$

Check:
5 × 4 = 20
20 + 3 = 23

There are 5 rows of band members with 3 band members left.

Problem Solving

For **23–25**, use the table at the right that shows all members of the band.

Clayton School Marching Band

Instrument	Number of Band Members
Drum	23
Flute	14
Clarinet	18
Trumpet	12

23. The flute players march in rows of 3. How many rows of flute players are there? How many flute players are left?

24. The drummers march in rows of 6. How many rows of drummers are there? How many drummers are left?

25. How many band members are there in all?

26. A group of 68 people will be going rafting. Each raft can hold 8 people. The group will fill each raft before using the next one. How many rafts will be needed?

27. **Writing to Explain** Together, Nick and Leslie need to make 9 sandwiches. Nick thinks they will have enough if they each make 4 sandwiches. Do you agree? Explain.

28. **Number Sense** What is the greatest possible remainder you can have if you divide a number by 7? Explain.

29. Melanie has $20. She wants to buy as many cartons of juice as she can. Each carton costs $3. How many cartons of juice can she buy?

A 6 **B** 7 **C** 17 **D** 23

30. If each skateboard has 4 wheels, how many skateboards can Julian make with 38 wheels? How many wheels are left?

Lesson

19-6

Understand It!
Some multiple-step problems have hidden questions.

Problem Solving

Multiple-Step Problems

You have learned that some problems have hidden questions to be answered before you can solve the problem.

A museum collection of 36 dragonflies and 54 butterflies will be used in 2 new displays. There will be the same number of insects in both displays. How many insects will be in each display?

36 dragonflies

54 butterflies

Another Example What is the hidden question?

A store has boxed sets of DVDs for sale. In each box, the DVDs are in 2 rows with 3 DVDs in each row. The total cost of a boxed set is $72. Each DVD costs the same. What is the cost of one DVD?

Plan and Solve

What is the hidden question? What is the total number of DVDs in each box?

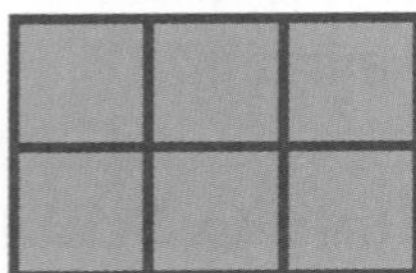

$2 \times 3 = 6$

There are 6 DVDs in each box.

Solve

Use the answer to the hidden question to solve the problem.

What is the cost of each DVD?

$$\begin{array}{r} 12 \\ 6\overline{)72} \\ -\underline{6} \\ 12 \\ -\underline{12} \\ 0 \end{array}$$

Each DVD costs $12.

Explain It

1. How do you know what the hidden question is in the problem above?
2. Explain how to check the solution to the problem above.

First, you need to find and solve the hidden question.

What is the total number of insects in the museum collection?

? insects in all

36 dragonflies	54 butterflies

$$\begin{array}{r} \scriptstyle 1 \\ 36 \\ +\ 54 \\ \hline 90 \end{array}$$

There are 90 insects in all.

Use the answer to the hidden question to solve the problem.

How many insects will be in each display?

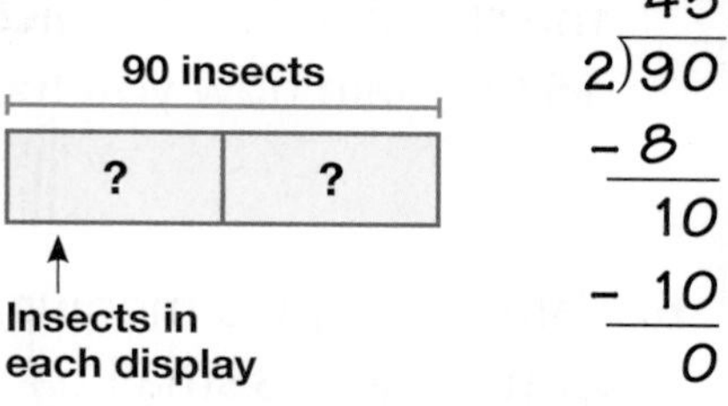

$$\begin{array}{r} 45 \\ 2\overline{)90} \\ -\ 8 \\ \hline 10 \\ -\ 10 \\ \hline 0 \end{array}$$

There will be 45 insects in each of the new displays.

Guided Practice*

Do you know HOW?

Answer the hidden question. Then solve.

1. Twelve friends went camping. All except 4 of them went on a hike. The hikers carried 32 water bottles. Each hiker carried the same number of water bottles. How many water bottles did each hiker carry?

   HINT: Hidden Question—How many went on the hike?

Do you UNDERSTAND?

2. What operations did you use to solve Problem 1?

3. **Write a Problem** Write a problem that can be solved by finding and answering a hidden question.

Independent Practice

Leveled Practice Solve. Answer the hidden question first.

4. Mrs. Lum bought 12 rolls of pink ribbon and some rolls of yellow ribbon. The total cost of the rolls of ribbon is $45. Each roll costs $3. How many rolls of yellow ribbon did Mrs. Lum buy?

   HINT: Hidden Question—What is the total number of rolls of ribbon Mrs. Lum bought?

Stuck? Try this....

- What do I know?
- What am I asked to find?
- What diagram can I use to help understand the problem?
- Can I use addition, subtraction, multiplication, or division?
- Is all of my work correct?
- Did I answer the right question?
- Is my answer reasonable?

For another example, see Set D on page 455.

Independent Practice

5. Writing to Explain There were 24 students in a class. All of the students, except 2, went bowling. What is the total cost the students paid if each person who went bowling paid \$5? Explain how you found your answer.

6. Vanya bought 5 medium packages of buttons and 3 small packages of beads. What was the total number of buttons she bought? Use the table at the right.

Data

Number of Items in Package

Item	Small	Medium	Large
Beads	32	64	96
Buttons	18	38	56

7. Mr. Alton wants to buy tickets for a show. The tickets are for seats in 3 rows with 3 seats in each row. The total cost of the tickets is \$108. Each ticket costs the same. What is the cost of one ticket?

8. Estimation Each stripe of the world's largest American flag is more than 19 feet wide. There are 7 red stripes and 6 white stripes. Each stripe is the same width. About how wide is this flag? Explain your answer.

9. Use the table at the right. Mrs. Casey bought one adult admission ticket and one child admission ticket. Then she bought one adult ticket and one child ticket for a boat ride. What was the total amount Mrs. Casey spent?

Data

County Fair

Kind of Ticket	Adult	Child
Admission	\$8	\$4
Boat Rides	\$2	\$1

10. Think About the Process Elio had \$36 in his wallet. He used \$9 to buy a book. Which number sentence shows how to find the amount of money he has left?

A $36 + 9 = \square$

B $36 - 9 = \square$

C $36 \times 9 = \square$

D $39 \div 9 = \square$

11. Think About the Process Martin raked 3 lawns yesterday and 4 lawns today. He earned a total of \$42. He earned the same amount for each lawn. Which number sentence shows how to find how much he earned for each lawn he raked?

A $42 - 4 = \square$

B $42 + 4 = \square$

C $42 \times 3 = \square$

D $42 \div 7 = \square$

Write the fraction in simplest form.

1. $\frac{4}{8}$ **2.** $\frac{4}{10}$ **3.** $\frac{8}{12}$ **4.** $\frac{2}{4}$

Find each sum or difference.

5. $\begin{array}{r} \$3.82 \\ +\ 1.47 \\ \hline \end{array}$ **6.** $\begin{array}{r} \$7.08 \\ +\ 2.93 \\ \hline \end{array}$ **7.** $\begin{array}{r} \$5.86 \\ -\ 1.29 \\ \hline \end{array}$ **8.** $\begin{array}{r} \$4.00 \\ -\ 1.38 \\ \hline \end{array}$

Find each product.

9. $\begin{array}{r} 39 \\ \times\ 8 \\ \hline \end{array}$ **10.** $\begin{array}{r} 56 \\ \times\ 7 \\ \hline \end{array}$ **11.** $\begin{array}{r} 97 \\ \times\ 3 \\ \hline \end{array}$ **12.** $\begin{array}{r} 86 \\ \times\ 5 \\ \hline \end{array}$ **13.** $\begin{array}{r} 300 \\ \times\ 4 \\ \hline \end{array}$

Find each quotient.

14. $3\overline{)78}$ **15.** $6\overline{)96}$ **16.** $2\overline{)56}$ **17.** $4\overline{)76}$

Error Search Find each product that is not correct. Write it correctly and explain the error.

18. $\begin{array}{r} 76 \\ \times\ 4 \\ \hline 300 \end{array}$ **19.** $\begin{array}{r} 39 \\ \times\ 6 \\ \hline 234 \end{array}$ **20.** $\begin{array}{r} 17 \\ \times\ 2 \\ \hline 16 \end{array}$ **21.** $\begin{array}{r} 86 \\ \times\ 3 \\ \hline 258 \end{array}$ **22.** $\begin{array}{r} 15 \\ \times\ 9 \\ \hline 135 \end{array}$

Number Sense

Estimating and Reasoning Write whether each statement is true or false. If the statement is false, explain why.

23. The sum of 128 and 292 is greater than 300.

24. The sum of 910 and 100 is less than 1,000.

25. The difference between 713 and 509 is less than 100.

26. The product of 4 and 29 is greater than 100.

27. The product of 5 and 86 is greater than 500.

28. The quotient of 82 ÷ 2 is greater than 40.

Test

1. An auditorium has 2,000 seats in 5 sections. Each section has the same number of seats. How many seats are in each section? (19-1)

   A 20

   B 40

   C 400

   D 10,000

2. Mr. Ortiz earned $6,496 by selling 8 paintings for the same price each. Which number sentence shows the best way to estimate the amount he earned for each painting? (19-2)

   A 8 × $6,400 = $51,200

   B $5,600 ÷ 8 = $700

   C $6,400 ÷ 10 = $640

   D $6,400 ÷ 8 = $800

3. What is 87 ÷ 7? (19-5)

   A 11 R1

   B 11 R7

   C 12

   D 12 R3

4. Don bought $76 in plants. He spent $24 on daisies and the rest on rose bushes. If Don bought 4 rose bushes that all had the same price, how much did each rose bush cost? (19-6)

   A $6

   B $13

   C $19

   D $52

5. Which number sentence does the diagram show? (19-3)

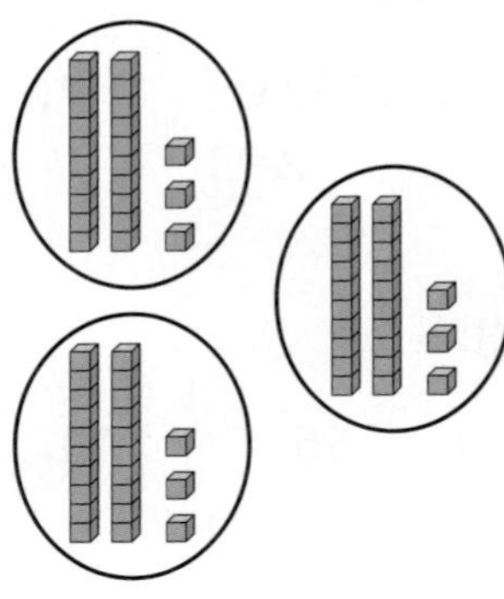

   A 69 ÷ 3 = 22

   B 69 ÷ 3 = 23

   C 69 ÷ 3 = 20

   D 60 ÷ 3 = 20

6. For the water balloon toss, 75 students were divided equally into 5 groups. How many students were in each group? (19-4)

   A 375

   B 25

   C 15

   D 14 groups with 5 left over

7. Four students stapled 84 school newsletters. How many newsletters did each student staple if they shared the work evenly? (19-4)

   A 336

   B 92

   C 21

   D 12

8. The art teacher has 240 cotton balls to use in her art classes. She has 3 classes in the morning and 1 in the afternoon. If she splits the cotton balls evenly among the classes, how many cotton balls would each class have? (19-6)

A 6

B 60

C 80

D 960

9. What is the quotient? (19-4)

$$\begin{array}{r} \square\square \\ 3\overline{)78} \\ -\ \square \\ \hline \square\square \\ -\ \square\square \\ \hline 0 \end{array}$$

A 16

B 23

C 24

D 26

10. Juan practiced the tuba for a total of 235 minutes this week. If he practiced an equal amount of time on 6 different nights, about how many minutes did he practice each night? (19-2)

A 40 minutes

B 55 minutes

C 60 minutes

D 240 minutes

11. What is 38 ÷ 9? (19-5)

A 4 R2

B 4 R3

C 4 R4

D 5 R3

12. To find 96 ÷ 4, Tim first divided the tens into 4 equal groups. What should Tim do next? (19-3)

$$\begin{array}{r} 2 \\ 4\overline{)96} \\ 8 \\ \hline \end{array}$$

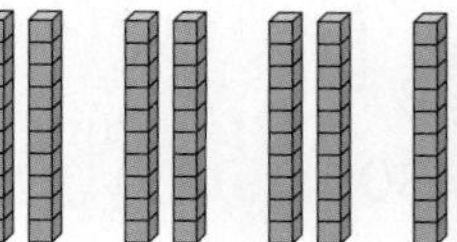

A Divide the ones.

B Subtract 8 tens from 9 tens.

C Regroup the two extra tens as ones.

D Nothing, he is finished.

13. Montgomery uses 7 beads to make a keychain. If she bought a package with 300 beads, about how many key chains will she be able to make? (19-2)

A 60

B 50

C 40

D 4

14. What is 2,400 ÷ 2? (19-1)

A 1,200

B 1,002

C 120

D 12

Reteaching

Set A, pages 436–439

Estimate 1,326 ÷ 4.

Use numbers that are close to the numbers in the problem and easy to divide.

1,200 is close to 1,326. 1,200 can be evenly divided by 4.

Think $12 \div 4 = 3$

Find 1,200 ÷ 4.

You can use patterns and mental math.

$12 \div 4 = 3$
$120 \div 4 = 30$
$1{,}200 \div 4 = 300$

Remember that you can use numbers that are close to the actual numbers and easy to divide.

Estimate each quotient.

1. 26 ÷ 3 **2.** 203 ÷ 2

3. 438 ÷ 6 **4.** 3,971 ÷ 5

5. 47 ÷ 8 **6.** 215 ÷ 4

7. 2,946 ÷ 7 **8.** 2,632 ÷ 9

Set B, pages 440–445

Find 57 ÷ 3.

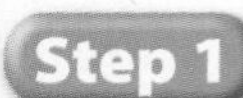

Divide the tens.

5 tens ÷ 3 = ▢
1 ten in each group → 1
3)57
3 tens used → − 3
27 left → 27

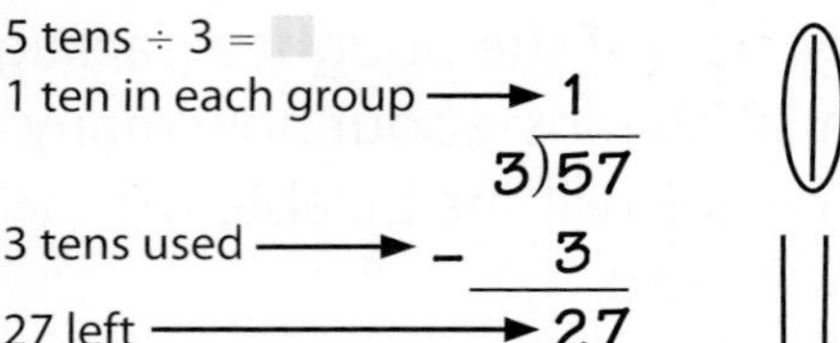

Divide the ones.

27 ones ÷ 3 = ▢
19 ← 9 ones in each group
3)57
− 3
27
− 27 ← 27 ones used
0 ← Nothing left

57 ÷ 3 = 19

Remember to first divide the tens by the divisor. Then regroup any extra tens as ones and divide the ones by the divisor.

Copy and complete. You may use place-value blocks or pictures to help find each quotient. Check your answers.

1. 2)38: quotient 1▢; − 2; 1▢; − ▢▢; 0

2. 4)68: quotient 1▢; − 4; 2▢; − ▢▢; 0

3. 3)45: quotient 1▢; − 3; ▢▢; − ▢▢; 0

4. 7)91: quotient 1▢; − 7; ▢▢; − ▢▢; 0

Set C, pages 446–447

Mrs. Anderson has 95 ounces of punch for a party. How many glasses can she fill if each glass holds 4 ounces of punch? Is any punch left?

Find 95 ÷ 4.

Step 1

Divide the tens.

$$\begin{array}{r} 2 \\ 4\overline{)95} \\ -\underline{8} \\ 15 \end{array}$$

Step 2

Divide the ones. Write the remainder.

$$\begin{array}{r} 23\text{ R3} \\ 4\overline{)95} \\ -\underline{8} \\ 15 \\ -\underline{12} \\ 3 \end{array}$$

She can fill 23 glasses. There are 3 ounces of punch left.

Remember to write the remainder in the quotient.

Copy and complete.

1. $\begin{array}{r} 1\square\text{ R}\square \\ 6\overline{)79} \\ -\underline{6} \\ \square\square \\ -\underline{\square\square} \\ \square \end{array}$

2. $\begin{array}{r} 2\square\text{ R}\square \\ 2\overline{)49} \\ -\underline{4} \\ \square\square \\ -\underline{\square\square} \\ \square \end{array}$

3. $4\overline{)81}$

4. $3\overline{)42}$

5. $5\overline{)79}$

6. $7\overline{)88}$

7. $8\overline{)98}$

8. $6\overline{)61}$

Set D, pages 448–450

There are 13 girls and 14 boys that will form volleyball teams. Each team needs 6 players. Extra players will be alternates. How many teams can be formed? How many players will be alternates?

First find the total number of children.

13 + 14 = 27

Step 2

Use the answer to the hidden question to solve the problem.

Step 3

Solve the problem. Divide 27 by 6 to find the number of teams.

$$\begin{array}{r} 4\text{ R3} \\ 6\overline{)27} \\ -\underline{24} \\ 3 \end{array}$$

There will be 4 teams with 3 players left to be alternates.

Remember to answer the hidden question and use the answer to solve the problem.

Solve.

1. Three friends ordered 2 pizzas. Each pizza was cut into 8 slices. If each person ate the same number of slices, how many slices did each person eat? How many slices were left over?

Topic 20

Data, Graphs, and Probability

Morse Code

M	▬ ▬	Y	▬ • ▬ ▬
N	▬ •	Z	▬ ▬ • •
O	▬ ▬ ▬	Ä	• ▬ • ▬
P	• ▬ ▬ •	Ö	▬ ▬ ▬ •
Q	▬ ▬ • ▬	Ü	• • ▬ ▬
R	• ▬ •	Ch	▬ ▬ ▬ ▬
S	• • •	0	▬ ▬ ▬ ▬ ▬
T	▬	1	• ▬ ▬ ▬ ▬
U	• • ▬	2	• • ▬ ▬ ▬
V	• • • ▬	3	• • • ▬ ▬
	• ▬ ▬	4	• • • • ▬
	▬ • • ▬	5	• • • • •

1 How fast can a peregrine falcon fly? You will find out in Lesson 20-4.

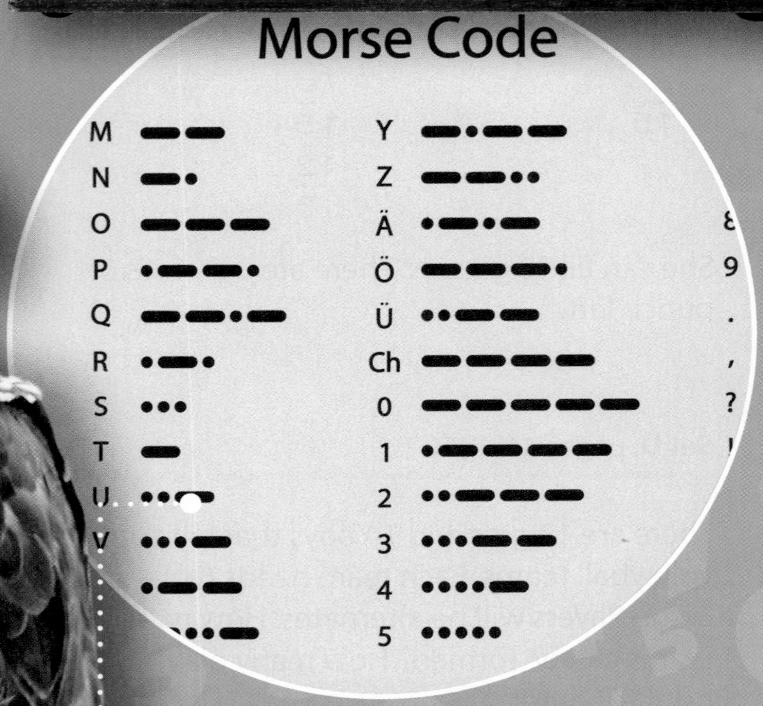

2 In the 1800s, Morse code used a series of dots and dashes to send messages over a telegraph or other machine. How many letters of the alphabet are sent using only dots in Morse code? You will find out in Lesson 20-6.

3

If you put each of the letters in this sign in a bag and took one without looking, which letter are you most likely to get? You will find out in Lesson 20-7.

4

How many gold, silver, and bronze medals did athletes from the United States win in the 2006 Winter Olympic Games? You will find out in Lesson 20-1.

Review What You Know!

Vocabulary

Choose the best term from the box.

- data
- less likely
- more likely
- tally

1. A graph can be used to compare __?__.
2. Elisa is at a library. It is __?__ that she will look at a book than eat lunch.
3. The time is 4 A.M. It is __?__ that you are playing soccer than sleeping.

Order Numbers

Write in order from least to greatest.

4. 56, 47, 93, 39, 10
5. 20, 43, 23, 19, 22
6. 24, 14, 54, 34, 4
7. 65, 33, 56, 87, 34

Skip Counting

Find the next two numbers in each pattern. Write a rule for the pattern.

8. 5, 10, 15, 20, ▢, ▢
9. 2, 4, 6, 8, ▢, ▢
10. 10, 20, 30, 40, ▢, ▢
11. 4, 8, 12, 16, ▢, ▢

Comparing

12. **Writing to Explain** Explain how to use place value to compare 326 and 345.

Lesson

20-1 Organizing Data

Understand It!
A tally chart can be used to organize information.

How can you collect and organize data?

A survey asked students, "What is your favorite after-school sport?"

Information you collect is called data. To take a survey, collect data by asking many people the same question.

Data

Favorite After-School Sport		
Swimming	Swimming	Soccer
Softball	Soccer	Swimming
Softball	Softball	Softball
Soccer	Swimming	Softball
Softball	Soccer	Softball
Soccer	Softball	Soccer

Guided Practice*

Do you know HOW?

In **1–2**, use the survey data below.

Data

Favorite Color			
Blue	Red	Blue	Blue
Red	Yellow	Red	Green
Blue	Red	Red	Red
Red	Red	Red	Blue

1. Make a tally chart for the data.

2. How many more students chose red than blue as their favorite color?

Do you UNDERSTAND?

In **3–5**, use the tally chart above.

3. What does the chart show?

4. How many students in all answered the survey?

5. Later, six more students answered the survey. Here are their answers.

Softball	Soccer	Softball
Swimming	Softball	Soccer

Make a new tally chart that includes their answers.

Independent Practice

For **6–9**, use the survey data at the right.

6. Make a tally chart for the data.

7. How many people answered the survey?

8. Which kinds of pet were the favorite of the same number of people?

9. Which pet was chosen most often?

Data

Favorite Kind of Pet			
Cat	Cat	Dog	Hamster
Fish	Bird	Dog	Dog
Dog	Bird	Hamster	Bird
Dog	Cat	Bird	Fish
Cat	Dog	Dog	Cat
Bird	Cat	Dog	Dog

*For another example, see Set A on page 486.

Step 1

A tally chart is one way to record data. A tally mark is a mark used to record data on a tally chart.

Title the tally chart. Label the columns.

Favorite After-School Sport

Sport	Tally	Number

Step 2

Make a tally mark for each answer given.

Favorite After-School Sport

Sport	Tally	Number
Soccer	𝍸 |	
Softball	𝍸 |||	
Swimming	||||	

Step 3

Count the tally marks. Record the number.

Favorite After-School Sport

Sport	Tally	Number
Soccer	𝍸 |	6
Softball	𝍸 |||	8
Swimming	||||	4

Problem Solving

For **10** and **11**, use the tally chart at the right.

Favorite Sport to Watch (Data)

Sport	Tally	Number
Football	𝍸 𝍸 |	
Baseball	𝍸 𝍸 𝍸 ||	
Hockey		8
Basketball		15

10. Copy and complete the chart.

11. Write the sports in order from most to least favorite.

12. Number Sense What number is shown by 𝍸 𝍸 𝍸 𝍸 𝍸?

13. Make a tally chart to show how many times the letters *a*, *e*, *i*, *o*, and *u* are used in this exercise.

14. Writing to Explain How would you make a tally chart to show what kind of pizza your classmates like most?

15. Reasoning Dennis is 2 inches taller than Mica and 1 inch shorter than Rosa. Is Rosa shorter than Mica or taller than Mica? How much shorter or taller?

16. In the 2006 Winter Olympic Games, the United States won 9 gold medals, 9 silver medals, and 7 bronze medals. Which tally chart shows these results?

A

U.S. Medals

Medal	Tally
Gold	𝍸 |||
Silver	𝍸 |||
Bronze	𝍸 |

B

U.S. Medals

Medal	Tally
Gold	𝍸 ||||
Silver	𝍸 ||||
Bronze	𝍸 ||

C

U.S. Medals

Medal	Tally
Gold	𝍸 𝍸 |
Silver	𝍸 𝍸 |
Bronze	𝍸 |||

D

U.S. Medals

Medal	Tally
Gold	𝍸 𝍸 ||
Silver	𝍸 𝍸 ||
Bronze	𝍸 𝍸

Lesson
20-2

Understand It!
Pictographs and bar graphs make it easy to compare data.

Reading Pictographs and Bar Graphs

How can you read graphs?

A pictograph uses pictures or symbols to show data.

Number of Hockey Teams in Each League

East Falls	X X X /
North Falls	X X /
South Falls	X X
West Falls	X X X X X /

Each X = 2 teams. Each / = 1 team.

The key explains what each picture represents.

Another Example How can you read a bar graph?

A bar graph uses bars to compare information. This bar graph shows the number of goals scored by different players on a hockey team.

The scale shows the units used.

On this graph, each grid line represents one unit. But only every other grid line is labeled: 0, 2, 4, and so on. For example, the line halfway between 4 and 6 represents 5 goals.

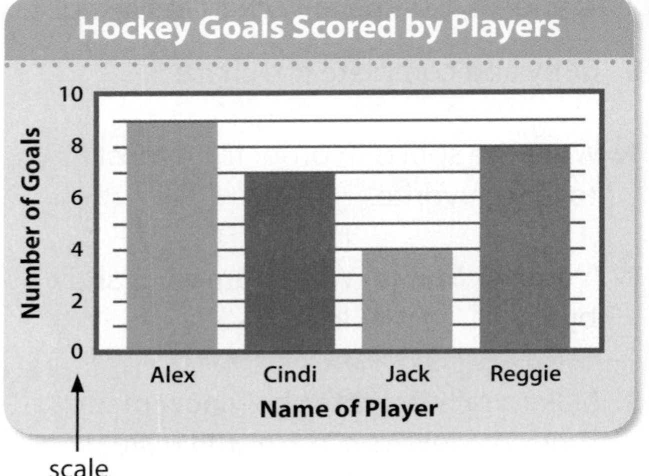

How many goals did Cindi score?

Find Cindi's name. Use the scale to find how high the bar reaches. Cindi scored 7 goals.

Who scored the fewest goals?

Find the shortest bar. The bar for Jack is shortest. He scored the fewest goals.

Explain It

1. Explain how to find how many more goals Alex scored than Cindi.
2. Who scored 8 goals?
3. How many goals in all did Alex and Reggie score?

How many teams are in the East Falls League?

Use the key.

Each [crossed hockey sticks] represents 2 teams.

Each [hockey stick] represents 1 team.

There are 3 [crossed hockey sticks] and 1 [hockey stick].

$2 + 2 + 2 + 1 = 7$

There are 7 teams in the East Falls League.

How many more teams does the East Falls League have than the South Falls League?

Compare the two rows.

East Falls League

3 more teams

South Falls League

The East Falls League has 3 more teams than the South Falls League.

Guided Practice*

Do you know HOW?

1. Which hockey league in the pictograph above has 5 teams?

2. Which league has the most teams? How many teams are in that league?

Do you UNDERSTAND?

In **3** and **4**, use the pictograph above.

3. Explain how to find which league has the fewest teams.

4. How many teams in all are in the North Falls and West Falls Leagues?

Independent Practice

In **5–7**, use the pictograph at the right.

5. Which area has lights on for the most hours in a week?

6. Which area of the Tri-Town Sports Center has lights on for 50 hours each week?

7. In one week, how many more hours are lights on in the exercise room than in the swimming pool?

*For another example, see Set A on page 486.

Problem Solving

In **8–12**, use the bar graph at the right.

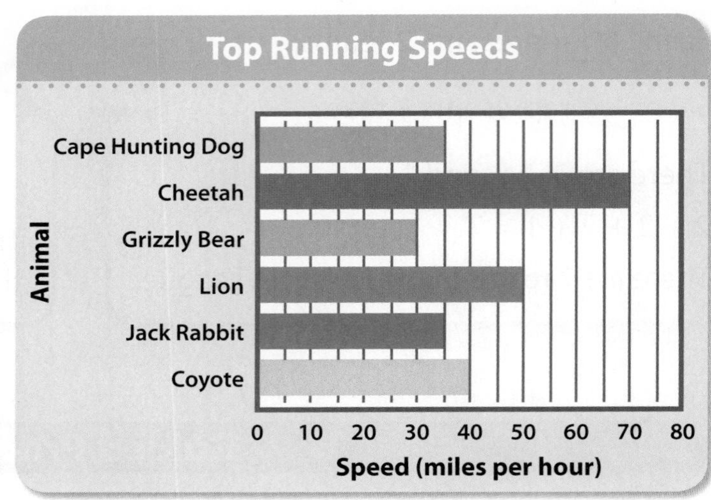

8. How fast can a jack rabbit run?

9. Which animal has the greatest top running speed?

10. Which animal has a top running speed of 50 miles per hour?

11. How much greater is the top running speed of a coyote than that of a grizzly bear?

12. Which animals have the same top running speed?

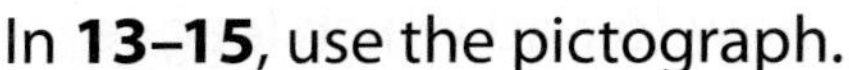

In **13–15**, use the pictograph.

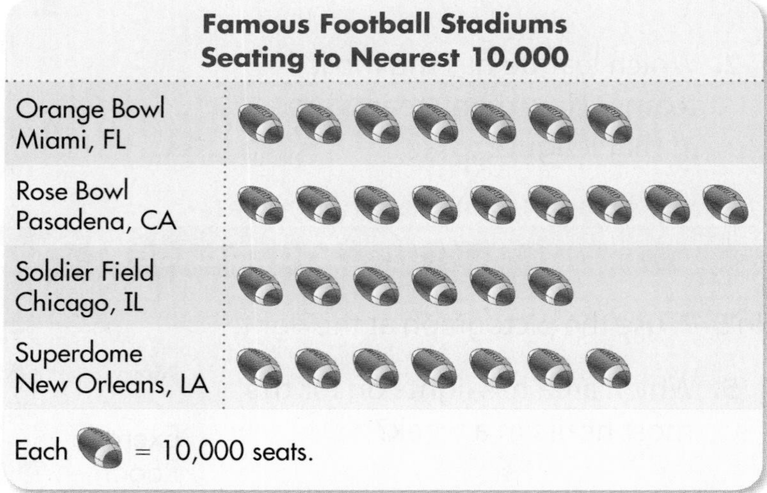

13. To the nearest 10,000, how many seats are in the Rose Bowl?

14. Estimation Which two stadiums have about the same number of seats?

15. Writing to Explain Maria says Soldier Field has about 6,000 seats. Is she correct? Explain.

In **16** and **17**, use the bar graph.

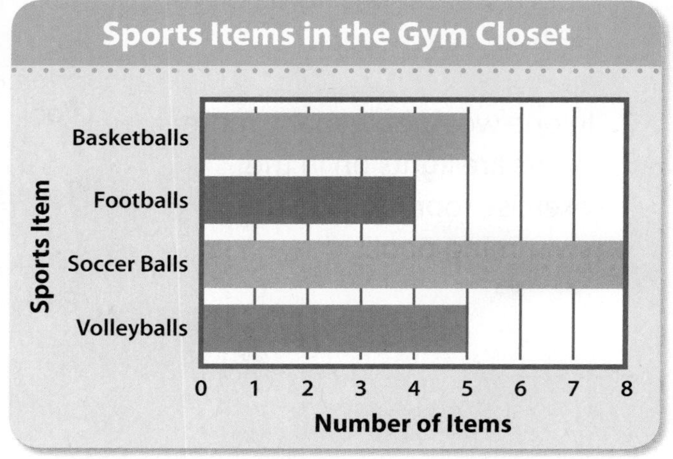

16. How many more soccer balls than basketballs are in the gym closet?

A 8 **C** 4

B 5 **D** 3

17. How many balls in all are in the gym closet?

Mixed Problem Solving

The government where you live uses money from the taxes that people pay to provide different kinds of services. The bar graph at the right shows how much money different departments in Park Town receive. Use the graph to answer the questions.

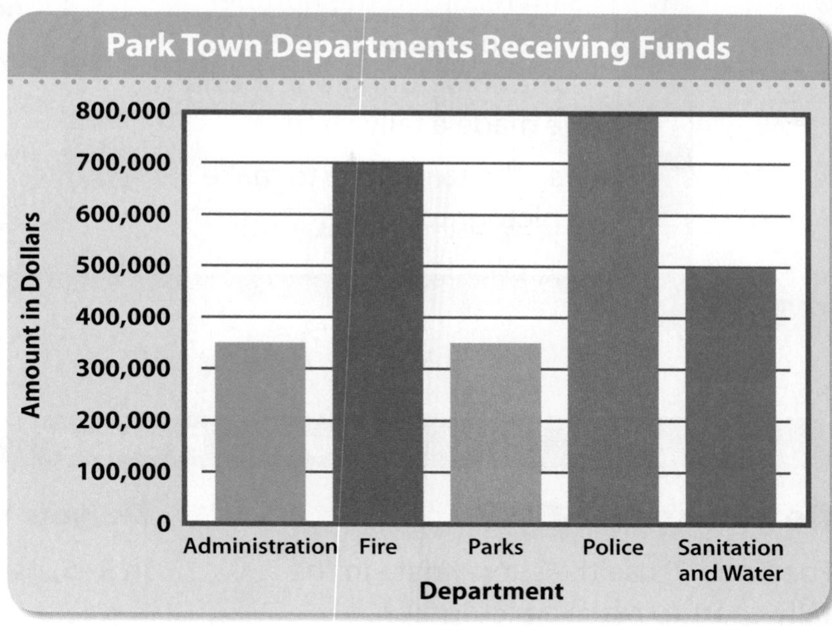

1. Which service in Park Town will receive the most funds?

2. Which two departments will get the same amount?

3. About how much money will the Parks Department and the Sanitation and Water Department receive in all?

4. How much more will the Police Department receive than the Fire Department?

5. Use the table below that shows how the Police Department money is used.

Police Department (Data)

Expenses	Amount
Cars	$42,000
Computers	$14,000
Police Equipment	$88,000
Salaries	$643,000
Station Expenses	$13,000

Which expenses are less than $50,000?

6. **Strategy Focus** Solve. Use the strategy Write a Number Sentence.

The state representatives voted on a budget plan. Each representative has 1 vote. There were 86 votes for the plan and 34 votes against the plan. How many representatives voted in all?

Lesson **20-3**

Understand It!
The key for a pictograph determines the number of symbols you need to show data.

Making Pictographs

How do you make a pictograph?

Sam recorded the number of each kind of bicycle the store sold during one month. He made a tally chart.

Use the tally chart to make a pictograph.

Data

Kind of Bicycle	Tally	Number
Boy's	𝍸 𝍸	10
Girl's	𝍸 𝍸 𝍸 𝍸	20
Training	𝍸 𝍸 𝍸	15
Tricycle	𝍸 𝍸	10

Guided Practice*

Do you know HOW?

For **1** and **2**, use the survey data in the tally chart to make a pictograph.

Data

Which is your favorite school lunch?		
Lunch	**Tally**	**Number**
Taco	‖	2
Pizza	𝍸 |||	8
Salad	|||	3
Sandwich	𝍸		6

1. What is the title? What is the symbol for the key? How many votes will each symbol stand for?

2. List the lunch choices. Draw the symbols to complete the graph.

Do you UNDERSTAND?

In **3–5**, use the pictograph above.

3. Explain the symbols that were used for the number of training bicycles that were sold.

4. Suppose 25 mountain bicycles were also sold. Draw symbols to show a row in the graph for mountain bicycles.

5. If the key was △ = 2 bicycles, how many symbols would be used for the boy's bicycles sold? How many symbols would be used for girl's bicycles sold?

Independent Practice

Data

Goals Each Kickball Team Has Scored		
Team Name	**Tally**	**Number**
Cubs	𝍸 𝍸	10
Hawks	𝍸 𝍸 𝍸 𝍸	20
Lions	𝍸 𝍸 𝍸 𝍸 𝍸 𝍸	30
Roadrunners	𝍸 𝍸 𝍸	15

For **6** and **7**, use the chart.

6. Make a pictograph to show the data.

7. Explain how you decided the number of symbols to draw to show the goals for the Roadrunners.

*For another example, see Set A on page 486.

Write a title for the pictograph.

The title is Kinds of Bicycles Sold.

Choose a symbol for the key. Decide what each symbol and half-symbol will represent.

Each △ means 10 bicycles.

Each half-△ means 5 bicycles.

Set up the graph and list the kinds of bicycles. Decide how many symbols you need for each number sold. Draw the symbols.

Kinds of Bicycles Sold	
Boy's	△
Girl's	△ △
Training	△ half-△
Tricycle	△

Each △ = 10 bicycles.
Each half-△ = 5 bicycles.

Problem Solving

Ed made a tally chart of the items he picked from the plants in his garden.

8. Make a pictograph to show the data in Ed's chart. Write a title and the key.

9. How many green peppers and red peppers did Ed pick in all?

Vegetables from Garden		
Kind	Tally	Number of Items
Green Pepper	||||	4
Red Pepper	||	2
Tomato	~~||||~~	5

10. **Geometry** Ed's garden has a square shape. Each side is 9 feet long. What is the area of Ed's garden?

In **11** and **12**, suppose you are going to make a pictograph to show Simon's Book Shop data.

11. Choose a symbol to stand for 5 books sold. Draw the row for fiction books sold.

12. **Reasoning** Why is 5 a good number to use in the key?

Simon's Book Shop	
Kind of Book	Number Sold
Fiction	25
Nonfiction	40
Poetry	20
Dictionary	15

Plants Sold at Garden Shop	
April	🪴 🪴 🪴 🪴 🪴
May	🪴 🪴 🪴 🪴 🪴 🪴
June	

Each 🪴 = 5 plants

13. Marisol is making a pictograph to show plant sales. There were 35 plants sold in June. How many symbols should Marisol draw for June?

A 5 **B** 7 **C** 11 **D** 35

Lesson
20-4

Understand It!
The lengths of the bars in a bar graph can be used to compare data.

Making Bar Graphs

Hands-On
grid paper

How do you make a bar graph?

Greg made a table to show the amount of money he saved each month.

Use the data in the table to make a bar graph on grid paper. A bar graph can make it easy to compare data.

Data

Month	Amount Saved
January	$25
February	$50
March	$65
April	$40

Guided Practice*

Do you know HOW?

Use the chart to make a bar graph.

Data

Class	Tally	Number of People Signed Up
Chess	𝍸 I	6
Guitar	𝍸 𝍸	10
Painting	𝍸 II	7
Writing	𝍸 IIII	9

1. Write a title. Choose the scale. What does each grid line represent?

2. Set up the graph with the scale, each class, and labels. Draw each bar.

Do you UNDERSTAND?

In **3–5**, use the bar graph above.

3. In the bar graph above, explain why the bar for January ends between 20 and 30.

4. In which month did Greg save the most money?

5. Suppose Greg saved $35 in May. Between which grid lines would the bar for May end?

Independent Practice

In **6** and **7**, use the tally chart.

Data

Favorite Store for Clothes		
Store	**Tally**	**Number of Votes**
Deal Mart	𝍸 𝍸 𝍸	15
Jane's	𝍸 𝍸 𝍸 𝍸 𝍸 𝍸	30
Parker's	𝍸 𝍸 𝍸 𝍸	20
Trends	𝍸	5

6. Make a bar graph to show the data.

7. Explain how to use the bar graph to find the store that received the most votes.

*For another example, see Set B on page 486.

Write a title.

The title of this bar graph is Amount Greg Saved Each Month.

Choose the scale. Decide how many units each grid line will represent.

Each grid line will represent $10.

Set up the graph with the scale, each month listed in the table, and labels. Draw a bar for each month.

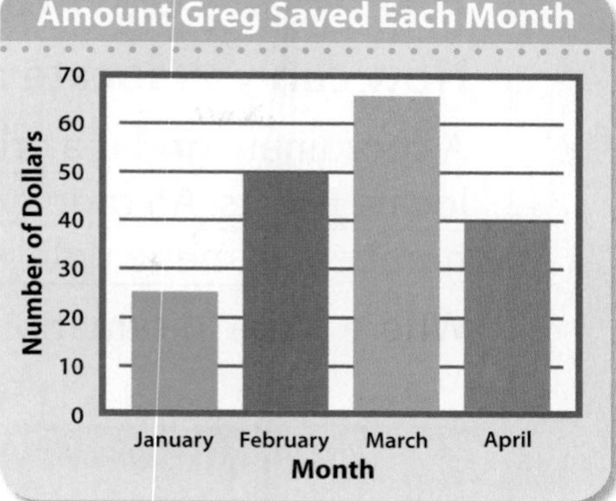

Problem Solving

For **8** and **9**, use the table at the right.

8. Make a bar graph. Write a title. Choose the scale. Draw bars that go across.

Favorite Kind of Movie

Kind of Movie	Adventure	Cartoon	Comedy	Science Fiction
Number of Votes	16	8	10	7

9. Number Sense Which two kinds of movies received about the same number of votes?

10. Strategy Focus Solve. Use the strategy Draw a Picture.

Each movie ticket costs $8. What is the total cost of tickets for a family of 6 people?

In **11** and **12**, suppose you are going to make a bar graph to show the data in the table.

11. Writing to Explain What scale would you choose? Explain.

12. Which would be the longest bar?

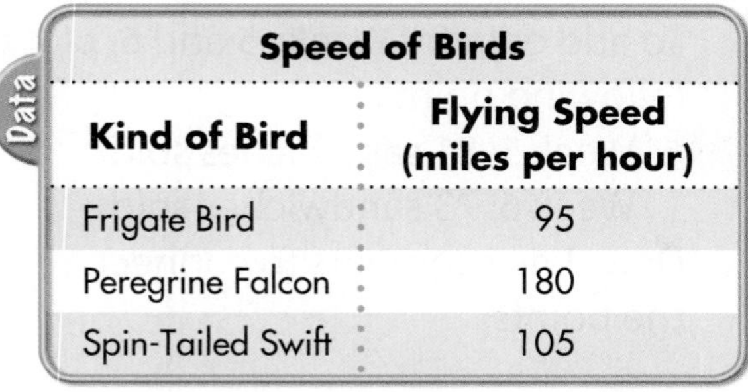

Speed of Birds

Kind of Bird	Flying Speed (miles per hour)
Frigate Bird	95
Peregrine Falcon	180
Spin-Tailed Swift	105

13. Luz made this graph to show how many friends wore each color of shoe. Which information does Luz need to complete the graph?

A How many friends wore black shoes

B The color of shoes with the longest bar

C The color of shoes worn by exactly 8 friends

D The color of shoes worn by exactly 7 friends

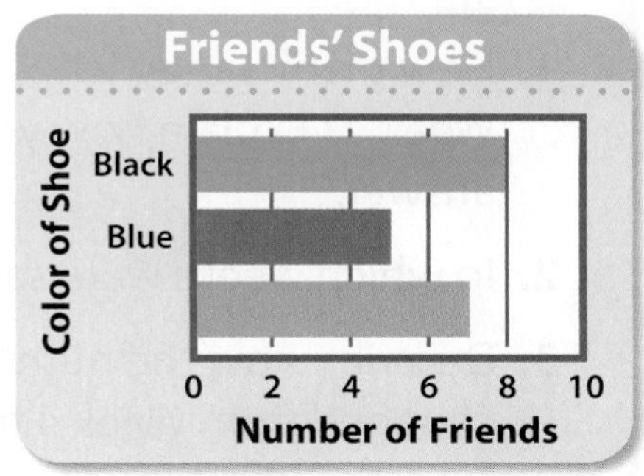

Lesson
20-5

Understand It!
Data can be displayed on a coordinate grid by using ordered pairs to make a line graph.

Ordered Pairs and Line Graphs

How can you locate a point?

A coordinate grid is a grid used to locate points. An ordered pair of numbers names a point on the grid.

Where is the Information desk?

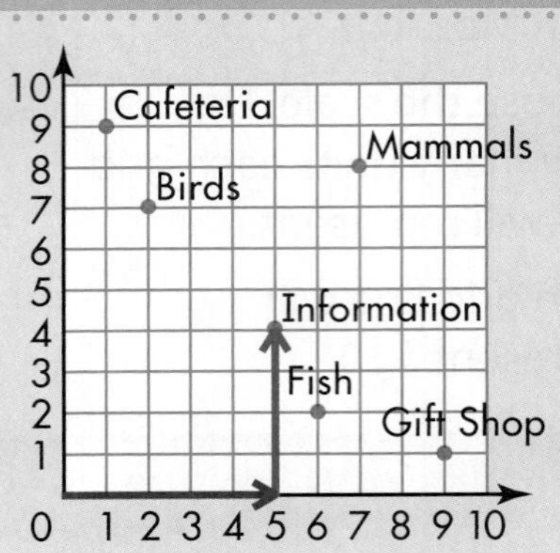

Another Example How can you read and make a line graph?

A line graph shows how data changes over a period of time.

Look at the *Lunchroom Sandwich Sales* graph. To read the data for Week 1, start at 0 and move right until you reach *Week 1*. Move up to the point. Move left to read that 50 sandwiches were sold.

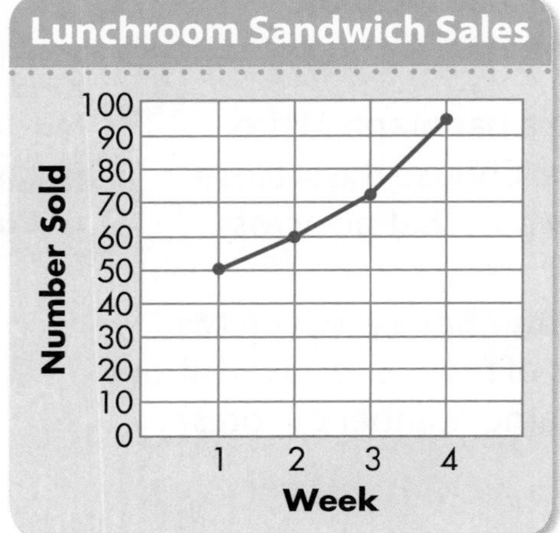

The line graph shows that the number of sandwiches sold increased each week.

To add data for Weeks 5 and 6, plot the following points.

Week 5: 81 sandwiches sold
Week 6: 73 sandwiches sold

Draw line segments to connect the points.

Explain It

1. How many sandwiches were sold in Week 2? Explain how you found your answer.
2. In which weeks were sandwich sales about the same?
3. Describe how the number of sandwiches sold changed from Week 4 to Week 5.

To name the location of a point:

- Start at 0. Move right until you are under the point labeled *Information*. Count the spaces you moved: **5**.
- Move up to the point. Count the spaces you moved: **4**.

The Information desk is at (5, 4).

To plot a point means to locate and mark the point using the given ordered pair. Plot a point to locate *Reptiles* at (1, 2).

Start at 0. Move 1 space to the right. Move up 2 spaces. Mark a point and label it *Reptiles*.

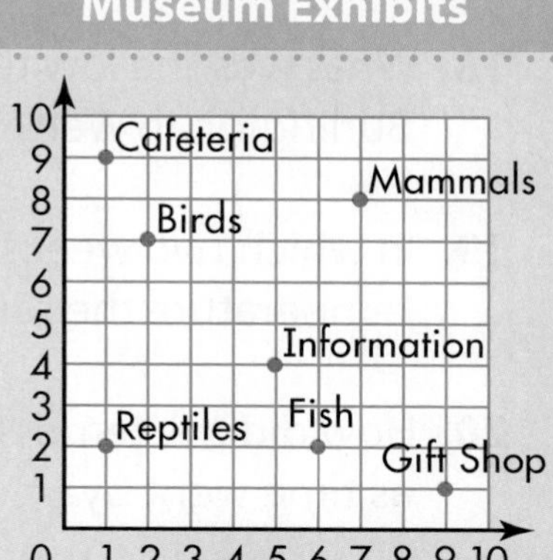

Guided Practice*

Do you know HOW?

For **1–4**, use the *Museum Exhibits* grid above. For **1–3**, write the ordered pair for the location of each exhibit.

1. Fish **2.** Birds **3.** Mammals

4. What is located at (9, 1)?

For **5** and **6**, use the *Luncheon Sandwich Sales* graph in Another Example.

5. About how many sandwiches were sold in Week 4?

6. Between which two weeks did the number of sandwiches sold increase the most?

Do you UNDERSTAND?

For **7–9**, use the *Museum Exhibits* grid.

7. In which direction do you move first to plot a point? In which direction do you move next?

8. Would it be correct to say that the bird exhibit is at (7, 2)? Explain.

9. Explain how to plot a point for the amphibians exhibit at (8, 6).

Independent Practice

For **10–13**, write the ordered pair for each point on the grid.

10. *A* **11.** *C* **12.** *E* **13.** *G*

For **14–17**, write the letter that names each point.

14. (1, 5) **15.** (3, 1) **16.** (2, 4) **17.** (1, 3)

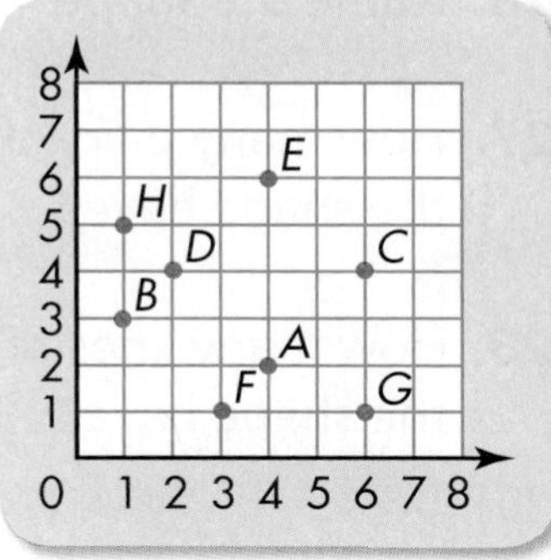

*For another example, see Set C on page 487.

Independent Practice

For **18–21**, use the line graph on the right.

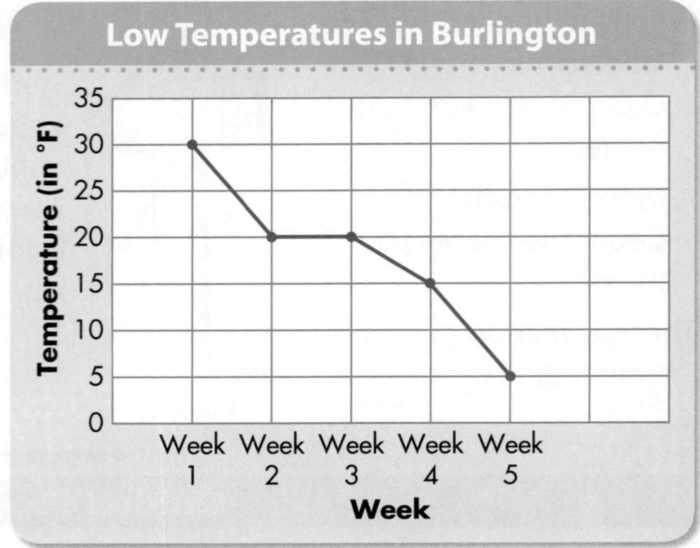

18. What was the low temperature in Burlington in Week 4?

19. In which two weeks was the low temperature the same?

20. How did the temperature change as time went by?

21. Copy and complete the graph to show the Week 6 low temperature of 10°F.

Problem Solving

City maps sometimes use a grid to show where places are located. Use the grid on the right for **22–25**.

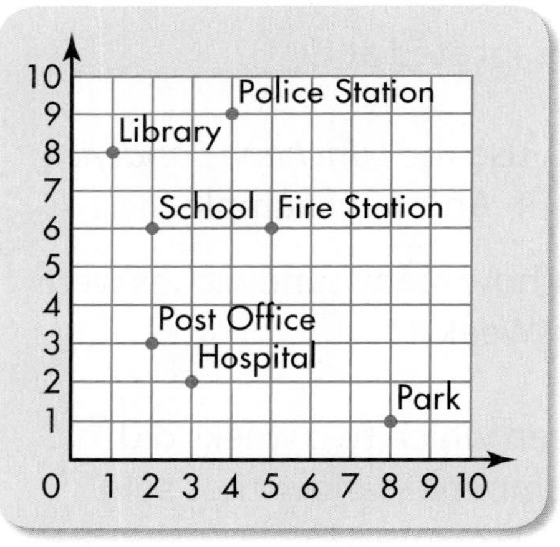

22. What is located at point (3, 2)?

23. What is the ordered pair that names the location of the police station?

24. Which building is located three units to the right of the school?

25. **Writing to Explain** Which is closer to the school, the park or the library? Explain how you know.

Geometry Jamal drew the shape below. Use the shape for **26–28**.

26. Name the shape.

27. How many pairs of parallel sides does the shape have?

28. How many lines of symmetry does the shape have?

Use the line graph to the right for **29–31**.

29. Copy the line graph that has been started.

a Plot these points on the graph.
8 months: 12 pounds
12 months: 14 pounds

b Draw line segments to connect the points.

30. What was the weight of the puppy at birth?

31. **Writing to Explain** How did the puppy's weight change as time passed?

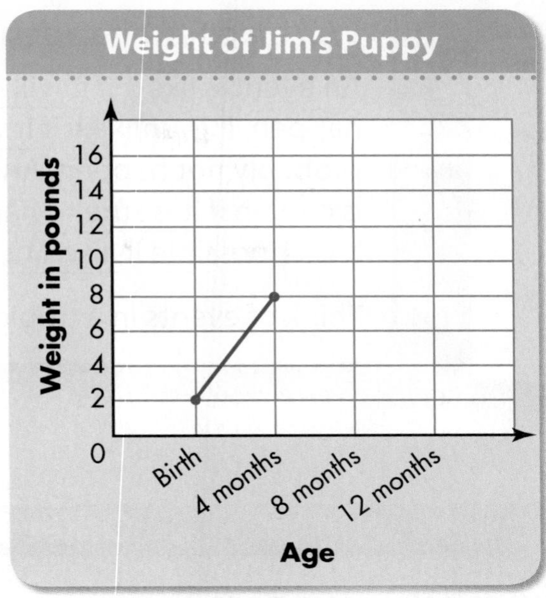

32. Toby has 75 cents. How is 75 cents written as a decimal?

33. The line graph below shows the low temperature each month in Springfield. Which statement best tells how the temperature changed as time passed?

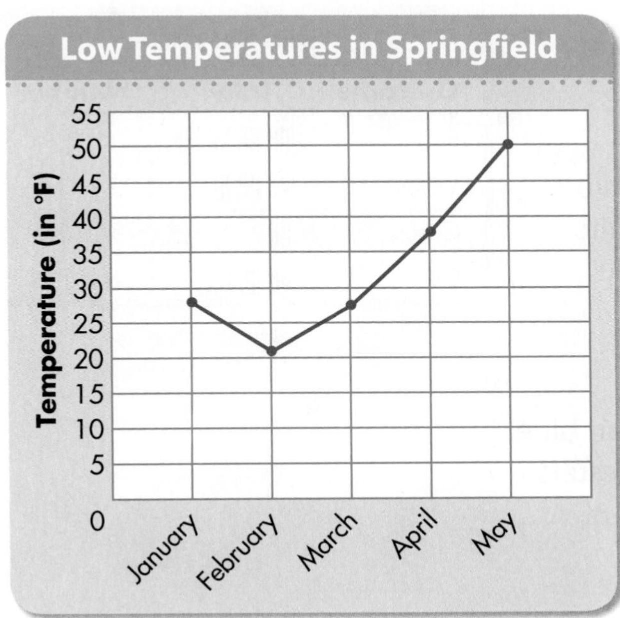

A The low temperature decreased from February to May.

B The low temperature did not change from March to May.

C The low temperature decreased from January to May.

D The low temperature increased from February to May.

Lesson
20-6

Understand It!
There are words that are used to describe the chance that something will happen.

How Likely?

Will an event happen?

An event is likely if it will probably happen. It is unlikely if it will probably not happen. An event is certain if it is sure to happen. It is impossible if it will never happen.

Think of events in a tropical rainforest.

Certain event: seeing green plants

Impossible event: seeing a polar bear

Likely event: seeing colorful birds

Unlikely event: seeing dry soil

Other Examples

How can you compare chances?

Outcomes with the same chance of happening are equally likely.

Sometimes you compare two outcomes.
The outcome with a greater chance of happening is more likely.
The outcome with the lesser chance of happening is less likely.

The tally chart shows the results of 48 spins of the spinner above.

Which outcome is more likely than blue?

A bigger part of the spinner is red than blue. Also, the tally chart shows more red results than blue. So, red is more likely than blue.

Data

Spin Results

Outcome	Tally	Number
Red	卌 卌 卌 IIII	19
Yellow	卌 卌 III	13
Green	卌	5
Blue	卌 卌 I	11

Which outcome is less likely than blue?

A smaller part of the spinner is green than blue. Also, the tally chart shows fewer green results than blue. So, green is less likely than blue.

Which outcomes are equally likely?

The yellow and blue parts of the spinner are the same size. Also, the yellow and blue results are nearly equal. So, yellow and blue are equally likely outcomes.

A possible result of a game or experiment is called an outcome.

What are the outcomes of spinning this spinner?

When you spin the spinner, the outcome might be blue, red, yellow, green, or a line.

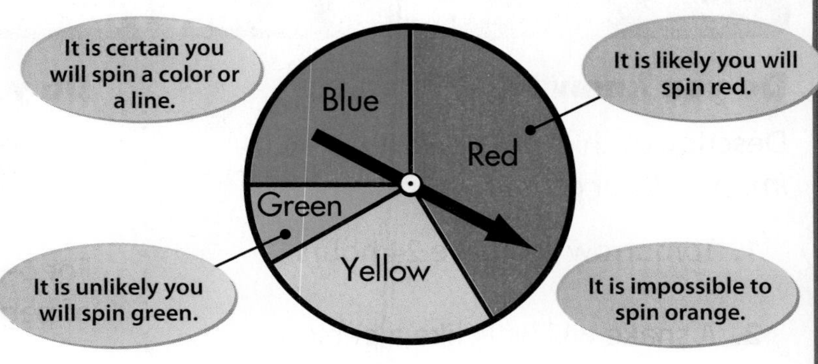

Another Example

Look at the spinner at the right. Which tally chart shows the most likely results of 25 spins?

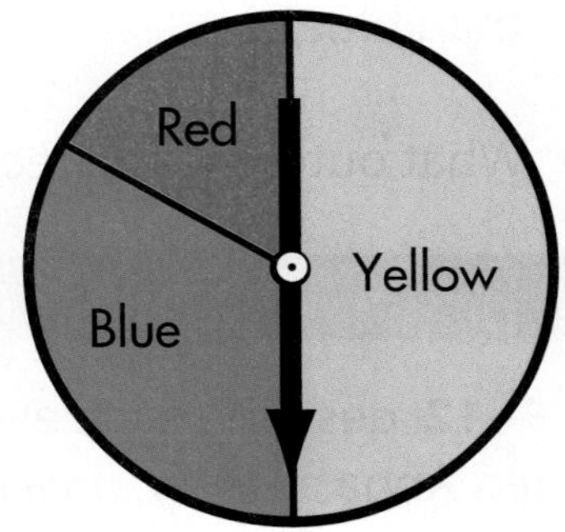

A

Color	Spin Results
Red	卌 IIII
Blue	卌 III
Yellow	卌 III

C

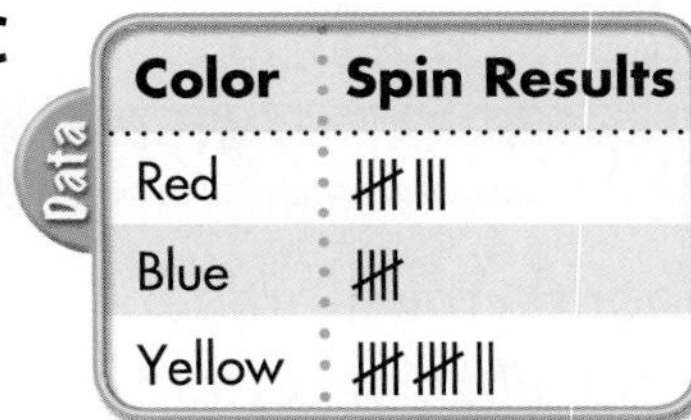

Color	Spin Results
Red	卌 III
Blue	卌
Yellow	卌 卌 II

B

Color	Spin Results
Red	卌
Blue	卌 IIII
Yellow	卌 卌 I

D

Color	Spin Results
Red	卌
Blue	卌 卌 II
Yellow	卌 III

Red is the smallest part of the spinner, so red should have the fewest tally marks. So, **A** and **C** are not good choices.

Look at choices **B** and **D**. The yellow part of the spinner is bigger than the blue part, so yellow should have more tally marks than blue. So, **D** is not a good choice.

Choice **B** shows the most likely results of 25 spins.

Explain It

1. Suppose a tally chart shows spin results. How can you tell if one part of the spinner is much larger than the others?

Guided Practice*

Do you know HOW?

Describe each event as *likely*, *unlikely*, *impossible*, or *certain*.

1. Tomorrow will have 24 hours.
2. A snake will walk like a person.

There are 6 white counters, 12 black counters, 2 red counters, and 6 blue counters in a bag. You take one counter from the bag without looking.

3. What outcome is more likely than blue?
4. What outcomes are equally likely?

Do you UNDERSTAND?

5. What is the difference between a certain event and a likely event?

For **6–8**, use the spinner at the top of page 473.

6. Which outcome is less likely than yellow?
7. Is purple a more likely or less likely outcome than blue?
8. Which outcome is more likely than yellow?

Independent Practice

For **9–12**, describe each event about a third-grader named Anna as *likely*, *unlikely*, *impossible*, or *certain*.

9. Anna will need food to grow.
10. Anna will grow to be 100 feet tall.
11. Anna will travel to the moon.
12. Anna will watch television tonight.

For **13–17**, use the spinner at the right.

13. What outcome is less likely than yellow?
14. What outcomes are equally likely?
15. What outcome is most likely?
16. Name an outcome that is certain.
17. Name an outcome that is impossible.

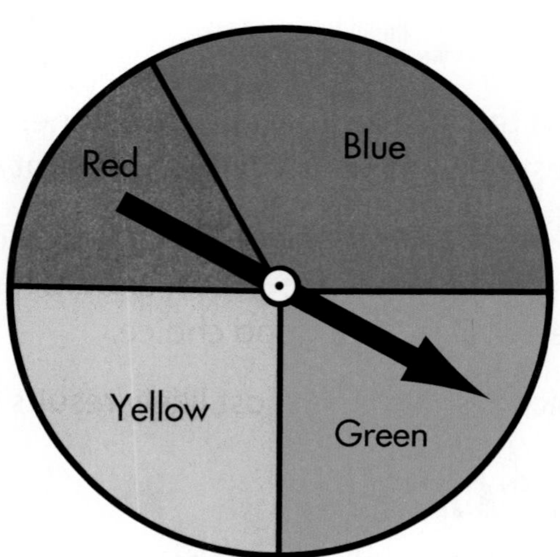

*For another example, see Set D on page 487.

Problem Solving

18. The table shows which letters use only dots and which letters use only dashes in Morse code. All the other letters of the alphabet use both dots and dashes. If you pick one letter from a bag with all 26 letters in the alphabet, are you more likely to pick a letter that uses dots only, dashes only, or both dots and dashes?

Morse Code	
Dots Only	**Dashes Only**
E, H, I, S	M, O, T

19. **Writing to Explain** How can you tell by looking at a spinner that one outcome is more likely than another outcome?

20. There are 4 medium boxes inside a large box. Inside each medium box, there are 3 small boxes. How many boxes are there in all?

21. Look at the spinner at the right. Which tally chart shows the most likely results of 30 spins?

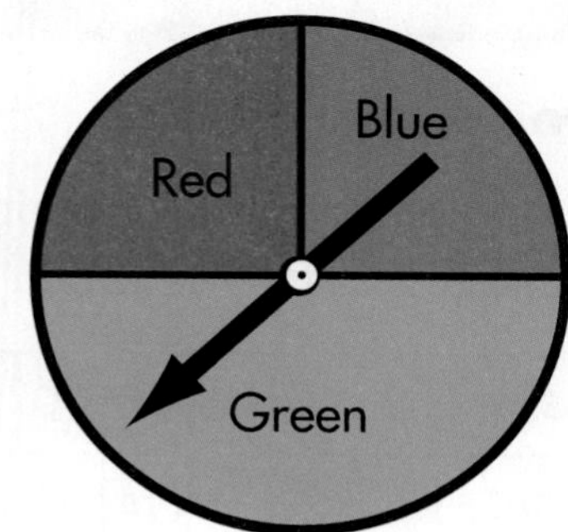

A

Color	Spin Results
Red	𝍸 ||||
Blue	𝍸 ||
Green	𝍸 𝍸 ||||

C

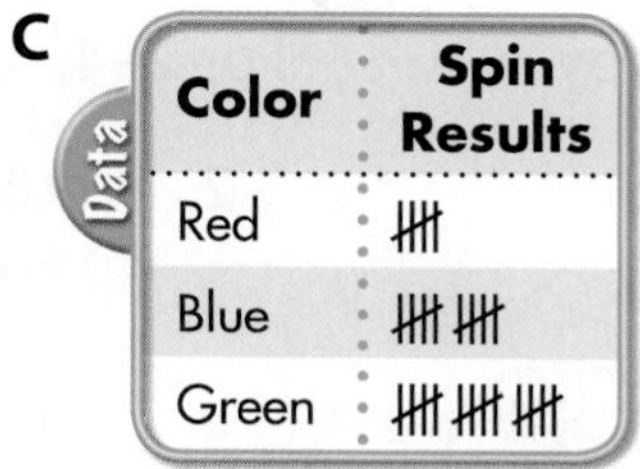

Color	Spin Results
Red	𝍸
Blue	𝍸 𝍸
Green	𝍸 𝍸 𝍸

B

Color	Spin Results
Red	𝍸 𝍸
Blue	𝍸 𝍸
Green	𝍸 𝍸

D

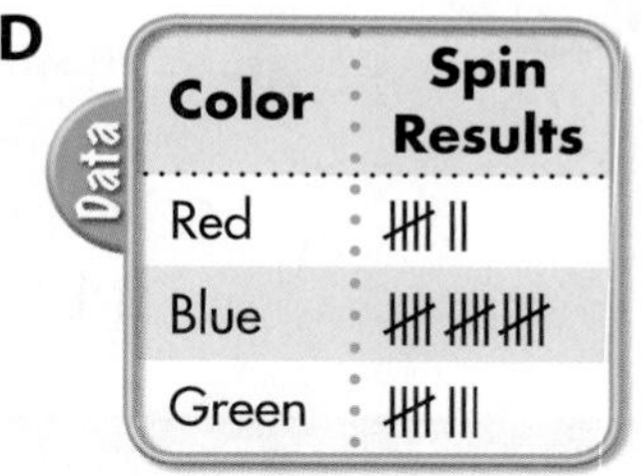

Color	Spin Results
Red	𝍸 ||
Blue	𝍸 𝍸 𝍸
Green	𝍸 |||

In **22** and **23**, use the table that shows the colors of paper clips in a box. Mary will take 1 paper clip out of the box without looking.

Paper Clip Colors	
Color	**Number in the Box**
Green	27
Red	38
Yellow	21
Blue	27

22. Which colors does Mary have an equally likely chance of taking?

A Green and red

B Red and blue

C Green and blue

D Red and yellow

23. Which of the four colors is Mary least likely to choose?

Lesson

20-7

Understand It!
Results from experiments can be used to make predictions.

Outcomes and Experiments

Hands-On
spinner

How do outcomes compare to predictions?

In 30 spins, how many times would you expect to spin red? blue?

Spin the spinner. Then compare the results to what you thought would happen.

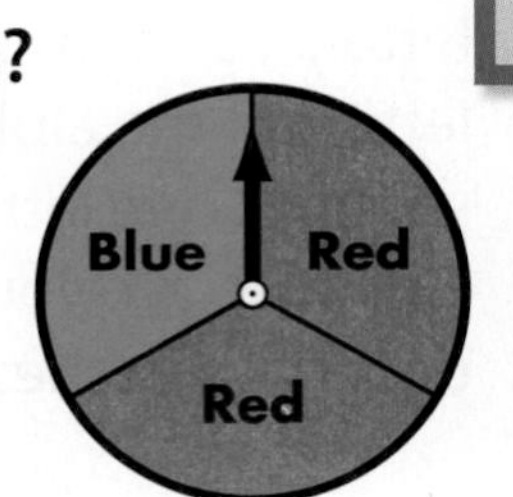

Guided Practice*

Do you know HOW?

1. Use the spinner at the right. Copy and complete the table.

Blue	2	4	6	8	10	20
Green	1	2	3	4	5	10
Red	1	2	3		5	
Total Spins	4	8	12	16		40

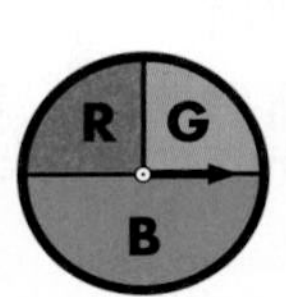

Do you UNDERSTAND?

For **2–4**, use the experiment above.

2. Predict what is likely to happen in 40 spins.

3. Do the experiment. Spin the spinner 40 times. How do the results compare to your prediction?

4. Why should you expect 2 reds and 1 blue in 3 spins?

Independent Practice

In **5–6**, use the table of letter tiles picked from a bag.

A	5	10	15	20	25	30	35	40
B	3	6	9		15	18	21	24
C	2	4	6	8			14	
Total Picks	10	20	30		50		70	

5. Copy and complete the table.

6. Predict what is likely to happen in 90 picks.

*For another example, see Set D on page 487.

Step 1

Predict the results of 30 spins.

To predict is to tell what may happen using information you know.

Red	2	4	6	8	10	20	40	60	80
Blue	1	2	3	4	5	10	20	30	40
Total Spins	3	6	9	12	15	30	60	90	120

The prediction for 30 spins is the spinner will land on red 20 times and on blue 10 times.

Step 2

Spin the spinner 30 times. Do this test 4 times. Compare the results to what you predicted.

Test	1	2	3	4	Total
Red	22	21	21	20	84
Blue	8	9	9	10	36
Total Spins	30	30	30	30	120

When there are more tests, the results get closer to the prediction.

Problem Solving

In **7–9**, use the spinner to the right and the table below.

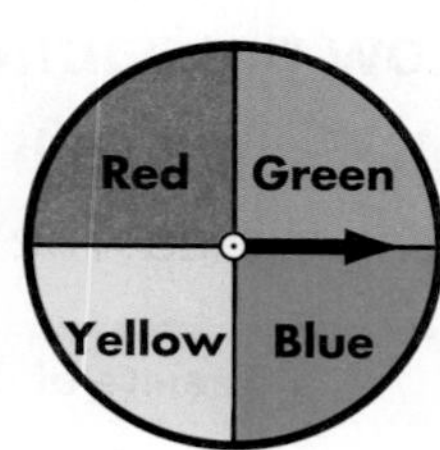

Blue	1	2	3	4		6		8
Green	1	2	3	4	5			
Red	1	2	3	4	5		7	
Yellow	1	2	3			6		
Total Spins	4	8	12	16		24		32

7. Copy and complete the table.

8. Predict the results of 40 spins. Then spin the spinner 40 times. How do the results compare to your prediction?

9. Reasonableness Danny says it is likely that in 40 spins, green will be spun more times than yellow. Do you agree? Explain.

10. Writing to Explain Look at the sign at the right. Suppose you put each of the five letters in a box and take one out without looking. Which outcome is most likely? Explain.

11. In an experiment, the spinner results were 16 blue, 32 green, and 16 red. Which spinner most likely gave these results?

A

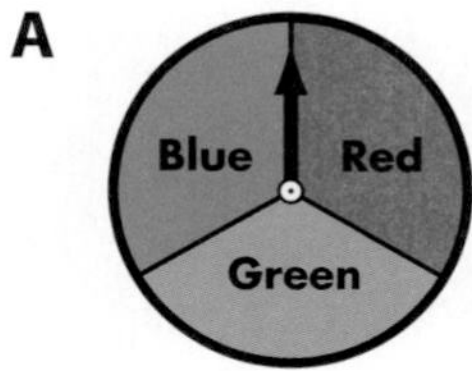

B

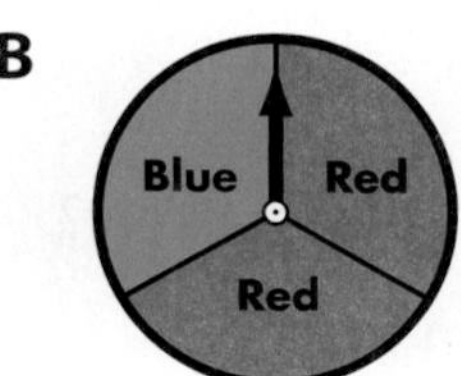

C

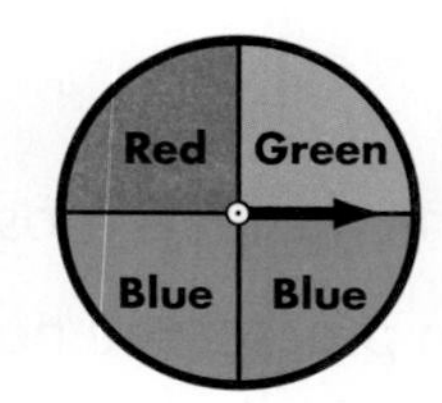

D

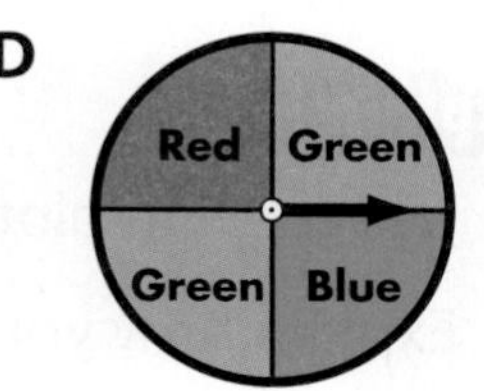

Lesson
20-8

Understand It!
Line plots can be used to organize and compare data.

Line Plots and Probability

How can you use line plots?

For each day in April, Dara recorded the high temperature on a line plot. What temperature occurred as the high temperature most often in April?

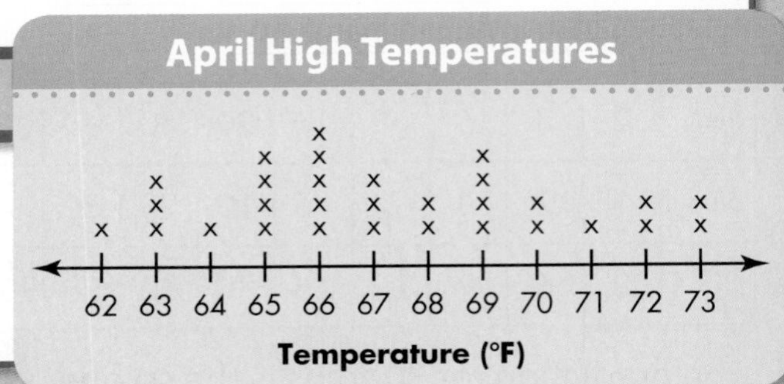

Another Example
How can you make a line plot to show probability data?

Ian tossed two number cubes with sides labeled 1 to 6 and added the numbers he tossed. The table shows his results.

Data

Results of 30 Tosses

Toss	Sum	Toss	Sum	Toss	Sum	Toss	Sum	Toss	Sum	Toss	Sum
1	8	6	5	11	10	16	7	21	10	26	8
2	8	7	5	12	7	17	6	22	8	27	9
3	7	8	7	13	9	18	8	23	4	28	7
4	12	9	11	14	6	19	5	24	7	29	7
5	6	10	3	15	9	20	5	25	6	30	7

Steps to make a line plot:

- Draw a line.
- Below the line, list in order all the possible outcomes of the sum of the two number cubes.
- Write a title for the line plot.
- Use the data table. Mark an X for each time that sum was the outcome.

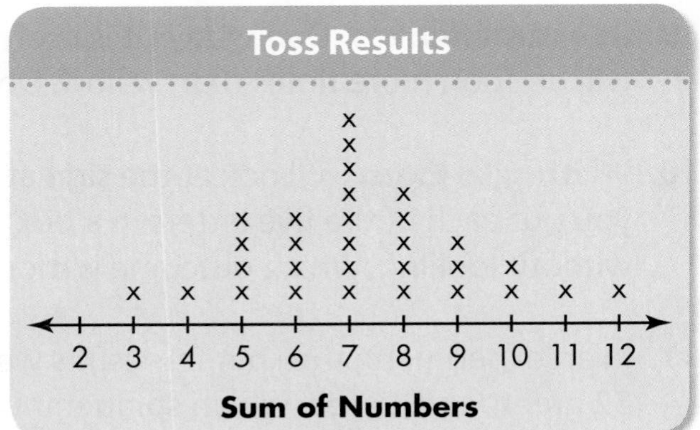

Explain It

1. Use the line plot. Which sum is most likely? least likely?
2. Explain how you can predict the next sum tossed.

A line plot is a way to organize data on a number line.

To read a line plot, look at the numbers below the line. Then count the Xs above each number.

On Dara's line plot, each temperature is labeled below the line. Each X represents one day.

Since there are 2 Xs above the 68, the high temperature was 68° on two days.

Which temperature has the most Xs?

There are 5 Xs above the 66, so the high temperature was 66° on five days.

The temperature that occurred as the high temperature most often in April was 66°.

Guided Practice*

Do you know HOW?

Sixteen 3rd-grade students entered the long jump event. The results are shown in the table below. Use the data for **1–3.**

Student	Distance (Inches)	Student	Distance (Inches)
1	27	9	30
2	31	10	26
3	28	11	28
4	26	12	30
5	30	13	31
6	33	14	26
7	29	15	33
8	31	16	30

1. Make a line plot to show the data.

2. How many Xs should be drawn for the number of students who jumped 33 inches?

3. Suppose another 3rd-grade student enters the long jump event. Predict the distance that student will jump. Explain.

Do you UNDERSTAND?

4. In the example above, what was the highest temperature recorded in April?

5. Use the line plot below. Which high temperature occurred most often in August?

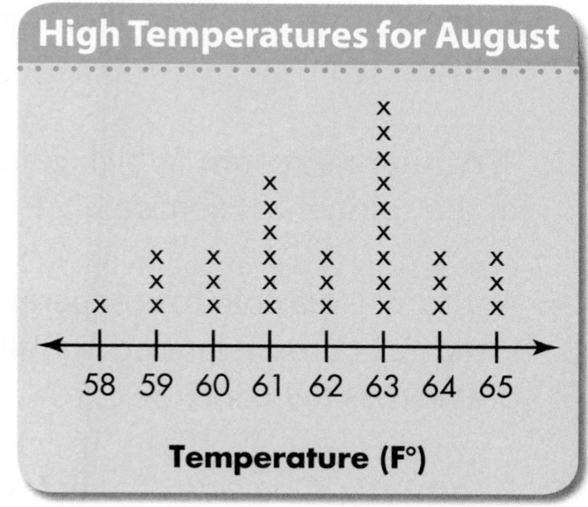

6. In Exercise 5, which high temperature occurred least often?

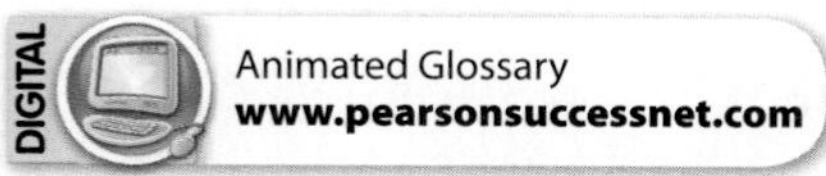

For another example, see Set E on page 487.

Independent Practice

Amelia recorded the number of people riding in each of 30 cars that passed by. Use the data to the right for **7–11**.

7. Make a line plot to show the data.

8. How many Xs should be drawn for 3 people in a car?

9. Which number of people occurred in two cars?

10. Which number of people in each car occurred most often?

11. What do you predict will be the number of people in the next car?

Data

Number of People in Each Car

Car	Number of People	Car	Number of People	Car	Number of People
1	2	11	3	21	1
2	3	12	1	22	2
3	2	13	2	23	2
4	1	14	4	24	4
5	4	15	1	25	1
6	1	16	3	26	3
7	1	17	1	27	1
8	5	18	2	28	1
9	4	19	6	29	5
10	1	20	1	30	2

Problem Solving

12. A spinner has two unequal parts. Janice spun the spinner 10 times. The spinner landed on Red 2 times. It landed on Green 8 times. What do you predict will be the outcome of the next spin?

13. **Writing to Explain** Which color is most likely the larger part of the spinner in Exercise 12? Explain your answer.

14. Anthony did a coin toss experiment. The coin landed on Heads 27 times. It landed on Tails 35 times. How many times did he toss the coin?

15. **Geometry** One side of a rectangle is 5 inches long. Another side of the rectangle is 7 inches long. What are the lengths of the other 2 sides of the rectangle?

16. **Algebra** One print of a photograph costs 36¢. Two prints cost 72¢. Three prints cost $1.08. If the cost of each print remains the same, how much would 4 prints cost?

Use the line plot at the right for **17-21.** It shows how long it took each of 28 people to run a mile.

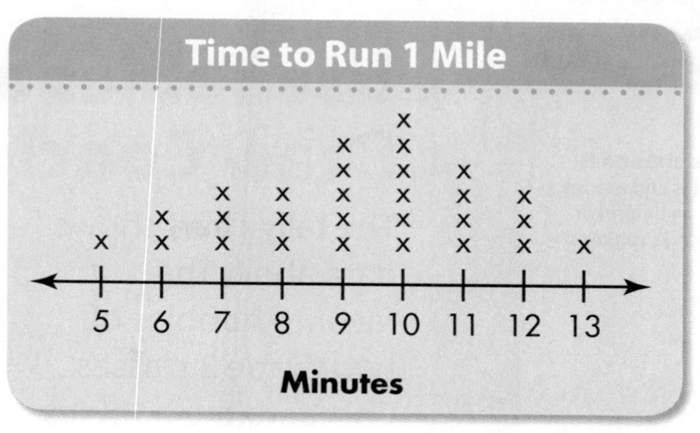

17. Which amount of time was used by the greatest number of people?

18. How many more people took 10 minutes than 5 minutes?

19. How many people took less than 8 minutes to run a mile? more than 8 minutes?

20. Suppose another runner joined this group. Predict that runner's time for 1 mile.

21. **Number Sense** Cory said that the fastest runner in this group took 13 minutes to run a mile. Is this reasonable? Explain.

22. **Algebra** Copy and complete each number sentence by writing <, >, or =.

a $3 \times 18 \bigcirc 6 \times 9$ **b** $76 \div 4 \bigcirc 64 \div 4$

23. In an experiment, with a spinner that had 4 numbered sections, results were 3, 1, 4, 1, 4, 2, 1, 3, 4, 4, 3, 2. Which line plot matches the data?

A

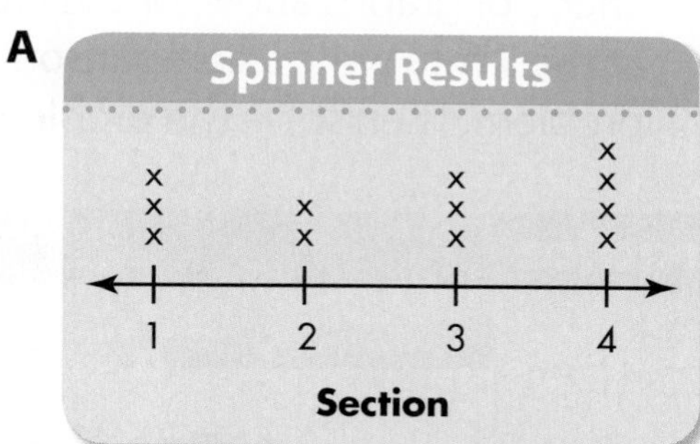

C

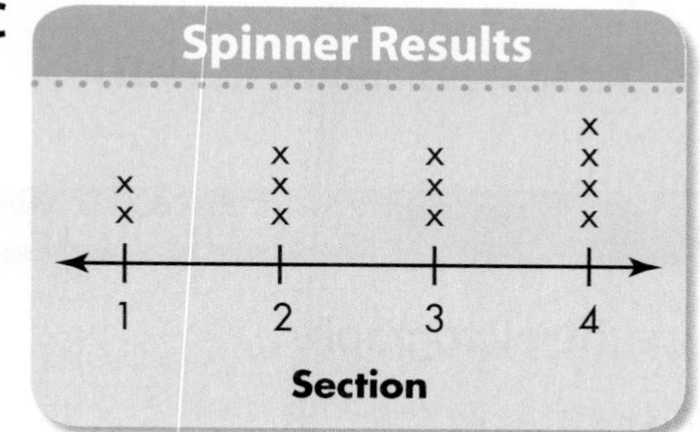

B

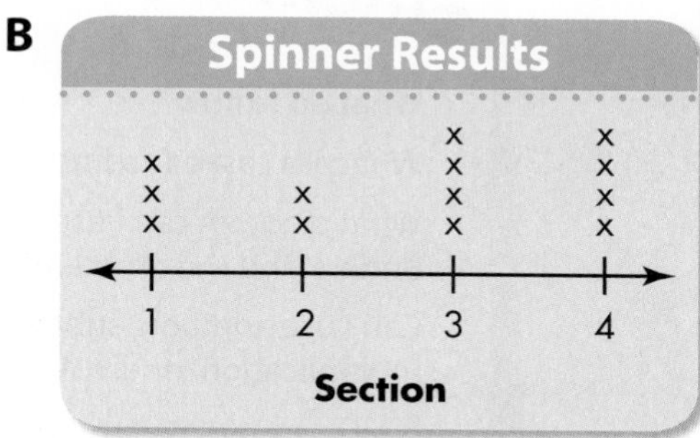

D

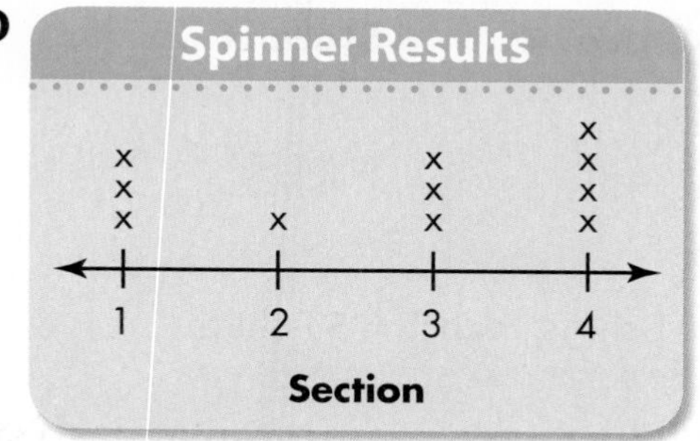

24. Which digit is used most often in whole numbers less than 20?

A 9 **B** 1 **C** 5 **D** 2

Lesson

20-9

Understand It!
Tables and graphs can be helpful in solving problems.

Problem Solving

Use Tables and Graphs to Draw Conclusions

The tally chart shows data about the favorite hobbies of two Grade 3 classes. Compare the hobbies of the two classes.

Data

Favorite Hobbies

	Class A		Class B	
Hobby	**Tally**	**Number**	**Tally**	**Number**
Model Building	|||	3	~~||||~~	5
Drawing	~~||||~~ ~~||||~~ ||	12	~~||||~~ ||	7
Rock Collecting	||||	4	||||	4
Reading	~~||||~~ |	6	~~||||~~ ||||	9

Guided Practice*

Do you know HOW?

Data

Bicycle Club Miles

Member	Victor	Rosita	Gary	Hal
Number of Miles	20	35	30	20

1. Which club member rode exactly 10 miles more than Hal?

2. Who rode the same distance as Hal?

Do you UNDERSTAND?

3. How do the bars on a bar graph help you to compare data?

4. What is the favorite hobby of Class A above? of Class B?

5. **Write a Problem** Use the tally charts or graphs above or the table at the left to write a comparison problem. Then solve the problem.

Independent Practice

For **6** and **7**, use the pictograph.

T-Shirt Sales

	Store A	Store B
Blue	👕 👕 half	👕
Red	👕 👕	👕 👕 half
Green	half	half

Each 👕 = 10 T-shirts. Each half = 5 T-shirts.

6. What color was sold most often at each store? equally at both stores?

7. Where was blue sold more often?

Stuck? Try this....

- What do I know?
- What am I asked to find?
- What diagram can I use to help understand the problem?
- Can I use addition, subtraction, multiplication, or division?
- Is all of my work correct?
- Did I answer the right question?
- Is my answer reasonable?

*For another example, see Set B on page 486.

Plan

Make a bar graph for each class.

Favorite Hobbies of Class A

Hobby: Model Building, Drawing, Rock Collecting, Reading

0 2 4 6 8 10 12 14

Number of Students

Favorite Hobbies of Class B

Hobby: Model Building, Drawing, Rock Collecting, Reading

0 2 4 6 8 10 12 14

Number of Students

Solve

Now read the graphs and make comparisons.

- More students in Class B like model building than in Class A.
- The same number of students in each class like rock collecting.

For **8–10**, use the bar graph at the right.

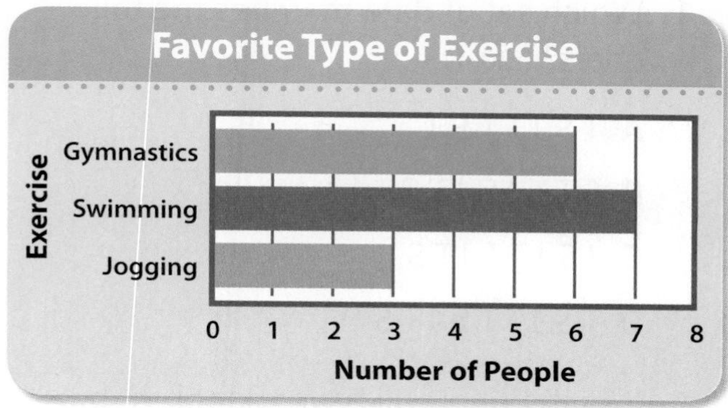

8. How many people in all voted for their favorite type of exercise?

9. How many more people voted for gymnastics than for jogging?

10. **Write a Problem** Write and solve a word problem different from Exercises 8 and 9.

For **11–13**, use the tally chart.

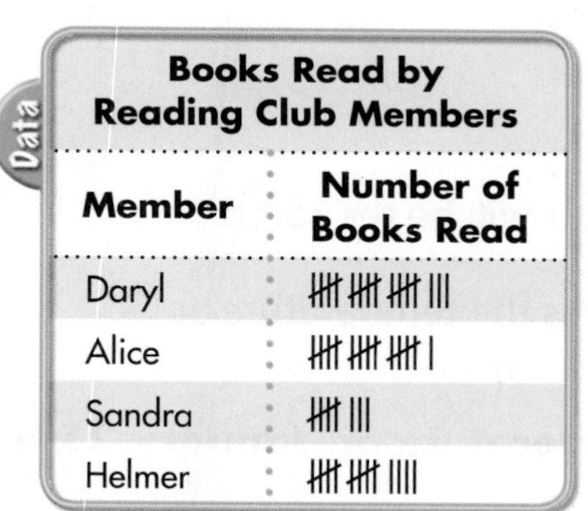

Data

Books Read by Reading Club Members

Member	Number of Books Read
Daryl	𝍸 𝍸 𝍸 |||
Alice	𝍸 𝍸 𝍸	
Sandra	𝍸 |||
Helmer	𝍸 𝍸 ||||

11. Make a graph to show the data. Choose a pictograph or a bar graph.

12. Who read exactly ten more books than Sandra?

13. Write the members in order from most to fewest books read.

14. **Strategy Focus** Solve. Use the strategy Make a Table.

At the farmer's market, Matt gives 2 free apples for every 6 apples the customer buys. If Lucinda buys 24 apples, how many free apples will she get?

15. **Write to Explain** What kinds of comparisons can you make when you look at a bar graph or a pictograph?

Test

Trudy took a survey and made the tally chart shown. Use the chart for **1** and **2**.

First Initials

Initial	Tally
J	‖
S	‖|
T	‖‖

1. Which set of data matches the tally chart? (20-1)

A T S J T T S J

B S T T J S J T S

C J S J T T J T S

D T S J T T S J T S

2. Which initial will have the tallest bar on a bar graph of Trudy's data? (20-4)

A J

B S

C T

D S and T will be the same.

3. What was the temperature at 9 A.M.? (20-5)

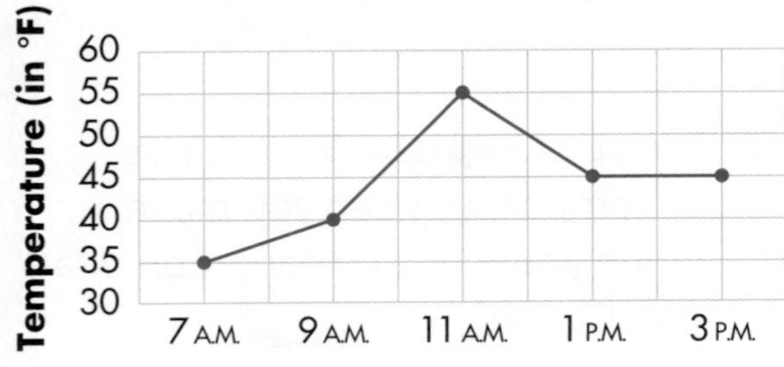

A 35°F

B 40°F

C 45°F

D 50°F

Use the pictograph for **4–6**.

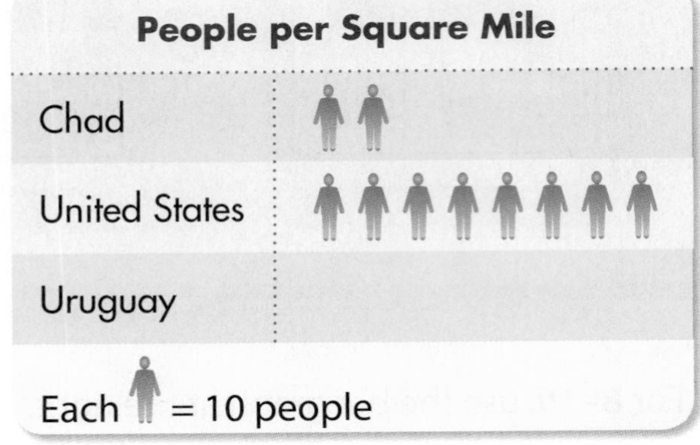

4. How many people per square mile does Chad have? (20-2)

A 80

B 20

C 10

D 2

5. How many more people per square mile does the United States have than Chad? (20-2)

A 6

B 20

C 60

D 100

6. If Pedro knows Uruguay has 50 people for each square mile, how many symbols should he draw for Uruguay? (20-3)

A 5

B 10

C 25

D 50

7. Use the bag of tiles and the table to answer the question below.

Heart	3	6	9		15	
Moon	2	4	6	8		12
Star	1	2	3			6
Total Picks	6	12	18	24	30	36

Which is the best prediction for how many moons will be picked in 30 total picks? (20-7)

A 12 moons

B 10 moons

C 8 moons

D 5 moons

8. Jose spun a spinner 12 times. The line plot below shows his results.

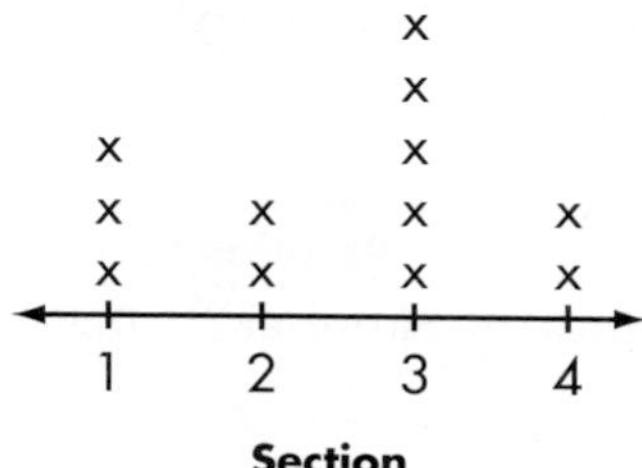

Which is the best prediction of the section Jose will spin next? (20-8)

A 1

B 2

C 3

D 4

9. Which statement is true about the data in the graphs? (20-9)

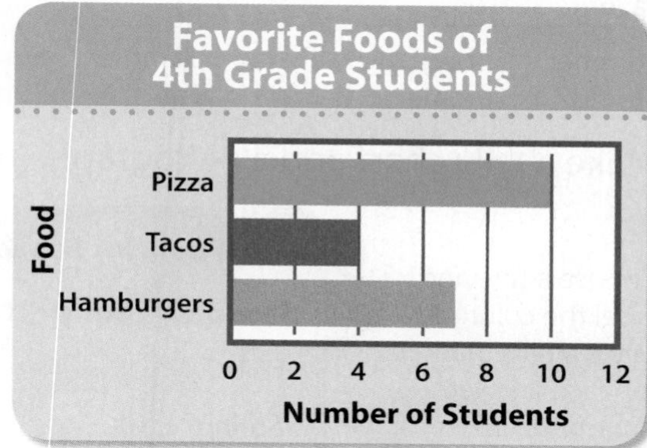

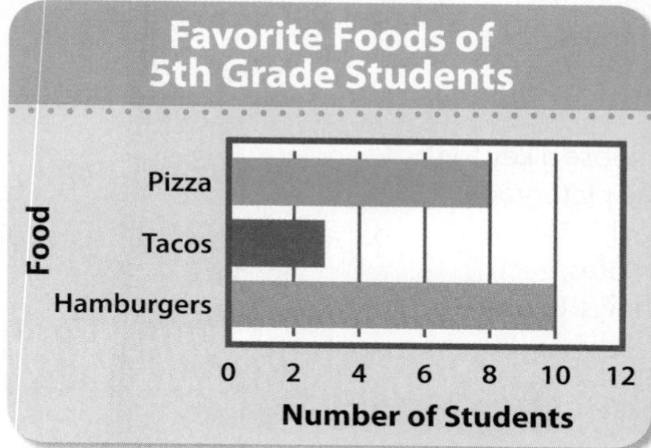

A Pizza is the favorite in both grades.

B The same number of students in each grade like tacos.

C More students in Grade 4 than in Grade 5 like hamburgers.

D More students in Grade 4 than in Grade 5 like pizza.

10. At the fair, the fish pond has 15 red fish, 9 blue fish, 10 yellow fish, and 5 orange fish. If Tammy hooks a fish without looking, what color fish is she most likely to get? (20-6)

A Blue

B Orange

C Red

D Yellow

Topic 20
Reteaching

Set A, pages 458–462, 464–465

What is the favorite season of these students?

Favorite Season

Summer	Spring	Fall	Summer	Summer
Spring	Summer	Winter	Fall	Summer

Make a tally chart and a pictograph.

Choose a title and label the columns. Make a tally mark for each answer. Count the tally marks. Record the number.

Data

Favorite Season		
Season	**Tally**	**Number**
Fall	||	2
Spring	||	2
Summer	𝍸	5
Winter	|	1

Choose a key for the pictograph. Each ● shows 2 votes; each ◖ shows 1 vote.

Season	Votes
Fall	●
Spring	●
Summer	● ● ◖
Winter	◖

Remember to make sure your tally marks and the symbols in the pictograph match the data.

For **1–3**, use the Team Name data.

Votes for Team Name

Aces	Fire	Aces	Fire	Aces
Aces	Fire	Fire	Aces	Stars
Fire	Stars	Fire	Fire	Fire
Aces	Aces	Aces	Fire	Stars
Fire	Fire	Fire	Aces	Fire
Stars	Fire	Stars	Fire	Aces

1. Make a tally chart for the data.

2. How many more players voted for Fire than Stars for their team name?

3. Choose a key and make a pictograph to show the data.

Set B, pages 466–467, 482–483

How can you make a bar graph to draw conclusions about how much Don saved?

Data

Month	Amount	Month	Amount
January	$20	March	$30
February	$35	April	$15

Choose 10 for the scale. Amounts with a 5 in the ones place will be halfway between 2 grid lines.

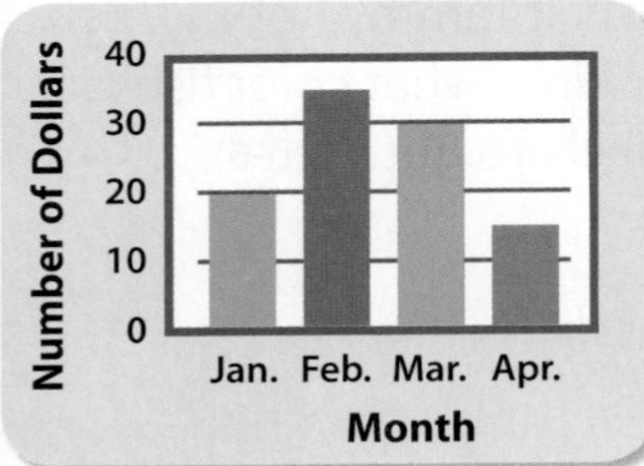

The longest bar in February shows the most.

The shortest bar in April shows the least.

Remember that you can compare the bars to draw conclusions.

1. Make a bar graph for the data below.

Data

Pennies Saved			
Day	**Number**	**Day**	**Number**
Mon.	25	Wed.	15
Tues.	20	Thurs.	10

2. Suppose the bar for Friday is as long as the bar for Tuesday. What conclusion can you draw?

Set C, pages 468–471

Add $15 earned in July to the line graph.

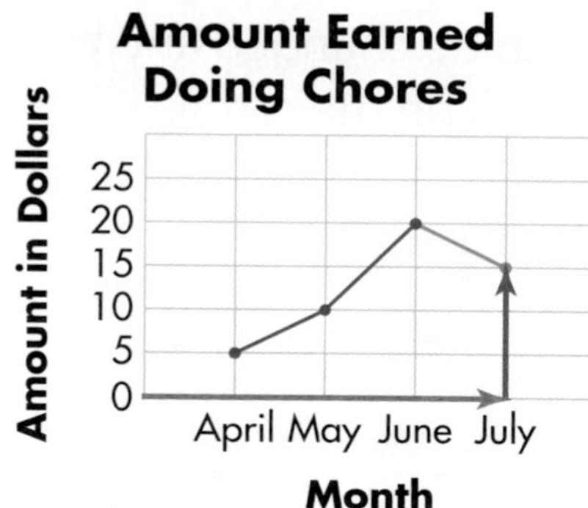

- Start at 0. Move along the bottom to July.
- Move up to the line for 15. Mark a point.
- Connect the points with a line segment.

Remember that to plot a point, go across, then up.

1. Explain how to plot (3, 2).
2. Copy and complete the graph to show the data for Friday.
   Friday: 20 books collected

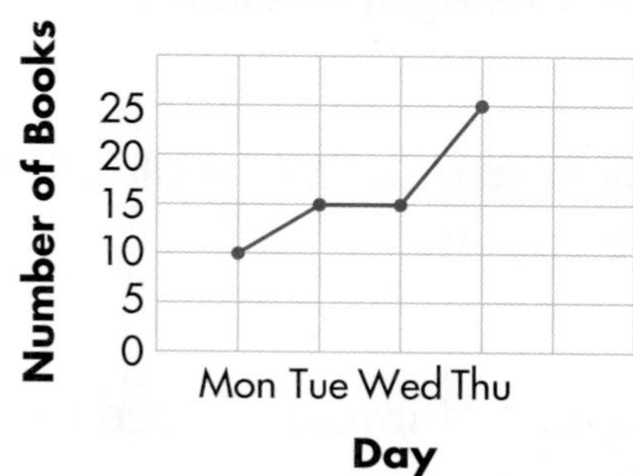

Set D, pages 472–477

When you spin this spinner, what outcome is likely? unlikely? impossible? certain?

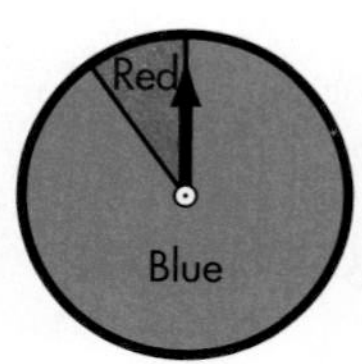

It is likely you will spin Blue.
It is unlikely you will spin Red.
It is impossible to spin Green.
It is certain you will spin a color or a line.

Remember that you are deciding what will probably happen.

1. What outcome is likely on this spinner?

2. In 3 spins, Lisa spun 2 Gs and 1 Y. Predict what is likely in 30 spins.

Set E, pages 478–481

Which high temperature occurred most often in June?

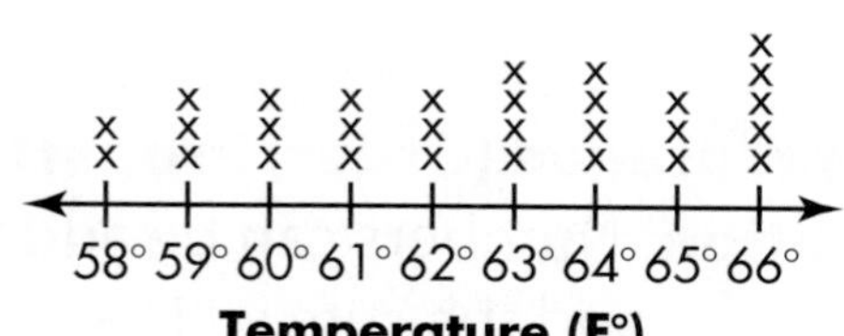

A high temperature of 66° occurred most often.

Remember that each outcome gets an X on a line plot.

Spin Results

Spin	Section	Spin	Section	Spin	Section
1	3	4	2	7	1
2	2	5	1	8	2
3	2	6	2	9	2

1. Make a line plot of the data. Then predict the section of Spin 10.

A.M. Time between midnight and noon.

acute angle An angle that measures less than a right angle.

acute triangle A triangle with three acute angles.

addends Numbers added together to give a sum.
Example: $2 + 7 = 9$
(2 and 7 are each labeled "Addend".)

angle A figure formed by two rays that have the same endpoint.

area The number of square units needed to cover a region.

array A way of displaying objects in rows and columns.

Associative (Grouping) Property of Addition The grouping of addends can be changed and the sum will be the same.

Associative (Grouping) Property of Multiplication The grouping of factors can be changed and the product will be the same.

bar graph A graph using bars to show data.

benchmark fraction A commonly used fraction such as $\frac{1}{4}$, $\frac{1}{3}$, $\frac{1}{2}$, $\frac{2}{3}$, and $\frac{3}{4}$.

capacity The volume of a container measured in liquid units.

centimeter (cm) A metric unit of length.

certain event An event that is sure to happen.

Commutative (Order) Property of Addition Numbers can be added in any order and the sum will be the same.

Commutative (Order) Property of Multiplication Numbers can be multiplied in any order and the product will be the same.

compare To decide if one number is greater than or less than another number.

compatible numbers Numbers that are easy to add, subtract, multiply or divide mentally.

cone A solid figure with a circle as its base and a curved surface that meets at a point.

congruent figures Figures that have the same shape and size.

coordinate grid A grid used to show ordered pairs.

corner The point where 3 or more edges meet in a solid figure.

cube A solid figure with six faces that are congruent squares.

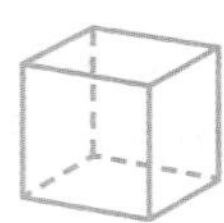

cubic unit A cube with edges 1 unit long, used to measure volume.

cup A customary unit of capacity.

cylinder A solid figure with two congruent circles as bases.

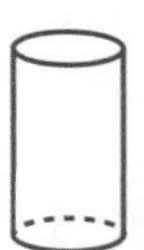

D

data Pieces of information.

decimal A number with one or more digits to the right of the decimal point.

decimal point A dot used to separate dollars from cents in money and ones from tenths in a number.

decimeter (dm) A metric unit of length. 1 decimeter equals 10 centimeters.

degree Celsius (°C) A metric unit of temperature.

degree Fahrenheit (°F) A customary unit of temperature.

denominator The number below the fraction bar in a fraction, the total number of equal parts in all.

difference The answer when subtracting two numbers.

digits The symbols 0, 1, 2, 3, 4, 5, 6, 7, 8, and 9 used to write numbers.

Distributive Property One factor in a multiplication problem can be broken apart to find partial products. The sum of the partial products is the product of the two factors.
Example: $(4 \times 28) = (4 \times 20) + (4 \times 8)$

dividend The number to be divided.
Example: $63 \div 9 = 7$
↑
Dividend

divisible Can be divided by another number without leaving a remainder.
Example: 10 is divisible by 2.

division An operation that tells how many equal groups there are or how many are in each group.

divisor The number by which another number is divided.
Example: $63 \div 9 = 7$
↑
Divisor

dollar sign ($) A symbol used to indicate money.

edge A line segment where two faces of a solid figure meet.

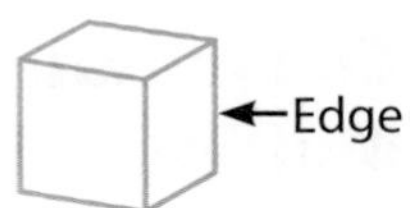

eighth One of 8 equal parts of a whole.

elapsed time Total amount of time that passes from the beginning time to the ending time.

equally likely outcomes Outcomes that have the same chance of happening.

equation A number sentence that uses = (is equal to).

equilateral triangle A triangle with all sides the same length.

equivalent fractions Fractions that name the same part of a whole, same part of a set, or same location on a number line.

estimate To give an approximate number or answer.

even number A whole number that has 0, 2, 4, 6, or 8 in the ones place; A number that is a multiple of 2.

expanded form A number written as the sum of the values of its digits.
Example: $2{,}476 = 2{,}000 + 400 + 70 + 6$

face A flat surface of a solid that does not roll.

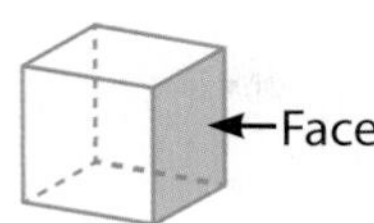

fact family A group of related facts using the same numbers.

factors Numbers that are multiplied together to give a product.
Example: $7 \times 3 = 21$

Factor Factor

fifth One of 5 equal parts of a whole.

flip (reflection) The change in the position that picks up and moves a figure to give a mirror image.
Example:

A B

Figure A is flipped to make figure B.

foot (ft) A customary unit of length. 1 foot equals 12 inches.

fourth One of 4 equal parts of a whole.

fraction A symbol, such as $\frac{2}{8}$, $\frac{5}{1}$, or $\frac{5}{5}$, used to name a part of a whole, a part of a set, or a location on a number line.

gallon (gal) A customary unit of capacity. 1 gallon equals 4 quarts.

gram (g) A metric unit of mass, the amount of matter in an object.

half (plural, halves) One of 2 equal parts of a whole.

half hour A unit of time equal to 30 minutes.

hexagon A polygon with 6 sides.

hour A unit of time equal to 60 minutes.

hundredth One of 100 equal parts of a whole, written as 0.01 or $\frac{1}{100}$.

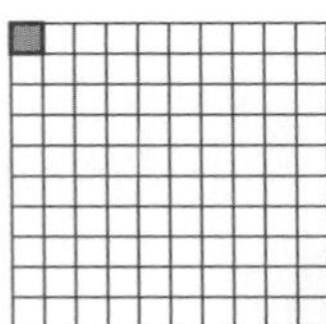

Identity (One) Property of Multiplication The product of any number and 1 is that number.

Identity (Zero) Property of Addition The sum of any number and zero is that same number.

impossible event An event that will never happen.

inch (in.) A customary unit of length.

inequality A number sentence that uses $<$ (is less than) or $>$ (is greater than).

intersecting lines Lines that cross at one point.

isosceles triangle A triangle with at least two sides the same length.

K

key Explanation of what each symbol represents in a pictograph.

kilogram (kg) A metric unit of mass, the amount of matter in an object. 1 kilogram equals 1,000 grams.

kilometer (km) A metric unit of length. 1 kilometer equals 1,000 meters.

likely event An event that will probably happen.

line A straight path of points that is endless in both directions.

line graph A graph that shows how data changes over a period of time.

line of symmetry A line on which a figure can be folded so that both parts match exactly.

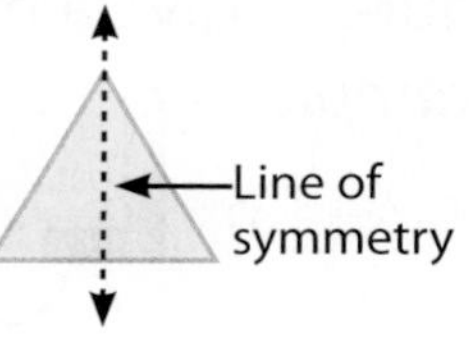

line plot A way to organize data on a line.

line segment A part of a line that has two endpoints.

liter (L) A metric unit of capacity. 1 liter equals 1,000 milliliters.

mass A measure of the amount of matter in an object.

meter (m) A metric unit of length. 1 meter equals 100 centimeters.

mile (mi) A customary unit of length. 1 mile equals 5,280 feet.

milliliter (mL) A metric unit of capacity. 1,000 milliliters equals 1 liter.

millimeter (mm) A metric unit of length. 1,000 millimeters equals 1 meter.

minute A unit of time equal to 60 seconds.

mixed number A number with a whole number part and a fraction part.
Example: $2\frac{3}{4}$

multiple The product of the number and any other whole number.
Example: 0, 4, 8, 12, and 16 are multiples of 4.

multiplication An operation that gives the total number when you put together equal groups.

number line A line that shows numbers in order using a scale.
Example: 0 1 2 3 4

numerator The number above the fraction bar in a fraction.

numerical expression An expression that contains numbers and at least one operation. A numerical expression is also called a number expression.

obtuse angle An angle that measures more than a right angle.

obtuse triangle A triangle with one obtuse angle.

octagon A polygon with 8 sides.

odd number A whole number that has 1, 3, 5, 7, or 9 in the ones place; A number not divisible by 2.

order To arrange numbers from least to greatest or from greatest to least.

ordered pair Two numbers used to name a point on a coordinate grid.

ordinal numbers Numbers used to tell the order of people or objects.

ounce (oz) A customary unit of weight.

outcome A possible result of a game or experiment.

P.M. Time between noon and midnight.

parallel lines Lines that never intersect.

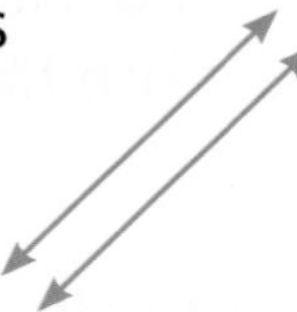

parallelogram A quadrilateral in which opposite sides are parallel.

pentagon A polygon with 5 sides.

perimeter The distance around a figure.

period A group of three digits in a number, separated by a comma.

perpendicular lines Two lines that intersect to form right angles.

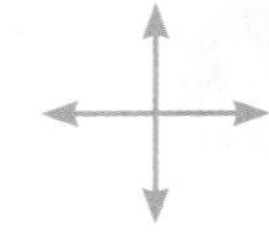

pictograph A graph using pictures or symbols to show data.

pint (pt) A customary unit of capacity. 1 pint equals 2 cups.

place value The value given to the place a digit has in a number. *Example:* In 3,946, the place value of the digit 9 is *hundreds.*

plot Locate and mark a point on a coordinate grid using a given ordered pair.

point An exact position often marked by a dot.

polygon A closed figure made up of straight line segments.

possible event An event that might or might not happen.

pound (lb) A customary unit of weight. 1 pound equals 16 ounces.

probability The chance an event will happen.

product The answer to a multiplication problem.

pyramid A solid figure whose base is a polygon and whose faces are triangles with a common point.

Q

quadrilateral A polygon with 4 sides.

quart (qt) A customary unit of capacity. 1 quart equals 2 pints.

quarter hour A unit of time equal to 15 minutes

quotient The answer to a division problem.

R

ray A part of a line that has one endpoint and continues endlessly in one direction.

rectangle A quadrilateral with four right angles.

rectangular prism A solid figure with faces that are rectangles.

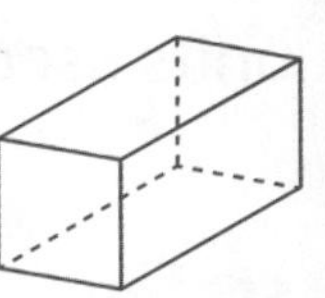

regroup To name a whole number in a different way.
Example: 28 = 1 ten 18 ones.

remainder The number that is left over after dividing.
Example: 31 ÷ 7 = 4R3

rhombus A quadrilateral with opposite sides parallel and all sides the same length.

right angle An angle that forms a square corner.

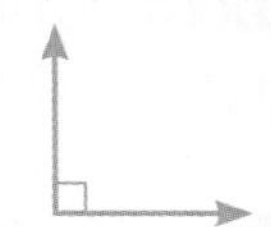

right triangle A triangle with one right angle.

round To replace a number with a number that tells about how much or how many to the nearest ten, hundred, thousand, and so on.
Example: 42 rounded to the nearest 10 is 40.

scale The numbers that show the units used on a graph.

scalene triangle A triangle with no sides the same length.

second A unit of time. 60 seconds equal 1 minute.

side A line segment forming part of a polygon.

simplest form A fraction with a numerator and denominator that cannot be divided by the same divisor, except 1.

sixth One of 6 equal parts of a whole.

slide (translation) The change in the position of a figure that moves it up, down, or sideways.
Example:

solid figure A figure that has length, width, and height.

sphere A solid figure in the shape of a ball.

square A quadrilateral with four right angles and all sides the same length.

square unit A square with sides 1 unit long, used to measure area.

standard form A way to write a number showing only its digits.
Example: 3,845

sum The answer to an addition problem.

survey Collect information by asking a number of people the same question and recording their answers.

symmetry A figure has symmetry if it can be folded along a line so that both parts match exactly.

tally chart A chart on which data is recorded.

tally mark A mark used to record data on a tally chart.
Example: 𝍸 = 5

tenth One of 10 equal parts of a whole, written as 0.1 or $\frac{1}{10}$.

thermometer A tool used to measure temperature.

third One of 3 equal parts of a whole.

ton (T) A customary unit of weight. 1 ton = 2,000 pounds.

trapezoid A quadrilateral with only one pair of parallel sides.

triangle A polygon with 3 sides.

turn (rotation) The change in the position of a figure that moves it around a point.
Example:

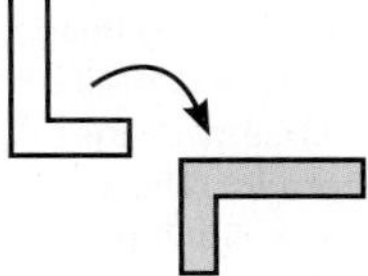

twelfth One of 12 equal parts of a whole.

twice Two times a number.

unit fraction A fraction with a numerator of 1.
Example: $\frac{1}{2}$

unlikely event An event that probably won't happen.

vertex (plural, vertices) The point where two rays meet to form an angle. The points where the sides of a polygon meet. The points where 3 or more edges meet in a solid figure that does not roll. The pointed part of a cone.

volume The number of cubic units needed to fill a solid figure.

week A unit of time equal to 7 days.

weight A measure of how heavy an object is.

word form A number written in words.
Example: 9,325 = nine thousand, three hundred twenty-five

yard (yd) A customary unit of length. 1 yard equals 3 feet or 36 inches.

Zero Property of Multiplication The product of any number and zero is zero.

Scott Foresman • Addison Wesley

enVisionMATH™

Illustrations:

8, 12, 16, 38, 54, 146, 350 Dick Gage; 10, 11, 76, 88, 117, 122, 123, 140, 143, 144, 166, 168, 237, 265, 267, 271, 281, 282, 283, 298, 301, 302, 345, 369, 386, 414, 422, 446, 448 Leslie Kell; 55, 92, 124, 146, 174, 331, 336, 351, 352, 353, 360, 386 Neil Stewart; 195, 279, 280 Joe LeMonnier; 251 Rob Schuster.

Photographs:

Every effort has been made to secure permission and provide appropriate credit for photographic material. The publisher deeply regrets any omission and pledges to correct errors called to its attention in subsequent editions.

Unless otherwise acknowledged, all photographs are the property of Pearson Education, Inc.

Photo locators denoted as follows: Top (T), Center (C), Bottom (B), Left (L), Right (R), Background (Bkgd)

Cover:

Luciana Navarro Powell

Front Matter:

X ©Corbis/SuperStock, Getty Images/Jupiterimages/Thinkstock, (TL) surpasspro/Fotolia; xi (TL) Getty Images/Jupiterimages/Thinkstock; xii (TL) Gallery of the Republic, (BR, BC) Glass Crab Sculpture by Jackie Leatherbury, assisted by John Douglass/©Jackie Douglass; xiii (BL) Getty Images, (TR) megasquib/Fotolia; xiv (TCR) Mark Markau/Fotolia, (BR) thinkstock/Getty Images; xv (T) Sven Weber/Fotolia; xxiv Getty Images/Jupiterimages/Thinkstock;

2 (TR) 2010/Photos to Go/Photolibrary, (CL) Comstock/Thinkstock; 3 (L) sculpies/Fotolia; 6 (TR) Eric Isselée/Fotolia; 14 (CR) ©Brad Perks Lightscapes/Alamy, (CR) Comstock/Thinkstock, (BC) Getty Images, (BC) Jupiter Images; 17 (R) ©WizData, inc./Alamy, (CC) 2010/Photos to Go/Photolibrary, (CL) Comstock/Thinkstock, (CC) steve estvanik/Fotolia; 21 (TR) Labrador/Fotolia; 30 (B) Getty Images, (CL) John Foxx/Thinkstock, (TR) Ken Usami/Getty Images; 31 (L) Goodshoot/Thinkstock; 35 (BL) 2010/Photos to Go/Photolibrary; 38 (C) Getty Images, (CL) IT Stock Free/Jupiter Images; 42 (BR) Goodshoot/Thinkstock, (CR) Thinkstock; 44 (TR) ©Royalty-Free/Corbis; 49 (BR, BL) ©photolibrary/Index Open, (BL) Getty Images, (C) Index Open, (CL) Stockdisc; 56 (TR, CR) ©imagebroker/Alamy, (TC) hotshotsworldwide/Fotolia; 57 (BR) ©John Luke/Index Open; 64 (BL) DM7/Fotolia, (L) Michael Rosskothen/Fotolia, (TR) NASA Image Exchange; 65 Getty Images, (TL) Getty Images/Thinkstock, (BL) Jefery/Fotolia; 70 (BL) Getty Images, (BL) Getty Images/Thinkstock; 73 (CR) Jefery/Fotolia; 84 David R. Frazier Photolibrary, Inc./Alamy Images, (TR) Getty Images, (CR) Hemera Technologies/Thinkstock; 85 (TL) 2010/Photos to Go/Photolibrary, (BL) 2011/Photos to Go/Photolibrary; 94 (B) David R. Frazier Photolibrary, Inc./Alamy Images; 106 (TR) ©Jill Stephenson/Alamy, (B) 2010/Photos to Go/Photolibrary; 107 (BL) 2010/Photos to Go/Photolibrary, (TL) Dusty Cline/Fotolia; 115 (BR) Photos to Go/Photolibrary; 138 (TL) ©Geoff du Feu/Alamy, (B) Dmitriy Elyuseev/Fotolia; 139 (BC) Getty Images/Thinkstock, (BL) Hemera Technologies/Thinkstock, (TL) NASA/JPL-Caltech/M. Kelley (Univ. of Minnesota)/NASA; 162 (TR) Getty Images, (B) NASA; 163 (C) Thinkstock/Getty Images; 182 (Inset) Library of Congress, (TC) Living Legend/Fotolia, (B) Saty Bha/Fotolia; 183 (BL) Getty Images, (TL) Rubberball/Getty Images; 184 (TL) Getty Images; 185 (TR) Getty Images; 198 (C) hotshotsworldwide/Fotolia, (CR) PB/Fotolia; 204 (TR) ©Directphoto/Alamy, (B) Ablestock/Thinkstock, (CL) Photos to Go/Photolibrary; 205 (L) Getty Images; 209 (CR) ©Directphoto/Alamy; 210 (TR) Jupiter Images; 214 (CR) Eric Isselée/Fotolia; 232 (B) 2010/Photos to Go/Photolibrary, (TL) poco_bw/Fotolia; 233 (CL) Henryk Sadura/Fotolia; 234 (BR) ©photolibrary/Index Open, (BL) Jupiter Images; 235 (BC) ©photolibrary/Index Open, (BL) ©Vstock/Index Open; 236 (BR, BC) Getty Images, (CR) Jupiter Images, (C) Stockdisc; 243 2010/Photos to Go/Photolibrary; 247 (BL) Henryk Sadura/Fotolia; 258 (B) Getty Images, (CL) Photos to Go/Photolibrary, (B) Photos/Thinkstock; 259 (T) Getty Images, (BL) Index Open; 267 (BL) Index Open; 274 (TCR) 2010/Photos to Go/Photolibrary, (BL) Getty Images, (TR) Michael Pettigrew/Fotolia; 275 (BL) Dream Maker Software, (T) Photos to Go/Photolibrary; 281 (BL) Keith Levit Photography/Photos to Go/Photolibrary; 283 (BC) Photos to Go/Photolibrary; 293 (TR) ©Creatas, (TC) ©Stefan Sollfors Insects/Alamy, (TRC,) Hemera Technologies/Thinkstock, (CR) Jupiterimages/Thinkstock; 297 (BC) 2010/Photos to Go/Photolibrary, (BR) Cathy Keifer/Fotolia; 305 (TL) ©Simon Belcher/Alamy; 308 (TR) ©Vstock/Index Open; 310 (BL) Getty Images; 327 (BL) 2010/Photos to Go/Photolibrary, (BCL) Eric Isselée/Fotolia, (TL) Library of Congress; 329 Jupiter Images; 332 ©photolibrary/Index Open, (CL) Corbis, (BL) Getty Images; 333 (B) ©Mistral Images/Index Open, (CR, CL) Index Open, (TR) Jupiter Images; 335 (TL) Getty Images; 338 (CR) ©Image Source Limited, (BL) Comstock Inc., (BR) Jupiter Images; 339 (CR) ©Simple Stock Shots; 340 (BR) ©D. Hurst/Alamy, (T) ©Mark Duffy/Alamy, (TR) ©Royalty-Free/Corbis, (CL, BR, BL) Getty Images, (BL) Jupiter Images; 341 (BC) 2010/Photos to Go/Photolibrary, (BCL) Eric Isselée/Fotolia; 344 (TCR) ©Vstock/Index Open, (BR) Corbis, (BC) Getty Images; 345 (BR) Corbis, (TR) Getty Images; 346 (BR) Getty Images, (CR) Index Open, (TR) Stockdisc; 347 (BR) ©Lew Robertson/Corbis, (CR) Index Open, (CL) Jupiter Images, (TR) Stockdisc; 348 (TC) EcoView/Fotolia, (B) Getty Images; 349 (BL) Frogkick/Fotolia, (TL) Getty Images; 350 (TR) ©Creatas, (CL) ©photolibrary/Index Open, (BR) Foodcollection/Getty Images, (CL) Getty Images, (BL) Hemera Technologies; 351 (TR) ©Creatas, (C) Frogkick/Fotolia, (C, BL) Getty Images, (R) Jupiter Images, (CL) Pat Lalli/Fotolia; 354 (BR) Pat Lalli/Fotolia; 356 (CL) ©photolibrary/Index Open, (BR) ©Simple Stock Shots; 357 (BR) Amur/Fotolia, (BC) Simple Stock Shots; 358 (BC) Getty Images, (BL) Jupiter Images, (CR) Stockdisc; 364 (CR) MIXA/Getty Images; 365 (C) ©photolibrary/Index Open, (TL) Getty Images; 366 (CL) Christopher Dodge/Fotolia, (BL) Photo courtesy of Pleasant Time Industries; 367 (BL) Anup Shah/Thinkstock, (TL) Jupiterimages/Thinkstock; 371 Jupiterimages/Thinkstock; 390 (Inset) Geza Farkas/Fotolia, (B) Thinkstock/Jupiter Images, (T) unamarina/Fotolia; 391 (BL) Getty Image/Photos/Thinkstock, (TL) NASA Image Exchange; 398 (TR) Getty Images; 403 (TR, T) Getty Images, (B) Jupiter Images; 410 (BR) Getty Images/Comstock/Thinkstock, (BL) Julia Mashkova/Fotolia, (TC) NASA Image Exchange; 411 (TR) ©Mike Hill/Alamy Images, (BR) Stockbyte/Thinkstock; 424 ©Mike Hill/Alamy Images; 434 (CL) Getty Images, (CL) judwick/Fotolia, (B) Photodisc/Thinkstock; 435 (BL) 2010/Photos to Go/Photolibrary, (TL) 2011/Photos to Go/Photolibrary; 456 (TR) ©Hot Ideas/Index Open, (C) cristi180884/Fotolia, (BL) Sir_Eagle/Fotolia; 457 (B) Galina Barskaya/Fotolia, (TL) Ingram Publishing/Jupiter Images; 472 (TR) Getty Images/Thinkstock; 477 (BR) Ingram Publishing/Jupiter Images.

Index